Advertising and Promotion

An Integrated Marketing Communications Perspective

Fourth Edition

George E. Belch & Michael A. Belch
Both of San Diego State University

Boston, Massachusetts   Burr Ridge, Illinois   Dubuque, Iowa
Madison, Wisconsin   New York, New York   San Francisco, California   St. Louis, Missouri

Irwin/McGraw-Hill

A Division of The McGraw·Hill Companies

ADVERTISING AND PROMOTION: AN INTEGRATED MARKETING COMMUNICATIONS PERSPECTIVE
International Editions 1999

Previously published under the title *Introduction to Advertising and Promotion: An Integrated Marketing Communications Perspective*

Exclusive rights by McGraw-Hill Book Co – Singapore for manufacture and export. This book cannot be re-exported from the country to which it is consigned by McGraw-Hill.

Credits appear on pages 744–46, and on this page by reference.

1 2 3 4 5 6 7 8 9 0 SLP PMP 2 0 9 8

Cover photos: **Airwalk:** Courtesy of Lambesis, Inc. **Curve:** Courtesy of Liz Claiborne Cosmetics. **ESPN:** Courtesy of ESPN, Inc. **Levi.com:** ©Levi Strauss & Co. 1996, 1997. All Rights Reserved. We would like to thank the following companies for their work in the development and management of the Levi's Web Site: TN Technologies Inc. and Jon Bains Lateral, Obsolete Studios.

Library of Congress Cataloging-in-Publication Data

Belch, George E. (George Eugene)
    Advertising and promotion : an integrated marketing communications
Perspective / George E. Belch, Michael A. Belch.–4th ed.
       p.   cm. – (Irwin/McGraw-Hill series in marketing)
    Rev. ed. of: Introduction to advertising and promotion. 3rd ed.
1995.
    Includes bibliographical references and index.
    ISBN 0-256-21899-4
    1. Advertising.   2. Sales promotion.   3. Communication in
marketing.   I. Belch, Michael A.   II. Belch, George E. (George
Eugene). Introduction to advertising and promotion.   III. Title.
    IV.   Series.
    HF5823.B387   1998
    659.1–dc21   97-28715

www.mhhe.com

When ordering this title, use ISBN 0-07-116088-4

Printed in Singapore

To Gayle, Derek, and Danny and to
Melanie, Jessica, and Trevor Milos

With a special dedication to Mom
for providing us with the proper
perspectives

Preface

THE CHANGING WORLD OF ADVERTISING AND PROMOTION

Nearly everyone in the modern world is influenced to some degree by advertising and other forms of promotion. Organizations in both the private and public sectors have learned that the ability to communicate effectively and efficiently with their target audiences is critical to their success. Advertising and other types of promotional messages are used to sell products and services as well as to promote causes, market political candidates, and deal with societal problems such as the AIDS crisis and alcohol and drug abuse. Consumers are finding it increasingly difficult to avoid the efforts of marketers, who are constantly searching for new ways to communicate with them.

Most of the people involved in advertising and promotion will tell you that there is no more dynamic and fascinating a field to either practice or study. However, they will also tell you that the field is undergoing dramatic changes that are changing advertising and promotion forever. The changes are coming from all sides—clients demanding better results from their advertising and promotional dollars; lean but highly creative smaller ad agencies; sales promotion and direct-marketing firms who want a larger share of the billions of dollars companies spend each year promoting their products and services; consumers who no longer respond to traditional forms of advertising; and new technologies that may reinvent the very process of advertising.

For decades the advertising business was dominated by large, full-service Madison Avenue-type agencies. The advertising strategy for a national brand involved creating one or two commercials that could be run on network television, a few print ads that would run in general interest magazines, and some sales promotion support such as coupons or premium offers. However, in today's world there are a myriad of media outlets—print, radio, cable and satellite TV, and now the Internet—competing for consumers' attention. Marketers are looking beyond the traditional media to find new and better ways to communicate with their customers. They no longer accept on faith the value of conventional advertising placed in conventional media. The large agencies are recognizing that they must change if they hope to survive into the 21st century. Keith Reinhard, chairman and CEO of DDB Needham Worldwide, notes that the large agencies

"have finally begun to acknowledge that this isn't a recession we're in, and that we're not going back to the good old days."

In addition to redefining the role and nature of their advertising agencies, marketers are changing the way they communicate with consumers. They know they are operating in an environment where advertising messages are everywhere, consumers channel-surf past most commercials, and brands promoted in traditional ways often fail. New-age advertisers are redefining the notion of what an ad is and where it runs. Stealth messages are being woven into the culture and embedded into movies and TV shows or made into their own form of entertainment.

Marketers are also changing the ways they allocate their promotional dollars. Spending on sales promotion activities targeted at both consumers and the trade has surpassed advertising media expenditures for years and continues to rise. In a recent article titled "Agencies: Change or Die," Joe Cappo, *Advertising Age* senior vice president, wrote, "What is happening in the advertising industry right now is a massive revolution that is changing the rules of marketing. This revolution is taking place not only in the United States, but in all affluent countries where advertising and media are well developed."

A number of factors are fueling this revolution. The audiences that marketers seek, along with the media and methods for reaching them, have become increasingly fragmented. Advertising and promotional efforts have become more regionalized and targeted to specific audiences. Retailers have become larger and more powerful, forcing marketers to shift money from advertising budgets to sales promotion. Marketers expect their promotional dollars to generate immediate sales and are demanding more accountability from their agencies. Many companies are coordinating all their communications efforts so they can send cohesive messages to their customers. Many advertising agencies have acquired, started, or become affiliated with sales promotion, direct-marketing, and public relations companies to better serve their clients' marketing communications needs.

This text will introduce students to this fast-changing field of advertising and promotion. While advertising is its primary focus, it is more than just an introductory advertising text because there is more to most organizations' promotional programs than just advertising. The changes discussed above are leading marketers and their agencies to approach advertising and promotion from an integrated marketing communications (IMC) perspective, which calls for a "big picture" approach to planning marketing and promotion programs and coordinating the various communication functions. To understand the role of advertising and promotion in today's business world, one must recognize how a firm can use all the promotional tools to communicate with its customers.

TO THE STUDENT: PREPARING YOU FOR THE NEW WORLD OF ADVERTISING AND PROMOTION

Some of you are taking this course to learn more about this fascinating field; many of you hope to work in advertising or some other promotional area. The changes in the industry have profound implications for the way today's student is trained and educated. You will not be working for the same kind of communication agencies that existed 5 or 10 years ago. If you work on the client side of the business, you will find that the way they approach advertising and promotion is changing dramatically.

Today's student is expected to understand all the major marketing communication functions: advertising, direct marketing, sales promotion, public relations, and personal selling. You will also be expected to know how to research and evaluate a company's marketing and promotional situation and how to use these various functions in developing effective communication strategies and programs. This book will help prepare you for these challenges.

As professors we were, of course, once students ourselves. In many ways we are perpetual students in that we are constantly striving to learn about and explain how advertising and promotion work. We share many of your interests and concerns and are often excited (and bored) by the same things. Having taught in the advertising and promotion area for a combined 40-plus years, we have developed an understanding of what makes a book in this field interesting to students. In writing this book, we have tried to remember how we felt about the various texts we used throughout the years and to incorporate the good things and minimize those we felt were of little use. We have tried not to overburden you with definitions, although we do call out those that are especially important to your understanding of the material.

We also remember that as students we were not really excited about theory. But to fully understand how integrated marketing communications works, it is necessary to establish some theoretical basis. The more you understand about how things are supposed to work, the easier it will be for you to understand why they do or do not turn out as planned.

Perhaps the question students ask most often is, "How do I use this in the real world?" In response, we provide numerous examples of how the various theories and concepts in the text can be used in practice. A particular strength of this text is the integration of theory with practical application. Nearly every day an example of advertising and promotion in practice is reported in the media. We have used many sources, such as *Advertising Age, AdWeek, BrandWeek, The Wall Street Journal, Business Week, Fortune, Forbes, Marketing Tools, Sales & Marketing Management, Business Marketing, Promo,* and many others, to find practical examples that are integrated throughout the text. We have spoken with hundreds of people about the strategies and rationale behind the ads and other types of promotions we use as examples. Each chapter begins with a vignette that presents an example of an advertising or promotional campaign or other interesting insights. Every chapter also contains several **IMC Perspectives** that present in-depth discussions of particular issues related to the chapter material and show how companies are using integrated marketing communications. **Global Perspectives** are presented throughout the text in recognition of the increasing importance of international marketing. **Ethical Perspectives** focus attention on important social issues and show how advertisers must take ethical considerations into account when planning and implementing advertising and promotional programs. New to this edition are a number of **Career Profiles** which highlight successful individuals working in the field of advertising and promotion.

Each chapter features beautiful four-color illustrations showing examples from many of the most current and best-integrated marketing communication campaigns being used around the world. We have included more than 350 advertisements and examples of numerous other types of promotion, all of which were carefully chosen to illustrate a particular idea, theory, or practical application. Please take time to read the opening vignettes to each chapter, the IMC, Global, and Ethical Perspectives, and the Career Profiles and study the diverse ads and illustrations. We think they will stimulate your interest and relate to your daily life as a consumer and a target of advertising and promotion.

TO THE INSTRUCTOR: A TEXT THAT REFLECTS THE CHANGES IN THE WORLD OF ADVERTISING AND PROMOTION

Our goal in writing the fourth edition of this text was to focus on the many changes that are occurring in the advertising industry and how they influence advertising and promotional strategies and tactics. We have done this by continuing with the *integrated marketing communications perspective* we introduced in the second edition. More and more companies are approaching advertising and promotion from an IMC perspective, coordinating the various promotional mix elements with other marketing activities that communicate with a firm's customers. A recent study found that an overwhelming majority of marketing managers believe IMC can enhance the effectiveness and impact of their marketing communications efforts. Many advertising agencies are also developing expertise in direct marketing, sales promotion, event sponsorship, the Internet, and other areas so they can meet all their clients' integrated marketing communication needs— and, of course, survive.

The text is built around an integrated marketing communications planning model and recognizes the importance of coordinating all of the promotional mix elements to develop an effective communications program. Although media advertising is often the most visible part of a firm's promotional program, attention must also be given to direct marketing, sales promotion, public relations, interactive media, and personal selling.

This text integrates theory with planning, management, and strategy. To effectively plan, implement, and evaluate IMC programs, one must understand the overall marketing process, consumer behavior, and communications theory. We draw from the extensive research in advertising, consumer behavior, communications, marketing, sales promotion, and other fields to give students a basis for understanding the marketing communications process, how it influences consumer decision making, and how to develop promotional strategies.

While this is an introductory text, we do treat each topic in some depth. We believe the marketing and advertising student of today needs a text that provides more than just an introduction to terms and topics. The book is positioned primarily for the introductory advertising, marketing communications, or promotions course as taught in the business/marketing curriculum. It can also be used in journalism/communications courses that take an integrated marketing communications perspective. In addition to its thorough coverage of advertising, this text has chapters on sales promotion, direct marketing and marketing on the Internet, personal selling, and publicity/public relations. These chapters stress the integration of advertising with other promotional mix elements and the need to understand their role in the overall marketing program.

ORGANIZATION OF THIS TEXT

This book is divided into seven major parts. In Part 1 we examine the role of advertising and promotion in marketing and introduce the concept of integrated marketing communications. Chapter 1 provides an overview of advertising and promotion and its role in modern marketing. The concept of IMC and the factors that have led to its growth are discussed. Each of the promotional mix elements is defined and an IMC planning model shows the various steps in the promotional planning process. This model provides a framework for developing the integrated marketing communications program and is followed throughout the text. Chapter 2 examines the role of advertising and promotion in the overall marketing program, with attention to the various elements of the marketing mix and how they interact with advertising and promotional strategy. We have also included coverage of market segmentation and positioning in this chapter so students can understand how these concepts fit into the overall marketing programs as well as their role in the development of an advertising and promotional program.

In Part 2 we cover the promotional program situation analysis. Chapter 3 describes how firms organize for advertising and promotion and examines the role of ad agencies and other firms that provide marketing and promotional services. We discuss how ad agencies are selected, evaluated, and compensated as well as the changes occurring in the agency business. We also consider whether responsibility for integrating the various communication functions lies with the client or the agency. Chapter 4 covers the stages of the consumer decision-making process and both the internal psychological factors and the external factors that influence consumer behavior. The focus of this chapter is on how advertisers can use an understanding of buyer behavior to develop effective advertising and other forms of promotion.

Part 3 analyzes the communications process. Chapter 5 examines various communication theories and models of how consumers respond to advertising messages, while Chapter 6 considers source, message, and channel factors.

In Part 4 we consider how firms develop goals for their integrated marketing communications programs and determine how much money to spend trying to achieve them. Chapter 7 stresses the importance of knowing what to expect from advertising, the differences between advertising and communication objectives, characteristics of good objectives, and problems in setting objectives. We have also integrated the discussion of various methods for determining and allocating the promotional budget into this chapter. These first four sections of the text provide students with a solid background in the areas of marketing, consumer behavior, communications, planning, objective setting, and budgeting. This foundation lays the foundation for the next section where we discuss the development of the integrated marketing communication program.

Part 5 examines the various promotional mix elements that form the basis of the integrated marketing communications program. Chapter 8 discusses the planning and development of the creative strategy and advertising campaign and examines the creative process. In Chapter 9 we turn our attention to ways to execute the creative strategy and some criteria for evaluating creative work. Chapters 10 through 13 cover media strategy and planning and the various advertising media. Chapter 10 introduces the key principles of media planning and strategy and examines how a media plan is developed. Chapter 11 discusses the advantages and disadvantages of the broadcast media (TV and radio) as well as issues regarding the purchase of radio and TV time and audience measurement. Chapter 12 considers the same issues for the print media (magazines and newspapers). Chapter 13 examines the role of support media such as outdoor and transit advertising and some of the many new media alternatives.

In Chapters 14 through 17 we continue the IMC emphasis by examining other promotional tools that are used in the integrated marketing communications process. Chapter 14 looks at the rapidly growing areas of direct marketing and marketing on the Internet. The first part of this chapter examines database marketing and the way by which companies communicate directly with target customers. In the second part of the chapter we added a detailed discussion of marketing on the Internet and how companies are using the World Wide Web as a medium for promoting and marketing their products and services. Chapter 15 examines both consumer-oriented sales promotion and programs targeted to the trade. Chapter 16 covers the role of publicity and public relations in IMC as well as corporate advertising. Basic issues regarding personal selling and its role in promotional strategy are presented in Chapter 17.

Part 6 of the text consists of Chapter 18, where we discuss ways to measure the effectiveness of various elements of the integrated marketing communications program, including methods for pretesting and posttesting advertising messages and campaigns. In Part 7 we turn our attention to special markets, topics, and perspectives that are becoming increasingly important in contemporary marketing. Chapter 19, on business-to-business marketing, examines how advertising and other forms of promotion are used to help one company sell its products and/or services to another firm. In Chapter 20 we examine the global marketplace and the role of advertising and other promotional mix variables in international marketing.

The text concludes with a discussion of the regulatory, social, and economic environments in which advertising and promotion operate. Chapter 21 examines industry self-regulation and regulation of advertising by governmental agencies such as the Federal Trade Commission, as well as the governing of sales promotion and direct marketing. Because advertising's role in society is constantly changing, our discussion would not be complete without a look at the criticisms frequently levied, so in Chapter 22 we consider the social, ethical, and economic aspects of advertising and promotion.

CHAPTER FEATURES

The following features in each chapter enhance students' understanding of the material as well as their reading enjoyment.

Chapter Objectives

Objectives are provided at the beginning of each chapter to identify the major areas and points covered in the chapter and guide the learning effort.

Chapter Opening Vignettes

Each chapter begins with a vignette that shows the effective use of integrated marketing communications by a company or ad agency or discusses an interesting issue that is relevant to the chapter. These opening vignettes are designed to draw the students into the chapter by presenting an interesting example, development, or issue that relates to the material covered in the chapter. Some of the companies whose advertising and promotion programs are profiled in the opening vignettes include Airwalk, Liz Claiborne, Saturn, Samsung Electronics, Fila, Nissan, Chevrolet trucks, ESPN, *Spin* magazine, Holiday Inn, General Electric, Procter & Gamble, Hewlett Packard, and the Fallon McElligott advertising agency.

IMC Perspectives

These boxed items feature in-depth discussions of interesting issues related to the chapter material and the practical application of integrated marketing communications. Each chapter contains several of these insights into the world of integrated marketing communications. Some of the companies/brands whose IMC programs are discussed in these perspectives are BMW, Adidas, General Motors, Coca-Cola, Air Canada, Apple Computer, Absolut vodka, Sears, Land O' Lakes, Procter & Gamble, Kraft Foods, DirecTV, and Intel.

Global Perspectives

These boxed sidebars provide information similar to that in the IMC Perspectives, with a focus on international aspects of advertising and promotion. Some of the companies/brands whose international advertising programs are covered in the Global Perspectives are Microsoft, Coca-Cola, Pepsi, Nestlé, Nike, IBM, Colgate, and Levi Strauss & Co.

Ethical Perspectives

These boxed items discuss the moral and/or ethical issues regarding practices engaged in by marketers and are also tied to the material presented in the particular chapter. Issues covered in the Ethical Perspectives include subliminal advertising, the use of shock ads by companies such as Calvin Klein and Benetton, invasion of consumer privacy by direct marketers, the controversy over use of the Joe Camel character in ads for Camel cigarettes, and the targeting of underage drinkers by alcoholic beverage companies

Career Profiles

Also included are eight items profiling the career path of successful individuals working in the communications industry. Some examples of the individuals featured in the Career Profiles are a president of integrated marketing at an agency, an account executive, a creative director, a group director of strategic planning and research and a vice president of global marketing. A director of research for a television network and individuals in sales promotion and public relations are also included.

Key Terms

Important terms are highlighted in boldface throughout the text and listed at the end of each chapter with a page reference. These terms help call students' attention to important ideas, concepts, and definitions and help them review their learning progress.

Chapter Summaries

These synopses serve as a quick review of important topics covered and a very helpful study guide.

Discussion Questions

Questions at the end of each chapter give students an opportunity to test their understanding of the material and to apply it. These questions can also serve as a basis for class discussion or assignments.

Four-Color Visuals

Print ads, photoboards, and other examples appear throughout the book. More than 400 ads, charts, graphs, and other types of illustrations are included in the text.

CHANGES IN THE FOURTH EDITION

We have made a number of changes in the fourth edition to make it as relevant and current as possible, as well as more interesting to students.

- **A Stronger Emphasis on Integrated Marketing Communications** The fourth edition puts an even stronger emphasis on approaching the field of advertising and promotion from an integrated marketing communications perspective. We continue to focus on how the various elements of an organization's promotional mix are combined to develop a total marketing communications program that sends a consistent message to customers. The first chapter now includes a discussion of the evolution of IMC and additional discussion of the factors that have contributed to the increased attention to IMC on both the client and agency side. Chapter 3 focuses on other communication agencies, such as sales promotion and direct-response firms, as well as interactive agencies. More attention is also given to setting objectives for IMC programs (Chapter 7) and measuring their effectiveness (Chapter 18).
- **Detailed Coverage of Marketing on the Internet** The fourth edition has detailed coverage of marketing on the Internet and how companies are using this new medium. This chapter discusses objectives and strategies for using the Internet and integrating it into marketing communications programs. Advantages and disadvantages of Web advertising are discussed, along with issues such as audience measurement and methods for determining the effectiveness of Internet advertising. Discussion of the Internet as a marketing communications tool is also integrated throughout the book.
- **New Chapter Opening Vignettes** All of the chapter opening vignettes in the fourth edition are new and were chosen for their currency and relevance to students. They demonstrate how various companies and advertising agencies use advertising and other IMC tools. They also provide interesting insights into some of the current trends and developments that are taking place in the advertising world.
- **New and Updated IMC Perspectives** All of the boxed items focusing on specific examples of how companies and their communications agencies are using integrated marketing communications are new or updated and provide insight into many of the most current and popular advertising and promotional campaigns being

used by marketers. The IMC Perspectives also address interesting issues related to advertising, sales promotion, direct marketing, marketing on the Internet, and personal selling.

- **New and Updated Global and Ethical Perspectives** Most of the boxed items focusing on global and ethical issues of advertising and promotion are new; those retained from the third edition have been updated. The Global Perspectives examine the role of advertising and other promotional areas in international markets. The Ethical Perspectives discuss specific issues, developments, and problems that call into question the ethics of marketers and their decisions as they develop and implement their advertising and promotional programs.
- **Career Profiles** A new feature has been added to the fourth edition called Career Profiles. These items profile the career path of successful individuals working in advertising and related fields. They provide the students with insight into various types of careers that are available in the area of advertising and promotion on the client and agency side as well as in media. The Career Profiles describe some of the responsibilities and requirements of these positions and also discuss the career path these individuals have taken as well as their educational background.
- **Contemporary Examples** The field of advertising and promotion changes very rapidly, and we tried to keep pace with it. Wherever possible we updated the statistical information presented in tables, charts, and figures throughout the text. We reviewed the most current academic and trade literature to ensure that this text reflects the most current perspectives and theories on advertising, promotion, and the rapidly evolving area of integrated marketing communications. We also updated most of the examples and ads throughout the book. *Advertising and Promotion* continues to be the most contemporary text on the market, offering students as timely a perspective as possible.
- **Fewer Chapters and More Concise Writing** In response to requests from instructors and students, we reduced the length of the text. The fourth edition has 22 chapters versus 24 in the previous two editions. One chapter was eliminated by integrating the material on market segmentation and positioning into Chapter 2 rather than having an entire chapter on these topics. Some of the material that appeared in Chapter 2 on the marketing environment has been dropped, since most instructors feel their students have covered this information in introductory marketing or other courses. A second chapter was eliminated by combining the chapters on setting objectives and budgeting for advertising and promotion. The fourth edition has been carefully edited to continue making the writing style tighter and more concise. In making these changes, we were careful not to reduce relevant content or the many examples that

are such a popular feature of this text. However, students will find the writing in the new edition more active, direct, and succinct and thus easier to read.

SUPPORT MATERIAL

A high-quality package of instructional supplements supports the fourth edition. Nearly all of the supplements have been developed by the authors to ensure their coordination with the text. We offer instructors a support package that facilitates the use of our text and enhances the learning experience of the student.

Instructor's Manual

The instructor's manual is a valuable teaching resource that includes learning objectives, chapter and lecture outlines, answers to all end-of-chapter discussion questions, transparency masters, and further insights and teaching suggestions. Additional discussion questions are also presented for each chapter. These questions can be used for class discussion or as short-answer essay questions for exams.

Manual of Tests

A test bank of more than 1,500 multiple-choice questions has been developed to accompany the text. The questions provide thorough coverage of the chapter material, including opening vignettes and IMC, Global, and Ethical Perspectives, and are categorized by level of learning (definitional, conceptual, or application).

Computerized Test Bank

A computerized version of the test bank is available to adopters of the text.

Instructor CD-ROM

This exciting presentation CR-ROM allows the professor to customize a multimedia lecture with original material from the supplements package. It includes video clips, commercials, ads and art from the text, electronic slides and acetates, the computerized test bank, and the print supplements.

Electronic Slides

A disk containing nearly 300 PowerPoint® slides is available to adopters of the fourth edition for electronic presentations. These slides contain lecture notes, charts, graphs, and other instructional materials.

Home Page

A home page on the Internet can be found at

www.mhhe.business/marketing/

It contains Web Exploration Links (hot links to other Web sites) as well as various other items of interest. For instructors, the home page will offer updates of examples; chapter opener vignettes; IMC, Global, and Ethical Perspectives; additional sources of advertising and promotion information; and downloads of key supplements. Adopters will be able to communicate directly with the authors through the site (contact your McGraw-Hill/Irwin representative for your password).

Internet Exercises

This supplement offers exercises and applications related to key topics in the fourth edition. These exercises and applications coincide with each chapter of the text and are page-referenced for maximum utility.

Four-Color Transparencies

Each adopter may request a set of 100 four-color acetate transparencies that present print ads, photoboards, sales promotion offers, and other materials that do not appear in the text. A number of important models or charts appearing in the text are also provided as color transparencies. Slipsheets are included with each transparency to give the instructor useful background information about the illustration and how it can be integrated into the lecture.

Video Supplements

A video supplement package has been developed specifically for classroom use with this text. The first video contains nearly 200 commercials that are examples of creative advertising. It can be used to help the instructor explain a particular concept or principle or give more insight into how a company executes its advertising strategy. Most of the commercials are tied to the chapter openings, IMC and Global Perspectives, or specific examples cited in the text. The video includes commercials for Airwalk footwear, No Fear, the California Fluid Milk Processors ("Got Milk?"), CompuServe, Westin Hotels, Motel 6, Nissan Infiniti and Porsche automobiles, Subaru Outback sport utility vehicles, Chevrolet trucks, Compaq computers, Taster's Choice coffee, Chips Ahoy! cookies, Nestlé, and Continental Airlines. A number of international commercials are included, as well as those used in public service campaigns for such organizations as the American Indian College Fund and the Partnership for a Drug-Free America. Insights and/or background information about each commercial are provided in the instructor's manual written specifically for the videos.

The second video contains longer segments on the advertising and promotional strategies of various companies and industries. Included on this video is a segment from the Advertising Educational Foundation, "Good-Bye Guesswork: How Research Guides Today's Advertisers, which examines how research is used to solve three specific advertising/marketing situations. Other segments include highlights of several promotions that won the 1996 and 1997 Reggie Awards (given each year to the best sales promotion campaigns), and case studies of the integrated marketing communications programs used by Airwalk Footwear, Southwest Airlines, Levi Strauss & Co., and Sprint to introduce its voice-activated FONCARD.

ACKNOWLEDGMENTS

While this fourth edition represents a tremendous amount of work on our part, it would not have become a reality without the assistance and support of many other people. Authors tend to think they have the best ideas, approach, examples, and organization for writing a great book. But we quickly learned that there is always room for our ideas to be improved on by others. A number of colleagues provided detailed, thoughtful reviews that were immensely helpful in making this a better book. We are very grateful to the following individuals who worked with us on earlier editions. They include Lauranne Buchanan, *University of Illinois*; Roy Busby, *University of North Texas*; Lindell Chew, *University of Missouri—St. Louis*; Catherine Cole, *University of Iowa*; John Faier, *Miami University*; Raymond Fisk, *Oklahoma State University*; Geoff Gordon, *University of Kentucky*; Donald Grambois, *Indiana University*; Stephen Grove, *Clemson University*; Ron Hill, *American University*; Paul Jackson, *Ferris State College*; Don Kirchner, *California State University—Northridge*; Clark Leavitt, *Ohio State University*; Charles Overstreet, *Oklahoma State University*; Paul Prabhaker, *Depaul University, Chicago*; Scott Roberts, *Old Dominion University*; Harlan Spotts, *Northeastern University*; Mary Ann Stutts, *Southwest Texas State University*; Terrence Witkowski, *California State University—Long Beach*; and Robert Young, *Northeastern University*.

We are particularly grateful to the individuals who provided constructive comments on how to make this edition better: Terry Bristol, *Oklahoma State University*; Roberta Ellins, *Fashion Institute of Technology*; Robert Erffmeyer, *University of Wisconsin—Eau Claire*; Alan Fletcher, *Louisiana State University*; Jon B. Freiden, *Florida State University*; Patricia Kennedy, *University of Nebraska*; Don Kirchner, *California State University—Northridge*; Susan Kleine, *Arizona State University*; Tina Lowry, *Rider University*; Elizabeth Moore-Shay, *University of Illinois*; Notis Pagiavlas, *University of Texas—Arlington*; William Pride, *Texas A&M University*; Joel Reedy, *University of South Florida*; Denise D. Schoenbachler, *Northern Illinois University*; Mary Ann Stutts, *Southwest Texas State University*; and James Swartz, *California State University—Pomona*.

We received very valuable comments and ideas from the reviewers of the fourth edition: Robert H. Ducoffe, *Baruch College*; Robert Gulonsen, *Washington University*; and Denise D. Schoenbachler, *Northern Illinois University*.

We would also like to acknowledge the cooperation we received from many people in the business, advertising, and media communities. This book contains several hundred ads, illustrations, charts, and tables that have been provided by advertisers and/or their agencies, various publications, and other advertising and industry organizations. Many individuals took time from their busy schedules to provide us with requested materials and gave us permission to use them. A special thanks to Sharon Lee and Chad Farmer of the Lambesis agency for their extraordinary assistance.

A manuscript does not become a book without a great deal of work on the part of a publisher. Various individuals at Irwin/McGraw-Hill have been involved with this project over the past several years. Our editor on the fourth edition, Karen Westover, provided valuable guidance and was instrumental in making sure this was much more than just a token revision. A special thanks goes to Libby Rubenstein, our developmental editor, for all of her efforts and for being so great to work with. Thanks also to Sue Trentacosti for doing a superb job of managing the production process.

We would like to acknowledge the support we have received from the College of Business at San Diego State University. We also want to thank Jennifer Labs for all of her help and the great job she did on the library research, and Charlotte Goldman for her assistance in getting many of the ads that appear throughout the book.

On a more personal note, a great deal of thanks goes to our families for putting up with us over the past few years while we were revising this book. Gayle, Danny, Derek, Melanie, and Jessica have had to endure the deviation from our usually pleasant personalities and dispositions for a fourth time, while Trevor is on his first round. We also wish to thank our cousin Gaetano for his expert opinions on anything and everything. Once again we look forward to returning to normal. Finally, we would like to acknowledge each other for making it through this ordeal a fourth time. Our mother will be happy to know that we still get along after all this—though it is definitely getting tougher—most of the time.

George E. Belch
Michael A. Belch

Contents in Brief

Contents

The Role of IMC
in Marketing

PART

1

CHAPTER 1

An Introduction to Integrated Marketing Communications

Chapter Objectives

- To examine the promotional function and the growing importance of advertising and other promotional elements in the marketing programs of domestic and foreign companies.

- To introduce the concept of integrated marketing communications (IMC) and consider how it has evolved.

- To examine reasons for the increasing importance of the IMC perspective in planning and executing advertising and promotional programs.

- To introduce the various elements of the promotional mix and consider their roles in an IMC program.

- To examine how various marketing and promotional elements must be coordinated to communicate effectively.

- To introduce a model of the IMC planning process and examine the steps in developing a marketing communications program.

AIRWALKS:
THE COOLEST SHOES ARE HOT

Over the past two decades, one of the most interesting and visible marketing battles has been waged by companies competing for a share of the athletic footwear market. Since the mid-1980s, the major battle in the sneaker wars has been waged between industry giants Nike and Reebok. Together the two account for more than half of the $11 billion spent on athletic shoes in the United States and over 40 percent of the $7 billion in sneaker sales outside the United States.

A major reason for Nike's and Reebok's success is that they recognize their business is no longer about just selling shoes. It's about sports, entertainment, style, and fashion. It's about creating a cool image for their products. Nike in particular has mastered the hard-to-define concept known as "cool," and scores points with the under-30 crowd for its attitude and irreverent ads. However, while Nike personifies cool to many, among impressionable young consumers a relatively new brand called Airwalk is fast becoming the coolest sneaker of all.

Airwalk footwear was founded in 1986 as a technical skateboard-shoe company. Its high-quality, stylish shoes soon became the number one skate shoe in the industry. In 1988, Airwalk was the first footwear company to enter the snowboard boot market; it is still the number one brand in this market as well. In 1989, Airwalk used its strong brand base in these sports to launch its casual footwear line, targeted at youths ages 7 to 25. By 1994, Airwalk was declared "the next big shoe" by *Esquire* magazine and sales tripled over the previous year. When Airwalk launched its first consumer-brand image advertising campaign in 1995, sales increased 400 percent to nearly $200 million. In 1996, sales soared to more than $300 million! Retailers named Airwalk the top brand they wanted to add in 1996 and the hottest brand at retail after Nike.

Airwalk's phenomenal growth stems from its ability to connect with its target audience. The casual footwear purchase decisions of young people around the world are based on style, image, and what's cool or hip. Airwalk's advertising agency, Lambesis, Inc., has established Airwalk as the harbinger of style in casual footwear. The marketing strategy for the brand rests on the tripod of sports, style, and entertainment. Airwalk's product line consists of original designs and colors that lead the customer and complement the alternative looks that have become popular among young people.

Airwalk TV commercials and print ads cut through the media clutter with humor, irreverence, and unrestrained attitude. Kids say they collect Airwalk ads because they are cool. In many countries, young people even steal Airwalk's bus shelter posters and hang them in their rooms. The best skateboarders, snowboarders, mountain-bike riders, and surfers are Airwalk team riders and represent the company in key competitions around the world. Influential bands and musicians such as the Beastie Boys, Green Day, Pearl Jam, and R.E.M. wear Airwalks and lend credibility to the brand. Airwalk's agency gets product placement in movies, music videos, skateboard/BMX camps, and fashion magazine photos. Airwalk sponsors events such as Board-Aid (a celebrity snowboard event), the U.S. Surf Open, the World Skate Competition, Destination Extreme, and the Lollapalooza concert tour.

A few years ago Airwalk was virtually unknown beyond skateboarders, snowboarders, and other action sports enthusiasts. But now Teen Research Unlimited reports that Airwalk is among the top 20% of "coolest" brands and still climbing up the TRU cool-meter. The only thing rising faster appears to be Airwalk's sales!

Source: Jeff Jensen, "Airwalk Plans Futuristic Ads for Hip New Shoe Line," *Advertising Age*, January 20, 1997, p. 10; Lambesis Advertising.

The opening vignette illustrates how the roles of advertising and promotion are changing in modern marketing. In the past, marketers such as Airwalk often relied primarily on advertising through the mass media to promote their products. Today many companies are taking a new approach to marketing and promotion: they integrate their advertising efforts with a variety of other communication techniques such as sales promotion, direct marketing, publicity and public relations (PR), and event sponsorships. They are also recognizing that advertising and other forms of promotion are most effective when coordinated with other elements of the marketing program.

The various marketing communication tools used by Airwalk to promote its shoes show how marketers are using an *integrated marketing communications* approach to gain a competitive advantage. Advertising is done in a variety of media, including television, magazines, outdoor posters, and wall paintings. Airwalk has a website on the Internet that provides updated information about its products, events and competitions the company sponsors, retailers, and other interesting items (see Exhibit 1–1). Publicity for the brand is generated through press releases and PR activities as well as key product placements in movies, music videos, and fashion photos. Airwalk sponsors concerts, action sports events, and fashion shows to reach members of its target audience as well as others who can influence the image and popularity of its shoes. Promotional efforts for Airwalk shoes are also carried to the store level with point-of-purchase displays and materials as well as training, contests, gifts, and incentives for retail store personnel.

Airwalk and thousands of other companies recognize that the way they must market their products and services is changing rapidly. The fragmentation of mass markets, the

EXHIBIT 1–1
Airwalk provides consumers with information through its website on the Internet

Sharon Lee is the account director at Lambesis, the agency in Del Mar, CA, that is credited for putting the Airwalk brand on the map and was recently named the "Best Agency on the West Coast" by the American Advertising

SHARON LEE

"To communicate with young people you must know what they think and how they think."

Federation. As the Airwalk account director, Sharon was instrumental in shaping and developing an image for Airwalk, and positioning the brand for international recognition. Her creativity and innovative thinking lead the development of IMC programs that helped catapult Airwalk from a virtually unknown brand to one of the hottest brands at retail. Airwalk established such credibility with consumers and the trade that it is immediately grouped in the same category with major brands such as Nike, Reebok, and Converse.

When Sharon joined Lambesis in 1993, there were only seven employees in a small office. While the agency was small in size, its ambitions and thinking were big. Sharon remembers that everyone had to wear several hats when she first joined Lambesis, but even today she never stops looking at the big picture noting that "To be an effective account manager, it is critical to be an expert in all departments including planning, media, production, and creative. The new renaissance account person is a deft thinker in all the areas that contribute to shaping the brand identity."

Sharon Lee credits most of her success to her ability to think "outside the box" and her unrelenting belief in advocating the best strategies and executions for the agency's clients. "Much of my job is properly articulating the goals and thinking of the agency to the client. They must believe in the agency's thinking to allow us to spend their money and produce creative executions that they may not personally agree with." Sharon also feels it is her role to be an advocate for the consumer's opinion as well as the client's and the agency's. As such, she spends a lot of her time working with Lambesis' consumer research department to remain knowledgeable about her client's customers, many of whom are teenagers. She notes that "to effectively communicate with the youth audience, it is important to earn their respect by knowing what they think and how they think. You must stay one step ahead of them by constantly studying what they are reading, doing, listening to, playing, and watching."

Sharon takes great pride in the advertising Lambesis created for Airwalk. She knows it played a key role in achieving the strategic objective she and the agency set for the brand—for Airwalk to be a cultural icon for the youth market. She feels the Airwalk strategy was very innovative and provided a firm foundation that allowed the agency to produce its best creative work. The print campaign created a great stir because of its arresting visuals of youth attitude, angst, and style while the television spots created a new genre of youth lifestyle advertising. Both executions were produced at the quality level of entertainment—not advertising. The TV spots use feature film directors, sound designers, production engineers, wardrobe designers, editors, and cinematographers. Sharon notes: "We took the production to this level because we know that we have to make the consumer want to watch the commercial. We are competing with programming for their attention, not just other commercials." This strategy has been extremely successful. She proudly notes that "Young people are taking Airwalk posters out of bus shelters, collecting the magazine ads, and discussing the latest commercial with their friends as if they were speaking about a favorite TV show or movie. That is when we know that the brand has become a part of their culture—when they accept it into their everyday lives and have an emotional attachment to it."

Sharon started her career in advertising as a print production manager at Ketchum Advertising in Los Angeles where she worked for two years. She made the move into account service to take on new challenges and to have an opportunity to develop and shape the image of brands. In addition to Airwalk, she has been instrumental in shaping the image for brands such as Guess Jeans, Baby Guess, Guess Kids, Charles David Footwear, Josten's Learning Software, Jonathan Martin Clothing, and Mattel Sports. She is one of the youngest account directors in the industry and her innovative thinking is helping to redefine the role of account service.

Sharon has a BA with honors from Claremont McKenna College.

explosion of new technologies, economic uncertainties, and the emergence of global markets and competition are all changing the way companies approach marketing as well as advertising and promotion. Developing marketing communications programs that are responsive to these changes is critical to the success of many organizations. Advertising and other forms of promotion will continue to play an important role in their integrated marketing programs.

THE GROWTH OF ADVERTISING AND PROMOTION

Advertising and promotion are an integral part of our social and economic systems. In our complex society, advertising has evolved into a vital communications system for both consumers and businesses. The ability of advertising and other promotional methods to deliver carefully prepared messages to target audiences has given them a major role in the marketing programs of most organizations. Companies ranging from large multinational corporations to small retailers increasingly rely on advertising and promotion to help them market products and services. In market-based economies, consumers have learned to rely on advertising and other forms of promotion for information they can use in making purchase decisions.

Evidence of the increasing importance of advertising and promotion comes from the growth in expenditures in these areas. In 1980, advertising expenditures in the United States were $53 billion, and $49 billion was spent on sales promotion techniques such as product samples, coupons, contests, sweepstakes, premiums, rebates, and allowances and discounts to retailers. By 1996, an estimated $174 billion was spent on local and national advertising, while sales promotion expenditures increased to more than $200 billion![1] Companies bombarded the U.S. consumer with messages and promotional offers, collectively spending more than $12 a week on every man, woman, and child in the country—nearly 50 percent more per capita than in any other nation.

Promotional expenditures in international markets have grown as well. Advertising expenditures outside the United States increased from $55 billion in 1980 to nearly $220 billion by 1996.[2] Both foreign and domestic companies spend billions more on sales promotion, personal selling, direct marketing, event sponsorships, and public relations, all important parts of a firm's marketing communications program.

The tremendous growth in expenditures for advertising and promotion reflects in part the growth of the U.S. and global economies. For example, Global Perspective 1–1 discusses how expansion-minded marketers are taking advantage of growth opportunities in various regions of the world. The growth in promotional expenditures also reflects the fact that marketers around the world recognize the value and importance of advertising and promotion. Promotional strategies play an important role in the marketing programs of companies as they attempt to communicate with and sell their products to their customers. To understand the roles advertising and promotion play in the marketing process, let us first examine the marketing function.

WHAT IS MARKETING?

Before reading on, stop for a moment and think about how you would define marketing. Chances are that each reader of this book will come up with a somewhat different answer, since marketing is often viewed in terms of individual activities that constitute the overall marketing process. One popular conception of marketing is that it primarily involves sales. Other perspectives view marketing as consisting of advertising or retailing activities. For some of you, market research, pricing, or product planning may come to mind.

While all these activities are part of marketing, it encompasses more than just these individual elements. The American Marketing Association, which represents marketing professions in the United States and Canada, defines **marketing** as

> the process of planning and executing the conception, pricing, promotion, and distribution of ideas, goods, and services to create exchanges that satisfy individual and organizational objectives.[3]

Effective marketing requires that managers recognize the interdependence of such activities as sales and promotion and how they can be combined to develop a marketing program.

Global Perspective 1–1
Reaching Consumers around the World

When Microsoft Corp. launched Windows 95, its new operating system for personal computers, the company turned its debut into a worldwide marketing event. On the day the product was introduced, a four-story-high Windows 95 balloon sailed over Sydney Harbor in Australia as musicians and dancers performed. Across the globe, the *Times* of London printed its first fully sponsored edition in its 307-year history. All 1.5 million copies of the paper were bought by Microsoft and distributed free along with an advertising supplement. In New York City, a Windows 95 light show was created for the Empire State Building. Consumers lined up at retail stores around the world to be the first to buy the new software the moment the clock struck midnight on August 23, the first day it was available.

Microsoft's worldwide launch of Windows 95 is another example of how companies are looking beyond their borders and developing marketing and promotional programs for global markets. Nearly 80 percent of the world's population lives in developing areas, and consumers in these countries represent an enormous market for all kinds of products and services.

The world's largest markets are developing in Asia and marketers are using a variety of integrated marketing communication techniques to pursue the opportunities in countries like China, India, and Thailand. Intel is placing television and billboard ads throughout China to establish brand awareness for its microprocessors, which serve as the brains of personal computers. The company also distributed nearly a million bike reflectors—which glow in the dark with the words "Intel Inside Pentium Processor"—in China's biggest cities. Citicorp's Citibank unit has captured 40 percent of Thailand's credit-card market, relying primarily on a sales force of 600 part-timers who are paid a fee for each applicant approved.

Global marketers are also recognizing the tremendous opportunities for selling sports in Asia. From Bombay to Beijing to Bangkok, foreign sports promoters, broadcasters, and consumer-product companies are pouring millions of dollars into sports. Companies are lining up to take advantage of the integrated marketing opportunities associated with corporate sponsorship of sporting events. Yonex Corp. pays $2 million annually to be the exclusive equipment sponsor for Indonesia's national badminton team. Hiram Walker, R. J. Reynolds, and Rado Uhren sponsor golf, tennis, and auto-racing events. MasterCard, Pepsi, Gillette, and Canon have all signed four-year, $2.6 million deals to sponsor Asian soccer. Nike sponsors four teams in China's new professional soccer league—including one owned by the People's Liberation Army. Broadcasters such as the Fox Sports Network (which is part of Rupert Murdoch's Star TV Asian satellite network) and ESPN are purchasing the broadcast rights for popular Asian sports such as badminton, cricket, and soccer, as well as golf and volleyball.

Companies are recognizing that emerging markets in Asia as well as other parts of the world offer tremendous opportunities for growth. They also know that advertising and other promotional tools will play an important role in reaching the new global consumers.

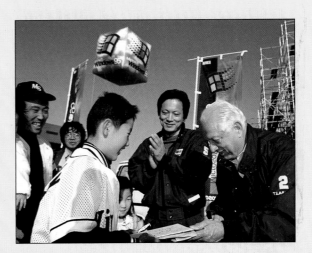

Sources: Fara Warner and Karen Hsu, "Intel Gets a Free Ride in China by Sticking Its Name on Bicycles," *The Wall Street Journal*, August 7, 1996, p. B5; "Sticky Wickets, But What a Future," *Business Week*, August 7, 1995, pp. 72–73; Leslie Helm, "Global Hype Raises the Curtain on Windows 95," *Los Angeles Times*, August 24, 1995, p. A1.

Marketing Focuses on Exchange

The AMA definition recognizes that **exchange** is a central concept in marketing.[4] For exchange to occur, there must be two or more parties with something of value to one another, a desire and ability to give up that something to the other party, and a way to communicate with each other. Advertising and promotion play an important role in the exchange process by informing consumers of an organization's product or service and convincing them of its ability to satisfy their needs or wants.

Not all marketing transactions involve the exchange of money for a tangible product or service. Nonprofit organizations such as charities, religious groups, the arts, and colleges and universities (probably including the one you are attending) receive millions of dollars in donations every year. Nonprofits often use ads like the one in Exhibit 1–2 to solicit contributions from the public. Donors generally do not receive any material benefits for their contributions; they donate in exchange for intangible social and psychological satisfactions such as feelings of goodwill and altruism.

EXHIBIT 1–2
Nonprofit organizations use advertising to solicit contributions and support

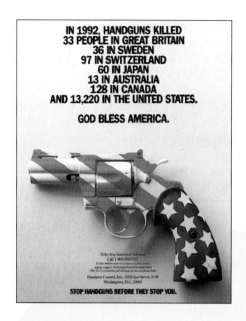

Relationship Marketing

Today, most marketers are seeking more than just a one-time exchange or transaction with customers. The focus of market-driven companies is on developing and sustaining *relationships* with their customers. This has led to a new emphasis on **relationship marketing**, which involves creating, maintaining, and enhancing long-term relationships with individual customers as well as other stakeholders for mutual benefit.[5]

The movement toward relationship marketing is due to several factors. First, companies recognize that customers have become much more demanding. They want personalized products and services tailored to their specific needs and wants. They also desire *superior value,* which they define as high-quality products that are competitively priced and supported by excellent customer service.

Another major reason why marketers are emphasizing relationships is that it is often more cost effective to retain customers than to acquire new ones. Marketers are giving more attention to the *lifetime value* of a customer because studies have shown that reducing customer defections by just 5 percent can increase future profit by as much as 30 to 90 percent.[6] Exhibit 1–3 shows an ad for the Zurich-American Insurance Group, a company that recognizes the importance of developing long-term relationships with its customers.

The Marketing Mix

Marketing facilitates the exchange process and the development of relationships by carefully examining the needs and wants of consumers, developing a product or service that satisfies these needs, offering it at a certain price, making it available through a particular place or channel of distribution, and developing a program of promotion or communication to

EXHIBIT 1–3
Zurich-American Insurance Group recognizes the importance of developing relationships with customers

create awareness and interest. These four Ps—product, price, place (distribution), and promotion—are elements of the **marketing mix.** The basic task of marketing is combining these four elements into a marketing program to facilitate the potential for exchange with consumers in the marketplace.

The proper marketing mix does not just happen. Marketers must be knowledgeable about the issues and options involved in each element of the mix. They must also be aware of how these elements can be combined to provide an effective marketing program. The market must be analyzed through consumer research and this information used to develop an overall marketing strategy and mix.

The primary focus of this book is on one element of the marketing mix: the promotional variable. However, the promotional program must be part of a viable marketing strategy and coordinated with other marketing activities. A firm can spend large sums on advertising or sales promotion, but it stands little chance of success if the product is of poor quality, is priced improperly, or does not have adequate distribution to consumers. Marketers have long recognized the importance of combining the elements of the marketing mix into a cohesive marketing strategy. Many companies also recognize the need to integrate their various marketing communication efforts, such as media advertising, direct marketing, sales promotion, and public relations, to achieve more effective marketing communications.

INTEGRATED MARKETING COMMUNICATIONS

For many years, the promotional function in most companies was dominated by mass media advertising. Companies relied primarily on their advertising agencies for guidance in nearly all areas of marketing communication. Most marketers did use additional promotional and marketing communication tools, but sales promotion and direct marketing agencies as well as package design firms were generally viewed as auxiliary services and often used on a per-project basis. Public relations agencies were used to manage the organization's publicity, image, and affairs with relevant publics on an ongoing basis but were not viewed as integral participants in the marketing communications process.

Many marketers built strong barriers around the various marketing and promotional functions and planned and managed them as separate practices, with different budgets, different views of the market, and different goals and objectives. These companies failed to recognize that the wide range of marketing and promotional tools must be coordinated to communicate effectively and present a consistent image to target markets.

The Evolution of IMC

During the 1980s, many companies came to see the need for more of a strategic integration of their promotional tools. These firms began moving toward the process of **integrated marketing communications (IMC),** which involves coordinating the various promotional elements and other marketing activities that communicate with a firm's customers.[7] As marketers embraced the concept of integrated marketing communications, they began asking their ad agencies to coordinate the use of a variety of promotional tools rather than relying primarily on media advertising. A number of companies also began to look beyond traditional advertising agencies and use other types of promotional specialists to develop and implement various components of their promotional plans.

Many agencies responded to the call for synergy among the various promotional tools by acquiring PR, sales promotion, and direct marketing companies and touting themselves as IMC agencies that offer one-stop shopping for all of their clients' promotional needs.[8] Some agencies became involved in these nonadvertising areas to gain control over their clients' promotional programs and budgets and struggled to offer any real value beyond creating advertising. However, the advertising industry soon recognized that IMC was more than just a fad. Terms such as *new advertising, orchestration,* and *seamless communication* were used to describe the concept of integration.[9] A task force from the American Association of Advertising Agencies (the 4As) developed one of the first definitions of integrated marketing communications:

a concept of marketing communications planning that recognizes the added value of a comprehensive plan that evaluates the strategic roles of a variety of communication disciplines—for example, general advertising, direct response, sales promotion, and public relations—and combines these disciplines to provide clarity, consistency, and maximum communications impact.[10]

The 4As' definition focuses on the process of using all forms of promotion to achieve maximum communications impact. However, advocates of the IMC concept, such as Don Schultz of Northwestern University, argue for an even broader perspective that considers *all sources of brand or company contact* that a customer or prospect has with a product or service.[11] Schultz and others note that integrated marketing communications calls for a "big picture" approach to planning marketing and promotion programs and coordinating the various communication functions. It requires firms to develop a total marketing communications strategy that recognizes how all of a firm's marketing activities, not just promotion, communicate with its customers.

Consumers' perceptions of a company and/or its various brands are a synthesis of the bundle of messages they receive or contacts they have (such as media advertisements, price, package design, direct marketing efforts, publicity, sales promotions, messages on the Internet, point-of-purchase displays, and even type of store where a product or service is sold). Integrated marketing communications seeks to have all of a company's marketing and promotional activities project a consistent, unified image to the marketplace.

For example, a high price may symbolize quality to customers, as may the shape or design of a product, its packaging, brand name, or the image of the stores in which it is sold. Vanderbilt perfume is one product that uses a distinctive package and brand name as well as a high price to connote a quality, upscale image that is reinforced by its advertising (Exhibit 1–4). Although the product is available in mass retail outlets, its positioning is premium, as reflected in both the package and the price.

Many companies have adopted this broader perspective of IMC. They see it as a way to coordinate and manage their marketing communication programs to ensure that they give customers a consistent message about the company and/or its brands. For these companies, the IMC approach represents an improvement over the traditional method of treating the various communication elements as virtually separate activities. However, as marketers become more sophisticated in their understanding of IMC, they recognize that it offers more than just ideas for coordinating all of the elements of the marketing and promotional program. The IMC approach helps companies identify the most appropriate and effective methods to contact customers as well as other stakeholders such as employees, suppliers, investors, media, and the general public.

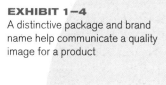

EXHIBIT 1—4
A distinctive package and brand name help communicate a quality image for a product

Reasons for the Growing Importance of IMC

The move toward integrated marketing communications has been called one of the most significant marketing developments of the 90s.[12] There are a number of reasons why marketers are adopting the concept. A fundamental reason is that they understand the value of strategically integrating the various communication functions rather than having them operate autonomously. By coordinating their marketing communication efforts, companies can avoid duplication, take advantage of synergy among various communication tools, and develop more efficient and effective marketing communication programs. Advocates of IMC argue that it is one of the easiest ways a company can maximize the return on its investment in marketing and promotion.[13]

The move to integrated marketing communications also reflects an adaptation by marketers to a changing environment, particularly with respect to consumers, technology, and media. Major changes have occurred among consumers with respect to demographics, lifestyles, media use, and buying and shopping patterns. For example, cable TV and more recently digital satellite systems have vastly expanded the number of channels available to households. Some of these channels offer 24-hour shopping networks; others contain 30- or 60-minute direct response appeals known as *infomercials*, which look more like TV shows than ads. Every day more consumers are surfing the Internet's World Wide Web. Online services such as CompuServe, America Online, and Prodigy provide information and entertainment as well as the opportunity to shop for and order a vast array of products and services. Marketers are responding by developing home pages where they can advertise their products and services interactively as well as transact sales. For example, American Airlines offers its AAccess Interactive Travel Network through its website. Travelers can use AAccess to plan flights and purchase tickets on American and other major airlines, as well as to make hotel and rental-car reservations.

Even as new technologies and formats create new ways for marketers to reach consumers, they are affecting the more traditional media. Television, radio, magazines, and newspapers are becoming more fragmented and reaching smaller and more selective audiences. A recent survey of leading U.S. advertising executives on trends that will shape the industry into the next century identified the segmentation of media audiences by new media technologies as the most important development.[14] In addition to the decline in audience size for many media, marketers are facing the problem that consumers are less responsive to traditional advertising. These factors are prompting many marketers to look for alternative ways to communicate with their customers. IMC Perspective 1–2 discusses just how far marketers are going in their efforts to find new ways to reach consumers and disguise their advertising messages by making them part of popular culture.

The integrated marketing communications movement is also being driven by changes in the ways companies market their products and services. A major reason for the growing importance of the IMC approach is the ongoing revolution that is changing the rules of marketing and the role of the traditional advertising agency.[15] Major characteristics of this marketing revolution include:

- A shifting of marketing dollars from media advertising to other forms of promotion, particularly consumer and trade-oriented sales promotions. Many marketers feel that traditional media advertising has become too expensive and is not cost effective. Also, escalating price competition in many markets has resulted in marketers pouring more of their promotional budgets into price promotions rather than media advertising.

IMC Perspective 1–2
Postmodern Advertising: Making Messages Part of Popular Culture

Consumers have long had a love/hate relationship with advertising. We enjoy watching music- and celebrity-laden commercials that are often more entertaining, humorous, and/or interesting than the programs they are sponsoring. We purchase magazines such as *Glamour, Vogue,* and *GQ,* which contain more ad pages than articles.

But many consumers, especially the younger generation, are turned off by advertising. They are tired of being bombarded with sales messages—and for good reason. The networks air over 6,000 commercials a week and nearly 15 minutes of every prime-time hour is devoted to ads or promotions for upcoming shows. Moreover, marketers are putting advertising messages everywhere: in theaters and toilet stalls, on shopping carts, computer screens, and airline ticket jackets, at self-serve gasoline pumps, and anywhere else they can reach consumers. Snapple slapped ads for its beverages on kiwis and mangoes as well as on the arms that sweep away toppled pins in bowling alleys. Lingerie maker Bamboo Inc. stenciled messages on Manhattan sidewalks that said "From here, it looks like you could use some new underwear."

Marketers recognize that consumers are growing tired of the nonstop sellathon and becoming cynical about their sales pitches. To get around this problem, many are obliterating the lines between advertising and entertainment by creating ads that appear to be part of popular culture rather than sales messages. These new age advertisers are redefining the notion of what an ad is and where it runs. In this era of postmodern advertising, stealth messages are being woven into the culture and embedded into movies and TV shows or made into their own form of entertainment.

Marketers hire product placement firms to make their brands part of TV shows and movies. The characters on "Seinfeld" talk about shopping at the Price Club, chew Junior Mints, and eat Kellogg's cereals. MGM/United Artists created special scenes in the James Bond movie *GoldenEye* to feature BMW's new Z3 roadster. BMW used the movie tie-in to develop a full-scale promotional campaign to launch the new sports car. Martha Stewart, queen of the domestic arts, signed copies of her real-life cookbook in a guest spot on the sitcom "Ellen." The Elizabeth Arden Co. got more exposure than a multimillion-dollar ad budget could buy when the plots for four CBS sitcoms were written around actress Elizabeth Taylor (playing herself) and her new perfume Black Pearls.

Marketers also work to create, imitate, or capitalize on grassroots trends and fads. To help revive its aging Hen-

nessy cognac, Hiram Walker & Sons' ad agency hired cool-looking models and actors to sit in trendy clubs and talk up a new drink made with the brand. The company bought a license from Spelling Entertainment Group sanctioning its Kahlua Royale Cream brand as host for "Melrose Place" parties, which were springing up spontaneously in bars around the country on Monday nights when the popular soap opera aired. The head of integrated communications for the brand's ad agency, Lois/EJL, developed a marketing kit that was sent to bar owners so they could host Kahlua-sponsored viewing parties.

In addition to infiltrating TV shows and movies, marketers are creating commercials that look like shows rather than ads. These 30- and 60-minute infomercials are no longer the domain of self-improvement products and exercise equipment. Microsoft, Apple Computer, Volvo, Procter & Gamble, and many other Fortune 500 firms use infomercials to sell their products.

Marketers know they are operating in an environment where advertising is everywhere, consumers often channel-surf past commercials, and what is advertised in traditional ways is immediately uncool. They also know that nearly everything, from sports arenas and stadiums to the clothing worn by athletes, is now for sale. And if it isn't, enjoy it while it lasts—because somebody will be sponsoring it soon.

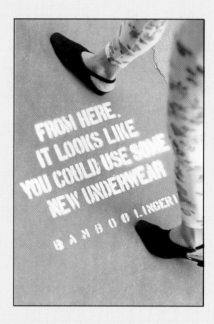

Sources: "The New Hucksterism," *Business Week,* July 1, 1996, pp. 76–84; "Brand Builders," *BrandWeek,* March 11, 1996, pp. 21–22.

- The fragmentation of media markets, which has resulted in less emphasis on mass media like network TV and more attention to smaller, targeted media alternatives like direct mail and event sponsorships.
- A shift in marketplace power from manufacturers to retailers. Due to consolidation in the retail industry, small local retailers are being replaced by regional, national, and international chains. These large retailers are using their clout to demand promotional fees and allowances from manufacturers, which often siphons monies away from advertising. Moreover, new technologies such as checkout scanners give retailers information on the effectiveness of manufacturers' promotional programs. This is leading many marketers to shift their focus to promotional tools that can produce short-term results, such as sales promotions.
- The rapid growth and development of database marketing. Many companies are using computers to build databases containing customer names; geographic, demographic, and psychographic profiles; purchase patterns; media preferences; credit ratings; and other characteristics. Marketers are using this information to target consumers through a variety of direct-marketing methods, such as telemarketing and direct-response advertising, rather than relying on mass media.
- Changes in media buying practices. Many companies are taking media buying inhouse or are turning to independent media buying services that offer discounted rates. Those that have kept media buying with their ad agencies are demanding reduced commissions and more accountability. They are also telling their agencies to consider less expensive alternatives to mass media advertising.

This marketing revolution is affecting everyone involved in the marketing and promotional process. Companies are recognizing that they must change the ways they market and promote their products and services. They can no longer be tied to a specific communications tool (such as media advertising); rather, they should use whatever contact methods offer the best way of delivering the message to their target audiences. Ad agencies continue to reposition themselves as offering more than just advertising expertise and convince their clients that they can manage all or any part of their integrated communications needs. Most agencies recognize that their future success depends on their ability to understand all areas of promotion and help their clients develop and implement integrated marketing communications programs.

A successful IMC program requires that a firm find the right combination of promotional tools and techniques, define their role and the extent to which they can or should be used, and coordinate their use. To accomplish this, those responsible for the company's communications efforts must understand the role of promotion in the marketing program.

The Role of Promotion

Promotion has been defined as the coordination of all seller-initiated efforts to set up channels of information and persuasion to sell goods and services or promote an idea.[16] While implicit communication occurs through the various elements of the marketing mix, most of an organization's communications with the marketplace take place in a carefully planned and controlled promotional program. The basic tools used to accomplish an organization's communication objectives are often referred to as the **promotional mix**. They are advertising, direct marketing, sales promotion, publicity/public relations, and personal selling (Figure 1–1).

FIGURE 1–1
Elements of the promotional mix

The Promotional Mix

Advertising | Direct marketing | Sales promotion | Publicity/public relations | Personal selling

In this text, we view direct marketing as a major promotional mix element marketers can use to communicate with their target markets. Each element of the promotional mix plays a distinctive role in an integrated marketing communications program. Each may take on a variety of forms. And each has certain advantages.)

THE PROMOTIONAL MIX: THE TOOLS FOR IMC

Advertising

Advertising is defined as any paid form of nonpersonal communication about an organization, product, service, or idea by an identified sponsor.[17] The *paid* aspect of this definition reflects the fact that the space or time for an advertising message generally must be bought. An occasional exception to this is the public service announcement (PSA), whose advertising space or time is donated by the media.

The *nonpersonal* component means advertising involves mass media (e.g., TV, radio, magazines, newspapers) that can transmit a message to large groups of individuals, often at the same time. The nonpersonal nature of advertising means there is generally no opportunity for immediate feedback from the message recipient (except in direct-response advertising). Therefore, before the message is sent, the advertiser must consider how the audience will interpret and respond to it.

Advertising is the best-known and most widely discussed form of promotion, probably because of its pervasiveness. It is also a very important promotional tool, particularly for companies whose products and services are targeted at mass consumer markets. More than 130 companies each spend over $100 million a year on advertising in the United States every year. Figure 1–2 shows the advertising expenditures of the 25 leading national advertisers for 1995.

FIGURE 1–2
25 leading advertisers in 1995

Rank	Advertiser	Ad Spending
01	Procter & Gamble Co.	$2,777.1
02	Philip Morris Cos.	2,576.9
03	General Motors Corp.	2,046.9
04	Time Warner	1,307.1
05	Walt Disney Co.	1,296.0
06	Sears, Roebuck & Co.	1,225.7
07	Chrysler Corp.	1,222.4
08	PepsiCo	1,197.0
09	Johnson & Johnson	1,173.3
10	Ford Motor Co.	1,149.2
11	AT&T Corp.	1,063.5
12	Warner-Lambert Co.	978.9
13	Grand Metropolitan	950.5
14	McDonald's Corp.	880.0
15	Unilever NV	858.3
16	Kellogg Co.	739.7
17	Toyota Motor Corp.	733.4
18	Sony Corp.	674.3
19	Viacom	647.0
20	American Home Products Corp.	634.4
21	JCPenney Co.	602.1
22	Honda Motor Co.	534.2
23	Anheuser-Busch Cos.	534.1
24	Federated Department Stores	509.6
25	General Mills	489.9

Note: Figures are in millions of dollars.

Source: Reprinted with permission from the September 30, 1996, issue of *Advertising Age*. Copyright Crain Communications, Inc. 1996.

There are several reasons why advertising is such an important part of many marketers' promotional mix. First, it can be a very cost-effective method for communicating with large audiences. For example, during the 1996–97 television season, the average 30-second spot on prime-time network television reached nearly 10 million households. The cost per thousand households reached was $11.18.[18]

Advertising can also be used to create images and symbolic appeals for a company or brand, a very important capability for companies selling products and services that are difficult to differentiate on functional attributes. For example, since 1962 advertising for Marlboro cigarettes has used the cowboy and "Marlboro country" advertising theme to create a masculine image for the brand (Exhibit 1–5). The campaign is one of the most successful and recognizable in marketing history and has made Marlboro one of the strongest brand franchises in the consumer market. The campaign's ability to transcend geographic borders has helped make Marlboro the world's most popular brand of cigarette as well as one of the world's best-selling packaged goods.

Another advantage of advertising is its ability to strike a responsive chord with consumers when differentiation across other elements of the marketing mix is difficult to achieve. Popular advertising campaigns attract consumers' attention and can help generate sales. These popular campaigns can also sometimes be leveraged into successful integrated marketing communication programs. For example, Eveready used the popularity of its Energizer bunny campaign to generate support from retailers in the form of shelf space, promotional displays, and other merchandising activities (Exhibit 1–6). Consumer promotions such as in-store displays, premium offers, and sweepstakes feature the pink bunny. Pictures of the bunny appear on Energizer packages to ensure brand identification and extend the campaign's impact to the point of purchase. Eveready has extended its integrated marketing efforts to include tie-ins with sports marketing and sponsorships.

EXHIBIT 1—5   Marlboro became the most popular brand of cigarettes in the world by developing a masculine image for the product

EXHIBIT 1—6   Eveready uses the popularity of its pink bunny campaign to generate support from retailers

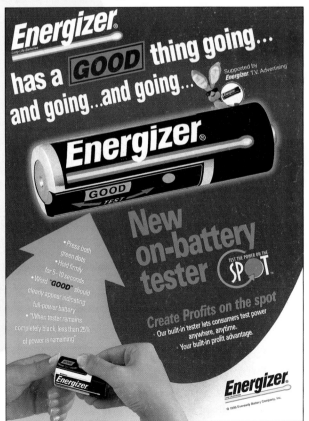

IMC Perspective 1–3
Changing Attitudes toward Milk

Per-capita milk consumption in the United States has been declining for nearly three decades. By 1995, it had reached an all-time low. Numerous ad campaigns (e.g., "Milk. It does a body good," and "America's Favorite Health Kick") sponsored by industry trade groups such as the American Dairy Association and the National Dairy Board failed to reverse the decline, and the product had little appeal to anyone over the age of 12. Although milk has many nutritional benefits, many consumers perceived it as boring and high in calories and fat.

In 1995, yet another industry trade group, the National Fluid Milk Processor Promotion Board, took on the challenge of trying to convince consumers of the benefits of drinking milk. The aim of this campaign, which is referred to as the Milk Processor Education Program, is to reverse the 30-year decline in per-capita milk consumption by changing consumers' attitudes and increasing their awareness of the nutritional value of the product.

Bozell Worldwide, the agency awarded the account, decided to make women aged 25 to 44 the target audience for the new milk campaign since they are often shoppers for their families, are the largest segment of lapsed milk drinkers, and are most at risk for osteoporosis and thus in need of milk's health benefits. The initial theme chosen for the ad campaign was "Milk, What a Surprise!" (now "Milk, Where's Your Mustache?") and features celebrities appearing in print ads sporting a milk mustache. Famous portrait photographer Annie Liebowitz was retained to take portraits of over 50 celebrities, who include athletes (Steve Young, Pete Sampras, Gabriela Sabatini), models (Christie Brinkley, Kate Moss, Iman), actresses (Jennifer Aniston, Lauren Bacall, Daisy Fuentes), and musicians (Tony Bennett, Billy Ray Cyrus). The celebrities play to their own natural audience with their own views on why milk is good. Models and actresses emphasize skim milk for developing bones without adding fat. Athletes tout milk's rejuvenating abilities after a grueling workout. The objectives of the campaign are to communicate important health messages while also assigning glamour to the product.

Bozell decided to spend the entire budget for the campaign on magazine ads, since TV would use up the budget too quickly and the ads might get lost among all the other beverage commercials. In its first year, the campaign focused on nearly 60 national and regional magazines; the agency's media director believed this would surround the target audience and dominate the medium. Magazines also provided integrated communications opportunities as publishers provided value-added programs to expand the campaign message into their editorial content.

For example, *Vanity Fair* published a booklet featuring personal trainers discussing how they keep Hollywood stars in shape. *People* ran a 50-page magazine-within-a-magazine on celebrity diets and fitness (20 pages of which were milk mustache ads). *In Style* magazine picked up the supermodel images and put them on postcards that showed up at trendy restaurants and clubs. Bozell extended the IMC efforts further by developing partnerships with package-goods companies such as Fujifilm and Keebler to get the message to stores. Millions of milk brochures were sent to doctors, dieticians, health clubs, and stores.

The milk mustache campaign appears to have struck a responsive chord with contemporary consumers. Based on a survey of 20,000 consumers, Video Storyboard Tests declared it the top print campaign of the year for 1995. More importantly, research studies have shown significant shifts in awareness of milk and its nutritional benefits, perceptions of milk as an adult beverage and a "cool, contemporary" drink, and intentions to drink milk. Attitude change was the major goal of the first phase of the campaign and was clearly accomplished. The goal of the second phase of the campaign, which includes a broader target audience, is to reverse the sales decline. With such a creative ad campaign, increases in milk's sales would come as no surprise!

Sources: Chad Rubel, "Mustache Ads Change Attitude toward Milk," *Marketing News*, August 26, 1996, p. 10; T. L. Stanley, "The Gods of the Milk," *Mediaweek*, May 20, 1996, pp. 44–45.

The nature and purpose of advertising differ from one industry to another and/or across situations. The targets of an organization's advertising efforts often vary, as do its role and function in the marketing program. One advertiser may seek to generate immediate response or action from the customer; another may want to develop awareness or a positive image for its products over a longer period. For example, IMC Perspective 1–3 discusses a recent ad campaign whose goal is to change the image of milk and help reverse the 30-year decline in per-capita milk consumption in the United States.

Marketers advertise to the consumer market with national and retail/local advertising, which may stimulate primary or selective demand. For business/professional markets, they use business-to-business, professional, and trade advertising. Figure 1–3 describes the most common types of advertising.

Direct Marketing

One of the fastest-growing sectors of the U.S. economy is **direct marketing,** in which organizations communicate directly with target customers to generate a response and/or a transaction. Traditionally, direct marketing has not been considered an element of the promotional mix. However, because it has become such an integral part of the IMC program of many organizations and often involves separate objectives, budgets, and strategies, we view direct marketing as a component of the promotional mix.

Direct marketing is much more than direct mail and mail-order catalogs. It involves a variety of activities, including database management, direct selling, telemarketing, and direct-response ads through direct mail and various broadcast and print media. Some companies, such as Tupperware, Discovery Toys, and Encyclopaedia Britannica, do not use any other distribution channels, relying on independent contractors to sell their products directly to consumers. Companies such as L.L. Bean, Lands' End, and The Sharper Image have been very successful through their direct-mail and phone-order business. Dell Computer and Gateway have experienced tremendous growth in the computer industry by selling a full line of personal computers through direct marketing (Exhibit 1–7).

One of the major tools of direct marketing is **direct-response advertising,** whereby a product is promoted through an ad that encourages the consumer to purchase directly from the manufacturer. Traditionally, direct mail has been the primary medium for direct-response advertising, although television is becoming an increasingly important medium. Direct-response advertising and other forms of direct marketing have become very popular in recent years, owing primarily to changing lifestyles, particularly the increase in two-income households. This has meant more discretionary income but less time for in-store shopping. The convenience of shopping by mail or phone has led to the tremendous increase in direct-response advertising. Credit cards and toll-free phone numbers have also facilitated the purchase of products from direct-response ads.

Direct-marketing tools and techniques are also being used by companies that distribute their products through traditional distribution channels or have their own sales force. Direct marketing plays a big role in the integrated marketing communication programs of consumer products companies and business-to-business marketers. These companies spend large amounts of money each year developing and maintaining databases containing the addresses and/or phone numbers of present and prospective customers. They use telemarketing to call customers directly and attempt to sell them products and services or qualify them as sales leads. Marketers also send out direct-mail pieces ranging from simple letters and flyers to detailed brochures, catalogs, and videotapes to give potential customers information about their products or services. Direct-marketing techniques are also used to distribute product samples or target users of a competing brand.

Sales Promotion

The next variable in the promotional mix is **sales promotion,** which is generally defined as those marketing activities that provide extra value or incentives to the sales force, distributors, or the ultimate consumer and can stimulate immediate sales. Sales promotion is generally broken into two major categories: consumer-oriented and trade-oriented activities.

Consumer-oriented sales promotion is targeted to the ultimate user of a product or service and includes couponing, sampling, premiums, rebates, contests, sweepstakes, and various

FIGURE 1–3
Classifications of advertising

ADVERTISING TO CONSUMER MARKETS

National Advertising

Advertising done by large companies on a nationwide basis or in most regions of the country. Most of the ads for well-known companies and brands that are seen on prime-time TV or in other major national or regional media are examples of national advertising. The goals of national advertisers are to inform or remind consumers of the company or brand and its features, benefits, advantages, or uses and to create or reinforce its image so consumers will be predisposed to purchase it.

Retail/Local Advertising

Advertising done by retailers or local merchants to encourage consumers to shop at a specific store, use a local service, or patronize a particular establishment. Retail or local advertising tends to emphasize specific patronage motives such as price, hours of operation, service, atmosphere, image, or merchandise assortment. Retailers are concerned with building store traffic, so their promotions often take the form of direct action advertising designed to produce immediate store traffic and sales.

Primary versus Selective Demand Advertising

Primary demand advertising is designed to stimulate demand for the general product class or entire industry. Selective demand advertising focuses on creating demand for a specific company's brands. Most advertising for various products and services is concerned with stimulating selective demand and emphasizes reasons for purchasing a particular brand.

An advertiser might concentrate on stimulating primary demand when, for example, its brand dominates a market and will benefit the most from overall market growth. Primary demand advertising is often used as part of a promotional strategy to help a new product gain market acceptance, since the challenge is to sell customers on the product concept as much as to sell a particular brand. Industry trade associations also try to stimulate primary demand for their members' products, among them cotton, milk, orange juice, pork, and beef.

ADVERTISING TO BUSINESS AND PROFESSIONAL MARKETS

Business-to-Business Advertising

Advertising targeted at individuals who buy or influence the purchase of industrial goods or services for their companies. Industrial goods are products that either become a physical part of another product (raw material or component parts), are used in manufacturing other goods (machinery), or are used to help a company conduct its business (e.g., office supplies, computers). Business services such as insurance, travel services, and health care are also included in this category.

Professional Advertising

Advertising targeted to professionals such as doctors, lawyers, dentists, engineers, or professors to encourage them to use a company's product in their business operations. It might also be used to encourage professionals to recommend or specify the use of a company's product by end-users.

Trade Advertising

Advertising targeted to marketing channel members such as wholesalers, distributors, and retailers. The goal is to encourage channel members to stock, promote, and resell the manufacturer's branded products to their customers.

point-of-purchase materials (Exhibit 1–8). These promotional tools encourage consumers to make an immediate purchase and thus can stimulate short-term sales. *Trade-oriented sales promotion* is targeted toward marketing intermediaries such as wholesalers, distributors, and retailers. Promotional and merchandising allowances, price deals, sales contests, and trade shows are some of the promotional tools used to encourage the trade to stock and promote a company's products.

Sales promotion expenditures in the United States exceeded $200 billion in 1996 and accounted for more promotional dollars than advertising.[19] Among many consumer package-

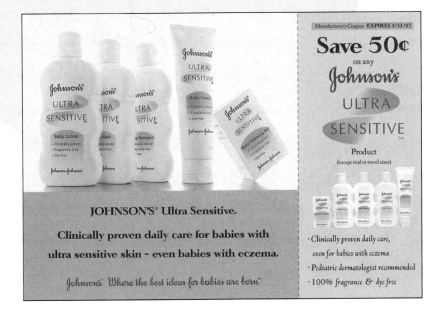

goods companies, sales promotion is often 60 to 70 percent of the promotional budget.[20] In recent years many companies, including H. J. Heinz Co. and Scott Paper, have shifted the emphasis of their promotional strategy from advertising to sales promotion.[21] Reasons for the increased emphasis on sales promotion include declining brand loyalty and increased consumer sensitivity to promotional deals. Another major reason is that retailers have become larger and more powerful and are demanding more trade promotion support from companies.

Promotion and *sales promotion* are two terms that often create confusion in the advertising and marketing fields. As noted, promotion is an element of the marketing by which firms communicate with their customers and includes all the promotional mix elements we have just discussed. However, many marketing and advertising practitioners use the term more narrowly to refer to sales promotion activities to either consumers or the trade (retailers, wholesalers). In this book, *promotion* is used in the broader sense to refer to the various marketing communications activities of an organization.

Publicity/Public Relations

Another important component of an organization's promotional mix is publicity/public relations.

PUBLICITY

Publicity refers to nonpersonal communications regarding an organization, product, service, or idea not directly paid for or run under identified sponsorship. It usually comes in the form of a news story, editorial, or announcement about an organization and/or its products and services. Like advertising, publicity involves nonpersonal communication to a mass audience, but unlike advertising, publicity is not directly paid for by the company. The company or organization attempts to get the media to cover or run a favorable story on a product, service, cause, or event to affect awareness, knowledge, opinions, and/or behavior. Techniques used to gain publicity include news releases, press conferences, feature articles, photographs, films, and videotapes.

An advantage of publicity over other forms of promotion is its credibility. Consumers generally tend to be less skeptical toward favorable information about a product or service when it comes from a source they perceive as unbiased. For example, the success (or failure) of a new movie is often determined by the reviews it receives from film critics, who are viewed by many moviegoers as objective evaluators. Another advantage of publicity is its low cost, since the company is not paying for time or space in a mass medium such as TV, radio, or newspapers. While an organization may incur some costs in developing publicity items or maintaining a staff to do so, these expenses will be far less than for the other promotional programs.

Publicity is not always under the control of an organization and is sometimes unfavorable. Negative stories about a company and/or its products can be very damaging. For example, in September 1996, negative stories about abdominal exercise machines appeared on ABC's "20/20" and NBC's "Dateline" newsmagazine TV shows. Before these stories aired, more than $3 million worth of the machines were being sold each week, primarily through infomercials. After the negative stories aired, sales of the machines dropped immediately; within a few months the product category was all but dead.[22]

PUBLIC RELATIONS

It is important to recognize the distinction between publicity and public relations. When an organization systematically plans and distributes information in an attempt to control and manage its image and the nature of the publicity it receives, it is really engaging in a function known as public relations. **Public relations** is defined as "the management function which evaluates public attitudes, identifies the policies and procedures of an individual or organization with the public interest, and executes a program of action to earn public understanding and acceptance."[23] Public relations generally has a broader objective than publicity, as its purpose is to establish and maintain a positive image of the company among its various publics.

Public relations uses publicity and a variety of other tools—including special publications, participation in community activities, fund-raising, sponsorship of special events, and

various public affairs activities—to enhance an organization's image. Organizations also use advertising as a public relations tool. For example, Exhibit 1–9 shows a corporate ad for State Farm Insurance Companies.

Traditionally, publicity and public relations have been considered more supportive than primary to the marketing and promotional process. However, many firms have begun making PR an integral part of their predetermined marketing and promotional strategies. PR firms are increasingly touting public relations as a communications tool that can take over many of the functions of conventional advertising and marketing.[24]

Personal Selling

The final element of an organization's promotional mix is **personal selling,** a form of person-to-person communication in which a seller attempts to assist and/or persuade prospective buyers to purchase the company's product or service or to act on an idea. Unlike advertising, personal selling involves direct contact between buyer and seller, either face to face or through some form of telecommunications such as telephone sales. This interaction gives the marketer communication flexibility; the seller can see or hear the potential buyer's reactions and modify the message accordingly. The personal, individualized communication in personal selling allows the seller to tailor the message to the customer's specific needs or situation.

Personal selling also involves more immediate and precise feedback because the impact of the sales presentation can generally be assessed from the customer's reactions. If the feedback is unfavorable, the salesperson can modify the message. Personal selling efforts can also be targeted to specific markets and customer types who are the best prospects for the company's product or service.

PROMOTIONAL MANAGEMENT

In developing a promotional strategy, a company combines the promotional mix elements, balancing the strengths and weaknesses of each, to produce an effective promotional campaign. **Promotional management** involves coordinating the promotional mix elements to develop a controlled, integrated program of effective marketing communications. The marketer must consider which promotional tools to use and how to combine them to achieve its marketing and promotional objectives. Companies also face the task of distributing the total promotional budget across the promotional mix elements. What percentage of the budget should they allocate to advertising, sales promotion, direct marketing, and personal selling?

Companies consider many factors in developing their promotional mix, including the type of product, the target market, the buyer's decision process, the stage of the product life cycle, and the channels of distribution. Companies selling consumer products and services

You May Not Know Us, But We Help
The North Face Satisfy Their Off-The-Wall Customers.

When The North Face, America's premier outdoor gear company, wanted to make a sleeping bag that could protect even their most high-minded customers, they turned to Hoechst Celanese. Always up to a challenge, Hoechst created Polarguard®, a remarkable insulating fiber that allows a sleeping bag weighing next to nothing to keep a body warm and dry down to 30 degrees below zero.

It's no wonder companies all over the world trust Hoechst Celanese for solutions and a never-say-never attitude. For whether it's creating the fabrics that keep you warm, the medicines that keep you well, or ways to protect the earth we share, at Hoechst Celanese, we take all our responsibilities very seriously. And with a partner like that, what company wouldn't rest comfortably?

Hoechst Celanese   Hoechst 🅱

The Name Behind The Names You Know

An advertisement from the April 16, 1992 issue of FORTUNE

generally rely on advertising through mass media to communicate with ultimate consumers. Business-to-business marketers, who generally sell expensive, risky, and often complex products and services, more often use personal selling. Business-to-business marketers such as Hoechst Celanese do use advertising to perform important functions such as building awareness of the company and its products, generating leads for the sales force, and reassuring customers about the purchase they have made.

Conversely, personal selling also plays an important role in consumer product marketing. A consumer-goods company retains a sales force to call on marketing intermediaries (wholesalers and retailers) that distribute the product or service to the final consumer. While the company sales reps do not communicate with the ultimate consumer, they make an important contribution to the marketing effort by gaining new distribution outlets for the company's product, securing shelf position and space for the brand, informing retailers about advertising and promotion efforts to users, and encouraging dealers to merchandise and promote the brand at the local market level.

Advertising and personal selling efforts vary depending on the type of market being sought, and even firms in the same industry may differ in the allocation of their promotional efforts. For example, in the cosmetics industry, Avon and Mary Kay Cosmetics concentrate on direct selling, whereas Revlon and Max Factor rely heavily on consumer advertising. Firms also differ in the relative emphasis they place on advertising and sales promotion. Companies selling high-quality brands use advertising to convince consumers of their superiority, justify their higher prices, and maintain their image. Brands of lower quality, or those that are hard to differentiate, often compete more on a price or "value for the money" basis and may rely more on sales promotion to the trade and/or to consumers.

The marketing communications program of an organization is generally developed with a specific purpose in mind and is the end product of a detailed marketing and promotional planning process. We will now look at a model of the promotional planning process that shows the sequence of decisions made in developing and implementing the IMC program.

THE PROMOTIONAL PLANNING PROCESS

As with any business function, planning plays a fundamental role in the development and implementation of an effective promotional program. The individuals involved in promotion design a **promotional plan** that provides the framework for developing, implementing, and controlling the organization's integrated marketing communication programs and activities. Promotional planners must decide on the role and function of the specific elements of the promotional mix, develop strategies for each element, and implement the plan. Promotion is but one part of, and must be integrated into, the overall marketing plan and program.

A model of the IMC planning process is shown in Figure 1–4. The remainder of this chapter presents a brief overview of the various steps involved in this process.

Review of the Marketing Plan

The first step in the IMC planning process is to review the marketing plan and objectives. Before developing a promotional plan, marketers must understand where the company (or the brand) has been, its current position in the market, where it intends to go, and how it plans to get there. Most of this information should be contained in the **marketing plan,** a written document that describes the overall marketing strategy and programs developed for an organization, a particular product line, or a brand. Marketing plans can take several forms but generally include five basic elements:

1. A detailed situation analysis that consists of an internal marketing audit and review and an external analysis of the market competition and environmental factors.

FIGURE 1—4   An integrated marketing communications planning model

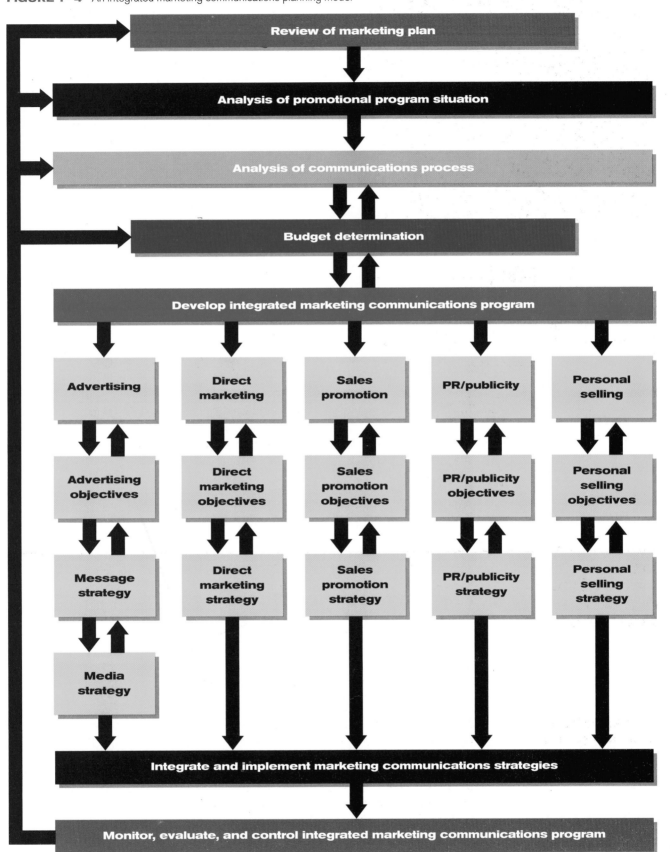

FIGURE 1–4
Concluded

Review of Marketing Plan

Examine overall marketing plan and objectives
Role of advertising and promotions
Competitive analysis
Assess environmental influences

Analysis of Promotional Program Situation

Internal analysis
   Promotional department
     organization
   Firm's ability to implement
     promotional program
   Agency evaluation and selection
   Review of previous program
     results

External analysis
   Consumer behavior analysis
   Market segmentation and target
     marketing
   Market positioning

Analysis of Communications Process

Analyze receiver's response processes
Analyze source, message, channel factors
Establish communications goals and objectives

Budget Determination

Set tentative marketing communications budget
Allocate tentative budget

Develop Integrated Marketing Communications Program

Advertising
   Set advertising objectives
   Determine advertising budget
   Develop message strategies
   Develop media strategies
Direct marketing
   Set direct marketing objectives
   Determine direct marketing
     budget
   Develop direct marketing
     strategies

Sales promotion
   Set sales promotion objectives
   Determine sales promotion
     budget
   Develop sales promotion
     strategies
Public relations/publicity
   Set PR/publicity objectives
   Determine PR/publicity budget
   Develop PR/publicity functions
Personal selling
   Set personal selling objectives
   Determine personal selling
     budget
   Develop selling roles and
     responsibilities

Integrate and Implement Marketing Communications Strategies

Integrate promotional mix strategies
Create and produce ads
Purchase media time, space, etc.
Design and implement direct marketing programs
Design and distribute sales promotion materials
Design and implement public relations/publicity programs

**Monitor, Evaluate, and Control Integrated Marketing
Communications Program**

Evaluate promotional program results/effectiveness
Take measures to control and adjust promotional strategies

2. Specific marketing objectives that provide direction, a time frame for marketing activities, and a mechanism for measuring performance.
3. A marketing strategy and program that include selection of target market(s) and decisions and plans for the four elements of the marketing mix.
4. A program for implementing the marketing strategy, including determining specific tasks to be performed and responsibilities.
5. A process for monitoring and evaluating performance and providing feedback so proper control can be maintained and any necessary changes made in the overall marketing strategy or tactics.

For most firms, the promotional plan is an integral part of the marketing strategy. Thus, the promotional planners must know the roles advertising and other promotional mix elements will play in the overall marketing program. The promotional plan is developed similarly to the marketing plan and often uses its detailed information. Promotional planners focus on information in the marketing plan that is relevant to the promotional strategy.

Promotional Program Situation Analysis

After the overall marketing plan is reviewed, the next step in developing a promotional plan is to conduct the situation analysis. In the IMC program, the situation analysis focuses on those factors that influence or are relevant to development of a promotional strategy. Like the overall marketing situation analysis, the promotional program situation analysis includes both an internal and an external analysis.

INTERNAL ANALYSIS

The **internal analysis** assesses relevant areas involving the product/service offering and the firm itself. The capabilities of the firm and its ability to develop and implement a successful promotional program, the organization of the promotional department, and the successes and failures of past programs should be reviewed. The analysis should study the relative advantages and disadvantages of performing the promotional functions in-house as opposed to hiring an external agency (or agencies). For example, the internal analysis may indicate the firm is not capable of planning, implementing, and managing certain areas of the promotional program. If this is the case, it would be wise to look for assistance from an advertising agency or some other promotional facilitator. If the organization is already using an ad agency, the focus will be on the quality of the agency's work and the results achieved by past and/or current campaigns.

This text will examine the functions ad agencies perform for their clients, the agency selection process, compensation, and considerations in evaluating agency performance. We will also discuss the role and function of other promotional facilitators such as sales promotion firms, direct-marketing companies, public relations agencies, and marketing and media research firms.

Another aspect of the internal analysis is assessing the strengths and weaknesses of the firm or the brand from an image perspective. Often, the image the firm brings to the market will have a significant impact on its promotional program. A firm with a strong corporate image, such as Rubbermaid, Citibank, Johnson & Johnson, or Sony, is already a step ahead when it comes to marketing its products or services. Companies or brands that are new to the market and those with a negative image may have to concentrate on their image, not just on the benefits or attributes of the specific product. For example, the Adolph Coors Co. is well known but not well liked by some groups, which have boycotted its products. So the company has spent a considerable amount of money on corporate image advertising in addition to its basic product-oriented ads (Exhibit 1–10).[25]

The internal analysis also assesses the relative strengths and weaknesses of the product or service, its advantages and disadvantages; any unique selling points or benefits it may have; its packaging, price, and design; and so on. This information is particularly important to the creative personnel who must develop the advertising message for the brand.

Figure 1–5 is a checklist of some of the areas one might consider when performing analyses for promotional planning purposes. Addressing internal areas may require information the company does not have available internally and must gather as part of the external analysis.

EXTERNAL ANALYSIS

The **external analysis** focuses on factors such as characteristics of the firm's customers, market segments, positioning strategies, and competitors, as shown in Figure 1–5. An important part of the external analysis is a detailed consideration of customers' characteristics and buying patterns, their decision processes, and factors influencing their purchase decisions. Attention must also be given to consumers' perceptions and attitudes, lifestyles, and criteria for making purchase decisions. Often, marketing research studies are needed to answer some of these questions.

A key element of the external analysis is an assessment of the market. The attractiveness of various market segments must be evaluated and the segments to target identified. Once the target markets are chosen, the emphasis will be on determining how the product should be positioned. What image or place should it have in consumers' minds?

The external phase of the promotional program situation analysis also includes an in-depth examination of both direct and indirect competitors. While competitors were analyzed in the overall marketing situation analysis, even more attention is devoted to promotional aspects at this phase. Focus is on the firm's primary competitors: their specific strengths and weaknesses; their segmentation, targeting, and positioning strategies; and the promotional strategies they employ. The size and allocation of their promotional budgets, their media strategies, and the messages they are sending to the marketplace should all be considered.

Analysis of the Communications Process

This stage of the promotional planning process examines how the company can effectively communicate with consumers in its target markets. The promotional planner must think about the process consumers will go through in responding to marketing communications. The response process for products or services where consumer decision making is characterized by a high level of interest is often different from that for low-involvement or routine purchase decisions. These differences will influence the promotional strategy.

FIGURE 1–5 Areas covered in the situation analysis

Internal Factors	External Factors
Assessment of firm's promotional organization and capabilities	**Customer analysis**
Organization of promotional department	Who buys our product or service?
Capability of firm to develop and execute promotional programs	Who makes the decision to buy the product?
Determination of role and function of ad agency and other promotional facilitators	Who influences the decision to buy the product?
Review of firm's previous promotional programs and results	How is the purchase decision made? Who assumes what role?
Review previous promotional objectives	What does the customer buy? What needs must be satisfied?
Review previous promotional budgets and allocations	Why do customers buy a particular brand?
Review previous promotional mix strategies and programs	Where do they go or look to buy the product or service?
Review results of previous promotional programs	When do they buy? Any seasonality factors?
Assessment of firm or brand image and implications for promotion	What are customers' attitudes toward our product/service?
Assessment of relative strengths and weaknesses of product/service	What social factors might influence the purchase decision?
What are the strengths and weaknesses of product or service?	Do the customers' lifestyles influence their decisions?
What are its key benefits?	How is our product/service perceived by customers?
Does it have any unique selling points?	How do demographic factors influence the purchase decision?
Assessment of packaging/labeling/brand image	**Competitive analysis**
How does our product/service compare with competition?	Who are our direct and indirect competitors?
	What key benefits and positioning are used by our competitors?
	What is our position relative to the competition?
	How big are competitors' ad budgets?
	What message and media strategies are competitors using?
	Environmental analysis
	Are there any current trends or developments that might affect the promotional program?

Communication decisions regarding the use of various source, message, and channel factors must also be considered. The promotional planner should recognize the different effects various types of advertising messages might have on consumers and whether they are appropriate for the product or brand. Issues such as whether a celebrity spokesperson should be used and at what cost may also be studied. Preliminary discussion of media mix options (print, TV, radio, newspaper, direct marketing) and their cost implications might also occur at this stage.

An important part of this stage of the promotional planning process is establishing communication goals and objectives. In this text, we stress the importance of distinguishing between communication and marketing objectives. **Marketing objectives** refer to what is to be accomplished by the overall marketing program. They are often stated in terms of sales, market share, or profitability.

Communication objectives refer to what the firm seeks to accomplish with its promotional program. They are often stated in terms of the nature of the message to be communicated or what specific communication effects are to be achieved. Communication objectives may include creating awareness or knowledge about a product and its attributes or benefits; creating an image; or developing favorable attitudes, preferences, or purchase intentions. Communication objectives should be the guiding force for development of the overall marketing communications strategy and of objectives for each promotional mix area.

Budget Determination

After the communication objectives are determined, attention turns to the promotional budget. Two basic questions are asked at this point: What will the promotional program cost? How will these monies be allocated? Ideally, the amount a firm needs to spend on promotion should be determined by what must be done to accomplish its communication objectives. In reality, promotional budgets are often determined using a more simplistic approach, such as how much money is available or a percentage of a company's or brand's sales revenue. At this stage, the budget is often tentative. It may not be finalized until specific promotional mix strategies are developed.

Developing the Integrated Marketing Communications Program

Developing the IMC program is generally the most involved and detailed step of the promotional planning process. As discussed earlier, each promotional mix element has certain advantages and limitations. At this stage of the planning process, decisions have to be made regarding the role and importance of each element and their coordination with one another. As Figure 1–4 shows, each promotional mix element has its own set of objectives and a budget and strategy for meeting them. Decisions must be made and activities performed to implement the promotional programs. Procedures must be developed for evaluating performance and making any necessary changes.

For example, the advertising program will have its own set of objectives, usually involving the communication of some message or appeal to a target audience. A budget will be determined, providing the advertising manager and the agency with some idea of how much money is available for developing the ad campaign and purchasing media to disseminate the ad message.

Two important aspects of the advertising program are development of the message and the media strategy. Message development, often referred to as *creative strategy*, involves determining the basic appeal and message the advertiser wishes to convey to the target audience. This process, along with the ads that result, is to many students the most fascinating aspect of promotion. *Media strategy* involves determining which communications channels will be used to deliver the advertising message to the target audience. Decisions must be made regarding which types of media will be used (e.g., newspapers, magazines, radio, TV, billboards) as well as specific media selections (e.g., a particular magazine or TV program). This task requires careful evaluation of the media options' advantages and limitations, costs, and ability to deliver the message effectively to the target market.

Once the message and media strategies have been determined, steps must be taken to implement them. Most large companies hire advertising agencies to plan and produce their messages and to evaluate and purchase the media that will carry their ads. However, most agencies work very closely with their clients as they develop the ads and select media, because it is the advertiser that ultimately approves (and pays for) the creative work and media plan.

Monitoring, Evaluation, and Control

The final stage of the promotional planning process is monitoring, evaluating, and controlling the promotional program. It is important to determine how well the promotional program is meeting communications objectives and helping the firm accomplish its overall marketing goals and objectives. The promotional planner wants to know not only how well the promotional program is doing but also why. For example, problems with the advertising program may lie in the nature of the message or in a media plan that does not reach the target market effectively. The manager must know the reasons for the results in order to take the right steps to correct the program.

This final stage of the process is designed to provide managers with continual feedback concerning the effectiveness of the promotional program, which in turn can be used as input into the planning process. As Figure 1–4 shows, information on the results achieved by the promotional program is used in subsequent promotional planning and strategy development.

PERSPECTIVE AND ORGANIZATION OF THIS TEXT

Traditional approaches to teaching advertising, promotional strategy, or marketing communications courses have often treated the various elements of the promotional mix as separate functions. As a result, many people who work in advertising, sales promotion, direct marketing, or public relations tend to approach marketing communications problems from the perspective of their particular specialty. An advertising person may believe marketing communications objectives are best met through the use of media advertising; a promotional specialist argues for a sales promotion program to motivate consumer response; a public relations person advocates a PR campaign to tackle the problem. These orientations are not surprising, since each person has been trained to view marketing communications problems primarily from one perspective.

In the contemporary business world, however, individuals working in marketing, advertising, and other promotional areas are expected to understand and use a variety of marketing communications tools, not just the one in which they specialize. Ad agencies no longer confine their services to the advertising area. Many are involved in sales promotion, public relations, direct marketing, event sponsorship, and other marketing communications areas. Individuals working on the client or advertiser side of the business, such as brand, product, or promotional managers, are developing marketing programs that use a variety of marketing communications methods.

This text views advertising and promotion from an integrated marketing communications perspective. We will examine all of the promotional mix elements and their roles in an organization's integrated marketing communications efforts. Although media advertising may be the most visible part of the communications program, understanding its role in contemporary marketing requires attention to other promotional areas such as direct marketing, sales promotion, public relations, and personal selling. Not all the promotional mix areas are under the direct control of the advertising or marketing communications manager. For example, personal selling is typically a specialized marketing function outside the control of the advertising or promotional department. Likewise, publicity/public relations is often assigned to a separate department. All of these departments should, however, communicate to coordinate all of the organization's marketing communications tools.

The purpose of this book is to provide you with a thorough understanding of the field of advertising and other elements of a firm's promotional mix and show how they are combined to form an integrated marketing communications program. To plan, develop, and implement an effective IMC program, those involved must understand marketing, consumer behavior, and the communications process. The first part of this book is designed to provide this foundation by examining the roles of advertising and other forms of promotion in the marketing process. We examine the process of market segmentation and positioning and consider their part in developing an IMC strategy. We also discuss how firms organize for IMC and make decisions regarding ad agencies and other firms that provide marketing and promotional services.

We then focus on consumer behavior considerations and analyze the communications process. We discuss various communications models of value to promotional planners in developing strategies and establishing goals and objectives for advertising and other forms of promotion. We also consider how firms determine and allocate their marketing communications budget.

After laying the foundation for the development of a promotional program, this text will follow the integrated marketing communications planning model presented in Figure 1–4. We examine each of the promotional mix variables, beginning with advertising. Our detailed examination of advertising includes a discussion of creative strategy and the process of developing the advertising message, an overview of media strategy, and an evaluation of the various media (print, broadcast, and support media). The discussion then turns to the other areas of the promotional mix: direct marketing and the use of the Internet as a marketing tool, sales promotion, public relations/publicity, and personal selling. Our examination of the IMC planning process concludes with a discussion of how the promotional program is monitored, evaluated, and controlled. Particular attention is given to measuring the effectiveness of advertising and other forms of promotion.

The final part of the text looks at special topic areas and perspectives that are becoming increasingly important in contemporary marketing, including business-to-business communications and international advertising and promotion. The text concludes with an examination of the environment in which advertising and promotion operate, including the regulatory, social, and economic factors that influence and are influenced by a firm's promotional program.

SUMMARY

Advertising and other forms of promotion are an integral part of the marketing process in most organizations. Over the past decade, the amount of money spent on advertising, sales promotion, direct marketing, and other forms of marketing communication has increased tremendously, both in the United States and in foreign markets. To understand the role of advertising and promotion in a marketing program, one must understand the role and function of marketing in an organization. The basic task of marketing is to combine the four controllable elements, known as the marketing mix, into a comprehensive program that facilitates exchange with a target market. The elements of the marketing mix are the product or service, price, place (distribution), and promotion.

For many years, the promotional function in most companies was dominated by mass media advertising. However, more and more companies are recognizing the importance of integrated marketing communications, coordinating the various marketing and promotional elements to achieve more efficient and effective communication programs. A number of factors underlie the move toward IMC by marketers as well as ad agencies and other promotional facilitators. Reasons for the growing importance of the integrated marketing communications perspective include a rapidly changing environment with respect to consumers, technology and media. The IMC movement is also being driven by changes in the ways companies market their products and services. A shift in marketing dollars from advertising to sales promotion, the rapid growth and development of database marketing, and the fragmentation of media markets are among the key changes taking place.

Promotion is best viewed as the communication function of marketing. It is accomplished through a promotional mix that includes advertising, personal selling, publicity/public relations, sales promotion, and direct marketing. The inherent advantages and disadvantages of each of these promotional mix elements influence the roles they play in the overall marketing program. In developing the promotional program, the marketer must decide which tools to use and how to combine them to achieve the organization's marketing and communication objectives.

Promotional management involves coordinating the promotional mix elements to develop an integrated program of effective marketing communication. The model of the IMC planning process in Figure 1–4 contains a number of steps: a review of the marketing plan; promotional program situation analysis; analysis of the communications process; budget determination; development of an integrated marketing communications program; integration and implementation of marketing communications strategies; and monitoring, evaluation, and control of the promotional program.

KEY TERMS

marketing, 6
exchange, 7
relationship marketing, 8
marketing mix, 9
integrated marketing
    communications
    (IMC), 9

promotion, 13
promotional mix, 13
advertising, 14
direct marketing, 17
direct-response
    advertising, 17
sales promotion, 17

publicity, 20
public relations, 20
personal selling, 21
promotional
    management, 21
promotional plan, 22
marketing plan, 22

internal analysis, 25
external analysis, 26
marketing objectives, 27
communication
    objectives, 27

DISCUSSION QUESTIONS

1. Analyze the role of integrated marketing communications in the marketing of trendy sneakers like Airwalks. How might each element of the promotional mix be used to market Airwalks?
2. Discuss the roles advertising and promotion will play as companies continue to focus their attention on global markets. What are some of the challenges marketers will face in promoting their products to consumers in developing countries?
3. What is relationship marketing? Discuss how integrated marketing communications might be used as part of relationship marketing.

4. It has been argued that the way an organization communicates with its customers is not limited to promotion, because all marketing activities send a message. Discuss how an organization communicates with its customers through marketing activities other than promotion. Cite several examples.
5. What is meant by the concept of integrated marketing communications? How might a firm that is using IMC differ from one that looks at advertising and promotion in a more traditional way?
6. Discuss the reasons why the integrated marketing communications approach is becoming so popular among mar-

keters. Do you think the growth of IMC will continue? Why or why not?

7. Figure 1–3 shows classifications of advertising to consumer and business-to-business markets. Choose one type of advertising to consumer markets and one to the business-to-business market, and find an ad that is an example of each. Explain the specific goals and objectives each company might have for the ad.

8. What are the advantages and disadvantages of the five elements of the promotional mix? Identify some situations where a firm might rely heavily on a particular element.

9. Discuss how publicity/public relations differs from other elements of the promotional mix. Identify a product, service, or cause that has been negatively or positively affected by publicity in recent years. Analyze any responses the company or organization took to deal with the problems or opportunities created by the publicity.

10. Why is it important for people who work in the field of promotion to appreciate and understand all elements of the promotional mix, not just the one in which they specialize?

2

The Role of IMC in the Marketing Process

Chapter Objectives

- To examine the marketing process and the role of advertising and promotion in an organization's integrated marketing program.

- To examine the various decision areas under each element of the marketing mix and how they influence and interact with advertising and promotional strategy.

- To examine the concept of target marketing in an integrated marketing communications program.

- To explain market segmentation and its use in an integrated marketing communications program.

- To understand the use of positioning and repositioning strategies.

For years Liz Claiborne was the hottest women's apparel brand in department stores nationwide and a favorite among working women, who liked its contemporary but not gaudy styles, high quality, and moderate prices. But in the early 1990s the company's growth began to stall as spending on women's apparel declined, new competitors entered the market, and working women grew more independent of fashion whims. Liz Claiborne recognized that it had to update an image that had become somewhat staid and reach out to a broader target market, particularly younger people.

Stop by the Liz Claiborne Curve fragrance counter. We're giving away twenty Chrysler Sebring JXi convertibles between September 1st and December 31st. Don't miss your chance to win one of these $25,000 cars.

see where it takes you.
curve for women and curve for men new from Liz claiborne

LORD & TAYLOR • HECHT'S • FOLEY'S • ROBINSON'S MAY • KAUFMANN'S
FILENE'S • FAMOUS-BARR • L.S.AYRES • MEIER & FRANK

titudes and lifestyles, these 20-somethings are a favorite target of a variety of companies who will spend billions of dollars in advertising, including perfume and cosmetics, automobile, soft drink, and detergent manufacturers. Liz Claiborne will spend $5 million on Curve alone—and many marketers think this is not enough.

Liz believes that its integrated marketing communications program for Curve will spell success. Based on extensive marketing research, the strategy was to develop a completely new brand rather than attempt to reposition the existing Liz fragrances. Spiro said, "We tried to tie everything back to what we learned in our research about this group. There has to be strong synergy between the ad campaign, the packaging, the name, and the actual fragrance." Two scents that "interact together" were developed, as were two distinct bottles and package designs. The fragrance's name came out of research showing that Xers are facing situations that previous generations didn't have to face, but they still maintain a positive attitude.

Long known as the brand of working women, the company launched a $25 million campaign designed to build brand awareness and attract a younger audience. Liz decided to compete for the highly desirable target market known as Generation X. The competition—Calvin Klein and Tommy Hilfiger, among many others—is formidable, but Liz Claiborne believes that its new brand called Curve (two new fragrances with the same name, targeted at both males and females) can go far in promoting the new image. What makes the company think it can succeed? A number of factors, including high market potential, a substantial advertising budget, and a solid integrated mar-keting communications program.

Generation X, the 36.8 million shoppers ages 20–29, constitutes a sizable market segment, with estimated spending power in excess of $125 billion a year. According to Art Spiro, Liz Claiborne's vice president of marketing, Gen X will be the primary market for virtually every product category in the new millennium, and Liz wants its share. A group with their own at-

The national print, outdoor, radio, and TV campaign uses the tag line "See where it will take you" in an attempt to portray the brand as hip and at the same time appeal to the countercultural values of Generation Xers. The ads feature a cool (rad?) young couple cruising around in a convertible; the goal is to convey the child of the eighties as aware, ambitious yet unsure of the road ahead, committed yet free. The 30- and 60-second TV spots will appear on cable networks, including MTV, VH-1, and E! (Entertainment). Print media include *Rolling Stone*, *Details*, and *Swing*. The ads were shot on the curving roads of the California Pacific Coast Highway to convey the feeling of freedom and beauty. The convertible is no accident either, as the sales promotion program includes a sweepstakes in which five Sebring JXi convertibles will be given away each month for four months to kick off the campaign. (The cars are prominently featured on the point-of-purchase displays and sample cards as well.)

The cars will be displayed in malls across the United States, with sweepstakes information available on site as well as in the media. Fragrance samples will be passed out on college campuses, and a website—a popular source of information for this target audience—will be created. All of the right things seem to have been done: strong research, selective target marketing, and an integrated marketing communications plan. Now the question is, can Liz make it work?

Sources: Cyndee Miller, "Liz Claiborne Throws a Curve with New Brand for Gen Xers," *Marketing News*, July 1, 1996, p. 1; Jennifer DeCoursey, "Claiborne Throws a Curve at Young Men and Women," *Advertising Age*, April 15, 1996, p. 20.

The Liz Claiborne example demonstrates a number of important marketing strategies that will be discussed in this chapter. These include the identification of market opportunities, market segmentation, target marketing and positioning, and marketing program development. Liz Claiborne's reliance on a marketing plan that is based on marketing research and uses all of the marketing mix variables in an IMC program reflects the solid marketing orientation required to be successful in today's marketplace.

In this chapter, we take a closer look at how marketing strategies influence the role of promotion and how promotional decisions must be coordinated with other areas of the marketing mix. In turn, all elements of the marketing mix must be consistent in a strategic plan that results in an integrated marketing communications program. We use the model in Figure 2–1 as a framework for analyzing how promotion fits into an organization's marketing strategy and programs.

This model consists of four major components: the organization's marketing strategy and analysis, the target marketing process, the marketing planning program development

FIGURE 2–1 Marketing and promotions process model

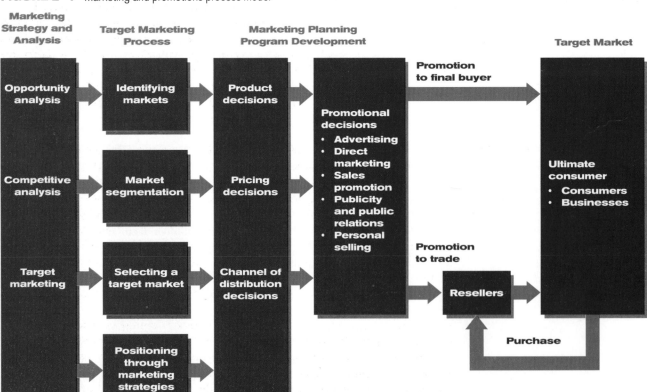

(which includes the promotional mix), and the target market. As the model shows, the marketing process begins with the development of a marketing strategy and analysis in which the company decides the product or service areas and particular markets where it wants to compete. The company must then coordinate the various elements of the marketing mix into a cohesive marketing program that will reach the target market effectively. Note that a firm's promotion program is directed not only to the final buyer but also to the channel or "trade" members that distribute its products to the ultimate consumer. These channel members must be convinced there is a demand for the company's products so they will carry them and will aggressively merchandise and promote them to consumers. Promotions play an important role in the marketing program for building and maintaining demand not only among final consumers but among the trade as well.

As noted in Chapter 1, all elements of the marketing mix—price, product, distribution, and promotions—must be integrated to provide consistency and maximum communications impact. Development of a marketing plan is instrumental in achieving this goal.

As Figure 2–1 shows, development of a marketing program requires an in-depth analysis of the market. This analysis may make extensive use of marketing research as an input into the planning process (as exemplified by Liz Claiborne's introduction of Curve). This analysis, in turn, provides the basis for the development of marketing strategies in regard to product, pricing, distribution, and promotion decisions. Each of these steps requires a detailed analysis, since this plan serves as the road map to follow in achieving marketing goals. Once the detailed market analysis has been completed and marketing objectives have been established, each element in the marketing mix must contribute to a comprehensive integrated marketing program. Of course, the promotional program element (the focus of this text) must be combined with all other program elements in such a way as to achieve maximum impact.

MARKETING STRATEGY AND ANALYSIS

Any organization that wants to exchange its products or services in the marketplace successfully should have a **strategic marketing plan** to guide the allocation of its resources. A strategic marketing plan usually evolves from an organization's overall corporate strategy and serves as a guide for specific marketing programs and policies. For example, Liz Claiborne's decision to launch the Curve fragrances is part of the overall corporate effort to attract a younger audience to the brand. As we noted earlier, marketing strategy is based on a situation analysis—a detailed assessment of the current marketing conditions facing the company, its product lines, or its individual brands. From this situation analysis, a firm develops an understanding of the market and the various opportunities it offers, the competition, and the **market segments** or target markets the company wishes to pursue. We examine each step of the marketing strategy and *planning* in this chapter.

Opportunity Analysis

A careful analysis of the marketplace should lead to alternative market opportunities for existing product lines in current or new markets, new products for current markets, or new products for new markets. **Market opportunities** are areas where there are favorable demand trends, where the company believes customer needs and opportunities are not being satisfied, and where it can compete effectively. For example, the number of people who exercise has increased tremendously in recent years, and the market for athletic shoes has reached nearly $6.8 billion.[1] Athletic-shoe companies such as Nike, Reebok, and L.A. Gear see the shoe market as an opportunity to broaden their customer base both domestically and internationally (Exhibit 2–1). To capitalize on this opportunity, Nike boosted its advertising and promotions budget by 161 percent to $495 million between 1990 and 1995.[2] Adidas and Fila have also increased their expenditures.

A company usually identifies market opportunities by carefully examining the marketplace and noting demand trends and competition in various market segments. A market can rarely be viewed as one large homogeneous group of customers; rather, it consists of many heterogeneous groups, or segments. In recent years, many companies have recognized the importance of tailoring their marketing to meet the needs and demand trends of different market segments.[3]

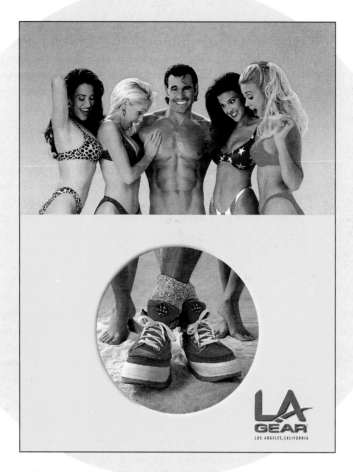

For example, different market segments in the personal computer industry include the home, education, science, and business markets. These segments can be even further divided. The business market consists of both small companies and large corporations; the education market can range from elementary schools to colleges and universities. A company that is marketing its products in the PC industry must decide in which particular market segment or segments it wishes to compete. This decision depends on the amount and nature of competition the brand will face in a particular market. For example, Apple Computer is firmly entrenched in the education market. Now it is also targeting the business segment, where IBM and Compaq are strong competitors. IBM, in turn, has gained market share in the education segment. A competitive analysis is an important part of marketing strategy development and warrants further consideration.

Competitive Analysis

In developing the firm's marketing strategies and plans for its products and services, the manager must carefully analyze the competition to be faced in the marketplace. This may range from direct brand competition (which can also include its own brands) to more indirect forms of competition, such as product substitutes. For example, when Lay's introduced Baked Lay's low-fat chips, the product ended up taking away sales from the regular Lay's potato chip brand. At the same time, new consumers were gained from competing brands of potato chips.

In addition to the direct potato chip competitors, Lay's faces competition from other types of snack foods, such as pretzels and crackers. One might argue that other low-fat products also offer the consumer a choice and compete with Lay's as well (for example, fruits).

At a more general level, marketers must recognize they are competing for the consumer's discretionary income, so they must understand the various ways potential customers choose to spend their money. For example, sales of motorcycles in the United States have declined significantly in recent years. This decline reflects shifting demographic patterns; aging baby boomers are less inclined to ride motorcycles, and the number of 18- to 34-year-old males has been declining. The drop in sales can also be attributed to the number of other options consumers can spend their discretionary income on, including Jet Skis, dirt bikes, home fitness equipment, spas, and home entertainment systems such as large-screen TVs and stereos. Thus, motorcycle marketers like Honda and Harley-Davidson must convince potential buyers that a motorcycle is worth a sizable portion of their disposable income in comparison to other purchase options.

An important aspect of marketing strategy development is the search for a **competitive advantage**, something special a firm does or has that gives it an edge over competitors. Ways to achieve a competitive advantage include having quality products that command a premium price, providing superior customer service, having the lowest production costs and lower prices, or dominating channels of distribution. Competitive advantage can also be achieved through advertising that creates and maintains product differentiation and brand equity, as shown by the advertising for Michelin tires which stresses security as well as performance. For example, the strong brand images of Colgate toothpaste, Campbell's soup, Nike shoes, Compaq computers, and Miller beer give them a competitive advantage in their respective markets.

Recently, there has been concern that some marketers have not been spending enough money on advertising to allow leading brands to sustain their competitive edge.[4] Advertising proponents have been calling for companies to protect their brand equity and franchises by investing more money in advertising instead of costly trade promotions. Some companies, recognizing the important competitive advantage strong brands provide, have been increasing their advertising investment in them. For example, Liz Claiborne announced it would increase its advertising spending by at least 25 percent in 1996.[5] KFC and Taco Bell also recently boosted their marketing and advertising spending by a combined $150 million, and L'Oreal increased its 1996 ad budget by 50 percent over 1995—an amount almost three times the 1994 budget.[6] Heineken USA increased its 1997 advertising budget by 50 percent in order to solidify brand awareness and reinforce its strong brand equity.[7]

Companies must be concerned with the ever-changing competitive environment. Competitors' marketing programs have a major impact on the firm's marketing strategy, so they must be analyzed and monitored. The reactions of competitors to a company's marketing and promotional strategy are also very important. Competitors may cut price, increase promotional spending, develop new brands, or attack one another through comparative advertising. One of the more intense competitive rivalries is the battle between Coca-Cola and Pepsi. The latest round of the "cola wars" has gone international, as discussed in Global Perspective 2–1.

A final aspect of competition is the growing number of foreign companies penetrating the United States market and taking business from domestic firms. In products ranging from beer to cars to electronics, imports are becoming an increasingly strong form of competition with which United States firms must contend. As we move to a more global economy, U.S. companies must not only defend their domestic markets but also learn how to compete effectively in the international marketplace.

Target Market Selection

After evaluating the opportunities presented by various market segments, including a detailed competitive analysis, the company may select one or more as a *target market*. This target market becomes the focus of the firm's marketing effort, and goals and objectives are set according to where the company wants to be and what it hopes to accomplish in this market. As noted in Chapter 1, these goals and objectives are set in terms of specific performance variables such as sales, market share, and profitability. The *selection* of the target market (or markets) in which the firm will compete is an important part of its marketing strategy and has direct implications for its advertising and promotional efforts.

Recall from our discussion of the integrated marketing communications planning program that the situation analysis is conducted at the beginning of the promotional planning process. Specific objectives—both marketing and communications—are derived from the

Global Perspective 2–1
Turning the World
Coca-Cola Red

For more than two decades, The Coca-Cola Company and its archrival, PepsiCo, have been battling for control of the global soft-drink market. During the 1970s and 80s, most of the battles in the cola wars were fought in the U.S. market. In 1975 Pepsi launched its Pepsi Challenge, which showed consumers preferring the taste of Pepsi over Coke in blind taste tests, and by 1984 it had achieved a 2 percent market share lead over Coke in supermarket sales. Pepsi's success was a major factor in Coca-Cola's controversial decision to change the formula of its 99-year-old flagship brand and launch New Coke in 1985. Consumers loyal to the old formula protested, prompting the company to reintroduce the original Coke as Coca-Cola Classic.

Pepsi's success prompted its top executive, Roger Enrico, to write a book about the New Coke debacle titled *The Other Guy Blinked: How Pepsi Won the Cola Wars.* Pepsi continued to challenge Coke throughout the 1980s and into the 90s as the battle shifted to the fast-growing diet segment of the soft-drink market. Creative advertising such as the campaign for Diet Pepsi that featured Ray Charles singing "You've got the right one baby, uh-huh" seemed to give Pepsi the edge in advertising for a while. However, Enrico's proclamation of victory in the cola wars was premature. Coke has emerged the victor in both the U.S. and worldwide markets in the most recent and fiercest battle yet of the cola titans.

Coca-Cola's assault on Pepsi actually began in 1993 when the company recognized that it needed to revitalize its advertising and overcome the perception that Pepsi is the hip soft drink for the youth market. The advertising for Coke Classic was turned over to the Hollywood talent firm Creative Artists Agency (CAA) who came up with the popular "Always Coca-Cola" campaign. Many analysts feel that commercials from the "Always" campaign, many of which are seen worldwide, are Coke's most successful advertising in over a decade. The new ad campaign has helped The Coca-Cola Company expand its market share lead in the United States to 42 percent versus Pepsi's 31 percent, the largest in 20 years.

While Coke has widened its lead over Pepsi in the United States, its real leadership is even more evident internationally, where Coke's market share has increased to nearly 50 percent while Pepsi's remains flat at 16 percent. Coke is not only increasing its global lead, it is helping itself to some of Pepsi's prime territories. In 1996 Coke overtook Pepsi in Russia, erasing the 10-year head start Pepsi enjoyed as the Official Party Cola. In India, a market Pepsi has owned for decades, Coke bought the leading soft-drink maker in 1994 and now has 58 percent of the market versus 26 percent for Pepsi. Russia and India are not the only markets that have chosen to go red. For 50 years, Pepsi was the choice of generations of Venezuelans and held a 40 percent market share in the company's showcase South American market. But in August 1996, Pepsi's independent bottler switched its 18 plants and 2,500 trucks to Coca-Cola, putting Pepsi out of business there literally overnight. Coke also leads Pepsi in many other large foreign markets, including Mexico, Germany, Japan, and Brazil.

Soft-drink analysts attribute Coca-Cola's worldwide leadership to several factors. While PepsiCo diversified into fast-food restaurants (Taco Bell, Pizza Hut, KFC) and snack foods (Frito-Lay), Coca-Cola kept focusing on soft drinks. Over the past decade or so, Coke has invested billions of dollars into its worldwide soft-drink infrastructure of bottling plants and distributors. Coke's global soft-drink business is also much more profitable; it pockets 30 cents for every dollar's worth of product it sells outside the United States, while Pepsi earns less than 7 cents. This means Coke has more money to invest in its foreign operations as well as advertising and promotion.

Although Pepsi is seeing a lot more Coca-Cola red than it ever expected, both at home and abroad, the company does not intend to surrender. Pepsi plans on targeting emerging markets like India, China, and Eastern Europe—all spots where Coke leads Pepsi but where there is room for both to grow. Both companies are advertising heavily in foreign markets, introducing new brands and using a variety of other promotional tools, including sponsorship of concerts and sporting events. In 1996 Pepsi launched a $500 million marketing campaign, called Pepsi Blue, to introduce a new sky-hued can in 24 countries and to reinforce Pepsi's image as the coolest cola in the cosmos. As part of this program, Pepsi is overhauling its packaging, logo, and graphics with electric-blue colors for all Pepsi brands. Pepsi plans to take the program worldwide to update its image and unify its global marketing efforts. However, as the world keeps turning Coca-Cola red, it may be Pepsi management who really turns blue.

Source: Patricia Sellers, "How Coke Is Kicking Pepsi's Can," *Fortune*, October 28, 1996, pp. 70–84; Bill Saporito, "Parched for Growth," *Time*, September 2, 1996, pp. 48–49; Robert Frank, "Pepsi Losing Overseas Fizz to Coca-Cola," *The Wall Street Journal*, August 22, 1996, p. C1.

situation analysis, and the promotional mix strategies are developed to achieve these objectives. Marketers rarely go after the entire market with one product, brand, or service offering. Rather, they pursue a number of different strategies, breaking the market into segments and targeting one or more of these segments for marketing and promotional efforts. This means different objectives may be established, different budgets may be used, and the promotional mix strategies may vary, depending on the market approach used.

THE TARGET MARKETING PROCESS

Because few, if any, products can satisfy the needs of all consumers, companies often develop different marketing strategies to satisfy different consumer needs. The process by which marketers do this (presented in Figure 2–2) is referred to as **target marketing** and involves four basic steps: identifying markets with unfulfilled needs, segmenting the market, targeting specific segments, and positioning one's product or service through marketing strategies.

Identifying Markets

When employing a target marketing strategy, the marketer identifies the specific needs of groups of people (or segments), selects one or more of these segments as a target, and develops marketing programs directed to each. This approach has found increased applicability in marketing for a number of reasons, including changes in the market (consumers are becoming much more diverse in their needs, attitudes, and lifestyles); increased use of segmentation by competitors; and the fact that more managers are trained in segmentation and realize the advantages associated with this strategy. Perhaps the best explanation, however, comes back to the basic premise that you must understand as much as possible about consumers to design marketing programs that meet their needs most effectively.

Target market identification isolates consumers with similar lifestyles, needs, and the like, and increases our knowledge of their specific requirements. The more marketers can establish this common ground with consumers, the more effective they will be in addressing these requirements in their communications programs and informing and/or persuading potential consumers that the product or service offering will meet their needs.

Let's use the beer industry as an example. Years ago, beer was just beer, with little differentiation, many local distributors, and few truly national brands. The industry began consolidating; many brands were assumed by the larger brewers or ceased to exist. As the number of competitors decreased, competition among the major brewers increased. To compete more effectively, brewers began to look at different tastes, lifestyles, and so on of beer drinkers and used this information in their marketing strategies. This process resulted in the identification of many market segments, each of which corresponds to different customers' needs, lifestyles, and other characteristics.

As you can see in Figure 2–3, the beer market has become quite segmented, offering super premiums, premiums, populars (low price), imports, lights (low calorie), and malts. Low-alcohol and nonalcoholic brands have also been introduced, as has draft beer in bottles and cans. And there are now imported lights, super premium drafts, dry beers, and on and on. As you can see in Exhibit 2–2, to market to these various segments, Anheuser-Busch pursues a strategy whereby it offers a variety of products from which consumers can choose, varying the marketing mix for each. Each appeals to a different set of needs. Taste is certainly one; others include image, costs, and the size of one's waistline. A variety of other reasons for purchasing are also operating, including the consumer's social class, lifestyle, and economic status.

Marketers competing in nearly all product and service categories are constantly searching for ways to segment their market, in an attempt to better satisfy customers' needs. The remainder of this section discusses ways to approach this task.

FIGURE 2–2 The target marketing process

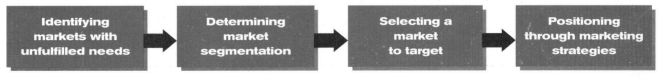

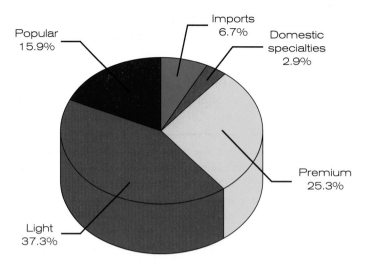

Imports
6.7%

Domestic
specialties
2.9%

Popular
15.9%

Premium
25.3%

Light
37.3%

Source: R. S. Weinberg & Associates, *Beverage Industry,* January 1997.

Market Segmentation

It is not possible to develop marketing strategies for every consumer. Rather, the marketer attempts to identify broad classes of buyers who have the same needs and will respond similarly to marketing actions. As noted by Eric N. Berkowitz, Roger A. Kerin, and William Rudelius, **market segmentation** is "dividing up a market into distinct groups that (1) have common needs and (2) will respond similarly to a marketing action."[8] The segmentation process involves five distinct steps:

1. Finding ways to group consumers according to their needs.
2. Finding ways to group the marketing actions—usually the products offered—available to the organization.
3. Developing a market-product grid to relate the market segments to the firm's products or actions.
4. Selecting the target segments toward which the firm directs its marketing actions.
5. Taking marketing actions to reach target segments.

The more marketers segment the market, the more precise is their understanding of it. But the more the market becomes divided, the fewer consumers are in each segment. Thus, a key decision is: How far should one go in the segmentation process? Where does the process stop? As you can see by the strategy taken in the beer industry, it can go far!

In planning the promotional effort, managers consider whether the target segment will support individualized strategies. More specifically, they consider whether this group is accessible. Can it be reached with a communications program? For example, you will see in Chapter 10 that in some instances there are no media that can be used to reach some targeted groups. Or the promotions manager may identify a number of segments but be unable to develop the required programs to reach them. The firm may have insufficient funds to develop the required advertising campaign, inadequate sales staff to cover all areas, or other promotional deficiencies. After determining that a segmentation strategy is in order, the marketer

must establish the basis on which it will address the market. The following section discusses some of the bases for segmenting markets and demonstrates advertising and promotions applications.

BASES FOR SEGMENTATION

As shown in Figure 2–4, several methods are available for segmenting markets. Marketers may use one of the segmentation variables or a combination of approaches. Consider the market segmentation strategy that might be employed to market snow skis. The consumer's lifestyle—active, fun-loving, enjoys outdoor sports—is certainly important. But so are other factors, such as age (participation in downhill skiing drops off significantly at about age 30) and income (Have you seen the price of a lift ticket lately?). Let us review the bases for segmentation and examine some promotional strategies employed in each.

Geographic Segmentation

In the **geographic segmentation** approach, markets are divided into different geographic units. These units may include nations, states, counties, or even neighborhoods. Consumers often have different buying habits depending on where they reside. For example, General Motors, among other car manufacturers, considers California a very different market from the rest of the United States and has developed specific marketing programs targeted to the consumers in that state. Other companies have developed programs targeted at specific regions. Exhibit 2–3 shows an ad for Big Red, just one of the regional soft drink "cult" brands—along with Cheerwine (the Carolinas), Vernors (Michigan), and Moxie (New England)—that have found success by marketing in regional areas (in this case Texas).

Demographic Segmentation

Dividing the market on the basis of demographic variables such as age, sex, family size, education, income, and social class is called **demographic segmentation**. Secret deodorant and the Lady Schick shaver are products that have met with a great deal of success by using the demographic variable of sex as a basis for segmentation. Lange Boots has effectively targeted women as well (Exhibit 2–4)

Although market segmentation on the basis of demographics may seem obvious, companies sometimes discover that they need to focus more attention on a specific demographic group. For example, Kodak and Procter & Gamble, among others, have had to redo their images for the Generation X market. The ad in Exhibit 2–5 is designed to give Nail Fetish a different look and increase its appeal to youth.

Other products that have successfully employed demographic segmentation include Virginia Slims cigarettes (sex), *IBM* (age), Coke and Saks Fifth Avenue (age), Mercedes-Benz and BMW cars (income), and prepackaged dinners (family size).

While demographics may still be the most common method of segmenting markets, it is important to recognize that other factors may be the underlying basis for homogeneity and/or consumer behavior (see IMC Perspective 2–2). The astute marketer will identify additional bases for segmenting and will recognize the limitations of demographics.

Psychographic Segmentation

Dividing the market on the basis of personality and/or lifestyles is referred to as **psychographic segmentation**. While there is some disagreement as to whether personality is a useful basis for segmentation, lifestyle factors have been used effectively. Many consider lifestyle the most effective criterion for segmentation.

The determination of lifestyles is usually based on an analysis of the activities, interests, and opinions (AIOs) of consumers. These lifestyles are then correlated with the consumers' product, brand, and/or media usage. For many products and/or services, lifestyles may be the best discriminator between use and nonuse, accounting for differences in food, clothing, and car selections, among numerous other consumer behaviors.[9]

Psychographic segmentation has been increasingly accepted with the advent of the values and lifestyles program (VALS) (although marketers employed lifestyle segmentation long be-

FIGURE 2—4 Some bases for market segmentation

Main Dimension	Segmentation Variables	Typical Breakdowns
A. Segmentation variables and breakdowns for consumer markets		
Customer Characteristics		
Geographic	Region	Pacific; Mountain; West North Central; West South Central; East North Central; East South Central; South Atlantic; Middle Atlantic; New England
	City or metropolitan statistical area (MSA) size	Under 5,000; 5,000 to 19,999; 20,000 to 49,999; 50,000 to 99,999; 100,000 to 249,999; 250,000 to 499,999; 500,000 to 999,999; 1,000,000 to 3,999,999; 4,000,000 or over
	Density	Urban; suburban; rural
	Climate	Northern; southern
Demographic	Age	Infant, under 6; 6 to 11; 12 to 17; 18 to 24; 25 to 34; 35 to 49; 50 to 64; 65 or over
	Sex	Male; female
	Family size	1 to 2; 3 to 4; 5 or over
	Stage of family life cycle	Young single; young married, no children; young married, youngest child under 6; young married, youngest child 6 or older; older married, with children; older married, no children under 18; older single; other older married, no children under 18
	Ages of children	No child under 18; youngest child 6 to 17; youngest child under 6
	Children under 18	0; 1; more than 1
	Income	Under $5,000; $5,000 to $14,999; $15,000 to $24,999; $25,000 to $34,999; $35,000 to $49,999; $50,000 or over
	Education	Grade school or less; some high school; high school graduate; some college; college graduate
	Race	Asian; black; Hispanic; white; other
	Home ownership	Own home; rent home
Psychographic	Personality	Gregarious; compulsive; extroverted; aggressive; ambitious
	Lifestyle	Use of one's time; values and importance; beliefs
Buying Situations		
Benefits sought	Product features	Situation specific; general
	Needs	Quality; service; economy
Usage	Rate of use	Light user; medium user; heavy user
	User states	Nonuser; ex-user; prospect; first-time user; regular user
Awareness and intentions	Readiness to buy	Unaware; aware; informed; interested; intending to buy
	Brand familiarity	Insistence; preference; recognition; nonrecognition; rejection
Buying condition	Type of buying activity	Minimum effort buying; comparison buying; special effort buying
	Kind of store	Convenience; wide breadth; specialty
B. Segmentation variables and breakdowns for industrial markets		
Customer Characteristics		
Geographic	Region	Pacific; Mountain; West North Central; West South Central; East North Central; East South Central; South Atlantic; Middle Atlantic; New England
	Location	In MSA; not in MSA
Demographic	SIC code	2-digit; 3-digit; 4-digit categories
	Number of employees	1 to 19; 20 to 99; 100 to 249; 250 or over
	Number of production workers	1 to 19; 20 to 99; 100 to 249; 250 or over
	Annual sales volume	Less than $1 million; $1 million to $10 million; $10 million to $100 million; over $100 million
	Number of establishments	With 1 to 19 employees; with 20 or more employees
Buying situations		
Nature of good	Kind	Product or service
	Where used	Installation; component of final product; supplies
	Application	Office use; limited production use; heavy production use
Buying condition	Purchase location	Centralized; decentralized
	Who buys	Individual buyer; group
	Type of buy	New buy; modified rebuy; straight rebuy

EXHIBIT 2–3 Big Red markets to a specific geographic region

EXHIBIT 2–4 Lange USA initiated a campaign targeted at women

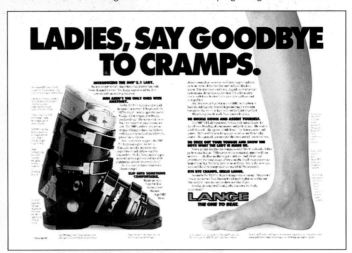

fore VALS). Developed by the Stanford Research Institute (SRI), VALS has become a very popular method for applying lifestyle segmentation. VALS 2 divides Americans into eight lifestyle segments that exhibit distinctive attitudes, behaviors, and decision-making patterns.[10] SRI believes that when combined with an estimate of the resources the consumer can draw on (education, income, health, energy level, self-confidence, and degree of consumerism), the VALS 2 system is an excellent predictor of consumer behaviors. A variety of companies, including Chevron, Mercedes, and Eastman Kodak, have employed the VALS 2 program.

VALS 2 is not the only lifestyle system available to marketers. While it is not possible to detail all the alternatives here, we will mention a few:

- *ClusterPlus.* This market segmentation system uses as its basis 47 lifestyle clusters. The Donnelley Marketing Information Services assigns each neighborhood in the country to one of the lifestyle clusters, representing groups of people with similar demographic characteristics and consumer behavior patterns.
- *Prizm.* Claritas' system classifies every neighborhood in the United States (more than half a million) by demographic characteristics and consumer behavior patterns, resulting in 62 distinct lifestyle clusters. Prizm claims to be the most widely used lifestyle segmentation system in the United States today.
- *MicroVision.* Equifax/National Decision Systems classifies all U.S. consumer households into 50 distinctive lifestyle segments at the Zip+4 level of geography, providing insight into purchase behavior, media habits, attitudes, and lifestyle activities.

Behavioristic Segmentation

Dividing consumers into groups according to their usage, loyalties, or buying responses to a product is **behavioristic segmentation**. For example, product or brand usage, degree of use (heavy versus light), and/or brand loyalty are combined with demographic and/or psychographic criteria to develop profiles of market segments. In the case of usage, the marketer assumes that nonpurchasers of a brand or product who have the same characteristics as purchasers hold greater potential for adoption than nonusers with different characteristics. A profile (demographic or psychographic) of the user is developed, which serves as the basis for promotional strategies designed to attract new users. For example, teenagers share certain similarities in their consumption behaviors. Those who do not currently own a Sony Discman are more likely to be potential buyers than people in other age groups.

Degree of use relates to the fact that a few consumers may buy a disproportionate amount of many products or brands. Industrial marketers, refer to the **80–20 rule**, meaning 20 percent of their buyers account for 80 percent of their sales volume. Again, when the characteristics of these users are identified, targeting them allows for a much greater concentration of efforts and less wasted time and money. The same heavy-half strategy is possible in the consumer market as well. The majority of purchases of many products (for example, soaps and detergents, shampoos, cake mixes, beer, dog food, colas, bourbon, and toilet tissue—yes, toilet tissue!) is accounted for by a small proportion of the population. Perhaps you can think of some additional examples.

Benefit Segmentation

In purchasing products, consumers are generally trying to satisfy specific needs and/or wants. These consumers are looking for products that provide specific benefits to satisfy these needs. The grouping of consumers on the basis of attributes sought in a product is known as **benefit segmentation** and is widely used.

Consider the purchase of a wristwatch. While you might buy a watch for particular benefits such as accuracy, water resistance, or stylishness, others may seek a different set of benefits. Watches are commonly given as gifts for birthdays, Christmas, and graduation. Certainly some of the same benefits are considered in the purchase of a gift, but the benefits the purchaser derives are different from those the user will obtain. Ads that portray watches as good gifts stress different criteria to consider in the purchase decision. The next time you see an ad or commercial for a watch, think about the basic appeal and the benefits it offers.

Another example of benefit segmentation can be seen in the toothpaste market. Some consumers want a product with fluoride (Crest, Colgate); others prefer one that freshens their breath (Close-Up, Aqua-Fresh). More recent benefit segments offer tartar control (Crest) and plaque reduction (Viadent). The Den-Mat Corp. introduced Rembrandt whitening toothpaste for consumers who want whiter teeth (Exhibit 2–6).

IMC Perspective 2–2
Does Anyone Really Care about Demographics Anymore?

Review almost any consumer products marketing plan and you are almost certain to see a market segmentation strategy based on demographics. More often than not, the demographic variables used are sex, age, and income. Target markets are often defined as women ages 18–49, or men 25–54. Media sources provide "demographic profiles" of their viewing and/or listening audience—again by categories such as men 18+, 18–34, and 35–54. (It has been estimated that roughly 25 percent of all advertising dollars spent on prime time TV are targeted to women 25–54!) These breakdowns supposedly provide us with segmentation criteria. But do they really?

In the women 18–49 category, is an 18-year-old the same as a 49-year-old? Are there any differences between the 25-year-old man and the 54-year-old man? It would certainly seem so. The definition of segmentation includes criteria such as "distinct groups" with "common needs" who "respond similarly to a marketing action"—not exactly exemplified by such broad demographic ranges as these.

As marketers become more sophisticated, they are recognizing the weaknesses associated with segmenting purely on the basis of demographics. Many recognize that attitudes and behaviors are not demographically driven. Not all baby boomers are health conscious, not all Generation Xers are detached. Says Lyle Schwartz of the ad agency Young & Rubicam, "When you come right down to it, talking about a demo like women 25–54 means absolutely nothing."

So why do marketers continue to use such imprecise segmentation criteria? A number of reasons have been offered: (1) tradition (that's the way it has always been done); (2) uncertainty (smaller segments seem to provide too small a market); (3) television dominates the media and that's how the networks set the buying segments; and (4) demos are the currency upon which ad rates are priced. While all of these reasons may be true to some extent, none provide a valid reason for continuing to segment this way.

So what can and should be done? David Reuff, director of marketing at Minneapolis advertising agency Clarity Coverdale and Rueff, suggests the following: (1) stop pretending that demographics does more than define anything beyond primal boundaries; (2) understand and use psychographics; (3) understand the whys and hows of consumer behavior; and (4) have the courage to target narrow segments. Betsy Frank, VP and director of television information and new media at Saatchi & Saatchi advertising in New York, believes that the new media appearing on the market will force advertisers to abandon demographics. Frank believes marketers will learn more about their consumers' buying habits and brand preferences from interactive TV. She says marketers will be able to reach only the households they want, for example, single-parent families, Cadillac owners, frequent fliers, or any other consumer profile. "The universe will be as few as one or as many as an advertiser would like," notes Jim Birschbach, director of ad sales at TCI. These experts and many others believe that the traditional media breaks now defined by the media—and subscribed to by marketers—will become obsolete. Demographics will be a dinosaur!

Sources: Joe Mandese, "Death Knell for Demo? Buyers Set to Move On," *Advertising Age*, July 25, 1994, p. S2; Robert Rueff, "Demographics Won't Find the Bull's-eye," *Advertising Age*, February 4, 1991, p. 20. Reprinted with permission from the July 25, 1994 and February 4, 1991 issues of *Advertising Age*. Copyright Crain Communications, Inc. 1991, 1994.

THE PROCESS OF SEGMENTING A MARKET

The segmentation process develops over time and is an integral part of the situation analysis. It is in this stage that marketers attempt to determine as much as they can about the market: What needs are not being fulfilled? What benefits are being sought? What characteristics distinguish among the various groups seeking these products and services? A number of alternative segmentation strategies may be used. Each time a specific segment is identified, additional information is gathered to help the marketer understand this group.

For example, once a specific segment is identified based on benefits sought, the marketer will examine lifestyle characteristics and demographics to help characterize this group and to further its understanding of this market. Behavioristic segmentation criteria will also be examined. In the purchase of ski boots, for example, specific benefits may be sought—flexibility or stiffness—depending on the type of skiing the buyer does. All this information will be combined to provide a complete profile of the skier.

A number of companies now offer research services to help marketing managers define their markets and develop strategies targeting them. The VALS, MicroVision, and ClusterPlus systems discussed earlier are just a few of the services offered. As you can see by examining the clusters shown in Exhibit 2–7, MicroVision uses demographic, socioeconomic, and geographic data to cluster consumer households into 50 distinctive "microgeographic"

EXHIBIT 2–6 Rembrandt toothpaste stresses the benefit of its superior whitening ability

EXHIBIT 2–7 50 market segments of MicroVision

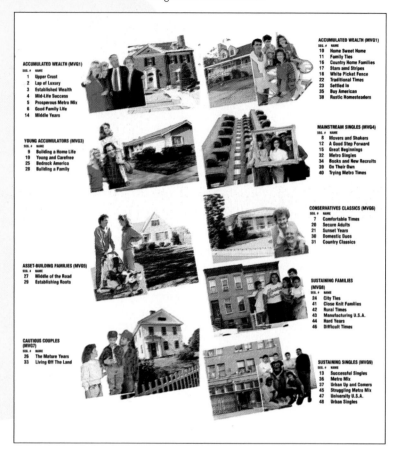

segments. These are built at the Zip+4 level of geography for precision market analysis and targeting.

Whether these microunits meet the criteria for useful segmentation is determined by the user of the system. A national company might not attempt to define such small segments, but it could be useful for companies operating within one city or geographic area.

After completing the segmentation analysis, the marketer moves to the third phase shown in Figure 2–2: targeting a specific market.

Selecting a Target Market

The outcome of the segmentation analysis will reveal the market opportunities available. The next phase in the target marketing process involves two steps: (1) determining how many segments to enter and (2) determining which segments offer the most potential.

DETERMINING HOW MANY SEGMENTS TO ENTER

Three market coverage alternatives are available. **Undifferentiated marketing** involves ignoring segment differences and offering just one product or service to the entire market. For example, when Henry Ford brought out the first assembly-line automobile, all potential consumers were offered the same basic product: a black Ford. For many years, Coca-Cola offered only one product version. While this standardized strategy saves the company money, it does not allow the opportunity to offer different versions of the product to different markets.

Differentiated marketing involves marketing in a number of segments, developing separate marketing strategies for each. The Dewar's ads in Exhibit 2–8 reflect this strategy. Notice how the two ads differ given alternate target markets and media.

While an undifferentiated strategy offers reduced costs through increased production, it does not allow for variety or tailoring to specific needs. Through differentiation, products—or advertising appeals—may be developed for the various segments, increasing the opportunity to satisfy the needs and wants of various groups.

EXHIBIT 2–8   Dewar's uses different appeals for the same product

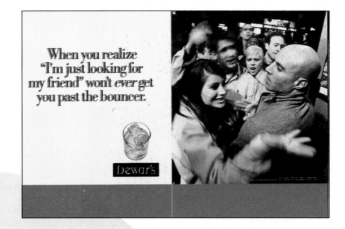

The third alternative, **concentrated marketing**, is used when the firm selects one segment and attempts to capture a large share of this market. Volkswagen used this strategy in the 1950s when it was the only major automobile company competing in the economy car segment in the United States. While Volkswagen has now assumed a more differentiated strategy, other companies have found the concentrated strategy effective. For example, Above the Rim markets only basketball clothing and accessories. The company has built a loyal following among young consumers who like its functional features (Exhibit 2–9.)

DETERMINING WHICH SEGMENTS OFFER POTENTIAL

The second step in selecting a market involves determining the most attractive segment. The firm must examine the sales potential of the segment, the opportunities for growth, the competition, and its own ability to compete. Then it must decide whether it can market to this group. Stories abound of companies that have entered new markets only to find their lack of resources or expertise would not allow them to compete successfully. For example, Royal Crown (RC) Cola has often been quite successful in identifying new segment opportunities but because of limited resources has been less able to capitalize on them than Coke and Pepsi. RC was the first to bring to market diet colas and caffeine-free colas, but it has not been able to establish itself as a market leader in either market. After selecting the segments to target and determining that it can compete, the firm proceeds to the final step in Figure 2–2: the market positioning phase.

EXHIBIT 2–9
Above the Rim pursues a
concentrated marketing strategy

Market Positioning

Positioning has been defined as "the art and science of fitting the product or service to one or more segments of the broad market in such a way as to set it meaningfully apart from competition."[11] As you can see, the position of the product, service, or even store is the image that comes to mind and the attributes consumers perceive as related to it. This communication occurs through the message itself—which explains these benefits—as well as the media strategy employed to reach the target group. Take a few moments to think about how some products are positioned and how their position is conveyed to you. For example, what comes to mind when your hear the name Mercedes, Dr. Pepper, or United Airlines? What about department stores such as Neiman-Marcus, Sears, and JCPenney? Now think of the ads for each of these products and companies. Are their approaches different from their competitors'? When and where are these ads shown?

APPROACHES TO POSITIONING

Positioning strategies generally focus on either the consumer or the competition. While both approaches involve the association of product benefits with consumer needs, the former does so by linking the product with the benefits the consumer will derive or creating a favorable brand image, as shown in Exhibit 2–10. The latter approach positions the product by comparing it and the benefit it offers to the competition, as shown in Exhibit 2–11. Products like Scope mouthwash (positioning itself as better tasting than Listerine) and Now cigarettes (comparing their nicotine content to several other brands') have employed this strategy successfully.

Many advertising practitioners consider market positioning the most important factor in establishing a brand in the marketplace. David Aaker and John Myers note that the term *position* has recently been used to indicate the brand's or product's image in the marketplace.[12] Jack Trout and Al Ries suggest that this brand image must contrast with competitors'. They say, "In today's marketplace, the competitors' image is just as important as your own. Some-

EXHIBIT 2–10 Positioning that focuses on the consumer

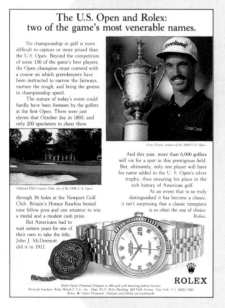

EXHIBIT 2–11 Positioning that focuses on the competition

times more important."[13] Thus, **positioning**, as used in this text, relates to the image of the product and or brand relative to competing products or brands. The position of the product or brand is the key factor in communicating the benefits it offers and differentiating it from the competition. Let us now turn to strategies marketers use to position a product.

DEVELOPING A POSITIONING STRATEGY

To create a position for a product or service, Trout and Ries suggest that managers ask themselves six basic questions:[14]

1. What position, if any, do we already have in the prospect's mind? (This information must come from the marketplace, not the managers' perceptions.)
2. What position do we want to own?
3. What companies must be outgunned if we are to establish that position?
4. Do we have enough marketing money to occupy and hold the position?
5. Do we have the guts to stick with one consistent positioning strategy?
6. Does our creative approach match our positioning strategy?

A number of positioning strategies might be employed in developing a promotional program. David Aaker and J. Gary Shansby discuss six such strategies: positioning by product attributes, price/quality, use, product class, users, and competitor.[15] Aaker and Myers add one more approach, positioning by cultural symbols.[16]

Positioning by product attributes and benefits

A common approach to positioning is setting the brand apart from competitors based on specific characteristics or benefits offered. Sometimes a product may be positioned on more than one product benefit. Marketers attempt to identify **salient attributes** (those that are important to consumers and are the basis for making a purchase decision). For example, when Apple first introduced its computers, the key benefit stressed was ease of use—an effective strategy, given the complexity of computers in the market at that time.

Positioning by price/quality

Marketers often use price/quality characteristics to position their brands. One way they do it is with ads that reflect the image of a high-quality brand where cost, while not irrelevant, is considered secondary to the quality benefits derived from using the brand. Premium brands positioned at the high end of the market use this approach to positioning.

Another way to use price/quality characteristics for positioning is to focus on the quality or value offered by the brand at a very competitive price. For example, the Oneida ad shown in Exhibit 2–12 uses this strategy by suggesting that quality need not be unaffordable. Remember that although price is an important consideration, the product quality must be comparable to, or even better than, competing brands for the positioning strategy to be effective.

Positioning by use or application

Another way to communicate a specific image or position for a brand is to associate it with a specific use or application. For example, Black & Decker introduced the SnakeLight as an innovative solution to the problem of trying to hold a flashlight while working. A TV commercial showed various uses for the product, while creative packaging and in-store displays were used to communicate the uses (Exhibit 2–13).

While this strategy is often used to enter a market based on a particular use or application, it is also an effective way to expand the usage of a product. For example, Arm & Hammer baking soda has been promoted for everything from baking to relieving heartburn to eliminating odors in carpets and refrigerators (Exhibit 2–14).

Positioning by product class

Often the competition for a product comes from outside the product class. For example, airlines know that while they compete with other airlines, trains and buses are also viable alternatives. Amtrak has positioned itself as an alternative to airplanes, citing cost savings,

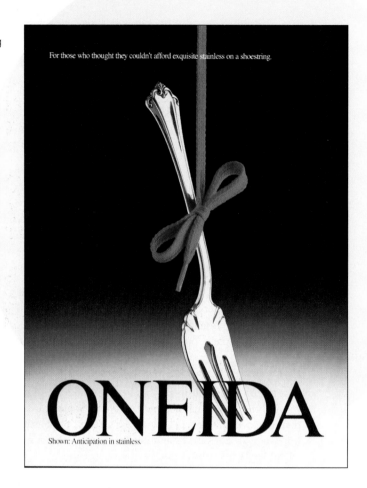

enjoyment, and other advantages. Manufacturers of music CDs must compete with the cassette industry; many margarines position themselves against butter. Rather than positioning against another brand, an alternative strategy is to position oneself against another product category, as shown in Exhibit 2–15.

Positioning by product user

Positioning a product by associating it with a particular user or group of users is yet another approach. An example would be the Dewar's ads shown earlier in Exhibit 2–8. These campaigns emphasize identification or association with a specific group, as reflected by the audience of the magazine.

Positioning by competitor

Competitors may be as important to positioning strategy as a firm's own product or services. As Trout and Ries observe, the old strategy of ignoring one's competition no longer works.[17] (Advertisers used to think it was a cardinal sin to mention a competitor in their advertising.) In today's market, an effective positioning strategy for a product or brand may focus on specific competitors. This approach is similar to positioning by product class, although in this case the competition is within the same product category. Perhaps the best-known example of this strategy was Avis, which positioned itself against the car-rental leader, Hertz, by stating, "We're number two, so we try harder." The Kleenex ad shown earlier (Exhibit 2–11) is an example of positioning a brand against the competition. When positioning by competitor, a marketer must often employ another positioning strategy as well to differentiate the brand.

Positioning by cultural symbols

Aaker and Myers include an additional positioning strategy in which cultural symbols are used to differentiate brands. Examples are the Jolly Green Giant, the Keebler elves, Speedy Alka-Seltzer, Bud Man, Buster Brown, Ronald McDonald, Chiquita Banana, and Mr.

Peanut. Each of these symbols has successfully differentiated the product it represents from competitors' (Exhibit 2–16).

The use of cultural symbols has become so common in our society that psychologists and sociologists have examined the mythological foundations underlying many characters and dissected the inherent meanings consumers ascribe to them. A museum of modern mythology that features 20th-century cultural symbols of advertising has been started in

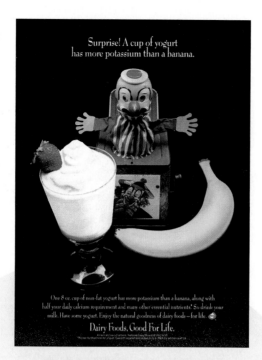

San Francisco. Part of the museum's attraction is that it traces the evolution of the characters over time, considering the changing culture of the United States and its impact on such symbols.

Repositioning

One final positioning strategy involves altering or changing a product's or brand's position. **Repositioning** a product usually occurs because of declining or stagnant sales or because of anticipated opportunities in other market positions. Repositioning is often difficult to accomplish because of entrenched perceptions about and attitudes toward the product or brand. Many companies' attempts to change their positions have met with little or no success. For example, K-mart (the store) and Goldstar (the brand) have both attempted to reposition themselves to a level of higher quality, appealing to more well-to-do customers. Both have met with limited success.

One extremely successful effort at repositioning was employed by *Rolling Stone* magazine. In an attempt to change advertisers' image of the type of person who reads *Rolling Stone*, the company embarked on an extensive advertising campaign directed at potential advertisers. The ad shown in Exhibit 2–17 is just one example of how this strategy was successfully implemented.

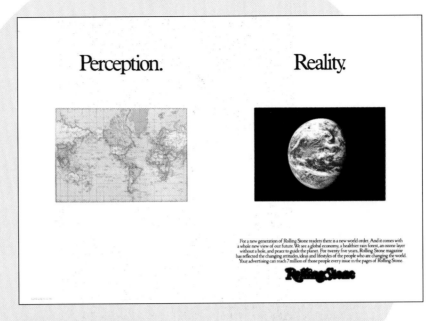

IMC Perspective 2–3 describes how other companies have also been successful in their repositioning efforts.

DETERMINING THE POSITIONING STRATEGY

Having explored the alternative positioning strategies available, the marketer must determine which strategy is best suited for the firm or product and begin developing the positioning platform. As you remember from the promotional planning process in Chapter 1, the input into this stage will be derived from the situation analysis—specifically, the marketing research conducted therein. Essentially, the development of a positioning platform can be broken into a six-step process:[18]

1. *Identifying competitors.* This process requires broad thinking. Competitors may not be just those products and/or brands that fall into your product class or with which you compete directly. For example, a red wine competes with other red wines of various positions. It may also compete with white, sparkling, and nonalcoholic wines. Wine coolers provide an alternative, as do beer and other alcoholic drinks. Other nonalcoholic drinks may come into consideration at various times and/or situations. The marketer must consider all likely competitors, as well as the various effects of use and situations on the consumer.

2. *Assessing consumers' perceptions of competitors.* Once we define the competition, we must determine how they are perceived by consumers. Which attributes are important to consumers in evaluating a product and/or brand? As you might expect, for many products, they consider a wide variety of attributes or product benefits —most if not all of which are important. Much of marketing firms' research is directed at making such determinations. Consumers are asked to take part in focus groups and/or complete surveys indicating which attributes are important in their purchase decisions. For example, attributes considered important in the selection of a bank may include convenience, teller friendliness, financial security, and a host of other factors. This process establishes the basis for determining competitive positions.

3. *Determining competitors' positions.* After identifying the relevant attributes and their relative importance to consumers, we must determine how each competitor (including our own entry) is positioned with respect to each attribute. This will also show how the competitors are positioned relative to each other. Consumer research is required to make this assessment.

4. *Analyzing the consumers' preferences.* Our discussion of segmentation noted various factors that may distinguish among groups of consumers, including lifestyles, purchase motivations, and demographic differences. Each of these segments may have different

IMC Perspective 2–3
Repositioning Success Stories

As markets change and brands progress through their product life cycles, companies often choose to reposition in an attempt to breathe new life into their products. Their efforts range from changing the product to changing the promotions to even going after completely new markets. Often this strategy fails, because consumers already have an image of the product that is not easily changed. For example, Oldsmobile has had to overcome the image of being an older person's car (remember the ad "It's not your father's Oldsmobile"?) and Cadillac is currently dealing with the same problem. While Oldsmobile focused efforts on advertising, Cadillac is trying to reposition the entire line through a new product introduction, the Catera, as well as younger-oriented advertisements. Oldsmobile has had little success; Cadillac is just beginning its repositioning effort. Some others to watch in their repositioning attempts:

- *Avon.* Remember the Avon Lady? Well, she's back, but in a very different form. Avon is attempting to shed its housewife image in favor of "Just another Avon lady," who is the most unlikely woman—for example, a fashion designer or a synchronized swimmer. To lose the image of dainty Avon ladies, Avon salespeople are now referred to as "representatives." Doubling its ad budget to $30 million, Avon will place eight-page ad spreads in *Vogue*, *Allure*, and *Martha Stewart Living*, and will present a new TV ad, the first in nearly two decades.
- *No Excuses.* The jeans company best known for its use of the notorious Marla Maples and Donna Rice and its in-your-face attitude is trying to move closer to the young female market through socially conscious ads targeted to young women's media like *Seventeen*, *Mouth2Mouth*, and *Marie Claire*. TV ads will air on CNN and TBS supporting social harmony and the Goodwill Games. Can No Excuses go socially conscious?
- *Betty Crocker.* Betty Crocker has been updated—on her 75th birthday. The eighth version of the General Mills cake-mix model is a blend of the features of 75 women who were chosen in a contest from among over 1,000 entries. The new Betty looks more like a working woman. Gone are the bow tie and prim face; in are a collarless blouse and generous smile. Betty is also multicultural—nonblonde, with a hint of Asian and Hispanic genes. The new Betty is re-created in the new image of the new General Mills.

- *Adidas.* Once the world's dominant athletic shoe company, Adidas enjoyed seeing its trademark three-stripe shoes worn by a number of the world's high-profile athletes, dating back as far as Jesse Owens and Muhammed Ali. In the 1980s, newcomers Nike and Reebok blew by Adidas in the shoe race. In the early 1990s, Adidas reported losses of nearly $100 million. Now armed with a new $270 million ad budget and a new approach, Adidas is trying to turn it all around. Sales in the United States have nearly doubled to $355 million as a result of a new positioning that features Adidas as not only a quality shoe, but "cool to wear" as well. NBA rookies Kobe Bryant (Los Angeles Lakers), Antoine Walker (Boston Celtics), and Jermaine O'Neal (Portland Trailblazers) will all be wearing Adidas on the NBA courts. Endorsements were also signed with the Nebraska Cornhuskers football team, Troy Aikman of the Dallas Cowboys, and Keyshawn Johnson of the New York Jets. The number of track and field athletes wearing Adidas increased by 30 percent in the 1996 Olympics. Supporting all of these endorsements are a worldwide advertising campaign and increased incentives for retailers to push the brand. The question is, can Adidas become cool again?
- *Kraft.* Managers at Kraft Foods are in the process of repositioning a wide variety of their brands to revitalize sales. Examples are: Crystal Light drinks (new package), Philadelphia Cream Cheese (new uses: smear it on toast, not just bagels), Oscar Mayer hot dogs and Maxwell House coffee (new distribution outlets), and Giorno Pizza (new product formulation). Kraft is also considering consolidating all of its $3.1 billion reduced-fat foods under one (health conscious) label.

Many more companies are joining the repositioning game, including Volkswagen (youthful, fun image), Poeme by Lancome (a perfume to relax with), Jello (fun and healthy), and Lotus (groupware). As you can see, the ways they go about it differ, but the goal they seek is the same. They all want a new image. Keep your eye on the market, as only time will tell whether they succeed.

Sources: Tom Lowry, "Sports Shoemaker Goes for Rebound," *USA Today*, October 21, 1996, pp. B1–2; Jack Trout and Steve Rivkin, "The New Positioning," *Soundview Executive Book Summaries*, Vol 18(2), February 1996, p. 5; Sara Olkon, "Kraft Crafts New Mold for Jello, Designs It for Kids, Young Women," *The Wall Street. Journal*, February 29, 1996, p. B2; Raymond Serafin, "Volkswagen Retools Brand Image in United States," *Ad Age*, July 17, 1985, p. 34; Rebecca Quick, "Betty Crocker Plans to Mix Ethnic Looks for Her New Face," *The Wall Street Journal*, September 11, 1995, p., A1; Yumiko Ono, "Remember the Avon Lady? She's Back," *The Wall Street Journal*, January 22, 1996, p. B2.

purchase motivations and different attribute importance ratings. One way to determine these differences is to consider the ideal brand or product, defined as the object the consumer would prefer over all others, including objects that can be imagined but do not exist. Identifying the ideal product can help you identify different ideals among segments or identify segments with similar or the same ideal points.

5. *Making the positioning decision.* Going through the first four steps should let us decide which position to assume in the marketplace. Such a decision is not always clear and well

defined, however, and research may provide only limited input. In that case, the marketing manager or groups of managers must make some subjective judgments. These judgments raise a number of questions:

- Is the segmentation strategy appropriate? Positioning usually entails a decision to segment the market. Consider whether the market segment sought will support an entry and whether it is in the best interests of the company to de-emphasize the remaining market. When a specific position is chosen, consumers may believe this is what the product is for. Those not looking for that specific benefit may not consider the brand. If the marketer decides on an undifferentiated strategy, it may be possible to be general in the positioning platform. For example, Toyota's slogan, "I love what you do for me—Toyota," allows consumers to assume they will get what they are looking for in the brand, whatever that may be.

- Are there sufficient resources available to communicate the position effectively? It is very expensive to establish a position. One ad, or even a series of ads, is not likely to be enough. The marketer must commit to a long-range effort in all aspects of the marketing campaign to make sure the objectives sought are obtained. Too often, the firm abandons a position and/or advertising campaign long before it can establish a position successfully. The *Rolling Stone* repositioning discussed earlier is an excellent example of sticking with a campaign: The basic theme has been running for a number of years. In contrast, Sears has switched campaigns so often in the past few years it has been impossible to establish a distinct position in the consumer's mind. Further, once a successful position is attained, it is likely to attract competitors. It may become expensive to ward off me-too brands and continue to hold on to the brand distinction.

- How strong is the competition? The marketing manager must ask whether a position sought is likely to be maintained, given the strengths of the competition. For example, General Foods often makes it a practice not to be the first entry into a market. When competitors develop new markets with their entries, General Foods simply improves on the product and captures a large percentage of the market share. This leads to two basic questions: First, if our firm is first into the market, will we be able to maintain the position (in terms of quality, price, etc.)? Second, if a product is positioned as finest quality, it must be. If it is positioned as lowest cost, it has to be. Otherwise, the position claimed is sure to be lost.

- Is the current positioning strategy working? There is an old saying, "If it ain't broke, don't fix it." If current efforts are not working, it may be time to consider an alternative positioning strategy. But if they are working, a change is usually unwise. Sometimes executives become bored with a theme and decide it is time for a change, but this change causes confusion in the marketplace and weakens a brand's position. Unless there is strong reason to believe a change in positioning is necessary, stick with the current strategy.

6. *Monitoring the position.* Once a position has been established, we want to monitor how well it is being maintained in the marketplace. Tracking studies measure the image of the product or firm over time. Changes in consumers' perceptions can be determined, with any slippage immediately noted and reacted to. At the same time, the impact of competitors can be determined.

Before leaving this section, you might stop to think for a moment about the positioning (and repositioning) strategies pursued by different companies. Any successful product that comes to mind probably occupies a distinct market position.

DEVELOPING THE MARKETING PLANNING PROGRAM

The development of the marketing strategy and selection of a target market(s) tell the marketing department which customers to focus on and what needs to attempt to satisfy. The next stage of the marketing process involves combining the various elements of the marketing mix into a cohesive, effective marketing program. Each marketing mix element is multi-dimensional and includes a number of decision areas. Likewise, each must consider and contribute to the overall IMC program. We now examine product, price, and distribution channels and how each influences and interacts with the promotional program.

Product Decisions

An organization exists because it has some product, service, or idea to offer consumers, generally in exchange for money. This offering may come in the form of a physical product (such as a soft drink, pair of jeans, or car), a service (banking, airlines, or legal assistance), a cause (United Way, March of Dimes), or even a person (a political candidate). The product is anything that can be marketed and that, when used or supported, gives satisfaction to the individual.

A product is not just a physical object; it is a bundle of benefits or values that satisfies the needs of consumers. The needs may be purely functional or they may include social and psychological benefits. For example, the ad for Michelin tires shown earlier stresses the quality built into Michelin tires (value) as well as their performance and durability (function). The term **product symbolism** refers to what a product or brand means to consumers and what they experience in purchasing and using it.[19] For many products, strong symbolic features and social and psychological meaning may be more important than functional utility.[20] For example, designer clothing such as Guess?, Calvin Klein, and Jordache is often purchased on the basis of its symbolic meaning and image, particularly by teenagers and young adults. Advertising plays an important role in developing and maintaining the image of these brands (Exhibit 2–18).

Product planning involves decisions not only about the item itself, such as design and quality, but also about aspects such as service and warranties as well as brand name and package design. Consumers look beyond the reality of the product and its ingredients. The product's quality, branding, packaging, and even the company standing behind it all contribute to consumers' perceptions.[21] In an effective IMC program, advertising, branding, and packaging are all designed to portray the product as more than just a bundle of attributes. All are coordinated to present an image or positioning of the product that extends well beyond its physical attributes. Think for a minute about the ads for Nike; the product benefits and attributes are usually not even mentioned—yet information about the brand is communicated effectively.

BRANDING

Choosing a brand name for a product is important from a promotional perspective because brand names communicate attributes and meaning. Marketers search for brand names that can communicate product concepts and help position the product in customers' minds. Names such as Safeguard (soap), I Can't Believe It's Not Butter! (margarine), Easy-Off (oven cleaner), Arrid (antiperspirant), and Spic and Span (floor cleaner) all clearly communicate the benefits of using these products and at the same time create images extending beyond the names themselves.

One important role of advertising in respect to branding strategies is creating and maintaining **brand equity**, which can be thought of as an intangible asset of added value or goodwill that results from the favorable image, impressions of differentiation, and/or the strength of consumer attachment to a company name, brand name, or trademark. Brand equity allows a brand to earn greater sales volume and/or higher margins than it could without the name, providing the company with a competitive advantage. The strong equity position a company and/or its brand enjoys is often reinforced through advertising. For example, Godiva Chocolates command a premium price because of their high quality as well as the strong brand equity they have developed through advertising (Exhibit 2–19).

PACKAGING

Packaging is another aspect of product strategy that has become increasingly important. Traditionally, the package provided functional benefits such as economy, protection, and storage. However, the role and function of the package have changed because of the self-service emphasis of many stores and the fact that more and more buying decisions are made at the point of purchase. One study estimated that as many as two-thirds of all purchases made in the supermarket are unplanned. The package is often the consumer's first exposure to the product, so it must make a favorable first impression. A typical supermarket has more than 20,000 items competing for attention. Not only must a package attract and hold the con-

EXHIBIT 2–18 Advertising for designer clothing

EXHIBIT 2–19
Godiva creates strong brand equity
through advertising

SAY IT LIKE YOU MEAN IT.

Nothing expresses your gratitude more elegantly than our indulgent mammoths of rich, luscious truffles.
Wrapped with true beauty and grace, they speak all the words you can't. Stop in or call 1-800-643-1579.

GODIVA
Chocolatier

sumer's attention, but it must also communicate information on how to use the product, divulge its composition and content, and satisfy any legal requirements regarding disclosure. Moreover, many firms design the package to carry a sales promotion message such as a contest, sweepstakes, or premium offer.

Many companies view the package as an important way to communicate with consumers and create an impression of the brand in their minds. Notice the effective use of the battery tester on the Duracell package shown in Exhibit 2–20. Besides offering value-added attributes beyond the product itself, the packaging gives Duracell a unique way to convey the claim that its batteries last longer. Design factors such as size, shape, color, and lettering all contribute to the appeal of a package and can be as important as a commercial in determining what goes from the store shelf to the consumer's shopping cart. Many products use packaging to create a distinctive brand image and identity. The next time you walk by a perfume counter, stop to look at the many unique package designs (see Exhibit 2–21). Packaging can also make a product more convenient to use. For example, Procter & Gamble introduced its Crest Neat Squeeze dispenser, which sucks the extra toothpaste back into the container when you let go.

Introducing
another
first
from
the first
toothpaste
to fight
tartar
and cavities.

Every time you squeeze out toothpaste this new squeezable Crest does something neat.

Oh boy.

The new Crest Neat Squeeze. Squeeze out what you want,

and when you let go.

what you don't want gets pulled back in.

Less mess. What an incredibly neat idea.

Price Decisions

The *price variable* refers to what the consumer must give up to purchase a product or service. While price is discussed in terms of the dollar amount exchanged for an item, the cost of a product to the consumer includes time, mental activity, and behavioral effort.[22] The marketing manager is usually concerned with establishing a price level, developing pricing policies, and monitoring competitors' and consumers' reactions to prices in the marketplace. A firm must consider a number of factors in determining the price it charges for its product or service, including costs, demand factors, competition, and perceived value. From an IMC perspective, the price must be consistent with the perceptions of the product, as well as the communications strategy. Higher prices, of course, will communicate a higher product quality, while lower prices reflect bargain or "value" perceptions (Exhibit 2–22). A product positioned as highest quality but carrying a lower price than competitors will only confuse consumers. In other words, the price, the advertising, and the distribution channels must present one unified voice speaking to the product's positioning.

RELATING PRICE TO ADVERTISING AND PROMOTION

Factors such as product quality, competition, and advertising all interact in determining what price a firm can and should charge. The relationship among price, product quality, and advertising was examined in one study using information on 227 consumer businesses from the PIMS (Profit Impact of Marketing Strategies) project of the Strategic Planning Institute.[23] Several interesting findings concerning the interaction of these variables emerged from this study:

- Brands with high relative advertising budgets were able to charge premium prices, whereas brands that spent less than their competitors on advertising charged lower prices.
- Companies with high-quality products charged high relative prices for the extra quality, but businesses with high quality and high advertising levels obtained the highest prices. Conversely, businesses with low quality and low advertising charged the lowest prices.
- The positive relationship between high relative advertising and price levels was stronger for products in the late stage of the product life cycle, for market leaders, and for low-cost products (under $10).
- Companies with relatively high prices and high advertising expenditures showed a higher return on investment than companies with relatively low prices and high advertising budgets.
- Companies with high-quality products were hurt the most, in terms of return on investment, by inconsistent advertising and pricing strategies.

The study concluded that pricing and advertising strategies go together. High relative ad expenditures should accompany premium prices, and low relative ad expenditures should be tailored to low prices. These results obviously support the IMC perspective that one voice must be conveyed.

EXHIBIT 2–21
The packaging shows product image

Distribution Channel Decisions

As consumers, we generally take for granted the role of marketing intermediaries or channel members. If we want a six-pack of soda or a box of detergent, we can buy it at a supermarket, a convenience store, or even a drugstore. Manufacturers understand the value and importance of these intermediaries.

One of a marketer's most important marketing decisions involves the way it makes its products and services available for purchase. A firm can have an excellent product at a great price, but it will be of little value unless it is available where the customer wants it, when the customer wants it, and with the proper support and service. **Marketing channels**, the place element of the marketing mix, are "sets of interdependent organizations involved in the process of making a product or service available for use or consumption."[24]

Channel decisions involve selecting, managing, and motivating intermediaries such as wholesalers, distributors, brokers, and retailers that help a firm make a product or service available to customers. These intermediaries, sometimes called **resellers**, are critical to the success of a company's marketing program.

The distribution strategy should also take into consideration the communication objectives and the impact that the channel strategy will have on the IMC program. Stewart and colleagues discuss the need for "integrated channel management," which "reflects the blurring of the boundaries of the communications and distribution functions."[25] Consistent with the product and pricing decisions, where the product is distributed will send a communications message. Does the fact that a product is sold at Nieman Marcus or Saks convey a different message regarding its image than if it were distributed at K–Mart or Wal–Mart? If you think about it for a moment, the mere fact that the product is distributed in these channels communicates an image about it in your mind. Stewart gives examples of how channel elements contribute to communications—for example, grocery store displays, point-of-purchase merchandising, and shelf footage. The distribution channel in a well-integrated marketing program serves as a form of reminder advertising. The consumer sees the brand

EXHIBIT 2–22
Some products compete on the basis
of quality rather than price

name and recalls the advertising. (Think about the last time you passed a McDonald's. Did it remind you of any of McDonald's ads?)

A company can choose not to use any channel intermediaries and sell to its customers through **direct channels**. This type of channel arrangement is sometimes used in the consumer market by firms using direct-selling programs, such as Avon, Tupperware, and Fuller Brush, or firms that use direct-response advertising or telemarketing to sell their products. Direct channels are also frequently used by manufacturers of industrial products and services, which are often selling expensive and complex products that require extensive negotiations and sales efforts, as well as service and follow-up calls after the sale. Most consumer product companies distribute through **indirect channels**, usually using a network of wholesalers (institutions that sell to other resellers) and/or retailers (which sell primarily to the final consumer).

**Developing
Promotional
Strategies:
Push or Pull?**

Most of you are aware of advertising and other forms of promotion directed toward ultimate consumers or business customers. We see these ads in the media and are often part of the target audience for the promotions. In addition to developing a consumer marketing mix, a company must have a program to motivate the channel members. Programs designed to persuade the trade to stock, merchandise, and promote a manufacturer's products are part of a **promotional push strategy**. The goal of this strategy is to push the product through the channels of distribution by aggressively selling and promoting the item to the resellers, or trade.

Promotion to the trade includes all the elements of the promotional mix. Company sales representatives call on resellers to explain the product, discuss the firm's plans for building demand among ultimate consumers, and describe special programs being offered to the trade, such as introductory discounts, promotional allowances, and cooperative ad programs. The company may use **trade advertising** to interest wholesalers and retailers and motivate them to purchase its products for resale to their customers. Trade advertising usually appears in publications that serve the particular industry.

A push strategy tries to convince resellers they can make a profit on a manufacturer's product and encourage them to order the merchandise and push it through to their customers. Sometimes manufacturers face resistance from channel members who do not want to take on an additional product line or brand. In these cases, companies may turn to a **promotional pull strategy**, spending money on advertising and sales promotional efforts directed toward the ultimate consumer. The goal of a pull strategy is to create demand by consumers and encourage them to request the product from the retailer. Seeing the consumer demand, retailers will order the product from wholesalers (if they are used), which in turn will request it from the manufacturer. Thus, stimulating demand at the end-user level pulls the product through the channels of distribution.

Whether to emphasize a push or a *pull strategy* depends on a number of factors, including the company's relations with the trade, its promotional budget, and demand for the firm's products. Companies that have favorable channel relationships may prefer to use a push strategy and work closely with channel members to encourage them to stock and promote their products. A firm with a limited promotional budget may not have the funds for advertising and sales promotion that a pull strategy requires and may find it more cost effective to build distribution and demand by working closely with resellers. When the demand outlook for a product is favorable because it has unique benefits, is superior to competing brands, or is very popular among consumers, a pull strategy may be appropriate. Companies often use a combination of push and pull strategies, with the emphasis changing as the product moves through its life cycle.

THE ROLE OF ADVERTISING AND PROMOTION

As shown in the marketing model in Figure 2–1, the marketing program includes promotion both to the trade (channel members) and to the company's ultimate customers. Marketers use the various promotional mix elements—advertising, sales promotion, direct marketing, publicity/public relations, and personal selling—to inform consumers about their products, prices, and places where they are available. Each promotional mix variable helps marketers achieve their promotional objectives, and each must work together to achieve an integrated marketing communications program.

To this point, we have discussed the various elements of the marketing plan that serves as the basis for the IMC program. The development and implementation of an IMC program is based on a strong foundation that includes market analysis, target marketing and positioning, and coordination of the various marketing mix elements. Throughout the following chapters of this text, we will explore the role of advertising and promotion in helping to achieve marketing objectives.

SUMMARY

Promotion plays an important role in an organization's efforts to market its product, service, or ideas to its customers. Figure 2–1 shows a model for analyzing how promotions fit into a company's marketing program. The model includes a marketing strategy and analysis, target marketing, program development, and the target market. The marketing process begins with a marketing strategy that is based on a detailed situation analysis and guides for target market selection and development of the firm's marketing program.

In the planning process, the situation analysis requires the marketing strategy to be assumed. The promotional program is developed with this strategy as a guide. One of the key decisions to be made regards the target marketing process,

which includes identifying, segmenting, target, and positioning to target markets. There are several bases for segmenting the market and various ways to position a product.

Once the target marketing process has been completed, marketing program decisions regarding product, price, distribution, and promotions must be made. All of these must be coordinated to provide an integrated marketing communications perspective, in which the positioning strategy is supported by one voice. Thus all product strategies, pricing strategies, and distribution choices must be made with the objective of contributing to the overall image of the product or brand. Advertising and promotion decisions, in turn, must be integrated with the other marketing mix decisions to accomplish this goal.

KEY TERMS

strategic marketing plan, 35
market segments, 35
market opportunities, 35
competitive advantage, 37
target marketing, 39
market segmentation, 40
geographic segmentation, 41
demographic
    segmentation, 41

psychographic
    segmentation, 41
behavioristic
    segmentation, 43
80-20 rule, 44
benefit segmentation, 44
undifferentiated
    marketing, 46

differentiated marketing,
    46
concentrated marketing,
    47
positioning, 49
salient attributes, 49
repositioning, 52
product symbolism, 56
brand equity, 56

marketing channels, 59
resellers, 59
direct channels, 60
indirect channels, 60
promotional push
    strategy, 60
trade advertising, 60
promotional pull strategy,
    61

DISCUSSION QUESTIONS

1. Discuss the concept of competitive advantage. Pick three brands or products and discuss the specific competitive advantage that they stress.

2. Many organizations segment on the basis of demographics. Discuss three products that might segment on this basis, then explain what other segmentation criteria they might also employ.

3. Generation Xers have their own purchasing motives. One such motive may be to differentiate themselves from others through the projection of a specific image. Describe one product that has been adopted by this market segment, and what image it creates.

4. Explain how the distribution channel may affect the image of a brand.

5. Describe how the positioning strategy adopted for a brand would need to be supported by all other elements of the marketing mix.

6. Discuss the differences between a promotional push strategy and a promotional pull strategy. What factors influence a firm's decision on which strategy to use?

7. Discuss the concept of target marketing. Why is it so important to marketers?

8. Discuss the process involved in segmenting a market. What are some factors one must consider in determining how to segment the market?

9. What is meant by positioning? Discuss the various approaches to positioning and give examples of companies or brands that use each approach.

10. What factors would lead a marketer to the use of a repositioning strategy? Find a product or service that has been repositioned recently and analyze the strategy.

Integrated Marketing Program Situation Analysis

2

3

Organizing for Advertising and Promotion: The Role of Ad Agencies and Other Marketing Communication Organizations

Chapter Objectives

- To understand how companies organize for advertising and other aspects of integrated marketing communications.

- To examine methods for selecting, compensating, and evaluating advertising agencies.

- To explain the role and functions of specialized marketing communications organizations.

- To examine various perspectives on the use of integrated services and responsibilities of advertisers versus agencies.

FALLON MCELLIGOTT SHOWS BIG IS NOT ALWAYS BETTER

The BMW CyberDrive.
Coming in May.

www.bmwusa.com BMW
The Ultimate Driving Machine.

©1997 BMW of North America, Inc.
The BMW name and logo are registered trademarks. For information 1-800-334-4BMW.

In July of 1996, executives at the Leo Burnett Co. in Chicago were shocked to learn that after 31 years with the agency, United Airlines, its prized account, had decided to put itself up for review. News that the $100 million-plus account was up for grabs spurred a mad dash among the major ad agencies who hoped to add United to their rosters. Four months later, United Airlines ended one of the most closely watched agency "shootouts" in years by announcing it was splitting its account between two agencies. Its North American business, which accounts for about two-thirds of the total billings, was awarded to Fallon McElligott, a mid-size agency based in Minneapolis, while its international advertising would be handled by Young & Rubicam, New York.

United Airlines' decision to award the bulk of its advertising to Fallon McElligott surprised many advertising people who thought it would opt for a larger agency. However, United has joined the ranks of a number of major companies who have chosen Fallon to handle some or all of their advertising and other forms of marketing communications, including BMW, Ameritech Corp., McDonald's, and Coca-Cola.

Fallon McElligott was founded in 1981 and has become one of the most respected agencies in the country in a relatively short time. At the beginning of the 80s, Fallon was a small start-up doing bold creative work—mostly print with clever headlines—that gained national attention for regional clients. The agency's strong creative work helped transform Fallon from a highly regarded regional print agency into a highly regarded national agency with clients such as Lee Jeans, *The Wall Street Journal*, *Rolling Stone* magazine, and Timex.

Although Fallon McElligott experienced strong growth in the 80s, by the early 90s, the flow of new business had begun to slow. After losing a close competition for the $40 million

MasterCard account, agency chair Pat Fallon realized that some major changes were needed for Fallon McElligott to compete at the higher levels. One area that needed strengthening was account planning, which was becoming increasingly important in the agency business. A new director of account planning, Rob White, was hired and immediately began building a planning department.

The new emphasis on account planning has paid off as the ability to transform a brand by redirecting its existing strength has become a Fallon specialty. For example, when Fallon pitched the Nikon camera account, the company told the agency not to meddle with the longtime slogan, "We take the world's greatest pictures." However, the agency felt the tagline wasn't right because it spoke only to professional photographers. The solution penned by Fallon's creative director consisted of one word: "Yours." By adding the word at the end of the existing tagline, the agency was able to speak to amateurs without alienating professionals—and win the Nikon account.

Another change that has been instrumental in Fallon McElligott's recent success is its commitment to finding integrated marketing communications solutions to its clients' problems. In 1993, Fallon hired Mark Goldstein as its president of integrated marketing and also took full control of its sister design agency, Joe Duffy Design, in order to have full integration of marketing services under one roof.

Goldstein has helped Fallon McElligott expand its capabilities in areas such as PR, promotion, events, and interactive advertising. Fallon developed a website for BMW of North America that impressed Apple Computer so much that it featured the site in print ads and commercials designed to showcase Apple technology. Fallon also won the 1996 Super Reggie Award from the Promotional Marketing Association of America for a sales promotion campaign it developed for BMW's new Z3 roadster.

Winning awards is becoming commonplace for Fallon McElligott; it was selected *Advertising Age*'s agency of the year for 1995 and *Adweek*'s National Agency of the Year in 1996. Fallon also won five Effie awards for advertising effectiveness from the American Marketing Association in 1996, including the Grand Effie for its Purina Dog Chow campaign. Other agencies should be aware that Fallon McElligott does not plan to rest on its laurels. It recently requested permission to repitch its Purina account with an integrated marketing campaign.

Sources: Mark Gleason, "Solid Creative Strengths Put Fallon in the Driver's Seat," *Advertising Age*, April 15, 1996, pp. S4, 5, 35; Mark Gleason, "United Opts for Team Approach with Fallon, Y&R," *Advertising Age*, October 21, 1996, pp. 1, 58. Reprinted with permission from the April 15, 1996 and October 21, 1996 issues of *Advertising Age*. Copyright Crain Communications, Inc. 1996.

Developing and implementing an integrated marketing communications program is usually a complex and detailed process involving the efforts of many persons. As consumers, we generally give little thought to the individuals or organizations that create the clever advertisements that capture our attention or the contests or sweepstakes we hope to win. But for those involved in the marketing process, it is important to understand the nature of the industry and the structure and functions of the organizations involved. As you can see in the opening to this chapter, the advertising and promotions business is changing as marketers search for better ways to communicate with their customers.

This chapter examines the various organizations that participate in the IMC process, their roles and responsibilities, and their relationship to one another. We discuss how companies organize internally for advertising and promotion. For most companies, advertising is planned and executed by an outside ad agency. Many large agencies offer a variety of other IMC capabilities, including public relations, sales promotion, and direct marketing. Thus, we will devote particular attention to the ad agency's role and the overall relationship between company and agency.

Other participants in the promotional process (such as direct-response, sales promotion, and interactive agencies and public relations firms) are becoming increasingly important as more companies take an integrated marketing communications approach to promotion. We examine the role of these specialized marketing communications organizations in the promotional process as well. The chapter concludes with a discussion of whether marketers are best served by using the integrated services of one large agency or a variety of communications specialists.

PARTICIPANTS IN THE INTEGRATED MARKETING COMMUNICATIONS PROCESS: AN OVERVIEW

Before discussing the specifics of the industry, we'll provide an overview of the entire system and identify some of the players. As shown in Figure 3–1, participants in the integrated marketing communications process can be broken into five major groups: the advertiser (or client), advertising agencies, media organizations, specialized communication services, and collateral services. Each group has specific roles in the promotional process.

The advertisers, or **clients**, are the key participants in the process. They have the products, services, or causes to be marketed, and they provide the funds that pay for advertising and promotions. The advertisers also assume major responsibility for developing the marketing program and making the final decisions regarding the advertising and promotional program to be employed. The organization may perform most of these efforts itself, either through its own advertising department or by setting up an in-house agency.

However, many organizations use an **advertising agency**, an outside firm that specializes in the creation, production, and/or placement of the communications message and that may provide other services to facilitate the marketing and promotions process. Many large advertisers retain the services of a number of agencies, particularly when they market a number of products. For example, Kraft Foods uses as many as eight advertising agencies for its various brands, while Procter & Gamble uses 10 promotional agencies for its Canadian business alone. More and more, ad agencies are acting as partners with advertisers and assuming more responsibility for developing the marketing and promotional programs.

Media organizations are another major participant in the advertising and promotions process. The primary function of most media is to provide information or entertainment to their subscribers, viewers, or readers. But from the perspective of the promotional planner,

FIGURE 3–1   Participants in the integrated marketing communications process

the purpose of media is to provide an environment for the firm's marketing communications message. The media must have editorial or program content that attracts consumers so advertisers and their agencies want to buy time or space with them. One Canadian publication's attempt to convince buyers of its value as a media vehicle is shown in Exhibit 3–1. While the media perform many other functions that help advertisers understand their markets and their customers, a medium's primary objective is to sell itself as a way for companies to reach their target markets with their messages effectively.

The next group of participants are organizations that provide **specialized marketing communications services.** They include direct marketing agencies, sales promotion agencies, interactive agencies, and public relations firms. These organizations provide services in their areas of expertise. A direct-response agency develops and implements direct

EXHIBIT 3–1
L'Actualité advertises the value of its medium

marketing programs, while sales promotion agencies develop promotional programs such as contests and sweepstakes, premium offers, or sampling programs. Interactive agencies are being retained to develop websites for the Internet and help marketers as they move deeper into the realm of interactive media. Public relations firms are used to generate and manage publicity for a company and its products and services as well as to focus on its relationships and communications with its relevant publics.

The final participants shown in the promotions process of Figure 3–1 are those that provide **collateral services**, the wide range of support functions used by advertisers, agencies, media organizations, and specialized marketing communications firms. These individuals and companies perform specialized functions the other participants use in planning and executing advertising and other promotional functions. We will now examine the role of each participant in more detail. (Media organizations will be examined in Chapters 10 through 14.)

ORGANIZING FOR ADVERTISING AND PROMOTION IN THE FIRM: THE CLIENT'S ROLE

Virtually every business organization uses some form of marketing communications. However, the way a company organizes for these efforts depends on several factors, including its size, the number of products it markets, the role of advertising and promotion in its marketing mix, the advertising and promotion budget, and its marketing organization structure. Many individuals throughout the organization may be involved in the promotions decision-making process. Marketing personnel have the most direct relationship with advertising and are often involved in many aspects of the decision process, such as providing input to the campaign plan, agency selection, and evaluation of proposed programs. Top management is usually interested in how the advertising program represents the firm, which may also mean being involved in advertising decisions even when these decisions are not part of its day-to-day responsibilities.

While many people both inside and outside the organization have some input into the advertising and promotion process, direct responsibility for administering the program must be assumed by someone within the firm. Many companies have an advertising department headed by an advertising or communications manager operating under a marketing director. An alternative used by many large multiproduct firms is a decentralized marketing (brand management) system. A third option is to form a separate agency within the firm, an in-house agency. Each of these alternatives is examined in more detail in the following sections.

The Centralized System

In many organizations, marketing activities are divided along functional lines, with advertising placed alongside other marketing functions such as sales, marketing research, and product planning, as shown in Figure 3–2. **The advertising manager** is responsible for all promotions activities except sales. In the most common example of a **centralized system**, the advertising manager controls the entire promotions operation, including budgeting, coordinating creation and production of ads, planning media schedules, and monitoring and administering the sales promotions programs for all the company's products or services.

FIGURE 3–2 The advertising department under a centralized system

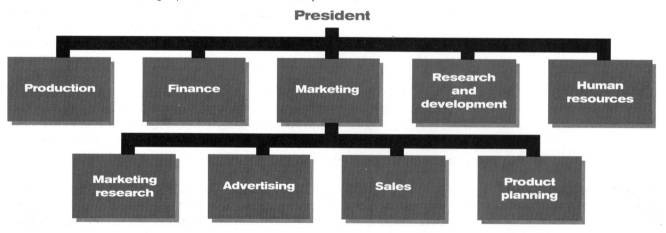

The specific duties of the advertising manager depend on the size of the firm and the importance it places on promotional programs. Basic functions the manager and staff perform include the following.

PLANNING AND BUDGETING

The advertising department is responsible for developing advertising and promotions plans that will be approved by management and recommending a promotions program based on the overall marketing plan, objectives, and budget. Formal plans are submitted annually or when a program is being changed significantly, as when a new campaign is developed. While the advertising department develops the promotional budget, the final decision on allocating funds is usually made by top management.

ADMINISTRATION AND EXECUTION

The manager must organize the advertising department and supervise and control its activities. The manager also supervises the execution of the plan by subordinates and/or the advertising agency. This requires working with such departments as production, media, art, copy, and sales promotion. If an outside agency is used, the advertising department is relieved of much of the executional responsibility; however, it must review and approve the agency's plans.

COORDINATION WITH OTHER DEPARTMENTS

The manager must coordinate the advertising department's activities with those of other departments, particularly those involving other marketing functions. For example, the advertising department must communicate with marketing research and/or sales to determine which product features are important to customers and should be emphasized in the company's communications. Research may also provide profiles of product users and nonusers for the media department before it selects broadcast or print media. The advertising department may also be responsible for preparing material the sales force can use when calling on customers, such as sales promotions tools, advertising materials, and point-of-purchase displays.

COORDINATION WITH OUTSIDE AGENCIES AND SERVICES

Many companies have an advertising department but still use many outside services. For example, companies may develop their advertising programs in-house while employing media buying services to place their ads and/or use collateral services agencies to develop brochures, point-of-purchase materials, and so on. The department serves as liaison between the company and any outside service providers and also determines which ones to use. Once outside services are retained, the manager will work with other marketing managers to coordinate their efforts and evaluate their performances.

A centralized organizational system is often used when companies do not have many different divisions, product or service lines, or brands to advertise. For example, airlines such as American and Continental have centralized advertising departments. Many companies prefer a centralized advertising department because developing and coordinating advertising programs from one central location facilitates communication regarding the promotions program, making it easier for top management to participate in decision making. A centralized system may also result in a more efficient operation because fewer people are involved in the program decisions, and as their experience in making such decisions increases, the process becomes easier.

At the same time, problems are inherent in a centralized operation. First, it is difficult for the advertising department to understand the overall marketing strategy for the brand. The department may also be slow in responding to specific needs and problems of a product or brand. As companies become larger and develop or acquire new products, brands, or even divisions, the centralized system may become impractical.

The Decentralized System

In large corporations with multiple divisions and many different products, it is very difficult to manage all the advertising, promotional, and other functions through a centralized department. These types of companies generally have a **decentralized system** with separate manufacturing, research and development, sales, and marketing departments for various divisions, product lines, or businesses. Many companies that use a decentralized system, such as Procter & Gamble, Gillette Co., and Nestlé, assign each product or brand to a **brand manager** who is responsible for the total management of the brand, including planning, budgeting, sales, and profit performance. (The term *product manager* is also used to describe this position.) The brand manager, who may have one or more assistant brand managers, is also responsible for the planning, implementation, and control of the marketing program.

Under this system, the responsibilities and functions associated with advertising and promotions are transferred to the brand manager, who works closely with the outside advertising agency and other marketing communications specialists as they develop the promotional program.[1] In a multiproduct firm, each brand may have its own ad agency and may compete against other brands within the company, not just against outside competitors. For example, Exhibit 3–2 shows ads for Cheer and Tide, which are both Procter & Gamble products that compete for a share of the laundry detergent market.

As shown in Figure 3–3, the advertising department is part of marketing services and provides support for the brand managers. The role of marketing services is to assist the brand managers in planning and coordinating the integrated marketing communications program. In some companies, the marketing services group may include sales promotion. The brand managers may work with sales promotion people to develop budgets, define strategies, and implement tactical executions for both trade and consumer promotions. Marketing services may also provide other types of support services, such as package design and merchandising.

Some companies may have an additional layer(s) of management above the brand managers to coordinate the efforts of all of the brand managers handling a related group of products. An example is the organizational structure of Procter & Gamble, shown in Figure 3–4. This system—generally referred to as a **category management system**—includes category managers as well as brand and advertising managers. The category manager oversees management of the entire product category and focuses on the strategic role of the various brands in order to build profits and market share.[2]

The advertising manager may review and evaluate the various parts of the program and advise and consult with the brand managers. This person may have the authority to override the brand manager's decisions on advertising. In some multiproduct firms that spend a lot on advertising, the advertising manager may coordinate the work of the various agencies to obtain media discounts for the firm's large volume of media purchases.

An advantage of the decentralized system is that each brand receives concentrated managerial attention, resulting in faster response to both problems and opportunities. The brand manager system is also more flexible and makes it easier to adjust various aspects of the ad-

EXHIBIT 3–2
Many of Procter & Gamble's brands compete against each other

FIGURE 3—3 A decentralized brand management system

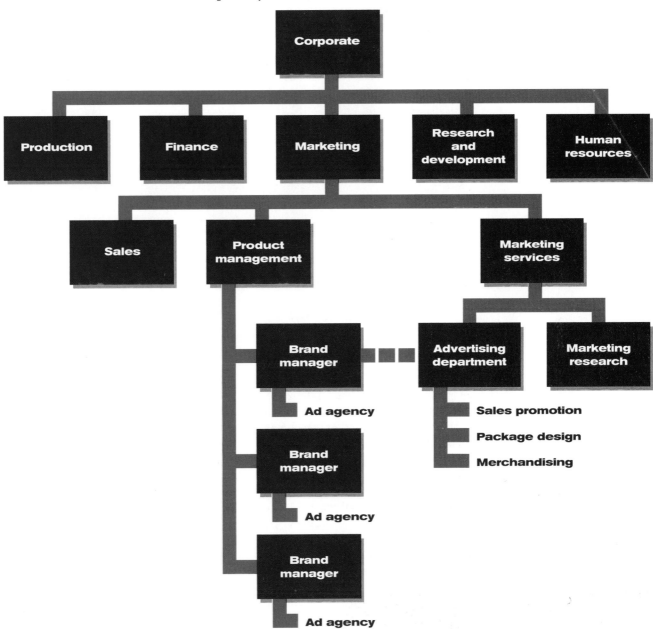

vertising and promotional program, such as creative platforms and media and sales promotion schedules.[3] IMC Perspective 3–1 discusses how General Motors recently adopted a brand management system to focus more attention on individual models and create stronger identities for them.

There are some drawbacks to the decentralized approach. Brand managers often lack training and experience. The promotional strategy for a brand may be developed by a brand manager who does not really understand what advertising or sales promotion can and cannot do and how each should be used. Brand managers may focus too much on short-run planning and administrative tasks, neglecting the development of long-term programs.

Another problem is that individual brand managers often end up competing for management attention, marketing dollars, and other resources, which can lead to unproductive rivalries and potential misallocation of funds. The manager's persuasiveness may become a bigger factor in determining budgets than the long-run profit potential of the brands. These types of problems were key factors in Procter & Gamble's decision to switch to a category management system.

FIGURE 3—4

A Procter & Gamble division using the category management system

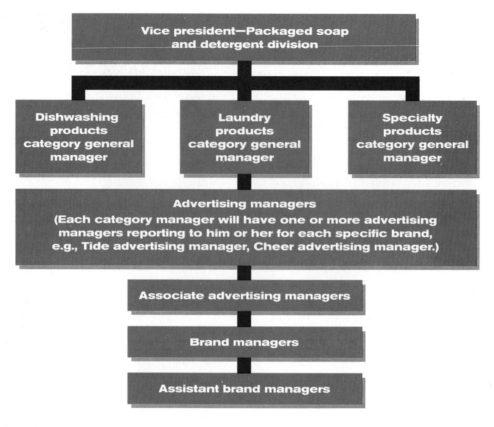

Finally, the brand management system has been criticized for failing to provide brand managers with authority over the functions needed to implement and control the plans they develop.[4] Some companies have dealt with this problem by expanding the role and responsibility of the advertising and sales promotion managers and their staff of specialists. The staff specialists counsel the individual brand managers, and advertising or sales promotion decision making involves the advertising and/or sales promotion manager, the brand manager, and the marketing director.

In-House Agencies

Some companies, in an effort to reduce costs and maintain greater control over agency activities, have set up their own advertising agencies internally. An **in-house agency** is an advertising agency that is set up, owned, and operated by the advertiser. Some in-house agencies are little more than advertising departments, but in other companies they are given a separate identity and are responsible for the expenditure of large sums of advertising dollars. Large advertisers that use in-house agencies include Calvin Klein, Radio Shack, and Benetton. Many companies use in-house agencies exclusively; others combine in-house efforts with those of outside agencies. For example, No Fear handles most of its advertising in-house, but it does use an outside agency for some of its creative work (Exhibit 3–3). (The specific roles performed by in-house agencies will become clearer when we discuss the functions of outside agencies.)

A major reason for using an in-house agency is to reduce advertising and promotion costs. Companies with very large advertising budgets pay a substantial amount to outside agencies in the form of media commissions. With an internal structure, these commissions go to the in-house agency. An in-house agency can also provide related work such as sales presentations and sales force materials, package design, and public relations at a lower cost than outside agencies. A study by M. Louise Ripley found that creative and media services were the most likely functions to be performed outside, while merchandising and sales promotion were the most likely to be performed in-house.[5]

Saving money is not the only reason companies use in-house agencies. Time savings, bad experiences with outside agencies, and the increased knowledge and understanding of the market that come from working on advertising and promotion for the product or service day by day are also reasons. Companies can also maintain tighter control over the process and

IMC Perspective 3-1
Brand Managers Take the Wheel at General Motors

The brand management organizational system has been around since 1927, when Procter & Gamble pioneered the concept by assigning a manager to work exclusively on Camay soap. Since then the practice of making a single manager a brand's internal champion with responsibility for all of its marketing has become commonplace in most large consumer and industrial product companies. Some companies, including P&G, are moving away from the traditional brand management approach. However, General Motors, the largest corporation in the U.S., is adopting the same brand management techniques used to sell cereal, toothpaste, soap, and thousands of other products in hopes of selling more cars.

The goal of General Motors founder Alfred P. Sloan was to "build a car for every purse and purpose," and for many years GM created some of the strongest brand names in the auto industry, among them Cadillac, Pontiac, Chevrolet, Oldsmobile, and Buick. However, over the past few decades, fuzzy advertising and marketing as well as lookalike models from competing GM divisions helped blur the identity of many of these brands. The problem was compounded by a system where dozens of managers in marketing, sales, and planning would work on various aspects of marketing for many different models. Moreover, GM's traditional divisional managers had too many responsibilities and could not give enough attention to the individual brands.

To address these problems and once again create strong identities for its 40-plus brands of cars, trucks, minivans and sport utility vehicles, GM appointed brand managers who work under the divisional general manager but are accountable for the sales success of such individual brands as the Chevrolet Malibu or Buick Century. The GM brand managers have full responsibility for marketing their vehicles, including pricing, advertising, and promotion. They are responsible for developing target markets as well as conceiving, implementing, and managing marketing campaigns that will differentiate their brands.

To put the system into practice, GM has named more than 40 brand managers, including a number of outsiders from package-goods companies like Nabisco and Procter & Gamble. The head of GM's North American marketing operations wants the brand managers to distill their model's key attributes or personality into a succinct mes-

sage and positioning platform. For example, the brand manager for the Pontiac Grand Prix is attempting to take the mid-size car back to its sporty, macho roots with advertising again touting a wide-track stance.

The brand manager for the Catera, a new entry-level luxury sports sedan introduced by the Cadillac division as a 1997 model, rejiggered Cadillac's traditional "wreath and crest" emblem. He took one of the six birds facing left, turned it around, colored it red, and made it a cartoon mascot in both TV and print ads. The goal is to attract baby boomers by projecting an irreverent image and showing that the Catera is far removed from the more traditional and stodgy Cadillac line of old.

Initially, GM's brand managers' primary influence will be in the advertising and promotion areas. However, GM's ultimate goal is to have the brand managers intimately involved in design as well so they can better meet their target customers' needs. As one management consultant has noted, "The cornerstone of brand management is to stop chasing your competition and start chasing your customer." GM has gotten the message." GM hopes that the results of proper brand management will be an array of well-defined brands that even Alfred Sloan would be proud of.

Sources: Kathleen Kerwin, "GM Warms Up the Branding Iron," *Business Week*, September 23, 1996, pp. 153–4; Warren Brown and Fran Swoboda, "A Revolution in Pieces," *Washington Post*, October 27, 1996, pp. H1, 4.

more easily coordinate promotions with the firm's overall marketing program. Some companies use an in-house agency simply because they believe they can do a better job than an outside agency could.[6]

Opponents of in-house agencies say they cannot give the advertiser the experience and objectivity of an outside agency, nor the range of services. They argue that outside agencies have more highly skilled specialists and attract the best creative talent, and that using an external firm gives a company a more varied perspective on its advertising problems as well as greater flexibility. In-house personnel may become narrow or grow stale while working on the same product line, but outside agencies may have different people with a variety of back-

grounds and ideas working on the account. Flexibility is greater because an outside agency can be dismissed if the company is not satisfied, whereas changes in an in-house agency could be slower and more disruptive.

The cost savings of an in-house agency must be evaluated against these considerations. For many companies, high-quality advertising is critical to their marketing success and should be the major criterion in determining whether to use in-house services. Companies like L.A. Gear and Redken Laboratories have moved their in-house work to outside agencies in recent years. Redken cited the need for a "fresh look" and objectivity as the reasons, noting that management gets too close to the product to come up with different creative ideas.[7]

The ultimate decision as to which advertising organization to use depends on which arrangement works best for the company. The advantages and disadvantages of the three systems are summarized in Figure 3–5. We now turn our attention to the functions of outside agencies and their roles in the promotional process.

ADVERTISING AGENCIES

Many major companies use an advertising agency to assist them in developing, preparing, and executing their promotional programs. An ad agency is a service organization that specializes in planning and executing advertising programs for its clients. Over 10,000 agencies are listed in the *Standard Directory of Advertising Agencies* (the "Red Book"); however, most are individually owned small businesses employing fewer than five people. The U.S. ad agency business is highly concentrated. Nearly half of the domestic **billings** (the amount of client money agencies spend on media purchases and other equivalent activities) are handled by the top 500 agencies. In fact, just 10 U.S. agencies handle nearly 30 percent of the total volume of business done by the top 500 agencies in the United States. The top agencies also have foreign operations that generate substantial billings and income. The top 25 agencies, ranked by their U.S. gross income, are shown in Figure 3–6. The figure shows that the advertising business is also geographically concentrated, with 18 of the top 25 agencies head-

FIGURE 3–5
Comparison of advertising
organization systems

Organizational system	Advantages	Disadvantages
Centralized	• Facilitated communications • Fewer personnel required • Continuity in staff • Allows for more top-management involvement	• Less involvement with and understanding of overall marketing goals • Longer response time • Inability to handle multiple product lines
Decentralized	• Concentrated managerial attention • Rapid response to problems and opportunities • Increased flexibility	• Ineffective decision making • Internal conflicts • Misallocation of funds • Lack of authority
In-house agencies	• Cost savings • More control • Increased coordination	• Less experience • Less objectivity • Less flexibility

FIGURE 3–6 Top 25 Agencies Ranked by U.S. Gross Income ($ in millions)

Rank 1995	Agency	Headquarters	Gross Income 1995	Volume 1995
1	Leo Burnett Co.	Chicago	$370.6	$2,484.8
2	J. Walter Thompson Co.	New York	347.0	2,419.9
3	Grey Advertising	New York	326.7	2,178.9
4	DDB Needham Worldwide	New York	284.7	2,546.0
5	McCann-Erickson Worldwide	New York	279.6	1,865.0
6	Saatchi & Saatchi Advertising	New York	275.5	2,204.1
7	BBDO Worldwide	New York	259.5	2,621.8
8	Foote, Cone & Belding Communications	Chicago	244.2	2,827.0
9	Ogilvy & Mather Worldwide	New York	209.5	2,091.7
10	Young & Rubicam	New York	205.8	2,142.6
11	Bozell Worldwide	New York	200.3	1,585.0
12	D'Arcy Masius Benton & Bowles	New York	191.4	1,960.4
13	Bates Worldwide	New York	152.1	1,217.1
14	TMP Worldwide	New York	137.4	16.7
15	TBWA Chiat/Day	New York	130.7	1,046.5
16	Ammirati Puris Lintas	New York	113.8	870.0
17	Gage Marketing Group	Minneapolis	108.5	723.8
18	Wunderman Cato Johnson	New York	101.0	842.6
19	N. W. Ayer & Partners	New York	94.1	851.9
20	Well Rich Greene BDDP	New York	89.2	850.3
21	Alcone Marketing Group	Irvine, Calif.	84.3	551.8
22	Campbell-Ewald	Warren, Mich.	81.8	843.6
23	Rapp Collins Worldwide	New York	80.1	594.8
24	Campbell Mithum Esty	Minneapolis	79.2	633.2
25	CommonHealth USA	Parsippany, N.J.	73.2	417.1

Source: Reprinted with permission from the April 14, 1996 issue of *Advertising Age*, p. S–8. Copyright Crain Communications, Inc. 1996.

quartered in New York City. Nearly 40 percent of U.S. agency business is handled by New York-based agencies. Other leading advertising centers in the United States include Chicago, Los Angeles, Detroit, San Francisco, and Minneapolis.

During the late 1980s, the advertising industry became even more concentrated as large agencies merged with or acquired other agencies and support organizations to form large advertising organizations, or **superagencies**. These superagencies were formed so that agencies could provide clients with integrated marketing communications services worldwide. Some advertisers became disenchanted with the superagencies and moved to smaller agencies that were more flexible and responsive.[8] However, in the mid-90s the agency business went through another wave of consolidation and a number of the mid-size agencies were acquired by large agency groups. For example, the Interpublic Group, which includes McCann-Erickson Worldwide and the Lowe group, acquired Ammirati & Puris, which was a very successful mid-size agency. The agency was merged with Interpublic's Lintas Worldwide agency to form Ammirati Puris Lintas.[9] A number of mid-size agencies have been forging alliances with larger agencies because they are feeling the pressures of globalization. Many of their clients want an agency with international advertising capabilities, so they are aligning with larger groups that have a network of agencies around the world.[10]

The Ad Agency's Role

The functions performed by advertising agencies might be conducted by the clients themselves through one of the designs discussed earlier in this chapter, but most large companies use outside firms. This section discusses some reasons advertisers use external agencies.

REASONS FOR USING AN AGENCY

Probably the main reason outside agencies are used is that they provide the client with the services of highly skilled individuals who are specialists in their chosen fields. An advertising agency staff may include artists, writers, media analysts, researchers, and others with specific skills, knowledge, and experience who can help market the client's products or services. Many agencies specialize in a particular type of business and use their knowledge of the industry to assist their clients. For example, Quill Communications Inc. is an agency that specializes in developing advertising and communications for the health care industry.

An outside agency can also provide an objective viewpoint of the market and its business that is not subject to internal company policies, biases, or other limitations. The agency can draw on the broad range of experience it has gained while working on a diverse set of marketing problems for various clients. For example, an ad agency that is handling a travel-related account may have individuals who have worked with airlines, cruise ship companies, travel agencies, hotels, and other travel-related industries. The agency may have experience in this area or may even have previously worked on the advertising account of one of the client's competitors. Thus, the agency can provide the client with insight into the industry (and, in some cases, the competition).

Types of Ad Agencies

Since ad agencies can range in size from a one- or two-person operation to large organizations with over 1,000 employees, the services offered and functions performed will vary. This section examines the different types of agencies, the services they perform for their clients, and how they are organized.

FULL-SERVICE AGENCIES

Many companies employ what is known as a **full-service agency**, which offers its clients a full range of marketing, communications, and promotions services, including planning, creating, and producing the advertising; performing research; and selecting media. A full-service agency may also offer nonadvertising services such as strategic market planning; production of sales promotions, sales training, and trade show materials; package design; and public relations and publicity.

The full-service agency is made up of departments that provide the activities needed to perform the various advertising functions and serve the client, as shown in Figure 3–7.

ACCOUNT SERVICES

Account services, or account management, is the link between the ad agency and its clients. Depending on the size of the client and its advertising budget, one or more account executives serve as liaison. The **account executive** is responsible for understanding the advertiser's marketing and promotions needs and interpreting them to agency personnel. He or she coordinates agency efforts in planning, creating, and producing ads. The account executive also presents agency recommendations and obtains client approval.

As the focal point of agency–client relationships, the account executive must know a great deal about the client's business and be able to communicate this to specialists in the agency working on the account.[11] The ideal account executive has a strong marketing background as well as a thorough understanding of all phases of the advertising process.

MARKETING SERVICES

Over the past two decades, use of marketing services has increased dramatically. One service gaining increased attention is research, as agencies realize that to communicate effectively

FIGURE 3–7 Full-service agency organizational chart

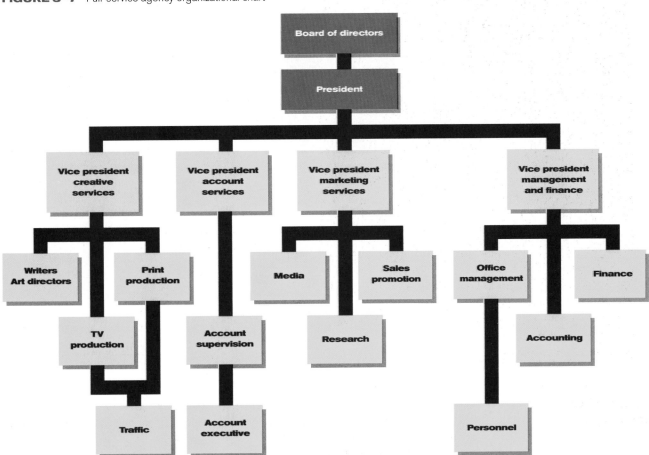

MARK GOLDSTEIN

When *Advertising Age* selected Fallon McElligott as Agency of the Year for 1995, the headline read "Integrated approach lets shop build roster, hold inventive edge." The person responsible for creating and sharpening that integrated marketing communications edge at Fallon McElligott is Mark Goldstein. Mark joined Fallon McElligott as president of integrated marketing in 1993. His role in transforming Fallon McElligott

into an integrated marketing company has helped Fallon garner the Agency of the Year award as well as *AD-WEEK*'s Hottest New Business agency. He has also developed the new business presentations that have helped the agency land an impressive list of new clients including United Airlines, BMW, Holiday Inn Worldwide, Miller Lite, and the USA Network.

Mark Goldstein is recognized as one of the leading experts on IMC. His expertise in integrated marketing has helped Fallon McElligott expand its services to include such areas as public relations, direct marketing, retail promotion, and interactive media. One area where he has had a major impact is in interactive media. When he joined Fallon McElligott, the agency had a loosely gathered interactive task force. Goldstein recalls that "Everyone thought it was cool but no one knew what to do with it." However, under his direction that group has evolved into a 21-person team with four management supervisors, who are regularly asked to speak about interactive media to other companies.

Mark Goldstein admits he has a crush on the Internet because in his career he has never seen anything that let him do so many things at one time. The Internet allows agencies and companies to talk directly to consumers and get immediate responses to questions. He says what he really likes is being able to reach out and touch customers via the Web noting: "I love it for its ability to create and nurture relationships. Because it's so new, it's like a giant sandbox. There are no rules." He cruises the Web looking for things that interest him professionally and otherwise. (One of his

> "We are not in the Web development business, we're in the surround-the-brand business."

favorite is www.hothothot.com—a hot sauce site.) But he also thinks a lot of websites fail to engage their audience, putting up little more than on-line brochures.

Mark Goldstein feels Fallon McElligott has a competitive edge because his interactive group understands that the Web is about marketing, not about technology. However, companies can forget about trying to have Fallon McElligott to build their Website unless they plan on naming them as agency of record. Goldstein notes that "We are not in the Web development business, we're in the surround-the-brand business."

With his education and advertising experience Mark Goldstein knows a great deal about how to surround a brand. He began his career in 1970 as a copywriter at Gerson, Howe and Johnson in Chicago and then became a creative supervisor at Leo Burnett, Chicago, from 1971 to 1975 where he was responsible for much of the copywriting on Virginia Slims, Wilson Tennis Racquets, and Kentucky Fried Chicken. In 1975 he joined Earle Palmer Brown (EPB) as creative director and became the president of the agency. In his 18 years at EPB he helped build the agency from $3 million in billings to over $400 million. Mark received his bachelor's and master's degrees in advertising from the Medill School of Journalism at Northwestern University. In 1992 he was elected to the prestigious Medill Board of Visitors and in 1996 he was among the first class of inductees in the Medill Hall of Achievement.

with their clients' customers, they must have a good understanding of the target audience. As shown in Chapter 1, the advertising planning process begins with a thorough situation analysis, which is based on research and information about the target audience.

Most full-service agencies maintain a *research department* whose function is to gather, analyze, and interpret information that will be useful in developing advertising for their clients. This can be done through primary research—where a study is designed, executed, and interpreted by the research department—or through the use of secondary (previously published) sources of information. Sometimes the research department acquires studies conducted by independent syndicated research firms or consultants. The research staff then interprets these reports and passes on the information to other agency personnel working on that account.

The research department may also design and conduct research to pretest the effectiveness of advertising the agency is considering. For example, copy testing is often conducted to determine how messages developed by the creative specialists are likely to be interpreted by the receiving audience.

The *media department* of an agency analyzes, selects, and contracts for space or time in the media that will be used to deliver the client's advertising message. The media department is expected to develop a media plan that will reach the target market and effectively communicate the message. Since most of the client's ad budget is spent on media time and/or space, this department must develop a plan that both communicates with the right audience and is cost effective.

Media specialists must know what audiences the media reach, their rates, and how well they match the client's target market. The media department reviews information on demographics, magazine and newspaper readership, radio listenership, and consumers' TV viewing patterns to develop an effective media plan. The media buyer implements the media plan by purchasing the actual time and space.

The media department is becoming an increasingly important part of the agency business as many large advertisers consolidate their media buying with one or a few agencies to save money and improve media efficiency. For example, for many years Nestlé had as many as 11 agencies purchasing media time for its products. Then Nestlé consolidated its $250 million to $300 million media buying into one agency, which gave the company more clout in the media buying market and saved a considerable amount of money.[12] General Motors, Campbell Soup, and Coca-Cola are other large advertisers who have consolidated their media buying with one or two agencies.[13] An agency's strategic ability to negotiate prices and effectively use the vast array of media vehicles available is becoming as important as its ability to create ads.

The research and media departments perform most of the functions that full-service agencies need to plan and execute their clients' advertising programs. Some agencies offer additional marketing services to their clients to assist in other promotional areas. An agency may have a sales promotion department, or merchandising department, that specializes in developing contests, premiums, promotions, point-of-sale materials, and other sales materials. It may have direct-marketing specialists and package designers, as well as a PR/publicity department. Many agencies have developed interactive media departments to create websites for their clients. The growing popularity of integrated marketing communications has prompted many full-function agencies to develop capabilities and offer services in these other promotional areas. Exhibit 3–4 shows how CKS Partners promotes its ability to do more than just advertising.

CREATIVE SERVICES

The creative services department is responsible for the creation and execution of advertisements. The individuals who conceive the ideas for the ads and write the headlines, subheads, and body copy (the words constituting the message) are known as **copywriters**. They may also be involved in determining the basic appeal or theme of the ad campaign and often prepare a rough initial visual layout of the print ad or television commercial.

While copywriters are responsible for what the message says, the *art department* is responsible for how the ad looks. For print ads, the art director and graphic designers prepare

EXHIBIT 3-4
CKS Partners offers its clients more than just advertising

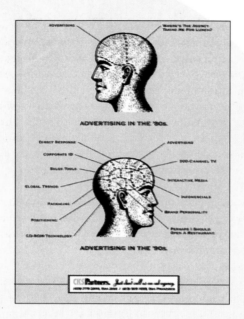

layouts, which are drawings that show what the ad will look like and from which the final artwork will be produced. For TV commercials, the layout is known as a *storyboard*, a sequence of frames or panels that depict the commercial in still form.

Members of the creative department work together to develop ads that will communicate the key points determined to be the basis of the creative strategy for the client's product or service. Writers and artists generally work under the direction of the agency's creative director, who oversees all the advertising produced by the organization. The director sets the creative philosophy of the department and may even become directly involved in creating ads for the agency's largest clients.

Once the copy, layout, illustrations, and mechanical specifications have been completed and approved, the ad is turned over to the *production department*. Most agencies do not actually produce finished ads; they hire printers, engravers, photographers, typographers, and other suppliers to complete the finished product. For broadcast production, the approved storyboard must be turned into a finished commercial. The production department may supervise the casting of people to appear in the ad and the setting for the scenes as well as choosing an independent production studio. The department may hire an outside director to turn the creative concept into a commercial. For example, Nike has used film director Spike Lee to direct a number of its commercials; Airwalk shoes has used John Glen, who directed many of the James Bond films, for its TV spots. Copywriters, art directors, account managers, people from research and planning, and representatives from the client side may all participate in production decisions, particularly when large sums of money are involved.

Creating an advertisement often involves many people and takes several months. In large agencies with many clients, coordinating the creative and production processes can be a major problem. A *traffic department* coordinates all phases of production to see that the ads are completed on time and that all deadlines for submitting the ads to the media are met. The traffic department may be located in the creative services area of the agency, or be part of media or account management, or be separate.

MANAGEMENT AND FINANCE

Like any other business, an advertising agency must be managed and perform basic operating and administrative functions such as accounting, finance, and human resources. It must also attempt to generate new business. Large agencies employ administrative, managerial, and clerical people to perform these functions. The bulk of an agency's income (approximately 64 percent) goes to salary and benefits for its employees. Thus, an agency must manage its personnel carefully and get maximum productivity from them.

AGENCY ORGANIZATION AND STRUCTURE

Full-function advertising agencies must develop an organizational structure that will meet their clients' needs and serve their own internal requirements. Most medium-size and large agencies are structured under either a departmental or a group system. Under the **departmental system**, each of the agency functions shown in Figure 3–7 is set up as a separate department and is called on as needed to perform its specialty and serve all of the agency's clients. Ad layout, writing, and production are done by the creative department, marketing services is responsible for any research or media selection and purchases, and the account services department handles client contact. Some agencies prefer the departmental system because it gives employees the opportunity to develop expertise in servicing a variety of accounts.

Many large agencies use the **group system**, in which individuals from each department work together in groups to service particular accounts. Each group is headed by an account executive or supervisor and has one or more media people, including media planners and buyers; a creative team, which includes copywriters, art directors, artists, and production personnel; and one or more account executives. The group may also include individuals from other departments such as marketing research, direct marketing, or sales promotion. The size and composition of the group varies depending on the client's billings and the importance of the account to the agency. For very important accounts, the group members may be assigned exclusively to one client. In some agencies, they may serve a number of smaller clients. Many agencies prefer the group system because employees become very knowledgeable about the client's business and there is continuity in servicing the account.

Other Types of Agencies and Services

Not every agency is a large full-service agency. Many smaller agencies expect their employees to handle a variety of jobs. For example, account executives may do their own research, work out their own media schedule, and coordinate the production of ads written and designed by the creative department. Many advertisers, including some large companies, are not interested in paying for the services of a full-service agency but are interested in some of the specific services agencies have to offer. Over the past few decades, several alternatives to full-service agencies have evolved, including creative boutiques and media buying services.

CREATIVE BOUTIQUES

A **creative boutique** is an agency that provides only creative services. These specialists have developed in response to some clients' desires to use only the creative talent of an outside provider while maintaining the other functions internally. The client may seek outside creative talent because it believes an extra creative effort is required or because its own employees do not have sufficient skills in this regard. For example, IMC Perspective 3–2 discusses how some advertisers and agencies have been bypassing traditional agencies and tapping into the movie industry for creative ideas for their commercials.

Full-service agencies often subcontract work to creative boutiques when they are very busy or want to avoid adding full-time employees to their payroll. Creative boutiques are usually founded by members of the creative departments of full-service agencies who leave the firm and take with them clients who want to retain their creative talents. These boutiques usually perform the creative function on a fee basis.

MEDIA BUYING SERVICES

Media buying services are independent companies that specialize in the buying of media, particularly radio and television time. The task of purchasing advertising media has grown more complex as specialized media proliferate, so media buying services have found a niche by specializing in the analysis and purchase of advertising time and space. Agencies and clients usually develop their own media strategies and hire the buying service to execute them. Some media buying services do help advertisers plan their media strategy. Because media buying services purchase such large amounts of time and space, they receive large discounts and can save the small agency or client money on media purchases. Media buying services are paid a fee or commission for their work.

IMC Perspective 3-2
Advertising Goes Hollywood

As the 1990s began, the Coca-Cola Co. faced a serious problem: sales of its flagship brand, Coke Classic, were stagnant in the U.S. market, and archrival Pepsi's ads were consistently rating higher among consumers. The company began a secret and unorthodox study, called Project Balance, which sought the views of a number of unconventional thinkers on how best to reach consumers in a media-saturated age. The first report from the group posed a provocative premise: "A brand advertised in a normal way, with normal media, is likely to develop a normal image, and not something special." The experts' advice: Don't be normal!

To help break away from normal advertising, Coca-Cola turned to Hollywood talent agent Michael Ovitz's Creative Artists Agency (CAA) for some new creative ideas, while retaining McCann-Erickson Worldwide, its agency for the past 38 years. Several Coke top executives were reportedly intrigued by CAA's pipeline into pop culture and Hollywood's "raw creativity."

Coca-Cola's decision to move much of its advertising to CAA sent shock waves through Madison Avenue. Many traditional advertising people were critical of it and argued that it was only a matter of time until Coke returned to a traditional full-service agency. However, just a week into his job, Coca-Cola's new director of worldwide marketing rejected McCann-Erickson's ideas for the company's global marketing campaign and announced that CAA would do Coke Classic's entire campaign. Many critics say the "Always" campaign, which has included a number of very popular TV commercials such as the computer-generated polar bears spots, is Coke's most successful advertising in over a decade. In addition to vaulting Coke back to the top of the advertising popularity charts, CAA has helped increase worldwide sales of Coke Classic by more than 500 million cases in 1995.

Many thought the Coke Classic account might return to a traditional agency when Michael Ovitz left CAA in late 1995 to become president of the Walt Disney Co. However, Coca-Cola stunned the advertising world again by entering into a joint venture with Disney and three former CAA executives to create an in-house agency called Edge Creative to develop commercials for its flagship brand.

Coke is not the only company looking outside of traditional agencies for creative ideas. To reach younger consumers in the United Kingdom, PepsiCo retained Planet 24, the Bob Geldof-linked film and TV production company, to produce a series of three-minute TV commercials in the style of a talk show. Sony Corp. of America solicited ideas from its Columbia Pictures division on how to advertise its new point-and-shoot camcorder.

Some advertising agencies are also taking steps to make sure they are not left behind by ever-demanding clients searching for new ways to entertain consumers. In another merger of Hollywood and Madison Avenue, DDB Needham Worldwide and film director Spike Lee (who has directed commercials for Snapple, Levi's, Nike, and ESPN, among others) recently formed a new agency named Spike/DDB. DDB Needham believes the venture with Lee will help clients like McDonald's, Frito-Lay, and Anheuser-Busch tap into urban trends and bolster the presence of their brands among minorities.

The vice president of brand management for Anheuser-Busch says, "The creative process can't always be structured in conventional ways. Agencies that don't follow that philosophy are the ones that are going to be left behind." Traditional ad agencies beware. Normal is out!

Sources: Sally Goll Beatty, "Spike Lee, DDB Join to Create New Ad Agency," *The Wall Street Journal*, December 5, 1996, pp. B1, 13; Robert Frank, "Coca-Cola, Disney Venture Mines Creative Artists Agency Talent," *The Wall Street Journal*, November 10, 1995, p. B8; "How CAA Bottled Coca-Cola," *Fortune*, November 15, 1993, p. 156.

Media buying services have been experiencing strong growth in recent years as clients seek alternatives to full-service agency relationships. Many companies have been unbundling agency services and consolidating media buying to get more clout from their advertising budgets. Nike, Bugle Boy, and Pennzoil are among those that have switched some or all of their media buying from full-service agencies to independent media buyers.[14] Exhibit 3–5 shows an ad promoting the services of Western International Media, the leading independent media buying company in the United States.

AGENCY COMPENSATION

As you have seen, the type and amount of services an agency performs vary from one client to another. As a result, agencies use a variety of methods to get paid for their services. Agencies are typically compensated in three ways: through commissions, some type of fee arrangement, or percentage charges.

Commissions from Media

The traditional method of compensating agencies is through a **commission system**, where the agency receives a specified commission (usually 15 percent) from the media on any advertising time or space it purchases for its client. (For outdoor advertising, the commission is $16\frac{2}{3}$ percent.) This system provides a simple method of determining payments, as shown in the following example.

Assume an agency prepares a full-page magazine ad and arranges to place the ad on the back cover of a magazine at a cost of $100,000. The agency places the order for the space and delivers the ad to the magazine. Once the ad is run, the magazine will bill the agency for $100,000, less the 15 percent ($15,000) commission. The media will also offer a 2 percent cash discount for early payment, which the agency may pass along to the client. The agency will bill the client $100,000 less the 2 percent cash discount on the net amount, or a total of $98,300, as shown in Figure 3–8. The $15,000 commission represents the agency's compensation for its services.

APPRAISAL OF THE COMMISSION SYSTEM

Use of the commission system to compensate agencies has been quite controversial for many years. A major problem centers on whether the 15 percent commission represents equitable compensation for services performed. Two agencies may require the same amount of effort to create and produce an ad. However, one client may spend $200,000 in commissionable media, which results in $30,000 agency income, while the other spends $2 million, generating $300,000 in commissions. Critics argue that the commission sys-

FIGURE 3–8
Example of commission system
payment

Media Bills Agency		Agency Bills Advertiser	
Costs for magazine space	$100,000	Costs for magazine space	$100,000
Less 15% commission	−15,000	Less 2% cash discount	−1,700
Cost of media space	85,000	Advertiser pays agency	98,300
Less 2% cash discount	−1,700		
Agency pays media	$ 83,300	Agency income	$ 15,000

tem encourages agencies to recommend high media expenditures to increase their commission level.

Another criticism of the commission system is that it ties agency compensation to media costs. In periods of media cost inflation, the agency is (according to the client) disproportionately rewarded. The commission system has also been criticized for encouraging agencies to ignore cost accounting systems to justify the expenses attributable to work on a particular account. Still others charge that this system tempts the agency to avoid noncommissionable media such as direct mail, sales promotions, or advertising specialties, unless they are requested by the client.

Defenders of the commission system argue that it is easy to administer and it keeps the emphasis in agency competition on nonprice factors such as the quality of the advertising developed. Proponents argue that agency services are proportional to the size of the commission, since more time and effort are devoted to the large accounts that generate high revenue for the agency. They also say the system is more flexible than it appears because agencies often perform other services for large clients at no extra charge, justifying such actions by the large commission they receive.

The commission system has become a heated topic among advertisers. Its opponents have been called traitors by their colleagues, who argue that their lack of support costs everyone in the business money and is nothing more than a competitive strategy designed to gain accounts.[15] However, those who support an alternative system contend that the old system is outdated and must be changed. The chair of the Leo Burnett agency has spoken out against the commission system: "It's incenting us to do the wrong thing, to recommend network TV and national magazines when other forms of communication like direct marketing or public relations might do the job better."[16]

Many advertisers have gone to a **negotiated commission**. This commission structure can take the form of reduced percentage rates, variable commission rates, and commissions with minimum and maximum profit rates. Negotiated commissions are designed to consider the needs of the client as well as the amount of time and effort exerted by the agency, avoiding some of the problems inherent in the traditional system. Some of the leading agencies now receive an average of 8 to 10 percent commission on media versus the traditional 15 percent.[17] Agencies are also relying less on media commissions for their income as their clients expand their integrated marketing communication programs to other forms of promotion and cut back on traditional mass media advertising. It is estimated that only 40 percent of advertising agencies' income now comes from the fixed commission, with the balance coming from a mix of fees and other charges.[18]

Fee, Cost, and Incentive-Based Systems

Since many believe the standard 15 percent commission system is not equitable to all parties, many agencies and their clients have developed some type of fee arrangement or cost-plus agreement for agency compensation. Some are using incentive-based compensation, which is a combination of a commission and a fee system.

FEE ARRANGEMENT

There are two basic types of fee arrangement systems. In the straight or **fixed-fee method**, the agency charges a basic monthly fee for all of its services and credits to the client any media commissions earned. Agency and client agree on the specific work to be done and the amount the agency will be paid for it. Sometimes agencies are compensated through a **fee-commission combination**, in which the media commissions received by the agency are credited against the fee. If the commissions are less than the agreed-on fee, the client must make up the difference. If the agency does much work for the client in noncommissionable media, the fee may be charged over and above the commissions received.

Both types of fee arrangements require the agency to carefully assess its costs of serving the client for the specified period, or for the project, plus a desired profit margin. To avoid any later disagreement, a fee arrangement should specify exactly what services the agency is expected to perform for the client.

COST-PLUS AGREEMENT

Under a **cost-plus system**, the client agrees to pay the agency a fee based on the costs of its work plus some agreed-on profit margin (often a percentage of total costs). This system requires the agency to keep detailed records of the costs it incurs in working on the client's account. Direct costs (personnel time and out-of-pocket expenses) plus an allocation for overhead and a markup for profits determine the amount the agency bills the client.

Fee agreements and cost-plus systems are commonly used in conjunction with a commission system. The fee-based system can be advantageous to both the client and the agency, depending on the size of the client, advertising budget, media used, and services required. Many clients prefer fee or cost-plus systems because they receive a detailed breakdown of where and how their advertising and promotion dollars are being spent. However, these arrangements can be difficult for the agency, as they require careful cost accounting and may be difficult to estimate when bidding for an advertiser's business. Agencies are also reluctant to let clients see their internal cost figures.

INCENTIVE-BASED COMPENSATION

Many clients these days are demanding more accountability from their agencies and tying agency compensation to performance through some type of **incentive-based system**. While there are many variations, the basic idea is that the agency's ultimate compensation level will depend on how well it meets predetermined performance goals. These goals often include objective measures such as sales or market share as well as more subjective measures such as evaluations of the quality of the agency's creative work. Companies using incentive-based systems determine agency compensation through media commissions, fees, bonuses, or some combination of these methods. Some clients use a sliding scale whereby the agency's base compensation is less than the 15 percent commission but it can earn extra commissions or bonuses depending on how it meets sales or other performance goals.

Recognizing the movement toward incentive-based systems, some agencies have offered to tie their compensation to performance. For example, a few years ago DDB Needham Worldwide announced a guaranteed results program: the agency receives a bonus in addition to the agreed-on compensation if its integrated marketing program improves the sales of the client's product. If sales do not improve, the agency rebates a substantial amount of its fee to the client.[19] Another agency that ties its compensation to a campaign's success is Calet, Hirsch & Ferrell.[20] Exhibit 3–6 shows an ad the agency ran promoting its guaranteed idea program.

Percentage Charges   Another way to compensate an agency is by adding a markup of **percentage charges** to various services the agency purchases from outside providers. These may include market research, artwork, printing, photography, and other services or materials. Markups usually range from 17.65 to 20 percent and are added to the client's overall bill. Since suppliers of these services do not allow the agency a commission, percentage charges cover administrative costs while allowing a reasonable profit for the agency's efforts. (A markup of 17.65 percent of costs added to the cost would yield a 15 percent commission. For example, research costs of $100,000 times 17.65% equals $100,000 plus $17,650 equals $117,650. The $17,650 markup is about 15 percent of $117,650.)

The Future of Agency Compensation   As you can see, there is no one method of compensation to which everyone subscribes. Cost-conscious advertisers are rebelling against the traditional commission system. A 1995 study on agency compensation by the Association of National Advertisers found that only 14 percent of full-service agencies receive a full 15 percent commission. Most advertisers using full-service agencies pay commissions ranging from 8 to 15 percent, with larger advertisers paying an average of 13 percent. An increasing number prefer set fees or an incentive-based system and nearly 20 percent now include incentives as part of total compensation.[21]

EXHIBIT 3–6
The Calet, Hirsch & Ferrell agency promotes its guaranteed idea program

THE TOP 100 AGENCIES OF 1992

Rank	Agency	Headquarters	1992	1991	% Change
1	Foote, Cone & Belding	Chicago	2,288,469	2,165,753	+5.7
2	Leo Burnett Co.	Chicago	2,104,073	2,040,268	+3.1
3	J. Walter Thompson	New York	1,944,000	1,753,000	+10.9
4	D'Arcy, Masius, Benton & Bowles	New York	1,929,000	1,962,000	-1.7
5	DDB Needham	New York	1,910,721	2,015,342	-5.2
6	Young & Rubicam	New York	1,842,000	1,852,600	-0.6
7	Saatchi & Saatchi Advertising	New York	1,750,000	1,762,000	-0.7
8	Grey Advertising	New York	1,719,000	1,623,200	+5.9
9	BBDO	New York	1,634,768	1,531,316	+6.8
10	McCann-Erickson	New York	1,567,800	1,400,000	+12.0
11	Ogilvy & Mather	New York	1,545,000	1,533,200	+0.8
12	CME KHBB	Minneapolis	1,008,542	975,180	+3.4
13	Backer Spielvogel Bates	Dallas	976,029	1,085,000	-10.0
14	Lintas:USA	New York	920,000	912,000	+0.9
15	Wells Rich Greene BDDP	New York	919,900	923,700	-0.4
16	Ayer	New York	855,300	754,413	+13.4
17	Bozell	New York	850,000	779,000	+9.1
18	Chiat/Day	Venice, CA	620,000	568,000	+9.2
19	Ketchum	Pittsburgh	612,490	604,800	+1.3
20	MVBMS/Euro RSCG	New York	500,635	405,641	+23.4
21	Earle Palmer Brown	Bethesda	408,640	417,600	-2.1
22	Temerlin McClain	Dallas	405,000	350,000	+15.7
23	Jordan, McGrath, Case & Taylor	New York	370,000	350,000	+5.7
24	Tatham Euro RSCG	Chicago	349,563	324,679	+7.7
25	Hill, Holliday, Connors, Cosmopulos	Boston	338,049	357,293	-5.4
26	Hal Riney & Partners	San Francisco	335,000	325,000	+3.1
27	Admarketing	Los Angeles	329,700	317,200	+3.9
28	TBWA	New York	325,597	303,728	+7.2
29	Lowe & Partners	New York	325,000	325,000	0.0
30	Ammirati & Puris	New York	325,000	250,000	+30.0
31	W.B. Doner	Southfield, MI	295,746	296,823	-0.4
32	Ally & Gargano	New York	275,000	284,000	-3.2
33	Anrett, Free & Ginsberg	New York	260,000	245,000	+6.1
34	Lois/USA	New York	246,000	237,000	+3.8
35	Wieden & Kennedy	Portland, OR	240,000	168,000	+42.9
36	Arnold Fortuna Lawner & Cabot	Boston	217,705	195,000	+11.6
37	Bloom FCA	New York	215,000	189,100	+13.7
38	Rubin Postaer & Associates	Los Angeles	210,800	180,700	+16.7
39	Laurence, Charles, Free & Lawson	New York	208,723	215,234	-3.0
40	GSD&M	Austin	201,083	149,500	+34.5
41	Team One	El Segundo, CA	197,000	183,500	+7.4
42	Tucker Wayne/Luckie & Co.	Atlanta	196,000	167,000	+17.4
45	The Richards Group	Dallas	182,500		
49	Goodby Berlin & Silverstein	San Francisco	166,445	117,300	+41.9
50	Berenstein-Rein	Kansas City	159,112	135,395	+17.5
51	Fallgren Martin	Parkersburg, WV	158,808	144,105	+10.2
52	Lord, Dentsu & Partners	New York	158,000	152,000	+3.9
53	Bayer Bess Vanderwarker	Chicago	151,338	125,312	+20.8
54	McCaffrey and McCall	New York	150,000	274,503	-45.4
55	Warwick Baker & Fiore	New York	150,000	153,000	-2.0
56	Dailey & Associates	Los Angeles	149,000	155,664	-4.3
57	The Martin Agency	Richmond	148,043	113,497	+30.4
58	Davis, Ball & Colombatto	Los Angeles	141,720	148,692	-4.7
59	Cramer-Krasselt	Milwaukee	141,460	126,240	+12.1
60	Ingalls, Quinn & Johnson	Boston	140,069	139,028	+0.7
61	Calet, Hirsch & Ferrell	New York	135,000	135,000	0.0
62	Deutsch/Dworin	New York	135,000	90,000	+50.0
63	Wyse Advertising	Cleveland	133,000	130,000	+2.3
64	Eisaman, Johns & Laws	Los Angeles	131,000	131,000	0.0
65	Rosenfeld, Sirowitz, Humphrey & Strauss	New York	129,000	135,000	-4.4
66	Fallon McElligott	Minneapolis	125,098	126,095	-0.8
67	Martin/Williams	Minneapolis	125,000	119,000	+5.0
68	Margeotes Fertitta & Weiss	New York	122,000	103,000	+18.4
69	Meldrum & Fewsmith	Cleveland	119,827	116,211	+3.1
70	Long Haymes & Carr	Winston-Salem	115,300	87,700	+36.0
71	Valentine-Radford	Kansas City	119,060	92,950	+28.1
72	Doremus & Co.	New York	111,914	86,457	+29.4
73	Carmichael Lynch	Minneapolis	110,700	109,700	+0.9
74	Mullen	Wenham, MA	108,300	96,210	+12.6
75	The Weightman Group	Philadelphia	108,000	104,000	+3.8
76	Angotti, Thomas, Hedge	New York	105,000	90,000	+16.7
77	Cliff Freeman & Partners	New York	105,000	80,800	+30.0
78	Kirshenbaum & Bond	New York	105,000	65,000	+61.5
79	CHC & M.E.O.	Woodbridge, NJ	103,000	140,000	-26.4
80	McKinney & Silver	Raleigh, NC	101,886	90,750	+12.3
81	Rotando Lerch & Iafelice	Stamford, CT	100,300	85,800	+16.9
82	Cadwell Davis Partners	New York	98,000	100,400	-2.4
83	Kresser Craig	Los Angeles	96,773	92,166	+5.0
84	Venet Advertising	Union, NJ	94,500	124,900	-24.3
85	Goldberg Moser O'Neill	San Francisco	89,600	81,000	+10.6
86	Gianettino & Meredith	Short Hills, NJ	89,000	81,200	+9.6
87	Fogarty & Klein/Wnius-Brandon	Houston	87,777	87,389	+0.4
88	Rumrill-Hoyt	Rochester	85,636	99,350	-13.6
89	Towne,Silverstein,Rotter	New York	85,000	85,000	0.0
90	Gray Kirk/Van Sant	Baltimore	80,750	75,500	+7.0
91	Laughlin/Constable	Milwaukee	80,500	68,440	+17.7
95	Cole & Weber	Seattle	79,000	83,246	-5.1
99	Jack Levy & Associates	Chicago	77,400	68,724	+12.6
100	Asher/Gould	Los Angeles	76,000	74,000	+2.7

There are 81 advertising agencies billing over $100,000,000. Only one of them is willing to guarantee its ideas.

As more companies adopt IMC approaches, they are reducing their reliance on traditional media advertising and thus changing their compensation systems. Usually some combination of payment methods is agreed on, such as a negotiated set fee plus incentives. For example, General Motors recently changed to an incentive-based compensation system that does not include media commissions with Leo Burnett, the agency for its Oldsmobile division, and Hal Riney & Partners, the agency for Saturn.[22] GM made the change to encourage its agencies to look beyond traditional mass media advertising and develop other ways of reaching consumers.[23]

Many companies are trying to reduce agency compensation, but most recognize that their account must be profitable for the agency if they want quality work. Nestlé and Unilever, two of the world's largest consumer product marketers, recently revised their compensation policies to make sure that their agencies receive a reasonable profit and that they get the best results from their agencies.[24]

EVALUATING AGENCIES

Given the substantial amounts of monies being spent on advertising and promotion, demand for accountability of the expenditures has increased. Regular reviews of the agency's performance are necessary. The agency evaluation process usually involves two types of assessments, one financial and operational and the other more qualitative. The **financial audit** focuses on how the agency conducts its business. It is designed to verify costs and expenses, the number of personnel hours charged to an account, and payments to media and outside suppliers. The **qualitative audit** focuses on the agency's efforts in planning, developing, and implementing the client's advertising programs and considers the results achieved.

The agency evaluation is often done on a subjective, informal basis, particularly in smaller companies where ad budgets are low or advertising is not seen as the most critical factor in the firm's marketing performance. Some companies have developed formal, systematic evaluation systems, particularly when budgets are large and the advertising function receives much emphasis. As advertising costs continue to rise, the top management of these companies wants to be sure money is being spent efficiently and effectively.

One example of a formal agency evaluation system is that used by Borden Foods Corporation, which markets a variety of consumer products.[25] Borden's brand teams meet once a

EXHIBIT 3—7   Borden's ad agency performance evaluation

IV. CREATIVE SERVICES
1. Agency regularly produces fresh ideas and original approaches
Poor   **Average**   **Excellent**
1   2   3   4   5   6   7   8   9   10
2. Creative executions are consistently on strategy
1   2   3   4   5   6   7   8   9   10
3. Research is effectively used in strategic development and in pre- and post-testing of advertising
1   2   3   4   5   6   7   8   9   10
4. Creative group is knowledgeable about Company's products, markets, and strategies
1   2   3   4   5   6   7   8   9   10
5. Borden is encouraged to participate in creative development
1   2   3   4   5   6   7   8   9   10
6. Creative group is concerned with good and consistent advertising communications, and develops campaigns/ads that exhibit this concern
1   2   3   4   5   6   7   8   9   10
7. Creative group produces on time and submits for review in time to permit orderly revisions
1   2   3   4   5   6   7   8   9   10
8. Creative group performs well under pressure
1   2   3   4   5   6   7   8   9   10
9. Agency presentations are well-organized with sufficient examples of proposed executions
1   2   3   4   5   6   7   8   9   10
10. Creative group participates in major campaign presentations
1   2   3   4   5   6   7   8   9   10
11. Agency presents ideas and executions not requested but which they feel are good opportunities
1   2   3   4   5   6   7   8   9   10
12. Creative group takes constructive criticism and redirection
1   2   3   4   5   6   7   8   9   10
13. Creative group effectively controls costs
1   2   3   4   5   6   7   8   9   10
14. Overall evaluation of creative services
1   2   3   4   5   6   7   8   9   10

VI. MEDIA SERVICES
1. Media group actively explores new uses of the various media available
Poor   **Average**   **Excellent**
1   2   3   4   5   6   7   8   9   10
2. Agency media recommendations are objective and reflect sufficient knowledge of Company's markets, target consumers, services and objectives
1   2   3   4   5   6   7   8   9   10
3. Agency exhibits a broad capability in media as opposed to specializing in one particular medium
1   2   3   4   5   6   7   8   9   10
4. Agency keeps Client up-to-date on trends and developments in the field of media
1   2   3   4   5   6   7   8   9   10
5. Agency subscribes to and makes use of available and applicable syndicated media services
1   2   3   4   5   6   7   8   9   10
6. Agency engages in original research relating to the selection and use of media
1   2   3   4   5   6   7   8   9   10
7. Agency provides Client with regular review and analysis of competition's media usage
1   2   3   4   5   6   7   8   9   10
8. Agency media administrative practices are adequate, including coordination of media schedules, contracts, checking media to verify advertising has run, etc.
1   2   3   4   5   6   7   8   9   10
9. Agency regularly conducts post-buy analysis on all media placements in a timely manner
1   2   3   4   5   6   7   8   9   10
10. Agency is effective in media negotiations for best possible rates and position for Company advertising
1   2   3   4   5   6   7   8   9   10
11. Media plans provide sufficient flexibility for opportunistic buys or other cost-saving strategies
1   2   3   4   5   6   7   8   9   10
12. Agency communicates plan objectives and rationale effectively to brand management
1   2   3   4   5   6   7   8   9   10
13. Media strategies establish specific and measurable goals for reach, frequency and other objectives
1   2   3   4   5   6   7   8   9   10

year with the company's agencies to review their performance. Brand management completes the advertising agency performance evaluation, part of which is shown in Exhibit 3–7. These reports are compiled and reviewed with the agency at each annual meeting. Borden's evaluation process consists of eight areas of performance.

Borden and the agency develop an action plan to correct areas of deficiency. But some companies doubt whether advertising effectiveness can be directly related to sales and have developed their own evaluation procedures. R. J. Reynolds emphasizes creative development and execution, marketing counsel and ideas, promotion support, and cost controls, without any mention of sales figures. Sears focuses on the performance of the agency as a whole in an effort to establish a partnership between the agency and the client.

These and other evaluation methods are being used more regularly by advertisers. As fiscal controls tighten, clients will require more accountability from their providers and adopt formal evaluation procedures.

Gaining and Losing Clients

The evaluation process results in outcomes that may or may not be favorable to the agency. As shown in Figure 3–9, some of the world's most valuable brands have had very long term relationships with their agencies. However, long-term relationships are becoming less common. A 1996 survey by the American Association of Advertising Agencies found that the average tenure of client-agency relationships has declined from 7.2 years to 5.3 years since 1984.[26]

There are a number of reasons clients switch agencies. Understanding these potential problems can help the agency avoid them.[27] In addition, it is important to understand the process agencies go through in trying to gain new clients.

	Age of Brand	Length of Agency Relationship
Marlboro	43	Leo Burnett Co./43 years
McDonald's	42	DDB Needham Worldwide/27 years
Kodak	105	J. Walter Thompson Co./67 years
Kellogg's	91	JWT/67 years
Gillette	94	BBDO Worldwide/31 years
General Electric	101	BBDO/77 years
Pepsi-Cola	99	BBDO/37 years
Frito-Lay	65	DDB Needham/43 years
Levi's	145	Foote, Cone & Belding/67 years

Note: From the top 20 as defined by *Financial World*, July 1996.

Note: For brands that split their accounts fairly evenly, agency with longer tenure is listed.

Source: Mark Gleason, "MIA on Madison Avenue: Agency, Client Loyalty," *Advertising Age*, January 27, 1997, p. 3.

WHY AGENCIES LOSE CLIENTS

Some of the more common reasons agencies lose clients follow.

- *Poor performance or service.* The client becomes dissatisfied with the quality of the advertising and/or the service provided by the agency.
- *Poor communication.* The client and agency personnel fail to develop or maintain the level of communication necessary to sustain a favorable working relationship.
- *Unrealistic demands by the client.* The client places demands on the agency that exceed the amount of compensation received and reduce the account's profitability.
- *Personality conflicts.* People working on the account on the client and agency sides do not have enough rapport to work well together.
- *Personnel changes.* A change in personnel at either the agency or the advertiser can create problems. New managers may wish to use an agency with whom they have established ties. Agency personnel often take accounts with them when they switch agencies or start their own.
- *Changes in size of the client or agency.* The client may outgrow the agency or decide it needs a larger agency to handle its business. If the agency gets too large, the client may represent too small a percentage of its business to command attention.
- *Conflicts of interest.* A conflict may develop when an agency merges with another agency or when a client is part of an acquisition or merger. In the United States, an agency cannot handle two accounts that are in direct competition with each other. In some cases, even indirect competition will not be tolerated.
- *Changes in the client's corporate and/or marketing strategy.* A client may change its marketing strategy and think a new agency is needed to carry out the new program. For example, AT&T decided to change agencies following a major restructuring of the company that included the divestment of its NCR computer division and Lucent Technologies, its phone-equipment business. AT&T felt that a new agency was needed to develop a corporate image campaign that positions the company as a supplier of long-distance and other telecommunications services.[28]
- *Declining sales.* When sales of the client's product or service are stagnant or declining, advertising may be seen as contributing to the problem. A new agency may be sought for a new creative approach.
- *Conflicting compensation philosophies.* Disagreement may develop over the level or method of compensation. As more companies move toward incentive-based compensation systems, disagreement over compensation is becoming more commonplace.
- *Changes in policies.* Policy changes may result when either party reevaluates the importance of the relationship, the agency acquires a new (and larger) client, or either side undergoes a merger or acquisition.

If the agency recognizes these warning signs, it can try to adapt its programs and policies to make sure the client is satisfied. Some of the situations discussed here are unavoidable and others are beyond the agency's control. But to maintain the account, problems within the agency's control must be addressed.

The time may come when the agency decides it is no longer in its best interest to continue to work with the client. Personnel conflicts, changes in management philosophy, and/or insufficient financial incentives are just a few of the reasons for such a decision. Then the agency may terminate the account relationship.

HOW AGENCIES GAIN CLIENTS

Competition for accounts in the agency business is intense, since most companies have already organized for the advertising function and only a limited number of new businesses require such services each year. While small agencies may be willing to work with a new company and grow along with it, larger agencies often do not become interested in these firms until they are able to spend at least $1 million per year on advertising. Many of the top 15 agencies won't accept an account that spends less than $5 million per year. Once that expenditure level is reached, competition for the account intensifies.

In large agencies, most new business results from clients that already have an agency but decide to change their relationships. Thus, agencies must constantly search and compete for new clients. Some of the ways they do this follow.

Referrals

Many good agencies obtain new clients as a result of referrals from existing clients, media representatives, and even other agencies. These agencies maintain good working relationships with their clients, the media, and outside parties that might provide business to them.

Solicitations

One of the more common ways to gain new business is through direct solicitation. In smaller agencies, the president may solicit new accounts. In most large agencies, a new business development group seeks out and establishes contact with new clients. The group is responsible for writing solicitation letters, making cold calls, and following up on leads.

Presentations

A basic goal of the new business development group is to receive an invitation from a company to make a presentation. This gives the agency the opportunity to sell itself—to describe its experience, personnel, capabilities, and operating procedures, as well as to demonstrate its previous work.

The agency may be asked to make a speculative presentation, in which it examines the client's marketing situation and proposes a tentative communications campaign. Because presentations require a great deal of time and preparation and may cost the agency a considerable amount of money without a guarantee of gaining the business, many firms refuse to participate in "creative shootouts." They argue that agencies should be selected based on their experience and the services and programs they have provided for previous clients.[29]

Nevertheless, most agencies do participate in this form of solicitation, either by choice or because they must do so to gain accounts.

Due in part to the emphasis on speculative presentations, a very important role has developed for *presentation consultants*, who specialize in helping clients choose ad agencies. Because their opinions are respected by clients, the entire agency review process may be structured according to their guidelines. As you might imagine, these consultants wield a great deal of power with both clients and agencies.

Public relations

Agencies also seek business through publicity/public relations efforts. They often participate in civic and social groups and work with charitable organizations pro bono (at cost, without pay) to earn respect in the community. Participation in professional associations such as the American Association of Advertising Agencies and the Advertising Research Foundation can also lead to new contacts. Successful agencies often receive free publicity throughout the industry as well as in the mass media.

Image and reputation

Perhaps the most effective way an agency can gain new business is through its reputation. Agencies that consistently develop excellent campaigns are often approached by clients. Agencies may enter their work in award competitions or advertise themselves to enhance their image in the marketing community (as shown here).

SPECIALIZED SERVICES

Many companies assign the development and implementation of their promotional programs to an advertising agency. But several other types of organizations provide specialized services that complement the efforts of ad agencies. Direct-response agencies, sales promotion agencies, and public relations firms are important to marketers in developing and executing IMC programs in the United States as well as international markets. Global Perspective 3–3 discusses specialized services for companies that want to adapt their integrated marketing communications to the Canadian marketplace. Let us examine the functions these organizations perform.

Direct-Response Agencies

One of the fastest-growing areas of IMC is direct marketing, where companies communicate with consumers through telemarketing, direct mail, and other forms of direct-response advertising. As this industry has grown, numerous direct-response agencies have evolved that offer companies their specialized skills in both the consumer and business markets. Figure 3–10 shows the top 10 direct-response agencies (several of which, including Ogilvy & Mather Direct, DraftDirect, and Grey Direct, are divisions or subsidiaries of large ad agencies).

Direct-response agencies provide a variety of services, including database management, direct mail, research, media services, and creative and production capabilities. While direct mail is their primary weapon, many direct-response agencies are expanding their services to include such areas as infomercial production and database management. Database development and management is becoming one of the most important services provided by direct-response agencies. Many companies are using database marketing to pinpoint new customers and build relationships and loyalty among existing customers.[30]

Global Perspective 3–3
Integrated Marketing Communications North of the Border

If you ask most people who the United States' largest trading partner is, they are likely to name a European country or Japan. But Canada has been our largest trading partner for years, and the Canadian market took on even more importance with the passage of the North American Free Trade Agreement (NAFTA), which eliminated many of the trade barriers among the United States, Canada, and Mexico. As more and more U.S. companies adopt the concept of integrated marketing communications, many want to approach the Canadian market the same way.

Companies hoping to use IMC in Canada will find that our northern neighbor has all of the services, technologies, and message delivery systems needed to utilize this approach fully. Virtually every major U.S. ad agency has offices or affiliations in Canada. There are a number of excellent Canadian agencies throughout the country, which are particularly important in adapting IMC to the specialized needs of French Canada.

Direct marketing is becoming an integral part of successful IMC programs in Canada. Some direct marketers knowledgeable about trends on both sides of the border claim Canadians are not bombarded with as much direct mail as Americans. With less clutter in their mailboxes, Canadians respond better to mail solicitations. A number of companies, among them CMAC, R. L. Polk, Compusearch, and Tetrad, provide special software and databases to target those of the Canada Post Corp.'s 25,000-plus mail walks that match a marketer's customer profile. There are also plenty of good mailing lists available. Much of the software used in the United States to support marketing databases can be used in Canada. Several U.S.-based database marketing companies have established a strong presence in Canada, and there are numerous Canadian direct-marketing agencies.

Canada offers broadcast and print media measurement services that closely resemble those used in the United States. For example, A. C. Nielsen and the Bureau of Broadcast Measurement in Toronto provide meter and diary results to subscribers for most broadcast programming, including U.S. stations that reach Canadians. For companies seeking information on the Canadian market, there are a number of professional survey research companies throughout Canada. Larger companies like Gallup of Canada and Market Facts of Canada offer syndicated tracking surveys similar to their U.S. counterparts. Canada's census bureau is also an excellent source of information. The bureau's Statistics Canada's *Survey of Family Expenditures* provides a wealth of detail on virtually all classes of consumer purchases across 17 metropolitan areas in Canada.

Canada has many demographic, cultural, and lifestyle diversities that must be recognized. Its 28.5 million people live in about 10 million households, and nearly 70 percent are within a two-hour drive of the U.S. border. About 40 percent of the Canadian population doesn't use English as its preferred language. Of the non-English speakers, about 60 percent are French Canadians, with the balance spread among a dozen or so other languages. Like the United States, Canada has seen the ethnic composition of its immigrants change. More than half of the country's immigrants now come from Asia and China in particular. Estimates are that by the year 2001, Canada's Chinese community will number nearly 1.2 million, with most settling in either Vancouver or Toronto. The Canadian Chinese are well-educated, affluent, and easy to reach through Chinese-language media including TV, radio, and three major daily newspapers.

Companies doing business in Canada will find all the resources and services they need for customer-focused IMC. However, U.S. companies must not assume that Canadians are simply Americans living north of the 49th parallel, and that what works in the United States should fit Canada. Canadians feel different from their neighbors to the south and want that difference recognized. The creative director of the Toronto office of J. Walter Thompson notes that: "We have specific marketing conditions in this country. We are temperamentally different from Americans and we have governmental regulations which differ from the U.S."

Sources: Stephen Barrington, "Canada Speaks to Chinese Markets," *Advertising Age International*, January 1997, pp. I12, 14; Jon Kalina, "'Vive la différence': Learning Trade North of the 49th Parallel," *Advertising Age International*, September 18, 1995, pp. I23, 30; Dan Hulk and Martin Dunphy, "Adapting IMC to Canada Requires a Custom Fit," *Marketing News*, August 16, 1993, p. 2.

Rank	Agency, Headquarters	
1	Wunderman Cato Johnson, New York	$669,335
2	Rapp Collins Worldwide, New York	486,294
3	Bronner Slosberg Humphrey, Boston	450,192
4	DraftDirect Worldwide, Chicago	413,500
5	Ogilvy & Mather Direct, New York	346,000
6	Barry Blau & Partners, Fairfield, CT	332,653
7	Dimac Direct, Bridgeton, MO	315,600
8	Customer Development Corp., Peoria, IL	201,826
9	Grey Direct Marketing, New York	186,100
10	Targetbase Marketing, Irving, TX	171,089

Source: Reprinted with permission from the August 5, 1996 issue of *Advertising Age*, p. S3. Copyright Crain Communications, Inc. 1996.

A typical direct-response agency is divided into three main departments: account management, creative, and media. Some agencies also have a department whose function is to develop and manage databases for their clients. The account managers work with their clients to plan direct-marketing programs and determine their role in the overall integrated marketing communications process. The creative department consists of copywriters, artists, and producers. Creative is responsible for developing the direct-response message, while the media department is concerned with its placement.

Like advertising agencies, direct-response agencies must solicit new business and have their performance reviewed by their existing clients, often through formal assessment programs. Most direct-response agencies are compensated on a fee basis, although some large advertisers still prefer the commission system.

Sales Promotion Agencies

Developing and managing sales promotion programs such as contests, sweepstakes, refunds and rebates, premium and incentive offers, and sampling programs is a very complex task. Most companies use a **sales promotion agency** to develop and administer these programs. Some large ad agencies have created their own sales promotion department or acquired a sales promotion firm. However, most sales promotion agencies are independent companies that specialize in providing the services needed to plan, develop, and execute a variety of sales promotion programs (Exhibit 3–8).

Sales promotion agencies often work in conjunction with the client's advertising and/or direct-response agencies to coordinate their efforts with the advertising and direct-marketing programs. Services provided by large sales promotion agencies include promotional planning, creative, research, tie-in coordination, fulfillment, premium design and manufacturing, catalog production, and contest/sweepstakes management. Many sales promotion agencies are also developing direct/database marketing and telemarketing to expand their integrated marketing services capabilities. Sales promotion agencies are generally compensated on a fee basis.

Public Relations Firms

Many large companies use both an advertising agency and a PR firm. The **public relations firm** develops and implements programs to manage the organization's publicity, image, and affairs with consumers and other relevant publics, including employees, suppliers, stockholders, government, labor groups, citizen action groups, and the general public. The PR firm analyzes the relationships between the client and these various publics, determines how the client's policies and actions relate to and affect these publics, develops PR strategies and programs, implements these programs using various public relations tools, and evaluates their effectiveness.

The activities of a public relations firm include planning the PR strategy and program, generating publicity, conducting lobbying and public affairs efforts, becoming involved in community activities and events, preparing news releases and other communications, conducting research, promoting and managing special events, and managing crises. As compa-

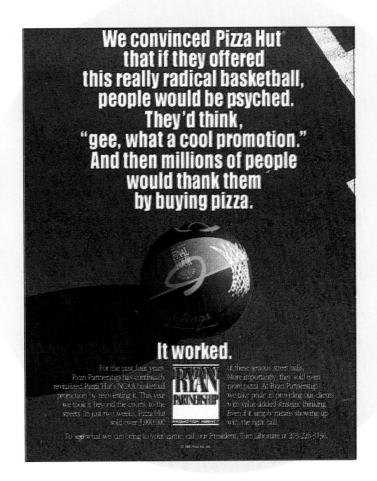

nies adopt an IMC approach to promotional planning, they are coordinating their PR activities with advertising and other promotional areas. Many companies are integrating public relations and publicity into the marketing communications mix to increase message credibility and save media costs.[31] Public relations firms are generally compensated by retainer. We will examine their role in more detail in Chapter 16.

Interactive Agencies

With the rapid growth of the Internet and other forms of interactive media, a new type of specialized marketing communication organization has evolved—the interactive agency. Many marketers are using **interactive agencies** that specialize in the creation of interactive media such as CD-ROMs, kiosks, and websites on the section of the Internet known as the World Wide Web (WWW). Many traditional ad agencies have established interactive capabilities, ranging from a few specialists within the agency to entire interactive divisions.[32] For example, the Leo Burnett agency has an interactive marketing group that developed media ranging from CD-ROMs for clients like Oldsmobile to entire websites for Maytag and Kellogg.

While many agencies have or are developing interactive capabilities, a number of marketers are turning to more specialized firms to develop interactive media. They feel these companies have more expertise in creating digitized sites that combine audio, animation, and video. For example, website developers such as Dimension X, On-Ramp Inc., and Organic Online are being used by major companies such as Fox Broadcasting, Sega of America, and McDonald's to develop high-impact sites. As the Internet becomes an increasingly important marketing tool, more companies will be looking to interactive agencies for assistance. Exhibit 3–9 shows an ad promoting the services of an interactive agency.

COLLATERAL SERVICES

The final participants in the promotional process are those that provide various collateral services. They include marketing research companies, package design firms, consultants, media buying services, photographers, printers, video production houses, and event marketing services companies.

EXHIBIT 3—9
An interactive agency promotes its services

Marketing Research Companies

One of the more widely used collateral service organizations is the marketing research firm. Companies are increasingly turning to marketing research to help them understand their target audiences and to gather information that will be of value in designing and evaluating their advertising and promotions programs. Even companies with their own marketing research departments often hire outside research agencies to perform some services. Marketing research companies offer specialized services and can gather objective information that is valuable to the advertiser's promotional programs. They conduct *qualitative* research such as in-depth interviews and focus groups, as well as *quantitative* studies such as market surveys.

INTEGRATED MARKETING COMMUNICATIONS SERVICES

You have seen that marketers can choose from a variety of specialized organizations to assist them in planning, developing, and implementing an integrated marketing communications program. But companies must decide whether to use a different organization for each marketing communications function or consolidate them with a large advertising agency that offers all of these services under one roof.

As noted in Chapter 1, during the 1980s many of the large agencies realized that their clients were shifting their promotional dollars away from traditional advertising to other forms of promotion and began developing IMC capabilities.[33] Some did this through mergers and acquisitions and became superagencies consisting of advertising, public relations, sales promotion, and direct-response agencies.

Many large agencies are continuing to expand their IMC capabilities by acquiring specialists in various fields. For example, the Interpublic Group, the world's third-largest advertising company, recently purchased DraftDirect Worldwide, one of the largest direct-response agencies. One of Interpublic's agencies, McCann-Erickson Worldwide, purchased Ad:vent, a leading specialist in the event marketing business, and merged the company with its existing event marketing operation, Momentum IMC.[34]

While some agencies are expanding their IMC capabilities by acquiring specialized firms and services, others are doing so internally. For example, Leo Burnett became one of the leaders in integrated marketing communications services by developing IMC skills internally. First it hired senior-level marketing specialists in a variety of disciplines whose job was to develop integrated strategic thinking and execution for the agency's clients in the U.S. and abroad. Then it brought in more than 100 direct-marketing, sales promotion, event marketing, interactive, and public relations professionals and dispersed them throughout the agency, rather than isolating them in a separate department. These IMC specialists are fully integrated with the agency's client services, creative, media, research, database, and production departments. They teach other agency personnel how to use the various promotional tools in their clients' campaigns.[35] Exhibit 3–10 shows promotional materials from the IMC campaign Leo Burnett developed to launch the Oldsmobile Aurora.

The Leo Burnett approach is an example of what Anders Gronstedt and Esther Thorson call an *integrated organization structure,* where the ad agency incorporates various communication specialists into its structure rather than forming separate departments for each.[36] The various communications specialists work for a particular client rather than a specific department. The integrated structure is also common among small and medium-size agencies that do not have the resources to hire specialists but rather have a group of generalists who handle a wide range of communication services.

Pros and Cons of Integrated Services

It has been argued that the concept of integrated marketing is nothing new, particularly in smaller companies and communication agencies that have been coordinating a variety of promotional tools for years. And larger advertising agencies have been trying to gain more of their clients' promotional business for over 20 years. However, in the past, the various services were run as separate profit centers. Each was motivated to push its own expertise and

EXHIBIT 3–10
Leo Burnett developed an integrated campaign for the Oldsmobile Aurora

pursue its own goals rather than develop truly integrated marketing programs. Moreover, the creative specialists in many agencies resisted becoming involved in sales promotion or direct marketing. They preferred to concentrate on developing magazine ads or television commercials rather than designing coupons or direct-mail pieces.

Proponents of the integrated marketing services agency (the one-stop shop) contend that past problems are being solved and the various individuals in the agencies and subsidiaries are learning to work together to deliver a consistent message to the client's customers. They argue that maintaining control of the entire promotional process achieves greater synergy among each of the communications program elements. They also note that it is more convenient for the client to coordinate all of its marketing efforts—media advertising, direct mail, special events, sales promotions, and public relations—through one agency. An agency with integrated marketing capabilities can create a single image for the product or service and address everyone, from wholesalers to consumers, with one voice.

But not everyone wants to turn the entire IMC program over to one agency. Opponents say the providers become involved in political wrangling over budgets, do not communicate with each other as well and as often as they should, and do not achieve synergy. They also claim that agencies' efforts to control all aspects of the promotional program are nothing more than an attempt to hold on to business that might otherwise be lost to independent providers. They note that synergy and economies of scale, while nice in theory, have been difficult to achieve, and competition and conflict among agency subsidiaries have been a major problem.[37]

Many companies, such as Miller Brewing and Reebok, use a variety of vendors for communication functions, choosing the specialist they believe is best suited for each promotional task, be it advertising, sales promotion, or public relations. Many marketers agree with the vice president of advertising at Reebok, who noted, "Why should I limit myself to one resource when there is a tremendous pool of fresh ideas available?"[38]

Responsibility for IMC: Agency versus Client

Surveys of advertisers and agency executives have shown that both groups believe integrated marketing is important to their organization's success and that it will be even more important in the future.[39] However, marketers and agency executives have very different opinions regarding who should be in charge of the integrated marketing communications process. Many advertisers prefer to set strategy for and coordinate their own IMC campaigns, but most agency executives see this as their domain.

While agency executives believe their shops are capable of handling the various elements an integrated campaign requires, many marketers, particularly larger firms, disagree. Marketing executives say the biggest obstacle to implementing IMC is the lack of people with the broad perspective and skills to make it work. Agencies are felt to lack expertise in database marketing, marketing research, and information technology. Internal turf battles, agency egos, and fear of budget reductions are also cited as major barriers to successful integrated marketing campaigns.[40]

Many ad agencies are adding more resources to offer their clients a full line of services. They are expanding their agencies' capabilities in interactive and multimedia advertising, database management, direct marketing, public relations, and sales promotion. However, many marketers still want to set the strategy for their IMC campaigns and seek specialized expertise, more quality and creativity, and greater control and cost efficiency by using multiple providers.

Most marketers do recognize that ad agencies will no longer stick primarily to advertising and will continue to expand their IMC capabilities. There is an opportunity for agencies to broaden their services beyond advertising—but they will have to develop true expertise in a variety of integrated marketing communications areas. They will also have to create organizational structures that make it possible for individuals with expertise in a variety of communications areas to work well together both internally and externally. One thing is certain: as companies continue to shift their promotional dollars away from media advertising to other forms of promotion, agencies will continue to explore ways to keep these monies under their roofs.

SUMMARY

The development, execution, and administration of an advertising and promotions program involve the efforts of many individuals, both within the company and outside it. Participants in the integrated marketing communications process include the advertiser or client, ad agencies, media organizations, specialized marketing communications firms, and providers of collateral services.

Companies use three basic systems to organize internally for advertising and promotion. Centralized systems offer the advantages of facilitated communications, lower personnel requirements, continuity in staff, and more top-management involvement. Disadvantages include a lower involvement with overall marketing goals, longer response times, and difficulties in handling multiple product lines.

Decentralized systems offer the advantages of concentrated managerial attention, more rapid responses to problems, and increased flexibility, though they may be limited by ineffective decision making, internal conflicts, misallocation of funds, and a lack of authority. In-house agencies, while offering the advantages of cost savings, control, and increased coordination, have the disadvantage of less experience, objectivity, and flexibility.

Many firms use advertising agencies to help develop and execute their programs. These agencies may take on a variety of forms, including full-service agencies, creative boutiques, and media buying services. The first offers the client a full range of services (including creative, account, marketing, and financial and management services); the other two specialize in creative services and media buying, respectively. Agencies are compensated through commission systems, percentage charges, and fee- and cost-based systems. Recently, the emphasis on agency accountability has increased. Agencies are being evaluated on both financial and qualitative aspects, and some clients are using incentive-based compensation systems that tie agency compensation to performance measures such as sales and market share.

In addition to ad agencies, marketers use the services of other marketing communication specialists, including direct marketing agencies, sales promotion agencies, public relations firms, and interactive agencies. A marketer must decide whether to use a different specialist for each promotional function or have all of its integrated marketing communications done by an advertising agency that offers all of these services under one roof.

Recent studies have found that most marketers believe it is their responsibility, not the ad agency's, to set strategy for and coordinate IMC campaigns. The lack of a broad perspective and specialized skills in nonadvertising areas is seen as the major barrier to agencies' increased involvement in integrated marketing communications.

KEY TERMS

clients, 66
advertising agency, 66
media organizations, 66
specialized marketing
    communications
    services, 67
collateral services, 68
advertising manager, 68
centralized system, 68
decentralized system, 69

brand manager, 70
category management
    system, 70
in-house agency, 72
billings, 74
superagencies, 76
full-service agency, 77
account executive, 77
copywriters, 79

departmental system, 81
group system, 81
creative boutique, 81
media buying services, 81
commission system, 83
negotiated commission, 84
fixed-fee method, 84
fee-commission
    combination, 84

cost-plus system, 85
incentive-based system, 85
percentage charges, 85
financial audit, 86
qualitative audit, 86
direct-response agency, 90
sales promotion agency, 92
public relations firm, 92
interactive agencies, 93

DISCUSSION QUESTIONS

1. What are some of the reasons companies are switching from large superagencies to mid-sized agencies such as Fallon McElligott? Find an article on a company that has recently switched its account to Fallon McElligott and discuss the reasons given for the change.

2. Who are the major participants in the integrated marketing communications process? Briefly discuss the roles and responsibilities of each.

3. What are some of the specific responsibilities and duties of the advertising manager under a centralized advertising department structure? Is an advertising manager needed if a company uses an outside agency?

4. Analyze General Motors' decision to switch to a brand management system as discussed in IMC Perspective 3–1. How will this affect the advertising function? Do you think adoption of a brand management system will help GM

stabilize its declining market share or are other changes needed?

5. Discuss the pros and cons of using an in-house agency. Why do companies such as No Fear, Benetton, and Calvin Klein use in-house agencies?

6. Discuss the reasons companies use outside agencies. What things should a company consider when selecting an agency?

7. Analyze the decision by the Coca-Cola Co. to switch its creative assignment from McCann-Erickson to Creative Artists Agency and then to Edge Creative. Do you think more companies will use the services of nontraditional agencies in the future?

8. Discuss the various methods by which advertising agencies are compensated. What factors will determine the type of compensation system a company uses with an agency?

9. A number of companies have implemented incentive-based compensation systems whereby agencies are paid based on performance measures such as sales or market share. Do you believe this system is fair? Would you accept it if you were an agency?

10. What factors influence the relationship between a client and an agency? Why might an advertiser decide to switch from a long-term relationship with the same agency?

11. Who should have responsibility for development of the integrated marketing communications strategy, the agency or the client? Why?

Perspectives on Consumer Behavior

Chapter Objectives

- To examine the role consumer behavior plays in the development and implementation of advertising and promotional programs.

- To examine the consumer decision-making process and how it varies for different types of purchases.

- To understand various internal psychological processes, their influence on consumer decision making, and implications for advertising and promotion.

- To examine various approaches to studying the consumer learning process and their implications for advertising and promotion.

- To examine external factors such as culture, social class, group influences, and situational determinants and how they affect consumer behavior.

- To introduce alternative approaches to studying consumer behavior.

SATURN: A DIFFERENT KIND OF CAR

Back in the 1980s, General Motors recognized that American consumers had turned away from American-made cars in favor of Japanese imports. Sales of cars made in the United States had steadily declined from a high of 80 percent in the 1940s to 50 percent in the 1960s and now were down to 25 percent. Small cars accounted for much of this shift in preference. GM decided that drastic action was called for. It would develop a completely new auto division, the first since it introduced the Pontiac in 1926. The new subsidiary—called Saturn—was formed in 1985, and the first car rolled off the assembly line at Spring Hill, Tennessee, in 1990. By the end of its first decade, Saturn had sold over a million cars.

What has made Saturn so successful? It all started with an in-depth study of American car buyers: their attitudes toward American and foreign autos, how they made their automotive decisions, and who influenced these decisions. What the study found was not pretty. People felt that American-made cars were inferior to those made by the Japanese. They didn't like the whole buying process of having to visit a number of showrooms, negotiate with dealers, and so on. In general, they expressed a great deal of animosity toward car buying.

Saturn knew that to be successful it would have to be "a different kind of car company" with a "different kind of car." Based on this knowledge, it developed a new kind of program and a new "Saturn philosophy." Some of the program philosophies:

- *A new target market.* The new market would be one ignored by traditional auto dealers: first-car buyers and buyers who were female, younger, single, or blue collar.
- *Partnering.* Saturn formed partnerships with ad agencies, the United Auto Workers, suppliers, and retailers (dealers). The focus was on the consumer as the center of all partnership efforts. The philosophy was that no one partner had all the answers.
- *Sales training.* All retail salespeople were trained in a seven-step process ranging from reception of the customer to follow-up.
- *No-dicker pricing.* There was no need to negotiate; the price was on the sticker.
- *Innovative advertising.* "Partner" Hal Riney & Partners' ads featured satisfied Saturn owners rather than automobile attributes and "the left front fender syndrome." The ads were designed to create an interest in the car and encouraged visits to showrooms, where a relaxed selling atmosphere prevailed.
- *Public relations.* Retailers held customer picnics and service clinics to cement relationships between the owners and providers. (All customers—600,000 at the time—were invited to a "homecoming" at Saturn's factory in 1994. Over 44,000 came, and another 130,000 participated at dealerships around the United States.)

Saturn's success was phenomenal. As noted, it sold over a million cars in the first decade. It has received awards from almost every major automotive magazine each year since inception. *Advertising Age* acclaimed it as one of the most successful brands ever introduced in the United States. And perhaps most important of all, satisfied customers w[...] to purchase Saturns in the future.

Sources: Chad Rubel, "Partnerships Steer Saturn t[...] News, January 29, 1996, p. 5; "GM Pulled Out[...] Brand in 64 Years," *Automotive News*, Ap[...]

The Saturn story reveals that the development of successful marketing communication programs begins with understanding why consumers behave as they do. Those who develop advertising and other promotional strategies begin by identifying relevant markets and then analyzing the relationship between target consumers and the product/service or brand. The decision process for cars had undergone some major changes over the years, and drastic measures were required to turn things around. These new strategies would require an in-depth understanding of how and why consumers made choices regarding automobiles. Their motives for purchasing, attitudes toward American and foreign cars, and lifestyles needed to be understood before marketing strategies could be formulated.

These are just a few of the aspects of consumer behavior that promotional planners must consider in developing integrated marketing communication programs. As you will see, consumer choice is influenced by a variety of factors.

It is beyond the scope of this text to examine consumer behavior in depth. However, promotional planners need a basic understanding of consumer decision making, factors that influence it, and how this knowledge can be used in developing promotional strategies and programs. We begin with an overview of consumer behavior.

AN OVERVIEW OF CONSUMER BEHAVIOR

A challenge faced by all marketers is how to influence the purchase behavior of consumers in favor of the product or service they offer. For companies like American Express, this means getting consumers to charge more purchases on their AmEx cards. For BMW, it means getting them to purchase or lease a car; for business-to-business marketers like Canon or Ricoh, it means getting organizational buyers to purchase more of their copiers or fax machines. While their ultimate goal is to influence consumers' purchase behavior, most marketers understand that the actual purchase is only part of an overall process.

EXHIBIT 4–1
New Balance appeals to the active lifestyle

Monday: Father. Husband. Banker. Friend. Runner.
Tuesday: Husband. Banker. Father. Runner. Friend.
Wednesday: Banker. Banker. Banker. Banker. Banker.
Thursday: Runner. Husband. Father. Friend. Banker.
Friday: ?

Achieve New Balance.

new balance

The M825, our newest and most advanced men's running shoe. For a dealer call 1-800-253-SHOE or visit http://www.newbalance.com

Consumer behavior can be defined as the process and activities people engage in when searching for, selecting, purchasing, using, evaluating, and disposing of products and services so as to satisfy their needs and desires. For many products and services, purchase decisions are the result of a long, detailed process that may include an extensive information search, brand comparisons and evaluations, and other activities. Other purchase decisions are more incidental and may result from little more than seeing a product prominently displayed at a discount price in a store. Think of how many times you have made impulse purchases in stores.

Marketers' success in influencing purchase behavior depends in large part on how well they understand consumer behavior. Marketers need to know the specific needs customers are attempting to satisfy and how they translate into purchase criteria. They need to understand how consumers gather information regarding various alternatives and use this information to select among competing brands. They need to understand how customers make purchase decisions. Where do they prefer to buy a product? How are they influenced by marketing stimuli at the point of purchase? Marketers also need to understand how the consumer decision process and reasons for purchase vary among different types of customers. For example, purchase decisions may be influenced by the personality or lifestyle of the consumer.[1] Notice how the ad shown in Exhibit 4–1 reflects the various roles in the life of the target audience member.

The conceptual model in Figure 4–1 will be used as a framework for analyzing the consumer decision process. We will discuss what occurs at the various stages of this model and how advertising and promotion can be used to influence decision making. We will also examine the influence of various psychological concepts, such as motivation, perception, attitudes, and integration processes. Variations in the consumer decision-making process will be examined, as will perspectives regarding consumer learning and external influences on the consumer decision process. The chapter concludes with a consideration of alternative means of studying consumer behavior.

THE CONSUMER DECISION-MAKING PROCESS

As shown in Figure 4–1, the consumer's purchase decision process is generally viewed as consisting of steps through which the buyer passes in purchasing a product or service. This model shows that decision making involves a number of internal psychological processes. Motivation, perception, attitude formation, integration, and learning are important to promotional planners, since they influence the general decision-making process of the consumer. We will examine each stage of the purchase decision model and discuss how the various subprocesses influence what occurs at this step of the consumer behavior process. We will also discuss how promotional planners can influence this process.

Problem Recognition

Figure 4–1 shows that the first stage in the consumer decision-making process is **problem recognition**, when the consumer perceives a need and becomes motivated to solve the problem. The problem recognition stage initiates the subsequent decision processes.

Problem recognition is caused by a difference between the consumer's *ideal state* and *actual state*. A discrepancy exists between what the consumer wants the situation to be like

FIGURE 4–1   A basic model of consumer decision making

A. Stages in the Consumer Decision-Making Process

Problem recognition → Information search → Alternative evaluation → Purchase decision → Postpurchase evaluation

B. Relevant Internal Psychological Processes

Motivation → Perception → Attitude formation → Integration → Learning

and what the situation is really like. (Note that *problem* does not always imply a negative state. A goal exists for the consumer, and this goal may be the attainment of a more positive situation.)

SOURCES OF PROBLEM RECOGNITION

The causes of problem recognition may be very simple or very complex and may result from changes in the consumer's current and/or desired state. These causes may be influenced by both internal and external factors.

Out of Stock

Problem recognition occurs when consumers use their existing supply of a product and must replenish their stock. The purchase decision is usually simple and routine and is often resolved by choosing a familiar brand or one to which the consumer feels loyal.

Dissatisfaction

Problem recognition is created by the consumer's dissatisfaction with the current state of affairs and/or the product or service being used. For example, a consumer may think her ski boots are no longer comfortable or stylish enough. Advertising may be used to help consumers recognize when they have a problem and/or need to make a purchase. For example, Oral-B added a feature to its toothbrush to help consumers recognize when it is time to buy a new brush (Exhibit 4–2).

New Needs/Wants

Changes in consumers' lives often result in new needs, triggering problem recognition. Changes in one's financial situation, employment status, or lifestyle may create new needs and trigger problem recognition. For example, when you graduate from college and begin

EXHIBIT 4–2
The new Oral-B toothbrush helps consumers recognize when they need to replace it

your professional career, your new job may necessitate a change in your wardrobe. (Good-bye blue jeans and T-shirts, hello suits and ties.)

Not all product purchases are based on needs. Some products or services sought by consumers are not essential but are nonetheless desired. A **want** has been defined as a felt need that is shaped by a person's knowledge, culture, and personality.[2] Many products sold to consumers satisfy their wants rather than their basic needs.

Related Products/Purchases

Problem recognition can also be stimulated by the purchase of a product. For example, the purchase of a new camera may lead to the recognition of a need for accessories, such as additional lenses or a carrying case. The purchase of a personal computer may prompt the need for software programs or upgrades.

Marketer-Induced Problem Recognition

Another source of problem recognition is marketers' actions that encourage consumers not to be content with their current state or situation. Ads for personal hygiene products such as mouthwash, deodorant, and foot sprays may be designed to create insecurities that consumers can resolve through the use of these products (Exhibit 4–3). Marketers change fashions and clothing designs and create perceptions among consumers that their wardrobes are out of style.

Marketers also take advantage of consumers' tendency toward *novelty-seeking behavior*, which leads them to try different brands. Consumers often try new products or brands even when they are basically satisfied with their regular brand. Marketers encourage brand switching by introducing new brands into markets that are already saturated and by using advertising and sales promotion techniques such as free samples, introductory price offers, and coupons.

New Products

Problem recognition can also occur when innovative products are introduced and brought to the attention of consumers. Marketers are constantly introducing new products and services and telling consumers about the types of problems they solve. For example, marketers of cellular phones tell us why we need telephones in our cars and stress the time savings, convenience, and security they offer. Communicating by fax is becoming so prevalent that even consumers who work at home are finding they need fax machines (Exhibit 4–4).

Marketers' attempts to create problem recognition among consumers are not always successful. Consumers may not see a problem or need for the product the marketer is selling. A

EXHIBIT 4–3
This ad for Tartar Control Crest shows how marketers can use advertising to stimulate problem recognition

If you don't clean your teeth with Tartar Control Crest, objects in mirror may be closer than they appear.

It's not a pretty sight. You go in for a checkup thinking your teeth are clean, and the next thing you know, you've got tartar. What's going on? You're constantly brushing. You even rinse and floss.

And still your teeth aren't clean? That's right, because you're probably using the wrong toothpaste. Get the right one. Tartar Control Crest. It fights tartar buildup between dental

visits. So for a better reflection of the way you brush, start using Tartar Control Crest.

Crest

Tartar Control Crest. The Dentists' & Hygienists' Choice.

"Tartar Control Crest has been shown to be an effective decay-preventive dentifrice that can be of significant value when used as directed in a conscientiously applied program of oral hygiene and regular professional care. It has been shown to reduce the formation of tartar above the gumline, but has not been shown to have a therapeutic effect on periodontal diseases." - Council on Dental Therapeutics, American Dental Association. © P&G 1994

EXHIBIT 4—4
Innovative products such as fax
machines are being purchased for
the home as well as the office

main reason many consumers have been reluctant to purchase personal computers is that
they fail to see what problems owning one will solve. One way PC manufacturers have attempted to activate problem recognition is by stressing how a computer helps children improve their academic skills and do better in school.

In most instances, the marketer is trying to respond to consumers' attempts to solve
problems. Global Perspective 4–1 discusses some of the demands consumers are making and
marketers' methods of responding to them.

**Examining
Consumer
Motivations**

Marketers recognize that while problem recognition is often a basic, simple process, the way
a consumer perceives a problem and becomes motivated to solve it will influence the remainder of the decision process. For example, one consumer may perceive the need to purchase a
new watch from a functional perspective and focus on reliable, low-priced alternatives. Another consumer may see the purchase of a watch as more of a fashion statement and focus on
the design and image of various brands. To better understand the reasons underlying consumer purchases, marketers devote considerable attention to examining **motives**—that is,
those factors that compel a consumer to take a particular action.

HIERARCHY OF NEEDS

One of the most popular approaches to understanding consumer motivations is based on the
classic theory of human motivation popularized many years ago by psychologist Abraham
Maslow.[3] His **hierarchy of needs** theory postulates five basic levels of human needs,
arranged in a hierarchy based on their importance. As shown in Figure 4–2, the five needs
are (1) *physiological*—the basic level of primary needs for things required to sustain life, such
as food, shelter, clothing, and sex; (2) *safety*—the need for security and safety from physical
harm; (3) *social/love and belonging*—the desire to have satisfying relationships with others
and feel a sense of love, affection, belonging, and acceptance; (4) *esteem*—the need to feel a
sense of accomplishment and gain recognition, status, and respect from others; and (5) *self-
actualization*—the need for self-fulfillment and a desire to realize one's own potential.

Global Perspective 4—1
Demanding Consumers Keep Marketers on Their Toes

Consumers around the world are becoming more sophisticated and more complex when it comes to making purchase decisions. As a result, marketers have had to change the way they think and do business as well. As consumers' decision processes evolve, smart companies' communications programs are evolving as well.

The company that hopes to compete internationally must constantly monitor the consumer and understand the factors involved in the purchase decision. Consider the following:

- Germans are considered the toughest customers to sell on athletic footwear, avidly perusing the specifications and expecting proof that the materials deliver the promised shoe. They are obsessed with the automobile. They prefer hot cereals to cold.
- Japanese are considered the toughest customers when it comes to selling automobiles, disposable diapers, irons, and refrigerators. In the purchase of a car, appearance is critical. They are similar to the Germans in making shoe decisions, buy only Japanese-made cosmetics, and will not eat cold cereals.
- Americans are brand conscious and demand comfort in athletic shoes. But they are much more forgiving when it comes to automobiles. They are increasingly concerned with nutrition in breakfast cereals and demand value for their money when purchasing cosmet-

ics. They are considered the toughest customers for VCRs.
- In the Czech Republic, the husband initiates the decision to purchase an automobile and has almost exclusive authority in determining when, where, and what model to buy and how much to spend. In the United States, spouses typically make such decisions jointly.

In addition to changing the choice criteria, consumers are becoming smarter and making more demands. They complain more, bombarding companies with letters, griping in focus groups, and even organizing boycotts. They are not as loyal as in the past.

Many manufacturers view smarter shoppers as an opportunity. In both the consumer and business-to-business markets, these companies have redesigned their programs to satisfy customer needs. Improved quality at lower costs, everyday low price strategies, and better customer service are just some of the ways these companies are adapting. Toll-free phone numbers provide more information and service to customers, and customer relations reps are more sophisticated. Smart companies, like smart consumers, are changing how the game is played.

Sources: Roger J. Baran, "Patterns of Decision Making Influence for Selected Products and Services among Husbands and Wives Living in the Czech Republic," *European Advances in Consumer Research*, 2, 1995, pp. 193–200; Rahul Jacob, "Beyond Quality and Value," *Fortune*, Autumn/Winter 1993, pp. 8–11; Faye Rice, "How to Deal with Tougher Customers," *Fortune*, December 3, 1990, pp. 38–40.

FIGURE 4—2

Maslow's hierarchy of needs

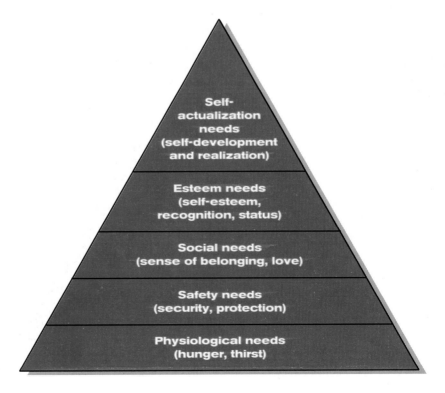

According to Maslow's theory, the lower-level physiological and safety needs must be satisfied before the higher-order needs become meaningful. Once these basic needs are satisfied, the individual moves on to attempting to satisfy higher-order needs such as self-esteem. In reality, it is unlikely that people move through the needs hierarchy in a stairstep manner. Lower-level needs are an ongoing source of motivation for consumer purchase behavior. However, since basic physiological needs are met in most developed countries, marketers often sell products that fill basic physiological needs by appealing to consumers' higher-level needs. For example, in marketing its condensed soups, Campbell Soup Co. focuses on the love between a parent and child (social needs) in addition to the nutritional value of the product (Exhibit 4–5).

While Maslow's need hierarchy has flaws, it offers a framework for marketers to use in determining what needs they want their products and services to be shown satisfying. Advertising campaigns can then be designed to show how a brand can fulfill these needs. Marketers also recognize that different market segments emphasize different need levels. For example, a young single person may be attempting to satisfy social or self-esteem needs in purchasing a car, while a family with children will focus more on safety needs. Buick has used ads like the one in Exhibit 4–6 to position its cars as meeting the safety needs of consumers with children.

PSYCHOANALYTIC THEORY

A somewhat more controversial approach to the study of consumer motives is the **psychoanalytic theory** pioneered by Sigmund Freud.[4] Although Freud's work dealt with the structure and development of personality, he also studied the underlying motivations for human behavior. Psychoanalytic theory had a strong influence on the development of mod-

EXHIBIT 4–5 Campbell appeals to needs for love and belonging in this ad

BOY SINGS: (VO) There's nothing like getting to the bottom of a bowl of soup.
Puts me in a real good mood.

There's nothing like getting to the bottom of a bowl of soup.
ANNCR: (VO) Campbell's Chicken Noodle Soup.
So good, and like most of Campbell's soups so low in cholesterol

BOY SINGS: (VO) Cause at the bottom of it all soup is good food.
BOY: (VO) Campbell's!

ern psychology and on explanations of motivation and personality. It has also been applied to the study of consumer behavior by marketers interested in probing deeply rooted motives that may underlie purchase decisions.

Those who attempt to relate psychoanalytic theory to consumer behavior believe consumers' motivations for purchasing are often very complex and unclear to the casual observer—and to the consumers themselves. Many motives for purchase and/or consumption may be driven by deep motives one can determine only by probing the subconscious.

Among the first to conduct this type of research in marketing, Ernest Dichter and James Vicary were employed by a number of major corporations to use psychoanalytic techniques to determine consumers' purchase motivations. The work of these researchers and others who continue to use this approach assumed the title of **motivation research**.

MOTIVATION RESEARCH IN MARKETING

Motivation researchers use a variety of methodologies to gain insight into the underlying causes of consumer behavior. Methods employed include in-depth interviews, projective techniques, association tests, and focus groups in which consumers are encouraged to bring out associations related to products and brands (see Figure 4–3). As one might expect, such associations often lead to interesting insights as to why people purchase. For example:

- A man buys a convertible as a substitute mistress.
- Women like to bake cakes because they feel like they are giving birth to a baby.
- Women wear perfume to "attract a man" and "glorify their existence."
- Men like frankfurters better than women do because cooking them (frankfurters, not men!) makes women feel guilty. It's an admission of laziness.
- When people shower, their sins go down the drain with the soap as they rinse.[5]

FIGURE 4–3

Some of the marketing research
methods employed to probe the mind
of the consumer

In-depth interviews
Face-to-face situations in which an interviewer asks a consumer to talk freely in an unstructured interview using specific questions designed to obtain insights into his or her motives, ideas, or opinions.

Projective techniques
Efforts designed to gain insights into consumers' values, motives, attitudes, or needs that are difficult to express or identify by having them project these internal states upon some external object.

Association tests
A technique in which an individual is asked to respond as to the first thing that comes to mind when he or she is presented with a stimulus; the stimulus may be a word, picture, ad, and so on.

Focus groups
A small number of people with similar backgrounds and/or interests are brought together to discuss a particular product, idea, or issue.

As you can see from these examples, motivation research has led to some very interesting, albeit controversial, findings and to much skepticism from marketing managers. However, major corporations and advertising agencies continue to use motivation research to help them market their products.

PROBLEMS AND CONTRIBUTIONS OF PSYCHOANALYTIC THEORY AND MOTIVATION RESEARCH

Psychoanalytic theory has been criticized as being too vague, unresponsive to the external environment, and too reliant on the early development of the individual. It also uses a small sample for drawing conclusions. Because of the emphasis on the unconscious, results are difficult if not impossible to verify, leading motivation research to be criticized for both the conclusions drawn and its lack of experimental validation. Since motivation research studies typically use so few participants, there is also concern that it really discovers the idiosyncracies of a few individuals and its findings are not generalizable to the whole population.

Still, it is difficult to ignore the psychoanalytic approach in furthering our understanding of consumer behavior. These insights can often be used as a basis for advertising messages aimed at buyers' deeply rooted feelings, hopes, aspirations, and fears. These strategies are often more effective than rationally based appeals.

Some advertising agencies have used motivation research to gain further insights into how consumers think. Examples include the following:[6]

• McCann-Erickson asked women to draw and describe how they felt about roaches. The agency concluded that many women associated roaches with men who had abandoned them. The agency concluded that was why women preferred roach killers that let them see the roaches die.

• Saatchi & Saatchi used psychological probes to conclude that Ronald McDonald created a more nurturing mood than did the Burger King (who was perceived as more aggressive and distant).

• Foote, Cone & Belding gave consumers stacks of photographs of faces and asked them to associate the faces with the kinds of people who might use particular products.

While often criticized, motivation research has also contributed to the marketing discipline. The qualitative nature of the research is considered important in assessing how and why consumers buy. Focus groups and in-depth interviews are valuable methods for gaining insights into consumers' feelings, and projective techniques are often the only way to get around stereotypical or socially desirable responses. In addition, motivation research is the forerunner of psychographics (discussed in Chapter 2).

Finally, we know that buyers are sometimes motivated by symbolic as well as functional drives in their purchase decisions. (Thus, we see the use of sexual appeals and symbols in ads like Exhibit 4–7.)

Information Search

The second step in the consumer decision-making process is *information search*. Once consumers perceive a problem or need that can be satisfied by the purchase of a product or service, they begin to search for information needed to make a purchase decision. The initial search effort often consists of an attempt to scan information stored in memory to recall past experiences and/or knowledge regarding various purchase alternatives.[7] This information retrieval is referred to as **internal search**. For many routine, repetitive purchases, previously acquired information that is stored in memory (such as past performance or outcomes from using a brand) is sufficient for comparing alternatives and making a choice.

If the internal search does not yield enough information, the consumer will seek additional information by engaging in **external search**. External sources of information include:

- *Personal sources*, such as friends, relatives, or co-workers.
- *Marketer-controlled (commercial) sources*, such as information from advertising, salespeople, or point-of-purchase displays and materials.
- *Public sources*, including articles in magazines or newspapers and reports on TV.
- *Personal experience*, such as actually handling, examining, or testing the product.

Determining how much and which sources of external information to use involves several factors, including the importance of the purchase decision, the effort needed to acquire information, the amount of past experience relevant, the degree of perceived risk associated with the purchase, and the time available. For example, the selection of a movie to see on a

EXHIBIT 4–7
Guess uses sexual appeal in its ads

Friday night might entail simply talking to a friend or checking the movie guide in the daily newspaper. A more complex purchase, such as a new car, might use a number of information sources—perhaps a review of *Road & Track, Motortrend,* or *Consumer Reports;* discussion with family members and friends; and test driving of cars. At this point in the purchase decision, the information-providing aspects of advertising are extremely important.

Perception

Knowledge of how consumers acquire and use information from external sources is important to marketers in formulating communication strategies. Marketers are particularly interested in (1) how consumers sense external information, (2) how they select and attend to various sources of information, and (3) how this information is interpreted and given meaning. These processes are all part of **perception**, the process by which an individual receives, selects, organizes, and interprets information to create a meaningful picture of the world.[8] Perception is an individual process; it depends on internal factors such as a person's beliefs, experiences, needs, moods, and expectations. The perceptual process is also influenced by the characteristics of a stimulus (such as its size, color, and intensity) and the context in which it is seen or heard.

SENSATION

Perception involves three distinct processes. **Sensation** is the immediate, direct response of the senses (taste, smell, sight, touch, and hearing) to a stimulus such as an ad, package, brand name, or point-of-purchase display. Perception uses these senses to create a representation of the stimulus. Marketers recognize that it is important to understand consumers' physiological reactions to marketing stimuli. For example, the visual elements of an ad or package design must attract consumers' favorable attention.

Marketers sometimes try to increase the level of sensory input so that their advertising messages will get noticed. For example, marketers of colognes and perfumes often use strong visuals as well as scent strips to appeal to multiple senses and attract the attention of magazine readers. Some advertisers have even inserted microcomputer chips into their print ads to play a song or deliver a message.

SELECTING INFORMATION

Sensory inputs are important but are only one part of the perceptual process. Other determinants of whether marketing stimuli will be attended to and how they will be interpreted include internal psychological factors such as the consumer's personality, needs, motives, expectations, and experiences. These psychological inputs explain why people focus attention on some things and ignore others. Two people may perceive the same stimuli in very different ways because they select, attend, and comprehend differently. An individual's perceptual processes usually focus on elements of the environment that are relevant to his or her needs and tune out irrelevant stimuli. Think about how much more attentive you are to advertising for personal computers, tires, or stereos when you are in the market for one of these products (a point that is made by the message from the American Association of Advertising Agencies in Exhibit 4–8).

INTERPRETING THE INFORMATION

Once a consumer selects and attends to a stimulus, the perceptual process focuses on organizing, categorizing, and interpreting the incoming information. This stage of the perceptual process is very individualized and is influenced by internal psychological factors. The interpretation and meaning an individual assigns to an incoming stimulus also depend in part on the nature of the stimulus. For example, many ads are objective, and their message is clear and straightforward. Other ads are more ambiguous, and their meaning is strongly influenced by the consumer's individual interpretation.

Selectivity occurs throughout the various stages of the consumer's perceptual process. Perception may be viewed as a filtering process in which internal and external factors influence what is received and how it is processed and interpreted. The sheer number and complexity of the marketing stimuli a person is exposed to in any given day require that this

filtering occur. **Selective perception** may occur at the exposure, attention, comprehension, or retention stage of perception, as shown in Figure 4–4.

SELECTIVE PERCEPTION

Selective exposure occurs as consumers choose whether or not to make themselves available to information. For example, a viewer of a television show may change channels or leave the room during commercial breaks.

Selective attention occurs when the consumer chooses to focus attention on certain stimuli while excluding others. One study of selective attention estimates the typical consumer is exposed to nearly 1,500 ads per day yet perceives only 76 of these messages.[9] This means advertisers must make considerable effort to get their messages noticed. Advertisers often use the creative aspects of their ads to gain consumers' attention. For example, some advertisers set their ads off from others by showing their products in color against a black-and-white background. This creative tactic has been used in advertising for many products, among them Cherry 7UP, Nuprin, and Pepto-Bismol.[10]

Even if the consumer does notice the advertiser's message, there is no guarantee it will be interpreted in the intended manner. Consumers may engage in **selective comprehension**, interpreting information based on their own attitudes, beliefs, motives, and experiences. They often interpret information in a manner that supports their own position. For example, an ad that disparages a consumer's favorite brand may be seen as biased or untruthful, and its claims may not be accepted.

The final screening process shown in Figure 4–4 is **selective retention**, which means consumers do not remember all the information they see, hear, or read even after attending to and comprehending it. Advertisers attempt to make sure information will be retained in the consumer's memory so as to be available when it is time

FIGURE 4—4 The selective perception process

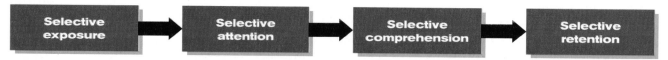

to make a purchase. **Mnemonics** such as symbols, rhymes, associations, and images that assist in the learning and memory process are helpful. Many advertisers use telephone numbers that spell out the company name and are easy to remember. Eveready put pictures of its pink bunny on packages to remind consumers at the point of purchase of its creative advertising.

SUBLIMINAL PERCEPTION

Advertisers know consumers use selective perception to filter out irrelevant or unwanted advertising messages, so they employ various creative tactics to get their messages noticed. One controversial tactic advertisers have been accused of using is appealing to consumers' subconscious. **Subliminal perception** refers to the ability to perceive a stimulus that is below the level of conscious awareness. Psychologists generally agree it is possible to perceive things without being consciously aware of them.

As you might imagine, the possibility of using hidden persuaders such as subliminal audio messages or visual cues to influence consumers might be intriguing to advertisers but would not be welcomed by consumers. The idea of marketers influencing consumers at a subconscious level has strong ethical implications. Ethical Perspective 4–2 discusses researchers' mixed opinions as to whether subliminal messages are likely to be effective in influencing consumer behavior. The use of subliminal techniques is *not* a creative tactic we would recommend to advertisers.

Alternative Evaluation

After acquiring information during the information search stage of the decision process, the consumer moves to alternative evaluation. In this stage, the consumer compares the various brands or products and services he or she has identified as being capable of solving the consumption problem and satisfying the needs or motives that initiated the decision process. The various brands identified as purchase options to be considered during the alternative evaluation process are referred to as the consumer's *evoked set*.

THE EVOKED SET

The evoked set is generally only a subset of all the brands of which the consumer is aware. The consumer reduces the number of brands to be reviewed during the alternative evaluation stage to a manageable level. The exact size of the evoked set varies from one consumer to another and depends on such factors as the importance of the purchase and the amount of time and energy the consumer wants to spend comparing alternatives.

The goal of most advertising and promotional strategies is to increase the likelihood that a brand will be included in the consumer's evoked set and considered during alternative evaluation. Marketers use advertising to create *top-of-mind awareness* among consumers so their brands are part of the evoked set of their target audiences. Popular brands with large advertising budgets use *reminder advertising* to maintain high awareness levels and increase the likelihood they will be considered by consumers in the market for the product. Marketers of new brands or those with a low market share need to gain awareness among consumers and break into their evoked sets. They can do this through methods such as comparative advertising, where their brand is compared to market leaders. The ad promoting Los Angeles as a better place to do business (Exhibit 4–9) shows this strategy being used in a different context from products and brands. The ad compares Los Angeles to four other cities and encourages prospective businesses to consider it in their evoked set of places to locate or relocate.

Advertising is a valuable promotional tool for creating and maintaining brand awareness and making sure a brand is included in the evoked set. However, marketers also work to pro-

Ethical Perspective 4–2
Subliminal Perception:
Fact or Fiction?

One of the most controversial topics in all of advertising is subliminal advertising. Rooted in psychoanalytic theory, subliminal advertising supposedly influences consumer behaviors by subconsciously altering perceptions or attitudes toward products without the knowledge—or consent—of the consumer. Marketers have promoted subliminal self-help audiotapes, weight-loss videos, and golf game improvement tapes. Studies have shown that the majority of American consumers believe that advertisers sometimes use subliminal advertising, and that it works.

The concept of subliminal advertising was introduced in 1957 when James Vicary, a motivational researcher, reported that he increased the sales of popcorn and Coke by subliminally flashing "Eat popcorn" and "Drink Coca-Cola" across the screen during a movie in New Jersey. Since then, numerous books and research studies have been published regarding the effectiveness of this advertising form. Some of these have reported on the use of this technique by advertisers to manipulate consumers.

Numerous articles have reviewed the research in this area. In 1982, Timothy Moore reported that the effects of subliminal advertising are so weak that they pose serious difficulties for any marketing applications. In 1988, after additional research in this area, Moore said, "There continues to be no evidence that subliminal messages can influence motivation or complex behavior." Again in 1992, Moore concluded that "recent research in subliminal perception has provided very little evidence that stimuli below observers' subjective thresholds influence motives, attitudes, beliefs, or choices." Joel Saegart and Jack Haberstroh have supported Moore's conclusions in their studies. On the other hand, in 1994 Kathryn Theus concluded after an extensive review of the literature that "certain themes might be effectively applied by advertising or marketing specialists."

When Jack Haberstroh asked ad agency executives in 1984 if they had ever deliberately used subliminal advertising, 96 percent said no, 94 percent said they had never supervised the use of implants, and 91 percent denied knowing anyone who had ever used this technique. A study by Rogers and Seiler in 1994 supported these results, with over 90 percent denying any use of this technique. Thus, while most consumers believe subliminal techniques are used and effective, and researchers are divided among its effects, it seems few people in the advertising world think subliminal advertising works and even fewer claim to use it. Now if they could only convince consumers!

Sources: Kathryn Theus, "Subliminal Advertising and the Psychology of Processing Unconscious Stimuli: A Review of Research," *Psychology & Marketing* 11, no. 3, 1994, pp. 271–90; Martha Rogers and Christine Seiler, "The Answer Is NO," *Journal of Advertising Research*, March/April 1994, pp. 36–45; Martha Rogers and Kirk H. Smith, "Public Perceptions of Subliminal Advertising," *Journal of Advertising Research*, March/April 1993, pp. 10–17; Timothy Moore, "Subliminal Perception: Facts and Fallacies," *Skeptical Inquirer* 1, Spring 1992, pp. 273–80; Jack Haberstroh, "Can't Ignore Subliminal Ad Charges," *Advertising Age*, September 17, 1984, pp. 3, 42–44; Timothy Moore, "Subliminal Advertising: What You See Is What You Get," *Journal of Marketing* 46, no. 2 (Spring 1982), pp. 38–47; Timothy Moore, "The Case against Subliminal Manipulation," *Psychology and Marketing* 5, no. 4 (Winter 1988), pp. 297–316; Joel Saegert, "Why Marketing Should Quit Giving Subliminal Advertising the Benefit of the Doubt," *Psychology and Marketing* 4, pp. 107–20.

EXHIBIT 4–9

Los Angeles wants to be in the evoked set of business locations

mote their brands in the actual environment where purchase decisions are made. Point-of-purchase materials and promotional techniques such as in-store sampling, end-aisle displays, or shelf tags touting special prices encourage consumers to consider brands that may not have initially been in their evoked set.

EVALUATIVE CRITERIA AND CONSEQUENCES

Once consumers have identified an evoked set and have a list of alternatives, they must evaluate the various brands. This involves comparing the choice alternatives on specific criteria important to the consumer. **Evaluative criteria** are the dimensions or attributes of a product or service that are used to compare different alternatives. Evaluative criteria can be objective or subjective. For example, in buying an automobile, consumers use objective attributes such as price, warranty, and fuel economy as well as subjective factors such as image, styling, and performance.

Evaluative criteria are usually viewed as product or service attributes. Many marketers view their products or services as *bundles of attributes*, but consumers tend to think about products or services in terms of their *consequences* instead. J. Paul Peter and Jerry Olson define consequences as specific events or outcomes that consumers experience when they purchase and/or consume a product or service.[11] They distinguish between two broad types of consequences. **Functional consequences** are concrete outcomes of product or service usage that are tangible and directly experienced by consumers. The taste of a soft drink or a potato chip, the acceleration of a car, and the clarity of a fax transmission are examples of functional consequences. **Psychosocial consequences** refer to abstract outcomes that are more intangible, subjective, and personal, such as how a product makes you feel or how you think others will view you for purchasing or using it.

Marketers should distinguish between product/service attributes and consequences, because the importance and meaning consumers assign to an attribute are usually determined by its consequences for them. Moreover, advertisers must be sure consumers understand the link between a particular attribute and a consequence. For example, the Top-Flite ad in Exhibit 4–10 focuses on the consequences of using the new Top-Flite XL golf ball, such as more distance and lower scores. Note how the highlighted scorecard is used to reinforce the point that the Top-Flite XL can help golfers achieve better scores.

Product/service attributes and the consequences or outcomes consumers think they will experience from a particular brand are very important, for they are often the basis on which consumers form attitudes and purchase intentions and decide among various choice alternatives. Two subprocesses are very important during the alternative evaluation stage: (1) the

EXHIBIT 4–10

This ad emphasizes the positive consequences of using the Top Flight XL golf ball

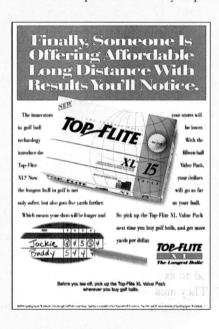

process by which consumer attitudes are created, reinforced, and changed and (2) the consumer decision rules or integration strategies consumers use to compare brands and make purchase decisions. We will examine each of these processes in more detail.

Attitudes

Attitudes are one of the most heavily studied concepts in consumer behavior. According to Gordon Allport's classic definition, "attitudes are learned predispositions to respond to an object."[12] More recent perspectives view attitudes as a summary construct that represents an individual's overall feelings toward or evaluation of an object.[13] Consumers hold attitudes toward a variety of objects that are important to marketers, including individuals (celebrity endorsers such as Dennis Rodman or Michael Jordan), brands (Cheerios, Kix), companies (Texaco, Microsoft), product categories (beef, pork, tuna), retail stores (Kmart, Sears), or even advertisements (the Energizer bunny ads).

Attitudes are important to marketers because they theoretically summarize a consumer's evaluation of an object (or brand or company) and represent positive or negative feelings and behavioral tendencies. Marketers' keen interest in attitudes is based on the assumption that they are related to consumers' purchase behavior. Considerable evidence supports the basic assumption of a relationship between attitudes and behavior.[14] The attitude–behavior link does not always hold; many other factors can affect behavior.[15] But attitudes are very important to marketers. Advertising and promotion are used to create favorable attitudes toward new products/services or brands, reinforce existing favorable attitudes, and/or change negative attitudes. An approach to studying and measuring attitudes that is particularly relevant to advertising is multiattribute attitude models.

MULTIATTRIBUTE ATTITUDE MODELS

Consumer researchers and marketing practitioners have been using multiattribute attitude models to study consumer attitudes for two decades.[16] A **multiattribute attitude model** views an attitude object, such as a product or brand, as possessing a number of attributes that provide the basis on which consumers form their attitudes. According to this model, consumers have beliefs about specific brand attributes and attach different levels of importance to these attributes. Using this approach, an attitude toward a particular brand can be represented as

$$A_B = \sum_{i=1}^{n} B_i \times E_i$$

where
A_B = attitude toward a brand
B_i = beliefs about the brand's performance on attribute i
E_i = importance attached to attribute i
n = number of attributes considered

For example, a consumer may have beliefs (B_i) about various brands of toothpaste on certain attributes. One brand may be perceived as having fluoride and thus preventing cavities, tasting good, and helping control tartar buildup. Another brand may not be perceived as having these attributes, but consumers may believe it performs well on other attributes such as freshening breath and whitening teeth.

To predict attitudes, one must know how much importance consumers attach to each of these attributes (E_i). For example, parents purchasing toothpaste for their children may prefer a brand that performs well on cavity prevention, which leads to a more favorable attitude toward the first brand. Teenagers and young adults may prefer a brand that freshens their breath and makes their teeth white and thus prefer the second brand.

Consumers may hold a number of different beliefs about brands in any product or service category. However, not all of these beliefs are activated in forming an attitude. Beliefs concerning specific attributes or consequences that are activated and form the basis of an attitude are referred to as **salient beliefs**. Marketers should identify and understand these salient beliefs. They must also recognize that the saliency of beliefs varies among different market segments, over time, and across different consumption situations.

Ordinary tap water
may be fine for bathing
and brushing your teeth.
But this is your coffee
we're talking about.

Introducing the Braun FlavorSelect with water filter.

BRAUN

ATTITUDE CHANGE STRATEGIES

Multiattribute models help marketers understand and diagnose the underlying basis of consumers' attitudes. By understanding the beliefs that underlie consumers' evaluations of a brand and the importance of various attributes or consequences, the marketer is better able to develop communication strategies for creating, changing, or reinforcing brand attitudes. The multiattribute model provides insight into several ways marketers can influence consumer attitudes, including:

- Increasing or changing the strength or belief rating of a brand on an important attribute.
- Changing consumers' perceptions of the importance or value of an attribute.
- Adding a new attribute to the attitude formation process.
- Changing perceptions of belief ratings for a competing brand.

The first strategy is commonly used by advertisers. They identify an attribute or consequence that is important and remind consumers how well their brand performs on this attribute. In situations where consumers do not perceive the marketer's brand as possessing an important attribute or the belief strength is low, advertising strategies may be targeted at changing the belief rating. Even when belief strength is high, advertising may be used to increase the rating of a brand on an important attribute. BMW's "The Ultimate Driving Machine" campaign is a good example of a strategy designed to create a belief and reinforce it through advertising.

Marketers often attempt to influence consumer attitudes by changing the relative importance of a particular attribute. This second strategy involves getting consumers to attach more importance to the attribute in forming their attitude toward the brand. Marketers using this strategy want to increase the importance of an attribute their particular brand has.

The third strategy for influencing consumer attitudes is to add or emphasize a new attribute that consumers can use in evaluating a brand. Marketers often do this by improving their products or focusing on additional benefits or consequences associated with using the brand. Exhibit 4–11 shows how Braun is stressing a new attribute in an attempt to influence consumers' attitudes.

A final strategy marketers use is to change consumer beliefs about the attributes of competing brands or product categories. This strategy has become much more common with the increase in comparative advertising, where marketers compare their brands to competitors' on specific product attributes. An example of this is the Geze ad shown in Exhibit 4–12, where the company compares a number of important attributes of its ski bindings to those of competitors.

Integration Processes and Decision Rules

Another important aspect of the alternative evaluation stage is the way consumers combine information about the characteristics of brands to arrive at a purchase decision. **Integration processes** are the way product knowledge, meanings, and beliefs are combined to evaluate two or more alternatives.[17] Analysis of the integration process focuses on the different types of *decision rules* or strategies consumers use to decide among purchase alternatives.

Consumers often make purchase selections by using formal integration strategies or decision rules that require examination and comparison of alternatives on specific attributes. This process involves a very deliberate evaluation of the alternatives, attribute by attribute. When consumers apply such formal decision rules, marketers need to know which attributes are being considered so as to provide the information the consumers require.

Sometimes consumers make their purchase decision using more simplified decision rules known as **heuristics**. Peter and Olson note that heuristics are easy to use and are highly adaptive to specific environmental situations (such as a retail store).[18] For familiar products that are purchased frequently, consumers may use price-based heuristics (buy the least expensive brand) or promotion-based heuristics (choose the brand for which I can get a price reduction through a coupon, rebate, or special deal).

One type of heuristic is the **affect referral decision rule**,[19] in which consumers make a selection on the basis of an overall impression or summary evaluation of the various alter-

natives under consideration. This decision rule suggests that consumers have affective impressions of brands stored in memory that can be accessed at the time of purchase. How many times have you gone into a store and made purchases based on your overall impressions of the brands rather than going through detailed comparisons of the alternatives' specific attributes?

Marketers selling familiar and popular brands may appeal to an affect referral rule by stressing overall affective feelings or impressions about their products. Market leaders, whose products enjoy strong overall brand images, often use ads that promote the brand as the best overall. Coke's campaign "Always Coca-Cola," Diet Pepsi's "You've got the right one baby, uh-huh!" and Budweiser's "The king of beers" are all examples of this strategy (Exhibit 4–13).

Purchase Decision

At some point in the buying process, the consumer must stop searching for and evaluating information about alternative brands in the evoked set and make a *purchase decision*. As an outcome of the alternative evaluation stage, the consumer may develop a **purchase intention** or predisposition to buy a certain brand. Purchase intentions are generally based on a matching of purchase motives with attributes or characteristics of brands under consideration. Their formation involves many of the personal subprocesses discussed in this chapter, including motivation, perception, attitude formation, and integration.

A purchase decision is not the same as an actual purchase. Once a consumer chooses which brand to buy, he or she must still implement the decision and make the actual purchase. Additional decisions may be needed, such as when to buy, where to buy, and how much money to spend. Often, there is a time delay between the formation of a purchase intention or decision and the actual purchase, particularly for highly involved and complex purchases such as automobiles, personal computers, and consumer durables.

For nondurable products, which include many low-involvement items such as consumer package goods, the time between the decision and the actual purchase may be short. Before

leaving home, the consumer may make a shopping list that includes specific brand names because the consumer has developed **brand loyalty**—a preference for a particular brand that results in its repeated purchase. Marketers strive to develop and maintain brand loyalty among consumers. They use reminder advertising to keep their brand names in front of consumers, maintain prominent shelf positions and displays in stores, and run periodic promotions to deter consumers from switching brands.

Maintaining consumers' brand loyalty is not easy. Competitors use many techniques to encourage consumers to try their brands, among them new product introductions and free samples. As Figure 4–5 shows, for many products fewer than 50 percent of consumers are loyal to one brand. Marketers must continually battle to maintain their loyal consumers while at the same time replacing those who switch brands.

Purchase decisions for nondurable, convenience items sometimes take place in the store, almost simultaneous with the purchase. Marketers must ensure that consumers have top-of-mind awareness of their brands so they are quickly recognized and considered. These types of decisions are influenced at the actual point of purchase. Packaging, shelf displays, point-of-purchase materials, and promotional tools such as on-package coupons or premium offers can influence decisions made through constructive processes at the time of purchase.

Postpurchase Evaluation

The consumer decision process does not end with the purchase. After using the product or service, the consumer compares the level of performance with expectations and is either satisfied or dissatisfied. *Satisfaction* occurs when the consumer's expectations are either met or exceeded; *dissatisfaction* results when performance is below expectations. The postpurchase evaluation process is important because the feedback acquired from actual use of a product will influence the likelihood of future purchases. Positive performance means the brand is retained in the evoked set and increases the likelihood it will be purchased again. Unfavorable outcomes may lead the consumer to form negative attitudes toward the brand, lessening the likelihood it will be purchased again or even eliminating it from the consumer's evoked set.

Another possible outcome of purchase is **cognitive dissonance**, a feeling of psychological tension or postpurchase doubt that a consumer experiences after making a difficult purchase choice. Dissonance is more likely to occur in important decisions where the consumer must choose among close alternatives (especially if the unchosen alternative has unique or desirable features that the selected alternative does not have).

Consumers experiencing cognitive dissonance may use a number of strategies to attempt to reduce it. They may seek out reassurance and opinions from others to confirm the wisdom of their purchase decision, lower their attitudes or opinions of the unchosen alternative, deny or distort any information that does not support the choice they made, or look for

FIGURE 4–5 Faithful or fickle? Percentage of users of these products who are loyal to one brand

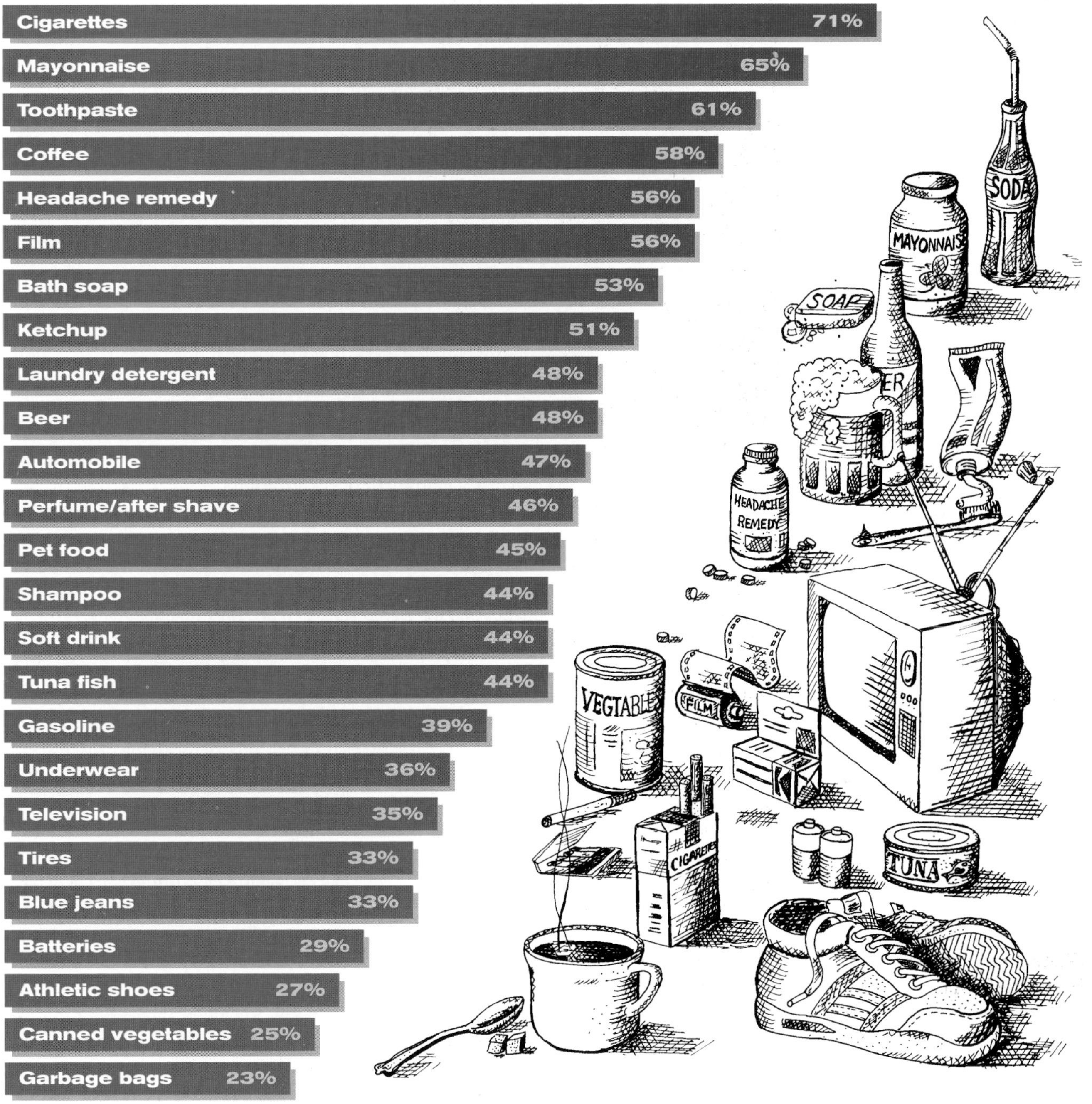

Cigarettes 71%
Mayonnaise 65%
Toothpaste 61%
Coffee 58%
Headache remedy 56%
Film 56%
Bath soap 53%
Ketchup 51%
Laundry detergent 48%
Beer 48%
Automobile 47%
Perfume/after shave 46%
Pet food 45%
Shampoo 44%
Soft drink 44%
Tuna fish 44%
Gasoline 39%
Underwear 36%
Television 35%
Tires 33%
Blue jeans 33%
Batteries 29%
Athletic shoes 27%
Canned vegetables 25%
Garbage bags 23%
SODA
MAYONNAISE
SOAP
HEADACHE REMEDY
VEGTABLES
FILM
CIGARETTES
TUNA

information that does support their choice. An important source of this supportive information is advertising; consumers tend to be more attentive to advertising for the brand they have chosen.[20] Thus, it may be important for companies to advertise to reinforce consumer decisions to purchase their brands.

Marketers must recognize the importance of the postpurchase evaluation stage. Dissatisfied consumers who experience dissonance are not only unlikely to repurchase the marketer's product, but they may also spread negative word-of-mouth information that deters others from purchasing the product or service. The best guarantee of favorable postpurchase evaluations is to provide consumers with a quality product or service that always meets their expectations. Marketers must be sure their advertising and other forms of promotion do not create unreasonable expectations their products cannot meet.

Marketers have come to realize that postpurchase communication is also important. Some companies send follow-up letters and brochures to reassure buyers and reinforce the wisdom of their decision. Many companies have set up toll-free numbers for consumers to call if they need information or have a question or complaint regarding a product. Marketers also offer liberalized return and refund policies and extended warranties and guarantees to ensure customer satisfaction. For example, this ad promotes Ford Motor Co.'s commitment to customer service.

Variations in Consumer Decision Making

The preceding pages describe a general model of consumer decision making. But consumers do not always engage in all five steps of the purchase decision process or proceed in the sequence presented. They may minimize or even skip one or more stages if they have previous experience in purchasing the product or service or if the decision is of low personal, social, or economic significance. To develop effective promotional strategies and programs, marketers need some understanding of the problem-solving processes their target consumers use to make purchase decisions.[21]

Many of the purchase decisions we make as consumers are based on a habitual or routine choice process. For many low-priced, frequently purchased products, the decision process consists of little more than recognizing the problem, engaging in a quick internal search, and making the purchase. The consumer spends little or no effort engaging in external search or alternative evaluation.

Marketers of products characterized by a routine response purchase process need to get and/or keep their brands in the consumer's evoked set and avoid anything that may result in their removal from consideration. Established brands that have strong market share position are likely to be in the evoked set of most consumers. Marketers of these brands want consumers to follow a routine choice process and continue to purchase their products. This means maintaining high levels of brand awareness through reminder advertising, periodic promotions, and prominent shelf positions in retail stores.

Marketers of new brands or those with a low market share face a different challenge. They must find ways to disrupt consumers' routine choice process and get them to consider different alternatives. High levels of advertising may be used to encourage trial or brand switching, along with sales promotion efforts in the form of free samples, special price offers, high-value coupons, and the like.

A more complicated decision-making process may occur when consumers have limited experience in purchasing a particular product or service and little or no knowledge of the brands available and/or the criteria to use in making a purchase decision. They may have to learn what attributes or criteria should be used in making a purchase decision and how the various alternatives perform on these dimensions. For products or services characterized by problem solving, whether limited or extensive, marketers should make information available that will help consumers decide. Advertising that provides consumers with detailed information about a brand and how it can satisfy their purchase motives and goals is important. Marketers may also want to give consumers information at the point of purchase, through either displays or brochures. Distribution channels should have knowledgeable salespeople available to explain the features and benefits of the company's product or service and why it is superior to competing products.

The IBM ad in Exhibit 4–14 is a good example of how advertising can appeal to consumers who may be engaging in extended problem solving when considering corporate security. Notice how the ad communicates with consumers who know little about how to purchase this product. The ad also makes more detailed information available by offering a free booklet and a website.

EXHIBIT 4–14
This ad for IBM shows how marketers can appeal to consumers engaging in extended problem solving

THE CONSUMER LEARNING PROCESS

The discussion of the decision process shows that the way consumers make a purchase varies depending on a number of factors, including the nature of the product or service, the amount of experience they have with the product, and the importance of the purchase. One factor in the level of problem solving to be employed is the consumer's *involvement* with the product or brand. Chapter 5 examines the meaning of involvement, the difference between low- and high-involvement decision making, and the implications of involvement for developing advertising and promotional strategies.

Our examination of consumer behavior thus far has looked at the decision-making process from a *cognitive orientation*. The five-stage decision process model views the consumer as a problem solver and information processor who engages in a variety of mental processes to evaluate various alternatives and determine the degree to which they might satisfy needs or purchase motives. There are, however, other perspectives regarding how consumers acquire the knowledge and experience they use in making purchase decisions. To understand these perspectives, we examine various approaches to learning and their implications for advertising and promotion.

Consumer learning has been defined as "the process by which individuals acquire the purchase and consumption knowledge and experience they apply to future related behavior."[22] Two basic approaches to learning are the behavioral approach and cognitive learning theory.

Behavioral Learning Theory

Behavioral learning theories emphasize the role of external, environmental stimuli in causing behavior; they minimize the significance of internal psychological processes. Behavioral learning theories are based on the *stimulus–response orientation* (S–R), the premise that learning occurs as the result of responses to external stimuli in the environment. Behavioral learning theorists believe learning occurs through the connection between a stimulus and a response. We will examine the basic principles of two behavioral learning theory approaches: classical conditioning and operant conditioning.

CLASSICAL CONDITIONING

Classical conditioning assumes that learning is an *associative process* with an already existing relationship between a stimulus and a response. Probably the best-known example of this type of learning comes from the studies done with animals by the Russian psychologist Pavlov.[23] Pavlov noticed that at feeding times, his dogs would salivate at the sight of food. The connection between food and salivation is not taught; it is an innate reflex reaction. Because this relationship exists before the conditioning process, the food is referred to as an *unconditioned stimulus* and salivation is an *unconditioned response.* To see if salivation could be conditioned to occur in response to another neutral stimulus, Pavlov paired the ringing of a bell with the presentation of the food. After a number of trials, the dogs learned to salivate at the sound of the bell alone. Thus, the bell became **a conditioned stimulus** that elicited **a conditioned response** resembling the original unconditioned reaction.

Two factors are important for learning to occur through the associative process. The first is *contiguity,* which means the unconditioned stimulus and conditioned stimulus must be close in time and space. In Pavlov's experiment, the dog learns to associate the ringing of the bell with food because of the contiguous presentation of the two stimuli. The other important principle is *repetition,* or the frequency of the association. The more often the unconditioned and conditioned stimuli occur together, the stronger the association between them will be.

Applying Classical Conditioning

Learning through classical conditioning plays an important role in marketing. Buyers can be conditioned to form favorable impressions and images of various brands through the associative process. Advertisers strive to associate their products and services with perceptions, images, and emotions known to evoke positive reactions from consumers. Many products are promoted through image advertising, in which the brand is shown with an unconditioned stimulus that elicits pleasant feelings. When the brand is presented simultaneously with this unconditioned stimulus, the brand itself becomes a conditioned stimulus that elicits the same favorable response.

Figure 4–6 provides a diagram of this process, and the ad for Brita in Exhibit 4–15 shows an application of this strategy. Notice how this ad associates Brita freshness with the freshness of a waterfall. The company's positioning plays off this association.

Classical conditioning can also associate a product or service with a favorable emotional state. A study by Gerald Gorn used this approach to examine how background music in ads influences product choice.[24] He found that subjects were more likely to choose a product when it was presented against a background of music they liked rather than music they disliked. These results suggest the emotions generated by a commercial are important because they may become associated with the advertised product through classical conditioning. Kellaris and colleagues also showed that music that was congruent with the message enhanced both ad recall and recognition.[25] Advertisers often attempt to pair a neutral product or service stimulus with an event or situation that arouses positive feelings, such as humor, an exciting sports event, or popular music.

OPERANT CONDITIONING

Classical conditioning views the individual as a passive participant in the learning process who simply receives stimuli. Conditioning occurs as a result of exposure to a stimulus that occurs before the response. In the **operant conditioning** approach, the individual must actively *operate* or act on some aspect of the environment for learning to occur. Operant conditioning is sometimes referred to as *instrumental conditioning* because the individual's response is instrumental in getting a positive reinforcement (reward) or negative reinforcement (punishment).

FIGURE 4–6
The classical conditioning process

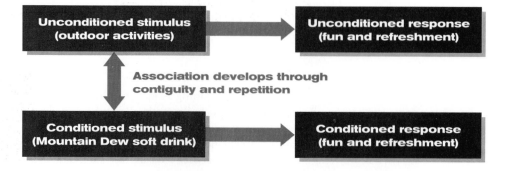

Reinforcement, the reward or favorable consequence associated with a particular response, is an important element of instrumental conditioning. Behavior that is reinforced strengthens the bond between a stimulus and a response. Thus, if a consumer buys a product in response to an ad and experiences a positive outcome, the likelihood that the consumer will use this product again increases. If the outcome is not favorable, the likelihood of buying the product again decreases.

The principles of operant conditioning can be applied to marketing, as shown in Figure 4–7. Companies attempt to provide their customers with products and services that satisfy their needs and reward them to reinforce the probability of repeat purchase. Reinforcement

FIGURE 4–7
Instrumental conditioning in marketing

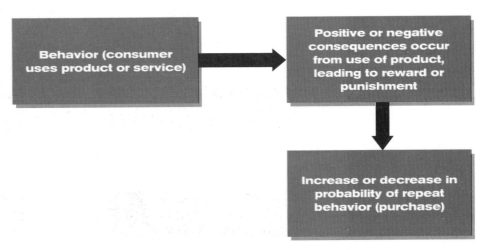

can also be implied in advertising; many ads emphasize the benefits or rewards a consumer will receive from using a product or service. Reinforcement also occurs when an ad encourages consumers to use a particular product or brand to avoid unpleasant consequences. For example, the ad for Dixie bathroom cups in Exhibit 4–16 shows how using this product will help avoid negative consequences.

Two concepts that are particularly relevant to marketers in their use of reinforcement through promotional strategies are schedules of reinforcement and shaping. Different **schedules of reinforcement** result in varying patterns of learning and behavior. Learning occurs most rapidly under a *continuous reinforcement schedule*, in which every response is rewarded—but the behavior is likely to cease when the reinforcement stops. Marketers must provide continuous reinforcement to consumers or risk their switching to brands that do.

Learning occurs more slowly but lasts longer when a *partial* or *intermittent reinforcement schedule* is used and only some of the individual's responses are rewarded. Promotional programs have partial reinforcement schedules. A firm may offer consumers an incentive to use the company's product. The firm does not want to offer the incentive every time (continuous reinforcement), because consumers might become dependent on it and stop buying the brand when the incentive is withdrawn. A study that examined the effect of reinforcement on bus ridership found that discount coupons given as rewards for riding the bus were as effective when given on a partial schedule as on a continuous schedule.[26] The cost of giving the discount coupons under the partial schedule, however, was considerably less.

Reinforcement schedules can also be used to influence consumer learning and behavior through a process known as **shaping**, the reinforcement of successive acts that lead to a desired behavior pattern or response. Rothschild and Gaidis argue that shaping is a very useful concept for marketers:

> Shaping is an essential process in deriving new and complex behavior because a behavior cannot be rewarded unless it first occurs; a stimulus can only reinforce acts that already occur. New, complex behaviors rarely occur by chance in nature. If the only behavior to be rewarded were the final com-

EXHIBIT 4—16
This ad shows how Dixie bathroom cups can help consumers avoid negative consequences

FIGURE 4–8
Application of shaping procedures in marketing

Plex sought behavior, one would probably have to wait a long time for this to occur by chance. Instead, one can reward simpler existing behaviors; over time, more complex patterns evolve and these are rewarded. Thus the shaping process occurs by a method of successive approximations.[27]

In a promotional context, shaping procedures are used as part of the introductory program for new products. Figure 4–8 provides an example of how samples and discount coupons can be used to introduce a new product and take a consumer from trial to repeat purchase. Marketers must be careful in their use of shaping procedures: if they drop the incentives too soon, the consumer may not establish the desired behavior, but if they overuse them, the consumer's purchase may become contingent on the incentive rather than the product or service.

Cognitive Learning Theory

Behavioral learning theories have been criticized for assuming a mechanistic view of the consumer that puts too much emphasis on external stimulus factors. They ignore internal psychological processes such as motivation, thinking, and perception; they assume that the external stimulus environment will elicit fairly predictable responses. Many consumer researchers and marketers disagree with the simplified explanations of behavioral learning theories and are more interested in the complex mental processes that underlie consumer decision making. The cognitive approach to studying learning and decision making has dominated the field of consumer behavior in recent years. Figure 4–9 shows how cognitive theorists view the learning process.

Since consumer behavior typically involves choices and decision making, the cognitive perspective has particular appeal to marketers, especially those whose product/service calls for important and involved purchase decisions. Cognitive processes such as perception, formation of beliefs about brands, attitude development and change, and integration are important to understanding the decision-making process for many types of purchases. The

FIGURE 4–9   The cognitive learning process

subprocesses examined during our discussion of the five-stage decision process model are all relevant to a cognitive learning approach to consumer behavior.

ENVIRONMENTAL INFLUENCES ON CONSUMER BEHAVIOR
Culture

The consumer does not make purchase decisions in isolation. A number of external factors have been identified that may influence consumer decision making. They are shown in Figure 4–10 and examined in more detail in the next sections.

The broadest and most abstract of the external factors that influence consumer behavior is **culture**, or the complexity of learned meanings, values, norms, and customs shared by members of a society. Cultural norms and values offer direction and guidance to members of a society in all aspects of their lives, including their consumption behavior. It is becoming increasingly important to study the impact of culture on consumer behavior as marketers expand their international marketing efforts. Each country has certain cultural traditions, customs, and values that marketers must understand as they develop marketing programs.

Marketers must also be aware of changes that may be occurring in a particular culture and the implications of these changes for their advertising and promotional strategies and programs. American culture continually goes through many changes that have direct implications for advertising. Marketing researchers monitor these changes and their impact on the ways companies market their products and services.

While marketers recognize that culture exerts a demonstrable influence on consumers, they often find it difficult to respond to cultural differences in different markets. The subtleties of various cultures are often difficult to understand and appreciate, but marketers must understand the cultural context in which consumer purchase decisions are made and adapt their advertising and promotional programs accordingly. Global Perspective 4–3 demonstrates some of the issues that U.S. companies confront in marketing to other cultures.

Subcultures

Within a given culture are generally found smaller groups or segments whose beliefs, values, norms, and patterns of behavior set them apart from the larger cultural mainstream. These **subcultures** may be based on age, geographic, religious, racial, and/or ethnic differences. A number of subcultures exist within the United States. The three largest racial/ethnic subcultures are African-Americans, Hispanics, and various Asian groups. These racial/ethnic subcultures are important to marketers because of their size, growth, purchasing power, and distinct purchasing patterns. Marketers develop specific marketing programs for various products and services for these target markets. The ads in Exhibit 4–17 are just two of the many specifically designed to appeal to U.S. subcultures—in these

FIGURE 4–10
External influences on consumer behavior

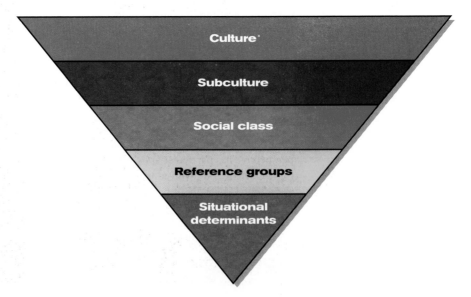

Global Perspective 4–3
Cultural Differences Challenge U.S. Advertisers

Push-up bras and racy G-strings are the hottest products of 1997. Where? Asia—particularly Singapore, a country with one of the most conservative governments in the free world (it's illegal to chew gum there). Flashy lingerie departments are the rage in Shanghai and Beijing, China, and Wonderbra is developing a special product line targeted to the slim Asian body. What's surprising about all of this is that Asian countries have generally been thought of as ultraconservative and family-oriented, while concern with one's body was the opiate of Western cultures. Has the Western influence made that much of an impact? Not necessarily.

The Discovery Channel has met with much less success in Asia—even though it was warmly received. It has also had limited success in Europe and Latin America. EuroDisney has had a hard time of it, and U.S. ad agencies have stumbled with their appeals in Europe and throughout the world. Many of these surprising results can be attributed to cultural differences. Consider the following:

- The Energizer bunny campaign failed in Hungary because consumers thought the bunny toy was being touted—not batteries.
- Lipton Tea's use of Tom Selleck as a macho man standing on a mountain drinking tea was not understood by Europeans. The concept just didn't come across.
- A baby soap company ad in which a mother held a baby in her arms was considered scandalous in Hun-

gary. The reason? The mother had her wedding ring on her left hand—the sign of an unwed mother. (Hungarians wear their rings on their right hands.)
- In Saudi Arabia, it's illegal to mix men and women in focus groups. In Spain, it's discourteous to say negative things about products, even in focus groups.
- After slow growth, the Discovery Channel learned that viewers in Mexico prefer programs about history and architecture, Russians like do-it-yourself series, Indians like travel shows, and Australian viewers prefer science and technology.

What advertisers are finding is that it is very difficult to assume anything when it comes to cultures. While many believe that the world is getting smaller and that cultural diversity will decline as a result (as the adoption of Western fashions in Asia suggests), others are finding that differences between cultures remain steadfast. The European Union, in which many of Europe's countries were to band together in a common market with similar values and purchasing behaviors, has not met expectations due to stereotypes, history, and schooling.

Advertisers are finding that to succeed in these markets they need to adapt before local agencies, stressing their understanding of the local cultures, take away their clients. So these agencies are increasing their consumer research efforts and localizing their campaigns. They are also paying particular attention to cultural nuances such as which hand one wears a wedding ring on!

Sources: Wayne Walley, "Programming Globally—with Care," *Advertising Age*, October 18, 1996, p. 18; Tara Parker-Pope, "Ad Agencies Are Stumbling in East Europe," *The Wall Street Journal*, May 19, 1996, p. B1; Tyler Marshall, "The United States of Europe," *Los Angeles Times*, May 10, 1996, p. 1.

EXHIBIT 4–17
Ads targeted to subcultures

cases, blacks and Hispanics. Many others can easily be found that target teens, Generation Xers, the elderly, and so on.

Social Class

Virtually all societies exhibit some form of stratification whereby individuals can be assigned to a specific social category based on criteria important to members of that society. **Social class** refers to relatively homogeneous divisions in a society into which people sharing similar lifestyles, values, norms, interests, and behaviors can be grouped. While a number of methods for determining social class exist, class structures in the United States are generally based on occupational status, educational attainment, and income. Sociologists generally agree there are three broad levels of social classes in the United States: the upper(14 percent), middle (70 percent), and lower (16 percent) classes.[28]

Social class is an important concept to marketers, since consumers within each social stratum often have similar values, lifestyles, and buying behavior. Thus, the various social class groups provide a natural basis for market segmentation. Consumers in the different social classes differ in the degree to which they use various products and services and in their leisure activities, shopping patterns, and media habits. Marketers respond to these differences through the positioning of their products and services, the media strategies they use to reach different social classes, and the types of advertising appeals they develop. The ad for Concord's Saratoga watch in Exhibit 4–18 shows how a product attempts to appeal to the upper classes in both copy and illustration.

Reference Groups

Think about the last time you attended a party. As you dressed for the party, you probably asked yourself (or someone else) what others would be wearing. Your selection of attire may have been influenced by those likely to be present. This simple example reflects one form of impact that groups may exert on your behavior.

A *group* has been defined as "two or more individuals who share a set of norms, values, or beliefs and have certain implicitly or explicitly defined relationships to one another such that their behavior is interdependent."[29] Groups are one of the primary factors influencing learning and socialization, and group situations constitute many of our purchase decisions.

A **reference group** is "a group whose presumed perspectives or values are being used by an individual as the basis for his or her judgments, opinions, and actions." Consumers use reference groups as a guide to specific behaviors, even when the groups are not present.[30] In the party example, your peers—although not present—provided a standard of dress that you referred to in your clothing selection. Likewise, your college classmates, fam-

EXHIBIT 4–18
Concord targets the upper classes

As grand
as the season.
As gala
as the ball.
A celebration of
excellence.
That's the beauty
of Saratoga.

CONCORD.
WATCH
MAKERS
TO
THE GENTRY.

ily, co-workers, or even a group to which you aspire may serve as referents, and your consumption patterns will typically conform to the expectations of the groups that are most important to you.

Marketers use reference group influences in developing advertisements and promotional strategies. The ads in Exhibit 4–19 are examples of aspirational reference groups (to which we might like to belong) and disassociative groups (to which we do not wish to belong), respectively.

FAMILY DECISION MAKING: AN EXAMPLE OF GROUP INFLUENCES

In some instances, the group may be involved more directly than just as a referent. Family members may serve as referents to each other, or they may actually be involved in the purchase decision process—acting as an individual buying unit. As shown in Figure 4–11, family members may assume a variety of roles in the decision-making process.[31] Each role has implications for marketers.[32]

First, the advertiser must determine who is responsible for the various roles in the decision-making process, so messages can be targeted at that person (or those people). These roles will also dictate media strategies, since the appropriate magazines, newspapers, or TV or radio stations must be used. Second, understanding the decision-making process and the use of information by individual family members is critical to the design of messages and choice of promotional program elements. In sum, a marketer must have an overall understanding of how the decision process works and the role that each family member plays to create an effective promotional program.

EXHIBIT 4—19   The ad on the left shows an aspirational reference group; the one on the right stresses a disassociative reference group

FIGURE 4–11
Roles in the family decision-making
process

The initiator. The person responsible for initiating the purchase decision process; for example, the mother who determines she needs a new car.

The information provider. The individual responsible for gathering information to be used in making the decision; for example, the teenage car buff who knows where to find product information in specific magazines or collects it from dealers.

The influencer. The person who exerts influence as to what criteria will be used in the selection process. All members of the family may be involved. The mother may have her criteria, whereas others may each have their own input.

The decision maker(s). That person(s) who actually makes the decision. In our example, it may be the mother alone or in combination with another family member.

The purchasing agent. That individual who performs the physical act of making the purchase. In the case of a car, a husband and wife may decide to choose it together and sign the purchase agreement.

The consumer. The actual user of the product. In the case of a family car, all family members are consumers. For a private car, only the mother might be the consumer.

Situational Determinants

The final external factor is the purchase and usage situation. The specific situation in which consumers plan to use the product or brand directly affects their perceptions, preferences, and purchasing behaviors.[33] Three types of **situational determinants** may have an effect: the specific usage situation, the purchase situation, and the communications situation.

Usage refers to the circumstance in which the product will be used. For example, purchases made for private consumption may be thought of differently from those that will be obvious to the public. The *purchase* situation more directly involves the environment operating at the time of the purchase. Time constraints, store environments, and other factors may all have an impact. The *communications* situation is the condition in which an advertising exposure occurs (in a car listening to the radio, with friends, etc.). This may be most relevant to the development of promotional strategies, because the impact on the consumer will vary according to the particular situation. For example, a consumer may pay more attention to a commercial that is heard alone at home than in the presence of friends, at work, or anywhere distractions may be present. If advertisers can isolate a particular time when the listener is likely to be attentive, they will probably earn his or her undivided attention.

In sum, situational determinants may either enhance or detract from the potential success of a message. To the degree that advertisers can assess situational influences that may be operating, they will increase the likelihood of successfully communicating with their target audiences.

ALTERNATIVE APPROACHES TO CONSUMER BEHAVIOR

The preceding discussion of consumer behavior focused on consumer decision making as viewed from several psychological perspectives. However, in the past decade, a growing number of consumer researchers have examined this process from a different perspective, often referred to as *alternative*, *interpretive*, *postmodern*, or *postpositivist*. Regardless of the name, *alternative* ways of attempting to understand consumer behavior assume a cross-disciplinary approach. Consumer decision making is viewed from different perspectives and nonquantitative research methodologies are used to broaden the discipline from a sociopsychological focus. Multisensory, fantasy, and emotive aspects of consumer behavior are examined through research techniques such as individual interviews, ethnographic participant observer studies, and interpretative analyses commonly employed in disciplines outside the psychological arena (semiotics, literary criticism, philosophy, history). This orientation is shaped by research with roots in anthropological, sociological, and historical studies.

Those who conduct research from this perspective believe that consumers' decision-making processes do not occur in isolation. Rather, they view consumer decision making as influenced by cultural, linguistic, and historical factors. They use historical and situational contexts to add insights to our understanding of consumer behavior. In examining the significance of communications, they have adopted three perspectives:

- *Sociocultural.* Avertising and other forms of communication are viewed as both influencing and being influenced by culture. That is, consumers' interpretations of ads are shaped by their cultural values, and in turn, these ads will (over time) shape the culture themselves.
- *Structural.* Consumption behaviors are examined to discover underlying meanings. For example, the symbolic meanings of advertising are examined in regard to their association with the cultural stack of stories and myths.
- *Semiotic.* Products and ads are examined for their symbolic meanings to consumers—for example, the meanings of words. In addition, consumer "rituals" such as fashion codes, gift giving, and rumormongering are studied.

As you can see, the variety of titles assigned to this domain of consumer behavior research reflects the multidimensional perspectives from which consumers are viewed. Studies of how consumers make decisions and the impact of communications (both *on* the consumer and *by* the consumer) are shedding new light in consumer research.

SUMMARY

This chapter introduced you to the field of consumer behavior and examined its relevance to promotional strategy. Consumer behavior is best viewed as the process and activities that people engage in when searching for, selecting, purchasing, using, evaluating, and disposing of products and services to satisfy their needs and desires. A five-stage model of the consumer decision-making process consists of problem recognition, information search, alternative evaluation, purchase, and postpurchase evaluation. Internal psychological processes that influence the consumer decision-making process include motivation, perception, attitude formation and change, and integration processes.

The decision process model views consumer behavior primarily from a cognitive orientation. The chapter considered other perspectives by examining various approaches to consumer learning and their implications for advertising and promotion. Behavioral learning theories such as classical conditioning and operant (instrumental) conditioning were discussed. Problems with behavioral learning theories were noted, and the alternative perspective of cognitive learning was discussed.

The chapter also examined relevant external factors that influence consumer decision making. Culture, subculture, social class, reference groups, and situational determinants were discussed, along with their implications for the development of promotional strategies and programs. The chapter concluded with an introduction to alternative perspectives on the study of consumer behavior (also called interpretive, postmodern, or postpositivist perspectives).

KEY TERMS

consumer behavior, 103
problem recognition, 103
want, 105
motives, 106
hierarchy of needs, 106
psychoanalytic theory, 108
motivation research, 109
internal search, 111
external search, 111
perception, 112
sensation, 112
selective perception, 113

selective exposure, 113
selective attention, 113
selective comprehension, 113
selective retention, 113
mnemonics, 114
subliminal perception, 114
evaluative criteria, 116
functional consequences, 116
psychosocial consequences, 116

multiattribute attitude model, 117
salient beliefs, 117
integration processes, 118
heuristics, 118
affect referral decision rule, 118
purchase intention, 119
brand loyalty, 120
cognitive dissonance, 120
classical conditioning, 123
conditioned stimulus, 124

conditioned response, 124
operant conditioning, 124
reinforcement, 125
schedules of reinforcement, 126
shaping, 126
culture, 128
subcultures, 128
social class, 130
reference group, 130
situational determinants, 132

DISCUSSION QUESTIONS

1. The text discusses alternative approaches to studying consumer behavior. Explain how these approaches differ from those described earlier in the chapter.

2. Why is it important for promotional planners to understand consumer behavior? What are some aspects of consumer behavior they need to understand?

3. Discuss some of the problems and contributions associated with the application of psychoanalytic theory to consumer behavior.

4. Explain how the screening processes involved in selective perception might impact a viewer of television commercials.

5. What is subliminal perception? Describe how marketers are attempting to use this concept in the marketing of goods and services.

6. Discuss the three variations of the consumer decision-making process. What is the importance of communications in each type?

7. Explain how reference groups influence buyers' behaviors. Give an example of how both aspirational and disassociative groups might have an impact.

8. Postmodern research often involves a sociological perspective to understanding consumer behavior. Give examples as to how sociology might impact purchase behaviors.

9. Discuss the various attitude change strategies recognized by the multiattribute model. How could an airline use some of these attitude change strategies in its marketing and advertising programs?

10. Discuss how promotional planners can use the principles of various behavioral learning theories, such as classical and operant conditioning and modeling, in the design of advertising and promotional strategies.

Analyzing the
Communication
Process

PART

3

CHAPTER 5

The Communication Process

Chapter Objectives

- To understand the basic elements of the communication process and the role of communications in marketing.

- To examine various models of the communication process.

- To analyze the response processes of receivers of marketing communications, including alternative response hierarchies and their implications for promotional planning and strategy.

- To examine the nature of consumers' cognitive processing of marketing communications.

SAMSUNG REMAKES ITS IMAGE

If asked to name some of the world's largest electronic product companies, consumers in the United States and Canada would probably mention Japanese firms such as Sony, Panasonic, and Sharp. Most would probably not name Samsung Electronics, the Korean company that makes more computer monitors than anyone else in the world and is the number-two maker of microwave ovens and VCRs. Samsung Electronics is a subsidiary of the Samsung Group, Korea's mammoth industrial conglomerate that makes and sells just about everything that plugs into a wall outlet. In 1996 Samsung Electronics sold more than $21 billion of electronics around the world, with nearly a third of its sales coming from North America. But because many of its products are marketed here by other companies under other names, Samsung is a relatively unknown brand name. However, the company is hard at work to change that.

Samsung Electronics' North American subsidiary, Samsung Electronics America (SEA), has recently embarked on a major integrated marketing communications campaign designed to increase awareness of the company, improve its corporate image, and gain more acceptance of its products in North America. Samsung plans to spend nearly $60 million a year on everything from billboards, bus posters, and postcards to magazine ads and TV commercials announcing its existence with the tagline "Simply Samsung." The new campaign is the brainchild of Peter Arnell, chair of the Arnell Group, an agency known for its heavily image-driven advertising for clients such as Anne Klein, Chanel, Banana Republic, and Donna Karan's DKNY brand, with its striking black-and-white ads.

The first series of ads in the campaign could easily be mistaken as advertising designer clothing or a fragrance rather than computer electronics. The black-and-white ads present Samsung's "sexy but simple" new look and feature physically flawless models flaunting burnished body parts. One shows a man cradling a microwave next to his washboard abs; another shows a beautiful woman who appears to be seducing a television set. Peter Arnell notes that the ads are designed to change perceptions of Samsung and make the company appear more consumer friendly. He says, "The ads look at SEA, who they really are, and reflect what they're about. They're honest, clean and bold." SEA's senior vice president for sales and marketing steers clear of trying to define the ads but says the campaign "is about simplicity, uniqueness, wistfulness. You have only got two seconds to make an image."

The Arnell Group's effort to update and sharpen Samsung's image among upscale buyers involves more than creating sexy ads. The agency is assisting SEA in everything from marketing strategy, advertising, branding, corporate identification, and strategic alliance planning all the way through to product and package design. The agency's industrial design division, A3-D, is involved in the design and development of new products and the identification of new product categories for SEA. In addition to handling the advertising for Samsung's consumer products, the agency now handles SEA's Information Services Division (ISD) which includes products such as notebook computers and CD-ROM drives.

A Samsung executive describes the company as a sleeping giant, a $70 billion corporation that most people don't know much about. The Arnell Group's hip, image-conscious advertising may give Samsung the image makeover it needs to become a major player in the lucrative North American market.

Source: John Spooner, "Remake, Remodel," *Marketing Computers*, June 1996, pp. 51–55; Joshua Levine, "You've Got Just Two Seconds . . . ," *Forbes*, July 1, 1996, p. 74.

The function of all elements of the promotional mix is to communicate. An organization's advertising and promotional strategy is implemented through the communications it sends to current or prospective customers. Thus, advertising and promotional planners need to understand the communication process. As you can see from the opening vignette, the way marketers communicate with their customers depends on many factors, including how much consumers know about their company and the image they hope to create. Developing an effective marketing communications program is far more complicated than just choosing a product feature or attribute to emphasize. Marketers must understand how consumers will perceive and interpret their messages and how these reactions will shape their responses toward the product or service.

This chapter reviews the fundamentals of communication and examines various perspectives regarding how consumers respond to promotional messages. Our goal is to demonstrate how valuable an understanding of the communication process can be in planning, implementing, and evaluating the marketing communications program.

THE NATURE OF COMMUNICATION

Communication has been variously defined as the passing of information, the exchange of ideas, or the process of establishing a commonness or oneness of thought between a sender and a receiver.[1] These definitions suggest that for communication to occur, there must be some common thinking between two parties and information must be passed from one person to another (or from one group to another). As you will see in this chapter, establishing this commonality in thinking is not always as easy as it might seem; many attempts to communicate are unsuccessful.

The communication process is often very complex. Success depends on such factors as the nature of the message, the audience's interpretation of it, and the environment in which it is received. The receiver's perception of the source and the medium used to transmit the message may also affect the ability to communicate, as do many other factors. Words, pictures, sounds, and colors may have different meanings to different audiences, and people's perceptions and interpretations of them vary. For example, if you ask for a soda on the East Coast or West Coast, you'll receive a soft drink such as Coke or Pepsi. However, in parts of the Midwest and South, a soft drink is referred to as pop. If you ask for a soda, you may get a glass of pop with ice cream in it. Marketers must understand the meanings that words and symbols take on and how they influence consumers' interpretation of products and messages. This can be particularly challenging to companies marketing their products in foreign countries, as discussed in Global Perspective 5–1.

A BASIC MODEL OF COMMUNICATION

Over the years, a basic model of the various elements of the communication process has evolved, as shown in Figure 5–1.[2] Two elements represent the major participants in the communication process, the sender and the receiver. Another two are the major communication tools, message and channel. Four others are the major communication functions and processes: encoding, decoding, response, and feedback. The last element, noise, refers to any extraneous factors in the system that can interfere with the process and work against effective communication.

Source Encoding

The sender, or **source**, of a communication is the person or organization that has information to share with another person or group of people. The source may be an individual (say, a salesperson or hired spokesperson, such as a celebrity, who appears in a company's advertisements) or a nonpersonal entity (such as the corporation or organization itself). For example, the source of the ad in Exhibit 5–1 is Motorola, since no specific spokesperson or source is shown. But in Exhibit 5–2, the source is golfer Lee Trevino, as Motorola's advertising spokesperson.

Because the receiver's perceptions of the source influence how the communication is received, marketers must be careful to select a communicator the receiver believes is knowledgeable and trustworthy or with whom the receiver can identify or relate in some manner. (How these characteristics influence the receiver's responses is discussed further in Chapter 6.)

Global Perspective 5—1
Communication Problems in International Marketing

Communication is a major problem facing U.S. companies that market their products in foreign countries. International marketers must be aware of the connotation of the words, signs, symbols, and expressions they use as brand names or logos or in various forms of promotion. Advertising copy, slogans, and symbols do not always transfer well into other languages. This not only impedes communication but also sometimes results in embarrassing blunders that can damage a company's or brand's credibility or image and cost it customers.

Mistranslations and faulty word choices have often created problems for firms engaging in international marketing. For example, the slogan "Come alive with Pepsi" translated too literally in some countries. The German translation was "Come out of the grave," while in Chinese it read, "Pepsi brings your ancestors back from the dead." An American airline competing in Brazil advertised "rendezvous lounges" in its jets—until it discovered that in the Brazilian dialect of Portuguese this meant a place to make love. Budweiser's long-time slogan "King of Beers" translates in Spanish as "Queen of Beers" because the noun *cerveza* (beer) has a feminine ending.

International marketers can also have linguistic problems with brand names and their meaning or pronunciation, as when Coca-Cola introduced its product to China. The Chinese characters sounded like Coca-Cola but meant "bite the wax tadpole." With the help of a language specialist, the company substituted four Mandarin characters that still sound like Coca-Cola but mean "Can happy, mouth happy."

International marketers may also encounter problems with the way certain cultures interpret visual signs and symbols. For example, AT&T found that the thumbs-up sign used in its "I plan" campaign presented a problem. Thumbs up signifies affirmation to most Americans, but to Russians and Poles, the fact that the person's palm was visible gave the ad an offensive meaning. AT&T hired YAR Communications, a company that specializes in translations, to reshoot the graphic element in the ad so that only the back of the person's hand showed, conveying the intended meaning.

Merrill Lynch & Co. also encountered problems when it tried to use its trademark bull symbol in advertising for the Russian market. YAR placed ads in Russian newspapers and magazines describing the company's services and explaining that the trademark bull stands for strength and is not, as some Russian consumers thought, a source of meat. The ads used a stylized image of a bull and a new Merrill Lynch logo.

Even company names can get lost in translation. The fast-food chain Wienerschnitzel (which in Germany means breaded veal cutlet rather than hot dog) had to deal with the fact that its name is a mouthful, particularly for Spanish-speaking consumers. When the chain expanded into Mexico, its franchisee shortened the name to Wieners so people could pronounce it. Disc jockeys doing radio ads were told to read the name slowly and identify Wienerschnitzel as "the place with the big red W" on its sign. Many multinational companies are trying to develop world brands that can be marketed internationally using the same brand name and advertising. However, they must be careful that brand names, advertising slogans, and other forms of marketing communications don't lose something in the translation.

Sources: Greg Johnson, "Fast-Food Firms Learn Lessons of El Mercado," *Los Angeles Times*, October 8, 1996, pp. A1,16; Riccardo A. Davis, "Many Languages—One Ad Message," *Advertising Age*, September 20, 1993, p. 50; "We Are the World," *Adweek's Marketing Week*, September 1990, pp. 61–68.

The communication process begins when the source selects words, symbols, pictures, and the like to represent the message that will be delivered to the receiver(s). This process, known as **encoding,** refers to putting thoughts, ideas, or information into a symbolic form. The sender's goal is to encode the message in such a way that it will be understood by the receiver. This means using words, signs, or symbols that are familiar to the target audience. Many symbols have universal meaning, such as the familiar circle with a line through it to denote no parking, no smoking, and so forth. Many companies also have highly recognizable symbols—such as McDonald's golden arches, Nike's swoosh, or the Coca-Cola trademark—that are known to consumers around the world.

FIGURE 5–1   A model of the communication process

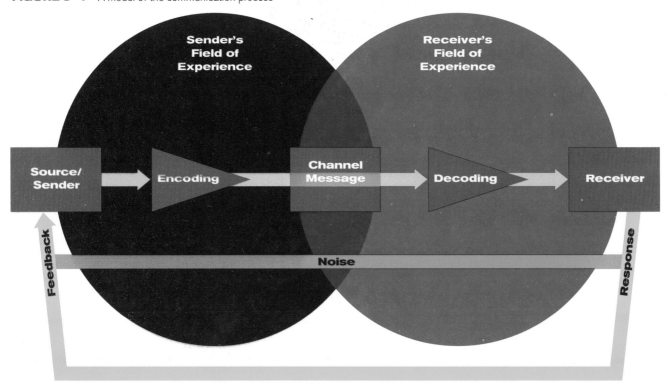

Message

The encoding process leads to development of a **message** that contains the information or meaning the source hopes to convey. The message may be verbal or nonverbal, oral or written, or symbolic. Messages must be put into a transmittable form that is appropriate for the channel of communication being used. In advertising, this may range from simply writing some words or copy that will be read as a radio message to producing an expensive television commercial. For many products, it is not the actual words of the message that determine its communication effectiveness but rather the impression or image the ad creates. Notice how Spellbound perfume in Exhibit 5–3 uses only a picture to deliver its message. However, the product name and picture help communicate a feeling of attraction and fascination between the couple shown in the ad.

EXHIBIT 5–1
The source of this ad is Motorola

EXHIBIT 5—2
Motorola uses Lee Trevino as a
spokesperson

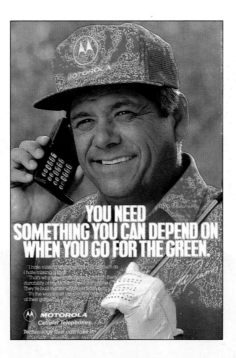

To better understand the symbolic meaning that might be conveyed in a communication, advertising and marketing researchers have begun focusing attention on **semiotics**, which studies the nature of meaning and asks how our reality—words, gestures, myths, products/services, theories—acquires meaning.[3] Marketers are using individuals trained in semiotics to better understand the conscious and subconscious meanings the nonverbal signs and symbols in their ads transmit to consumers.

Look at the ad for Snuggle fabric softener shown in Exhibit 5–4 and think about what the teddy bear might symbolize. Lever Brothers conducted a semiotic analysis to help understand the meaning of Snuggle, the huggable teddy bear that has become such a successful advertising symbol. The semiologist concluded Snuggle is a "symbol of tamed aggression," a perfect symbol for a fabric softener that "tames" the rough texture of clothing.[4]

Some advertising and marketing people are skeptical about the value of semiotics. They question whether social scientists read too much into advertising messages and are overly intellectual in interpreting them. However, the meaning of an advertising message or other form of marketing communication lies not in the message, but with the people who see and interpret it. Moreover, consumers behave based on the meanings they ascribe to marketplace

EXHIBIT 5—3
The image projected by an ad often
communicates more than words

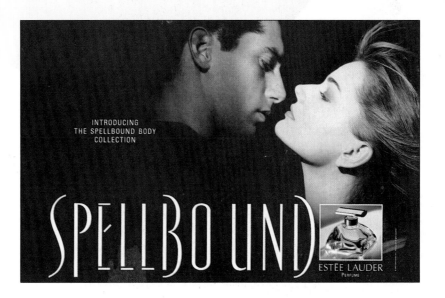

EXHIBIT 5—4
Semiotic research suggests that the Snuggle bear symbolizes tamed aggression

stimuli. Thus, marketers must consider the meanings consumers attach to the various signs and symbols. Semiotics may be helpful in analyzing how various aspects of the marketing program—such as advertising messages, packaging, brand names, and even the nonverbal communications of salespeople (gestures, mode of dress)—are interpreted by receivers.[5]

Channel

The **channel** is the method by which the communication travels from the source or sender to the receiver. At the broadest level, channels of communication are of two types, personal and nonpersonal. *Personal channels* of communication are direct interpersonal (face-to-face) contact with target individuals or groups. Salespeople serve as personal channels of communication when they deliver their sales message to a buyer or potential customer. Social channels of communication such as friends, neighbors, associates, co-workers, or family members are also personal channels. They often represent *word-of-mouth communication*, a powerful source of information for consumers.[6]

Nonpersonal channels of communication are those that carry a message without interpersonal contact between sender and receiver. Nonpersonal channels are generally referred to as the **mass media** or mass communications, since the message is sent to many individuals at one time. For example, a TV commercial broadcast on a prime-time show may be seen by 20 million households in a given evening. Nonpersonal channels of communication consist of two major types, print and broadcast. Print media include newspapers, magazines, direct mail, and billboards; broadcast media include radio and television.

Receiver/Decoding

The **receiver** is the person(s) with whom the sender shares thoughts or information. Generally, receivers are the consumers in the target market or audience who read, hear, and/or see the marketer's message and decode it. **Decoding** is the process of transforming the sender's message back into thought. This process is heavily influenced by the receiver's frame of reference or **field of experience**, which refers to the experiences, perceptions, attitudes, and values he or she brings to the communication situation.

For effective communication to occur, the message decoding process of the receiver must match the encoding of the sender. Simply put, this means the receiver understands and correctly interprets what the source is trying to communicate. As Figure 5–1 showed, the source and the receiver each have a frame of reference (the circle around each) that they bring to the communication situation. Effective communication is more likely when there is some *common ground* between the two parties. (This is represented by the overlapping of the two circles.) The more knowledge the sender has about the receivers, the better it can understand their needs, empathize with them, and communicate effectively.

While this notion of common ground between sender and receiver may sound basic, it often causes great difficulty in the advertising communications process. Marketing and advertising people often have very different fields of experience from the consumers who constitute the mass markets with whom they must communicate. Most advertising and marketing people are college educated and work and/or reside in large urban areas such as New York, Chicago, or Los Angeles. Yet they are attempting to develop commercials that will effectively communicate with millions of consumers who have never attended college, work in blue-collar occupations, and live in rural areas or small towns. The executive creative director of a large advertising agency described how advertising executives become isolated from the cultural mainstream: "We pull them in and work them to death. And then they begin moving in sushi circles and lose touch with Velveeta and the people who eat it."[7]

Another factor that can lead to problems in establishing common ground between senders and receivers is age. IMC Perspective 5–2 discusses some interesting findings from a study that considered problems younger advertising professionals have in developing ads for older consumers.

Advertisers spend millions of dollars every year to understand the frames of reference of the target markets who receive their messages. They also spend much time and money pretesting messages to make sure consumers understand and decode them in the manner the advertiser intended.

Noise

Throughout the communication process, the message is subject to extraneous factors that can distort or interfere with its reception. This unplanned distortion or interference is known as **noise**. Errors or problems that occur in the encoding of the message, distortion in a radio or television signal, or distractions at the point of reception are examples of noise. When you are watching your favorite commercial on TV and a problem occurs in the signal transmission, this will obviously interfere with your reception, lessening the impact of the commercial.

Noise may also occur because the fields of experience of the sender and receiver don't overlap. Lack of common ground may result in improper encoding of the message—using a sign, symbol, or words that are unfamiliar or have different meaning to the receiver. The more common ground there is between the sender and the receiver, the less likely it is this type of noise will occur.

Response/Feedback

The receiver's set of reactions after seeing, hearing, or reading the message is known as a **response**. Receivers' responses can range from nonobservable actions such as storing information in memory to immediate action such as dialing a toll-free number to order a product advertised on television. Marketers are very interested in **feedback**, that part of the receiver's response that is communicated back to the sender. Feedback, which may take a variety of forms, closes the loop in the communications flow and lets the sender monitor how the intended message is being decoded and received.

For example, in a personal selling situation, customers may pose questions, comments, or objections or indicate their reactions through nonverbal responses such as gestures and frowns.[8] The salesperson has the advantage of receiving instant feedback through the customer's reactions. But this is generally not the case when mass media are used. Because advertisers are not in direct contact with the customers, they must use other means to determine how their messages have been received. While the ultimate form of feedback occurs through sales, it is often hard to show a direct relationship between advertising and pur-

IMC Perspective 5–2
Is Ageism a Problem in Advertising?

It has often been argued that people who work in advertising are different from the typical consumers who represent the target markets for their clients' products and services. Some say advertising may better reflect those who work in the industry than the consuming public. Critics argue that most advertising is really about the people who create it, not about the consumers who actually buy the products being advertised.

A recent study on ageism in advertising considered potential problems that might arise because of age differences between agency personnel and older consumers. The study, which was conducted by High-Yield Marketing in conjunction with the Association of Advertising Agencies International, found that the median age of ad agency employees is much lower than that of people in law, accounting, banking, and insurance. The study noted that "the majority of advertising agency professionals are in early adulthood, when empathic understanding for people of different generations is relatively unknown" and "most agency professionals are most comfortable advertising to younger consumers like themselves."

Advertisers who are unable to connect with the so-called mature market may be squandering opportunities to reach a valuable market. People who are 50 or older and head a household account for 43 percent of the U.S. population and control more than 40 percent of discretionary income. However, myths persist about the older consumer, among both agencies and clients. Older people are stereotyped as unlikely to change brands and try something new and as less affluent than younger consumers. Judith Langer, president of Langer Associates, a New York market research and trend consulting company, says, "The myths rule, and reality doesn't intrude when marketing to those over 50." However, she notes that the fault often lies with clients who want to focus on the younger generation.

Of course, not everyone in the advertising industry agrees with the findings of the ageism study. One agency executive calls the conclusion ridiculous, noting that "We have people of every age segment here." The president of the American Association of Advertising Agencies says, "Clearly in the case of the top 20 or 30 agencies, they have a balanced population that reflects the ages of the country's population. I'm not sure that is the case with smaller and mid-size agencies, nor with the new hotshot creative agencies simply because of who they would attract."

There are examples of excellent advertising targeted at mature consumers. A commercial for Kellogg's All-Bran cereal features the rock classic "Wild Thing" accompanied by shots of older people performing vigorous activities such as water skiing. A series of Nike ads features senior athletes. Quaker Oats recently dropped its growly, paunchy, oatmeal pitchman Wilford Brimley for "George," a 60-something model who wears a muscle shirt revealing biceps that would be the envy of anyone 20 years younger. Compaq Computer has two grandmotherly types using their computers to fax recipes back and forth.

Many believe that good ads aimed at older consumers are still too few and far between and the advertising industry's youthfulness is indeed a problem. However, others feel that it has finally dawned on Madison Avenue, and on marketing people in general, that they ought to follow the green—which is quickly going gray. As one agency executive noted: "After all, Mick Jagger is 52 and a grandfather."

Sources: Lisa Gubernick and Luisa Kroll, "Gray Hair Is Cool," *Forbes*, May 6, 1996, p. 116; Kevin Goldman, "Study Finds Agency Employees Favor Ads Directed at the Young," *The Wall Street Journal*, May 4, 1995, p. B8.

chase behavior. So marketers use other methods to obtain feedback, among them customer inquiries, store visits, coupon redemptions, and reply cards. Research-based feedback analyzes readership and recall of ads, message comprehension, attitude change, and other forms of response. With this information, the advertiser can determine reasons for success or failure in the communication process and make adjustments.

Successful communication is accomplished when the marketer selects an appropriate source, develops an effective message or appeal that is encoded properly, and then selects the channels or media that will best reach the target audience so that the message can be effectively decoded and delivered. In Chapter 6, we will examine the source, message, and channel decisions and see how promotional planners work with these controllable variables to develop communication strategies. Since these decisions must consider how the target audience will respond to the promotional message, the remainder of this chapter examines the receiver and the process by which consumers respond to advertising and other forms of marketing communications.

ANALYZING THE RECEIVER

To communicate effectively with their customers, marketers must understand who the target audience is, what (if anything) it knows or feels about the company's product or service, and how to communicate with the audience to influence its decision-making process. Marketers must also know how the market is likely to respond to various sources of communication or different types of messages. Before they make decisions regarding source, message, and channel variables, promotional planners must understand the potential effects associated with each of these factors. This section focuses on the receiver of the marketing communication. It examines how the audience is identified and the process it may go through in responding to a promotional message. This information serves as a foundation for evaluating the controllable communication variable decisions in the next chapter.

Identifying the Target Audience

The marketing communication process really begins with identifying the audience that will be the focus of the firm's advertising and promotions efforts. The target audience may consist of individuals, groups, niche markets, market segments, or a general public or mass audience (Figure 5–2). Marketers approach each of these audiences differently.

The target market may consist of individuals who have specific needs and for whom the communication must be specifically tailored. This often requires person-to-person communication and is generally accomplished through personal selling. Other forms of communication, such as advertising, may be used to attract the audience's attention to the firm, but the detailed message is carried by a salesperson who can respond to the specific needs of the individual customer. Life insurance, financial services, and real estate are examples of products and services promoted this way.

A second level of audience aggregation is represented by the group. Marketers often must communicate with a group of people who make or influence the purchase decision. For example, organizational purchasing often involves buying centers or committees that vary in size and composition. Companies marketing their products and services to other businesses or organizations must understand who is on the purchase committee, what aspect of the decision each individual influences, and the criteria each member uses to evaluate a product. Advertising may be directed at each member of the buying center, and multilevel personal selling may be necessary to reach those individuals who influence or actually make decisions.

Marketers look for customers who have similar needs and wants and thus represent some type of market segment that can be reached with the same basic communication strategy.

FIGURE 5–2
Levels of audience aggregation

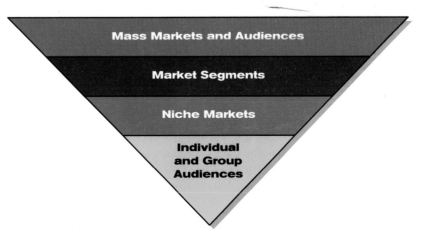

Mass Markets and Audiences

Market Segments

Niche Markets

Individual and Group Audiences

Very small, well-defined groups of customers are often referred to as *market niches*. They can usually be reached through personal selling efforts or highly targeted media such as direct mail. The next level of audience aggregation is market segments, broader classes of buyers who have similar needs and can be reached with similar messages. As we saw in Chapter 2, there are various ways of segmenting markets and reaching the customers in these segments. As market segments get larger, marketers usually turn to broader-based media such as newspapers, magazines, and TV to reach them.

Marketers of most consumer products attempt to attract the attention of large numbers of present or potential customers (mass markets) through mass communication such as advertising or publicity. Mass communication is a one-way flow of information from the marketer to the consumer. Feedback on the audience's reactions to the message is generally indirect and difficult to measure.

TV advertising, for example, lets the marketer send a message to millions of consumers at the same time. But this does not mean effective communication has occurred. This may be only one of several hundred messages the consumer is exposed to that day. There is no guarantee the information will be attended to, processed, comprehended, or stored in memory for later retrieval. Even if the advertising message is processed, it may not interest consumers or may be misinterpreted by them. Studies by Jacob Jacoby and Wayne D. Hoyer have shown that nearly 20 percent of all print ads and even more TV commercials are miscomprehended by readers.[9]

Unlike personal or face-to-face communications, mass communications do not offer the marketer an opportunity to explain or clarify the message to make it more effective. The marketer must enter the communication situation with knowledge of the target audience and how it is likely to react to the message. This means the receiver's response process must be understood, along with its implications for promotional planning and strategy.

THE RESPONSE PROCESS

Perhaps the most important aspect of developing effective communication programs involves understanding the *response process* the receiver may go through in moving toward a specific behavior (like purchasing a product) and how the promotional efforts of the marketer influence these responses. In many instances, the marketer's only objective may be to create awareness of the company or brand name, which may trigger interest in the product. In other situations, the marketer may want to convey detailed information to change consumers' knowledge of and attitudes toward the brand and ultimately change their behavior.

Traditional Response Hierarchy Models

A number of models have been developed to depict the stages a consumer may pass through in moving from a state of not being aware of a company, product, or brand to actual purchase behavior. Figure 5–3 shows four of the best-known response hierarchy models. While these response models may appear similar, they were developed for different reasons.

The **AIDA model** was developed to represent the stages a salesperson must take a customer through in the personal selling process.[10] This model depicts the buyer as passing successively through attention, interest, desire, and action. The salesperson must first get the customer's attention and then arouse some interest in the company's product or service. Strong levels of interest should create desire to own or use the product. The action stage in the AIDA model involves getting the customer to make a purchase commitment and closing the sale. To the marketer, this is the most important stage in the selling process, but it can also be the most difficult. Companies train their sales reps in closing techniques to help them complete the selling process.

Perhaps the best known of these response hierarchies is the model developed by Robert Lavidge and Gary Steiner as a paradigm for setting and measuring advertising objectives.[11] Their **hierarchy of effects model** shows the process by which advertising works and assumes a consumer passes through a series of steps in sequential order from initial awareness of a product or service to actual purchase. A basic premise of this model is that advertising effects occur over a period of time. Advertising communication may not lead to immediate behavioral response or purchase; rather, a series of effects must occur, with each step fulfilled before the consumer can move to the next stage in the hierarchy. As we will see in

FIGURE 5–3   Models of the response process

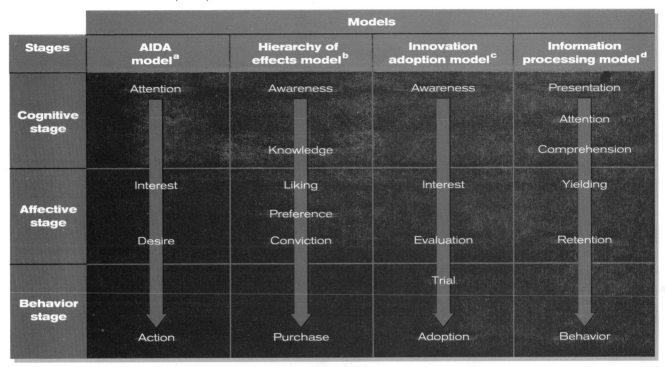

		Models		
Stages	**AIDA model**[a]	**Hierarchy of effects model**[b]	**Innovation adoption model**[c]	**Information processing model**[d]
Cognitive stage	Attention	Awareness Knowledge	Awareness	Presentation Attention Comprehension
Affective stage	Interest Desire	Liking Preference Conviction	Interest Evaluation	Yielding Retention
Behavior stage	Action	Purchase	Trial Adoption	Behavior

Sources: (a) E. K. Strong, *The Psychology of Selling* (New York: McGraw-Hill, 1925), p. 9; (b) Robert J. Lavidge and Gary A. Steiner, "A Model for Predictive Measurements of Advertising Effectiveness," *Journal of Marketing* (October 1961), p. 61; (c) Everett M. Rogers, *Diffusion of Innovations* (New York: Free Press, 1962), pp. 79–86; (d) William J. McGuire, "An Information Processing Model of Advertising Effectiveness," in *Behavioral and Management Science in Marketing,* ed. Harry L. Davis and Alvin J. Silk (New York: Ronald/Wiley, 1978), pp. 156–80; and Philip Kotler, *Marketing Management,* 5th ed. (Englewood Cliffs, NJ: Prentice Hall, 1984), p. 612.

Chapter 7, the hierarchy of effects model has become the foundation for objective setting and measurement of advertising effects in many companies.

The **innovation adoption model** evolved from work on the diffusion of innovations.[12] This model represents the stages a consumer passes through in adopting a new product or service. Like the other models, it says potential adopters must be moved through a series of steps before taking some action (in this case deciding to adopt a new product). The steps preceding adoption are awareness, interest, evaluation, and trial. The challenge facing companies introducing new products is to create awareness and interest among consumers and then get them to evaluate the product favorably. The best way to evaluate a new product is through actual use so that performance can be judged. Marketers often encourage trial by using demonstration or sampling programs or allowing consumers to use a product with minimal commitment (Exhibit 5–5). After trial, consumers either adopt the product or reject it.

The final hierarchy model shown in Figure 5–3 is the **information processing model** of advertising effects, developed by William McGuire.[13] This model assumes the receiver in a persuasive communication situation like advertising is an information processor or prob-

EXHIBIT 5–5

Sampling or demonstration programs encourage trial of new products such as disposable contact lenses

FIGURE 5—4
Methods of obtaining feedback in the
response hierarchy

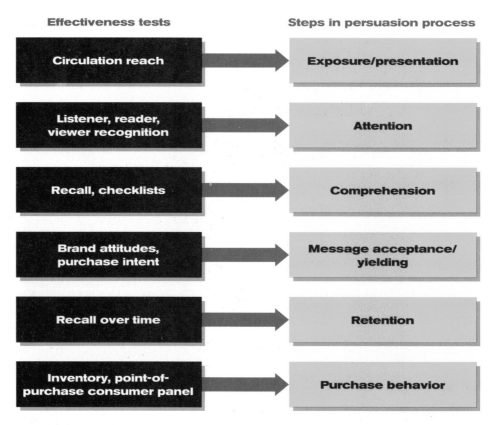

lem solver. McGuire suggests the series of steps a receiver goes through in being persuaded constitutes a response hierarchy. The stages of this model are similar to the hierarchy of effects sequence; attention and comprehension are similar to awareness and knowledge, and yielding is synonymous with liking. McGuire's model includes a stage not found in the other models: retention, or the receiver's ability to retain that portion of the comprehended information that he or she accepts as valid or relevant. This stage is important since most promotional campaigns are designed not to motivate consumers to take immediate action but rather to provide information they will use later when making a purchase decision.

Each stage of the response hierarchy is a dependent variable that must be attained and that may serve as an objective of the communications process. As shown in Figure 5–4, each stage can be measured, providing the advertiser with feedback regarding the effectiveness of various strategies designed to move the consumer to purchase. The information processing model may be an effective framework for planning and evaluating the effects of a promotional campaign.

IMPLICATIONS OF THE TRADITIONAL HIERARCHY MODELS

The hierarchy models of communication response are useful to promotional planners from several perspectives. First, they delineate the series of steps potential purchasers must be taken through to move them from unawareness of a product or service to readiness to purchase it. Second, potential buyers may be at different stages in the hierarchy, so the advertiser will face different sets of communication problems. For example, a company introducing an innovative product like Philips' digital compact cassette system (DCC) may need to devote considerable effort to making people aware of the product, how it works, and its benefits. Marketers of a mature brand that enjoys customer loyalty may need only supportive or reminder advertising to reinforce positive perceptions and maintain the awareness level for the brand.

The hierarchy models can also be useful as intermediate measures of communication effectiveness. The marketer needs to know where audience members are on the response hierarchy. For example, research may reveal that one target segment has low awareness of the advertiser's brand, whereas another is aware of the brand and its various attributes but has a low level of liking or brand preference.

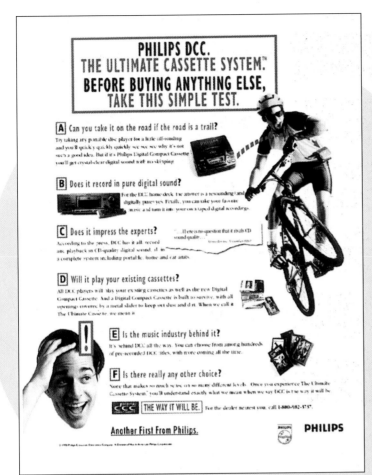

For the first segment of the market, the communication task involves increasing the awareness level for the brand. The number of ads may be increased or a product sampling program may be used. For the second segment, where awareness is already high but liking and preference are low, the advertiser must determine the reason for the negative feelings and then attempt to address this problem in future advertising.

When research or other evidence reveals a company is perceived favorably on a particular attribute or performance criterion, the company may want to take advantage of this in its advertising. Global Perspective 5–3 discusses how Air Canada addressed a problem: It had high brand recognition but a negative image resulting from misperceptions that it was a government-owned airline.

EVALUATING TRADITIONAL RESPONSE HIERARCHY MODELS

As you saw in Figure 5–3, the four models presented all view the response process as consisting of movement through a sequence of three basic stages. The *cognitive stage* represents what the receiver knows or perceives about the particular product or brand. This state includes awareness that the brand exists and knowledge, information, or comprehension about its attributes, characteristics, or benefits. The *affective stage* refers to the receiver's feelings or affect level (like or dislike) for the particular brand. This stage also includes stronger levels of affect such as desire, preference, or conviction. The *conative* or *behavioral stage* refers to the consumer's action toward the brand: trial, purchase, adoption, or rejection.

All four models assume a similar ordering of these three stages. Cognitive development precedes affective reactions, which precede behavior. One might assume that consumers become aware of and knowledgeable about a brand, develop feelings toward it, form a desire or preference, and then make a purchase. While this logical progression is often accurate, the response sequence does not always operate this way.

Over the past two decades, considerable research in marketing, social psychology, and communications has led to questioning of the traditional cognitive → affective → behavioral sequence of response. Several other configurations of the response hierarchy have been theorized.

Alternative Response Hierarchies

Michael Ray has developed a model of information processing that identifies three alternative orderings of the three stages based on perceived product differentiation and product involvement.[14] These alternative response hierarchies are the standard learning, dissonance/attribution, and low-involvement models (Figure 5–5).

THE STANDARD LEARNING HIERARCHY

In many purchase situations, the consumer will go through the response process in the sequence depicted by the traditional communication models. Ray terms this a **standard learning model**, which consists of a learn → feel → do sequence. Information and knowledge acquired or *learned* about the various brands are the basis for developing affect, or *feelings*, that guide what the consumer will *do* (e.g., actual trial or purchase). In this hierarchy, the consumer is viewed as an active participant in the communication process who gathers information through active learning.

Ray suggests the standard learning hierarchy is likely when the consumer is highly involved in the purchase process and there is much differentiation among competing brands.

Global Perspective 5–3
Changing the Image of Air Canada

Before reading this vignette, answer the following questions: What is the name of Canada's government-owned airline? What markings do its planes carry? Most Americans and nearly 80 percent of Canadians will answer Air Canada in response to the first question. Moreover, most people even remotely familiar with Canada know that the airline has white planes with bright-red lettering and a big red maple leaf on the tail—a symbol synonymous with Canada itself.

While most airlines would love to have this kind of instant brand recognition, the strong image has been a real problem for Air Canada. Why? According to Air Canada's chief operating officer, "Canadians think of their government as stodgy, bureaucratic, and dull." A poll of citizens found that 49 percent of Canadians were "very dissatisfied" with their government, the highest dissatisfaction rating of the 16 developed nations surveyed. The negative association with the Canadian government would be bad enough if Air Canada really were state-owned, but it is not. The airline was privatized in 1988 and today is as private as American Airlines, United, or Delta.

To better compete against its chief rival, Canadian Airlines International, in 1992 Air Canada hired the U.S. design firm of Diefenbach Elkins to develop a corporate identity that would sever its perceived ties to the government. While Air Canada still wants to be perceived as the country's flag carrier, it does not want its image to be tarnished by association with the government bureaucracy.

Before Diefenbach Elkins could begin revamping the image of the airline, it had to figure out how Canadians really felt about Canada. Marketing research discovered that Canadians adore Canada but dislike its politicians. Canadians attribute a variety of values to themselves and their country, including compassion, friendliness, a progressive outlook, and a law-abiding nature. The design firm concluded that it should play up the Canadianness of Air Canada while scotching any association with the government. It also decided to ignore altogether the deep rift between English- and French-speaking Canadians. The firm recommended that Air Canada portray the country it serves as a modern melting pot—a kind of innocent America, untainted by ethnic tensions and urban blight.

To help execute this strategy, Air Canada's ad agency produced a TV commercial depicting Canada as a diverse nation of Indians, Greeks, Chinese, and other immigrant groups, all of whom happily coexist. The image portrayed in the ad seems appropriate, since Canadians of non-European descent have risen from 2 percent of the population 20 years ago to nearly 40 percent today.

As part of the image makeover, Diefenbach Elkins came up with a new design for Air Canada's fleet of 103 planes. After much debate, the design firm decided to keep the ubiquitous maple leaf (which adorns nearly everything in Canada) but to render it in a more natural earthy red on a new evergreen tail. The logic was that the old, stark red-on-white design smacked more of the big government bureaucracy. While the new paint job retains the vibrant red lettering, the firm believes the overall effect makes the planes look a lot less like flying Mounties.

The makeover of Air Canada appears to be working; it is emerging the winner in a long and costly battle with Canadian Airlines for air supremacy. After losing over $1 billion between 1989 and 1992, Air Canada returned to profitability in 1993 and in 1996 reported record earnings. Air Canada launched an aggressive marketing campaign outside Canada in 1996, targeting the lucrative business market. The airline is capitalizing on the open-skies agreement between Canada and the United States and has expanded its service between cities in the two countries. An Air Canada executive says, "Canadians would rather fly a Canadian carrier than a U.S. carrier." It appears the new image is helping to make Air Canada the airline Canadians prefer to fly.

Sources: Brenda Russell, "Unfriendly Skies," *Maclean's*, November 18, 1996, p. 34; Joshua Levine, "Ah, Canada," *Forbes*, January 3, 1994, p. 74.

High-involvement purchase decisions such as those for industrial products and services and consumer durables like personal computers, VCRs, and cars are areas where a standard learning hierarchy response process is likely. Ads for products and services in these areas are usually very detailed and attempt to give consumers a great deal of information about the brand.

THE DISSONANCE/ATTRIBUTION HIERARCHY

A second response hierarchy proposed by Ray involves situations where consumers first behave, then develop attitudes or feelings as a result of that behavior, and then learn or process

FIGURE 5–5
Alternative response hierarchies: the three-orders model of information processing

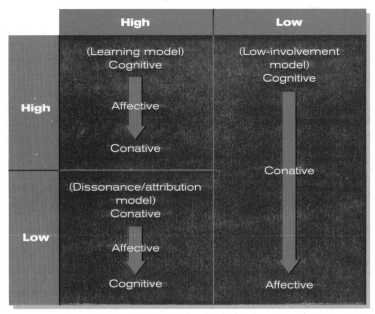

information that supports the behavior. This **dissonance/attribution model**, or do → feel → learn, occurs in situations where consumers must choose between two alternatives that are similar in quality but are complex and may have hidden or unknown attributes. The consumer may purchase the product based on the recommendation of some nonmedia source and then attempt to support the decision by developing a positive attitude toward the brand and perhaps even developing negative feelings toward the rejected alternative(s). This reduces any *postpurchase dissonance* or anxiety the consumer may experience resulting from doubt over the purchase (as discussed in Chapter 4). Dissonance reduction involves *selective learning*, whereby the consumer seeks information that supports the choice made and avoids information that would raise doubts about the decision.

According to this model, marketers need to recognize that in some situations, attitudes develop *after* purchase, as does learning from the mass media. Ray suggests that in these situations the main effect of the mass media is not so much to promote original choice behavior and attitude change but rather to reduce dissonance by reinforcing the wisdom of the purchase or providing supportive information.

As with the standard learning model, this response hierarchy is likely to occur when the consumer is involved in the purchase situation; it is particularly relevant for postpurchase situations. For example, a consumer may purchase tires recommended by a friend and then develop a favorable attitude toward the company and pay close attention to its ads to reduce dissonance.

Some marketers resist this view of the response hierarchy because they can't accept the notion that the mass media have no effect on the consumer's initial purchase decision. But it doesn't claim the mass media have no effect, just that their major impact occurs after the purchase has been made. Marketing communications planners must be aware of the need for advertising and promotion efforts not just to encourage brand selection but to reinforce choices and ensure that a purchase pattern will continue.

THE LOW-INVOLVEMENT HIERARCHY

Perhaps the most intriguing of the three response hierarchies proposed by Ray is the **low-involvement hierarchy**, in which the receiver is viewed as passing from cognition to behavior to attitude change. This learn → do → feel sequence is thought to characterize situations of low consumer involvement in the purchase process. Ray suggests this hierarchy tends to occur when involvement in the purchase decision is low, there are minimal differences among brand alternatives, and mass media (especially broadcast) advertising is important.

The notion of a low-involvement hierarchy is based in large part on Herbert Krugman's theory explaining the effects of television advertising.[15] Krugman wanted to find out why TV advertising produced a strong effect on brand awareness and recall but little change in consumers' attitudes toward the product. He hypothesized that TV is basically a low-involvement medium and the viewer's perceptual defenses are reduced or even absent during commercials. In a low-involvement situation, the consumer does not compare the message with previously acquired beliefs, needs, or past experiences. The commercial results in subtle changes in the consumer's knowledge structure, particularly with repeated exposure. This change in the consumer's knowledge does not result in attitude change but is related to learning something about the advertised brand, such as a brand name, ad theme, or slogan. According to Krugman, when the consumer enters a purchase situation, this information may be sufficient to trigger a purchase. The consumer will then form an attitude toward the purchased brand as a result of experience with it. Thus, in the low-involvement situation the response sequence is as follows:

Message exposure under low involvement →

Shift in cognitive structure → Purchase →

Positive or negative experience → Attitude formation

In the low-involvement hierarchy, the consumer engages in passive learning and random information catching rather than active information seeking. The advertiser must recognize that a passive, uninterested consumer may focus more on nonmessage elements such as music, characters, symbols, and slogans or jingles than actual message content. The advertiser might capitalize on this situation by developing a catchy jingle that is stored in the consumer's mind without any active cognitive processing and becomes salient when he or she enters the actual purchase situation.

Advertisers of low-involvement products also repeat simple product claims such as a key copy point or distinctive product benefit. A study by Scott Hawkins and Stephen Hoch found that under low-involvement conditions, repetition of simple product claims increased consumers' memory of and belief in those claims.[16] They concluded that advertisers of low-involvement products might find it more profitable to pursue a heavy repetition strategy than to reach larger audiences with lengthy, more detailed messages. For example, Heinz has dominated the ketchup market for over 20 years by repeatedly telling consumers that its brand is the thickest and richest. Heinz has used a variety of advertising campaigns over the years, but they all repeat the same basic theme and focus on the consistent quality of the brand.

Low-involvement advertising appeals prevail in much of the advertising we see for frequently purchased consumer products: Wrigley's Doublemint gum invites consumers to "Double your pleasure." Bounty paper towels claim to be the "quicker picker-upper." Oscar Mayer uses the catchy jingle, "I wish I were an Oscar Mayer wiener." Each of these appeals is designed to help consumers make an association without really attempting to formulate or change an attitude.

Another popular creative strategy used by advertisers of low-involvement products is what advertising analyst Harry McMahan calls VIP, or visual image personality.[17] Advertisers often use symbols like the Pillsbury doughboy, Morris the cat, Tony the tiger, Speedy Alka-Seltzer, and Mr. Clean to develop visual images that will lead consumers to identify and retain ads. The campaign featuring Morris has helped make 9-Lives a leading brand of cat food, and the feline has become so popular that he even has his own fan club (Exhibit 5–6).

EXHIBIT 5–6 Morris the cat has been a very effective VIP for 9-Lives cat food

The Integrated Information Response Model

Advertising and consumer researchers recognize that not all response sequences and behaviors are explained adequately by either the traditional or alternative response hierarchies. Advertising is just one source of information consumers use in forming attitudes and/or making purchase decisions. Moreover, for many consumers, purchase does not reflect commitment to a brand but is merely a way to obtain firsthand information from trial use of a product.

Robert Smith and William Swinyard developed a revised interpretation of the advertising response sequence.[18] Their **integrated information response model**, shown in Figure 5–6, integrates concepts from both the traditional and low-involvement response hierarchy perspectives. It also accounts for the effects of direct experience and recognizes that different levels of belief strength result from advertising versus personal experience with a product.

The integrated information response model suggests several different response patterns that can result from advertising. For low-involvement purchases, a cognition → trial → affect → commitment response sequence may be operating. This can be seen in the top line of Figure 5–6. According to this sequence, advertising generally leads to low information acceptance, lower-order beliefs, and low-order affect. However, as repetitive advertising builds awareness, consumers become more likely to engage in a trial purchase to gather information. The direct experience that results from trial purchase leads to high information acceptance and higher-order beliefs and affect, which can result in commitment or brand loyalty.

Advertising generally leads only to lower-order beliefs and affect because it is seen as a biased source of interest, subject to much source and message discounting and/or rejection. But in some situations, such as when perceived risk and involvement are low, advertising may move consumers directly to purchase.

If consumers are involved with the product, they may seek additional information from other external sources (for example, more advertising, word of mouth, salespeople) and/or from direct experience. This means the response sequence is similar to the traditional hierarchy of effects model (cognition → affect → commitment). The higher-order response path (bottom line of Figure 5–6) shows that direct experience, and in some cases advertising, is accepted at higher-order magnitudes, which results in higher-order beliefs and affect. This strong affect is more likely to result in preferences and committed purchases.

FIGURE 5–6   Integrated information response model

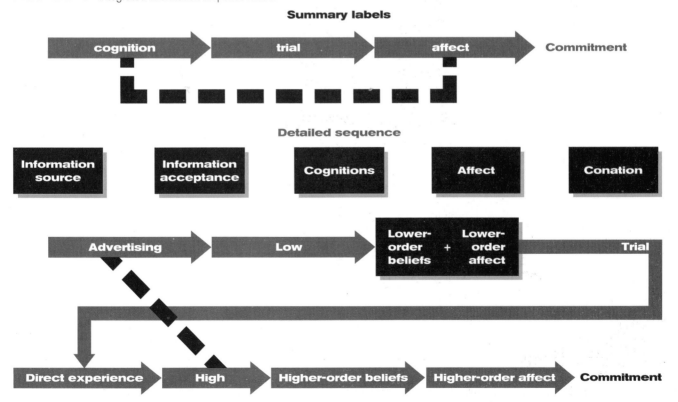

Smith and Swinyard discuss the implications of the integrated response model regarding promotional strategy for low- versus high-involvement products. For example, they recommend less enthusiastic promotional goals for low-involvement products, because advertising has a limited ability to form or change higher-order beliefs and affect:

> Low-involvement products, for example, could benefit from advertisements oriented to inducing trial by creating generally favorable lower order beliefs. This could be accomplished with campaigns designed to reduce perceived risk through repetition and familiarity, or those directly advocating a trial purchase. In addition, the integrated response model suggests that other marketing strategies designed to facilitate trial should be coupled with the advertising campaign. Free samples, coupons, price cuts, or effective point-of-purchase displays could all be integrated with media advertising to produce an environment highly conducive to trial. So too, because low-involvement products are frequently homogeneous, subsequent advertisements might be designed to reaffirm the positive aspects of trial. If successful, these efforts might generate brand loyalty based upon higher order beliefs and affect. This could be a major advantage for advertisers of low-involvement products where frequent brand switching may be based on the absence of antecedents for commitment (i.e., higher order beliefs and affect).[19]

For high-involvement products, more basic attitude change strategies are warranted. However, Smith and Swinyard note that the higher-order response sequence focuses attention on message acceptance as a prerequisite for affect development:

> In this instance, the advertising manager should attempt to isolate the conditions facilitating the formation of higher order beliefs. Factors influential in this process could include whether the message claims are easily verifiable (e.g., price) and/or demonstrable (e.g., styling), whether the individual knows the sponsoring company and its reputation/credibility, selection of a credible spokesperson to deliver the message, whether the message is consistent with already established beliefs, etc. It also is likely that interactions could exist between acceptance factors, and that certain message configurations would be much more successful than others.[20]

Smith and Swinyard point out that communication strategies for high-involvement products may be difficult to implement since media advertising often has little effect on higher-order attitude formation or change. Thus, they suggest that marketing communications focus on achieving a product demonstration rather than a direct urge to purchase. Product demonstrations and information received from compelling personal communication sources, such as knowledgeable and well-trained in-store sales personnel, are more likely to change higher-order beliefs and affect and lead to purchase.

An important implication of the integrated information response model is that consumers are likely to integrate information from advertising, other sources, and direct experience in forming judgments about a brand. For example, in a recent study Robert Smith found that advertising can lessen the negative effects of an unfavorable trial experience on brand evaluations when the ad is processed before the trial. However, when a negative trial experience precedes exposure to an ad, cognitive evaluations of the ad are more negative.[21] Thus it is important to consider how consumers integrate advertising with other brand information sources, both before and after trial or purchase.

IMPLICATIONS OF THE ALTERNATIVE RESPONSE MODELS

The various response models offer an interesting perspective on the ways consumers respond to advertising and other forms of marketing communications. They also provide insight into promotional strategies marketers might pursue in different situations. A review of these alternative models of the response process shows that the traditional standard learning model does not always apply. The notion of a highly involved consumer who engages in active information processing and learning and acts on the basis of higher-order beliefs and a well-formed attitude may be inappropriate for some types of purchases. Sometimes consumers make a purchase decision based on a general awareness resulting from repetitive exposure to advertising, and attitude development occurs after the purchase, if at all. The integrated information response model suggests that the role of advertising and other forms of promotion may be to induce trial, so consumers can develop brand preferences primarily on the basis of their direct experience with the product.

From a promotional planning perspective, it is important that marketers examine the communication situation for their product or service and determine which type of response process is most likely to occur. They should analyze involvement levels and product/service differentiation as well as consumers' use of various information sources and their levels of experience with the product or service. Once the manager has determined which response sequence is most likely to operate, the integrated marketing communications program can be designed to influence the response process in favor of the company's product or service. Because this requires that marketers determine the involvement level of consumers in their target markets, we examine the concept of involvement in more detail.

UNDERSTANDING INVOLVEMENT

Over the past two decades, consumer behavior and advertising researchers have extensively studied the concept of involvement.[22] Involvement is viewed as a variable that can help explain how consumers process advertising information and how this information might affect message recipients. One problem that has plagued the study of involvement has been agreeing on how to define and measure it. Advertising managers must be able to determine targeted consumers' involvement levels with their products.

Some of the problems in conceptualizing and measuring involvement have been addressed in extensive review by Judith Zaichkowsky. She has noted that although there is no single precise definition of involvement, there is an underlying theme focusing on *personal relevance*.[23] Zaichkowsky developed an involvement construct that includes three antecedents, or variables proposed to precede involvement (Figure 5–7). The first is traits of the person (value system, unique experiences, needs). The second factor is characteristics of the stimulus, or differences in type of media (TV, radio, or print), content of the communication, or product class variations. The third antecedent is situational factors, such as whether one is or is not in the market for a particular product.

FIGURE 5–7 Involvement concept

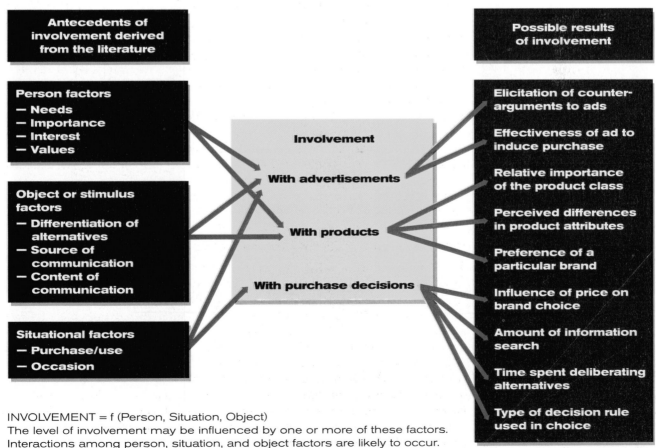

INVOLVEMENT = f (Person, Situation, Object)
The level of involvement may be influenced by one or more of these factors.
Interactions among person, situation, and object factors are likely to occur.

The various antecedents can influence the consumer's level of involvement in several ways, including the way the consumer responds to the advertising, the products being advertised, and the actual purchase decision. This involvement theory shows that a variety of outcomes or behaviors can result from involvement with advertising, products, or purchase decisions.

Several other advertising planning grids have been developed that consider involvement levels as well as several other factors, including response processes and motives that underlie attitude formation and subsequent brand choice.

The FCB Planning Model

An interesting approach to analyzing the communication situation comes from the work of Richard Vaughn of the Foote, Cone & Belding advertising agency. Vaughn and his associates developed an advertising planning model by building on traditional response theories such as the hierarchy of effects model and its variants and research on high and low involvement.[24] They added the dimension of thinking versus feeling processing at each involvement level by bringing in theories regarding brain specialization. The right/left brain theory suggests the left side of the brain is more capable of rational, cognitive thinking, while the right side is more visual and emotional and engages more in the affective (feeling) functions. Their model, which became known as the FCB grid, delineates four primary advertising planning strategies—informative, affective, habit formation, and satisfaction—along with the most appropriate variant of the alternative response hierarchies (Figure 5–8).

Vaughn suggests that the *informative strategy* is for highly involving products and services where rational thinking and economic considerations prevail and the standard learning hierarchy is the appropriate response model. The *affective strategy* is for highly involving/feeling purchases. For these types of products, advertising should stress psychological and emotional motives such as building self-esteem or enhancing one's ego or self-image.

The *habit formation strategy* is for low-involvement/thinking products with such routinized behavior patterns that learning occurs most often after a trial purchase. The response process for these products is consistent with a behavioristic learning-by-doing model (remember our discussion of operant conditioning in Chapter 4?). The *self-satisfaction strat-*

FIGURE 5–8
The Foote, Cone & Belding (FCB) grid

	Thinking	**Feeling**
High involvement	**1. Informative (thinker)** Car–house–furnishings–new products model: Learn–feel–do (economic?) **Possible implications** Test: Recall Diagnostics Media: Long copy format Reflective vehicles Creative: Specific information Demonstration	**2. Affective (feeler)** Jewelry–cosmetics–fashion apparel–motorcycles model: Feel–learn–do (psychological?) **Possible implications** Test: Attitude change Emotional arousal Media: Large space Image specials Creative: Executional Impact
Low involvement	**3. Habit formation (doer)** Food–household items model: Do–learn–feel (responsive?) **Possible implications** Test: Sales Media: Small space ads 10 second I.D.'s Radio; POS Creative: Reminder	**4. Self-satisfaction (reactor)** Cigarettes–liquor–candy model: Do–feel–learn (social?) **Possible implications** Test: Sales Media: Billboards Newspapers POS Creative: Attention

EXHIBIT 5–7
A think-type product is advertised by an appeal to feelings

egy is for low-involvement/feeling products where appeals to sensory pleasures and social motives are important. Again, the do → feel or do → learn hierarchy is operating, since product experience is an important part of the learning process. Vaughn acknowledges that some minimal level of awareness (passive learning) may precede purchase of both types of low-involvement products, but deeper, active learning is not necessary. This is consistent with the low-involvement hierarchy discussed earlier (learn → do → feel).

The FCB grid provides a useful way for those involved in the advertising planning process, such as creative specialists, to analyze consumer/product relationships and develop appropriate promotional strategies. Consumer research can be used to determine how consumers perceive products or brands on the involvement and thinking/feeling dimensions.[25] This information can then be used to develop effective creative options such as using rational versus emotional appeals, increasing involvement levels, or even getting consumers to evaluate a think-type product on the basis of feelings. The ad for the KitchenAid refrigerator in Exhibit 5–7 is an example of this latter strategy. Notice how it uses beautiful imagery to appeal to emotional concerns such as style and appearance. Appliances have traditionally been sold on the basis of more rational, functional motives.

COGNITIVE PROCESSING OF COMMUNICATIONS

The hierarchical response models were for many years the primary focus of approaches to study the receivers' responses to marketing communications. Attention centered on identifying relationships between specific controllable variables (such as source and message factors) and outcome or response variables (such as attention, comprehension, attitudes, and purchase intentions). This approach has been criticized on a number of fronts, including its black box nature, since it can't explain what is causing these reactions.[26] In response to these concerns, researchers began trying to understand the nature of cognitive reactions to persuasive messages. Several approaches have been developed to examine the nature of consumers' cognitive processing of advertising messages.

The Cognitive Response Approach

One of the most widely used methods for examining consumers' cognitive processing of advertising messages is assessment of their **cognitive responses**, the thoughts that occur to them while reading, viewing, and/or hearing a communication.[27] These thoughts are generally measured by having consumers write down or verbally report their reactions to a message. The assumption is that these thoughts reflect the recipient's cognitive processes or reactions and help shape ultimate acceptance or rejection of the message.

The cognitive response approach has been widely used in research by both academicians and advertising practitioners. Its focus has been to determine the types of responses evoked

FIGURE 5—9 A model of cognitive response

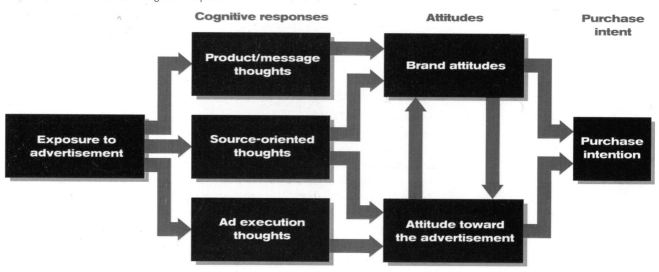

by an advertising message and how these responses relate to attitudes toward the ad, brand attitudes, and purchase intentions. Figure 5–9 depicts the three basic categories of cognitive responses researchers have identified—product/message, source-oriented, and ad execution thoughts—and how they may relate to attitudes and intentions.

PRODUCT/MESSAGE THOUGHTS

The first category of thoughts is those directed at the product or service and/or the claims being made in the communication. Much attention has focused on two particular types of responses, counterarguments and support arguments.

Counterarguments are thoughts the recipient has that are opposed to the position taken in the message. For example, consider the ad for Ultra Tide shown in Exhibit 5–8. A consumer may express disbelief or disapproval of a claim made in an ad. ("I don't believe that any detergent could get that stain out!") Other consumers who see this ad may generate **support arguments,** or thoughts that affirm the claims made in the message. ("Ultra Tide looks like a really good product—I think I'll try it.")

The likelihood of counterarguing is greater when the message makes claims that oppose the receiver's beliefs. For example, a consumer viewing a commercial that attacks a favorite

EXHIBIT 5—8
Consumers often generate support arguments in response to ads for quality products

brand is likely to engage in counterarguing. Counterarguments relate negatively to message acceptance; the more the receiver counterargues, the less likely he or she is to accept the position advocated in the message.[28] Support arguments, on the other hand, relate positively to message acceptance. Thus, the marketer should develop ads or other promotional messages that minimize counterarguing and encourage support arguments.

SOURCE-ORIENTED THOUGHTS

A second category of cognitive responses is directed at the source of the communication. One of the most important responses in this category is **source derogations**, or negative thoughts about the spokesperson or organization making the claims. Such thoughts generally lead to a reduction in message acceptance. If consumers find a particular spokesperson annoying or untrustworthy, they are less likely to accept what this source has to say.

Of course, source-related thoughts are not always negative. Receivers who react favorably to the source generate favorable thoughts, or **source bolsters**. As you would expect, most advertisers attempt to hire spokespeople their target audience likes so as to carry this effect over to the message. Considerations involved in choosing an appropriate source or spokesperson will be discussed in Chapter 6.

AD EXECUTION THOUGHTS

The third category of cognitive responses shown in Figure 5–9 is the individual's thoughts about the ad itself. Many of the thoughts receivers have when reading or viewing an ad do not concern the product and/or message claims directly. Rather, they are affective reactions representing the consumer's feelings toward the ad. These thoughts may include reactions to ad execution factors such as the creativity of the ad, the quality of the visual effects, colors, and voice tones. **Ad execution-related thoughts** can be either favorable or unfavorable. They are important because of their effect on attitudes toward the advertisement as well as the brand.

In recent years, much attention has focused on consumers' affective reactions to ads, especially TV commercials.[29] **Attitude toward the ad** (A → ad) represents the receivers' feelings of favorability or unfavorability toward the ad. Advertisers are interested in consumers' reactions to the ad because they know that affective reactions are an important determinant of advertising effectiveness, since these reactions may be transferred to the brand itself or directly influence purchase intentions. One study found that people who enjoy a commercial are twice as likely as those who are neutral toward it to be convinced that the brand is the best.[30]

Consumers' feelings about the ad may be just as important as their attitudes toward the brand (if not more so) in determining an ad's effectiveness.[31] The importance of affective reactions and feelings generated by the ad depend on several factors, among them the nature of the ad and the type of processing engaged in by the receiver.[32] Many advertisers now use emotional ads designed to evoke feelings and affective reactions as the basis of their creative strategy. The success of this strategy depends in part on the consumers' involvement with the brand and their likelihood of attending to and processing the message.

We end our analysis of the receiver by examining a model that integrates some of the factors that may account for different types and levels of cognitive processing of a message.

The Elaboration Likelihood Model (ELM)

Differences in the ways consumers process and respond to persuasive messages are addressed in the **elaboration likelihood model (ELM)** of persuasion, shown in Figure 5–10.[33] The ELM was devised by Richard Petty and John Cacioppo to explain the process by which persuasive communications (such as ads) lead to persuasion by influencing *attitudes*. According to this model, the attitude formation or change process depends on the amount and nature of *elaboration*, or processing, of relevant information that occurs in response to a persuasive message. High elaboration means the receiver engages in careful consideration, thinking, and evaluation of the information or arguments contained in the message. Low elaboration occurs when the receiver does not engage in active information processing or thinking but rather makes inferences about the position being advocated in the message based on simple positive or negative cues.

FIGURE 5—10
The elaboration likelihood model of
persuasion

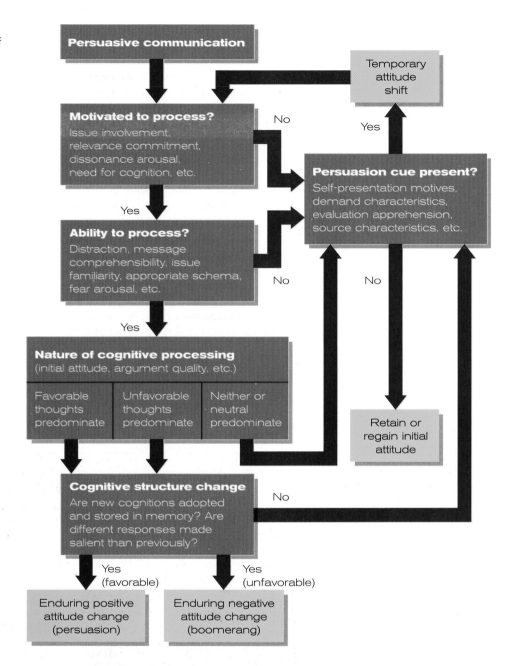

The ELM shows that elaboration likelihood is a function of two elements, motivation and ability to process the message. *Motivation* to process the message depends on such factors as involvement, personal relevance, and individuals' needs and arousal levels. *Ability* depends on the individual's knowledge, intellectual capacity, and opportunity to process the message. For example, an individual viewing a humorous commercial or one containing an attractive model may be distracted from processing the information about the product.

According to the ELM, there are two basic routes to persuasion or attitude change. Under the **central route to persuasion**, the receiver is viewed as a very active, involved participant in the communication process whose ability and motivation to attend, comprehend, and evaluate messages are high. When central processing of an advertising message occurs, the consumer pays close attention to message content and scrutinizes the message arguments. A high level of cognitive response activity or processing occurs, and the ad's ability to persuade the receiver depends primarily on the receiver's evaluation of the quality of the arguments presented. Predominantly favorable cognitive responses (support arguments and source bolsters) lead to favorable changes in cognitive structure, which lead to positive attitude change, or persuasion.

Conversely, if the cognitive processing is predominantly unfavorable and results in counterarguments and/or source derogations, the changes in cognitive structure are unfavorable and *boomerang*, or result in negative attitude change. Attitude change that occurs through central processing is relatively enduring and should resist subsequent efforts to change it.

Under the **peripheral route to persuasion**, shown on the right side of Figure 5–10, the receiver is viewed as lacking the motivation or ability to process information and is not likely to engage in detailed cognitive processing. Rather than evaluating the information presented in the message, the receiver relies on peripheral cues that may be incidental to the main arguments. The receiver's reaction to the message depends on how he or she evaluates these peripheral cues.

The consumer may use several types of peripheral cues or cognitive shortcuts rather than carefully evaluating the message arguments presented in an advertisement.[34] Favorable attitudes may be formed if the endorser in the ad is viewed as an expert or is attractive and/or likable, or if the consumer likes certain executional aspects of the ad such as the way it is made, the music, or the imagery. Notice how the ad in Exhibit 5–9 for Right Guard Clear Stick and Clear Gel deodorant and antiperspirant contains several positive peripheral cues, including a popular celebrity endorser (basketball star Scottie Pippen) and excellent visual imagery. These cues might help consumers form a positive attitude toward the brand even if they do not process the message portion of the ad.

Peripheral cues can also lead to rejection of a message. For example, ads that advocate extreme positions, use endorsers who are not well liked or have credibility problems, or are not executed well (such as low-budget ads for local retailers) may be rejected without any consideration of their information or message arguments. As shown in Figure 5–10, the ELM views attitudes resulting from peripheral processing as temporary. So favorable attitudes must be maintained by continual exposure to the peripheral cues, such as through repetitive advertising.

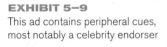

EXHIBIT 5–9
This ad contains peripheral cues, most notably a celebrity endorser

IMPLICATIONS OF THE ELM

The elaboration likelihood model has important implications for marketing communications, particularly with respect to involvement. For example, if the involvement level of consumers in the target audience is high, an ad or sales presentation should contain strong arguments that are difficult for the message recipient to refute or counterargue. If the involvement level of the target audience is low, peripheral cues may be more important than detailed message arguments.

An interesting test of the ELM showed that the effectiveness of a celebrity endorser in an ad depends on the receiver's involvement level.[35] When involvement was low, a celebrity endorser had a significant effect on attitudes. When the receiver's involvement was high, however, the use of a celebrity had no effect on brand attitudes; the quality of the arguments used in the ad was more important.

The explanation given for these findings was that a celebrity may serve as a peripheral cue in the low-involvement situation, allowing the receiver to develop favorable attitudes based on feelings toward the source rather than engaging in extensive processing of the message. A highly involved consumer, however, engages in more detailed central processing of the message content. The quality of the message claims becomes more important than the identity of the endorser.

The ELM suggests that the most effective type of message depends on the route to persuasion the consumer follows. Many marketers recognize that involvement levels are low for their product categories and consumers are not motivated to process advertising messages in any detail. That's why marketers of low-involvement products often rely on creative tactics that emphasize peripheral cues and use repetitive advertising to create and maintain favorable attitudes toward their brand.

A FINAL WORD ON THE RESPONSE PROCESS

As you have seen from our analysis of the receiver, the process consumers go through in responding to marketing communications can be viewed from a number of perspectives. We hope the various communication models presented in this chapter give you a better understanding of how consumers process persuasive messages. Promotional planners need to learn as much as possible about the company's target market and how it may respond to marketing communications efforts. Marketers who understand the process by which their target audience responds to persuasive communications will be able to make better decisions regarding the promotional program.

SUMMARY

The function of all elements of the promotional mix is to communicate, so promotional planners must understand the communication process. This process can be very complex; successful marketing communications depend on a number of factors, including the nature of the message, the audience's interpretation of it, and the environment in which it is received. For effective communication to occur, the sender must encode a message in such a way that it will be decoded by the receiver in the intended manner. Feedback from the receiver helps the sender determine whether proper decoding has occurred or whether noise has interfered with the communication process.

Promotional planning begins with the receiver or target audience, as marketers must understand how the audience is likely to respond to various sources of communication or types of messages. For promotional planning, the receiver can be analyzed both with respect to its composition (i.e., individual, group, or mass audiences) and the response process it goes through. Different orderings of the traditional response hierarchy include the standard learning, dissonance/attribution, and low-involvement models. The information response model integrates concepts from both the high- and low-involvement response hierarchy perspectives and recognizes the effects of direct experience with a product.

The cognitive response approach examines the thoughts evoked by a message and how they shape the receiver's ultimate acceptance or rejection of the communication. The elaboration likelihood model of attitude formation and change recognizes two forms of message processing, the central and peripheral routes to persuasion, which are a function of the receiver's motivation and ability to process a message.

KEY TERMS

communication, 138
source, 138
encoding, 139
message, 140
semiotics, 141
channel, 142
mass media, 142
receiver, 142
decoding, 142
field of experience, 142
noise, 143

response, 143
feedback, 143
AIDA model, 146
hierarchy of effects
    model, 146
innovation adoption
    model, 147
information processing
    model, 147
standard learning model,
    149

dissonance/attribution
    model, 151
low-involvement
    hierarchy, 151
integrated information
    response model, 153
cognitive responses, 157
counterarguments, 158
support arguments, 158
source derogations, 159

source bolsters, 159
ad execution-related
    thoughts, 159
attitude toward the ad, 159
elaboration likelihood
    model (ELM) , 159
central route to
    persuasion, 160
peripheral route to
    persuasion, 161

DISCUSSION QUESTIONS

1. What is your opinion of the "Simply Samsung" campaign discussed in the opening vignette? Do you feel that this image-driven approach will be effective for selling consumer electronics such as microwaves and television set? Why or why not?

2. What is meant by encoding? Discuss how the encoding process differs for radio versus television commercials.

3. How can companies marketing their products in a foreign country avoid some of the communications problems discussed in Global Perspective 5–1?

4. Discuss how the science of semiotics can be of value to the field of integrated marketing communications. Select a specific stimulus such as an advertisement, package, or other relevant marketing symbol and conduct a semiotic analysis of it.

5. Those responsible for most of the advertising and promotion decisions for consumer products are brand managers (client side) and account executives (agency side). These individuals are usually well-paid, well-educated marketing professionals living in urban areas. What differences might there be between marketing professionals and the consumers who are the primary users of Budweiser beer or Mennen aftershave? What problems could these differences present in developing an IMC program for these brands? How might these problems be overcome?

6. The study discussed in IMC Perspective 5–2 suggests that ageism is a problem in the advertising business. Do you think young professionals can create ads that connect with the mature market? Defend your position.

7. Discuss the various forms feedback might take in the following situations:
   * An office copier salesperson has just made a sales presentation to a potential account.
   * A consumer has just seen a direct-response ad for an exercise machine on late-night TV.
   * Millions of consumers are exposed to an ad for a sports car during a Sunday afternoon football game.

8. Explain how a company like Samsung might use the four models of the response process shown in Figure 5–3 to develop promotional strategies for its various products.

9. An implication of the integrated information response model is that consumers are likely to take information from advertising and integrate it with direct experience to form judgments about a product. Explain how advertising could lessen the negative outcomes a consumer might experience when trying a brand.

10. Select an ad you think would be processed by a central route and one where you think peripheral processing would occur. Show the ad to several people and ask them to write down the thoughts they have about the ad. Analyze their thoughts using the cognitive response categories discussed in the chapter.

CHAPTER 6

Source, Message, and Channel Factors

Chapter Objectives

- To study the major variables in the communications system and how they influence consumers' processing of promotional messages.

- To examine the considerations involved in selecting a source or communicator of a promotional message.

- To examine different types of message structures and appeals that can be used to develop a promotional message.

- To consider how the channel or medium used to deliver a promotional message influences the communication process.

WHEN IT COMES TO ENDORSEMENTS, NICE GUYS FINISH FIRST

Using popular athletes to endorse and pitch companies and their products has become commonplace in advertising. U.S. companies paid more than $1 billion to nearly 2,000 athletes for endorsement deals and licensing rights in 1996—a tenfold increase from just a decade ago. Nike alone spends more than $100 million a year on endorsement contracts. The average athlete on the *Forbes* super 40 list of top-earning athletes commands around $250,000 a year for a national endorsement. Superstar Michael Jordan, the athlete who makes the most from endorsements, considers only multiyear deals that pay at least $10 million. In addition to the endorsement fees, companies spend another $10 billion to advertise and promote their association to these athletes.

While companies are investing huge sums of money into the concept that athletes make good promoters, they are also recognizing that choosing a celebrity endorser is no longer a matter of personal taste and top-management whimsy. Several companies have been badly burned when their high-priced endorsers were involved in messy scandals and controversies. Hertz Corp. used O. J. Simpson as its spokesperson for 20 years and lost all of that equity when he was accused of murdering his ex-wife and her friend. Smaller companies face even greater risks when they entrust their name and image to an athlete. When Dallas Cowboys football star Michael Irvin was caught in a motel room with strippers and drugs, 13 Toyota dealerships that had paid him $120,000 to do a series of commercials had little choice but to pull the ads and swallow the $400,000 in production costs. When Irvin refused to return his payment, as well as a $50,000 car the dealerships had lent him, they sued. The case was settled out of court.

Risk management has become a major consideration for companies considering using athletes as endorsers. However, many marketers are willing to take chances on irreverent or rebellious athletes whose outlandish behavior draws attention to them. For example, basketball star Dennis Rodman has parlayed his bad boy image into endorsement contracts with Nike, McDonald's, Pizza Hut, Comfort Inn, and Converse. Rodman's sponsors believe he appeals to the elusive Generation X market that these companies are trying to reach. However, Rodman's antics have become too much for some companies. The Carl's Jr. fast-food chain temporarily suspended its relationship with Rodman in early 1997 when he was suspended for kicking a courtside photographer during a game.

Most companies are moving away from controversial athletes and looking for ones who will not just attract attention but enhance the image of the company or brand they are endorsing. Their goal is to achieve an endorser's halo effect—a positive association that bathes the product in good vibes after a popular sports celebrity has pitched it. Marketers have discovered that there are a number of "nice guys" available to endorse their products. Among them are tennis stars Pete Sampras and Michael Chang (who has emerged as the most popular athlete in Asia by far), San Francisco 49ers quarterback Steve Young, baseball iron man Cal Ripken Jr., Los Angeles Lakers basketball star Shaquille O'Neal, hockey star Wayne Gretzky, and golfer Tiger Woods. Even former stars with likable personalities and images as positive role models are still popular, including Arnold Palmer, Joe Montana, Jim Palmer, Nolan Ryan, and Chris Evert.

Perhaps nobody embodies the new breed of nice guy superstar better than basketball star Grant Hill. An All-American at Duke, he stayed all four years and graduated with his class. His father, Calvin, played football at Yale and was a star with the Dallas Cowboys. During his first two years in the NBA, Hall received more fan votes for a spot on the NBA All-Star team than any other player, including Michael Jordan.

The biggest benefactor of Grant Hill's nonabrasive, good-humored, All-American image has been Fila, an Italian company that signed Hill to an endorsement contract in 1994. Since signing Hill, Fila has become the third-largest sneaker maker in the United States. Sales shot up 37 percent in 1995 and another 40 percent in 1996 to $750 million. Hill's name-sake shoe trails only Nike's Air Jordans in sales. Fila officials readily acknowledge that Hill's "nice guy" image appeals to the current sensibilities of middle America.

Three years ago basketball star Charles Barkley appeared in a Nike commercial where he glowered at the camera and declared, "I am not a role model." Since then, his endorsement take has been cut in half. Hill readily acknowledges, "I am a role model." In addition to getting $6 million a year from Fila plus a 5 percent royalty on the sale of his shoes, Hill has endorsement contracts with Sprite, GMC trucks, Kellogg's, and McDonald's. It appears that nice guys are finishing first in the endorsement game.

Sources: Randall Lane, "Nice guys Finish First," *Forbes*, December 16, 1996, pp. 237–42; Joseph Pereira, "Fila Scores on an Assist from Grant Hill," *The Wall Street Journal*, November 5, 1996, p. B1; Otis Port, "Rebel with a Cachet," *Business Week*, July 17, 1995, pp. 74–75.

In this chapter, we analyze the major variables in the communication system: the source, the message, and the channel. We examine the characteristics of sources, how they influence reactions to promotional messages, and why one type of communicator is more effective than another. We then focus on the message itself and how structure and type of appeal influence its effectiveness. Finally, we consider how factors related to the channel or medium affect the communication process.

PROMOTIONAL PLANNING THROUGH THE PERSUASION MATRIX

To develop an effective advertising and promotional campaign, a firm must select the right spokesperson to deliver a compelling message through appropriate channels or media. Source, message, and channel factors are controllable elements in the communications model. The **persuasion matrix** (Figure 6–1) helps marketers see how each controllable element interacts with the consumer's response process.[1] The matrix has two sets of variables. Independent variables are the controllable components of the communication process, outlined in Chapter 5; dependent variables are the steps a receiver goes through in being persuaded. Marketers can choose the person or source who delivers the message, the type of message appeal used, and the channel or medium. And although they can't control the receiver, they can select their target audience. The destination variable is included because the initial message recipient may pass on information to others, such as friends or associates, through word of mouth.

Promotional planners need to know how decisions about each independent variable influence the stages of the response hierarchy so they don't enhance one stage at the expense of another. A humorous message may gain attention but result in decreased comprehension if consumers fail to process its content. Many ads that use humor, sexual appeals, or celebrities capture consumers' attention but result in poor recall of the brand name or message. The following examples, which correspond to the numbers in Figure 6–1, illustrate decisions that can be evaluated with the persuasion matrix.

1. **Receiver/comprehension: Can the receiver comprehend the ad?** Marketers must know their target market to make their messages clear and understandable. A less educated person may have more difficulty interpreting a complicated message. Jargon may be unfamiliar to some receivers. The more marketers know about the target market, the more they see which words, symbols, and expressions their customers understand.

FIGURE 6—1 The persuasion matrix

Dependent variables: Steps in being persuaded	Independent variables: The communication components				
	Source	Message	Channel	Receiver	Destination
Message presentation			(2)		
Attention	(4)				
Comprehension				(1)	
Yielding		(3)			
Retention					
Behavior					

2. Channel/presentation: Which media will increase presentation? A top-rated, prime-time TV program is seen by nearly 30 million households each week. *TV Guide* and *Reader's Digest* reach nearly 16 million homes with each issue. But the important point is how well they reach the marketer's target audience. CNN's "Moneyline" reaches only around a million viewers each weekday evening, but its audience consists mostly of upscale businesspeople who are prime prospects for expensive cars, financial services, and business-related products.

3. Message/yielding: What type of message will create favorable attitudes or feelings? Marketers generally try to create agreeable messages that lead to positive feelings toward the product or service. Humorous messages often put consumers in a good mood and evoke positive feelings that may become associated with the brand being advertised. Music adds emotion that makes consumers more receptive to the message. Many advertisers use explicit sexual appeals designed to arouse consumers or suggest they can enhance their attractiveness to the opposite sex. Some marketers compare their brand to the competition.

4. Source/attention: Who will be effective in getting consumers' attention? The large number of ads we are bombarded with every day makes it difficult for advertisers to break through the clutter. Marketers deal with this problem by using sources who will attract the target audience's attention—actors, athletes, rock stars, or attractive models. Each year, *Advertising Age* gives a star presenter award to the individual it believes has been the most effective advertising spokesperson. The winners for the past 18 years are shown in Figure 6–2. These star presenters don't just attract attention. They successfully influence other steps in the response hierarchy behavior, as measured by increased sales.

SOURCE FACTORS

The source component is a multifaceted concept. When Michael Jordan appears in a commercial for Wheaties, is the source Jordan himself, the company (General Mills), or some combination of the two? And, of course, consumers get information from friends, relatives, and neighbors; in fact, personal sources may be the most influential factor in a purchase decision. MCI has taken advantage of personal sources' ability to influence one another with its highly successful Friends & Family program (Exhibit 6–1).

FIGURE 6–2
Advertising Age star presenters

1996	No award
1995	No award
1994	Cast of "Seinfeld"
1993	Michael Jordan
1992	Candice Bergen
1991	John Cleese
1990	Ray Charles
1989	Bo Jackson
1988	Wilford Brimley
1987	Michael J. Fox
1986	Paul Hogan
1985	William Perry
1984	Cliff Robertson
1983	John Cleese
1982	Rodney Dangerfield
1981	John Houseman
1980	Brooke Shields
1979	Robert Morley
1978	James Garner and Mariette Hartley
1977	Bill Cosby

We use the term **source** to mean the person involved in communicating a marketing message, either directly or indirectly. A direct source is a spokesperson or endorser who delivers a message and/or demonstrates a product or service, like football coach Bill Walsh in Exhibit 6–2. An indirect source, say, a model, doesn't actually deliver a message but draws attention to and/or enhances the appearance of the ad. Some ads use neither a direct nor an indirect source; the source is the organization with the message to communicate. Since most research focuses on individuals as a message source, our examination of source factors follows this approach.

Companies are very careful when selecting individuals to deliver their selling messages. Many firms spend huge sums of money for a specific person to endorse their product or company. They also spend millions recruiting, selecting, and training salespeople to repre-

EXHIBIT 6–1
MCI's Friends & Family program
relies on interpersonal influence

EXHIBIT 6–2
Football coach Bill Walsh serves as a spokesperson for Sharp copiers

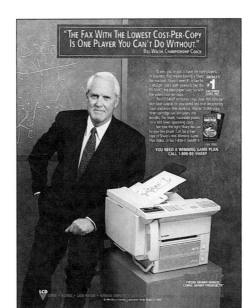

sent the company and deliver sales presentations. They recognize that the characteristics of the source affect the sales and advertising message.

Marketers try to select individuals whose traits will maximize message influence. The source may be knowledgeable, popular, and/or physically attractive; typify the target audience; or have the power to reward or punish the receiver in some manner. Herbert Kelman developed three basic categories of source attributes: credibility, attractiveness, and power.[2] Each influences the recipient's attitude or behavior through a different process (see Figure 6–3).

Source Credibility

Credibility is the extent to which the recipient sees the source as having relevant knowledge, skill, or experience and trusts the source to give unbiased, objective information. There are two important dimensions to credibility, expertise and trustworthiness.

A communicator seen as knowledgeable—someone with *expertise*—is more persuasive than one with less expertise. But the source also has to be *trustworthy*—honest, ethical, and believable. The influence of a knowledgeable source will be lessened if audience members think he or she is biased or has underlying personal motives for advocating a position (such as being paid to endorse a product).

One of the most reliable effects found in communications research is that expert and/or trustworthy sources are more persuasive than sources who are less expert or trustworthy.[3] Information from a credible source influences beliefs, opinions, attitudes, and/or behavior through a process known as **internalization**, which occurs when the receiver adopts the opinion of the credible communicator since he or she believes information from this source is accurate. Once the receiver internalizes an opinion or attitude, it becomes integrated into his or her belief system and may be maintained even after the source of the message is forgotten.

FIGURE 6–3
Source attributes and receiver processing modes

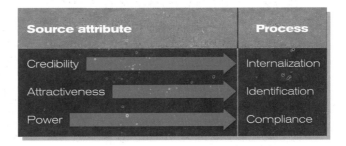

Source attribute	Process
Credibility	Internalization
Attractiveness	Identification
Power	Compliance

A highly credible communicator is particularly important when message recipients have a negative position toward the product, service, company, or issue being promoted, because the credible source is likely to inhibit counterarguments. As discussed in Chapter 5, reduced counterarguing should result in greater message acceptance and persuasion.

APPLYING EXPERTISE

Because attitudes and opinions developed through an internalization process become part of the individual's belief system, marketers want to use communicators with high credibility. Companies use a variety of techniques to convey source expertise. Sales personnel are trained in the product line, which increases customers' perceptions of their expertise. Marketers of highly technical products recruit sales reps with specialized technical backgrounds in engineering, computer science, and other areas to ensure their expertise.

Spokespeople are often chosen because of their knowledge, experience, and expertise in a particular product or service area. Endorsements from individuals or groups recognized as experts, such as doctors or dentists, are also common in advertising (Exhibit 6–3). The importance of using expert sources was shown in a study by Roobina Ohanian, who found that the perceived expertise of celebrity endorsers was more important in explaining purchase intentions than their attractiveness or trustworthiness. She suggests that celebrity spokespeople are most effective when they are knowledgeable, experienced, and qualified to talk about the product they are endorsing.[4]

APPLYING TRUSTWORTHINESS

While expertise is important, the target audience must also find the source believable. Finding celebrities or other figures with a trustworthy image is often difficult. Many trustworthy public figures hesitate to endorse products because of the potential impact on their reputation and image. It has been suggested that former CBS news anchor Walter Cronkite, who has repeatedly been rated one of the most trusted people in America, could command millions of dollars as a product spokesperson. Global Perspective 6-1 discusses how some American celebrities protect their image by endorsing products abroad rather than in the United States.

Advertisers use various techniques to increase the perception that their sources are trustworthy. Hidden cameras are used to show that the consumer is not a paid spokesperson and is making an objective evaluation of the product. Disguised brands are compared. (Of course, the sponsor's brand always performs better than the consumer's regular brand, and he or she is always surprised.) Most consumers are skeptical of these techniques, so they may have limited value in enhancing perceptions of credibility.

EXHIBIT 6–3
Dove promotes the fact that it is recommended by experts in skin care

USING CORPORATE LEADERS AS SPOKESPEOPLE

Another way of enhancing source credibility is to use the company president or chief executive officer as a spokesperson in the firm's advertising. Many companies believe the use of their president or CEO is the ultimate expression of the company's commitment to quality and customer service. In some cases, these ads have not only increased sales but also helped turn the company leaders into celebrities.[5] Lee Iacocca appeared in more than 60 commercials for Chrysler Corp. and became a national business hero for guiding the successful turnaround of the company. Another popular corporate spokesperson is Dave Thomas, the founder of Wendy's fast-food restaurants, who has been the company's pitchman since 1989. Thomas has appeared in more than 500 Wendy's commercials and is widely credited with having helped increase the restaurant chain's sales.[6]

Some research suggests the use of a company president or CEO can improve attitudes and increase the likelihood consumers will inquire about the company's product or service.[7] It is becoming common for local retailers to use the owner or president in their ads. Companies are likely to continue using their top executives in their advertising, particularly when they have celebrity value that helps enhance the firms' image. However, there can be problems with this strategy. CEO spokespeople who become very popular may get more attention than their company's product/service or advertising message. And if a firm's image becomes too closely tied to a popular leader, there can be problems if that person leaves the company.

LIMITATIONS OF CREDIBLE SOURCES

Several studies have shown that a high-credibility source is not always an asset, nor is a low-credibility source always a liability. High- and low-credibility sources are equally effective when they are arguing for a position opposing their own best interest.[8] A very credible source is more effective when message recipients are not in favor of the position advocated in the message.[9] However, a very credible source is less important when the audience has a neutral position and may even be less effective than a moderately credible source when the receiver's initial attitude is favorable.[10]

Another reason a low-credibility source may be as effective as a high-credibility source is the **sleeper effect**, whereby the persuasiveness of a message increases with the passage of time. The immediate impact of a persuasive message may be inhibited because of its association with a low-credibility source. But with time, the association of the message with the source diminishes and the receiver's attention focuses more on favorable information in the message, which results in more support arguing. However, many studies have failed to demonstrate the presence of a sleeper effect.[11] Many advertisers hesitate to count on the sleeper effect, since exposure to a credible source is a more reliable strategy.[12]

Source Attractiveness

A source characteristic frequently used by advertisers is **attractiveness**, which encompasses similarity, familiarity, and likability.[13] *Similarity* is a supposed resemblance between the source and the receiver of the message, while familiarity refers to knowledge of the source through exposure. *Likability* is an affection for the source as a result of physical appearance, behavior, or other personal traits. Even when these sources are not athletes or movie stars, consumers often admire their physical appearance, talent, and/or personality.

Source attractiveness leads to persuasion through a process of **identification**, whereby the receiver is motivated to seek some type of relationship with the source and thus adopts

Global Perspective 6–1
Selling Out, but Only Abroad

Many American celebrities make huge sums of money endorsing products and serving as advertising spokespeople. Some big stars won't do endorsements because they don't want fans to think they've sold out. But many stars who resist the temptation to cash in on their fame in the United States are only too happy to appear in ads in foreign countries.

Actress Kim Basinger models hosiery in Italy; Woody Allen wrote and directed a series of commercials for the country's largest grocery chain, Co-op Italia, for several million dollars. Sharon Stone, who became a superstar with her sexy roles in movies like *Basic Instinct* and *Casino*, received between $1 million and $2 million to star in a racy ad for Pirelli Tires in Europe. An executive for the agency that did the ads says "Pirelli's brand image is very Italian, quite sexy. We chose Sharon Stone because of who she is—very sexy, grown up, in control."

Nowhere are ads starring American celebrities more prevalent than in Japan. While the Japanese flood the United States with cars, TVs, and VCRs, the trade in celebrity endorsers flows the other way. Arnold Schwarzenegger pitches Nissin Cup Noodle and Chi Chin vitamin drink and can be seen straddling a rocket that blasts off and shoots him out of the frame in a commercial for Takeda Chemical Industries. Gene Hackman and Sylvester Stallone each received $1 million to represent Kirin beer. Bruce Willis appears on Japanese television selling Subarus and Post Water, while his wife, actress Demi Moore, pushes cosmetics. Japan's two major airlines have used Frank Sinatra and Richard Gere to fill seats. Actress Jodie Foster flirts with a group of men to the tune of the Fine Young Cannibals' "She Drives Me Crazy" in a Honda ad. Charlie Sheen praises Tokyo Gas, while Sigourney Weaver promotes the strengths of Nippon Steel.

Western celebrities are used to promote products in Japan for several reasons. Many Japanese identify with the Western style of life, and the celebrity endorsements give brands a certain international cachet. Also, Japanese advertising emphasizes style and mood rather than substance; consumers expect to be entertained by ads rather than bored by product testimonials. Because Japanese commercials commonly last only 15 seconds, advertisers find an instantly recognizable Western celebrity who can capture viewers' attention is well worth the money. According to an *Advertising Age* reporter, the movie studios also encourage celebrities to do ads in Japan because it boosts their visibility in the Far East. He says "Increasingly the market for films is becoming global and the more recognizable the star, the better the picture will do in the Asian market." The studio and the celebrity benefit along with the marketer.

Many celebrities cashing in on foreign commercials try to protect their image at home. The stars commonly have nondisclosure clauses in their contracts, specifying that the ads cannot be shown—or sometimes even discussed (oops!)—outside the country for which they were intended. The worldwide head of commercials at the William Morris talent agency says that actors "believe that knowledge of that endorsement should stay within that country." Sorry about that.

Sources: Stephen Rae, "How Celebrities Make Killings on Commercials," *Cosmopolitan*, January 1997, pp. 164–67; Lauren David Peden, "Seen the One Where Arnold Sells Noodles?" *The New York Times*, June 20, 1993, p. 28; David Kilburn, "Japanese Airlines Tap U.S. Stars," *Advertising Age*, April 8, 1991.

similar beliefs, attitudes, preferences, or behavior. Maintaining this position depends on the source's continued support for the position as well as the receiver's continued identification with the source. If the source changes position, the receiver may also change. Unlike internalization, identification does not usually integrate information from an attractive source into the receiver's belief system. The receiver may maintain the attitudinal position or behavior only as long as it is supported by the source or the source remains attractive.

Marketers recognize that receivers of persuasive communications are more likely to attend to and identify with people they find likable or similar to themselves. Similarity and likability are the two source characteristics marketers seek when choosing a communicator.

APPLYING SIMILARITY

Marketers recognize that people are more likely to be influenced by a message coming from someone with whom they feel a sense of similarity.[14] If the communicator and receiver have similar needs, goals, interests, and lifestyles, the position advocated by the source is better understood and received. Similarity is used in various ways in marketing communications. Companies select salespeople whose characteristics match well with their customers'. A sales position for a particular region may be staffed by someone local who has background and interests in common with the customers. Global marketers often hire foreign nationals as salespeople so customers can relate more easily to them.

IMC Perspective 6–2
Advertisers Turn to Everyday Guys to Pitch Products

When most people think of an advertising spokesperson, the image that usually comes to mind is a celebrity—a star athlete or a popular entertainer or a supermodel like Cindy Crawford. The use of celebrities and supermodels is, of course, commonplace in advertising. However, many companies feel that the best way to connect with consumers is by using regular-looking, everyday people with whom the average person can easily identify. And many of the top advertisers have found the Everyman for the 90s—Chris Dollard, a thirtyish actor with loose curls and a sweet, slightly nerdy demeanor.

Most people have never heard of Chris Dollard, but they've seen him in commercials. He's the father in the Isuzu ad who tries to drag his son out of a toy store until he spots an Isuzu Rodeo in a giant toy box. He's the JCPenney shoe salesman who turns his store into a mock football stadium, hurling shoe boxes across the room as he calls the play-by-play. He's the goofy Super Bowl fan munching Baked Tostitos while wearing a too-small leather football helmet, and a nervous groom contemplating marriage to a Radio Shack cellular phone dressed up as a bride.

The rise of the Everyman in advertising is an interesting phenomenon. In the 70s, commercials were filled with parents with perfect hair and gleaming teeth. In the 80s, attractive parents gave way to dress-for-success yuppies. But in the 90s many advertisers are clamoring for someone who can connect to average Americans struggling with downsizing, reduced expectations, and work/family juggling acts. Many advertisers feel that Dollard is the person with the face and personality that push America's buttons.

The casting director at the agency that chose Dollard over 1,000 other aspirants for the Tostitos spot says "A lot of people were starting to get frustrated by trying to live up to something that they were never going to be. By casting regular-looking folks like Mr. Dollard, advertisers are bet-

ting you can reach more people if you reach them on their level." The co-creative director at Goodby, Silverstein & Partners, the agency that made the Isuzu toy-store commercial, says he was explicitly looking for a "regular Joe who was quirky, someone you can relate to." The commercial has been Isuzu's most popular ad since the liar campaign featuring the smarmy car salesman Joe Isuzu.

The creative director at the Temerlin McClain agency looked at nearly 60 actors for the JCPenney ad and says "We were looking for just an average everyday guy. The minute we saw him on tape we said, 'That's our guy.'" The account director who helped cast Dollard as a bemused caller expressing wonderment at the pennies he can save by using MCI's collect calling says, "He presents a nonthreatening, noncommercial sort of personality people are more willing today to accept messages from." Marketers will continue to pay huge sums of money to celebrities to appear in their ads. However, many consumers really identify with an average Joe like Chris Dollard.

Source: Sally Goll Beatty, "Madison Avenue Picks an Average Joe as '90s Pitchman," *The Wall Street Journal*, September 11, 1996, pp. B1, 7. Reprinted by permission of *The Wall Street Journal*, ©1996 Dow Jones & Company, Inc. All Rights Reserved Worldwide.

Companies may also try to recruit former athletes to sell sporting goods or beer, since their customers usually have a strong interest in sports. Several studies have shown that customers who perceive a salesperson as similar to themselves are more likely to be influenced by his or her message.[15]

Similarity is also used to create a situation where the consumer feels empathy for the person shown in the commercial. In a slice-of-life commercial, the advertiser usually starts by presenting a predicament with the hope of getting the consumer to think, "I can see myself in that situation." This can help establish a bond of similarity between the communicator and the receiver, increasing the source's level of persuasiveness. IMC Perspective 6–2 describes how many advertisers are casting in their commercials average, regular-looking people with whom the typical consumer can identify.

APPLYING LIKABILITY: USING CELEBRITIES

Advertisers recognize the value of using spokespeople who are admired: TV and movie stars, athletes, musicians, and other popular public figures. More than 20 percent of all TV

commercials feature celebrities, and advertisers pay hundreds of millions of dollars for their services. One of the top celebrity endorsers, basketball superstar Michael Jordan, makes an estimated $40 million a year in endorsement fees from companies such as McDonald's, Nike, General Mills, Hanes, and Quaker Oats (makers of Gatorade) (Exhibit 6–4).[16] One of the hottest new celebrity endorsers is golfer Tiger Woods, who recently signed endorsement contracts worth more than $70 million with Nike, American Express, and the Achusuet Co. and Cobra Golf, subsidiaries of American Brands, Inc. (Exhibit 6–5).

Why do companies spend huge sums to have celebrities appear in their ads and endorse their products? They think celebrities have stopping power. That is, they draw attention to advertising messages in a very cluttered media environment. Marketers think a popular

EXHIBIT 6–6
Pro golfer Nick Price attracts attention and delivers a convincing message about the product

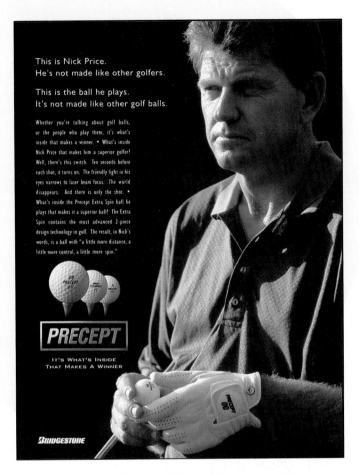

This is Nick Price.
He's not made like other golfers.

This is the ball he plays.
It's not made like other golf balls.

Whether you're talking about golf balls, or the people who play them, it's what's inside that makes a winner. • What's inside Nick Price that makes him a superior golfer? Well, there's this switch. Ten seconds before each shot, it turns on. The friendly light in his eyes narrows to laser beam focus. The world disappears. And there is only the shot. • What's inside the Precept Extra Spin ball he plays that makes it a superior ball? The Extra Spin contains the most advanced 2-piece design technology in golf. The result, in Nick's words, is a ball with "a little more distance, a little more control, a little more spin."

PRECEPT
IT'S WHAT'S INSIDE
THAT MAKES A WINNER

BRIDGESTONE

celebrity will favorably influence consumers' feelings, attitudes, and purchase behavior. And they believe celebrities can enhance the target audience's perceptions of the product in terms of image and/or performance. For example, a well-known athlete may convince potential buyers that the product will enhance their own performance, as Exhibit 6–6 shows.

A number of factors must be considered when a company decides to use a celebrity spokesperson, including the dangers of overshadowing the product and being overexposed, the target audience's receptivity, and risks to the advertiser.

Overshadowing the Product

How will the celebrity affect the target audience's processing of the advertising message? Consumers may focus their attention on the celebrity and fail to note the brand. Mazda dropped actor James Garner as its spokesperson to focus exclusively on its cars. Said Mazda's vice president of advertising, "We want the cars to be the stars."[17]

Overexposure

Consumers are often skeptical of endorsements because they know the celebrities are being paid.[18] This problem is particularly pronounced when a celebrity endorses too many products or companies and becomes overexposed. Advertisers can protect themselves against overexposure with an exclusivity clause limiting the number of products a celebrity can endorse. However, such clauses are usually expensive and most celebrities agree not to endorse similar products anyway. Many celebrities, knowing their fame is fleeting, try to earn as much endorsement money as possible, yet they must be careful not to damage their credibility by endorsing too many products. For example, singer/actress Cher damaged her credibility as an advertising spokesperson by appearing in too many infomercials. When she realized that appearing in all of the infomercials was devastating to her acting career as well, she ceased doing them.[19]

Target Audiences' Receptivity

Consumers who are particularly knowledgeable about a product or service or have strongly established attitudes may be less influenced by a celebrity than those with little knowledge or neutral attitudes. One study found that college-age students were more likely to have a positive attitude toward a product endorsed by a celebrity than were older consumers.[20] The teenage market segment is generally very receptive to celebrity endorsers, as evidenced by the frequent use of entertainers and athletes in ads targeted to this group for products like soft drinks, apparel, and cosmetics.

Some studies suggest that celebrity endorsements are becoming less important in influencing purchase decisions for a broad range of consumers.[21] In a survey of 30,000 consumers ages 13 to 75 conducted by the Athletic Footwear Association, celebrity endorsements were the least important factor for buying a particular brand of shoe (Figure 6–4).

One company that believes that celebrity endorsements are not worthwhile is New Balance, which has an across-the-board policy against them. The president of the company notes, "If you want the best shoe for yourself, you don't generally give a hoot if Michael Jordan wears it. We'd rather put the money into our factories than into the hands of celebrities."[22] New Balance's perspective on celebrity endorsers is summarized pretty well in the ad shown in Exhibit 6–7.

Risk to the Advertiser

A celebrity's behavior may pose a risk to a company. As noted in the opening vignette, a number of entertainers and athletes have been involved in activities that could embarrass the companies whose products they endorsed. For example, the Florida Citrus Commission had to drop actor Burt Reynolds as its spokesperson when his divorce from actress Loni Anderson became the talk of the tabloids.[23] Pepsi had a string of problems with celebrity endorsers; it severed ties to boxer Mike Tyson after his wife, Robin Givens, accused him of beating her and with singer Michael Jackson after he was accused of having sex with a 12-year-old boy. Pepsi dropped a TV ad featuring pop singer Madonna when some religious groups and consumers objected to her "Like a Prayer" video and threatened to boycott Pepsi products.[24] The ad ran only twice, but Pepsi still had to pay Madonna a reported $10 million. Recently Pepsi has chosen more wholesome types—supermodels Claudia Schiffer and Cindy Crawford—to appear in its Pepsi Blue campaign in various international markets. The Beef Industry Council suffered embarrassment when spokesperson Cybill Shepherd was quoted as saying that she didn't eat red meat.[25]

To avoid these problems, companies often research a celebrity's personal life and background. Many contracts include a morals clause allowing the company to terminate the contract if a controversy arises. However, marketers should remember that adding morals clauses to their endorsement contracts only gets them out of a problem; it does not prevent it.

FIGURE 6–4

Importance of various information sources in the purchase of athletic shoes

Information Source	Percent Who Consider It Important
All advertising	69%
Store displays	57
TV commercials	53
Friends	48
Observing others	41
Magazine articles	19
Salespeople	19
Newspaper articles	13
Mail-order catalogs	11
Celebrity endorsements	10

Source: Athletic Footwear Association.

EXHIBIT 6–7
New Balance does not believe in
using celebrities to promote its shoes

UNDERSTANDING THE MEANING OF CELEBRITY ENDORSERS

Advertisers must try to match the product or company's image, the characteristics of the target market, and the personality of the celebrity.[26] The image celebrities project to consumers can be just as important as their ability to attract attention. A new perspective on celebrity endorsement has been developed recently by Grant McCracken.[27] He argues that credibility and attractiveness don't sufficiently explain how and why celebrity endorsements work and offers a model based on *meaning transfer* (Figure 6–5).

According to this model, a celebrity's effectiveness as an endorser depends on the culturally acquired meanings he or she brings to the endorsement process. Each celebrity contains many meanings, including status, class, gender, and age as well as personality and lifestyle. In explaining stage 1 of the meaning transfer process, McCracken notes:

> Celebrities draw these powerful meanings from the roles they assume in their television, movie, military, athletic, and other careers. Each new dramatic role brings the celebrity into contact with a range of objects, persons, and contexts. Out of these objects, persons, and contexts are transferred meanings that then reside in the celebrity.[28]

Examples of meanings that have been acquired by celebrities include actor Bill Cosby as the perfect father (from his role on "The Cosby Show"), tennis star Andre Agassi as the defiant tennis star (from his antics and performance on and off the court), and actor Paul Hogan as the rugged tough guy from the Australian outback (from his roles in *Crocodile Dundee* and other films).

McCracken suggests celebrity endorsers bring their meanings into the ad and transfer them to the product they are endorsing (stage 2 of the model in Figure 6–5). For example, long-distance carrier Sprint's use of Candice Bergen as its spokesperson takes advantage of the glib, caustic (and cheap) journalist she plays on her popular television show. Murphy Brown's character embodies the irreverent, alternative image Sprint wants to project in

FIGURE 6–5 Meaning movement and the endorsement process

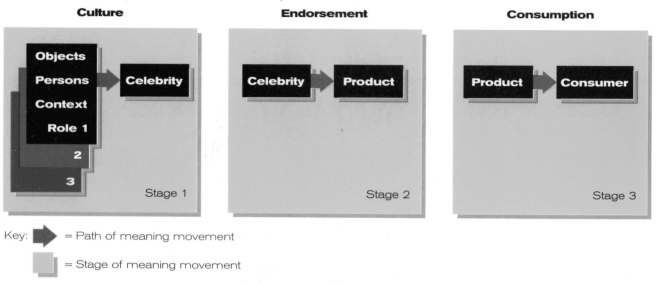

Key: = Path of meaning movement

= Stage of meaning movement

competing as the underdog, and it comes across in the ads when Bergen delivers sarcastic zingers at industry leader AT&T.

Marketers using a celebrity endorser try to capture the exact set of meanings being sought from the celebrity in the ad campaign and not to transfer unwanted meaning. For example, Subaru has done an excellent job of using Australian actor Paul Hogan in ads for its new Outback—a vehicle the company positioned as the first sport utility wagon (Exhibit 6–8).

In the final stage of McCracken's model, the meanings the celebrity has given to the product are transferred to the consumer. For example, Subaru touts the Outback as a vehicle that combines rough-terrain driving capability with the ride and comfort of a passenger car, and the use of Paul Hogan helps in creating this image. Subaru's vice president of marketing says "A lot of sport utility shoppers are buying the rugged, go-anywhere image. Paul Hogan not only gives us a nice play on the Outback name but also a chance to help rugged-ize the Outback image."[29] McCracken notes that this final stage is complicated and difficult to achieve. The way consumers take possession of the meaning the celebrity has transferred to a product is probably the least understood part of this process.

The meaning transfer model has some important implications for companies using celebrity endorsers. Marketers must first decide on the image or symbolic meanings important to their target audience for this particular product, service, or company. They must then determine which celebrity best represents the meaning or image to be projected. An advertising campaign must be designed that captures that meaning in the product and moves it to the consumer. Marketing and advertising personnel often rely on intuition in choosing celebrity endorsers for their companies or products, but some companies conduct research studies to determine consumers' perceptions of celebrities' meaning.

Marketers may also pretest ads to determine whether they transfer the proper meaning to the product. When celebrity endorsers are used, the marketer should track the campaign's effectiveness. Does the celebrity continue to be effective in communicating the proper meaning to the target audience? Celebrities who are no longer in the limelight may lose their ability to transfer any significant meanings to the product.

As we have seen, marketers must consider many factors when choosing a celebrity to serve as an advertising spokesperson for the company or a particular brand. IMC Perspective 6–3 discusses some interesting issues regarding the choice of celebrity endorsers.

APPLYING LIKABILITY: DECORATIVE MODELS

Advertisers often draw attention to their ads by featuring a physically attractive person who serves as a passive or decorative model rather than as an active communicator. Research sug-

EXHIBIT 6–8
Australian actor Paul Hogan helps position the Subaru Outback as a rugged, go-anywhere vehicle

gests that physically attractive communicators generally have a positive impact and generate more favorable evaluations of both ads and products than less attractive models.[30] The gender appropriateness of the model for the product being advertised and his or her relevance to the product are also important considerations.[31] Products such as cosmetics or fashionable clothing are likely to benefit from the use of an attractive model, since physical appearance is very relevant in marketing these items. For example, Revlon uses supermodel Cindy Crawford in advertising for various cosmetics products such as its new Fire & Ice fragrance (Exhibit 6–9).

Some models draw attention to the ad but not to the product or message. Studies show that an attractive model facilitates recognition of the ad but does not enhance copy readership or message recall.[32] Thus, advertisers must ensure that the consumer's attention will go beyond the model to the product and advertising message.

Source Power

The final characteristic in Kelman's classification scheme is **source power**. A source has power when he or she can actually administer rewards and punishments to the receiver. As a result of this power, the source may be able to induce another person(s) to respond to the request or position he or she is advocating. The power of the source depends on several factors. The source must be perceived as being able to administer positive or negative sanctions to the receiver (*perceived control*) and the receiver must think the source cares about whether or not the receiver conforms (*perceived concern*). The receiver's estimate of the source's ability to observe conformity is also important (*perceived scrutiny*).

When a receiver perceives a source as having power, the influence process occurs through a process known as **compliance**. The receiver accepts the persuasive influence of the source and acquiesces to his or her position in hopes of obtaining a favorable reaction or avoiding punishment. The receiver may show public agreement with the source's position but not have an internal or private commitment to this position. Persuasion induced through

IMC Perspective 6–3
Choosing a Celebrity Endorser

Obviously many marketers believe strongly in the value of celebrity spokespeople, as the amount of money paid to them has soared to record levels. Marketers look for a celebrity who will attract viewers' or readers' attention and enhance the image of their company or brand. But how do they choose the right one? While some executives rely on their own gut feeling, many turn to research that measures a celebrity's appeal.

Marketing Evaluations Inc.'s TVQ Services surveys more than 7,000 people each year to come up with recognizability scores and its well-known Q rating for TV and movie actors, athletes, authors, businesspeople, and other personalities. The recognizability score indicates what percentage of people recognize the celebrity. The Q score tells the percentages of people recognizing the celebrity who rate him or her as one of their favorite performers. Bill Cosby set a record a few years ago when 96 percent of those surveyed recognized him and he had a Q score of 71 (i.e., 71 percent of those who recognized him said he was one of their favorite performers). The average Q score for performers is 18. Marketing Evaluations' celebrity ratings are also broken down by various demographic groups such as age, income, occupation, education, and race. Thus, marketers have some idea of how a celebrity's popularity varies among different groups of consumers.

Video Storyboard Tests surveys more than 2,200 adult TV viewers annually to measure attitudes toward celebrities as endorsers and rate their persuasiveness and credibility. The table here shows consumers' ratings of the most popular entertainer and athlete endorsers for TV in 1995. The list is carefully scrutinized by ad executives and talent agencies to determine the most effective spokespeople for various companies.

Marketers also consider the celebrities' visibility and personalities. Among athletes, basketball players, tennis players, and golfers are popular spokespeople, since the public buys the footwear, clubs, balls, rackets, and clothing these highly visible athletes use. It also helps to be perceived as a winner. Most of the top athlete endorsers are current or former stars in their sports and have led their teams to championships. And, of course, physical attractiveness is always an asset, particularly for celebrities endorsing health and beauty products, such as Cybill Shepherd, Cindy Crawford, and Jaclyn Smith.

It is interesting to note that in recent years female stars have been outshining males. In 1985, males accounted for nine of the top 10 endorsers. However, in the 1995 poll the top 10 included only two men, perennial favorite Bill Cosby and comedian Jerry Seinfeld. David Vadehra, president of Video Storyboard Tests, notes that women endorsers are becoming more popular because today's more sophisticated consumers are not looking for traditional male authority figures. Conventional wisdom once favored using men in all ads, even those that were supposed to appeal to women. Vadehra says, "Now if you need to speak to a woman consumer, you hire a woman." He also notes that advertisers are turning away from male entertainers in favor of male athletes. "It's becoming obvious to advertisers that if you want to sell to men, use a jock. Athletes represent something men aspire to: perfection."

Selling power: Top celebrity endorsers ranked by consumer appeal

Rank			
1995	1994	Name	Endorsements
1	2	Candice Bergen	Sprint
2	3	Bill Cosby	Jell-O
3	4	Elizabeth Taylor	White Diamonds Perfume
4	–	Kathie Lee Gifford	Carnival Cruise Line
5	1	Cindy Crawford	Pepsi-Cola, Revlon
6	6	Whitney Houston	AT&T
7	5	Jerry Seinfeld	American Express
8	–	Jaclyn Smith	Kmart
9	10	Cybill Shepherd	L'Oreal
10	–	Kate Jackson	Lincoln-Mercury

Source: Video Storyboard Tests.

Sources: Kevin Goldman, "Women Endorsers More Credible than Men, a Survey Suggests," *The Wall Street Journal*, October 12, 1995, p. B1; Kevin Goldman, "Athletes Find Endorsements Hard to Win," *The Wall Street Journal*, January 27, 1994, p. B10. Reprinted by permission of *The Wall Street Journal*, ©1994, 1995 Dow Jones & Company, Inc. All Rights Reserved Worldwide.

compliance may be superficial and last only as long as the receiver perceives that the source can administer some reward or punishment.

Power as a source characteristic is very difficult to apply in a nonpersonal influence situation such as advertising. A communicator in an ad generally cannot apply any sanctions to the receiver or determine whether compliance actually occurs. An indirect way of using power is by using an individual with an authoritative personality as a spokesperson. Actor Charles Bronson, who typifies this image, has appeared in public service campaigns commanding people not to pollute or damage our natural parks (Exhibit 6–10).

EXHIBIT 6–9
Revlon makes effective use of
supermodel Cindy Crawford in this ad

EXHIBIT 6–10   Actor Charles
Bronson's authoritative image makes
him an effective source

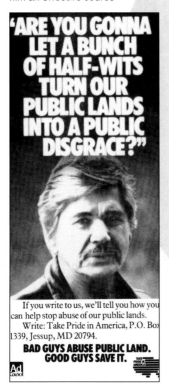

The use of source power applies more in situations involving personal communication and influence. For example, in a personal selling situation, the sales rep may have some power over a buyer if the latter anticipates receiving special rewards or favors for complying with the salesperson. Some companies provide their sales reps with large expense accounts to spend on customers for this very purpose. Representatives of companies whose product demand exceeds supply are often in a position of power; buyers may comply with their requests to ensure an adequate supply of the product. Sales reps must be very careful in their use of a power position, since abusing a power base to maximize short-term gains can damage long-term relationships with customers.

MESSAGE FACTORS

The way marketing communications are presented is very important in determining their effectiveness. Promotional managers must consider not only the content of their persuasive messages but also how this information will be structured for presentation and what type of message appeal will be used. Advertising, in all media except radio, relies heavily on visual as well as verbal information. Many options are available with respect to the design and presentation of a message. This section examines the structure of messages and considers the effects of different types of appeals used in advertising.

Message Structure

Marketing communications usually consist of a number of message points that the communicator wants to get across. An important aspect of message strategy is knowing the best way to communicate these points and overcome any opposing viewpoints audience members may hold. Extensive research has been conducted on how the structure of a persuasive message can influence its effectiveness, including order of presentation, conclusion drawing, message sidedness, refutation, and verbal versus visual message characteristics.

ORDER OF PRESENTATION

A basic consideration in the design of a persuasive message is the arguments' order of presentation. Should the most important message points be placed at the beginning of the message, in the middle, or at the end? Research on learning and memory generally indicates that items presented first and last are remembered better than those presented in the middle (see Figure 6–6).[33] This suggests that a communicator's strongest arguments should be presented early or late in the message but never in the middle.

Presenting the strongest arguments at the beginning of the message assumes a **primacy effect** is operating, whereby information presented first is most effective. Putting the strong points at the end assumes a **recency effect**, whereby the last arguments presented are most persuasive.

Whether to place the strongest selling points at the beginning or the end of the message depends on several factors. If the target audience is opposed to the communicator's position, presenting strong points first can reduce the level of counterarguing. Putting weak arguments first might lead to such a high level of counterarguing that strong arguments that followed would not be believed. Strong arguments work best at the beginning of the message if the audience is not interested in the topic, so they can arouse interest in the message. When the target audience is predisposed toward the communicator's position or is highly interested in the issue or product, strong arguments can be saved for the end of the message. This may result in a more favorable opinion as well as better retention of the information.

The order of presentation can be critical when a long, detailed message with many arguments is being presented. Most effective sales presentations open and close with strong selling points and bury weaker arguments in the middle. For short communications, such as a 15- or 30-second TV or radio commercial, the order may be less critical. However, many product and service messages are received by consumers with low involvement and minimal interest. Thus, an advertiser may want to present the brand name and key selling points early in the message and repeat them at the end to enhance recall and retention.

CONCLUSION DRAWING

Marketing communicators must decide whether their messages should explicitly draw a firm conclusion or allow the audience to draw their own conclusions. Research suggests that, in general, messages with explicit conclusions are more easily understood and effective in influencing attitudes. However, other studies have shown that the effectiveness of conclusion drawing may depend on the target audience, the type of issue or topic, and the nature of the situation.[34]

More highly educated people prefer to draw their own conclusions and may be annoyed at an attempt to explain the obvious or to draw an inference for them. But stating the conclusion may be necessary for a less educated audience, who may not draw any conclusion or may make an incorrect inference from the message. Marketers must also consider the audience's level of involvement in the topic. For highly personal or ego-involving issues, message recipients may want to make up their own minds and resent any attempts by the communicator to draw a conclusion. A recent study found that open-ended ads (without explicit con-

FIGURE 6–6

Ad message recall as a function of order of presentation

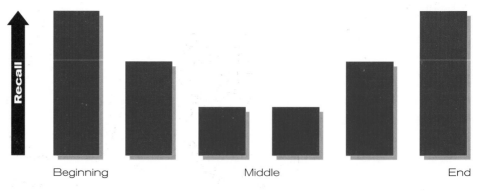

clusions) were more effective than closed-ended arguments that did include a specific conclusion—but only for involved audiences.[35]

Whether to draw a conclusion for the audience also depends on the complexity of the topic. Even a highly educated audience may need assistance if its knowledge level in a particular area is low. Does the marketer want the message to trigger immediate action or a more long-term effect? If immediate action is an objective, the message should draw a definite conclusion. This is a common strategy in political advertising, particularly for ads run close to election day. When immediate impact is not the objective and repeated exposure will give the audience opportunities to draw their own conclusion, an open-ended message may be used.

Drawing a conclusion in a message may make sure the target audience gets the point the marketer intended. But many advertisers believe that letting customers draw their own conclusions reinforces the points being made in the message. For example, a health services agency in Kentucky found that open-ended ads were more memorable and more effective in getting consumers to use health services than ads stating a conclusion. Ads that posed questions about alcohol and drug abuse and left them unanswered resulted in more calls by teenagers to a help line for information than did a message offering a resolution to the problem.[36] The ad for Hewlett-Packard personal computers in Exhibit 6–11 is a very good example of an open-ended ad. The questions encourage individuals choosing a PC for their company to consider the benefits of purchasing from a well-known corporation like Hewlett-Packard rather than from a smaller, less reliable company.

MESSAGE SIDEDNESS

Another message structure decision facing the marketer involves message sidedness. A **one-sided message** mentions only positive attributes or benefits. A **two-sided message** presents both good and bad points. One-sided messages are most effective when the target audience already holds a favorable opinion about the topic. They also work better with a less educated audience.[37]

Two-sided messages are more effective when the target audience holds an opposing opinion or is highly educated. Two-sided messages may enhance the credibility of the source.[38] A better-educated audience usually knows there are opposing arguments, so a communicator who presents both sides of an issue is likely to be seen as less biased and more objective.

Most advertisers use one-sided messages. They are concerned about the negative effects of acknowledging a weakness in their brand or don't want to say anything positive about their competitors. There are exceptions, however. Sometimes advertisers compare brands on several attributes and do not show their product as being the best on every one.

REFUTATION

In a special type of two-sided message known as a **refutational appeal**, the communicator presents both sides of an issue and then refutes the opposing viewpoint. Since refutational appeals tend to "inoculate" the target audience against a competitor's counterclaims, they

EXHIBIT 6–11
Hewlett-Packard makes effective use of an open-ended approach

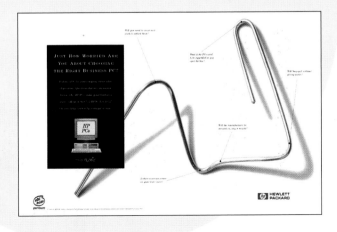

are more effective than one-sided messages in making consumers resistant to an opposing message.[39]

Refutational messages may be useful when marketers wish to build attitudes that resist change and must defend against attacks or criticism of their products or the company. For example, Exhibit 6–12 shows one of a series of ads from Apple Computer that were run in response to negative publicity the company had been receiving regarding the company's long-term viability and position in the PC market. Market leaders, who are often the target of comparative messages, may find that acknowledging competitors' claims and then refuting them can help build resistant attitudes and customer loyalty.

VERBAL VERSUS VISUAL MESSAGES

Thus far our discussion has focused on the information, or verbal, portion of the message. However, the nonverbal, visual elements of an ad are also very important. Many ads provide minimal amounts of information and rely on visual elements to communicate. Pictures are commonly used in advertising to convey information or reinforce copy or message claims.

Both the verbal and visual portions of an ad influence the way the advertising message is processed.[40] Consumers may develop images or impressions based on visual elements such as an illustration in an ad or the scenes in a TV commercial. In some cases, the visual portion of an ad may reduce its persuasiveness, since the processing stimulated by the picture may be less controlled and consequently less favorable than that stimulated by words.[41]

Pictures affect the way consumers process accompanying copy. A recent study showed that when verbal information was low in imagery value, the use of pictures providing examples increased both immediate and delayed recall of product attributes.[42] However, when the verbal information was already high in imagery value, the addition of pictures did not increase recall. Advertisers often design ads where the visual image supports the verbal appeal to create a compelling impression in the consumer's mind. Notice how the ad for Mammoth Mountain ski resort uses visual elements to support the claims made in the copy regarding the size of Mammoth versus other ski areas (Exhibit 6–13).

EXHIBIT 6–12
Apple used a refutational appeal to address concerns about the company

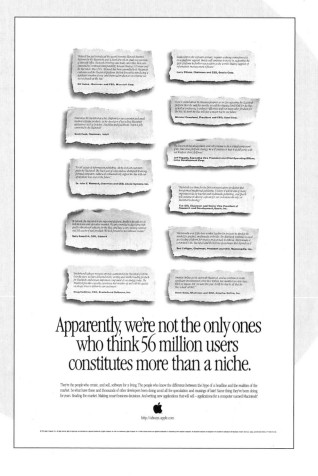

Sometimes advertisers use a different strategy; they design ads in which the visual portion is *incongruent* with or contradicts the verbal information presented. The logic behind this strategy is that the use of an unexpected picture or visual image will grab consumers' attention and get them to engage in more effortful or elaborative processing.[43] A number of studies have shown that the use of a visual that is inconsistent with the verbal content leads to more recall and greater processing of the information presented.[44]

Message Appeals

One of the advertiser's most important creative strategy decisions involves the choice of an appropriate appeal. Some ads are designed to appeal to the rational, logical aspect of the consumer's decision-making process; others appeal to feelings in an attempt to evoke some emotional reaction. Many believe that effective advertising combines the practical reasons for purchasing a product with emotional values. In this section we will examine several common types of message appeals, including comparative advertising, fear, and humor.

COMPARATIVE ADVERTISING

Comparative advertising refers to the practice of either directly or indirectly naming competitors in an ad and comparing one or more specific attributes.[45] This form of advertising became popular after the Federal Trade Commission (FTC) began advocating its use in 1972. The FTC reasoned that direct comparison of brands would provide better product information, giving consumers a more rational basis for making purchase decisions. Television networks cooperated with the FTC by lifting their ban on comparative ads, and the result was a flurry of comparative commercials.

Initially, the novelty of comparative ads resulted in greater attention. But since they have become so common, their attention-getting value has probably declined. Some studies show that recall is higher for comparative than noncomparative messages, but comparative ads are generally not more effective for other response variables, such as brand attitudes or purchase intentions.[46] Advertisers must also consider how comparative messages affect credibility.

Users of the brand being attacked in a comparative message may be especially skeptical about the advertiser's claims.

Comparative advertising may be particularly useful for new brands, since it allows a new market entrant to position itself directly against the more established brands and to promote its distinctive advantages. Direct comparisons can help position a new brand in the evoked, or choice, set of brands the customer may be considering. In the comparative ad shown in Exhibit 6–14, California Slim compares its brand to Ultra Slim-Fast, the leading brand in the meal replacement drink market.

Comparative advertising is often used for brands with a small market share. They compare themselves to an established market leader in hopes of creating an association and tapping into the leader's market. Market leaders, on the other hand, often hesitate to use comparison ads, as most believe they have little to gain by featuring competitors' products in their ads. There are exceptions, of course; Coca-Cola resorted to comparative advertising in response to challenges made by Pepsi that were reducing Coke's market share.

FEAR APPEALS

Fear is an emotional response to a threat that expresses, or at least implies, some sort of danger. Ads sometimes use **fear appeals** to evoke this emotional response and arouse individuals to take steps to remove the threat. Some, like the antidrug ads used by the Partnership for a Drug-Free America, stress physical danger that can occur if behaviors are not altered. Others—like those for deodorant, mouthwash, or dandruff shampoos—threaten disapproval or social rejection.

How Fear Operates

Before deciding to use a fear appeal-based message strategy, the advertiser should consider how fear operates, what level to use, and how different target audiences may respond. One theory suggests that the relationship between the level of fear in a message and acceptance or persuasion is *curvilinear*, as shown in Figure 6–7.[47] This means that message acceptance increases as the amount of fear used rises—to a point. Beyond that point, acceptance decreases as the level of fear rises.

FIGURE 6–7
Relationship between fear levels and
message acceptance

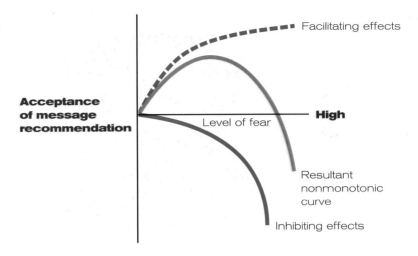

This relationship between fear and persuasion can be explained by the fact that fear appeals have both facilitating and inhibiting effects.[48] A low level of fear can have *facilitating effects;* it attracts attention and interest in the message and may motivate the receiver to act to resolve the threat. Thus, increasing the level of fear in a message from low to moderate can result in increased persuasion. High levels of fear, however, can produce *inhibiting effects;* the receiver may emotionally block the message by tuning it out, perceiving it selectively, or denying its arguments outright. Figure 6–7 illustrates how these two countereffects operate to produce the curvilinear relationship between fear and persuasion.

A recent study by Anand-Keller and Block provides support for this perspective on how fear operates.[49] They examined the conditions under which low- and high-fear appeals urging people to stop smoking are likely to be effective. Their study indicated that a communication using a low level of fear may be ineffective because it results in insufficient motivation to elaborate on the harmful consequences of engaging in the destructive behavior (smoking). However, an appeal arousing high levels of fear was ineffective because it resulted in too much elaboration on the harmful consequences. This led to defensive tendencies such as message avoidance and interfered with processing of recommended solutions to the problem.

Another approach to the curvilinear explanation of fear is the *protection motivation model.*[50] According to this theory, four cognitive appraisal processes mediate the individual's response to the threat: appraising (1) the information available regarding the severity of the perceived threat, (2) the perceived probability the threat will occur, (3) the perceived ability of a coping behavior to remove the threat, and (4) the individual's perceived ability to carry out the coping behavior.

This model suggests that both the cognitive appraisal of the information in a fear appeal message and the emotional response mediate persuasion. An audience is more likely to continue processing threat-related information, which increases the likelihood that a coping behavior will occur.

The protection motivation model suggests that ads using fear appeals should give the target audience information about the severity of the threat, the probability of its occurrence, the effectiveness of a coping response, and the ease with which the response can be implemented.[51] For example, this ad for the Havrix hepatitis A vaccine discusses how tourists can pick up hepatitis A when traveling to high-risk areas outside the United States and describes the severity of the problem. However, the ad reduces anxiety by offering a solution to the problem—a vaccination with Havrix.

It is also important to consider how the target audience may respond. Fear appeals are more effective when the message recipient is self-confident and prefers to cope with dangers rather than avoid them.[52] They are also more effective among nonusers of a product than among users. Thus, a fear appeal may be better at keeping nonsmokers from starting than persuading smokers to stop.

HUMOR APPEALS

Humorous ads are often the best known and best remembered of all advertising messages. The humorous commercials for Miller Lite beer featuring ex-athletes and other celebrities were the basis of one of the most effective, longest-running ad campaigns ever developed. Many other advertisers, among them FedEx, Little Caesar's pizza, Pepsi, and Budweiser, have also used humor appeals effectively (Exhibit 6–15).

Advertisers use humor for many reasons. Humorous messages attract and hold consumers' attention. They enhance effectiveness by putting consumers in a positive mood, increasing their liking of the ad itself and their feeling toward the product or service. And humor can distract the receiver from counterarguing against the message.[53]

Critics argue that funny ads draw people to the humorous situation but distract them from the brand and its attributes. Also, effective humor can be difficult to produce and some attempts are too subtle for mass audiences. And, as discussed in IMC Perspective 6–4, there is concern that humorous ads may wear out faster than serious appeals.

Clearly, there are valid reasons both for and against the use of humor in advertising. Not every product or service lends itself to a humorous approach. A number of studies have found that the effectiveness of humor depends on several factors, including the type of product and audience characteristics.[54] For example, humor has been more prevalent and more effective with low-involvement, feeling products than high-involvement, thinking products.[55] An interesting study surveyed the research and creative directors of the top 150 advertising agencies.[56] They were asked to name which communications objectives are facilitated through the appropriate situational use of humor in terms of media, product, and audience factors. The general conclusions of this study are shown in Figure 6–8.

EXHIBIT 6–15
Little Caesar's has used humor very effectively in its commercials

IMC Perspective 6—4
Do Humorous Ads Wear Out Too Fast?

An issue of much concern to advertisers is the problem of commercial wearout, or the tendency of a message to lose its effectiveness when it is seen repeatedly. Wearout may occur for several reasons. One is inattention; consumers may no longer attend to an ad after several exposures, so the message loses its effectiveness. Another reason is that consumers may become annoyed at seeing an ad many times.

While wearout is a problem for any type of commercial, some advertising experts argue that humorous ads wear out much sooner than other formats because once the viewer gets the joke, the ad becomes boring. However, advocates of humor argue that ads filled with yuks are effective longer because consumers can tolerate a well-executed humorous commercial again and again.

So who is right? Well, a study conducted by Research Systems Corp. concludes that neither view is correct. Humorous ads wear out at the same rate as other types of ads, whether the commercials include comparative messages, celebrity spokespeople, or other approaches. According to the study, the average ad's effectiveness wears out within eight weeks.

Not everyone agrees with this study. Another research firm, Video Storyboard Tests, claims that humorous ads lose their effectiveness faster than other ads. Says the company's president, "The first time the ad is funny, the second time the ad is acceptable, and the third time it is a bore."

While individual humorous ads may get old fast, advertisers often get around this problem by using humorous campaigns consisting of many different commercials. For example, the Little Caesar's pizza chain has run more than 35 humorous ads in the past five years. FedExpress, Energizer batteries, Pepsi, and Anheuser-Busch (Budweiser and Bud Light beer) have also made effective use of humor by constantly developing new commercials and working them into the ad rotation.

Some individual humorous commercials seem to have been immune to wearout. "Where's the beef?" which was used heavily by Wendy's in the mid-1980s, is a classic example of how to use humor to sell a product and not get in the way of the message.

One media consultant argues that it's quite simple to determine if a humorous spot or campaign is wearing out. "If the viewers laugh with you, you can be in it for the long haul. It's when they laugh at you that you're in trouble."

Sources: Dottie Enrico, "Humorous Touch Resonates with Consumers," *USA Today*, May 13, 1996, p 3B; Kevin Goldman, "Ever Hear the One about the Funny Ad?" *The Wall Street Journal*, November 2, 1993, p. B11.

FIGURE 6—8

Summary of top ad agency research and creative directors' opinions regarding humor

- Humor does aid awareness and attention, which are the objectives best achieved by its use.
  - Humor may harm recall and comprehension in general.
  - Humor may aid name and simple copy registration.
  - Humor may harm complex copy registration.
  - Humor may aid retention.
- Humor does not aid persuasion in general.
  - Humor may aid persuasion to switch brands.
  - Humor creates a positive mood that enhances persuasion.
- Humor does not aid source credibility.
- Humor is generally not very effective in bringing about action/sales.
- Creatives are more positive on the use of humor to fulfill all the above objectives than research directors are.
- Radio and TV are the best media in which to use humor; direct mail and newspapers are least suited.
- Consumer nondurables and business services are best suited to humor; corporate advertising and industrial products are least suited.
- Humor should be related to the product.
- Humor should not be used with sensitive goods or services.
- Audiences that are younger, better educated, upscale, male, and professional are best suited to humor; older, less educated, and downscale groups are least suited to humor appeals.

CHANNEL FACTORS

The final controllable variable of the communication process is the channel, or medium, used to deliver the message to the target audience. While a variety of methods are available to transmit marketing communications, as noted in Chapter 5 they can be classified into two broad categories, personal and nonpersonal media.

Personal versus Nonpersonal Channels

There are a number of basic differences between personal and nonpersonal communications channels. Information received from personal influence channels is generally more persuasive than information received via the mass media. Reasons for the differences are summarized in the following comparison of advertising versus personal selling:

> From the standpoint of persuasion, a sales message is far more flexible, personal, and powerful than an advertisement. An advertisement is normally prepared by persons having minimal personal contact with customers. The message is designed to appeal to a large number of persons. By contrast, the message in a good sales presentation is not determined in advance. The salesman has a tremendous store of knowledge about his product or service and selects appropriate items as the interview progresses. Thus, the salesman can adapt this to the thinking and needs of the customer or prospect at the time of the sales call. Furthermore, as objections arise and are voiced by the buyer, the salesman can treat the objections in an appropriate manner. This is not possible in advertising.[57]

Effects of Alternative Mass Media

The various mass media that advertisers use to transmit their messages differ in many ways, including the number and type of people they reach, costs, information processing requirements, and qualitative factors. The mass media's costs and efficiency in exposing a target audience to a communication will be evaluated in chapters 10 through 12. However, we should recognize differences in how information is processed and how communications are influenced by context or environment.

DIFFERENCES IN INFORMATION PROCESSING

There are basic differences in the manner and rate at which information from various forms of media is transmitted and can be processed. Information from ads in print media, such as newspapers, magazines, or direct mail, is *self-paced;* readers process the ad at their own rate and can study it as long as they desire. In contrast, information from the broadcast media of radio and television is *externally paced;* the transmission rate is controlled by the medium.

The difference in the processing rate for print and broadcast media has some obvious implications for advertisers. Self-paced print media make it easier for the message recipient to process a long, complex message. Advertisers often use print ads when they want to present a detailed message with a lot of information. Broadcast media are more effective for transmitting shorter messages or, in the case of TV, presenting pictorial information along with words.

While there are limits to the length and complexity of broadcast messages, advertisers can deal with this problem. One strategy is to use a radio or TV ad to get consumers' attention and direct them to specific print media for a more detailed message. For example, home builders use radio ads to draw attention to new developments and direct listeners to the real estate section of the newspaper for more details. Some advertisers develop broadcast and print versions of the same message. The copy portion is similar in both media, but the print ad can be processed at a rate comfortable to the receiver.

Effects of Context and Environment

Interpretation of an advertising message can be influenced by the context or environment in which the ad appears. Communication theorist Marshall McLuhan's thesis, "The medium is the message," implies that the medium communicates an image that is independent of any message it contains.[58] A **qualitative media effect** is the influence the medium has on a message. The image of the media vehicle can affect reactions to the message. For example, an ad for a high-quality men's clothing line might have more of an impact in a fashion magazine like *GQ* than in *Sports Afield.* Airlines, destination resorts, and travel-related services

EXHIBIT 6—16
Travel & Leisure magazine creates
an excellent reception environment
for travel-related ads

advertise in publications such as *Travel & Leisure* partly because the articles, pictures, and other ads help to excite readers about travel (Exhibit 6–16).

A media environment can also be created by the nature of the program in which a commercial appears. One study found that consumers reacted more positively to commercials seen during a happy TV program than a sad one.[59] Advertisers pay premium dollars to advertise on popular programs that create positive moods, like the Olympic Games and Christmas specials. Conversely, advertisers tend to avoid programs that create a negative mood among viewers or may be detrimental to the company or its products. Many companies won't advertise on programs with excessive violence or sexual content. As a corporate policy, Coca-Cola never advertises on TV news programs because it thinks bad news is inconsistent with Coke's image as an upbeat, fun product.

Clutter

Another aspect of the media environment is the problem of **clutter**, which refers to all the nonprogram material that appears in the broadcast environment—commercials, promotional messages for shows, public service announcements (PSAs), and the like. Clutter is of increasing concern to advertisers since there are so many messages competing for the consumer's attention. This annoys consumers and makes it difficult for ads to communicate effectively.[60] The problem has become compounded in television advertising by increases in nonprogram time and the trend toward shorter commercials. While the 30-second commercial replaced 60-second spots as the industry standard in the 1970s, many advertisers are now using 15-second spots.

The advertising industry continues to express concern over the highly cluttered commercial viewing environment. An industry-sponsored study found that the amount of clutter had increased as much as 14 percent over the past 10 years and averaged around 11 minutes per prime time hour on the major networks.[61] The problem is even greater during popular shows, to which the networks add more commercials because they can charge more. And, of course, advertisers and their agencies perpetuate the problem by pressuring the networks to squeeze their ads into top-rated shows with the largest audiences.

Advertisers and agencies want the networks to commit to a minimum amount of program time and then manage the nonprogram portion however they see fit. If the networks wanted to add more commercials, it would come out of their promos, PSAs, or program credit time. The problem is not likely to go away, however, and advertisers will continue to search for ways to break through the clutter, such as using humor, celebrity spokespeople, or novel, creative approaches.[62]

SUMMARY

This chapter focused on the controllable variables that are part of the communication process—source, message, and channel factors. Decisions regarding each of these variables should consider their impact on the various steps of the response hierarchy the message receiver passes through. The persuasion matrix helps assess the effect of controllable communication decisions on the consumer's response process.

Selection of the appropriate source or communicator to deliver a message is an important aspect of communications strategy. Three important attributes are source credibility, attractiveness, and power. Marketers enhance message effectiveness by hiring communicators who are experts in a particular area and/or have a trustworthy image. The use of celebrities to deliver advertising messages has become very popular; advertisers hope they will catch the receivers' attention and influence their attitudes or behavior through an identification process. The chapter discusses the meaning a celebrity brings to the endorsement process and the importance of matching the image of the celebrity with that of the company or brand.

The design of the advertising message is a critical part of the communication process. There are various options regarding message structure, including order of presentation of message arguments, conclusion drawing, message sidedness, refutation, and verbal versus visual traits. The advantages and disadvantages of different message appeal strategies were considered, including comparative messages and emotional appeals such as fear and humor.

Finally, the channel or medium used to deliver the message was considered. Differences between personal and nonpersonal channels of communication were discussed. Alternative mass media can have an effect on the communication process as a result of information processing and qualitative factors. The context in which an ad appears and the reception environment are important factors to consider in the selection of mass media. Clutter has become a serious problem for advertisers, particularly on TV, where commercials have become shorter and more numerous.

KEY TERMS

persuasion matrix, 166
source, 168
credibility, 169
internalization, 169
sleeper effect, 171

attractiveness, 171
identification, 171
source power, 179
compliance, 179
primacy effect, 182

recency effect, 182
one-sided message, 183
two-sided message, 183
refutational appeal, 183
comparative advertising, 185

fear appeals, 186
qualitative media effect, 190
clutter, 191

DISCUSSION QUESTIONS

1. The opening vignette discusses how some companies use athletes with a negative reputation or image as a spokesperson in their advertisements. Why do you think these companies use controversial athletes such as Dennis Rodman as spokespersons? What risks are they taking?

2. Choose a current print ad or TV commercial and use the persuasion matrix to analyze how it might influence consumers' response process.

3. What are the differences between the source credibility components of expertise and trustworthiness? Provide an example of an ad or other form of marketing communications that uses these source characteristics.

4. Do you feel companies such as American Brands, Inc., which makes Titleist golf balls and Cobra clubs, and Nike can justify paying golfer Tiger Woods $20 million and $40 million respectively to endorse their products? Why or why not?

5. Discuss the ethics of celebrities endorsing products in foreign countries but not in the United States to protect their image. Do you think celebrities hurt their reputations by doing endorsements? Why or why not?

6. Analyze the decision by Subaru to use Australian actor Paul Hogan as an endorser for its Outback sport utility vehicle using the meaning transfer model presented in Figure 6–5.

7. Discuss the pros and cons of using celebrities as advertising spokespeople. Provide examples of two celebrities you believe are very appropriate (or inappropriate) for the brands they are endorsing and explain why.

8. Discuss the pros and cons of using an open-ended message that does not draw specific conclusions versus a closed-ended message that does make explicit conclusions for the message recipient.

9. Evaluate the pros and cons of using humor as the basis for an advertising campaign. Find an example of a campaign that supports your arguments for and against the use of humor.

10. Assume that you have been asked to consult for a government agency that wants to use a fear appeal message to encourage college students not to drink and drive. Explain how fear appeals might affect persuasion and what factors should be considered in developing the ads.

Objectives and Budgeting for Integrated Marketing Communications Programs

7

*Establishing Objectives and Budgeting
for the Promotional Program*

4

CHAPTER 7

Establishing Objectives and Budgeting for the Promotional Program

Chapter Objectives

- To analyze the importance and value of setting specific objectives for advertising and promotion.

- To examine the role objectives play in the IMC planning process and the relationship of promotional objectives to marketing objectives.

- To consider the differences between sales and communications objectives and issues regarding the use of each.

- To examine some problems marketers encounter in setting objectives for their IMC programs.

- To understand the process of budgeting for IMC.

- To understand theoretical issues involved in budget setting.

- To examine various methods of budget setting.

CEREAL MAKERS CHANGE OBJECTIVES AND SLASH BUDGETS ON "GRAPE-NUTS MONDAY"

A variety of factors can account for changes in the advertising and promotional budgets companies establish. One of the most common of these is a drop in sales. Take the cereal industry for example. When Post Cereal found itself losing market share to the number one and two companies—Kellogg and General Mills, respectively—it tried to bring consumers back by slashing prices on its 22 cereal brands by an average of 20 percent (about a dollar). Kellogg immediately followed suit, as did General Mills (which had already announced a smaller price cut two years earlier).

How will these companies finance the lower prices? One way is by reducing advertising and promotional spending. As cereal prices continued to climb faster than the grocery price index in almost every year since 1983, much of the revenue was used to fund the advertising and promotions campaigns. (One estimate is that $1.02 of a $3.39 box of Kellogg's Corn Flakes goes to advertising.) Now that these revenues will be reduced, these expenditures will be reduced. Judann Pollack notes that if the cereal manufacturers maintained their price cuts for a year, advertising and promotional spending would decrease by $70 million (from $353 million) at Kellogg and $40 million (from $203 million) at Post.

But isn't it counterintuitive to decrease advertising and promotional spending when sales go down? Post doesn't think so. The cuts are an attempt to make the name brands more price competitive with store brands, which have experienced a 7 percent gain in market share over the past seven years, due in part to the fact that they cost about a third as much as the Post and Kellogg offerings. Post cites the success its parent brand, Philip Morris, had when it employed the same strategy with Marlboro cigarettes. Brand managers consider the cuts a "return to rational marketing," noting that in the past price increases were often offset by heavy couponing and promotional incentives offered to dealers. These programs will be the first to feel the impact; Post will now offer a single coupon good for any of its cereals, thereby reducing promotional costs. Advertising will also feel it. Media spending on Kellogg's Frosted Flakes (now over $51 million) and Frosted Mini-Wheats (approximately $49 million) will certainly see reductions.

But not everyone agrees with the advertising and promotional budget cuts. Rance Crain, the editor of *Advertising Age*, notes that with over 200 competitors in the cereal category and competition from breakfast alternatives such as muffins and bagels on the rise, the cereal makers cannot afford to maintain such cuts for very long. Crain notes that brand identity is critical to keep cereals from becoming a commodity category. Securities analyst William Leach agrees, noting that it would be a mistake for the industry to neglect building quality and image. Industry suppliers and ad agencies are already feeling the pinch and are encouraging a return to past spending levels. Opponents of the price cuts suggest their own alternative: more effective advertising and promotions.

Thomas Knowlton, Kellogg's North America president, claims that the advertising and promotional spending cuts will be a short-term strategy. He says that with the price cuts, "We can't afford advertising that isn't working. We are going to be more demanding with our brands, and only proven ad campaigns will get full funding." More testing of ads and media will take place to help determine what is and is not working, says Knowlton. Only time will tell whether the cereal makers are embarking on a short- or long-term strategy.

Sources: John Greenwald, "Cereal Showdown," *Time*, April 29, 1996, pp. 60–61; Judann Pollack, "Cereals to Pare Ad Plans," *Advertising Age*, June 24, 1996 , p. 1; Rance Crain, "Cereals Shouldn't Squeeze Ad Bucks," *Advertising Age*, July 1, 1996, p. 15.

We think shopping with kids shouldn't be harder than raising them.

{So we lowered our prices and made our new special coupons good on *any* Post® cereal.}

Let's face it, they want what they want. Try explaining to them which one's on sale or which one you happen to have a coupon for. So, at Post we lowered the price on every cereal we make. And our new special coupons are good on all our cereals. The choice is yours. Or your kids'. Either way, we hope it will make shopping with the kids go a bit more smoothly. We know what it's like. After all, we're parents too.

Post

Breakfast made right™

The price-cutting strategy employed by the cereal manufacturers is just one example of companies reducing advertising and promotional spending in exchange for price cuts. Delta Airlines and Procter & Gamble (among others) have also taken significant steps to "control growth in marketing spending."[1] In each of these instances, the overall objectives of increasing sales and market share have remained the same. But the role of advertising and promotions has been redefined, with new objectives and budgets being established. This chapter will examine how the goals for the integrated marketing communications program follow the company's overall marketing strategy and how these goals determine and are determined by the promotional budget.

Unfortunately, many companies have difficulty with the most critical step in the promotional planning process—setting realistic objectives that will guide the development of the IMC program. Complex marketing situations, conflicting perspectives regarding what advertising and other promotional mix elements are expected to accomplish, and uncertainty over resources make the setting of marketing communications objectives "a job of creating order out of chaos."[2] While the task of setting objectives can be complex and difficult, it must be done properly, because specific goals and objectives are the foundation on which all other promotional decisions are made. Budgeting for advertising and other promotional areas, as well as creative and media strategies and tactics, evolve from these objectives. They also provide a standard against which performance can be measured.

Why Volvo believes no child should sit in the front seat of a car. It's quite simple, really. A front air bag is a very powerful device designed, by law, to help protect an adult. Because of the size of the air bag and its speed of inflation, a child should never be placed in the front seat, even if he or she is properly belted or strapped into a child safety seat. Volvo has been an innovator in safety for over fifty years, and we'll continue to do our part. But we need your help. Please remember to put your children in the back seat, and buckle them up. Drive safely.   **VOLVO**

Setting specific objectives should be an integral part of the planning process. However, many companies either fail to use specific marketing communications objectives or set ones that are inadequate for guiding the development of the promotional plan or measuring its effectiveness. Many marketers are uncertain as to what integrated marketing communications should be expected to contribute to the marketing program. The goal of their company's advertising and promotional program is simple: to generate sales. They fail to recognize the specific tasks that advertising and other promotional mix variables must perform in preparing customers to buy a particular product or service.

As we know, advertising and promotion are not the only marketing activities involved in generating sales. Moreover, it is not always possible or necessary to measure the effects of advertising in terms of sales. For example, the Georgia-Pacific ad in Exhibit 7–1 is designed to promote the company's concern for the environment.

Consider the Volvo ad shown here. What objectives (other than generating sales) might the company have for this ad? How might its effectiveness be measured?

This chapter examines the nature and purpose of objectives and the role they play in guiding the development, implementation, and evaluation of an IMC program. Attention is given to the various types of objectives appropriate for different situations. We will also examine the budget-setting process and the interdependence of objective setting and budgeting.

THE VALUE OF OBJECTIVES

Perhaps one reason many companies fail to set specific objectives for their integrated marketing communications programs is that they don't recognize the value of doing so. Advertising and promotional objectives are needed for several reasons, including the functions they serve in communication, planning and decision making, and measurement and evaluation.

Communications

Specific objectives for the IMC program facilitate coordination of the various groups working on the campaign. Many people are involved in the planning and development of an integrated marketing communications program on the client side as well as in the various promotional agencies. The advertising and promotional program must be coordinated within the company, inside the ad agency, and between the two. Any other parties involved in the promotional campaign, such as public relations and/or sales promotion firms, research specialists, or media buying services, must also know what the company hopes to accomplish

EXHIBIT 7–1
The objective of this ad is to promote Georgia-Pacific's concern for the environment

"There's a stretch along the Lower Roanoke River in North Carolina

21,008 magnificent acres,

that's been called one of America's last great places. It's where I grew up, and now I bring my

400 plant varieties,

kids here to teach them what nature's all about. My company, Georgia-Pacific, owns this land

214 species of birds

and we did something no forest products company has ever done before. We formed a partnership

and one partnership making sure

with The Nature Conservancy to co-manage and protect this place. We all want a better world

it all stays that way.

for our kids. It just feels good to be working for a company that's doing something about it."

Mason Lilley, Forester

Georgia-Pacific
The Forest Products Company

through its marketing communications program. Many problems can be avoided if all parties have written, approved objectives to guide their actions and serve as a common base for discussing issues related to the promotional program.

Planning and Decision Making

Specific promotional objectives also guide development of the integrated marketing communications plan. All phases of a firm's promotional strategy should be based on the established objectives, including budgeting, creative, and media decisions as well as supportive programs such as direct marketing, public relations/publicity, sales promotion, and/or reseller support.

Meaningful objectives can also be a useful guide for decision making. Promotional planners are often faced with a number of strategic and tactical options in terms of choosing creative options, selecting media, and allocating the budget among various elements of the promotional mix. Choices should be made based on how well a particular strategy matches the firm's promotional objectives.

Measurement and Evaluation of Results

An important reason for setting specific objectives is that they provide a benchmark against which the success or failure of the promotional campaign can be measured. Without specific objectives, it is extremely difficult to determine what the firm's advertising and promotion efforts accomplished. One characteristic of good objectives is that they are *measurable;* they specify a method and criteria for determining how well the promotional program is working. By setting specific and meaningful objectives, the promotional planner provides a measure(s) that can be used to evaluate the effectiveness of the marketing communications program. Most organizations are concerned about the return on their promotional investment, and comparing actual performance against measurable objectives is the best way to determine if the return justifies the expense—a position obviously advocated by Kellogg's Knowlton.

DETERMINING PROMOTIONAL OBJECTIVES

Integrated marketing communications objectives should be based on a thorough situation analysis that identifies the marketing and promotional issues facing the company or a brand. The situation analysis is the foundation on which marketing objectives are determined and the marketing plan is developed. Promotional objectives evolve from the company's overall marketing plan and are rooted in its marketing objectives. Advertising and promotion objectives are not the same as marketing objectives (although many firms tend to treat them as synonymous).

Marketing versus Communications Objectives

Marketing objectives are generally stated in the firm's marketing plan and are statements of what is to be accomplished by the overall marketing program within a given time period. Marketing objectives are usually defined in terms of specific, measurable outcomes such as sales volume, market share, profits, or return on investment. Good marketing objectives are *quantifiable;* delineate the target market and note the time frame for accomplishing the goal (often one year). For example, a copy machine company may have as its marketing objective "to increase sales by 10 percent in the small business segment of the market during the next 12 months." To be effective, objectives must also be *realistic* and *attainable.*

A company with a very high market share may seek to increase its sales volume by stimulating growth in the product category. It might accomplish this by increasing consumption by current users or encouraging nonusers to use the product. Some firms have as their marketing objectives expanding distribution and sales of their product in certain market areas. Companies often have secondary marketing objectives that are related to actions they must take to solve specific problems and thus achieve their primary objectives. For example, in the early 1990s San Antonio–based Pace Foods began a promotional campaign to expand its business beyond its traditional Texas base. To achieve this objective, its agency set out to establish a position of authenticity and make Mexican food seem fun. An advertising campaign for Pace picante sauce pokes fun at the New York City origins of a fictitious rival brand. Pace's vice president of sales and marketing says the idea behind the campaign was that Pace's sauce is created by people who live "where folks know what salsa should be." Pace also uses various sales promotion tools such as coupons, promotional tie-ins, and point-of-purchase displays to generate sales (Exhibit 7–2). Sales of Pace picante sauce have tripled and its 28 percent brand share makes it the market leader in a category that has surpassed ketchup.[3]

Once the marketing communications manager has reviewed the marketing plan, he or she should understand where the company hopes to go with its marketing program, how it intends to get there, and the role advertising and promotion will play. Marketing goals defined in terms of sales, profit, or market share increases are usually not appropriate promotional objectives. They are objectives for the entire marketing program, and achieving them depends on the proper coordination and execution of all the marketing mix elements, including not just promotion but product planning and production, pricing, and distribution.

EXHIBIT 7–2
Pace Foods' New York City campaign has helped expand sales beyond the Texas market

Integrated marketing communications objectives are statements of what various aspects of the IMC program will accomplish. They should be based on the particular communications tasks required to deliver the appropriate messages to the target audience. Managers must be able to translate general marketing goals into communications goals and specific promotional objectives. Some guidance in doing this may be available from the marketing plan, as the situation analysis should provide important information on

- The market segments the firm wants to target and the target audience (demographics, psychographics, and purchase motives).
- The product and its main features, advantages, benefits, uses, and applications.
- The company's and competitors' brands (sales and market share in various segments, positioning, competitive strategies, promotional expenditures, creative and media strategies, and tactics).
- Ideas on how the brand should be positioned and specific behavioral responses being sought (trial, repurchase, brand switching, and increased usage).

For example, the ads for Del Monte stewed tomatoes and snack cups in Exhibit 7–3 were part of the company's marketing strategy to increase sales and market share for its various food products by targeting existing or lapsed users as well as new, younger customers. The 12-month, $20 million advertising campaign used a series of four-color ads featuring new recipe ideas and serving suggestions. All of the ads used the same graphic format to help build the overall franchise for Del Monte brands while promoting individual products. The campaign resulted in increased market share for all four of the advertised categories.

Sometimes companies do not have a formal marketing plan, and the information needed may not be readily available. In this case, the promotional planner must attempt to gather as much information as possible about the product and its markets from sources both inside and outside the company.

After reviewing all the information, the promotional planner should see how integrated marketing communications fits into the marketing program and what the firm hopes to achieve through advertising and other promotional elements. The next step is to set objectives in terms of specific communications goals or tasks.

Many promotional planners approach promotion from a communications perspective and believe the objective of advertising and other promotional mix elements is usually to communicate information or a selling message about a product or service. Other managers argue that sales or some related measure, such as market share, is the only meaningful goal for advertising and promotion and should be the basis for setting objectives. These two perspectives have been the topic of considerable debate and are worth examining further.

EXHIBIT 7–3
These ads for Del Monte food products were part of a marketing strategy designed to increase sales and market share

SALES VERSUS COMMUNICATIONS OBJECTIVES
Sales-Oriented Objectives

To many managers, the only meaningful objective for their promotional program is sales. They take the position that the basic reason a firm spends money on advertising and promotion is to sell its product or service. Promotional spending represents an investment of a firm's scarce resources that requires an economic justification. Rational managers generally compare investment options on a common financial basis, such as return on investment (ROI). As we'll discuss later in this chapter, determining the specific return on advertising and promotional dollars is often quite difficult. However, many managers believe that monies spent on advertising and other forms of promotion should produce measurable results, such as increasing sales volume by a certain percentage or dollar amount or increasing the brand's market share. They believe objectives (as well as the success or failure of the campaign) should be based on the achievement of sales results.

Some managers prefer sales-oriented objectives to make the individuals involved in advertising and promotion think in terms of how the promotional program will influence sales. Or they may confuse marketing objectives with advertising and promotional objectives. For example, for Kellogg and Post, the goal was to increase sales and market share versus store brands. This goal not only became the basis of the marketing plan but carried over as the primary objective of the promotional program. The success of the advertising and promotional campaign is judged only by attainment of these goals.

PROBLEMS WITH SALES OBJECTIVES

If Kellogg and Post fail to reverse their sales declines, does this mean the advertising and promotional program was ineffective? Or does it mean the price cuts didn't work? It might help to compare this situation to a football game and think of advertising as a quarterback. The quarterback is one of the most important players on the team but can be effective only with support from the other players. If the team loses, is it fair to blame the loss entirely on the quarterback? Of course not. Just as the quarterback is but one of the players on the football team, promotion is but one element of the marketing program, and there are many other reasons why the targeted sales level was not reached. The quarterback can lead his team to victory only if the linemen block, the receivers catch his passes, and the running backs help the offense establish a balanced attack of running and passing. Even if the quarterback plays an outstanding game, the team can still lose if the defense gives up too many points.

In the business world, poor sales results could be due to any of the other marketing mix variables, including product design or quality, packaging, distribution, or pricing. Advertising can make consumers aware of and interested in the brand, but it can't make them buy it, particularly if it is not readily available or is priced higher than a competing brand. As shown in Figure 7–1, sales are a function of many factors, not just advertising and promotion. IMC Perspective 7–1 discusses Nissan Motor Co.'s search for an advertising campaign that will help increase sales of its Infiniti automobiles in the highly competitive luxury segment of the U.S. market.

Another problem with sales objectives is that the effects of advertising often occur over an extended period. Many experts recognize that advertising has a lagged or **carryover effect**; monies spent on advertising do not necessarily have an immediate impact on sales.[4] Advertising may create awareness, interest, and/or favorable attitudes toward a brand, but these feelings will not result in an actual purchase until the consumer enters the market for the product, which may occur later. A review of econometric studies that examined the duration of cumulative advertising effects found that for mature, frequently purchased, low-priced products, advertising's effect on sales lasts up to nine months.[5] Models have been developed to account for the carryover effect of advertising and to help determine the long-term effect of advertising on sales.[6] The carryover effect adds to the difficulty of determining the precise relationship between advertising and sales.

Another problem with sales objectives is that they offer little guidance to those responsible for planning and developing the promotional program. The creative and media people working on the account need some direction as to the nature of the advertising message the company hopes to communicate, the intended audience, and the particular effect or response sought. As you will see shortly, communications objectives are recommended be-

FIGURE 7–1
Factors influencing sales

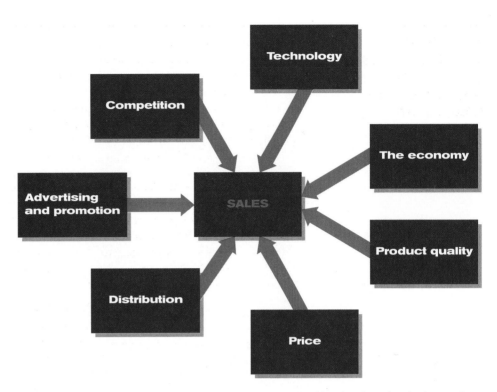

cause they provide operational guidelines for those involved in planning, developing, and executing the advertising and promotional program.

WHERE SALES OBJECTIVES ARE APPROPRIATE

While there can be many problems in attempting to use sales as objectives for a promotional campaign, there are situations where sales objectives are appropriate. Certain types of promotion efforts are direct action in nature; they attempt to induce an immediate behavioral response from the prospective customer. A major objective of most sales promotion programs is to generate short-term increases in sales. When Microsoft introduced its Windows 95 operating system, it spent an estimated $200 million in the first year to create awareness and interest in the new product. A 30-minute "info-show," tie-in promotions with Cracker Jack, prelaunch parties and public relations activities around the world, point-of-sale displays, and millions of dollars in advertising were all part of the introduction. At the same time, Microsoft expected to sell over 82 million copies of Win95 in the first year[7] (Exhibit 7–4).

EXHIBIT 7–4
Microsoft spent $200 million to
launch Windows 95

IMC Perspective 7—1
Relaunching Infiniti

In 1989, Nissan Motor Co.'s Infiniti division introduced its two new luxury automobiles to the U.S. market. The Infiniti division was formed to manufacture and market cars to compete in the luxury sports sedan segment, which includes the established European imports such as BMW, Mercedes, and Volvo, as well as two Japanese luxury cars, Acura (a division of Honda Motors) and Lexus (a division of Toyota).

Many ad agencies introduce new automobiles by immediately focusing on the cars and saying great things about them. But Hill, Holliday, Connors, Cosmopulos, the original agency for Infiniti, decided to take an unconventional approach by creating commercials and print ads that showed scenes of rocks, trees, clouds, the ocean, and even flying geese—but never the cars. The ads aimed to explain the philosophy behind the design of the new cars and to position the Infiniti as a new kind of luxury car with a "Japanese sense of luxury."

The teaser campaign used to launch the Infiniti was very successful from several perspectives. The ads generated requests for information about the cars and visits to dealer showrooms. They also scored very high in surveys of advertising awareness; consumers still cited them a year after they stopped running. Yet initial sales of the Infiniti were well below forecast, so the company responded to dealer demands for more product-oriented advertising.

Ensuing campaigns focused on the cars and hammered home the performance theme, but by March of 1993 Infiniti had only a 3.9 percent share of the U.S. luxury market, compared with Lexus's 7.7 percent and Mercedes' 4.5 percent. The company aimed to change this with its Q45, which was redesigned to move Infiniti into the mainstream of the market, with more than enhancements intended to push the traditional luxury car buyer's hot button. Infiniti also embarked on a new advertising approach that represented a sharp change from earlier campaigns.

A new agency, Chiat/Day Advertising, Inc., was hired, and a new strategy was developed. The new strategy involves presenting the car, and the company, in a series of individual ads that each highlighted a single Infiniti feature. The look of the campaign was sparse: a dramatically lit car on a sweeping expanse of white background. Jonathan Pryce was chosen as a celebrity spokesperson for the campaign. Unfortunately, sales of the Q45 lagged far behind those of rival Lexus LS 400.

In 1996 Infiniti announced that it was dramatically changing its ad campaign to launch the 1997 Q45. While Jonathan Pryce would be kept, the new campaign "Everything has changed but the soul," clearly repositions the Q45 as a luxurious automobile. With ads (now in color) depicting elegance and set in Prague and Barcelona, Infiniti hoped to build upon the emotional atmosphere of elegance and sophistication provided in earlier campaigns. Pryce informs the viewer that "one of the world's best-performing luxury cars has an almost entirely new identity."

Some critics say the original campaign and subsequent advertising for the Infiniti did not send the right message to luxury car buyers. Others offer other reasons for the less-than-hoped-for results. Infiniti hoped that the reinventing of its image would change all that starting in 1997, but apparently it did not as in April 1997 Infiniti again announced a change in strategy. A new campaign created by TBWA Chiat/Day dispensed with ad spokesman Pryce in favor of a focus on the Infiniti ownership experience. The new campaign titled "Own One and You'll Understand" is intended to reconnect with consumers through straight talk about Infiniti's high customer satisfaction. Infiniti hopes to finally shift into drive with a new approach once again.

Sources: Steve Gelsi, "Pryce Slashed: Infiniti to Refocus on Ownership, Value," *Brandweek* February 3, 1997, p. 1; Michelle Krebs, "Behind the Wheel/Infiniti Q45"; Even the Spirit Is Scaled Down," *The New York Times*, October 20, 1996, p. 1; "It's No Masquerade—Infiniti Unveils the New Q45 Ad Campaign; Everything Has Changed But the Soul," *PR Newswire*, September 18, 1996, p. 7; "Infiniti Ad Trigger Auto Debate," *Advertising Age*, January 22, 1990, p. 49; and Larry Armstrong, "Infiniti: If at First You Don't Succeed," *Business Week*, May 3, 1993, pp. 126–27.

Direct-response advertising is one type of advertising that evaluates its effectiveness on the basis of sales. Merchandise is advertised in material mailed to customers, in newspapers and magazines, or on television. The consumer purchases the merchandise by mail or by calling a toll-free number. The direct-response advertiser generally sets objectives and measures success in terms of the sales response generated by the ad. For example, objectives for and the evaluation of a direct-response ad on TV are based on the number of orders received each time a station broadcasts the commercial. Because advertising is really the only form of communication and promotion used in this situation and response is generally immediate, setting objectives in terms of sales is appropriate. The Fast Track™ exerciser shown in Exhibit 7–5 is an example of a product sold through direct-response advertising.

Retail advertising, which accounts for a significant percentage of all advertising expenditures, is another area where the advertiser often seeks a direct response, particularly when sales or special events are being promoted. The ad for Service Merchandise's Valentine's Day

EXHIBIT 7–5
Sales results are an appropriate objective for direct-response advertising

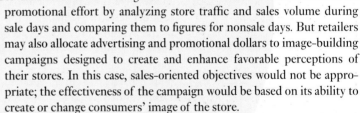

sale shown here is designed to attract consumers to stores during the sales period (and to generate sales volume). Service Merchandise management can determine the effectiveness of its promotional effort by analyzing store traffic and sales volume during sale days and comparing them to figures for nonsale days. But retailers may also allocate advertising and promotional dollars to image-building campaigns designed to create and enhance favorable perceptions of their stores. In this case, sales-oriented objectives would not be appropriate; the effectiveness of the campaign would be based on its ability to create or change consumers' image of the store.

Sales-oriented objectives are also used when advertising plays a dominant role in a firm's marketing program and other factors are relatively stable. For example, many package-goods products compete in mature markets with established channels of distribution, stable competitive prices and promotional budgets, and products of similar quality. They view advertising and sales promotion as the key determinants of a brand's sales or market share, so it may be possible to isolate the effects of these promotional mix variables.[8] Many companies have accumulated enough market knowledge with their advertising, sales promotion, and direct marketing programs to have considerable insight into the sales levels that should result from their promotional efforts. Thus, they believe it is reasonable to set objectives and evaluate the success of their promotional efforts in terms of sales results. Established brands are often repositioned (as discussed in Chapter 2) with the goal of improving their sales or relative market share.

Advertising and promotional programs tend to be evaluated in terms of sales, particularly when expectations are not being met. Marketing and brand managers under pressure to show sales results often take a short-term perspective in evaluating advertising and sales promotion programs. They are often looking for a quick fix for declining sales or loss of market share. They ignore the pitfalls of making direct links between advertising and sales, and campaigns, as well as ad agencies, may be changed if sales expectations are not being met. As discussed in Chapter 3, many companies want their agencies to accept incentive-based compensation systems tied to sales performance. Thus, while sales may not be an appropriate objective in many advertising and promotional situations, managers are inclined to keep a close eye on sales and market share figures and make changes in the promotional program when these numbers become stagnant.

Communications Objectives

Some marketers do recognize the problems associated with sales-oriented objectives. They recognize that the primary role of an IMC program is to communicate and that planning should be based on communications objectives. Advertising and other promotional efforts are designed to achieve such communications as brand knowledge and interest, favorable attitudes and image, and purchase intentions. Consumers are not expected to respond immediately; rather, advertisers realize they must provide relevant information and create favorable predispositions toward the brand before purchase behavior will occur.

For example, the ad for Dooney & Bourke leather goods in Exhibit 7–6 is designed to inform consumers of the product's tradition and craftsmanship. While there is no call for immediate action, the ad creates favorable impressions about the product so that consumers will consider it when they enter the market for leather products.

Advocates of communications-based objectives generally use some form of the hierarchical models discussed in Chapter 5 when setting advertising and promotion objectives. In all these models, consumers pass through three successive stages: cognitive, affective, and conative. As consumers proceed through the three stages, they move closer to making a purchase. Figure 7–2 shows the various steps in the Lavidge and Steiner hierarchy of effects model as the consumer moves from awareness to purchase, along with examples of types of promotion or advertising relevant to each step.

COMMUNICATIONS EFFECTS PYRAMID

Advertising and promotion perform communications tasks as a pyramid is built, by first accomplishing lower-level objectives such as awareness and knowledge or comprehension.[9] Subsequent tasks involve moving consumers who are aware of or knowledgeable about the product or service to higher levels in the pyramid (Figure 7–3). The initial stages, at the base of the pyramid, are easier to accomplish than those toward the top, such as trial and repurchase or regular use. Thus, the percentage of prospective customers will decline as they move up the pyramid. Figure 7–4 shows how a company introducing a new brand of shampoo targeted at 18- to 34-year-old females might set its IMC objectives using the communications effects pyramid.

The communications pyramid can also be used to determine promotional objectives for an established brand. The promotional planner must determine where the target audience

EXHIBIT 7–6
Dooney & Bourke creates an image of quality products

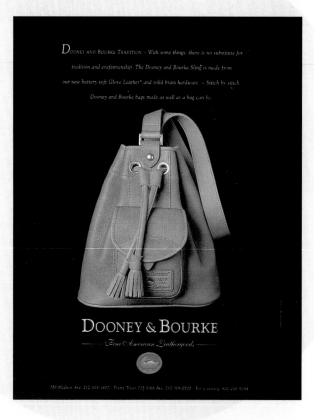

FIGURE 7–2
Effect of advertising on consumers:
movement from awareness to action

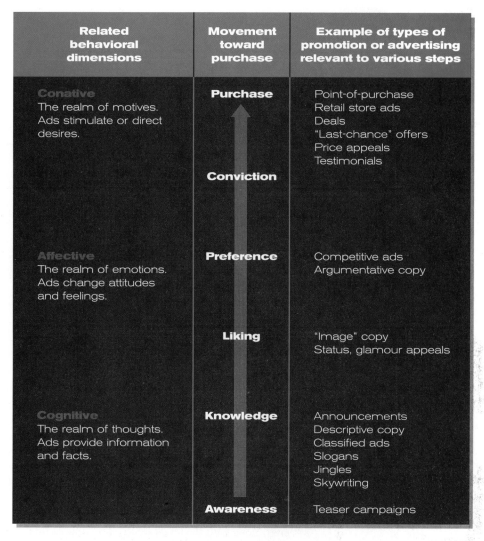

Related behavioral dimensions	Movement toward purchase	Example of types of promotion or advertising relevant to various steps
Conative The realm of motives. Ads stimulate or direct desires.	**Purchase** **Conviction**	Point-of-purchase Retail store ads Deals "Last-chance" offers Price appeals Testimonials
Affective The realm of emotions. Ads change attitudes and feelings.	**Preference** **Liking**	Competitive ads Argumentative copy "Image" copy Status, glamour appeals
Cognitive The realm of thoughts. Ads provide information and facts.	**Knowledge** **Awareness**	Announcements Descriptive copy Classified ads Slogans Jingles Skywriting Teaser campaigns

lies with respect to the various blocks in the pyramid. If awareness levels for a brand and knowledge of its features and benefits are low, the communications objective should be to increase them. If these blocks of the pyramid are already in place, but liking or preference is low, the advertising goal may be to change the target markets' image of the brand and move them through to purchase.

PROBLEMS WITH COMMUNICATIONS OBJECTIVES

Not all marketing and advertising managers accept communications objectives; some say it is too difficult to translate a sales goal into a specific communications objective. But at some point a sales goal must be transformed into a communications objective. If the marketing plan for an established brand has as an objective increasing sales by 10 percent, the promotional planner will eventually have to think in terms of the message that will be communicated to the target audience to achieve this. Possible objectives include the following:

- Increasing the percentage of consumers in the target market who associate specific features, benefits, or advantages with our brand.
- Increasing the number of consumers in the target audience who prefer our product over the competition's.
- Encouraging current users of the product to use it more frequently or in more situations.
- Encouraging consumers who have never used our brand to try it.

In some situations, promotional planners may gain insight into communications objectives' relationship to sales from industry research. Evalucom, Inc., conducted a study of

effects pyramid

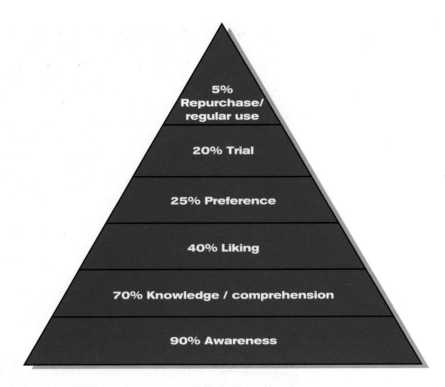

commercials for new products. Some succeeded in stimulating anticipated levels of sales; others did not. Figure 7–5 shows four factors the study identified that affect whether a commercial for a new product is successful in generating sales.

In attempting to translate sales goals into specific communications objectives, promotional planners often are not sure what constitutes adequate levels of awareness, knowledge, liking, preference, or conviction. There are no formulas to provide this information. The promotional manager will have to use his or her personal experience and that of the brand or product managers, as well as the marketing history of this and similar brands. Average scores on various communications measures for this and similar products should be considered, along with the levels achieved by competitors' products. This information can be related to the amount of money and time spent building these levels as well as the resulting sales or market share figures.

At some point, sales-oriented objectives must be translated into what the company hopes to communicate and to whom it hopes to communicate it. For example, Milwaukee-based Midwest Express Airlines found itself in a situation where business travelers, its primary

FIGURE 7–4
Setting objectives using the communications effects pyramid

Product: Backstage Shampoo

Time period: Six months

Objective 1: Create awareness among 90 percent of target audience. Use repetitive advertising in newspapers, magazines, TV and radio programs. Simple message.

Objective 2: Create interest in the brand among 70 percent of target audience. Communicate information about the features and benefits of the brand—i.e., that it contains no soap and improves the texture of the hair

Objective 3: Create positive feelings about the brand among 40 percent and preference among 25 percent of the target audience. Create favorable attitudes by conveying information, promotions, sampling, etc.

Objective 4: Obtain trial among 20 percent of the target audience. Use sampling and cents-off coupons along with advertising and promotions.

Objective 5: Develop and maintain regular use of Backstage Shampoo among 5 percent of the target audience. Use continued reinforcement advertising, fewer coupons and promotions

FIGURE 7–5
Factors related to success of
advertising for new products

- **Communicating that something is different about the product.** Successful introductory commercials communicated some point of difference for the new product.

- **Positioning the brand difference in relation to the product category.** Successful commercials positioned their brand's difference within a specific product category. For example, a new breakfast product was positioned as the "crispiest cereal" or a new beverage as the "smoothest soft drink."

- **Communicating that the product difference is beneficial to consumers.** Nearly all of the successful commercials linked a benefit directly to the new product's difference.

- **Supporting the idea that something about the product is different and/or beneficial to consumers.** All the successful commercials communicated support for the product's difference claim or its relevance to consumers. Support took the form of demonstrations of performance, information supporting a uniqueness claim, endorsements, or testimonials.

Source: Kirby Andrews, "Communications Imperatives for New Products," *Journal of Advertising Research* 26, no. 5 (October/November 1986), pp. 29–32.

market, assumed that the airline's high level of service meant premium prices. To combat this perception, the "Best care. Same fare" campaign was developed. In the commercials, a man claimed Midwest's fares were higher, only to be told flatly by a female colleague that he was wrong. The conversations occurred in humorous settings, such as one where a man scrambles up a down escalator to keep up with a woman (Exhibit 7–7). Midwest was able to communicate its competitive fares and achieve its sales objective. The number of people who thought Midwest cost more than competitors declined by 17 percent within six months, while the airline's market share grew from 19 percent to 25 percent.[10]

Many marketing and promotional managers recognize the value of setting specific communications objectives and their important role as operational guidelines to the planning,

EXHIBIT 7–7
Midwest Express increased its
market share by advertising its
competitive fares

execution, and evaluation of the promotional program. Communications objectives are the criteria used in the DAGMAR approach to setting advertising goals and objectives, which has become one of the most influential approaches to the advertising planning process.

DAGMAR: AN APPROACH TO SETTING OBJECTIVES

In 1961, Russell Colley prepared a report for the Association of National Advertisers titled *Defining Advertising Goals for Measured Advertising Results* (DAGMAR).[11] In it, Colley developed a model for setting advertising objectives and measuring the results of an ad campaign. The major thesis of the **DAGMAR** model is that communications effects are the logical basis for advertising goals and objectives against which success or failure should be measured. Colley's rationale for communications-based objectives was as follows:

> Advertising's job, purely and simply, is to communicate to a defined audience information and a frame of mind that stimulates action. Advertising succeeds or fails depending on how well it communicates the desired information and attitudes to the right people at the right time and at the right cost.[12]

Under the DAGMAR approach, an advertising goal involves a **communications task** that is specific and measurable. A communications task, as opposed to a marketing task, can be performed by, and attributed to, advertising rather than to a combination of several marketing factors. Colley proposed that the communications task be based on a hierarchical model of the communications process with four stages:

- *Awareness*—making the consumer aware of the existence of the brand or company.
- *Comprehension*—developing an understanding of what the product is and what it will do for the consumer.
- *Conviction*—developing a mental disposition in the consumer to buy the product.
- *Action*—getting the consumer to purchase the product.

As discussed earlier, other hierarchical models of advertising effects can be used as a basis for analyzing the communications response process. Some advertising theorists prefer the Lavidge and Steiner hierarchy of effects model, since it is more specific and provides a better way to establish and measure results.[13]

While the hierarchical model of advertising effects was the basic model of the communications response process used in DAGMAR, Colley also studied other specific tasks that advertising might be expected to perform in leading to the ultimate objective of a sale. He developed a checklist of 52 advertising tasks to characterize the contribution of advertising and serve as a starting point for establishing objectives.

Characteristics of Objectives

A second major contribution of DAGMAR to the advertising planning process was its definition of what constitutes a good objective. Colley argued that advertising objectives should be stated in terms of concrete and measurable communications tasks, specify a target audience, indicate a benchmark starting point and the degree of change sought, and specify a time period for accomplishing the objective(s).

CONCRETE, MEASURABLE TASKS

The communications task specified in the objective should be a precise statement of what appeal or message the advertiser wants to communicate to the target audience. Advertisers generally use a copy platform to describe their basic message. The objective or copy platform statement should be specific and clear enough to guide the creative specialists who develop the advertising message. In the Midwest Express example, the objective was to combat the perception that its fares were higher than competitors'.

According to DAGMAR, the objective must also be measurable. There must be a way to determine whether the intended message has been communicated properly. Midwest Express measured its communications objective by asking airline travelers whether they thought Midwest's airfares were higher than those of competing airlines.

TARGET AUDIENCE

Another important characteristic of good objectives is a well-defined target audience. The primary target audience for a company's product or service is described in the situation analysis. It may be based on descriptive variables such as geography, demographics, and psychographics (on which advertising media selection decisions are based) as well as on behavioral variables such as usage rate or benefits sought. For example, Sonance, a company that makes architectural audio systems that include in-wall speakers and controls, defines its target audience as "affluent audio enthusiasts who are also design trendsetters." To reach this target market and communicate its message of "total audio ambiance," Sonance advertises in upscale, design-oriented magazines such as *Architectural Digest* (Exhibit 7–8).

BENCHMARK AND DEGREE OF CHANGE SOUGHT

To set objectives, one must know the target audience's present status concerning response hierarchy variables such as awareness, knowledge, image, attitudes, and intentions, and then determine the degree to which consumers must be changed by the advertising campaign. Determining the target market's present position regarding the various response stages requires **benchmark measures**. Often a marketing research study must be conducted to determine prevailing levels of the response hierarchy. In the case of a new product or service, the starting conditions are generally at or near zero for all the variables, so no initial research is needed.

Establishing benchmark measures gives the promotional planner a basis for determining what communications tasks need to be accomplished and for specifying particular objectives. For example, a preliminary study for a brand may reveal that awareness is high but consumer perceptions and attitudes are negative. The objective for the advertising campaign must then be to change the target audience's perceptions of and attitudes toward the brand. IMC Perspective 7–2 discusses how Hush Puppies shoes developed a new advertising campaign in response to this situation.

Quantitative benchmarks are not only valuable in establishing communications goals and objectives but essential to determining whether the campaign was successful. Objectives provide the standard against which the success or failure of a campaign is measured. An ad campaign that results in a 90 percent awareness level for a brand among its target audience cannot really be judged effective unless one knows what percentage of the consumers were aware of the brand before the campaign began. A 70 percent precampaign awareness level would lead to a different interpretation of the campaign's success than would a 30 percent level.

EXHIBIT 7–8
Sonance's target audience is the upscale audio enthusiast and design trendsetter

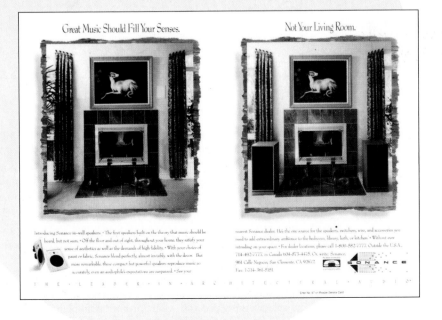

IMC Perspective 7–2
Selling Hush Puppies to a New Generation

For more than 30 years, the cuddly, rumpled, droopy-eyed Hush Puppies basset hound has been an advertising icon familiar to most consumers. But the brand has suffered from image problems for nearly as long. To many consumers, Hush Puppies are old-fashioned, conservative, fuzzy pigskin loafers. The last time Hush Puppies were considered hip, John F. Kennedy was president. Now Wolverine Worldwide, Inc., the maker of Hush Puppies, is out to change this.

Wolverine's CEO, Geoff Bloom, says, "We want to see those nifty, natural, contemporary younger people wearing our shoes." To achieve this goal, the company developed a new mix of products and recently launched a $3 million print ad campaign aimed at casting aside Hush Puppies' loafer image and appealing to Americans who are more familiar with MTV than Ed Sullivan. Advertising spending was increased fourfold; ads in magazines such as *Details*, *Wired*, *Glamour*, and even *GQ* show Hush Puppies on the feet of youthful models whom Wolverine calls "aspirational" people who tout the tagline "We invented casual." The new ads, and the magazines in which they appear, are a big departure from Hush Puppies' more familiar lifestyle ads, and even the brand's signature mascot has been shrunk and relegated to the bottom of the ads.

So far the campaign seems to be working. The shoes are back on the fast track. "Duke" loafer and oxford sales are up to over 400,000 pairs from 60,000. The biggest sales are coming from upscale stores like Nordstrom and Barneys New York. Fashion designers put Hush Puppies on the feet of Forrest Gump and in the Broadway play *Damn Yankees*. Anna Sui, one of New York's most famous fashion designers, had her models walk down the runway in several Hush Puppies styles. Young people in 60 countries buy Hush Puppies for their American cachet.

But shoe manufacturers know that fashion can be a faddish thing, and Wolverine is taking no chances. New ads are being developed, new versions of the classic styles are being designed, and TV and movie actors are being courted, including Jerry Seinfeld and Tom Hanks. In 1997 Hush Puppies began its first television advertising in a decade with a campaign targeting 18- to 34-year olds. The offbeat spots show only the feet of reclining Hush Puppies wearers, whose views of the world are favorably changed by moving their feet. All of the spots in the campaign use the "We invented casual" slogan.

Wolverine also has a major Hush Puppies push underway in the United Kingdom, where it recently bought back the license to the brand name. The company is exporting its fashion positioning by using print ads for the hot-colored suedes. Having now successfully changed attitudes toward Hush Puppies, Wolverine wants to make sure they remain changed.

Sources: Jean Halliday, "Hush Puppies Unleashes TV Effort," *Advertising Age*, February 24, 1997, pp. 16–17; Teri Agins, " As Casual Gets Hip, Hush Puppies Embarks on a New Ad Campaign," *The Wall Street Journal*, November 1, 1995, p. B9; Oscar Suris, "Ads Aim to Sell Hush Puppies to New Yuppies," *The Wall Street Journal*, July 28, 1993, p. B1. Reprinted by permission of *The Wall Street Journal*, ©1995, 1993 Dow Jones & Company, Inc. All Rights Reserved Worldwide.

SPECIFIED TIME PERIOD

A final consideration in setting advertising objectives is specifying the time period in which they must be accomplished. Appropriate time periods can range from a few days to a year or more. Most ad campaigns specify time periods from a few months to a year, depending on the situation facing the advertiser and the type of response being sought. For example, awareness levels for a brand can be created or increased fairly quickly through an intensive media schedule of widespread, repetitive advertising to the target audience. Repositioning of a product requires a change in consumers' perceptions and takes much more time. The repositioning of Marlboro cigarettes from a feminine brand to one with a masculine image, for instance, took several years.

Assessment of DAGMAR

The DAGMAR approach to setting objectives has had considerable influence on the advertising planning process. Many promotional planners use this model as a basis for setting objectives and assessing the effectiveness of their promotional campaigns. DAGMAR also focused advertisers' attention on the value of using communications-based rather than sales-based objectives to measure advertising effectiveness and encouraged the measurement of stages in the response hierarchy to assess a campaign's impact. Colley's work has led to improvements in the advertising and promotional planning process by providing a better understanding of the goals and objectives toward which planners' efforts should be directed. This usually results in less subjectivity and also leads to better communication and relationships between the client and its agency.

CRITICISMS OF DAGMAR

While DAGMAR has contributed to the advertising planning process, it has not been totally accepted by everyone in the advertising field. A number of problems have led to questions regarding its value as an advertising planning tool.[14]

- *Problems with the response hierarchy.* A major criticism of the DAGMAR approach is its reliance on the hierarchy of effects model. The fact that consumers do not always go through this sequence of communications effects before making a purchase has been recognized, and alternative response models have been developed.[15] DAGMAR MOD II recognizes that the appropriate response model depends on the situation and emphasizes identifying the sequence of decision-making steps that apply in a buying situation.[16]
- *Sales objectives.* Another objection to DAGMAR comes from those who argue that the only relevant measure of advertising objectives is sales. They have little tolerance for ad campaigns that achieve communications objectives but fail to increase sales. Advertising is seen as effective only if it induces consumers to make a purchase.[17] The problems with this logic were addressed in our discussion of communications objectives.
- *Practicality and costs.* Another criticism of DAGMAR concerns the difficulties involved in implementing it. Money must be spent on research to establish quantitative benchmarks and measure changes in the response hierarchy. This is costly and time consuming and can lead to considerable disagreement over method, criteria, measures, and so forth. Many critics argue that DAGMAR is practical only for large companies with big advertising and research budgets. Many firms do not want to spend the money needed to use DAGMAR effectively.
- *Inhibition of creativity.* A final criticism of DAGMAR is that it inhibits advertising creativity by imposing too much structure on the people responsible for developing the advertising. Many creative personnel think the DAGMAR approach is too concerned with quantitative assessment of a campaign's impact on awareness, brand name recall, or specific persuasion measures. The emphasis is on passing the numbers test rather than developing a message that is truly creative and contributes to brand equity.

PROBLEMS IN SETTING OBJECTIVES

Although the DAGMAR model suggests a logical process for advertising and promotion planning, most advertisers and their agencies fail to follow these basic principles. They fail to set specific objectives for their campaigns and/or do not have the proper evidence to determine the success of their promotional programs. A classic study conducted by Stewart H. Britt examined problems with how advertisers set objectives and measure their accomplishment.[18] The study showed that most advertising agencies did not state appropriate objectives for determining success and thus could not demonstrate whether a supposedly successful campaign was really a success. Even though these campaigns may have been doing something right, they generally did not know what it was.

Although this study was conducted in 1969, the same problems exist in advertising today. A more recent study examined the advertising practices of business-to-business marketers to determine whether their ads used advertising objectives that met Colley's four DAGMAR criteria.[19] Entries from the annual Business/Professional Advertising Association Gold Key Awards competition, which solicits the best marketing communications efforts from business-to-business advertisers, were evaluated with respect to their campaigns' objectives and summaries of results. Most of these advertisers did not set concrete advertising objectives, specify objective tasks, measure results in terms of stages of a hierarchy of effects, or match objectives to evaluation measures. The authors concluded: "Advertising practitioners have only partially adopted the concepts and standards of objective setting and evaluation set forth 25 years ago."[20]

Improving Promotional Planners' Use of Objectives

As we have seen, it is important that advertisers and their agencies pay close attention to the objectives they set for their campaigns. They should strive to set specific and measurable objectives that not only guide promotional planning and decision making but also can be used as a standard for evaluating performance. Unfortunately, many companies do not set appropriate objectives for their integrated marketing communications programs.

Many companies fail to set appropriate objectives because top management has only an abstract idea of what the firm's IMC program is supposed to be doing. In a study by the American Business Press that measured the attitudes of chairs, presidents, and other senior managers of business-to-business advertising companies, more than half of the 427 respondents said they did not know whether their advertising was working and less than 10 percent thought it was working well.[21] This study showed overwhelmingly that top management did not even know what the company's advertising was supposed to do, much less how to measure it.

Few firms will set objectives that meet all the criteria set forth in DAGMAR. However, promotional planners should set objectives that are specific and measurable and go beyond basic sales goals. Even if specific communications response elements are not always measured, meeting the other criteria will sharpen the focus and improve the quality of the IMC planning process.

Setting Objectives for the IMC Program

One reason so much attention is given to advertising objectives is that for many companies advertising has traditionally been the major way of communicating with target audiences. Other promotional mix elements such as sales promotion, direct marketing, and publicity are used intermittently to support and complement the advertising program.

Another reason is that traditional advertising-based views of marketing communications planning, such as DAGMAR, have dominated the field for so long. These approaches are based on a hierarchical response model and consider how marketers can develop and disseminate advertising messages to move consumers along an effects path. This approach, shown in Figure 7–6, is what professor Don Schultz calls *inside-out planning*. He says, "It focuses on what the marketer wants to say, when the marketer wants to say it, about things the marketer believes are important about his or her brand, and in the media forms the marketer wants to use."[22]

Schultz advocates an *outside-in planning* process for IMC that starts with the customer and builds backward to the brand. This means that promotional planners study the various media customers and prospects use, when the marketer's messages might be most relevant to customers, and when they are likely to be most receptive to the message.

A similar approach is suggested by Professor Tom Duncan, who argues that IMC should use **zero-based communications planning**, which involves determining what tasks need

FIGURE 7–6
Traditional advertising-based view of marketing communications

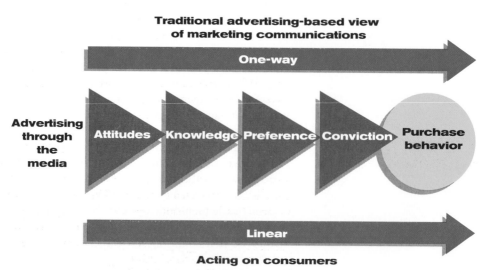

Traditional advertising-based view of marketing communications

One-way

Advertising through the media

Attitudes   Knowledge   Preference   Conviction   Purchase behavior

Linear

Acting on consumers

to be done and which marketing communications functions should be used and to what extent.[23] This approach focuses on the task to be done and searches for the best ideas and media to accomplish it. He notes that as with a traditional advertising campaign, the basis of an IMC campaign is a big idea. However, in IMC the big idea can be public relations, direct response, packaging, or sales promotion. Duncan suggests that an effective IMC program should lead with the marketing communications function that most effectively addresses the company's main problem or opportunity and should use a promotional mix that draws on the strengths of whichever communications functions relate best to the particular situation.

Many of the considerations for determining advertising objectives are relevant to setting goals for other elements of the integrated marketing communications program. The promotional planner should determine what role various sales promotion techniques, publicity and public relations, direct marketing, and personal selling will play in the overall marketing program and how they will interact with advertising as well as with one another.

ALL SEALS, OUT OF THE POOL.

This summer, the world's greatest divers aren't in Atlanta. You can see them at the World Famous San Diego Zoo's newest and coolest exhibit, opening June 29. At Polar Bear Plunge, we've created a natural summer arctic environment with a spectacular 125,000-gallon pool as its centerpiece. Through a huge window, you can watch as our polar bears splash, dive and swim underwater. And nearby are more new exhibits for arctic foxes, reindeer and birds. It's an arctic adventure you'll never forget.

World-Famous San Diego Zoo

For example, the marketing communications program for the San Diego Zoological Society has a number of objectives. First, it must provide funding for the society's programs and maintain a large and powerful base of supporters for financial and political strength. The program must educate the public about the society's various programs and maintain a favorable image on a local, regional, national and even international level. A major objective of the IMC program is drawing visitors to the two attractions.

To achieve these objectives, the San Diego Zoological Society and its advertising agency developed an IMC program. As can be seen in Figure 7–7, this program employed a variety of promotional tools. (See Figure 7–7 for a sample IMC program.) When setting objectives for these promotional elements, planners must consider what the firm hopes to communicate through the use of this element, among what target audience, and during what time period. As with advertising, results should be measured and evaluated against the original objectives, and attempts should be made to isolate the effects of each promotional element. Objectives for marketing communications elements other than advertising are discussed more thoroughly in Part 5 of the text.

ESTABLISHING AND ALLOCATING THE PROMOTIONAL BUDGET

If you take a minute to look back at Figure 1–4 on page 23, you will see that while the arrows from the review of the marketing plan and the promotional situation analysis to analysis of the communications process are *unidirectional*, the flow between the communications analysis and budget determination is a *two-way interaction*. What this means is that while establishing objectives is an important part of the planning process, the limitations of the budget are important too. No organization has an unlimited budget, so objectives must be set with the budget in mind.

Often when we think of promotional expenditures of firms, we think only about the huge amounts being spent. We don't usually take the time to think about how these monies are being allocated and about the recipients of these dollars. The budgeting decisions have a significant impact not only on the firm itself but also on numerous others involved either directly or indirectly. The remainder of this chapter provides insight into some underlying theory with respect to budget setting, discusses how companies budget for promotional efforts, and demonstrates the inherent strengths and weaknesses associated with these approaches. Essentially, we focus on two primary budgeting decisions: establishing a budget amount and allocating the budget.

Establishing the Budget

The size of a firm's advertising and promotions budget can vary from a few thousand dollars to more than a billion. When companies like Procter & Gamble and General Motors spend over a billion dollars per year to promote their products, they expect such expenditures to accomplish their stated objectives. (Think back to the comments of Kellogg's North America president in the chapter opener.) The budget decision is no less critical to a firm spending only a few thousand dollars; its ultimate success or failure may depend on the monies spent. One of the most critical decisions facing the marketing manager is how much to spend on the promotional effort.

FIGURE 7–7   The San Diego Zoo sets objectives for various promotional elements

Advertising

Objectives:	Drive attendance to Zoo and Wild Animal Park. Uphold image and educate target audience and inform them of new attractions and special events and promotions.
Audience:	Members and nonmembers of Zoological Society. Households in primary and secondary geographic markets consisting of San Diego County and 5 other counties in southern California. Tertiary markets of 7 western states. Tourist and group sales markets.
Timing:	As allowed and determined by budget. Mostly timed to coincide with promotional efforts.
Tools/media:	Television, radio, newspaper, magazines, direct mail, outdoor, tourist media (television and magazine).

Sales Promotions

Objectives:	Use price, product, and other variables to drive attendance when it might not otherwise come.
Audience:	Targeted, depending on co-op partner, mostly to southern California market.
Timing:	To fit needs of Zoo and Wild Animal Park and cosponsoring partner.
Tools/media:	Coupons, sweepstakes, tours, broadcast tradeouts, direct mail: statement stuffers, fliers, postcards.

Public Relations

Objectives:	Inform, educate, create, and maintain image for Zoological Society and major attractions; reinforce advertising message.
Audience:	From local to international, depending on subject, scope, and timing.
Timing:	Ongoing, although often timed to coincide with promotions and other special events. Spur-of-the-moment animal news and information such as acquisitions, births, etc.
Tools/media:	Coverage by major news media, articles in local, regional, national and international newspapers, magazines and other publications such as visitors guides, tour books and guides, appearances by Zoo spokesperson Joanne Embery on talk shows (such as "The Tonight Show").

Cause Marketing/Corporate Sponsorships/Events Underwriting

Objectives:	To provide funding for Zoological Society programs and promote special programs and events done in cooperation with corporate sponsor. Must be win-win business partnership for Society and partner.
Audience:	Supporters of both the Zoological Society and the corporate or product/service partner.
Timing:	Coincides with needs of both partners, and seasonal attendance generation needs of Zoo and Wild Animal Park.
Tools:	May involve advertising, publicity, discount co-op promotions, ticket trades, hospitality centers. Exposure is directly proportional to amount of underwriting by corporate sponsor, both in scope and duration.

Direct Marketing

Objectives:	Maintain large powerful base of supporters for financial and political strength.
Audience:	Local, regional, national and international. Includes children's program (Koala Club), seniors (60+), couples, single memberships, and incremental donor levels.
Timing:	Ongoing, year-round promotion of memberships.
Tools:	Direct mail and on-grounds visibility.

Group Sales

Objectives:	Maximize group traffic and revenue by selling group tours to Zoo and Wild Animal Park.
Audience:	Conventions, incentive groups, bus tours, associations, youth, scouts, schools, camps, seniors, clubs, military, organizations, domestic and foreign travel groups.
Timing:	Targeted to drive attendance in peak seasons or at most probable times such as convention season.
Tools:	Travel and tourism trade shows, telemarketing, direct mail, trade publication advertising.

Unfortunately, many managers fail to realize the value of advertising and promotion. They treat the communications budget as an expense rather than an investment. Instead of viewing the dollars spent as contributing to additional sales and market share, they see budget expenses as cutting into profits. As a result, when times get tough, the advertising and promotional budget is the first to be cut—even though there is strong evidence that exactly the opposite should occur, as Exhibit 7–9 argues. Moreover, the decision is not a one-time responsibility. A new budget is formulated every year, each time a new product is introduced, or when either internal or external factors necessitate a change to maintain competitiveness.

While it is one of the most critical decisions, budgeting has perhaps been the most resistant to change. A comparison of advertising and promotional texts over the past 10 years would reveal the same methods for establishing budgets. The theoretical basis for this process remains rooted in economic theory and marginal analysis. (Advertisers also use an approach based on **contribution margin**—the difference between the total revenue generated by a brand and its total variable costs. But, as Robert Steiner says, marginal analysis and contribution margin are essentially synonymous terms.)[24] We begin our discussion of budgeting with an examination of these theoretical approaches.

THEORETICAL ISSUES IN BUDGET SETTING

Most of the models used to establish advertising budgets can be categorized as taking an economic or a sales response perspective.

EXHIBIT 7–9
The AAAA promotes the continued use of advertising in a recession

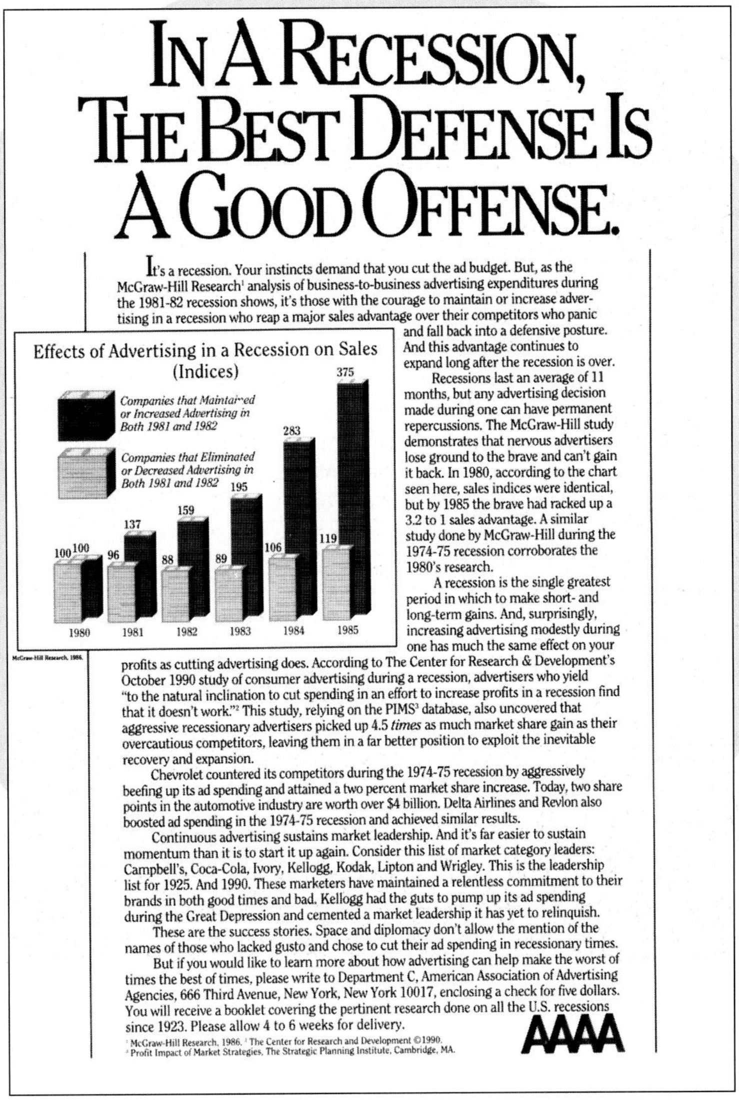

Marginal Analysis

Figure 7–8 graphically represents the concept of **marginal analysis**. As advertising/promotional expenditures increase, sales and gross margins also increase to a point, but then they level off. Profits are shown to be a result of the gross margin minus advertising expenditures. Using this theory to establish its budget, a firm would continue to spend advertising/promotional dollars as long as the marginal revenues created by these expenditures exceeded the incremental advertising/promotional costs. As shown on the graph, the optimal expenditure level is the point where marginal costs equal the marginal revenues they generate (point *A*). If the sum of the advertising/promotional expenditures exceeded the revenues they generated, one would conclude the appropriations were too high and scale down the budget. If revenues were higher, a higher budget might be in order. (We will see later in this chapter that this approach can also be applied to the allocation decision.)

While marginal analysis seems logical intuitively, certain weaknesses limit its usefulness. These weaknesses include the assumptions that (1) sales are a direct result of advertising and promotional expenditures and this effect can be measured and (2) advertising and promotion are solely responsible for sales. Let us examine each of these assumptions in more detail.

1. *Assumption that sales are a direct measure of advertising and promotions efforts.* Earlier in this chapter we discussed the fact that the advertiser needs to set communications objectives that contribute to accomplishing overall marketing objectives but at the same time are separate. One reason for this strategy is that it is often difficult, if not impossible, to demonstrate the effects of advertising and promotions on sales. In studies using sales as a direct measure, it has been almost impossible to establish the contribution of advertising and promotion. As noted by Frank Bass, "There is no more difficult, complex, or controversial problem in marketing than measuring the influence of advertising on sales."[25] In the words of David Aaker and James Carman, "Looking for the relationship between advertising and sales is somewhat worse than looking for a needle in a haystack."[26] Thus, to try to show that the size of the budget will directly affect sales of the product is misleading. A more logical approach would be to examine the impact of various budgets on the attainment of communications objectives.

As we saw in the discussion of communications objectives, sales are not the only goal of the promotional effort. Awareness, interest, attitude change, and other communications objectives are often sought, and while the bottom line may be to sell the product, these objectives may serve as the basis on which the promotional program is developed.

2. *Assumption that sales are determined solely by advertising and promotion.* This assumption ignores the remaining elements of the marketing mix—price, product, and distribution—which do contribute to a company's success. Environmental factors may also affect the promotional program, leading the marketing manager to assume the advertising was or was not effective when some other factor may have helped or hindered the accomplishment of the desired objectives.

FIGURE 7–8
Marginal analysis

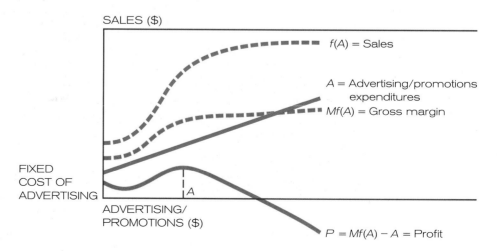

Overall, you can see that while the economic approach to the budgeting process is a logical one, the difficulties associated with determining the effects of the promotional effort on sales and revenues limit its applicability. Marginal analysis is seldom used as a basis for budgeting (except for direct-response advertising).

Sales Response Models

You may have wondered why the sales curve in Figure 7–8 shows sales leveling off even though advertising and promotions efforts continue to increase. The relationship between advertising and sales has been the topic of much research and discussion designed to determine the shape of the response curve.

Almost all advertisers subscribe to one of two models of the advertising/sales response function: the concave-downward function or the S-shaped response curve.

- *The concave-downward function.* After reviewing more than 100 studies of the effects of advertising on sales, Julian Simon and Johan Arndt concluded that the effects of advertising budgets follow the microeconomic law of diminishing returns.[27] That is, as the amount of advertising increases, its incremental value decreases. The logic is that those with the greatest potential to buy will likely act on the first (or earliest) exposures, while those less likely to buy are not likely to change as a result of the advertising. For those who may be potential buyers, each additional ad will supply little or no new information that will affect their decision. Thus, according to the **concave-downward function model**, the effects of advertising quickly begin to diminish, as shown in Figure 7–9A. Budgeting under this model suggests that fewer advertising dollars may be needed to create the optimal influence on sales.

- *The S-shaped response function.* Many advertising managers assume the **S-shaped response curve** (Figure 7–9B), which projects an S-shaped response function to the budget outlay (again measured in sales). Initial outlays of the advertising budget have little impact (as indicated by the essentially flat sales curve in range A). After a certain budget level has been reached (the beginning of range B), advertising and promotional efforts begin to have an effect, as additional increments of expenditures result in increased sales. This incremental gain continues only to a point, however, because at the beginning of range C additional expenditures begin to return little or nothing in the way of sales. This model suggests a small advertising budget is likely to have no impact beyond the sales that may have been generated through other means (for example, word of mouth). At the other extreme, more does not necessarily mean better: additional dollars spent beyond range B have no additional impact on sales and for the most part can be considered wasted. As with marginal analysis, one would attempt to operate at that point on the curve in area B where the maximum return for the money is attained.

FIGURE 7–9   Advertising sales/response functions

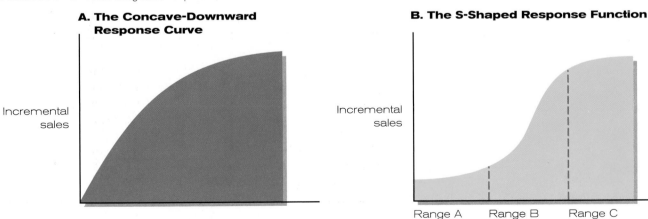

Weaknesses in these sales response models render them of limited use to practitioners for direct applications. Many of the problems seen earlier—the use of sales as a dependent variable, measurement problems, and so on—limit the usefulness of these models. At the same time, keep in mind the purpose of discussing such models. Even though marginal analysis and the sales response curves may not apply directly, they give managers some insight into a theoretical basis of how the budgeting process should work. Some empirical evidence indicates the models may have validity. One study, based on industry experience, has provided support for the S-shaped response curve; the results indicate that a minimum amount of advertising dollars must be spent before there is a noticeable effect on sales.[28]

The studies discussed in earlier chapters on learning and the hierarchy of effects also demonstrate the importance of repetition on gaining awareness and on subsequent higher-order objectives such as adoption. Thus, while these models may not provide a tool for setting the advertising and promotional budget directly, we can use them to guide our appropriations strategy from a theoretical basis. As you will see later in this chapter, such a theoretical basis has advantages over many of the methods currently being used for budget setting and allocation.

ADDITIONAL FACTORS IN BUDGET SETTING

While the theoretical bases just discussed should be considered in establishing the budget appropriation, a number of other issues must also be considered. A weakness in attempting to use sales as a *direct* measure of response to advertising is that various situational factors may have an effect. In one comprehensive study, 20 variables were shown to affect the advertising/sales ratio. Figure 7–10 lists these factors and their relationships.[29] For a product characterized by emotional buying motives, hidden product qualities, and/or a strong basis for differentiation, advertising would have a noticeable impact on sales (see Exhibit 7–10). Products characterized as large dollar purchases and those in the maturity or decline stages

FIGURE 7–10   Factors influencing advertising budgets

Factor	Relationship of Advertising/Sales	Factor	Relationship of Advertising/Sales
Product factors		**Customer factors**	
Basis for differentiation	+	Industrial products users	−
Hidden product qualities	+	Concentration of users	+
Emotional buying motives	+	**Strategy factors**	
Durability	−	Regional markets	−
Large dollar purchase	−	Early stage of brand life cycle	+
Purchase frequency	Curvilinear	High margins in channels	−
Market factors		Long channels of distribution	+
Stage of product life cycle		High prices	+
Introductory	+	High quality	+
Growth	+	**Cost factors**	
Maturity	−	High profit margins	+
Decline	−		
Inelastic demand	+		
Market share	−		
Competition			
Active	+		
Concentrated	+		
Pioneer in market	−		

Note: + relationship means the factor leads to a positive effect of advertising on sales; − relationship indicates little or no effect of advertising on sales.

EXHIBIT 7–10
A strong basis for differentiation could show a noticeable effect of advertising on sales

of the product would be less likely to benefit. The study showed that other factors involving the market, customer, costs, and strategies employed have different effects.

The results of this study are interesting but limited, since they relate primarily to the percentage of sales dollars allocated to advertising and the factors influencing these ratios. As we will see later in this chapter, the percentage-of-sales method of budgeting has inherent weaknesses in that the advertising and sales effects may be reversed. So we cannot be sure whether the situation actually led to the advertising/sales relationship or vice versa. Thus, while these factors should be considered in the budget appropriation decision, they should not be the sole determinants of where and when to increase or decrease expenditures.

The *Advertising Age* Editorial Sounding Board consists of 92 executives of the top 200 advertising companies in the United States (representing the client side) and 130 executives of the 200 largest advertising agencies and 11 advertising consultants (representing the agency side). A survey of the board yielded the factors shown in Figure 7–11 that are gaining and losing importance in budget setting. Clearly, there is little consensus. While clients most commonly cite intended changes in advertising strategy and/or creative approaches as important in setting the ad budget, those on the agency side are more likely to cite *profit contribution goals* or other financial targets of the client as growing in importance. Regarding which factors are decreasing in importance, only the level of the previous year's spending is a key factor to both groups.

Overall, the responses of these two groups reflect in part their perceptions as to how budgets are set. To understand the differences in the relative importance of these factors, it is important to understand the approaches currently employed in budget setting. The next section examines these approaches.

Budgeting Approaches

The theoretical approaches to establishing the promotional budget are seldom employed. In smaller firms, they may never be used. Instead, a number of methods developed through practice and experience are implemented. This section reviews some of the more traditional methods of setting budgets and the relative advantages and disadvantages of each. First, you must understand two things: (1) Many firms employ more than one method, and (2) budgeting approaches vary according to the size and sophistication of the firm.

TOP-DOWN APPROACHES

The approaches discussed in this section may be referred to as **top-down approaches** because a budgetary amount is established (usually at an executive level) and then the monies are passed down to the various departments (as shown in Figure 7–12). These budgets are essentially predetermined and have no true theoretical basis. Top-down methods include the

FIGURE 7–11
Importance of factors in budget setting

Advertisers—Referring to Own Companies	
Increasing in Importance	
Intended changes in advertising strategy and/or creative approach	51%
Competitive activity and/or spending levels	47
Profit contribution goal or other financial target	43
Decreasing in Importance	
Level of previous year's spending, with adjustment	17
Senior management dollar allocation or set limit	11
Volume share projections	8
Agencies—Referring to Client Companies	
Increasing in Importance	
Profit contribution goal or other financial target	56%
Competitive activity and/or spending levels	43
Intended changes in advertising strategy and/or creative approach	37
Decreasing in Importance	
Projections/assumptions on media cost increases	25
Level of previous year's spending, with adjustment	24
Modifications in media strategy and/or buying techniques	17

FIGURE 7–11
Importance of factors in budget setting

affordable method, arbitrary allocation, percentage of sales, competitive parity, and return on investment (ROI).

The Affordable Method

In the **affordable method** (often referred to as the all-you-can-afford method), the firm determines the amount to be spent in various areas such as production and operations. Then it allocates what's left to advertising and promotion, considering this to be the amount it can afford. The task to be performed by the advertising/promotions function is not considered, and the likelihood of under- or overspending is high, as no guidelines for measuring the effects of various budgets are established.

FIGURE 7–12
Top-down versus bottom-up approaches to budget setting

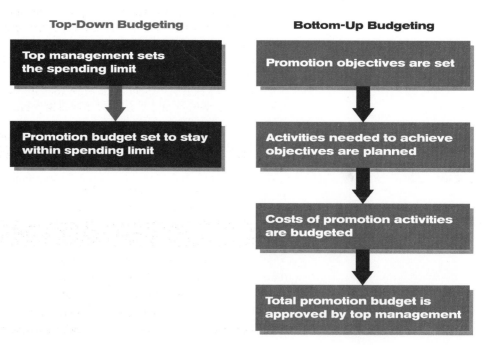

Top-Down Budgeting

Top management sets the spending limit

Promotion budget set to stay within spending limit

Bottom-Up Budgeting

Promotion objectives are set

Activities needed to achieve objectives are planned

Costs of promotion activities are budgeted

Total promotion budget is approved by top management

Strange as it may seem, this approach is common among small firms. Unfortunately, it is also used in large firms, particularly those that are not marketing driven and do not understand the role of advertising and promotion. For example, many high-tech firms focus on new product development and engineering and assume that the product, if good enough, will sell itself. In these companies, little money may be left for performing the advertising and promotions tasks.

The logic for this approach stems from "We can't be hurt with this method" thinking. That is, if we know what we can afford and we do not exceed it, we will not get into financial problems. While this may be true in a strictly accounting sense, it does not reflect sound managerial decision making from a marketing perspective. Often this method does not allocate enough money to get the product off the ground and into the market. In terms of the S-shaped sales response model, the firm is operating in range A. Or the firm may be spending more than necessary, operating in range C. When the market gets tough and sales and/or profits begin to fall, this method is likely to lead to budget cuts at a time when the budget should be increased.

Arbitrary Allocation

Perhaps an even weaker method than the affordable method for establishing a budget is **arbitrary allocation**, in which virtually no theoretical basis is considered and the budgetary amount is often set by fiat. That is, the budget is determined by management solely on the basis of what is felt to be necessary. In a discussion of how managers set advertising budgets, Melvin Salveson reported that these decisions may reflect "as much upon the managers' psychological profile as they do economic criteria."[30] While Salveson was referring to larger corporations, the approach is no less common in small firms and nonprofit organizations.

The arbitrary allocation approach has no obvious advantages. No systematic thinking has occurred, no objectives have been budgeted for, and the concept and purpose of advertising and promotion have been largely ignored. Other than the fact that the manager believes some monies must be spent on advertising and promotion and then picks a number, there is no good explanation why this approach continues to be used. Yet budgets continue to be set this way, and our purpose in discussing it is to point out only that this method is used—not recommended.

Percentage of Sales

Perhaps the most commonly used method for budget setting (particularly in large firms) is the **percentage-of-sales method**, in which the advertising and promotions budget is based on sales of the product. Management determines the amount by either (1) taking a percentage of the sales dollars or (2) assigning a fixed amount of the unit product cost to promotion and multiplying this amount by the number of units sold. These two methods are shown in Figure 7–13.

A variation on the percentage-of-sales method uses a percentage of projected future sales as a base. This method also uses either a straight percentage of projected sales or a unit cost

FIGURE 7–13

Alternative methods for computing percentage of sales for Entree Cologne

Method 1: Straight Percentage of Sales		
1996	Total dollar sales	$1,000,000
	Straight % of sales at 10%	$100,000
1997	Advertising budget	$100,000
Method 2: Percentage of Unit Cost		
1996	Cost per bottle to manufacturer	$4.00
	Unit cost allocated to advertising	1.00
1997	Forecasted sales, 100,000 units	
1997	Advertising budget (100,000 × $1.00)	$100,000

projection. In the straight percentage method, sales are projected for the coming year based on the marketing manager's estimates. The budget is a percentage of these sales, often an industry standard percentage like those presented in Figure 7–14.

One advantage of using future sales as a base is that the budget is not based on last year's sales. As the market changes, management must factor the effect of these changes on sales into next year's forecast rather than relying on past data. The resulting budget is more likely to reflect current conditions and be more appropriate.

Figure 7–14 reveals that the percentage allocated varies from one industry to the next. Some firms budget a very small percentage (for example, 0.2 percent in lumber and wood products), and others spend a much higher proportional amount (18.1 percent in the games and toy industry). Actual dollar amounts spent vary markedly according to the company's total sales figure. Thus, a smaller percentage of sales in the construction machinery industry may actually result in significantly more advertising dollars being spent.

Proponents of the percentage-of-sales method cite a number of advantages. It is financially safe and keeps ad spending within reasonable limits, as it bases spending on the past year's sales or what the firm expects to sell in the upcoming year. Thus, there will be sufficient monies to cover this budget, with increases in sales leading to budget increases and sales decreases resulting in advertising decreases. The percentage-of-sales method is simple, straightforward, and easy to implement. Regardless of which basis—past or future sales—is employed, the calculations used to arrive at a budget are not difficult. Finally, this budgeting approach is generally stable. While the budget may vary with increases and decreases in sales, as long as these changes are not drastic the manager will have a reasonable idea of the parameters of the budget.

At the same time, the percentage-of-sales method has some serious disadvantages, including the basic premise on which the budget is established: sales. Letting the level of sales determine the amount of advertising and promotions dollars to be spent reverses the cause-and-effect relationship between advertising and sales. It treats advertising as an expense associated with making a sale rather than an investment. As discussed in IMC Perspective 7–3, companies that consider promotional expenditures an investment reap the rewards.

A second problem with this approach was actually cited as an advantage earlier: stability. Proponents say that if all firms use a similar percentage, that will bring stability to the marketplace. But what happens if someone varies from this standard percentage? The problem is that this method does not allow for changes in strategy either internally or from competitors. An aggressive firm may wish to allocate more monies to the advertising and promotions budget, a strategy that is not possible with a percentage-of-sales method unless the manager is willing to deviate from industry standards.

The percentage-of-sales method of budgeting may result in severe misappropriation of funds. If advertising and promotion have a role to perform in marketing a product, then allocating more monies to advertising will, as shown in the S-shaped curve, generate incremental sales (to a point). If products with low sales have smaller promotion budgets, this will hinder sales progress. At the other extreme, very successful products may have excess budgets, some of which may be better appropriated elsewhere.

The percentage-of-sales method is also difficult to employ for new product introductions. If no sales histories are available, there is no basis for establishing the budget. Projections of future sales may be difficult, particularly if the product is highly innovative and/or has fluctuating sales patterns.

Finally, if the budget is contingent on sales, decreases in sales will lead to decreases in budgets when they most need to be increased. Continuing to cut the advertising and promotion budgets may just add impetus to the downward sales trend. On the other hand, some of the more successful companies have allocated additional funds during hard times or downturns in the cycle of sales. Companies that maintain or increase their ad expenditures during recessions achieve increased visibility and higher growth in both sales and market share (compared to those that reduce advertising outlays). For example, Sunkist can attribute at least some of its success in maintaining its strong image to the fact that it has maintained consistent levels of advertising expenditures over 80 years, despite recessions.[31]

FIGURE 7–14
A sampling of advertising ratios by industry

Industry	Ad Dollars as		Annual Growth Rate (%)
	% of Sales	% of Margin	
Food and kindred products	6.5	16.7	5.4
Food stores	4.3	10.5	13.4
Footwear, except rubber	3.8	10.2	5.6
Furniture stores	6.1	13.3	5.9
Games, toys child veh, ex dolls	18.1	34.6	8.4
Gen med & surgical hospitals	1.0	4.9	30.4
General indus. mach and eq, NEC	0.7	2.1	4.8
General industrial mach and eq	2.0	6.9	9.0
Glass, glassware-pressed, blown	1.2	2.7	10.2
Grain mill products	8.7	17.1	−0.3
Greeting cards	5.3	7.6	9.1
Groceries and related prods-whls	3.5	24.6	10.2
Grocery stores	1.1	4.1	1.2
Hardware, plumb, heat eq-whsl	2.0	31.4	7.3
Health services	1.5	7.2	4.6
Help supply services	0.8	3.9	2.7
Hobby, toy and game shops	1.4	4.3	10.1
Home furniture and equip stores	2.8	7.7	12.2
Hospital and medical svc plan	1.0	4.0	16.4
Hospitals	4.1	32.2	11.0
Hotels, motels, tourist courts	3.6	11.0	10.1
Household appliances	2.6	8.5	−2.2
Household audio and video equip	3.2	10.7	6.9
Household furniture	4.5	14.0	10.6
Ice cream & frozen desserts	6.8	20.4	13.4
In vitro, in vivo diagnostics	2.5	6.4	17.3
Indiv. ceiling fans, blowers, etc	1.0	4.2	14.4
Indl trucks, tractors, trailers	0.9	3.7	7.2
Industrial measurement instr	0.6	1.6	−9.8
Industrial organic chemicals	0.8	3.0	6.3
Insurance agents, brokers	1.2	5.6	7.3
Investment advice	5.1	14.3	14.3
Iron and steel foundries	1.1	4.0	7.4
Jewelry stores	3.9	6.3	−9.2
Jewelry, precious metals	4.6	9.6	1.1
Knit outerwear mills	3.3	10.1	12.0
Knitting mills	3.8	12.8	3.5
Lab analytical instruments	1.8	3.2	−1.0
Lawn, garden, tractors, equip	3.2	8.4	8.4
Leather and leather prods.	8.2	17.1	−7.9
Lumber/other bldg matl-retail	1.0	3.5	8.0
Lumber and wood pds, ex furn.	0.2	0.9	1.6
Machine tools, metal cutting	1.1	3.3	3.7
Magnetic, optic recording media	2.8	8.0	5.0
Malt beverages	4.9	12.9	3.5

Source: Schonfeld & Associates, Inc.

IMC Perspective 7–3
Investing in Advertising and Promotions

Many marketers think of advertising and promotions as an expense of making a sale. When it comes time to cut costs, the promotional budget often takes the big hit. More astute companies take a different perspective. They consider advertising and promotion an investment that will pay off in the long run—sometimes years later (see chart). Consider the following examples:

- **Charles Schwab.** In an attempt to change the way people purchase mutual funds, Charles Schwab initiated an advertising campaign designed to show existing and potential companies the fees that they might pay at other brokerage houses. The campaign generated over 140,000 mail leads and increased assets to over $2 billion during a three-month period. One-Source mutual funds holders increased by 34 percent and assets by 54 percent.
- **Residence Inn by Marriott.** Marriott ran an IMC campaign that proved so successful in the first three months that it continued for two years. A single print ad, reminder postcards targeted to existing customers, direct-mail pitches, and point-of-purchase displays led to a 12 percent increase in occupancy rates during the time period.
- **Zantac.** This ulcer medication introduced by Glaxo was predicted to gain no more than a 10 percent share against the incumbent Tagamet. As a result of an aggressive, investment-driven campaign, Zantac achieved a 50 percent share, replacing Tagamet as the leading brand.
- **Hawaiian Punch.** After spending $10 to $20 million a year on promotions throughout the 1980s, Del Monte cut expenditures to less than $2 million. Even though sales eroded as a result, they remained above $100 million a year. In addition, consumers remembered the character Punchy three years after the ads ran, reflecting carryover from the larger budget.
- **Philip Morris.** Introduced in the 1920s, Marlboro cigarettes had only a 1 percent brand share 30 years later. In 1954, the company invested in a distinctive brand image (the cowboy) it has maintained into the present. Marlboro now holds a 60 to 70 percent brand share among young smokers in the United States, and the cowboy image is recognized around the world.
- **AT&T.** In 1995, four months before President Clinton signed into law a new telecommunications bill, AT&T— one of the country's most well-known brands—an-

nounced that the company would split into three companies. Many predicted disaster for the new companies due to lack of name awareness, negative publicity from the loss of 40,000 jobs, and increased competition. However, AT&T took an aggressive stance. By repositioning itself, and increasing advertising and promotions outlays to over $620 million, AT&T hoped to fend off potential market share declines. By the end of 1996, it appeared that the gloomy forecasts were unfounded, as AT&T successfully held share in all areas, while increasing in others.

Derrith Lambka, corporate advertising manager for Hewlett-Packard, says there is more and more pressure on marketing departments to prove that advertising and promotions are a good investment. He says managers are looking at spending to receive the "greatest return possible." If they are patient and look at the investment strategies of Ivory soap and Ritz crackers, as well as those mentioned above, they just may find that advertising and promotions fit the bill.

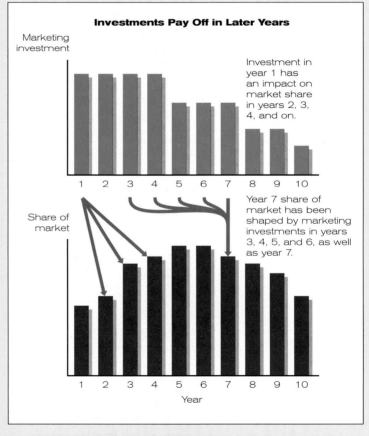

Investments Pay Off in Later Years

Marketing investment

Investment in year 1 has an impact on market share in years 2, 3, 4, and on.

Share of market

Year 7 share of market has been shaped by marketing investments in years 3, 4, 5, and 6, as well as year 7.

Year

Sources: Hillary Rosner, "AT&T's New Esprit de Core," *Brandweek*, February 19, 1996, pp. 22–28; "The 1994 Effies," *Brandweek*, June 13, 1994; Adrian J. Slywotzky and Benson P. Shapiro, "Leveraging to Beat the Odds: The New Marketing Mind-Set," *Harvard Business Review*, September/October 1993, pp. 97–107; Mary Welch, "Upbeat Marketers Wield Bigger Budgets, Shift Marketing Mix," *Business Marketing*, February 1993, p. 23.

While the percentage-of-future-sales method has been proposed as a remedy for some of the problems discussed here, the reality is that problems with forecasting, cyclical growth, and uncontrollable factors limit its effectiveness.

Competitive Parity

If you asked marketing managers if they ever set their advertising and promotions budgets based on what their competitors allocate, they would probably deny it. Yet if you examined the advertising expenditures of these companies, both as a percentage of sales and in respect to the media where they are allocated, you would see little variation in the percentage-of-sales figures for firms within a given industry. Such results do not happen by chance alone. Companies that provide competitive advertising information, trade associations, and other advertising industry periodicals are sources for competitors' expenditures. Larger corporations often subscribe to services such as Competitive Media Reporting, which estimates the top 1,000 companies' advertising in 10 media and in total. Smaller companies often use a **clipping service,** which clips competitors' ads from local print media, allowing the company to work backward to determine the cumulative costs of the ads placed.

In the **competitive parity method,** managers establish budget amounts by matching the competition's percentage-of-sales expenditures. The argument is that setting budgets in this fashion takes advantage of the collective wisdom of the industry. It also takes the competition into consideration, which leads to stability in the marketplace by minimizing marketing warfare. If companies know that competitors are unlikely to match their increases in promotional spending, they are less likely to take an aggressive posture to attempt to gain market share. This minimizes unusual or unrealistic ad expenditures.

The competitive parity method has a number of disadvantages, however. For one, it ignores the fact that advertising and promotions are designed to accomplish specific objectives by addressing certain problems and opportunities. Second, it assumes that because firms have similar expenditures, their programs will be equally effective. This assumption ignores the contributions of creative executions and/or media allocations, as well as the success or failure of various promotions. Further, it ignores possible advantages of the firm itself; some companies simply make better products than others.

Also, there is no guarantee that competitors will continue to pursue their existing strategies. Since competitive parity figures are determined by examination of competitors' previous years' promotional expenditures (short of corporate espionage), changes in market emphasis and/or spending may not be recognized until the competition has already established an advantage. Further, there is no guarantee that a competitor will not increase or decrease its own expenditures, regardless of what other companies do. Finally, competitive parity may not avoid promotional wars. Coke versus Pepsi and Anheuser-Busch versus Miller have been notorious for their spending wars, each responding to the other's increased outlays.

In summary, few firms employ the competitive parity method as a sole means of establishing the promotional budget. This method is typically used in conjunction with the percentage-of-sales or other methods. It is never wise to ignore the competition; managers must always be aware of what competitors are doing. But they should not just emulate them in setting goals and developing strategies.

Return on Investment (ROI)

In the percentage-of-sales method, sales dictate the level of advertising appropriations. But advertising causes sales. In the marginal analysis and S-shaped curve approaches, incremental investments in advertising and promotions lead to increases in sales. The key word here is *investment.* In the **ROI budgeting method,** advertising and promotions are considered investments, like plant and equipment. Thus, the budgetary appropriation (investment) leads to certain returns. Like other aspects of the firm's efforts, advertising and promotion are expected to earn a certain return.

While the ROI method looks good on paper, the reality is that it is rarely possible to assess the returns provided by the promotional effort—at least as long as sales continue to be the basis for evaluation. Thus, while managers are certain to ask how much return they are getting for such expenditures, the question remains unanswered, and ROI remains a virtually unused method of budgeting.

Summary of Top-Down Budgeting Methods

You are probably asking yourself why we even discussed these budgeting methods if they are not recommended for use or have severe disadvantages that limit their effectiveness. But you must understand the various methods used in order to recognize their limitations, especially since these flawed methods are commonly employed by marketers throughout the United States, Europe, and Canada, as demonstrated in the results of a number of research studies shown in Figure 7–15. Tradition and top management's desire for control are probably the major reasons why top-down methods continue to be popular.

As shown in Figure 7–15, the use of percentage-of-sales methods remains high, particularly that based on anticipated sales. Unfortunately, the affordable method appears to be on the increase. On the decrease are two methods not yet discussed: quantitative modes and the objective and task method. Let us now turn our discussion to these methods as well as one other, payout planning.

BUILD-UP APPROACHES

The major flaw associated with the top-down methods is that these judgmental approaches lead to predetermined budget appropriations often not linked to objectives and the strategies designed to accomplish them. A more effective budgeting strategy would be to consider the firm's communications objectives and budget what is deemed necessary to attain these goals. As noted earlier, the promotional planning model shows the budget decision as an interactive process, with the communications objectives on one hand and the promotional mix alternatives on the other. The idea is to budget so these promotional mix strategies can be implemented to achieve the stated objectives.

FIGURE 7–15 Comparison of methods for budgeting

Study	San Augustine and Foley (1975)	Patti and Blasko (1981)	Lancaster and Stern (1983)	Blasko and Patti (1984)	Hung and West (1991)
Population	Large consumer/ industrial advertisers	Large consumer/ services advertisers	Large consumer advertisers	Large industrial advertisers	Large & medium advertisers in U.K., U.S., & Canada
Sample	50/50	54	60	64	100
Methods					
• Quantitative models	2/4	51	20	3	NA
• Objective and task	6/10	63	80	74	61
• Percent anticipated sales	50/28	53	53	16	32
• Unit anticipated sales	8/10	22	28	NA	9
• Percent past year's sales	14/16	20	20	23	10
• Unit past year's sales	6/4	NA	15	2	NA
• Affordable	30/26	20	13	33	41
• Arbitrary	12/34	4	NA	13	NA
• Competitive parity	NA	24	33	21	25
• Previous budget	NA	NA	3	NA	NA
• Share of voice	NA	NA	5	NA	NA
• Others	26/10	NA	12	NA	NA

Note: Figures exceed 100% due to multiple responses.   NA = No answer.

Objective and Task Method

It is important that objective setting and budgeting go hand in hand rather than sequentially. It is difficult to establish a budget without specific objectives in mind, and setting objectives without regard to how much money is available makes no sense. For example, a company may wish to create awareness among X percent of its target market. A minimal budget amount will be required to accomplish this goal, and the firm must be willing to spend this amount.

The **objective and task method** of budget setting uses a **build-up approach** consisting of three steps: (1) defining the communications objectives to be accomplished, (2) determining the specific strategies and tasks needed to attain them, and (3) estimating the costs associated with performance of these strategies and tasks. The total budget is based on the accumulation of these costs.

Implementing the objective and task approach is somewhat more involved. The manager must monitor this process throughout and change strategies depending on how well objectives are attained. As shown in Figure 7–16, this process involves several steps.

1. *Isolate objectives.* When the promotional planning model is presented, a company will have two sets of objectives to accomplish—the marketing objectives for the product and the communications objectives. After the former are established, the task involves determining what specific communications objectives will be designed to accomplish these goals. Communications objectives must be specific, attainable, and measurable, as well as time limited.

2. *Determine tasks required.* A number of elements are involved in the strategic plan designed to attain the objectives established. (These strategies constitute the remaining chapters in this text.) These tasks may include advertising in various media, sales promotions, and/or other elements of the promotional mix, each with its own role to perform.

3. *Estimate required expenditures.* Build-up analysis requires determining the estimated costs associated with the tasks developed in the previous step. For example, it involves costs for developing awareness through advertising, trial through sampling, and so forth.

4. *Monitor.* As you will see in Chapter 18 on measuring effectiveness, there are ways to determine how well one is attaining established objectives. Performance should be monitored and evaluated in light of the budget appropriated.

5. *Reevaluate objectives.* Once specific objectives have been attained, monies may be better spent on new goals. Thus, if one has achieved the level of consumer awareness sought, the budget should be altered to stress a higher-order objective such as evaluation or trial.

The major advantage of the objective and task method is that the budget is driven by the objectives to be attained. The managers closest to the marketing effort will have specific strategies and input into the budget-setting process.

FIGURE 7–16

The objective and task method

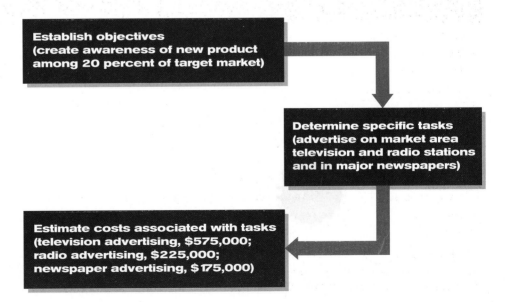

The major disadvantage of this method is the difficulty of determining which tasks will be required and the costs associated with each. For example, specifically what tasks are needed to attain awareness among 50 percent of the target market? How much will it cost to perform these tasks? While these decisions are easier to determine for certain objectives—for example, estimating the costs of sampling required to stimulate trial in a defined market area—it is not always possible to know exactly what is required and/or how much it will cost to complete the job. This process is easier if there is past experience to use as a guide, with either the existing product or a similar one in the same product category. But it is especially difficult for new product introductions. As a result, budget setting using this method is not as easy to perform or as stable as some of the methods discussed earlier. Given this disadvantage, many marketing managers have stayed with those top-down approaches for setting the total expenditure amount.

The objective and task method offers advantages over methods discussed earlier but is more difficult to implement when there is no track record for the product. The following section addresses the problem of budgeting for new product introductions.

Payout Planning

The first months of a new product's introduction typically require heavier than normal advertising and promotion appropriations to stimulate higher levels of awareness and subsequent trial. After studying more than 40 years of Nielsen figures, James O. Peckham estimated that the average share of advertising to sales ratio necessary to launch a new product successfully is approximately 1.5:2.0.[32] This means that a new entry should be spending at approximately twice the desired market share, as shown in the two examples in Figure 7–17. For example, in the food industry, brand 101 gained a 12.6 percent market share by spending 34 percent of the total advertising dollars in this category. Likewise, brand 401 in the toiletry industry had a 30 percent share of advertising dollars to gain 19.5 percent of sales.

To determine how much to spend, marketers often develop a **payout plan** that determines the investment value of the advertising and promotion appropriation. The basic idea is to project the revenues the product will generate, as well as the costs it will incur, over two to three years. Based on an expected rate of return, the payout plan will assist in determining how much advertising and promotions expenditure will be necessary when the return might be expected. A three-year payout plan is shown in Figure 7–18. The product would lose money in year 1, almost break even in year 2, and finally begin to show substantial profits by the end of year 3.

The advertising and promotion figures are highest in year 1 and decline in years 2 and 3. This appropriation is consistent with Peckham's findings and reflects the additional outlays needed to make as rapid an impact as possible. (Keep in mind that shelf space is limited, and store owners are not likely to wait around for a product to become successful.) The budget also reflects the firm's guidelines for new product expenditures, since companies generally have established deadlines by which the product must begin to show a profit. Finally, keep in mind that building market share may be more difficult than maintaining it—thus the substantial dropoff in expenditures in later years.

While the payout plan is not always perfect, it does guide the manager in establishing the budget. When used in conjunction with the objective and task method, it provides a much more logical approach to budget setting than the top-down approaches previously discussed. Yet based on the studies reported on in Figure 7–15, payout planning does not seem to be a widely employed method.

Quantitative Models

Attempts to apply *quantitative models* to budgeting have met with limited success. For the most part, these methods employ **computer simulation models** involving statistical techniques such as multiple regression analysis to determine the relative contribution of the advertising budget to sales. Because of problems associated with these methods, their acceptance has been limited, as demonstrated in the figures reported earlier in Figure 7–15.

FIGURE 7–17
Share of advertising/sales relationship (two-year summary)

A. New Brands of Food Products

Brand	Average share of advertising	Attained share of sales	Ratio of share of advertising to share of sales
101	34%	12.6%	2.7
102	16	10.0	1.6
103	8	7.6	1.1
104	4	2.6	1.5
105	3	2.1	1.4

B. New Brands of Toiletry Products

Brand	Average share of advertising	Attained share of sales	Ratio of share of advertising to share of sales
401	30%	19.5%	1.5
402	25	16.5	1.5
403	20	16.2	1.2
404	12	9.4	1.3
405	16	8.7	1.8
406	19	7.3	2.6
407	14	7.2	1.9
408	10	6.0	1.7
409	7	6.0	1.2
410	6	5.9	1.0
411	10	5.9	1.7
412	6	5.2	1.2

Quantitative models have yet to reach their potential. As computers continue to find their way into the advertising domain, better models may be forthcoming. Specific discussion of these models is beyond the scope of this text, however. Such methods do have merit but may need more refinement before achieving widespread success.

SUMMARY OF BUDGETING METHODS

There is no universally accepted method of setting a budget figure. Weaknesses in each method may make it unfeasible or inappropriate. As Figure 7–15 shows, the use of the objective and task method continues to increase, whereas less sophisticated methods are declining in favor. More advertisers are also employing the payout planning approach.

FIGURE 7–18
Example of three-year payout plan ($ millions)

	Year 1	Year 2	Year 3
Product sales	15.0	35.50	60.75
Profit contribution (@ $0.50/case)	7.5	17.75	30.38
Advertising/promotions	15.0	10.50	8.50
Profit (loss)	(7.5)	7.25	21.88
Cumulative profit (loss)	(7.5)	(0.25)	21.63

By using these approaches in combination with the percentage-of-sales methods, these advertisers are likely to arrive at a more useful, accurate budget. For example, many firms now start the budgeting process by establishing the objectives they need to accomplish and then limit the budget by applying a percentage-of-sales or other method to decide whether or not it is affordable. Competitors' budgets may also influence this decision.

Allocating the Budget

Once the budget has been appropriated, the next step is to allocate it. The allocation decision involves determining which markets, products, and/or promotional elements will receive which amounts of the funds appropriated.

ALLOCATING TO ADVERTISING AND PROMOTION ELEMENTS

As noted earlier, advertisers have begun to shift some of their budget dollars away from traditional advertising media and into sales promotions targeted at both the consumer and the trade. Direct marketing and other promotional tools are also receiving increased attention and competing for more of the promotional budget. The advantage of more target selectivity has led to an increased emphasis on direct marketing, while a variety of new media (which will be discussed in Chapter 13) have given marketers new ways to reach prospective customers. Rapidly rising media costs, the ability of sales promotions to motivate trial, maturing of the product and/or brand, and the need for more aggressive promotional tools have also led to shifts in strategy.[33] (We will discuss consumer and trade promotions and the reasons for some of these changes in Chapter 15.)

Some marketers have also used the allocation decision to stretch their advertising dollar and get more impact from the same amount of money. For example, General Motors recently reevaluated its advertising and promotional expenditures and made significant shifts in allocations by both media and product.[34] Other companies have reevaluated as well, including Procter & Gamble, Apple Computer, and Dow Chemical.

CLIENT/AGENCY POLICIES

Another factor that may influence budget allocation is the individual policy of the company or the advertising agency. The agency may discourage the allocation of monies to sales promotion, preferring to spend them on the advertising area. The agency position is that promotional monies are harder to track in terms of effectiveness and may be used improperly if not under its control. (In many cases commissions are not made on this area, and this fact may contribute to the agency's reluctance.)[35]

The orientation of the agency or the firm may also directly influence where monies are spent. Many ad agencies are managed by officers who have ascended through the creative ranks and are inclined to emphasize the creative budget. Others may have preferences for specific media. For example, BBDO Worldwide, one of the largest advertising agencies in the United States, has positioned itself as an expert in cable TV programming and often spends more client money in this medium. McCann-Erickson is spending more monies on the Internet. Both the agency and the client may favor certain aspects of the promotional program, perhaps based on past successes, that will substantially influence where dollars are spent.

MARKET SIZE

While the budget should be allocated according to the specific promotional tools needed to accomplish the stated objectives, the *size* of the market will affect the decision. In smaller markets, it is often easier and less expensive to reach the target market. Too much of an expenditure in these markets will lead to saturation and a lack of effective spending. In larger markets, the target group may be more dispersed and thus more expensive to reach. Think about the cost of purchasing media in Chicago or New York City versus a smaller market like Columbus, Ohio, or Birmingham, Alabama. The former would be much more costly and would require a higher budget appropriation.

MARKET POTENTIAL

For a variety of reasons, some markets hold more potential than others. Marketers of snow skis would find greater returns on their expenditures in Denver, Colorado, than in Fort Lauderdale, Florida. Imported Mexican beers sell better in the border states (Texas, Arizona, California) than in the Midwest. A disproportionate number of imported cars are sold in California and New England. When particular markets hold higher potential, the marketing manager may decide to allocate additional monies to them. (Keep in mind that just because a market does not have high sales does not mean it should be ignored. The key is *potential*—and a market with low sales but high potential may be a candidate for additional appropriations.)

There are several methods for estimating marketing potential. Many marketers conduct research studies to forecast demand and/or use secondary sources of information such as those provided by government agencies or syndicated services like Dun & Bradstreet, A. C. Nielsen, and Audits and Surveys. One source for consumer goods information is the *Survey of Buying Power*, published annually by *Sales & Marketing Management* magazine. The survey contains population, income, and retail sales data for states, counties, metropolitan statistical areas, and cities in the United States and Canada with populations of 40,000 or more.

MARKET SHARE GOALS

Two recent studies in the *Harvard Business Review* discussed advertising spending with the goal of maintaining and increasing market share.[36] John Jones compared the brand's share of market with its share of advertising voice (the total value of the main media exposure in the product category). Jones classified the brands as "profit taking brands, or underspenders" and "investment brands, those whose share of voice is clearly above their share of market." His study indicated that for those brands with small market shares, profit takers are in the minority; however, as the brands increase their market share, nearly three out of five have a proportionately smaller share of voice.

Jones noted that three factors can be cited to explain this change. First, new brands generally receive higher than average advertising support. Second, older, more mature brands are often "milked"—that is, when they reach the maturity stage, advertising support is reduced. Third, there's an advertising economy of scale whereby advertising works harder for well-established brands, so a lower expenditure is required. Jones concluded that for larger brands, it may be possible to reduce advertising expenditures and still maintain market share. Smaller brands, on the other hand, have to continue to maintain a large share of voice.

James Schroer addressed the advertising budget in a situation where the marketer wishes to increase market share. His analysis suggests that marketers should:

- Segment markets, focusing on those markets where competition is weak and/or underspending instead of on a national advertising effort.
- Determine their competitors' cost positions (how long the competition can continue to spend at the current or increased rate).
- Resist the lure of short-term profits that result from ad budget cuts.
- Consider niching strategies as opposed to long-term wars.

Figure 7–19 shows Schroer's suggestions for spending priorities in various markets.

ECONOMIES OF SCALE IN ADVERTISING

Some studies have presented evidence that firms and/or brands maintaining a large share of the market have an advantage over smaller competitors and thus can spend less money on advertising and realize a better return.[37] Larger advertisers can maintain advertising shares that are smaller than their market shares because they get better advertising rates, have declining average costs of production, and accrue the advantages of advertising several products jointly. In addition, they are likely to enjoy more favorable time and space positions, cooperation of middlepeople, and favorable publicity. These advantages are known as **economies of scale.**

FIGURE 7–19
The share of voice (SOV) effect and ad spending: priorities in individual markets

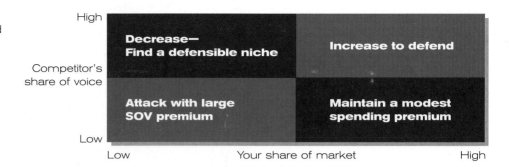

Reviewing the studies in support of this position and then conducting research over a variety of small package products, Kent Lancaster found that this situation did not hold true and that in fact larger brand share products might actually be at a disadvantage.[38] His results indicated that leading brands spend an average of 2.5 percentage points more than their brand share on advertising. More specifically, his study concluded:

1. There is no evidence that larger firms can support their brands with lower relative advertising costs than smaller firms.
2. There is no evidence that the leading brand in a product group enjoys lower advertising costs per sales dollar than do other brands.
3. There is no evidence of a static relationship between advertising costs per dollar of sales and the size of the advertiser.

The results of this and other studies suggest there really are no economies of scale to be accrued from the size of the firm or the market share of the brand.[39]

ORGANIZATIONAL CHARACTERISTICS

In a review of the literature on how allocation decisions are made between advertising and sales promotion, George Low and Jakki Mohr concluded that organizational factors play an important role in determining how communications dollars are spent.[40] The authors note that the following factors influence the allocation decision. These factors vary from one organization to another, and each influences the relative amounts assigned to advertising and promotion.

• The organization's structure–centralized versus decentralized, formalization, and complexity.
• Power and politics in the organizational hierarchy.
• The use of expert opinions (for example, consultants).
• Characteristics of the decision maker (preferences and experience).
• Approval and negotiation channels.
• Pressure on senior managers to arrive at the optimal budget.

One example of how these factors might influence allocations relates to the level of interaction between marketing and other functional departments, such as accounting and operations. The authors note that the relative importance of advertising versus sales promotion might vary from department to department. Accountants, being dollars-and-cents minded, would argue for the sales impact of promotions, while operations would argue against sales promotions because the sudden surges in demand that might result would throw off production schedules. The marketing department might be influenced by the thinking of either of these groups in making its decision.

The use of outside consultants to provide expert opinions might also affect the allocation decision. Trade journals, academic journals, and even books might also be valuable inputs into the decision maker's thinking. In sum, it seems obvious that many factors must be taken into account in the budget allocation decision. Market size and potential, specific objectives sought, and previous company and/or agency policies and preferences all influence this decision.

SUMMARY

This chapter has examined the role of objectives in the planning and evaluation of the IMC program and how firms budget in an attempt to achieve these objectives. Specific objectives are needed to guide the development of the promotional program, as well as to provide a benchmark against which performance can be measured and evaluated. Objectives serve important functions as communications devices, as a guide to planning the IMC program and deciding on various alternatives, and for measurement and evaluation.

Objectives for IMC evolve from the organization's overall marketing plan and are based on the roles various promotional mix elements play in the marketing program. Many managers use sales or a related measure such as market share as the basis for setting objectives. However, many promotional planners believe the role of advertising and other promotional mix elements is to communicate because of the various problems associated with sales-based objectives. They use communications-based objectives like those in the response hierarchy as the basis for setting goals.

Much of the emphasis in setting objectives has been on traditional advertising-based views of marketing communications. However, many companies are moving toward zero-based communications planning, which focuses on what tasks need to be done, which marketing communication functions should be used, and to what extent. Many of the principles used in setting advertising objectives can be applied to other elements in the promotional mix.

As you have probably concluded, the budget decision is not typically based on supporting experiences or strong theoretical foundations. Nor is it one of the more soundly established elements of the promotional program. The budgeting methods used now have some major problems. Economic models are limited, often try to demonstrate the effects on sales directly, and ignore other elements of the marketing mix. Some of the methods discussed have no theoretical basis and ignore the roles advertising and promotion are meant to perform.

One possible way to improve the budget appropriation is to tie the measures of effectiveness to communications objectives rather than to the broader-based marketing objectives. Using the objective and task approach with communications objectives may not be the ultimate solution to the budgeting problem, but it is an improvement over the top-down methods. Marketers often find it advantageous to employ a combination of methods.

As with determining the budget, managers must consider a number of factors when allocating advertising and promotions dollars. Market size and potential, agency policies, and the preferences of management itself may influence the allocation decision.

KEY TERMS

marketing objectives, 200
integrated marketing
    communications
    objectives, 201
carryover effect, 202
DAGMAR, 210
communications task, 210
benchmark measures, 211

zero-based communications
    planning, 214
contribution margin, 217
marginal analysis, 218
concave-downward
    function model, 219
S-shaped response curve, 219
top-down approaches, 221

affordable method, 222
arbitrary allocation, 223
percentage-of-sales
    method, 223
clipping service, 227
competitive parity
    method, 227
ROI budgeting method, 227

objective and task
    method, 229
build-up approach, 228
payout plan, 230
computer simulation
    models, 230
economies of scale,
    233–34

DISCUSSION QUESTIONS

1. Discuss the alternative points of view regarding the cutting of advertising budgets in the cereal industry. Cite potential advantages and disadvantages.
2. Discuss the value of setting objectives for the integrated marketing communications program. What important functions do objectives serve?
3. What are the differences between marketing objectives and communications objectives? Why do so many managers confuse the two?

4. What are some of the problems associated with using sales objectives?
5. What is meant by an advertising carryover effect? Discuss the problems carryover creates for managers who are trying to determine the impact of their advertising on sales.
6. What is the difference between outside-in planning for IMC versus inside-out planning?
7. Explain the difference between investing in advertising and spending. Cite examples of companies that have successfully invested.

8. Compare the S-shaped response curve and the concave-downward sales response models. What types of products and/or services are most likely to be characterized by each?

9. Discuss how you would explain to a small business owner why he or she needs to budget a larger amount to advertising and promotion. Base your argument on the S-shaped response function.

10. Some advertisers believe economies of scale are accrued in the advertising process. Discuss their reasons for taking this position. Does research evidence support it?

Developing the Integrated Marketing Communications Program

PART

5

CHAPTER 8

Creative Strategy: Planning and Development

Chapter Objectives

- To discuss what is meant by advertising creativity and examine the role of creative strategy in advertising.

- To examine creative strategy development and the roles of various client and agency personnel involved in it.

- To consider the process that guides the creation of advertising messages and the research inputs into the stages of the creative process.

- To examine various approaches used for determining major selling ideas that form the basis of an advertising campaign.

SELLING THE BRAND, NOT THE PRODUCT

Life is a journey.

Enjoy the ride. NISSAN

In 1957 social critic Vance Packard wrote his best-seller *The Hidden Persuaders*, in which he purported to reveal all of the secret techniques used by advertisers to manipulate consumers. Critics of advertising loved it. For example, *New Yorker* magazine wrote that the hucksters wanted to "turn the American mind into a kind of catatonic dough that will buy, give or vote at their command." Today Packard, now 82, is still fuming over what he sees coming out of Madison Avenue. It is not because the advertisers have sharpened their brainwashing skills. He is puzzled by modern-day advertising because, as he says, "Commercials seem totally unrelated to selling any product at all."

Packard has noticed the change in the way advertisers are selling their products. There is an obsession with images and feelings and an almost total lack of any concrete claims about the product or why anyone should buy it. Today we have ads for blue jeans that say nothing about blue jeans, ads for watches that say nothing about watches, ads for shoes that say nothing about shoes. A company that personifies this new genre of advertising is Nike, whose ads often say little if anything about athletic shoes and apparel but rather center on concepts such as self-sacrifice, racial harmony, the unimportance of age, and the unifying spirit of sports. Nike's marketing formula is to integrate its brand name and image into the cultural fabric of sports and harness its emotional power. The formula has proven successful: the Nike name ranks among the world's top 10 brands.

Another example of advertising in which making a point and selling a product seem irrelevant is the popular campaign for Levi's wide-leg jeans. One of the commercials is a 60-second spot called "Elevator-Fantasy" in which a young man eyes an attractive young woman in an elevator and instantly their imaginations run wild toward dream dates, love dens—and a screaming newborn. When the doors to the elevator open, the fantasies end and they go separate ways. Another spot is a sidesplitting "ER" parody set to the tune of Soft Cell's "Tainted Love" in which an emergency room is transformed into a funky party room.

This new genre of advertising is quite different from the traditional approaches espoused by the Madison Avenue experts. At the heart of the old credo was what legendary adman Rosser Reeves called the unique selling proposition, or USP. Advocates of the USP approach argue that advertising should highlight that aspect of a product that distinguishes it from its rivals and repeatedly trumpet the value of that attribute. However, the director of brand planning at the J. Walter Thompson agency says, "USP is a great theory, but what do you do when most products come to the market without a visible point of difference? We're communicating a different type of information today—a feeling of what the world is like, and if you identify with that feeling, maybe you identify with the advertised brand."

Image-oriented advertising is being used to sell all types of products and services. Nissan recently launched a $200 million ad campaign aimed at establishing its name as a prominent U.S. brand. One of the spots in the campaign, set to the tune of Van Halen's rock song "You Really Got Me," shows a male doll leaving a playroom in his sporty coupe and picking up a silver-lamé-clad doll from her dull, preppie companion. The message is clear. The right wheels always win you the girl—so drive a Nissan or be left behind. Punctuating all of the ads in the campaign is an elderly, twinkly eyed Japanese man who represents Yutaka Katayama, known as "Mr. K" to his colleagues and friends, the founder of Nissan's American subsidiary in 1960.

The head of the Nissan account at the TBWA Chiat/Day agency claims its research shows that consumers detest hearing about dual-side airbags and wishbone suspensions; the only real difference is how they see the brand image. He says,

"The product is no longer just what's between the bumpers—anybody can copy that. The brand is the only thing that is truly unique anymore."

It used to be that the brand identified the product and advertisers would get your attention with an appealing image. Once they had your attention, they would boast about the product's features and benefits and other virtues. However, in today's world of advertising it appears that the brand is the product. No wonder Vance Packard is puzzled.

Sources: Joshua Levine, "Brands with Feeling," *Forbes*, December 16, 1996, pp. 292–94; Jeff Jensen, "Marketer of the Year," *Advertising Age*, December 16, 1996, pp. 1, 16; Ken Tucker, "Yuks Mark the Spots," *Entertainment Weekly*, January 10, 1997, pp. 44–45.

As the opening vignette shows, one of the most important components of an integrated marketing communications program is the advertising message. While the fundamental role of an advertising message is to communicate information, it does much more. The commercials we watch on TV or hear on radio and the print ads we see in magazines and newspapers are a source of entertainment, motivation, fascination, fantasy, and sometimes irritation as well as information. Ads and commercials appeal to, and often create or shape, consumers' problems, desires, and goals. From the marketer's perspective, the advertising message is a way to tell consumers how the product or service can solve a problem or help satisfy desires or achieve goals. Advertising can also be used to create images or associations and position a brand in the consumer's mind as well as transform the experience of buying and/or using a product or service. Many consumers who have never driven or even ridden in a BMW perceive it as "the ultimate driving machine" (Exhibit 8–1). Many people feel good about sending Hallmark greeting cards because they have internalized the company's advertising theme, "when you care enough to send the very best."

One need only watch an evening of commercials or peruse a few magazines to realize there are a myriad of ways to convey an advertising message. Underlying all of these messages, however, are a **creative strategy** that determines what the advertising message will say or communicate and **creative tactics** for how the message strategy will be executed. In this chapter, we focus on advertising creative strategy. We consider what is meant by creativity, particularly as it relates to advertising, and examine a well-known approach to creativity in advertising.

We also examine the creative strategy development process and various approaches to determining the *big idea* that will be used as the central theme of the advertising campaign and translated into attention-getting, distinctive, and memorable messages. Creative specialists are finding it more and more difficult to come up with big ideas that will break through the clutter and still satisfy the concerns of their risk-averse clients. Yet their clients are continu-

EXHIBIT 8–1
Excellent advertising helps create an image for BMW automobiles as "the ultimate driving machine"

WHAT MICHELANGELO WOULD HAVE CREATED IF HE WORKED WITH GALVANIZED STEEL.

ally challenging them to find the creative message that will strike a responsive chord with their target audience.

Some of you may not be directly involved in the design and creation of ads; you may choose to work in another agency department or on the client side of the business. However, because creative strategy is often so crucial to the success of the firm's promotional effort, everyone involved in the promotional process should understand the creative strategy and tactics that underlie the development of advertising campaigns and messages, as well as the creative options available to the advertiser. Also, individuals on the client side as well as agency people outside the creative department must work with the creative specialists in developing the advertising campaign, implementing it, and evaluating its effectiveness. Thus, marketing and product managers, account representatives, researchers, and media personnel must appreciate the creative process and develop a productive relationship with creative personnel.

THE IMPORTANCE OF CREATIVITY IN ADVERTISING

For many students, as well as many advertising and marketing practitioners, the most interesting aspect of advertising is the creative side. We have all at one time or another been intrigued by an ad and admired the creative insight that went into it. A great ad is a joy to behold and often an epic to create, as the cost of producing a TV commercial can exceed $1 million. Many companies see this as money well spent. They realize that the manner in which the advertising message is developed and executed is often critical to the success of the promotional program, which in turn can influence the effectiveness of the entire marketing program. Procter & Gamble, Levi Strauss, Nissan, Compaq, Coke, Pepsi, Nike, McDonald's, and many other companies spend millions of dollars each year to produce advertising messages and hundreds of millions more to purchase media time and space to run them. While these companies make excellent products, they realize creative advertising is also an important part of their marketing success.

Good creative strategy and execution can often be central to determining the success of a product or service or reversing the fortunes of a struggling brand. Conversely, an advertising campaign that is poorly conceived or executed can be a liability. Many companies have solid marketing and promotional plans and spend substantial amounts of money on advertising, yet have difficulty coming up with a creative campaign that will differentiate them from their competitors. For example, Burger King changed its advertising campaign theme 18 times in the past 20 years and changed agencies 7 times in search of an advertising approach that would give the chain a strong identity in the fast-food market (Figure 8–1). Market share dropped and franchisees were unhappy with the company's inability to come up with an effective campaign.[1] Burger King has finally hit pay dirt with the "Get your burger's worth" campaign that has been running since 1994.[2]

Just because an ad or commercial is creative or popular does not mean it will increase sales or revive a declining brand. Many ads have won awards for creativity but failed to increase sales. In some instances, the failure to generate sales has cost the agency the account. For example, many advertising people believe some of the best ads of all time were those done for Alka-Seltzer years ago, including the classic "Mama Mia! That's a spicy meatball!" and "I can't believe I ate the whole thing" (Exhibit 8–2). While the commercials won numerous creative awards, Alka-Seltzer sales still declined and the agencies lost the account.[3]

Many advertising and marketing people have become ambivalent toward, and in some cases even critical of, advertising awards.[4] They argue that agency creative people are often more concerned with creating ads that win awards than ones that sell their clients' products. Other advertising people believe awards are a good way to recognize creativity that often does result in effective advertising. Global Perspective 8–1 discusses how the emphasis on creative awards has shifted to the international arena with awards like the Cannes Gold Lion trophies.

As we saw in Chapter 7, the success of an ad campaign cannot always be judged in terms of sales. However, many advertising and marketing personnel, particularly those on the client

FIGURE 8–1
Hungry for a winning campaign

Burger King's ad path, from "Have it your way" to "Get your burger's worth"

- Burger King dismisses BBDO, creator of its most famous slogan, "Have it your way," and hires J. Walter Thompson, New York (Aug. 1976)
- "America loves burgers, and we're America's Burger King" (Nov. 1977–Feb. 1978)
- "Who's got the best darn burger?" (Feb. 1978–Jan. 1980)
- "Make it special. Make it Burger King." (Jan. 1980–Jan. 1982)
- "Aren't you hungry for Burger King now?" (Jan. 1982–Sept. 1982)
- "Battle of the burgers" (Sept. 1982–March 1983)
- "Broiling vs. frying" campaign tied to "Aren't you hungry?" (March 1983–Sept. 1983)
- "The big switch" campaign (Sept. 1983–Nov. 1985)
- "Search for Herb" campaign (Nov. 1985–June 1986)
- "This is a Burger King town" (June 1986–Jan. 1987)
- "The best food for fast times" (Jan. 1987–Oct. 1987)
- BK hires NW Ayer, New York, and fires JWT (Oct. 1987)
- "We do it like you'd do it" (April 1988–May 1989)
- BK hires D'Arcy Masius Benton & Bowles, and Saatchi & Saatchi, New York, firing Ayer (May 1989)
- "Sometimes you gotta break the rules" (Oct. 1989–April 1991)
- "Your way. Right away." (April 1991–Oct. 1992)
- "BK Tee Vee: I love this place!" (Oct. 1992–1994)
- "Get your burger's worth." (1994–present)

Source: Jeanne Whalen, "BK Caters to Franchisees with New Review," *Advertising Age*, October 25, 1993, p. 3.

EXHIBIT 8–2 Alka-Seltzer's creative advertising was not effective in reversing the brand's sales decline

Global Perspective 8–1
Cannes Lions Become Advertising's New Status Symbol

For many years the most coveted prize for creativity in advertising was a Clio award. But in recent years the Clios have lost much of their prestige, particularly after financial problems resulted in cancellation of the 1992 awards ceremony. There are a number of other popular and well-respected advertising award competitions to recognize creative excellence. These include the Kelley Awards given by the Magazine Publishers of America, the Best Awards competition sponsored by *Advertising Age*, and the Addys, the prize given to winners of the American Advertising Awards (sponsored by the American Advertising Federation).

While these contests remain very popular in the United States, on a global level the Cannes International Advertising Film Festival is now widely considered the most prestigious advertising award competition. The Cannes competition receives entries from agencies around the world hoping to win Lions (the name of the award) in each of the two major categories—television and print and poster. Many of the top U.S. agencies do not enter the print contest, which is usually dominated by agencies from the United Kingdom, whose style of advertising is considered more popular among the Cannes jury. In the 1996 competition, U.K. agencies won 43 of the print Lions, compared to only 13 for U.S. agencies.

Agencies from the United States generally focus their entries on the TV part of the competition. In 1996, U.S. agencies won the most Gold Lions for TV, 7 of the 17 awarded, and 18 of the 78 total Lions for TV. The U.S. Gold Winners included DDB Needham Worldwide's popular "Clydesdales" spot for Anheuser-Busch, which features the horses playing football; Cliff Freeman & Partners' commercial for Little Caesar's Pizza called "Training Camp," which features a battalion of delivery trainees going through vigorous drills such as ringing doorbells, knocking on doors, running from a mechanical dog, and shouting "Pizza, pizza" as screaming drill sergeants spur them on.

Two Amersterdam agencies fought it out for the International Advertising Festival's Grand Prix for the best overall commercial. A charming and humorous commercial for Nestlés Rolo candy edged out the "Nike vs. Evil" spot from Wieden & Kennedy's Amsterdam office, which features a team of Nike's soccer endorsers taking on a team of Satanic opponents. The Grand Prix winner was done by Lintas. It features a little boy who teases a baby elephant with his last Rolo and then snatches it away. Years later, the grown man, wearing an identical sweater and watching another circus parade, gets trunk-whipped by the same elephant, now full-grown and with a very long memory. The print Grand Prix was awarded to Dentsu Young & Rubicam, Tokyo, for Volvo. The ad stressed Volvo's well-known safety heritage by simply showing a safety pin bent into the shape of a car.

While many advertising people are critical of creative awards, the 1996 Cannes competition attracted 4,391 TV entries and 4,855 in the print category, so someone must think they are important. Agencies know that the prestige of a Cannes Gold Lion award enhances their image and can help attract new business.

Sources: Claudia Penteado, "Rolo's Elephant Snares Grand Prix at Cannes," *Advertising Age*, July 1, 1996, pp. 1, 26; Jennifer Comiteau, "Cannes: Grand Results," *Adweek*, July 8, 1996, p. 6.

---

side, believe advertising must ultimately lead the consumer to purchase the product or service. Finding a balance between creative advertising and effective advertising is difficult. To better understand this dilemma, we turn to the issue of creativity and its role in advertising.

ADVERTISING CREATIVITY
What Is Creativity?

Creativity is probably one of the most commonly used terms in advertising. Ads are often called creative. The people who develop ads and commercials are known as creative types. And advertising agencies develop reputations for their creativity. Perhaps so much attention is focused on the concept of creativity because many people view the specific challenge given to those who develop an advertising message as being creative. It is their job to turn all of the information regarding product features and benefits, marketing plans, consumer research, and communication objectives into a creative concept that will bring the advertising message to life. This begs the question: What is meant by *creativity* in advertising?

Different Perspectives on Advertising Creativity

Perspectives on what constitutes creativity in advertising differ. At one extreme are those who argue that advertising is creative only if it sells the product. An advertising message's or campaign's impact on sales counts more than whether it is innovative or wins awards. At the other end of the continuum are those who judge the creativity of an ad in terms of its artistic or aesthetic value and originality. They contend creative ads can break through the competitive clutter, grab the consumer's attention, and have some impact.

As you might expect, perspectives on advertising creativity often depend on one's role. A study by Elizabeth Hirschman examined the perceptions of various individuals involved in the creation and production of TV commercials, including management types (brand managers and account executives) and creatives (art director, copywriter, commercial director, and producer).[5] She found that product managers and account executives view ads as promotional tools whose primary purpose is to communicate favorable impressions to the marketplace. They believe a commercial should be evaluated in terms of whether it fulfills the client's marketing and communicative objectives. The perspective of those on the creative side was much more self-serving, as Hirschman noted:

> In direct contrast to this client orientation, the art director, copywriter, and commercial director viewed the advertisement as a communication vehicle for promoting their own aesthetic viewpoints and personal career objectives. Both the copywriter and art director made this point explicitly, noting that a desirable commercial from their standpoint was one which communicated their unique creative talents and thereby permitted them to obtain "better" jobs at an increased salary.[6]

In her interviews, Hirschman also found that brand managers were much more risk averse and wanted a more conservative commercial than the creative people, who wanted to maximize the impact of the message.

What constitutes creativity in advertising is probably somewhere between the two extremes. To break through the clutter and make an impression on the target audience, an ad often must be unique and entertaining. As noted in Chapter 5, research has shown that a major determinant of whether a commercial will be successful in changing brand preferences is its "likability," or the viewer's overall reaction.[7] TV commercials and print ads that are well designed and executed and generate emotional responses can create positive feelings that are transferred to the product or service being advertised. Many creative people believe this type of advertising can come about only if they are given considerable latitude in developing advertising messages. But ads that are creative only for the sake of being creative often fail to communicate a relevant or meaningful message that will lead consumers to purchase the product or service.

Everyone involved in planning and developing an advertising campaign must understand the importance of balancing the "it's not creative unless it sells" perspective with the novelty/uniqueness and impact position. Marketing and brand managers or account executives must recognize that imposing too many sales- and marketing-oriented communications objectives on the creative team can result in mediocre advertising, which is often ineffective in today's competitive, cluttered media environment. At the same time, the creative specialists must recognize that the goal of advertising is to assist in selling the product or service and good advertising must communicate in a manner that helps the client achieve this goal.

Advertising creativity is the ability to generate fresh, unique, and appropriate ideas that can be used as solutions to communications problems. To be *appropriate* and effective, a creative idea must be relevant to the target audience. Many ad agencies recognize the importance of developing advertising that is creative and different yet communicates relevant information to the target audience. Figure 8–2 shows D'Arcy, Masius Benton & Bowles's universal advertising standards, nine principles that the agency developed to guide its creative efforts and help achieve superior creativity consistently. The agency views a creative advertising message as one built around a creative core or power idea and using excellent design and execution to communicate information that interests the target audience. It has used these principles in doing outstanding creative work for Procter & Gamble's Charmin and Pampers brands, Norelco, and many other popular brands.

Advertising creativity is not the exclusive domain of those who work on the creative side of advertising. The nature of the business requires creative thinking from everyone involved

FIGURE 8–2   D'Arcy, Masius Benton & Bowles's universal advertising standards

1. *Does this advertising position the product simply and with unmistakable clarity?*

   The target audience for the advertised product or service must be able to see and sense in a flash *what* the product is for, *whom* it is for, and *why* they should be interested in it.

   Creating this clear vision of how the product or service fits into their lives is the first job of advertising. Without a simple, clear, focused positioning, no creative work can begin.

2. *Does this advertising bolt the brand to a clinching benefit?*

   Our advertising should be built on the most compelling and persuasive consumer benefit—not some unique-but-insignificant peripheral feature.

   Before you worry about how to say it, you must be sure you are saying *the right thing.* If you don't know what the most compelling benefit is, you've got to find out before you do anything else.

3. *Does this advertising contain a Power Idea?*

   The Power Idea is the vehicle that transforms the strategy into a dynamic, creative communications concept. It is the core creative idea that sets the stage for brilliant executions to come. The ideal Power Idea should:

   • Be describable in a simple word, phrase, or sentence without reference to any final execution.

   • Be likely to attract the prospect's attention.

   • Revolve around the clinching benefit.

   • Allow you to brand the advertising.

   • Make it easy for the prospect to vividly experience our client's product or service.

4. *Does this advertising design in Brand Personality?*

   The great brands tend to have something in common: the extra edge of having a Brand Personality. This is something beyond merely identifying what the brand does for the consumer; all brands *do* something, but the great brands also *are* something.

   A brand can be whatever its designers want it to be—and it can be so from day one.

5. *Is this advertising unexpected?*

   Why should our clients pay good money to wind up with advertising that looks and sounds like everybody else's in the category? They shouldn't.

   We must dare to be different, because sameness is suicide. We can't be outstanding unless we first stand out.

   The thing is not to *emulate* the competition but to *annihilate* them.

6. *Is this advertising single-minded?*

   If you have determined the right thing to say and have created a way to say it uncommonly well, why waste time saying anything else?

   If we want people to remember one big thing from a given piece of advertising, let's not make it more difficult than it already is in an overcommunicated world.

   The advertising should be all about that one big thing.

7. *Does this advertising reward the prospect?*

   Let's give our audience something that makes it easy—even pleasurable—for our message to penetrate: a tear, a smile, a laugh. An emotional stimulus is that special something that makes them want to see the advertising again and again.

8. *Is this advertising visually arresting?*

   Great advertising you remember—and can play back in your mind—is unusual to look at: compelling, riveting, a nourishing feast for the eyes. If you need a reason to strive for arresting work, go no further than Webster: "Catching or holding the attention, thought, or feelings. Gripping. Striking. Interesting."

9. *Does this advertising exhibit painstaking craftsmanship?*

   You want writing that is really written. Visuals that are designed. Music that is composed.

   Lighting, casting, wardrobe, direction—all the components of the art of advertising are every bit as important as the science of it. It is a sin to nickel-and-dime a great advertising idea to death.

   Why settle for good, when there's great? We should go for the absolute best in concept, design, and execution.

   This is our craft—the work should sparkle.

   "Our creative standards are not a gimmick," Steve emphasizes. "They're not even revolutionary. Instead, they are an explicit articulation of a fundamental refocusing on our company's only reason for being.

   "DMB&B's universal advertising standards are the operating link between our vision today—and its coming reality."

IMC Perspective 8–2
Getting Everyone Involved in Developing Creative Strategies

When the term *creative* comes up in the world of advertising, most people think of the so-named department of the ad agency and the individuals who come up with ideas for the ads. *Creative media planning* traditionally has meant finding an offbeat way to help an advertiser's message break through the competitive clutter. However, today the phrase has evolved to mean much more, including finding synergy between the creative and media departments.

In most companies and ad agencies, the usual approach is to create print ads and TV commercials and then determine where to place them. Now many agencies and their clients are realizing that synergy between the media and creative departments, as well as creative thinking by clients and even the media themselves, are important in developing a successful ad campaign.

Perhaps the best example of an advertiser/agency team that recognizes the value of using media-driven creative strategies is Absolut vodka and its longtime agency, TBWA Advertising. More than 15 years ago TBWA developed an ad campaign that plays off the distinctive shape of the Absolut bottle and made it the hero of the ads by depicting it with visual puns and witty headlines. The campaign's objective has been to build awareness of the brand and make Absolut a "fashionable symbol of smartness and sophistication that consumers would want to be associated with."

This goal has been accomplished through outstanding creative execution and a spirit of cooperation between the media and creative departments of TBWA. They recognized early on that they could carry the advertising campaign further by playing on the name Absolut, highlighting the distinctive shape of the bottle, and tailoring the print ads for the magazines or regions where they appear. For example, for New York media, the agency created "Absolut Manhattan," showing Central Park in the shape of a vodka bottle. Ads in skiing magazines show ski slopes curving around pine trees formed in the shape of the bottle, with the tagline "Absolut Peak."

Absolut's annual media schedule may cover 100 magazines, including various consumer and business publications. The creative and media departments work together selecting magazines and deciding on ads that will appeal to the readers of each publication. The creative department is often asked to create media-specific ads to run in a particular publication. Recently TBWA even got the media involved in the creative process. It challenged all of the magazines that carry Absolut ads to come up with cutting-edge concepts that go beyond pure advertising and tell the Absolut story in an interesting way to their readers.

One of the first new Absolut ads whose format was suggested by a magazine appeared in *Atlantic*. The ad, which is titled "The Tradition," features four paragraphs of copy and a soothing illustration of a wheat field and accompanying scenery that form the familiar bottle. The ad was the first in a four-part series developed to tell the story of the Absolut brand to the publication's cerebral readers.

A media-inspired creative concept that was suggested by the ad department at *Rolling Stone* featured a six-page pullout of recording artists, including Tony Bennett and Iggy Pop, who painted original Absolut ads. Another example suggested by *Saveur*, a tony food magazine, showed an ad for Absolut Kurant Black Currant flavored vodka that allows the reader to pull a tab and smell black currant.

Absolut has also gotten media experts involved in the design of its website. In May 1996 it unveiled "Absolut Kelly," a website that was designed in part by Kevin Kelly, the executive editor of *Wired*, a magazine where Absolut is a prominent advertiser. He is the first of several media experts who will create Internet content for Absolut.

The media-driven creative strategy for Absolut has paid off. Its ads are always among the most popular print campaigns in consumer surveys and the brand is the number-one imported vodka and tenth most popular liquor brand in the United States.

Sources: Debra Aho Williamson, "Absolut Web: Site with a Twist," *Advertising Age*, May 20, 1996, p. 48; Kevin Goldman, "Asolut Tones Down Its Familiar Bottle," *The Wall Street Journal*, July 27, 1995, p. B6; Valerie H. Free, "Absolut Original," *Marketing Insights*, Summer 1991, pp. 64–72.

in the promotional planning process. Agency people, such as account executives, media planners, researchers, and attorneys, as well as those on the client side, such as marketing and brand managers, must all seek creative solutions to problems encountered in planning, developing, and executing an advertising campaign. IMC Perspective 8–2 discusses how creative synergy between the media and creative departments as well as with the client is becoming more commonplace.

PLANNING CREATIVE STRATEGY
The Creative Challenge

Those who work on the creative side of advertising often face a real challenge. They must take all the research, creative briefs, strategy statements, communications objectives, and other input and transform them into an advertising message. Their job is to write copy, design layouts and illustrations, or produce commercials that effectively communicate the central theme on which the campaign is based. Rather than simply stating the features or benefits of a product or service, they must put the advertising message into a form that will engage the audience's interest and make the ads memorable.[8]

The job of the creative team is challenging because every marketing situation is different and each campaign or advertisement may require a different creative approach. Numerous guidelines have been developed for creating effective advertising,[9] but there is no magic formula. As copywriter Hank Sneiden notes in his book, *Advertising Pure and Simple*:

> Rules lead to dull stereotyped advertising, and they stifle creativity, inspiration, initiative, and progress. The only hard and fast rule that I know of in advertising is that there are no rules. No formulas. No right way. Given the same problem, a dozen creative talents would solve it a dozen different ways. If there were a sure-fire formula for successful advertising, everyone would use it. Then there'd be no need for creative people. We would simply program robots to create our ads and commercials and they'd sell loads of product—to other robots.[10]

Taking Creative Risks

Many creative people follow proven formulas when creating ads because they are safe. Clients often feel uncomfortable with advertising that is too different. Bill Tragos, chair of TBWA, the advertising agency noted for its excellent creative work for Absolut vodka, Evian, and many other clients, says, "Very few clients realize that the reason that their work is so bad is that they are the ones who commandeered it and directed it to be that way. I think that at least 50 percent of an agency's successful work resides in the client."[11]

Many creative people say it is important for clients to take some risks if they want breakthrough advertising that gets noticed. One agency that has been successful in getting its clients to take risks is Wieden & Kennedy, best known for its excellent creative work for companies such as Nike and Microsoft (Exhibit 8–3). The agency's founders believe a key element to their success has been a steadfast belief in taking risks when most agencies and their clients have been retrenching and becoming more conservative.[12] The agency can develop great advertising partly because clients like Nike are willing to take risks and go along with the agency's priority system, which places the creative work first and the client-agency relationship second. The agency has even terminated relationships with large clients like Gallo when they interfered too much with the creative process.

Not all companies or agencies agree that advertising has to be risky to be effective, however. Many marketing managers are more comfortable with advertising that simply communicates product or service features and benefits and gives the consumer a reason to buy. They see their ad campaigns as multimillion-dollar investments whose goal is to sell the product rather than finance the whims of their agency's creative staff. They argue that some creative people have lost sight of advertising's bottom line: Does it sell?

The issue of how much latitude creative people should be given and how much risk the client should be willing to take is open to considerable debate. However, clients and agency personnel generally agree that the ability to develop novel yet appropriate approaches to communicating with the customer makes the creative specialist valuable—and often hard to find.

Creative Personnel

The image of the creative advertising person perpetuated in novels, movies, and TV shows is often one of a freewheeling, freethinking, eccentric personality. The educational background of creative personnel is often in nonbusiness areas such as art, literature, music, humanities, or journalism, so their interests and perspectives tend to differ from those of managers with a business education or background. Creative people tend to be more abstract and less structured, organized, or conventional in their approach to a problem, relying on intuition more often than logic.

Advertising creatives are sometimes stereotyped as odd, perhaps because they dress differently and do not always work the conventional 9-to-5 schedule. Of course, from the perspective of the creatives, it is the marketing or brand managers and account executives (the

EXHIBIT 8–3 Wieden & Kennedy's belief in taking risks has resulted in creative advertising for clients like Nike

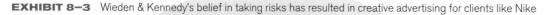

EXHIBIT 8–3 Wieden & Kennedy's belief in taking risks has resulted in creative advertising for clients like Nike

"suits") who are strange. In many agencies, you can't tell the creative personnel from the executives by their dress or demeanor. Yet the differences between creative and managerial personalities and perspectives must be recognized and tolerated so creative people can do their best work and all those involved in the advertising process can cooperate.

Most agencies thrive on creativity, for it is the major component in the product they produce. Thus, they must create an environment that fosters the development of creative thinking and creative advertising. Clients must also understand the differences between the perspectives of the creative personnel and marketing and product managers. While the client has ultimate approval of the advertising, the opinions of creative specialists must be respected when advertising ideas and content are evaluated. (Evaluation of the creative's ideas and work is discussed in more detail in Chapter 9.)

THE CREATIVE PROCESS

Some advertising people say creativity in advertising is best viewed as a process and creative success is most likely when some organized approach is followed. This does not mean there is an infallible blueprint to follow to create effective advertising; as we saw earlier, many advertising people reject attempts to standardize creativity or develop rules. However, most do follow a process when developing an ad.

One of the most popular approaches to creativity in advertising was developed by James Webb Young, a former creative vice president at the J. Walter Thompson agency. Young said, "The production of ideas is just as definite a process as the production of Fords; the production of ideas, too, runs an assembly line; in this production the mind follows an operative technique which can be learned and controlled; and that its effective use is just as much a matter of practice in the technique as in the effective use of any tool."[13] Young's model of the creative process contains five steps:

1. *Immersion.* Gathering raw material and information through background research and immersing yourself in the problem.
2. *Digestion.* Taking the information, working it over, and wrestling with it in the mind.
3. *Incubation.* Putting the problems out of your conscious mind and turning the information over to the subconscious to do the work.
4. *Illumination.* The birth of an idea—the "Eureka! I have it!" phenomenon.
5. *Reality or verification.* Studying the idea to see if it still looks good or solves the problem, then shaping the idea to practical usefulness.

Young's process of creativity is similar to a four-step approach outlined much earlier by English sociologist Graham Wallas:

1. *Preparation.* Gathering background information needed to solve the problem through research and study.
2. *Incubation.* Getting away and letting ideas develop.
3. *Illumination.* Seeing the light or solution.
4. *Verification.* Refining and polishing the idea and seeing if it is an appropriate solution.

Models of the creative process are valuable to those working in the creative area of advertising, since they offer an organized way to approach an advertising problem. Preparation or gathering of background information is the first step in the creative process. As we saw in earlier chapters, the advertiser and agency start by developing a thorough understanding of the product or service, the target market, and the competition. They also focus on the role of advertising in the marketing and promotional program.

These models do not say much about how this information will be synthesized and used by the creative specialist because this part of the process is unique to the individual. In many ways, it's what sets apart the great creative minds and strategists in advertising. The following section examines how various types of research and information can provide input to the creative process of advertising.

Inputs to the Creative Process: Preparation, Incubation, Illumination

BACKGROUND RESEARCH

Only the most foolish creative person or team would approach an assignment without first learning as much as possible about the client's product or service, the target market, the competition, and any other relevant background information. The creative specialist should also be knowledgeable about general trends, conditions, and developments in the marketplace, as well as research on specific advertising approaches or techniques that might be effective. The creative specialist can acquire background information in numerous ways. Some informal fact-finding techniques have been noted by Sandra Moriarty:

- Reading anything related to the product or market—books, trade publications, general interest articles, research reports, and the like.
- Asking everyone involved with the product for information—designers, engineers, salespeople, and consumers.
- Listening to what people are talking about. Visits to stores, malls, restaurants, and even the agency cafeteria can be informative. Listening to the client can be particularly valuable, since he or she often knows the product and market best.
- Using the product or service and becoming familiar with it. The more you use a product, the more you know and can say about it.
- Working in and learning about the client's business to understand better the people you're trying to reach.[14]

To assist in the preparation, incubation, and illumination stages, many agencies provide creative people with both general and product-specific preplanning input. **General preplanning input** can include books, periodicals, trade publications, scholarly journals, pictures, and clipping services, which gather and organize magazine and newspaper articles on the product, the market, and the competition, including the latter's ads. This input can also come from research studies conducted by the client, agency, media, or other sources.

Another useful general preplanning input concerns trends, developments, and happenings in the marketplace. Information is available from a variety of sources, including local, state, and federal governments, secondary research suppliers, and various industry trade associations, as well as advertising and media organizations. For example, advertising industry groups like the American Association of Advertising Agencies and media organizations like the National Association of Broadcasters (NAB) and Magazine Publishers of America (MPA) publish research reports and newsletters that provide information on market trends and developments and how they might affect consumers. Those involved in developing creative strategy can also gather relevant and timely information by reading publications like *Advertising Age, Brand Week,* and *The Wall Street Journal* (Exhibit 8–4).

PRODUCT/SERVICE-SPECIFIC RESEARCH

In addition to general background research and preplanning input, creative people receive **product/service-specific preplanning input**. This information generally comes in the form of specific studies conducted on the product or service, the target audience, or a combination of the two. Quantitative and qualitative consumer research such as attitude studies; market structure and positioning studies such as perceptual mapping and lifestyle research; focus group interviews; and demographic and psychographic profiles of users of a particular product, service, or brand are examples of product-specific preplanning input.

Many product- or service-specific studies helpful to the creative team are conducted by the client or the agency. A number of years ago, the BBDO ad agency developed an approach for finding ideas around which creative strategies could be based called **problem detection**.[15] This research technique involves asking consumers familiar with a product (or service) to generate an exhaustive list of things that bother them or problems they encounter when using it. The consumers rate these problems in order of importance and evaluate various brands in terms of their association with each problem. A problem detection study can provide valuable input for product improvements, reformulations, or new products. It can also give the creative people ideas regarding attributes or features to emphasize and guidelines for positioning new or existing brands.

Some agencies conduct psychographic studies annually and construct detailed psychographic or lifestyle profiles of product or service users. DDB Needham conducts a large-scale psychographic study each year using a sample of 4,000 U.S. adults. The agency's Life Style Study provides its creative teams with a better understanding of the target audience for whom they are developing ads.

For example, information from its Life Style Study was used by DDB Needham's creative department in developing a recent advertising campaign for Westin. The agency's Life

EXHIBIT 8—4
Industry publications like *Advertising Age* are excellent sources of information on market trends

MARTY HORN

Marty Horn is a rare breed among agency people: he's been at the same agency, albeit one that has undergone several name and organizational changes, for over 20 years. Why so long at one agency? "It's a combination of liking where I am, trying to make sure that what I do is valued by the agency and clients, getting along with people, and a little luck," he muses. In his role as a researcher and strategic planner, Marty oversees all agency research for building communication strategies and guiding creative development for clients such as Tyson Foods, Wilson Sporting Goods, Ameritech, and various Frito Lay snack food brands. He notes that "in 20 years I've worked on a lot of different accounts, from on-line services to laxatives, dog food to fast food, shampoo to salt. My career path has crossed with Lassie on Recipe Dog Food, the Energizer Bunny, Chester Cheetah on Cheetos, and Ronald McDonald."

"The great thing about the Life Style Study is that it gives us deeper insights into our client's consumers."

The research Marty does for DDB Needham's accounts runs the gamut from one-on-one interviews to focus groups to large scale studies that model advertising's effects. He feels the biggest challenge of his job is trying to synthesize a tangled web of data, find the insight, and communicate it in a way that is informative, interesting, and clearly *actionable*. "One thing I try to discipline myself to do, and it's something all researchers should do, is to 'think backwards.' When beginning a research project, I do not start with the method, sample size, and composition, questionnaire items and the like. Rather I begin with the marketing or advertising decision that needs to be made and ask what do we need to know to take the appropriate action? When I have answered that question I begin to work on the research design."

Marty notes that once the data are in and analyzed, he faces the hardest part of his job—presenting the research so it is clear, concise, and compelling. "My audience usually is not other researchers, but rather marketing executives and agency creative people who don't really care much about the research details. All they want to know is what the research found and what they should do as a result. Moreover, I have to communicate the findings and implications in a way that makes people sit up, take notice, and take action. While researchers draw on data to develop insights and ideas, in the end we have to be fascinating, motivating storytellers, not data mongers."

In addition to his client responsibilities, Marty Horn oversees *The DDB Needham Life Style Study*, an annual survey of American's attitudes, interests, and opinions as well as their product usage and ownership, media habits, and demographics. The information from this yearly survey of 4,000 men and women is used for all of the agency's clients and as a tool for attracting new business. Marty says that "the great thing about the Life Style Study is that it gives us deeper insights into our client's consumers. Information from the Life Style Study helps the creative teams develop advertising that will speak the language of our target audience and be more relevant to them."

Marty also spearheads *The Marketing Olympics*, a study which has tracked the value of corporate sponsorship of the Summer Olympics since 1984. The study helps companies determine whether their Olympic sponsorships were a success and, more important, what strategic and tactical steps they might take to better utilize their sponsorship. It also is valuable to companies considering involvement in Olympic sponsorships.

Marty is an active member of the Association for Consumer Research (ACR), an organization of academics and practitioners who study various aspects of consumer behavior. He notes, "the organization is an eclectic mix of very bright people who address advertising and marketing issues in unique, innovative ways. I often attend the annual ACR conference where I always gain new perspectives that help me in my own job." He has presented papers at the conference, chaired sessions, and serves on the ACR Advisory Board. He has also co-authored articles in *Journal of Advertising* and *Journal of Advertising Research*.

Marty received his Bachelors and Masters degrees in communications from the University of Connecticut. Before joining DDB Needham, he worked for one year at Burke Marketing Research in Cincinnati.

Style Study showed that the younger business travelers the luxury hotel chain was targeting are highly confident, intelligent, assertive, classy, and considered themselves to be a "winner." Rather than using the traditional images that feature buildings and golf courses, the creative team decided to "brand the user" by playing to their ego and reinforcing their strong self-image. The new ad campaign uses the tagline "Who is he/she sleeping with? Westin. Choose your travel partner wisely." (Exhibit 8–5.) Since the campaign began in mid-1996, Westin's call volumes have increased by 25 percent.

QUALITATIVE RESEARCH INPUT

Many agencies, particularly larger ones with strong research departments, have their own research programs and specific techniques they use to assist in the development of creative strategy and provide input to the creative process. In addition to the various quantitative research studies, qualitative research techniques such as in-depth interviews or focus groups can provide the creative team with valuable insight at the early stages of the creative process. **Focus groups** are a research method whereby consumers (usually 10 to 12 people) from the target market are led through a discussion regarding a particular topic. Focus groups give insight as to why and how consumers use a product or service, what is important to them in choosing a particular brand, what they like and don't like about various products or services, and any special needs they might have that aren't being satisfied. A focus group session might also include a discussion of types of ad appeals to use or evaluate the advertising of various companies.

Focus group interviews bring the creative people and others involved in creative strategy development into contact with the customers. Listening to a focus group gives copywriters, art directors, and other creative specialists a better sense of who the target audience is, what the audience is like, and who the creatives need to write, design, or direct to in creating an advertising message. Focus groups can also be used to evaluate the viability of different creative approaches under consideration and suggest the best direction to pursue.[16]

EXHIBIT 8–5
DDB Needham's Life Style Study provided valuable input in the development of this campaign for Westin

Generally, creative people are open to any research or information that will help them understand the client's target market better and assist in generating creative ideas. The advertising industry is recognizing the importance of using research to guide the creative process. The Advertising Research Foundation recently initiated the David Ogilvy Awards, named after the advertising legend who founded Ogilvy & Mather. These awards are presented to teams of advertising agencies, client companies, and research companies in recognition of research that has been used successfully to determine the strategy and effectiveness of ad campaigns. IMC Perspective 8–3 discusses how the California Milk Processor Board, which won the David Ogilvy Award in 1996, used both quantitative and qualitative research in developing the popular "Got milk?" advertising campaign.

Inputs to the Creative Process: Verification, Revision

The verification and revision stage of the creative process evaluates ideas generated during the illumination stage, rejects inappropriate ones, refines and polishes those that remain, and gives them final expression. Techniques used at this stage include directed focus groups to evaluate creative concepts, ideas, or themes; message communication studies; portfolio tests; and evaluation measures such as viewer reaction profiles.[17]

At this stage of the creative process, members of the target audience may be asked to evaluate rough creative layouts and to indicate what meaning they get from the ad, what they think of its execution, or how they react to a slogan or theme. The creative team can gain insight into how a TV commercial might communicate its message by having members of the target market evaluate the ad in storyboard form. A **storyboard** is a series of drawings used to present the visual plan or layout of a proposed commercial. It contains a series of sketches of key frames or scenes along with the copy or audio portion for each scene (Exhibit 8–6).

Testing a commercial in storyboard form can be difficult because storyboards are too abstract for many consumers to understand. To make the creative layout more realistic and easier to evaluate, the agency may produce an **aniamatic**, a videotape of the storyboard along with an audio soundtrack. Storyboards and aniamatics are useful for research purposes as well as for presenting the creative idea to other agency personnel or to the client for discussion and approval.

At this stage of the process, the creative team is attempting to find the best creative approach or execution style before moving ahead with the campaign themes and going into actual production of the ad. The verification/revision process may include more formal, extensive pretesting of the ad before a final decision is made. Pretesting and related procedures are examined in detail in Chapter 18.

CREATIVE STRATEGY DEVELOPMENT

Like any other area of the marketing and promotional process, the creative aspect of advertising is guided by specific goals and objectives. A creative strategy that focuses on what must be communicated will guide the development of all messages used in the ad campaign. Creative strategy is based on several factors, including an identification of the target audience; the basic problem, issue, or opportunity the advertising must address; the major selling idea or key benefit the message needs to communicate; and any supportive information that needs to be included in the ad. Once these factors are determined, a creative strategy statement should describe the message appeal and execution style that will be used. Many ad agencies outline these elements in a document known as the copy or creative platform.

Copy Platform

The written **copy platform** specifies the basic elements of the creative strategy. Different agencies may call this document a creative platform or work plan, creative blueprint, or creative contract. The account representative or manager assigned to the account usually prepares the copy platform. In larger agencies, an individual from research or the strategic planning department may write it. People from the agency team or group assigned to the account, including creative personnel as well as representatives from media and research, have input. The advertising manager and/or the marketing and brand managers from the client side ultimately approve the copy platform. Figure 8–3 is a sample copy platform outline that can be used to guide the creative process. Just as there are different names for the platform, there are variations in the outline and format used and in the level of detail included.

IMC Perspective 8–3
Understanding How People Really Drink Milk Leads to a Creative Advertising Campaign

If you are like most consumers, when you need to quench a thirst you probably reach for a soft drink, a glass of juice, iced tea, or just a plain glass of water. However, if you have a peanut butter-and-jelly sandwich, a chocolate-chip cookie, or a brownie in front of you, or are about to have a bowl of cereal, there is really only one choice: milk. Nothing else will do. That is the idea behind the "Got milk?" advertising campaign created by Goodby, Silverstein & Partners for the California Milk Processor Board.

Milk consumption has been declining across the country for nearly three decades. The decline has been particularly bad in California where overall consumption fell an average of 2 to 3 percent per year between the late 1980s and early 1990s. Alarmed by this trend, milk processors in the state formed the board in 1993, hired executive director Jeff Manning to develop a marketing program to increase sales and gave him three years to turn things around. When Manning hired Goodby, Silverstein, he made it clear that the goal of the ad campaign was increased milk sales, not image enhancement.

Manning had a strong hunch that would prove remarkably accurate. In previous ads, milk had been shown as a beverage that was consumed alone. But Manning thinks most people drink milk in combination with other foods: "If you ask people when milk is crucial, they'll tell you it's when they have cereal in the bowl or cookies in their mouth. The driver is not the milk. It's the food." Manning's hypothesis became a guiding force for the qualitative and quantitative research conducted to develop the campaign. The team decided to target people who were already milk drinkers and encourage them to drink more, rather than try to convert nonusers.

A telephone survey of Californians over the age of 11 found that 88 percent of milk is consumed at home and it is usually accompanied by other foods, most frequently cereal. Other key companion foods included cookies, pastries, brownies, and peanut butter-and-jelly sandwiches. While the quantitative information was valuable in identifying the best foods to feature in the ads, the agency wanted to determine which situations prompt a strong desire for milk and how people feel when they are deprived of it.

To observe the effects of this "milk deprivation," the agency added a unique twist to its focus groups. In return for extra payment, people agreed not to drink any milk for a week before the focus group and to keep a diary of everything they ate or drank in that time. The participants found that this was easier said than done. One man described his usual pattern of waking up bleary-eyed at 7 A.M. and pouring a bowl of cereal, only to find no milk in the fridge. Others identified with his plight. One said, "It's so bad, you'd even steal milk from your kid." Another respondent noted, "Never mind your kid. You're so desperate, you'd even steal it from your cat."

The focus group stories formed the basis for a series of humorous TV commercials emphasizing the agony that awaits those who run out of milk. One spot shows a milk-less man agonizing over a bowl of cereal, deciding whether to rob his baby's bottle or his pet's bowl. In a Christmas spot, Santa enters a home, consumes a brownie, finds no milk, and takes his presents away. Each spot ends with the tagline "Got milk?"

Although television advertising is the largest and most visible part of the campaign, an entire integrated marketing strategy has been built around the "got milk" theme. Radio ads remind people to stop for milk on their way home. Billboards are strategically placed around shopping malls and grocery and convenience stores. Point-of-purchase displays are set up in aisles containing cookies, cereals, and other companion foods. There have been joint promotions with companion food companies such as Nestlé, General Mills, and Nabisco.

The "got milk" campaign is widely recognized for its creative excellence, and it seems to be increasing sales as well. In the first year of the campaign, milk sales rose just about 1 percent over the previous year; in 1996, sales were about 1 percent higher than in 1995. These increases were achieved despite higher milk prices and a shaky California economy. Another important result of the campaign is that per capita consumption stabilized at 23 gallons from 1994 to 1996. The Milk Processor Board voted to extend the campaign through 1998 and it has been expanded to other areas of the country.

Sources: Paula Mergenhagen, "How 'Got milk?' Got Sales," *Marketing Tools*, September 1996, pp. 4–7; "Got Milk?" *Adweek*, August 5, 1996, p. 6.

EXHIBIT 8–6   Marketers can gain insight into consumers' reactions to a commercial by showing them a storyboard

SFX: CAR AND FOOT TRAFFIC AMBIENCE

VO: Why did the chicken cross the road? To open a 7/24 Savings Plan at San Diego Trust.

Because with $500 in savings . . . he can avoid getting henpecked by monthly charges on a checking account.

What's more, he can access his nest egg through our huge ATM network . . .

SFX: BANK AMBIENCE

. . . and round-the-clock phone service.

VO: And of course, the interest he'll earn on savings isn't just chicken feed.

So open a 7/24 Savings Plan at San Diego Trust.

And give yourself a good reason to . . .

SFX: COCKA DOODLE DOO

1. Basic problem or issue the advertising must address.
2. Advertising and communications objectives.
3. Target audience.
4. Major selling idea or key benefits to communicate.
5. Creative strategy statement (campaign theme, appeal, and execution technique to be used).
6. Supporting information and requirements.

Several components of the copy platform were discussed in previous chapters. For example, Chapter 7 examined the DAGMAR model and showed how the setting of advertising objectives requires specifying a well-defined target audience and developing a communications task statement that spells out what message must be communicated to this audience. Determining what problem the product or service will solve or what issue must be addressed in the ad helps in establishing communications objectives for the message to accomplish. Many copy platforms also include supporting information and requirements (brand identifications, disclaimers, and the like). The final two components of the copy platform, development of the major selling idea and creative strategy development, are often the responsibility of the creative team or specialist and form the basis of the advertising campaign.

Advertising Campaigns

Most ads are part of a series of messages that make up an **advertising campaign**, which often consists of multiple messages in a variety of media that center on a single theme or idea. Determining the central theme, idea, position, or image is a critical part of the creative process, as it sets the tone for the individual ads that make up the campaign. Some campaigns last only a short time, usually because they are ineffective or market conditions change. A successful campaign theme and creative strategy may last for years. Philip Morris has been using the "Marlboro country" campaign for over 35 years, while Campbell Soup Co. first began airing radio spots using the familiar "M'm! M'm! Good!" theme in radio spots in the 1930s.[18] Recruitment advertising for the United States Army has used "Be all you can be" for many years (Exhibit 8–7). Figure 8–4 lists some of the more enduring ad campaign themes.

Once the creative theme is established and approved, attention turns to what type of appeal and creative execution approach to use. Before considering these parts of creative strategy, we examine how major selling ideas are determined.

If you'd like a career with a high-tech company, start with one of ours.

From telecommunications centers to laser technology to advanced radar systems, you'll work with the most sophisticated technology in the world, as a member of an Army company. Which means you'll gain the skills it takes to get an edge on the high-tech job market. And you'll gain the confidence, self-discipline and capacity for leadership the best employers insist on.

So call 1-800-USA-ARMY and get the training you'll need to get an edge on life. And your future.

ARMY. BE ALL YOU CAN BE.

Company or Brand	Campaign Theme
Nike	"Just do it."
Allstate Insurance	"You're in good hands with Allstate."
Hallmark cards	"When you care enough to send the very best."
De Beers	"A diamond is forever."
BMW	"The ultimate driving machine."
State Farm Insurance	"Like a good neighbor, State Farm is there."
Timex watches	"It takes a licking and keeps on ticking."
Dial soap	"Aren't you glad you use Dial? Don't you wish everyone did?"

The Search for the Major Selling Idea

An important part of creative strategy is determining the central theme that will become the **major selling idea** of the ad campaign. As A. Jerome Jeweler states in his book *Creative Strategy in Advertising*:

> The major selling idea should emerge as the strongest singular thing you can say about your product or service. This should be the claim with the broadest and most meaningful appeal to your target audience. Once you determine this message, be certain you can live with it; be sure it stands strong enough to remain the central issue in every ad and commercial in the campaign.[19]

Some advertising experts argue that for an ad campaign to be effective it must contain a big idea that attracts the consumer's attention, gets a reaction, and sets the advertiser's product or service apart from the competition's. Well-known adman John O'Toole describes the *big idea* as "that flash of insight that synthesizes the purpose of the strategy, joins the product benefit with consumer desire in a fresh, involving way, brings the subject to life, and makes the reader or audience stop, look, and listen."[20]

Of course, the real challenge to the creative team is coming up with the big idea to use in the ad. Many products and services offer virtually nothing unique, and it can be difficult to find something interesting to say about them. David Ogilvy, generally considered one of the most creative advertising copywriters ever to work in the business, has stated:

> I doubt if more than one campaign in a hundred contains a big idea. I am supposed to be one of the more fertile inventors of big ideas, but in my long career as a copywriter I have not had more than 20, if that.[21]

While really great ideas in advertising are difficult to come by, there are many examples of big ideas that became the basis of very creative, successful advertising campaigns. Classic examples include "we try harder," which positioned Avis as the underdog rental car company that provided better service than Hertz; "tastes great, less filling," used for over 20 years for Miller Lite beer; the "Pepsi generation" theme and subsequent variations like "the taste of a new generation" and "GenerationNext"; and BMW's "ultimate driving machine." More recent big ideas that have resulted in effective advertising include the "Intel Inside" campaign for Intel computer microprocessors, Nike's "just do it," and the "like a rock" theme for GMC trucks.

Big ideas are important in business-to-business advertising as well. For example, Beacon Manufacturing Co. was unimpressed with the way blankets were advertised and wanted to do something different to get the attention of retail stores' buyers and mer-

chandise managers. Beacon and its agency, Easterby & Associates, leveraged the popularity of the company's vice president of sales, Ted Smith, into an advertising campaign. "Adventures of Teddy" elevated Smith into an Everyman willing to go the extra mile to prove his product's superiority. The ads have shown Smith being tossed in the air by a Beacon blanket, hanging from a helicopter with a Beacon blanket, using one as a parachute, and keeping sharks at bay with one. The idea resulted in great advertising that has helped Beacon increase sales three times the industry average.

It is difficult to pinpoint the inspiration for a big idea or to teach advertising people how to find them. However, several approaches can guide the creative team's search for a major selling idea and offer solutions for developing effective advertising. Some of the best-known approaches follow:

- Using a unique selling proposition.
- Creating a brand image.
- Finding the inherent drama.
- Positioning.

UNIQUE SELLING PROPOSITION

The concept of the **unique selling proposition (USP)**, which was mentioned in the opening vignette, was developed by Rosser Reeves, former chair of the Ted Bates agency, and is described in his influential book *Reality in Advertising*. Reeves noted three characteristics of unique selling propositions:

1. Each advertisement must make a proposition to the consumer. Not just words, not just product puffery, not just show window advertising. Each advertisement must say to each reader: "Buy this product and you will get this benefit."
2. The proposition must be one that the competition either cannot or does not offer. It must be unique either in the brand or in the claim.
3. The proposition must be strong enough to move the mass millions, that is, pull over new customers to your brand.[22]

Reeves said the attribute claim or benefit that forms the basis of the USP should dominate the ad and be emphasized through repetitive advertising. An example of advertising based on a USP is the campaign for Castrol Syntec synthetic motor oil. Other companies had marketed synthetic oils with little success. But a unique feature of Castrol Syntec is its ability to offer superior protection because it bonds to the engine. A TV commercial was created showing dozens of revving engines running on conventional motor oil and one on Syntec. The oil was drained from the engines and they were restarted. While the conventional ones ground to a halt, the engine using Syntec kept going thanks to its unique bonding properties (Exhibit 8–8).

For Reeves's approach to work, there must be a truly unique product or service attribute, benefit, or inherent advantage that can be used in the claim. This may require considerable research on the product and consumers, not only to determine the USP but also to document the claim. As we shall see in Chapter 21, the Federal Trade Commission objects to ad-

EXHIBIT 8–8
Advertising for Castrol Syntec motor oil uses a unique selling proposition

vertisers making claims of superiority or uniqueness without supporting data. Also, some companies have sued their competitors for making unsubstantiated uniqueness claims.[23]

Advertisers must also consider whether the unique selling proposition affords them a *sustainable competitive advantage* that competitors cannot easily copy. In the package-goods field in particular, companies quickly match a brand feature for feature, so advertising based on USPs becomes obsolete. For example, a few years ago Procter & Gamble invented a combination shampoo and conditioner to rejuvenate its struggling Pert brand. The reformulated brand was called Pert Plus and its market share rose from 2 percent to 12 percent, making it the leading shampoo. But competing brands like Revlon and Suave quickly launched their own two-in-one formula products.[24]

CREATING A BRAND IMAGE

In many product and service categories, competing brands are so similar it is very difficult to find or create a unique attribute or benefit to use as the major selling idea. Many of the package-goods products that account for most of the advertising dollars spent in the United States are difficult to differentiate on a functional or performance basis. The creative strategy used to sell these products is based on the development of a strong, memorable identity for the brand through **image advertising**.

David Ogilvy popularized the idea of brand image in his famous book *Confessions of an Advertising Man*. Ogilvy said that with image advertising, "Every advertisement should be thought of as a contribution to the complex symbol which is the brand image." He argued that the image or personality of the brand is particularly important when brands are similar:

> The greater the similarity between brands, the less part reason plays in brand selection. There isn't any significant difference between the various brands of whiskey, or cigarettes, or beer. They are all about the same. And so are the cake mixes and the detergents and the margarines. The manufacturer who dedicates his advertising to building the most sharply defined personality for his brand will get the largest share of the market at the highest profit. By the same token, the manufacturers who will find themselves up the creek are those shortsighted opportunists who siphon off their advertising funds for promotions.[25]

As noted in the opening vignette, image advertising has become increasingly popular and is used as the main selling idea for a variety of products and services, including soft drinks, liquor, cigarettes, cars, airlines, financial services, perfume/colognes, and clothing. Many consumers wear designer jeans or Ralph Lauren polo shirts or drink certain brands of beer or soft drinks because of the image of these brands. The key to successful image advertising is developing an image that will appeal to product users. For example, the sports apparel company No Fear uses the advertising theme "Face your fears, live your dreams" to create a unique image for the brand as representing the outer limits of human performance. Ads like this one have helped create this image for No Fear.

FINDING THE INHERENT DRAMA

Another approach to determining the major selling idea is finding the **inherent drama** or characteristic of the product that makes the consumer purchase it. The inherent drama approach expresses the advertising philosophy of Leo Burnett, founder of the Leo Burnett agency in Chicago. Burnett said inherent drama "is often hard to find but it is always there, and once found it is the most interesting and believable of all advertising appeals."[26] He believed advertising should be based on a foundation of consumer benefits with an emphasis on the dramatic element in expressing these benefits.

They say you can tell a man's fears by looking him in the eyes.

See anything?

NO FEAR

Burnett advocated a down-home type of advertising that presents the message in a warm and realistic way. Some of the more famous ads developed by his agency using the inherent drama approach are for McDonald's, Maytag appliances, Kellogg's cereals, and Hallmark cards. Notice how the Hallmark commercial shown in Exhibit 8–9 uses this approach to deliver a poignant message.

POSITIONING

The concept of *positioning* as a basis for advertising strategy was introduced by Jack Trout and Al Ries in the early 1970s and has become a popular basis of creative development.[27] The basic idea is that advertising is used to establish or "position" the product or service in a particular place in the consumers' mind. For example, the Copper Mountain Resort in Colorado positions itself as an area for serious skiers with its "Where the skiers ski" campaign (Exhibit 8–10).

Trout and Ries originally described positioning as the image consumers had of the brand in relation to competing brands in the product or service category, but the concept has been expanded beyond direct competitive positioning. As discussed in Chapter 2, products can be positioned on the basis of product attributes, price/quality, usage or application, product users, or product class. Any of these can spark a major selling idea that be-

EXHIBIT 8–9

This Hallmark commercial uses an inherent drama approach

comes the basis of the creative strategy and results in the brand occupying a particular place in the minds of the target audience. Since positioning can be done on the basis of a distinctive attribute, the positioning and unique selling proposition approaches can overlap. Positioning approaches have been used as the foundation for a number of successful creative strategies.

Positioning is often the basis of a firm's creative strategy when it has multiple brands competing in the same market. For example, Procter & Gamble markets more than 10 brands of laundry detergents—and positions each one differently, as shown in Figure 8–5.

The USP, brand image, inherent drama, and positioning approaches are often used as the basis of the creative strategy for ad campaigns. These creative styles have become associated with some of the most successful creative minds in advertising and their agencies.[28] However, many other creative approaches are available.

Specific agencies are by no means limited to any one creative approach. For example, the famous Marlboro country campaign, a classic example of image advertising, was developed by Leo Burnett Co. Many different agencies have followed the unique selling proposition approach advocated by Rosser Reeves at Ted Bates. The challenge to the creative specialist or team is to find a major selling idea—whether it is based on a unique selling proposition,

FIGURE 8–5
A P&G detergent for every washday need

Brand	Positioning	Share
Tide	Tough, powerful cleaner	31.1%
Cheer	Tough cleaner and color protection	8.2
Bold	Detergent plus fabric softener	2.9
Gain	Sunshine scent and odor-removing formula	2.6
Era	Stain pretreatment and stain removal	2.2
Dash	Value brand	1.8
Oxydol	Bleach-boosted formula, whitening	1.4
Solo	Detergent and fabric softener in liquid form	1.2
Dreft	Outstanding cleaning for baby clothes, safe for tender skin	1.0
Ivory Snow	Fabric and skin safety on baby clothes and fine washables	0.7
Ariel	Tough cleaner, aimed at Hispanics	0.1

Source: Jennifer Lawrence, "Don't Look for P&G to Pare Detergents," p. 3. Reprinted with permission from the May 31, 1993 issue of *Advertising Age*. Copyright Crain Communications, Inc. 1993.

Ethical Perspective 8–4
Calvin Klein and Benetton Create Controversies with Shock Ads

In recent years, many creative people complain, advertising has become bland and boring because advertisers are too concerned about offending someone and restrict themselves to ads that are politically correct. However, not all advertisers are worried about their ads offending; some are even deliberately creating controversial ads. Critics call this genre *shock advertising* and claim that its intent is to elicit attention for a brand name by jolting consumers.

The companies best known for using shock ads are Calvin Klein and Benetton, both of which do their advertising in-house. For Calvin Klein, shock tactics and controversy go hand in hand. In 1980, Klein caused an outcry with two of his jeans commercials, "The Feminist," featuring a teenage Brook Shields saying, "Nothing comes between me and my Calvins," and a spot called "The Teenager" in which a young model proclaims: "If my jeans could talk, I'd be ruined." Although the ads were banned by some TV stations, Klein noted that "jeans are about sex" and continued using shocking ads.

In 1995, Klein created one of the greatest furors in the history of American advertising with a campaign for CK Jeans featuring childlike models in provocative poses. Public outcry, led by professional moralist Donald Wildmon's American Family Association, led to an investigation whether Klein and his in-house agency, CRK, had violated child pornography laws. The Justice Department found no evidence of wrongdoing. However, Klein still had to contend with threats of consumer boycotts of stores where CK Jeans were sold, retailers who refused to stock the brand, and intense criticism from the media.

Although the campaign was canceled not long after it first aired, it was still considered a sales success. Klein has continued to push the shock envelope with his ads. A campaign for CK Be fragrance features pierced, tattooed, stringy-haired, and generally grungy models.

Benetton, the Italian-based clothing manufacturer whose ads are well known worldwide for their shock value, says it has a different reason for using this type of advertising. Benetton's creative director, Oliviero Toscani, says the controversial images are designed to raise public awareness of social issues and position the company as a cutting-edge, socially conscious marketer.

Benetton has been regarded as a renegade of the advertising world since 1989, when it ran a print ad featuring a black woman nursing a white baby. Other shock ads have featured such images as a black man's hand handcuffed to a white man's, a priest kissing a nun, an AIDS patient and his family moments before his death, a boatload of refugees, a car ablaze after being bombed, naked adults with naked children, and the blood-soaked uniform of a young soldier killed in the war in Bosnia. One of the latest Benetton ads stirring up controversy features a double-page spread of a black horse mounting a white horse. The company's response: "What is natural is never vulgar."

Critics argue that the real goal of the Benetton ads is to generate publicity. Some accuse Benetton of exploiting human suffering to sell its products. The Benetton ads are controversial even in more liberal European countries. Advertising self-regulatory bodies in Britain, France, and Spain have condemned the ads and urged magazines in these countries to reject many of them. In Germany, Benetton's second-largest market, a group of retailers that carried the Benetton line took the company to court, charging that the controversial ads had caused a drop in their sales. Germany's highest court eventually ruled against the controversial ads.

Toscani sees the negative reactions to the Benetton ads as nothing less than a debate between advertising and art. He argues that in the art world, debatably offensive images are accepted. An attorney for France's self-regulating advertising body replies, "Advertising versus art or whatever, Benetton always has an explanation. That's not the point. The point is they've broken the rules."

It is likely that Benetton will continue breaking the rules and shocking people. Of course, it may also get them to think about some of the world's problems in the process.

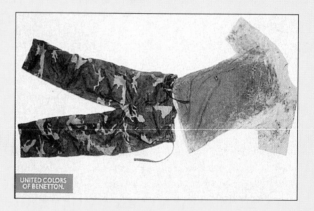

UNITED COLORS OF BENETTON.

Sources: Stephanie Bentley, "Benetton Risks Fresh Outrage," *Marketing Week*, September 13, 1996, p. 9; Robert Gustafson, Johan Yssel, and Lea Witta, "Ad Agency Employees Give Views on Calvin Klein, Benetton Ads," *Marketing News*, September 23, 1996, p. 16; Gary Levin, "Benetton Ad Lays Bare the Bloody Toll of War," *Advertising Age*, February 21, 1994, p. 38.

brand image, inherent drama, position in the market, or some other approach—and use it as a guide in developing an effective creative strategy.

In their search for a big idea, advertisers consider many different creative options that might grab consumers' attention. However, as discussed in Ethical Perspective 8–4, many people believe some advertisers are going too far in their efforts to break through the advertising clutter and have an impact on consumers.

SUMMARY

The creative development and execution of the advertising message are a crucial part of a firm's integrated marketing communications program and are often the key to the success of a marketing campaign. Marketers generally turn to ad agencies to develop, prepare, and implement their creative strategy since they are specialists in the creative function of advertising. The creative specialist or team is responsible for developing an effective way to communicate the marketer's message to the customer. Other individuals on both the client and agency sides work with the creative specialists to develop the creative strategy, implement it, and evaluate its effectiveness.

The challenge facing the writers, artists, and others who develop ads is to be creative and come up with fresh, unique, and appropriate ideas that can be used as solutions to communications problems. Creativity in advertising is a process of several stages, including preparation, incubation, illumi-

nation, verification, and revision. Various sources of information are available to help the creative specialists determine the best campaign theme, appeal, or execution style.

Creative strategy development is guided by specific goals and objectives and is based on a number of factors, including the target audience, the basic problem the advertising must address, the objectives the message seeks to accomplish, and the major selling idea or key benefit the advertiser wants to communicate. These factors are generally stated in a copy platform, which is a work plan used to guide development of the ad campaign. An important part of creative strategy is determining the major selling idea that will become the central theme of the campaign. There are several approaches to doing this, including using a unique selling proposition, creating a brand image, looking for inherent drama in the brand, and positioning.

KEY TERMS

creative strategy, 240
creative tactics, 240
advertising creativity, 244
general preplanning
   input, 249

product/service-specific
   preplanning input, 250
problem detection, 250
focus groups, 252
storyboard, 253

eniamatic, 253
copy platform, 253
advertising campaign, 256
major selling idea, 257

unique selling proposition
   (USP), 258
image advertising, 259
inherent drama, 259

DISCUSSION QUESTIONS

1. The opening vignette discusses how many companies such as Nissan and Levi's are making brand image the major focus of their advertising, rather than product features and benefits. Discuss the pros and cons of this strategy. Do you feel consumers purchase products such as automobiles primarily on the basis of brand image?

2. Discuss the role of creativity in advertising. How should advertising creativity be judged and who should be responsible for judging it—clients or agency creative personnel?

3. What is your opinion of advertising awards, such as the Cannes Lions, that are based solely on creativity? Should agencies pride themselves on their creative awards? Why or why not?

4. Many advertising and marketing experts feel that Burger King has finally come up with an effective advertising approach with the "Get your burger's worth" campaign. Why do you think Burger King had such a difficult time finding an effective advertising campaign? Should Burger King continue to use this campaign theme?

5. The text discusses two perspectives of advertising creativity—the "it's not creative unless it sells" approach and the perspective that creativity should be based on aesthetic value

and originality. Discuss the argument for and against each perspective. Which do you support?

6. Assume you have been assigned to work on the development of an advertising campaign for a new brand of cereal. Describe the various types of general and product-specific preplanning input you might provide for the creative team.

7. IMC Perspective 8–3 discusses the success of the "Got Milk?" campaign developed for the California Milk Processor Board. How would you compare this campaign to the "Milk, Where's Your Mustache?" campaign discussed in IMC Perspective 1–3? Do you feel the two campaigns complement one another? Why or why not?

8. Find an example of an ad campaign theme that has been around for a very long time. Why do you think the advertiser has been able to use this theme for so long?

9. What is meant by a unique selling proposition? Find an example of an ad that uses a USP as its major selling idea. Evaluate this ad against the three characteristics of USPs discussed in the chapter.

10. Evaluate the use of shock advertising by companies such as Calvin Klein and Benetton. Why do these companies use this type of advertising? Evaluate the pros and cons of using these types of advertising messages.

CHAPTER 9

Creative Strategy: Implementation and Evaluation

Chapter Objectives

- To analyze various types of appeals that can be used in the development and implementation of an advertising message.

- To analyze the various creative execution styles that advertisers can use and the advertising situations where they are most appropriate.

- To analyze various tactical issues involved in the creation of print advertising and TV commercials.

- To consider how clients evaluate the creative work of their agencies and discuss guidelines for the evaluation and approval process.

CHEVY TRUCKS FIND A ROCK-SOLID ADVERTISING THEME

In 1990 the Chevrolet truck line was in a battle for survival. Sales were down, factories were closing. R. M. "Mac" Whisner, manager of Chevy truck advertising, and Don Gould of Campbell-Ewald Advertising knew they had to find a way to bolster the Chevy truck line, which accounts for well over half of all Chevrolet sales. The marketing research showed that Chevy trucks performed well and were viewed as good-looking, but they were also perceived as least dependable, least durable, and wimpy. These perceptions had to be changed.

THE MOST DEPENDABLE, LONGEST-LASTING TRUCKS ON THE ROAD.

Chevy Trucks
LIKE A ROCK

Gould and his colleagues had two campaigns ready to test, but he didn't like either one. Desperate, he spent a weekend hunting through his music collection looking for inspiration and noticed an old tape of Bob Seger's. Gould recalls, "Right on the cover it said "Like a Rock," and I thought, 'That is *exactly* what we need.'" He patched together a mock-up commercial using old videotape with the song and rushed it to California for a focus group test.

One of the participants in the focus group was a carpenter named Fred. In the taped interviews before the presentation, Fred described himself as the most vocal critic of American trucks. He considered them shoddy. However, after viewing the mock-up commercial, Fred was a changed man. "You got me!" he shouted. He and the rest of the group said there was no way they could ever buy another truck without at least looking at a Chevy. Gould says, "Good old Fred sold this. When he talked about goosebumps, we knew we had a hit." They got the same response from every focus group test they did. They didn't just have a great commercial, they had one that was making audiences stand up and cheer.

There was still one problem, however. Chevrolet did not have the rights to air it. In the rush to put the test commercial together, there had been no time to acquire the rights to use the lyrics from Seger, and when they asked he turned them down. For six months Seger kept saying no, as he did not want to do any commercials. Gould finally convinced Seger's manager, Punch Andrews, to watch the ad. After 15 seconds Andrews was convinced. Seger, a workaday rocker with blue-collar Michigan roots, recalls Andrews telling him: "I know I've been bringing you these commercials for years and you have always said no. But this one makes sense. This is trucks. You drive them. It's very American." Seger adds, "There was this feeling that the Japanese were running us off our heels and maybe we could help."

But Seger was not swayed until one night when he was dining with his wife at a restaurant in Detroit. An autoworker came up to the table and politely asked him to do something to help the auto industry. Seger had just read that GM had lost over $1 billion in a single quarter and decided that if he could do something to help, he would. The next day he called Andrews and told him to accept (but not before first checking to make sure the autoworker was legitimate and not working for the ad agency).

The "Like a Rock" song has propelled one of the most successful and long-lasting campaigns in automotive advertising and has become a three-word mission statement for the entire Chevrolet truck division. The manager for Chevy trucks says, "It is not just a marketing campaign. It captures the soul of the brand. It is how to build a truck, it is how to run a company."

It is also the foundation of a great ad campaign for selling trucks. General Motors has been producing Chevy trucks at or near capacity for several years. Chevy has become a strong number-two truck brand in the United States and annual sales have increased 33 percent since 1991. Marketing and strategy consultant Jack Trout says of the campaign, "There is a handful of brilliant positioning ideas in the auto business—Volvo and safety, BMW and driving—and this is one of them: Chevy trucks, like a rock. I would never change it."

Sources: Joe Urschel, "Three Words that Evolved into a Corporate Hymn," *USA Today*, January 5, 1996, pp. 1, 2A; Dottie Enrico, "Chevy Campaign Is Solid 'Like a Rock,'" *USA Today*, February 19, 1996, p. 6B.

In Chapter 8, we discussed the importance of advertising creativity and examined the various steps in the creative process. We focused on determining *what* the advertising message should communicate. This chapter focuses on *how* the message will be executed. It examines various appeals and execution styles that can be used to develop the ad and tactical issues involved in the design and production of effective advertising messages. We conclude by presenting some guidelines clients can use to evaluate the creative work of their agencies.

APPEALS AND EXECUTION STYLES

The **advertising appeal** refers to the approach used to attract the attention of consumers and/or to influence their feelings toward the product, service, or cause. An advertising appeal can also be viewed as "something that moves people, speaks to their wants or needs, and excites their interest."[1] The **creative execution style** refers to the way a particular appeal is turned into an advertising message presented to the consumer. According to William Weilbacher:

> The appeal can be said to form the underlying content of the advertisement, and the execution the way in which that content is presented. Advertising appeals and executions are usually independent of each other; that is, a particular appeal can be executed in a variety of ways and a particular means of execution can be applied to a variety of advertising appeals. Advertising appeals tend to adapt themselves to all media, whereas some kinds of executional devices are more adaptable to some media than others.[2]

Advertising Appeals

Hundreds of different appeals can be used as the basis for advertising messages. At the broadest level, these approaches are generally broken into two categories: informational/rational appeals and emotional appeals. In this section, we focus on ways to use rational and emotional appeals as part of a creative strategy. We also consider how rational and emotional appeals can be combined in developing the advertising message.

INFORMATIONAL/RATIONAL APPEALS

Informational/rational appeals focus on the consumer's practical, functional, or utilitarian need for the product or service and emphasize features of a product or service and/or the benefits or reasons for owning or using a particular brand. The content of these messages emphasizes facts, learning, and the logic of persuasion.[3] Rational-based appeals tend to be informative, and advertisers using them generally attempt to convince consumers that their product or service has a particular attribute(s) or provides a specific benefit that satisfies their needs. Their objective is to persuade the target audience to buy the brand because it is the best available or does a better job of meeting consumers' needs. For example, the Quaker Oats company uses a rational appeal in noting how fiber from oatmeal may help reduce the risk of heart disease (Exhibit 9–1).

Many rational motives can be used as the basis for advertising appeals, including comfort, convenience, economy, health, and sensory benefits such as touch, taste, and smell. Other rational motives or purchase criteria commonly used in advertising include quality, dependability, durability, efficiency, efficacy, and performance. The particular features, benefits, or evaluative criteria that are important to consumers and can serve as the basis of an informational/rational appeal vary from one product or service category to another as well as among various market segments.

Weilbacher identified several types of advertising appeals that fall under the category of rational approaches, among them feature, competitive advantage, favorable price, news, and product/service popularity appeals.

Ads that use a *feature appeal* focus on the dominant traits of the product or service. These ads tend to be highly informative and present the customer with a number of important product attributes or features that will lead to favorable attitudes and can be used as the basis for a

rational purchase decision. Technical and high-involvement products often use this advertising approach. This type of appeal can also be used for a service. Notice how the Continental Airlines ad in Exhibit 9–2 focuses on the various features of its BusinessFirst class of service.

When a *competitive advantage appeal* is used, the advertiser makes either a direct or an indirect comparison to another brand (or brands) and usually claims superiority on one or more attributes. This type of appeal was discussed in Chapter 6 under comparative advertising.

A *favorable price appeal* makes the price offer the dominant point of the message. Price appeal advertising is used most often by retailers to announce sales, special offers, or low everyday prices. Price appeal ads are often used by national advertisers during recessionary times. Many fast-food chains have made price an important part of their marketing strategy through promotional deals and "value menus" or lower overall prices, and their advertising strategy is designed to communicate this. Many other types of advertisers use price appeals as well. In Exhibit 9–3, Denny's restaurants uses a price appeal to promote big breakfast deals.

News appeals are those where some type of news or announcement about the product, service, or company dominates the ad. This type of appeal can be used for a new product or service or to inform consumers of significant modifications or improvements. This appeal works best when a company has important news it wants to communicate to its target market. The Quaker Oatmeal ad shown in Exhibit 9–1, which announced the news from the Food and Drug Administration regarding the health benefits of eating oatmeal, is an example of a news appeal.

Product/service popularity appeals stress the popularity of a product or service by pointing out the number of consumers who use the brand, the number who have switched to it, or its leadership position in the market. The main point of this advertising appeal is that the wide use of the brand proves its quality or value and other customers should consider using it. The Minolta ad in Exhibit 9–4 uses this type of advertising appeal.

EMOTIONAL APPEALS

Emotional appeals relate to the customers' social and/or psychological needs for purchasing a product or service. Many of consumers' motives for their purchase decisions are emotional, and their feelings about a brand can be more important than knowledge of its features or attributes. Advertisers for many products and services view rational, information-based appeals as dull. Many advertisers believe appeals to consumers' emotions work better at selling brands that do not differ markedly from competing brands, since rational differentiation of them is difficult.[4]

Many feelings or needs can serve as the basis for advertising appeals designed to influence consumers on an emotional level, as shown in Figure 9–1. These appeals are based on the psychological states or feelings directed to the self (such as pleasure or excitement), as well

FIGURE 9–1
Bases for emotional appeals

Personal States or Feelings	Social-Based Feelings
Safety	Recognition
Security	Status
Love	Respect
Affection	Involvement
Happiness	Embarrassment
Joy	Affiliation/belonging
Nostalgia	Rejection
Sentiment	Acceptance
Excitement	Approval
Arousal/stimulation	
Sorrow/grief	
Pride	
Achievement/accomplishment	
Self-esteem	
Actualization	
Pleasure	
Ambition	
Comfort	

as those with a more social orientation (such as status or recognition). The "Like a rock" campaign for Chevrolet trucks discussed at the beginning of this chapter relies on an emotional appeal; a goal of these ads is to evoke a positive emotional response, such as pride or sentiment, that carries over to the product.

Advertisers can use emotional appeals in many ways in their creative strategy. Kamp and Macinnis note that commercials often rely on the concept of *emotional integration*, whereby they portray the characters in the ad as experiencing an emotional benefit or outcome from using a product or service.[5] Ads using humor, sex, and other appeals that are very entertaining, arousing, upbeat, and/or exciting can affect the emotions of consumers and put them in a favorable frame of mind. Many TV advertisers use poignant ads that bring a lump to viewers' throats. Hallmark, AT&T, Kodak, and McDonald's often create commercials that evoke feelings of warmth, nostalgia, and/or sentiment.

Marketers use emotional appeals in hopes that the positive feelings they evoke will transfer to the brand. Research shows that positive mood states created by advertising can have a favorable effect on consumers' evaluation of a product.[6] It also shows that emotional advertising is better remembered than nonemotional messages.[7]

Another reason for using emotional appeals is to influence consumers' interpretations of their product usage experience. One way of doing this is through what is known as transformational advertising. A **transformational ad** is defined as "one which associates the experience of using (consuming) the advertised brand with a unique set of psychological characteristics which would not typically be associated with the brand experience to the same degree without exposure to the advertisement."[8]

Transformational ads create feelings, images, meanings, and beliefs about the product or service that may be activated when consumers use it, transforming their interpretation of the usage experience. Christopher Puto and William Wells note that a transformational ad has two characteristics:

1. It must make the experience of using the product richer, warmer, more exciting, and/or more enjoyable than that obtained solely from an objective description of the advertised brand.
2. It must connect the experience of the advertisement so tightly with the experience of using the brand that consumers cannot remember the brand without recalling the experience generated by the advertisement.[9]

IMC Perspective 9–1
The Vacation You Take in Your Mind

Most advertising for cruises pushes the obvious, with shots of buffet tables with mountains of food, entertaining shows, and people sipping drinks and relaxing at poolside—the staples of most industry ads. Norwegian Cruise Lines (NCL), in contrast, has been very successful in painting a different image of the cruise experience and standing out from the competition with the creative "It's different out here" advertising campaign.

Once the leader in the Caribbean cruise market, Norwegian Cruises had slipped to fourth by 1993, overtaken by aggressive fleet expansion. Following the debut of two new ships and an extensive renovation of the fleet flagship, the *Norway*, new management was brought in to operate the company. Programs were immediately implemented to increase the level of on-board quality and the ad agency, Goodby, Silverstein & Partners, was instructed to create a campaign and image consistent with the new ships and service upgrades.

In the briefing, the agency was told that NCL wanted to attract younger people to its cruises. Norwegian's new president, Adam Aron, had a very clear vision of what he wanted the campaign to be. He spoke about sex and the rekindling of relationships as key reasons why people take cruises and said, "You know, on a cruise ship, you can make love at 4:00 on a Tuesday afternoon." He thought that a campaign capturing that idea would reflect a previously unspoken truth and would stand out despite a limited media budget.

The challenge for the agency team was to find a way to capture Aron's idea and produce truly different cruise advertising, without crossing the lines of taste and acceptability with an overtly sexual message. The agency conducted focus groups on the ships and found that while passengers wanted good food and service, they also wanted something different: an escape, the fantasy of taking an "abnormal" vacation. An idea video or "living creative brief" was produced that combined black-and-white imagery with a sensual music track and poetic copy designed to capture and enhance the feelings of freedom the passengers had described. Further consumer research with the video helped identify the fine line between sexuality and sensuality and confirmed that the sensual possibilities of a cruise were the result of a broader idea: On a Norwegian cruise, there are no rules.

This idea was executed in a campaign that was stylistically similar to the idea video but focused on the idea there are no restrictions on a Norwegian cruise. Your imagination can become reality. The tagline "It's really different out here" was chosen as the theme. The campaign uses black-and-white images and beautiful music to hearken back to the golden age of cruises and create a sense of escape and romance. Most of the ads are targeted at women, the key decision makers on vacations and cruises. The romance angle was emphasized over sex, because the agency believed women are more inclined toward romance. However, one of the most popular ads in the campaign uses the memorable line suggested by Arons: "There's no law that says you can't make love at four o'-clock in the afternoon on a Tuesday."

The campaign has been very successful and has allowed NCL to establish a brand personality with only a fraction of the media budget of its largest competitors. NCL has become the most recognizable cruise line next to Carnival, which outspends it by an 8-to-1 margin. For the first time in years, Norwegian has been able to fill all its berths while its major competitors' load factors actually declined. It looks as if Norwegian has successfully transformed the idea of a cruise with cerebral advertising.

Sources: "It's Different Out Here," *Adweek*, August 5, 1996, p. 7; Chad Rubel, "Out of Ideas? Try Thinking 'Out of the Dots,'" *Marketing News*, November 20, 1995, p. 19.

Transformational advertising can differentiate a product or service by making the consumption experience more enjoyable. The "reach out and touch someone" campaign used by AT&T for many years to encourage consumers to keep in touch with family and friends by phone is an example of the successful use of transformational advertising. McDonald's has also used transformational advertising very effectively to position itself as the fast-food chain where parents (or grandparents) can enjoy a warm, happy experience with their children. IMC Perspective 9–1 discusses how Norwegian Cruise Lines used transformational advertising to create a unique image of cruises and differentiate itself from competitors with the "It's different out here" campaign.

COMBINING RATIONAL AND EMOTIONAL APPEALS

In many advertising situations, the decision facing the creative specialist is not whether to choose an emotional or a rational appeal but rather determining how to combine the two approaches. As noted copywriters David Ogilvy and Joel Raphaelson have stated:

> Few purchases of any kind are made for entirely rational reasons. Even a purely functional product such as laundry detergent may offer what is now called an emotional benefit—say, the satisfaction of seeing one's children in bright clean clothes. In some product categories the rational element is small. These include soft drinks, beer, cosmetics, certain personal care products, and most old-fashioned products. And who hasn't experienced the surge of joy that accompanies the purchase of a new car?[10]

Consumer purchase decisions are often made on the basis of both emotional and rational motives, and attention must be given to both elements in developing effective advertising. Exhibit 9–5 shows a very clever ad that uses the Freudian concepts of id and superego to suggest that there are both emotional and rational reasons for purchasing the Lexus SC 400 coupe.

Advertising researchers and agencies have given considerable thought to the relationship between rational and emotional motives in consumer decision making and how advertising influences both. McCann-Erickson Worldwide, in conjunction with advertising professor Michael Ray, developed a proprietary research technique known as *emotional bonding*. This technique evaluates how consumers feel about brands and the nature of any emotional rapport they have with a brand compared to the ideal emotional state they associate with the product category.[11]

The basic concept of emotional bonding is that consumers develop three levels of relationships with brands, as shown in Figure 9–2. The most basic relationship indicates how consumers *think* about brands in respect to product benefits. This occurs, for the most part, through a rational learning process and can be measured by how well advertising communicates product information. Consumers at this stage are not very brand loyal, and brand switching is common.

At the next stage, the consumer assigns a *personality* to a brand. For example, a brand may be thought of as self-assured, aggressive, and adventurous, as opposed to compliant and timid. The consumer's judgment of the brand has moved beyond its attributes or delivery of product/service benefits. In most instances, consumers judge the personality of a brand based on an assessment of overt or covert cues found in its advertising.

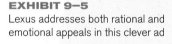

EXHIBIT 9–5
Lexus addresses both rational and emotional appeals in this clever ad

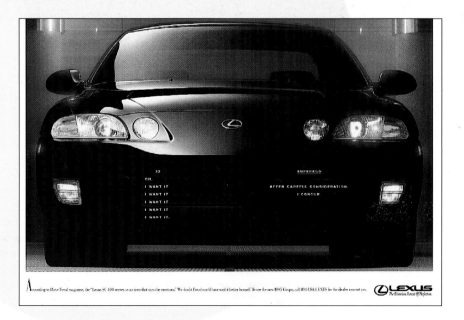

FIGURE 9–2
Levels of relationships with brands

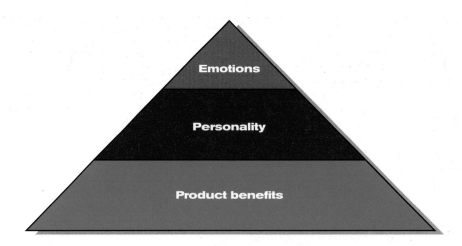

Emotions

Personality

Product benefits

McCann-Erickson researchers believe the strongest relationship that develops between a brand and the consumer is based on feelings or emotional attachments to the brand. Consumers develop *emotional bonds* with certain brands, which result in positive psychological movement toward them. The marketer's goal is to develop the greatest emotional linkage between its brand and the consumer. McCann-Erickson believes advertising can develop and enrich emotional bonding between consumers and brands. McCann and its subsidiary agencies use emotional bonding research to provide strategic input into the creative process and determine how well advertising is communicating with consumers. Global Perspective 9–2 discusses how McCann-Erickson used this approach in developing a popular and long-running advertising campaign for Taster's Choice instant coffee, the idea for which was borrowed from the agency's London office.

ADDITIONAL TYPES OF APPEALS

Not every ad fits neatly into the categories of rational or emotional appeals. For example, the ad for Hershey's Kisses in Exhibit 9–6 can be classified as **reminder advertising**. This ad does not rely on any specific type of appeal; its only objective is to keep the brand name in readers' minds. Well-known brands and market leaders often use reminder advertising, especially for products and services that have a seasonal pattern to their consumption. For example, candy sales are highest before Halloween and Valentine's Day, Christmas, and Easter.

EXHIBIT 9–6 This ad serves as a reminder for Hershey's chocolate kisses during the holiday season

Three cheers for the holidays.

———— HERSHEY'S KISSES. ————

Advertisers introducing a new product often use **teaser advertising**, which is designed to build curiosity, interest, and excitement about a product or brand by talking about it but not showing it. Teaser ads are often used for new movies or TV shows and for major product launches. They are especially popular among automotive advertisers when they introduce a new model or make significant changes in a car. For example, Chrysler used a series of teaser ads to introduce its Neon subcompact a few years ago. The teasers were lighthearted and whimsical and helped position the brand. One showed a helicopter with a crate coming in for a landing. When the crate was opened, it was empty. The national ad campaign that followed the teasers featured a mischievous little car with the word "Hi!" written above it.

Teaser advertising is also used by marketers to draw attention to upcoming advertising campaigns and generate publicity for them. For example, in 1995 Taco Bell used teaser ads featuring basketball stars Shaquille O'Neal and Hakeem Olajuwon to launch its new Double Decker taco. The ads ran a few weeks after O'Neal's team at the time, the Orlando Magic, lost to Olajuwon's team, the Houston Rockets, in the NBA finals. The first teaser ad featured a letter from O'Neal telling Olajuwon, "it ain't over between you and me," and challenging him to a one-on-one game. Olajuwon's response: "Anywhere, any way, any time at all" (Exhibit 9–7). The two anonymous full-page ads were run in *USA Today*, *The New York Times*, and a few other newspapers and sent sports fans and the media into a frenzy. More than 1,000 calls flooded the NBA offices and Taco Bell as well as Pepsi and Reebok, which also

Global Perspective 9–2
Still Using Romance to Sell Coffee around the World

In 1990, Nestlé Corp. and its agency, McCann-Erickson, were looking for a new advertising approach for Taster's Choice instant coffee. For more than 20 years advertising for the brand had focused primarily on the product, positioning Taster's Choice as "tasting closest to fresh brewed." But there was concern that U.S. consumers were beginning to perceive coffee as a commodity and becoming highly responsive to price and sales promotion. The agency recommended abandoning the product-oriented advertising and developing a more emotionally driven campaign.

McCann-Erickson conducted emotional bonding research among instant-coffee drinkers and found that typical users of Taster's Choice were discriminating, self-assured, and sophisticated. These personality traits matched well with the premium image of Taster's Choice. The agency recommended a campaign that would involve consumers emotionally in the advertising and in the brand. Some competitors, such as General Foods International Coffees, were already using emotional appeals. But one emotional dimension that was absent in coffee advertising was romance. Thus, the client and agency decided the new campaign for Taster's Choice would add a touch of romance to the brand's sophisticated image.

Generally, at this point, an ad agency would have to begin thinking about how to execute the creative strategy. However, McCann-Erickson's London office had created a campaign for Nestlé U.K.'s Gold Blend instant-coffee brand that fit very well with the creative strategy chosen for Taster's Choice in the United States. The campaign was based on soap opera-style commercials featuring two flirtatious neighbors, Tony and Sharon, whose relationship develops in each episode. The coffee plays a background role to the evolving romantic tension between them.

The "brewing romance" campaign was introduced in the United Kingdom in 1987 and quickly developed an avid following. British tabloids chronicled the series; viewers wrote in for autographs of the actors who played the couple and even sent in script suggestions. Nestlé had the whole country anticipating their wedding. The campaign lasted for six years and 12 episodes and as the romance heated up so did Gold Blend's sales, which soared by 40 percent and helped the brand become the United Kingdom's number-two instant coffee. The U.K. campaign finally ended in 1993 with Sharon and Tony driving happily off into the sunset.

The agency extended the U.K. campaign with a love triangle involving the girlfriend of the straitlaced young man who has taken over Sharon's apartment. She is tempted by a young artiste.

The campaign's success in the United Kingdom inspired Nestlé and McCann-Erickson to take the ads to the United States, Canada, Chile, Australia, New Zealand, and Japan. Nestlé began using the campaign in the United States in 1991, and initial consumer reactions were nearly as feverish as in the United Kingdom. The first two commercials generated more positive mail and phone calls than any other campaign in Nestlé's history. The debut of each new "episode" became a major media event, often premiering on network shows such as ABC's "Good Morning America." By 1997, thirteen episodes of the brewing romance had aired in the United States and the couple had survived a misunderstanding about a brother, shared a first kiss in Paris, endured unexpected visits from Sharon's son and ex-husband, and continued to exchange looks hotter than a pot of coffee.

Many people in the United States, as well as many other countries, are waiting eagerly for Tony and Sharon to tie the knot. However, as long as the campaign is capturing consumer interest and anticipation and selling coffee, Nestlé will keep it moving slowly. The campaign helped Taster's Choice gain several market share points in the United States and was one of the most popular TV campaigns.

But by 1996, there were signs that consumers might be losing interest in the romance. The McCann-Erickson creative director insists the problem is not a lack of interest in the plot as much as a reduced media budget. He thinks the campaign still can generate excitement as new twists are added to the relationship and if the budget is increased to show viewers what is new between the couple. If the campaign is as successful in other countries as it has been in the United Kingdom and United States, Nestlé is likely to keep the romance brewing around the world for quite a long time.

Sources: Bradley Johnson, "Romance Warms," *Advertising Age*, February 24, 1992, p. 4; Bradley Johnson and Joe Mandes, "Nestlé, ABC Strike Taster's Choice Deal," *Advertising Age*, February 3, 1992, p. 3; Laurel Wentz, "New Coffee Romance: Same Old Problem," *Advertising Age*, November 29, 1993, p. 3; Dave Vadehra, "Taster's Choice Ads Lose Flavor with Consumers," *Advertising Age*, August 5, 1996, p. 21.

EXHIBIT 9—7 Taco Bell's teaser ads generated a great deal of curiosity and publicity

Hakeem-

The series may be a done deal,
but it ain't over between you and me.
Sure, you're pretty good with your team
behind you, but I want you one on one.

-Shaq

Shaq-

You want to go one on one? No problem.
Anywhere, any way, any time at all.

-Hakeem

use O'Neal. Everyone wanted to know whose ad it was and whether the two superstars would play a one-on-one basketball game. The challenge turned out to be for a taco-eating match rather than a basketball game. However, Taco Bell estimated that the $250,000 spent on teaser ads generated more than $10 million worth of publicity from the media.[12]

Teaser campaigns can generate interest in a new product, but advertisers must be careful not to extend them too long or they will lose their effectiveness.[13] Many advertising experts thought the teaser campaign used by Infiniti to introduce its cars to the U.S. market in 1989 ran too long and created confusion among consumers.[14] As one advertising executive says, "Contrary to what we think, consumers don't hold seminars about advertising. You have to give consumers enough information about the product in teaser ads to make them feel they're in on the joke."[15]

Many ads are not designed to sell a product or service but rather to enhance the image of the company or meet other corporate goals such as soliciting investment or recruiting employees. These are generally referred to as corporate image advertising and are discussed in detail in Chapter 16.

Advertising Execution

Once the specific advertising appeal that will be used as the basis for the advertising message has been determined, the creative specialist or team begins its execution. *Creative execution* refers to the way an advertising appeal is presented. While it is obviously important for an ad to have a meaningful appeal or message to communicate to the consumer, the manner in which the ad is executed is also important.

One of the best-known advocates of the importance of creative execution in advertising was William Bernbach, founder of the Doyle Dane Bernbach agency. In his famous book on the advertising industry, *Madison Avenue*, Martin Mayer notes Bernbach's reply to David Ogilvy's rule for copywriters that "what you say in advertising is more important than how you say it."

Bernbach replied, "Execution can become content, it can be just as important as what you say. A sick guy can utter some words and nothing happens; a healthy vital guy says them and they rock the world."[16]

An advertising message can be presented in numerous ways:

- Straight sell or factual message
- Scientific/technical evidence
- Demonstration
- Comparison
- Testimonial
- Slice of life
- Animation
- Personality symbol
- Fantasy
- Dramatization
- Humor
- Combinations

We now examine these formats and considerations involved in their use.

STRAIGHT SELL OR FACTUAL MESSAGE

One of the most basic types of creative executions is the straight sell or factual message. This type of ad relies on a straightforward presentation of information concerning the product or service. This execution is often used with informational/rational appeals, where the focus of the message is the product or service and its specific attributes and/or benefits.

Straight-sell executions are commonly used in print ads. A picture of the product or service occupies part of the ad and the factual copy takes up the rest of the space. (See the ad for Valvoline motor oil in Exhibit 9–8.) They are also used in TV advertising, with an announcer generally delivering the sales message while the product/service is shown on the screen. Ads for high-involvement consumer products as well as industrial and other business-to-business products generally use this format.

SCIENTIFIC/TECHNICAL EVIDENCE

In a variation of the straight sell, scientific or technical evidence is presented in the ad. Advertisers often cite technical information, results of scientific or laboratory studies, or endorsements by scientific bodies or agencies to support their advertising claims. For example, an endorsement from the American Council on Dental Therapeutics on how fluoride helps prevent cavities was the basis of the campaign that made Crest the leading brand on the market. The ad for Dermasil Pharmaceutical Dry Skin Treatment shown in Exhibit 9–9 uses this execution style to emphasize the breakthrough from Vaseline Research.

DEMONSTRATION

Demonstration advertising is designed to illustrate the key advantages of the product/service by showing it in actual use or in some staged situation. Demonstration executions can

EXHIBIT 9–8   Valvoline uses a straight-sell execution style in this ad

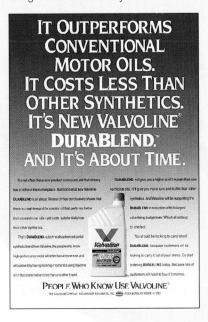

EXHIBIT 9–9   This Dermasil ad cites a scientific study

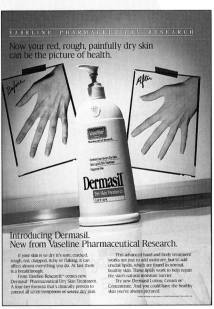

be very effective in convincing consumers of a product's utility or quality and of the benefits of owning or using the brand. TV is particularly well suited for demonstration executions, since the benefits or advantages of the product can be shown right on the screen. Although perhaps a little less dramatic than TV, demonstration ads can also work in print, as shown in the ad for Du Pont's Teflon® Bakeware Liners (Exhibit 9–10).

COMPARISON

Brand comparisons can also be the basis for the advertising execution. The comparison execution approach is increasingly popular among advertisers, since it offers a direct way of communicating a brand's particular advantage over its competitors or positioning a new or lesser-known brand with industry leaders. Comparison executions are often used to execute competitive advantage appeals, as discussed earlier.

TESTIMONIAL

Many advertisers prefer to have their messages presented by way of a testimonial, where a person praises the product or service based on his or her personal experience with it (Exhibit 9–11). Testimonial executions can have ordinary satisfied customers discuss their own experiences with the brand and the benefits of using it. This approach can be very effective when the person delivering the testimonial is someone with whom the target audience can identify or who has an interesting story to tell. The testimonial must be based on actual use of the product or service to avoid legal problems, and the spokesperson must be credible.

Testimonials can be particularly effective when they come from a recognizable or popular source. Ultra Slim-Fast has used a variety of celebrities, including former Los Angeles Dodgers manager Tommy Lasorda, talk-show host Kathie Lee Gifford, and her husband, sportscaster Frank Gifford, to deliver testimonials on its effectiveness in weight loss. The company has also used actress Brooke Shields to reach a younger market.[17]

EXHIBIT 9–10
This ad demonstrates the benefits of Du Pont's Teflon® Bakeware Liners

A related execution technique is the endorsement, where a well-known or respected individual such as a celebrity or expert in the product or service area speaks on behalf of the company or the brand. When endorsers promote a company or its products or services, the message is not necessarily based on their personal experiences.

SLICE OF LIFE

A widely used advertising format, particularly for package-goods products, is the slice-of-life execution, which is generally based on a problem/solution approach. This type of ad portrays a problem or conflict that consumers might face in their daily lives. The ad then shows how the advertiser's product or service can resolve the problem.

Slice-of-life executions are often criticized for being unrealistic and irritating to watch because they are often used to remind consumers of problems of a personal nature, such as dandruff, bad breath, body odor, and laundry problems. Often these ads come across as contrived, silly, phony, or even offensive to consumers. However, many advertisers still prefer this style because they believe it is effective at presenting a situation to which most consumers can relate and at registering the product feature or benefit that helps sell the brand.

For many years, Procter & Gamble was known for its reliance on slice-of-life advertising executions. In 1980, two-thirds of the company's commercials used either the slice-of-life or testimonial format. However, P&G has begun using humor, animation, and other less traditional execution styles. Now only one in four of the company's ads relies on slice-of-life or testimonials.[18]

Slice-of-life or problem/solution execution approaches are not limited to consumer product advertising. Many business-to-business marketers use a variation of this style to demonstrate how their products and services can be used to solve business problems. In the late 1980s and early 90s, a new advertising genre that some advertising people refer to as *slice of death* became popular. One well-known example was the "business realities" campaign used by AT&T Business Systems. The campaign was targeted toward businesspeople pur-

EXHIBIT 9–12   Slice-of-death ads remind executives of the consequences of making bad business decisions

chasing a phone system for their company (Exhibit 9–12). The director of advertising at AT&T says, "Businesspeople are not always nice and polite to one another. They operate under a great deal of confusion and decisions are critical to their careers. What we're saying is don't make a mistake."[19] Slice-of-death ads have also been used by other business-to-business advertisers such as Apple Computer and FedEx.

ANIMATION

An advertising execution approach that has become popular in recent years is animation. With this technique, animated scenes are drawn by artists or created on the computer, and cartoons, puppets, or other types of fictional characters may be used. Cartoon animation is especially popular for commercials targeted at children.

Animated cartoon characters have also been used successfully by the Leo Burnett agency in campaigns for Green Giant vegetables (the Jolly Green Giant) and Keebler cookies (the Keebler elves). Another successful example of animation execution was the ad campaign developed for the California Raisin Advisory Board. A technique called Claymation was used to create the dancing raisin characters used in these ads.

The use of animation as an execution style may increase as creative specialists discover the possibilities of computer-generated graphics and other technological innovations. Will Vinton, the developer of Claymation, came up with a new technique called dimensional animation that combines three forms of production: Claymation, stop-motion animation, and computer

EXHIBIT 9–13 The Maytag repairman is an example of an advertising personality symbol

EXHIBIT 9–13 The Maytag repairman is an example of an advertising personality symbol

animation. The technique was used for the first time by Nabisco in a commercial for Chips Ahoy! cookies.[20]

Some advertisers have begun using Roger Rabbit-style ads that mix animation with real people. Nike has used this technique to develop several creative, entertaining commercials. One featured Michael Jordan and Bugs Bunny trouncing a foursome of bullies on the basketball court and was the inspiration for the movie *Space Jam.*

PERSONALITY SYMBOL

Another type of advertising execution involves developing a central character or personality symbol that can deliver the advertising message and with which the product or service can be identified. This character can be a person, like Mr. Whipple, who asked shoppers, "Please don't squeeze the Charmin," or the Maytag repairman, who sits anxiously by the phone but is never needed because the company's appliances are so reliable (Exhibit 9–13). Advertising for the Jack in the Box fast-food restaurant chain uses "Jack," a character with a large plastic clown head who is portrayed as the CEO of the company (Exhibit 9–14). The "Jack is back" advertising campaign has been very effective in creating a strong identity for the restaurant chain and increasing sales.[21]

Personality symbols can also be based on fantasy characters or animals. As discussed in Chapter 5, visual image personalities (VIPs) can create interest for low-involvement products. Morris, the finicky feline, has been promoting 9–Lives cat food since 1969, Charlie the Tuna first started tricking fishermen into catching him in Starkist tuna commercials in 1961, and Tony the Tiger has been touting Kellogg's Frosted Flakes as Grrreat for over three decades.

One of the most popular advertising personality symbols was Spuds MacKenzie, the bull terrier who was used to promote Bud Light beer for several years. However, Anheuser-Busch had to deal with complaints from some groups that it was using Spuds to appeal to minors—a charge the company strongly denied. Actually, the controversy over Spuds MacKenzie was mild compared to the furor over the use of Old Joe, the cartoon camel who

EXHIBIT 9–14
"Jack" is a very popular personality symbol for Jack in the Box restaurants

Ethical Perspective 9–3
The Controversy over Joe Camel Comes to an End

In late 1987, RJR Nabisco launched the "smooth character" advertising campaign featuring Old Joe, a cartoon camel. The campaign was soon criticized as an effort by RJR to reposition Camels to appeal to young people. Critics argued that ads showing Old Joe accompanied by beautiful women, race cars, jet airplanes, and other appealing images are particularly intriguing to children. They also suggested the campaign was another example of the tobacco industry's efforts to sustain sales by attracting teenagers, since 90 percent of people who smoke start before they reach the age of 21.

The controversy surrounding the campaign heated up in 1991, when three studies published in the *Journal of the American Medical Association* concluded the smooth character ads were more successful at marketing Camels to children than to adults. One of the studies concluded the ad campaign boosted RJR's share of the children's cigarette market from less than 1 percent to 32.8 percent. Another found that 91.6 percent of six-year-olds associated Old Joe with cigarettes, a level nearly equal to the number who associated Mickey Mouse with the Disney Channel.

These findings led a powerful coalition of health groups—formed by the American Medical Association, the American Cancer Society, and the American Lung Association—to petition the Federal Trade Commission (FTC) to take immediate action to stop RJR's use of the smooth character ads. In 1992, Antoine Novella, the U.S. Surgeon General at the time, urged RJR to voluntarily stop using the Joe Camel ads because of their appeal to children. She also asked billboard companies and magazine and newspaper publishers to stop running the ads. In 1993, FTC staff recommended an outright ban of the campaign on the grounds that it entices minors to smoke. However, in 1994, the FTC voted 3–2 not to ban the Joe Camel ads.

RJR officials have characterized some of the conclusions of the *JAMA* studies as absurd. The company says the campaign is targeted at adults and any appeal to children is unintentional. An RJR spokeswoman noted that the company has studies showing that despite a high awareness of Joe Camel among children, kids still don't like smoking, and that the company does not want them to smoke. In 1994, RJR released the results of a survey of young people ages 10 to 17 conducted by the research firm of Roper Starch; only 3 percent of the youths who recognized Joe Camel said they had a positive attitude toward smoking, and those respondents were all 16- to 17-year-olds. The study also found that while 73 percent of the children surveyed recognized Joe Camel, he was actually among the least recognized of nine major advertising symbols. More recognized symbols included the Energizer Bunny, Ronald McDonald, and Tony the Tiger.

Despite all the criticism, RJR continued the campaign, arguing that its responsibility is to its shareholders and it would be wrong to stop it solely because of criticism from antismokers. The company spent over $48 million to advertise Camels in 1996 and sales increased by 7.4 percent. In the first quarter of 1997 Camel's market share increased to 5 percent.

While the Joe Camel campaign was increasing Camel sales, it was also continuing to create problems for RJR. In May of 1997 the FTC filed an unfair advertising complaint against the company charging that the campaign caused substantial injury to children and is seeking an irrevocable guarantee that the ads would never be used again. In June 1997, the federal government negotiated a landmark settlement accord with the tobacco industry which will forbid the use of the cartoon in cigarette ads if it goes into effect.

In July 1997, RJR announced that it was phasing out the Joe Camel ads and would begin a new campaign using the theme "What you're looking for." RJR insists that scrapping Joe Camel was entirely a marketing decision that was not affected by the tobacco agreement or the FTC investigation. Whatever the reason, it appears that antismoking advocates and the FTC may finally have found what they have been looking for—an end to the Joe Camel campaign.

Sources: Yumiko Ono and Bruce Ingersoll, "RJR Retires Joe Camel, Adds Sexy Smokers," *The Wall Street Journal*, July 11, 1997, p. B1, 5; Stuart Elliott, "Joe Camel, Spokesbeast to the Smoking Set, Is Trying Menthol," *New York Times*, January 17, 1997, p. C4; Eben Shapiro, "FTC Staff Recommends Ban of Joe Camel Campaign," *The Wall Street Journal*, August 11, 1993, p. B1; Ira Teinowitz, "Joe Camel Is No Tony Tiger to Kids," *Advertising Age*, February 21, 1994, p. 36.

appears in ads for Camel cigarettes. Ethical Perspective 9–3 discusses the continuing controversy surrounding the "smooth character" campaign for Camels.

FANTASY

An execution technique that is popular for emotional types of appeals such as image advertising is fantasy. Fantasy executions are particularly well suited for television, as the commercial can become a 30-second escape for the viewer into another lifestyle. The product or service becomes a central part of the situation created by the advertiser. Cosmetics ads often use fantasy appeals to create images and symbols that become associated with the brand.

DRAMATIZATION

Another execution technique particularly well suited to television is dramatization, where the focus is on telling a short story with the product or service as the star. Dramatization is somewhat akin to slice-of-life execution in that it often relies on the problem/solution approach, but it uses more excitement and suspense in telling the story. The purpose of using drama is to draw the viewer into the action it portrays. Advocates of drama note that when it is successful, the audience becomes lost in the story and experiences the concerns and feelings of the characters.[22] According to Sandra Moriarty, there are five basic steps in a dramatic commercial:

> First is exposition, where the stage is set for the upcoming action. Next comes conflict, which is a technique for identifying the problem. The middle of the dramatic form is a period of rising action where the story builds, the conflict intensifies, the suspense thickens. The fourth step is the climax, where the problem is solved. The last part of a drama is the resolution, where the wrap-up is presented. In advertising that includes product identification and call to action.[23]

The real challenge facing the creative team is how to encompass all these elements in a 30-second commercial. A good example of the dramatization execution technique is the ad for Zerex antifreeze in Exhibit 9–15, which shows a woman's sense of relief when her car starts at the airport on a cold winter night. The ad concludes with a strong identification slogan, "The temperature never drops below Zerex," that connects the brand name to its product benefit.

HUMOR

Like comparisons, humor was discussed in Chapter 6 as a type of advertising appeal, but this technique can also be used as a way of presenting other advertising appeals. Humorous executions are particularly well suited to television or radio, although some print ads attempt to use this style. The pros and cons of using humor as an executional technique are similar to those associated with its use as an advertising appeal.

EXHIBIT 9–15
This Zerex ad uses a dramatization execution

COMBINATIONS

Many of the execution techniques can be combined to present the advertising message. For example, animation is often used to create personality symbols or present a fantasy. Slice-of-life ads are often used to demonstrate a product or service. Comparisons are sometimes made using a humorous approach. FedEx uses humorous executions of the slice-of-death genre depicting businesspeople experiencing dire consequences when they use another delivery service and an important document doesn't arrive on time. It is the responsibility of the creative specialist(s) to determine whether more than one execution style should be used in creating the ad.

CREATIVE TACTICS

Our discussion thus far has focused on the development of creative strategy and various appeals and execution styles that can be used for the advertising message. Once the creative approach, type of appeal, and execution style have been determined, attention turns to creating the actual advertisement. The design and production of advertising messages involve a number of activities, among them writing copy, developing illustrations and other visual elements of the ad, and bringing all of the pieces together to create an effective message. In this section, we examine the verbal and visual elements of an ad and discuss tactical considerations in creating print ads and TV commercials.

Creative Tactics for Print Advertising

The basic components of a print ad are the headline, the body copy, the visual or illustrations, and the layout (the way they all fit together). The headline and body copy portions of the ad are the responsibility of the copywriters; artists, often working under the direction of an art director, are responsible for the visual presentation. Art directors also work with the copywriters to develop a layout, or arrangement of the various components of the ad: headlines, subheads, body copy, illustrations, captions, logos, and the like. We briefly examine the three components of a print ad and how they are coordinated.

HEADLINES

The **headline** refers to the words in the leading position of the ad—the words that will be read first or are positioned to draw the most attention.[24] Headlines are usually set in larger, darker type and are often set apart from the body copy or text portion of the ad to give them prominence. Most advertising people consider the headline the most important part of a print ad.

The most important function of a headline is attracting readers' attention and interesting them in the rest of the message. While the visual portion of an ad is obviously important, the headline often shoulders most of the responsibility of attracting readers' attention. Research has shown the headline is generally the first thing people look at in a print ad, followed by the illustration. Only 20 percent of readers go beyond the headline and read the body copy.[25] So in addition to attracting attention, the headline must give the reader good reason to read the copy portion of the ad, which contains more detailed and persuasive information about the product or service. To do this, the headline must put forth the main theme, appeal, or proposition of the ad in a few words. Some print ads contain little if any body copy, so the headline must work with the illustration to communicate the entire advertising message.

Headlines also perform a segmentation function by engaging the attention and interest of consumers who are most likely to buy a particular product or service. Advertisers begin the segmentation process by choosing to advertise in certain types of publications (e.g., a travel, general interest, or fashion magazine). An effective headline goes even further in selecting good

Ready to sell products on the Internet? Count on us for the technology and security. You just count the sales.

POWERED BY
AT&T SecureBuy Service

Presenting AT&T SecureBuy℠ Service – available at special introductory pricing.

Now there's a quick, low-risk way to ring up new sales, by putting your business on the Internet and selling your products through your own state-of-the-art electronic store. And our special pricing makes it more affordable than ever to back your online efforts with advanced AT&T technology!

Everything you need to set up shop on the Web

AT&T SecureBuy Service, integrated with AT&T Easy World Wide Web℠ Service, offers one stop shopping to create, host and manage your Web site and store – including catalog creation tools, full support for credit card purchases and back-office operations, and even integration with legacy systems.

Co-branding with AT&T adds customer confidence

As one of our merchants, your storefront displays our "Powered by AT&T SecureBuy Service" logo. This association with AT&T, experienced leaders in building advanced and reliable network infrastructures, adds to consumer confidence in the security of your site and their willingness to buy.

Commerce building and purchasing incentives drive customers to your store

You get a free listing in our merchant directory with hotlink connections to your store... and consumers get 100 free minutes of AT&T calls with their first $25 purchase using the service.

Plus, our special low introductory pricing also includes 500 free transactions per month, along with our "Never Miss An Order Guarantee" and our "Server Availability Guarantee."*

So whether you're new to the 'Net – or you already have a site but now you're ready to sell – it's as easy as AT&T SecureBuy Service to put AT&T technology, reliability and world-class service and support behind your efforts.

For more information
Call toll-free 1 800 746-7846
(1 800 7-HOSTIN) Dept. 125
E-mail us at hostinfo@attmail.com
www.securebuy.com

© 1997 AT&T. All rights reserved.

AT&T

Chad Farmer is the creative director and a partner at Lambesis, Inc., a small agency in Del Mar, CA, whose cutting-edge creative work is attracting the attention of national and international accounts. Like other hot advertising shops, Lambesis is be-

CHAD FARMER

"Our biggest clients come to us because of Chad. They know where the talent is."

coming known for its excellent creative work. The agency's founder, Nick Lambesis, credits Chad Farmer with its growing notoriety noting that: "Our biggest clients come to us because of Chad. They know where the talent is."

Chad's shooting-star ascension through the advertising ranks comes as no surprise, given his family heritage. His father owned a number of agencies in Phoenix and while he was growing up he often created his own ad campaigns at his father's office. "Since I was old enough to draw I'd hang out at the office and sketch storyboards. He'd say 'make me a story in six frames,' and I thought it was like making a cartoon." His father recommended fashion design as a career choice, but Chad opted for graphic design. He enrolled at Arizona State University to study graphic design and film and transferred during his junior year to the Art Center in Pasadena.

His first advertising job was with Lord Dentsu & Partners, Los Angeles, where he started out working on the Suzuki motorcycles account. One memorable Suzuki TV spot he created featured portentous shots of a Suzuki motorcycle surrounded by giant mirrors in the middle of the desert. The idea was to accentuate the beauty of the bike. While at Lord Dentsu, Farmer learned a great deal about how advertising and other forms of communication can be used to build an image for a brand. "The most valuable thing I gained was building brand image via type, color, and the characters. Whatever direction you decide to take that image, it needs to work in every avenue of media and still retain the same quality of communication."

He was briefly lured away from Lord Dentsu by DDB Needham in Chicago where he worked on major accounts such as Bud Lite, SeaWorld, and McDonald's. However after a few months Farmer realized he did not like working for a big agency with large accounts. He found the agency and client bureaucracy too restricting and felt it lessened the purity of his ideas. He returned to Lord Dentsu for another two years before being lured away by Lambesis, a small agency just outside of San Diego. He notes that the decision to leave the world of high-profile, big agencies for a small agency was a no brainer. He was tired of big companies altering his work or rejecting it out-

right because of its edgy tone. He yearned for more creative control, the flexibility to pick and choose his own accounts, and the opportunity to co-direct his own agency. So the promise from Lambesis of complete artistic control, plus a partnership, was more than enough incentive to get him to move south.

Since joining Lambesis, Farmer's cutting-edge creative work has helped transform Lambesis into a hot advertising shop and smash the old maxim that you have to work for a big agency to land major national and international accounts. In addition to Airwalk, the agency's roster now includes major accounts such as Guess?, Rossignol In-line skates, Charles David footwear, and Renaissance cosmetics. Farmer is best known for his knack for tapping into the wavelength of today's youth. He feels the younger generation can be reached through advertising but that today's youth detest the "Generation X" label. Farmer notes that "To reach them you have to be truthful with them. Cut through the B.S. Don't talk at them, talk with them and they will react."

Surfing and alternative music, his prime hobbies, have been getting less attention these days as Chad Farmer wrestles with his expanding workload. The relatively little time he spends away from advertising is often work-related. He says that many of his best ideas have come while grocery shopping, driving on the freeway, or lying awake in bed in the middle of the night. For inspiration he reads newspapers, watches films, listens to music, and reads about 60 magazines a month, many of them fashion publications (he avoids television). Or he talks to his teenage sister who gave him some ideas for the Sorrel Junior ads, which are aimed at 14- to 20-year-old girls.

Chad Farmer's guiding principle is never to live in fear of losing an account noting that "you should be giving so much that they are deliriously happy." Thanks to Chad Farmer's creative talent, Lambesis has a lot of happy accounts these days.

prospects for the product by addressing their specific needs, wants, or interests. For example, the headline in the ad for AT&T's SecureBuy Service catches the attention of readers whose companies are considering selling their products over the Internet.

Types of Headlines

There are numerous headline possibilities. The type used depends on several factors, including the creative strategy, the particular advertising situation (e.g., product type, media vehicle(s) being used, timeliness), and its relationship to other components of the ad, such as the illustration or body copy. Headlines can be categorized as direct and indirect. **Direct headlines** are straightforward and informative in terms of the message they are presenting and the target audience they are directed toward. Common types of direct headlines include those offering a specific benefit, making a promise, or announcing a reason the reader should be interested in the product or service.

Indirect headlines are not straightforward about identifying the product or service or getting to the point. But they are often more effective at attracting readers' attention and interest because they provoke curiosity and lure readers into the body copy to learn an answer or get an explanation. Techniques for writing indirect headlines include using questions, provocations, how-to statements, and challenges.

Indirect headlines rely on their ability to generate curiosity or intrigue so as to motivate readers to become involved with the ad and read the body copy to find out the point of the message. This can be risky if the headline is not provocative enough to get the readers' interest. Advertisers deal with this problem by using a visual appeal that helps attract attention and offers another reason for reading more of the message. For example, in Exhibit 9–16, the headline is accompanied by an amusing illustration that entices travelers to read the message to learn more about the Fresca® World Ski Card and how to get it. Do you think this ad would have been as effective with a more traditional illustration such as a skier?

EXHIBIT 9—16
This ad combines an indirect headline with an amusing illustration to attract readers' attention

Subheads

While many ads have only one headline, it is also common to see print ads containing the main head and one or more secondary heads, or **subheads**. Subheads are usually smaller than the main headline but larger than the body copy. They may appear above or below the main headline, or within the body copy. The AT&T ad on page 282 uses subheads within the body copy.

Subheads are often used to enhance the readability of the message by breaking up large amounts of body copy and highlighting key sales points. Their content reinforces the headline and advertising slogan or theme.

BODY COPY

The main text portion of a print ad is referred to as the **body copy** (or sometimes just copy). While the body copy is usually the heart of the advertising message, getting the target audience to read it is often difficult. The copywriter faces a dilemma: the body copy must be long enough to communicate the advertiser's message yet short enough to hold readers' interest.

Body copy content often flows from the points made in the headline or various subheads, but the specific content depends on the type of advertising appeal and/or execution style being used. For example, straight-sell copy that presents relevant information, product features and benefits, or competitive advantages is often used with the various types of rational appeals discussed earlier in the chapter. Emotional appeals often use narrative copy that tells a story or provides an interesting account of a problem or situation involving the product.

Advertising body copy can be written to go along with various types of creative appeals and executions—comparisons, price appeals, demonstrations, humor, dramatizations, and the like. Copywriters choose a copy style that is appropriate for the type of appeal being used and effective for executing the creative strategy and communicating the advertiser's message to the target audience.

VISUAL ELEMENTS

The third major component of a print ad is the visual element. The illustration is often a dominant part of a print ad and plays an important role in determining its effectiveness. The visual portion of an ad must attract attention, communicate an idea or image, and work in a synergistic fashion with the headline and body copy to produce an effective message. Notice how the visual portion of the British Airways ad in Exhibit 9–17 helps reinforce the message announcing the airline's new arrival facilities for passengers at the two London airports.

Many decisions have to be made regarding the visual portion of the ad: what identification marks should be included (brand name, company or trade name, trademarks, logos); whether to use photos or hand-drawn or painted illustrations; what colors to use (or even perhaps black and white or just a splash of color); and what the focus of the visual should be.

LAYOUT

While each individual component of a print ad is important, the key factor is how these elements are blended into a finished advertisement. A **layout** is the physical arrangement of the various parts of the ad, including the headline, subheads, body copy, illustrations, and any identifying marks. The layout shows where each part of the ad will be placed and gives guidelines to the people working on the ad. For example, the layout helps the copywriter determine how much space he or she has to work with and how much copy should be written. The layout can also guide the art director in determining the size and type of photos. Layouts are often done in rough form and presented to the client so the advertiser can visualize what the ad will look like before giving preliminary approval. The agency should get client approval of the layout before moving on to the more costly stages of print production.

Creative Tactics for Television

As consumers, we see so many TV commercials that it's easy to take for granted the time, effort, and money that go into making them. Creating and producing commercials that break through the clutter on TV and communicate effectively is a detailed, expensive

EXHIBIT 9–17
The visual portion of this ad interacts
very well with the message

process. On a cost-per-minute basis, commercials are the most expensive productions seen on television.[26]

TV is a unique and powerful advertising medium because it contains the elements of sight, sound, and motion, which can be combined to create a variety of advertising appeals and executions. Unlike print, the viewer does not control the rate at which the message is presented, so there is no opportunity to review points of interest or reread things that are not communicated clearly. As with any form of advertising, one of the first goals in creating TV commercials is to get the viewers' attention and then maintain it. This can be particularly challenging because of the clutter and because people often view TV commercials while doing other things (reading a book or magazine, talking).

Like print ads, TV commercials have several components. The video and audio must work together to create the right impact and communicate the advertiser's message.

VIDEO

The video elements of a commercial are what is seen on the TV screen. The visual portion generally dominates the commercial, so it must attract viewers' attention and communicate an idea, message, and/or image. A number of visual elements may have to be coordinated to produce a successful ad. Decisions have to be made regarding the product, the presenter, action sequences, demonstrations, and the like, as well as the setting(s), the talent or characters who will appear in the commercial, and such other factors as lighting, graphics, color, and identifying symbols.

AUDIO

The audio portion of a commercial includes voices, music, and sound effects. Voices are used in different ways in commercials. They may be heard through the direct presentation of a spokesperson or as a conversation among various people appearing in the commercial. A common method for presenting the audio portion of a commercial is through a **voiceover**, where the message is delivered or action on the screen is narrated or described by an announcer who is not visible. A recent trend among major advertisers is to have distinctive celebrities do voiceovers for their commercials.[27] Actor Gene Hackman does many of the voiceovers for United Airlines spots, Jack Lemmon does Honda commercials, Adam Arkin is the voice in many Compaq computer ads and Johnny Cash does Folgers coffee.

Music is also an important part of many TV commercials and can play a variety of roles.[28] In many commercials, the music provides a pleasant background or helps create the appropriate mood. Advertisers often use needledrop, which Linda Scott describes as follows:

> Needledrop is an occupational term common to advertising agencies and the music industry. It refers to music that is prefabricated, multipurpose, and highly conventional. It is, in that sense, the musical equivalent of stock photos, clip art, or canned copy. Needledrop is an inexpensive substitute for original music; paid for on a one-time basis, it is dropped into a commercial or film when a particular normative effect is desired.[29]

In other commercials, such as the "Like a Rock" campaign for Chevy trucks, music is much more central to the advertising message. It can be used to get attention, break through the advertising clutter, communicate a key selling point, help establish an image or position, or add feeling.[30] For example, music can work through a classical conditioning process to create positive emotions that become associated with the advertised product or service. Music can also create a positive mood that makes the consumer more receptive toward the advertising message.[31]

Because music can play such an important role in the creative strategy, many companies have paid large sums for the rights to use popular songs in their commercials. For example, Microsoft paid a reported $4 million to use the Rolling Stones' classic "Start Me Up" to introduce the advertising campaign for Windows 95.[32] Mercedes-Benz bought the rights to Janis Joplin's antimaterialist anthem of the same name. A number of advertisers have developed commercials around classic songs from the 1960s and 70s. Figure 9–3 lists some of the advertisers and the songs they have used.

Another important musical element in both TV and radio commercials is **jingles**, catchy songs about a product or service that usually carry the advertising theme and a simple message. For example, Doublemint gum has used the well-known "Double your pleasure, double your fun with Doublemint, Doublemint gum" for years. The jingle is very memorable and serves as a good reminder of the product's minty flavor. Ace Hardware recently brought back the "Ace is the place with the friendly hardware man" jingle and updated it by changing the last three words to "friendly hardware folks" and having Jimmy Buffett sing it. The jingle was reintroduced to create a friendly image for the dealer-owned Ace stores and help them compete against superstores like Home Depot and Builder's Square.[33]

Jingles can be used by themselves as the basis for a musical commercial. For example, commercials for Diet Pepsi have been built around Ray Charles singing the jingle for the brand, which incorporates the "You've got the right one, baby! Uh-huh!" slogan (Exhibit 9–18). Diet Coke recently brought back its old slogan "Just for the taste of it," set it to a luxurious musical score, and made it the basis of a multimillion-dollar ad campaign. In some commercials, jingles are used more as a form of product identification and appear at the end of the message. Jingles are often composed by companies that specialize in writing commercial music for advertising. These jingle houses work with the creative team to determine the role music will play in the commercial and the message that needs to be communicated.

PLANNING AND PRODUCTION OF TV COMMERCIALS

One of the first decisions that has to be made in planning a TV commercial is the type of appeal and execution style that will be used. Television is well suited to both rational and emotional advertising appeals or combinations of the two. Various execution styles used with rational appeals, such as a straight sell or announcement, demonstration, testimonial, or comparison, work well on TV.

Advertisers recognize that they need to do more than talk about, demonstrate, or compare their products or services. Their commercials have to break through the clutter and grab viewers' attention; they must often appeal to emotional, as well as rational, buying mo-

FIGURE 9–3
Classic songs that have been used in commercials

It finally happened—Bob Dylan has allowed "The Times They Are A-Changin'" to be used in an advertisement on television. The ad went on the air this month, but it is not the first—only the most amazing—example of the commercial use of a rebellious classic.

- Song: "The Times They Are A-Changin'," **Bob Dylan**
- Product: **Coopers & Lybrand**, accountants

For an undisclosed sum, Dylan permitted the Big Six firm to use folkie Richie Havens's rendition of his protest anthem. The company cannot use Dylan's name, even when discussing the spot.

- Song: "Teach Your Children," **Crosby, Stills, Nash, & Young**
- Product: **Fruit of the Loom** underwear

For $1.5 million, Fruit of the Loom used 30 seconds of the song, with writer Nash himself rerecording it. "I'm not that precious about my music. We're not talking Mozart here," he said.

- Song: "Revolution," **the Beatles**
- Product: **Nike** athletic shoes

Michael Jackson owned the rights to the Lennon and McCartney composition, Capitol Records owned the original masters, and so for $500,000 Nike was allowed to use the actual voices of the Beatles.

- Song: "Born to Be Wild," **Steppenwolf**
- Product: The **Ford Mercury Cougar**

With a yuppie, his leather jacket, and his cougar, the ad was part of a campaign that also used "Proud Mary" and the Beatles' "Help." In three years the average age of Cougar buyers fell from 44 to 35.

- Song: "Satisfaction," **the Rolling Stones**
- Product: **Snickers** candy bars

Mick Jagger and Keith Richards, the songwriters, and ABKCO, the owner of the rights to the song, were made an irresistible offer in 1991: $4 million, with $2.8 million going to the composers.

- Song: "Turn! Turn! Turn!" **the Byrds**
- Product: *Time*, the weekly newsmagazine

Folk legend Pete Seeger set words from the Book of Ecclesiastes to music, and the Byrds' version became a huge early hippie hit. In the ad it segued into "Hi, I'm Nancy, and operator here at *Time*."

Source: *Time*, January 31, 1994, p. 23.

tives. Television is essentially an entertainment medium, and many advertisers recognize that their commercials are most successful when they entertain as well as inform. Figure 9–4 shows the 10 most popular TV campaigns of 1995. Many of these campaigns are characterized by commercials with strong entertainment value, like the Budweiser spots that featured an army of ants drinking an entire bottle of Bud, the humorous spots for Little Caesar's Pizza (Exhibit 6–15), and the "Got Milk?" ads discussed in Chapter 8. TV is particularly well suited to drama; no other advertising medium can touch emotions as well. Various emotional appeals such as humor, fear, and fantasy work well on TV, as do dramatizations and slice-of-life executions.

Planning the Commercial

The various elements of a TV commercial are brought together in a **script**, a written version of a commercial that provides a detailed description of its video and audio content. The script shows the various audio components of the commercial—the copy to be spoken by

EXHIBIT 9—18   Diet Pepsi commercials featured Ray Charles singing the popular jingle

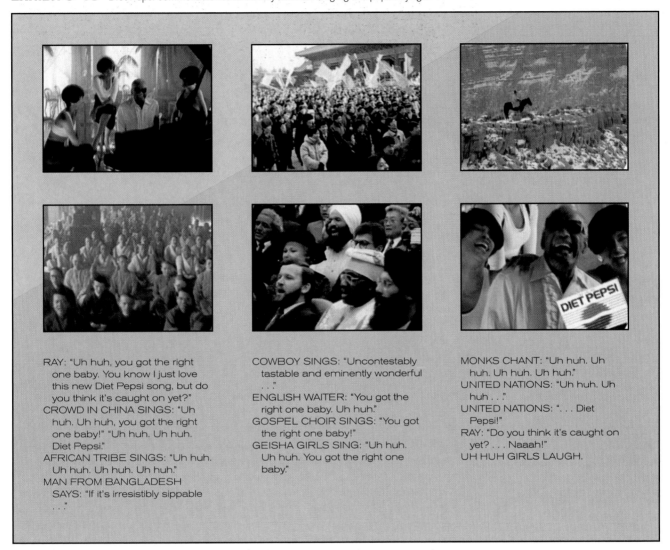

RAY: "Uh huh, you got the right one baby. You know I just love this new Diet Pepsi song, but do you think it's caught on yet?"
CROWD IN CHINA SINGS: "Uh huh. Uh huh, you got the right one baby!" "Uh huh. Uh huh. Uh huh. Diet Pepsi."
AFRICAN TRIBE SINGS: "Uh huh. Uh huh. Uh huh. Uh huh."
MAN FROM BANGLADESH SAYS: "If it's irresistibly sippable . . ."

COWBOY SINGS: "Uncontestably tastable and eminently wonderful . . ."
ENGLISH WAITER: "You got the right one baby. Uh huh."
GOSPEL CHOIR SINGS: "You got the right one baby!"
GEISHA GIRLS SING: "Uh huh. Uh huh. You got the right one baby."

MONKS CHANT: "Uh huh. Uh huh. Uh huh. Uh huh."
UNITED NATIONS: "Uh huh. Uh huh . . ."
UNITED NATIONS: ". . . Diet Pepsi!"
RAY: "Do you think it's caught on yet? . . . Naaah!"
UH HUH GIRLS LAUGH.

FIGURE 9—4
Top 10 television campaigns of 1995

Rank	Brand	Ad Agency
1	Budweiser	DDB Needham
2	McDonald's	Leo Burnett
3	Pepsi	BBDO
4	Little Caesar's	Cliff Freeman & Partners
5	Coca-Cola	Creative Artists Agency
6	Pizza Hut	BBDO Worldwide
7	AT&T	FCB Leber Katz/NW Ayer & Partners/ McCann-Erickson/Young & Rubicam
8	Milk	Goodby, Silverstein
9	Bud Light	DDB Needham
10	Edy's/Dryers	Goldberg Moser O'Neill

Sources: Video Storyboard Tests; Sally Goll Beatty, "Omnicom Menagerie Tops Poll of Most Popular TV Ads," *The Wall Street Journal*, March 11, 1996, pp. B1, 5.

voices, music, and sound effects. The video portion of the script provides the visual plan of the commercial—camera actions and angles, scenes, transitions, and other important descriptions. The script also shows how the video corresponds to the audio portion of the commercial.

Once the basic script has been conceived, the writer and art director get together to produce a storyboard, a series of drawings used to present the visual plan or layout of a proposed commercial. The storyboard contains still drawings of the video scenes and descriptions of the audio that accompanies each scene. Like layouts for print ads, storyboards provide those involved in the production and approval of the commercial with a good approximation of what the final commercial will look like. In some cases an aniamatic (a videotape of the storyboard along with the soundtrack) may be produced if a more finished form of the commercial is needed for client presentations or pretesting.

Production

Once the storyboard or aniamatic of the commercial is approved, it is ready to move to the production phase, which involves three stages:

1. *Preproduction*—all the work and activities that occur before the actual shooting/recording of the commercial.
2. *Production*—the period during which the commercial is filmed or videotaped and recorded.
3. *Postproduction*—activities and work that occur after the commercial has been filmed and recorded.

The various activities of each phase are shown in Figure 9–5. Before the final production process begins, the client must usually review and approve the creative strategy and the various tactics that will be used in creating the advertising message.

CLIENT EVALUATION AND APPROVAL OF CREATIVE WORK

While the creative specialists have much responsibility for determining the advertising appeal and execution style to be used in a campaign, the client must evaluate and approve the creative approach before any ads are produced. A number of people on the client side may be involved in evaluating the creative work of the agency, including the advertising or communications manager, product or brand managers, marketing director or vice president, representatives from the legal department, and sometimes even the president or chief executive officer (CEO) of the company or the board of directors.

The amount of input each of these individuals has in the creative evaluation and approval process varies depending on the company's policies, the importance of the product to the company, the role of advertising in the marketing program, and the advertising approach being recommended. IMC Perspective 9–4 discusses how Chiat/Day had to convince Apple's board of directors to air the "1984" commercial used to introduce the Macintosh personal computer.

FIGURE 9–5 The three phases of production for electronic media

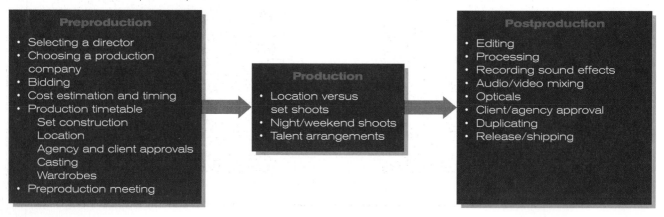

IMC Perspective 9–4
The Commercial that Changed Advertising—and Why We almost Didn't See It

In 1983, Apple Computer was planning the introduction of its line of Macintosh personal computers, designed to take on its main competitor, corporate giant IBM. Apple had just lost its lead in the PC market to IBM and its previous product introduction, the $10,000 Lisa, had not been very successful. Some analysts suggested that the survival of Apple might depend on the market's response to the Mac.

Apple's marketing strategy called for the introduction of the Macintosh to be a major event that would generate immediate support for the new product. The advertising agency, Chiat/Day, was given the creative challenge of coming up with a blockbuster idea that would result in a dramatic commercial to introduce the Mac. Chiat/Day's creative team developed a commercial based on the concept of Big Brother (purportedly symbolizing IBM) from George Orwell's classic novel *1984*. The ad used stark images of Orwell's dystopia and a dramatic scene of a young woman throwing a mallet through a movie screen to destroy the controlling force. More than $500,000 was spent to produce the "1984" commercial, which was filmed in London by well-known film director Ridley Scott and contained a cast of more than 200.

When the commercial was first shown at Apple's annual sales meeting in October 1983, there was stunned silence followed by a 15-minute standing ovation. Apple was ready to showcase the 60-second commercial in two spots during the 1984 Super Bowl that would cost $500,000 each. But there was still one problem—getting approval from Apple's board of directors for the avant-garde ad and the million-dollar media purchase.

The board thought the commercial was too controversial and might be detrimental to Apple's image, particularly in the business market. The cost-conscious board also thought the Super Bowl rates were too expensive and directed the agency to sell off the two spots. The agency began working to sell off the media time while simultaneously lobbying Apple not to cancel the ad. The agency did manage to sell one of the 60-second spots but could not attract a reasonable offer for the other. Two days before the game, the Apple board reluctantly approved airing the commercial.

The Super Bowl showing of "1984" was the only time it ever appeared as a commercial spot on network TV. The impact of the ad was tremendous. It was the focus of attention in the media and the talk of the advertising and marketing industries. Perhaps most important, the ad helped Apple achieve a very ambitious sales goal. Apple projected sales of 50,000 Macs in the first 100 days; actual sales surpassed 72,000 units.

Over time the "1984" spot became one of the most talked-about commercials ever. In 1990, *Advertising Age*, the ad industry's leading trade publication, chose it as the commercial of the decade and named Chiat/Day agency of the decade. Ten years after the commercial first ran, it still receives numerous accolades. In January 1994, *Advertising Age* published a feature story that said the "1984" spot had changed the nature of advertising forever. It helped turn the Super Bowl from a mere football game into advertising's super event of the year. And it ushered in the era of advertising as news: the three major TV networks replayed parts or all of the spot as a story on nightly news programs. John O'Toole, president of the American Association of Advertising Agencies, said "1984" was the beginning of a new era of integrated marketing communications as event marketing, with sales promotion and PR built in.

Many view the Macintosh PC as one of the most significant new products ever introduced, since it revolutionized personal computing and transformed the production of graphics around the world. The "computer for the rest of us" is also credited with helping to bring computing power to the people. As *Advertising Age* critic Bob Garfield said, "This is what happens when breakthrough technology is given the benefit of the greatest TV commercial ever made."

In 1986 Apple moved its account to BBDO Worldwide, which handled its advertising for more than 10 years. However, the company and agency that created "1984" were reunited in 1997 when Apple announced that it was returning its account to TBWA/Chiat Day.

Sources: Bradley Johnson, "Apple Ready to Return Account to TBWA Chiat," *Advertising Age*, August 4, 1997, pp. 1, 42. Bradley Johnson, "10 Years after '1984': The Commercial and the Product that Changed Advertising," *Advertising Age*, June 1994, pp. 1, 12–14; Bob Garfield, "Breakthrough Product Gets Greatest TV Spot," *Advertising Age*, January 10, 1994, p. 14; Cleveland Horton, "Apple's Bold '1984' Scores on All Fronts," *Advertising Age*, January 1, 1990, p. 12. Reprinted with permission from the June 1994, January 10, 1994, and January 1, 1990 issues of *Advertising Age*. Copyright Crain Communications, Inc. 1990, 1994.

Earlier in this chapter, we noted that Procter & Gamble has been moving away from testimonials and slice-of-life advertising executions to somewhat riskier and more lively forms of advertising. But the company remains very conservative and has been slow to adopt the avant-garde ads used by many of its competitors. Agencies that do the advertising for various P&G brands recognize that quirky executions that challenge the company's subdued corporate culture are not likely to be approved.[34]

In many cases, top management is involved in selecting an ad agency and must approve the theme and creative strategy for the campaign. Evaluation and approval of the individual ads proposed by the agency often rest with the advertising and product managers who are primarily responsible for the brand. The account executive and a member of the creative team present the creative concept to the client's advertising and product and/or marketing managers for their approval before beginning production. A careful evaluation should be made before the ad actually enters production, since this stage requires considerable time and money as suppliers are hired to perform the various functions required to produce the actual ad.

The client's evaluation of the print layout or commercial storyboard can be difficult, since the advertising or brand manager is generally not a creative expert and must be careful not to reject viable creative approaches or accept ideas that will result in inferior advertising. However, personnel on the client side can use the guidelines discussed next to judge the efficacy of creative approaches suggested by the agency.

Guidelines for Evaluating Creative Output

Advertisers use numerous criteria to evaluate the creative approach suggested by the ad agency. In some instances, the client may want to have the rough layout or storyboard pretested to get quantitative information to assist in the evaluation. However, the evaluation process is usually more subjective; the advertising or brand manager relies on qualitative considerations. Basic criteria for evaluating creative approaches are discussed next.

- *Is the creative approach consistent with the brand's marketing and advertising objectives?* One of the most important factors the client must consider is whether the creative appeal and execution style recommended by the agency are consistent with the marketing strategy for the brand and the role advertising and promotion have been assigned in the overall marketing program. This means the creative approach must be compatible with the image of the brand and the way it is positioned in the marketplace and should contribute to the marketing and advertising objectives.
- *Is the creative approach consistent with the creative strategy and objectives? Does it communicate what it is supposed to?* The advertising appeal and execution must meet the communications objectives laid out in the copy platform, and the ad must say what the advertising strategy calls for it to say. Creative specialists can lose sight of what the advertising message is supposed to be and come up with an approach that fails to execute the advertising strategy. Individuals responsible for approving the ad should ask the creative specialists to explain how the appeal or execution style adheres to the creative strategy and helps meet communications objectives.
- *Is the creative approach appropriate for the target audience?* Generally, much time has been spent defining, locating, and attempting to understand the target audience for the advertiser's product or service. Careful consideration should be given to whether the ad appeal or execution recommended will appeal to, be understood by, and communicate effectively with the target audience. This involves studying all elements of the ad and how the audience will respond to them. Advertisers do not want to approve advertising that they believe will receive a negative reaction from the target audience. For example, it has been suggested that advertising targeted to older consumers should use models who are 10 years younger than the average age of the target audience, since most people feel younger than their chronological age.[35] Advertisers also face a considerable challenge developing ads for the teen market because their styles, fashions, language, and values change so rapidly. They may find they are using an advertising approach, a spokesperson, or even an expression that is no longer popular among teens.
- *Does the creative approach communicate a clear and convincing message to the customer?* Most ads are supposed to communicate a message that will help sell the brand. Many ads

fail to communicate a clear and convincing message that motivates consumers to use a brand. While creativity is important in advertising, it is also important that the advertising communicate information attributes, features and benefits, and/or images that give consumers a reason to buy the brand.

• *Does the creative execution keep from overwhelming the message?* A common criticism of advertising, and TV commercials in particular, is that so much emphasis is placed on creative execution that the advertiser's message gets overshadowed. Many creative, entertaining commercials have failed to register the brand name and/or selling points effectively.

For example, a few years ago the agency for North American Philips Lighting Corp. developed an award-winning campaign that focused on the humorous results when lightbulbs fail at just the wrong time. The spots included a woman who appears to accidentally vacuum up her screeching cat after a lightbulb blows out and an elderly couple using Philips Pastel bulbs to create a romantic mood (Exhibit 9–19). While the purpose of the campaign was to help Philips make inroads into General Electric's dominance in the lightbulb market, many consumers did not notice the Philips brand name. A Video Sto-

EXHIBIT 9—19 Some advertising experts think these Philips Lighting commercials may have been too creative and overwhelmed the message

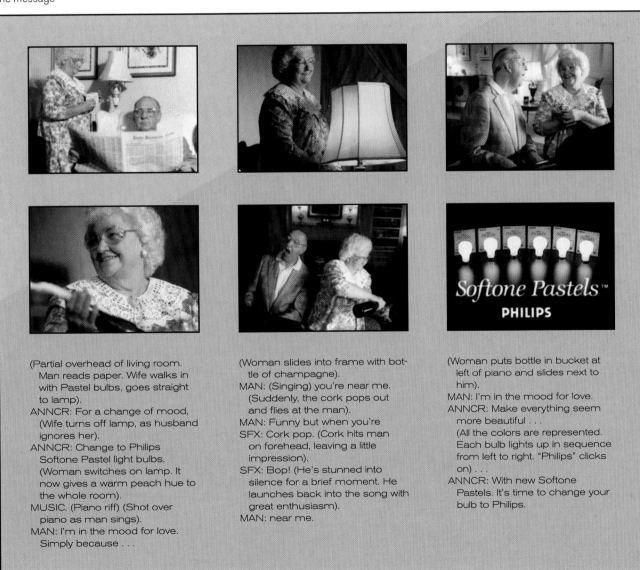

(Partial overhead of living room. Man reads paper. Wife walks in with Pastel bulbs, goes straight to lamp).
ANNCR: For a change of mood, (Wife turns off lamp, as husband ignores her).
ANNCR: Change to Philips Softone Pastel light bulbs. (Woman switches on lamp. It now gives a warm peach hue to the whole room).
MUSIC. (Piano riff) (Shot over piano as man sings).
MAN: I'm in the mood for love. Simply because . . .

(Woman slides into frame with bottle of champagne).
MAN: (Singing) you're near me. (Suddenly, the cork pops out and flies at the man).
MAN: Funny but when you're
SFX: Cork pop. (Cork hits man on forehead, leaving a little impression).
SFX: Bop! (He's stunned into silence for a brief moment. He launches back into the song with great enthusiasm).
MAN: near me.

(Woman puts bottle in bucket at left of piano and slides next to him).
MAN: I'm in the mood for love.
ANNCR: Make everything seem more beautiful . . .
(All the colors are represented. Each bulb lights up in sequence from left to right. "Philips" clicks on) . . .
ANNCR: With new Softone Pastels. It's time to change your bulb to Philips.

ryboard survey showed that many viewers thought the ads were for GE lightbulbs. Surveys taken a year later by the agency that created the campaign showed that brand awareness and sales had increased considerably, but some advertising people still think the ad was so creative and entertaining that it overwhelmed the message.[36]

With the increasing amount of clutter in most advertising media, it may be necessary to use a novel creative approach to gain the viewer's or reader's attention. However, the creative execution cannot overwhelm the message. Clients must walk a fine line: make sure the sales message is not lost, but be careful not to stifle the efforts of the creative specialists and force them into producing dull, boring advertising.

• *Is the creative approach appropriate for the media environment in which it is likely to be seen?* Each media vehicle has its own specific climate that results from the nature of its editorial content, the type of reader or viewer it attracts, and the nature of the ads it contains. Consideration should be given to how well the ad fits into the media environment in which it will be shown. For example, the Super Bowl has become a showcase for commercials. People who care very little about advertising know how much a 30-second commercial costs and pay as much attention to the ads as to the game itself. So many advertisers feel compelled to develop new ads for the Super Bowl or to save new commercials for the game.

• *Is the ad truthful and tasteful?* The ultimate responsibility for determining whether an ad deceives or offends the target audience lies with the client. It is the job of the advertising or brand manager to evaluate the approach suggested by the creative specialists against company standards. The firm's legal department may be asked to review the ad to determine whether the creative appeal, message content, or execution could cause any problems for the company. It is much better to catch any potential legal problems before the ad is shown to the public.

The advertising manager, brand manager, or other personnel on the client side can use these basic guidelines in reviewing, evaluating, and approving the ideas offered by the creative specialists. There may be other factors specific to the firm's advertising and marketing situation. Also, there may be situations where it is acceptable to deviate from the standards the firm usually uses in judging creative output. As we shall see in Chapter 18, the client may want to move beyond these subjective criteria and use more sophisticated pretesting methods to determine the effectiveness of a particular approach suggested by the creative specialist or team.

SUMMARY

In this chapter, we examined how the advertising message will be implemented and executed. Once the creative strategy that will guide the ad campaign has been determined, attention turns to the specific type of advertising appeal and execution format to carry out the creative plan. The appeal is the central message used in the ad to elicit some response from consumers or influence their feelings. Appeals can be broken into two broad categories, rational and emotional. Rational appeals focus on consumers' practical, functional, or utilitarian need for the product or service; emotional appeals relate to social and/or psychological reasons for purchasing a product or service. Numerous types of appeals are available to advertisers within each category.

The creative execution style is the way the advertising appeal is presented in the message. A number of common execution techniques were examined in the chapter, along with considerations for their use. Attention was also given to tactical issues involved in creating print and TV advertising. The components of a print ad include headlines, body copy, illustrations, and layout. We also examined the video and audio components of TV commercials and various considerations involved in the planning and production of commercials.

Creative specialists are responsible for determining the advertising appeal and execution style as well as the tactical aspects of creating ads. However, the client must review, evaluate, and approve the creative approach before any ads are produced or run. A number of criteria can be used by advertising, product, or brand managers and others involved in the promotional process to evaluate the advertising messages before approving final production.

KEY TERMS

advertising appeal, 266
creative execution style, 266
informational/rational
   appeals, 266
emotional appeals, 268

transformational ad, 269
reminder advertising, 272
teaser advertising, 272
headline, 282

direct headlines, 284
indirect headlines, 284
subheads, 285
body copy, 285

layout, 285
voiceover, 286
jingles, 287
script, 288

DISCUSSION QUESTIONS

1. Analyze the "Like a Rock" campaign for Chevrolet trucks discussed in the opening vignette. Why do you think this campaign has been so successful in striking a responsive chord with truck buyers? How long do you think Chevy can use this campaign theme?

2. Discuss the differences between an advertising appeal and a creative execution style. Choose several ads and analyze the particular appeal and execution style used in each.

3. What are the differences between informational/rational and emotional advertising appeals and the factors that would favor the use of one over the other? Find examples of advertising campaigns that use each type of appeal and discuss the reasons why you feel they are effective or ineffective.

4. What is meant by transformational advertising? Analyze the "It's different out here" advertising campaign for Norwegian Cruise Lines discussed in IMC Perspective 9–1 from a transformational advertising perspective.

5. Some advertising critics believe the Taster's Choice "brewing romance" campaign is no longer effective, since it is difficult to keep a serial theme going for several years. The creative director for the agency argues that the problem is a drastic cut in the media budget rather than declining interest

in the romance. Do you think this campaign is still effective? Why or why not? Would you recommend increasing the media budget for the campaign?

6. Why do advertisers such as Procter & Gamble and other consumer package-goods marketers use slice-of-life executions so often?

7. Analyze R. J. Reynolds's decision to stop using the Joe Camel cartoon character ad campaign. Do you think Camel cigarettes can retain their market share without this campaign?

8. What are the various roles of the headline in a print ad? Find examples of print ads that use direct and indirect headlines.

9. Why do many advertisers pay large sums of money to celebrities to do the voiceovers for their commercials? Do you think consumers recognize the voices of the celebrities doing the commercials? Is it necessary that they recognize them for the commercials to be effective?

10. Choose a current advertising campaign and analyze it with respect to the creative criteria discussed in the last section of the chapter. Do you think the advertising meets all of the guidelines?

10

Media Planning and Strategy

Chapter Objectives

- To introduce the key terminology needed to understand media planning.

- To provide an understanding of how a media plan is developed.

- To explain the process of developing and implementing media strategies.

- To introduce sources of media information and characteristics of media.

INTERACTIVE TV: BOOM OR BUST?

Imagine that you are watching a television program like "Friends" and you like the blouse Rachel is wearing. You click on it with your remote control, and a menu appears asking if you wish to buy it. You click on "yes." More menus appear asking how you would like to pay for it, where it should be sent, and in what color. (Your size and credit card information are already programmed in.) When you finish ordering, the menus disappear and "Friends" continues—and your blouse arrives at your home the next day. Such is the vision of Microsoft's Bill Gates for what lies ahead in interactive television. Is this vision a dream or close to reality? It appears to be a little of both.

In addition to Microsoft, Time Warner, NBC, and Bell Atlantic are just a few of the companies that believe the future for interactive TV is promising. But companies like US West, Nordstrom, Ford, and Hallmark are not so sure; they have discontinued efforts into interactive shopping, at least in the short run. The reason? Sophisticated programming is years away, and costs are too prohibitive at this time.

Mike Mills, a writer for the *Washington Post*, agrees that interactive television has a way to go. Mills notes that of the 136 interactive licenses granted by the Federal Communications Commission (FCC), 23 have defaulted on payments—including the top three. The 113 remaining are urging the FCC to relax its stringent rules for payment and construction of the system. Mills says the technology is just not ready and there is no evidence that people want to interact with their TV sets.

You knead dough for therapy.
You julienne vegetables for meditation.
You decorate cupcakes with rainbow sprinkles to console your inner child.
You e-mail a chef in the south of France for enlightenment.

webtv

The Internet. The ultimate resource. Now showing on a TV near you. You don't even need a computer. You just need a subscription to the WebTV Network, an Internet terminal from Sony or Philips Magnavox and a few basic remote control skills. Simply click on the Explore button and go to an area like "Lifestyle." Then try "The Kitchen." From there, you'll find all kinds of specific sites. Like "Food of the Godz." Or, conduct your own search. And e-mail it to a friend. WebTV. Offering extra helpings of possibilities.

Tune into what you're into.

©1996 WebTV Networks, Inc. WebTV and the WebTV Network are trademarks of WebTV Networks, Inc. All other company brand and product names may be registered trademarks of their respective holdings and hereby recognized. Price of service is $19.95 per month for unlimited use. For more information, call 1-800-GOWEBTV or visit us at our Web site at http://webtv.net

Still others are pushing ahead. Kim Cleland of *Advertising Age* says, "Interactive TV is alive and kicking." But, she notes, "It's not called that anymore. Instead, it's Internet TV." Time Warner, Sega, and Zenith are all working to offer Internet services by way of the TV—either as an add-on box or integrated into the set itself. The numbers seem to support this new "interactive TV 2," according to Joan Rigdon of *The Wall Street Journal*. While only a few thousand people subscribe to interactive TV, there are over 24 million Internet subscribers in North America alone and many more worldwide. All expectations are that this number will continue to increase. They believe that the Internet will adapt successfully to television interactivity.

In yet another twist, @Home is taking an opposite approach. Instead of turning the TV into an Internet monitor, the company aims to bring TV-style programming to the PC. Live programming will appear in one window while menu information is provided in another.

While there are supporters and skeptics on both sides, interactive media continue to be explored. New hardware companies, new programmers, and even new advertising sources are entering the arena. Skeptics say interactivity is a long time away because habits change slowly. Supporters say to get on board now before it's too late. We'll see who is right.

Sources: Kim Cleland, "NBC Adding Interactive Slant to Some Shows/Ads," *Advertising Age*, June 30, 1997, p. 1, and "Interactive TV, Round Two," *Advertising Age*, July 1, 1996, p. 18; Joan Rigdon, "Interactive TV from Internet May Be in Sight," *The Wall Street Journal*, December 7, 1995, p. B1; Mike Mills, "Interactive TV: The Leap Looks a Long Way Off," *Washington Post*, July 2, 1995, p. H1.

A great deal of uncertainty and controversy exists regarding interactive TV. At the same time, an apparently more successful new medium—the Internet—also has its critics and supporters, with a wide range of predictions as to the value of this interactive tool. New and evolving media contribute to the already difficult task of media planning. Planning when, where, and how the advertising message will be delivered is a complex and involved process. The primary objective of the media plan is to develop a framework that will deliver the message to the target audience in the most efficient, cost-effective manner possible—that will communicate what the product, brand, and/or service can do.

This chapter presents the various methods of message delivery available to marketers, examines some key considerations in making media decisions, and discusses the development of media strategies and plans. Later chapters will explore the relative advantages and disadvantages of the various media and examine each in more detail.

AN OVERVIEW OF MEDIA PLANNING

The media planning process is not an easy one. Options include mass media such as television, newspapers, radio, and magazines (and the choices available within each of these categories) as well as out-of-the-home media such as outdoor advertising, transit advertising, and electronic billboards. A variety of support media such as direct marketing, interactive media, promotional products advertising, and in-store point-of-purchase options must also be considered.

While at first glance the choices among these alternatives might seem relatively straightforward, this is rarely the case. Part of the reason media selection becomes so involved is due to the nature of the media themselves. TV combines both sight and sound, an advantage not offered by other media. Magazines can convey more information and may keep the message available to the potential buyer for a much longer time. Newspapers also offer their own advantages, as do outdoor, direct media, and each of the others. The characteristics of each alternative must be considered, along with many other factors. This process becomes even more complicated when the manager has to choose between alternatives within the same medium—for example, between *Time* and *Newsweek* or between "Roseanne" and "Mad About You."

The potential for achieving effective communications through a well-designed media strategy warrants the added attention. The power of an effective media strategy was demonstrated by PC Flowers, at one time the smallest of the 25,000 members in the Florists' Transworld Delivery Association. The company then started to advertise its services on Prodigy, the interactive computer service. Within four months, PC Flowers moved into the top 10; now it consistently ranks as one of the top two FTD members in the world.[1] Likewise, MCI, the number-two long-distance company, was losing market share to AT&T until it began blitzing the market with promotions and other ad messages. In one year, MCI ran more than 50 different TV commercials in addition to specialized spots on Chinese, Hispanic, and Russian television. The company effectively stemmed the market share erosion.[2]

The product and/or service being advertised affects the media planning process. As demonstrated in Figure 10–1, firms have found some media more useful than others in conveying their messages to specific target audiences. For example, MCI tends to rely more heavily on broadcast media, while Hewlett-Packard prefers print media. The result is placement of advertising dollars in these preferred media—and significantly different media strategies.

Some Basic Terms and Concepts

Before beginning our discussion of media planning, we review some basic terms and concepts used in the media planning and strategy process.

Media planning is the series of decisions involved in delivering the promotional message to the prospective purchasers and/or users of the product or brand. Media planning is a process, which means a number of decisions are made, each of which may be altered or abandoned as the plan develops.

The media plan is the guide for media selection. It requires development of specific **media objectives** and specific **media strategies** (plans of action) designed to attain these

FIGURE 10-1   Expenditures of top business-to-business advertisers in various media

						1996 Top 10 Business-to-Business Advertisers						
Rank	Company	Total $000	Maga-zines	Sunday maga-zines	News-papers	Outdoor	Network television	Spot television	Syndi-cated television	Cable	National radio	National spot radio
1.	AT&T Corp.	$248,345	46,742	330	27,178	189	76,041	49,534	13,999	18,570	8,020	7,742
2.	IBM Corp.	228,054	137,822	288	21,831	297	50,446	10,138	727	4,876	0	1,629
3.	Microsoft Corp.	124,221	85,279	165	8,062	60	22,020	249	49	7,092	1,012	233
4.	MCI Communications Corp.	108,208	3,037	5	3,005	300	58,650	12,032	3,655	15,830	5,169	6,524
5.	Hewlett-Packard Co.	84,181	62,068	0	9,052	6	5,746	3,450	0	5,610	0	1,255
6.	Sprint Corp.	77,340	9,851	45	7,152	92	31,005	12,131	2,902	14,105	0	57
7.	United Parcel Service of America	66,838	10,980	0	3,227	3	41,629	8,548	0	1,405	0	1,047
8.	Compaq Computer Corp.	59,185	44,532	0	3,502	49	10,540	78	65	406	0	14
9.	American Express Co.	58,430	8,469	539	5,035	18	20,045	10,524	731	12,208	23	838
10.	Canon	55,056	30,973	0	6,056	4	11,328	461	365	4,332	1,359	178

Source: Copyright 1996 by Competitive Media Reporting, and Publishers Information Bureau, Inc.

objectives. Once the decisions have been made and the objectives and strategies formulated, this information is organized into the media plan.

The **medium** is the general category of available delivery systems, which includes broadcast media (like TV and radio), print media (like newspapers and magazines), direct mail, outdoor advertising, and other support media. The **media vehicle** is the specific carrier within a medium category. For example, *Time* and *Newsweek* are print vehicles; "20/20" and "60 Minutes" are broadcast vehicles. As you will see in later chapters, each vehicle has its own characteristics as well as its own relative advantages and disadvantages. Specific decisions must be made as to the value of each in delivering the message.

Reach is a measure of the number of different audience members exposed at least once to a media vehicle in a given period of time. *Coverage* refers to the potential audience that might receive the message through a vehicle. Coverage relates to potential audience; reach refers to the actual audience delivered. The importance of this distinction will become clearer later in this chapter.) Finally, *frequency* refers to the number of times the receiver is exposed to the media vehicle in a specified period.

The Media Plan

The media plan determines the best way to get the advertiser's message to the market. In a basic sense, the goal of the media plan is to find that combination of media that enables the marketer to communicate the message in the most effective manner to the largest number of potential customers at the lowest cost.

The activities involved in developing the media plan and the purposes of each are presented in Figure 10–2. As you can see, a number of decisions must be made throughout this process. As the plan evolves, events may occur that necessitate changes. Many advertisers find it necessary to alter and update their objectives and strategies frequently.

Problems in Media Planning

Unfortunately, the media strategy decision has not become a standardized task. A number of problems contribute to the difficulty of establishing the plan and reduce its effectiveness. These problems include insufficient information, inconsistent terminologies, time pressures, and difficulty measuring effectiveness.

INSUFFICIENT INFORMATION

While a great deal of information about markets and the media exists, media planners often require more than is available. Some data are just not measured, either because they cannot be or because measuring them would be too expensive. For example, continuous measures of radio listenership exist, but only periodic listenership studies are reported due to sample size and cost constraints. There are problems with some measures of audience size in TV and print as well, as demonstrated by IMC Perspective 10–1.

The timing of measurements is also a problem; some audience measures are taken only at specific times of the year. (For example, **sweeps periods** in February, May, July, and No-

FIGURE 10–2 Activities involved in developing the media plan

The situation analysis

Purpose: To understand the marketing problem. An analysis is made of a company and its competitors on the basis of:

1. Size and share of the total market.
2. Sales history, costs, and profits.
3. Distribution practices.
4. Methods of selling.
5. Use of advertising.
6. Identification of prospects.
7. Nature of the product.

The marketing strategy plan

Purpose: To plan activities that will solve one or more of the marketing problems. Includes the determination of:

1. Marketing objectives.
2. Product and spending strategy.
3. Distribution strategy.
4. Which elements of the marketing mix are to be used.
5. Identification of "best" market segments.

The creative strategy plan

Purpose: To determine what to communicate through advertisements. Includes the determination of:

1. How product can meet consumer needs.
2. How product will be positioned in advertisements.
3. Copy themes.
4. Specific objectives of each advertisement.
5. Number and sizes of advertisements.

Setting media objectives

Purpose: To translate marketing objectives and strategies into goals that media can accomplish.

Determining media strategy

Purpose: To translate media goals into general guidelines that will control the planner's selection and use of media. The best strategy alternatives should be selected.

Selecting broad media classes

Purpose: To determine which broad class of media best fulfills the criteria. Involves comparison and selection of broad media classes such as newspapers, magazines, radio, television, and others. The analysis is called intermedia comparisons. Audience size is one of the major factors used in comparing the various media classes.

Selecting media within classes

Purpose: To compare and select the best media within broad classes, again using predetermined criteria. Involves making decisions about the following:

1. If magazines were recommended, then which magazines?
2. If television was recommended, then
   a. Broadcast or cable television?
   b. Network or spot television?
   c. If network, which program(s)?
   d. If spot, which markets?
3. If radio or newspapers were recommended, then
   a. Which markets shall be used?
   b. What criteria shall buyers use in making purchases of local media?

Media use decisions— broadcast

1. What kind of sponsorship (sole, shared, participating, or other)?
2. What levels of reach and frequency will be required?
3. Scheduling: On which days and months are commercials to appear?
4. Placement of spots: In programs or between programs?

Media use decisions— print

1. Number of ads to appear and on which days and months.
2. Placements of ads: Any preferred position within media?
3. Special treatment: Gatefolds, bleeds, color, etc.
4. Desired reach or frequency levels.

Media use decisions— other media

1. Billboards
   a. Location of markets and plan of distribution.
   b. Kinds of outdoor boards to be used.
2. Direct mail or other media: Decisions peculiar to those media.

IMC Perspective 10-1
Media Services Companies under Attack

Advertising costs are determined by how many people can be reached through the medium. In print media, such costs are based on circulation and readership figures; in broadcast, the basis is ratings. As in any industry, firms compete directly to provide advertisers with these audience numbers. Because so many billions of dollars are spent on advertising each year, the figures the services provide are critical. One would expect that competing firms' information would be valid and consistent. Those in the magazine and newspaper industries believe that it isn't, and they are unhappy about it.

The two primary providers of information on magazine readership are Mediamark Research Inc. (MRI) and Simmons Market Research Bureau (SMRB). Because of the importance media buyers place on these figures, they have become crucial to individual publications. As the vice president of one top ad agency noted, "If the readership numbers shift just a hair, there is a big shift in the number of ad pages." Yet MRI's and SMRB's numbers rarely agree, causing many to question their validity.

A recent dispute involved *USA Today*, *The Wall Street Journal*, and MRI. The MRI readership survey showed dramatic gains in audience counts for both newspapers. But MRI, citing problems associated with its new measurement system, discarded the new results, calling them "statistically unbalanced." It said it would return to the old measurement methodology. The newspapers sent a joint letter of protest noting that they were "alarmed" over this "arbitrary decision." A comparison of the MRI and SMRB numbers added to the controversy. According to SMRB, the *Journal*'s adult readership was 4.8 million—29 percent higher than MRI's 3.4 million. *USA Today* had 5.9 million adult readers according to Simmons, but 34 percent fewer according to MRI (3.9 million).

SMRB was also under attack. Hearst and Condé Nast refused to use the audience measuring company, citing

methodology problems. The Magazine Publishers of America research committee noticed what appeared to be illogical numbers in the SMRB research materials. Like MRI, SMRB said it would change its research methods—to those previously employed by MRI.

At least part of the problem stems from the methodologies used. Both companies interview over 10,000 adults. But some magazine readership profiles are based on only a few hundred responses. SMRB previously employed a "through the book" measure that required respondents to flip through an entire magazine to explain how much they actually read. This method was both costly and time consuming. The MRI (and new Simmons) method employs "recent reading," which merely requires respondents to say whether they've read a recent issue. The latter technique is considered less comprehensive but is less expensive and time consuming and allows for more titles to be measured. The measures for newspapers are different from those for magazines.

Almost everyone in the industry knows there are problems with print audience measurement. However, it appears that no one has a better solution. *USA Today* and *The Wall Street Journal* have argued with MRI. Hearst, Condé Nast, and the *New Yorker* dropped SMRB (though some of their magazines recently resubscribed). In 1996 Audits & Surveys Worldwide began to offer its services—using yet another methodology, primary readers versus total audience. Roper/Starch and Arbitron (other measurement companies) are presenting new measurement proposals, but a solution does not seem to be around the corner. Says Alan Jurmain, executive director of media services at Lowe & Partners/SMS, "There are flaws with both Simmons and MRI . . . but until someone comes up with something better—well, it's better to be partially right than precisely wrong." So it will apparently be business as usual for the foreseeable future.

Sources: Keith J. Kelly, "New Player, New Idea in Readership Fray," *Advertising Age*, April 29, 1996, p. 51; Keith J. Kelly, "Simmons Research Repairs Reputation," *Advertising Age*, October 2, 1996, p. 46; Keith J. Kelly, "*USA Today*, *Journal*, Fume at MRI," *Advertising Age*, March 25, 1996, p. 1.

vember are used for measuring TV audiences and setting advertising rates.) This information is then generalized to succeeding months, so future planning decisions must be made on past data that may not reflect current behaviors. Think about planning for TV advertising for the fall season. There are no data on the audiences of new shows, and audience information taken on existing programs during the summer may not indicate how these programs will do in the fall because summer viewership is generally much lower. While the advertisers can review these programs before they air, they do not have actual audience figures.

The lack of information is even more of a problem for small advertisers, who may not be able to afford to purchase the information they require. As a result, their decisions are based on limited or out-of-date data or no data at all.

INCONSISTENT TERMINOLOGIES

Problems arise because the cost bases used by different media often vary and the standards of measurement used to establish these costs are not always consistent. For example, print media may present cost data in terms of the cost to reach a thousand people (cost per thousand, or CPM), broadcast media use the cost per ratings point (CPRP), and outdoor media use the number of showings. Audience information that is used as a basis for these costs has also been collected by different methods. Finally, terms that actually mean something different (such as reach and coverage) may be used synonymously, adding to the confusion.

TIME PRESSURES

It seems that advertisers are always in a hurry—sometimes because they need to be, other times because they *think* they need to be. Actions by a competitor—for example, the cutting of airfares by one carrier—require immediate response. But sometimes a false sense of urgency dictates time pressures. In either situation, media selection decisions may be made without proper planning and analyses of the markets and/or media.

DIFFICULTY MEASURING EFFECTIVENESS

Because it is so hard to measure the effectiveness of advertising and promotions in general, it is also difficult to determine the relative effectiveness of various media or media vehicles. While progress is being made in this regard (particularly in the area of direct-response advertising), the media planner must usually guess at the impact of these alternatives.

Because of these problems, not all media decisions are quantitatively determined. Sometimes managers have to assume the image of a medium in a market with which they are not familiar, anticipate the impact of recent events, or make judgments without full knowledge of all the available alternatives.

While these problems complicate the media decision process, they do not render it an entirely subjective exercise. The remainder of this chapter explores in more detail how media strategies are developed and ways to increase their effectiveness.

DEVELOPING THE MEDIA PLAN

The promotional planning model in Chapter 1 discussed the process of identifying target markets, establishing objectives, and formulating strategies for attaining them. The development of the media plan and strategies follows a similar path, except that the focus is more specifically keyed to determining the *best* way to deliver the message. The process, shown in Figure 10–3, involves a series of stages: (1) market analysis, (2) establishment of media objectives, (3) media strategy development and implementation, and (4) evaluation and follow-up. Each of these is discussed in turn, with specific examples. Appendix B to this chapter is an actual media plan, which we refer to throughout the remainder of the chapter to exemplify each phase further.

MARKET ANALYSIS AND TARGET MARKET IDENTIFICATION

The situation analysis stage of the overall promotional planning process involves a complete review of internal and external factors, competitive strategies, and the like. In the development of a media strategy, a market analysis is again performed, although this time the focus is on the media and delivering the message. The key questions at this stage are these: To whom shall we advertise (who is the target market)? What internal and external factors may influence the media plan? Where (geographically) and when should we focus our efforts?

To Whom Shall We Advertise?

While a number of target markets might be derived from the situation analysis, to decide which specific groups to go after the media planner may work with the client, account representative, marketing department, and creative directors. A variety of factors can assist media

FIGURE 10–3 Developing the media plan

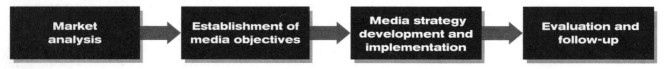

planners in this decision. Some will require primary research, whereas others will be available from published (secondary) sources.

The Simmons Market Research Bureau (SMRB) provides secondary information: syndicated data on audience size and composition for approximately 100 publications, as well as broadcast exposure and data on usage of over 800 consumer products and services. This information comes in the form of raw numbers, percentages, and indexes. As seen in Figure 10–4, information is given on (1) the number of adults in the United States by each category under consideration; (2) the number of users; (3) the percentage of users falling into each

FIGURE 10–4 Market research profile of cola users

	TOTAL U.S. '000	ALL USERS A '000	B % DOWN	C % ACROSS	D INDX	HEAVY USERS EIGHT OR MORE A '000	B % DOWN	C % ACROSS	D INDX	BOTTLED A '000	B % DOWN	C % ACROSS	D INDX	CANNED A '000	B % DOWN	C % ACROSS	D INDX
TOTAL ADULTS	182456	107986	100.0	59.2	100	34162	100.0	18.7	100	64427	100.0	35.3	100	77735	100.0	42.6	100
MALES	87118	57364	53.1	65.8	111	19037	55.7	21.9	117	33966	52.7	39.0	110	41533	53.4	47.7	112
FEMALES	95338	50622	46.9	53.1	90	15125	44.3	15.9	85	30461	47.3	32.0	90	36202	46.6	38.0	89
18-24	25530	17961	16.6	70.4	119	7633	22.3	29.9	160	11523	17.9	45.1	128	13715	17.6	53.7	126
25-34	44118	29093	26.9	65.9	111	10646	31.2	24.1	129	17994	27.9	40.8	116	22039	28.4	50.0	117
35-44	37521	23183	21.5	61.8	104	6716	19.7	17.9	96	13883	21.5	37.0	105	17172	22.1	45.8	107
45-54	25346	14302	13.2	56.4	95	4240	12.4	16.7	89	8281	12.9	32.7	93	9798	12.6	38.7	91
55-64	21009	11029	10.2	52.5	89	2655	7.8	12.6	67	5946	9.2	28.3	80	7563	9.7	36.0	84
65 OR OLDER	28934	12419	11.5	42.9	73	2271	6.6	7.8	42	6801	10.6	23.5	67	7449	9.6	25.7	60
18-34	69647	47054	43.6	67.6	114	18279	53.5	26.2	140	29517	45.8	42.4	120	35754	46.0	51.3	120
18-49	120585	78177	72.4	64.8	110	27394	80.2	22.7	121	48074	74.6	39.9	113	58377	75.1	48.4	114
25-54	106984	66577	61.7	62.2	105	21603	63.2	20.2	108	40158	62.3	37.5	106	49009	63.0	45.8	108
35-49	50938	31123	28.8	61.1	103	9115	26.7	17.9	96	18557	28.8	36.4	103	22623	29.1	44.4	104
50 OR OLDER	61871	29810	27.6	48.2	81	6768	19.8	10.9	58	16353	25.4	26.4	75	19358	24.9	31.3	73
GRADUATED COLLEGE	35347	18823	17.4	53.3	90	4256	12.5	12.0	64	10728	16.7	30.4	86	13919	17.9	39.4	92
ATTENDED COLLEGE	35167	20303	18.8	57.7	98	6323	18.5	18.0	96	11597	18.0	33.0	93	15374	19.8	43.7	103
GRADUATED HIGH SCHOOL	70823	43928	40.7	62.0	105	15062	44.1	21.3	114	26676	41.4	37.7	107	31808	40.9	44.9	105
DID NOT GRADUATE HIGH SCHOOL	41119	24932	23.1	60.6	102	8521	24.9	20.7	111	15426	23.9	37.5	106	16634	21.4	40.5	95
EMPLOYED MALES	67846	46006	42.6	67.8	115	15993	46.8	23.6	126	27566	42.8	40.6	115	33752	43.4	49.7	117
EMPLOYED FEMALES	57394	30497	28.2	53.1	90	9317	27.3	16.2	87	18245	28.3	31.8	90	22414	28.8	39.1	92
EMPLOYED FULL-TIME	112285	69201	64.1	61.6	104	22930	67.1	20.4	109	41409	64.3	36.9	104	50475	64.9	45.0	106
EMPLOYED PART-TIME	12955	7302	6.8	56.4	95	2380	7.0	18.4	98	4402	6.8	34.0	96	5692	7.3	43.9	103
NOT EMPLOYED	57216	31483	29.2	55.0	93	8852	25.9	15.5	83	18616	28.9	32.5	92	21569	27.7	37.7	88
PROFESSIONAL/MANAGER	31819	17101	15.8	53.7	91	4515	13.2	14.2	76	10036	15.6	31.5	89	12604	16.2	39.6	93
TECHNICAL/CLERICAL/SALES	39581	22672	21.0	57.3	97	7008	20.5	17.7	95	13089	20.3	33.1	94	16905	21.7	42.7	100
PRECISION/CRAFT	14839	10235	9.5	69.0	117	4012	11.7	27.0	144	6535	10.1	44.0	125	7470	9.6	50.3	118
OTHER EMPLOYED	39001	26494	24.5	67.9	115	9775	28.6	25.1	134	16151	25.1	41.4	117	19187	24.7	49.2	115
SINGLE	40179	26098	24.2	65.0	110	10217	29.9	25.4	136	16252	25.2	40.4	115	19644	25.3	48.9	115
MARRIED	108808	64055	59.3	58.9	99	18481	54.1	17.0	91	37570	58.3	34.5	98	45904	59.1	42.2	99
DIVORCED/SEPARATED/WIDOWED	33469	17834	16.5	53.3	90	5464	16.0	16.3	87	10606	16.5	31.7	90	12188	15.7	36.4	85
PARENTS	60855	40631	37.6	66.8	113	13482	39.5	22.2	118	25180	39.1	41.4	117	30061	38.7	49.4	116
WHITE	156458	90780	84.1	58.0	98	28116	82.3	18.0	96	53093	82.4	33.9	96	65803	84.7	42.1	99
BLACK	20509	13774	12.8	67.2	113	5160	15.1	25.2	134	9041	14.0	44.1	125	9432	12.1	46.0	108
OTHER	5489	3432	3.2	62.5	106	885	2.6	16.1	86	2293	3.6	41.8	118	2500	3.2	45.5	107
NORTHEAST-CENSUS	38593	22160	20.5	57.4	97	5368	15.7	13.9	74	16028	24.9	41.5	118	14293	18.4	37.0	87
MIDWEST	44281	24898	23.1	56.2	95	7327	21.4	16.5	88	12677	19.7	28.6	81	19201	24.7	43.4	102
SOUTH	62591	39118	36.2	62.5	106	14519	42.5	23.2	124	24320	37.7	38.9	110	26905	34.6	43.0	101
WEST	36991	21811	20.2	59.0	100	6947	20.3	18.8	100	11402	17.7	30.8	87	17337	22.3	46.9	110
COUNTY SIZE A	75891	43359	40.2	57.1	97	12309	36.0	16.2	87	26324	40.9	34.7	98	30712	39.5	40.5	95
COUNTY SIZE B	54708	33119	30.7	60.5	102	10665	31.2	19.5	104	19543	30.3	35.7	101	24116	31.0	44.1	103
COUNTY SIZE C	27729	16793	15.6	60.5	102	5938	17.4	21.4	114	9674	15.0	34.9	99	12452	16.0	44.9	105
COUNTY SIZE D	24127	14715	13.6	61.0	103	5250	15.4	21.8	116	8886	13.8	36.8	104	10456	13.5	43.3	102
METRO CENTRAL CITY	57518	35162	32.6	61.1	103	11223	32.9	19.5	104	19989	31.0	34.8	99	26734	34.4	46.5	109
METRO SUBURBAN	85780	49004	45.4	57.1	97	14390	42.1	16.8	90	29956	46.5	34.9	99	34168	44.0	39.8	93
NON METRO	39158	23820	22.1	60.8	103	8549	25.0	21.8	117	14482	22.5	37.0	105	16834	21.7	43.0	101
TOP 5 ADI'S	40412	23079	21.4	57.1	96	6233	18.2	15.4	82	15097	23.4	37.4	106	15727	20.2	38.9	91
TOP 10 ADI'S	57709	32644	30.2	56.6	96	9067	26.5	15.7	84	21381	33.2	37.0	105	22081	28.4	38.3	90
TOP 20 ADI'S	83116	47625	44.1	57.3	97	13722	40.2	16.5	88	29571	45.9	35.6	101	33506	43.1	40.3	95
HSHLD. INC. $75,000 OR MORE	21409	11472	10.6	53.6	91	3137	9.2	14.7	78	6677	10.4	31.2	88	8465	10.9	39.5	93
$60,000 OR MORE	36836	20296	18.8	55.1	94	5450	16.0	14.8	79	11854	18.4	32.2	91	14883	19.1	40.4	95
$50,000 OR MORE	53155	29435	27.3	55.4	94	8401	24.6	15.8	84	17518	27.2	33.0	93	21230	27.3	39.9	94
$40,000 OR MORE	75291	42438	39.3	56.4	95	12102	35.4	16.1	86	24710	38.4	32.8	93	31064	40.0	41.3	97
$30,000 OR MORE	102396	59510	55.1	58.1	98	17769	52.0	17.4	93	35324	54.8	34.5	98	43174	55.5	42.2	99
$30,000 - $39,999	27105	17072	15.8	63.0	106	5667	16.6	20.9	112	10614	16.5	39.2	111	12111	15.6	44.7	105
$20,000 - $29,999	30317	18768	17.4	61.9	105	6373	18.7	21.0	112	10822	16.8	35.7	101	13883	17.9	45.8	107
$10,000 - $19,999	29855	18353	17.0	61.5	104	6479	19.0	21.7	116	11297	17.5	37.8	107	13108	16.9	43.9	103
UNDER $10,000	19888	11355	10.5	57.1	96	3541	10.4	17.8	95	6808	10.6	35.1	99	7571	9.7	38.1	89
HOUSEHOLD OF 1 PERSON	23383	11336	10.5	48.5	82	2915	8.5	12.5	67	6621	10.3	28.3	80	7727	9.9	33.0	78
2 PEOPLE	59547	31809	29.5	53.4	90	9263	27.1	15.6	83	17730	27.5	29.8	84	22690	29.2	38.1	89
3 OR 4 PEOPLE	72643	46028	42.6	63.4	107	15192	44.5	20.9	112	28128	43.7	38.7	110	33353	42.9	45.9	108
5 OR MORE PEOPLE	26884	18813	17.4	70.0	118	6793	19.9	25.3	135	11948	18.5	44.4	126	13965	18.0	51.9	122
NO CHILD IN HSHLD.	109702	59165	54.8	53.9	91	17626	51.6	16.1	86	33808	52.5	30.8	87	41560	53.5	37.9	89
CHILD(REN) UNDER 2 YEARS	15048	10548	9.8	70.1	118	4030	11.8	26.8	143	6875	10.7	45.7	129	7752	10.0	51.5	121
2 - 5 YEARS	25473	17985	16.7	70.6	119	6250	18.3	24.5	131	11774	18.3	46.2	131	13493	17.4	53.0	124
6 - 11 YEARS	34011	23085	21.4	67.9	115	7433	21.8	21.9	117	14221	22.1	41.8	118	17375	22.4	51.1	120
12 - 17 YEARS	33774	22110	20.5	65.6	111	7394	21.6	21.9	117	13733	21.3	40.7	115	16230	20.9	48.1	113
RESIDENCE OWNED	124747	69384	64.3	55.6	94	19886	58.2	15.9	85	40350	62.6	32.3	92	49466	63.6	39.7	93
VALUE: $70,000 OR MORE	69554	36947	34.2	53.1	90	9297	27.2	13.4	71	21652	33.6	31.1	88	26509	34.1	38.1	89
VALUE: UNDER $70,000	55193	32437	30.0	58.8	99	10588	31.0	19.2	102	18699	29.0	33.9	96	22957	29.5	41.6	98

category (for example, the percentage who are female); (4) the percentage of each category that uses the product (for example, the percentage of all females using); (5) an index number; and (6) the same information classified by heavy, medium, and light users. (Both Simmons and its major competitor, Mediamark Research, Inc. (MRI), also provide lifestyle information and media usage characteristics of the population.)

Media planners are often more concerned with the percentage figures and index numbers than with the raw numbers. This is largely due to the fact that they may have their own data from other sources, both primary and secondary; the numbers provided may not be specific enough for their needs; or they question the numbers provided because of the methods by

FIGURE 10–5

Cellular phones purchased in the past year—MRI report

3.1% of all adults purchased a cellular phone in the past year. Of this group, women account for 51.1%; 36.4% graduated from college; 26.0% are ages 25–34; 15.1% have $50,000–$59,999 household income and members of this group are 62% more likely than average adults to have purchased a cellular phone in the past year.

Base: All adults	Population (000) 5,863 Percent of Target	Percent of Base 3.1% Index
Men	48.9	102
Women	51.1	98
Household heads	54.3	89
Homemakers	58.9	95
Graduated college	36.4	176
Attended college	29.8	112
Graduated high school	26.7	79
Did not graduate high school	7.2	38
18–24	11.9	92
25–34	26.0	117
35–44	27.7	128
45–54	20.5	132
55–64	9.2	82
65 or over	4.6	28
18–34	37.9	108
18–49	78.1	119
25–54	74.3	125
Employed full-time	74.8	137
Employed part-time	10.8	112
Sole wage earner	15.3	87
Not employed	14.4	40
Professional	16.1	166
Executive/admin/managerial	15.5	172
Clerical/sales/technical	26.6	141
Precision/crafts/repair	9.4	132
Other employed	18.0	92
H/D income $75,000 or more	38.5	239
H/D income $60,000–$74,999	15.7	162
H/D income $50,000–$59,999	15.1	162
H/D income $40,000–$49,999	13.5	119
H/D income $30,000–$39,999	8.5	62
H/D income $20,000–$29,999	5.0	33
H/D income $10,000–19,999	3.2	22
H/D income less than $10,000	0.4	4

FIGURE 10–6
How high indexes can be misleading

Age Segment	Population in Segment (percent)	Product Use in Segment (percent)	Index
18–24	15.1	18.0	119
25–34	25.1	25.0	100
35–44	20.6	21.0	102
45+	39.3	36.0	91

which they were collected. (See IMC Perspective 10–1.) The total (raw) numbers provided by Simmons and MRI are used in combination with the media planner's own figures.

On the other hand, the **index number** is considered a good indicator of the potential of the market. This number is derived from the formula:

$$\text{Index} = \frac{\text{Percentage of users in a demographic segment}}{\text{Percentage of population in the same segment}} \times 100$$

An index number over 100 means use of the product is proportionately greater in that segment than in one that is average (100) or less than 100. For example, the MRI data in Figure 10–5 show that people in the age groups 45–54, 35–44, and 25–34, respectively, are more likely to purchase cellular phones than those in the other age segments, as are those with a household income of $40,000 or more. Most occupation groups are users, though executive/managerial and professionals are more likely to be. College graduates also have a high index. Depending on their overall strategy, marketers may wish to use this information to determine which groups are now using the product and target them or to identify a group that is currently using the product less and attempt to develop that segment.

While the index is helpful, it should not be used alone. Percentages and product usage figures are also needed to get an accurate picture of the market. Just because the index for a particular segment of the population is very high, that doesn't always mean this is an attractive segment to target. The high index may be a result of a low denominator (a very small proportion of the population in this segment). In Figure 10–6, the 18- to 24-year-old age segment has the highest index, but it also has both the lowest product usage and the lowest population percentage. A marketer who relied solely on the index would be ignoring a full 82 percent of product users.

Keep in mind that while Simmons and MRI provide demographic, geographic, and psychographic information, other factors may be more useful in defining specific markets.

What Internal and External Factors Are Operating?

Media strategies are influenced by both internal and external factors operating at any given time. *Internal factors* may involve the size of the media budget, managerial and administrative capabilities, or the organization of the agency, as demonstrated in Figure 10–7. *External factors* may include the economy (the rising costs of media), changes in technology (the availability of new media), competitive factors, and the like. While some of this information may require primary research, much information is available through secondary sources, including magazines, syndicated services, and even the daily newspaper.

One service's competitive information was shown in Figure 10–1. The Competitive Media Reporting Service provides media spending figures for various brands competing in the same market. Competitive information is also available from many other sources, as shown in Appendix A to this chapter.

Where to Promote?

The question of where to promote relates to geographic considerations. As noted in Chapter 7, companies often find that sales are stronger in one area of the country than another and may allocate advertising expenditures according to the market potential of an area. For years, Whirlpool has had a much greater brand share of the appliance market in the East and Midwest than in the Southeast and West. The question is, where will the ad dollars be more wisely spent? Should Whirlpool allocate additional promotional monies to those markets where the brand is already the leader to maintain market share, or does more potential exist

FIGURE 10—7 Organizing the media buying department

While various firms and ad agencies have different ways of organizing the media buying department, three seem to be the most common. The first form employs a product/media focus, the second places more emphasis on the market itself, and the third organizes around media classes alone.

Form 1 In this organizational arrangement, the media buyers and assistant media buyers are responsible for a product or group of products and/or brands. Their media planner both plans and buys for these products/brands in whichever geographic areas they are marketed. For example, if the agency is responsible for the advertising of Hart skis, the media planners determine the appropriate media in each area for placing the ads for these skis. The logic underlying this approach is that the planner knows the product and will identify the best media and vehicles for promoting it.

Form 2 In this approach, the market is the focal point of attention. Media planners become "experts" in a particular market area and are responsible for planning and buying for all products/brands the firm and/or agency markets in those areas. For example, a planner may be responsible for the Memphis, Tennessee, market. If the agency has more than one client who wishes to market in this area, media selection for all of the brands/products is the responsibility of the same person. The logic is that his or her knowledge of the media and vehicles in the area allows for a more informed media choice. The nonquantitative characteristics of the media get more attention under this approach.

Form 3 Organizing around a specific class of media—for example, print or broadcast—is a third alternative. The purchasing and development unit handles all the agency print or broadcast business. Members of the media department become specialists who are brought in very early in the promotional planning process. Planners perform only planning functions, while buyers are responsible for all purchases. The buying function itself may be specialized with specific responsibilities for specialty advertising, national buys, local buys, and so on. Knowledge of the media and the audience each serves is considered a major benefit. Also, people who handle all the media buys can negotiate better deals.

As to which strategy works best, who's to say? Each has been in use for some time. The second approach requires that the agency be big enough and have enough clients to support the geographic assignment. The third alternative seems to be the most common design.

in those markets where the firm is not doing as well and there is more room to grow? Perhaps the best answer is that the firm should spend advertising and promotion dollars where they will be the most effective—that is, in those markets where they will achieve the desired objectives. Unfortunately, as we have seen so often, it is not always possible to measure directly the impact of promotional efforts. At the same time, certain tactics can assist the planner in making this determination.

USING INDEXES TO DETERMINE WHERE TO PROMOTE

In addition to the indexes from Simmons and MRI, three other indexes may also be useful:

1. **The Survey of Buying Power Index,** published annually by *Sales and Marketing Management* magazine, is conducted for every major metropolitan market in the United States and is based on a number of factors, including population, effective buying income, and total retail sales in the area. Each of these factors is individually weighted to drive a buying power index that charts the potential of a particular metro area, county, or city relative to the United States as a whole. The resulting index gives media planners insight into the relative value of that market, as shown in Figure 10–8. When used in combination with other market information, the survey of buying power index helps the marketer determine which geographic areas to target.

2. **The Brand Development Index (BDI)** helps marketers factor the rate of product usage by geographic area into the decision process.

$$\text{BDI} = \frac{\text{Percentage of brand to total U.S. sales in the market}}{\text{Percentage of total U.S. population in the market}} \times 100$$

The BDI compares the percentage of the brand's total U.S. sales in a given market area with the percentage of the total population in the market to determine the sales potential for that brand in that market area. An example of this calculation is shown in Figure 10–9. The higher the index number, the more market potential exists. In this case, the index number indicates this market has high potential for brand development.

3. **The Category Development Index (CDI)** is computed in the same manner as the BDI, except it uses information regarding the product category (as opposed to the brand) in the numerator:

FIGURE 10–8
Survey of buying power index

Rhode Island

POPULATION

S&MM ESTIMATES: 12/31/90

METRO AREA County City	Total Population (Thousands)	% Of U.S.	Median Age Of Pop.	18-24 Years	25-34 Years	35-49 Years	50 & Over	Households (Thousands)	Total Retail Sales ($000)	Food ($000)	Eating & Drinking Places ($000)	General Mdse. ($000)	Furniture/ Furnish. Appliance ($000)	Automotive ($000)	Drug ($000)
PROVIDENCE–PAWTUCKET–WOONSOCKET	921.4	.3674	34.1	11.8	17.0	20.1	28.4	347.2	6,621,140	1,390,972	740,007	750,465	291,612	1,175,964	301,155
Bristol	49.0	.0196	35.9	10.9	15.5	20.9	30.5	17.6	239,949	66,787	27,747	2,630	6,814	53,545	13,682
Kent	162.1	.0646	35.9	8.9	16.9	22.3	29.2	62.4	1,687,207	275,155	168,616	307,478	55,278	301,666	58,221
Warwick	85.9	.0342	36.9	8.7	16.7	21.4	31.5	33.6	1,241,231	159,242	114,017	300,202	47,168	189,376	34,648
Providence	598.9	.2388	33.8	12.2	17.3	19.2	28.7	227.4	3,832,852	814,370	442,223	400,598	197,994	690,435	198,710
Cranston	76.4	.0305	37.3	9.5	17.5	20.7	32.8	29.5	513,493	116,552	55,772	21,447	43,116	94,507	34,699
East Providence	50.6	.0202	36.9	9.1	16.9	19.4	33.3	20.0	405,889	72,226	38,188	22,368	20,077	130,818	20,625
• Pawtucket	73.0	.0291	33.7	10.2	19.1	17.8	29.7	29.9	514,684	105,502	42,451	110,785	21,226	73,536	34,132
• Providence	161.4	.0644	29.6	18.0	17.6	16.5	24.0	59.1	931,996	174,406	126,906	59,502	63,388	169,702	39,520
• Woonsocket	44.1	.0176	33.3	10.9	17.9	17.9	28.9	17.7	292,009	70,461	20,413	36,712	12,715	72,514	14,174
Washington	111.4	.0444	32.6	14.2	16.2	21.9	24.3	39.8	861,132	234,660	101,421	39,759	31,526	130,318	30,542
SUBURBAN TOTAL	642.9	.2563	35.5	10.5	16.6	21.4	29.3	240.5	4,882,451	1,040,603	550,237	543,466	194,283	860,212	213,329
OTHER COUNTIES															
Newport	87.5	.0349	33.8	11.8	17.6	22.3	25.5	32.8	703,842	121,062	118,031	34,174	29,726	176,816	18,994
TOTAL METRO COUNTIES	921.4	.3674	34.1	11.8	17.0	20.1	28.4	347.2	6,621,140	1,390,972	740,007	750,465	291,612	1,175,964	301,155
TOTAL STATE	1,008.9	.4023	34.1	11.8	17.0	20.3	28.1	380.0	7,324,982	1,512,034	858,038	784,639	321,338	1,352,780	320,149

EFFECTIVE BUYING INCOME

S&MM ESTIMATES: 12/31/90

METRO AREA County City	Total EBI ($000)	Median Hsld. EBI	(A) $10,000-$19,999	(B) $20,000-$34,999	(C) $35,000-$49,999	(D) $50,000 & Over	Buying Power Index
PROVIDENCE–PAWTUCKET–WOONSOCKET	13,161,017	28,441	19.4	25.5	18.6	20.9	.3714
Bristol	727,359	30,275	19.2	26.8	17.6	23.9	.0182
Kent	2,422,662	30,869	17.0	27.8	21.2	21.1	.0756
Warwick	1,322,227	31,519	16.5	27.6	21.5	21.8	.0463
Providence	8,427,416	27,115	20.2	24.4	17.8	20.3	.2319
Cranston	1,237,230	31,764	17.7	24.6	19.9	25.2	.0323
East Providence	777,080	30,763	18.3	25.3	21.5	22.1	.0219
• Pawtucket	997,942	25,377	21.5	26.0	17.8	16.3	.0286
• Providence	1,924,178	20,802	24.2	23.5	13.4	14.8	.0558
• Woonsocket	566,843	23,811	22.3	24.4	16.8	15.5	.0165
Washington	1,583,580	30,461	18.6	28.1	19.4	22.3	.0457
SUBURBAN TOTAL	9,672,054	31,087	17.8	26.1	20.0	23.3	.2705
OTHER COUNTIES							
Newport	1,414,978	31,746	17.5	24.8	19.4	25.8	.0388
TOTAL METRO COUNTIES	13,161,017	28,441	19.4	25.5	18.6	20.9	.3714
TOTAL STATE	14,575,995	28,696	19.2	25.5	18.6	21.3	.4102

$$CDI = \frac{\text{Percentage of product category total sales in market}}{\text{Percentage of total U.S. population in market}} \times 100$$

The CDI provides information on the potential for development of the total product category rather than specific brands. When this information is combined with the BDI, a much more insightful promotional strategy may be developed. For example, consider the market potential for coffee in the United States. One might first look at how well the product category does in a specific market area. In Utah and Idaho, for example, the category potential is low (see Figure 10–10). The marketer analyzes the BDI to find how the brand is doing relative to other brands in this area. This information can then be used in determining how well a particular product category and a particular brand are performing and figuring what media weight (or quantity of advertising) would be required to gain additional market share, as shown in Figure 10–11.

While these indexes provide important insights into the market potential for the firm's products and/or brands, this information is supplemental to the overall strategy determined earlier in the promotional decision-making process. In fact, much of this information may have already been provided to the media planner. Since it may be used more specifically to determine the media weights to assign to each area, this decision ultimately affects the budget allocated to each area as well as other factors such as reach, frequency, and scheduling.

FIGURE 10–9
Calculating BDI

$$BDI = \frac{\text{Percentage of brand sales in South Atlantic region}}{\text{Percentage of U.S. population in South Atlantic region}} \times 100$$

$$= \frac{50\%}{16\%} \times 100$$

$$= 312$$

FIGURE 10–10
Using CDI and BDI to determine
market potential

$$CDI = \frac{\text{Percentage of product category sales in Utah/Idaho}}{\text{Percentage of total U.S. population in Utah/Idaho}} \times 100$$

$$= \frac{1\%}{1\%} \times 100$$

$$= 100$$

$$BDI = \frac{\text{Percentage of total brand sales in Utah/Idaho}}{\text{Percentage of total U.S. population in Utah/Idaho}} \times 100$$

$$= \frac{2\%}{1\%} \times 100$$

$$= 200$$

FIGURE 10–11
Using BDI and CDI indexes

	High BDI	Low BDI
High CDI	High market share Good market potential	Low market share Good market potential
Low CDI	High market share Monitor for sales decline	Low market share Poor market potential

High BDI and high CDI	This market usually represents good sales potential for both the product category and the brand.
High BDI and low CDI	The category is not selling well, but the brand is; probably a good market to advertise in but should be monitored for declining sales.
Low BDI and high CDI	The product category shows high potential but the brand is not doing well; the reasons should be determined.
Low BDI and low CDI	Both the product category and the brand are doing poorly; not likely to be a good place for advertising.

ESTABLISHING MEDIA OBJECTIVES

Just as the situation analysis leads to establishment of marketing and communications objectives, the media situation analysis should lead to determination of specific media objectives. The media objectives are not ends in themselves. Rather, they are designed to lead to the attainment of communications and marketing objectives. Media objectives are the goals for the media program and should be limited to those that can be accomplished through media strategies. An example of media objectives is this: Create awareness in the target market through the following:

- Use broadcast media to provide coverage of 80 percent of the target market over a six-month period.
- Reach 60 percent of the target audience at least three times over the same six-month period.
- Concentrate heaviest advertising in winter and spring, with lighter emphasis in summer and fall.

DEVELOPING AND IMPLEMENTING MEDIA STRATEGIES

Having determined what is to be accomplished, media planners consider how to achieve these objectives. That is, they develop and implement media strategies, which evolve directly from the actions required to meet objectives and involve the criteria in Figure 10–12.

The Media Mix

A wide variety of media and media vehicles are available to advertisers. While it is possible that only one medium and/or vehicle might be employed, it is much more likely that a num-

FIGURE 10–12
Criteria considered in the development of media plans

- The media mix
- Target market coverage
- Geographic coverage
- Scheduling
- Reach versus frequency
- Creative aspects and mood
- Flexibility
- Budget considerations

Target Market Coverage

ber of alternatives will be used. The objectives sought, the characteristics of the product or service, the size of the budget, and individual preferences are just some of the factors that determine what combination of media will be used.

As an example, consider a promotional situation in which a product requires a visual demonstration to be communicated effectively. In this case, TV may be the most effective medium. If the promotional strategy calls for coupons to stimulate trial, print media will be necessary.

By employing a media mix, advertisers can add more versatility to their media strategies, since each medium contributes its own distinct advantages (as demonstrated in later chapters). By combining media, marketers can increase coverage, reach, and frequency levels while improving the likelihood of achieving overall communications and marketing goals.

The media planner determines which target markets should receive the most media emphasis. (In the media plan for WD-40 penetrating oil in Appendix B, this was determined to be core markets of adults, 25+, blue collar, and "do-it-yourselfers.") Developing media strategies involves matching the most appropriate media to this market by asking, "Through which media and media vehicles can I best get my message to prospective buyers?" The issue here is to get coverage of the market, as shown in Figure 10–13. The optimal goal is full market coverage, shown in the second pie chart. But this is a very optimistic scenario. More realistically, conditions shown in the third and fourth charts are most likely to occur. In the third chart, the coverage of the media does not allow for coverage of the entire market, leaving some potential customers without exposure to the message. In the fourth chart, the marketer is faced with a problem of overexposure (also called **waste coverage**) in which the media coverage exceeds the targeted audience. If media coverage reaches people who are not sought as buyers and are not potential users, then it is wasted. (This term is used for coverage that reaches people who are not potential buyers and/or users. Consumers may not be part of the intended target market but may still be considered as potential—for example, those who buy the product as a gift for someone else.)

The goal of the media planner is to extend media coverage to as many of the members of the target audience as possible while minimizing the amount of waste coverage. The situation usually involves trade-offs. Sometimes one has to live with less coverage than desired; other times, the most effective media expose people not sought. In this instance, waste coverage is justified because the media employed are likely to be the most effective means of delivery available and the cost of the waste coverage is exceeded by the value gained from their use.

When watching football games on TV, you may have noticed commercials for stock brokerage firms such as Dean Witter Reynolds and Merrill Lynch. Not all viewers are candidates for stock market services, but a very high percentage of potential customers can be reached with this strategy. So the program is considered a good media buy because the ability to generate market coverage outweighs the disadvantages of high waste coverage.

FIGURE 10–13
Marketing coverage possibilities

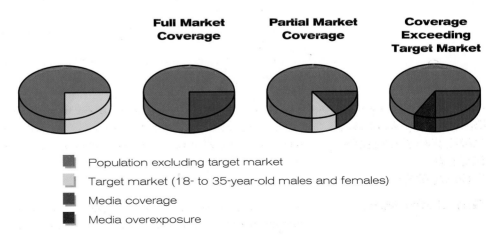

Full Market Coverage   **Partial Market Coverage**   **Coverage Exceeding Target Market**

- Population excluding target market
- Target market (18- to 35-year-old males and females)
- Media coverage
- Media overexposure

FIGURE 10–14
Magazines purchased by people who do aerobics

	TOTAL U.S. '000	AEROBICS				20 OR MORE DAYS			
		A '000	B % DOWN	C % ACROSS	D INDX	A '000	B % DOWN	C % ACROSS	D INDX
REDBOOK	10533	1074	9.1	10.2	157	760	10.1	7.2	174
ROAD & TRACK	3838	*133	1.1	3.5	53	**55	0.7	1.4	35
ROLLING STONE	6154	496	4.2	8.1	124	317	4.2	5.2	124
SCIENTIFIC AMERICAN	1835	*137	1.2	7.5	115	**57	0.8	3.1	75
SELF	2957	594	5.0	20.1	310	466	6.2	15.8	381
SESAME STREET MAGAZINE	3606	444	3.8	12.3	190	292	3.9	8.1	196
SEVENTEEN	3532	259	2.2	7.3	113	*165	2.2	4.7	113
SHAPE	1664	252	2.1	15.1	234	*185	2.4	11.1	269
SKI	1764	*176	1.5	10.0	154	**102	1.4	5.8	140
SKIING	1535	*161	1.4	10.5	162	**86	1.1	5.6	135
SMITHSONIAN	6299	464	3.9	7.4	114	219	2.9	3.5	84
SOAP OPERA DIGEST	6437	756	6.4	11.7	181	433	5.7	6.7	162
SOUTHERN LIVING	7213	675	5.7	9.4	144	506	6.7	7.0	169
SPORT	3012	**153	1.3	5.1	78	**67	0.9	2.2	54
THE SPORTING NEWS	3348	*179	1.5	5.3	82	**128	1.7	3.8	92
SPORTS AFIELD	3370	**91	0.8	2.7	42	**37	0.5	1.1	27
SPORTS ILLUSTRATED	21035	1002	8.5	4.8	73	611	8.1	2.9	70
STAR	10704	814	6.9	7.6	117	470	6.2	4.4	106
SUNDAY MAGAZINE NETWORK	34831	2761	23.3	7.9	122	1828	24.2	5.2	127
SUNSET	3255	269	2.3	8.3	127	185	2.4	5.7	137
TV GUIDE	39127	2620	22.1	6.7	103	1565	20.7	4.0	97
TENNIS	1548	**102	0.9	6.6	102	**82	1.1	5.3	128
TIME	24413	1734	14.7	7.1	110	1165	15.4	4.8	115
TRAVEL & LEISURE	2520	189	1.6	7.5	116	*144	1.9	5.7	138
TRUE STORY	3060	*312	2.6	10.2	157	**234	3.1	7.6	185
USA TODAY	6199	459	3.9	7.4	114	328	4.3	5.3	128
USA WEEKEND	34618	2192	18.5	6.3	98	1369	18.1	4.0	96
U.S. NEWS & WORLD REPORT	13465	830	7.0	6.2	95	596	7.9	4.4	107
US	4059	453	3.8	11.2	172	311	4.1	7.7	185
VANITY FAIR	1974	292	2.5	14.8	228	*173	2.3	8.8	212

Figure 10–14 shows how information provided by Simmons can be used to match media to target markets. It profiles magazines read and TV shows watched by people who do aerobics. (You can practice using index numbers here.) From Figure 10–14, you can see that *Shape*, *Self*, and *Vanity Fair* magazines would likely be wise selections for aerobics ads, whereas *Road and Track*, *Sports Afield*, or *Sport* would be less likely to lead to the desired exposures.

Geographic Coverage

Snow skiing is much more popular in some areas of the country than in others. It would not be the wisest of strategies to promote skis in those areas where interest is not high, unless you could generate an increase in interest. It may be possible to promote an interest in skiing in the Southeast, but a notable increase in sales of ski equipment is not very likely, given the market's distance from snow. The objective of weighting certain geographic areas more than others makes sense, and the strategy of exerting more promotional efforts and dollars in these areas follows naturally.

Scheduling

Obviously, companies would like to keep their advertising in front of consumers at all times as a constant reminder of the product and/or brand name. In reality, this is not possible for a variety of reasons (not the least of which is the budget). Nor is it necessary. The primary objective of *scheduling* is to time promotional efforts so they will coincide with the highest potential buying times. For some products these times are not easy to identify; for others they are very obvious. Three scheduling methods available to the media planner—continuity, flighting, and pulsing—are shown in Figure 10–15.

Continuity refers to a continuous pattern of advertising, which may mean every day, every week, or every month. The key is that a regular (continuous) pattern is developed without gaps or nonadvertising periods. Such strategies might be used for advertising for food products, laundry detergents, or other products consumed on an ongoing basis without regard for seasonality.

A second method, **flighting**, employs a less regular schedule, with intermittent periods of advertising and nonadvertising. At some time periods there are heavier promotional expenditures, and at others there may be no advertising. Many banks, for example, spend no monies on advertising in the summer but maintain advertising throughout the rest of the year. Snow skis are advertised heavily between October and April; less in May, August, and September; and not at all in June and July.

FIGURE 10–15
Three methods of promotional
scheduling

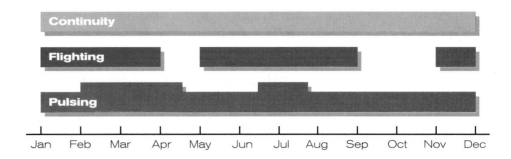

Pulsing is actually a combination of the first two methods. In a pulsing strategy, continuity is maintained, but at certain times promotional efforts are stepped up. In the automobile industry, advertising continues throughout the year but may increase in April (income-tax refund time), September (when new models are brought out), and the end of the model year. The scheduling strategy depends on the objectives, buying cycles, and the budget, among other factors. There are certain advantages and disadvantages to each scheduling method, as shown in Figure 10–16. (Notice that in the WD-40 media plan in Appendix B, flighting is recommended for the consumer advertising strategy, but a continuous schedule is employed for the industrial market.)

**Reach versus
Frequency**

Since advertisers have a variety of objectives and face budget constraints, they usually must trade off reach and frequency. They must decide whether to have the message be seen or heard by more people (reach) or by fewer people more often (frequency).

HOW MUCH REACH IS NECESSARY?

Thinking back to the hierarchies discussed in Chapter 5, you will recall that the first stage of each model requires awareness of the product and/or brand. The more people are aware, the more are likely to move to each subsequent stage. Achieving awareness requires reach—

FIGURE 10–16
Characteristics of scheduling
methods

Continuity	
Advantages	Serves as a constant reminder to the consumer
	Covers the entire buying cycle
	Allows for media priorities (quantity discounts, preferred locations, etc.)
Disadvantages	Higher costs
	Potential for overexposure
	Limited media allocation possible

Flighting	
Advantages	Cost efficiency of advertising only during purchase cycles
	May allow for inclusion of more than one medium or vehicle with limited budgets
Disadvantages	Weighting may offer more exposure and advantage over competitors
	Increased likelihood of wearout
	Lack of awareness, interest, retention of promotional message during nonscheduled times
	Vulnerability to competitive efforts during nonscheduled periods

Pulsing	
Advantages	All of the same as the previous two methods
Disadvantages	Not required for seasonal products (or other cyclical products)

that is, exposing potential buyers to the message. New brands or products need a very high level of reach, since the objective is to make all potential buyers aware of the new entry. High reach is also desired at later stages of the hierarchy. For example, at the trial stage of the adoption hierarchy, a promotions strategy might use cents-off coupons or free samples. An objective of the marketer is to reach a larger number of people with these samples, in an attempt to make them learn of the product, try it, and develop favorable attitudes toward it. (In turn, these attitudes may lead to purchase.)

The problem arises because there is no known way of determining how much reach is required to achieve levels of awareness, attitude change, or buying intentions, nor can we be sure an ad placed in a vehicle will actually reach the intended audience. (There has been some research on the first problem, which will be discussed in the section on effective reach.)

If you buy advertising time on "60 Minutes," does this mean everyone who is tuned to this program will see the ad? No. Many viewers will leave the room, be distracted during the commercial, and so on, as shown in Figure 10–17 (which also provides a good example of the difference between reach and coverage). If I expose everyone in my target group to the message once, will this be sufficient to create a 100 percent level of awareness? The answer again is no. This leads to the next question: What frequency of exposure is necessary for the ad to be seen and to have an impact?

WHAT FREQUENCY LEVEL IS NEEDED?

With respect to media planning, *frequency* carries a slightly different meaning. (Remember when we said one of the problems in media planning is that terms often take on different meanings?) Here frequency refers to the number of times one is exposed to the media vehicle, not necessarily to the ad itself. While one study has estimated the actual audience for the commercial may be as much as 30 percent lower than that for the program, not all researchers agree.[3] Figure 10–17 demonstrates that depending on the program, this number may range from 12 percent to 40 percent.

Most advertisers do agree that a 1:1 exposure ratio does not exist. So while your ad may be placed in a certain vehicle, the fact that a consumer has been exposed to that vehicle does not ensure that your ad has been seen. As a result, the frequency level expressed in the media

FIGURE 10–17 Who's still there to watch the ads?

How many viewers actually watch a commercial? R. D. Percy & Co. reports that its advanced people meters, equipped with heat sensors that detect viewers present, indicate that spots retain, on average, 82 percent of the average-minute ratings for the quarter hour. During early morning news programs, "commercial efficiency" (as Percy calls it) is lower because so many people are bustling about, out of the room (yellow), but the rate rises at night.

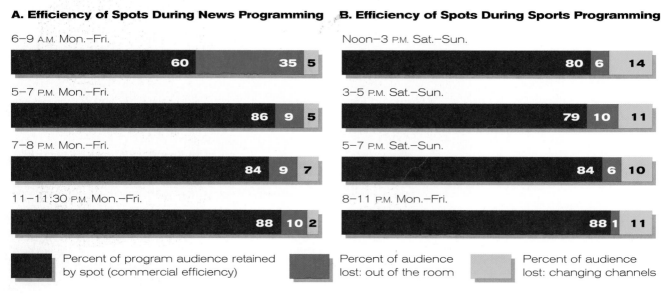

A. Efficiency of Spots During News Programming

6–9 A.M. Mon.–Fri.
60 | 35 | 5

5–7 P.M. Mon.–Fri.
86 | 9 | 5

7–8 P.M. Mon.–Fri.
84 | 9 | 7

11–11:30 P.M. Mon.–Fri.
88 | 10 | 2

B. Efficiency of Spots During Sports Programming

Noon–3 P.M. Sat.–Sun.
80 | 6 | 14

3–5 P.M. Sat.–Sun.
79 | 10 | 11

5–7 P.M. Sat.–Sun.
84 | 6 | 10

8–11 P.M. Mon.–Fri.
88 | 1 | 11

■ Percent of program audience retained by spot (commercial efficiency)

■ Percent of audience lost: out of the room

□ Percent of audience lost: changing channels

plan overstates the actual level of exposure to the ad. This overstatement has led some media buyers to refer to the reach of the media vehicle as "opportunities to see" an ad rather than actual exposure to it.

Because the advertiser has no sure way of knowing whether exposure to a vehicle results in exposure to the ad, the media and advertisers have adopted a compromise: one exposure to the vehicle constitutes reach, given that this exposure must occur for the viewer even to have an opportunity to see the ad. Thus, the exposure figure is used to calculate reach and frequency levels. But this compromise does not help determine the frequency required to make an impact. The creativity of the ad, the involvement of the receiver, noise, and many other intervening factors confound any attempts to make a precise determination.

At this point, you may be thinking, "If nobody knows this stuff, how do they make these decisions?" That's a good question, and the truth is that the decisions are not always made on hard data. Says Joseph Ostrow, executive vice president/director of communications services with Young and Rubicam, "Establishing frequency goals for an advertising campaign is a mix of art and science but with a definite bias toward art."[4] Let us first examine the process involved in setting reach and frequency objectives and then discuss the logic of each.

ESTABLISHING REACH AND FREQUENCY OBJECTIVES

It is possible to be exposed to more than one media vehicle with an ad, resulting in repetition (frequency). If one ad is placed on one TV show one time, the number of people exposed is the reach. If the ad is placed on two shows, the total number exposed once is **unduplicated reach**. Some people will see the ad twice. The reach of the two shows, as depicted in Figure 10–18, includes a number of people who were reached by both shows (C). This overlap is referred to as **duplicated reach.**

Both unduplicated and duplicated reach figures are important. Unduplicated reach indicates potential new exposures, while duplicated reach provides an estimate of frequency. Most media buys include both forms of reach. Let us consider an example.

A measure of potential reach in the broadcast industry is the TV (or radio) **program rating**. This number is expressed as a percentage. For an estimate of the total number of homes reached, multiply this percentage times the number of homes with TV sets. For example, if there are 96.9 million homes with TV sets in the United States and the program has a rating of 30, then the calculation is 0.30 times 96.9, or 29.07 million homes. (We go into much more detail on ratings and other broadcast terms in Chapter 11.)

FIGURE 10–18
Representation of reach and frequency

A. Reach of One TV Program

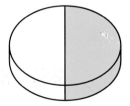

Total market audience reached

B. Reach of Two Programs

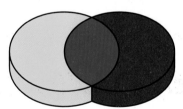

Total market audience reached

C. Duplicated Reach

Total market reached
with both shows

D. Unduplicated Reach

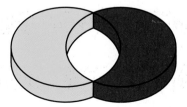

Total reach less
duplicated reach

USING GROSS RATINGS POINTS

The media buyer typically uses a numerical indicator to know how many potential audience members may be exposed to a series of commercials. A summary measure that combines the program rating and the average number of times the home is reached during this period (frequency of exposure) is a commonly used reference point known as **gross ratings points (GRPs)**.

GRP = Reach × Frequency

GRPs are based on the total audience the media schedule may reach; they use a duplicated reach estimate. **Target ratings points (TRPs)** refer to the number of people in the primary target audience the media buy will reach—and the number of times. Unlike GRP, TRP does not include waste coverage.

Given that GRPs do not measure actual reach, the advertiser must ask: How many GRPs are needed to attain a certain reach? How do these GRPs translate into effective reach? For example, how many GRPs must one purchase to attain an unduplicated reach of 50 percent, and what frequency of exposure will this schedule deliver? The following example may help you to understand how this process works.

First you must know what these ratings points represent. A purchase of 100 GRPs could mean 100 percent of the market is exposed once or 50 percent of the market is exposed twice or 25 percent of the market is exposed four times, and so on. As you can see, this information must be more specific for the marketer to use it effectively. To know how many GRPs are necessary, the manager needs to know how many members of the intended audience the schedule actually reaches. The chart in Figure 10–19 helps make this determination.

In Figure 10–19, a purchase of 100 TRPs on one network would yield an estimated reach of 32 percent of the total households in the target market. This figure would climb to 37.2 percent if two networks were used and 44.5 percent on three. Working backward through the formula for GRPs, the estimate of frequency of exposure—3.125, 2.688, and 2.247, respectively—demonstrates the trade-off between reach and frequency.

As an example of a media buy, Denny's purchased 1,300 GRPs in a 10-week period to introduce a new Grand Slam promotion. This purchase employed TV spots in 28 markets and was estimated to reach 40 percent of the target audience an average of 17 times. To determine if this was a wise media buy, we need to know whether this was an effective reach figure. Certainly, reaching 40 percent of the target market is attractive. But why was the frequency level so high? And was it likely to be effective? In other words, does this level of GRPs affect awareness, attitudes, and purchase intentions?

A number of researchers have explored this issue. David Berger, vice president and director of research at Foote, Cone & Belding, has determined that 2,500 GRPs are likely to lead to roughly a 70 percent probability of high awareness, 1,000 to 2,500 would yield about a 33 percent probability, and less than 1,000 would probably result in almost no awareness.[5] David Olson obtained similar results and further showed that as awareness increased, trial of the product would also increase, although at a significantly slower rate.[6] In both cases, it was evident that high numbers of GRPs were required to make an impact.

FIGURE 10–19
Estimates of reach for network TRPs

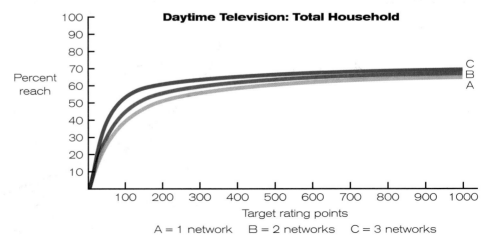

Daytime Television: Total Household

A = 1 network   B = 2 networks   C = 3 networks

EXHIBIT 10–20
The effects of reach and frequency

1. One exposure of an ad to a target group within a purchase cycle has little or no effect in most circumstances.

2. Since one exposure is usually ineffective, the central goal of productive media planning should be to enhance frequency rather than reach.

3. The evidence suggests strongly that an exposure frequency of two within a purchase cycle is an effective level.

4. Beyond three exposures within a brand purchase cycle or over a period of four or even eight weeks, increasing frequency continues to build advertising effectiveness at a decreasing rate but with no evidence of decline.

5. Although there are general principles with respect to frequency of exposure and its relationship to advertising effectiveness, differential effects by brand are equally important.

6. Nothing we have seen suggests that frequency response principles or generalizations vary by medium.

7. The data strongly suggest that wearout is not a function of too much frequency; it is more of a creative or copy problem.

Figure 10–20 summarizes the effects that can be expected at different levels of exposure, based on research in this area. A number of factors may be operating, and direct relationships may be difficult to establish.[7] In addition to the results shown in Figure 10–20, Joseph Ostrow has shown that while the number of repetitions increases awareness rapidly, it has much less impact on attitudinal and behavioral responses.[8]

You can imagine how expensive it was for Denny's to purchase 1,300 gross ratings points on TV. Now that you have additional information, we will ask again, "Was this a good buy?"

DETERMINING EFFECTIVE REACH

Since marketers have budget constraints, they must decide whether to increase reach at the expense of frequency or increase the frequency of exposure but to a smaller audience. A number of factors influence this decision. For example, a new product or brand introduction will attempt to maximize reach, particularly unduplicated reach, to create awareness in as many people as possible as quickly as possible. At the same time, for a high-involvement product or one whose benefits are not obvious, a certain level of frequency is needed to achieve effective reach.

Effective reach represents the percentage of a vehicle's audience reached at each effective frequency increment. This concept is based on the assumption that one exposure to an ad may not be enough to convey the desired message. As we saw earlier, no one knows the exact number of exposures necessary for an ad to make an impact, although advertisers have settled on three as the minimum. Effective reach (exposure) is shown in the shaded area in Figure 10–21 in the range of 3 to 10 exposures. Fewer than three exposures is considered insufficient reach, while more than 10 is considered overexposure and thus ineffective reach.

FIGURE 10–21
Graph of effective reach

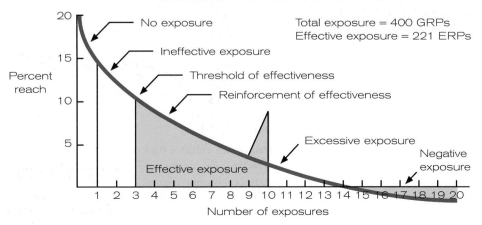

Total Exposure versus Effective Exposure of a Prime-Time Television Schedule

This exposure level is no guarantee of effective communication; different messages may require more or fewer exposures. IMC Perspective 10–2 provides some additional insight into effective reach.

Since they do not know how many times the viewer will actually be exposed, advertisers typically purchase GRPs that lead to more than three exposures to increase the likelihood of effective reach and frequency.

Determining effective reach is further complicated by the fact that when calculating GRPs, advertisers use a figure that they call **average frequency**, or the average number of times the target audience reached by a media schedule is exposed to the vehicle over a specified period. The problem with this figure is revealed in the following scenario.

Consider a media buy in which:
    50 percent of audience is reached 1 time.
    30 percent of audience is reached 5 times.
    20 percent of audience is reached 10 times.
    Average frequency = 4.0

In this media buy, the average frequency is 4.0, which is slightly more than the number established as effective. Yet a full 50 percent of the audience receives only one exposure. Thus, the average frequency number can be misleading, and using it to calculate GRPs might result in underexposing the audience.

Although GRPs have their problems, they can provide useful information to the marketer. A certain level of GRPs is necessary to achieve awareness, and increases in GRPs are likely to lead to more exposures and/or more repetitions—both of which are necessary to have an effect on higher-order objectives. Perhaps the best advice for purchasing GRPs is offered by Ostrow, who recommends the following strategies:[9]

1. Instead of using average frequency, the marketer should decide what minimum frequency goal is needed to reach the advertising objectives effectively and then maximize reach at that frequency level.
2. To determine effective frequency, one must consider marketing factors, message factors, and media factors. (See Figure 10–22, page 318.)

In summary, the reach versus frequency decision, while critical, is very difficult to make. A number of factors must be considered, and concrete rules do not always apply. The decision is often more of an art than a science.

Creative Aspects and Mood

The context of the medium in which the ad is placed may also affect viewers' perceptions. A specific creative strategy may require certain media. Because TV provides both sight and sound, it may be more effective in generating emotions than other media; magazines may create different perceptions from newspapers. In developing a media strategy, marketers must consider both creativity and mood factors. Let us examine each in more detail.

CREATIVE ASPECTS

It is possible to increase the success of a product significantly through a strong creative campaign. But to implement this creativity, you must employ a medium that will support such a strategy. For example, the Absolut vodka campaign discussed in Chapter 8 and the campaign for Obsession cologne shown in Chapter 4 used print media to communicate their messages effectively. Kodak and McDonald's, among many others, have effectively used TV to create emotional appeals. In some situations, the media strategy to be pursued may be the driving force behind the creative strategy, as the media and creative departments work closely together to achieve the greatest impact with the audience of the specific media.

MOOD

Certain media enhance the creativity of a message because they create a mood that carries over to the communication. For example, think about the moods created by the following magazines: *Gourmet, Skiing, Travel,* and *House Beautiful.* Each of these special-interest ve-

IMC Perspective 10–2
Exactly What Is the Right Frequency?

One of the more spirited debates among and between media planners and academicians involves the number of exposures necessary to make an effective impression. As you might imagine, it is one of the more critical decisions planners face in putting together a media strategy, yet it's like arguing politics or religion—no one ever wins. Abbott Wool, senior vice president and media director at Siboney Advertising, claims one exposure may be enough. Wool stresses the theory of *propinquity*, which states that the message received closest to the purchase decision is the one that affects brand sales the most. Thus, if we could reach the consumer with the ad very close to purchase time, we could lower the frequency levels required and save advertising dollars. Wool advises studying the geographic concentration of prospects, the seasonality of purchases, purchase times and dates, and demographics to time ads optimally. Professor John Philip Jones, in his book *When Ads Work*, agrees with Wool's contention that one exposure is enough, and suggests one exposure a week with continuity throughout the year (or as long as one can afford).

Others are not inclined to agree. Jack Myers, president of Myers Reports and a media consultant, says Krugman's work "Why Three Exposures May Be Enough" was valid 20 years ago but is not any more. Myers notes that when Krugman conducted his research the consumer was exposed to *only* 1,000 ads per day. Now that exposure is probably 3,000 to 5,000 ads per day. Throw in the fragmentation of television, the increase in the number of magazines, and the new alternative media options now being used, and Myers argues that there is less chance of one ad being noticed. He thinks 12 times may be the bare minimum frequency required to achieve the equivalent of Krugman's three exposures. Myers suggests that a new movie release, for example, may require exposures of 24 to 36 times during a 10-day period to duplicate the impact of 6 to 10 ads in 1980. He expects that in the future, brand marketers will establish average frequency levels of 24 to 36 ads, with exposure levels exceeding 100 during the course of a one-year campaign.

Jim Surmanek, VP of the International Communications Group (a media planning and buying agency) also believes that one exposure is not enough. Surmanek contends, "For nearly all products there is a 'magic range' of advertising pressure below which the sales effect is minimal, and above which advertising simply does not pay out. The same happens with reach and frequency." He says consumers' motivation to buy, purchase cycles, the type of product, complexity of the message, message length, and other factors all influence the required frequency level.

Both sides do agree on a few points. One is that the importance attached to determining effective reach is on the increase among media planners. In a study by academicians Leckenby and Kim, over the past 10 years the number of practitioners who consider effective reach to be important in their media plan increased significantly—among both U.S. and international agencies. Also, practitioners are concerned about their ability to determine what constitutes effective reach. In addition, Wool agrees that the difficulty of reaching the consumer close to the purchase decision makes it unlikely that one exposure will be effective. Myers agrees that the timing of the presentation is critical, and the closer to the action the exposure takes place the more likely it is to be effective.

So there appears to be consensus—if you don't look too closely.

Sources: Jim Surmanek, "One-Hit or Miss: Is a Frequency of One Frequently Wrong?" *Advertising Age*, November 27, 1995, p. 46; John P. Jones, *When Ads Work* (New York: Lexington Books, 1995); John D. Leckenby and Heejin Kim, "How Media Directors View Reach/Frequency Estimation: Now and a Decade Ago," *Journal of Advertising Research*, September/October 1994, pp. 9–21; Abbott Wool, "Frequency vs. Propinquity," *MediaWeek*, July 26, 1993, p. 19; Jack Myers, "More Is Indeed Better," *MediaWeek*, September 6, 1993, pp. 14–18.

FIGURE 10–22
Factors important in determining frequency levels

Marketing Factors

- *Brand history* — Is the brand new or established? New brands generally require higher frequency levels.
- *Brand share* — An inverse relationship exists between brand share and frequency. The higher the brand share, the lower the frequency level required.
- *Brand loyalty* — An inverse relationship exists between loyalty and frequency. The higher the loyalty, the lower the frequency level required.
- *Purchase cycles* — Shorter purchasing cycles require higher frequency levels to maintain top-of-mind awareness.
- *Usage cycle* — Products used daily or oftener need to be replaced quickly, so a higher level of frequency is desired.
- *Competitive share of voice* — Higher frequency levels are required when a lot of competitive noise exists and when the goal is to meet or beat competitors.
- *Target group* — The ability of the target group to learn and to retain messages has a direct effect on frequency.

Message or Creative Factors

- *Message complexity* — The simpler the message, the less frequency required.
- *Message uniqueness* — The more unique the message, the lower the frequency level required.
- *New versus continuing campaigns* — New campaigns require higher levels of frequency to register the message.
- *Image versus product sell* — Creating an image requires higher levels of frequency than does a specific product sell.
- *Message variation* — A single message requires less frequency; a variety of messages requires more.
- *Wearout* — Higher frequency may lead to wearout. This effect must be tracked and used to evaluate frequency levels.
- *Advertising units* — Larger units of advertising require less frequency than smaller ones to get the message across.

Media Factors

- *Clutter* — The more advertising that appears in the media used, the more frequency is needed to break through the clutter.
- *Editorial environment* — The more consistent the ad is with the editorial environment, the less frequency is needed.
- *Attentiveness* — The higher the level of attention achieved by the media vehicle, the less frequency is required. Low attention-getting media require more repetitions.
- *Scheduling* — Continuous scheduling requires less frequency than does flighting or pulsing.
- *Number of media used* — The fewer media used, the lower the level of frequency required.
- *Repeat exposures* — Media that allow for more repeat exposures (for example, monthly magazines) require less frequency.

hicles puts the reader in a particular mood. The promotion of fine wines, ski boots, luggage, and home products is enhanced by this mood. What different images might be created for your product if you advertised it in these media?

> *The New York Times* versus the *National Enquirer*
>
> *Architectural Digest* versus *Reader's Digest*
>
> A highly rated prime-time TV show versus an old rerun

The message may require a specific medium and a certain media vehicle to achieve its objectives. Likewise, certain media and vehicles have images that may carry over to the perceptions of messages placed within them.

Flexibility

An effective media strategy requires a degree of flexibility. Because of the rapidly changing marketing environment, strategies may need to be modified. If the plan has not built in some flexibility, opportunities may be lost and/or the company may not be able to address new threats. Flexibility may be needed to address the following:

1. *Market opportunities*   Sometimes a market opportunity arises that the advertiser wishes to take advantage of. For example, the development of a new advertising medium may offer an opportunity that was not previously available.

2. *Market threats*   Internal or external factors may pose a threat to the firm, and a change in media strategy is dictated. For example, a competitor may alter its media strategy to gain an edge. Failure to respond to this challenge could create problems for the firm.

3. *Availability of media*   Sometimes a desired medium (or vehicle) is not available to the marketer. Perhaps the medium does not reach a particular target segment or has no time or space available. There are still some geographic areas where certain media do not reach. Even when the media are available, limited advertising time or space may have already been sold or cutoff dates for entry may have passed. Alternative vehicles or media must then be considered.

4. *Changes in media or media vehicles*   A change in the medium or in a particular vehicle may require a change in the media strategy. For example, the advent of cable TV opened up new opportunities for message delivery, as will the introduction of interactive media. Likewise, a drop in ratings or a change in editorial format may lead the advertiser to use different programs or print alternatives.

Fluctuations in these factors mean the media strategy must be developed with enough flexibility to allow the manager to adapt to specific market situations.

Budget Considerations

One of the more important decisions in the development of media strategy is cost estimating. The value of any strategy can be determined by how well it delivers the message to the audience with the lowest cost and the least waste. We have already explored a number of factors, such as reach, frequency, and availability, that affect this decision. The marketer tries to arrive at the optimal delivery by balancing cost with each of these. (Again, the WD-40 plan in Appendix B demonstrates how this issue is addressed.) As the following discussion shows, understanding cost figures may not be as easy as it seems.

Advertising and promotional costs can be categorized in two ways. The **absolute cost** of the medium or vehicle is the actual total cost required to place the message. For example, a full-page four-color ad in *Newsweek* magazine costs about $144,000. **Relative cost** refers to the relationship between the price paid for advertising time or space and the size of the audience delivered; it is used to compare media vehicles. Relative costs are important because the manager must try to optimize audience delivery within budget constraints. Since a number of alternatives are available for delivering the message, the advertiser must evaluate the relative costs associated with these choices. The way media costs are provided and problems in comparing these costs across media often make such evaluations difficult.

DETERMINING RELATIVE COSTS OF MEDIA

To evaluate alternatives, advertisers must compare the relative costs of media as well as vehicles within these media. Unfortunately, the broadcast, print, and out-of-home media do not always provide the same cost breakdowns, nor necessarily do vehicles within the print media. Following are the cost bases used.

1. **Cost per thousand (CPM)**   For years the magazine industry has provided cost breakdowns on the basis of cost per thousand people reached. The formula for this computation is

$$\text{CPM} = \frac{\text{Cost of ad space (absolute cost)}}{\text{Circulation}} \times 1,000$$

Figure 10–23 provides an example of this computation for two vehicles in the same medium—*Time* and *Newsweek*—and shows that (all other things being equal) *Time* is a

FIGURE 10–23
Cost per thousand computations:
Time versus *Newsweek*

	Time	Newsweek
Per-page cost	$156,000	$144,000
Circulation	4.0 million	3.1 million
Calculation of CPM	$\dfrac{156,000 \times 1,000}{4,000,000}$	$\dfrac{144,000 \times 1,000}{3,100,000}$
CPM	$39.00	$46.45

more cost-effective buy, even though its absolute cost is higher. (We will come back to "all other things being equal" in a moment.)

2. **Cost per ratings point (CPRP)**   The broadcast media provide a different comparative cost figure, referred to as cost per ratings point or cost per point (CPP), based on the following formula:

$$\text{CPRP} = \frac{\text{Cost of commercial time}}{\text{Program rating}}$$

An example of this calculation for a spot ad in a local TV market is shown in Figure 10–24. It indicates that "Touched by an Angel" would be more cost effective than "Murphy Brown."

3. **Daily inch rate**   For newspapers, cost effectiveness is based on the daily inch rate, which is the cost per column inch of the paper. Like magazines, newspapers now use the cost per thousand formula discussed earlier to determine relative costs. As shown in Figure 10–25, the *Boston Globe* costs significantly more to advertise in than does the *Boston Herald* (again, all other things being equal).

As you can see, it is difficult to make comparisons across various media. What is the broadcast equivalent of cost per thousand or the column inch rate? In an attempt to standardize relative costing procedures, the broadcast and newspaper media have begun to provide costs per thousand, using the following formulas:

$$\text{Television:} \frac{\text{Cost of 1 unit of time} \times 1,000}{\text{Program rating}} \qquad \text{Newspapers:} \frac{\text{Cost of ad space} \times 1,000}{\text{Circulation}}$$

While the comparison of media on a cost per thousand basis is important, intermedia comparisons can be misleading. The ability of TV to provide both sight and sound, the longevity of magazines, and other characteristics of each medium make direct comparisons difficult. The media planner should use the cost per thousand numbers but must also consider the specific characteristics of each medium and each media vehicle in the decision.

The cost per thousand may overestimate or underestimate the actual cost effectiveness. Consider a situation where some waste coverage is inevitable. The circulation (using the *Time* magazine figures to demonstrate our point) exceeds the target market. If the people reached by this message are not potential buyers of the product, then having to pay to reach them results in too low a cost per thousand, as shown in scenario A of Figure 10–26. We must use the potential reach to the target market—the destination sought—rather than the overall circulation figure. A medium with a much higher cost per thousand may be a wiser buy if it is reaching more potential receivers.

FIGURE 10–24
Comparison of cost per ratings point:
"Murphy Brown" versus "Touched by an Angel"

	"Murphy Brown"	"Touched by an Angel"
Cost per spot ad	$3,500	$4,000
Rating	11	15
Reach (households)	109,000	135,000
Calculation	$3,500/11	$4,000/15
CPRP (CPP)	$318.18	$266.67

FIGURE 10–25
Comparative costs in newspaper advertising

FIGURE 10–25
Comparative costs in newspaper advertising

	Boston Globe	Boston Herald
Cost per page	$32,205	$15,135
Cost per inch	$268.60	$216.50
Circulation	499,000	308,000

Calculation

$$CPM = \frac{Page\ cost \times 1,000}{Circulation}$$

$$CPM = \frac{\$32,205 \times 1,000}{499,000}$$	$$\frac{\$15,135 \times 1,000}{308,000}$$
$64.54	$49.14

CPM may also underestimate cost efficiency. Magazine advertising space sellers have argued for years that because more than one person may read an issue, the actual reach is underestimated. They want to use the number of **readers per copy** as the true circulation. This would include a **pass-along rate**, estimating the number of people who read the magazine without buying it. Scenario B in Figure 10–26 shows how this underestimates cost efficiency. Consider a family in which a father, mother, and two teenagers read each issue of *Time*. Assume such families constitute 33 percent of *Time*'s circulation base. While the circulation figure includes only one magazine, in reality there are four potential exposures in these households, increasing the total reach to 7.96 million.

While the number of readers per copy makes intuitive sense, it has the potential to be extremely inaccurate. The actual number of times the magazine changes hands is difficult to determine. How many people in a fraternity read each issue of *Sports Illustrated* or *Playboy* that is delivered? How many people in a sorority or on a dorm floor read each issue of *Cosmopolitan* or *Self*? How many of either group read each issue of *Business Week*? While research is conducted to make these determinations, pass-along estimates are very subjective and using them to estimate reach is speculative. These figures are regularly provided by the media, but managers are selective about using them. At the same time, the art of media buy-

FIGURE 10–26
Cost per thousand estimates

Scenario A: Overestimation of Efficiency

Target market:	18–49
Magazine circulation:	4,000,000
Circulation to target market:	65% (2,600,000)
Cost per page:	$156,000

$$CPM = \frac{\$156,000 \times 1,000}{4,000,000} = \$39.00$$

$$CPM\ (actual\ target\ audience) = \frac{\$156,000 \times 1,000}{2,600,000} = \$60.00$$

Scenario B: Underestimation of Efficiency

Target market:	All age groups, male and female
Magazine circulation:	4,000,000
Cost per page:	$156,000
Pass-along rate:	3* (33% of households)

$$CPM\ (based\ on\ readers\ per\ copy) = \frac{Page\ cost \times 1,000}{Circulation + 3(1,320,000)} = \frac{\$156,000 \times 1,000}{7,960,000}$$

$$= \$19.60$$

*Assuming pass-along was valid.

ing enters, for many magazines' managers have a good idea how much greater the reach is than their circulation figures provided.

In addition to the potential for over- or underestimation of cost efficiencies, CPMs are limited in that they make only *quantitative* estimates of the value of media. While they may be good for comparing very similar vehicles (such as *Time* and *Newsweek*), they are less valuable in making intermedia comparisons. We have already noted some differences among media that preclude direct comparisons.

You can see that the development of a media strategy involves many factors. Ostrow may be right when he calls this process an art rather than a science, as so much of it requires going beyond the numbers.

EVALUATION AND FOLLOW-UP

All plans require some evaluation to assess their performance. The media plan is no exception.

In outlining the planning process, we stated that objectives are established and strategies developed for them. Having implemented these strategies, marketers need to know whether or not they were successful. Measures of effectiveness must consider two factors: (1) How well did these strategies achieve the media objectives? (2) How well did this media plan contribute to attaining the overall marketing and communications objectives? If the strategies were successful, they should be used in future plans. If not, their flaws should be analyzed.

The problem with measuring the effectiveness of media strategies is probably obvious to you at this point. At the outset of this chapter, we suggested the planning process was limited by problems with measurements and lack of consistent terminology (among others). While these problems limit the degree to which we can assess the relative effectiveness of various strategies, that does not mean it is impossible to make such determinations. Sometimes it is possible to show that a plan has worked. Even if the evaluation procedure is not foolproof, it is better than no attempt.

COMPUTERS IN MEDIA PLANNING

Attempts to improve on the media buying process through the use of computers have received a great deal of attention. While advanced planning models have been around since at least 1963, for the most part these models have met with limited success. Programs based on linear programming, simulation, and iteration have been adopted by a number of agencies, but there remains a great deal of skepticism regarding their practicality.[10]

Computers have been used, however, to automate each of the four steps involved in planning and strategy development. While the art of media strategy has not been mechanized, advances in the quantitative side have significantly improved managers' decision-making capabilities while saving substantial time and effort. Let us briefly examine some of these methods.

Computers in Market Analysis

Earlier in this chapter, we provided examples of Simmons and MRI data. In Chapter 2, we reviewed the information in Prizm, VALS, Vision, and other such systems. All these data can be accessed either through an interactive system or on the agency's own PC. For example, MRI offers its clients interactive capabilities with its mainframe or its MEMRI software database that can be used on a PC to cross-tabulate media and demographic data, estimate reach and frequency, and rank costs, in addition to numerous other applications. The databases can also interface with Prizm, VALS, and Vision data. Simmons also allows access to Prizm, Acorn, VALS, and others.

Other market analysis programs are also available. ClusterPlus and Market America include demographic, geographic, psychographic, and product and media use information that can be used for media planning. Census tract information and socioeconomic data are also accessible. These systems are linked to Nielsen data for scheduling and targeting to specific groups.

Analyses of these data can help planners determine which markets and which groups should be targeted for advertising and promotions. By using this information along with other data, the marketer can also define media objectives.

Computers in Media Strategy Development

In the strategy development phase, we discussed the need to make decisions regarding coverage, scheduling, costs, and the trade-off between reach and frequency, among others. Of primary benefit to media planners are the programs that assist in development of these strategies. While there are far too many of these programs to review here, we will provide a small sampling to demonstrate our point.

REACH AND FREQUENCY ANALYSES ON THE COMPUTER

Figure 10–27 demonstrates how software programs are being used to determine reach and frequency levels and assist in deciding which alternative is best. The Telmar program computes various media mixes for TV and radio at different TRPs, with reach and frequency estimates, the number of people reached three or more times, and the costs. The program has determined that a mix of 125 TRPs on TV and 150 TRPs on radio would result in the best buy. Keep in mind that this recommendation considers only the most efficient combination of quantifiable factors and does not allow for the art of media buying.

Figure 10–27 shows just one of the many examples of how computer programs are being used in media strategy development. Other computer-based media planning programs are available: the following list is just a small sample.

- **ADplus** provides for media planning, reach and frequency analysis, media mix information, budgeting, and more.
- **Adware** provides Arbitron and Nielsen information, calculates media costs, projects GRPs, and more.
- **IMS** offers a fully integrated suite of software that performs market analysis, target identification, print and broadcast planning, and more. It also provides access to over 600 databases, including syndicated and proprietary, media and marketing, consumer, trade, domestic, and international data.
- **Media Control by Control G Software** has a Print Media Control Module and Broadcast Media Control. The software packages help to manage media planning by controlling deadlines, station and spot mix, contract usage, and much more.
- **Media Management Plus** ranks stations in each market according to delivery potential and costs, and calculates projected ratings.
- **Neilsen SAVIE** (formerly AdExpress) provides a full picture of cable TV alternatives and the value of each by using multiple databases, such as product purchasing data, customer preference cluster data, Neilsen audience data, and specific systems data.
- **Tapscan** uses syndicated data useful in radio media planning, including ratings data and reach and frequency analysis.

FIGURE 10–27
Telmar media plan for a local bank

Media Mix (A 25–54)	Reach Frequency (%/X)	3+ Level (%)	1st Quarter Weekly Cost
TV (125)	84/4.5	51	$21,480
TV (125) R (125)	91/8.2	71	29,450
TV (125) R (150)*	92/9.0	73	31,045
TV (150)	86/5.2	57	25,660
TV (150) R (125)	92/9.0	73	33,625
TV (150) R (150)	92/9.8	74	35,220
TV (175)	89/5.9	61	29,930
TV (175) R (125)	93/9.7	75	37,900
TV (175) R (150)	93/10.5	76	39,490
TV (200)	90/6.7	65	34,255
TV (200) R (125)	93/10.5	76	42,225
TV (200) R (150)	93/11.3	78	43,820

Note: Based on a three-week flight.
*Recommended.

- **Telmar** allows planners to analyze media data, devise media plans, and create flowcharts. It is linked to major syndicated data services.
- **TVscan** provides information like Tapscan's for TV.
- **TV Conquest** combines Nielsen, Donnelley, and Simmons data to provide demographic, product usage, and ratings information.

In addition to these, media models have been developed to show the effects of media selection on advertising responses.

1. *Evaluation models* are exposure distribution models that estimate the reach and frequency of media vehicles based on probability theories.
2. *Allocation models* are comprehensive models used to optimize advertising budget allocation.
3. *Interaction models* consider the interaction effects between copy and media selection in predicting advertising effects.

Unfortunately, these models also have weaknesses that limit their adoption.[11]

The one area where computers have not yet provided a direct benefit is in the evaluation stage of the media plan. While these programs do generate what they consider to be optimal TRP, GRP, and media mixes and allow for pre- and postbuy analyses, the true test is what happens when the plan is implemented. We reserve our discussion of the evaluation process for Chapter 18 on measuring effectiveness.

CHARACTERISTICS OF MEDIA

To this point, we have discussed the elements involved in the development of media strategy. One of the most basic elements in this process is the matching of media to markets. In the following chapters, you will see that each medium has its own characteristics that make it better or worse for attaining specific objectives. First, Figure 10–28 is an overall comparison of media and some of the characteristics by which they are evaluated. This is a very general comparison, and the various media options must be analyzed for each situation. However, it provides a good starting point.

Interactive Media

Much has been written about the new **interactive media**. Articles have appeared everywhere from *Time* to *Business Week* to *MediaWeek*. *Advertising Age* has a regular interactive section every week, and as noted in Chapter 3, interactive agencies have been established. When most people think of interactive media, they think of television and the promise of 500 channels ranging from home shopping to news and information services to classified ads. But interactive involves more media than just TV. BBDO, one of the world's largest advertising agencies, categorizes interactive media into five areas: online, Internet, CD-ROM, kiosks, and interactive TV. Figure 10–29 provides an expanded list, with a brief description of each medium.

Figure 10–30 summarizes some of the information provided by an *Advertising Age* study of consumers' awareness and usage of interactive media. As this study clearly indicates, both awareness and usage of interactive media are increasing, as users see significant advantages over traditional media.

Interactive media move the receivers from being passive participants to active ones. Says Hanna Liebman, a writer for *MediaWeek*, these new media will "allow anybody to get information of any kind to anybody else at any time."[12] Interactive media allow the consumer to literally interact with the source, offering a number of advantages (Figure 10–28). Advertisers are attracted to these media due to their ability to target specific market segments, as well as to deal directly with the user. At the same time, not everyone is enamored with interactive media. In a test of interest in interactive services conducted by British Telecommunications PLC and Deutsche Telekom AG, the companies found that:

- Only 19 percent of consumers in France and Britain said they were "very interested in video-on-demand services," versus 43 percent in the United States.
- While 75 percent of U.S. consumers rent at least one movie a month, the number drops to less than 40 percent in Western Europe.

FIGURE 10–28
Media characteristics

Media	Advantages	Disadvantages
Television	Mass coverage High reach Impact of sight, sound, and motion High prestige Low cost per exposure Attention getting Favorable image	Low selectivity Short message life High absolute cost High production costs Clutter
Radio	Local coverage Low cost High frequency Flexible Low production costs Well-segmented audiences	Audio only Clutter Low attention getting Fleeting message
Magazines	Segmentation potential Quality reproduction High information content Longevity Multiple readers	Long lead time for ad placement Visual only Lack of flexibility
Newspapers	High coverage Low cost Short lead time for placing ads Ads can be placed in interest sections Timely (current ads) Reader controls exposure Can be used for coupons	Short life Clutter Low attention-getting capabilities Poor reproduction quality Selective reader exposure
Outdoor	Location specific High repetition Easily noticed	Short exposure time requires short ad Poor image Local restrictions
Direct mail	High selectivity Reader controls exposure High information content Opportunities for repeat exposures	High cost/contact Poor image (junk mail) Clutter
Interactive media	User selects product information User attention and involvement Interactive relationship Direct selling potential Flexible message platform	Limited creative capabilities Websnarl (crowded access) Technology not advanced No valid measurement techniques

- Germans are most likely to order food for home delivery (21 percent), but this number is far less than the 45 percent in the United States.

This information coupled with ancedotal research led the companies to conclude that Europeans are not quite ready for the information highway to invade their homes.[13] And, as noted in the introduction to this chapter, the media themselves have limitations that slow down the adoption process.

We could expand the list of media in Figure 10–29 since it seems virtually all media are thinking interactive (yes, even outdoor). The important point is to recognize that interactive media will forever change the way marketers communicate with their audiences. The ability to target media will be greatly enhanced, traditional media may have to adapt, and media planners will have a lot of learning to do. Throughout the following chapters you will read more on each of these interactive media, with more detail regarding specific uses, advantages, and disadvantages.

FIGURE 10–29 An interactive glossary

Audiotex. These automated telephone information services are already widely used by publishers to deliver "soaps and scopes," stock quotes, sports scores, and other information to directory users. Audiotex is evolving into a more advertiser-oriented product with sponsored "tips" services and in-the-ad audiotex numbers that callers use to get more timely information on an advertiser's product or service. Many tips services are offering call completion to sponsoring advertisers, making the medium more transactional and measurable.

CD-ROM. Compact disk-read only memory. The CD-ROM player is a computer disk drive that runs CDs instead of magnetic floppy disks. The advantage: CDs have vastly greater storage capacity than floppies, and offer high quality and versatility. Uses include databases, catalogs, magazines, and product information, among others.

Fax on demand. A relatively low-tech service recognized for its ease of entry and potential for widespread use, given the proliferation of fax machines. Callers can request information that is timely, such as a restaurant menu or a research report from a financial services firm. Prepared material is then faxed to callers' fax machines.

Interactive TV. This platform has gotten the most attention in the relentless hype of the information superhighway. Interactive TV, whether delivered through cable, telephone, or wireless, could revolutionize the way Americans shop, pay their bills, learn, and entertain themselves. Customers could access information through one of the predicted 500 cable TV channels, select listings, and possibly explore multimedia ads for businesses. Transaction processing capabilities are another likely component of interactive TV. This platform offers perhaps the greatest capability to measure usage and consumer response to advertisements.

Internet. Developed in 1969 as a communications system robust enough to survive a nuclear war, the Internet was opened to commercial and public access in 1991. A section of the Net known as the World Wide Web is a network of networks accessible through computers. Websites provide information ranging from libraries and museums to government documents. Over 25,000 commercial websites provide product and service information.

Kiosks. Available in hotels, shopping malls, and other public places, interactive kiosks are another promising delivery point for electronic directory products. Using touch-screen technology, users can menu-drive their way into directory or catalog listings, banking services, and more.

Online services. America Online, CompuServe, Prodigy, and other online services deliver news, information, access to the Internet, and shopping services. Thousands of product and service advertisers use online services as an advertising medium.

Screen telephony. Telephones equipped (in most cases) with a keyboard and an LED display panel permit callers to enter and access data more easily than through a regular telephone. Considered a promising delivery vehicle by many because of its ease of use and low cost of entry, screen telephony could serve as a transitional platform until interactive TV gains sufficient penetration and consumer acceptance.

Source: Adapted from *Link* 6, no. 1, January 1994, p. 24; updated 1997.

FIGURE 10–30
Awareness and usage of interactive media

Advertising Age's third annual survey of 1,000 U.S. adults revealed the following information regarding awareness and use of interactive media.

	1994	1995
Heard of concept of interactive media	19.1%	44.7%
Aware of the Internet	NA	82.0
Aware of World Wide Web	NA	44.7
Have used video games	46.0	60.7
Have used CD-ROMs	9.0	35.5
Have used online services	15.7	23.6
Have used kiosks	17.7	12.6
Agree media should include advertising	29.7	29.7
Willing to pay for interactive services	48.0	41.3
Interested in interactive on home TV	34.0	44.8
Interested in interactive on home PC	25.3	36.5
Willing to pay for online services	39.4	46.1

NA: Not asked due to expected low level of awareness.
Source: *Advertising Age*—Articles and Opinions, January 15, 1997 (online).

SUMMARY

This chapter has presented an overview of the determination of media objectives, development of the media strategy, and the formalization of them in the form of a media plan. Sources of media information, characteristics of media, and an actual plan were also provided.

The media strategy must be designed to supplement and support the overall marketing and communications objectives. The objectives of this plan are designed to deliver the message the program has developed.

The basic task involved in the development of media strategy is to determine the best matching of media to the target market, given the constraints of the budget. The media planner attempts to balance reach and frequency and to deliver the message to the intended audience with a minimum of waste coverage. At the same time, a number of additional factors affect the media decision. Media strategy development has been called more of an art than a science because while many quantitative data are available, the planner also relies on creativity and nonquantifiable factors.

This chapter discussed many factors, including developing a proper media mix, determining target market and geographic coverage, scheduling, and balancing reach and frequency. Creative aspects, budget considerations, the need for flexibility in the schedule, and the use of computers in the media planning process were also considered.

An introduction to the new interactive media was provided. Specific interactive media will be discussed in more detail in later chapters.

KEY TERMS

media planning, 298
media objectives, 298
media strategies, 298
medium, 299
media vehicle, 299
reach, 299
sweeps periods, 299
index number, 305

waste coverage, 309
continuity, 310
flighting, 310
pulsing, 311
unduplicated reach, 313
duplicated reach, 313
program rating, 313

gross ratings points (GRPs), 314
target ratings points (TRPs), 314
effective reach, 315
average frequency, 316
absolute cost, 319
relative cost, 319

cost per thousand (CPM), 319
cost per ratings point (CPRP), 320
daily inch rate, 320
readers per copy, 321
pass-along rate, 321
interactive media, 324

DISCUSSION QUESTIONS

1. Why do many advertisers believe that interactive media offer advantages over more traditional media?
2. What is a brand development index? A category development index? How can marketers use these indexes?
3. Explain the difference between CPM and TPCM. Which would be of more relevance to the marketer?
4. What level of frequency is necessary to achieve an impact on the receiver?
5. Discuss some of the factors that are important in determining frequency levels. Give examples of each factor.
6. What is meant by readers per copy? How is this figure derived? What are some of the problems associated with this number?

7. Discuss the market situation being described by each of the following: high BDI and high CDI; high BDI and low CDI; low BDI and high CDI; and low BDI and low CDI.
8. Describe the four stages of developing the media plan. Briefly describe what occurs at each stage.
9. Obtain cost, circulation, and ratings information for some of your local media. Using the relative cost formulas provided in the text, compare the efficiencies of each.
10. Explain why more media are now presenting their relative cost figures as CPM. Discuss advantages and disadvantages of this.

APPENDIXES

A. Sources of Media Information

B. Media Plan for WD-40

APPENDIX A: SOURCES OF MEDIA INFORMATION

Cross-reference guide to advertising media sources

	General Information	Competitive Activities	Market Information (Geographic)	Audience Information (Target Groups)	Advertising Rates
Nonmedia information (general marketing)	1, 10, 15, 16, 21, 22, 23	1, 19	10, 11, 15, 16, 18, 20, 21, 24	15, 16, 21	
Multimedia or intermedia	1, 15, 16, 21	1, 13	18	2, 25	2
Daily newspapers				5, 15, 16, 21	2, 24
Weekly newspapers					24
Consumer magazines	14	13		15, 16, 21	2, 24
Farm publications				5, 26	2, 24
Business publications			6, 8	6, 26	2, 24
Network television		7, 13		4, 15, 16, 17, 21	2
Spot television		7, 13		4, 15, 16, 17, 21	2, 24
Network radio		7		12, 15, 16, 17, 21, 27	2
Spot radio				4, 5, 12, 17, 21	2, 24
Direct mail					2, 24
Outdoor		13			2, 9
Transit					2

1. *Advertising Age*
2. Advertising agency media estimating guides
3. American Business Press, Inc. (ABP)
4. Arbitron Ratings Company
5. Audit Bureau of Circulations (ABC)
6. Business/Professional Advertising Association (B/PAA) Media Data
7. Broadcast Advertisers Reports (BAR)
8. Business Publications Audit of Circulation (BPA)
9. *Buyer's Guide to Outdoor Advertising*
10. *State and Metropolitan Area Data Book*
11. *Editor & Publisher Market Guide*
12. Survey of World Advertising Expenditures, Stach/Inra/Heeper
13. Leading National Advertisers (LNA), Inc.
14. Magazine Publishers Association of America (MPA)
15. Mediamark Research, Inc. (MRI)
16. Mendelsohn Media Research, Inc. (MMR)
17. Nielsen Media Research Company
18. Prizm
19. SAMI Burke, Inc.
20. *Sales and Marketing Management Survey of Buying Power*
21. Simmons Market Research Bureau: *Study of Media and Markets*
22. *Standard Directory of Advertisers*
23. *Standard Directory of Advertising Agencies*
24. Standard Rate and Data Service
25. Telmar
26. Verified Audit Circulation Corporation (VAC)

Source: Adapted from Arnold M. Bantam, Donald W. Jugenheimer, and Peter B. Turk, *Advertising Media Sourcebook*, 3rd ed. (Lincolnwood, Ill.: NTC Business Books), pp. 8–9.

APPENDIX B: MEDIA PLAN FOR WD-40

WD–40
1997 Advertising Plan
Preliminary Strategic Direction

Phillips–Ramsey

WD-40 COMPANY: CONSUMER MEDIA PLANNING, 1997

WD-40's defined audience publication ranking was reviewed for selection of viable publication alternatives that provide coverage of the target in suitable editorial environments with satisfactory composition.

The resulting final plan will include a mixture of high-target-coverage publications to provide the cost efficiency and reach for the campaign companioned with high-composition publications with appropriate editorial environments to provide reach in WD-40's primary target niches (home improvement, automotive, and outdoor).

The attached plan outlines the publications that are recommended for initial negotiation. The plan provides circulation, open rate info, male/female ratios, readers per copy, WD-40 Target Audience delivery, and coverage and composition percentages for WD-40's target audience.

Estimated rates are provided at both the $\frac{1}{3}$-page and $\frac{1}{2}$-page ad size to estimate an anticipated schedule based on the calendar budget and also provide a benchmark for negotiations.

High-target *coverage* publications include:

Reader's Digest

Sports Illustrated

Field & Stream/Outdoor Life

High-target composition publications include:

Hot Rod

Popular Science

Field & Stream/Outdoor Life (indexes well in both areas!)

Sports Afield

North American Outdoor Group (will include *American How-To* as group negotiation)

Guns & Ammo

Family Handyman (can be packaged with *Reader's Digest*)

Home Mechanix

High-coverage publications that were discussed and eliminated include:

Parade and *USA Weekend*	High out-of-pocket ad unit cost does not serve continuity/frequency objective for the campaign. Weekly issue does not allow for build of reach via pass-along audience due to shelf life of the publications.

TV Guide	Editorial environment deemed not suitable for the industrial creative message. Weekly issue does not allow for build of reach via pass-along audience due to timely nature of the editorial product.
Better Homes & Gardens	Editorial environment deemed not suitable for the industrial creative message.
People	Editorial environment deemed not suitable for the industrial creative message.
National Geographic	Editorial environment deemed not suitable for the industrial creative message.
Good Housekeeping	Editorial environment deemed not suitable for the industrial creative message.
Popular Mechanics	Cannot be considered due to licensed lubricant product.

Given that some of the high-composition publications fall into publication groups, the following group buys will also be negotiated with final decision based on discounts offered. Groups to be negotiated and publication titles include:

Peterson Network	**Trade Press Group**
Hot Rod	*North American Hunter*
Sport	*North American Fisherman*
Guns & Ammo	*American How-To*
4 Wheel & Off-Road	

Times Mirror Group

Field & Stream

Outdoor Life

Home Mechanix

Popular Science

Marketing Objective

Increase consumption of WD-40 among end users.

Marketing Strategy

- Use advertising, public relations, and promotional programs to increase awareness of new uses for WD-40 among consumer segments with the highest propensity to adopt.
- Focus new use education programs on uses with the highest volume potential (i.e., cleaning/removing functions).

Advertising Objectives

- Increase awareness of new uses for WD-40, focusing on applications with the highest volume potential.
- Reinforce WD-40's position as an "industrial strength" product.

Target Audience

Current users of WD-40 who use WD-40 at work, at home, and at play. This target will provide WD-40 with the highest volume per capita consumption upon recognition of new uses because they will be able to apply the new uses to various activities. Additionally, this target can act as influencers to a broader market.

Advertising Strategy	• Continue running the "Proving Ground" campaign against key industrial segments where end users can be reached effectively with trade publications. • Develop a campaign that maximizes reach to the target with consumer media, but delivers a message that is credible and relevant to work situations. "Work" applications will reinforce the industrial positioning and provide credibility and transferability to home and leisure/hobby uses.
Media Objective	Maximize reach to the target audience while providing advertising program continuity throughout 1997.
Media Target Audience	Blue-collar workers who are also automotive do-it-yourselfers (DIY), home do-it-yourselfers, and/or outdoor enthusiasts (hunters, fishers, boaters).
Media Strategy	• Use industrial/trade publications to target key industrial segments who can be reached by this medium effectively. • Select media that will most cost-effectively reach the target, provide an appropriate environment for "at work" uses, and also provide overall impact against a minimum of 25 percent of the target. • Cable TV and magazines have been considered as viable options.
Media Elements Discussion	• Magazines and cable TV have been recommended as the viable alternatives for 1997 advertising. • Magazines provide the opportunity to narrowly define the target audience via use of selected publication titles. • Cable TV also provides the opportunity to select specific programming to enhance the selling message in appropriate environment. • Local media alternatives (including newspaper, spot radio, and outdoor) are not applicable to WD-40's national coverage objectives and would be utilized in market-specific emphasis situations only. • Network television is cost-prohibitive and does not serve the continuity objective of the campaign. • Network radio is also cost-prohibitive (proposed budget would yield 10 weeks at a minimal 50 points per week level) and does not serve the continuity objective of the campaign. • Traffic radio (10-second messages to emphasize specific uses) was explored but also did not serve the continuity objective.
Media Alternatives Discussion	Cross-tabulations were prepared for both the blue-collar worker audience and the composite do-it-yourself and outdoor enthusiast audience to determine media elements that index well for reach to these target audiences. Findings are as follows: • Cable networks that index well for both audiences include ESPN, TNN, TBS, Discover, the Learning Channel, and the Sci Fi Channel. • Television sporting events indexed high, but other television dayparts contained indices of 100 or below. • Radio index was high for the blue-collar worker (140), and a little above average (109) for the DIY and outdoor audiences. • Radio formats with high indices included album-oriented rock, country, and classic rock. • National radio networks with high indices included ABC Excel, ABC Galaxy, ABC Genesis, American Urban Network, Westwood, The Source, and ESPN.

- Newspaper usage did not have a high index for the blue-collar worker but was slightly above average for the DIY/outdoor target.

Industrial Advertising

It is recommended that key industrial categories that provide reach to the industrial end user be retained for the 1997 campaign.

MANUFACTURING

- *Industrial Maintenance & Plant Operation*, given its product tabloid format, provides the best alternative to reach the manufacturing plant floor.
- *Purchasing* magazine provides reach to the key manufacturing purchasing function in the plant.

AUTOMOTIVE

Motor Age reached the mechanics in repair shops via pass-along circulation. Ad placement inside training editorial enchances exposure to this target audience.

AVIATION

Aircraft Maintenance Technology delivers the hands-on mechanics and technicians in the aviation industry.

HVAC

Refrigeration Service & Contracting provides reach to the service technicians and contractors.

MAINTENANCE/CLEANING

Maintenance Solutions provides a new product tabloid format to reach the end user in this industry.

BICYCLE DEALERS

Bicycle Dealer Showcase provides reach to the bicycle dealers in a targeted editorial format that includes features on new products.

TRUCKING

- The publications in this category reach a primary management-focused subscriber base.
- Participation in the *Rand McNally Motor Carrier's Atlas* is recommended for continuation in 1997 for reach to the drivers in this industry.
- Industrial categories that have a retail emphasis in audience and ancillary categories are not recommended for participation in 1997. These categories include:
  - Marine (retail emphasis).
  - Gun (retail emphasis).
  - Rental equipment (ancillary category).
  - Locksmith (ancillary category).
  - Construction (end user audience better reached via consumer books).
  - Trucking (end user audience better reached via consumer books with the exception of the annual atlas).

Media readership profile

Target market: Blue-collar worker and composite DIYer or automotive DIYer or enthusiast
Population = 63,371 (000)
Percent of base = 33.59%

Rank	Media	UnWgt	Avg Aud (000)	Cov%	Rank Cov%	Comp%	Index
1	American Hunter	443	2,466	3.9	75	57.5	171
2	Sports Afield	463	2,676	4.2	70	57.5	171
3	North Amer Hunter	305	1,776	2.8	108	56.6	169
4	Workbench	387	1,829	2.9	106	56.5	168
5	Yachting	141	555	0.9	238	56.4	168
6	Home Mechanix	244	1,075	1.7	169	56.4	168
7*	North Amer Outdoor G	546	3,520	5.6	55	56.3	168
8	North Amer Fishermn	309	1,743	2.8	111	56.0	167
9	American Rifleman	566	2,972	4.7	66	55.8	166
10	Bassmaster	382	2,124	3.4	87	54.6	163
11	Outside	181	873	1.4	200	53.8	160
12	Outdoor Life	620	3,533	5.6	54	53.5	159
13	Boating	285	1,246	2.0	153	53.2	159
14	4 Wheel & Off Road	242	1,499	2.4	131	53.0	158
15	Motor Btg & Sailing	150	644	1.0	228	53.0	158
16	Backpacker	95	517	0.8	243	53.0	158
17	Four Wheeler	193	1,184	1.9	160	52.7	157
18	Circle Track	93	548	0.9	239	52.7	157
19*	Field & Stream/Outdoor	1,522	10,432	16.5	17	51.7	154
20	Flying	197	866	1.4	201	51.6	154
21	Easyriders	218	1,243	2.0	156	51.5	153
22	Popular Mechanics	1,073	4,993	7.9	39	51.4	153
23	Saltwater Sportsman	144	701	1.1	222	51.4	153
24	Popular Hot Rodding	287	1,648	2.6	118	51.1	152
25	Field & Stream	1,252	6,899	10.9	29	50.8	151
26	Family Handyman	471	2,024	3.2	91	50.7	151
27*†	Snow Country	1,912	935	1.5	192	50.7	151
28	Popular Science	806	3,805	6.0	51	50.5	150
29	Dirt Rider	85	616	1.0	232	50.4	150
30	Hot Rod	555	3,174	5.0	63	50.2	150
31	Car Craft	237	1,319	2.1	149	50.1	149
32	Guns & Ammo	564	3,217	5.1	62	49.9	149
33	Handguns	334	1,977	3.1	95	49.8	148
34*	Times Mirror Group	3,083	21,855	34.5	4	49.5	147

*Gross audience.   †Prototype.   Composition based on: Adults.
Source: 1995 MRI Doublebase. Weighted by population. ©MRI All rights reserved.

IMS modal reach and frequency report

Target: Adults
Pop (000): 191,663
Schedule: A

Media Summary	Inserts	Avg Aud (000)	Coverage (%)
Readers' Digest	4	51925	27.09
Family Handyman	6	3705	1.93
Sports Illustrated	7	21602	11.27
Hot Rod	6	6865	3.58
4 Wheel & Off Road	6	2700	1.41
Field & Stream	6	12769	6.66
Outdoor Life	6	5344	2.79
Sports Afield	4	3038	1.59

Calculations		Calculations	
Total inserts	45		
Gross impressions	559363	Gross rating points	292
		Net reach	111039
Reach percent	57.93		
Effective reach: 3+	80761	Eff. reach percent	42.14
		Average frequency	5.04
Median frequency	3.99		

IMS modal frequency report

Target: Adults
Pop (000): 191,663
Schedule: A

Frequency Level	Number Fx	% of Pop Fx	% of Reach Fx	Gross Imps Fx	% of Pop F+	% of Reach F+
0	80624	42.07	NA	NA	NA	NA
1	18323	9.56	16.50	18323	57.93	100.00
2	11954	6.24	10.77	23908	48.37	83.50
3	11261	5.88	10.14	33784	42.14	72.73
4	28333	14.78	25.52	113331	36.26	62.59
5	7805	4.07	7.03	39023	21.48	37.07
6	7003	3.65	6.31	42016	17.41	30.05
7	6298	3.29	5.67	44088	13.75	23.74
8	3529	1.84	3.18	28229	10.47	18.07
9	3038	1.58	2.74	27340	8.63	14.89

Fx = Average.   F+ = Effective.

IMS net/duplication report

Target: Adults
Pop (000): 191662

Media	Net Reach (000)	Reach %	Dup (000)	Dup % of Net
Reader's Digest Family Handyman	53733	28.04	1897	3.53
Reader's Digest Sports Illustrated	66828	34.87	6698	10.02
Reader's Digest Hot Rod	57160	29.82	1631	2.85
Reader's Digest 4 Wheel & Off Road	53820	28.08	805	1.50
Reader's Digest Field & Stream	59738	31.17	4956	8.30
Reader's Digest Outdoor Life	55153	28.78	2115	3.84
Reader's Digest Sports Afield	53636	27.98	1327	2.47
Family Handyman Sports Illustrated	24708	12.89	599	2.42
Family Handyman Hot Rod	10232	5.34	338	3.31
Family Handyman 4 Wheels & Off Road	6108	3.19	296	4.85
Family Handyman Field & Stream	15882	8.29	592	3.73
Family Handyman Outdoor Life	8662	4.52	387	4.47
Family Handyman Sports Afield	6628	3.46	115	1.74
Sports Illustrated Hot Rod	26789	13.98	1678	6.26
Sports Illustrated 4 Wheel & Off Road	23433	12.23	868	3.71
Sports Illustrated Field & Stream	31287	16.32	3084	9.86
Sports Illustrated Outdoor Life	25611	13.36	1334	5.21
Sports Illustrated Sports Afield	23660	12.34	980	4.14
Hot Rod 4 Wheel & Off Road	8381	4.37	1184	14.13
Hot Rod Field & Stream	18232	9.51	1403	7.69
Hot Rod Outdoor Life	11644	6.08	566	4.86
Hot Rod SportsAfield	9787	5.11	117	1.19
4 Wheel & Off Road Field & Stream	14742	7.69	727	4.93
4 Wheel & Off Road Outdoor Life	7626	3.98	418	5.49
4 Wheel & Off Road Sports Afield	5558	2.90	180	3.24
Field & Stream Outdoor Life	14762	7.70	3352	22.70
Field & Stream Sports Afield	14139	7.38	1668	11.80

Source: 1996 MRI Spring. Weighted by population. ©MRI All rights reserved.

WD-40 consumer media calendar 1997

Publication	Jan	Feb	Mar	Apr	May	Jun	Jul	Aug	Sep	Oct	Nov	Dec
Reader's Digest		X				X					X	
Family Handyman									X	X		
Sports Illustrated			X		X				X	X		
Hot Rod											X	X
4 Wheel & Off-Road		X		X		X						
Field & Stream			X					X				
Outdoor Life								X				
Sports Afield								X				

WD-40 industrial media calendar 1997

Publication	Jan	Feb	Mar	Apr	May	Jun	Jul	Aug	Sep	Oct	Nov	Dec
IMPO												X
Purchasing	X											
Plant Engineering		X	X		X				X			X
Plant Services			X									X
Motor Age					X			X		X		X
Motor	X					X						
Aircraft Maintenance & Technology		X					X					
Refrigeration Service & Contracting				X							X	
Maintenance Solutions		X			X				X			
Cleaning & Maintenance Management						X				X		
Bicycle Dealer Showcase			X									
Rand McNally Motor Carriers' Road Atlas 1997 issue (on sale 10/96)		X										

11

Evaluation of Broadcast Media

Chapter Objectives

- To examine the structure of the television and radio industries and the role of each medium in the advertising program.

- To consider the advantages and limitations of TV and radio as advertising media.

- To explain how advertising time is purchased for the broadcast media, how audiences are measured, and how rates are determined.

- To consider future trends in TV and radio and how they will influence the use of these media in advertising.

THE BOOM IN SPORTS PROGRAMMING

For many years, TV sports programming consisted primarily of football, baseball, and, to a lesser extent, basketball. When ESPN, the first cable network devoted entirely to sports programming, was launched in 1979 the critics declared that "all the good sports are already on the three networks." They ridiculed the network for broadcasting sports like stock-car racing, which was described as "two hours of left turns." No one is laughing at ESPN today. It is now one of the top cable networks with nearly 70 million subscribers and televises more than 4,800 live or original hours of sports programming that includes over 65 different sports. It has spawned two other U.S. sports networks—ESPN2, a combination of traditional and emerging sports, and ESPNEWS—and is planning a fourth network, which some speculate may be devoted to a single sport such as the once-ridiculed auto-racing (somebody likes watching all those left turns). There are also ESPN Radio Network, with 420 affiliates, and the ESPN SportsZone website, one of the most visited in cyberspace with over 20 million hits a week.

The success of the ESPN franchise is largely responsible for the current explosion in sports programming. Fans' hunger for all types of televised sports shows no signs of abating, and sports programming has become the key to the growth plans of most big media companies, including the Walt Disney Co. (which owns ABC and ESPN), Time Warner Inc., and News Corp.'s Fox Broadcasting Co.

The latest battleground in the sports programming war is 24-hour news, aimed at sports fiends who can't wait another minute for news from the sports world. ESPNEWS made its debut in November 1996; Time Warner's CNN/SI debuted a month later. The latter is an effort to weld the news-gathering prowess of CNN to the sports-journalism credibility of *Sports Illustrated* magazine.

Both Time Warner and Disney recognize that it will take time to build their sports-news networks because the field is so crowded. More than 20 national networks, both cable and broadcast, now carry significant sports programming and sports news is especially abundant. Numerous channels, including ESPN2 and CNN Headline News, "crawl" continuously updated scores across the bottom of the screen. Some services now beam a continuous stream of updates directly to a subscriber's personal pager, while the Internet also offers instant sports news. Both ESPNEWS and CNN/SI say they will break up the flow of scores and highlights by carrying live sports-news events such as press conferences.

While critics complain about a surfeit of sports, veteran sports programmers argue that they are expanding the size of the sports market rather than slicing it thinner. They point to the fact that the number of subscribers to national cable sports networks has jumped nearly 77 percent, from 253.6 million in late 1989 to 450.4 million at the end of 1996. They see the market expanding beyond the traditional adult male audience to include more women and children.

The boom in sports programming has led to frequent complaints about the proliferation of "junk sports" that seem to have sprung up merely to be televised. However, executives like ESPN president and CEO Steven M. Bornstein say that by offering viewers a variety of choices, their companies can attract viewers and make a tidy profit. The question is not really the size of the niche but rather the costs of providing the programming. A good case in point is the Winter X Games, an "extreme sports" event that ESPN created for a fraction of the multimillion rights to broadcast a major sport. Such events draw substantial audiences and have attracted major advertisers.

With digital television and its expanded channel capacity on the horizon, some say the sports-TV boom may just be

warming up and more sports offerings will be thrust on a seemingly ever-receptive public. This means women may face a greater challenge than ever in getting their husbands or boyfriends away from the TV set. Or vice versa!

Sources: Bruce Orwall, "Field Is Crowded, but Sports Still Score on TV," *The Wall Street Journal*, January 13, 1997, pp. B1, 8; Jeff Jensen, "Cable TV Marketer of the Year," *Advertising Age*, December 9, 1996, pp. S1–2.

The developments in sports programming are very important to marketers because they affect our primary form of entertainment, television. TV has virtually saturated households throughout the United States and most other countries and has become a mainstay in the lives of most people. The average American household watches nearly seven hours of TV a day, and the tube has become the predominant source of news and entertainment for many people. Nearly 80 percent of the TV households in the United States have a VCR, and many people have entertainment centers with big-screen TVs, VCRs, and stereos. On any given evening during the prime-time hours of 8 to 11 PM, more than 90 million people are watching TV. Popular shows like "Home Improvement" and "Seinfeld" may have more than 40 million viewers. The large numbers of people who watch television are important to the TV networks and stations because they can sell time on these programs to marketers who want to reach that audience with their advertising messages. Moreover, the qualities that make TV a great medium for news and entertainment also encourage creative ads that can have a strong impact on customers.

Radio is also an integral part of our lives. Many of us wake up to clock radios in the morning and rely on radio programs to inform and/or entertain us while we drive to work or school. For many people, radio is a constant companion in their cars, at home, even at work. The average American listens to the radio more than three hours each day.[1] Like TV viewers, radio listeners are an important audience for marketers.

In this chapter, we examine the broadcast media of TV and radio, including the general characteristics of each as well as their specific advantages and disadvantages. We examine how advertisers use TV and radio as part of their advertising and media strategies, how they buy TV and radio time, and how audiences are measured and evaluated for each medium. We also examine the factors that are changing the role of TV and radio as advertising media.

TELEVISION

It has often been said that television is the ideal advertising medium. Its ability to combine visual images, sound, motion, and color presents the advertiser with the opportunity to develop the most creative and imaginative appeals of any medium. However, TV does have certain problems that limit or even prevent its use by many advertisers.

Advantages of Television

TV has numerous advantages over other media, including creativity and impact, coverage and cost effectiveness, captivity and attention, and selectivity and flexibility.

CREATIVITY AND IMPACT

Perhaps the greatest advantage of TV is the opportunity it provides for presenting the advertising message. The interaction of sight and sound offers tremendous creative flexibility and makes possible dramatic, lifelike representations of products and services. TV commercials can be used to convey a mood or image for a brand as well as to develop emotional or entertaining appeals that help make a dull product appear interesting.

Television is also an excellent medium for demonstrating a product or service. For example, print ads are effective for showing a car and communicating information regarding its

features, but only a TV commercial can put you in the driver's seat and give you the sense of actually driving, as shown by the Porsche commercial in Exhibit 11–1.

COVERAGE AND COST EFFECTIVENESS

Television advertising makes it possible to reach large audiences. Nearly everyone, regardless of age, sex, income, or educational level, watches at least some TV. Most people do so on a regular basis. According to Nielsen estimates, over 267 million people, 77 percent of whom are 18 or older, are in TV households.[2]

Marketers selling products and services that appeal to broad target audiences find that TV lets them reach mass markets, often very cost efficiently. The average prime-time TV show reaches 11 million homes; a top-rated show like "ER" may reach nearly 20 million homes and perhaps twice that many viewers. In 1997, the average cost per thousand (CPM) homes reached was $11.18 for network evening shows and $3.85 for daytime weekly shows.[3]

Because of its ability to reach large audiences in a cost-efficient manner, TV is a popular medium among companies selling mass consumption products. Companies with widespread distribution and availability of their products and services use TV to reach the mass market and deliver their advertising messages at a very low cost per thousand. Television has become indispensable to large consumer package-goods companies, carmakers, and major retailers. Companies like Procter & Gamble and Coca-Cola spend more than 80 percent of their media advertising budget on various forms of TV—network, spot, cable, and syndicated programs. Figure 11–1 shows the top 25 network TV advertisers and their expenditures.

CAPTIVITY AND ATTENTION

Television is basically intrusive in that commercials impose themselves on viewers as they watch their favorite programs. Unless we make a special effort to avoid commercials, most of

Rank	Advertiser	Expenditures ($ millions)
1	Procter & Gamble Co.	$641.3
2	General Motors Corp.	500.9
3	Philip Morris Co.	475.3
4	Johnson & Johnson	388.6
5	PepsiCo	362.1
6	Ford Motor Co.	360.3
7	McDonald's Corp.	322.4
8	Kellogg Co.	271.7
9	Chrysler Corp.	239.7
10	Unilever NV	232.6
11	AT&T Corp.	227.6
12	Walt Disney Co.	209.0
13	Warner-Lambert Co.	200.9
14	American Home Products Corp.	182.9
15	MCI Communications Corp.	168.2
16	Grand Metropolitan	164.6
17	Toyota Motor Corp.	156.8
18	Anheuser-Busch Cos.	156.0
19	Sears, Roebuck & Co.	137.0
20	JCPenney Co.	126.0
21	Time Warner	123.0
22	Honda Motor Co.	120.0
23	Bristol-Myers Squibb Co.	113.2
24	Coca-Cola Co.	112.8
25	Nissan Motor Co.	110.5

Source: Reprinted with permission from the September 30, 1996 issue of *Advertising Age*, p. S38. Copyright Crain Communications, Inc. 1996.

us are exposed to thousands of them each year. The increase in viewing options and the penetration of VCRs, remote controls, and other automatic devices have made it easier for TV viewers to avoid commercial messages. Studies of consumers' viewing habits found that as much as a third of program audiences may be lost during commercial breaks.[4] However, the remaining viewers are likely to devote some attention to many advertising messages. As discussed in Chapter 5, the low-involvement nature of consumer learning and response processes may mean TV ads have an effect on consumers simply through heavy repetition and exposure to catchy slogans and jingles.

SELECTIVITY AND FLEXIBILITY

Television has often been criticized for being a nonselective medium, since it is difficult to reach a precisely defined market segment through the use of TV advertising. But some selectivity is possible due to variations in the composition of audiences as a result of program content, broadcast time, and geographic coverage. For example, Saturday morning TV caters to children; Saturday and Sunday afternoon programs are geared to the sports-oriented male; and weekday daytime shows appeal heavily to homemakers.

With the growth of cable TV, advertisers refine their coverage further by appealing to groups with specific interests such as sports, news, history, the arts, or music. Exhibit 11–2 shows an ad promoting Animal Planet, a new cable network launched by the Discovery Channel, that focuses solely on animals.

Advertisers can also adjust their media strategies to take advantage of different geographic markets through local or spot ads in specific market areas. Ads can be scheduled

to run repeatedly or to take advantage of special occasions. For example, companies such as Anheuser-Busch and Gillette are major sponsors during baseball's World Series, which allows them to advertise heavily to men who constitute the primary market for their products.

Limitations of Television

Although television is unsurpassed from a creative perspective, the medium has several disadvantages that limit or preclude its use by many advertisers. These problems include high costs, the lack of selectivity, the fleeting nature of a television message, commercial clutter, limited viewer attention, and distrust of TV ads.

COSTS

Despite the efficiency of TV in reaching large audiences, it is an expensive medium in which to advertise. The high cost of TV stems not only from the expense of buying air time but also from the costs of producing a quality commercial. Production costs for a national brand 30-second spot average nearly $300,000 and can reach over a million for more elaborate commercials.[5] Many advertisers such as Burger King, Coca-Cola, and others develop commercials specifically for certain ethnic markets such as African-Americans and Hispanics.[6] More advertisers are using media-driven creative strategies that require production of a variety of commercials, which drive up their costs. Even local ads can be expensive to produce and often are not of high quality. The high costs of producing and airing commercials often price small- and medium-size advertisers out of the market.

LACK OF SELECTIVITY

Some selectivity is available in television through variations in programs and cable TV. But advertisers who are seeking a very specific, often small, target audience find the coverage of TV often extends beyond their market, reducing its cost effectiveness (as discussed in Chapter 10). Geographic selectivity can be a problem for local advertisers such as retailers, since a station bases its rates on the total market area it reaches. For example, stations in Pittsburgh, Pennsylvania, reach viewers in western and central Pennsylvania, eastern Ohio, northern West Virginia, and even parts of Maryland. The small company whose market is limited to the immediate Pittsburgh area may find TV an inefficient media buy, since the stations cover a larger geographic area than the merchant's trade area.

Audience selectivity is improving as advertisers target certain groups of consumers through the type of program or day and/or time when they choose to advertise. However, TV still does not offer as much audience selectivity as radio, magazines, newspapers, or direct mail for reaching precise segments of the market.

FLEETING MESSAGE

TV commercials usually last only 30 seconds or less and leave nothing tangible for the viewer to examine or consider. Commercials have become shorter and shorter as the demand for a limited amount of broadcast time has intensified and advertisers try to get more impressions from their media budgets. As shown in Figure 11–2, 30-second commercials became the norm in the mid-1970s. In September 1986, the three networks began accepting 15-second spots across their full schedules (except during children's viewing time). Since 1987, these shorter spots have been accounting for about a third of all network commercials.

An important factor in the decline in commercial length has been the spiraling inflation in media costs over the past decade. With the average cost of a prime-time spot reaching over $100,000, many advertisers see shorter commercials as the only way to keep their media costs in line. A 15-second spot typically sells for half the price of a 30-second spot. By using 15- or even 10-second commercials, advertisers think they can run additional spots to reinforce the message or reach a larger audience. Many advertisers believe shorter commercials can deliver a message just as effectively as longer spots for much less money.

Several years ago, many advertising people predicted 15-second spots would become the dominant commercial unit by the early 1990s. However, the growth in the use of 15-second commercials peaked at 38 percent in 1989 and has now declined to 32 percent. The decline may be due to several factors, including creative considerations, lower prices for network time, and a desire by the networks to restrict clutter.[7]

CLUTTER

The problems of fleeting messages and shorter commercials are compounded by the fact that the advertiser's message is only one of many spots and other nonprogramming material seen during a commercial break, so it may have trouble being noticed. One of advertisers' greatest concerns with TV advertising is the potential decline in effectiveness because of such *clutter*.

The next time you watch TV, count the number of commercials, promotions for the news or upcoming programs, or public service announcements that appear during a station break and you will appreciate why clutter is a major concern. A study sponsored by the advertising industry found that the three major networks ran more than 13 minutes of nonprogramming material in a one-hour period during prime time; on some cable networks, the amounts exceeded 17 minutes.[8] With all of these messages competing for our attention, it is easy to

FIGURE 11–2 Changes in percentage of network commercials by length

Commercial Length	1965	1975	1980	1985	1987	1988	1989	1990	1994	1995
15	–	–	–	10	31	36	38	35	30	32
30	23	93	96	84	65	61	57	60	66	65
60	77	6	2	2	2	2	2	2	2	1
All others	–	1	2	4	2	1	3	3	2	2

understand why the viewer comes away confused or even annoyed and unable to remember or properly identify the product or service advertised.

One cause of clutter is the use of shorter commercials and **split-30s**, 30-second spots in which the advertiser promotes two different products with separate messages. Clutter also results when the networks and individual stations run promotional announcements for their shows, making more time available for commercials and redistributing time to popular programs. For many years, the amount of time available for commercials was restricted by the Code Authority of the National Association of Broadcasters to 9.5 minutes per hour during prime time and 12 minutes during nonprime time. The Justice Department suspended the code in 1982 on the grounds that it violated antitrust law. At first the networks did not alter their time standards, but in recent years they have increased the number of commercial minutes in their schedules. The networks argue that they must increase commercial inventory or raise their already steep rates. Advertisers and agencies have been pressuring the networks to cut back on the commercials and other sources of clutter.

LIMITED VIEWER ATTENTION

When advertisers buy time on a TV program, they are not purchasing guaranteed exposure but rather the opportunity to communicate a message to large numbers of consumers. But there is increasing evidence that the size of the viewing audience shrinks during a commercial break. People leave the room to go to the bathroom or to get something to eat or drink, or they are distracted in some other way during commercials.

Getting consumers to pay attention to commercials has become an even greater challenge in recent years. The increased presence of VCRs and remote controls has led to the problems of zipping and zapping. **Zipping** occurs when customers fast-forward through commercials as they play back a previously recorded program. A study by Nielsen Media Research found that while 80 percent of recorded shows are actually played back, viewers zip past more than half of the commercials.[9] Another study found that most viewers fully or partially zipped commercials when watching a prerecorded program.[10]

Zapping refers to changing channels to avoid commercials. Over three-quarters of homes in the U.S. now have television sets with remote controls, which enable viewers to switch channels easily. An observational study conducted by John Cronin found as much as a third of program audiences may be lost to electronic zapping when commercials appear.[11] The Nielsen study found that most commercial zapping occurs at the beginning and, to a lesser extent, the end of a program. Zapping at these points is likely to occur because commercial breaks are so long and predictable. Zapping has also been fueled by the emergence of 24-hour continuous format programming on cable channels such as CNN, MTV, and ESPN. Viewers can switch over for a few news headlines, sports scores, or a music video and then switch back to the program. Research shows that young adults zap more than older adults, and men are more likely to zap than women.[12]

How to inhibit zapping? The networks use certain tactics to hold viewers' attention, such as previews of the next week's show or short closing scenes at the end of a program. Some programs start with action sequences before the opening credits and commercials. A few years ago, Anheuser-Busch began using the Bud Frame, in which the ad frames live coverage of a sporting event. Some advertisers believe that producing different executions of a campaign theme is one way to maintain viewers' attention. Others think the ultimate way to zap-proof commercials is to produce creative advertising messages that will attract and hold viewers' attention, such as the Nissan spot in Exhibit 11–3. However, this is easier said than done, as many consumers just do not want to watch commercials. As more viewers gain access to remote controls and the number of channels increases, the zapping problem is likely to continue.

DISTRUST AND NEGATIVE EVALUATION

To many critics of advertising, TV commercials personify everything that is wrong with the industry. Critics often single out TV commercials because of their pervasiveness and the intrusive nature of the medium. Consumers are seen as defenseless against the barrage of TV

EXHIBIT 11–3
Developing creative commercials that hold viewers' attention is one answer to the zapping problem

ads, since they cannot control the transmission of the message and what appears on their screens. Viewers dislike TV advertising when they believe it is offensive, uninformative, or shown too frequently, or when they do not like its content.[13] Studies have shown that of the various forms of advertising, distrust is generally the highest for TV commercials.[14] Also, concern has been raised about the effects of TV advertising on specific groups, such as children or the elderly.[15]

BUYING TELEVISION TIME

A number of options are available to advertisers that choose to use TV as part of their media mix. They can purchase time in a variety of program formats that appeal to various types and sizes of audiences. They can purchase time on a national, regional, or local basis. Or they can sponsor an entire program, participate in the sponsorship, or use spot announcements during or between programs.

The purchase of TV advertising time is a highly specialized phase of the advertising business, particularly for large companies spending huge sums of money. Large advertisers that do a lot of TV advertising generally use agency media specialists or specialized media buying services to arrange the media schedule and purchase TV time. Decisions have to be made regarding national or network versus local or spot purchases, selection of specific stations, sponsorship versus participation, different classes of time, and appropriate programs. Local advertisers may not have to deal with the first decision, but they do face all the others.

Network versus Spot

A basic decision for all advertisers is allocating their TV media budget to network versus local or spot announcements. Most national advertisers use network schedules to provide national coverage and supplement this with regional or local spot purchases to reach markets where additional coverage is desired.

NETWORK ADVERTISING

A common way advertisers disseminate their messages is by purchasing air time from a **television network**. A network assembles a series of affiliated local TV stations, or **affiliates**, to which it supplies programming and services. These affiliates, most of which are independently owned, contractually agree to preempt time during specified hours for programming provided by the networks and to carry the national advertising within the program. The networks share the advertising revenue they receive during these time periods with the affiliates. The affiliates are also free to sell commercial time in nonnetwork periods and during station breaks in the preempted periods to both national and local advertisers.

The three traditional major networks are NBC, ABC, and CBS. The Fox Broadcasting Co. broadcasts its programs over a group of affiliated independent stations and has become

"It is important to understand how co-workers at Fox apply the research and marketing strategies we develop."

Barbara is the head of affiliate research and marketing for Fox Broadcasting, where she supervises a staff of three. She and her staff are responsible for providing research on 169 Fox affiliates throughout the U.S. to Fox management and stations. They analyze ratings and market research information for each affiliate's news, prime-time programs, and Fox Kids programs. Barbara's position carries a great deal of responsibility and requires considerable expertise. She is responsible for assisting individual Fox stations in marketing and program analysis in their market. She gets involved in the promotion of these programs and helps to title them to achieve optimal ratings success. In working with the Nielsen numbers, her department analyzes trends and sets up tracking programs to help the affiliates understand Nielsen's methodology and the impact of sampling or other changes in their particular markets. When there are problems, particularly with the ratings, Barbara is very involved with helping find a resolution.

Barbara is responsible for helping the Fox affiliate stations develop sales programs and presentations. Her department prepares presentations and tapes that are sent to all affiliates on topics such as new program audience estimates, sweeps performance, reaching upscale markets, and product usage patterns. Presentations are also developed for Network Distribution representatives explaining various Fox initiatives such as strategies for the Fox Kids Network, Fox SummerBlast, and ratings performance. She is also responsible for planning and executing annual sales seminars which are attended by over 1,300 salespeople from the 169 Fox affiliates.

Barbara's marketing and media career began after she received a Marketing degree from the University of Oregon. Her first job was part of a four-person marketing team responsible for promoting a local bus service. She then took a position as an account executive at GMA research, a Seattle-based research organization, where she conducted full-service research projects for media, adver-

tising, political, retail, and manufacturing clients. Striking out on her own, Barbara started a consulting firm, with clients like GMA, Seattle University, and Golden Grain (Rice a Roni and Giardelli brands). She then moved on to become the research manager at KING TV-5, a Seattle NBC affiliate. At KING she was responsible for analyzing ratings information and developing sales and marketing presentations. While working in Seattle, Barbara earned her MBA degree at Seattle University.

In 1990 Barbara moved to Los Angeles to become the research manager for KNBC TV4. In 1994 she moved to New York to head the NBC-TV stations research department which provides research information, analysis, and recommendations to management, sales, and marketing for the NBC-owned local TV stations. One interesting project she was involved with was determining whether NBC-owned stations should maintain their local identities or assume the NBC name (for example, NBC TV4). She concluded that local stations often have their own identities which are important to maintain to maximize ratings. She also worked on projects such as researching whether the popular "Days of Our Lives" soap opera should switch time slots to help NBC achieve higher ratings in its daytime programming.

While at NBC Barbara was on the advisory team for TV Azteca, which is the second largest Mexican television network. She was also a member of the 1996 Olympic Sales and Marketing Team, where she managed development, execution, and distribution of materials, tapes, and presentations for NBC-TV's national Olympics sales efforts.

Now with Fox Broadcasting, Barbara maintains her management philosophy of giving credit where credit is due. She believes that recognizing employees for jobs well done means that more jobs are done well. Barbara's marketing philosophy of taking a strong customer orientation is very effective internally. Her co-workers are considered customers and she strives to understand their needs and how they use and apply the products she develops, such as research and marketing strategies, to maximize results for the company.

the fourth major network (Exhibit 11–4). A number of Fox's programs, such as "The Simpsons," "Melrose Place," and "The X-Files," are quite popular. Fox has also become a major player in sports programming with its contracts to broadcast major sporting events such as the Super Bowl and the World Series.[16]

The networks have affiliates throughout the nation for almost complete national coverage. When an advertiser purchases air time from one of these four national networks, the commercial is transmitted across the nation through the affiliate station network. Network advertising truly represents a mass medium, as the advertiser can broadcast its message simultaneously throughout the country.

A major advantage of network advertising is the simplification of the purchase process. The advertiser has to deal with only one party or media representative to air a commercial nationwide. The networks also offer the most popular programs and generally control prime-time programming. Advertisers interested in reaching huge nationwide audiences generally buy network time during the prime viewing hours of 8 to 11 PM eastern time.

The major drawback is the high cost of network time. Figure 11–3 shows cost estimates for a 30-second spot on the three networks' prime-time shows during the 1996–97 television season.[17] Many of the popular prime-time shows charge $200,000 or more for a 30-second spot; the highest-rated shows, like "Seinfeld" and "ER," can command half a million dollars. Thus, only advertisers with large budgets can afford to use network advertising on a regular basis.

Availability of time can also be a problem as more advertisers turn to network advertising to reach mass markets. Traditionally, most prime-time commercial spots, particularly on the popular shows, are sold during the **up-front market**, a buying period that occurs before the TV season begins. Advertisers hoping to use prime-time network advertising must plan their media schedules and often purchase TV time as much as a year in advance. Demands from large clients who are heavy TV advertisers force the biggest agencies to participate in the up-front market. However, TV time is also purchased during the **scatter market** that runs through the TV season. Some key incentives for buying up front, such as cancellation options and lower prices, are becoming more available in the quarterly scatter market. Network TV can also be purchased on a regional basis, so

EXHIBIT 11—4
Fox has become the fourth major network with popular shows and sports programming

FOX
Broadcasting Company
The **new** #2.

•FOX is the #2 television network among Adults 18–49.

Source: Nielsen NTI average audience estimates, including preliminary estimates, to head-to-head common hours of prime time. Broadcast season-to-date (9/16/96–2/23/97) and February sweep (1/30–2/26/97). Subject to qualification.

©1997 FOX BROADCASTING COMPANY

FIGURE 11–3

What TV shows cost: estimated price of a 30-second spot on the four major networks

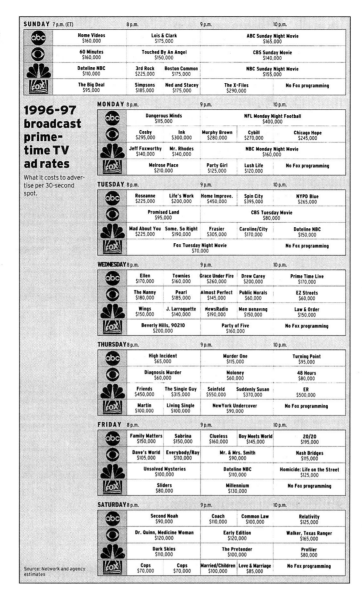

SPOT AND LOCAL ADVERTISING

Spot advertising refers to commercials shown on local TV stations, with time negotiated and purchased directly from the individual stations. All nonnetwork advertising done by a national advertiser is known as **national spot advertising**; air time sold to local firms such as retailers, restaurants, banks, and auto dealers is known as **local advertising**. Local advertisers want media whose coverage is limited to the geographic markets in which they do business. This may be difficult to accomplish with TV, but many local businesses are large enough to make efficient use of TV advertising.

Spot advertising offers the national advertiser flexibility in adjusting to local market conditions. The advertiser can concentrate commercials in areas where market potential is greatest or where additional support is needed. This appeals to advertisers with uneven distribution or limited advertising budgets, as well as those interested in test marketing or introducing a product in limited market areas. National advertisers often use spot television advertising through local retailers or dealers as part of their cooperative advertising programs and to provide local dealer support.

that an advertiser's message can be aired in certain sections of the country with one media purchase.

A major problem for national advertisers is that spot advertising can be more difficult to acquire, since the time must be purchased from a number of local stations. Moreover, there are more variations in the pricing policies and discount structure of individual stations than of the networks. However, this problem has been reduced somewhat by the use of **station reps**, individuals who act as sales representatives for a number of local stations in dealings with national advertisers.

Spot ads are subject to more commercial clutter, since local stations can sell time on network-originated shows only during station breaks between programs, except when network advertisers have not purchased all the available time. Viewership generally declines during station breaks, as people may leave the room, zap to another channel, attend to other tasks, or stop watching TV.

While spot advertising is mostly confined to station breaks between programs on network-originated shows, local stations sell time on their own programs, which consist of news, movies, syndicated shows, or locally originated programs. Most cities have independent stations that spot advertisers use. Local advertisers find the independent stations attractive because they generally have lower rates than the major network affiliates.

The decision facing most national advertisers is how to combine network and spot advertising to make effective use of their TV advertising budget. Another factor that makes spot advertising attractive to national advertisers is the growth in syndication.

SYNDICATION

Advertisers may also reach TV viewers by advertising on **syndicated programs**, shows that are sold or distributed on a station-by-station, market-by-market basis. A syndicator seeks to sell its program to one station in every market. There are several types of syndicated programming. *Off-network syndication* refers to reruns of network shows that are bought by individual stations. Shows that are popular in off-network syndication include "Seinfeld" "Roseanne," and "The Simpsons." The FCC prime-time access rule forbids large-market network affiliates from carrying these shows from 7 to 8 PM, but independent stations are not affected by this restriction. A show must have a minimum number of episodes before it is eligible for syndication, and there are limits on network involvement in the financing or production of syndicated shows.

Off-network syndication shows are very important to local stations because they provide quality programming with an established audience. The syndication market is also very important to the studios that produce programs and sell them to the networks. Most prime-time network shows initially lose money for the studios, since the licensing fee paid by the networks does not cover production costs. Over four years (the time it takes to produce the 88 episodes needed to break into syndication), half-hour situation comedies often run up a deficit of nearly $12 million, and losses on a one-hour drama show can reach $30 million. However, the producers recoup their money when they sell the show to syndication.

First-run syndication refers to shows produced specifically for the syndication market. The first-run syndication market is made up of a variety of shows, including some that did not make it as network shows and are moved into syndication while new episodes are being produced. Examples of popular first-run syndication shows include talk shows like "Live with Regis & Kathie Lee," "Jerry Springer," and "Rosie O"Donnell" and dramas such as "Star Trek: Voyager" and "Highlander."

Advertiser-supported or *barter syndication* is the practice of selling shows to stations in return for a portion of the commercial time in the show, rather than (or in addition to) cash. The commercial time from all stations carrying the show is packaged into national units and sold to national advertisers. The station sells the remaining time to local and spot advertisers. Both off-network and first-run syndicated programs are offered through barter syndication. Usually, more than half of the advertising time is presold, and the remainder is available for sale by the local advertiser. Barter syndication allows national advertisers to participate in the syndication market with the convenience of a network-type media buy, while local stations get free programming and can sell the remainder of the time to local or spot advertisers. Recently, the straight barter deal has given way to more barter/cash arrange-

ments, where the station pays for a program at a reduced rate and accepts a number of preplaced bartered ads. Top-rated barter syndicated programs include "Wheel of Fortune," "Jeopardy," and "The Oprah Winfrey Show."

Syndication now accounts for more than a third of the national broadcast audience and has become a very big business, generating ad revenue comparable to any of the big three networks. Syndicated shows have become more popular than network shows in certain dayparts, such as daytime, early prime time, and late fringe (Figure 11–4). In some markets, syndicated shows like "Wheel of Fortune" draw a larger audience than the network news.

Many national advertisers use syndicated shows to broaden their reach, save money, and target certain audiences. For example, "Baywatch" is one of the most popular shows in syndication because it reaches the highly sought after, and often difficult to reach, young adult audience (ages 18 to 34) and is more cost effective than network shows. Figure 11–5 shows the top 10 syndicated programs in 1997.

Syndication has certain disadvantages, such as more commercial time and thus more clutter. The audience for syndicated shows is often older and more rural, and syndicators do not supply as much research information as the networks do. Syndication also creates more problems for media buyers, since a syndicated show may not be seen in a particular market or may be aired during an undesirable time period. Thus, media buyers have to look at each market and check air times and other factors to put together a syndication schedule.

FIGURE 11–4
Syndication delivers big audiences in many dayparts

Daypart	Hours	Share of National Broadcast
Daytime	M–F 9 AM–4 PM	45%
Early prime	M–F 4–8 PM	85
Prime time	M–S 8–11 PM	7
Late fringe	M–S 11 PM–1 AM	26
Children	M–F and weekends	40

Sources: Nielsen, NTI, NSS, 4th quarter 1995.

FIGURE 11–5
Top ten regularly scheduled syndicated programs

Rank	Program	Rating %
1	Wheel of Fortune	14.1
2	Jeopardy	11.3
3	Wheel of Fortune (weekend)	9.2
4	Oprah Winfrey Show	8.3
5	Seinfeld	8.0
6	Home Improvement	8.0
7	Jeopardy (weekend)	7.2
8	Entertainment Tonight	6.5
9	Rosie O'Donnell	6.0
10	Inside Edition	5.4

Source: Nielsen Report on Syndicated Programs, February 1997.

Methods of Buying Time

In addition to deciding whether to use network versus spot advertising, advertisers must decide whether to sponsor an entire program, participate in a program, or use spot announcements between programs. Sponsorship of a program and participations are available on either a network or a local market basis, whereas spot announcements are available only from local stations.

SPONSORSHIP

Under a **sponsorship** arrangement, an advertiser assumes responsibility for the production and usually the content of the program as well as the advertising that appears within it. In the early days of TV, most programs were produced and sponsored by corporations and were identified by their name, for example, "Texaco Star Theater" and "The Colgate Comedy Hour." Today most shows are produced by either the networks or independent production companies that sell them to a network.

Some companies are becoming more involved in the production business. For example, in 1995 Procter & Gamble, which has been producing soap operas since 1950, entered into a three-year agreement with Paramount Television Groups to develop shows for network TV and first-run syndication. P&G executives say this will help them deal with threats from new media such as the Internet, pay-per-view, and interactive TV. A consortium of nine major advertisers—AT&T, Campbell Soup, General Motors, Coca-Cola, Sears, McDonald's, Clorox, Coors, and Reebok—recently joined Television Production Partners, a new venture to develop movies, specials, and limited-run series. Each company will choose which programs it wants to be involved with and take a portion of the commercial spots.[18]

Several major companies have been sponsoring special programs for many years, such as the Kraft Masterpiece Theater and Hallmark Hall of Fame dramatic series. In 1994 Hallmark acquired RHI Entertainment Inc., the company that produces its wholesome Hall of Fame productions as well as TV miniseries and movies. Sole sponsorship of programs, which is usually limited to specials, has been declining steadily since the mid-1970s. Some companies, including Ford, AT&T, General Electric, IBM, and Chrysler, do still use program sponsorships.

A company might choose to sponsor a program for several reasons. Sponsorship allows the firm to capitalize on the prestige of a high-quality program, enhancing the image of the company and its products. Ethical Perspective 11–1 discusses the favorable publicity Ford received when it sponsored the commercial-free television debut of the Holocaust movie *Schindler's List*. Companies also sponsor programs to gain more control over the shows carrying their commercials. For example, Wendy's International has been involved in sponsorship of family-oriented programs.

Another reason is that the sponsor has control over the number, placement, and content of its commercials. Commercials can be of any length as long as the total amount of commercial time does not exceed network or station regulations. Advertisers introducing a new product line often sponsor a program and run commercials that are several minutes long to introduce and explain the product. IBM used this strategy to introduce its new generation of personal computers. While these factors make sponsorship attractive to some companies, the high costs of sole sponsorship limit this option to large firms. Most commercial time is purchased through other methods, such as participations.

PARTICIPATIONS

Most advertisers either cannot afford the costs of sponsorship or want greater flexibility than sole sponsorship permits. Nearly 90 percent of network advertising time is sold as **participations**, with several advertisers buying commercial time or spots on a particular program. An advertiser can participate in a certain program once or several times on a regular or irregular basis. Participating advertisers have no financial responsibility for production of the program; this is assumed by the network or individual station that sells and controls the commercial time.

There are several advantages to participations. First, the advertiser has no long-term commitment to a program, and expenditures can be adjusted to buy whatever number of

Ethical Perspective 11–1
NBC and Ford Take a Risk on Schindler's List

On a Sunday evening in February 1997, NBC aired *Schindler's List*, Steven Spielberg's Academy Award-winning movie, for the first time on network television. The 3½-hour drama is based on Oskar Schindler, a Nazi war profiteer who saved the lives of more than 1,000 Jewish people during the Holocaust. NBC's airing of *Schindler's List* marked a major breakthrough for network TV in terms of both programming and advertising. It was the first movie aired on network TV to receive a TV-M rating and it was shown with no commercial interruptions.

The TV-M rating, which is based on the industry's new ratings system, cautions viewers: "This program may contain mature themes, profane language, graphic violence and explicit sexual content." Only a few scenes were edited from the film's original version, and it contained some profane language, nudity, and numerous violent scenes. Many people in the TV industry felt NBC took a major risk in showing the movie on Sunday night, which has traditionally been reserved for relatively light family fare.

NBC's gamble paid off. *Schindler* earned a 23.8 in the overnight ratings, putting it in the same league as "Seinfeld" and "ER," which are usually ranked as the most-watched shows in the country. The film attracted more than 65 million viewers for NBC's best Sunday of regular programming since it began tracking overnight ratings 14 years ago.

NBC wasn't the only company to take a risk airing *Schindler's List*. It was also a winning gamble for the Ford Motor Co., which was the only sponsor of the movie and aired it without commercials. Ford broadcast a 60-second image ad before and after the movie. The Ford logo also appeared on two short intermissions during the film, though no commercials were shown. Ford's decision not to show any ads was praised by television and film critics, who noted that commercial interruptions would have violated the film's extremely serious nature. Although Ford declined to reveal its budget for the sponsorship, estimates were that it was around $5 million.

Advertising experts say Ford's sole sponsorship could have backfired if people perceived it as cashing in on the Holocaust victims. It is well known that the company's founder, Henry Ford, was a virulent anti-Semite who feared a Jewish plot to rule the world. Ford Motor Co.'s North American news manager says, "We thought this was a perfect thing for us to sponsor. We believe in learning from the past."

Ford officials said the company received nearly three dozen calls the day after *Schindler's List* aired on NBC thanking the company for its sponsorship. Ford also received a great deal of favorable publicity in the media for its willingness to sponsor the film and forgo the commercials. As one network media buyer says, "In the end, it was handled magnificently. It really was a very big media coup for Ford."

Sources: Kyle Pope, "Sunday TV Fare May Get Serious after *Schindler*," *The Wall Street Journal*, February 25, 1997, pp. B1, 8; John Freeman, "For TV, Ford Alike, *List* a Landmark," *San Diego Union*, February 25, 1997, pp. E1, 6.

participation spots fit within the budget. This is particularly important to small advertisers with a limited budget. The second advantage is that the TV budget can be spread over a number of programs, which provides for greater reach in the media schedule.

The disadvantage of participations is that the advertiser has little control over the placement of ads, and there may also be problems with availability. Preference is given to advertisers willing to commit to numerous spots, and the firm trying to buy single spots in more than one program may find that time is unavailable in certain shows, especially during prime time.

SPOT ANNOUNCEMENTS

As discussed earlier, spot announcements are bought from the local stations and generally appear during time periods adjacent to network programs (hence the term **adjacencies**), rather than within them. Spot announcements are most often used by purely local advertisers but are also bought by companies with no network schedule (because of spotty or limited distribution) and by large advertisers that use both network and spot advertising.

Selecting Time Periods and Programs

Another consideration in buying TV time is selecting the right period and program for the advertiser's commercial messages. The cost of TV advertising time varies depending on the time of day and the particular program, since audience size varies as a function of these two factors. TV time periods are divided into **dayparts**, which are specific segments of a broadcast day.

The time segments that make up the programming day vary from station to station. However, a typical classification of dayparts for a weekday is shown in Figure 11–6. The var-

FIGURE 11–6
Common television dayparts

Morning	7:00 AM–9:00 AM, Monday through Friday
Daytime	9:00 AM–4:30 PM, Monday through Friday
Early fringe	4:30 PM–7:30 PM, Monday through Friday
Prime-time access	7:30 PM–8:00 PM, Sunday through Saturday
Prime-time	8:00 PM–11:00 PM, Monday through Saturday, and 7:00 PM–11 PM, Sunday
Late news	11:00–11:30 PM, Monday through Friday
Late fringe	11:30–1:00 AM, Monday through Friday

ious daypart segments attract different audiences in both size and nature, so advertising rates vary accordingly. Prime-time draws the largest audiences, with 8:30 to 9 PM being the most watched half-hour time period and Sunday the most popular night for television. Since firms that advertise during prime time must pay premium rates, this daypart is dominated by the large national advertisers.

The various dayparts are important to advertisers since they attract different demographic groups. For example, daytime TV generally attracts women; early morning attracts women and children. The late-fringe (late-night) daypart period has become popular among advertisers trying to reach young adults who tune into "The Late Show with David Letterman" on CBS and NBC's "The Tonight Show with Jay Leno." Audience size and demographic composition also vary depending on the type of program. Situation comedies attract the largest prime-time audiences, with women 18 to 34 comprising the greatest segment of the audience. Feature films rank second, followed by general drama shows. Women 55 and older are the largest audience segment for these programs.

Cable Television

THE GROWTH OF CABLE

Perhaps the most significant development in the broadcast media has been the expansion of **cable television**. Cable, or CATV (community antenna television), which delivers TV signals through wire rather than the airways, was developed to provide reception to remote areas that couldn't receive broadcast signals. Cable then expanded to metropolitan areas and grew rapidly due to the improved reception and wider selection of stations it offered subscribers. Cable has experienced substantial growth during the past two decades. In 1975, only 13 percent of TV households had cable. By 1996, cable penetration reached 68 percent, or 65.4 million households.[19]

Cable subscribers pay a monthly fee for which they receive an average of more than 30 channels, including the local network affiliates and independent stations, various cable networks, superstations, and local cable system channels. Cable networks and channels have a dual revenue stream; they are supported by both subscriber fees and ad revenue. Cable operators also offer programming that is not supported by commercial sponsorship and is available only to households willing to pay a fee beyond the monthly subscription charge. These premium channels include HBO, Showtime, and the Movie Channel.

Cable TV broadens the program options available to the viewer as well as the advertiser by offering specialty channels, including all-news, pop music, country music, sports, weather, educational, and cultural channels as well as children's programming. Figure 11–7 shows the most popular cable channels along with the types of programming they carry and their number of subscribers. Many cable systems also carry **superstations**, independent local stations that send their signals nationally via satellite to cable operators to make available to subscribers. The five superstations in the United States are WWOR and WPIX in New York, WGN in Chicago, WSBK in Boston, and WTBS in Atlanta (which, like CNN, is part of the Turner Broadcasting System). Programming on superstations generally consists of sports, movies, and reruns of network shows. The superstations do carry national advertising and are a relatively inexpensive option for cable households across the country.

Cable has had a considerable influence on the nature of television as an advertising medium. First, the expanded viewing options have led to considerable audience fragmenta-

FIGURE 11–7
Major cable networks

Network	Estimated Coverage (Millions)	Type of Programming
TBS	73.0	Entertainment/movies/sports
TNT	72.0	Movies/sports
USA Network	72.0	Entertainment/movies/sports
CNN	71.0	News/information
A&E	70.0	Family/variety/mysteries/specials
Nickelodeon	69.3	Youth interest
ESPN	68.6	Sports
TNN (The Nashville Network)	68.0	Country music
The Family Channel	68.0	Family/general/original
The Discovery Channel	67.9	Family/health/technology/science
MTV	66.7	Music video and entertainment
Lifetime	66.7	News/information/women's interests
The Weather Channel	65.0	National/regional/local weather
Headline News	64.0	News/information
CNBC	60.8	News/information
VH-1	56.3	Music (video)
The Learning Channel	49.5	Information
BET Networks	45.2	Entertainment/information for African-Americans
Comedy Central	45.0	Comedy
Sci-Fi Channel	39.0	Science fiction
The Cartoon Network	38.0	Cartoons
CMT (Country Music TV)	37.0	Country music (videos)
ESPN2	35.2	Sports
E! Entertainment	35.0	Entertainment/news/gossip
Courtroom TV Network	33.3	Court/legal
MSNBC	30.0	News/information
fX Network	30.0	Entertainment
Television Food Network	29.0	Food/health/nutrition
The History Channel	28.0	Historical documentaries/movies
The Travel Channel	20.0	World travel

Source: *1997 Cable TV Facts*, New York: Cable Advertising Bureau.

tion. Much of the growth in cable audiences has come at the expense of the three major networks. Cable channels now have about 27 percent of the prime-time viewing audience, while the total share of the three networks has declined to around 57 percent. Many cable stations have become very popular among consumers, leading advertisers to reevaluate their media plans and the prices they are willing to pay for network and spot commercials on network affiliate stations. The networks, recognizing the growing popularity of cable, are becoming involved with the cable industry. ABC purchased ESPN, while NBC started two cable channels in the early 90s—the Consumer News and Business Channel (CNBC) and Sports Channel America—and in 1996 entered in a joint venture with MicroSoft to launch MSNBC, a 24-hour news channel.[20]

ADVERTISING ON CABLE

As shown in Figure 11–8, cable advertising revenues have increased steadily since the mid-1980s and exceeded $6 billion in 1996. Much of this growth has come from advertising on the national cable networks such as CNN, ESPN, USA, and MTV. However, many na-

FIGURE 11—8   Cable advertising revenue growth ($ millions)

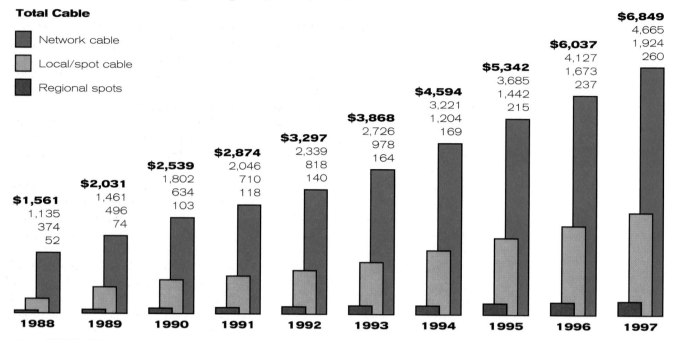

Source: *1997 Cable TV Facts*, Cable Television Advertising Bureau, New York, NY.

tional advertisers have been shifting some of their advertising budgets to spot cable and purchasing through local operators as well as the national cable networks. Over the past four years, spot cable revenues have averaged 20 percent annual growth, reaching nearly $2 billion in 1997.

Like broadcast TV, cable time can be purchased on a national, regional, or local (spot) level. Many large marketers advertise on cable networks to reach large numbers of viewers across the country with a single media buy. Regional advertising on cable is available primarily through sports and news channels that cover a certain geographic area.

Many national advertisers are turning to spot advertising on local cable systems to reach specific geographic markets. Spot cable affords them more precision in reaching specific markets, and they can save money by using a number of small, targeted media purchases rather than making one network buy. The growth in spot cable advertising is also being facilitated by the use of **interconnects**, where a group of cable systems in a geographic area are joined for advertising purposes. These interconnects increase the size of the audience an advertiser can reach with a spot cable buy. For example, WNYI: New York Interconnect reaches more than 4.3 million subscribers in the greater New York metropolitan area; the ADLINK Digital Interconnect delivers 3 million cable subscribers in Los Angeles and four surrounding counties. More sophisticated interconnect systems are developing that will pool large numbers of cable systems and allow spot advertisers to reach more viewers. These new systems will also allow local advertisers to make more selective cable buys, since they can purchase the entire interconnect or one of several zones within the system.

While spot cable is becoming very popular among national advertisers, it has some of the same problems as spot advertising on broadcast TV. The purchasing process is very complicated and time consuming; media buyers must contact hundreds of cable systems to put together a media schedule consisting of spot cable buys. Local cable systems also do not provide advertisers with strong support or much information on demographics, lifestyle, or viewership patterns.

ADVANTAGES OF CABLE

Cable TV has experienced tremendous growth as an advertising medium because it has some important advantages. A primary one is selectivity. Cable subscribers tend to be younger, more affluent, and better educated than nonsubscribers and have greater purchasing power. Moreover, the specialized programming on the various cable networks reaches very specific target markets.

Many advertisers have turned to cable because of the opportunities it offers for **narrowcasting,** or reaching very specialized markets. For example, ESPN is very popular among advertisers whose primary target audience is male sports enthusiasts. MTV is used by advertisers in the United States and many other countries that want to reach teenagers and young adults. Nickelodeon claims to have more viewers of kids' programs than the three networks combined and has become very popular among advertisers targeting this market (Exhibit 11–5).

Advertisers are also interested in cable because of its low cost and flexibility. It costs substantially less to produce a program for cable TV than for a network. A two-hour network program may cost about $2.5 million, but a half-hour cable show can be produced for anywhere from $15,000 to $25,000. Even if the advertiser does not produce the program, spot announcements are considerably cheaper on most cable stations. This makes TV a much more viable media option for smaller advertisers with limited budgets and those interested in targeting their commercials to a well-defined target audience. Also, cable advertisers generally do not have to make the large up-front commitments, which may be as much as a year in advance, the networks require.

In addition to lower costs, cable gives advertisers much greater flexibility in the type of commercials that can be used. While most network commercials are 30- or 15-second spots, commercials on cable are often longer. **Infomercials,** commercials that range from 3 to 30 minutes in length, are common on cable. Direct-response advertisers often use these longer ads to describe their products or services and encourage consumers to call in their orders during the commercial. The use of infomercials by direct-response advertisers is discussed in Chapter 14.

The low costs of cable make it a very popular advertising medium among local advertisers. Car dealers, furniture stores, restaurants, and many other merchants are switching advertising spending from traditional media such as radio, newspapers, and even magazines to take advantage of the low rates of local cable channels. Local cable advertising is one of the fastest-growing segments of the advertising market, and cable systems are increasing the percentage of revenue they earn from local advertising.

EXHIBIT 11–5
Nickelodeon promotes its coverage of the kids' market

LIMITATIONS OF CABLE

While cable has become increasingly popular among national, regional, and local advertisers, it still has a number of drawbacks. One major problem is that cable is overshadowed by the major networks, as households with basic cable service still watch considerably more network and syndicated programming than cable shows. This stems from the fact that cable generally has less desirable programming than broadcast TV.

Another drawback of cable is audience fragmentation. Although cable's share of the TV viewing audience has increased significantly, these viewers are spread out among the large number of channels available to cable subscribers. The number of viewers who watch any one cable channel is generally quite low. Even MTV, ESPN, and CNN have prime-time ratings of only about 1 or 2. The large number of cable stations has fragmented audiences and made buying procedures more difficult, since numerous stations must be contacted to reach the majority of the cable audience in a market. There are also problems with the quality and availability of local ratings for cable stations as well as research on audience characteristics.

Cable also lacks penetration, especially in the major markets. As of September 1996, cable penetration was 69 percent in the New York City designated market area, 62 percent in Los Angeles, and 60 percent in Chicago. While cable now penetrates 68 percent of all U.S. television households, this still means that nearly a third of the market cannot be reached by advertising on cable.

THE FUTURE OF CABLE

Cable TV should continue to experience strong growth as its audience share increases and advertisers spend more money to reach cable viewers. However, the cable industry faces several challenges: increases in the number of channels, leading to fragmentation of the audience, changes in government regulations, and competition in the programming distribution business from other telecommunications companies and direct broadcast satellite services. Advances in technology such as digital video compression and fiber optics, coupled with massive investments in system upgrades, are making it possible for cable operators to offer more channels and thus subject existing cable channels to greater competition. In 1996, over 30 million U.S. homes could receive at least 54 channels. An average 95 percent of cable subscribers could receive 30 channels or more.[21] Increases in the number of channels available lead to further fragmentation of the cable audience and make it more difficult for cable networks to charge the ad rates needed to finance original programming. Some of the growth in cable channels will come from **multiplexing**, or multiple channels transmitted from one network. Several major cable networks, including ESPN, the Nashville Network, and the Discovery Channel, own several channels.

The cable industry has also been affected by changes in government regulation. In the early 90s, concerns over poor service and high rates led to a revolt against the cable industry. As a result, Congress passed legislation in 1993 that rolls back the provisions of the Cable Television Act of 1984, allows local governments to regulate basic cable rates, and forces cable operators to pay licensing fees for local broadcast programming they used to retransmit for free. The Telecommunications Act of 1996 allows local phone companies to offer cable service.[22] The biggest threat facing the cable industry is competition from direct broadcast satellite (DBS) services, discussed in IMC Perspective 11–2.

The future of cable as an advertising medium will ultimately depend on the size and qualities of the audiences cable stations can reach with their programs. This in turn will depend on cable's ability to offer programs that attract viewers and subscribers. Cable's role as a stepchild in program development and acquisition has changed. For example, CNN has become the authoritative source for news throughout the world. Cable networks like A&E, the Discovery Channel, and the Learning Channel provide outstanding cultural and educational programming.

Cable TV will continue to be a popular source of sports programming and is very important to advertisers interested in reaching the male market. There are 23 regional cable sports networks, and with companies such as Fox Sports, advertisers can buy multiple regions with one media buy. Cable networks are also paying large sums for the rights to sports programming. Deals by ESPN and TBS for exclusive Sunday night coverage of National Football

IMC Perspective 11—2
DBS Systems Challenge Cable

For years, the only way viewers could get MTV, CNN, ESPN, and other cable channels was by subscribing to a local cable service. With a virtual monopoly in most markets, cable operators wired more than 65 million homes by 1996, making cable the dominant provider of television access in the U.S. Now, for the first time in its history, the cable TV industry is facing stiff competition in the programming distribution business. The competition is coming from local phone companies such as the RBOCs (Regional Bell Operating Companies) and, more notably, from direct broadcast satellite (DBS) services.

A few years ago, Stanley S. Hubbard, chair of U.S. Satellite Broadcasting, was laughed out of cable conventions when he promised to offer a direct broadcast satellite service on an 18-inch dish he held under his arm. Hubbard recalls that cable operators would say, "DBS stands for Don't be stupid" and the audience would roar. But nobody in the cable industry is laughing today. After years of false starts, the direct broadcast satellite industry is giving cable a run for its money. By June 1995, sales of DBS dishes hit one million units—making it the most successful first-year rollout of any consumer electronics product. By 1997, DBS had more than 4 million subscribers.

Several factors are driving the growth of DBS. Prices for the pizza-pan-size dishes have plunged to $200 from $600 and DBS subscribers, who pay a monthly programming fee, can get as many as 200 channels of movies, news, music, and sports in crisp, digital video and CD-quality sound. Sports programming is a major selling point for DBS. DirecTV, the market leader, offers an exclusive package of all regular season NFL football games for $10, as well as 18 regional sports channels. Cable subscribers are also being lured away by more than 50 channels of pay-per-view movies available on DBS at $2.99 a film.

The DBS industry has attracted some of the communications industry's most powerful players. DirecTV is a unit of General Motors' Hughes Electronics subsidiary and AT&T owns a 2.5 percent stake in the company with an option to purchase up to 30 percent. Primestar Partners is a joint venture of some of the largest cable operators—including Time Warner, TCI, Comcast, and Cox Communications—who formed the DBS venture as a hedge against their own cable business. In early 1997, Rupert Murdock's News Corp. and MCI Communications purchased controlling interest in EchoStar Communications Corp., the fourth-largest DBS company. The two companies plan to invest $2.5 billion and offer a new DBS service called Sky.

The DBS companies have been aggressively marketing their service, superior picture quality, and greater channel choice. DirecTV and Primestar spent a combined $300 million on ads promoting their DBS systems. Traditional cable operators still command the overwhelming majority of the cable distribution business. However, industry estimates are that the number of DBS subscribers will quadruple by the year 2000, taking a major bite out of cable's 65-million-customer base.

The cable industry is not about to surrender its market and is hammering away at the shortcomings of DBS. The dishes come with ownership and maintenance responsibilities and do not get local channels, only feeds of network affiliates from selected cities. And DBS doesn't allow unlimited high-speed access to the Internet or other interactive services, which cable operators are now starting to provide with cable modem and digital-cable boxes. The cable operators are also upgrading their systems, paying more attention to customer service, and investing more in consumer marketing.

Cable operators argue that DBS's growth has expanded the overall market for cable and is not a major threat to their business. They say the current growth has come from those viewers who were easiest to pull in and the DBS industry will have a harder time attracting more customers. But no one in the cable industry is laughing at those funny little dishes any longer.

Sources: "News Corp. to Acquire 50% Stake in EchoStar," *Los Angeles Times*, January 25, 1997, pp. D1, 11; Laurie Freeman, "Improving Customer Service Becomes MSO's Major Objective," *Advertising Age*, December 9, 1996, p. S8; Mark Robichaux, "Once a Laughingstock, Direct-Broadcast TV Gives Cable a Scare," *The Wall Street Journal*, November 7, 1996, pp. A1, 7.

League games have proved that cable networks can compete with the major networks in a sports bidding war.[23]

As cable penetration increases, its programming improves, and more advertisers discover its efficiency and ability to reach targeted market segments, cable's popularity as an advertising medium should continue to grow. Many agencies have developed specialists to examine the use of cable in their clients' media schedules. Cable networks are also looking to international markets as a source of future growth. Both ESPN and MTV have expanded into

EXHIBIT 11–6
CNN International is the authoritative source for news throughout the world

South America, Europe, and Asia, while TV viewers throughout the world tune to CNN International for news (Exhibit 11–6).

Measuring the TV Audience

One of the most important considerations in TV advertising is the size and composition of the viewing audience. Audience measurement is critical to advertisers as well as to the networks and stations. Advertisers want to know the size and characteristics of the audience they are reaching when they purchase time on a particular program. And since the rates they pay are a function of audience size, advertisers want to be sure audience measurements are accurate.

Audience size and composition are also important to the network or station, since they determine the amount it can charge for commercial time. Shows are frequently canceled because they fail to attract enough viewers to make their commercial time attractive to potential advertisers. Determining audience size is not an exact science and has been the subject of considerable controversy through the years. In this section, we examine how audiences are measured and how advertisers use this information in planning their media schedules.

AUDIENCE MEASURES

The size and composition of television audiences are measured by ratings services. The sole source of network TV and local audience information is the A. C. Nielsen Co. For many years local audience information was also available from the Arbitron Co., but Arbitron exited the local TV ratings business at the end of 1993 due to steep financial losses.[24] Nielsen gathers viewership information from a sample of TV homes and then projects this information to the total viewing area. The techniques used to gather audience measurement information include diaries, electronic meters or recorders, and personal interviews. Nielsen provides various types of information that can be used to measure and evaluate a station's audience. These measures are important to media planners as they weigh the value of buying commercial time on a program.

Television Households

The number of households in the market that own a TV is sometimes referred to as the *universe estimate* (UE). Nielsen estimates that 96.9 million U.S. households owned at least one TV set as of September 1996. Since over 98 percent of U.S. households own a TV set, **television households** generally correspond to the number of households in a given market.

Program Rating

Probably the best known of all audience measurement figures is the **program rating**, the percentage of TV households in an area that are tuned to a specific program during a specific time period. The program rating is calculated by dividing the number of households tuned to a particular show by the total number of households in the area. For example, if 12 million households (HH) watched the "CBS Evening News," the national rating would be 12.4, calculated as follows:

$$\text{Rating} = \frac{\text{HH tuned to show}}{\text{Total U.S. HH}} = \frac{12,000,000}{96,900,000} = 12.4$$

A **ratings point** represents 1 percent of all the television households in a particular area tuned to a specific program. On a national level, one ratings point represents 969,000 households. Thus, a top-rated program like "Home Improvement," which has an average rating of 19, reaches 18.4 million households each week ($19 \times 969,000$).

The program rating is the key number to the stations, since the amount of money they can charge for commercial time is based on it. Ratings points are very important to the networks as well as to individual stations. A 1 percent change in a program's ratings over the course of a viewing season can gain or lose millions of dollars in advertising revenue. Advertisers also follow ratings closely, since they are the key measure for audience size and commercial rates.

Households Using Television

The percentage of homes in a given area where TV is being watched during a specific time period is called **households using television (HUT)**. This figure, sometimes referred to as *sets in use*, is always expressed as a percentage. For example, if 50 million of the U.S. TV households have their sets turned on at 10 PM on a Wednesday night, the HUT figure is 51.5 percent (50 million out of 96.9 million). Television usage varies widely depending on the time of day and season of the year.

Share of Audience

Another important audience measurement figure is the **share of audience**, which refers to the percentage of households using TV in a specified time period that are tuned to a specific program. This figure considers variations in the number of sets in use and the total size of the potential audience, since it is based only on those households that have their sets turned on. Audience share is calculated by dividing the number of households (HH) tuned to a show by the number of households using television (HUT). Thus, if 51.5 percent (or 50 million) of U.S. households had their sets turned on for the "CBS Evening News," the share of audience would be 24, calculated as follows:

$$\text{Share} = \frac{\text{HH tuned to show}}{\text{U.S. households using TV}} = \frac{12,000,000}{50,000,000} = 24$$

Audience share is always higher than the program rating unless all the households have their sets turned on (in which case they would be equal). Share figures are important since they reveal how well a program does with the available viewing audience. For example, late at night the size of the viewing audience drops substantially, so the best way to assess the popularity of a late-night program is to examine the share of the available audience it attracts relative to competing programs.

Ratings services also provide an audience statistic known as **total audience**, the total number of homes viewing any five-minute part of a telecast. This number can be broken down to provide audience composition figures that are based on the distribution of the audience into demographic categories.

NETWORK AUDIENCE INFORMATION

Nielsen Television Index

The source of national and network TV audience information is the Nielsen Television Index (NTI), which provides daily and weekly estimates of TV viewing and national sponsored network and major cable program audiences. For more than 25 years, Nielsen provided this information using a two-pronged system consisting of a national sample of metered households along with a separate sample of diary households. In the metered households, an electronic measurement device known as the **audimeter** (audience meter) was hooked up to the TV set to continuously measure the channels to which the set was tuned. Network viewing for the country (the famous Nielsen ratings) was based on the results provided by audimeters placed in a national sample of homes carefully selected to represent the population of U.S. households. The metered households were supported by a separate panel of households that recorded viewing information in diaries. Since the audimeter could measure only the channel to which the set was tuned, the diary panel was used to gather demographic data on the viewing audience.

For many years, the television and advertising industries expressed concern over the audimeter/diary system. The information from diaries was not available to the network and advertising analysts for several weeks, and studies indicated the method was overstating the size of some key demographic audiences. Cooperation rates among diary keepers declined, and often the person who kept a household's diary did not note what other family members watched when he or she wasn't home. The complex new video environment and explosion in viewing options also made it difficult for diary keepers to maintain accurate viewing records.

As a result of these problems, and in response to competitive pressure from an audience measurement company from England, AGB, in 1987 Nielsen made the people meter the sole basis of its national rating system and eliminated the use of the diary panel.

The People Meter

The **people meter** is an electronic measuring device that incorporates the technology of the old-style audimeter in a system that records not only what is being watched but also by whom in 5,000 homes. The actual device is a small box with eight buttons—six for the family and two for visitors—that can be placed on the top of the TV set (Exhibit 11–7). A remote control unit permits electronic entries from anywhere in the room. Each member of the sample household is assigned a button that indicates his or her presence as a viewer. The device is also equipped with a sonar sensor to remind viewers entering or leaving the room to log in or out on the meter.

The viewership information the people meter collects from the household is stored in the home system until it is retrieved by Nielsen's computers. Data collected include when the set is turned on, which channel is viewed, when the channel is changed, and when the set is off, in addition to who is viewing. The demographic characteristics of the viewers are also in the system, and viewership can be matched to these traits. Nielsen's operation center processes all this information each week for release to the TV and advertising industries. Nielsen uses a sample of metered households in the nation's largest markets (New York, Los Angeles, and Chicago) to provide overnight viewing results.

LOCAL AUDIENCE INFORMATION

Information on local audiences is important to both local advertisers and firms making national spot buys. The Nielsen Station Index (NSI) measures TV station audiences in 211 local markets known as **designated market areas (DMAs)**. DMAs are nonoverlapping

EXHIBIT 11–7 Nielsen uses the people meter to measure national TV audiences

areas used for planning, buying, and evaluating TV audiences and are generally a group of counties in which stations located in a metropolitan or central area achieve the largest audience share. NSI reports information on viewing by time periods and programs and includes audience size and estimates of viewing over a range of demographic categories for each DMA.

Nielsen measures viewing audiences in every television market at least four times a year. The major markets (New York, Chicago, Los Angeles) are covered six times a year. The ratings periods when all 211 DMAs are surveyed are known as **sweeps**. The networks and local stations use numbers gathered during the sweeps rating periods in selling TV time. Exhibit 11–8 shows how KFMB, the CBS affiliate in San Diego, promotes its dominance of the sweeps ratings for local news.

However, as discussed in IMC Perspective 11–3, many advertising professionals believe the audience estimates gathered during the sweeps are overestimated because of special programming and promotions that occur during these periods.

DEVELOPMENTS IN AUDIENCE MEASUREMENT

For years the advertising industry has been calling for changes in the way TV viewing audiences are measured, at both the national and local levels.[25] Many people believe people meters are only the first step in improving the way audiences are measured. While the people meter is seen as an improvement over the diary method, it still requires cooperation on an ongoing basis from people in the metered homes. Viewers in the Nielsen households, including young children, must punch a preassigned number on the remote control device each time they start or stop watching. Media researchers argue that kids forget and adults tire of the task over the two years they are in the Nielsen sample. Nielsen has been trying to develop passive measurement systems that require less involvement by people in metered homes and can produce more accurate measures of the viewing audience. However, such a system does not appear to be forthcoming in the near future.

EXHIBIT 11–8
KFMB promotes its dominance of the sweeps rating period for local news

IMC Perspective 11–3
Is It Time to Do Away with Sweeps Ratings?

The cornerstone of selling local television time is the sweeps rating periods, which are held in November, February, May, and, to a lesser extent, August by Nielsen Media Research to determine what stations and shows are being watched. The numbers gathered during the sweeps periods are used as guideposts in the buying and selling of TV ad time during the rest of the year. However, many people in the advertising industry are enraged over the TV stations' practice of artificially bolstering their ratings during sweeps periods with special programming and contests, games, and other nontypical promotions.

Advertisers and their agencies have become accustomed to the usual tactics used to beef up program schedules during the sweeps months, from blockbuster network programming to lurid sensationalism in local newscasts. Of much greater concern, however, is the blatant use of ratings grabbers such as big-prize sweepstakes, contests, and giveaways during sweeps. Nielsen Media Research says the number of unusual sweeps-period station promotions—most often giveaway contests on local newscasts—is growing faster than ever and was up 55 percent from November 1995 to May 1996. Six stations, an unusually high number, were cited by Nielsen for appealing directly to Nielsen households with special promotion spots. The number of station-sponsored contests reached an all-time high of 234 during the May 1996 ratings period.

After the February 1996 sweeps, Nielsen told the American Association of Advertising Agencies (4As) that its research had found that giveaway promotions substantially affect TV station audience share. The 4As is becoming involved in the controversy by developing a position paper it hopes will check local TV stations' rampant use of viewer watch-and-win contests during sweeps periods.

Nielsen is working with the advertising industry to solve the sweeps problem. It provides *red flags* in its printed reports when stations use special promotions to bump up their ratings. However, the computer tapes that are fed into the agencies' media department computers contain only the ratings. Alert buyers can spot unusual blips in continuously metered TV markets, but in other markets the sweeps period numbers are the only numbers available and they have no benchmark. One proposal made by Nielsen is that the computer tape used by many agencies be highlighted in some way so media buyers know which stations are running the contests and when.

Advertisers, agencies, and the major TV networks argue that the long-term solution to the problem is for Nielsen to switch to continuous measurement, 13-week averages reported four times a year, rather than relying on the artificially hyped numbers from the sweeps periods. However, Nielsen argues that such a service would be costly and the TV and advertising industries would have to be willing to pay a higher price for ratings information. There may also be some resistance from the local stations that have grown accustomed to getting higher ad rates year-round from the sweeps numbers. They also save money by compressing the bulk of their promotional spending into a few specific sweeps periods.

Sources: Michael Wilke, "4As Lobbies to Kill TV Sweeps; 13-Week Averages Offered as One Possible Solution," *Advertising Age*, November 11, 1996, p.59; Mark Gimein, "4As Rips Sweeps Contest: Station Giveaway Games Intentionally 'Distort' Ratings, Group Says," *MediaWeek*, April 8, 1996, p. 6; "Agencies Right to Battle Hype," *Advertising Age*, March 4, 1996, p. 18.

Much of the concern over the Nielsen measurements involves the diary system used to measure viewing in the 211 local markets. This system requires that every 15 minutes viewers write down station call letters, channel numbers, programs, and who is watching. Many homes do not return completed diaries and many of those that are returned are often not filled out correctly. Nielsen executives acknowledge the problems with its measurement system for local markets and is trying to correct them. The company is testing new diaries, sending out more of them, and working to improve the response rates.[26] Nielsen is also considering switching to a continuous measurement system for local markets rather than relying solely on the sweeps measurement system. (See IMC Perspective 11–3.)[27]

Nielsen has been battling with the networks, local TV stations, and ad agencies for years over the accuracy of its numbers. Many in the industry suspect that Nielsen is not moving fast enough to improve its audience measurement systems because it has a virtual monopoly in both the national and local ratings business. They would like to see some competition.

The networks are actively exploring alternatives to Nielsen through the Committee on Nationwide Television Audience Measurement, a research group that allows the networks to collaborate on ratings methodology without violating antitrust laws. The three major networks have invested $40 million to test an alternative ratings system in the Philadelphia area. The test is being run by Statistical Research Inc. (SRI), a firm that has been used for years to double-check Nielsen's accuracy. SRI's System for Measuring and Reporting Television (Smart-TV) involves a type of people meter that reads a code embedded in the TV signal that is collected by a sensor on the screen, transmitted to a data-collection box, and sent via phone line to SRI's computer.[28]

SRI claims its Smart-TV service has many advantages over Nielsen's people meter and is considering using the test project as the basis for a rival ratings service that could be ready by the end of the decade. But the company faces a number of hurdles. Estimates are that the Smart-TV system would cost as much as $100 million to develop on a nationwide level, and it is uncertain whether the television industry will provide financial support for it. Advertisers would also have to be convinced to accept a new TV viewership system. SRI received a major boost in its efforts to challenge in early 1997 when three major advertisers—Procter & Gamble, AT&T, and General Motors—agreed to provide financial support for start-up efforts for Smart-TV.[29] However, no other attempt to develop TV rating services to compete with Nielsen has proved successful.

Many advertising professionals hope that a focus of new technology for measuring viewing audiences will be on developing rating systems for commercials, not just for programs. The Nielsen system and Smart-TV measure the audiences for the programs surrounding the commercials rather than the commercials themselves. But with zipping, zapping, people leaving the room, and people being distracted from the TV during commercial breaks, there is a need to develop accurate ratings of more than just program audience viewing.

For over 50 years consumers passively received TV programming and commercials. This is changing rapidly, however, as the major cable operators, telecommunications companies, and others bring various entertainment, information, and interactive services into homes via television. Researchers argue that the Nielsen system is being overwhelmed by the explosion in the number of TV sets, delivery systems, and program options available. These developments must be carefully monitored by advertisers and media planners as well as by people in the TV industry, as they can have a profound impact on audience size and composition, and the way advertisers use and pay for the use of TV as an advertising medium. Improvements in measurement technology are needed to accommodate these developments.

RADIO

Television has often been referred to as the ideal advertising medium, and to many people it personifies the glamour and excitement of the industry. Radio, on the other hand, has been called the Rodney Dangerfield of media because it gets no respect from many advertisers.[30] Dominated by network programming and national advertisers before the growth of TV, radio has evolved into a primarily local advertising medium. In 1995, network advertising accounted for less than 4 percent of radio's revenue.[31] Radio has also become a medium characterized by highly specialized programming appealing to very narrow segments of the population.

The importance of radio is best demonstrated by the numbers. There are more than 11,000 radio stations in this country, including 4,906 commercial AM stations and 5,285 commercial FM stations. There are over 576 million radios in use in the United States, an average of 5.6 per household. Radio reaches 77 percent of all Americans over the age of 12 each day and has grown into a ubiquitous background to many activities, among them reading, driving, running, working, and socializing. The average American listens to radio 3 hours and 18 minutes every weekday and nearly 6 hours every weekend.[32] The pervasiveness of this medium has not gone unnoticed by advertisers; radio advertising revenue grew from $3.5 billion in 1980 to $11.5 billion in 1995.

Radio has survived and flourished as an advertising medium because it offers advertisers certain advantages for communicating messages to their potential customers. However, radio has inherent limitations that affect its role in the advertiser's media strategy.

Advantages of Radio

Radio has many advantages over other media, including cost and efficiency, selectivity, flexibility, mental imagery, and integrated marketing opportunities.

COST AND EFFICIENCY

One of the main strengths of radio as an advertising medium is its low cost. Radio commercials are very inexpensive to produce. They require only a script of the commercial to be read by the radio announcer or a copy of a prerecorded message that can be broadcast by the station. The cost for radio time is also low. A minute on network radio may cost only $5,000, which translates into a cost per thousand of only $3 to $4. The low relative cost of radio makes it one of the most efficient of all advertising media, and the low absolute cost means the budget needed for an effective radio campaign is often lower than for other media.

The low cost of radio also means advertisers can build more reach and frequency into their media schedules within a certain budget. They can use different stations to broaden the reach of their messages and multiple spots to ensure adequate frequency. Many national advertisers have begun to recognize the cost efficiency of radio. For example, the Motel 6 chain has had tremendous success with its "We'll leave the light on for you" campaign, featuring Tom Bodett delivering down-home, humorous messages that poke fun at expensive hotels and the perils of travel (Figure 11–9).

SELECTIVITY

Another major advantage of radio is the high degree of audience selectivity available through the various program formats and geographic coverage of the numerous stations. Radio lets companies focus their advertising on specialized audiences such as certain demographic and lifestyle groups. Most areas have radio stations with formats such as adult contemporary, easy listening, classical music, country, news/talk shows, jazz, and all news, to name a few. Figure 11–10 shows the age composition of four of the more common radio formats. Talk radio, for example, reaches the adult market effectively. Elusive consumers like teenagers, college students, and working adults can be reached more easily through radio than most other media.

Radio can reach consumers other media can't. Light television viewers spend considerably more time with radio than with TV and are generally an upscale market in terms of income and education level. Light readers of magazines and newspapers also spend more time listening to radio. Radio has become a popular way to reach specific non-English-speaking ethnic markets. Los Angeles, New York City, Dallas, and Miami have several radio stations that broadcast in Spanish and reach these areas' large Hispanic markets. As mass marketing gives way to market segmentation and regional marketing, radio will continue to grow in importance.

FLEXIBILITY

Radio is probably the most flexible of all the advertising media because it has a very short closing period, which means advertisers can change their message almost up to the time it goes on the air. Radio commercials can usually be produced and scheduled on very short notice. Radio advertisers can easily adjust their messages to local market conditions and marketing situations.

FIGURE 11–9
Sample Motel 6 radio spot

"Hi. Tom Bodett for Motel 6 with a plan for anyone whose kids are on their own now. Take a drive, see some of the country and visit a few relatives. Like your sister Helen and her husband Bob. They're wonderful folks and always happy to pull the hide-a-bed out for you, but somehow the smell of mothballs just isn't conducive to gettin' a good night's sleep. And since Bob gets up at 5:30, well that means you do too. So here's the plan. Check into Motel 6. 'Cause for around 22 bucks, the lowest prices of any national chain, you'll get a clean, comfortable room, and Helen and Bob'll think you're mighty considerate. Well you are, but maybe more important, you can sleep late and not have to wonder if the towels in their bathroom are just for decoration. My rule of thumb is, if they match the tank and seat cover, you better leave 'em alone. Just call 505-891-6161 for reservations. I'm Tom Bodett for Motel 6. Give my best to Helen and Bob and we'll leave the light on for you."

One of the 100-plus radio spots for Motel 6 created by The Richards Group.

FIGURE 11–10
Age composition of some common radio formats

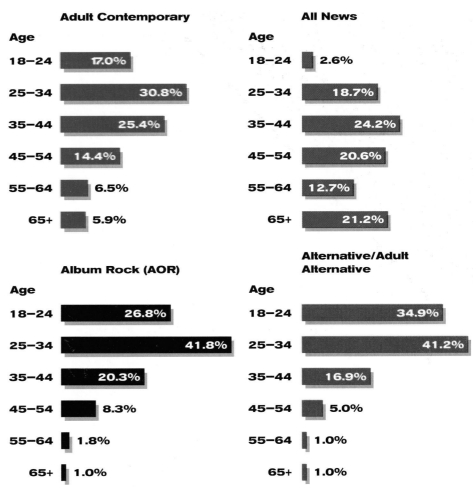

Adult Contemporary

Age
18–24 | 17.0%
25–34 | 30.8%
35–44 | 25.4%
45–54 | 14.4%
55–64 | 6.5%
65+ | 5.9%

All News

Age
18–24 | 2.6%
25–34 | 18.7%
35–44 | 24.2%
45–54 | 20.6%
55–64 | 12.7%
65+ | 21.2%

Album Rock (AOR)

Age
18–24 | 26.8%
25–34 | 41.8%
35–44 | 20.3%
45–54 | 8.3%
55–64 | 1.8%
65+ | 1.0%

Alternative/Adult Alternative

Age
18–24 | 34.9%
25–34 | 41.2%
35–44 | 16.9%
45–54 | 5.0%
55–64 | 1.0%
65+ | 1.0%

Source: Imagery Transfer, © Strategic Research Inc., 1993, 1996.

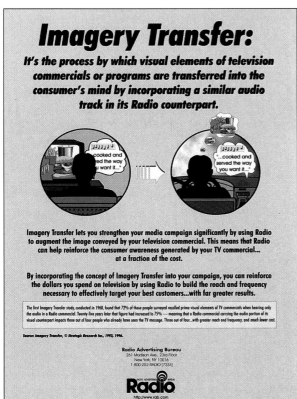

MENTAL IMAGERY

A potential advantage of radio that is often overlooked is that it encourages listeners to use their imagination when processing a commercial message. While the creative options of radio are limited, many advertisers take advantage of the absence of a visual element to let consumers create their own picture of what is happening in a radio message.

Radio may also reinforce television messages through a technique called **image transfer**, where the images of a TV commercial are implanted into a radio spot.[33] First the marketer establishes the video image of a TV commercial. Then it uses a similar, or even the same, audio portion (spoken words and/or jingle) as the basis for the radio counterpart. The idea is that when consumers hear the radio message, they will make the connection to the TV commercial, reinforcing its video images. Image transfer offers advertisers a way to make radio and TV ads work together synergistically. This promotional piece put out by the Radio Advertising Bureau shows how the image transfer process works.

INTEGRATED MARKETING OPPORTUNITIES

Radio provides marketers with a variety of integrated marketing opportunities. Radio stations become an integral part of many communities, and the deejays and program hosts may become popular figures. Advertisers often use radio stations and personalities to enhance their involvement with a local market and to gain influence

EXHIBIT 11–9
Banana Boat uses live radio
broadcasts to promote its suncare
products

with local retailers. Radio also works very effectively in conjunction with place-based/point-of-purchase promotions. Retailers often use on-site radio broadcasts combined with special sales or promotions to attract consumers to their stores and get them to make a purchase. Live radio broadcasts are also used in conjunction with event marketing. For example, Banana Boat Suncare often sponsors live broadcast promotions at beaches, sporting events, and festivals, setting up product booths for sampling and giveaways. (Exhibit 11–9).

Limitations of Radio

Several factors limit the effectiveness of radio as an advertising medium, among them creative limitations, fragmentation, chaotic buying procedures, limited research data, limited listener attention, and clutter. The media planner must consider them in determining the role the medium will play in the advertising program.

CREATIVE LIMITATIONS

A major drawback of radio as an advertising medium is the absence of a visual image. The radio advertiser cannot show the product, demonstrate it, or use any type of visual appeal or information. A radio commercial is, like a TV ad, a short-lived and fleeting message that is externally paced and does not allow the receiver to control the rate at which it is processed. Because of these creative limitations many companies tend to ignore radio, and agencies often assign junior people to the development of radio commercials.

FRAGMENTATION

Another problem with radio is the high level of audience fragmentation due to the large number of stations. The percentage of the market tuned to any particular station is usually very small. The top-rated radio station in many major metropolitan areas with a number of AM and FM stations may attract less than 10 percent of the total listening audience. Advertisers that want a broad reach in their radio advertising media schedule have to buy time on a number of stations to cover even a local market.

CHAOTIC BUYING PROCEDURES

It should be readily apparent how chaotic the media planning and purchasing process can become for the advertiser that wants to use radio on a nationwide spot basis. Acquiring information and evaluating and contracting for time with even a fraction of the 10,200 commercial stations that operate across the country can be very difficult and time consuming. This problem has diminished somewhat in recent years as the number of radio networks and of syndicated programs offering a package of several hundred stations increases.

LIMITED RESEARCH DATA

Audience research data on radio are often limited, particularly compared with TV, magazines, or newspapers. Most radio stations are small operations and lack the revenue to support detailed studies of their audiences. And most users of radio are local companies that cannot support research on radio listenership in their markets. Thus, media planners do not have as much audience information available to guide them in their purchase of radio time as they do with other media.

LIMITED LISTENER ATTENTION

Another problem that plagues radio is that it is difficult to retain listener attention to commercials. Radio programming, particularly music, is often the background to some other activity and may not receive the listeners' full attention. Thus they may miss all or some of the commercials. One environment where radio has a more captive audience is in cars. But getting listeners to pay attention to commercials can still be difficult. Most people preprogram their car radio and change stations during commercial breaks. A study by Avery Abernethy found large differences between exposure to radio programs versus advertising for listeners in cars. They were exposed to only half of the advertising broadcast and changed stations frequently to avoid commercials.[34]

CLUTTER

Clutter is just as much a problem with radio as with other advertising media. Most radio stations carry an average of nearly 10 minutes of commercials every hour. During the popular morning and evening rush hours, the amount of commercial time may exceed 12 minutes. Advertisers must create commercials that break through the clutter or use heavy repetition to make sure their messages reach consumers.

Buying Radio Time

The purchase of radio time is similar to that of television, as advertisers can make either network, spot, or local buys. Since these options were reviewed in the section on buying TV time, they are discussed here only briefly.

NETWORK RADIO

Advertising time on radio can be purchased on a network basis using one of the national networks. In 1987, the Westwood One Network purchased Mutual Broadcasting Network and NBC Radio Network, leaving four major networks: Westwood One, ABC, CBS, and Unistar. There are also more than 100 regional radio networks across the country. Using networks minimizes the amount of negotiation and administrative work needed to get national or regional coverage, and the costs are lower than for individual stations. However, the number of affiliated stations on the network roster and the types of audiences they reach can vary considerably, so the use of network radio reduces advertisers' flexibility in selecting stations.

An important trend in radio is the increasing number of radio networks and syndicated programs that offer advertisers a package of several hundred stations. For example, conservative Rush Limbaugh's radio show is syndicated nationally and is carried by more than 500 stations, reaching more than 11 million people weekly (Exhibit 11–10). Syndication reduces

EXHIBIT 11–10
Rush Limbaugh's talk radio show is syndicated nationally

FIGURE 11–11
Radio's top national advertisers, 1995 ($ millions)

		Total	Network	Spot
1.	Sears	$71.637	$67.398	$ 4.240
2.	AT&T Corp.	59.558	34.288	25.271
3.	General Motors Corp.	51.264	30.318	20.945
4.	Chrysler Corp.	49.143	16.932	32.211
5.	U.S. government	36.552	29.474	7.078
6.	News Corp. LTD (Fox TV)	35.809	4.977	30.838
7.	MCI Communications	33.540	14.768	18.773
8.	Tandy Corp. (Radio Shack)	32.243	15.846	16.397
9.	Sunsource Health Products (Ginsana)	30.158	30.158	–
10.	Philip Morris Corp (Maxwell House, Miller Beer, Stovetop, Shake 'n' Bake)	28.249	13.230	15.020
11.	Warner-Lambert	23.190	23.190	–
12.	Visa International	23.076	17.188	5.887
13.	Montgomery Ward	21.261	–	21.261
14.	Kmart Corp.	20.309	9.550	10.759
15.	U.S. West, Inc.	18.468	–	18.468
16.	CompUSA	18.023	–	18.023
17.	Bayer Group (Alka-Seltzer)	17.502	17.502	–
18.	Ito-Yokado Co. Ltd. (7-Eleven)	16.861	–	16.861
19.	Procter & Gamble	15.866	15.866	–
20.	William Wrigley, Jr.	15.529	15.529	–
21.	American Stores Co. (Lucky)	14,594	–	14.594
22.	Capital Cities/ABC	13.314	6.219	7.095
23.	Walt Disney Co.	13.229	–	13.229
24.	Goodyear Tire & Rubber	12.849	12.849	–
25.	Grand Metropolitan (Burger King)	12.630	–	12.630

Sources: Competitive Media Reporting—Copyright 1996; *1997 Radio Marketing Guide and Fact Book for Advertising*, Radio Advertising Bureau, New York, NY.

audience fragmentation and purchasing problems and increases radio's appeal to national advertisers.

SPOT RADIO

National advertisers can also use spot radio to purchase air time on individual stations in various markets. The purchase of spot radio provides greater flexibility in selecting markets, individual stations, and air time and adjusting the message for local market conditions. Spot radio accounts for about 20 percent of radio time sold. Figure 11–11 shows the top 25 national advertisers and how they allocate their radio budgets between network and spot radio.

LOCAL RADIO

By far the heaviest users of radio are local advertisers; nearly 79 percent of radio advertising time is purchased from individual stations by local companies. Auto dealers, retailers, restaurants, and financial institutions are among the heaviest users of local radio advertising. But a number of radio advertisers are switching to local cable TV because the rates are comparable and there is the added advantage of TV's visual impact.

Time Classifications

As with television, the broadcast day for radio is divided into various time periods or dayparts, as shown in Figure 11–12. The size of the radio listening audience varies widely across the dayparts, and advertising rates follow accordingly. The largest radio audiences (and thus

FIGURE 11–12
Dayparts for radio

Morning drive time	6:00–10:00 AM
Daytime	10:00 AM–3:00 PM
Afternoon/evening drive time	3:00–7:00 PM
Nighttime	7:00 PM–12:00 AM
All night	12:00–6:00 AM

the highest rates) occur during the early morning and late afternoon drive times. Radio rates also vary according to the number of spots or type of audience plan purchased, the supply and demand of time available in the local market, and the ratings of the individual station. Rate information is available directly from the stations and is summarized in Standard Rate and Data Service's (SRDS) *Spot Radio Rates and Data* for both local stations and radio networks. Some stations issue rate cards like the one shown in Figure 11–13. But many stations do not adhere strictly to rate cards and the rates published in SRDS. Their rates are negotiable and depend on factors such as availability, time period, and number of spots purchased.

**Audience
Information**

One problem with radio is the lack of audience information. Because there are so many radio stations and thus many small, fragmented audiences, the stations cannot support the expense of detailed audience measurement. Also, owing to the nature of radio as incidental or background entertainment, it is difficult to develop precise measures of who listens at various time periods and for how long. There are now two major radio ratings services: Arbitron is the primary supplier of audience information for local stations and the RADAR (Radio's All-Dimension Audience Research) studies supply information on network audiences.

ARBITRON

Arbitron covers 260 local radio markets with one to four ratings reports per year. Arbitron has a sample of representative listeners in each market maintain a diary of their radio listening for seven days. Audience estimates for the market are based on these diary records and

FIGURE 11–13
Sample radio rate card

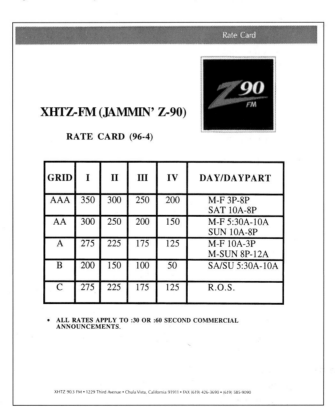

Rate Card

XHTZ-FM (JAMMIN' Z-90)

RATE CARD (96-4)

GRID	I	II	III	IV	DAY/DAYPART
AAA	350	300	250	200	M-F 3P-8P SAT 10A-8P
AA	300	250	200	150	M-F 5:30A-10A SUN 10A-8P
A	275	225	175	125	M-F 10A-3P M-SUN 8P-12A
B	200	150	100	50	SA/SU 5:30A-10A
C	275	225	175	125	R.O.S.

• **ALL RATES APPLY TO :30 OR :60 SECOND COMMERCIAL
ANNOUNCEMENTS.**

XHTZ 90.3 FM • 1229 Third Avenue • Chula Vista, California 91911 • FAX (619) 426-3690 • (619) 585-9090

FIGURE 11–14   Partial sample page from Arbitron radio ratings report

	Target Audience, Persons 18–49							
	Monday–Friday 6–10 AM				Monday–Friday 10 am–3 PM			
	AQH (OO)	CUME (OO)	AQH RTG	AQH SHR	AQH (OO)	CUME (OO)	AQH RTG	AQH SHR
KCBQ								
METRO	25	263	.2	.8	40	365	.3	1.3
TSA	25	263			40	365		
KCBQ-FM								
METRO	101	684	.7	3.1	117	768	.9	3.7
TSA	101	684			117	768		
KCEO								
METRO	11	110	.1	.3	8	81	.1	.3
TSA	11	110			8	81		
KFMB								
METRO	171	790	1.3	5.3	106	678	.8	3.3
TSA	171	790			106	678		

reported by time period and selected demographics in the *Arbitron Ratings/Radio* book, to which clients subscribe. Figure 11–14 provides a sample page from the Arbitron ratings report for people in the 18–49 age target audience across the various dayparts. The three basic estimates in the Arbitron report are

- Person estimates—the estimated number of people listening.
- Rating—the percentage of listeners in the survey area population.
- Share—the percentage of the total estimated listening audience.

These three estimates are further defined by using quarter-hour and cume figures. The **average quarter-hour (AQH) figure** expresses the average number of people estimated to have listened to a station for a minimum of five minutes during any quarter-hour in a time period. For example, station KCBQ has an average quarter-hour listenership of 2,500 during the weekday 6–10 AM daypart. This means that any weekday, for any 15-minute period during this time period, an average of 2,500 people between the ages of 18 and 49 are tuned to this station. This figure helps to determine the audience and cost of a spot schedule within a particular time period.

Cume stands for cumulative audience, the estimated total number of different people who listened to a station for at least five minutes in a quarter-hour period within a reported daypart. In Figure 11-14, the cumulative audience of people 18 to 49 for station KCBQ during the weekday morning daypart is 26,300. Cume estimates the reach potential of a radio station.

The **average quarter-hour rating** (AQH RTG) expresses the estimated number of listeners as a percentage of the survey area population. The **average quarter-hour share** (AQH SHR) is the percentage of the total listening audience tuned to each station. It shows the share of listeners each station captures out of the total listening audience in the survey area. The average quarter-hour rating of station KCBQ during the weekday 6–10 AM daypart is 0.2, while the average quarter-hour share is 0.8.

RADAR

Another rating service is Statistical Research Inc.'s RADAR (Radio's All-Dimension Audience Research) studies, which are sponsored by the major radio networks. Audience esti-

FIGURE 11–14   Concluded

	Target Audience, Persons 18–49											
	Monday–Friday 3–7 PM				Monday–Friday 7 PM–Mid				Weekend 10 AM–7 PM			
	AQH (OO)	CUME (OO)	AQH RTG	AQH SHR	AQH (OO)	CUME (OO)	AQH RTG	AQH SHR	AQH (OO)	CUME (OO)	AQH RTG	AQH SHR
KCBQ												
METRO	36	340	.3	1.4	6	138		.5	51	356	.4	2.4
TSA	36	340			6	138			51	356		
KCBQ-FM												
METRO	83	736	.6	3.2	23	354	.2	2.1	67	616	.5	3.2
TSA	83	736			23	354			67	616		
KCEO												
METRO	10	95	.1	.4		8			1	8		
TSA	10	95				8			1	8		
KFMB												
METRO	141	1092	1.0	5.4	87	827	.6	7.9	92	567	.7	4.4
TSA	141	1092			87	827			92	567		

mates are collected twice a year based on 12,000 daily telephone interviews covering seven days of radio listening behavior. Each listener is called daily for a week and asked about radio usage from the day before until that moment. RADAR provides network audience measures, along with estimates of audience size for all stations and various segments. The audience estimates are time-period measurements for the various dayparts. RADAR also provides estimates of network audiences for all commercials and commercials within various programs. The research is conducted year-round and is published annually in *Radio Usage and Network Radio Audiences.*

As with TV, media planners must use the audience measurement information to evaluate the value of various radio stations in reaching the advertiser's target audience and their relative cost. The media buyer responsible for the purchase of radio time works with information on target audience coverage, rates, time schedules, and availability to optimize the advertiser's radio media budget.

OTHER RATINGS SERVICES

Several other companies have begun offering radio audience measurement services. Symmetrical Resources focuses on measuring radio audiences in markets other than the top 50. The company uses telephone surveys to measure radio listenership as well as product consumption data in these markets. Symmetrical Resources is targeting advertisers and stations with its MATRIX (Marketing and Target Ratings Index) report in 200 smaller markets.[35]

Strategic Radio Research's AccuRatings is another new radio ratings service for local markets. The company uses telephone surveys to develop its ratings, including information on radio listening behavior, demographics, and selected qualitative characteristics of respondents. AccuRatings is currently measuring radio audiences in 20 markets throughout the country.

While Arbitron focuses primarily on local audience measurement, the company has made several proposals to the major radio networks to begin tracking network radio audiences. Arbitron is proposing to offer more frequent, quarterly reports and an annual sample of 1 million diaries versus the 12,000 phone interviews done by RADAR.[36]

SUMMARY

Television and radio, or the broadcast media, are the most pervasive media in most consumers' daily lives and offer advertisers the opportunity to reach vast audiences. Both broadcast media are time rather than space oriented and organized similarly in that they use a system of affiliated stations belonging to a network, as well as individual stations, to broadcast their programs and commercial messages. Advertising on radio or TV can be done on national or regional network programs or purchased in spots from local stations.

TV has grown faster than any other advertising medium in history and has become the leading medium for national advertisers. No other medium offers its creative capabilities; the combination of sight, sound, and movement give the advertiser a vast number of options for presenting a commercial message with high impact. Television also offers advertisers mass coverage at a low relative cost. Variations in programming and audience composition, along with the growth of cable, are helping TV offer more audience selectivity to advertisers. While television is often viewed as the ultimate advertising medium, it has several limitations, including the high cost of producing and airing commercials, a lack of selectivity relative to other media, the fleeting nature of the message, and the problem of commercial clutter. The latter two problems have been compounded in recent years by the trend toward shorter commercials.

Information regarding the size and composition of national and local TV audiences is provided by the A. C. Nielsen Co. The amount of money networks or stations can charge for commercial time on their programs is based on these audience measurement figures. This information is also important to media planners, as it is used to determine the combination of shows needed to attain specific levels of reach and frequency with the advertiser's target market. Statistical Research Inc. (SRI) is testing a TV audience measurement system that could become a rival to Nielsen if it receives adequate financial support from advertisers, agencies, and the networks.

Future trends in television include the continued growth of cable, competition to local cable operators from direct broadcast satellite systems, and a resulting increase in channels available to television households. Changes are also likely to occur in the measurement of viewing audiences—for example, continuous measurement of audiences.

The role of radio as an entertainment and advertising medium has changed with the rapid growth of television. Radio has evolved into a primarily local advertising medium that offers highly specialized programming appealing to narrow segments of the market. Radio offers advertisers the opportunity to build high reach and frequency into their media schedules and to reach selective audiences at a very efficient cost. It also offers opportunities for integrated marketing programs such as place-based promotions and event sponsorships.

The major drawback of radio is its creative limitations owing to the absence of a visual image. The short and fleeting nature of the radio commercial, the highly fragmented nature of the radio audience, and clutter are also problems.

As with TV, the rate structure for radio advertising time varies with the size of the audience delivered. The primary sources of information are Arbitron for local radio audiences and RADAR studies for network audiences.

KEY TERMS

split-30s, 345
zipping, 345
zapping, 345
television network, 346
affiliates, 346
up-front market, 348
scatter market, 348
spot advertising, 349
national spot advertising, 349
local advertising, 349
station reps, 350

syndicated programs, 350
sponsorship, 352
participations, 352
adjacencies, 353
dayparts, 353
cable television, 354
superstations, 354
interconnects, 356
narrowcasting, 357
infomercials, 357
multiplexing, 358

television households, 361
program rating, 361
ratings point, 361
households using
    television (HUT), 361
share of audience, 361
total audience, 362
audimeter, 362
people meter, 362
designated market areas
    (DMAs), 362

sweeps, 363
image transfer, 367
average quarter-hour
    (AQH) figure, 372
cume, 372
average quarter-hour
    rating, 372
average quarter-hour
    share, 372

DISCUSSION QUESTIONS

1. Analyze the reasons for the boom in televised sports programming discussed in the opening vignette. How can marketers capitalize on the growth of sports programming in developing IMC programs?

2. Television is often described as a mass medium that offers little selectivity to advertisers. Do you agree with this statement? What are some of the ways selectivity can be achieved through TV advertising?

3. Choose a network prime-time show and a local program such as a news broadcast and analyze it in terms of clutter. How might advertisers on these programs break through the clutter?

4. Explain what is meant by zipping and zapping and how they affect TV advertising. Discuss some ways advertisers can deal with the zapping problem.

5. Ethical Perspective 11–1 discusses the decision by the Ford Motor Co. to sponsor the network premiere of the movie *Schindler's List* without any commercial interruptions. Evaluate Ford's decision to pay $5 million to sponsor a program and not advertise any of its products.

6. Choose a particular television daypart other than prime time and analyze the products and services being advertised during this period. Why do you think these firms have chosen to advertise during this daypart?

7. Discuss the developments occurring in the distribution of cable TV programming. How are these developments likely to affect the advertising industry?

8. Discuss the methods used to measure network and local TV viewing audiences. Do you believe the measurement methods being used for each are producing valid estimates of program audiences? How can they be improved and who should pay the costs of these improvements?

9. What are the advantages and limitations of advertising on radio? What types of advertisers are most likely to use radio?

10. Discuss how the concept of image transfer can be used in radio advertising. Describe a radio campaign that is using this concept and evaluate it.

Evaluation of Print Media

Chapter Objectives

- To examine the structure of the magazine and newspaper industries and the role of each medium in the advertising program.

- To analyze the advantages and limitations of magazines and newspapers as advertising media.

- To examine the various types of magazines and newspapers and the value of each as an advertising medium.

- To discuss how advertising space is purchased in magazines and newspapers, how readership is measured, and how rates are determined.

- To consider future developments in magazines and newspapers and how these trends will influence their use as advertising media.

SPIN CONNECTS WITH READERS AND ADVERTISERS

Thousands of new consumer magazines have been introduced over the past decade, each with high hopes of attracting large numbers of readers and in turn attracting the advertisers and the ad revenue needed to survive and prosper. Many of these magazines failed to survive and others are struggling to keep their circulation base and number of ad pages high enough to stay out of the red. However, those whose editorial platform appeals to the needs, interests, and lifestyles of certain groups are finding success. One publication that is doing this particularly well recently is the music magazine *Spin*.

Though most of its articles are dedicated to the music scene, the monthly magazine's editorial focus has been firmly fixed on pop culture and its effect on the magazine's readers. *Spin* hasn't shied away from investigative journalism, news topics, politics, and controversy. The magazine has run an AIDS column in each issue since 1986 and caused a stir in 1988 by distributing condoms with one issue. Current-event stories in recent years have dealt with subjects such as the whereabouts of Moammer Gadhafi and the thoughts of the inventors of the atomic bomb 50 years after Hiroshima and the war in Bosnia.

Spin was started in 1986 by Bob Guccione, Jr., whose father is the publisher of *Penthouse*. Guccione admits that he modeled *Spin* after *Rolling Stone*, noting that the aging of the latter's core baby-boomer audience has allowed his magazine to focus on 18- to 25-year-olds. Guccione says, "My model for *Spin* was *Rolling Stone* of the 70s which meant something to me when I was a young man. My romanticism was to parallel what *Rolling Stone* meant to me when I was 18 and have *Spin* be that to today's people who are 18."

Spin is best known for its coverage of alternative music, and its profile has grown with the current interest in the music genre. The number of radio stations carrying the alternative music format has nearly tripled in the last three years. *Spin*'s music criticism and coverage has given it a reputation of being an insightful publication that is in tune with readers as well as the artists featured. Its cover stories in recent years have included PJ Harvey, Michael Stipe, Aerosmith, and Green Day. On the cover of its 10th-anniversary issue was the late Kurt Cobain, lead singer of the former band Nirvana and a central figure in the explosion of alternative rock's popularity.

The focus on pop culture has helped *Spin* connect with its readers and as alternative rock has grown, so has *Spin*'s circulation, which was up nearly 17 percent in 1995 and 13 percent in 1996 to nearly 467,000. The rise in circulation has been accompanied by increases in advertising as Spin has steadily increased its annual ad page totals through the 90s. New *Spin* advertisers in recent years have included blue-chip marketers IBM, Intel, Apple Computer, General Motors' Pontiac Division, Eastman Kodak, Sprint, and Calvin Klein. The associate media director at J. Walter Thompson USA, San Francisco, put its client Sprint into *Spin* for the first time to broaden its ways of reaching the college market.

Although pop music trends have come and gone, the fact that the alternative music craze may also die out doesn't bother Mr. Guccione or his prospects for *Spin*. He notes: "I look at the magazine like a boat. If it looks like it's going up and down, left and right, it's not because the boat doesn't know where it's going, it's because it's moving with the waves. If you're doing your job right, you should be going in different ways a bit." It appears that *Spin* is clearly doing a great job of catching the waves. The magazine was named one of *Advertising Age*'s Best Magazines in 1996, and its focus on alternative rock and the pop culture–reader connection has caught the attention of the younger generation, as well as the advertisers who want to reach them. Bob Guccione, Jr., appears to have fulfilled his dream of establishing *Spin* as the *Rolling Stone* of the under-25 set.

Source: Junu Bryan Kim, "Putting 'Spin' on Pop Culture," *Advertising Age*, March 11, 1996, p. S8; and Keith J. Kelly, "Magazines Stay on Downward Course in 1st Half," *Advertising Age*, August 26, 1996, p. 25.

Magazines and newspapers have been advertising media for more than two centuries; for many years, they were the only major media available to advertisers. With the growth of the broadcast media, particularly television, reading habits declined. More consumers turned to TV viewing not only as their primary source of entertainment but also for news and information. But despite the competition from the broadcast media, newspapers and magazines have remained important media vehicles to both consumers and advertisers.

Thousands of magazines are published in the United States and throughout the world. They appeal to nearly every specific consumer interest and lifestyle, as well as to thousands of businesses and occupations. By becoming a highly specialized medium that reaches specific target audiences, the magazine industry has prospered. Newspapers are still the primary advertising medium in terms of both ad revenue and number of advertisers. Newspapers are particularly important as a local advertising medium for hundreds of thousands of retail businesses and are often used by large national advertisers as well.

Magazines and newspapers are an important part of our lives. For many consumers, newspapers are their primary source of product information. They would not think of going shopping without checking to see who is having a sale or clipping coupons from the weekly food section or Sunday inserts. Many people read a number of different magazines each week or month to become better informed or simply entertained. Individuals employed in various occupations rely on business magazines to keep them current about trends and developments in their industries as well as in business in general.

While most of us are very involved with the print media, it is important to keep in mind that few newspapers or magazines could survive without the support of advertising revenue. Consumer magazines generate an average of 47 percent of their revenues from advertising; business publications receive nearly 73 percent.[1] Newspapers generate 70 percent of their total revenue from advertising. In many cities, the number of daily newspapers has declined because they could not attract enough advertising revenue to support their operations. The print media must be able to attract large numbers of readers or a very specialized audience to be of interest to advertisers.

THE ROLE OF MAGAZINES AND NEWSPAPERS

The role of magazines and newspapers in the advertiser's media plan differs from that of the broadcast media because they allow the presentation of detailed information that can be processed at the reader's own pace. The print media are not intrusive like radio and TV, and they generally require some effort on the part of the reader for the advertising message to have an impact. For this reason, newspapers and magazines are often referred to as *high-involvement media*.[2]

Newspapers are received in nearly two-thirds of American households daily. Most magazines, however, reach a very selective audience. Like radio, they can be valuable in reaching specific types of consumers and market segments. While both magazines and newspapers are print media, the advantages and disadvantages of the two are quite different, as are the types of advertising each attracts. This chapter focuses on these two major forms of print media. It examines the specific advantages and limitations of each, along with factors that are important in determining when and how to use newspapers and magazines in the media plan.

MAGAZINES

Over the past several decades, magazines have grown rapidly to serve the educational, informational, and entertainment needs of a wide range of readers in both the consumer and business markets. Magazines are the most specialized of all advertising media. While some magazines—such as *Reader's Digest*, *Time*, and *TV Guide*—are general mass-appeal publications, most are targeted to a very specific audience. There is a magazine designed to appeal to nearly every type of consumer in terms of demographics, lifestyle, activities, interests, or fascination. Numerous magazines are targeted toward specific businesses and industries as well as toward individuals engaged in various professions (Exhibit 12–1).

The wide variety makes magazines an appealing medium to a vast number of advertisers. Although TV accounts for the largest dollar amount of advertising expenditures among national advertisers, more companies advertise in magazines than in any other medium. Users of magazines range from large consumer products companies such as Philip Morris Co. and General Motors, which spend nearly $400 million a year on magazine advertising, to a small company advertising scuba equipment in *Skin Diver* magazine.

Classifications of Magazines

To gain some perspective on the various types of magazines available and the advertisers that use them, consider the way magazines are generally classified. Standard Rate and Data Service (SRDS), the primary reference source on periodicals for media planners, divides magazines into three broad categories based on the audience to which they are directed: consumer, farm, and business publications. Each category is then further classified according to the magazine's editorial content and audience appeal.

CONSUMER MAGAZINES

Consumer magazines are bought by the general public for information and/or entertainment. SRDS divides 2,700 domestic consumer magazines into 51 classifications, among them general interest, sports, travel, and women's. Another way of classifying consumer magazines is by distribution: they can be sold through subscription or circulation, store distribution, or both. *Time* and *Newsweek* are sold both through subscription and in stores; *Woman's World* is sold only through stores. *People* magazine was originally sold only through stores but then added subscription sales as it gained in popularity. Figure 12–1 shows the top 10 magazines in terms of subscriptions and single-copy sales, respectively. Magazines can also be classified by frequency; weekly, monthly, and bimonthly are the most common.

EXHIBIT 12–1
Magazines targeted to a specific industry or profession

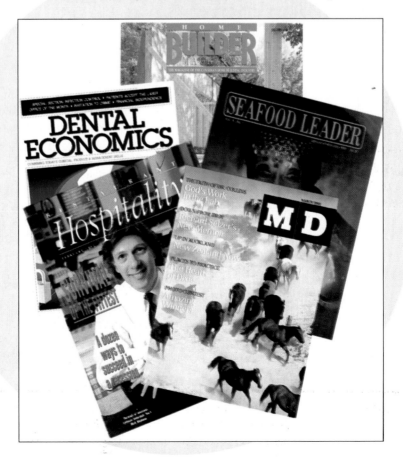

FIGURE 12–1

Top magazines by subscriptions and single-copy sales

By Subscriptions		By Single-Copy Sales	
1. *Modern Maturity*	20,528,786	1. *TV Guide*	4,058,548
2. *Reader's Digest*	14,295,228	2. *Family Circle*	2,275,500
3. *TV Guide*	8,955,390	3. *Woman's Day*	2,171,750
4. *National Geographic*	8,870,395	4. *National Enquirer*	2,104,913
5. *Better Homes & Gardens*	7,212,825	5. *Star*	1,910,141
6. *Time*	3,941,757	6. *Cosmopolitan*	1,676,918
7. *Ladies' Home Journal*	3,916,249	7. *Woman's World*	1,504,067
8. *McCall's*	3,860,383	8. *People*	1,440,276
9. *Good Housekeeping*	3,574,354	9. *Good Housekeeping*	1,376,886
10. *Sports Illustrated*	3,080,167	10. *First for Women*	1,185,800

Note: Figures are averages for six months ended December 31, 1996.

Source: Audit Bureau of Circulations.

Consumer magazines represent the major portion of the magazine industry, accounting for nearly two-thirds of all advertising dollars spent in magazines. The distribution of advertising revenue in consumer magazines is highly concentrated; the top 25 magazines receive more than 70 percent of total consumer magazine advertising. Consumer magazines are best suited to marketers interested in reaching general consumers of products and services as well as to companies trying to reach a specific target market. The most frequently advertised categories in consumer magazines are automotive, direct response, toiletries and cosmetics, computers, office equipment and stationery, and business and consumer services. Marketers of tobacco products spend much of their media budget in magazines, since they are prohibited from advertising in the broadcast media.

While large national advertisers tend to dominate consumer magazine advertising in terms of expenditures, the more than 2,000 consumer magazines are also important to smaller companies selling products that appeal to specialized markets. Special-interest magazines assemble consumers with similar lifestyles or interests and offer marketers an efficient way to reach these people with little wasted coverage or circulation. For example, a manufacturer of ski equipment such as Nordica, Rossignol, or Salomon might find *Powder* the best vehicle for advertising to serious skiers.

Not only are these specialty magazines of value to firms interested in reaching a specific market segment, but their editorial content often creates a very favorable advertising environment for relevant products and services. For example, avid skiers cannot wait for the first snowfall after reading the season's first issues of *Powder* or *Skiing* magazine and may be quite receptive to the ads they carry for skiing products and destination ski resorts.

FARM PUBLICATIONS

The second major SRDS category consists of all the magazines directed to farmers and their families. About 270 publications are tailored to nearly every possible type of farming or agricultural interest. Standard Rate and Data Service breaks farm publications into 11 classifications, ranging from general-interest magazines aimed at all types of farmers (e.g., *Farm Journal*, *Successful Farmer*, *Progressive Farmer*) to those in specialized agricultural areas such as poultry (*Gobbles*), hog

farming (*National Hog Farmer*), or cattle raising (*Beef*—see Exhibit 12–2). A number of farm publications are directed at farmers in specific states or regions, such as *Nebraska Farmer* or *Montana Farmer Stockman*. Farm publications are not classified with business publications because historically farms were not perceived as businesses.

BUSINESS PUBLICATIONS

Business publications are those magazines or trade journals published for specific businesses, industries, or occupations. Standard Rate and Data Service breaks down over 7,500 U.S. magazines and trade journals into 159 categories. The major categories include

1. Magazines directed at specific professional groups, such as *National Law Review* for lawyers and *Architectural Forum* for architects.
2. Industrial magazines directed at businesspeople in various manufacturing and production industries—for example, *Iron Age*, *Chemical Week*, and *Industrial Engineering*.
3. Trade magazines targeted to wholesalers, dealers, distributors, and retailers, among them *Progressive Grocer*, *Drug Store News*, *Women's Wear Daily*, and *Restaurant Business*.
4. General business magazines aimed at executives in all areas of business, such as *Forbes*, *Fortune*, and *Business Week*. (General business publications are also included in SRDS's consumer publications edition.)

The numerous business publications reach specific types of professional people with particular interests and give them important information relevant to their industry, occupation, and/or careers. Business publications are important to advertisers because they provide an efficient way of reaching the specific types of individuals who constitute their target market. Much marketing occurs at the trade and business-to-business level, where one company sells its products or services directly to another. We examine the role of advertising in business-to-business marketing in greater detail in Chapter 19.

Advantages of Magazines

Magazines have a number of characteristics that make them attractive as an advertising medium. Strengths of magazines include their selectivity, excellent reproduction quality, creative flexibility, permanence, prestige, readers' high receptivity and involvement, and services they offer to advertisers.

SELECTIVITY

One of the main advantages of using magazines as an advertising medium is their **selectivity,** or ability to reach a specific target audience. Magazines are the most selective of all media except direct mail. Most magazines are published for special-interest groups. The thousands of magazines published in the United States reach all types of consumers and businesses and allow advertisers to target their advertising to segments of the population who buy their products. For example, *Modern Photography* is targeted toward camera buffs, *Stereo Review* reaches those with an avid interest in music, and *Ebony* focuses on the upscale African-American market. Many new magazines each year are targeted at new interests and trends. *PC Gamer*, for example, is a new publication that is capitalizing on the increasing popularity of electronic sports games played on computers.

In addition to selectivity based on interests, magazines can provide advertisers with high demographic and geographic selectivity. *Demographic selectivity,* or the ability to reach specific demographic groups, is available in two ways. First, most magazines are, as a result of editorial content, aimed at fairly well-defined demographic segments. *Ladies' Home Journal, Ms., Self,* and *Cosmopolitan* are read predominantly by women; *Esquire, Playboy,* and *Sports Illustrated* are read mostly by men. Teenage girls can be reached through *Seventeen* or *Sassy,* while older consumers can be reached through publications like *Modern Maturity.*

A second way magazines offer demographic selectivity is through special editions. Even magazines that appeal to broader audiences, such as *Reader's Digest, Time,* or *Newsweek,* can provide a high degree of demographic selectivity through their special demographic editions. Most of the top consumer magazines publish different editions targeted at different demographic markets. Exhibit 12–3 describes *Newsweek 50 Plus*, a specific demographic edition offered by *Newsweek* magazine.

Geographic selectivity lets an advertiser focus ads in certain cities or regions. One way to achieve geographic selectivity is by using a magazine that is targeted toward a particular area. Magazines devoted to regional interests include *Yankee* (New England), *Southern Liv-*

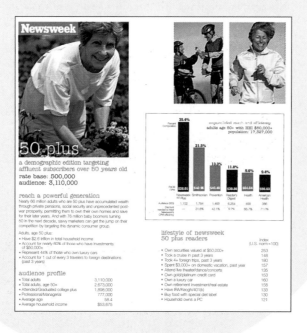

EXHIBIT 12–3
This special edition of *Newsweek* allows advertisers to reach a specific demographic group

ing (South), *Sunset* (West), and *Texas Monthly* (guess where?), among many others. One of the more successful media developments of recent years has been the growth of city magazines in most major American cities.[3] *Los Angeles Magazine*, *Philadelphia*, and *Denver*, to name a few, provide residents of these areas with articles concerning lifestyle, events, and the like in these cities and their surrounding metropolitan areas.

Another way to achieve geographic selectivity in magazines is through purchasing ad space in specific geographic editions of national or regional magazines. A number of publications divide their circulation into groupings based on regions or major metropolitan areas and offer advertisers the option of concentrating their ads in these editions. For example, *Newsweek* breaks the United States into 11 geographic areas and offers regional editions for each, as shown in Exhibit 12–4. *Newsweek* also offers advertisers their choice of editions directed to the top 40, 20, or 10 metropolitan areas. Many magazines allow advertisers to combine regional or metropolitan editions to best match the geographic market of interest to them.

Standard Rate and Data Service lists over 350 consumer magazines offering geographic and/or demographic editions. Regional advertisers can purchase space in editions that reach only areas where they have distribution, yet still enjoy the prestige of advertising in a major national magazine. National advertisers can use the geographic editions to focus their advertising on areas with the greatest potential or those needing more promotional support. They can also use regional editions to test-market products or alternative promotional campaigns in various regions of the country.

Ads in regional editions can also list the names of retailers or distributors in various markets, thus encouraging greater local support from the trade. The trend toward regional marketing is increasing the importance of having regional media available to marketers. The availability of regional and demographic editions can also reduce the cost per thousand for reaching desired audiences.

REPRODUCTION QUALITY

One of the most valued attributes of magazine advertising is the reproduction quality of the ads. Magazines are generally printed on high-quality paper stock and use printing processes that provide excellent reproduction in black and white or color. Since magazines are a visual medium where illustrations are often a dominant part of an ad, this is a very important property. The reproduction quality of most magazines is far superior to that offered by the other major print medium of newspapers, particularly when color is needed. The use of color has become a virtual necessity in most product categories, and more than two-thirds of all magazine ads now use color.

EXHIBIT 12–4
Geographic editions of *Newsweek* magazine

CREATIVE FLEXIBILITY

In addition to their excellent reproduction capabilities, magazines also offer advertisers a great deal of flexibility in terms of the type, size, and placement of the advertising material. Some magazines offer (often at extra charge) a variety of special options that can enhance the creative appeal of the ad and increase attention and readership. Examples include gatefolds, bleed pages, inserts, and creative space buys.

Gatefolds enable an advertiser to make a striking presentation by using a third page that folds out and gives the ad an extra-large spread. Gatefolds are often found at the inside cover of large consumer magazines or on some inside pages. Advertisers use gatefolds to make a very strong impression, especially on special occasions such as the introduction of a new product or brand. For example, automobile advertisers often use gatefolds to introduce new versions of their cars each model year. Not all magazines offer gatefolds, however, and they must be reserved well in advance and are sold at a premium.

Bleed pages are those where the advertisement extends all the way to the end of the page, with no margin of white space around the ad. Bleeds give the ad an impression of being larger and make a more dramatic impact. Many magazines charge an extra 10 to 20 percent for bleeds.

In addition to gatefolds and bleed pages, creative options available through magazines include unusual page sizes and shapes. Some advertisers have grabbed readers' attention by developing three-dimensional pop-up ads that jump off the page. Exhibit 12–5 shows a pop-up ad from Transamerica Corp. depicting the city of San Francisco and the company's corporate symbol, the Transamerica pyramid tower. The ad, which cost nearly $1 million to produce and run once in *Time* magazine, was designed to promote Transamerica Insurance Cos. as leaders in providing innovative insurance services.

Various other *inserts* are used in many magazines. These include return cards, recipe booklets, coupons, records, and even product samples. Cosmetic companies use scratch-and-sniff inserts to introduce new fragrances, and some companies use them to promote deodorants, laundry detergents, or other products whose scent is important. Inserts are also used in conjunction with direct-response ads and as part of sales promotion strategies.

Scented ads, pop-ups, singing ads, and other techniques are ways to break through the clutter in magazines and capture consumers' attention. However, there recently has been some backlash against various types of *printaculars*. Critics argue that they alter the appearance and feel of a magazine and the reader's relationship to it. Advertisers do not want to run regular ads that have to compete against heavy inserts, pop-ups, talking ads, or other distractions. Some advertisers and agencies are even asking publishers to notify them when they plan to run any spectacular inserts so they can decide whether to pull their regular ads from the issue.[4]

Creative space buys are another option of magazines. Some magazines let advertisers purchase space units in certain combinations to increase the impact of their media budget. For

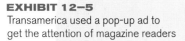

EXHIBIT 12–5
Transamerica used a pop-up ad to get the attention of magazine readers

example, WD-40, an all-purpose lubrication product, uses quarter-page ads on four consecutive pages of several magazines, mentioning a different use for the product on each page, as shown in Exhibit 12–6. (For more about WD-40's media plan, see Chapter 10's Appendix B). This strategy gave the company greater impact for its media dollars and was helpful in promoting the product's variety of uses.

PERMANENCE

Another distinctive advantage offered by magazines is their long life span. TV and radio are characterized by fleeting messages that have a very short life span; newspapers are generally discarded soon after being read. Magazines, however, are generally read over several days and are often kept for reference. They are retained in the home longer than any other medium and are generally referred to on several occasions. A study of magazine audiences found that readers devote an hour or more over a period of two or three days to reading an average magazine.[5] Studies have also found that nearly 75 percent of consumers retain magazines for future reference.[6] One benefit of the longer life of magazines is that reading occurs at a less hurried pace and there is more opportunity to examine ads in considerable detail. This means ads can use longer and more detailed copy, which can be very important for high-involvement and complex products or services. The permanence of magazines also means readers can be exposed to ads on multiple occasions and can pass magazines along to other readers.

PRESTIGE

Another positive feature of magazine advertising is the prestige the product or service may gain from advertising in publications with a favorable image. Companies whose products rely heavily on perceived quality, reputation, and/or image often buy space in prestigious publications with high-quality editorial content whose consumers have a high level of interest in the advertising pages. For example, *Esquire* and *GQ* cover men's fashions in a very favorable environment, and a clothing manufacturer may advertise its products in these magazines to enhance the prestige of its lines. *Architectural Digest* provides an impressive editorial environment that includes high-quality photography and artwork. The magazine's upscale readers are likely to have a favorable image of the publication that may transfer to the products advertised on its pages. *Good Housekeeping* provides a unique consumer's refund or replacement policy for products that bear the limited warranty seal or advertise in the magazine. This can increase a consumer's confidence in a particular brand and reduce the amount of perceived risk associated with a purchase.

While most media planners recognize that the environment created by a publication is important, it can be difficult to determine the image a magazine provides. Subjective estimates based on media planners' experience are often used to assess a magazine's prestige, as are objective measures such as reader opinion surveys.[7]

CONSUMER RECEPTIVITY AND INVOLVEMENT

With the exception of newspapers, consumers are more receptive to advertising in magazines than in any other medium. Magazines are generally purchased because the information they contain interests the reader, and ads provide additional information that may be of value in making a purchase decision. A study conducted for the Magazine Publishers Association of America (MPA) examined the various media as sources of knowledge and usable ideas for various products. It found that magazines are consumers' primary source of information for a variety of products and services, including cars, money matters, clothing and fashions, beauty and grooming, and personal and business travel.[8] The MPA has been promoting the value of magazines in successful marketing programs with its "I'm glad we did this ad" and "I'm glad we spent *more* in magazines" series. Exhibit 12–7 shows one of the ads from the latter and discusses how Avon Products, Inc. uses magazines as part of its successful "Avon Ladies" campaign.

In addition to their relevance, magazine ads are likely to be received favorably by consumers because, unlike broadcast ads, they are nonintrusive and can easily be ignored. Studies show that the majority of magazine readers welcome ads; only a small percentage have negative attitudes toward magazine advertising.[9] Some magazines, such as bridal or fashion publications, are purchased as much for their advertising as for their editorial content. MPA-sponsored studies have shown that magazine readers are more likely to attend to and recall ads than are TV viewers.

EXHIBIT 12–7

This ad is part of a campaign by the Magazine Publishers of America promoting the value of magazine advertising

SERVICES

A final advantage of magazines is the special services some publications offer advertisers. Some magazines have merchandising staffs that call on trade intermediaries like retailers to let them know a product is being advertised in their publication and to encourage them to display or promote the item. Another service offered by magazines (usually the larger ones) is research studies that they conduct on consumers. These studies may deal with general consumer trends, changing purchase patterns, and media usage or may be relevant to a specific product or industry.

An important service offered by some magazines is **split runs**, where two or more versions of an ad are printed in alternate copies of a particular issue of a magazine. This service is used to conduct a split-run test, which allows the advertiser to determine which ad generates the most responses or inquiries, providing some evidence as to their effectiveness.

Disadvantages of Magazines

Although the advantages offered by magazines are considerable, they have certain drawbacks too. These include the costs of advertising, their limited reach and frequency, the long lead time required in placing an ad, and the problem of clutter and heavy advertising competition.

COSTS

The costs of advertising in magazines vary according to the size of the audience they reach and their selectivity. Advertising in large mass-circulation magazines like *TV Guide*, *Time*, or *Reader's Digest* can be very expensive. For example, a full-page, four-color ad in *Time* magazine's national edition (circulation 4.1 million) cost $162,000 in 1997. Popular positions such as the back cover cost even more. By contrast, a full-page, four-color ad in *Runner's World* (circulation 447,145) cost $36,850.

Like any medium, magazines must be considered not only from an absolute cost perspective but also in terms of relative costs. Most magazines emphasize their effectiveness in reaching specific target audiences at a low cost per thousand. Also, an increasing number of magazines are offering demographic and geographic editions, which helps lower their costs. Media planners generally focus on the relative costs of a publication in reaching their target audience. However, they may recommend a magazine with a high cost per thousand because of its ability to reach a small, specialized market segment. Of course, advertisers with limited budgets will be interested in the absolute costs of space in a magazine and the costs of producing quality ads for these publications.

LIMITED REACH AND FREQUENCY

Magazines are generally not as effective as other media in offering reach and frequency. While nearly 90 percent of adults in the United States read one or more consumer magazines each month, the percentage of adults reading any individual publication tends to be much smaller, so magazines have a thin penetration of households. For example, *TV Guide* has the third-highest circulation of any magazine, at just over 13 million, but this represents only 13.4 percent of the 97 million households in the United States.

As shown in Figure 12–2, only 33 magazines had a paid circulation over 2 million at the end of 1996. Thus, advertisers seeking broad reach must make media buys in a number of magazines, which means more negotiations and transactions. For a broad reach strategy, magazines are used in conjunction with other media. Since most magazines are monthly or at best weekly publications, the opportunity for building frequency through the use of the same publication is limited. Using multiple ads in the same issue of a publication is an inefficient way to build frequency. Most advertisers try to achieve frequency by adding other magazines with similar audiences to the media schedule.

LONG LEAD TIME

Another drawback of magazines is the long lead time needed to place an ad. Most major publications have a 30- to 90-day lead time, which means space must be purchased and the

FIGURE 12–2 Top 50 magazines in paid circulation

Rank	Magazine	Circulation	Rank	Magazine	Circulation
1.	Modern Maturity	20,528,786	26.	Motor Land	2,376,974
2.	Reader's Digest	15,072,260	27.	U.S. News & World Report	2,260,857
3.	TV Guide	13,013,938	28.	Star	2,220,711
4.	National Geographic	9,025,003	29.	NEA Today	2,168,447
5.	Better Homes & Gardens	7,605,325	30.	YM	2,153,815
6.	The Cable Guide	5,260,421	31.	Glamour	2,115,488
7.	Family Circle	5,239,074	32.	Smithsonian	2,095,819
8.	Good Housekeeping	4,951,240	33.	Martha Stewart Living	2,025,182
9.	Ladies' Home Journal	4,544,416	34.	Money	1,993,119
10.	Woman's Day	4,317,604	35.	V.F.W. Magazine	1,980,947
11.	McCall's	4,290,216	36.	Ebony	1,803,566
12.	Time	4,102,168	37.	Popular Science	1,793,192
13.	People	3,449,852	38.	Field & Stream	1,750,180
14.	Prevention	3,311,244	39.	Parents	1,737,249
15.	Playboy	3,236,517	40.	Country Living	1,674,925
16.	Newsweek	3,194,769	41.	Life	1,601,069
17.	Sports Illustrated	3,173,639	42.	American Rifleman	1,545,242
18.	Redbook	2,926,702	43.	Golf Digest	1,515,829
19.	The American Legion Magazine	2,777,351	44.	Woman's World	1,504,067
20.	Home and Away	2,719,931	45.	Soap Opera Digest	1,468,333
21.	Avenues	2,549,695	46.	Sunset	1,431,549
22.	Southern Living	2,490,542	47.	Popular Mechanics	1,428,356
23.	Cosmopolitan	2,486,393	48.	Cooking Light	1,379,055
24.	National Enquirer	2,480,349	49.	Men's Health	1,373,817
25.	Seventeen	2,442,090	50.	Secure Retirement	1,363,086

Note: Figures are averages for six months ended December 31, 1996.

Source: Audit Bureau of Circulations.

ad must be prepared well in advance of the actual publication date. No changes in the art or copy of the ad can be made after the closing date. This long lead time means magazine ads cannot be as timely as other media, such as radio or newspapers, in responding to current events or changing market conditions.

CLUTTER AND COMPETITION

While the problem of advertising clutter is generally discussed in reference to the broadcast media, magazines also have this drawback. The clutter problem for magazines is something of a paradox: the more successful a magazine becomes, the more advertising pages it attracts, which leads to greater clutter. In fact, magazines generally gauge their success in terms of the number of advertising pages they sell.

Magazine publishers do attempt to control the clutter problem by maintaining a reasonable balance of editorial pages to advertising. According to the Magazine Publishers of America, the average consumer magazine contains 48 percent advertising and 52 percent editorial.[10] However, many magazines contain ads on more than half of their pages. This clutter makes it difficult for an advertiser to gain readers' attention and draw them into the ad. Thus, many print ads use strong visual images, catchy headlines, or some of the creative techniques discussed earlier to grab the interest of magazine readers. Ethical Perspective 12–1 discusses how some advertisers are creating their own custom magazines to sidestep advertising clutter.

Ethical Perspective 12—1
Is It a Magazine or an Ad?

Advertising clutter is a problem in most media, and magazines are no exception. The average consumer magazine has ads on about half its pages, and in some publications the percentage is even higher. Some companies are dealing with the clutter problem by publishing their own custom magazines. Examples include *Know How*, a women's magazine sponsored by General Motors; *Tell*, a teen magazine published by the NBC TV network; and *Your Body & Your Health*, from weight-loss company Jenny Craig.

A number of companies have long published their own magazines, using them to build relationships with their customers. Farmer's Insurance sends its customers a magazine called *The Friendly Review* that contains useful articles on a variety of topics. FedExpress publishes *Via FedEx*, a free magazine full of career and office management tips for some of its most important customers, professional secretaries.

The new corporate magazines differ, however, in that they are produced by the same publishers as traditional magazines and readers must pay to read them. For example, *Sun* magazine, a publication of Ray-Ban sunglasses (a division of Bausch & Lomb), sells for $2.50 and bears more than a passing resemblance to the popular women's fashion magazine *Elle*. This is no coincidence, since it is published by Hachette Filipacchi Magazines, *Elle*'s publisher. Hachette Filipacchi has brought out seven custom-published magazines, including *Sony Style*, a twice yearly publication that sells for $4.95 and doubles as the company's catalog.

Philip Morris also recently hired the custom-publishing division of Hachette Filipacchi to produce a glossy new magazine called *Unlimited: Action, Adventure, Good Times*. The creators claim the new magazine, which debuted in late 1996, will reach close to two million men between the ages of 21 and 29. The magazine won't be available on newsstands. Instead, 1.5 million copies are being sent to Marlboro smokers plucked from Philip Morris's vast databases. Another one million issues will be mailed to anyone 21 or older who requests the magazine by signing an order form available at stores that sell Marlboros. The editor of *Unlimited* describes it as "a regular-guy magazine" aimed at Marlboro smokers who have broad interests but don't necessarily have a college education and a lot of disposable income. He says articles about smokers' rights will not be part of the editorial recipe. *Unlimited* will carry ads for a variety of other products aimed at young men, but Marlboro will be the only cigarette brand allowed to advertise in the publication.

While the custom magazines are growing in popularity, some people think advertisers and publishers are losing credibility by asking consumers to pay for what are at worst little more than long glossy ads and at best advertiser-controlled publications posing as independent media. One publishing consultant calls the custom magazines "phony publishing" and says they are no more credible than a TV infomercial.

While critics may debate whether these publications are really magazines or infomercials in print, advertisers see them as a viable alternative to traditional forms of advertising. The vice president of marketing at Bausch & Lomb's eyewear division notes that the purpose of *Sun* is to go beyond the limits of traditional advertising and bring readers several messages about the benefits of Ray-Ban sunglasses.

The ultimate question, of course, is whether consumers will pay to read these custom magazines. *Sun* has an abundance of fashion photographs (in which most of the models wear Ray-Bans), along with articles tangentially related to sunglasses, such as sports stories, celebrity profiles, tips on driving safety, and warnings about the dangers of ultraviolet rays. Some of the publications tackle sensitive topics that might make advertisers nervous. For example, NBC's *Tell* published an article about teens and sex. Ultimately, whether consumers will pay to read these custom magazines may be the real determinant of whether they are seen as interesting magazines or infomercials in print.

Sources: Sally Goll Beatty, "Philip Morris Starts Lifestyle Magazine," *The Wall Street Journal*, September 16, 1996, pp. B1,8; Laura Bird, "'Custom' Magazines Stir Credibility Issues," *The Wall Street Journal*, February 14, 1993, p. B10. Reprinted by permission of *The Wall Street Journal*, ©1996, 1993 Dow Jones & Company, Inc. All Rights Reserved Worldwide.

Clutter is not as serious an issue for the print media as for radio or TV, since consumers tend to be more receptive and tolerant of print advertising. They can also control their exposure to a magazine ad simply by turning the page.

Magazine Circulation and Readership

Two of the most important considerations in deciding whether to use a magazine in the advertising media plan are the size and characteristics of the audience it reaches. Media buyers evaluate magazines on the basis of their ability to deliver the advertiser's message to as many people as possible in the target audience. To do this, they must consider the circulation of the publication as well as its total readership and match these figures against the audience they are attempting to reach.

CIRCULATION

Circulation figures represent the number of individuals who receive a publication through either subscription or store purchase. The number of copies distributed to these original subscribers or purchasers is known as *primary circulation* and is the basis for the magazine's rate structure. Circulation fluctuates from issue to issue, particularly for magazines that rely heavily on retail or newsstand sales. Many publications base their rates on *guaranteed circulation* and give advertisers a rebate if the number of delivered magazines falls below the guarantee. To minimize rebating, most guaranteed circulation figures are conservative; that is, they are set safely below the average actual delivered circulation. Advertisers are not charged for any excess circulation.

Many publishers became unhappy with the guaranteed circulation concept, since it requires them to provide refunds if guarantees are not met but results in a bonus for advertisers when circulation exceeds the guarantee. Thus, many publications have gone to a circulation rate base system. Rates are based on a set average circulation that is nearly always below the actual circulation delivered by a given issue but carries no guarantee. However, circulation is unlikely to fall below the rate base, since this would reflect negatively on the publication and make it difficult to attract advertisers at prevailing rates.

Circulation Verification

Given that circulation figures are the basis for a magazine's advertising rates and one of the primary considerations in selecting a publication, the credibility of circulation figures is important. Most major publications are audited by one of the circulation verification services. Consumer magazines and farm publications are audited by the Audit Bureau of Circulations (ABC), which was organized in 1914 and is sponsored by advertisers, agencies, and publishers. ABC collects and evaluates information regarding the subscriptions and sales of magazines and newspapers to verify their circulation figures. Only publications with 70 percent or more paid circulation (which means the purchaser paid at least half the magazine's established base price) are eligible for verification audits by ABC. Certain business publications are audited by the Business Publications Audit (BPA) of Circulation. Many of these are published on a **controlled-circulation basis**, meaning copies are sent (usually free) to individuals the publisher believes can influence their company's purchases.

Circulation verification services provide media planners with reliable figures regarding the size and distribution of a magazine's circulation that help them evaluate its worth as a media vehicle. The ABC statement also provides other important information.[11] It shows how a magazine is distributed by state and size, as well as percentage of the circulation sold at less than full value and percentage arrears (how many subscriptions are being given away). Many advertisers believe that subscribers who pay for a magazine are more likely to read it than are those who get it at a discount or for free.

Media buyers are generally skeptical about publications whose circulation figures are not audited by one of the verification services, and some companies will not advertise in unaudited publications. Circulation data, along with the auditing source, are available from Standard Rate and Data Service or from the publication itself. Exhibit 12–8 shows a sample magazine publisher's statement which is subject to audit by Audit Bureau of Circulations.

EXHIBIT 12–8 Example of an Audit Bureau of Circulations publisher's statement

Audit Bureau of Circulations
900 North Meacham Road, Schaumburg, Illinois 60173-4968

MAGAZINE PUBLISHER'S STATEMENT

PROTOTYPE
ANYTOWN, IL 60000

AVERAGE PAID CIRCULATION
For Six Months Ended December 31, (Year)

404,790

Publisher's Compilation - Subject to Audit

Publisher's Statement For 6 Months Ended December 31, (Year)

PROTOTYPE

CLASS, INDUSTRY OR FIELD SERVED: Travel, customs of people, products and related human interest, subject to geographical and sociological nature.

1. AVERAGE PAID CIRCULATION FOR 6 MONTHS ENDED DECEMBER 31, (YEAR)

Subscriptions:		295,069
Single Copy Sales:		109,721
AVERAGE TOTAL PAID CIRCULATION		404,790
Advertising Rate Base		400,000
Average Total Non-Paid Distribution	12,050	

1a. AVERAGE PAID CIRCULATION of Regional, Metro and Demographic Editions

Edition & number of issues	
Eastern (6)	149,772
Central (6)	161,916
Western (6)	93,102

2. PAID CIRCULATION by Issues

Issue	Subscriptions	Single Copy Sales	Total Paid	Issue	Subscriptions	Single Copy Sales	Total Paid
July	285,960	116,637	402,597	Oct.	301,738	105,764	407,502
Aug.	297,181	107,749	404,930	Nov.	290,590	109,495	400,085
Sept.	300,315	102,700	403,015	Dec.	294,630	115,979	410,609

ANALYSIS OF TOTAL NEW AND RENEWAL SUBSCRIPTIONS

Sold during 6 Month Period Ended December 31, (Year)

3. AUTHORIZED PRICES

(a) Basic Prices: Single Copy: $1.50. Subscriptions: 1 yr. $12.00; 2 yrs. $22.00; 3 yrs. $30.00	19,431
(b) Higher than basic prices	None
(c) Lower than basic prices: 1 yr. $7.00, $8.00, $8.99; 2 yrs. $13.99	78,924
(d) Association subscription prices	None
Total Subscriptions Sold in Period	98,355

4. DURATION OF SUBSCRIPTIONS SOLD:

(a) One to six months (1 to 6 issues)	660
(b) Seven to twelve months (7 to 12 issues)	85,669
(c) Thirteen to twenty-four months	1,021
(d) Twenty-five to thirty-six months	143
(e) Thirty-seven to forty-eight months	9,100
(f) Forty-nine months and more	1,822
Total Subscriptions Sold in Period	98,355

5. CHANNELS OF SUBSCRIPTION SALES:

(a) Ordered by mail and/or direct request	68,501
(b) Ordered through salespeople:	
1. Catalog agencies and individual agents	8,644
2. Publisher's own and other publisher's salespeople	590
3. Independent agencies' salespeople	14,100
4. Newspaper agencies	None
5. Members of schools, churches, fraternal and similar organizations	6,317
(c) Association memberships	None
(d) All other channels, See Par. 11(a)	203
Total Subscriptions Sold in Period	98,355

READERSHIP AND TOTAL AUDIENCE

Advertisers are often interested in the number of people a publication reaches as a result of secondary, or pass-along, readership. **Pass-along readership** can occur when the primary subscriber or purchaser gives a magazine to another person or when the publication is read in doctors' waiting rooms or beauty salons, on airplanes, and so forth.

Advertisers generally attach greater value to the primary in-home reader than the pass-along reader or out-of-home reader, as the former generally spends more time with the publication, picks it up more often, and receives greater satisfaction from it. Thus, this reader is more likely to be attentive and responsive to ads. However, the value of pass-along readers should not be discounted. They can greatly expand a magazine's readership. *People* magazine commissioned a media research study to determine that its out-of-home audience spends as much time reading the publication as do its primary in-home readers.[12]

You can calculate the **total audience**, or **readership**, of a magazine by multiplying the readers per copy (the total number of primary and pass-along readers) by the circulation of an average issue. For example, a magazine that has a circulation of 1 million and 3.5 readers per copy has a total audience of 3.5 million. However, rate structures are generally based on the more verifiable primary circulation figures, and many media planners devalue pass-along readers by as much as 50 percent. Total readership estimates are reported by major syndicated magazine research services (discussed next), but media buyers view these numbers with suspicion.

Audience Research for Magazines

While circulation and total audience size are important in selecting a media vehicle, the media planner is also interested in the match between the magazine's readers and the advertiser's target audience. Information on readers is available from several sources, including the publication's own research and syndicated studies. Most magazines provide media planners with reports detailing readers' demographics, financial profile, lifestyle, and product usage characteristics. The larger the publication, the more detailed and comprehensive the information it usually can supply about its readers.

Syndicated research studies are also available. For consumer magazines, primary sources of information are Simmons Market Research Bureau's *Study of Media and Markets* and the studies of Mediamark Research Inc. (MRI). These studies provide a broad range of information on the audiences of major national and regional magazines, including demographics, lifestyle characteristics, and product purchase and usage data. Most large ad agencies and media buying services also conduct ongoing research on the media habits of consumers. All this information helps determine the value of various magazines in reaching particular types of product users.

Audience information is generally more limited for business publications than for consumer magazines. The widely dispersed readership and nature of business publication readers make audience research more difficult. Media planners generally rely on information provided by the publication or by sources such as Standard Rate and Data Service. SRDS's Business Publication Advertising Source provides the titles of individuals who receive the publication and the type of industry in which they work. This information can be of value in understanding the audiences reached by various business magazines.

Purchasing Magazine Advertising Space

COST ELEMENTS

Magazine rates are primarily a function of circulation. Other variables include the size of the ad, its position in the publication, the particular editions (geographic, demographic) chosen, any special mechanical or production requirements, and the number and frequency of insertions.

Advertising space is generally sold on the basis of space units such as full page, half page, and quarter page, although some publications quote rates on the basis of column inches. The larger the ad, the greater the cost. However, many advertisers use full-page ads since they result in more attention and readership. Studies have found that full-page ads generated 36 percent more readership than half-page ads.[13]

Ads can be produced or run using black and white, black and white plus one color, or four colors. The more color used in the ad, the greater the expense because of the increased printing costs. On average, a four-color ad costs 30 percent more than a black-and-white ad. Advertisers generally prefer color ads because they have greater visual impact and are superior for attracting and holding attention.[14] Starch INRA Hooper, Inc., analyzed the effect of various factors on the readership of magazine ads. The "noted" scores (the percentage of readers who remember seeing the ad in a publication they read) are 45 percent higher for a four-color full-page ad than for a black-and-white ad. A four-color spread (two facing pages) outperforms a black-and-white spread by 53 percent.[15] Ads requiring special mechanical production such as bleed pages or inserts may also cost extra.

Rates for magazine ad space can also vary according to the number of times an ad runs and the amount of money spent during a specific period. The more often an advertiser contracts to run an ad, the lower are the space charges. Volume discounts are based on the total space purchased within a contract year, measured in dollars. Advertisers can also save money by purchasing advertising in magazine combinations, or networks.

Magazine networks offer the advertiser the opportunity to buy space in a group of publications as a package deal. The publisher usually has a variety of magazines that reach audiences with similar characteristics. The ad for the Petersen Magazine Network shown in Exhibit 12–9 promotes its leisure-time publications' coverage of the adult male market. Networks can also be publishers of a group of magazines with diversified audiences or independent networks that sell space in groups of magazines published by different companies. For example, the News Network sells space in a group of news-oriented publications such as *Time*, *Newsweek*, and *U.S. News & World Report*. IMC Perspective 12–2 discusses how many advertisers are reaching upscale readers through the Ivy League Magazine Network.

The Future of Magazines

Magazines have gone through a very difficult period recently. Advertising revenue declined by 20 to 30 percent for some publications as marketers reduced their ad budgets during the recession, and discounting of advertising space became more pervasive. Mass circulation magazines have been particularly hard hit; 60 percent of the top 50 magazines registered de-

EXHIBIT 12–9
This publisher offers a network of
magazines that reach adult males

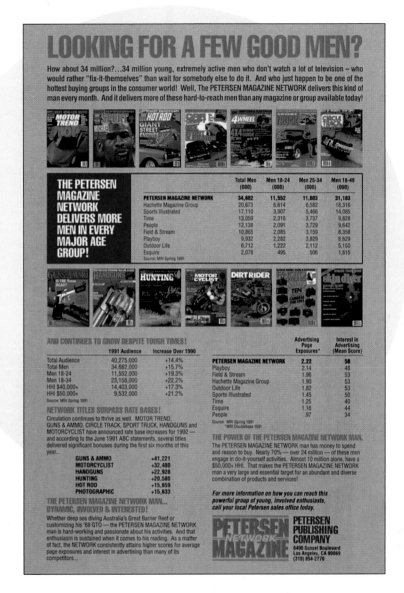

clines in circulation in the first half of 1996.[16] While ad revenue has declined, publishers' costs have increased. The cost of paper and ink continues to rise, and second-class postage rates have jumped. A number of well-known publications failed to survive the tough times, including *Savvy, Fame,* and *Connoisseur.* Many magazines have been reducing personnel, trimming circulation, and using computers to increase productivity of their editorial staffs.

A major problem facing many magazines is that they cannot increase their advertising rates to cover these increasing costs and declines in ad pages. Magazines are looking at a number of ways to improve their position—including stronger editorial platforms, better circulation management, cross-magazine and media deals, database marketing, technological advances, and electronic delivery methods—to make advertising in magazines more appealing to marketers.[17]

STRONGER EDITORIAL PLATFORMS

The number of magazines will probably shrink over the next several years because the economy and advertising industry cannot continue to support them all. Magazines with strong editorial platforms that appeal to the interests, lifestyles, and demographics of consumers and market trends of the 90s will have the best chance of attracting readers and advertisers. For example, *Martha Stewart Living* covers a mix of topics (including gardening, cooking, home, and entertainment) that appeal to the growing interest in do-it-yourself projects and

IMC Perspective 12–2
How to Reach Ivy Leaguers

Companies whose products and services are targeted at well-educated, affluent consumers generally find magazines the best medium for reaching them. They place ads in individual magazines that reach upscale readers such as *The Robb Report, The New Yorker,* or *Civilization.* However, many marketers are discovering yet another way to reach affluent readers is by advertising in alumni magazines of Ivy League schools: Brown, Cornell, Dartmouth, Harvard, Princeton, Yale, and the University of Pennsylvania. (Columbia, the eighth Ivy school, doesn't have a magazine.) And a ready-made way to advertise in all of these publications is by using the Ivy League Magazine Network, a consortium of the alumni magazines for the seven Ivy League schools and one non-Ivy, Stanford University. Advertisers can purchase ad space in the magazines of all eight schools with one media purchase through the network.

The Ivy League Network was founded in the mid-1970s but only recently began a full-blown marketing campaign to draw advertisers' attention to its elite readership. The idea of the Ivy network is strength in numbers combined with impeccable demographics. Advertisers can reach over a million readers whose median household income is $148,000 and net worth is $972,000. Nearly half of all Ivy alumni magazine readers are millionaires and have done postgraduate study. Only a few publications—such as *The Economist, Wine Spectator,* and *Worth*—boast readers with higher median household incomes.

Along with its demographics, the Ivy network markets the professed loyalty of its readers to their alma maters and the time they spend with the magazines reading about developments at the schools and keeping updated on campus news and classmates' comings and goings. Research shows the average reader spends 80 minutes with an issue and picks it up on more than two occasions.

The combination of upscale demographics and reader involvement has lured advertisers of a number of luxury products and services, including Lexus and Cadillac automobiles, Absolut vodka, Bermuda Tourism, Cunard Cruise Lines, and British Airways. Lexus began advertising in the network eight years ago. The company's marketing manager says, "It is a good, upscale, educated market that has always understood the essence of smart value." Lexus targets a similar crowd by advertising in *Smithsonian, The New Yorker,* and *The Atlantic Monthly.*

While each school sells space individually, the network offers a 10 percent discount for ad placements in at least three of the Ivy League publications. The network keeps about 15 percent of the ad revenue and distributes the rest among the individual magazines based on their circulation. The network increased ad sales 20 percent in both 1995 and 1996, and the revenue has helped buoy some of the publications during an era of skyrocketing paper prices and increases in postage costs. The extra revenue also allows the schools to send magazines to more of their alumni, which means the network can reach even more affluent Ivy Leaguers.

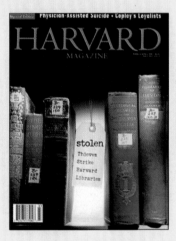

Source: Laura Gardner, "Advertisers Find New Upscale Audience," *The Philadelphia Inquirer,* March 22, 1996, p. C1; Alessandra Galloni, "Advertisers Enroll in Ivy League Network," *The Wall Street Journal,* August 4, 1995, p. B3.

fit the lifestyles of many consumers.[18] Another successful new magazine is *Men's Journal,* which focuses on the healthy, active, fun lifestyle of baby boomer men with stories on health, fitness, travel, and sex.[19]

CIRCULATION MANAGEMENT

Magazine publishers will also have to improve the quality of their circulation bases to remain profitable. Circulation is becoming the major source of revenue for many publications, and they must carefully consider the costs of attracting and maintaining additional readers or subscribers. For many years, magazines focused on increasing their circulation under the assumption that higher circulation meant higher advertising rates. However, publishers are now realizing that the cost of attracting and maintaining the last 10 to 15 percent of their circulation base is often greater than the additional revenue generated, since these subscribers require numerous direct-mail solicitations, premium offers, or discount subscriptions.

A number of magazines have reduced their circulation base in recent years. Hearst recently shed unprofitable circulation by cutting rate bases on 10 of its 16 monthly publications, which include *Cosmopolitan*, *Good Housekeeping*, and *Esquire*.[20] Many publishers believe they can pass on price increases more easily to their core readers or subscribers and offer advertisers a more loyal and focused audience. Many advertisers welcome the improvement in circulation management. They would rather reach a few hundred thousand fewer subscribers than pay for inefficient circulation and be hit with advertising rate increases each year. Many magazines are also using the monies saved on the circulation side to improve the editorial content of their publications, which should attract more readers—and advertisers.

CROSS-MAGAZINE AND MEDIA DEALS

Another important development involves the way ad space is sold; there will be more cross- or multimagazine and cross-media ad packages. **Multimagazine deals** involve two or more publishers offering their magazines to an advertiser as one package. For example, *Newsweek* offers cross-magazine deals with several other publishers, including Meredith and Times Mirror (Exhibit 12–10). Many magazines are also making **cross-media advertising** deals that include several different media opportunities from a single company or a partnership of media providers. For example, General Motors negotiated an $80 million cross-media deal with Time Warner that includes advertising in the magazines owned by the media conglomerate (among them *Time*, *Sports Illustrated*, and *Fortune*), on its cable TV stations, and in home videos. Cross-media deals may account for 20 percent of all media buys over the next several years.[21]

DATABASE MARKETING

Many advertisers are increasingly turning to magazines as a cost-efficient way of reaching specialized audiences. As marketers continue to move toward greater market segmentation, market niche strategies, and regional marketing, they are making greater use of magazines because of their high selectivity and ability to avoid wasted coverage or circulation. Magazines are using advances in technology and *database marketing* to divide their audiences on the basis of demographics, psychographics, or regions and to deliver more personalized advertising messages. Database marketing lets advertisers personalize their advertising by merging their own databases with those of a magazine. By selectively accessing information from a magazine's database, advertisers can choose from an array of information on consumers, such as product usage or purchase intention data. Marketers will increasingly advertise in magazines that are targeted specifically to narrow groups of subscribers.[22]

EXHIBIT 12–10
Newsweek offers cross-media opportunities with several other publications

ADVANCES IN TECHNOLOGY

Two important technological developments are making it possible for advertisers to deliver personalized messages to tightly targeted audiences: selective binding technology and ink-jet imaging. **Selective binding** is a computerized production process that allows the creation of hundreds of copies of a magazine in one continuous sequence. Selective binding enables magazines to target and address specific groups within a magazine's circulation base. They can then send different editorial or advertising messages to various groups of subscribers within the same issue of a publication. **Ink-jet imaging** reproduces a message by projecting ink onto paper rather than using mechanical plates. This process makes it possible to personalize an advertising message. Many publishers believe selective binding and ink-jet imaging will let advertisers target their messages more finely and let magazines compete more effectively with direct mail and other direct-marketing vehicles. Exhibit 12–11 shows how *Newsweek* promotes the capabilities of ink-jet imaging for targeting advertising messages.

Publishers are also developing new technologies that will enhance the creative opportunities available to magazine advertisers. Advertisers use a variety of techniques in print ads to capture readers' attention, including sound, scents, moving images, and pop-up ads. Current technologies are being refined and made more cost effective, and a number of new technologies will be incorporated into print ads soon. These include anaglyphic images (three-dimensional materials that are viewed with colored glasses); lenticular (color) images printed on finely corrugated plastic that seem to move when tilted; and pressure- or heat-sensitive inks that change color on contact. These new technologies will give advertisers ways to break through the advertising clutter. However, as shown in Figure 12–3, these new print technologies can be very costly. Moreover, many advertisers and agencies are concerned that ads that use these new technologies may do so at the expense of other ads in the magazine, so they may pressure publishers to control their use. Some creative people have also expressed concern that these new technologies are gimmicks being substituted for creative advertising ideas.[23]

ELECTRONIC DELIVERY METHODS

Many magazines are keeping pace with the electronic age and the continuing consumer interest in technology and new media by using alternative delivery methods such as CD-ROM and online computer services. Some magazines are providing CD-ROM versions of their print titles that integrate animation, video, audio, graphics, and text to provide an interactive medium. More and more magazines are also becoming available online. As of mid-1996 there were over 1,750 online magazines, and many more become available almost daily. The

EXHIBIT 12—11
Newsweek promotes the value of ink-jet imaging

FIGURE 12–3
High costs for high-tech wizardry
(per piece of print based on order of
1 million pieces)

Talking ads (6-second play)	$2.25*
Reflective light technology	$2.00+
Lenticular image 7 × 10	$1.00–$1.50*
Liquid-filled ads	$0.85
Singing ads	$0.81*
Heat-sensitive ink	$0.62
Stereo viewers	$0.55*
3-D images	$0.23

*Cost of printing ad not included.

Note: Costs do not include binding into magazines.

ads appearing in electronic magazines thus far tend to be text-based with some graphics. However, digital advertising in the interactive electronic environment can offer interactive hypertext or multimedia hyperlink opportunities. Many magazines and advertisers are still experimenting with ways to sell and use advertising on the new electronic media. As the presence of magazines online grows, the industry will have to address pressing questions regarding audience measurement and how to determine consumers' exposure to and interaction with advertising.

NEWSPAPERS

Newspapers, the second major form of print media, are the largest of all advertising media in terms of total dollar volume. In 1995 more than $36 billion was spent on newspaper advertising, or about 22 percent of the total advertising expenditures in the United States. Newspapers are an especially important advertising medium to local advertisers, particularly retailers. However, newspapers are also valuable to national advertisers. Many of the advertising dollars spent by local retailers are actually provided by national advertisers through cooperative advertising programs (discussed in Chapter 15). Newspapers vary in terms of their characteristics and their role as an advertising medium.

Types of Newspapers

The traditional role of newspapers has been to deliver prompt, detailed coverage of news as well as to supply other information and features that appeal to readers. The vast majority of newspapers are daily publications serving a local community. However, weekly, national, and special-audience newspapers have special characteristics that can be valuable to advertisers.

DAILY NEWSPAPERS

Daily newspapers, which are published each weekday, are found in cities and larger towns across the country. Many areas have more than one daily paper. Daily newspapers are read by nearly 84 million adults each weekday.[24] They provide detailed coverage of news, events, and issues concerning the local area as well as business, sports, and other relevant information and entertainment. Daily newspapers can further be classified as morning, evening, or Sunday publications. In 1996, there were 1,520 daily newspapers in the United States; of these, 55 percent were evening papers and 45 percent morning. There were also 890 Sunday newspapers, most of which were published by daily newspapers.

WEEKLY NEWSPAPERS

Most weekly newspapers originate in small towns or suburbs where the volume of news and advertising cannot support a daily newspaper. These papers focus primarily on news, sports, and events relevant to the local area and usually ignore national and world news, sports, and financial and business news. Weeklies are the fastest-growing class of newspapers; in 1996, there were 7,915 in the United States. Weeklies appeal primarily to local advertisers because of their geographic focus and lower absolute cost. Most national advertisers avoid weekly newspapers because of their duplicate circulation with daily or Sunday papers in the large metropolitan areas and problems in contracting for and placing ads in these publications. However, the contracting and scheduling problems associated with these papers have been reduced by the emergence of syndicates that publish them in a number of areas and sell ad space in all of their local newspapers through one office.

NATIONAL NEWSPAPERS

Newspapers in this country with national circulation include *The Wall Street Journal*, *The Christian Science Monitor*, and *USA Today*. All three are daily publications and have editorial content with a nationwide appeal. *The Wall Street Journal* has the largest circulation of any newspaper in the country, selling over 1.8 million copies a day, and is an excellent way to reach businesspeople (Exhibit 12–12). *USA Today*, the most recent successful national newspaper, has positioned itself as "the nation's newspaper." National newspapers appeal primarily to large national advertisers and to regional advertisers that use specific geographic editions of these publications. For example, *The Wall Street Journal* has 3 geographic editions covering 18 regions in which ads can be placed, while *USA Today* offers advertisers any combination of 25 national edition markets. While there are only a few newspapers in the United States with nationwide circulation, national newspapers are common in many other countries.

SPECIAL-AUDIENCE NEWSPAPERS

A variety of papers offer specialized editorial content and are published for particular groups, including labor unions, professional organizations, industries, and hobbyists. Many people working in advertising and marketing read *Advertising Age*, the leading trade publication for these industries. Specialized newspapers are also published in areas with large foreign-language-speaking ethnic groups, among them Polish, Chinese, Hispanics, Vietnamese, and Filipinos. In the United States, there are newspapers printed in more than 40 languages.

EXHIBIT 12–12
The Wall Street Journal is an excellent way to reach businesspeople

Newspapers targeted at various religious groups compose another large class of special-interest papers. For example, more than 140 Catholic newspapers are published across the United States. Another type of special-audience newspaper is one most of you probably read regularly during the school year, the college newspaper. More than 1,300 colleges and universities publish newspapers that offer advertisers an excellent medium for reaching college students.

NEWSPAPER SUPPLEMENTS

Although not a category of newspapers per se, many papers include magazine-type supplements, primarily in their Sunday editions. Sunday supplements have been part of most newspapers for many years and come in various forms. One type is the syndicated Sunday magazine, such as *Parade* or *USA Weekend*, distributed in hundreds of papers throughout the country. *Parade* has a circulation of over 37 million; *USA Weekend* is carried by more than 350 newspapers with a combined circulation of over 20 million. These publications are similar to national magazines and carry both national and regional advertising.

Some large newspapers publish local Sunday supplements distributed by the parent paper. These supplements contain stories of more local interest, and both local and national advertisers buy ad space. The *New York Times Sunday Magazine* is the best-known local supplement. The *Washington Post*, *San Francisco Examiner*, and *Los Angeles Times* have their own Sunday magazines.

In some areas, papers have begun carrying regional supplements as well as specialized weekday supplements that cover specific topics such as food, sports, or entertainment. Supplements are valuable to advertisers that want to use the newspaper yet get four-color reproduction quality in their ads.

Types of Newspaper Advertising

The ads appearing in newspapers can also be divided into different categories. The major types of newspaper advertising are display and classified. Other special types of ads and preprinted inserts also appear in newspapers.

DISPLAY ADVERTISING

Display advertising is found throughout the newspaper and generally uses illustrations, headlines, white space, and other visual devices in addition to the copy text. Display ads account for approximately 70 percent of the advertising revenue of the average newspaper. The two types of display advertising in newspapers are local and national (general).

Local advertising refers to ads placed by local organizations, businesses, and individuals who want to communicate with consumers in the market area served by the newspaper. Supermarkets and department stores are among the leading local display advertisers, along with numerous other retailers and service operations such as banks and travel agents. Local advertising is sometimes referred to as retail advertising because retailers account for 85 percent of local display ads.

National or *general advertising* refers to newspaper display advertising done by marketers of branded products or services that are sold on a national or regional level. These ads are designed to create and maintain demand for a company's product or service and to complement the efforts of local retailers that stock and promote the advertiser's products. Major retail chains, automakers, and airlines are heavy users of newspaper advertising.

CLASSIFIED ADVERTISING

Classified advertising also provides newspapers with a substantial amount of revenue. These ads are arranged under subheads according to the product, service, or offering being advertised. Employment, real estate, and automotive are the three major categories of classified advertising. While most classified ads are just text set in small type, some newspapers also accept classified display advertising. These ads are run in the classified section of the paper but use illustrations, larger type sizes, white space, borders, and even color to stand out.

SPECIAL ADS AND INSERTS

Special advertisements in newspapers include a variety of government and financial reports and notices and public notices of changes in business and personal relationships. Other types of advertising in newspapers include political or special-interest ads promoting a particular candidate, issue, or cause. **Preprinted inserts** are another type of advertising distributed through newspapers. These ads do not appear in the paper itself; they are printed by the advertiser and then taken to the newspaper to be inserted before delivery. Many retailers use inserts such as circulars, catalogs, or brochures in specific circulation zones to reach shoppers in their particular trade areas.

Advantages of Newspapers

Newspapers have a number of characteristics that make them popular among both local and national advertisers. These include their extensive penetration of local markets, flexibility, geographic selectivity, reader involvement, and special services.

EXTENSIVE PENETRATION

One of the primary advantages of newspapers is the high degree of market coverage, or penetration, they offer an advertiser. In most areas, 70 percent or more of households read a daily newspaper, and the reach figure may exceed 80 percent among households with higher incomes and education levels. Most areas are served by one or two daily newspapers and often the same company owns both, publishing a morning and an evening edition. By making one space buy, the advertiser can achieve a high level of overall reach in a particular market.

The extensive penetration of newspapers makes them a truly mass medium and provides advertisers with an excellent opportunity for reaching all segments of the population with their message. Also, since many newspapers are published and read daily, the advertiser can build a high level of frequency into the media schedule.

FLEXIBILITY

Another advantage of newspapers is the flexibility they offer advertisers. First, they are flexible in terms of requirements for producing and running the ads. Newspaper ads can be written, laid out, and prepared in a matter of hours. For most dailies, the closing time by which the ad must be received is usually only 24 hours before publication (although closing dates for special ads, such as those using color, and Sunday supplements are longer). The short production time and closing dates make newspapers an excellent medium for responding to current events or presenting timely information to consumers. For example, CompuServe used newspaper ads to respond quickly when subscribers to America Online, its major competitor, were experiencing problems getting through on the phone (Exhibit 12–13).

A second dimension of newspapers' flexibility stems from the creative options they make available to advertisers. Newspaper ads can be produced and run in various sizes, shapes, and formats; they can use color or special inserts to gain the interest of readers. Ads can be run in Sunday magazines or other supplements, and a variety of scheduling options are possible, depending on the advertiser's purpose.

GEOGRAPHIC SELECTIVITY

Newspapers generally offer advertisers more geographic or territorial selectivity than any other medium except direct mail. Advertisers can vary their coverage by choosing a paper—or combination of papers—that reaches the areas with the greatest sales potential. National advertisers take advantage of the geographic selectivity of newspapers to concentrate their advertising in specific areas they can't reach with other media or to take advantage of strong sales potential in a particular area. For example, BMW, Mercedes, and Volvo use heavy newspaper media schedules in California and New York/New Jersey to capitalize on the high sales potential for luxury import cars in these markets.

EXHIBIT 12–13
CompuServe used newspapers to
respond quickly and take advantage
of a competitor's problems

A number of companies, including General Motors, AT&T, and Campbell, use newspapers in their regional marketing strategies. Newspaper advertising lets them feature products on a market-by-market basis, respond and adapt campaigns to local market conditions, and tie into more retailer promotions, fostering more support from the trade.

Local advertisers like retailers are interested in geographic selectivity or flexibility within a specific market or trade area. Their media goal is to concentrate their advertising on the areas where most of their customers are. Many newspapers now offer advertisers various geographic areas or zones for this purpose. For example, the *Chicago Tribune* offers combinations of the 95 zip zones shown in Exhibit 12–14.

READER INVOLVEMENT AND ACCEPTANCE

Another important feature of newspapers is consumers' level of acceptance and involvement with papers and the ads they contain. The typical daily newspaper reader spends an average of 45 minutes a day reading the weekday newspaper and 62 minutes reading the Sunday paper.[25] Most consumers rely heavily on newspapers not only for news, information, and entertainment but also for assistance with consumption decisions.

Many consumers actually purchase a newspaper *because* of the advertising it contains. Consumers use retail ads to determine product prices and availability and to see who is having a sale. One aspect of newspapers that is helpful to advertisers is readers' knowledge about particular sections of the paper. Most of us know that ads for automotive products and sporting goods are generally found in the sports section, while ads for financial services are found in the business section. The weekly food section in many newspapers is popular for recipe and menu ideas as well as for the grocery store ads and coupons offered by many stores and companies.

The value of newspaper advertising as a source of information has been shown in several studies. One study found that consumers look forward to ads in newspapers more than in other media. In another study, 80 percent of consumers said newspaper ads were most helpful to them in doing their weekly shopping. Newspaper advertising has also been rated the most believable form of advertising in numerous studies.

SERVICES OFFERED

The special services newspapers offer can be valuable to advertisers. For example, many newspapers offer merchandising services and programs to manufacturers that make the trade aware of ads being run for the company's product and help convince local retailers they should stock, display, and promote the item.

Many newspapers are also excellent sources of local market information through their knowledge of market conditions and research like readership studies and consumer surveys.

EXHIBIT 12–14   The *Chicago Tribune* offers advertisers combinations of 95 different zip zones

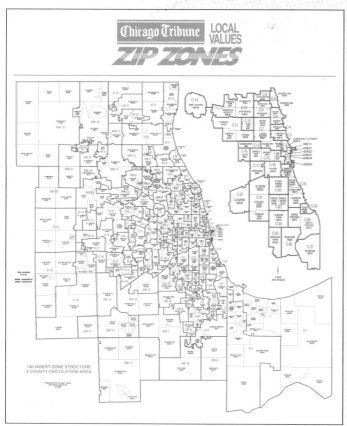

EXHIBIT 12–15   Newspaper publishers are often an excellent source for information on local markets

For example, the publisher of the *San Diego Union-Tribune*, the major daily newspaper in San Diego, provides information on the local market through reports such as the Marketbook (Exhibit 12–15).

Newspapers can also assist small companies through free copywriting and art services. Small advertisers without an agency or advertising department often rely on the newspaper to help them write and produce their ads.

Limitations of Newspapers

While newspapers have many advantages, like all media they also have disadvantages that media planners must consider. The limitations of newspapers include their reproduction problems, short life span, lack of selectivity, and clutter.

POOR REPRODUCTION

One of the greatest limitations of newspapers as an advertising medium is their poor reproduction quality. The coarse paper stock used for newspapers, the absence of color, and the lack of time papers have available to achieve high-quality reproduction limits the quality of most newspaper ads. Newspapers have improved their reproduction quality in recent years, and color reproduction has become more available. Also, advertisers desiring high-quality color in newspaper ads can turn to such alternatives as freestanding inserts or Sunday supplements. However, these are more costly and may not be desirable to many advertisers. As a general rule, if the visual appearance of the product is important, the advertiser will not rely on newspaper ads. Ads for food products and fashions generally use magazines to capitalize on their superior reproduction quality and color.

SHORT LIFE SPAN

Unlike magazines, which may be retained around the house for several weeks, a daily newspaper is generally kept less than a day. So an ad is unlikely to have any impact beyond the day

FIGURE 12—4   Daily newspaper pages or sections generally read

	Percent of Weekday Audience					
Reading Style	Adults	Men	Women	White	Black	Spanish/ Hispanic*
Read every page	59	58	59	60	53	48
Read some pages/sections	41	42	41	40	47	52
Section Readership						
General news	95	94	96	95	93	94
Editorial	76	75	78	77	71	68
Entertainment (movies, theater)	79	74	85	80	80	72
Sports	78	88	68	79	75	76
TV, radio listings	74	72	76	74	73	67
Food, cooking	73	65	81	74	70	62
Comics	72	71	74	73	67	67
Business, finance	75	77	74	77	68	62
Classified	73	73	74	74	70	69
Home (furnishings, gardening, etc.)	71	64	78	72	66	59

*Spanish or Hispanic origin or descent.

Sources: Simmons Market Research Bureau, Fall 1996 *Study of Media and Markets*, 1994.

of publication, and repeat exposure is very unlikely. Compounding this problem are the short amount of time many consumers spend with the newspaper and the possibility they may not even open certain sections of the paper. Media planners can offset these problems somewhat by using high frequency in the newspaper schedule and advertising in a section where consumers who are in the market for a particular product or service are likely to look. Figure 12–4 shows readership figures for various sections of newspapers by gender and ethnic background.

LACK OF SELECTIVITY

EXHIBIT 12—16   Island ads are a way to break through the clutter in newspaper advertising

While newspapers can offer advertisers geographic selectivity, they are not a selective medium in terms of demographics or lifestyle characteristics. Most newspapers reach broad and very diverse groups of consumers, which makes it difficult for marketers to focus on narrowly defined market segments. For example, manufacturers of fishing rods and reels will find newspapers very inefficient because of the wasted circulation that results from reaching all the newspaper readers who don't fish. Thus, they are more likely to use special-interest magazines such as *Field & Stream* or *Fishing World*. Any newspaper ads for their products will be done through cooperative plans whereby retailers share the costs or spread them over a number of sporting goods featured in the ad.

CLUTTER

Newspapers, like most other advertising media, suffer from clutter. Because 64 percent of the average daily newspaper in the United States is devoted to advertising, the advertiser's message must compete with numerous other ads for consumers' attention and interest. Moreover, the creative options in newspapers are limited by the fact that most ads are black and white. Thus, it can be difficult for a newspaper advertiser to break through the clutter without using costly measures such as large space buys or color. Some advertisers use creative techniques like *island ads*—ads surrounded by editorial material. Island ads are found in the middle of the stock market quotes on the financial pages of many newspapers. Exhibit 12–16 shows an island ad for Cathay Pacific Airways that targets business travelers to Hong Kong and other Asian destinations.

The Newspaper Audience

As with any medium, the media planner must understand the nature and size of the audience reached by a newspaper in considering its value in the media plan. Since newspapers as a class of media do an excellent job of penetrating their market, the typical daily newspaper gives advertisers the opportunity to reach most of the households in a market. But, while local advertisers aim to cover a particular market or trade area, national advertisers want to reach broad regions or even the entire country. They must purchase space in a number of papers to achieve the desired level of coverage.

The basic sources of information concerning the audience size of newspapers come from the circulation figures available through rate cards, publishers' statements, or Standard Rate and Data Service's *Newspaper Rates and Data*. Circulation figures for many newspapers are verified by one of the auditing services discussed earlier. Advertisers that use a number of papers in their media plan generally find SRDS the most convenient source.

Newspaper circulation figures are generally broken down into three categories: the city zone, the retail trading zone, and all other areas. The **city zone** is a market area composed of the city where the paper is published and contiguous areas similar in character to the city. The **retail trading zone** is the market outside the city zone whose residents regularly trade with merchants within the city zone. The "all other" category covers all circulation not included in the city or retail trade zone.

Sometimes circulation figures are provided only for the primary market, which is the city and retail trade zones combined, and the other area. Both local and national advertisers consider the circulation patterns across the various categories in evaluating and selecting newspapers.

National advertisers often buy newspapers based on the size of the market area they cover. For example, General Motors might decide to purchase advertising in the top 10 markets, the top 50 markets, the top 100 markets, and so on. A national advertiser gets different levels of market coverage depending on the number of market areas purchased.

AUDIENCE INFORMATION

Circulation figures provide the media planner with the basic data for assessing the value of newspapers and their ability to cover various market areas. However, the media planner also wants to match the characteristics of a newspaper's readers with those of the advertiser's target audience. Data on newspaper audience size and characteristics are available from commercial research services and from studies conducted by the papers.

Commercial studies providing readership information for the top 100 or so major markets are supplied by Simmons-Scarbough Syndicated Research Associates. These studies cover more than 150 daily newspapers and provide reach and frequency estimates for various demographic groups. Their audience information is valuable for comparing newspapers with other media vehicles, for which similar data are generally available. Many ad executives and media planners believe the newspaper industry must expand the amount of audience research data available or risk losing more advertising dollars to magazines and television.

Many newspapers commission their own audience studies to provide current and potential advertisers with information on readership and characteristics of readers such as demographics, shopping habits, and lifestyles. These studies are often designed to promote the effectiveness of the newspaper in reaching various types of consumers. Since they are sponsored by the paper itself, many advertisers are skeptical of their results. Careful attention must be given to the research methods used and conclusions drawn by these studies.

Purchasing Newspaper Space

Advertisers are faced with a number of options and pricing structures when purchasing newspaper space. The cost of advertising space depends not only on the newspaper's circulation but also on factors such as premium charges for color or special sections as well as discounts available. The purchase process and the rates paid for newspaper space differ for national and local advertisers.

NATIONAL VERSUS LOCAL RATES

The rates paid by national advertisers are, on average, 75 percent higher than those paid by local advertisers. Newspaper publishers claim the rate differential is justified for several reasons. First, they argue it costs more to handle national advertising since ad agencies get a 15 percent commission and commissions must also be paid to the independent sales reps who solicit nonlocal advertising. Second, they note that national advertising is less dependable than local advertising; national advertisers usually don't use newspapers on a continual basis like local advertisers do. Finally, newspaper publishers contend that demand for national advertising is inelastic—it will not increase if rates are lowered or decrease if rates are raised. This means there is no incentive to lower the national advertisers' rates.

National advertisers do not view these arguments as valid justification for the rate differential. They argue that the costs are not greater for handling national advertising than for local business and that many national advertisers use newspapers on a regular basis. Since they use an agency to prepare their ads, national advertisers are less likely to request special services. The large and costly staff maintained by many newspapers to assist in the design and preparation of advertising is used mostly by local advertisers.

The differential rate structure for national versus local advertising has been the source of considerable controversy. Some newspapers are making efforts to narrow the rate differential, as is the Newspaper Association of America (NAA). In late 1993, the NAA created the Newspaper National Network (NNN) to target national advertisers in six low-use categories: automotive, cosmetics and toiletries, food, household products, liquor and beverages, and drugs and remedies.[26] The network's goal is to attract more advertising dollars from national advertisers in these categories by promoting the strategic use of newspapers and facilitating the purchase of newspaper space with their one order/one bill model. Exhibit 12–17 shows an ad encouraging national advertisers to place their ads in newspapers through the NNN.

Many marketers sidestep the national advertiser label and the higher rates by channeling their newspaper ads through special category plans, cooperative advertising deals with retailers, and local dealers and distributors that pay local rates. However, the rate differential does keep many national advertisers from making newspapers a larger part of their media mix.

Newspaper Rates

Traditionally, newspaper space for national advertisers has been sold by the agate line. The problem is that newspapers use columns of varying width. Some have six columns per page, while others have eight or nine, which affects the size, shape, and costs of an ad. This results

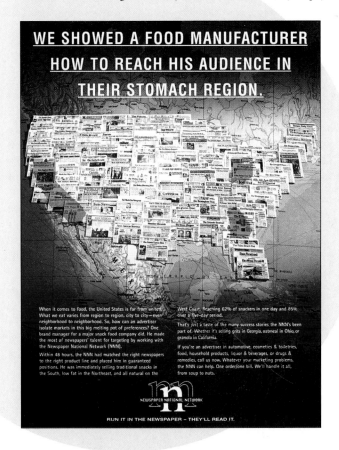

in a complicated production and buying process for national advertisers purchasing space in a number of newspapers.

To address this problem and make newspapers more comparable to other media that sell space and time in standard units, the newspaper industry switched to **standard advertising units (SAUs)** in 1984. All newspapers under this system use column widths $2\frac{1}{16}$ inches wide, with tabloid-size papers five columns wide and standard or broadcast papers six columns. The column inch is the unit of measurement to create the 57 standard units or format sizes shown in Figure 12–5.

A national advertiser can prepare one ad in a particular SAU, and it will fit every newspaper in the country that accepts SAUs. Rates are quoted on that basis. Since over 1,400 (about 90 percent) of daily newspapers use the SAU system, the purchase and production process has been simplified tremendously for national advertisers.

Newspaper rates for local advertisers continue to be based on the column inch, which is one inch deep by one column wide. Advertising rates for local advertisers are quoted per column inch, and media planners calculate total space costs by multiplying the ad's number of column inches by the cost per inch.

RATE STRUCTURES

While the column inch and SAU are used to determine basic newspaper advertising rates, the media planner must consider other options and factors. Many newspapers charge **flat rates**, which means they offer no discount for quantity or repeated space buys. Others have

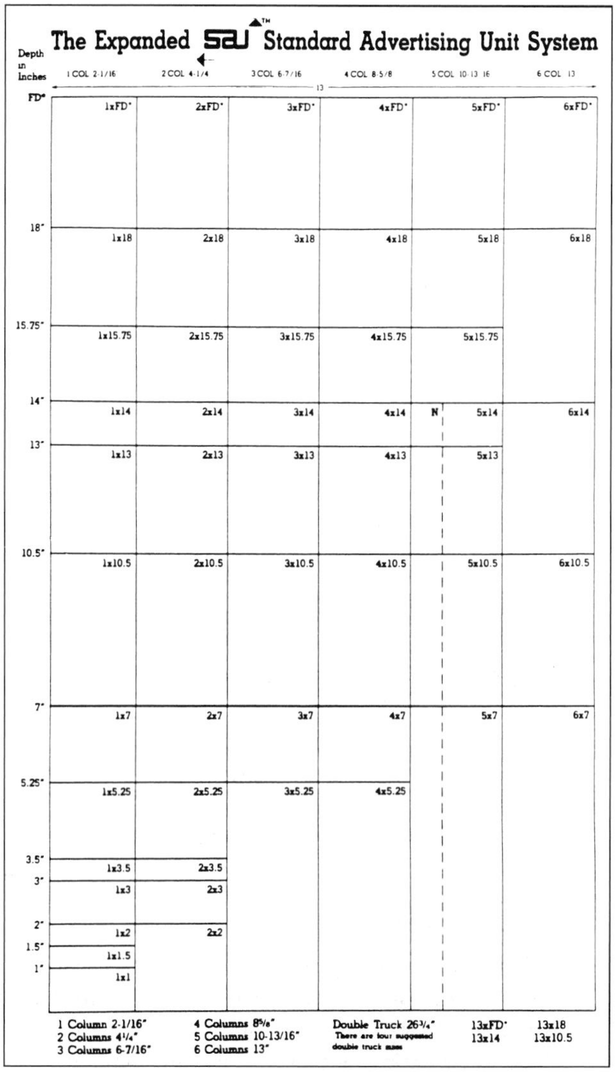

FIGURE 12–5
The standard advertising unit system

an **open-rate structure**, which means various discounts are available. These discounts are generally based on frequency or bulk purchases of space and depend on the number of column inches purchased in a year.

Newspaper space rates also vary with an advertiser's special requests, such as preferred position or color. The basic rates quoted by a newspaper are **run of paper (ROP)**, which means the paper can place the ad on any page or in any position it desires. While most newspapers try to place an ad in a requested position, the advertiser can ensure a specific section and/or position on a page by paying a higher **preferred position rate**. Color advertising is also available in many newspapers on an ROP basis or through preprinted inserts or Sunday supplements.

Advertisers can also buy newspaper space based on **combination rates**, where they get a discount for using several newspapers as a group. Typically, a combination rate occurs when a publisher owns both a morning and an evening newspaper in a market and offers a reduced single rate for running the same ad in both newspapers, generally within a 24-hour period. Combination discounts are also available when the advertiser buys space in several newspapers owned by the publisher in a number of markets or in multiple newspapers affiliated in a syndicate or newspaper group.

The Future of Newspapers

Newspapers remain the largest advertising medium in terms of total advertising volume, despite the tremendous growth of the broadcast media and cable advertising in particular. However, newspapers have fallen behind TV and magazines as a medium for national advertisers; they accounted for only 4.5 percent of the $95 billion spent by national advertisers in 1995. Newspapers' major strength lies in their role as a medium that can be used effectively by local advertisers on a continual basis. While it is unlikely that newspapers' importance to local advertisers will change in the near future, they will face greater competition from other advertising media and direct marketers. Newspapers must address a number of problems and issues.

COMPETITION FROM OTHER MEDIA

The newspaper industry's battle to increase its share of national advertising volume has been difficult. In addition to the problems of reproduction quality and rate differentials, newspapers face competition from other media for both national and local advertisers' budgets. The newspaper industry is particularly concerned about the *bypass*, or loss of advertisers to direct marketing and telemarketing.[27]

To deal with this problem, many newspapers will have to gear up to compete as direct marketers. Many papers are already building databases by collecting information from readers that potential advertisers can use to target specific groups or for direct marketing. Newspapers already have a distribution system that can reach nearly every household in a market every day. It is likely that many newspapers will find ways to make their extensive databases and distribution systems available to marketers that want to target consumers with direct-marketing efforts.[28] By supplementing newspaper advertising with direct mail, marketers can be encouraged to invest more of their advertising dollars with newspaper publishers.

The intermedia battle that newspapers find themselves involved in is no longer limited to national advertising. Many companies are investigating the Internet as a marketing tool and a place to invest advertising dollars that might otherwise go to newspapers. Local radio and TV stations (particularly cable stations), as well as the expanding number of Yellow Pages publishers, are aggressively pursuing local advertisers. Newspapers will have to fight harder to retain those advertisers. IMC Perspective 12–3 discusses how some newspapers are turning to relationship marketing to attract and retain more advertising revenue.

CIRCULATION

Like magazines, many newspapers are taking a closer look at their circulation and analyzing whether the cost of getting additional circulation is justified by the advertising revenue it generates. Many papers are raising newsstand and home delivery rates and circulation revenue is accounting for more of their total revenue.

IMC Perspective 12–3
Newspapers Turn to Relationship Marketing in Tough Times

These are tough times in the newspaper industry. More than 25 newspapers either folded or merged in the past two years, including major dailies such as the *Houston Post* and *New York Newsday*. The rising cost of newsprint forced many papers to hike prices in 1995, but consumer resistance to the rising prices resulted in circulation losses at over half of the 20 largest metropolitan newspapers in 1996. Since consumers appear to be taking longer than usual to adjust to the jump in newsstand and home delivery prices, many papers have implemented major cost-cutting programs. The Times Mirror Co. brought in Mark Willes, vice chair of General Mills, for some serious cost-cutting strategies. Dubbed the "cereal killer," Willes jolted the newspaper industry by shutting down *Newsday* and slashing 700 jobs at Times Mirror's flagship newspaper, the *Los Angeles Times*.

During this period of instability, many newspaper publishers have tried to bring back their profits by cutting back on the editorial product and raising advertising rates. However, many say this is a quick fix rather than a long-term solution and the industry is really left with only one option—change or lose its advertisers. Newspapers must become better marketers, which means treating their advertisers like customers and developing *relationships* with them.

For years, newspapers were accustomed to high profit margins that came with little effort. Their sales and marketing departments existed because advertisers needed people with whom to place their orders. Newspaper sales reps knew everything about the newspaper industry but little if anything about their customers' businesses. Now many newspapers are becoming more market driven.

The *Chicago Tribune*, which reported a 20 percent revenue growth over the past two years, is one paper that has taken steps to ensure that reps know more about customers than the size of their ads. The advertising department, which was traditionally organized by geographic areas, was recently split into four key account areas that use media in similar ways: home improvement, electronics, and home furnishings; fashion, financial, and technical; leisure and entertainment; and food, drugs, and discount. Five category division managers are encouraged to read industry trade magazines, become more familiar with their customers' needs, and develop marketing solutions for their problems.

Many newspapers have expanded their marketing in other ways. Some have created sophisticated databases and direct-mail capabilities they offer as value-added services. Some have added nonsubscriber products and special editions. The *Omaha World Herald* took advantage of an opportunity to cement a new customer relationship when the Dillard's department store chain expanded into the Omaha market five years ago. The paper researched sales in the retailer's Dallas market, extrapolated the data, and prepared a comprehensive marketing study for the new stores in Omaha. It outlined a media plan for Dillard's that included run-of-paper advertising and direct mail, two services the newspaper was able to provide. The plan also suggested TV advertising—advice that did not financially benefit the paper but strengthened its role as a media advisor and marketing partner.

The *Dallas Morning News*, which has been forced to pass on a portion of its 80 percent newsprint price increase to advertisers, offers them several niche vehicles, including a six-page weekly religious section and a bilingual Hispanic publication. *La Fuente* is mailed to 105,000 Hispanic households and gives advertisers in the Dallas market access to an important market segment.

The *Miami Herald* has also added new products to help advertisers and generate more ad revenue. The newspaper delivers *Vida Social*, a publication covering social events in Miami to 250,000 Hispanic households. The paper has also expanded into international markets to help advertisers who want to reach tourists from Latin America before they visit Florida. It has established partnerships with the leading papers in Venezuela, Columbia, Brazil, and Argentina to distribute a monthly circular in the countries' top demographic areas.

Newspapers are by no means obsolete; the medium is still considered the best way to cover mass markets, and its traditional benefits to advertisers are obvious. However, today's customers expect much more—and newspapers must deliver on these expectations if they want to avoid becoming yesterday's news.

Sources: Keith J. Kelly, "National Papers Record Healthy Circulation Gains," *Advertising Age*, November 11, 1996, p. 55; Michele Marchetti, "Extras!" *Sales and Marketing Management*, March 1996, pp. 56–61.

Several major metropolitan newspapers have found that advertisers use newspapers to reach consumers within specific geographic areas and do not want to pay for readers in outlying areas. Thus, some papers are eliminating what has been called ego circulation and focusing more on regional editions in their immediate trade area.

CROSS-MEDIA BUYS

Another area where newspapers may be following the lead of magazines is cross-newspaper and media buys. Newspapers within, as well as across, various regions are banding together to offer national advertisers a package of newspapers so they won't have to purchase space in individual papers. A number of newspaper networks are being formed to help newspapers compete for more of the media expenditures of national advertisers.

Cross-media buys involving newspapers with other media vehicles are also likely to become more prevalent. For example, the *Washington Post* has been involved in a cross-media deal with *Newsweek*, while large companies that own newspapers, magazines, and broadcast media are also offering cross-media packages to advertisers (Exhibit 12–18).

ATTRACTING AND RETAINING READERS

The growth of newspapers as an advertising medium may be limited by the reduced popularity of the medium itself. Newspaper readership has been on a steady decline for the past two decades. The percentage of the adult population reading a newspaper on the average weekday has declined from 78 percent in 1970 to just over 64 percent today. The percentage of U.S. households receiving a daily newspaper has declined from 77 percent in 1980 to 67 percent. The decline in newspaper readership can be attributed to several factors, including the fast-paced, time-poor lifestyle of the modern dual-income household and the continued growth, popularity, and viewing options of TV.

A number of newspapers have been redesigned to be more interesting and easier and faster to read. Changes include the increased use of color and graphics as well as expanded coverage of sports and entertainment. Some papers have begun providing short summaries of articles in each section of the paper so readers can skim them and decide what they want to read.

Of particular concern to publishers is the decline in newspaper readership among important market segments such as women and young adults. Surveys by Simmons Market Research Bureau show the percentage of women who read a newspaper on a typical day declined from 67 percent in 1981 to 62 percent in 1995.[29] Newspapers and advertisers are

EXHIBIT 12–18
Newsweek and the *Washington Post* offer advertisers a cross-media opportunity

concerned because women are far more likely than men to make buying decisions. Many newspapers are introducing new women's sections and revising old ones to make them more appealing to modern women. This means including articles on such issues as health, parenting, and careers—for example, how women with children and jobs manage their time.[30]

Newspapers are also concerned about where their future readers will come from, since young people in this country are very dependent on the broadcast media. Many newspapers are making special efforts to attract teenagers in hopes that they will become and remain regular newspaper readers. Some publishers are creating special sections that rely heavily on color and graphics and focus on topics relevant to young people, such as local issues, fashion, music, and entertainment.

The newspaper industry faces a serious challenge. To increase circulation and readership and continue to attract advertising revenue, it must make newspapers more interesting to readers by targeting specific groups and expand services to encourage advertisers to continue using newspapers.

The growth of the Internet and online services is likely to erode newspaper readership even further. Publishers are addressing this threat by making their papers available online. The number of U.S. newspapers available online or on the World Wide Web doubled to over 200 from 1995 to 1996. Internationally, about 750 publications are available. Many papers are developing innovative programs for advertisers to attract their interactive advertising dollars.[31] Networks are also forming to help local newspapers go online and to facilitate the sale and purchase of ad space on these sites. But as with magazines, audience measurement issues and user involvement are making it difficult for newspapers to attract advertisers to their online sites.[32]

SUMMARY

Magazines and newspapers, the two major forms of print media, play an important role in the media plans and strategy of many advertisers. Magazines are a very selective medium and are very valuable for reaching specific types of customers and market segments. The three broad categories of magazines are consumer, farm, and business publications. Each of these categories can be further classified according to the publication's editorial content and audience appeal.

In addition to their selectivity, the advantages of magazines include their excellent reproduction quality, creative flexibility, long life, prestige, and readers' high receptivity to magazine advertising, as well as the services they offer to advertisers. Disadvantages of magazines include their high cost, limited reach and frequency, long lead time, and the advertising clutter in most publications.

Advertising space rates in magazines vary according to a number of factors, among them the size of the ad, position in the publication, particular editions purchased, use of color, and number and frequency of insertions. Rates for magazines are compared on the basis of the cost per thousand, although other factors such as the editorial content of the publication and its ability to reach specific target audiences must also be considered.

Newspapers represent the largest advertising medium in terms of total volume, receiving nearly a fourth of all advertising dollars. Newspapers are a very important medium to local advertisers, especially retailers. They are also used by national advertisers, although the differential rate structure for national versus local advertisers is a source of controversy. Newspapers are a broad-based medium that reaches a large percentage of households in a particular area. Newspapers' other advantages include flexibility, geographic selectivity, reader involvement, and special services. Drawbacks of newspapers include their lack of high-quality ad reproduction, short life span, lack of audience selectivity, and clutter.

Trends toward market segmentation and regional marketing are prompting many advertisers to make more use of newspapers and magazines. However, both magazines and newspapers face increasing competition from such other media as radio, cable TV, direct marketing, and the Internet. Both magazines and newspapers are working to improve the quality of their circulation bases, offer database marketing services, and initiate cross-media deals. Rising costs and declining readership are problems for many magazines and newspapers. Both magazines and newspapers are making their publications available online, but problems with audience measurement and interactions with ads are important issues that must be resolved.

KEY TERMS

selectivity, 382
gatefolds, 384
bleed pages, 384
split runs, 387
controlled-circulation basis, 390
pass-along readership, 391

total audience/readership, 391
magazine networks, 392
multimagazine deals, 395
cross-media advertising, 395
selective binding, 396
ink-jet imaging, 396

display advertising, 399
classified advertising, 399
preprinted inserts, 400
city zone, 404
retail trading zone, 404
standard advertising units (SAUs), 406

flat rates, 406
open-rate structure, 407
run of paper (ROP), 407
preferred position rate, 407
combination rates, 407

DISCUSSION QUESTIONS

1. The vignette at the beginning of the chapter discusses the success of the magazine *Spin*. Why do you think this magazine has been so successful and been able to attract so many advertisers?

2. Discuss the role of magazines and newspapers in the development and implementation of an integrated marketing communications program.

3. Find either a consumer or business magazine targeted to a specific audience and analyze it using information from Standard Rate and Data Service (SRDS), which should be available in your library. How might a media planner be able to use the information in SRDS to evaluate the value of this magazine as an advertising medium?

4. Choose a specific target market that an advertiser might want to reach. Discuss how magazines and/or newspapers could be used to reach this particular market in a cost effective manner.

5. Explain why advertisers of products such as cosmetics or women's clothing would choose to advertise in a magazine like *Vogue*, which devotes most of its pages to ads rather than articles.

6. Discuss why companies like Ray-Ban, Sony, and Philip Morris choose to publish their own magazines. Do you agree or disagree with critics who call some of these custom magazines "phony publishing"?

7. If you were purchasing magazine ad space for a manufacturer of skiing equipment, what factors would you consider? Would your magazine selection be limited to skiing publications? Why or why not?

8. Do you agree or disagree with the policy of most newspapers to charge national advertisers a higher rate than local advertisers? Do you think this policy limits the amount of advertising newspapers can generate from national advertisers? How might newspapers attract more business from national advertisers?

9. Why do you think many newspapers are experiencing declines in circulation and readership? What can newspapers do to attract advertisers as well as readers?

10. Discuss the challenges and opportunities magazines and newspapers are facing from the growth of online services and the Internet.

13

Support Media

- To introduce the various support media available to the marketer in developing an IMC program.

- To provide an understanding of the advantages and disadvantages of support media.

- To explain how audiences for support media are measured.

ADS BECOME THE NEW STARS IN MOVIES AND TV

You may or may not know that soap operas derived their name because they were produced and sponsored by soap manufacturers like Procter & Gamble. Why would a soap company produce TV shows? They were a great place to advertise its products. Now advertisers are becoming part of TV shows and movies in very different ways, from sponsorships to product placements to starring roles. Consider the following:

- Elizabeth Taylor's Black Pearls fragrance was the beneficiary of a CBS-publicized "Liz Night," in which Ms. Taylor appeared on four back-to-back sitcoms whose scripts featured a running story line about the filming of a Black Pearls commercial and the disappearance of a strand of black pearls. Starting with "The Nanny," continuing on "Can't Hurry Love" and "Murphy Brown," and finally culminating on "High Society," Black Pearls perfume was mentioned "too many times to count," according to Teri Agins of *The Wall Street Journal*.
- Polaroid's new ad slogan was cast in a starring role in Fox Broadcasting's "Melrose Place." At the end of one show, the teaser invited viewers to "see what develops next week on Melrose Place." A camera's flash then flooded the screen, followed by the tagline "Brought to you by Polaroid." ABC followed with Polaroid tune-in spots for "Roseanne," "Home Improvement," and "The Dana Carvey Show."
- "The Taco Bell Dana Carvey Show" was originally designed to be a joint venture between PepsiCo and ABC. In each weekly episode, a member of the Pepsi family would serve as both "title and target" for Carvey's satire. For a variety of reasons, Taco Bell pulled out after only one episode. After the show was toned down, PepsiCo

sponsors with lower profiles became sponsors—for example, one episode was "The Mug Root Beer Dana Carvey Show."
- "Murphy Brown" wrote John F. Kennedy Jr. into a script so he could promote his new magazine, *George*.

In addition to these examples, Diet Coke ("Friends"), America's Dairy Farmers ("Party of Five") AT&T ("New York Undercover") and MCI ("Living Single") have also gotten their ads into TV shows.

Advertisers have made some cross-promotional deals with moviemakers as well. Beyond the ever-increasing product placements, products and brands are taking center stage. For example, Apple Computer joined with Paramount Pictures to feature the Apple PowerBook as Tom Cruise's sidekick in Mission Impossible. MGM/UA wrote in an entire scene for the BMW Z3 in the James Bond flick *GoldenEye*. When the American Dairy Farmers wanted Billy Zane to appear in the famous "milk moustache" ad campaign, he wore his outfit from the movie *Phantom*.

The relationships appear to be a good deal for both sides. The advertisers get their products featured, and the television and movie producers receive income that offsets some production costs—and maybe even a little help with the scripts. But do they have an impact on consumers? The answer is sometimes yes and sometimes no. BMW credits the James Bond movie for much of its initial success, but Sony's Mini Disk CD player received little benefit from its featured role in *The Last Action Hero*, starring Arnold Schwarzenegger. And Taco Bell was certainly not happy with Dana Carvey.

Sources: Leslie Savan, "Your Show of Shills," *Time*, April 1, 1996, pp. 70–71; "Cue the Soda Can," *Business Week*, June 24, 1996, pp. 64–66; Teri Agins, "Liz's Perfume Gets Star Role in Prime Time," *The Wall Street Journal*, February 15, 1996, p. B1; Sally Goll Beatty, "Polaroid Co-Stars in 'Melrose Place' Teaser," *The Wall Street Journal*, March 18, 1996, p. B9.

Ads in movies and as part of TV programs themselves are just a few of the many different ways that companies and organizations get their messages out. Ads have also appeared on manhole covers, inside restroom stalls, even on beepers. In this chapter, we review a number of support media, some that are new to the marketplace and others that have been around a while. We discuss the relative advantages and disadvantages, cost information, and audience measurement of each. We refer to them as **support media** because the media described in the previous chapters dominate the media strategies of large advertisers, particularly national advertisers. Support media are used to reach those people in the target market the primary media may not have reached and to reinforce, or support, their messages.

You may be surprised at how many different ways there are to deliver the message and how often you are exposed to them. Let's begin by examining the scope of the support media industry and some of the many alternatives available to marketers.

THE SCOPE OF THE SUPPORT MEDIA INDUSTRY

Support media are referred to by several titles, among them **alternative media, nonmeasured media,** and **nontraditional media.** These terms describe a vast variety of channels used to deliver communications and to promote products and services. In this chapter we will discuss many of these media (though, as you might imagine, it would be impossible for us to discuss them all).

Many advertisers, as well as the top 100 advertising agencies, have increased their use of nontraditional support media, and as new alternatives are developed, this use will continue to grow. Figures for nontraditional media do not include some of the most popular support media, such as out-of-home advertising, specialty advertising, and advertising in the Yellow Pages. Let us examine some of these in more detail.

OUT-OF-HOME MEDIA

Out-of-home advertising encompasses many advertising forms, including outdoor (billboards and signs), transit (both inside and outside the vehicle), skywriting, and a variety of other media. While outdoor advertising is used most often, as shown in Figure 13–1, the others are also increasing in use.

Outdoor Advertising

Outdoor advertising has probably existed since the days of cave dwellers. Both the Egyptians and the Greeks used it as early as 5,000 years ago. Outdoor is certainly one of the more pervasive communication forms, particularly if you live in an urban or suburban area.

Even though outdoor accounts for only about 2.3 percent of all advertising expenditures and the number of billboards has decreased, the medium has grown steadily in terms of dollars billed. In 1982, approximately $888 million was spent in this area; by 1995 this figure had risen to about $2.1 billion.[1] Outdoor expenditures are expected to increase in 1997.[2] Increased spending by companies like McDonald's, Anheuser-Busch, Nissan, and General Motors has compensated for decreased spending by the tobacco and spirits companies (the most frequent users of outdoor for many years). As shown in Figure 13–2, outdoor is used by a broad client base, a demonstration of its continued acceptance in the industry. The increase in the number of women in the work force has led to more advertising of products targeted to this segment. Travel companies, entertainment and amusement attractions, insurance companies, and board-game companies have also discovered outdoor advertising.

A major reason for the continued success of outdoor is its ability to remain innovative through technology. As Exhibit 13–1 shows, billboards are no longer limited to standard sizes and two dimensions; 3-D forms and extensions are now used to attract attention. Electronic billboards and inflatables, like the one in Exhibit 13–2 that was used to promote Burger King, have also opened new markets. You probably have been exposed to either signboards or electronic billboards at sports stadiums, in supermarkets, in the campus bookstore and dining halls, in shopping malls, on the freeways, or on the sides of buildings, from neon signs on skyscrapers in New York City to Mail Pouch Tobacco signs painted on the sides of barns in the Midwest. This is truly a pervasive medium.

FIGURE 13–1
Estimated gross billings by media category show that outdoor ads are still the most popular

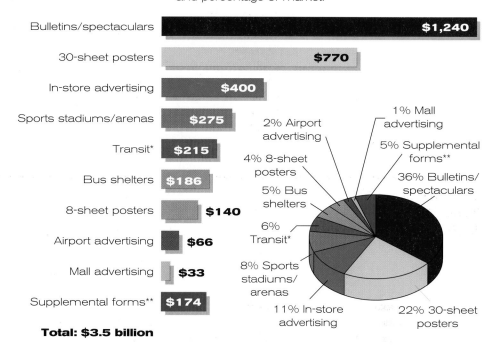

Bulletins Post the Best Numbers

Estimated gross billings by out-of-home media category (in millions) and percentage of market.

Bulletins/spectaculars — **$1,240**
30-sheet posters — **$770**
In-store advertising — **$400**
Sports stadiums/arenas — **$275**
Transit* — **$215**
Bus shelters — **$186**
8-sheet posters — **$140**
Airport advertising — **$66**
Mall advertising — **$33**
Supplemental forms** — **$174**

Total: $3.5 billion

1% Mall advertising
2% Airport advertising
5% Supplemental forms**
4% 8-sheet posters
36% Bulletins/spectaculars
5% Bus shelters
6% Transit*
8% Sports stadiums/arenas
11% In-store advertising
22% 30-sheet posters

* Includes bus, train, and cab advertising.

** Includes painted walls, mobile truck advertising, catering trucks, displays on college campuses, displays on military bases, air banner towing, airplane advertising, movie theater advertising, doctor's offices waiting rooms, health clubs, JumboTrons, golf course signage, ski resort signage, phone kiosks, truck stop advertising.

FIGURE 13–2
Outdoor spending by category (percent of total revenues)

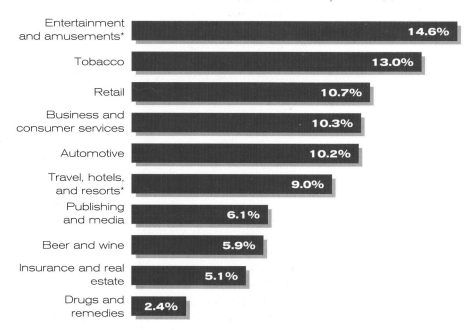

Entertainment and amusements* — **14.6%**
Tobacco — **13.0%**
Retail — **10.7%**
Business and consumer services — **10.3%**
Automotive — **10.2%**
Travel, hotels, and resorts* — **9.0%**
Publishing and media — **6.1%**
Beer and wine — **5.9%**
Insurance and real estate — **5.1%**
Drugs and remedies — **2.4%**

* Travel and tourism advertisers, comprised of these two categories, represent 23.6% of industry revenues.

EXHIBIT 13–1
Outdoor advertising goes beyond two
dimensions

Outdoor advertising does have its critics. Ever since Lady Bird Johnson tried to rid the interstate highways of billboard advertising during her husband's presidency with the Highway Beautification Act of 1965, there has been controversy regarding its use. A number of cities and states have passed or are considering legislation limiting the use of this advertising form, because they find it unsightly and obtrusive. In a study conducted by the University of Michigan Survey Research Center, 19 percent of those polled favored doing away with outdoor advertising, and 64.5 percent favored reasonable regulation.

Media buyers have not completely adopted outdoor, partially because of image problems and because of the belief that it is difficult to buy. (Approximately 80 percent of outdoor advertising is purchased by local merchants and companies.) Let us examine some of the advantages and disadvantages of the medium in more detail.

ADVANTAGES AND DISADVANTAGES OF OUTDOOR ADVERTISING

Outdoor advertising offers a number of advantages.

1. *Wide coverage of local markets.* With proper placement, a broad base of exposure is possible in local markets, with both day and night presence. A 100 GRP **showing** (the percentage of duplicated audience exposed to an outdoor poster daily) could yield exposure to an equivalent of 100 percent of the marketplace daily, or 3,000 GRPs over a month. This level of coverage is likely to yield high levels of reach.

EXHIBIT 13–2
Inflatables bring new meaning to
outdoor advertising

FIGURE 13–3
Higher sales from outdoor
advertising

Brand	Outdoor Used	Results
Hormel chili	#25 poster showing	Sales increased 8.5% Share grew 4.6%
Slice beverage	33 posters in Chicago positioned near Jewel stores	Sales at Jewel stores increased 18%
Neon automobile	#50 showing in 23 markets	60% of year one production sold out in 4 months
Shoney's Restaurants	47 posters in Nashville	Dessert sales up 27%
NFL on Fox network	Bulletins in 14 markets	Ratings up . . . no makegoods necessary

Source: Outdoor Advertising Association of America.

2. *Frequency.* Because purchase cycles are typically for 30-day periods, consumers are usually exposed a number of times, resulting in high levels of frequency.

3. *Geographic flexibility.* Outdoor can be placed along highways, near stores, or on mobile billboards, almost anywhere that laws permit. Local, regional, or even national markets may be covered.

4. *Creativity.* As shown in Exhibit 13–1, outdoor ads can be very creative. Large print, colors, and other elements attract attention.

5. *Ability to create awareness.* Because of its impact (and the need for a simple message), outdoor can lead to a high level of awareness.

6. *Efficiency.* Outdoor usually has a very competitive CPM when compared to other media.

7. *Effectiveness.* Outdoor advertising can often lead to sales, as demonstrated in Figure 13–3.

8. *Production capabilities.* Modern technologies have reduced production times for outdoor advertising to allow for rapid turnaround time.

At the same time, however, there are limitations to outdoor, many of them related to its advantages.

1. *Waste coverage.* While it is possible to reach very specific audiences, in many cases the purchase of outdoor results in a high degree of waste coverage. It is not likely that everyone driving past a billboard is part of the target market.

2. *Limited message capabilities.* Because of the speed with which most people pass by outdoor ads, exposure time is short, so messages are limited to a few words and/or an illustration. Lengthy appeals are not likely to be effective.

3. *Wearout.* Because of the high frequency of exposures, outdoor may lead to a quick wearout. People are likely to get tired of seeing the same ad every day.

4. *Cost.* Because of the decreasing signage available and the higher cost associated with inflatables, outdoor advertising can be expensive in both an absolute and a relative sense.

5. *Measurement problems.* One of the more difficult problems of outdoor advertising lies in the accuracy of measuring reach, frequency, and other effects. (As you will see in the measurement discussion, this problem is currently being addressed, though it has not been resolved.)

6. *Image problems.* Outdoor advertising has suffered some image problems as well as some disregard among consumers.

In sum, outdoor advertising has both advantages and disadvantages for marketers. Some of these problems can be avoided with other forms of out-of-home advertising.

Additional Out-of-Home Media

Several other forms of outdoor advertising are also available. As you read about them, keep in mind the advantages and disadvantages of outdoor in general mentioned earlier and consider whether these alternatives have the same advantages and/or provide a possible solution to the disadvantages.

EXHIBIT 13–3
Aerial advertising is used by a variety of marketers

EXHIBIT 13–4
An interesting and unusual example of a mobile billboard

AERIAL ADVERTISING

Airplanes pulling banners, skywriting (in letters as high as 1,200 feet), and blimps all constitute another form of outdoor advertising available to the marketer: **aerial advertising**. Generally these media are not expensive in absolute terms and can be useful for reaching specific target markets. For example, Coppertone has often used skywriting over beach areas to promote its tanning lotions, Gallo used skywriting to promote its wine coolers (Bartles & Jaymes), and local advertisers promote special events, sales, and the like. Exhibit 13–3 shows one of the many products, services, and/or events that have used this medium.

MOBILE BILLBOARDS

Another outdoor medium is **mobile billboards** (see Exhibit 13–4). Some companies paint Volkswagen Beetles with ads called Beetleboards; others paint trucks and vans. Still others put ads on small billboards, mount them on trailers, and drive around and/or park in the geographic areas being targeted. Costs depend on the area and the mobile board company's fees, though even small and large organizations have found the medium affordable. Valvoline, Citicorp, and Knott's Berry Farm are a few advertisers that have used this medium.[3]

In-Store Media

Advertisers spend an estimated $17 billion to promote their products in supermarkets and other stores with untypical media like displays, banners, and shelf signs. These point-of-purchase materials include video displays on shopping carts, kiosks that provide recipes and coupons at counters and cash registers, LED (light-emitting diode) boards, and ads that broadcast over in-house screens. IBM spends an estimated $15 million per year in this area. At one time, Miller Brewing Co. used 30 to 40 agencies to provide these services (it now uses 10). Figure 13–4 lists a few of the many **in-store media** options.

Much of the attraction of point-of-purchase media is based on figures from the Point of Purchase Advertising Institute (POPAI) that state approximately two-thirds of consumers' purchase decisions are made in the store; some impulse categories demonstrate an 80 percent rate.[4] Many advertisers are spending more of their dollars where decisions are made now that they can reach consumers at the point of purchase, providing additional product information while reducing their own efforts.

FIGURE 13–4
In-store media options

Company/Program	Medium
ActMedia	
Act Now	Co-op couponing/sampling
Aisle Vision	Ad posters inserted in stores' directory signs
Carts	Ad placed on frame inside/outside shopping cart
Impact	Customized in-store promotion events
Instant Coupon Machine	Coupon dispensers mounted in shelf channels
Act Radio	Live format in-store radio network
Shelf Take-One	Two-sided take-one offers in plastic see-thru cartridges placed at shelf
Shelf Talk	Plastic frames on shelf near product
Advanced Promotion Technologies	
Vision System	Scanner-driven, card-based promotion system using audio/video at checkout
Catalina Marketing	
Checkout Coupon	Scanner-driven coupon program that generates coupons at checkout
Checkout Message	Targeted ad messages delivered at checkout
Save Now	Instant electronic discounts
Donnelly Marketing	
Convert	Solo/customized promotion events
In-Store Advertising	Two-sided LED display units that hang above 5 high-traffic areas
News America	In-store couponing
Time In-Store	In-store couponing
Valassis In-Store	In-store couponing
SPAR Marketing Force	In-store demos & customized events
Media One, Inc.	
SuperAd	Backlit ads placed in checkout lanes
Stratmar Systems	
Field Services	In-store demos & customized events
StratMedia	Shopping cart ad program
Supermarket Communications Systems	
Good Neighbor Direct	Bulletin board distribution center

Sources: Dan Ailloni-Charas, "Beyond the Upheaval in In-Store Marketing," *Brandweek*, September 23, 1996, p. 18; 1997 Catalina Marketing Corp., www.catalinamktg.com.

Miscellaneous Outdoor Media

As shown in Figure 13–5, there are numerous outdoor media available, adding to the pervasiveness of this medium. The next time you are out, take a few moments to observe how many different forms of outdoor advertising you are exposed to. Global Perspective 13–1 demonstrates that this phenomenon is not limited to the U.S. marketplace.

Audience Measurement in Out-of-Home Media

A number of sources of audience measurement and other information are available:

- Competitive Media Reports (formerly BAR/LNA) provides information on expenditures on outdoor media by major advertisers.
- Simmons Market Research Bureau conducts research annually for the Institute of Outdoor Advertising, providing demographic data, exposures, and the like. Mediamark Research Inc. (MRI) provides similar data.
- Standard Rate & Data Service provides a sourcebook on rate information, production requirements, closing dates, etc.

FIGURE 13-5 Out-of-home advertising faces/vehicles

Medium	1995 Estimate	
30-sheet posters	200,000 posters	There are well over 30 types of out-of-home media vehicles in active use by advertisers today (many of which did not exist in 1970). The following media forms are also now available in various markets around the country:
8-sheet posters	140,000 posters	
Bulletins	56,000 bulletins	
Buses	37,100 buses*	
Commuter rail/subways	13,000 cars	
Bus shelters	32,000 **	
Airports	100 airports	
Shopping malls	1,200 malls	
Grocery store displays	24,000 stores	
Drugstores	10,000 stores	
Convenience stores	10,000 stores	
Professional sports stadiums/arenas	77 facilities	

- Painted walls
- Truck advertising
- Catering trucks
- Displays on college campuses
- Diplays on military bases
- Air banner towing
- Movie theater advertising

- Doctor's offices/waiting rooms
- Health clubs
- Jumbo Trons
- Golf course signage
- Ski resort signage
- Taxi signage
- Truck-stop advertising

*The United States has a total of 60,000 buses; 37,100 carry advertising.

**Includes shelter-size displays in parking lots/garages, approximately 1,500 in number.

Source: Outdoor Advertising Association of America.

- Eight-Sheet Outdoor Advertising Association provides a buyers' guide containing facts and figures regarding outdoor advertising.
- Shelter Advertising Association provides a buyers' guide containing facts and figures regarding shelter advertising.
- Audience Measurement by Market for Outdoor (AMMO) audience estimates are provided by Marketmath, Inc., for outdoor showings in over 500 markets. Published annually, the reports are based on a series of local market travel studies and circulation audits and provide demographic characteristics of audiences.
- The Institute of Outdoor Advertising is a trade organization of the outdoor advertising industry. It gathers cost data and statistical information for outdoor advertising space purchases.
- Harris-Donovan Media Systems employs a mathematical model using data supplied by the Traffic Audit Bureau and segmented by time period and billboard size. The data provide audience figures in the top 50 metropolitan areas and are available to subscribers on any IBM-compatible computer.
- The Point of Purchase Advertising Institute is a trade organization of point-of-purchase advertisers collecting statistical and other market information on POP advertising.
- The Outdoor Advertising Association of America (OAAA), the primary trade association of the industry, assists members with research, creative ideas, and more effective use of the medium.
- The Media Market Guide (MMG) provides physical dimensions, population characteristics, and media opportunities for the top 100 media markets.
- The Traffic Audit Bureau (TAB) is the auditing arm of the industry. TAB conducts traffic counts on which the published rates are based.
- The Traffic Audit Bureau for Media Measurement provides data regarding exposures to a variety of out-of-home media, including bus shelters, aerial banners, in-store media, and billboards. This organization was formed in response to complaints that current methodologies might overstate the reach provided by these media.
- Scarborough publishes local market studies providing demographic data, product usage, and outdoor media usage.
- Computer packages like Telmar, Donnelly, TAPSCAN, and IMS also provide information comparing outdoor with other media.

Global Perspective 13—1
Alternative Media Go International

Everyone knows that advertising is pervasive in the United States; ads appear everywhere from manhole covers to the inside of golf cups to trash cans. What you may not have realized is just how common these forms of advertising are in the international arena as well. As the world becomes smaller and support media continue to increase in use, foreign markets are adopting this form of communication almost as quickly as the United States.

- To increase brand awareness, Intel distributed a million bike reflectors in Shanghai and Beijing, China. The stickers, which say "Intel Inside Pentium Processor" are an attempt to help Intel capture part of the Chinese market of 1.8 million computers.
- Image Productions, an English company, is placing advertising for its clients on bus tickets, supermarket receipts, and phone cards throughout Europe. Polygram Records and Rock Circus (a British tourist attraction) are just two of the many European subscribers.
- Joop! Jeans advertises on taxis painted completely with ads. Even the interiors of some of the cabs are upholstered with the same ads.

- In Turkey, Pepsi, Coke, MasterCard, United Airlines, and M&M/Mars have painted entire buses with ads. US Air has plastered ads on commuter trains.
- In Hong Kong, Hertz painted a tram entirely in black and yellow; a camera company designed a tram's headlight into a camera lens. Delta, Cathay Pacific, and Qantas airlines are just a few of the many others employing this medium.

With all of these advertisers rushing out to find new ways to advertise, the big question is "Does it work?" A tram ad in Hong Kong currently costs about $2,900 (U.S.) a month, with a minimum one-year commitment. Advertisers must believe that it works—there is a waiting list to buy and there are plans to take the idea to Guangzhou, China. Intel is a believer; its Pentium processors account for 70 percent of sales, versus 50 percent prior to the bicycle campaign. So, as you can see, you can't escape ads by leaving the country anymore.

Sources: Fara Warner and Karen Hsu, "Intel Gets a Free Ride in China Sticking Its Name on Bicycles," *The Wall Street Journal*, July 23, 1996, p. B5; Allyson L. Stewart-Allen, "Creative New Media in Europe Here to Stay?" *Marketing News*, June 3, 1996, p. 15; Robert Goldsborough, "Hong Kong Trams Keep Ads Rolling," *Advertising Age*, May 8, 1995, p. 36.

One of the weaknesses associated with outdoor advertising is audience measurement. Space rates are usually based on the number of desired showings, as shown in Figure 13–6. For example, a 100 showing would theoretically provide coverage to the entire market. In San Diego, this would mean coverage of nearly 2 million people for a monthly rate of $30,600 to $37,200. Along with rate information, the companies offering outdoor billboards provide reach and frequency estimates—but there is no valid way to verify that the showings are performing as promised. The buyer is somewhat at the mercy of the selling agent.

In response to criticism, the industry has implemented a gross ratings point system similar to that used in the television industry. While the system has helped, problems associated with the use of GRPs (discussed earlier in this text) limit the usefulness of this information. Many experts think the new service provided by Harris Media Systems is a significant improvement over the AMMO system, resulting in more credible information.[5]

Transit Advertising

Another form of out-of-home advertising is **transit advertising**. While similar to outdoor in the sense that it uses billboards and electronic messages, transit is targeted at the millions of people who are exposed to commercial transportation facilities, including buses, taxis, commuter trains, elevators, trolleys, airplanes, and subways.

FIGURE 13—6
Posting space rates, San Diego market (per-month basis)

Showing Size	1 Month	3 Months	6 Months	12 Months
#25 (15 posters)	$10,650	$10,350	$10,050	$ 9,750
#50 (30 posters)	21,300	20,700	20,100	19,500
#75 (45 posters)	31,950	31,050	30,150	29,250
#100 (60 posters)	37,200	35,700	33,000	30,600

Transit advertising has been around for a long time, but recent years have seen a renewed interest in this medium. Due in part to the increased number of women in the work force (they can be reached on their way to work more easily than at home), audience segmentation, and the rising cost of TV advertising, transit ad spending increased from $43 million in 1972 to over $225 million in 1996.[6] Much of this spending has come from package-goods companies such as Colgate, H. J. Heinz, Kraft–General Foods, and Weight Watchers, which like transit's lower costs and improved frequency of exposures. Other retailers, movie studios, and business-to-business companies have also increased expenditures in this area.

TYPES OF TRANSIT ADVERTISING

There are actually three forms of transit advertising: (1) inside cards, (2) outside posters, and (3) station, platform, or terminal posters.

Inside Cards

If you have ever ridden a commuter bus, you have probably noticed the **inside cards** placed above the seats and luggage area advertising restaurants, TV or radio stations, or a myriad of other products and services. An innovation is the electronic message boards that carry current advertising information. The ability to change the message and the visibility provide the advertiser with a more attention-getting medium.

Transit cards can be controversial. For example, in the New York subway system, many of the ads for chewing gum, soup, and Smokey the Bear have given way to public service announcements about AIDS, unwanted pregnancies, rape, and infant mortality. While subway riders may agree that such issues are important, many of them complain that the ads are depressing and intrusive.

A variation on inside transit advertising is shown in Exhibit 13–5. The airline ticket holder is a very effective form of advertising communication. It takes advantage of a captive audience and keeps the message in front of the passenger the whole time he or she is holding the ticket.

EXHIBIT 13–5
Airline ticket holders are used to promote a variety of products

Outside Posters

Advertisers use various forms of outdoor transit posters to promote products and services. These **outside posters** may appear on the sides, backs, and/or roofs of buses, taxis, trains, and subway and trolley cars. Some examples are shown in the ad for Transportation Displays, Inc., a leading outdoor and transit advertising company.

The increased sophistication of this medium was demonstrated in a test market in Barcelona, Spain, during the 1992 Summer Olympics. Viatex—a joint venture among Atlanta-based Bevilaqua International (a sports marketing company), Saatchi & Saatchi Lifestyle Group, and Warrec Co., a Connecticut-based international business firm—mounted electronic billboards on the sides of buses. These monitors flashed Olympic news and ads that could change at scheduled times. Electronic beacons located throughout the city were activated as the buses drove by to change the message for the various locations.

Station, Platform, and Terminal Posters

Floor displays, island showcases, electronic signs, and other forms of advertising that appear in train or subway stations, airline terminals, and the like are all forms of transit advertising. As Exhibit 13–6 shows, **terminal posters** can be very attractive and attention getting. Bus shelters often provide the advertiser with expanded coverage where other outdoor boards may be restricted. Gannett Transit recently introduced electronic signs on subway platforms in New York.

ADVANTAGES AND DISADVANTAGES OF TRANSIT ADVERTISING

Advantages of using transit advertising include the following.

1. *Exposure.* Long length of exposure to an ad is one major advantage of indoor forms. The average ride on mass transit is 30 to 44 minutes, allowing for plenty of exposure time.[7] As with airline tickets, the audience is essentially a captive one, with nowhere else to go and nothing much to do. As a result, riders are likely to read the ads—more than once. A second form of exposure transit advertising provides is the absolute number of people exposed. About 9 million people ride mass transit every year, providing a substantial number of potential viewers.[8]

2. *Frequency.* Because our daily routines are standard, those who ride buses, subways, and the like are exposed to the ads repeatedly. If you rode the same subway to work and back every day, in one month you would have the opportunity to see the ad 20 to 40 times. The locations of station and shelter signs also afford high frequency of exposure.

EXHIBIT 13—6
Terminal posters can be used to attract attention

3. *Timeliness.* Many shoppers get to stores on mass transit. An ad promoting a product or service at a particular shopping area could be a very timely communication.

4. *Geographic selectivity.* For local advertisers in particular, transit advertising provides an opportunity to reach a very select segment of the population. A purchase of a location in a certain neighborhood will lead to exposure to people of specific ethnic backgrounds, demographic characteristics, and so on.

5. *Cost.* Transit advertising tends to be one of the least expensive media in terms of both absolute and relative costs. An ad on the side of a bus can be purchased for a very reasonable CPM.

Some disadvantages are also associated with transit.

1. *Image factors.* To many advertisers, transit advertising does not carry the image they would like to represent their products or services. Some advertisers may think having their name on the side of a bus or on a bus stop bench does not reflect well on the firm.

2. *Reach.* While an advantage of transit advertising is the ability to provide exposure to a large number of people, this audience may have certain lifestyles and/or behavioral characteristics that are not true of the target market as a whole. For example, in rural or suburban areas, mass transit is limited or nonexistent, so the medium is not very effective for reaching these people.

3. *Waste coverage.* While geographic selectivity may be an advantage, not everyone who rides a transportation vehicle or is exposed to transit advertising is a potential customer. For products that do not have specific geographic segments, this form of advertising incurs a good deal of waste coverage.

Another problem is that the same bus may not run the same route every day. To save wear and tear on the vehicles, some companies alternate city routes (with much stop and go) with longer suburban routes. Thus, a bus may go downtown one day and reach the desired target group, but spend the next day in the suburbs, where there may be little market potential.

4. *Copy and creative limitations.* It may be very difficult to place colorful, attractive ads on cards or benches. And while much copy can be provided on inside cards, on the outside of buses and taxis the message is fleeting and short copy points are necessary.

5. *Mood of the audience.* Sitting or standing on a crowded subway may not be conducive to reading advertising, let alone experiencing the mood the advertiser would like to create. Controversial ad messages may contribute to this less than positive feeling. Likewise, hurrying through an airport may create anxieties that limit the effectiveness of the ads placed there.

In summary, an advantage for one product or service advertiser may be a disadvantage for another. Transit advertising can be an effective medium, but one must understand its strengths and weaknesses to use it properly.

AUDIENCE MEASUREMENT IN TRANSIT ADVERTISING

As with outdoor advertising, the cost basis for transit is the number of showings. In transit advertising, a 100 showing means one ad appears on or in each vehicle in the system; a showing of 50 means half of the vehicles carry the ad. If you are placing such ads on taxicabs, it may be impossible to determine who is being exposed to them.

Rate information comes from the sellers of transit advertising, and audience information is very limited. So much of the information marketers need to purchase transit ads does not come from purely objective sources.

PROMOTIONAL PRODUCTS MARKETING

According to the Promotional Products Association International (PPA), **promotional products marketing** is "the advertising or promotional medium or method that uses promotional products, such as ad specialties, premiums, business gifts, awards, prizes, or commemoratives." Promotional products marketing is the more up-to-date name for what used to be called specialty advertising. **Specialty advertising** has now been provided with a new definition:

> A medium of advertising, sales promotion, and motivational communication employing imprinted, useful, or decorative products called advertising specialties, a subset of promotional products.
>
> Unlike premiums, with which they are sometimes confused (called advertising specialties), these articles are always distributed free—recipients don't have to earn the specialty by making a purchase or contribution.[9]

As you can see from these descriptions, specialty advertising is often considered both an advertising and a sales promotion medium. In our discussion, we treat it as a supportive advertising medium.

There are over 15,000 *advertising specialty* items, including ballpoint pens, coffee mugs, key rings, calendars, T-shirts, and matchbooks. Unconventional specialties such as plant holders, wall plaques, and gloves with the advertiser's name printed on them are also used to promote a company or its product; so are glassware, trophies, awards, and vinyl products, as shown in Exhibit 13–7. In fact, advertisers spend over $8 billion per year on specialty advertising items. The increased use of this medium makes it the fastest-growing of all advertising or sales promotion media.[10]

If you stop reading for a moment and look around your desk (or bed or beach blanket), you'll probably find some specialty advertising item nearby. It may be the pen you are using, a matchbook, or even a book cover with the campus bookstore name on it. (Figure 13–7 shows the percentage of sales by product category.) Specialty items are used for many promotional purposes: to thank a customer for patronage, keep the name of the company in front of consumers, introduce new products, or reinforce the name of an existing company, product, or service. Advertising specialties are often used to support other forms of product promotions.

EXHIBIT 13–7
Examples of specialty advertising items

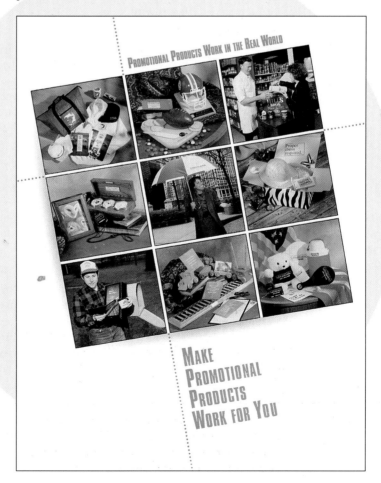

FIGURE 13–7
Sales of promotional products by category

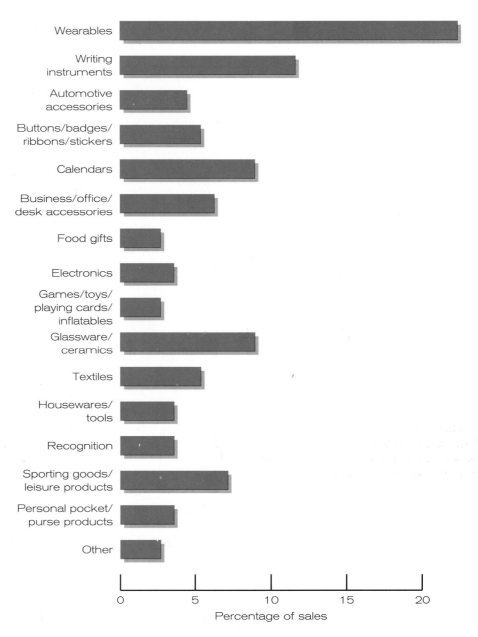

Percentage of sales

Advantages and Disadvantages of Promotional Products Marketing

Like any other advertising medium, promotional products marketing offers the marketer both advantages and disadvantages. Advantages include the following.

1. *Selectivity.* Because specialty advertising items are generally distributed directly to target customers, the medium offers a high degree of selectivity. The communication is distributed to the desired recipient, reducing waste coverage.

2. *Flexibility.* As the variety of specialty items in Exhibit 13–7 demonstrates, this medium offers a high degree of flexibility. A message as simple as a logo or as long as is necessary can be distributed through a number of means. Both small and large companies can employ this medium, limited only by their own creativity.

3. *Frequency.* Most forms of specialty advertising are designed for retention. Key chains, calendars, and pens remain with the potential customer for a long time, providing repeat exposures to the advertising message at no additional cost.

4. *Cost.* Some specialty items are rather expensive (for example, leather goods), but most are affordable to almost any size organization. While they are costly on a CPM basis when compared with other media, the high number of repeat exposures drives down the relative cost per exposure of this advertising medium.

5. *Goodwill.* Promotional products are perhaps the only medium that generates goodwill in the receiver. Because people like to receive gifts and many of the products are functional (key chains, calendars, etc.), consumers are grateful to receive them.

6. *Supplementing other media.* A major advantage of promotional products marketing is its ability to supplement other media. Because of its low cost and repeat exposures, the simplest message can reinforce the appeal or information provided through other forms. For example, the Cartoon Network, which includes two of the world's largest animated film libraries, used specialty products to target 500 cable TV stations featuring "Wile E. Coyote and the Roadrunner." It delivered a crowbar and a brown box whose lid read "One ACME Launch Assistance Tool" to each station. The crates contained promotional launch items such as ad slicks, literature, videos, and audiotapes describing the new network. Of the 500 networks, 480 signed up for the new program.

Disadvantages of promotional products marketing include the following.

1. *Image.* While most forms of specialty advertising are received as friendly reminders of the store or company name, the firm must be careful choosing the specialty item. The company image may be cheapened by a chintzy or poorly designed advertising form.

2. *Saturation.* With so many organizations now using this advertising medium, the marketplace may become saturated. While you can always use another ballpoint pen or book of matches, the value to the receiver declines if replacement is too easy, and the likelihood that you will retain the item or even notice the message is reduced. The more unusual the specialty, the more value it is likely to have to the receiver.

3. *Lead time.* The lead time required to put together a promotional products message is significantly longer than for most other media.

Audience Measurement in Promotional Products Marketing

Owing to the nature of the industry, specialty advertising has no established ongoing audience measurement system. Research has been conducted in an attempt to determine the impact of this medium, however, including the following reports.

A study by Schreiber and Associates indicated 39 percent of people receiving advertising specialties could recall the name of the company as long as six months later, and a study conducted by A. C. Nielsen found that 31 percent of respondents were still using at least one specialty they had received a year or more earlier.[11]

A study by Gould/Pace University found the inclusion of a specialty item in a direct-mail piece generated a greater response rate and 321 percent greater dollar purchases per sale than mail pieces without such items.[12] Studies at Baylor University showed that including an ad specialty item in a thank-you letter can improve customers' attitudes toward a company's sales reps by as much as 34 percent and toward the company itself by as much as 52 percent.[13] Finally, Richard Manville Research reported the average household had almost four calendars; if they had not been given such items free, two-thirds said they would purchase one, an indication of the desirability of this particular specialty item.[14]

The Promotional Products Association International is the trade organization of the field. The PPA helps marketers develop and use specialty advertising forms. It also provides promotional and public relations support for specialty advertising and disseminates statistical and educational information.

Yellow Pages Advertising

When we think of advertising media, many of us overlook one of the most popular forms in existence—the Yellow Pages. While most of us use the **Yellow Pages** frequently, we tend to forget they are advertising. Over 200 publishers produce more than 6,500 Yellow Pages throughout the United States, generating $10 billion in advertising expenditures. This makes the Yellow Pages the fifth-largest medium (just behind radio).[15]

More than 90 percent of the industry's ad revenues are accounted for by nine big operators: the seven regional Bell companies, the Donnelley Directory, and GTE Directories.[16] Local advertisers constitute the bulk of the ads in these directories (about 90 percent), though national advertisers such as U-Haul, Sears, and General Motors use them as well.[17]

Interestingly, there are several forms of Yellow Pages. (Because AT&T never copyrighted the term, any publisher can use it.) They include the following.

- *Specialized directories.* Directories are targeted at select markets such as Hispanics, blacks, Asians, and women. Also included in this category are toll-free directories, Christian directories, and many others.
- *Audiotex.* The "talking Yellow Pages" offer oral information on advertisers.
- *Interactive.* Consumers search the database for specific types of information. Advertisers can update their listings frequently.
- *Other services.* Some Yellow Pages directories offer coupons and freestanding inserts. In Orange County, California, telephone subscribers received samples of Golden Grahams and Cinnamon Toast Crunch cereals when their Yellow Pages were delivered.

AWARENESS ACTION

The Yellow Pages are often referred to as a **directional medium** because the ads do not create awareness or demand for products or services; rather, once consumers have decided to buy, the Yellow Pages point them in the direction where their purchases can be made.[18] The Yellow Pages are thus considered the final link in the buying cycle, as shown in this ad.

ADVANTAGES AND DISADVANTAGES OF YELLOW PAGES

The Yellow Pages offer the following advantages to advertisers.

1. *Wide availability.* A variety of directories are published. According to the Yellow Pages Publishers Association, consumers refer to the Yellow Pages more than 19.4 billion times yearly.[19]

2. *Action orientation.* Consumers use the Yellow Pages when they are considering, or have decided to take, action.

3. *Costs.* Ad space and production costs are relatively low compared to other media.

4. *Frequency.* Because of their longevity (Yellow Pages are published yearly), consumers return to the directories time and again. The average adult refers to the Yellow Pages about twice a week.[20]

5. *Nonintrusiveness.* Because consumers choose to use the Yellow Pages, they are not considered an intrusion. Studies show that most consumers rate the Yellow Pages very favorably.[21]

Disadvantages of the Yellow Pages include the following.

1. *Market fragmentation.* Since Yellow Pages are essentially local media, they tend to be very localized. Add to this the increasing number of specialized directories, and the net result is a very specific offering.

2. *Timeliness.* Because Yellow Pages are printed only once a year, they become outdated. Companies may relocate, go out of business, or change phone numbers in the period between editions.

3. *Lack of creativity.* While the Yellow Pages are somewhat flexible, their creative aspects are limited.

4. *Lead times.* Printing schedules require that ads be placed a long time before the publications appear. It is impossible to get an ad in after the deadline, and advertisers need to wait a long time before the next edition.

AUDIENCE MEASUREMENT IN THE YELLOW PAGES

Two forms of audience measurement are employed in the Yellow Pages industry. As with other print media, *circulation* is counted as the number of either individuals or households

FIGURE 13–8
The Yellow Pages use a usage rating system

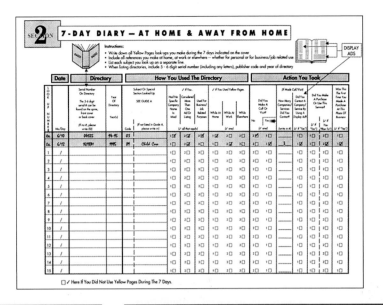

CPM Based on Directory Circulation			
Directory	Circulation	Cost for a Full-Page Ad	CPM
A	509,000	$28,000	$55.01
B	505,000	$21,000	$41.58

CPM Based on Directory Usage (Ratings)				
Directory	Total References per Year	Share of References	Cost for a Full-Page Ad	CPM
A	58,400,000	76.9%	$28,000	$ .48
B	17,500,000	23.1%	$21,000	$1.20

possessing a particular directory. But Yellow Pages advertisers have resisted the use of circulation figures for evaluating audience size, arguing that this number represents only *potential* exposures to an ad.[22] Given that households may possess more than one directory, advertisers argued for a figure based on *usage.* The National Yellow Pages Monitor (NYPM) now provides Yellow Pages directory ratings. Using a diary method similar to broadcast media, this ratings method allows advertisers to determine both the absolute and relative costs of advertising in different directories (see Figure 13–8).

The trade association for the Yellow Pages, the Yellow Pages Publishers Association, provides industry information, rates, educational materials, and assistance to advertisers and potential advertisers. The YPPA also disseminates educational and statistical information.

OTHER MEDIA

There are numerous other nontraditional ways to promote products. Some are reviewed here.

Advertising in Movie Theaters and Videos

Two methods of delivering the message that are increasing quickly (to the dismay of many) are the use of movie theaters and video rentals to promote products and/or services. Commercials shown before the film and previews, with both local and national sponsorships, have almost replaced cartoons. For example, Coca-Cola Co. has frequently advertised the Coke Classic brand in movie theaters and promoted Fruitopia with a 60-second spot in this medium. On videos, companies place ads before the movies as well as on the cartons they come in. Pepsi advertises on the video of *Casper.* Disney often promotes its upcoming movies as well as Disney World (10 minutes of advertising preceded *The Lion King* on video).[23] The Canadian government has shown "stay in school" spots, knowing that the movies are a good way to reach 12- to 17-year-olds. Dozens of other advertisers have also used this medium, including Sega, AT&T, and DeBeers.

Consumer reaction to ads in movie theaters and on videos is mixed. As shown in Figure 13–9, most people think ads on videos are annoying or very annoying (67.5 percent). But the same survey showed that as many as 57 percent watch these commercials. The same seems to

FIGURE 13–9
Consumer opinions about ads on video

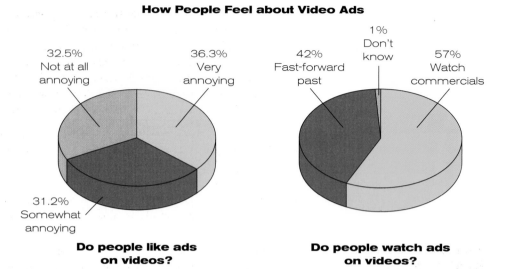

How People Feel about Video Ads

32.5% Not at all annoying

36.3% Very annoying

31.2% Somewhat annoying

42% Fast-forward past

1% Don't know

57% Watch commercials

Do people like ads on videos?

Do people watch ads on videos?

hold true for advertising in movie theaters. In an *Advertising Age*/Gallup national sample of moviegoers, 35 percent were against a ban on ads in movie theaters and another 21 percent were unsure whether such a ban should be enacted.[24] The survey was taken after Walt Disney Co. announced it would stop showing its movies in any theater that runs on-screen advertising along with the films. While advertisers were infuriated, Disney claimed its surveys showed customers were extremely irritated by such ads and as a result might quit coming to the theaters.[25]

Adam Snyder, writing in *Brandweek* magazine, believes that pushing movies is acceptable but beyond that consumers are likely to react negatively.[26] Nevertheless, Blake Thomas, marketing vice president for MGM/UA Home Entertainment, claims "We could conceivably sell as much air time as we want," since advertisers cannot resist the temptation of reaching tens of millions of viewers.[27]

ADVANTAGES OF MOVIE AND VIDEO ADVERTISING

Both movies and videos provide a number of advantages to advertisers, including the following.

1. *Exposure.* The number of people attending movies is substantial; ticket sales are approaching $5 billion per year.[28] At the same time, the number of households using VCRs is increasing. These growth figures mean that more people are likely to be exposed to the ads. These viewers constitute a captive audience who are also known to watch less television than the average.[29]
2. *Mood.* If viewers like the movie, the mood can carry over to the product advertised. For example, when BMW placed its Z3 in the movie *GoldenEye*, it hoped viewers' excitement and good feelings toward the movie would carry over to the car.
3. *Cost.* The cost of advertising in a theater varies from one setting to the next. However, it is low in terms of both absolute and relative costs per exposure.
4. *Recall.* Research indicates that the next day about 87 percent of viewers can recall the ads they saw in a movie theater. This compares with a 20 percent recall rate for television.[30]
5. *Clutter.* Lack of clutter is another advantage offered by advertising in movie theaters. Most theaters limit the number of ads.

DISADVANTAGES OF MOVIE AND VIDEO ADVERTISING

Some of the disadvantages associated with movies and videos as advertising media follow.

1. *Irritation.* Perhaps the major disadvantage is that many people do not wish to see advertising in these media. A number of studies suggest these ads may create a high degree

of annoyance.[31] This dissatisfaction may carry over to the product itself, to the movies, or to the theaters. Mike Stimler, president of the specialty video label Water Bearer Films, says, "People boo in movie theaters when they see product advertising."[32]

2. *Cost.* While the cost of advertising in local theaters has been cited as an advantage because of the low rates charged, ads exposed nationally cost up to $425,000 per minute to reach 25 million viewers. This rate is 20 percent higher than an equal exposure on television. CPMs also tend to be higher than in other media.

While only two disadvantages of theater advertising have been mentioned, the first is a strong one. Many people who have paid to see a movie (or rent a video) perceive advertising as an intrusion. In a study by Michael Belch and Don Sciglimpaglia, many moviegoers stated that not only would they not buy the product advertised, but they would consider boycotting it. So advertisers should be cautious in their use of this medium. If they want to use movies, they might consider an alternative—placing products in the movies.

Product Placements in Movies and TV

An increasingly common way to promote a product is by showing the actual product or an ad for it as part of a movie or TV show. While such **product placement** does not constitute a major segment of the advertising and promotions business, it has proved effective for some companies. (Note: Like specialty advertising, product placement is sometimes considered a promotion rather than an advertising form. This distinction is not a critical one, and we have decided to treat it as a form of advertising.)

A number of companies pay to have their products used in movies and music videos. For example, in the movie *Austin Powers*, the villain Dr. Evil's spacecraft was in the shape of a "Big Boy" from the Big Boy restaurant chain. In the movie *The Lost World*, the San Diego Zoo, Seaworld, and downtown shopping mall Horton Plaza were all part of the movie. Exhibit 13–8 shows how Cheer was able to get its product featured in the movie *Wayne's World II*; the effect is as if Kim Basinger had endorsed the product. Essentially, this form is advertising without an advertising medium. The audience doesn't realize a product promotion is going on. Viewers tend to see brand names in films as lending realism to the story. Yet the impact on the buying public is real. For example, when Reese's Pieces were used in the movie *E.T.*, sales rose 70 percent and the candies were added to the concessions of 800 movie theaters where they had previously not been sold.[33] Sales of Ray-Ban Wayfarer sunglasses tripled after Tom Cruise wore them in the movie *Risky Business* and Ray-Ban Aviator sales increased 40 percent after he wore them in *Top Gun*.[34]

The move to place products on TV programs is also on the increase. In 1988, CBS broke its long-standing tradition of not mentioning brand names in its programs. In addition to feature roles and product placements, free plugs are now becoming more common, as discussed in IMC Perspective 13–2.

EXHIBIT 13–8
Many companies use movies to promote their products

ADVANTAGES OF PRODUCT PLACEMENTS

A number of advantages of product tie-ins have been suggested.

1. *Exposure.* A large number of people see movies each year (over 1 billion admissions in 1996).[35] The average film is estimated to have a life span of three and one-half years (with 75 million exposures), and most of these moviegoers are very attentive audience members. When this is combined with the increasing home video rental market and network and cable TV (for example, HBO, Showtime, the Movie Channel), the potential exposure for a product placed in a movie is enormous. And this form of exposure is not subject to zapping, at least not in the theater.

High exposure numbers are also offered for TV tie-ins, based on the ratings and (at least in the case of soaps) the possibility to direct the ad to a defined target market.

2. *Frequency.* Depending on how the product is used in the movie (or program), there may be ample opportunity for repeated exposures (many, for those who like to watch a program or movie more than once). For example, if you are a regular watcher of "Seinfeld," you will be exposed to the products placed therein a number of times.

IMC Perspective 13–2
Free Ad Plugs on the Rise

"Better coffee a millionaire's money can't buy," the long-time jingle of Chock Full o' Nuts coffee is now a part of a circus act—New York's Big Apple Circus. So are a lot of other things about Chock, including a cart selling coffee, a Chock night for the coffee's trade customers, and an FSI drop that offered up to $21.35 worth of coffee and circus tickets. The jingle, part of an old-time radio spot well known to New Yorkers, will be revived in radio spots and played at the circus in an attempt to leverage the company's ties to New York.

It probably started long before *E.T.*, but the success Reese's enjoyed when its product was placed in that movie made a lot of marketers notice the potential of product placements. Since then product placements have appeared in dozens of movies, including *It Could Happen to You* (Rollerblade skates), *Forrest Gump* (*People* magazine), and *Angels in the Outfield* (Gatorade), among many others. This form of advertising has also increased on television.

For a mere $5,000 (most of it in beer shipped to the film crew), Red Stripe beer was able to have its product shown and mentioned in *The Firm*. Avery Tolar (Gene Hackman) told Mitch McDeere (Tom Cruise) to "grab a Red Stripe out of the fridge." Potential exposures? An estimated 7 million people saw the movie the first weekend alone. Millions more have seen it since and are still watching it on videotape.

The $5,000 paid by Red Stripe was a steal. Other companies have paid upwards of $50,000 just to have a mention or hands-on placement. Red Stripe's brand manager was much less successful at getting his imported beer Moretti into the Sharon Stone movie *Sliver*. The bottle was seen, but only at a distance and not too clearly.

Ad plugs on TV are also on the increase, according to a study conducted for *Advertising Age* by Northwestern University. As with movies, these plugs can take on a variety of forms. Jay Leno mentioning a Big Mac on the "Tonight Show," Kramer and Jerry on "Seinfeld" discussing Calvin Klein fragrances, and Bruce Springsteen on "Saturday Night Live" wearing blue jeans with a distinctive Levi's label are somewhat subtle approaches. Less subtly, Sweet 'n Low packages lie on a table on "One Life to Live" and Cap'n Crunch makes a pretty obvious appearance on "Melrose Place."

Do the free ad plugs work? A lot depends on the nature of the plug—how long it is shown, how casually it is mentioned, and how familiar viewers are with the brand (popular brands are more recognizable). According to Mark Weiner, managing partner of PR Data Systems, you can determine the value of the plug by comparing the length of exposure to the cost of a one-minute spot. So in the Seinfeld discussion, Calvin Klein racked up $347,000 of free ad time for every minute the conversation lasted. Stories on the top-selling Christmas toys are often perceived as endorsements, says Weiner. Once again, advertising appears inescapable!

Sources: "Coffee Ties to Circus Act," *Brandweek*, January 1, 1996, p. 15; "Cue the Soda Can," *Business Week*, June 24, 1996, pp. 64–66; Adrienne Ward Fawcett, "Free TV 'Ad Plugs' Are on the Rise," *Advertising Age*, July 12, 1993, p. 21; Laura Bird, "A Star Is Brewed as Obscure Beer Scores with Role in Hit Movie," *The Wall Street Journal*, July 8, 1993, p. B3.

Where and Who Gets the Ad Plugs

Percentage of 1,035 ad plugs measured over a recent 24-hour period

Type of Plug	
Brand name shown	49.8%
Brand name spoken	34.8%
Label/logo shown	9.5%
Design identifiable	6.0%

How Clear Was It?	
Very clear	74.9%
Somewhat clear	20.7%
Not very clear	4.4%

Where Are They?	
Evening news	39.9%
Morning news	15.5%
Talk show	15.2%
Hour dramatic series	7.1%
Newsmagazine	6.8%
Half-hour sitcom	4.8%
Game show	2.7%
Daytime soap opera	2.5%
Nonfictional drama	2.4%
Movie	1.7%
Feature news	1.1%
Children's program	0.3%

Which Network?	
ABC	31.6%
NBC	30.8%
CBS	24.9%
Fox	12.7%

Who Gets Plugs?	
Autos	18.3%
Businesses	14.5%
Movies and plays	13.4%
Print media	10.4%
Beverages	7.8%
Apparel	6.2%
Sports	5.7%
Food	5.0%
Restaurants	3.9%
Universities	3.5%
Appliances	3.3%
HBA	2.6%
Music	1.7%

Context of Plugs	
Editorial	48.1%
All other	51.9%

Sources: Northwestern University; *Advertising Age*, July 12, 1993, p. 21.

3. *Support for other media*. Ad placements may support other promotional tools. For example, Mirage Resorts ran four minutes of commercials promoting its Treasure Island Resort on an NBC special titled "Treasure Island: The Adventure Begins," a story about a boy's adventures at the Treasure Island Resort. Kimberly-Clark Corp. created a sweepstakes, coupon offer, and TV-based ad around its Huggies diapers, featured in the movie *Baby Boom*.

4. *Source association*. In Chapter 6, we discussed the advantages of source identification. When consumers see their favorite movie star wearing Keds, drinking Gatorade, or driving a Mercedes, this association may lead to a favorable product image. The purple dinosaur Barney achieved tremendous sales success as a result of its PBS show, "Barney & Friends." Thomas the Tank Engine never used paid commercials, yet it rivaled the sales of Teenage Mutant Ninja Turtles and G.I. Joe, thanks to its appearance on PBS.[36]

5. *Cost*. While the cost of placing a product may range from free samples to $1 million, these are extremes. As shown in Figure 13–10, the CPM for this form of advertising can be very low, owing to the high volume of exposures it generates.

6. *Recall*. A number of firms have measured the impact of product placements on next-day recall. Results ranged from Johnson's Baby Shampoo registering 20 percent to Kellogg's Corn Flakes registering 67 percent (in the movie *Raising Arizona*). Average recall is approximately 38 percent. Again, these scores are better than those reported for TV viewing.

DISADVANTAGES OF PRODUCT PLACEMENTS

Some disadvantages are also associated with product placements.

1. *High absolute cost*. While the CPM may be very low for product placement in movies, the absolute cost of placing the product may be very high, pricing some advertisers out of the market. For example in the Disney film *Mr. Destiny*, it cost $20,000 to have a product seen in the film, $40,000 for an actor to mention the product, and $60,000 for the actor to actually use it.[37]

2. *Time of exposure*. While the way some products are exposed to the audience has an impact, there is no guarantee viewers will notice the product. Some product placements are more conspicuous than others. When the product is not featured prominently, the advertiser runs the risk of not being seen (although, of course, the same risk is present in all forms of media advertising).

3. *Limited appeal*. The appeal that can be made in this media form is limited. There is no potential for discussing product benefits or providing detailed information. Rather, appeals are limited to source association, use, and enjoyment. The endorsement of the product is indirect, and the flexibility for product demonstration is subject to its use in the film.

FIGURE 13–10
CPMs for movie advertising

Title of Film	Theater Box Office	Audience*	Weeks in Release	Cost per Thousand†
Batman Returns	145,480,492	29,750,600	4	.16
Beauty and the Beast	141,838,563	29,000,500	35	.17
Lethal Weapon 3	135,799,341	27,770,820	9	.18
Wayne's World	121,115,040	24,767,900	22	.20
Hook	118,965,084	24,328,240	24	.21
The Addams Family	113,379,166	23,185,920	22	.22
Basic Instinct	110,987,913	22,696,910	17	.22

*Audience figure is based on average ticket price of $4.89 from Motion Picture Association of America, Inc., data and statistics, published in June 1992.

†CPM is the cost for reaching 1,000 consumers with an ad multiplied by 1,000, divided by the total audience (the average cost of a product placement is $5,000).

4. *Lack of control.* In many movies, the advertiser has no say over when and how often the product will be shown. Sony, as noted, found its placement in the movie *Last Action Hero* did not work as well as expected. Fabergé developed an entire Christmas campaign around its Brut cologne and its movie placement, only to find the movie was delayed until February.

5. *Public reaction.* Many TV viewers and moviegoers are incensed at the idea of placing ads in programs or movies. These viewers want to maintain the barrier between program content and commercials. If the placement is too intrusive, they may develop negative attitudes toward the brand. The FTC has explored options for limiting placements without consumer notification.

6. *Competition.* The appeal of product placements has led to increased competition to get one's product placed. BMW was originally placed in the movie *The Firm*—only to be ousted when Mercedes offered a higher bid. In *Wall Street*, Michael Douglas refers to *Fortune* magazine as the financial bible rather than *Forbes* because the former offered more money.[38] The result of this competition is higher prices and no guarantee that one's product will be placed.

7. *Negative placements.* Some products may appear in movie scenes that are disliked by the audience or create a less than favorable mood. For example, in the movie *Missing*, a very good, loyal father takes comfort in a bottle of Coke, while a Pepsi machine appears in a stadium where torturing and murders take place—not a good placement for Pepsi.

AUDIENCE MEASUREMENT FOR PRODUCT PLACEMENTS

To date, no audience measurement is available except from the providers. Potential advertisers often have to make decisions based on their own creative insights or rely on the credibility of the source. However, at least two studies have demonstrated the potential effectiveness of product placements.

In a study by Eva Steortz, viewers had an average recall for placements of 38 percent.[39] And Damon Darlin has provided evidence that an aura of glamour is added to products associated with celebrities.[40] Research companies like PR Data Systems (mentioned earlier) compare the amount of time a product is exposed in the program/movie to the cost of an equivalent ad spot to measure value. (As you will see in Chapter 18, however, we have problems with this measure of effectiveness.)

In-Flight Advertising

Another rapidly growing medium is **in-flight advertising**. As the number of flying passengers increases (to over 5 million per month on American, United, and Delta alone), so too does the attractiveness of this medium. In-flight advertising includes three forms:

- *In-flight magazines.* Free magazines (like the one in Exhibit 13–9) published by the airlines are offered on almost every plane in the air. Delta distributes over 500,000 of its *Sky* magazines each month and estimates potential exposures at 1.7 million.[41]
- *In-flight videos.* In-flight videos have been common on international flights for some time and are now being used on domestic flights. Commercials were not originally included in these videos. Now about $18 million in commercials is booked on flights per year ($12 million on international flights), and advertisers expect a 25 percent growth rate throughout the 1990s.[42] While not all airlines offer in-flight commercials, companies like Japan Air Lines, Delta, TWA, and British Airways are participating.
- *In-flight radio.* *USA Today*'s in-flight radio is run by the same people responsible for publishing its newspaper.

EXHIBIT 13–9
In-flight magazines are available on most carriers

ADVANTAGES AND DISADVANTAGES OF IN-FLIGHT ADVERTISING

Advantages of in-flight advertising include the following.

1. *A desirable audience.* The average traveler is 45 years old and has a household income over $83,700. Both business and tourist travelers tend to be upscale, an attractive audience to companies targeting these groups. Many of these passengers hold top manage-

The Reader

A truism among traditional media circles is that the best way to reach an upscale business audience is through publications such as *Forbes* and *Fortune*. But like a lot of other truisms, this has its myths. If you take a close look at the numbers that drive *Sky* magazine's editorial, you will find that we communicate quite effectively to the demographics you want to reach.

Upwardly Employed

Base: Adults

Target market: Professional/managerial

	MMR Rank	Percent Composition	Index
Sky magazine	16	69.48	126
The Wall Street Journal	19	68.57	124
Business Week	21	66.85	121
Fortune	24	65.99	120
Forbes	36	62.15	113

Corporate Influentials

Base: Adults

Target market: Top management

	MMR Rank	Percent Composition	Index
The Wall Street Journal	10	47.20	156
Business Week	12	46.31	153
Sky magazine	13	46.21	153
Fortune	15	45.92	152
Forbes	19	43.99	146

Business Travelers

Base: Adults

Target market: Spent 7+ nights in hotels for business during the past year

	MMR Rank	Percent Composition	Index
Sky magazine	04	63.74	216
The Wall Street Journal	15	49.51	168
Business Week	16	49.19	167
Forbes	22	47.13	160
Fortune	23	47.04	160

ment positions in their firms, and Delta estimates that as many as 60 percent are responsible for procuring products and/or services for their companies. Other demographics are favorable as well (see Figure 13–11).[43]

2. *A captive audience.* As noted in the discussion about ticket covers, the audience in an airplane cannot leave the room. Particularly on long flights, many passengers are willing (and even happy) to have in-flight magazines to read, news to listen to, and even commercials to watch.

3. *Cost.* The cost of in-flight commercials is lower than that of business print media. The CPM to reach adults with at least a $75,000 household income on United and

FIGURE 13–12 Place-based media make a comeback

Venture	Venue	Reach	Costs
Channel One	Secondary schools	350,000 classrooms; 8 million teens/day	$175–200K/unit CPM: $25 vs. teens
CNN Airport Network	Airports	25 airports, 1,100 gates; 9 million viewers/month	CPM: $30 vs. men 25–54
Channel M	Video arcades	100 mall arcades; 2 million kids age 7–24/month	$55K/unit CPM: N.A.
Cafe USA	Mall food courts	40 malls* 4 million people/month	$3K/mall/mo. CPM: $20 vs. women 18–49

Source: *Brandweek*, April 29, 1996, p. 25. ©1996 BRANDWEEK Magazine. Used with permission from ASM Communications, Inc.

Northwest Airlines with a 30-second commercial is approximately $82.60. A four-color spread in Forbes and Fortune would cost double that amount.

4. *Segmentation capabilities.* In-flight allows the advertiser to reach specific demographic groups, as well as travelers to a specific destination. For example, Martell cognac targeted only first-class passengers on JAL's New York to Tokyo route.[44]

Disadvantages of in-flight advertising include the following.

1. *Irritation.* Many consumers are not pleased with the idea of ads in general and believe they are already too intrusive. In-flight ads are just one more place, they think, where advertisers are intruding.

2. *Limited availability.* Many airlines limit the amount of time they allow for in-flight commercials. Japan Air Lines, for example, allows a mere 220 seconds per flight.

3. *Lack of attention.* Many passengers may decide to tune out the ads, not purchase the headsets required to get the volume, or simply ignore the commercials.

4. *Wearout.* Given projections for significant increases in the number of in-flight ads being shown, airline passengers may soon be inundated by these commercials.

Miscellaneous Other Media

As noted earlier in this chapter, the variety of advertising support media continues to increase, and discussing or even mentioning all is beyond the scope of this text. However, the following are provided just to demonstrate a few of the many options:

- *Place-based media.* The idea of bringing the advertising medium to the consumers wherever they may be underlies the strategy behind place-based media. TV monitors and magazine racks have appeared in classrooms, doctors' offices, and health clubs, among a variety of other locations. After an initial introduction and failure by Whittle Communications, K-III Communications acquired Channel One. As shown in Figure 13–12, place-based media have become a profitable venture for K-III and an attractive alternative for media buyers.
- *Kiosks.* The growth of interactive kiosks was briefly mentioned in Chapter 10. Advertisers pay rates ranging from $1,000 to $2,500 a month for signage and interactive ads on kiosks that are placed in malls, movie theaters, and other high-traffic areas. Additional charges may accrue for more complex interactive programs. Companies like Ameritech and North Communications have increased their involvement in this medium. Intel has deployed over 1,000 kiosks in computer stores to give consumers immediate access to the Internet.[45]
- *Others.* Just a few other examples of the use of support media: Motorola is advertising on pagers; Muzak, a provider of background music, has teamed with Tyme ATMs to broadcast ads at bank ATM sites; movie companies are advertising on popcorn bags in theaters; and MCI has offered Swedish phone customers free long-distance calling if they agree to listen to a commercial every 10 seconds. There are many such examples.

SUMMARY

This chapter introduced you to the vast number of support media available to marketers. These media, also referred to as nontraditional or alternative media, are just a few of the many ways advertisers attempt to reach their target markets. We have barely scratched the surface here. Support media include out-of-home advertising (outdoor, in-store, and transit), promotional products, product placements in movies and TV, and in-flight advertising, among many others.

Support media offer a variety of advantages. Cost, ability to reach the target market, and flexibility are just a few of those cited in this chapter. In addition, many of the media discussed here have effectively demonstrated the power of their specific medium to get results.

But each of these support media has disadvantages. Perhaps the major weakness with most is the lack of audience measurement and verification. Unlike many of the media discussed earlier in this text, most nontraditional media do not provide audience measurement figures. So the advertiser is forced to make decisions without hard data or based on information provided by the media.

As the number and variety of support media continue to grow, it is likely the major weaknesses will be overcome. When that occurs, these media may no longer be considered nontraditional or alternative.

KEY TERMS

support media, 414
alternative media, 414
nonmeasured media, 414
nontraditional media, 414
out-of-home advertising, 414

showing, 416
aerial advertising, 418
mobile billboards, 418
in-store media, 418
transit advertising, 421

inside cards, 422
outside posters, 423
terminal posters, 423
promotional products marketing, 424

specialty advertising, 425
Yellow Pages, 427
directional medium, 428
product placement, 431
in-flight advertising, 434

DISCUSSION QUESTIONS

1. A prevalent strategy among advertisers is to get themselves into television shows and movies. Discuss the possible advantages and disadvantages that might result from such exposures.

2. The text notes that users of transit advertising must rely on audience information provided by companies selling transit ad space. Discuss some of the problems this might create.

3. The YPPA has recently gone to the diary method for collecting information regarding Yellow Pages usage. Discuss some of the problems that might be associated with this methodology.

4. The Yellow Pages has been proven to be an extremely effective advertising medium for some firms. Explain why the Yellow Pages are so effective. Are there any limitations associated with this medium? If so, what are they?

5. Describe some of the sources available for audience measurement of out-of-home media.

6. Some research companies determine the value of product placements by comparing the time the product is shown to the cost of an ad on the same program. Discuss why this might not be an accurate measure.

7. What are some reasons in-store media may be effective in increasing sales?

8. Discuss advantages and disadvantages associated with advertising in movie theaters and on videotapes. For what types of products and/or services might these media be most effective?

9. What are place-based media? Explain what type of advertisers would most benefit from their use.

10. Discuss some of the reasons why in-flight advertising is becoming a more attractive medium to many advertisers.

CHAPTER 14

Direct Marketing and Marketing on the Internet

Chapter Objectives

- To introduce the area of direct marketing as a communications tool.

- To present the strategies and tactics involved in direct marketing.

- To demonstrate the use of direct-marketing media.

- To illustrate the scope and effectiveness of direct marketing.

- To examine the use of the Internet in the IMC program.

- To examine the effectiveness of the Internet as an IMC tool.

THE INTERNET: MEDIA HOPE OR MEDIA HYPE?

In the 1970s *Forbes* magazine, discussing catalogs, noted, "Mail order is the entrepreneur's paradise—perhaps the last such paradise." In fact, in the 1970s the growth of catalogs as a marketing medium seemed unstoppable. Indeed, fortunes were made and millionaires were born from the success of companies like L. L. Bean, Williams-Sonoma, and Lands' End.

Many feared that catalog shopping would be the death of retail stores as catalog sales increased at a faster rate than retail sales, more women entered the workplace, and consumers overall had less time to shop. Then came the shakeout. Sears dropped its catalog, and only one out of every four new start-ups survived. The growth (and the threat) was over.

The catalog story of the 1990s may very well be the Internet. Proponents of this new medium are singing a familiar tune—referring to the Net as "the most revolutionary tool of our lives" and predicting its absorption of advertising and promotions dollars from traditional media until those media become obsolete.

While online retailing accounted for slightly over $500 million in 1995, predictions range as high as $15 billion in sales by the year 2000. One estimate is that the number of households in North America with online access will grow from 15 million at the end of 1996 to over 38 million by 2000.

The attractiveness of the Internet comes in many forms. First and foremost is the ability to generate an immediate and direct response. The demographics of Internet users are appealing, as is the potential for growth. Businesses have certainly been attracted to the Internet. AT&T, MasterCard, American Airlines, and MCI are just a few of the very recognizable names in the top 10 list of Net advertisers. General

Electric predicted online sales would reach $1 billion in 1996 alone. Advertising on the World Wide Web (the commercial arm of the Net) was expected to reach $300 million by the end of 1996—a triple-digit increase over 1995. For many companies, the Net is seen as a provider of unlimited opportunity.

To many others, the Net is no more than the catalog of the 1990s—that is, more hype than substance. They note that after the initial burst of sales, catalogs (while remaining a solid business) saw sales level off and eventually begin to decline. They see history repeating itself with the Internet, and they have some pretty strong support for their convictions. Skeptics say the expected penetration of personal computers (PCs) into U.S. households is overly optimistic, the Net will never appeal to a mass market, and, like catalogs, shopping from home will never replace the social and recreational aspects of going to stores and/or malls. They also point out that many companies that thought they would be successful on the Net—like the National Association of Realtors and *Web Review* (a highly regarded web magazine)—discontinued their websites, and 29 of the major consumer products marketers polled by *Advertising Age* do not even have plans to participate. Many others have slashed their Internet ad budgets for 1997.

After a quarter of a century, the revolutionary medium of the 1970s has been able to achieve sales of $50 billion—only 2.5 percent of retail sales (excluding automobiles). Will the Internet be the catalog of the 1990s, or will it change the way consumers shop forever?

Sources: Zina Moukheiber, "Plus ça Change . . .," *Forbes*, February 10, 1997, pp. 46–47; Peter McGrath, "The Web: Infotopia or Marketplace?" *Newsweek*, January 27, 1997, pp. 82–83; "Is the Web Ubiquitous Yet?" *Web Marketing Update* 1, no. 1, November 1996, p. 1.

It seems that you can hardly pick up a newspaper, turn on the television, or read a magazine these days without seeing something about the Internet. As the lead-in to this chapter notes, the Internet has the potential to become an extremely powerful communications tool. Consulting companies, agencies specializing in Internet advertising, trade magazines, and books are springing up every day to assist organizations and individuals interested in promoting their products. (Some movie stars have their own websites.)

The uniqueness of this medium makes it both attractive and difficult to characterize. Because the Internet is an interactive medium and allows for a direct response, we could place our discussion of the Net in a variety of places in this text—in one of several media chapters, or as part of the chapter on direct marketing. But because so many Internet marketers, like direct marketers, market directly to the consumer with the goal of obtaining a direct response, we feel the subject matter fits well here. Yet we want you to know that the Net is not just a direct-response medium. As you will see, it is much broader; it provides many opportunities beyond direct response. However, let's reserve that discussion until later in this chapter, after we discuss another rapidly growing area: direct marketing.

DIRECT MARKETING

While most companies continue to rely primarily on the other promotional mix elements to move their products and services through intermediaries, an increasing number are going directly to the consumer. These companies believe that while the traditional promotional mix tools such as advertising, sales promotion, and personal selling are effective in creating brand image, conveying information, and/or creating awareness, going direct with these same tools can generate an immediate behavioral response. Direct marketing is a valuable tool in the integrated communications program, though it seeks somewhat different objectives.

In the first part of this chapter, we discuss direct marketing and its role as a communications tool. Direct marketing is one of the fastest-growing forms of promotion in terms of dollar expenditures, and for many marketers it is rapidly becoming the medium of choice for reaching consumers. Stan Rapp and Thomas Collins, in their book *Maximarketing*, propose that direct marketing be the driving force behind the overall marketing program.[1] They present a nine-step model that includes creating a database, reaching prospects, developing the sale, and developing the relationship. We begin by defining direct marketing and then examine direct-marketing media and their use in the overall communications strategy. The section concludes with a basis for evaluating the direct-marketing program and a discussion of the advantages and disadvantages of this marketing tool.

Defining Direct Marketing

As noted in Chapter 1, **direct marketing** refers to a system of marketing by which organizations communicate directly with target customers to generate a response or transaction. This response may take the form of an inquiry, a purchase, or even a vote. In his *Dictionary of Marketing Terms*, Peter Bennett defines direct marketing as:

> The total of activities by which the seller, in effecting the exchange of goods and services with the buyer, directs efforts to a target audience using one or more media (direct selling, direct mail, telemarketing, direct-action advertising, catalogue selling, cable TV selling, etc.) for the purpose of soliciting a response by phone, mail, or personal visit from a prospect or customer.[2]

First we must distinguish between direct marketing and direct-marketing media. As you can see in Figure 14–1, direct marketing is an aspect of total marketing—that is, it involves marketing research, segmentation, evaluation, and the like, just as our planning model in Chapter 1 did. Direct marketing uses a set of **direct-response media**, including direct mail, telemarketing, interactive TV, print, the Internet, and other media. These media are the tools by which direct marketers implement the communications process.

The purchases of products and services through direct-response advertising currently exceed $360 billion and are projected to reach $600 billion by the year 2000.[3] Firms that use this marketing method range from major retailers such as Montgomery Ward and Victoria's Secret to publishing companies to computer retailers to financial services. Business-to-business and industrial marketers have also significantly increased their direct-marketing efforts.

FIGURE 14–1
Direct marketing flowchart

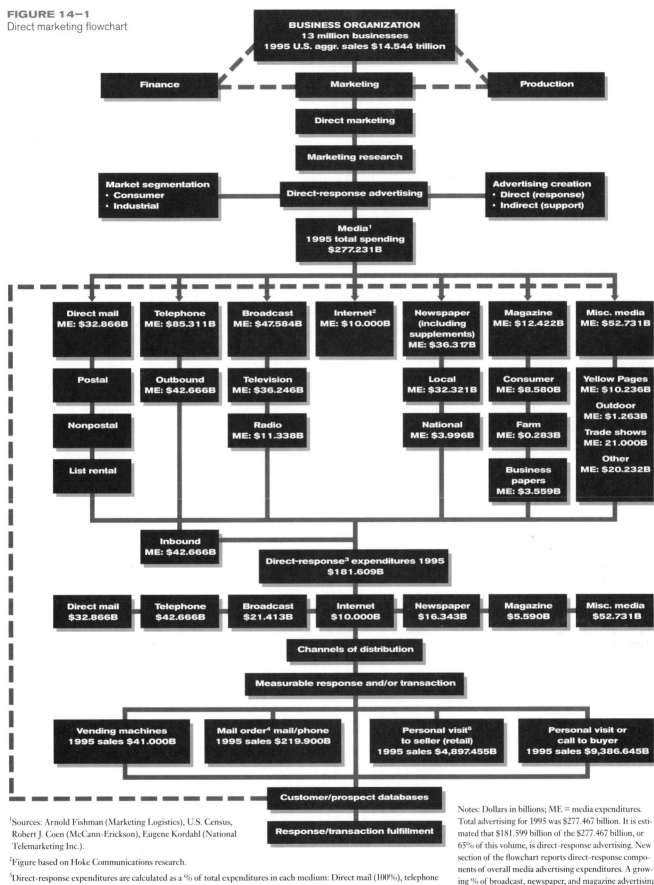

BUSINESS ORGANIZATION
13 million businesses
1995 U.S. aggr. sales $14.544 trillion

Finance — Marketing — Production

Direct marketing

Marketing research

Market segmentation
• Consumer
• Industrial

Direct-response advertising

Advertising creation
• Direct (response)
• Indirect (support)

Media[1]
1995 total spending
$277.231B

| Direct mail ME: $32.866B | Telephone ME: $85.311B | Broadcast ME: $47.584B | Internet[2] ME: $10.000B | Newspaper (including supplements) ME: $36.317B | Magazine ME: $12.422B | Misc. media ME: $52.731B |

Postal / Outbound ME: $42.666B / Television ME: $36.246B / Local ME: $32.321B / Consumer ME: $8.580B / Yellow Pages ME: $10.236B

Nonpostal / Radio ME: $11.338B / National ME: $3.996B / Farm ME: $0.283B / Outdoor ME: $1.263B

List rental / Business papers ME: $3.559B / Trade shows ME: 21.000B

Other ME: $20.232B

Inbound ME: $42.666B

Direct-response[3] expenditures 1995
$181.609B

| Direct mail $32.866B | Telephone $42.666B | Broadcast $21.413B | Internet $10.000B | Newspaper $16.343B | Magazine $5.590B | Misc. media $52.731B |

Channels of distribution

Measurable response and/or transaction

| Vending machines 1995 sales $41.000B | Mail order[4] mail/phone 1995 sales $219.900B | Personal visit[5] to seller (retail) 1995 sales $4,897.455B | Personal visit or call to buyer 1995 sales $9,386.645B |

Customer/prospect databases

Response/transaction fulfillment

[1]Sources: Arnold Fishman (Marketing Logistics), U.S. Census, Robert J. Coen (McCann-Erickson), Eugene Kordahl (National Telemarketing Inc.).

[2]Figure based on Hoke Communications research.

[3]Direct-response expenditures are calculated as a % of total expenditures in each medium: Direct mail (100%), telephone (50%), broadcast (45%), Yellow Pages (100%), newspaper (45%), magazine (45%), misc. (100%), Internet (100%).

[4]Mail-order sales figure excludes roughly $57.540 billion of charitable mail-order contributions, which are not included in the $14.544 trillion of U.S. aggregate sales.

[5]Personal visit to seller (retail) includes $2.349 trillion of consumer product sales at retail plus 90% of consumer services sales; 10% of consumer services sales are conducted by salespeople visiting the buyer.

Notes: Dollars in billions; ME = media expenditures. Total advertising for 1995 was $277.467 billion. It is estimated that $181.599 billion of the $277.467 billion, or 65% of this volume, is direct-response advertising. New section of the flowchart reports direct-response components of overall media advertising expenditures. A growing % of broadcast, newspaper, and magazine advertising dollars can be categorized as direct-response advertising. The % is growing rapidly as marketers learn the efficiency of measuring advertising performance.

Source: Reprinted with permission from Hoke Communications, Inc. Garden City, NY (516) 746-6700.

The Growth of Direct Marketing

Direct marketing has been around since the invention of the printing press in the 15th century. Ben Franklin was a very successful direct marketer in the early 1700s, and Warren Sears and Montgomery Ward (you may have heard of these guys) were using this medium in the 1880s.

The major impetus behind the growth of direct marketing may have been the development and expansion of the U.S. Postal Service, which made catalogs available to both urban and rural dwellers. Catalogs revolutionized America's buying habits; consumers could now shop without ever leaving their homes.

But catalogs alone do not account for the rapid growth of direct marketing. A number of factors in American society have led to the increased attractiveness of this medium for both buyer and seller.

- *Consumer credit cards.* There are now over 1 billion credit cards—bank, oil company, retail, and so on—in circulation in the United States. This makes it feasible for consumers to purchase both low- and high-ticket items through direct-response channels and assures sellers that they will be paid. It is projected that over $882 billion yearly will be charged on credit cards by the year 2000.[4] Of course, not all of this will be through direct marketing, but a high percentage of direct purchases do use this method of payment, and companies such as American Express, Diners Club, MasterCard, and Visa are among the heaviest direct advertisers.

- *Direct-marketing syndicates.* Companies specializing in list development, statement inserts, catalogs, and sweepstakes have opened many new opportunities to marketers. The number of these companies continues to expand, creating even more new users.

- *The changing structure of American society and the market.* One of the major factors contributing to the success of direct marketing is that so many Americans are now "money-rich and time-poor."[5] The rapid increase in dual-income families (in 1996 an estimated 62 percent of women were in the work force) has meant more income.[6] At the same time, the increased popularity of physical fitness, do-it-yourself crafts and repairs, and home entertainment have reduced the time available for shopping and have increased the attractiveness of direct purchases.

- *Technological advances.* The rapid technological advancement of the electronic media (discussed later in this chapter) and of computers has made it easier for consumers to shop and for marketers to be successful in reaching the desired target markets. Well over 110 million television homes receive home shopping programs, and home channel purchases total more than $2.55 billion.[7]

- *Miscellaneous factors.* A number of other factors have contributed to the increased effectiveness of direct marketing, including changing values, more sophisticated marketing techniques, and the industry's improved image. These factors will also assure the success of direct marketing in the future. The variety of companies employing direct marketing (see Figure 14–2) demonstrates its potential.

While some organizations rely on direct marketing solely to generate consumer response, in many others direct marketing is an integral part of the IMC program. They use direct marketing to achieve other than sales goals and integrate it with other program elements. We first examine the role of direct marketing in the IMC program and then consider its more *traditional* role.

The Role of Direct Marketing in the IMC Program

Long the stepchild of the promotional mix, direct marketing is now becoming an important component in the integrated marketing programs of many organizations. In fact, direct marketing activities support and are supported by other elements of the promotional mix.

COMBINING DIRECT MARKETING WITH ADVERTISING

Obviously, direct marketing is in itself a form of advertising. Whether through mail, print, or TV, the direct-response offer is an ad. It usually contains an 800 or 900 number or a form that requests mailing information. Sometimes the ad supports the direct selling effort. For example, Victoria's Secret runs image ads to support its store and catalog sales. Both Marl-

FIGURE 14–2
Top 10 direct-marketing industries
($ millions)

Industry	1997 ($)*	Compound Annual Growth	
		1991–1996	1996–2001
1. Nonstore retailers	$72.016	6.7%	6.7%
2. Nonprofit organizations	68.697	7.3	6.0
3. Auto dealers/service stations	67.054	7.1	6.1
4. Food stores	34.530	2.3	3.0
5. Food/kindred products	34.091	4.1	5.6
6. Insurance carriers/agents	33.464	8.2	12.8
7. Real estate	30.702	6.5	7.1
8. Health services	31.705	11.7	16.0
9. Specialty retailers	27.147	5.3	4.0
10. Personal/repair services	19.963	5.7	7.5

*These numbers have not been inflation adjusted; they represent current (nominal) dollars.

Note: Nonstore retailers, including catalog and mail-order houses and TV shopping channels, ranked highest in direct-marketing sales volume. Significant growth rates are shown in health services and insurance direct-marketing sales.

Source: DMA Report—*Economic Impact: U.S. Direct Marketing Today*, 1996. From the Direct Marketing Association *1997 Statistical Fact Book*, p. 339.

boro and Benson & Hedges advertise their cigarettes, achieving a carryover effect of their image to their direct-response merchandise catalogs. Direct-response ads or infomercials are also referred to in retail outlet displays.

COMBINING DIRECT MARKETING WITH PUBLIC RELATIONS

As you will see later in this text, public relations activities often employ direct-response techniques. Private companies may use telemarketing activities to solicit funds for charities or cosponsor charities that use these and other direct response techniques to solicit funds. Likewise, corporations and/or organizations engaging in public relations activities may include 800 or website numbers in their ads or promotional materials.

COMBINING DIRECT MARKETING WITH PERSONAL SELLING

Telemarketing and direct selling are two methods of personal selling (others will be discussed in Chapter 17). Nonprofit organizations like charities often use telemarketing to solicit funds. As you will see in Chapter 17, for-profit companies are also using telemarketing with much greater frequency to screen and qualify prospects (which reduces selling costs) and to generate leads. Direct-mail pieces are often used to invite prospective customers to visit auto showrooms to test-drive new cars; the salesperson then assumes responsibility for the selling effort.

COMBINING DIRECT MARKETING WITH SALES PROMOTIONS

How many times have you received a direct-mail piece notifying you of a sales promotion or event or inviting you to participate in a contest or sweepstakes? Ski shops regularly mail announcements of special end-of-season sales. Airlines send out mailers announcing promotional airfares. Nordstom and other retail outlets call their existing customers to notify them of special sales promotions. Each of these is an example of a company using direct-marketing tools to inform customers of sales promotions. In turn, the sales promotion event may support the direct-marketing effort. Databases are often built from the names and addresses acquired from a promotion, and direct mail and/or telemarketing calls follow. Carol Wright, one of the nation's leading direct mailers of coupons, participated with ABC's Daytime Emmy Awards Show in all major markets to mail coupons to 30 million households promoting the awards show and major programs. The joint venture promoted Carol Wright as well

as local radio station affiliates, while offering consumers a chance to win valuable prizes including a trip to the awards ceremony. (See Exhibit 14–1).[8]

To successfully implement direct-marketing programs, companies must make a number of decisions. As in other marketing programs, they must determine (1) what the program's objectives will be; (2) which markets to target (through the use of a list or marketing database); (3) what direct-marketing strategies will be employed; and (4) how to evaluate the effectiveness of the program.

Direct-Marketing Objectives

The direct marketer seeks a direct response. The objectives of the program are normally behaviors—for example, test drives, votes, contributions, and/or sales. A typical objective is defined through a set response, perhaps a 2 to 3 percent response rate.

Not all direct marketing seeks a behavioral response, however. Many organizations use direct marketing to build an image, maintain customer satisfaction, and inform and/or educate customers in an attempt to lead to future actions (Exhibit 14–2).

Developing a Database

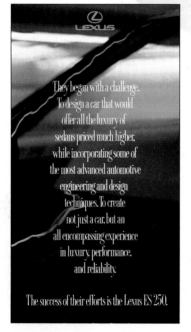

As we have discussed throughout this text, market segmentation and targeting are critical components of any promotional program. Direct-marketing programs employ these principles even more than others, since the success of a direct-marketing program is in large part tied to the ability to do *one-to-one marketing*. To segment and target their markets, direct marketers use a **database**, a listing of customers and/or potential customers. This database is a tool for **database marketing** —the use of specific information about individual customers and/or prospects to implement more effective and efficient marketing communications.[9]

Figure 14–3 demonstrates how database marketing works. As you can see, the database marketing effort must be an integral part of the overall IMC program. At the very least, this list contains names, addresses, and Zip codes; more sophisticated databases include information on demographics and psychographics, purchase transactions and payments, personal facts, neighborhood data, and even credit histories. This database serves as the foundation from which the direct-marketing programs evolve. Databases are used to perform the following functions.[10]

- *Improving the selection of market segments.* Some consumers are more likely to be potential purchasers, users, voters, and so on than others. By analyzing the characteristics of the database, a marketer can target a greater potential audience. For example, catalog companies have become very specialized. Companies such as Lands' End, Lilly's Kids, and Johnson & Murphy have culled their lists and become much more efficient, targeting only those who are most likely to purchase their products.
- *Stimulate repeat purchases.* Once a purchase has been made, the customer's name and other information are entered into the database. These people are proven direct-marketing users who offer high potential for repurchase. Magazines, for example, routinely send out renewal letters and/or call subscribers before the expiration date. Blockbuster Entertainment helps its video-rental customers select movies and locate additional

FIGURE 14–3
How database marketing works

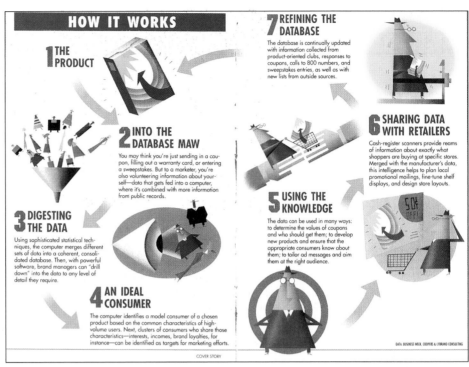

Source: Reprinted from the September 15, 1993 issue of *Business Week* by special permission, copyright ©1993 by McGraw-Hill, Inc.

Blockbuster locations. Companies from window cleaners to carpet cleaners to car dealers build a base of customers and contact them when they are "due" to repurchase.

- *Cross-sell.* Customers who demonstrate a specific interest also constitute strong potential for other products of the same nature. For example, the National Geographic Society has successfully sold globes, maps, videos, travel magazines, and an assortment of other products to subscribers who obviously have an interest in geography and/or travel. Likewise, Victoria's Secret has expanded its clothing lines primarily through sales to existing customers, and Kraft–GF has successfully cross-sold products in its varied food line.

Numerous other companies have established comprehensive databases on existing and potential customers both in the United States and internationally. Database marketing has become so ubiquitous that many people are concerned about invasion of privacy. Direct marketers are concerned as well. The Direct Marketing Association (DMA), the trade association for direct marketers, has asked its members to adhere to ethical rules of conduct in their marketing efforts. It points out that if the industry does not police itself, the government will.

SOURCES OF DATABASE INFORMATION

There are many sources of information for direct-marketing databases.

- *The U.S. Census Bureau.* Census data provide information on almost every household in the United States. Data include household size, demographics, income, and other information.
- *The U.S. Postal Service.* Postal Zip codes and the extended four-digit code provide information on both household and business locations.
- *List services.* Many providers of lists are available (one is shown in Exhibit 14–3). The accuracy and timeliness of the lists vary.
- *Standard Rate and Data Service.* SRDS provides information regarding both consumer and business lists. Published in two volumes, *Direct Mail List Rates and Data* contains over 50,000 list selections in hundreds of classifications.

EXHIBIT 14–3   An example of the variety of mail response lists available

Quantity		Price		Quantity		Price
Automotive				**Contributors**		
15,000,000	American Car Buyers/ Foreign/ or USA Models	Inquire		435,000	American Museum of Natural History	$75/M
208,000	AutoWeek Subscribers	$60/M		400,000	Animal Welfare Donors	$65/M
146,000	Babcox Business Leaders	$65/M		437,000	Greenpeace	$65/M
160,000	Beverly Hills Motoring Accessories Buyers	$95/M		4,000,000	Health	$65/M
165,000	4 Wheel & Off Road Subs	$60/M		1,313,000	Humanitarian	$65/M
48,000	Hearst Motor Bookbuyers	$50/M		226,000	National Foundation Cancer Research	$60/M
49,500	Hot Rod Magazine	$60/M		148,000	National Glaucoma Research	$75/M
328,000	Classic Motor Books	$55/M				
218,000	Auto/Truck Do-It-Yourselfers	$60/M		1,497,000	Political	$65/M
74,000	Cars & Parts Magazine	$70/M		248,000	Political/Conservative	$65/M
Beauty/Health/Diet				162,000	Political/Liberal	$65/M
800,000	American Health Magazine	$65/M		4,000,000	Religious	$65/M
1,000,000	Bio-Energetics Research Buyers	$70/M		586,000	Hands Across America Donors	$55/M
339,000	Comfortably Yours	$85/M		**Computers/Data Processing**		
1,700,000	Cosmetique Beauty Buyers	$55/M		2,800,000	Personal Computer Owners/Type of Brand	Inquire
32,000	Cardiac Alert Subs	$85/M		700,000	Business Computer Owners/Type of Brand	Inquire
33,000	Executive Fitness Letter	$75/M		260,000	Professionals Using Computers	Inquire
912,000	Health Magazine	$60/M		665,000	Brandon Computer Professionals	$75/M
480,000	Health Conscious Americans	$50/M		255,000	Byte Magazine	$100/M
224,000	Tufts University Newsletter	$65/M		113,000	Computerworld Magazine	$125/M
550,000	University of California–Berkeley Wellness Letter	$70/M		70,000	Computer Systems News	$87/M
				137,580	Computel Magazine	$80/M
135,000	Vegetarian Times	$65/M		160,000	Datamation	$80/M
200,000	Weider Health and Fitness	$65/M		400,000	Family and Home Office Computing	$80/M
2,400,000	Prevention Magazine	$60/M		135,000	MIS Week	$110/M
821,000	Weight Watchers Magazine	$65/M		453,000	PC Magazine	$100/M
Bookbuyers				**Consumer Magazines**		
2,200,000	Better Homes & Gardens	$60/M		250,000	Americana Magazine	$65/M
642,000	Barnes & Noble	$70/M		93,000	Art & Antiques Magazine	$80/M
840,000	Boardroom Bookbuyers	$85/M		380,000	Atlantic Monthly	$80/M
330,000	Warren, Gorham & Lamont	$90/M		148,000	American History Illustrated	$70/M
	Bantam Bookbuyers	Inquire		73,000	Birdwatchers Digest	$60/M
	Book of the Month Club	Inquire		110,000	Collectors Mart	$60/M
	CMG (College Bookbuyers)	Inquire		1,160,000	Contest Newsletter	$70/M
	Doubleday Bookbuyers	Inquire		1,100,000	Davis Publications	$55/M
	Literary Guild	Inquire		295,000	Early American Life	$70/M
	MacMillan Bookbuyers	Inquire		110,000	Fate Magazine	$65/M
	Prentice Hall, Inc.	Inquire		919,000	Insight Magazine	$55/M
	Time-Life—INQUIRE BY SUBJECT	Inquire		1,000,000	Life Magazine	$70/M
				112,000	New Age Journal	$75/M
				346,000	National Audubon Society	$70/M
				2,700,000	Newsweek	$60/M

Many types of **privately owned** specialty lists of people are available, such as:

- **MAIL-ORDER BUYERS** of various direct mail, TV or magazine products
- **SUBSCRIBERS** to magazines, newsletters
- **CONTRIBUTORS** to fund-raising campaigns
- **CREDIT CARD HOLDERS**, charge customers

These lists can be related to your specific product or purpose. If your offer is not in competitive conflict with such lists, the owner will authorize the use of his names for your mailing. **A SAMPLE MAILING PIECE MUST BE SUBMITTED WITH YOUR ORDER FOR APPROVAL.** These **RESPONSE LISTS** are an additional tool to target specific segments of your direct-mail market.

PRICES, QUANTITIES, AND MINI-MUMS (usually 5,000—Inquire) for such lists are completely at the discretion of the list owner, and are subject to change. *Please inquire for details and current prices before placing your order.* Orders for RESPONSE LISTS are not commissionable and cannot be charged on credit cards.

These two pages are a representative group of such private response lists. Many, many more are available.

• *Simmons Market Research Bureau.* SMRB conducts an annual study of customers who buy at home via mail or telephone (see Figure 14–4). It compiles information on total orders placed, types of products purchased, demographics, and purchase satisfaction, among others.

• *Direct Marketing Association.* The direct marketers' trade organization promotes direct marketing and provides statistical information on direct-marketing use. The DMA's *Fact Book of Direct Marketing* contains information regarding use, attitudes toward direct marketing, rules and regulations, and so forth.

Consumer-goods manufacturers, banks, credit bureaus, retailers, charitable organizations, and other business operations also sell lists and other selected information. Companies can build their own databases through completed warranty cards, surveys, and so on.

Direct-Marketing Strategies and Media

As with all other communications programs discussed in this text, marketers must decide the message to be conveyed, the size of the budget, and so on. Perhaps the major difference between direct-marketing programs and other promotional mix programs regards the use of media.

As shown in Figure 14–1, direct marketing employs a number of media, including direct mail, telemarketing, direct-response broadcasting, and print. Each medium is used to perform specific functions, although they generally follow a one- or two-step approach.

In the **one-step approach**, the medium is used directly to obtain an order. You've probably seen TV commercials for products like wrench sets, workout equipment, or magazine subscriptions in which the viewer is urged to phone a toll-free number to place an order immediately. Usually these ads accept credit cards or cash on delivery and give an address. Their goal is to generate an immediate sale when the ad is shown.

The **two-step approach** may involve the use of more than one medium. The first effort is designed to screen, or qualify, potential buyers. The second effort generates the response. For example, many companies use telemarketing to screen on the basis of interest, then follow up to interested parties with more information designed to achieve an order or use personal selling to close the sale.

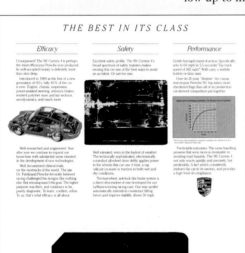

DIRECT MAIL

Direct mail is often called junk mail—the unsolicited mail you receive. More advertising dollars continue to be spent in direct mail than in almost any other advertising medium—an estimated $32.9 billion in 1996.[11] Mail-order sales exceeded $382.9 billion in 1996 ($239.8 in the consumer market).[12] Direct mail is not restricted to small companies seeking our business. Respected large companies such as General Electric, American Express, and Citicorp have increased their expenditures in this area, as have many others. Sales through direct mail in the business-to-business market are expected to reach over $208 billion by the year 2000.[13]

Many advertisers shied away from direct mail in the past, fearful of the image it might create or harboring the belief that direct mail was useful only for low-cost products. But this is no longer the case. For example, Porsche Cars North America, Inc., uses direct mail to target high-income, upscale consumers who are most likely to purchase its expensive sports cars. Porsche developed a direct-mail piece that was sent to a precisely defined target market: physicians in specialties with the highest income levels. This list was screened to match the demographics of Porsche buyers and narrowed further to specific geographic areas. The direct-mail piece was an x-ray of a Porsche 911 Carrera 4 written in the language of the medical audience. This creative campaign generated one of the highest response rates of any mailing Porsche has done in recent years.[14]

Keys to the success of direct mail are the **mailing list**, which constitutes the database from which names are generated, and the ability to segment mar-

FIGURE 14–4
SMRB provides information on consumers who ordered merchandise by mail or phone

	Total US 000	Ordered by Mail or Phone			
		A 000	B % Down	C Across %	D Indx
Total adults	185,822	97,715	100.0	52.6	100
Males	88,956	42,488	43.5	47.8	91
Females	96,866	55,227	56.5	57.0	108
Principal shoppers	112,018	60,697	62.1	54.2	103
18–24	23,965	9,846	10.1	41.1	78
25–34	42,832	22,434	23.0	52.4	100
35–44	39,908	23,902	24.5	59.9	114
45–54	27,327	16,047	16.4	58.7	112
55–64	21,238	10,939	11.2	51.5	98
65 or older	30,552	14,547	14.9	47.6	91
18–34	66,798	32,280	33.0	48.3	92
18–49	121,918	65,339	66.9	53.6	102
25–54	110,067	62,383	63.8	56.7	108
35–49	55,120	33,059	33.8	60.0	114
50 or older	63,905	32,376	33.1	50.7	96
Graduated college	36,463	23,374	23.9	64.1	122
Attended college	44,294	24,904	25.5	56.2	107
Graduated high school	66,741	34,408	35.2	51.6	98
Did not graduate high school	38,324	15,028	15.4	39.2	75
Employed males	65,500	32,228	33.0	49.2	94
Employed females	55,910	34,804	35.6	62.3	118
Employed full-time	110,363	60,402	61.8	54.7	104
Employed part-time	11,047	6,630	6.8	60.0	114
Not employed	64,412	30,682	31.4	47.6	91
Professional/manager	31,718	19,851	20.3	62.6	119
Technical/clerical/sales	37,895	22,703	23.2	59.9	114
Precision/craft	13,954	6,930	7.1	49.7	94
Other employed	37,843	17,548	18.0	46.4	88
Single	41,284	17,744	18.2	43.0	82
Married	109,023	62,594	64.1	57.4	109
Divorced/separated/widowed	35,515	17,376	17.8	48.9	93
Parents	62,342	35,701	36.5	57.3	109
White	158,841	87,327	89.4	55.0	105
Black	21,122	7,896	8.1	37.4	71
Other	5,859	2,492	2.6	42.5	81
Household income					
$75,000 or more	24,165	14,731	15.1	61.0	116
$60,000 or more	40,979	24,220	24.8	59.1	112
$50,000 or more	57,996	34,185	35.0	58.9	112
$40,000 or more	80,078	47,018	48.1	58.7	112
$30,000 or more	106,838	62,069	63.5	58.1	110
$30,000–$39,000	26,759	15,051	15.4	56.2	107
$20,000–$29,000	30,669	15,147	15.5	49.4	94
$10,000–$19,999	29,083	13,069	13.4	44.9	85
Under $10,000	19,232	7,430	7.6	38.6	73

kets. Lists have become more current and more selective, eliminating waste coverage. Segmentation on the basis of geography (usually through Zip codes), demographics, and lifestyles has led to increased effectiveness. The most commonly used lists are of individuals who have already purchased direct-mail products.

The importance of the list has led to a business of its own. In 1996 there were over 38 billion names on lists, and many companies have found it profitable to sell the names of purchasers of their products and/or services to list firms. Companies like A. B. Zeller and Metromail provide such lists on a national level, and in most metropolitan areas there are firms providing the same service locally. In 1996, the list business accounted for approximately $46 billion in sales of names.[15]

CATALOGS

Major participants in the direct-marketing business include catalog companies. The number of catalogs mailed and the number of catalog shoppers have increased significantly since 1984, with sales growing by an average of 5.5 percent each year between 1990 and 1995. Catalog sales are projected to reach $51.9 billion by the year 2000.[16]

Many companies use catalogs in conjunction with their more traditional sales and promotional strategies. For example, companies like Pottery Barn, Nordstrom, and JCPenney sell directly through catalogs but also use them to inform consumers of product offerings available in the stores. Some companies (for example, L.L. Bean) rely solely on catalog sales. Others that started out exclusively as catalog companies have branched into retail outlets, among them The Sharper Image, Lands' End, and Banana Republic. As you can see by the following examples, the products being offered through this medium have reached new heights as well.

- Victoria's Secret featured a $1 million Miracle Bra in its 1996 Christmas catalog. Modeled by supermodel Claudia Schiffer, the bra contained over 100 carats of real diamonds as well as hundreds of semiprecious stones.
- Saks' Holding Co., a division of Saks Fifth Avenue, offered a pair of Mercedes–Benz convertibles in a catalog, with bidding to start at $50,000.
- Hammacher Schlemmer featured a $43,000 taxicab and a $34,000 train set in its Christmas catalog.
- The Sharper Image offered a $375,000 silver saddle in its catalog (though it didn't sell any).[17]

In addition to the traditional hard copies, catalogs are now available through online services such as Prodigy, Genie, and CompuServe. The Merchant Co. offers an interactive CD-ROM catalog service with as many as 25 different mail-order catalogs on one disk. Spiegel, Lands' End, Brooks Brothers, and Books on Tape (among others) are all available through this medium.

BROADCAST MEDIA

The success of direct marketing in the broadcast industry has been truly remarkable; over 77 percent of the U.S. population report that they have viewed a direct-response appeal on TV.[18] Direct-response TV is estimated to have generated more than $3 billion in sales in 1995—an increase of almost 50 percent over 1993. However, failure by interactive TV, less triers, and alternative technologies such as the Internet have led to forecasts of slower growth in the next few years.[19]

Two broadcast media are available to direct marketers: television and radio. While radio was used quite extensively in the 1950s, its use and effectiveness have dwindled substantially in recent years. Thus, the majority of direct-marketing broadcast advertising now occurs on TV, which receives the bulk of our attention here.

Direct marketing in the broadcast industry involves both direct-response advertising and support advertising. In **direct-response advertising**, the product or service is offered and a sales response is solicited, through either the one- or two-step approach previously discussed. Examples include ads for Soloflex, Nordic Track, CDs and tapes, and tips on football or basketball betting. Toll-free phone numbers are included so the receiver can immediately call to order. **Support advertising** is designed to do exactly that—support

EXHIBIT 14—4 Dirt Devil uses infomercials to sell their products

other forms of advertising. Ads for Publishers Clearing House or *Reader's Digest* or other companies telling you to look in your mailbox for a sweepstakes entry are examples of support advertising.

Direct-response TV encompasses a number of media, including direct-response TV spots like those just mentioned, infomercials, and home shopping shows (teleshopping). And as noted in Chapter 10, Internet -TV has recently been introduced.

INFOMERCIALS

The lower cost of commercials on cable and satellite channels has led advertisers to a new form of advertising. An **infomercial** is a long commercial that ranges from 3 to 60 minutes. (Most are 30 minutes long, though the five-minute format is gaining in popularity.) Many infomercials are produced by the advertisers and are designed to be viewed as regular TV shows. Consumers dial a toll-free 800 or 900 number to place an order. Programs such as "Liquid Luster," "Amazing Discoveries," and "Stainerator" (the so-called miracle products shows) were the most common form of infomercial in the 1980s. While this form of show is still popular, the infomercial industry is welcoming many big, mainstream marketers (Exhibit 14–4). Apple Computer, Microsoft, Sony, Volvo, and Philips Electronics are just some of the many others now employing this method of communication (Exhibit 14–5).

As to their effectiveness, studies indicate that infomercials get watched and sell products. Figure 14–5 shows the results of a study by Naveen Donthu and David Gilliland profiling infomercial viewers and buyers. It demonstrates that this advertising medium is indeed effective with a broad demographic base, not significantly different from the in-

EXHIBIT 14—5
Volvo uses an infomercial to attract buyers

FIGURE 14–5

Here's who's watching (and buying from) infomercials

Hypothesis Number: Construct	Infomercial Shopper (n = 84)	Infomercial Nonshopper (n = 284)	Difference Significant at the 0.05 Level?
H1: Age[a]	2.6	2.8	N
H1: Education[b]	2.4	2.2	N
H1: Income[c]	2.8	2.7	N
H1: Gender[d]	1.4	1.5	N
H2: Importance of convenience	4.2	2.8	Y[e]
H3: Brand consciousness	3.5	3.0	Y[e]
H4: Price consciousness	4.1	3.6	Y
H5: Variety-seeking propensity	3.9	3.0	Y
H6: Impulsiveness	3.2	2.6	Y
H7: Innovativeness	3.8	3.0	Y
H8: Number of hours per week spent watching television	20	14	Y
H9: Risk aversion	2.1	3.5	Y
H10: Attitude toward shopping	1.8	3.1	Y
H11: Attitude toward direct marketing	3.1	2.1	Y
H12: Attitude toward advertising	3.5	2.9	Y

[a]Age: 1 = <20; 2 = 20–35; 3 = 36–50; 4 = 51–65; 5 = >65.
[b]Education: 1 = Some school; 2 = High school diploma; 3 = Some college; 4 = College degree; 5 = Postgraduate degree
[c]Income: 1 = <$15K; 2 = $15–30K; 3 = $31–45K; 4 = $46–60K; 5 = >$60K.
[d]Gender: 1 = female; 2 = male.
[e]Significant in opposite direction as hypothesized.
Source: *Journal of Advertising Research*, 1996, p. 75.

fomercial nonshopper in age, education, income, or gender. There are also a number of differences between infomercial shoppers and nonshoppers, as this figure shows. Infomercial sales in 1996 exceeded $1 billion, with an estimated $500 million spent in media billings.[20] Retail stores are benefiting from infomercials as well, as brand awareness leads to increased in-store purchases.[21]

However, some people are not sold on the idea of ads disguised as programs. For example, infomercials disguised as "ultrahip" TV shows have been targeted at teenagers, raising fears that kids under the age of 13 will be susceptible to their lure. Consumer complaints are on the rise, and the FTC has already levied fines for deceptive endorsements against infomercial sponsors. Four consumer groups (the Consumer Federation of America, Center for the Study of Commercialism, Center for Media Education, and Telecommunications Research and Action Center) have asked the FCC to require all infomercials to display a symbol that indicates a "paid ad" or "sponsored by" so viewers won't confuse them with regular programming.

TELESHOPPING

The development of toll-free telephone numbers, combined with the widespread use of credit cards, has led to a dramatic increase in the number of people who shop via their TV sets. Jewelry, kitchenware, fitness products, insurance, and a variety of items are now promoted (and sold) this way. The three major shopping channels in the United States (QVC, the Home Shopping Network (HSN), and ValueVision), account for over $3.4 billion worth of sales, though there are indications that this medium may have reached maturity.[22] Sales at HSN are declining, while the sales of the others are increasing less than forecasted. In a national research study, 55 percent of Americans stated that they had never purchased through TV shopping and do not intend to start. Another 65 percent said that they are buying less. A number of reasons for the maturing of this market have been offered; many believe that the primary cause is a shift of existing customers to the World Wide Web and limited success in attracting new audiences.[23] To address this latter problem, QVC is pursuing international markets (including the United Kingdom, Canada, Germany, and Japan), pursuing partnerships (United signed on as official airline of the "Quest for America's Best" program) and sponsorships (of, for example, Geoff Bodine on the Nascar circuit).

PRINT MEDIA

Magazines and newspapers are difficult media to use for direct marketing. Because these ads have to compete with the clutter of other ads and because the space is relatively expensive, response rates and profits may be lower than in other media. This does not mean these media are not used (as evidenced by the fact that expenditures total over $41 billion).[24] Exhibit 14–6 shows a direct ad that appeared in *Time* magazine. You can find many more in specific interest areas like financial newspapers or sports, sex, or hobby magazines.

TELEMARKETING

If you have a telephone, you probably do not have to be told about the rapid increase in the use of **telemarketing**, or sales by telephone. Both profit and charitable organizations have employed this medium effectively in both one- and two-step approaches. Over 118 million Americans receive nearly 3 billion telemarketing phone calls each year; approximately 6 percent of these result in a completed transaction.[25] While 6 percent may seem low, the fact is that telemarketing is a very big industry and still growing. Consider these facts:

- Over a million people are now employed in the telemarketing industry.[26]
- Sales now exceed $600 billion.[27]
- Marketers spend an estimated $55 billion a year on outbound telemarketing calls.[28]

Business-to-business marketers like Adobe Systems, Kaiser Permanente, and Hewlett-Packard are just a few of the many companies that use this direct-marketing medium effectively.

As telemarketing continues to expand in scope, a new dimension referred to as **audiotex** or **telemedia** has evolved. Tom Eisenhart defines telemedia as the "use of telephone and voice information services (900, 800, and 976 numbers) to market, advertise, promote, entertain, and inform."[29] Many telemedia programs are interactive. While many people still think of 900 and 976 numbers as rip-offs or "sex, lies, and phone lines," over 7,000 programs are carried on 900 numbers alone, including Tele-Lawyer, a legal information services organization; Bally's Health & Tennis Corp., the nation's largest health-club chain; and NutraSweet. Figure 14–6 shows more specifically how 800/900 numbers are used as marketing tools.[30]

Problems associated with telemarketing include its potential for fraud and deception and its potential for annoyance. (Doesn't it seem as if every time you sit down to dinner you re-

EXHIBIT 14—6
A direct-response print ad

These Aren't Just Mountain Bikes.
They're A $38.99 Bonus.

The GM Gold Card. Don't Spend More, Spend Smarter.
To apply, call **1-800-846-2273.**

Sheila Silver Library
Self Issue
Leeds Beckett University

Customer name: Shah, Syed Zeeshan (Mr)

Customer ID: 0771433939

Title: Advertising and promotion : an integrated marketing communications perspective
ID: 1702726563
Due: 18/5/2015,23:59

Total items: 1
Total fines: £1.20
03/05/2015 19:43
Checked out: 3
Overdue: 0
Hold requests: 1
Ready for pickup: 1

Need help? Why not Chat with Us 24/7?
See the Need Help? page on the library
website: library.leedsbeckett.ac.uk

FIGURE 14—6   800 and 900 numbers are used as marketing tools (percent of respondents)

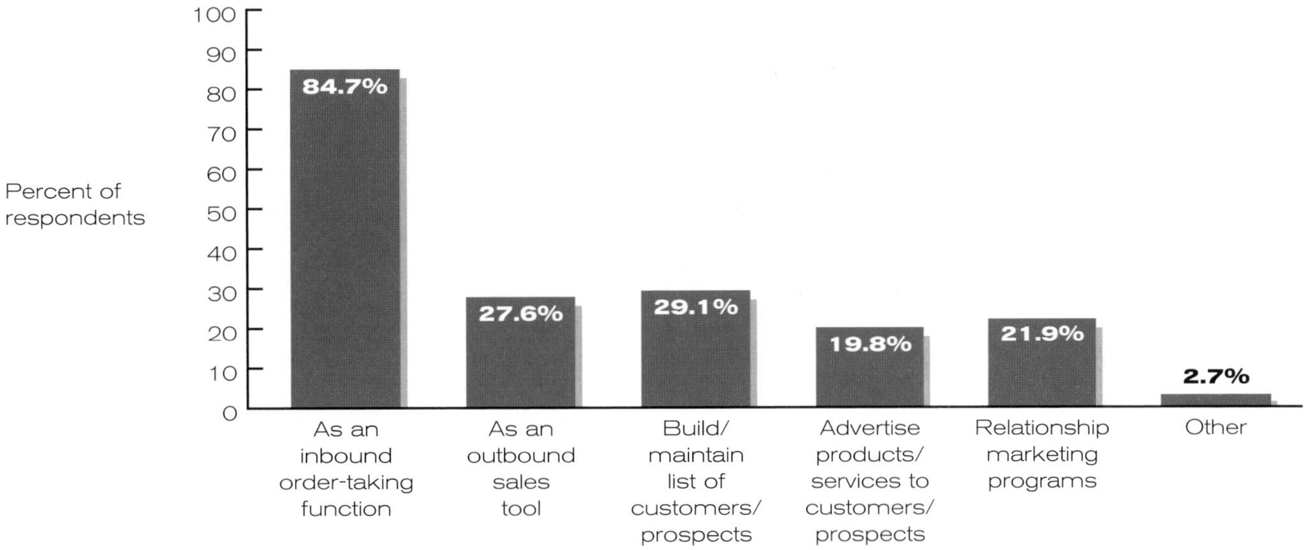

Note: *Direct* forecast survey was conducted by Jacobson Consulting Applications. The firm mailed a four-page questionnaire to direct-marketing executives, on an nth name basis from *Direct*'s circulation list. There were 565 responses.

Source: Direct Marketing Association *1996 Statistical Fact Book*, p. 146.

ceive a phone call from someone trying to sell you something or asking for a donation?) Ethical Perspective 14–1 discusses this problem in more detail.

Those in the telemarketing and telemedia industry have responded to public criticisms. Dial-a-Porn and its ilk hold a diminishing share of 800, 900, and 976 offerings. As more and more large companies use telemedia, its tarnished image will likely brighten up.

ELECTRONIC TELESHOPPING

Unlike infomercials and home shopping channels, which rely on broadcast or cable TV, **electronic teleshopping** is an online shopping and information retrieval service accessed through personal computers.

Home shoppers need only a minimal knowledge of computers to select the information they want as if using a book index. They can buy products, buy services such as airline tickets, play games, get stock market reports, view the latest headlines, pay bills, and access the Internet. Advertisers may provide their messages in the form of logos or names or in longer segments, depending on how much they want to pay and the message they wish to convey.

The country's leading information retrieval services companies—CompuServe, America Online, Microsoft Network, and Prodigy—have increased their information offerings in recent years, making this medium more attractive to marketers (Exhibit 14–7). As of 1996, these four services had over 15 million subscribers and featured such advertisers as Sharp Electronics, KLM Royal Dutch Airlines, Oldsmobile, Hallmark, and Panasonic.[31] Besides access to the Internet, these online providers offer another way to access direct-marketing companies. For example, AOL claims that on the day before Mother's Day 1996, the website 1-800-Flowers transacted 500 sales. The same company made 30,000 sales in AOL's *Marketplace* during the same time period.[32] So as you can see, online services offer more than just Internet access.

DIRECT SELLING

An additional element of the direct-marketing program is **direct selling**, the direct, personal presentation, demonstration, and sales of products and services to consumers in their homes. Avon, Amway, Mary Kay Cosmetics, and Tupperware are some of the best-known direct-selling companies in the United States (Exhibit 14–8). Close to 5 million people engage in direct selling throughout the world; 98 percent of them are independent contractors (not employees of the firm they represent). These 5 million generate approximately $12 billion in sales.[33]

Ethical Perspective 14–1
The Big Business
of Telemarketing Fraud

The potential for fraud exists in any business transaction. From the used-car salesman selling an automobile with defects to large-scale consumer deception through advertising, fraudulent communications are a big business. Unfortunately for the direct-marketing industry, one of the more common arenas for such acts is telemarketing. It has been estimated that telemarketing fraud reaps $40 billion a year in the United States alone, and the practice is catching on overseas as well. Because elderly people make up a disproportionate number of victims and this age group is growing in size, forecasts indicate an even larger market in the future.

According to Steven Michaels (pseudonym for a defrauder turned law enforcement cooperator) everyone is a potential victim. Michaels claims to have bilked millions of dollars out of unsuspecting buyers, including doctors, lawyers, state legislators, and even governors, over a 20-year period. He says the common traits that lead to a successful "hit" include gullibility, greed, and a willingness to be controlled. He notes that people's reluctance to be rude plays right into the seller's hands. Michaels says he has a tape of one of his phone solicitations in which the receiving party threatened to hang up 27 times—but never did—and he made the sale.

Citizen groups and government agencies are now starting to fight back against telemarketing fraud. The American Association of Retired People (AARP), the National Consumers League, postal inspectors, attorneys general, and sheriffs have banded together to find ways to curtail fraudulent activities. The groups obtain hit lists and preempt the telemarketers with warning calls advising potential victims of the scams. The National Consumers League has set up a fraud-reporting hot line (The National Fraud Information Center) and the FTC has passed new regulations designed to combat fraudulent activities. Under these new rules, telemarketers must:

- Call only between 8 A.M. and 9 P.M.
- Promptly say that they are selling something.
- Disclose total costs before they ask for money.
- Get written or taped authorization to take money from consumers' bank accounts.
- Specify the odds of winning for prize contests and say no purchase is necessary.
- Not call anyone who has asked not to be called.

Each violation is punishable by a $10,000 fine. Telemarketers can now also be banned from operating anywhere in the United States.

Will all of these efforts decrease the frequency of telemarketing scams? Maybe, if we take the advice of Steven Michaels and "don't talk to strangers."

Sources: Kathy M. Kristof, "Groups Band Together to Crack Down on Telemarketing Fraud," *Los Angeles Times*, January 19, 1997, p. D2; David J. Lynch, "New Telemarket Rules Aim to Save Consumers Billions," *USA Today*, August 17, 1995, p. 1a.

EXHIBIT 14–7
Some of the services offered by AOL

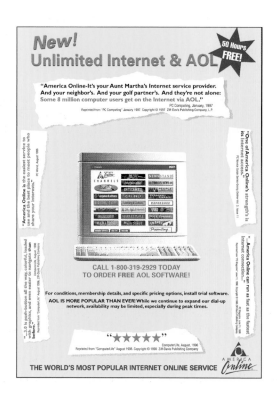

The three forms of direct selling are

1. *Repetitive person-to-person selling.* The salesperson visits the buyer's home, job site, or other location to sell frequently purchased products or services (for example, Amway).
2. *Nonrepetitive person-to-person selling.* The salesperson visits the buyer's home, job site, or other location to sell infrequently purchased products or services (for example, Encyclopaedia Britannica).
3. *Party plans.* The salesperson offers products or services to groups of people through home or office parties and demonstrations (for example, Tupperware and PartyLite Gifts).

EVALUATING THE EFFECTIVENESS OF DIRECT MARKETING

Because they generate a direct response, measuring the effectiveness of direct-marketing programs is not difficult. Using the **cost per order (CPO),** advertisers can evaluate the relative effectiveness of an ad in only a few minutes based on the number of calls generated. By running the same ad on different stations, a direct marketer can determine the relative effectiveness of the medium itself. For example, if the advertiser targets a $5 return per order and a broadcast commercial (production and print) costs $2,500, the ad is considered effective if it generates 500 orders. Similar measures have been developed for print and direct-mail ads.

For direct-marketing programs that do not have an objective of generating a behavioral response, traditional measures of effectiveness can be applied. (We discuss these measures in Chapter 18.)

Advantages and Disadvantages of Direct Marketing

Many of the advantages of direct marketing have already been presented. A review of these and some additions follow.

1. *Selective reach.* Direct marketing lets the advertiser reach a large number of people and reduces or eliminates waste coverage. Intensive coverage may be obtained through broadcast advertising or through the mail. While not everyone drives on highways where there are billboards or pays attention to TV commercials, virtually everyone receives mail. A good list allows for minimal waste, as only those consumers with the highest potential are targeted. For example, a political candidate can direct a message at a very select group of people (those living in a certain Zip code or members of the Sierra Club, say); a music club can target recent purchasers of CD players.
2. *Segmentation capabilities.* Marketers can purchase lists of recent product purchasers, car buyers, bank-card holders, and so on. These lists may allow segmentation on the basis of geographic area, occupation, demographics, and job title, to mention a few. Combin-

ing this information with the geocoding capabilities of Prizm or Vision (discussed in Chapter 2), marketers can develop effective segmentation strategies.

3. *Frequency*. Depending on the medium used, it may be possible to build frequency levels. The program vehicles used for direct-response TV advertising are usually the most inexpensive available, so the marketer can afford to purchase repeat times. Frequency may

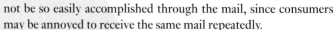
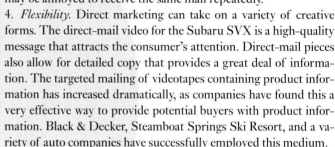

not be so easily accomplished through the mail, since consumers may be annoyed to receive the same mail repeatedly.

4. *Flexibility*. Direct marketing can take on a variety of creative forms. The direct-mail video for the Subaru SVX is a high-quality message that attracts the consumer's attention. Direct-mail pieces also allow for detailed copy that provides a great deal of information. The targeted mailing of videotapes containing product information has increased dramatically, as companies have found this a very effective way to provide potential buyers with product information. Black & Decker, Steamboat Springs Ski Resort, and a variety of auto companies have successfully employed this medium.

5. *Timing*. While many media require long-range planning and have long closing dates, direct-response advertising can be much more timely. Direct mail, for example, can be put together very quickly and distributed to the target population. TV programs typically used for direct-response advertising are older, less sought programs that are likely to appear on the station's list of available spots. Another common strategy is to purchase available time at the last possible moment to get the best price.

6. *Personalization*. No other advertising medium can personalize the message as well as direct mail. Parents with children at different age levels can be approached, with their child's name included in the appeal. Car owners are mailed letters congratulating them on their new purchase and offering accessories. Computer purchasers are sent software solicitations. Graduating college students receive very personalized information that recognizes their specific needs and offers solutions (such as credit cards).

7. *Costs*. While the CPM for direct mail may be very high on an absolute and a relative basis, its ability to specifically target the audience and eliminate waste coverage reduces the actual CPM. The ads used on TV are often among the lowest-priced available, and a video can be delivered for less than $1 (including postage).

A second factor contributing to the cost effectiveness of direct-response advertising is the cost per customer purchasing. Because of the low cost of media, each sale generated is very inexpensive.

8. *Measures of effectiveness*. No other medium can measure the effectiveness of its advertising efforts as well as direct response. Feedback is often immediate and always accurate.

Disadvantages of direct marketing include the following.

1. *Image factors*. As we noted earlier, the mail segment of this industry is often referred to as junk mail. Many people believe unsolicited mail promotes junk products, and others dislike being solicited. Even some senders of direct mail, including Motorola, GM, and Air Products & Chemicals, say they throw out most of the junk mail they receive. This problem is particularly relevant given the increased volume of mail being sent. (One study estimates the typical American receives 14 pieces of junk mail per week.)[34]

Likewise, direct-response ads on TV are often low-budget ads for lower-priced products, which contributes to the image that something less than the best products are marketed in this way. (Some of this image is being overcome by the home shopping channels, which promote some very expensive products.) As you saw in Ethical Perspective 14–1, other factors have also created image problems for the direct-marketing industry.

2. *Accuracy*. One of the advantages cited for direct mail and telemarketing was targeting potential customers specifically. But the effectiveness of these methods depends on the accuracy of the lists used. People move, change occupations, and so on, and if the lists are not kept current, selectivity will decrease. Computerization has greatly improved the currency of lists and reduced the incidence of bad names.

3. *Content support.* In our discussion of media strategy objectives in Chapter 10, we said the ability of magazines to create mood contributes to the overall effectiveness of the ads they carry. In direct-response advertising, mood creation is limited to the surrounding program and/or editorial content. Direct mail and online services are unlikely to create a desirable mood.

PROS AND CONS OF ELECTRONIC MEDIA

Given the lack of time experienced by so many people, the ability of the new electronic media to offer an alternative shopping medium holds great potential. The visual aspects of TV allow for demonstrations and product representations not available through catalogs and give potential consumers much more information for decision making. The information retrieval systems offer an almost unlimited opportunity for marketers.

Despite the growth in this industry, some marketers are still skeptical. They theorize that sales are not as high as projected because:

- Computers have not been adopted at the rate expected for home use.
- Many people are still not comfortable shopping without being able to handle the merchandise. They prefer to feel the material, see the colors, try on the product, and so on.
- Shopping may be a form of relaxation. To many people, a day in the mall or downtown is a form of entertainment. It gets them out of the house, takes their mind off work, and provides them with an opportunity to interact socially. Some people feel that since they work hard to earn their money, at least they can take the time to enjoy spending it.
- Many consumers prefer to get their news in the traditional manner: TV, radio, and newspapers. It's hard to change people's behaviors and habits.
- Information offerings are still limited.

According to Jon Berry, consumers just don't feel that they need this high-tech form of shopping and prefer to stick with their traditional shopping behaviors.[35] But Michael J. Major notes that many of these problems have been corrected and projections for electronic media are much more optimistic. In France, over 5.5 million videotext screens are in use (60 percent of phone subscribers) and the future for this service appears to be rosy.[36]

Online services also continue to increase in use in the industrial sector. When companies are bidding on government or private industry contracts that require meeting specifications, the electronic media offer distinct advantages. For example, where specifications previously had to be mailed to prospective bidders, these specs are now available immediately on the video screen. Changes in specs can be noted almost immediately, saving valuable time and effort for all parties involved.

In sum, while the electronic media may not be the answer for all marketers or for all shoppers, they do satisfy the needs of certain segments of society. The commitment made by the companies offering electronic services, and the success experienced by many of those who have advertised in these media, suggest that there is a bright future for advertisers in this area.

MARKETING ON THE INTERNET

As noted at the outset of this chapter, the hottest medium going right now seems to be the Internet. *The Economist* points out that no communication medium or electronic technology has ever grown as quickly, not even fax machines and PCs.[37] Some think everyone has discovered this new medium and its opportunities are limitless. Others are not inclined to agree. The remainder of this chapter discusses this new medium, its advantages and disadvantages, and its role in the IMC program.

Defining the Internet

The **Internet** is a worldwide means of exchanging information and communicating through a series of interconnected computers. Started as a U.S. Defense Department project, the Internet, or information superhighway, is now accessible to anyone with a computer and a modem. Features available on the Net are shown in Figure 14–7.

FIGURE 14–7
Features of the Internet

Feature	Use
Electronic mail (e-mail)	Allows users to send electronic mail anywhere in the world
Usenet	Discussion groups, newsgroups, and electronic bulletin boards, similar to those offered by online services
Telnet	Online databases, library catalogs, and electronic journals at hundreds of colleges and public libraries
File transfer protocol (ftp) or hypertext transfer protocol (http)	The ability to transfer files from one mainframe computer to another
Client server	Allows for the transfer of files from one mainframe computer to another
Gopher	A document retrieval system used to search for information
Wide Area Information Server (WAIS)	Enables one to use keywords in specific databases and retrieve full text information
World Wide Web (WWW)	Does much the same thing as gopher and WAIS, but combines sound, graphic images, video, and hypertext on a single page

While the Internet offers a variety of services to users, the most powerful and popular is the **World Wide Web (WWW)**, commonly referred to as the Web. In fact, many use the terms Internet and World Wide Web synonymously. For marketers, a number of Internet features offer potential, but it is the Web that has developed as the commercial component. (For that reason, the following discussion will focus on the Web as a communications tool.) First, however, it would be useful to examine Figure 14–8, which explains some of the Internet terminology that will be used in the remainder of this chapter.

Developing an Internet Program

As with other media discussed earlier in this text, using the Internet wisely requires development of a plan. This plan should consider target audiences (users of the Net) as well as specific objectives and strategies and a way to measure effectiveness.

WEB PARTICIPANTS

The Web, like other media, has both advertisers and potential customers. Unfortunately, the actual degree of use and profiles of these groups is extremely difficult to determine (a problem that will be discussed later).

Advertisers

Estimates of ad spending on the Web in the first half of 1996 vary, but most sources place this figure in the $66 to $71 million range, indicating triple-digit growth from the same period in 1995.[38] AT&T, MasterCard, American Airlines, MCI, and the Internet Shopping Network were some of the top advertisers, though many consumer and business-to-business companies participated. Most of the advertisers are companies offering computer and other technology products and services.

A variety of providers of Internet services have also surfaced. Traditional ad agencies have developed Internet advertising departments. New agencies that provide only Internet advertising assistance and website developers are also appearing in increasing numbers, as are companies that specialize in helping companies learn to market on the Web (Exhibit 14–9).

Users

An even harder profile to develop is that of the users of Internet and WWW services. Again, the estimated number of users constitutes a broad range, from as few as 8 million to over 40 million in the U.S. and from 23 million to 27 million worldwide. In six studies conducted in the United States and two worldwide, estimates varied by as much as 600 percent.[39] Demo-

FIGURE 14–8
Internet terminology

Browser	A graphic interface that provides simple access to documents on the World Wide Web (for example, Netscape is a browser).
Surfing	Slang word used to describe the act of searching for information on the Web.
Homepage	The first page on a website.
Website	The entire set of links that comprise the information compiled by a company, organization, or individual on the Web.
URL	Uniform resource locator—the "address" that tells the browser the specific place you want to go. It usually starts with http://, Telnet, gopher, or ftp.
Links	On Web documents, links are shaded or colored differently from text; when a link is selected, the browser will clear the window and retrieve the link document.
Provider	The company or institution that owns the server that you are accessing and regulates the access. It usually charges user fees.
HTML	Hypertext markup language; the language used to create Web pages with graphics, links, and text.

graphic profiles also vary, though most studies agree that the heaviest users are in their 30s and have above-average education and income. Males log on more frequently than females, and a disproportionate number of Web surfers are technology oriented, spending more than average amounts of time on the computer.

A more useful profile of Web users may come from looking at why they access rather than who accesses. Figure 14–9 reflects users' evaluations of the Web's offerings. It correlates highly with other studies of why users access this medium.[40]

While the exact profiles of advertisers and users of the Web may be difficult to obtain, most marketers remain optimistic about the potential for communicating with and selling to

EXHIBIT 14–9
One of the many organizations specializing in Internet marketing services

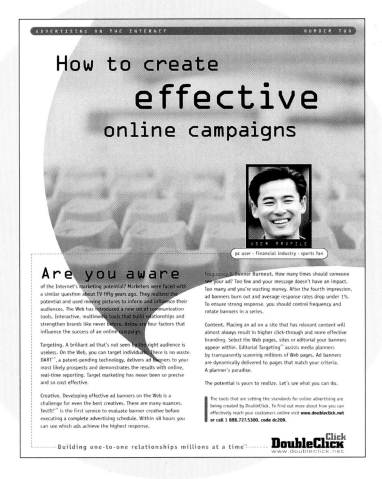

FIGURE 14–9
Users of all ages value the Internet's information, communication, and education offerings

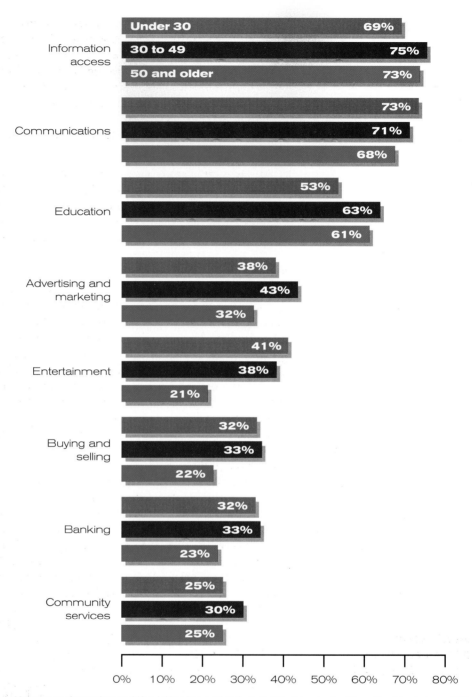

Note: percent of respondents aged 18 and older who rate selected aspects of the Internet as 9 or 10 on a 10-point scale, by age, 1995.

Source: *American Demographics*, July 1996, p. 52. Reprinted with permission. ©1996 *American Demographics*, Ithaca, New York.

consumers. They believe as the product itself matures, information and strategies will improve as well.

WEB OBJECTIVES

As noted at the outset of this chapter, the Web offers marketers an excellent opportunity to sell their products directly to the consumer. Thus, one of the primary objectives of advertising on the Internet is to generate sales *directly*. Advertisers on the Internet may have additional objectives in mind, including the following.

- *Disseminating information.* The website is an excellent place to provide in-depth information about a company's products and/or services.

- *Creating awareness.* Advertising on the Web can be useful in creating awareness of an organization in general as well as its specific product and service offerings.
- *Gathering research information.* The Web has been used by marketers to gain audience profile information. Cathay Pacific Airlines uses its website to interview frequent fliers to determine their preferences, buying habits, and so on.
- *Creating an image.* The website may be designed to project the image an organization or company wishes to have.
- *Stimulating trial.* Some websites offer electronic coupons to attempt to stimulate trial of their offerings.[41]

As you might imagine, it is possible to extend this list and generate even more potential objectives. As noted by Pierre Berthon and colleagues, "The Web is like a cross between an electronic trade show and community flea market." It has the capabilities to move customers and prospects through successive stages of the buying process.[42] Suffice it to say that advertising on the Internet can meet objectives beyond just selling products and services.

WEB STRATEGIES

Web advertising may take place through the use of display banners and the establishment of a website that provides more extensive information about the company or organization (see Exhibits 14–10 and 14–11). Some of these are used to stimulate sales directly, while others serve other communications objectives. For example, 1-800-Flowers, whose direct on-line shopping services were mentioned earlier, also has a website. Ragú greets website visitors with a new saying from "Mama" every 15 minutes and a variety of recipes, as well as product information. There are over 5,000 sports-related websites on the Net providing statistics, chat rooms, and products for sale. The NFL, NHL, NBA, and even the Harlem Globetrotters have sites designed to stimulate interest in their respective games. Procter & Gamble is increasing its ad expenditures in this area, and both McDonald's and Disney have established websites to reach the children's market. Exhibit 14–12 reflects the objectives and strategies for the website Foote, Cone & Beldings developed for Levi's. Other ad agencies—among them Ketchum, BBDO, and Ogilvy & Mather—are also active in Web advertising for their clients.

Having a website does not, in itself, guarantee a successful communications program. While the website can be valuable in providing information and even in making the sale, consumers must first be attracted to the site. A number of companies are now experimenting with a strategy of "**webcasting**"—pushing out site information to Web users rather than waiting for them to find the site on their own. These webcasters provide Web channels similar to TV or radio channels. Advertisers put their messages on the channels and have them sent to prospective interested parties.[43] Once a consumer visits a website, the site itself must be effective, as demonstrated in Exhibit 14–13.

Audience Measurement on the Internet

At least part of the problem in defining the Internet user is due to the infancy of this medium. In all media, audience measurement providers have become involved only after the medium has achieved a significant role in the marketplace. As Internet providers develop their offerings, audience data will improve. Several sources of audience information are now available or soon will be, among them the following.

- *Nielsen Media Research and CommerceNet.* These two organizations conduct joint surveys to determine Web demographics and usage characteristics.
- *IntelliQuest.* This firm conducts surveys of Web users to provide demographic, lifestyle, and usage information.

EXHIBIT 14–10   Banner advertising on the Net

Click to see the new ThinkPad 380.

EXHIBIT 14-11   An example of an Internet website

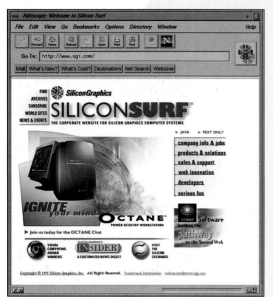

EXHIBIT 14-12   The objectives and strategies for Levi's website

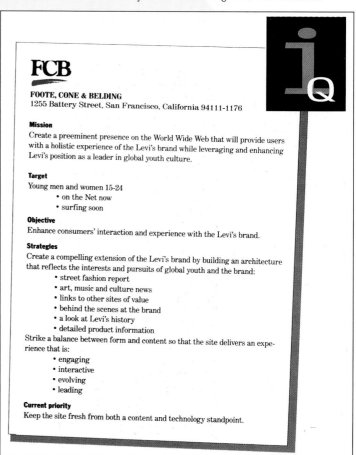

- *PC-Meter.* This metering service measures how much time computer users spend at their machines, what software and online services they access, and how long they spend online. It also provides demographic data.
- *Audit Bureau of Circulations.* This print agency is developing a product called WebFacts to certify Web counts.
- *Simmons Market Research Bureau.* SMRB provides viewership profiles of the Internet and other interactive media.
- *Arbitron.* Through its 4,000-sample Pathfinder Study, Arbitron provides demographic, media usage, and values and lifestyle data on users of the Internet and other interactive media.

In addition to these providers of audience information, *AdSpend* allows Web advertisers to track competitive spending and provides insights into marketing trends and performances of Web advertisers.

Measuring the Effectiveness of Web Advertising

No specific criteria for setting advertising rates or measuring effectiveness of the Web have been agreed on by all advertisers. Since ad rates are determined in part by potential exposures, advertisers have demanded information regarding the potential number of viewers of their banners and websites. Both Netscape and InfoSeek (the leading Web publishers) have used CPMs to establish rates. However, since there are no accurate figures on viewers, many companies (led by Procter & Gamble) have balked at this costing method.[44] P&G, Ziff-Davis, and others have demanded more concrete measures. They argue that the number of people who see a banner is irrelevant and that rates should be based on the number of visitors to a site. According to these advertisers, visits to a site (referred to as *hits* or click-throughs) are more indicative of consumer involvement. These demands, coupled with the desire of advertisers to measure the communications effectiveness of the medium, have led a number of companies to offer effectiveness measures.

EXHIBIT 14—13   Hot Hot Hot founders demonstrate what makes a website work

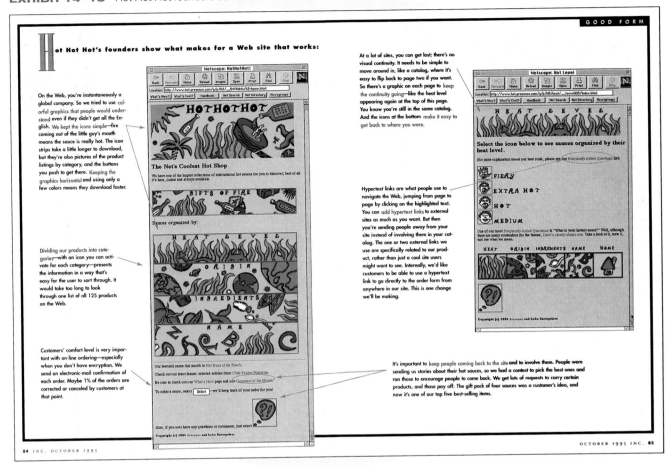

- *Orb Communications.* Orb works with clients to determine the measure sought. Impressions, click-throughs, leads, and even sales are tracked to determine value.
- *Firefly Network.* This group's software can watch users enter a site and observe what pages they view and what banners they see.
- *I/Pro.* This division of A. C. Neilsen measures site visits and provides data regarding the geographic area and institutional setting or even company where they originated.
- *NetCount.* This counts visits to a site and provides demographic profiles of the visitors.
- *AOL and Netscape.* Both America Online and Netscape provide advertisers with the number of hits on their sites.

As you can see, the number of hits, or visits to a website, is the most prevalent form of measuring effectiveness of advertising on the Web. Problems with this basis for measurement have led many advertisers to request more valid measures. But until these measures are provided, their lack will remain a disadvantage associated with Web advertising.

Advantages and Disadvantages of Internet Advertising

A number of advantages of advertising on the Web can be cited.

- *Target marketing.* A major advantage of the Web is the ability to target very specific groups of individuals with a minimum of waste coverage.
- *Message tailoring.* As a result of precise targeting, messages can be designed to appeal to the specific needs and wants of the target audience.
- *Interactive capabilities.* The interactive nature of the Web leads to a higher degree of customer involvement. Site visitors are already interested enough in the company and/or products to visit.
- *Information access.* Once users visit the website, they can garner a wealth of information regarding product specifications, purchase information, and more. New information can be made available almost immediately.

- *Sales potential.* Because this is a direct-response medium, the ability to generate sales is enhanced.
- *Creativity.* Proper design of a website can lead to repeat visits and generate interest in the company as well as its products and services (see the Ragú and Disney examples mentioned earlier). Banners and websites can be changed frequently to stimulate interest and meet consumers' needs.
- *Market potential.* The Internet keeps growing astronomically. As household penetration of PCs increases and awareness and interest in the Net continue to grow, the market potential will continue to increase.

There are also some disadvantages associated with advertising on the Internet.

- *Measurement problems.* Due to the novelty of this medium, sophisticated and universally adopted measures of audience and effectiveness have not yet been established.
- *Audience characteristics.* The Web is not for everybody. Most users are interested in computer- and technology-related products, so over half of all Web advertising is for computer-related products. Only 14 percent of advertising is for other consumer goods, with less than 10 percent for autos, travel, and financial services (all of them prime prospects for Internet sales).[45] The World Wide Web is not necessarily worldwide, as is demonstrated by Global Perspective 14–2.
- *WebSnarl.* A major complaint associated with the Web is the time required to access information. As more and more people enter the Web, this problem will get worse. There are already indications of high dropout rates due to the slowness of the Net.
- *Clutter.* As the number of ads proliferates, the likelihood of one ad being noticed drops accordingly. One study shows that only 7.2 percent of Net users say they click on banner ads for more information often or very often, while over half say that they never do so.[46] E-mail is already experiencing floods of marketing-related communications.
- *Potential for deception.* The Center for Media Education has referred to the Web as "a web of deceit" in reference to advertisers' attempts to target children with subtle advertising messages. They have called for the government to increase regulation on the Net.
- *Costs.* Many advertisers believe the Web is an effective medium for high-ticket items but less efficient for lower-priced consumer products like soups and candies. Relatively high costs of advertising and delivery limit the Web's appeal.
- *Limited production quality.* While it is improving, Net advertising does not offer the capabilities of many competitive media from a production standpoint. Websites do not reflect the high quality of TV and print graphics.[47]

In a survey of 29 major consumer products companies conducted by *Advertising Age* in 1996, nearly half stated that they had not created a media budget for Web advertising for 1997. Other studies show that many companies now advertising on the Web do not plan to keep doing so. Jim Savage, vice president and general manager of Ziff-Davis Publishing's ZD net, says "If the Web is really going to be a meaningful advertising channel, it's got to appeal beyond the narrow technology niches."[48]

Combining Internet Advertising with IMC Program Elements

The direct-response sales capabilities of the Internet are easily recognized. The potential for sales can be enhanced through integration with other program elements. Like the direct-response media discussed earlier, Web advertising both supports and is supported by other advertising media. As a support, the Web offers unlimited potential to provide interested consumers with product information. At the same time, effective advertising will lead to more awareness and subsequently more website visits.

SALES PROMOTIONS

To attract more visitors to their sites, Web advertisers are offering a variety of sales promotions. For example, the Burlington Coat Factory gives visitors coupons. Ragú offers

Global Perspective 14—2
Direct Marketing and the Web Go Worldwide

Infomercials have been adopted quite readily in Japan, New Zealand, Asia, and Europe. Telemarketing has proven extremely effective for AT&T in Asia, and a variety of direct-response methods are working in Latin America. So it would seem only natural for the Internet to be successful internationally as well. After all, it is the World Wide Web, isn't it?

While the Internet has experienced rapid growth in the United States, its adoption has been much slower internationally. A recent study conducted by *Internet* magazine found that over 73 percent of all Net users were from the United States, while Europeans constituted 10.8 percent, and Canada and Mexico accounted for 8.4 percent. Another study places the percentage of U.S. users at 85 percent. In either case, the percentage of foreign users (particularly in Asian countries) is quite low. In France, the Net has met with great resistance; many people see it as a threat to their culture. The British are also spending more time away from their screens (both TV and computer).

What are the reasons for the Net's slower adoption in foreign countries? A variety of explanations have been offered:

- *Cultural differences.* The English are spending more time going out to movies, eating, and shopping than in past years. The French see the predominantly English-speaking messages as a threat to anything French, and the Asians just seem to be less fascinated with technology (at least outside of Japan).
- *Technology.* While the Net is offered worldwide, a computer or specially wired TV is required for access. Computer penetration is lower in many foreign countries than in North America and Europe. The French are loyal to the Minitel, their own online system.
- *Competition.* France Telecom is offering customers wide discounts to keep them on the Minitel. Other local companies in other parts of the world have fought back against the outside influence of the English-speaking Internet ads, using local appeals and taking advantage of the language barrier.

So what can advertisers do to enhance the adoption process for the Internet? Perhaps they can borrow some of the strategies employed by other direct marketers:

- *Develop local appeals.* Many U.S. infomercial companies have found that to be successful in foreign countries, they must adapt their appeal to each market. TV Media, a Singapore-based infomercial company, says Asians are interested in the same products as Americans but local celebrities must be used to promote them successfully.
- *Form ventures with foreign companies.* Another infomercial company, Guthy-Renker, has been successful in Japan by joint venturing with Mitsui, Japan's largest cable company, and National Media, a U.S.-based company that dubs infomercials into local languages. The former provides household penetration, the latter a more tailored and accepted appeal.
- *Adapt to the market.* Some cultures may never be good targets for the Internet. The penetration of technology and cultural nuances may lengthen the process or even prohibit adoption but in other cultures, adapting to the market may be the key. AOL has been successful in some foreign markets by dumbing down—making its online product more user friendly than the Net. In other markets it has achieved success by joining the competition—providing the Net as part of their package.

Some experts think worldwide adoption of the Internet is just a matter of time. Others believe that it may always appeal only to certain markets, specifically the United States and parts of the Western world. For many advertisers on the Net, the success of other direct media forms kindles unbridled optimism.

Sources: Amy Harmon, "Why the French Hate the Internet," *Los Angeles Times*, January 27, 1997, p. A1; Kim Cleland, "Infomercial Audience Crosses over Cultures," *Advertising Age*, January 15, 1996, p. 18; Andrew Kantor and Michael Neubarth, "Off the Charts," *Internet World*, December 1996, pp. 44–51.

coupons, recipes, Italian lessons, and sweepstakes entries. Many marketers recognize the value of sales promotions in keeping their websites entertaining.[49]

PUBLIC RELATIONS

Some companies offer seminars and other forms of information content to their website visitors. Guinness allows visitors to download its latest TV commercial to use as a screensaver, thereby enhancing (it hopes) its corporate image.

PERSONAL SELLING

The website can be used effectively to generate qualified leads, identify customer inquiries, and direct personal selling efforts. Software developers are using their sites to allow consumers to voice complaints and offer suggestions about the product.

In sum, advertising on the Internet provides an excellent example of the value of an IMC program. As a stand-alone medium, the Net offers marketing potential. Combining it with other program elements greatly enhances this potential.

SUMMARY

This chapter introduced you to the rapidly growing field of direct marketing, which involves a variety of methods and media beyond direct mail and telemarketing. The versatility of direct marketing offers many different types of companies and organizations a powerful promotional and selling tool.

Direct marketing continues to outpace other advertising and promotional areas in growth; many of the Fortune 500 companies now use sophisticated direct-marketing strategies. Database marketing has become a critical component of many marketing programs.

Advantages of direct marketing include its selective reach, segmentation, frequency, flexibility, and timing. Personalized and custom messages, low costs, and the ability to measure program effectiveness are also advantages of direct-marketing programs.

At the same time, a number of disadvantages are associated with the use of direct marketing. Image problems, the proliferating sale and use of databases (some of them based on inaccurate lists), lack of content support, and the intrusive nature of the medium make some marketers hesitant to use direct-marketing tools. However, self-policing of the industry and involvement by large, sophisticated companies have led to significant improvements. As a result, the use of direct marketing will continue to increase.

The chapter also discussed marketing on the Internet, especially the World Wide Web, which is receiving much attention. While still in its early growth stage, the Net holds a lot of promise for marketers. Internet objectives and strategies were discussed, as were some of the advantages and disadvantages of this medium and sources of information. The role of direct marketing and the Internet in the IMC program were also discussed.

KEY TERMS

direct marketing, 440
direct-response media, 440
database, 444
database marketing, 444
one-step approach, 447

two-step approach, 447
mailing list, 447
direct-response advertising, 449
support advertising, 449

infomercial, 450
telemarketing, 452
audiotex, 452
telemedia, 452
electronic teleshopping, 453

direct selling, 453
cost per order (CPO), 455
Internet, 457
World Wide Web (WWW), 458
webcasting, 461

DISCUSSION QUESTIONS

1. Discuss some of the advantages and disadvantages of the Internet.

2. Describe what is meant by a database. What functions do databases perform?

3. There are conflicting viewpoints as to whether the WWW will be "the medium of the future" or just another tool in the promotional mix. Discuss both sides of this argument.

4. Discuss the evolution of infomercials. How are today's infomercials different from those of 10 years ago?

5. Direct marketing has been beset by a number of problems that have tarnished its image. Discuss some of these and what might be done to improve direct marketing's image.

6. Discuss some of the reasons direct marketing has been receiving more attention from marketers.

7. How do Internet marketers measure the effectiveness of this medium? Discuss the pros and cons of these measures.

8. How might business-to-business marketers use telemarketing effectively?

9. Name some companies that currently employ direct selling methods. What forms of direct selling do they use?

10. How is the effectiveness of a direct-marketing program measured?

CHAPTER 15

Sales Promotion

Chapter Objectives

- To understand the role of sales promotion in a company's integrated marketing communications program and to examine why it is increasingly important.

- To examine the various objectives of sales promotion programs.

- To examine the types of consumer- and trade-oriented sales promotion tools and factors to consider in using them.

- To understand how sales promotion is coordinated with advertising.

- To consider potential problems and abuse by companies in their use of sales promotion.

PROCTER & GAMBLE LEADS THE MOVEMENT TO SIMPLIFY PROMOTIONS

For decades, Procter & Gamble and many other consumer package goods companies prospered by bombarding both shoppers and retailers with promotional offers. The marketing system that developed during the 1980s was based on the assumption that what moved products was bigger and better promotions and pricing. Shoppers browsed through the aisles looking for specials, as popular brands would sell at full price one week and half-off the next. They clipped coupons, saved box tops, mailed in rebate or refund offers, and looked for packages with a toy or some other premium offer inside. Marketers pushed so many specials and price changes that it became difficult for them, as well as the retailers, to keep all of the paperwork straight. P&G made 55 price changes a day across 110 brands and offered 440 promotions a year.

But then P&G, perhaps the world's preeminent consumer products company, discovered that the marketing system that had evolved over the years had forgotten someone: the consumer. Today's average consumer, more often than not a woman, takes just 21 minutes to do her shopping. In that time she buys an average of 18 items out of 30,000 choices in a typical supermarket. She spends 25 percent less time browsing than she did five years ago and she doesn't bother to check prices. She wants the same product at the same price in the same row and shelf position week after week.

Durk Jager, P&G's president and chief operating officer, concedes that his company has been confusing consumers. "It's mind-boggling how difficult we've made it for them over the years," he says. Under Jager's direction, P&G is over-

hauling its sales and marketing programs as part of a larger strategy of simplification.

P&G began to simplify its promotional programs in 1991 by moving many of its brands to an everyday low pricing (EDLP) strategy, which vastly reduced the number of deals offered to retailers and distributors in favor of lower list prices. P&G argues that all of the allowances and deals are costly and confusing for retailers. Moreover, they cause shelf prices to fluctuate weekly and train consumers to buy on price instead of perceived value (which undermines brand loyalty). P&G's drive to simplify has been gaining momentum and has resulted in the elimination of 27 types of consumer promotions, including the traditional bonus packs, premiums, cents-off packs, and refund offers. The company is taking the ax to coupons as well, noting that with redemption rates declining, they are a less efficient way to draw new customers. So far it has cut its use of coupons in half and has been testing the total elimination of coupons in some markets. P&G is putting the money saved from these cuts into lower prices and other promotions such as sampling and in-store demonstrations.

Procter & Gamble, long a bellwether for the package-goods industry, is leading a broad movement to reduce the complexity of sales promotion programs. After a debilitating price war using endless coupons and buy-one-get-one-free offers, cereal makers like General Mills and Kellogg Co. have cut back on their weekly price promotions in favor of simplicity, stability, and lower list prices. Clorox has also simplified its trade promotions, cut back on coupons, and trimmed the number of products it sells.

A former P&G executive who is now a management consultant says, "When they write the next book on P&G, these initiatives will be the most important, most telling changes in the history of the company." However, Jager notes there is little time for P&G to relax; its rivals are working on how to better meet shoppers' needs and make things even simpler for them.

Sources: Raju Narisetti, "P&G, Seeing Shoppers Were Being Confused, Overhauls Marketing," *The Wall Street Journal*, January 15, 1997, pp. A1, 6; "Make It Simple," *Business Week*, September 9, 1996, pp. 96–104.

Marketers have come to recognize that advertising alone is not always enough to move their products off store shelves and into the hands of consumers. Companies also use sales promotion methods targeted at both consumers and the wholesalers and retailers that distribute their products to stimulate demand. Most companies' integrated marketing communications programs include consumer and trade promotions that are coordinated with advertising, direct marketing, and publicity/public relations campaigns as well as sales force efforts.

This chapter focuses on the role of sales promotion in a firm's IMC program. We examine how marketers use both consumer- and trade-oriented promotions to influence the purchase behavior of consumers as well as wholesalers and retailers. We explore the objectives of sales promotion programs and the various types of sales promotion tools that can be used at both the consumer and trade level. We also consider how sales promotion can be integrated with other elements of the promotional mix and look at problems that can arise when marketers become overly dependent on consumer and trade promotions, especially the latter.

THE SCOPE AND ROLE OF SALES PROMOTION

Sales promotion has been defined as "a direct inducement that offers an extra value or incentive for the product to the sales force, distributors, or the ultimate consumer with the primary objective of creating an immediate sale."[1] Keep in mind several important aspects of sales promotion as you read this chapter.

First, sales promotion involves some type of inducement that provides an *extra incentive* to buy. This incentive is usually the key element in a promotional program; it may be a coupon or price reduction, the opportunity to enter a contest or sweepstakes, a money-back refund or rebate, or an extra amount of a product. The incentive may also be a free sample of the product, given in hopes of generating a future purchase, or a premium that serves as a reminder of the brand and reinforces its image, such as the Trix hypnotic sunglasses offer (Exhibit 15–1). Most sales promotion offers attempt to add some value to the product or service. While advertising appeals to the mind and emotions to give the consumer a reason to buy, sales promotion appeals more to the pocketbook and provides an incentive for purchasing a brand.

Sales promotion can also provide an inducement to marketing intermediaries such as wholesalers and retailers. A trade allowance or discount gives retailers a financial incentive to stock and promote a manufacturer's products. A trade contest directed toward wholesalers or retail personnel gives them extra incentive to perform certain tasks or meet sales goals.

A second point is that sales promotion is essentially an *acceleration tool*, designed to speed up the selling process and maximize sales volume.[2] By providing an extra incentive, sales promotion techniques can motivate consumers to purchase a larger quantity of a brand or shorten the purchase cycle of the trade or consumers by encouraging them to take more immediate action.

Companies also use limited-time offers such as price-off deals to retailers or a coupon with an expiration date to accelerate the purchase process.[3] Sales promotion attempts to maximize sales volume by motivating customers who have not responded to advertising. The ideal sales promotion program generates sales that would not be achieved by other means. However, as we shall see later, many sales promotion offers end up being used by current users of a brand rather than attracting new users.

EXHIBIT 15–1   General Mills offers a premium to provide extra incentive to purchase Trix cereal

FIGURE 15–1

Types of sales promotion activities

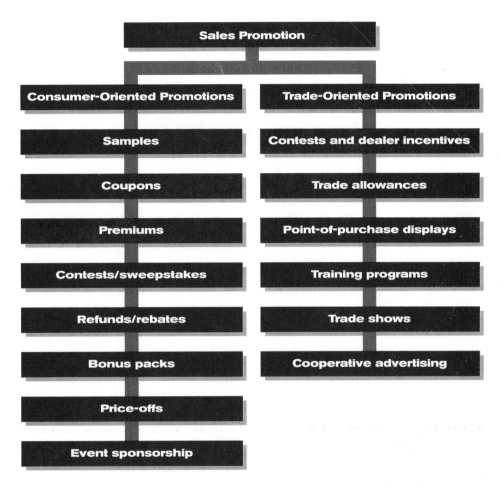

A final point regarding sales promotion activities is that they can be *targeted to different parties* in the marketing channel. As shown in Figure 15–1, sales promotion can be broken into two major categories: consumer-oriented and trade-oriented promotions. Activities involved in **consumer-oriented sales promotion** include sampling, couponing, premiums, contests and sweepstakes, refunds and rebates, bonus packs, price-offs, and event sponsorship. These promotions are directed at consumers, the end purchasers of goods and services, and are designed to induce them to purchase the marketer's brand.

As discussed in Chapter 2, consumer-oriented promotions are part of a promotional pull strategy; they work along with advertising to encourage consumers to purchase a particular brand and thus create demand for it. Consumer promotions are also used by retailers to encourage consumers to shop in their particular stores. Many grocery stores use their own coupons or sponsor contests and other promotions to increase store patronage.

Trade-oriented sales promotion includes dealer contests and incentives, trade allowances, point-of-purchase displays, sales training programs, trade shows, cooperative advertising, and other programs designed to motivate distributors and retailers to carry a product and make an extra effort to push it to their customers. Nearly two-thirds of all sales promotional dollars are spent on trade promotions. Many marketing programs include both trade- and consumer-oriented promotions, since motivating both groups maximizes the effectiveness of the promotional program.

THE GROWTH OF SALES PROMOTION

While sales promotion has been around for a long time, its role and importance in manufacturers' marketing programs have increased dramatically. Not only has the total amount of money spent on sales promotion increased, but the percentage of marketers' budgets allocated to promotion has skyrocketed. Annual studies by Carol Wright Promotions track the marketing spending of major package-goods companies in three categories: trade promo-

FIGURE 15–2   Long-term allocations to advertising, trade promotion, and consumer promotion

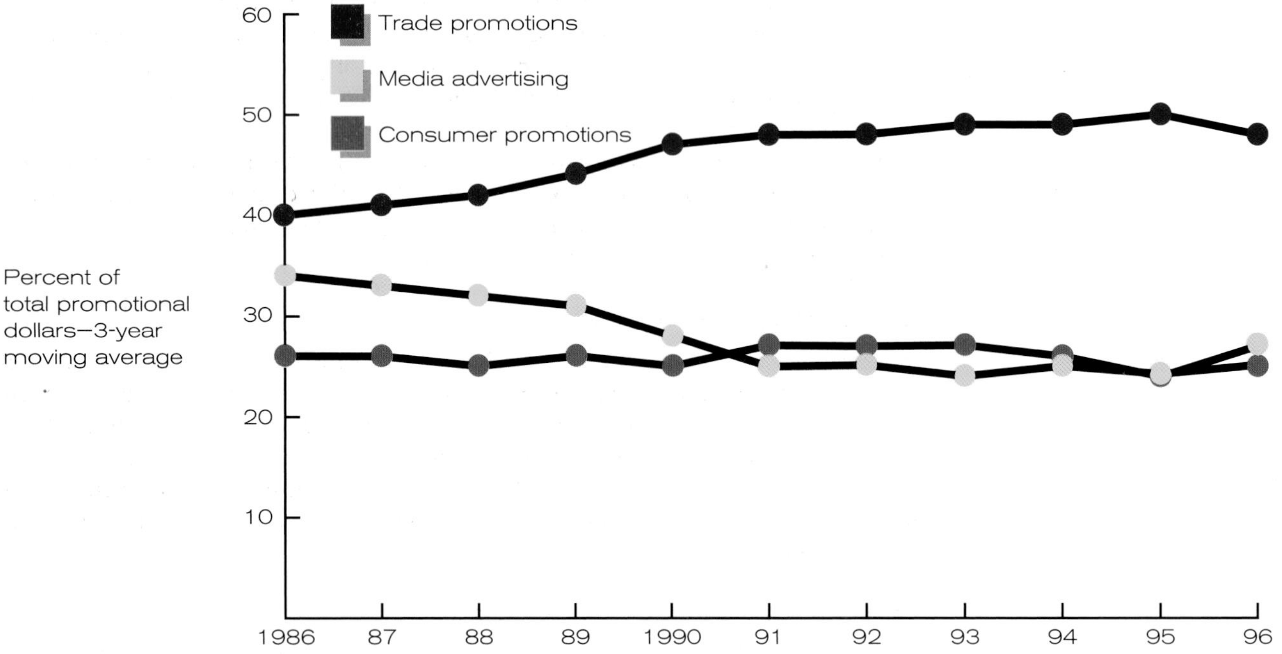

	1986	87	88	89	1990	91	92	93	94	95	96
Trade promotions	40	41	42	44	47	48	48	49	49	50	48
Media advertising	34	33	32	31	28	25	25	24	25	26	27
Consumer promotions	26	26	25	26	25	27	27	27	26	24	25

Source: Cox Direct 19th Annual Survey of Promotional Practices, 1997.

tion, consumer promotion, and media advertising. Figure 15–2 shows the long-term trend of allocations to each category. The percentage of the marketing budget spent on consumer promotions has held steady over the past decade, while the allocation to trade promotions has risen dramatically.

This increase in trade promotion spending has come almost totally at the expense of media advertising. Marketers say they expect trade spending to decline somewhat in the future, with corresponding increases in consumer promotions and media advertising. However, many marketing people believe it will be difficult to reverse the flow of marketing dollars to the trade, for the reasons discussed next.

Reasons for the Increase in Sales Promotion

A number of factors have led to the shift in marketing dollars to sales promotion from media advertising. Among them are the growing power of retailers, declining brand loyalty, increased promotional sensitivity, brand proliferation, fragmentation of the consumer market, short-term focus, increased accountability, competition, and clutter.

THE GROWING POWER OF RETAILERS

One reason for the increase in sales promotion is the power shift in the marketplace from manufacturers to retailers. For many years, manufacturers of national brands had the power and influence; retailers were just passive distributors of their products. Consumer products manufacturers created consumer demand for their brands by using heavy advertising and some consumer-oriented promotions, such as samples, coupons, and premiums, and exerted pressure on retailers to carry the products. Retailers did very little research and sales analysis; they relied on manufacturers for information regarding the sales performance of individual brands.

In recent years, however, several developments have helped to transfer power from the manufacturers to the retailers. With the advent of optical checkout scanners and sophisticated in-store computer systems, retailers gained access to data concerning how quickly products turn over, which sales promotions are working, and which products make money. Retailers use this information to analyze sales of manufacturers' products and then demand discounts and other promotional support from manufacturers of lagging brands. Companies that fail to comply with retailers' demands for more trade support often have their shelf space reduced or even their product dropped.

Another factor that has increased the power of retailers is the consolidation of the grocery store industry, which has resulted in larger chains with greater buying power and clout. These large chains have become accustomed to trade promotions and can pressure manufacturers to provide deals, discounts, and allowances.

DECLINING BRAND LOYALTY

Another major reason for the increase in sales promotion is that consumers have become less brand loyal and are purchasing more on the basis of price, value, and convenience. You may recall from Chapter 4 that the percentage of consumers who are brand loyal is under 50 percent for most product categories.[4] Many consumers switch back and forth among a set of brands they view as essentially equal. These brands are all perceived as being satisfactory and interchangeable, and consumers purchase whatever brand is on special or for which they have a coupon.

INCREASED PROMOTIONAL SENSITIVITY

Marketers are making greater use of sales promotion because consumers respond favorably to it. The percentage of purchases made in conjunction with some sort of promotional offer has increased sharply over the past decade.[5] In one study, consumers said 54 percent of their purchases were made under some promotional inducement, with price promotions, coupons, and point-of-purchase displays being the most important.[6] A national survey of 7,500 households found that over 90 percent of consumers had taken advantage of some form of promotion in the past month. Coupons were particularly popular as a way to get greater value.[7]

An obvious reason for consumers' increased sensitivity to sales promotion offers is that they save money. Another reason is that many purchase decisions are made at the point of purchase by consumers who are increasingly time sensitive and facing too many choices.[8] Some studies have found that up to 70 percent of purchase decisions are made in the store, where people are very likely to respond to promotional deals.[9] Buying a brand that is on special or being displayed can simplify the decision-making process and solve the problem of overchoice. Professor Leigh McAlister has described this process:

> As consumers go down the supermarket aisle they spend 3 to 10 seconds in each product category. They often don't know the regular price of the chosen product. However, they do have a sense of whether or not that product is on promotion. As they go down the aisle, they are trying to pensively fill their baskets with good products without tiresome calculations. They see a "good deal" and it goes in the cart.[10]

BRAND PROLIFERATION

A major aspect of many firms' marketing strategies over the past decade has been the development of new products. Consumer product companies are launching more than 20,000 new products each year, according to the trade publication *New Product News* (compared with only 2,689 in 1980).[11] The market has become saturated with new brands, which often lack any significant advantages that can be used as the basis of an advertising campaign. Thus, companies increasingly depend on sales promotion to encourage consumers to try these brands. In Chapter 4, we saw how sales promotion techniques can be used as part of the shaping process to lead the consumer from initial trial to repeat purchase at full price. Marketers are relying more on samples, coupons, rebates, premiums, and other innovative promotional tools to achieve trial usage of their new brands and encourage repeat purchase (Exhibit 15–2).

EXHIBIT 15—2
Sales promotion tools are often used
to encourage trial of a new brand

Promotions are also important in getting retailers to allocate some of their precious shelf space to new brands. The competition for shelf space for new products in stores is enormous. Supermarkets carry an average of 30,000 products (compared with 13,067 in 1982). Retailers favor new brands with strong sales promotion support that will bring in more customers and boost their sales and profits.[12] Many retailers require special discounts or allowances from manufacturers just to handle a new product. These slotting fees or allowances, which are discussed later in the chapter, can make it expensive for a manufacturer to introduce a new product.

FRAGMENTATION OF THE CONSUMER MARKET

As the consumer market becomes more fragmented and traditional mass media-based advertising less effective, marketers are turning to more segmented, highly targeted approaches. Many companies are tailoring their promotional efforts to specific regional markets.[13] Sales promotion tools have become one of the primary vehicles for doing this, through programs tied into local flavor, themes, or events. For example, Burger King spends nearly half of its advertising budget on local tie-ins and promotions designed to build traffic in its restaurants.

Marketers are also shifting more of their promotional efforts to direct marketing, which often includes some form of sales promotion incentive. Many marketers use information they get from premium offers, trackable coupons, rebates, and sweepstakes to build databases for future direct-marketing efforts. As marketers continue to shift from media advertising to direct marketing, promotional offers will probably be used even more to help build databases.

SHORT-TERM FOCUS

Many businesspeople believe the increase in sales promotion is motivated by marketing plans and reward systems geared to short-term performance and the immediate generation of sales volume.[14] Some think the package-goods brand management system has contributed to marketers' increased dependence on sales promotion. Brand managers use sales promotions routinely, not only to introduce new products or defend against the competition, but also to meet quarterly or yearly sales and market share goals. The sales force, too, may have short-term quotas or goals to meet and may also receive requests from retailers and wholesalers for promotions. Thus, reps may pressure marketing or brand managers to use promotions to help them move the products into the retailers' stores.

Many managers view consumer and trade promotions as the most dependable way to generate short-term sales, particularly when they are price related. The reliance on sales promotion is particularly high in mature and slow-growth markets, where it is difficult to stimulate consumer demand through advertising. This has led to concern that managers have become too dependent on the quick sales fix that can result from a promotion and that the brand franchise may be eroded by too many deals.

INCREASED ACCOUNTABILITY

In addition to pressuring their marketing or brand managers and sales force to produce short-term results, many companies are demanding to know what they are getting for their promotional expenditures. Sales promotion is more economically accountable than advertising. In companies struggling to meet their sales and financial goals, top management is demanding measurable, accountable ways to relate promotional expenditures to sales and profitability. For example, Philip Morris's Kraft General Foods unit is using computerized sales information from checkout scanners in determining compensation for marketing personnel. Part of the pay managers receive depends on the sales a promotion generates relative to its costs.[15]

Managers who are being held accountable to produce results often use price discounts or coupons, since they produce a quick and easily measured jump in sales. It takes longer for an ad campaign to show some impact and the effects are more difficult to measure. Marketers are also feeling pressure from the trade as powerful retailers demand sales performance from their brands.

COMPETITION

Another factor that led to the increase in sales promotion is manufacturers' reliance on trade and consumer promotions to gain or maintain competitive advantage. The markets for many products are mature and stagnant, and it is increasingly difficult to boost sales through advertising. Exciting, breakthrough creative ideas are difficult to come by, and consumers' attention to mass media advertising continues to decline. Rather than allocating large amounts of money to run dull ads, many marketers have turned to sales promotion.

Many companies are tailoring their trade promotions to key retail accounts and developing strategic alliances with retailers that include both trade and consumer promotional programs. A major development in recent years is **account-specific marketing**, whereby a manufacturer develops a customized promotion for individual retailers. For example, Hasbro teamed with toy retailer Toys "Я" Us to create direct-mail booklets offering discounts on Hasbro brands, good only at Toys "Я" Us stores. Estimates are that by the end of the decade, U.S. marketers will spend more than half of their promotion and advertising budgets on account-specific marketing.[16] Exhibit 15–3 shows an ad promoting the Carol Wright Account Specific marketing program.

Retailers may use a promotional deal with one company as leverage to seek an equal or better deal with its competitors. Consumer and trade promotions are easily matched by competitors, and many marketers find themselves in a promotional trap where they must continue using promotions or be at a competitive disadvantage. (We discuss this problem in more detail later in the chapter.)

CLUTTER

A promotional offer in an ad can break through the clutter that is prevalent in most media today. A premium offer may help attract consumers' attention to an ad, as will a contest or sweepstakes. Some studies have shown that readership scores are higher for print ads with coupons than for ads without them.[17] However, more recent studies by Starch INRA Hooper suggest that magazine ads with coupons do not generate higher readership.[18]

Concerns about the Increased Role of Sales Promotion

Many factors have contributed to the increased use of sales promotion by consumer product manufacturers. Marketing and advertising executives are concerned about how this shift in the allocation of the promotional budget affects brand equity. As noted in Chapter 2, *brand equity*, or consumer franchise, is an intangible asset of added value or goodwill that results from consumers' favorable image, impressions of differentiation, and/or strength of attachment to a brand.

Some critics argue that sales promotion increases come at the expense of brand equity and every dollar that goes into promotion rather than advertising devalues the brand.[19] They say trade promotions in particular contribute to the destruction of brand franchises and equity as they encourage consumers to purchase primarily on the basis of price. Studies conducted by ad agency DDB Needham Worldwide show that the percentage of consumers who say they purchase well-known brands declined from 77 percent in 1975 to 62 percent in the early 90s.[20]

Proponents of advertising argue that marketers must maintain strong franchises if they want to differentiate their brands and charge a premium price for them. They say advertising is still the most effective way to build the long-term franchise of a brand: it informs consumers of a brand's features and benefits, creates an image, and helps build and maintain brand loyalty. However, many marketers are not investing in their brands as they take monies away from media advertising to fund short-term promotions. If this trend continues, brands may lose the equity that advertising helped create and be forced to compete primarily on the basis of price. IMC Perspective 15–1 discusses how Heinz became too reliant on sales promotion and is increasing its advertising spending to rebuild brand equity.

Many of these concerns are justified, but not all sales promotion activities detract from the value of a brand. It is important to distinguish between consumer franchise-building and nonfranchise-building sales promotions.

Consumer Franchise-Building versus Nonfranchise-Building Promotions

Sales promotion activities that communicate distinctive brand attributes and contribute to the development and reinforcement of brand identity are **consumer franchise-building (CFB) promotions**.[21] Consumer sales promotion efforts cannot make consumers loyal to a brand that is of little value or does not provide them with a specific benefit. But they can make consumers aware of a brand and, by communicating its specific features and benefits, contribute to the development of a favorable brand image. Consumer franchise-building promotions are designed to build long-term brand preference and help the company achieve the ultimate goal of full-price purchases that do not depend on a promotional offer.

IMC Perspective 15–1
Heinz Tries to Rebuild Brand Equity

During the 1990s many companies have concentrated on consumer and trade promotions at the expense of advertising. But few have been as promotion prone as the H. J. Heinz Co., whose major products include ketchup and condiments, 9-Lives and Kibbles 'N Bits cat food, Starkist tuna, and Weight Watchers and Budget Gourmet frozen entrees. In 1992 Heinz increased its marketing spending by $100 million and allocated virtually all of the money to trade promotion while cutting back substantially on advertising. A Heinz executive said the move was made in response to a weak economy: "Price elasticity is what it's all about, and no amount of advertising will sell as well as price in this environment."

Over the past decade, trade and consumer promotion has played a much bigger role than advertising at Heinz, the advertising cellar dweller among food companies. The company's advertising stinginess, in fact, led the Leo Burnett agency to resign the Heinz account in November 1994. In 1996 Heinz had $9 billion in sales but spent only about $90 million advertising its brands in the United States—considerably less than it spent 10 years ago. And excluding the $16 million devoted to Weight Watchers' weight-loss centers, it spent only about $53 million on its 400 other brands. Commercials for Starkist featuring Charlie the tuna or 9-Lives spots with Morris the finicky feline are rarely seen anymore.

Some analysts argue that the lack of ad spending is turning the Heinz brands into commodities. In recent years Heinz has had difficulty raising prices, once an essential part of its growth strategy, and most of its brands took price cuts in 1996. Moreover, many of its brands face difficult competition. In pet foods, 9-Lives and Kibbles 'N Bits face an array of well-armed competitors from Mars, Ralston-Purina, and Carnation/Nestlé. In the frozen food aisle, Budget Gourmet and Weight Watchers have been battered by lower-priced rivals.

In early 1997 Heinz announced a major restructuring that includes cutting costs, upgrading manufacturing facilities, and pruning its product lines while boosting the company's anemic ad budget. Increases in advertising spending will go to Heinz's six core business categories: food service, pet foods, tuna, infant foods, ketchup/condiments, and weight control. The advertising accounts for several key brands were moved to DDB Needham Worldwide, a move industry insiders read to mean a new commitment to ad spending.

It remains to be seen if Heinz will be able to rebuild the equity many of its brands have lost over the past decade and reverse eroding profit margins. Most of its products compete in mature markets where consumers (and perhaps more importantly, retailers) have grown accustomed to promotions. However, many analysts are hoping that Heinz will reinvest any earnings increases back into the business through advertising and rebuild its big brands. Heinz may have learned that there is more to marketing than price elasticity. We may even start seeing Charlie the tuna and Morris the cat on TV again.

Sources: Matt Murray and Emily Nelson, "Heinz to Take Charge, Cut Staff by 6%," *The Wall Street Journal*, March 10, 1997, pp. A3, 11; Judan Pollack, "Heinz to Pare Products while It Boosts Ads," *Advertising Age*, March 3, 1997, pp. 3, 37.

For years, franchise or image building was viewed as the exclusive realm of advertising, and sales promotion was used only to generate short-term sales increases. But now marketers are recognizing the image-building potential of sales promotion and paying attention to its CFB value. A survey of senior marketing executives found that 88 percent believe consumer promotions can help build a brand's equity and 58 percent think trade promotions can contribute.[22] One sales promotion expert says:

IF YOUR TRADE PROMOTION DOLLARS AREN'T BUILDING YOUR BRAND, WHAT THE HELL ARE THEY BUILDING?

Today's marketers who appreciate the potential of sales promotion as an ongoing strategy that works to build a brand's franchise recognize that promotion's potential goes well beyond mere quick-fix, price-off tactics. The promotion professional is familiar with a variety of approaches to generating consumer involvement—that is, sweepstakes, special events, premiums, or rebates—and understands that the given campaign must work in harmony with long-term goals and brand positioning.[23]

Many sales promotion agencies, such as Ryan Partnership, recognize the importance of developing consumer and trade promotions that can help build brand equity.

Companies can use sales promotion techniques in a number of ways to contribute to franchise building. Rather than using a one-time offer, many companies are developing pro-

EXHIBIT 15–4   The bone china
sweepstakes is an excellent example
of a consumer franchise-building
promotion

motional programs that encourage repeat purchases and long-term patronage. Many credit cards have promotional programs where consumers earn bonus points every time they use their card to charge a purchase. These points can then be redeemed for various items. Most airlines and many hotel chains offer frequent flyer or guest programs to encourage repeat patronage. Fast-food chains such as McDonald's, Arby's, and Hardee's use frequency programs to build loyalty and encourage repeat purchases.[24]

Companies can also use sales promotion to contribute to franchise building by developing an offer consistent with the image of the brand. One successful consumer franchise-building promotion is the bone china sweepstakes for Palmolive dishwashing liquid and dishwasher detergent shown in Exhibit 15–4. For many consumers, an important factor in choosing a dishwashing product is that it will not harm their dishes. The "Trust your best to Palmolive" slogan helps to position the Palmolive products as being gentle enough to use on even the best dishes, like Royal Doulton bone china. Colgate-Palmolive has run this successful promotion for several years.

Nonfranchise-building (non-FB) promotions are designed to accelerate the purchase decision process and generate an immediate increase in sales. These activities do not communicate information about a brand's unique features or the benefits of using it, so they do not contribute to the building of brand identity and image. Price-off deals, bonus packs, and rebates or refunds are examples of non-FB sales promotion techniques. Trade promotions receive the most criticism for being nonfranchise building—for good reason. First, many of the promotional discounts and allowances given to the trade are never passed on to consumers. Most trade promotions that are forwarded through the channels reach consumers in the form of lower prices or special deals and lead them to buy on the basis of price rather than brand equity.

Many specialists in the promotional area stress the need for marketers to use sales promotion tools to build a franchise and create long-term continuity in their promotional programs.[25] Whereas non-FB promotions merely borrow customers from other brands, well-planned CFB activities can convert consumers to loyal customers. Short-term non-FB promotions have their place in a firm's promotional mix, particularly when competitive developments call for them. But their limitations must be recognized when a long-term marketing strategy for a brand is developed.

CONSUMER-ORIENTED SALES PROMOTION

In this section, we examine the various sales promotion tools and techniques marketers can use to influence consumers. We study the consumer-oriented promotions shown in Figure 15–2 and discuss their advantages and limitations. First, we consider some objectives marketers have for sales promotion programs targeted to the consumer market.

Objectives of Consumer-Oriented Sales Promotion

As the use of sales promotion techniques continues to increase, companies must consider what they hope to accomplish through their consumer promotions and how they interact with other promotional activities such as advertising, direct marketing, and personal selling. When marketers implement sales promotion programs without considering their long-term cumulative effect on the brand's image and position in the marketplace, they often do little more than create short-term spikes in the sales curve.

Not all sales promotion activities are designed to achieve the same objectives. As with any promotional mix element, marketers must plan consumer promotions by conducting a situation analysis and determining sales promotion's specific role in the integrated marketing communications program. They must decide what the promotion is designed to accomplish and to whom it should be targeted. Setting clearly defined objectives and measurable goals for their sales promotion programs forces managers to think beyond the short-term sales fix (although this can be one goal).

While the basic goal of most consumer-oriented sales promotion programs is to induce purchase of a brand, the marketer may have a number of different objectives for both new and established brands—for example, obtaining trial and repurchase, increasing consumption of an established brand, defending current customers, targeting a specific market segment, or enhancing advertising and marketing efforts.

OBTAINING TRIAL AND REPURCHASE

One of the most important uses of sales promotion techniques is to encourage consumers to try a new product or service. While thousands of new products are introduced to the market every year, as many as 90 percent of them fail within the first year. Many of these failures are due to the fact that the new product or brand lacks the promotional support needed either to encourage initial trial by enough consumers or to induce enough of those trying the brand to repurchase it. Many new brands are merely new versions of an existing product without unique benefits, so advertising alone cannot induce trial. Sales promotion tools have become an important part of new brand introduction strategies; the level of initial trial can be increased through techniques such as sampling, couponing, and refund offers.

The success of a new brand depends not only on getting initial trial but also on inducing a reasonable percentage of people who try the brand to repurchase it and establish ongoing purchase patterns. Promotional incentives such as coupons or refund offers are often included with a sample to encourage repeat purchase after trial. For example, when Lever Brothers introduced its Lever 2000 brand of bar soap, it distributed millions of free samples along with a 75-cent coupon. The samples allowed consumers to try the new soap, while the coupon provided an incentive to purchase it.

INCREASING CONSUMPTION OF AN ESTABLISHED BRAND

Many marketing managers are responsible for established brands competing in mature markets, against established competitors, where consumer purchase patterns are often well set. Awareness of an established brand is generally high as a result of cumulative advertising effects, and many consumers have probably tried the brand. These factors can create a challenging situation for the brand manager. Sales promotion can generate some new interest in an established brand to help increase sales or defend market share against competitors.

Marketers attempt to increase sales for an established brand in several ways, and sales promotion can play an important role in each. One way to increase product consumption is by identifying new uses for the brand. Sales promotion tools like recipe books or calendars that show various ways of using the product often can accomplish this. One of the best examples of a brand that has found new uses is Arm & Hammer baking soda. Exhibit 15–5 shows a clever freestanding insert (FSI) that promotes the brand's new fridge-freezer pack, which absorbs more odors in refrigerators and freezers.

Another strategy for increasing sales of an established brand is to use promotions that attract nonusers of the product category or users of a competing brand. Attracting nonusers of the product category can be very difficult, as consumers may not see a need for the product. Sales promotions can appeal to nonusers by providing them with an extra incentive to try the product, but a more common strategy for increasing sales of an established brand is to attract consumers who use a competing brand. This can be done by giving them an incentive to switch, such as a coupon, premium offer, bonus pack, or price deal. Marketers can also get users of a competitor to try their brand through sampling or other types of promotional programs.

EXHIBIT 15–5 Arm & Hammer used this FSI to promote a specific use for the product

One of the most successful promotions ever used to attract users of a competing brand was the Pepsi Challenge. In this campaign, Pepsi took on its archrival, industry leader Coca-Cola, in a hard-hitting comparative promotion that challenged consumers to taste the two brands in blind taste tests (Exhibit 15–6). The Pepsi Challenge promotion included national and local advertising, couponing, and trade support as part of a fully integrated promotional program. The campaign was used for several years and was instrumental in helping Pepsi move ahead of Coke to become the market share leader in supermarket sales. In response Coke launched a variety of counterattacks, including the controversial decision to change its formula and launch New Coke in 1986.

DEFENDING CURRENT CUSTOMERS

With more new brands entering the market every day and competitors attempting to take away their customers through aggressive advertising and sales promotion efforts, many companies are turning to sales promotion programs to hold present customers and defend their market share. A company can use sales promotion techniques in several ways to retain

EXHIBIT 15—6   The Pepsi Challenge was a very successful promotion for attracting users of a competing brand

ANNCR: All across America people are taking the Pepsi Challenge. In California here's what they are saying.
TRACY KUERBIS: Pepsi really is the better drink.
DAVE JOHNSON: I've proven to myself now that I like Pepsi better.
ANNCR: Nationwide more people

prefer the taste of Pepsi over Coca-Cola.
CHERIE BOOTH: I think today's test was very honest.
DAVE: Pepsi has a better product and that's probably why they are running a test like this because it's obvious how many people over here have picked Pepsi.

SUZANNE MACK: Being able to compare the two, I'd pick Pepsi.
CHERIE: If someone offered me either or, I choose the Pepsi.
ANNCR: What will you say? Take the Pepsi Challenge and find out.

its current customer base. One way is to load them with the product, taking them out of the market for a certain time. Special price promotions, coupons, or bonus packs can encourage consumers to stock up on the brand. This not only keeps them using the company's brand but also reduces the likelihood they will switch brands in response to a competitor's promotion.

TARGETING A SPECIFIC MARKET SEGMENT

Most companies focus their marketing efforts on specific market segments and are always looking for ways to reach these target audiences. Many marketers are finding that sales promotion tools such as event sponsorships, contests and sweepstakes, and sampling are very effective ways to reach specific geographic, demographic, psychographic, and ethnic markets.

Event sponsorship has become a good sales promotion tool for reaching specific target markets. Golf tournaments are a popular event for sponsorship by marketers of luxury automobiles and other upscale products and services. The golf audience is affluent and highly educated, and marketers believe that golfers care passionately about the game, leading them to form emotional attachments to brands they associate with the sport.

Marketers can also turn their sponsorships into effective integrated marketing opportunities. For example, Cadillac is an umbrella sponsor of the Senior PGA TOUR, which fits well with its attempt to target age 40-plus professionals with incomes exceeding $60,000. On-site signage and vehicle displays are part of the sponsorship deal. The 13 Team Cadillac golfers, including such notables as Lee Trevino and Arnold Palmer, wear the automaker's logo during tournaments and also help in public relations by giving media interviews and representing Cadillac at tie-in events (Exhibit 15–7). In the weeks preceding an event, dealers send out as many as 20,000 direct-mail pieces to owners and prospects inviting them to visit a dealership for a test drive and to pick up tournament tickets and hospitality passes. Response to the direct-mail offerings averages 16 percent. Cadillac also gets automotive advertising exclusivity on the ESPN telecasts and often airs commercials featuring the Team Cadillac members.

Cadillac attributes $250 million in vehicle sales directly to its involvement with the tour since 1990. The dollar figure comes from tracking sales to prospects who respond to Cadillac's direct-marketing programs built around the tournament.[26] IMC Perspective 15–2 discusses how marketers are using event sponsorships and other sales promotion tools to target ethnic markets.

EXHIBIT 15—7
Cadillac targets a specific market segment with its sponsorship of the Senior PGA TOUR

ENHANCING ADVERTISING AND MARKETING EFFORTS

A final objective for consumer trade promotions is to enhance or support the advertising and marketing effort for the brand. Sales promotion techniques such as contests or sweepstakes are often used to draw attention to an ad and increase the consumer's involvement with the message and the product. Sales promotion programs can also encourage retailers to stock, display, and promote a brand during the promotional period. Cooperation from the trade is important to the success of a promotional program.

CONSUMER-ORIENTED SALES PROMOTION TECHNIQUES
Sampling

Marketers use various sales promotional techniques to meet the objectives just discussed. Figure 15–3 shows the extent to which these consumer promotions are used by package-goods companies.

Sampling involves a variety of procedures whereby consumers are given some quantity of a product for no charge to induce trial. Sampling is generally considered the most effective way to generate trial, although it is also the most expensive. As a sales promotion technique, sampling is often used to introduce a new product or brand to the market. However, as Figure 15–3 shows, sampling is also used for established products as well. Some companies do not use sampling for established products, reasoning that samples may not induce satisfied users of a competing brand to switch and may just go to the firm's current customers, who would buy the product. This may not be true when significant changes (new and improved) are made in a brand.

Manufacturers of package-goods products such as food, health care items, cosmetics, and toiletries are heavy users of sampling since their products meet the three criteria for an effective sampling program:

1. The products are of relatively low unit value, so samples do not cost too much.
2. The products are divisible, which means they can be broken into small sample sizes that are adequate for demonstrating the brand's features and benefits to the user.
3. The purchase cycle is relatively short, so the consumer will consider an immediate purchase or will not forget about the brand before the next purchase occasion.

BENEFITS AND LIMITATIONS OF SAMPLING

Samples are an excellent way to induce a prospective buyer to try a product or service. One expert estimates approximately 75 percent of the households receiving a sample will try it.[27] Sampling generates much higher trial rates than advertising or other sales promotion techniques.

IMC Perspective 15-2
Using Sales Promotion to Target Ethnic Markets

Ethnic markets are becoming very important to marketers in the United States. African, Hispanic, and Asian-Americans now spend an estimated $800 billion a year on brands, from Kraft macaroni & cheese to MCI long-distance service. Traditionally, marketers have targeted ethnic markets by running ads in ethnic TV, radio, and print media. However, many marketers are discovering that sales promotion techniques are more effective.

Ethnic groups are assimilating into mainstream culture more slowly than in past decades and immigrants want to retain their language and culture. For example, 90 percent of Hispanics prefer to communicate in Spanish. Marketers are finding that the best way to reach these consumers is by spending more dollars on local promotions tied to cultural events in ethnic neighborhoods.

Sears has developed a two-pronged event marketing strategy for reaching ethnic consumers. First, it sponsors mainstream events that have significant ethnic implications. For example, the company sponsored Hispanic singer Gloria Estefan's 1996–97 concert tour. The sponsorship included a national sweepstakes giving away trips to Hawaii for the final concert. A Hispanic overlay was used in TV advertising and in-store signage support. Second, Sears hosts grassroots events at stores and ties in with local festivals using its "Fiestamobile," a 30-foot Winnebago party on wheels. The Fiestamobile ties in with radio stations for live remote broadcasts in Sears parking lots and brings games and live music to create a carnival atmosphere that brings traffic into the store.

Dairy marketer Land O Lakes signed on as a title sponsor of the Los Angeles Hispanic youth soccer league, which has 14,000 players. In a promotion similar to Campbell Soup's longtime Labels for Education program, teams save Land O Lakes and Lake-to-Lake cheese UPCs for team uniforms and equipment. The company also gets signage and does sampling at games, which are big family events.

Land O Lakes has also begun tailoring account-specific marketing tactics to ethnic markets. The company has partnered with grocery store chains in southern California for quarterly coupon drops in Hispanic neighborhoods. The coupon drops are supported by radio spots telling consumers to watch for the coupons and ads showing traditional and mainstream recipe ideas for cooking with cheese.

Marketers are also targeting African-Americans with local promotions. For example, AT&T and Ford Motor Co. are national sponsors of the Universal Big Top Circus (also dubbed the "Cirque du Soul"), the only circus owned and run by African-Americans. A number of other companies, including McDonald's, PepsiCo, and Kraft Foods, have developed local tie-ins for the circus's 10-city tour, which draws over 1.1 million people.

As sales promotion becomes a more integral part of sophisticated ethnic marketing, ethnic ad agencies are expanding into the promotional area as an outgrowth of their cultural expertise. Clients are asking their agencies to add capabilities and broaden their expertise in developing programs to target ethnic groups. Brand managers and ethnic marketing specialists will continue mapping ethnic promotion strategies around a growing pool of events or creating their own to reach these fast-growing market segments.

Source: Betsy Spethmann, "Here Comes the Neighborhood," *Promo*, January 1997, pp. 51–58.

Getting people to try a product leads to a second benefit of sampling: consumers experience the brand directly, gaining a greater appreciation for its benefits. This can be particularly important when a product's features and benefits are difficult to describe through advertising. Many foods, beverages, and cosmetics have subtle features that are most appreciated when experienced directly.

The brand must have some unique or superior benefits for a sampling program to be worthwhile. Otherwise, the sampled consumers revert back to other brands and do not be-

FIGURE 15–3
Types of consumer promotions used in 1996

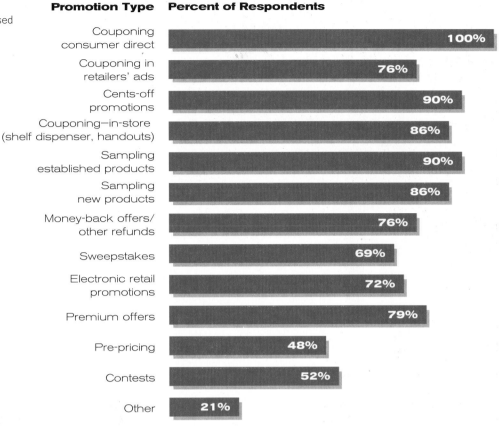

Promotion Type	Percent of Respondents
Couponing consumer direct	100%
Couponing in retailers' ads	76%
Cents-off promotions	90%
Couponing—in-store (shelf dispenser, handouts)	86%
Sampling established products	90%
Sampling new products	86%
Money-back offers/ other refunds	76%
Sweepstakes	69%
Electronic retail promotions	72%
Premium offers	79%
Pre-pricing	48%
Contests	52%
Other	21%

come repeat purchasers. The costs of a sampling program can be recovered only if it gets a number of consumers to become regular users of the brand at full retail price.

Another possible limitation to sampling is that the benefits of some products are difficult to gauge immediately, and the learning period required to appreciate the brand may require supplying the consumer with larger amounts of the brand than are affordable. An example would be an expensive skin cream that is promoted as preventing or reducing wrinkles but has to be used for an extended period before any effects are seen.

SAMPLING METHODS

One basic decision the sales promotion or brand manager must make is how the sample will be distributed. The sampling method chosen is important not only in terms of costs but also because it influences the type of consumer who receives the sample. The best sampling method gets the product to the best prospects for trial and subsequent repurchase. Some basic distribution methods include door-to-door, direct-mail, in-store, and on-package approaches.

Door-to-door sampling, in which the sample is delivered directly to the prospect's residence, is used when it is important to control where the samples are delivered. While virtually any type of product samples can be delivered this way, this method is on the decline because of the labor expense involved. Some companies have their samples delivered directly as part of a cooperative effort where several product samples are sent to a household together or through services such as Welcome Wagon, which calls on new residents in an area.

Sampling through the mail is common for small, lightweight, nonperishable products such as those shown in Exhibit 15–8. A major advantage of this method is that the marketer has control over where and when the product will be distributed and can target the sample to specific market areas. Many marketers are using information from target marketing programs such as Claritas's Prizm or Equifax/National Decision System's Microvision to better target their sample mailings. The main drawbacks to mail sampling are postal restrictions and increasing postal rates.

EXHIBIT 15–8   Product samples sent through the mail

EXHIBIT 15—9 Armor All uses on-package samples for related products

In-store sampling is increasingly popular, especially for food products. The marketer hires temporary demonstrators who set up a table or booth, prepare small samples of the product, and pass them out to shoppers. The in-store sampling approach can be very effective for food products, since consumers get to taste the item and the demonstrator can give them more information about the product while it is being sampled. Demonstrators may also give consumers a cents-off coupon for the sampled item to encourage immediate trial purchase. While this sampling method can be very effective, it can also be expensive and requires a great deal of planning, as well as the cooperation of retailers.

On-package sampling, where a sample of a product is attached to another item, is another common sampling method (see Exhibit 15–9). This procedure can be very cost effective, particularly for multiproduct firms that attach a sample of a new product to an existing brand's package. A drawback is that since the sample is distributed only to consumers who purchase the item to which it is attached, the sample will not reach nonusers of the carrier brand. Marketers can expand this sampling method by attaching the sample to multiple carrier brands and including samples with products not made by their company.

OTHER METHODS OF SAMPLING

The four sampling methods just discussed are the most common, but several other methods are also used. Marketers may insert packets in magazines or newspapers (particularly Sunday supplements). Some tobacco and cereal companies send samples to consumers who call toll-free numbers to request them or mail in sample request forms. As discussed in Chapter 14, these sampling methods are becoming popular because they can help marketers build a database for direct marketing.

Many companies also use specialized sample distribution services such as Advo Inc., Carol Wright Promotions, and D. L. Blair. These firms help the company identify consumers who are nonusers of a product or users of a competing brand and develop appropriate procedures for distributing a sample to them. Many college students receive sample packs at the beginning of the semester that contain trial sizes of such products as mouthwash, toothpaste, headache remedies, and deodorant.

Some companies cut back on their sampling programs in recent years because they felt they were too expensive, wasteful, and fraught with distribution problems. However, several factors have led to a resurgence in sampling recently. First, big companies like Advo and Time Warner have entered the sampling business, which creates more competition and helps keep sampling costs down. Also, a combination of technology and creativity is driving new sampling methods that let marketers target more efficiently. For example, Kendall-Futuro, the marketer of Curad adhesive strips, inserted kid-size bandage sample packs and coupons into 7.5 million McDonald's Happy Meals. The sampling promotion created so much exposure for the new brand, which was decorated with images of McDonald's characters, that the subsequent retail sell-in exceeded projections by 30 percent.[28]

Yet another factor may be the everyday low pricing strategies that have prompted companies such as Procter & Gamble to move away from coupons and other price promotions in favor of samples. Many marketers are finding that sampling meets the complementary goals of introducing consumers to their products and getting retailers to support their promotional programs.

Couponing

The oldest, most widely used, and most effective sales promotion tool is the cents-off coupon. Coupons have been around since 1895, when the C. W. Post Co. started using the penny-off coupon to sell its new Grape-Nuts cereal. In recent years, coupons have become increasingly popular with consumers, which may explain their explosive growth among manufacturers and retailers who use them as sales promotion incentives. As Figure 15–3 showed, coupons are the most popular sales promotion technique. They are used by nearly all the package-goods firms in the Carol Wright Promotions survey.

Coupon distribution rose dramatically in the last decade. The number of coupons distributed by marketers increased from 16 billion in 1968 to 310 billion in 1994 before falling to 268.5 billion in 1996. According to studies by NCH Promotional Services, over 80 per-

IMC Perspective 15–3
Marketers Cut Back on Coupons

Every year the average American household is barraged with nearly 3,000 coupons for everything from ketchup to kitty litter. Many marketers feel this is 3,000 too many and are cutting back dramatically on their use of coupons. According to NCH Promotional Services, which monitors coupon trends, the total number of coupons issued declined from 310 billion in 1994 to 268.5 billion in 1996. And while this means a lot of coupons are still being distributed, it is the lowest number since 1989.

Coupon promotions cost marketers roughly $8 billion a year, and more and more companies are questioning their value. Coupons have always been considered inefficient. Critics argue that they cost too much to print, distribute, and process and they don't benefit enough consumers. Fewer than 2 percent of the 268 billion coupons issued in 1996 were redeemed by consumers. According to coupon processor CMS Inc., the decline came partly because manufacturers, eager to limit their exposure, have cut the average time before expiration from 7.6 months in 1988 to 3.5. Durk Jager, president and chief operating officer at Procter & Gamble, echoes the sentiment of many consumer product companies when he says, "Who can argue for a practice that fails 98 percent of the time? It's ludicrous. We decided that coupons have to go."

Jager's company is leading the revolt against coupons. In early 1996 P&G reduced its total spending on coupons by 50 percent and eliminated all promotional coupons in three big New York test markets: Rochester, Syracuse, and Buffalo. Marketers have been watching to see whether P&G's test would spur a broad decline in the issuing of coupons by companies or whether competitors would increase coupon promotions in the test markets. P&G has refused to comment on its test. However, the company doesn't appear to have lost ground and competitors are not rushing to increase promotions.

P&G is actually finding that it has allies in the battle against coupons. Other consumer product companies have begun experimenting with different ways to wean consumers from coupons. Kimberly-Clark, P&G's archrival in diapers, is experimenting with a coupon cutback in the markets where the zero-coupon tests are being conducted. So are Clorox and Rubbermaid. Post Cereal, a division of Kraft Foods, has eliminated a plethora of coupons aimed at

individual cereals and now offers a single coupon good on any of its 23 cereals.

Despite the growing consensus among major marketers that coupons are inefficient and costly, very few companies, including P&G, are expected to abandon them entirely. Although most coupons never get used, shoppers have come to expect them. Some 83 percent of consumers use coupons some of the time, and 27 percent say they use them every time they shop. And die-hard coupon clippers won't give up without a fight. In Buffalo, one of P&G's zero coupon test markets, an Erie County legislator organized a petition drive calling on the company to rescind its decision.

With so many consumers eager for coupons, there will always be marketers willing to accommodate them—sometimes for good reasons. A coupon is still considered one of the best ways to get consumers to try a new product. Also, smaller companies with lesser-known brands have a better chance of attracting new users with a coupon offer. Advocates also argue that ads with coupons in them are read more closely. Even if the coupon isn't redeemed, it helps make the ad more effective. Love them or hate them, coupons have become a narcotic that neither marketers or consumers can easily kick.

Source: Raju Narisetti, "Many Companies Are Starting to Wean Shoppers Off Coupons," *The Wall Street Journal*, January 22, 1997, pp. B1, 10; "First Green Stamps. Now, Coupons?" *Business Week*, April 22, 1996, p. 68.

cent of U.S. households use coupons and 39 percent use five or more coupons per week. The average face value of coupons increased from 21 cents in 1981 to 67 cents in 1996.[29]

Adding additional fuel to the coupon explosion has been the vast number of coupons distributed through retailers that are not even included in these figures. In most markets, a number of grocery stores make manufacturers' coupons even more attractive to consumers by doubling their face value.

But now many companies are becoming less reliant on coupons and redemption rates are falling.[30] IMC Perspective 15–3 discusses why many companies are turning away from coupons.

ADVANTAGES AND LIMITATIONS OF COUPONS

Coupons have a number of advantages that make them popular sales promotional tools for both new and established products. First, coupons make it possible to offer a price reduction only to those consumers who are price sensitive. Such consumers generally purchase *because* of coupons, while those who are not as concerned about price buy the brand at full value. Coupons also make it possible to reduce the retail price of a product without relying on retailers for cooperation, which can often be a problem. Coupons are generally regarded as second only to sampling as a promotional technique for generating trial. Since a coupon lowers the price of a product, it reduces the consumer's perceived risk associated with trial of a new brand. Coupons can encourage repurchase after initial trial. Many new products include a cents–off coupon inside the package to encourage repeat purchase.

Coupons can also be useful promotional devices for established products. They can encourage nonusers to try a brand, encourage repeat purchase among current users, and get users to try a new, improved version of a brand. Coupons may also help coax users of a product to trade up to more expensive brands. In product categories such as disposable diapers, cereals, and detergents, coupons have become very popular. Figure 15–4 shows the most popular product categories for coupon users.

But there are a number of problems with coupons. First, it can be difficult to estimate how many consumers will use a coupon and when. Response to a coupon is rarely immediate; it typically takes anywhere from two to six months to redeem one. A study of coupon redemption patterns by Inman and McAlister found that many coupons are redeemed just before the expiration date rather than in the period following the initial coupon drop.[31] Many marketers are attempting to expedite redemption by shortening the time period before expiration. However, coupons remain less effective than sampling for inducing initial product trial in a short period.

A problem associated with using coupons to attract new users to an established brand is that it is difficult to prevent the coupons from being used by consumers who already use the brand. For example, General Foods decided to reduce its use of coupons for Maxwell House coffee when research revealed the coupons were being redeemed primarily by current users.

FIGURE 15–4

Percentage of purchases made with coupons in various product categories

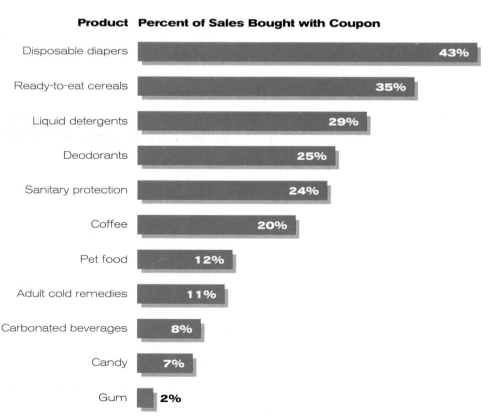

Product Percent of Sales Bought with Coupon

Product	Percent
Disposable diapers	43%
Ready-to-eat cereals	35%
Liquid detergents	29%
Deodorants	25%
Sanitary protection	24%
Coffee	20%
Pet food	12%
Adult cold remedies	11%
Carbonated beverages	8%
Candy	7%
Gum	2%

Rather than attracting new users, coupons can end up reducing the company's profit margins among consumers who would probably purchase the product anyway.

Other problems with coupons include low redemption rates and high costs. Couponing program expenses include the face value of the coupon redeemed plus costs for production, distribution, and handling of the coupons. Figure 15–5 shows the calculations used to determine the costs of a couponing program using an FSI (freestanding insert) in the Sunday newspaper and a coupon with an average face value of 67 cents. The marketer should track costs closely to ensure the promotion is economically feasible.

Another problem with coupon promotions is misredemption, or the cashing of a coupon without purchase of the brand. Coupon misredemption or fraud occurs in a number of ways, including:

- Redemption of coupons by consumers for a product or size not specified on the coupon.
- Redemption of coupons by salesclerks in exchange for cash.
- Gathering and redemption of coupons by store managers or owners without the accompanying sale of the product.
- Gathering or printing of coupons by criminals who sell them to unethical merchants, who in turn redeem them.

Estimates of coupon misredemption costs are as high as $500 million. Many manufacturers hold firm in their policy to not pay retailers for questionable amounts or suspicious types of coupon submissions. However, some companies are less aggressive, which affects their profit margins. Marketers must allow a certain percentage for misredemption when estimating the costs of a couponing program. Ways to identify and control coupon misredemption, such as improved coding, are being developed, but it still remains a problem.

COUPON DISTRIBUTION

Coupons can be disseminated to consumers in a number of ways, including freestanding inserts in Sunday newspapers, direct mail, newspapers (either in individual ads or as a group of coupons in a cooperative format), magazines, and packages. Distribution through newspaper *freestanding inserts* is by far the most popular method for delivering coupons to consumers, accounting for over 83 percent of all coupons distributed in 1996. This growth has come at the expense of vehicles such as manufacturers' ads in newspapers (newspaper ROP), newspaper co-op ads, and magazines.

There are a number of reasons why FSIs are the most popular way of delivering coupons, including their high-quality four-color graphics, competitive distribution costs,

FIGURE 15–5
Calculating couponing costs

Cost per Coupon Redeemed: An Illustration	
1. Distribution cost 55,000,000 circulation × $6.25/M	$343,750
2. Redemptions at 1.8%	990,000
3. Redemption cost 990,000 redemptions × $.67 face value	$663,300
4. Retailer handling cost and processor fees 990,000 redemptions × $.10	$99,000
5. Total program cost Items 1 + 3 + 4	$1,106,050
6. Cost per coupon redeemed Cost divided by redemptions	$1.12
7. Actual product sold on redemption (misredemption estimated at 20%) 990,000 × 80%	792,000
8. Cost per product moved Program cost divided by amount of product sold	$1.40

national same-day circulation, market selectivity, and the fact that they can be competition-free due to category exclusivity (by FSI company). Prices for a full-page FSI are currently about $6 to $7 per thousand, which makes FSI promotions very efficient and affordable. Because of their consumer popularity and predictable distribution, coupons distributed in FSIs are also a strong selling point with the retail trade.

The increased distribution of coupons through FSIs has, however, led to a clutter problem. Consumers are being bombarded with too many coupons, and although each FSI publisher offers product exclusivity in its insert, this advantage may be negated when there are three inserts in a Sunday paper. Redemption rates of FSI coupons have declined from 4 percent to only 1.4 percent and even lower for some products (Figure 15–6). These problems are leading many marketers to look at ways of delivering coupons that will result in less clutter and higher redemption rates, such as direct mail.

Direct mail accounts for about 3 percent of all coupons distributed. Most are sent by local retailers or through co-op mailings where a packet of coupons for many different products is sent to a household. These couponing programs include Cox Direct's Carol Wright Co-op, Metromail's Red Letter Day, Advo Systems' Mailbox Values, and Val-Pak Direct Marketing Systems.

Direct-mail couponing has several advantages. First, the mailing can be sent to a broad audience or targeted to specific geographic or demographic segments. Carol Wright Co-op, for example, has special mailings to teenagers, senior citizens, Hispanics, and other market segments. Firms that mail their own coupons can be quite selective about recipients. Another important advantage of direct-mail couponing is a redemption rate of nearly 4 percent, much higher than for FSIs. Direct-mail couponing can also be combined with a sample, which makes it a very effective way to gain the attention of consumers.

The major disadvantage of direct-mail coupon delivery is the expense relative to other distribution methods. The cost per thousand for distributing coupons through co-op mailings ranges from $10 to $15, and more targeted promotions can cost $20 to $25 or even more. Also, the higher redemption rate of mail-delivered coupons may result from the fact that

FIGURE 15–6

Coupon redemption rates by media

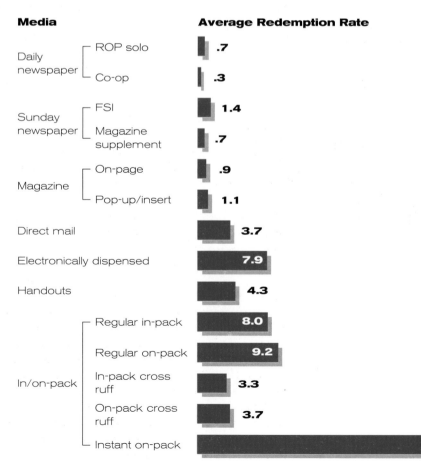

Media		Average Redemption Rate
Daily newspaper	ROP solo	.7
	Co-op	.3
Sunday newspaper	FSI	1.4
	Magazine supplement	.7
Magazine	On-page	.9
	Pop-up/insert	1.1
Direct mail		3.7
Electronically dispensed		7.9
Handouts		4.3
In/on-pack	Regular in-pack	8.0
	Regular on-pack	9.2
	In-pack cross ruff	3.3
	On-pack cross ruff	3.7
	Instant on-pack	31.8

many recipients are already users of the brand who take advantage of the coupons sent directly to them.

The use of *newspapers* and *magazines* as couponing vehicles has declined dramatically since the introduction of FSIs. In 1996 only 1.6 percent of coupons were distributed via newspapers. The advantages of newspapers as a couponing vehicle include market selectivity, shorter lead times with timing to the day, cooperative advertising opportunities that can lead to cost efficiencies, and promotional tie-ins with retailers. Other advantages of newspaper-delivered coupons are the broad exposure and consumer receptivity. Many consumers actively search the newspaper for coupons, especially on Sundays or "food day" (when grocery stores advertise their specials). This enhances the likelihood of the consumer at least noticing the coupon. Problems with newspapers as couponing vehicles include higher distribution costs, poor reproduction quality, clutter, and declining readership of newspapers; all contribute to low redemption rates.

The use of magazines as a couponing vehicle has also declined steadily since the introduction of FSIs. Magazines now account for only about 3 percent of the total number of coupons distributed each year. Distribution of coupons through magazines can take advantage of the selectivity of the publication to reach specific target audiences, along with enhanced production capabilities and extended copy life in the home. However, cost of distributing coupons through magazines is very high and redemption rates are low (just under 1 percent).

Placing coupons either *inside* or on the *outside* of the *package* is a distribution method that accounted for about 3 percent of the coupons distributed in 1996. The in/on package coupon has virtually no distribution costs and a much higher redemption rate than other couponing methods, averaging between 8 and 10 percent. An in/on pack coupon that is redeemable for the next purchase of the same brand is known as a **bounce-back coupon**. This type of coupon gives consumers an inducement to repurchase the brand.

Bounce-back coupons are often used with product samples to encourage the consumer to purchase the product after sampling. They may be included in or on the package during the early phases of a brand's life cycle to encourage repeat purchase, or they may be a defensive maneuver for a mature brand that is facing competitive pressure and wants to retain its current users. The main limitation of bounce-back coupons is that they go only to purchasers of the brand and thus do not attract nonusers. A bounce-back coupon placed on the package for Kellogg's Eggo brand waffles is shown here.

Another type of in/on pack coupon is the **cross-ruff coupon**, which is redeemable on the purchase of a different product, usually one made by the same company but occasionally through a tie-in with another manufacturer. Cross-ruff coupons have a redemption rate of 3 to 4 percent and can be effective in encouraging consumers to try other products or brands. Companies with wide product lines, such as cereal manufacturers, often use these coupons.

Yet another type of package coupon is the **instant coupon**, which is attached to the outside of the package so the consumer can rip it off and redeem it immediately at the time of purchase. Instant coupons have redemption levels of around 30 percent and give consumers an immediate point-of-purchase incentive. They can be selectively placed in terms of promotion timing and market region. Some companies prefer instant coupons to price-off deals because the latter require more cooperation from retailers and can be more expensive, since every package must be reduced in price.

Another distribution method that has experienced strong growth over the past 10 years or so is **in-store couponing**, which includes all co-op couponing programs distributed in a retail store environment. This medium now accounts for around 7 percent of total coupon distribution. Coupons are distributed to consumers in stores in several ways, including tear-off pads, handouts in the store (sometimes as part of a sampling demonstration), on-shelf dispensers, and electronic dispensers.

Most of the coupons distributed in stores are through ActMedia's Instant Coupon Machine. This coupon dispenser is mounted on the shelf in front of the product being promoted. It has blinking red lights to draw consumers' attention to the savings opportunity. These in-store coupons have several advantages: They can reach consumers when they are ready to make a purchase, increase brand awareness on the shelf, generate impulse buying, and encourage product trial. They also provide category exclusivity. In-store couponing removes the need for consumers to clip coupons from FSIs or print ads and then remember to bring them to the store. Redemption rates for coupons distributed by the Instant Coupon Machine are very high, averaging about 12 percent.

Another popular way to distribute in-store coupons is through electronic devices such as kiosks or at the checkout counter. Some electronically dispensed coupons, such as Catalina Marketing Corp.'s Checkout Coupon, are tied to scanner data at each grocery store checkout. When the specified product, such as a competitive brand, is purchased, the consumer receives a coupon at the checkout for the company's brand (Exhibit 15–10). Companies also use this system to link purchases of products that are related. For example, a consumer who purchases a caffeine-free cola might be issued a coupon for a decaffeinated coffee.

Major advantages of electronically dispensed checkout coupons are that they are cost effective and can be targeted to specific categories of consumers, such as users of competitive or complementary products. Since 65 to 85 percent of a manufacturer's coupons are used by current customers, marketers want to target their coupons to users of competitive brands. Redemption rates are also high for electronically dispensed coupons, averaging around 8 percent.

COUPONING TRENDS

Marketers are continually searching for more effective couponing techniques. General Mills, Kellogg, and Post recently replaced brand-specific coupons with universal coupons good for any of their cereal brands. For example, to make its couponing spending more efficient, Post began using universal coupons worth $1.50 off two boxes (matching the average cereal-coupon discount of 75 cents) and cut coupon distribution in half. Even though Post dropped only half as many coupons, redemption rates reached 6 percent, far exceeding the FSI average of less than 2 percent.[32]

Some marketers are broadening their use of account-specific direct-mail couponing, in which coupons are co-branded with individual retailers but can be used by consumers at any retail store. Procter & Gamble began using account-specific couponing with Tide detergent and has broadened the program to include mailings for a number of other brands.[33]

Some marketers and retailers are looking to the Internet as a medium for distributing coupons.[34] Several companies are testing online couponing services. Supermarkets Online, a division of Catalina Marketing, is extensively testing an online site in California where consumers can choose from a range of supermarkets and manufacturer- and retailer-sponsored downloadable coupons. Val-Pak, a company that distributes coupons by mail for local retailers, has had success in tests of online coupon distribution in several areas, including Richmond, Dayton, and Dallas, with each city site getting over 1,000 hits a day (Exhibit 15–11). A number of retailers, particularly supermarkets, are also using the Internet to distribute coupons to encourage consumers to shop at their stores.

Premiums

Premiums are a sales promotion device used by many marketers. A **premium** is an offer of an item of merchandise or service either free or at a low price that is an extra incentive for purchasers. Many marketers are eliminating toys and gimmicks in favor of value-added premiums that reflect the quality of the product and are consistent with its image and positioning in the market. Marketers spend over $20 billion a year on these value-added incentives. The two basic types of offers are the free premium and the self-liquidating premium.

FREE PREMIUMS

Free premiums are usually small gifts or merchandise included in the product package or sent to consumers who mail in a request along with a proof of purchase. In/on package free premiums include toys, balls, trading cards, or other items included in cereal packages, as

EXHIBIT 15—10 Catalina Marketing
promotes its checkout coupons

EXHIBIT 15—11 Coupons are now available online

well as samples of one product included with another. A recent survey found that in/on package premiums are consumers' favorite type of promotion.[35]

Package-carried premiums have high impulse value and can provide an extra incentive to buy the product. However, several problems are associated with their use. First, there is the cost factor, which results from the premium itself as well as from extra packaging that may be needed. Finding desirable premiums at reasonable costs can be difficult, particularly for adult markets, and using a poor premium may do more harm than good.

Another problem with these premiums is possible restrictions from regulatory agencies such as the Federal Trade Commission and the Food and Drug Administration or from industry codes regarding the type of premium used. The National Association of Broadcasters has strict guidelines regarding the advertising of premium offers to children. There is concern that premium offers will entice children to request a brand to get the promoted item and then never consume the product. Networks' policy on children's advertising is that a premium offer cannot exceed 15 seconds of a 30-second spot, and the emphasis must be on the product, not the premium.

Since most free mail-in premium offers require the consumer to send in more than one proof of purchase, they encourage repeat purchase and reward brand loyalty. But a major drawback of mail-in premiums is that they do not offer immediate reinforcement or reward to the purchaser, so they may not provide enough incentive to purchase the brand. Few consumers take advantage of mail-in premium offers; the average redemption rate is only 2 to 4 percent.[36]

Free premiums have become very popular in the restaurant industry, particularly among fast-food chains such as McDonald's and Burger King, which use premium offers in their kids' meals to attract children.[37] McDonald's has become the world's largest toymaker on a unit basis, commissioning about 750 million toys per year for its Happy Meals (Exhibit 15–12). Many of the premium offers used by the fast-food giants have cross-promotional tie-ins with popular movies and can be very effective at generating incremental sales. For example, Burger King's Kids Club meal sales doubled to more than 1,000 per week during the promotional tie-in with the hit Disney movie *Toy Story*. McDonald's gained a major competitive advantage in the movie tie-in premium wars recently when it signed an agreement with Disney giving McDonald's exclusive rights to promotional tie-ins with Disney movies.[38]

SELF-LIQUIDATING PREMIUMS

Self-liquidating premiums require the consumer to pay some or all of the cost of the premium plus handling and mailing costs. The marketer usually purchases items used as

EXHIBIT 15–12
McDonald's Happy Meals use toys to help attract children

self-liquidating premiums in large quantities and offers them to consumers at lower than retail prices. The goal is not to make a profit on the premium item but rather just to cover costs and offer a value to the consumer.

In addition to cost savings, self-liquidating premiums offer several advantages to marketers. Offering values to consumers through the premium products can create interest in the brand and goodwill that enhances the brand's image. These premiums can also encourage trade support and gain in-store displays for the brand and the premium offer. Self-liquidating premiums are often tied directly to the advertising campaign, so they extend the advertising message and contribute to consumer franchise building for a brand. For example, Philip Morris offers Western wear, outdoor items, and other types of Marlboro gear through its Marlboro Country catalog, which reinforces the cigarette brand's positioning theme.

Self-liquidating premium offers have the same basic limitations as mail-in premiums: a very low redemption rate. Fewer than 10 percent of U.S. households have ever sent for a premium, and fewer than 1 percent of self-liquidating offers are actually redeemed.[39] Low redemption rates can leave the marketer with a large supply of items with a logo or some other brand identification that makes them hard to dispose of. Thus, it is important to test consumers' reaction to a premium incentive and determine whether they perceive the offer as a value. Another option is to use premiums with no brand identification, but that detracts from their consumer franchise-building value.

The popularity of premium incentives as consumer motivators has declined as companies try to make their promotional programs more cost effective. Since 1991, the use of premium offers among package-goods manufacturers has fallen from 70 percent to 56 percent. Marketers are cutting back on stand-alone premium offers in favor of incentives that can be used as part of a strategic integrated marketing program.[40]

Contests and Sweepstakes

Contests and sweepstakes are an increasingly popular consumer-oriented promotion. Marketers spent $2.3 billion on these promotions in 1996, double the amount they spent five years ago. These promotions seem to have an appeal and glamour that tools like cents-off coupons lack. Contests and sweepstakes are exciting because, as one expert has noted, many consumers have a "pot of gold at the end of the rainbow mentality" and think they can win the big prizes being offered.[41]

There are differences between contests and sweepstakes. A **contest** is a promotion where consumers compete for prizes or money on the basis of skills or ability. The company determines winners by judging the entries or ascertaining which entry comes closest to some predetermined criteria (e.g., picking the winning teams and total number of points in the Super Bowl or NCAA basketball tournament). Contests usually provide a purchase incentive by requiring a proof of purchase to enter or an entry form that is available from a dealer or advertisement. Some contests require consumers to read an ad or package or visit a store display to gather information needed to enter. Marketers must be careful not to make their

Few promotions can generate as much excitement as a well-planned and executed contest, sweepstakes, or game. The lure of big money, travel, and merchandise prizes continues to entice consumers and exerts a strong pull for marketers looking to leverage the excitement that these chance promotions produce. At Kraft Foods, Inc., chance promotions are the fastest-growing promotional tools and

MONIQUE SOARES

play a major role in the integrated marketing strategies for brands such as Kraft Macaroni & Cheese, Kool-Aid, Jell-O, Oscar Mayer Lunchables, Tombstone Pizza, Post Cereals, and scores of others. The job of ensuring the promotions for the various Kraft Foods' brands are executed without a hitch belongs to Monique Soares, a senior associate promotions manager in Kraft's Promotions Resources Department.

Monique manages the execution of all chance promotions—contests, sweepstakes, and games for Kraft Foods. She coordinates all activities required to plan and execute a chance promotion. She notes: "You have to plan everything including rules development, odds generation, judging, prize fulfillment, and on-package disclaimers, and it all needs to happen within a short time frame." Monique works with brand managers, consumer promotion managers, and sales promotion agencies. She consults with the brand managers and consumer promotion managers when a promotion is being developed to understand its specific goals and objectives. Games, contests, and sweepstakes are used to achieve different objectives including building traffic, developing customer and prospect databases, and trade support. She notes it is often difficult to execute the creativity that marketing wants in a promotion, so her job is to find creative solutions for their ideas and concepts. She also works closely with Kraft Foods' sales promotion agencies, D.L. Blair and Simon Marketing, which handle the operations and execution aspects of chance promotions such as rules development, redemption, artwork review, and game piece printing.

Since joining Kraft Foods, Monique has used her expertise in chance promotions to help the company execute more than 60 national contests, sweepstakes, and games. She

"It's my job to ensure that the chance promotions for the various Kraft Food brands are executed without a hitch."

has worked on a variety of chance promotions for Kraft such as the "Jam with the Pros at School" Instant Win Game for Oscar Mayer Lunchables, where the winner gets to have an NBA basketball player come to his or her school to have lunch and play basketball. She has also been involved with Kraft's $60 million multibrand promotional partnership with Nickelodeon which is designed to establish a new brand mark: Kraft Kids Brands. The promotional alliance, backing 25 brands targeted at kids, began with a "Nick in the Afternoon" sweepstakes, which gave kids the chance to win a trip to the Nickelodeon studios in Orlando to host "Nick in the Afternoon" for a day.

Before joining Kraft Foods, Monique spent two years in the operational marketing division of Simon Marketing, Inc. where she managed the development and execution of promotions for McDonald's. She was involved with designing premium promotions for McDonald's Happy Meals, as well as the McDonald's Monopoly game. Monique's first marketing position was with Equity Management, Inc., a corporate trademark licensing firm, where she worked on the General Mills and Chevrolet Motor Division accounts.

Monique is a graduate of San Diego State University with a major in journalism and a minor in marketing. She is pursing her MBA in marketing while working at Kraft Foods, Inc. and plans to continue to specialize in the promotional area.

EXHIBIT 15—13   The Gillette 3-Point Challenge sweepstakes is tied to a popular sporting event

EXHIBIT 15—13   The Gillette 3-Point Challenge sweepstakes is tied to a popular sporting event

contests too difficult to enter, which might discourage participation among key prospects in the target audience.

A **sweepstakes** is a promotion where winners are determined purely by chance; it cannot require a proof of purchase as a condition for entry. Entrants need only submit their names for the prize drawing. While there is often an official entry form, handwritten entries must also be permitted. One form of sweepstakes is a **game**, which also has a chance element or odds of winning. Scratch-off cards with instant winners are a popular promotional tool. Some games occur over a longer period and require more involvement by consumers. Promotions where consumers must collect game pieces are popular among retailers and fast-food chains as a way to build store traffic and repeat purchases. For example, McDonald's has used promotions based on the game *Monopoly* several times in recent years.

Because they are easier to enter, sweepstakes attract more entries than contests. They are also easier and less expensive to administer, since every entry does not have to be checked or judged. Choosing the winning entry in a sweepstakes requires only the random selection of a winner from the pool of entries or generation of a number to match those held by sweepstakes entrants.

Contests and sweepstakes can get the consumer involved with a brand by making the promotion product relevant. For example, contests that ask consumers to suggest a name for a product or to submit recipes that use the brand can increase involvement levels. Nabisco developed an "Open a box, make up a snack," promotional contest for its three top cracker brands—Ritz, Triscuit, and Wheat Thins. Consumers sent in their favorite recipes, which were then made available on a dedicated website and at a toll-free number.

Sweepstakes and games can also be used to generate excitement by involving people with a popular and timely event. For example, the Gillette 3-Point Challenge offers consumers a chance to win a trip to the NCAA Men's or Women's Final Four basketball tournament and take a three-point shot worth $1 million (Exhibit 15–13).

PROBLEMS WITH CONTESTS AND SWEEPSTAKES

While the use of contests and sweepstakes continues to increase, there are some problems associated with these types of promotions. Many sweepstakes and/or contest promotions do little to contribute to consumer franchise building for a product or service and may even detract from it. The sweepstakes or contest often becomes the dominant focus rather than the brand, and little is accomplished other than giving away substantial amounts of money and/or prizes. Many promotional experts question the effectiveness of contests and sweepstakes. Some companies have cut back or even stopped using them because of concern over their effectiveness and fears that consumers might become dependent on them.

Numerous legal considerations affect the design and administration of contests and sweepstakes.[42] These promotions are regulated by several federal agencies, and each of the 50 states has its own rules. The regulation of contests and sweepstakes has helped clean up the abuses that plagued the industry in the late 1960s and has improved consumers' perceptions of these promotions. But companies must still be careful in designing a contest or sweepstakes and awarding prizes. Most firms use consultants that specialize in the design and administration of contests and sweepstakes to avoid any legal problems, but they may still run into problems with promotions, as discussed in Global Perspective 15–4.

A final problem with contests and sweepstakes is participation by professionals or hobbyists who submit many entries but have no intention of purchasing the product or service. Because most states make it illegal to require a purchase as a qualification for a sweepstakes entry, consumers can enter as many times as they wish. Professional players sometimes enter one sweepstakes several times, depending on the nature of the prizes and the number of entries the promotion attracts. Newsletters are even available that inform them of all the contests and sweepstakes being held, the entry dates, estimated probabilities of winning for various numbers of entries, how to enter, and solutions to any puzzles or other information that might be needed. The presence of these professional entrants not only defeats the purpose of the promotion but may also discourage entries from consumers who think their chances of winning are limited.

Global Perspective 15–4
Promotions Don't Always Go as Planned

Contests, sweepstakes, and other types of promotions are often used by marketers to give consumers an extra incentive to buy their products. However, when these promotions don't go as planned, they can embarrass a company or even create legal problems. Several major companies known for their marketing excellence have experienced major promotional blunders in recent years, both in the United States and abroad.

Coca-Cola lost millions of dollars and went through great turmoil in the summer of 1991 when its "Magi-can" promotion went awry. The liquid used to give the high-tech prize-bearing cans the same heft as Coke's regular cans leaked and the promotion had to be canceled. The Beatrice Co. ran into major legal problems when a computer buff cracked the contest code of a promotion tied to ABC's "Monday Night Football" and turned in 4,000 scratch-off cards worth $21 million in prize money. Millions of dollars in lawsuits were filed, although the case was eventually settled out of court.

Kraft also found out how expensive it can be when a promotion goes awry. A printing error resulted in tens of thousands of winning pieces being printed in a match-and-win sweepstakes for its cheese brands. Kraft canceled the promotion but still had to spend nearly $3.8 million to compensate the winners—versus the $36,000 budgeted for prizes. The snafu gave birth to what promotional professionals call "the Kraft clause," a disclaimer stating that a marketer reserves the right to cancel a promotion if there are problems and that a random drawing will be held if there are more winners than prizes.

These botched promotions were embarrassing for the companies and resulted in the loss of goodwill as well as money. But the consequences can be even worse, as PepsiCo discovered when a bottle-cap promotion went wrong in the Philippines. The local Pepsi bottler launched a Number Fever promotion offering a grand prize of 1 million pesos (about $36,000) to holders of bottle caps with the number 349 printed on them. Due to a computer glitch, the winning number appeared on more than 500,000 bottle caps, making the company liable for more than $18 billion in prize money.

When the error was discovered, Pepsi announced the problem and quickly offered to pay $19 for each winning cap. While more than 500,000 Filipinos have collected nearly $10 million from the company, thousands of others pursued the full amount in civil and criminal courts. The Filipino justice department found that Pepsi was not criminally liable and dismissed 7,000 lawsuits, but others are still pending. The furor caused by the botched promotion prompted anti-Pepsi rallies, death threats against Pepsi executives, and attacks on Pepsi trucks and bottling plants.

Sometimes marketers can run into problems when a promotion works too well. In April 1996 PepsiCo launched its Pepsi Stuff promotion, in which consumers collected award points from peel-off strips on Pepsi or Diet Pepsi. Some industry executives thought it might be too challenging for consumers. As it turned out, the contest wasn't challenging enough; redemptions were 50 percent higher than expected. This created a financial burden for bottlers, who had to pay half the costs of all prizes. Pepsi canceled the last phase of media advertising on the six-month campaign because too many consumers were claiming prizes.

Maytag Corp. also learned the hard way when it ran a promotion in the United Kingdom offering two free round-trip airline tickets with a purchase of a Hoover appliance for $150 or more. Nearly 100,000 consumers responded and it cost the company $48 million to cover the airfares. To make matters worse, Hoover's booking system couldn't order tickets fast enough, generating ill will among consumers and negative publicity for the company.

New technologies, especially the Internet, will provide new territory for various types of promotions. But as these examples show, marketers need to plan carefully when designing promotions at home or in foreign markets.

Sources: Glenn Heitsmith and Betsy Spethmann, "The Perils of Promotion," *Promo*, November 1996, pp. 22, 134; Robert Frank, "Pepsi Cancels an Ad Campaign as Customers Clamor for Stuff," *The Wall Street Journal*, June 27, 1996, pp. B1, 6; "Botched Pepsi Promotion Prompts Terrorist Attacks," *Promo*, September 1993, p. 10.

Refunds and Rebates

Refunds (also known as rebates) are offers by the manufacturer to return a portion of the product purchase price, usually after the consumer supplies some proof of purchase. Consumers are generally very responsive to rebate offers, particularly as the size of the savings increases. Rebates are used by makers of all types of products, ranging from package goods to major appliances and cars.

Package-goods marketers often use refund offers to induce trial of a new product or encourage users of another brand to switch. Consumers may perceive the savings offered through a cash refund as an immediate value that lowers the cost of the item, even though those savings are realized only if the consumer redeems the refund or rebate offer. Redemption rates for refund offers typically range from 1 to 3 percent for print and point-of-purchase offers and 5 percent for in/on package offers.[43]

Refund offers can also encourage repeat purchase. Many offers require consumers to send in multiple proofs of purchase. The size of the refund offer may even increase as the

EXHIBIT 15–14 Bonus packs provide more value for consumers

number of purchases gets larger. Some package-goods companies are switching away from cash refund offers to coupons or cash/coupon combinations. Using coupons in the refund offer enhances the likelihood of repeat purchase of the brand.

Rebates have become a widely used form of promotion for consumer durables. Products such as cameras, sporting goods, appliances, televisions, audio and video equipment, computers, and cars frequently use rebate offers to appeal to price-conscious consumers. The use of rebates for expensive items like cars was begun by Chrysler Corp. in 1981 to boost sales and generate cash for the struggling company. Rebates are now common not only in the auto industry and other durable products but for package-goods products as well.

EVALUATING REFUNDS AND REBATES

Rebates can help create new users and encourage brand switching or repeat purchase behavior, or they can be a way to offer a temporary price reduction. The rebate may be perceived as an immediate savings even though many consumers do not follow through on the offer. This perception can influence purchase even if the consumer fails to realize the savings, so the marketer can reduce price for much less than if it used a direct price-off deal.

Some problems are associated with refunds and rebates. Many consumers are not motivated by a refund offer because of the delay and the effort required to obtain the savings. They do not want to be bothered saving cash register receipts and proofs of purchase, filling out forms, and mailing in the offer.[44] A study of consumer perceptions found a negative relationship between the use of rebates and the perceived difficulties associated with the redemption process.[45] The study also found that consumers perceive manufacturers as offering rebates to sell products that are not faring well. Nonusers of rebates were particularly likely to perceive the redemption process as too complicated and to suspect manufacturers' motives. This implies that companies using rebates must simplify the redemption process and use other promotional elements such as advertising to retain consumer confidence in the brand.

When small refunds are being offered, marketers may find other promotional incentives such as coupons or bonus packs more effective. They must be careful not to overuse rebate offers and confuse consumers about the real price and value of a product or service. Also, consumers can become dependent on rebates and delay their purchases or purchase only brands for which a rebate is available. Many retailers have become disenchanted with rebates and the burden and expense of administering them.[46]

Bonus Packs

Bonus packs offer the consumer an extra amount of a product at the regular price by providing larger containers or extra units (Exhibit 15–14). Bonus packs result in a lower cost per unit for the consumer and provide extra value as well as more product for the money. There are several advantages to bonus pack promotions. First, they give marketers a direct way to provide extra value without having to get involved with complicated coupons or refund offers. The additional value of a bonus pack is generally obvious to the consumer and can have a strong impact on the purchase decision at the time of purchase.

Bonus packs can also be an effective defensive maneuver against a competitor's promotion or introduction of a new brand. By loading current users with large amounts of its product, a marketer can often remove these consumers from the market and make them less susceptible to a competitor's promotional efforts. Bonus packs may result in larger purchase orders and favorable display space in the store if relationships with retailers are good. They do, however, usually require additional shelf space without providing any extra profit margins for the retailer, so the marketer can encounter problems with bonus packs if trade relationships are not good. Another problem is that bonus packs may appeal primarily to current users who probably would have purchased the brand anyway or to promotion-sensitive consumers who may not become loyal to the brand.

Price-Off Deals

Another consumer-oriented promotion technique is the direct **price-off deal**, which reduces the price of the brand. Price-off reductions are typically offered right on the package through specially marked price packs, as shown in Exhibit 15–15. Typically, price-offs range from 10 to 25 percent off the regular price, with the reduction coming out of the manufac-

EXHIBIT 15—15 Examples of price-off packages

turer's profit margin, not the retailer's. Keeping the retailer's margin during a price-off promotion maintains its support and cooperation.

Marketers use price-off promotions for several reasons. First, since price-offs are controlled by the manufacturer, it can make sure the promotional discount reaches the consumer rather than being kept by the trade. Like bonus packs, price-off deals usually present a readily apparent value to shoppers, especially when they have a reference price point for the brand and thus recognize the value of the discount.[47] So price-offs can be a strong influence at the point of purchase when price comparisons are being made. Price-off promotions can also encourage consumers to purchase larger quantities, preempting competitors' promotions and leading to greater trade support.

Price-off promotions may not be favorably received by retailers, since they can create pricing and inventory problems. Most retailers will not accept packages with a specific price shown, so the familiar X amount off the regular price must be used. Also, like bonus packs, price-off deals appeal primarily to regular users instead of attracting nonusers. Finally, the Federal Trade Commission has regulations regarding the conditions that price-off labels must meet and the frequency and timing of their use.

Event Sponsorship

Another type of consumer-oriented promotion that has become popular in recent years is **event sponsorship**, in which a company develops sponsorship relations with a particular event. An estimated 4,800 companies spent nearly $5 billion on event sponsorships in 1996, nearly tripling the amount spent in 1988 (Figure 15–7). Sports receive two-thirds of the event sponsorship monies. Among the most popular sporting events for sponsorship are auto racing, golf and tennis tournaments, and running events. Professional sports leagues and teams as well as Olympic teams and competitions also receive large amounts of sponsorship money. Bicycle racing, beach volleyball, skiing, and various water sports are also attracting corporate sponsorship. Traditionally, tobacco, beer, and car companies have been among the largest sports event sponsors. Now a number of other companies have become involved in event sponsorships, including beverage companies, airlines, telecommunications and financial services companies, and high-tech firms.

Many marketers are attracted to event sponsorship because it gets their company and/or product names in front of consumers. By choosing the right events for sponsorship, companies can get visibility among their target market. For example, RJR Nabisco is heavily involved in sponsoring auto racing under its Winston and Camel cigarette brands. The company's market research showed that racing fans fit the demographic profile of users of these brands and consumers would purchase a product that sponsored their favorite sport.[48] For tobacco companies, which are prohibited from advertising on radio and TV, event sponsorship is also a way to have their brand names seen on TV. However, President Clinton issued an executive order in 1996 that would prohibit any form of advertising of tobacco

FIGURE 15—7 Breakdown of spending on event sponsorship

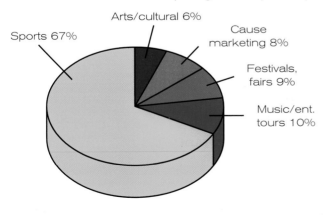

Where They Spend

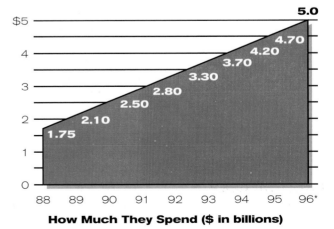

How Much They Spend ($ in billions)
*Projected.

sponsorships at sporting events after 1998. The tobacco companies are appealing this order in the courts on the grounds that to prohibit advertising a legal product violates free speech.[49]

Many companies are attracted to event sponsorships because effective IMC programs can be built around them and promotional tie-ins can be made to local, regional, national, and even international markets. Companies are finding event sponsorships an excellent platform from which to build equity and gain affinity with target audiences as well as a good public relations tool.

A major issue that continues to face the event sponsorship industry is incomplete research. As marketers become interested in targeted audiences, they will want more evidence that event sponsorship is effective and is a good return on their investment. Measuring the effectiveness of event sponsorships is discussed in Chapter 19.

TRADE-ORIENTED SALES PROMOTION
Objectives of Trade-Oriented Sales Promotion

Like consumer-oriented promotions, sales promotion programs targeted to the trade should be based on well-defined objectives and measurable goals and a consideration of what the marketer wants to accomplish. Typical objectives for promotions targeted to marketing intermediaries such as wholesalers and retailers include obtaining distribution and support for new products, maintaining support for established brands, encouraging retailers to display established brands, and building retail inventories.

OBTAIN DISTRIBUTION FOR NEW PRODUCTS

Trade promotions are often used to encourage retailers to give shelf space to new products. Manufacturers recognize that only a limited amount of shelf space is available in supermarkets, drugstores, and other major retail outlets. Thus, they provide retailers with financial incentives to stock new products. For example, Lever Brothers used heavy sampling and high-value coupons in the successful introduction of Lever 2000 bar soap. However, in addition to these consumer promotions, the company used discounts to the trade to encourage retailers to stock and promote the new brand.

While trade discounts or other special price deals are used to encourage retailers and wholesalers to stock a new brand, marketers may use other types of promotions to get them to push the brand. Merchandising allowances can get retailers to display a new product in high-traffic areas of stores, while incentive programs or contests can encourage wholesale or retail store personnel to push a new brand.

MAINTAIN TRADE SUPPORT FOR ESTABLISHED BRANDS

Trade promotions are often designed to maintain distribution and trade support for established brands. Brands that are in the mature phase of their product life cycle are vulnerable to losing wholesale and/or retail distribution, particularly if they are not differentiated or face competition from new products. Trade deals induce wholesalers and retailers to continue to carry weaker products because the discounts increase their profit margins. Brands with a smaller market share often rely heavily on trade promotions, since they lack the funds required to differentiate themselves from competitors through media advertising.

Even if a brand has a strong market position, trade promotions may be used as part of an overall marketing strategy. As discussed in IMC Perspective 15–1, Heinz has relied heavily on trade promotions to hold its market share position for many of its brands. Many consumer package-goods companies count on trade promotions to maintain retail distribution and support.

ENCOURAGE RETAILERS TO DISPLAY ESTABLISHED BRANDS

Another objective of trade-oriented promotions is to encourage retailers to display and promote an established brand. Marketers recognize that many purchase decisions are made in the store and promotional displays are an excellent way of generating sales. An important goal is to obtain retail store displays of a product away from its regular shelf location. A typical supermarket has approximately 50 display areas at the ends of aisles, near checkout counters, and elsewhere. Marketers want to have their products displayed in these areas to increase the probability shoppers will come into contact with them. Even a single display can increase a brand's sales significantly during a promotion.

Manufacturers often use multifaceted promotional programs to encourage retailers to promote their products at the retail level. For example, Exhibit 15–16 shows a brochure for a promotion Van Camp Seafood Co. used for its Chicken of the Sea brand tuna. The promotion included a variety of tools designed to increase retailer participation: manufacturer-sponsored advertising in local newspapers, display cards, and even free shoes for purchasing a specified number of cases. The program also encouraged retailers to participate by showing promotional offers targeted toward consumers, such as coupons, premiums, and rebate offers.

BUILD RETAIL INVENTORIES

Manufacturers often use trade promotions to build the inventory levels of retailers or other channel members. There are several reasons manufacturers want to load retailers with their products. First, wholesalers and retailers are more likely to push a product when they have high inventory levels rather than storing it in their warehouses or back rooms. Building channel members' inventories also ensures they will not run out of stock and thus miss sales opportunities.

Some manufacturers of seasonal products offer large promotional discounts so retailers will stock up on their products before the peak selling season begins. This enables the manufacturer to smooth out seasonal fluctuations in its production schedule and passes on some of the inventory carrying costs to retailers or wholesalers. When retailers stock up on a product before the peak selling season, they often run special promotions and offer discounts to consumers to reduce excess inventories.

Types of Trade-Oriented Promotions

Manufacturers use a variety of trade promotion tools as inducements for wholesalers and retailers. Next we examine some of the most often used types of trade promotions and some factors marketers must consider in using them. These promotions include contests and in-

EXHIBIT 15–16 Multifaceted promotional programs encourage retail participation and support for a brand

centives, trade allowances, displays and point-of-purchase materials, sales training programs, trade shows, and co-op advertising.

CONTESTS AND INCENTIVES

Manufacturers may develop contests or special incentive programs to stimulate greater selling effort and support from reseller management or sales personnel. Contests or incentive programs can be directed toward managers who work for a wholesaler or distributor as well as toward store or department managers at the retail level. Manufacturers often sponsor contests for resellers and use prizes such as trips or valuable merchandise as rewards for meeting sales quotas or other goals. Exhibit 15–17 shows a contest Van Camp sponsored for food-service distributors who call on restaurants.

Contests or special incentives are often targeted at the sales personnel of the wholesalers, distributors/dealers, or retailers. These salespeople are an important link in the distribution chain because they are likely to be very familiar with the market, more frequently in touch with the customer (whether it be another reseller or the ultimate consumer), and more numerous than the manufacturer's own sales organization. Manufacturers often devise incentives or contests for these sales personnel. These programs may involve cash payments made directly to the retailer's or wholesaler's sales staff to encourage them to promote and sell a manufacturer's product. These payments are known as **push money** (pm) or *spiffs*. For example, an appliance manufacturer may pay a $25 spiff to retail sales personnel for selling a certain model or size. In sales contests, salespeople can win trips or valuable merchandise for meeting certain goals established by the manufacturer. As shown in Figure 15–8, these incentives may be tied to product sales, new account placements, or merchandising efforts.

While contests and incentive programs can generate reseller support, they can also be a source of conflict between retail sales personnel and management. Some retailers want to maintain control over the selling activities of their sales staff. They don't want their salespeople devoting an undue amount of effort to trying to win a contest or receive incentives

EXHIBIT 15–17
This contest was targeted toward food-service distributors

FIGURE 15–8
Three forms of promotion targeted to reseller salespeople

- **Product or Program Sales**

  Awards are tied to the selling of a product, for example:

  Selling a specified number of cases

  Selling a specified number of units

  Selling a specified number of promotional programs

- **New Account Placements**

  Awards are tied to:

  The number of new accounts opened

  The number of new accounts ordering a minimum number of cases or units

  Promotional programs placed in new accounts

- **Merchandising Efforts**

  Awards are tied to:

  Establishing promotional programs (such as theme programs)

  Placing display racks, counter displays, and the like

offered by the manufacturer. Nor do they want their people becoming too aggressive in pushing products that serve their own interests instead of the product or model that is best for the customer.

Many retailers refuse to let their employees participate in manufacturer-sponsored contests or to accept incentive payments. Retailers that do allow them often have strict guidelines and require management approval of the program.

TRADE ALLOWANCES

Probably the most common trade promotion is some form of trade allowance, a discount or deal offered to retailers or wholesalers to encourage them to stock, promote, or display the manufacturer's products. Types of allowances offered to retailers include buying allowances, promotional or display allowances, and slotting allowances.

Buying Allowances

A buying allowance is a deal or discount offered to resellers in the form of a price reduction on merchandise ordered during a fixed period. These discounts are often in the form of an **off-invoice allowance**, which means a certain per-case amount or percentage is deducted from the invoice. A buying allowance can also take the form of *free goods*; the reseller gets extra cases with the purchase of specific amounts (for example, one free case with every 10 cases purchased).

Buying allowances are used for several reasons. They are easy to implement and are well accepted, and sometimes expected, by the trade. They are also an effective way to encourage resellers to buy the manufacturer's product, since they will want to take advantage of the discounts being offered during the allowance period. Manufacturers offer trade discounts expecting wholesalers and retailers to pass the price reduction through to consumers, resulting in greater sales. However, as discussed shortly, this is often not the case.

Promotional Allowances

Manufacturers often give retailers allowances or discounts for performing certain promotional or merchandising activities in support of their brands. These merchandising allowances can be given for providing special displays away from the product's regular shelf position, running in-store promotional programs, or including the product in an ad. The manufacturer generally has guidelines or a contract specifying the activity to be performed to qualify for the promotional allowance. The allowance is usually a fixed amount per case or a percentage deduction from the list price for merchandise ordered during the promotional period.

Slotting Allowances

In recent years, retailers have been demanding a special allowance for agreeing to handle a new product. Also called stocking allowances, introductory allowances, or street money, these are fees retailers charge for providing a slot or position to accommodate the new product. Retailers justify these fees by pointing out the costs associated with taking on so many new products each year, such as redesigning store shelves, entering the product into their computers, finding warehouse space, and briefing store employees on the new product.[50] They also note they are assuming some risk, since so many new product introductions fail.

Slotting fees can range from a few hundred dollars per store to $50,000 or more for an entire retail chain. Manufacturers that want to get their products on the shelves nationally can face several million dollars in slotting fees. Many marketers believe slotting allowances are a form of blackmail or bribery and say some 70 percent of these fees go directly to retailers' bottom lines.

Retailers can continue charging slotting fees because of their power and the limited availability of shelf space in supermarkets relative to the large numbers of products introduced each year. Some retailers have even been demanding **failure fees** if a new product does not hit a minimum sales level within a certain time. The fee is charged to cover the costs associated with stocking, maintaining inventories, and then pulling the product.[51] Large manufacturers with popular brands are less likely to pay slotting fees than smaller companies that lack leverage in negotiating with retailers.

Problems with Trade Allowances

Many companies are concerned about the abuse of trade allowances by wholesalers, retailers, and distributors. Marketers give retailers these trade allowances so the savings will be passed through to consumers in the form of lower prices, but companies such as Procter & Gamble claim that only 30 percent of trade promotion discounts actually reach consumers because 35 percent is lost in inefficiencies and another 35 percent is pocketed by retailers and wholesalers. Moreover, many marketers believe that the trade is taking advantage of their promotional deals and misusing promotional funds.

For example, many retailers and wholesalers engage in a practice known as **forward buying**, where they stock up on a product at the lower deal or off-invoice price and resell it to consumers after the marketer's promotional period ends. Another common practice is **diverting**, where a retailer or wholesaler takes advantage of the promotional deal and then sells some of the product purchased at the low price to a store outside its area or to a middleman who resells it to other stores.

Forward buying and diverting are widespread practices. Industry studies show that nearly 40 percent of wholesalers' and retailers' profits come from these activities. In addition to not passing discounts on to consumers, forward buying and diverting create other problems for manufacturers. They lead to huge swings in demand that cause production scheduling problems and leave manufacturers and retailers always building toward or drawing down from a promotional surge. Marketers also worry that the system leads to frequent price specials, so consumers learn to make purchases on the basis of what's on sale rather than developing any loyalty to their brands.

As mentioned in the chapter opener, the problems created by retailers' abuse led Procter & Gamble, one of the country's most powerful consumer products marketers, to adopt **everyday low pricing (EDLP)**, which lowers the list price of over 60 percent of its product line by 10 to 25 percent while cutting promotional allowances to the trade. The price cuts leave the overall cost of the product to retailers about the same as it would have been with the various trade allowance discounts.

P&G argues that EDLP eliminates problems such as deal buying, leads to regular low prices at the retail level, and helps build brand loyalty among consumers. Yet the EDLP strategy has caused great controversy in the trade, which depends heavily on promotions to attract consumers. Some retailers took P&G products off the shelf; others cut their ads and displays of the company's brands. Retailers prefer to operate on a *high/low strategy* of fre-

quent price specials and argue that EDLP puts them at a disadvantage against the warehouse stores and mass merchandisers that already use everyday low pricing. They also say that some products, such as those that are bought on impulse, thrive on promotions and don't lend themselves to EDLP. Retailers rely on promotions like end-of-aisle displays and price discounts to create excitement and generate incremental sales and profits from products like soft drinks, cookies, and candy.[52]

Critics of EDLP also note that while the strategy may work well for market leaders whose brands enjoy high loyalty, it is not effective for marketers trying to build market share or prop up lagging products. Moreover, many consumers are still motivated more by promotional deals and specials than by advertising claims from retailers promoting everyday low prices.

Despite the criticism, P&G says EDLP is paying off and volume is growing faster in its brands that have switched to the new pricing strategy. And it claims that market share in two-thirds of these product categories has increased. P&G recently extended its use of everyday low pricing to international markets, including the United Kingdom and Italy.[53]

DISPLAYS AND POINT-OF-PURCHASE MATERIALS

The next time you are in a store, take a moment to examine the various promotional materials used to display and sell products. Point-of-purchase displays are an important promotional tool because they can help a manufacturer obtain more effective in-store merchandising of products. Companies in the United States spend more than $12 billion a year on point-of-purchase materials, including end-of-aisle displays, banners, posters, shelf cards, motion pieces, and stand-up racks, among others. Exhibit 15–18 shows an award-winning point-of-purchase display for Top-Flite golf balls.

Many manufacturers help retailers use shelf space more efficiently through **planograms,** which are configurations of products that occupy a shelf section in a store. Some manufacturers are developing computer-based programs that allow retailers to input information from their scanner data and determine the best shelf layouts by experimenting with product movement, space utilization, profit yields, and other factors.[54]

SALES TRAINING PROGRAMS

Another form of manufacturer-sponsored promotional assistance is sales training programs for reseller personnel. Many products sold at the retail level require knowledgeable salespeople who can provide consumers with information about the features, benefits, and advantages of various brands and models. Cosmetics, appliances, computers, consumer electronics, and sporting equipment are examples of products for which consumers often rely on well-informed retail sales personnel for assistance.

Manufacturers provide sales training assistance to retail salespeople in a number of ways. They may conduct classes or training sessions that retail personnel can attend to increase their knowledge of a product or a product line. These training sessions present information and ideas on how to sell the manufacturer's product and may also include motivational components. Sales training classes for retail personnel are often sponsored by companies selling high-ticket items or complex products such as personal computers, cars, or ski equipment.

Another way manufacturers provide sales training assistance to retail employees is through their own sales force. Sales reps educate retail personnel about their product line and provide selling tips and other relevant information. The reps can provide ongoing sales training as they come into contact with retail sales staff on a regular basis and can update them on changes in the product line, market developments, competitive information, and the like.

Manufacturers also give resellers detailed sales manuals, product brochures, reference manuals, and other material. Many companies provide videocassettes for retail sales personnel that include product information, product-use demonstrations, and ideas on how to sell their product. These selling aids can often be used to provide information to customers as well. Exhibit 15–19 shows an example of sales training material that Cadillac provides for retail sales personnel.

EXHIBIT 15—19 An example of sales training material provided to retail sales personnel

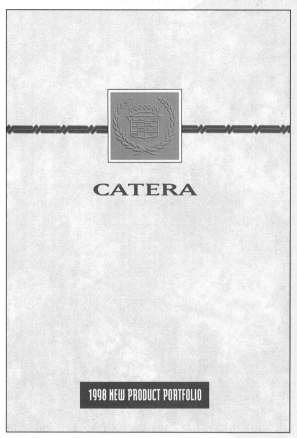

TRADE SHOWS

Another important promotional activity targeted to resellers is the **trade show**, a forum where manufacturers can display their products to current as well as prospective buyers. According to the Trade Show Bureau, nearly 100 million people attend the 5,000 trade shows each year in the United States and Canada, and the number of exhibiting companies exceeds 1.3 million. In many industries, trade shows are a major opportunity to display one's product lines and interact with customers. They are often attended by important management personnel from large retail chains as well as by distributors and other reseller representatives.

A number of promotional functions can be performed at trade shows, including demonstrating products, identifying new prospects, gathering customer and competitive information, and even writing orders for a product. Trade shows are particularly valuable for introducing new products, because resellers are often looking for new merchandise to stock. Shows can also be a source of valuable leads to follow up on through sales calls or direct marketing. The social aspect of trade shows is also important. Many companies use them to entertain key customers and to develop and maintain relationships with the trade. A recent academic study demonstrated that trade shows generate product awareness and interest and can have a measurable economic return.[55]

COOPERATIVE ADVERTISING

The final form of trade-oriented promotion we examine is **cooperative advertising**, where the cost of advertising is shared by more than one party. There are three types of cooperative advertising. Although the first two are not trade-oriented promotion, we should recognize their objectives and purpose.

Horizontal cooperative advertising refers to advertising sponsored in common by a group of retailers or other organizations providing products or services to the market. Ex-

EXHIBIT 15—20
Horizontal cooperative advertising is reflected in this ad for Colorado ski resorts

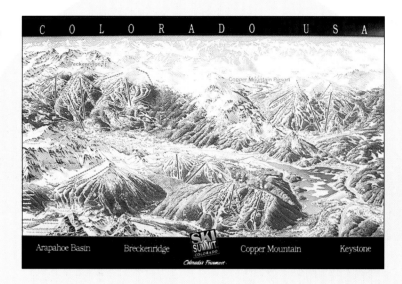

hibit 15–20 shows an ad representing a cooperative effort among ski resorts in Summit County, Colorado.

Ingredient-sponsored cooperative advertising is supported by raw materials manufacturers; its objective is to help establish end products that include the company's materials and/or ingredients. An example is the Intel Inside program sponsored by Intel Corp., which makes the microprocessors found in most personal computers. Intel provides PC makers with cooperative advertising monies based on the number of microprocessors they buy. In exchange, the computer companies display the Intel Inside logo in their ads.

The most common form of cooperative advertising is the trade-oriented form, **vertical cooperative advertising**, in which a manufacturer pays for a portion of the advertising a retailer runs to promote the manufacturer's product and its availability in the retailer's place of business. Manufacturers generally share the cost of advertising run by the retailer on a percentage basis (usually 50/50) up to a certain limit.

The amount of cooperative advertising the manufacturer pays for is usually based on a percentage of dollar purchases. If a retailer purchases $100,000 of product from a manufacturer, it may receive 3 percent, or $3,000, in cooperative advertising money. Large retail chains often combine their co-op budgets across all of their stores, which gives them a larger sum to work with and more media options.

Cooperative advertising can take on several forms. Retailers may advertise a manufacturer's product in, say, a newspaper ad featuring a number of different products, and the individual manufacturers reimburse the retailer for their portion of the ad. Or the ad may be prepared by the manufacturer and placed in the local media by the retailer. Exhibit 15–21 shows a cooperative ad format for New Balance athletic shoes that retailers in various market areas can use by simply inserting their store name and location.

Once a cooperative ad is run, the retailer requests reimbursement from the manufacturer for its percentage of the media costs. Manufacturers usually have specific requirements the ad must meet to qualify for co-op reimbursement, such as size, use of trademarks, content, and format. Verification that the ad was run is also required, in the form of a tearsheet (print) or an affidavit from the radio or TV station (broadcast) and an invoice.

As with other types of trade promotions, manufacturers have been increasing their cooperative advertising expenditures in recent years. Some companies have been moving money out of national advertising into cooperative advertising because they believe they can have greater impact with ad campaigns in local markets. There is also a trend toward more cooperative advertising programs initiated by retailers, who approach manufacturers with catalogs, promotional events they are planning, or advertising programs they have developed in conjunction with local media and ask them to pay a percentage of the cost. Manufacturers often go along with these requests, particularly when the retailer is large and powerful.[56]

EXHIBIT 15–21   An example of vertical cooperative advertising

Performance fit in a performance shoe.

new balance

Men's M851NV

STORE NAME HERE

COORDINATING SALES PROMOTION AND ADVERTISING

Those involved in the promotional process must recognize that sales promotion techniques usually work best in conjunction with advertising and that the effectiveness of an ad campaign can be enhanced by consumer-oriented sales promotion efforts. Rather than separate activities competing for a firm's promotional budget, advertising and sales promotion should be viewed as complementary tools. When properly planned and executed to work together, advertising and sales promotion can have a *synergistic effect* much greater than that of either promotional mix element alone.

Proper coordination of advertising and sales promotion is essential for the firm to take advantage of the opportunities offered by each tool and get the most out of its promotional budget. Successful integration of advertising and sales promotion requires decisions concerning not only the allocation of the budget to each area but also the coordination of the ad and sales promotion themes, the timing of the various promotional activities, and the target audience reached.

Budget Allocation

While many companies are spending more money on sales promotion than on media advertising, it is difficult to say just what percentage of a firm's overall promotional budget should be allocated to advertising versus consumer- and trade-oriented promotions. This allocation depends on a number of factors, including the specific promotional objectives of the campaign, the market and competitive situation, and the brand's stage in its life cycle.

Consider, for example, how allocation of the promotional budget may vary according to a brand's stage in the product life cycle. In the introductory stage, a large amount of the budget may be allocated to sales promotion techniques such as sampling and couponing to induce trial. In the growth stage, however, promotional dollars may be used primarily for advertising to stress brand differences and keep the brand name in consumers' minds.

When a brand moves to the maturity stage, advertising is primarily a reminder to keep consumers aware of the brand. Consumer-oriented sales promotions such as coupons, price-offs, premiums, and bonus packs may be needed periodically to maintain consumer loyalty, attract new users, and protect against competition. Trade-oriented promotions are needed to maintain shelf space and accommodate retailers' demands for better margins as well as encourage them to promote the brand. A study on the synergistic effects of advertising and promotion examined a brand in the mature phase of its life cycle and found that 80 percent of its sales at this stage were due to sales promotions. When a brand enters the decline stage of the product life cycle, most of the promotional support will probably be removed and expenditures on sales promotion are unlikely.

Coordination of Ad and Promotion Themes

To integrate the advertising and sales promotion programs successfully, the theme of consumer promotions should be tied in with the advertising and positioning theme wherever possible. Sales promotion tools should attempt to communicate a brand's unique attributes or benefits and to reinforce the sales message or campaign theme. In this way, the sales promotion effort contributes to the consumer franchise-building effort for the brand.

An example of this is the contest promotion for Taster's Choice coffee in Exhibit 15–22. Notice how this promotion is tied to the developing romance theme used in the TV campaign for Taster's Choice, which was discussed in Global Perspective 9–2.

Media Support and Timing

Media support for a sales promotion program is critical and should be coordinated with the media program for the ad campaign. Media advertising is often needed to deliver such sales promotion materials as coupons, sweepstakes, contest entry forms, premium offers, and even samples. It is also needed to inform consumers of a promotional offer as well as to create awareness, interest, and favorable attitudes toward the brand.

By using advertising in conjunction with a sales promotion program, marketers can make consumers aware of the brand and its benefits and increase their responsiveness to the promotion. Consumers are more likely to redeem a coupon or respond to a price-off deal for a brand they are familiar with than one they know nothing about. Moreover, product trial created through sales promotion techniques such as sampling or high-value couponing is more likely to result in long-term use of the brand when accompanied by advertising.[57]

Using a promotion without prior or concurrent advertising can limit its effectiveness and risk damaging the brand's image. If consumers perceive the brand as being promotion dependent or of lesser quality, they are not likely to develop favorable attitudes and long-term loyalty. Conversely, the effectiveness of an ad can be enhanced by a coupon, a premium offer, or an opportunity to enter a sweepstakes or contest.

An example of the effective coordination of advertising and sales promotion is the introductory campaign Lever Brothers developed for its Lever 2000 bar soap. As noted earlier in

EXHIBIT 15–22
This Taster's Choice contest is tied to the brand's ad campaign theme

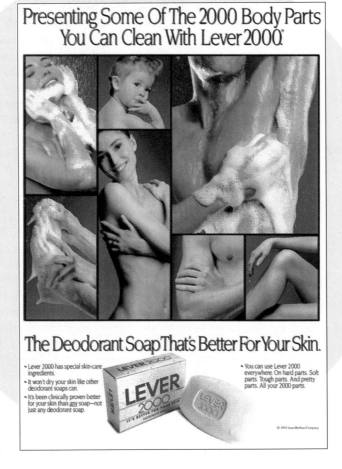

the chapter, Lever Brothers used high-value coupons, sent samples to half of U.S. house-holds, and offered discounts to retailers as part of its introductory marketing blitz. These sales promotion efforts were accompanied by heavy advertising in print and TV with the tagline "Presenting some of the 2000 body parts you can clean with Lever 2000" (Exhibit 15–23).

Sales promotion was important in inducing trial for Lever 2000 and continued after introduction in the form of couponing. But it was the strong positioning created through effective advertising that converted consumers to regular users. Repeat sales of the brand were at about 40 percent even after heavy discounting ended. Just six months after its introduction, Lever 2000 became the number-two deodorant soap in dollar volume, with an estimated 8.4 percent of the $1.5 billion bar-soap market.[58]

To coordinate their advertising and sales promotion programs more effectively, many companies are getting their sales promotion agencies more involved in the advertising and promotional planning process. Rather than hiring agencies to develop individual, nonfranchise-building types of promotions with short-term goals and tactics, many firms are having their sales promotion and advertising agencies work together to develop integrated promotional strategies and programs. Figure 15–9 shows how the role of sales promotion agencies is changing.

SALES PROMOTION ABUSE

The increasing use of sales promotion in marketing programs is more than a passing fad. It is a fundamental change in strategic decisions about how companies market their products and services. The value of this increased emphasis on sales promotion has been questioned by several writers, particularly with regard to the lack of adequate planning and management of sales promotion programs.[59]

Are marketers becoming too dependent on this element of the marketing program? Consumer and trade promotions can be a very effective tool for generating short-term increases

FIGURE 15–9

The shifting role of the promotion agency

Traditional	New and Improved
1. Primarily used to develop short-term tactics or concepts.	1. Used to develop long- and short-term promotional strategies as well as tactics.
2. Hired/compensated on a project-by-project basis.	2. Contracted on annual retainer, following formal agency reviews.
3. Many promotion agencies used a mix—each one hired for best task and/or specialty.	3. One or two exclusive promotion agencies for each division or brand group.
4. One or two contact people from agency.	4. Full team or core group on the account.
5. Promotion agency never equal to ad agency—doesn't work up front in annual planning process.	5. Promotion agency works on equal basis with ad agency—sits at planning table up front.
6. Not directly accountable for results.	6. Very much accountable—goes through a rigorous evaluation process.

in sales, and many brand managers would rather use a promotion to produce immediate sales than invest in advertising and build the brand's image over an extended time. As the director of sales promotion services at one large ad agency noted:

> There's a great temptation for quick sales fixes through promotions. It's a lot easier to offer the consumer an immediate price savings than to differentiate your product from a competitor's.[60]

Overuse of sales promotion can be detrimental to a brand in several ways. A brand that is constantly promoted may lose perceived value. Consumers often end up purchasing a brand because it is on sale, they get a premium, or they have a coupon, rather than basing their decision on a favorable attitude they have developed. When the extra promotional incentive is not available, they switch to another brand.

Alan Sawyer and Peter Dickson have used the concept of *attribution theory* to examine how sales promotion may affect consumer attitude formation.[61] According to this theory, people acquire attitudes by observing their own behavior and considering why they acted in a certain manner. Consumers who consistently purchase a brand because of a coupon or price-off deal may attribute their behavior to the external promotional incentive rather than to a favorable attitude toward the brand. By contrast, when no external incentive is available, consumers are more likely to attribute their purchase behavior to favorable underlying feelings about the brand.

Another potential problem with consumer-oriented promotions is that **a sales promotion trap** or spiral can result when several competitors use promotions extensively.[62] Often a firm begins using sales promotions to differentiate its product or service from the competition. If the promotion is successful and leads to a differential advantage (or even appears to do so), competitors may quickly copy it. When all the competitors are using sales promotions, it not only lowers profit margins for each firm but also makes it difficult for any one firm to hop off the promotional bandwagon.[63] This dilemma is shown in Figure 15–10.

A number of industries have fallen into this promotional trap. In the cosmetics industry, gift-with-purchase and purchase-with-purchase promotional offers were developed as a tac-

FIGURE 15–10

The sales promotion trap

All Other Firms	Our Firm Cut back promotions	Maintain promotions
Cut back promotions	Higher profits for all	Market share goes to our firm
Maintain promotions	Market share goes to all other firms	Market share stays constant; profits stay low

tic for getting buyers to sample new products. But they have become a common, and costly, way of doing business.[64] In many areas of the country, supermarkets have gotten into the trap of doubling or even tripling manufacturers' coupons, which cuts into their already small profit margins.

Fast-food chains have also fallen into the trap with promotions featuring popular menu items, such as Burger King's Whopper for 99 cents. In early 1997 McDonald's began another round of promotional wars with its Campaign 55, dropping the price of popular items like the Big Mac, Quarter Pounder, and Arch Deluxe to 55 cents with the purchase of french fries and a soft drink. If this promotion had been successful, the other fast-food chains may have had little choice but to match it.[65]

Marketers must consider both the short-term impact of a promotion and its long-term effect on the brand. The ease with which competitors can develop a retaliatory promotion and the likelihood of their doing so should also be considered. Marketers must be careful not to damage the brand franchise with sales promotions or to get the firm involved in a promotional war that erodes the brand's profit margins and threatens its long-term existence. Marketers are often tempted to resort to sales promotions to deal with declining sales and other problems when they should examine such other aspects of the marketing program as channel relations, price, packaging, product quality, or advertising.

SUMMARY

For many years, advertising was the major promotional mix element for most consumer product companies. Over the past decade, however, marketers have been allocating more of their promotional dollars to sales promotion. There has been a steady increase in the use of sales promotion techniques to influence consumers' purchase behavior. The growing power of retailers, erosion of brand loyalty, increase in consumers' sensitivity to promotions, increase in new product introductions, fragmentation of the consumer market, short-term focus of marketing and brand managers, and increase in advertising clutter are some of the reasons for this increase.

Sales promotions can be characterized as either franchise building or nonfranchise building. The former contribute to the long-term development and reinforcement of brand identity and image; the latter are designed to accelerate the purchase process and generate immediate increases in sales.

Sales promotion techniques can be classified as either trade or consumer oriented. A number of consumer-oriented sales promotion techniques were examined in this chapter, including sampling, couponing, premiums, contests and sweepstakes, rebates and refunds, bonus packs, price-off deals, and event sponsorships. The characteristics of these promotional tools were examined, along with their

advantages and limitations. Various trade-oriented promotions were also examined, including trade contests and incentives, trade allowances, displays and point-of-purchase materials, sales training programs, trade shows, and cooperative advertising.

Advertising and sales promotion should not be viewed as separate activities but rather as complementary tools. When planned and executed properly, advertising and sales promotion can produce a synergistic effect that is greater than the response generated from either promotional mix element alone. To accomplish this, marketers must coordinate budgets, advertising and promotional themes, media scheduling and timing, and target audiences.

Sales promotion abuse can result when marketers become too dependent on the use of sales promotion techniques and sacrifice long-term brand position and image for short-term sales increases. Many industries experience sales promotion traps when a number of competitors use promotions extensively and it becomes difficult for any single firm to cut back on promotion without risking a loss in sales. Overuse of sales promotion tools can lower profit margins and threaten the image and even the viability of a brand.

KEY TERMS

sales promotion, 470
consumer-oriented sales
   promotion, 471
trade-oriented sales
   promotion, 471

account-specific
   marketing, 475
consumer franchise-
   building (CFB)
   promotions, 476

nonfranchise-building
   (non-FB) promotions, 478
sampling, 481
bounce-back coupon, 489
cross-ruff coupon, 489

instant coupon, 489
in-store couponing, 489
premium, 490
self-liquidating
   premiums, 491

DISCUSSION QUESTIONS

1. The opening vignette discusses how Procter & Gamble and other consumer-product marketers are simplifying their marketing programs, particularly with regard to promotions. How will these simplification efforts affect their use of sales promotions?

2. What are the differences between consumer-oriented and trade-oriented sales promotions? Discuss the role of each in a firm's IMC program.

3. What is meant by account-specific marketing and how does it affect sales promotion strategies?

4. Discuss the various reasons sales promotion has become so important and is receiving an increasing portion of marketers' promotional budgets. Do you think the allocation trend toward sales promotion will continue? Why or why not?

5. IMC Perspective 15–1 discusses how Heinz cut back on advertising and allocated most of its promotional dollars to sales promotion. How much should a company like Heinz be spending on advertising versus sales promotion? How might an advertising manager at Heinz persuade top management to allocate more money to advertising?

6. What are the differences between consumer franchise-building and nonfranchise-building promotions? Find an example of a promotion you believe contributes to the franchise of the brand and explain why.

7. Do you think the sharp decline in coupon distribution will continue? How might marketers compete without coupons and/or become more efficient in their couponing strategies?

8. Discuss some of the reasons why event sponsorships are becoming so popular. How might a marketer build an IMC program around sponsorship of an event such as a tennis tournament?

9. Discuss how advertising and sales promotion can have a synergistic effect and what is required to create this effect.

10. What is meant by a sales promotion trap? Do you think McDonald's could have created a sales promotion spiral with its Campaign 55 promotional strategy? What are the options for a company involved in such a situation?

CHAPTER 16

Public Relations, Publicity, and Corporate Advertising

Chapter Objectives

- To demonstrate the roles of public relations, publicity, and corporate advertising in the promotional mix.

- To differentiate between public relations and publicity and demonstrate the advantages and disadvantages of each.

- To examine the reasons for corporate advertising and its advantages and disadvantages.

- To examine methods for measuring the effects of public relations, publicity, and corporate advertising.

PUBLICITY STUNTS OR SMART MARKETING?

The crowd standing in front of the window of NBC's "Today" show studio often looks like a series of walking TV commercials. People dressed like dogs, candy bars, and lima beans wait in line or meander about, while BMWs and WeinerMobiles cruise the streets. More conventionally dressed people often wave products and/or signs in front of the NBC cameras at every opportunity. What are they doing? They are trying to get free air time for their products, organizations, or ideas.

Trying to get free air time is nothing new, but it has never been so organized and sophisticated. Companies are trying everything they can to get their products on television without paying for it. And why not? A 30-second commercial on the "Today" show, for example, now costs over $25,000 and is seen by millions of viewers. Almost any exposure is valuable. Public relations agencies that achieve these goals pride themselves on their creativity and value to their clients, Consider these attempts to get on the "Today" show:

- Old Navy sent five people dressed as Old Navy candy bars.
- MGM/UA sent an employee dressed as a dog to get publicity for its movie *All Dogs Go to Heaven 2*.
- The Oscar Mayer WeinerMobile is a frequent visitor.
- Saatchi & Saatchi employees waved boxes of Cheerios until Katie Couric tasted them.

Even the chair of BMW's North American unit, Helmut Panke, got involved by pulling up to the NBC window to take Bryant Gumbel for a ride in the new BMW Z3 roadster on the opening day of the James Bond movie *GoldenEye*. (Bond drives the car in the movie.) Other companies that have crashed the "Today" show include Avon, Gap, McDonald's and the Soybean Council—to name a few.

But that's not the only way to get free publicity and air time. Ronald McDonald attended the Academy Awards, the Kentucky Derby, and a Chicago Bulls basketball game (courtside with Dennis Rodman) to tout the Arch Deluxe. Snapple sent out "samplers" (employees distributing free bottles of Snapple) to create events at Little League games, college sporting events, and other sites, giving away over 10 million bottles in 60 days. Taco Bell took out full-page ads to announce that it had purchased the Liberty Bell (an April Fool's day publicity stunt) and gave away a free Taco Bell franchise (valued at $1 million). Both generated a lot of free air time.

When these efforts are successful, the results benefit both the clients and the PR agencies that typically sponsor them. But they don't always work. NBC has become increasingly agitated by the number of attempts to get on the show. It says it is not in the business to give away free ad time and has taken steps to keep publicity seekers from being shown or mentioned. Other networks have taken similar positions. They ignore most attempts and denounce the rest as publicity ploys.

At the same time, however, NBC still can't avoid a good shtick. When Oscar Mayer sent its WeinerMobile around with "Happy Birthday Bryant" painted on its buns, it won a prominent appearance on the show. Larry Fowler of Fowler's clothing store in St. Louis was able to get an interview by bringing two silver Western-style belt buckles for the anchors. Beanie's efforts to gain attention by passing out chocolate-covered lima beans didn't fare as well. Maybe it all depends on what you're offering?

Sources: Judann Pollack, "New Marketing Spin: The PR 'Experience,'" *Advertising Age*, August 5, 1996, p. 33; David Kirkpatrick, "Advertisers Crash Crowd Outside *Today*," *The Wall Street Journal*, April 24, 1996, p. B1.

The attempt to generate free publicity cited in the lead-in are just some examples of the many ways organizations integrate public relations programs with other elements of the promotional mix to market their products more effectively. These efforts have become such an integral part of the IMC mix that many agencies have formed departments within the public relations area specifically for this purpose. McCann-Erickson refers to it as experiential branding, while Puris Lintas calls it idea engineering. Whatever you call it, such efforts are clearly on the increase.[1] Besides generating increased sales, the good publicity provides long-term benefits.

Publicity, public relations, and corporate advertising all have promotional program elements that may be of great benefit to marketers. They are integral parts of the overall promotional effort that must be managed and coordinated with the other elements of the promotion mix. However, these three tools do not always have the specific objectives of product and service promotion, nor do they always involve the same methods you have become accustomed to as you have read this text. Typically, these activities are designed more to change attitudes toward an organization or issue than to promote specific products or affect behaviors directly (though you will see that this role is changing in some organizations). This chapter explores the roles of public relations, publicity, and corporate advertising, the advantages and disadvantages of each, and the process by which they are employed. Examples of such efforts—both successful and unsuccessful—are also included.

PUBLIC RELATIONS

What is public relations? How does it differ from other elements of marketing discussed thus far? Perhaps a good starting point is to define what the term public relations has traditionally meant and then to introduce its new role.

The Traditional Definition of PR

A variety of books define **public relations**, but perhaps the most comprehensive definition is that offered by the *Public Relations News* (the weekly newsletter of the industry):

> the management function which evaluates public attitudes, identifies the policies and procedures of an organization with the public interest, and executes a program of action (and communication) to earn public understanding and acceptance.[2]

Public relations is indeed a management function. The term *management* should be used in its broadest sense; it is not limited to business managements but extends to other types of organizations, including nonprofit institutions.

In this definition, public relations requires a series of stages, including:

1. The determination and evaluation of public attitudes.
2. The identification of policies and procedures of an organization with a public interest.
3. The development and execution of a communications program designed to bring about public understanding and acceptance.

This process does not occur all at once. An effective public relations program continues over months or even years.

Finally, this definition reveals that public relations involves much more than activities designed to sell a product or service. The PR program may involve some of the promotional program elements previously discussed but use them in a different way. For example, press releases may be mailed to announce new products or changes in the organization, special events may be organized to create goodwill in the community, and advertising may be used to state the firm's position on a controversial issue.

The New Role of PR

In an increasing number of marketing-oriented companies, new responsibilities have been established for public relations. It takes on a much broader (and more marketing-oriented) perspective, designed to promote the organization as well as its products and/or services.

FIGURE 16—1
Four classes of marketing and public relations use

	Public Relations	
Marketing	**Weak**	**Strong**
Weak	**1** Example: Small social service agencies	**2** Example: Hospitals and colleges
Strong	**3** Example: Small manufacturing companies	**4** Example: Fortune 500 companies

Figure 16–1 demonstrates four relationships that marketing and public relations can assume in an organization. These relationships are defined by the degree of use of each function.

Class 1 relationships are characterized by a minimal use of either function. Organizations with this design typically have very small marketing and/or public relations budgets and devote little time and effort to them. Small social service agencies and nonprofit organizations are typically class 1.

Organizations characterized by a *class 2* relationship have a well-established public relations function but do very little in the way of formal marketing. Colleges and hospitals typically have such a design, although in both cases marketing activities are increasing. Both of these groups have moved in the direction of class 4 organizations in recent years, though PR activities still dominate.

Many small companies are typified by a *class 3* organization in which marketing dominates and the public relations function is minimal. Private companies (without stockholders) and small manufacturers with little or no public to appease tend to employ this design.

Class 4 enterprises have both strong marketing and strong public relations. These two departments often operate independently. For example, public relations may be responsible for the more traditional responsibilities described earlier, while marketing promotes specific products and/or services. Both groups may work together at times, and both report to top management. Many Fortune 500 companies employ multiple ad agencies and PR firms.

The new role of public relations might best be characterized as class 4, although with a slightly different relationship. Rather than each department operating independently, the two now work closely together, blending their talents to provide the best overall image of the firm and its product or service offerings. Public relations departments increasingly position themselves as a tool to both supplant and support traditional advertising and marketing efforts and as a key part of the IMC program.

Writing in *Advertising Age*, William N. Curry notes that organizations must use caution in developing class 4 relationships because PR and marketing are not the same thing, and when one becomes dominant, the balance required to operate at maximum efficiency is lost.[3] He says losing sight of the objectives and functions of public relations in an attempt to achieve marketing goals may be detrimental in the long run. Others take an even stronger view that if public relations and marketing distinctions continue to blur, the independence of the PR function will be lost and it will become much less effective.[4] In this book, we take the position that in a truly integrated marketing communications program, public relations must play an integral role.

Integrating PR into the Promotional Mix

Given the broader responsibilities of public relations, the issue is how to integrate it into the promotional mix. Philip Kotler and William Mindak suggest a number of alternative organizational designs: either marketing or public relations can be the dominant function; both can be equal but separate functions; or the two can perform the same roles.[5] While each of these designs has its merits, in this text we consider public relations a promotional program element. This means that its broad role must include traditional responsibilities.

Whether public relations takes on a traditional role or a more marketing-oriented one, PR activities are still tied to specific communications objectives. Assessing public attitudes and creating a favorable corporate image are no less important than promoting products or services directly.

Marketing Public Relations (MPR) Functions

Thomas L. Harris has referred to public relations activities designed to support marketing objectives as **marketing public relations (MPR)** functions.[6] Marketing objectives that may be aided by public relations activities include raising awareness, informing and educating, gaining understanding, building trust, giving consumers a reason to buy, and motivating consumer acceptance. MPR adds value to the integrated marketing program in a number of ways:

- Building marketplace excitement before media advertising breaks. The announcement of a new product, for example, is an opportunity for the marketer to obtain publicity and dramatize the product, thereby increasing the effectiveness of ads.
- Creating advertising news where there is no product news. Ads themselves can be the focus of publicity. Pepsi, Apple Computer, and others have received millions of dollars of free exposure through their public relations activities surrounding Michael Jackson, Madonna, Ray Charles, and the Apple Macintosh.
- Introducing a product with little or no advertising. You will see later in this chapter that this strategy has been implemented successfully by Hewlett-Packard and No Excuses jeans. Crayon manufacturer Crayola has also used this approach to its advantage.
- Providing a value-added customer service. Butterball established a hot line where people can call in to receive personal advice on how to prepare their turkeys. The company handled 25,000 calls during one holiday season. Many companies provide such services on their Internet sites.
- Building brand-to-customer bonds. The Pillsbury Bake-Off has led to strong brand loyalty among Pillsbury customers, who compete by submitting baked goods.
- Influencing the influentials—that is, providing information to opinion leaders.
- Defending products at risk and giving consumers a reason to buy. By taking constructive actions to defend a company's products, PR can actually give consumers a reason to buy. Harris notes that Heinz and McDonald's have worked with environmental groups and have been rewarded by consumers for it. As shown in Figure 16–2, a number of companies have employed these strategies successfully.

FIGURE 16–2

MPRs add value to marketing program

Campbell's Soup. The company's PR-only program for the 40th anniversary of Swanson frozen dinners produced a 44 percent sales and two-share-point increase without a dime of paid advertising. The program used press releases and a video news release.

WD-40. A two-month promotion to ask consumers how they used WD-40 led to over 1,200 entries, coverage on many TV stations, and a front-page write-up in *USA Today's* national and international editions. Even the tabloid *Sun* ran a front-page story.

Cabbage Patch Kids. The runaway success of the Cabbage Patch Kids dolls was the result of a sophisticated PR effort that saw them featured by every major TV station, newspaper, and general-interest magazine in the United States.

Ford Motor Co. Ford achieved 50 percent brand awareness and orders for 146,000 Tauruses and Sables before they were ever advertised or released for sale, due to a strong MPR campaign.

Cuisinart. An article in *Gourmet* magazine led to the launch of the food-processor category and more orders for Cuisinart than the company could handle.

Saucony. Hyde Athletic Industries doubled its sales when Consumer Reports awarded the Saucony Jazz 3000 running shoe with its top rating.

Goodyear. An effective publicity campaign sold 150,000 Aquatred tires before the first ads broke.

Sources: Judann Pollack, "New Marketing Spin: The PR 'Experience,'" *Advertising Age*, August 5, 1996, p. 33; Thomas L. Harris, "How MPR Adds Value to Integrated Marketing Communications," *Public Relations Quarterly* 38, no. 2 (Summer 1993), pp. 13–19.

THE PROCESS OF PUBLIC RELATIONS
Determining and Evaluating Public Attitudes

The actual process of conducting public relations and integrating it into the promotional mix involves a series of both traditional and marketing-oriented tasks.

You've learned that public relations is concerned with people's attitudes toward the firm or specific issues beyond those directed at a product or service. The first question you may ask is why. Why is the firm so concerned with the public's attitudes?

One reason is that these attitudes may affect sales of the firm's products. A number of companies have experienced sales declines as a result of consumer boycotts. Procter & Gamble, Coors, Nike, and Bumble Bee Seafoods are just a few companies that responded to organized pressures. When high-ranking Texaco officials were caught on tape allegedly making racial slurs, the negative publicity led to public outrage. Texaco was hit with a $520 million racial discrimination lawsuit, as well as a second lawsuit by shareholders against Texaco directors and executives for failing to check racist attitudes and practices in the company. The city of Philadelphia voted to sell more than $5.6 million in Texaco stock as a protest.[7] Exhibit 16–1 shows an ad run by Texaco in response to the controversy.

Second, no one wants to be perceived as a bad citizen. Corporations exist in communities, and their employees may both work and live there. Negative attitudes carry over to employee morale and may result in a less than optimal working environment internally and in the community.

Due to their concerns about public perceptions, many privately held corporations, publicly held companies, utilities, and the media survey public attitudes. The reasons for conducting this research are many.

1. It provides input into the planning process. Once the firm has determined public attitudes, they become the starting point in the development of programs designed to maintain favorable positions or change unfavorable ones.
2. It serves as an early warning system. Once a problem exists, it may require substantial time and money to correct. By conducting research, the firm may be able to identify potential problems and handle them effectively before they become serious issues.
3. It secures support internally. If research shows a problem or potential problem exists, it will be much easier for the public relations arm to gain the support it needs to address this problem.
4. It increases the effectiveness of the communication. The better it understands a problem, the better the firm can design communications to deal with it.[8]

Establishing a PR Plan

In a survey of 100 top and middle managers in the communications field, over 60 percent said their PR programs involved little more than press releases, press kits for trade shows, and new product announcements.[9] Further, these tools were not designed into a formal public relations effort but rather were used only as needed. In other words, no structured program was evident in well over half of the companies surveyed! As we noted earlier, the public relations process is an ongoing one, requiring formalized policies and procedures for dealing with problems and opportunities. Just as you would not develop an advertising and/or promotions program without a plan, you should not institute public relations efforts haphazardly. Moreover, the PR plan needs to be integrated into the overall marketing communications program. Figure 16–3 provides some questions marketers should ask to determine whether their PR plan is workable.

Cutlip, Center, and Broom suggest a four-step process for developing a public relations plan: (1) define public relations problems; (2) plan and program; (3) take action and communicate; and (4) evaluate the program.[10] These questions and the four-step planning process tie in with the promotional planning process stressed throughout this text.

Developing and Executing the PR Program

Because of the broad role that public relations may be asked to play, the PR program may need to extend beyond promotion. A broader definition of the target market, additional communications objectives, and different messages and delivery systems may be employed. Let us examine this process.

EXHIBIT 16–1
Texaco responds to negative publicity

Where we go from here...

Texaco is facing a vital challenge. It's broader than any specific words and larger than any lawsuit.

We are committed to begin meeting this challenge swiftly through specific programs with concrete goals and measurable timetables.

Our responsibility is to eradicate discriminatory behavior wherever and however it surfaces within our company. Our challenge is to make Texaco a company of limitless opportunity for all men and women. Our goal is to broaden economic access to Texaco for women and minorities and to increase the positive impact our investments can have in communities across America.

We have started down this road by reaching out to prominent minority and religious leaders to explore ways to make Texaco a model of diversity and workplace equality.

It is essential to this urgent mission that we work together to help solve the problems we face as a company - which, after all, echo the problems faced in society as a whole.

Discrimination will be extinguished only if we tackle it together - only if we join in a unified, common effort.

Together we can take Texaco into the 21st century as a model of diversity.

We can make Texaco a company of limitless opportunity.

We can and must make Texaco a leader in according respect to every man and woman.

Peter I. Bijur
Peter I. Bijur
Chairman & CEO

TEXACO

Visit our Web site: http://www.texaco.com

DETERMINING RELEVANT TARGET AUDIENCES

The targets of public relations efforts may vary, with different objectives for each. Some may be directly involved in selling the product; others may affect the firm in a different way (e.g., they may be aimed at stockholders or legislators). These audiences may be internal or external to the firm or, as Global Perspective 16–1 demonstrates, international.

Internal audiences may include the employees of the firm, stockholders and investors, members of the local community, suppliers, and current customers. Why are community members and customers of the firm considered internal rather than external? According to John Marston, it's because these groups are already connected with the organization in some way and the firm normally communicates with them in the ordinary routine of work.[11] **External audiences** are those people who are not closely connected with the organization (e.g., the public at large).

It may be necessary to communicate with these groups on an ongoing basis for a variety of reasons, ranging from ensuring goodwill to introducing new policies, procedures, or even products. A few examples may help.

FIGURE 16–3
Ten questions to evaluate public relations plans

1. Does the plan reflect a thorough understanding of the company's business situation?
2. Has the PR program made good use of research and background sources?
3. Does the plan include full analysis of recent editorial coverage?
4. Do the PR people fully understand the product's strengths and weaknesses?
5. Does the PR program describe several cogent, relevant conclusions from the research?
6. Are the program objectives specific and measurable?
7. Does the program clearly describe what the PR activity will be and how it will benefit the company?
8. Does the program describe how its results will be measured?
9. Do the research, objectives, activities, and evaluations tie together?
10. Has the PR department communicated with marketing throughout the development of the program?

Global Perspective 16–1
Public Relations around the World

We are probably all familiar with some form of public relations activities carried out in the United States. These range from local sponsorships of Little League baseball teams to support of charities to sponsorships of the Olympics. All of these are made possible by a capitalist society. But public relations activities are carried out throughout the world—in some places and ways that might surprise you. Consider:

- In the 1996 Russian elections, U.S. advertising and public relations experts were employed to assist Boris Yeltsin in his bid to gain reelection. The group conducted research studies, wrote press releases, and even helped write some of Yeltsin's speeches. Even though the government owns and controls the media in Russia, many nongovernment organizations successfully employ public relations techniques to get the word out. In fact, the effectiveness of their actions has contributed to the more liberal government policies there. The same is true in other former Eastern Bloc countries and Cuba.
- In France, Belgium, and the Netherlands, public relations messages from Philip Morris Europe S.A. regarding second-hand cigarette smoke were banned because the governments of these countries perceived them to be advertisements rather than public relations.
- In Brazil, entrance into the public relations profession requires a university degree in PR and a professionally awarded license. Because of the large bureaucratic government, public relations is little more than

a government lobbying effort. Corporate activities are almost nonexistent.
- In Turkey, the PR business is flourishing due to the desire of business and government to sell to the European Community and the United States. While the government still censors, unfavorable articles are tolerated.
- Public relations activities in Ghana use ancient channels of communications. Dance, songs, and storytelling are the most commonly employed PR tools for getting information to small towns and communities.

While the sophistication of public relations programs varies around the world, Ray E. Hiebert believes that the old ways of theorizing about these systems may be obsolete. (In the old system, the range was from total freedom of the press—in the United States, Canada, and the United Kingdom—to government censorship—in Russia, Cuba, and other communist countries.) Hiebert says the development of effective PR techniques, coupled with advances in communications technologies, requires new thinking. He thinks both extremes have moved more toward the center. Governments can't black out news anymore, given the proliferation of Internet hookups and fax machines. On the other hand, Western countries have passed laws that restrict the media's freedoms. The way the media reported on Watergate and Vietnam would not be permitted now. Which raises a question: Who is headed in the right direction here?

Sources: Martin du Bois and Tara Parker-Pope, "Philip Morris Campaign Stirs Uproar in Europe," *The Wall Street Journal*, July 1, 1996, p. B1; Michael Kramer, "Rescuing Boris," *Time*, July 15, 1996, pp. 28–37; Melvin L. Sharpe, "The Impact of Social and Cultural Conditioning on Global Public Relations," *Public Relations Review*, Summer 1992, pp. 103–8; Ray E. Hiebert, "Global Public Relations in a Post-Communist World: A New Model," *Public Relations Review*, Summer 1992, pp. 117–27.

Employees of the Firm

Maintaining morale and showcasing the results of employees' efforts are often prime objectives of the public relations program. Organizational newsletters, notices on bulletin boards, paycheck envelope stuffers, direct mail, and annual reports are some of the methods used to communicate with these groups. Exhibit 16–2 shows one such internal communication used by Brunswick Corp.

Personal methods of communicating may be as formal as an established grievance committee or as informal as an office Christmas party. Other social events, such as corporate bowling teams or picnics, are also used to create goodwill.

Stockholders and Investors

You may think an annual report like the one in Exhibit 16–3 just provides stockholders and investors with financial information regarding the firm. While this is one purpose, annual reports are also a communications channel for informing this audience about why the firm is or is not doing well, future plans, and other information that goes beyond numbers.

For example, McDonald's has successfully used annual reports to fend off potential PR problems. One year the report described McDonald's recycling efforts to alleviate consumers' concerns about waste; another report included a 12-page spread on food and nutrition. Other companies use similar strategies, employing shareholders' meetings, video presentations, and

EXHIBIT 16–2   An example of a newsletter used for internal corporate communication

EXHIBIT 16–3   Annual reports serve a variety of purposes

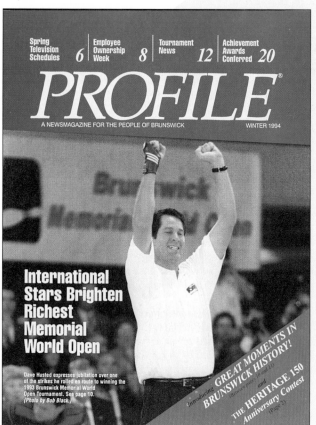

other forms of direct mail. General Motors' annual public interest report is sent to shareholders and community members to detail the company's high standards of corporate responsibility. Companies have used these approaches to generate additional investments, to bring more of their stocks "back home" (i.e., become more locally controlled and managed), and to produce funding to solve specific problems, as well as to promote goodwill.

Community Members

People who live and work in the community where a firm is located or doing business are often the target of public relations efforts. Such efforts may involve ads informing the community of activities that the organization is engaged in—for example, reducing air pollution, cleaning up water supplies or, as shown in Exhibit 16–4, protecting wildlife. (As you can see, the community can be defined very broadly.) Demonstrating to people that the organization is a good citizen with their welfare in mind may also be a reason for communicating to these groups.

Suppliers and Customers

An organization wishes to maintain *goodwill* with its suppliers as well as its consuming public. If consumers think a company is not socially conscious, they may take their loyalties elsewhere. Suppliers may be inclined to do the same.

Sometimes sponsoring a public relations effort results in direct evidence of success. For example, the "Just say no" to drugs campaign was a boon to companies manufacturing drug testing kits, hospitals offering drug rehabilitation programs, and TV news programs' ratings.[12] Indirect indications of the success of PR efforts may include more customer loyalty, less antagonism, or greater cooperation between the firm and its suppliers or consumers.

Sometimes a public relations effort is targeted to more than one group. For example, San Diego Gas & Electric (SDGE), the public utility company for the San Diego area, has suf-

EXHIBIT 16–4
Chevron demonstrates concern for the public

fered from extreme negative attitudes among its customers due to its high rates. This problem was aggravated when a series of management blunders resulted in even higher rates and SDGE announced plans to build a nuclear plant in one of the lagoons near the ocean, resulting in protests from consumers and environmentalists. Stockholders and potential investors lacked trust, and employee morale was low. (Company cars with the SDGE logo on the doors were vandalized and drivers were threatened to the point where the identifying logos had to be removed.)

The public relations plan developed to deal with these problems targeted a variety of publics and employed a number of channels. TV spots showed consumers how to save energy, print ads explained the reasons for the energy purchases made by management, and PR programs were developed to foster more community interaction. These programs have led to much more favorable attitudes among all the publics targeted. (At least employees can put the SDGE logo back on their cars.)

Relevant audiences may also include people not directly involved with the firm. The press, educators, civic and business groups, governments, and the financial community can be external audiences.

The Media

Perhaps one of the most critical external publics is the media, which determine what you will read in your newspapers or see on TV, and how this news will be presented. Because of the media's power, they should be informed of the firm's actions. Companies issue press releases and communicate through conferences, interviews, and special events. The media are generally receptive to such information so long as it is handled professionally; reporters are always interested in good stories.

In turn, the media are concerned about how the community perceives them. Exhibit 16–5 is a public relations piece distributed by a Dallas–Fort Worth TV station that describes a variety of ways the station benefits the community.

Educators

A number of organizations provide educators with information regarding their activities. The Direct Marketing Association, the Promotional Products Association, and the American Association of Yellow Pages Publishers, among others, keep educators informed in an attempt to generate goodwill as well as exposure for their causes. These groups and major corporations provide information regarding innovations, state-of-the-art research, and other items of interest.

Educators are a target audience because, like the media, they control the flow of information to certain parties—in this case, people like you.

Understanding Yellow Pages

Joel J. Davis

EXHIBIT 16–5
The media employ public relations to enhance their image in the community

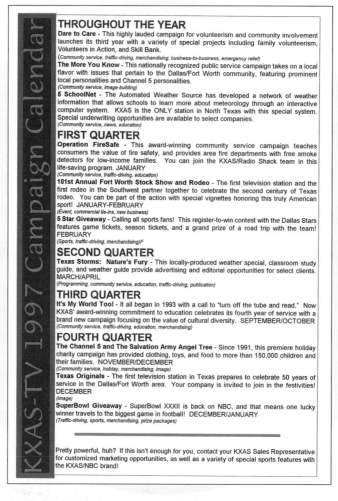

KXAS-TV 1997 Campaign Calendar

THROUGHOUT THE YEAR

Dare to Care - This highly lauded campaign for volunteerism and community involvement launches its third year with a variety of special projects including family volunteerism, Volunteers in Action, and Skill Bank.
(Community service, traffic-driving, merchandising, business-to-business, emergency relief)

The More You Know - This nationally recognized public service campaign takes on a local flavor with issues that pertain to the Dallas/Fort Worth community, featuring prominent local personalities and Channel 5 personalities.
(Community service, image-building)

5 SchoolNet - The Automated Weather Source has developed a network of weather information that allows schools to learn more about meteorology through an interactive computer system. KXAS is the ONLY station in North Texas with this special system. Special underwriting opportunities are available to select companies.
(Community service, news, education)

FIRST QUARTER

Operation FireSafe - This award-winning community service campaign teaches consumers the value of fire safety, and provides area fire departments with free smoke detectors for low-income families. You can join the KXAS/Radio Shack team in this life-saving program. JANUARY
(Community service, traffic-driving, education)

101st Annual Fort Worth Stock Show and Rodeo - The first television station and the first rodeo in the Southwest partner together to celebrate the second century of Texas rodeo. You can be part of the action with special vignettes honoring this truly American sport! JANUARY-FEBRUARY
(Event, commercial tie-ins, new business)

5 Star Giveaway - Calling all sports fans! This register-to-win contest with the Dallas Stars features game tickets, season tickets, and a grand prize of a road trip with the team! FEBRUARY
(Sports, traffic-driving, merchandising)F

SECOND QUARTER

Texas Storms: Nature's Fury - This locally-produced weather special, classroom study guide, and weather guide provide advertising and editorial opportunities for select clients. MARCH/APRIL
(Programming, community service, education, traffic-driving, publication)

THIRD QUARTER

It's My World Too! - It all began in 1993 with a call to "turn off the tube and read." Now KXAS' award-winning commitment to education celebrates its fourth year of service with a brand new campaign focusing on the value of cultural diversity. SEPTEMBER/OCTOBER
(Community service, traffic-driving, education, merchandising)

FOURTH QUARTER

The Channel 5 and The Salvation Army Angel Tree - Since 1991, this premiere holiday charity campaign has provided clothing, toys, and food to more than 150,000 children and their families. NOVEMBER/DECEMBER
(Community service, holiday, merchandising, image)

Texas Originals - The first television station in Texas prepares to celebrate 50 years of service in the Dallas/Fort Worth area. Your company is invited to join in the festivities! DECEMBER
(Image)

SuperBowl Giveaway - SuperBowl XXXII is back on NBC, and that means one lucky winner travels to the biggest game in football! DECEMBER/JANUARY
(Traffic-driving, sports, merchandising, prize packages)

Pretty powerful, huh? If this isn't enough for you, contact your KXAS Sales Representative for customized marketing opportunities, as well as a variety of special sports features with the KXAS/NBC brand!

Civic and Business Organizations

The local Jaycees, Kiwanis, and other nonprofit civic organizations also serve as gatekeepers of information. Companies' financial contributions to these groups, speeches at organization functions, and sponsorships are all designed to create goodwill. Corporate executives' service on the boards of nonprofit organizations also generates positive public relations.

Governments

Public relations often attempts to influence government bodies directly at both local and national levels. Successful lobbying may mean immediate success for a product, while regulations detrimental to the firm may cost it millions. Imagine for a moment what FDA approval of NutraSweet meant to Searle or what could happen to the beer and wine industries if TV advertising were banned. The bicycle helmet industry sometimes experiences sales increases of 200 to 400 percent in a state when it passes a helmet law.

Financial Groups

In addition to current shareholders, potential shareholders and investors may be relevant target markets. Financial advisors, lending institutions, and others must be kept abreast of new developments as well as financial information, since they offer the potential for new sources of funding. Press releases and corporate reports play an important role in providing information to these publics.

IMPLEMENTING THE PR PROGRAM

Once the research has been conducted and the target audiences identified, the public relations program must be developed and delivered to the receivers. A number of PR tools are available for this purpose, including press releases, press conferences, exclusives, interviews, and community involvement.

The Press Release

One of the most important publics is the press. To be used by the press, information must be factual, true, and of interest to the medium as well as to its audience. As shown in Figure 16–4, the source of the **press release** can do certain things to improve the likelihood that the "news" will be disseminated.

The information in a press release won't be used unless it's of interest to the readers of the medium it's sent to. For example, financial institutions may issue press releases to business trade media and to the editor of the business section of a general-interest newspaper. Information on the release of a new rock album is of more interest to radio disk jockeys than to TV newscasters; sports news also has its interested audiences.

Press Conferences

We are all familiar with **press conferences** held by political figures. While used less often by organizations and corporations, this form of delivery can be very effective. The topic must be of major interest to a specific group before it is likely to gain coverage. Usually major accomplishments (such as the awarding of the next Super Bowl or Olympics location), major breakthroughs (such as medical cures), emergencies, or catastrophes warrant a national press conference. On a local level, community events, local developments, and the like may receive coverage. Companies often call press conferences when they have significant news to announce, such as the introduction of a new product or advertising campaign. Pepsi held a press conference to announce the termination of its contract with Michael Jackson when the rock star was accused of child molestation. Hertz held two press conferences regarding O. J. Simpson when he was accused of murdering his wife—the first to announce that it would continue to support him as its spokesman, then later to announce that it would discontinue the relationship.

Exclusives

Although most public relations efforts seek a variety of channels for distribution, an alternative strategy is to offer one particular medium exclusive rights to the story if that medium reaches a substantial number of people in the target audience. Offering an **exclusive** may enhance the likelihood of acceptance. As you watch television over the next few weeks, look for the various networks' and local stations' exclusives. Notice how the media actually use these exclusives to promote themselves.

Interviews

When you watch TV or read magazines, pay close attention to the personal interviews. Usually someone will raise specific questions and a spokesperson provided by the firm will answer them. For example, when four people died from eating tainted hamburgers at Jack in the Box restaurants, the company's president gave personal interviews with the press to detail the corrective actions the company would take. Earvin (Magic) Johnson granted personal interviews when he announced his retirement as a pro basketball player and then later his resignation as

FIGURE 16–4
Getting the public relations story told

Jonathan Schenker of Ketchum Public Relations, New York, suggests four technological methods to make life easier for the press and to increase the likelihood that they will use your story.

1. *Telephone press conferences.* Since reporters cannot always get to a press conference, use the telephone to call them for coverage.

2. *In-studio media tours.* Satellite communications providing a story, and a chance to interview, from a central location such as a TV studio save broadcast journalists time and money by eliminating their need to travel.

3. *Multicomponent video news releases (VNRs).* A five-component package consisting of a complete script in print and on tape, a video release with a live reporter, a local contact source at which to target the video, and a silent video news release that allows the station to fill in with its own news reporter lend an advantage by saving the media money.

4. *Targeted newswire stories.* When the sender targets the public relations message, reporters are spared the need to read through volumes of news stories to select those of interest to their target audiences.

coach of the Los Angeles Lakers. Peter Bijur, the chair of Texaco, met with the press to discuss his plans to eliminate discriminatory practices within his corporation.

Community Involvement

Many corporations enhance their public images through involvement in the local community. This involvement may take many forms, including membership in local organizations like the Kiwanis or Jaycees and contributions to or participation in community events. For example, after the great flood created so much damage in the Midwest in 1993, Maytag issued press releases on how to deal with waterlogged appliances, Sara Lee provided frozen bagels and cheesecake, and Principal Mutual Life offered volunteer lawyers and actuaries to assess damages. State Farm Insurance established flood relief centers and catastrophe centers when the floods returned in 1997. Exhibit 16–6 is just one example of how companies pitched in to help Los Angeles residents after a major earthquake.

Other methods of distributing information include photo kits, bylined articles (signed by the firm), speeches, and trade shows. Of course, the specific mode of distribution is determined by the nature of the story and the interest of the media and its publics.

Advantages and Disadvantages of PR

Like the other program elements, public relations has both advantages and disadvantages. Advantages include the following.

• *Credibility.* Because public relations communications are not perceived in the same light as advertising—that is, the public does not realize the organization either directly or indirectly paid for them—they tend to have more credibility. The fact that the media are not being compensated for providing the information may lead receivers to consider the news more truthful and credible. For example, an article in newspapers or magazines discussing the virtues of aspirin may be perceived as much more credible than an ad for a particular brand of aspirin.

EXHIBIT 16–6
Sears ad offering assistance to earthquake victims

EXHIBIT 16–7 Olympus capitalizes on positive publicity in its advertising

EXHIBIT 16–8 The HP Pavilion launch relied heavily on public relations activities

Best Consumer Digital Camera
(MacUser EddyAwards, Jan.'97)
Product of the Year
(InfoWorld, Jan.'97)
Stellar
(Windows Sources, Jan.'97)
★★★★
(Computer Life, Feb.'97)

Any questions?

Plenty. How many pictures does the D-200L take?
Up to 80.

You're not sure?
You can shoot in both high-resolution or standard formats. And switch back and forth whenever you want. Even delete the shots you don't want at any time.

How do I know which ones to delete or keep?
You can instantly view the images you just captured.

Where?
On the color LCD screen. One at a time or nine at a time.

What's the resolution?
640 × 480. But you're not buying a pixel taker. It's pictures you're after. And

picture quality is where the D-200L really outperforms the competition.

Who says?
InfoWorld, for one: "The image quality far surpassed any of the other digital cameras." And *Windows Sources*: "It delivers the best images we've seen from a consumer-level camera."

What about the lens?
It's a razor sharp, wide angle, macro, Olympus glass lens.

Flash?
With red-eye reduction, fill flash and auto mode.

But does it feel like a camera?
With an optical viewfinder and Olympus design, it follows in the footsteps of the Stylus series, the most successful line of 35mm cameras in the world.

Okay. I take a color shot. Now what?
Download the image into a computer, either Windows™ PC or a Mac® Then go to town.

Talk to me.
Create multiple images from one image. Or combine several. Add and subtract color. Retouch. Crop.

Go on.
E-mail it across the Internet. Put it on a Web page. Store it on disk.

Suppose I want to be creative?
With the included Adobe PhotoDeluxe™ software you can make greeting cards and real estate listings, design layouts, put together mail-order catalogs and newsletters. All in full living color.

Hold it! How much is all of this going to cost me?
$599.

That's it?
That's it.

There must be a science to all this.
And an art.

To learn more about the D-200L and how it completes the ideal home or office imaging system, contact your Olympus Marketing Representative at 1-800-622-6372. They'll also tell you all about the new Olympus personal storage system and CD writer.

OLYMPUS
THE ART & SCIENCE OF IMAGING™

® and ™ All trademarks and registered trademarks mentioned herein are the property of the respective holders.
The Art and Science of Imaging is a trademark of Olympus America Inc.
InfoWorld & MacUser awards received 1/97. ©1997 Olympus America Inc.

Visit us at http://www.olympus.com/digital

Automotive awards presented in magazines such as *Motor Trend* have long been known to carry clout with potential car buyers. Now marketers have found that even lesser media mean a lot as well. General Motors' Pontiac division played up an award given to Pontiac as "the best domestic sedan" by *MotorWeek* in a 30-minute program carried by about 300 public broadcasting stations. Likewise, Chrysler trumpeted the awards given to its Jeep Cherokee by *4-Wheel & Off Road* magazine.[13] It has become a common practice for car companies to promote their achievements.

News about a product may in itself serve as the subject of an ad. Exhibit 16–7 demonstrates how Olympus used favorable publicity from a variety of sources to promote its digital camera. A number of auto manufacturers have also taken advantage in their ads of high customer satisfaction ratings reported by J. D. Powers & Associates, an independent research firm specializing in automotive research.

• *Cost.* In both absolute and relative terms, the cost of public relations is very low, especially when the possible effects are considered. While a firm can employ public relations agencies and spend millions of dollars on PR, for smaller companies this form of communication may be the most affordable alternative available.

When Hewlett-Packard launched its new line of Pavilion PCs, the launch team was told that it would receive the $15 million advertising budget promised only if it first brought the HP name to consumers. Armed with only public relations and point-of-purchase materials, the team and its PR agency created the tagline "It's not just a PC. It's an HP," which appeared on all communications pieces, packaging, and product literature (Exhibit 16–8). Press releases and product information were then disseminated to many consumer and trade media. When it came time to seek the advertising dollars, the HP

Pavilion (the name Pavilion never appeared alone) was firmly entrenched in the minds of the target market.[14]

Many public relations programs require little more than the time and expenses associated with putting the program together and getting it distributed, yet they still accomplish their objectives.

• *Avoidance of clutter.* Because they are typically perceived as news items, public relations messages are not subject to the clutter of ads. A story regarding a new product introduction or breakthrough is treated as a news item and is likely to receive attention. When Steven Jobs (the founder of Apple Computer) announced his return to Apple, all the networks covered it, as did major newspapers and magazines. Some (like CNN) devoted two- to three-minute segments to the story.

• *Lead generation.* Information about technological innovations, medical breakthroughs, and the like results almost immediately in a multitude of inquiries. These inquiries may give the firm some quality sales leads. For example, when Tiger Woods, one of the longest drivers on the PGA tour, was seen using a Cobra golf club in the internationally televised U.S. Open, the club manufacturer received inquiries from all over the United States and as far away as Europe and Japan.

• *Ability to reach specific groups.* Because some products appeal to only small market segments, it is not feasible to engage in advertising and/or promotions to reach them. If the firm does not have the financial capabilities to engage in promotional expenditures, the best way to communicate to these groups is through public relations.

• *Image building.* Effective public relations helps to develop a positive image for the organization. A strong image is insurance against later misfortunes. For example, in 1982, seven people in the Chicago area died after taking Extra Strength Tylenol capsules that had been laced with cyanide (after they reached the store). Within one week of the poisonings, Tylenol's market share fell from 35 to only 6.5 percent. Strong public relations efforts combined with an already strong product and corporate image helped the product rebound (despite the opinions of many experts that it had no chance of recovering). A brand or firm with a lesser image would never have been able to come back. The ad in Exhibit 16–9 demonstrates the power of a strong image.

Perhaps the major disadvantage of public relations is the potential for not completing the communications process. While public relations messages can break through the clutter of commercials, the receiver may not make the connection to the source. Many firms' PR efforts are never associated with their sponsors in the public mind.

Public relations may also misfire through mismanagement and a lack of coordination with the marketing department. When marketing and PR departments operate independently, there is a danger of inconsistent communications, redundancies in efforts, and so on.

The key to effective public relations is to establish a good program, worthy of public interest, and manage it properly. To determine if this program is working, the firm must measure the effectiveness of the PR effort.

Measuring the Effectiveness of PR

As with the other promotional program elements, it is important to evaluate the effectiveness of the public relations efforts. In addition to determining the contribution of this program element to attaining communications objectives, the evaluation offers other advantages:

1. It tells management what has been achieved through public relations activities.
2. It provides management with a way to measure public relations achievements quantitatively.
3. It gives management a way to judge the quality of public relations achievements and activities.

As shown in Figure 16–5, a number of criteria may be used to measure the effects of PR programs. Raymond Simon suggests additional means for accomplishing this evaluation process, including the following.

FIGURE 16–5

Criteria for measuring the effectiveness of PR

A system for measuring the effectiveness of the public relations program has been developed by Lotus HAL. The criteria used in the evaluation process follow.

• Total number of impressions over time
• Total number of impressions on the target audience
• Total number of impressions on specific target audiences
• Percentage of positive articles over time
• Percentage of negative articles over time
• Ratio of positive to negative articles
• Percentage of positive/negative articles by subject
• Percentage of positive/negative articles by publication or reporter
• Percentage of positive/negative articles by target audience

- *Personal observation and reaction.* Personal observation and evaluation by one's superiors should occur at all levels of the organization.
- *Matching objectives and results.* Specific objectives designed to attain the overall communications objectives should be related to actions, activities, or media coverage. For example, placing a feature story in a specific number of media is an objective, quantitative, and measurable goal.[15]
- *The team approach.* Harold Mendelsohn suggests that one way to achieve attitude and behavior modification through public information campaigns is the **team approach,** whereby evaluators are actually involved in the campaign.[16] By using research principles and working together, the team develops—and accomplishes—goals.
- *Management by objectives.* Executives and their managers act together to identify goals to be attained and the responsibilities of the managers. These goals are then used as a standard to measure accomplishments.
- *Public opinion and surveys.* Research in the form of public opinion surveys may be used to gather data to evaluate program goal attainment.
- *Audits.* Both internal and external audits may be used. **Internal audits** involve evaluations by superiors or peers within the firm to determine the performance of the employee (or his or her programs). **External audits** are conducted by consultants, the client (in the case of a PR agency), or other parties outside the organization.

A number of other bases for evaluation can be used. Walter Lindenmann says three levels of measures are involved: (1) the basic, which measures the actual PR activities undertaken; (2) the intermediate, which measures audience reception and understanding of the message; and (3) the advanced, which measures the perceptual and behavioral changes that result.[17]

Some organizations may use a combination of measures, depending on their specific needs. For example, Hewlett-Packard uses impression counts, awareness and preference studies, in-house assessments, press clippings counts, and tracking of studies.[18]

In summary, the role of public relations in the promotional mix is changing. As PR has become more marketing oriented, the criteria by which the programs are evaluated have also changed. At the same time, nonmarketing activities will continue to be part of the public relations department and part of the basis for evaluation.

PUBLICITY

Publicity refers to the generation of news about a person, product, or service that appears in broadcast or print media. To many marketers, publicity and public relations are synonymous. In fact, publicity is really a subset of the public relations effort.

But there are several major differences. First, publicity is typically a *short-term* strategy, while public relations is a concerted program extending over a period of time. Second, public relations is designed to provide positive information about the firm and is usually controlled by the firm or its agent. Publicity, on the other hand, is not always positive and is not always under the control of, or paid for by, the organization. Both positive and negative publicity often originates from sources other than the firm.

In most organizations, publicity is controlled and disseminated by the public relations department. In this section, we discuss the role publicity plays in the promotional program and some of the ways marketers use and react to these communications.

The Power of Publicity

One of the factors that most sets off publicity from the other program elements is the sheer power this form of communication can generate. Unfortunately for marketers, this power is not always realized in the way they would like it to be. Publicity can make or break a product or even a company, as evidenced by IMC Perspective 16–2.

Earlier we discussed the substantial drop in Tylenol sales after extensive media coverage of the tampering with its products while on store shelves. The Johnson & Johnson marketing efforts (including a strong public relations emphasis) designed to aid recovery were a model in proficiency that will be studied by students of marketing (in both the classroom and the boardroom) for many years. By January 1983, almost 100 percent of the original

SONJA POPP-STAHLY

Sonja Popp-Stahly is an Account Supervisor at DeVries Public Relations in New York City, which has been named one of the "15 Hot Creative Agencies" and "considered one of the best all-around marketing communications firms in New York" by *Inside PR* magazine. DeVries's clients range from beauty and fashion, food, entertainment and telecommunications companies. Since joining DeVries, Sonja has worked for a variety of clients including Oil of Olay skin care products, Pantene hair care products, Taster's Choice coffee, Bain de Soleil sunscreens, Donna Karan Beauty Company, and SnackWell's Chocolate Nonfat Yogurt.

"It's always surprising to me how many people do not really understand what public relations is."

Sonja has worked on numerous new product launches for most of her clients and has been responsible for obtaining publicity in a variety of media, including national magazines and television. This often begins with writing press releases and fact sheets, executing press events and mailings, and conducting proactive follow-up calls with the media to offer clients for interviews and provide them with product information. "It's always surprising to me how many people do not really understand what public relations is," says Sonja. "Although public relations is a communications field in its own right, it is often confused with advertising."

Sonja has seen first-hand the differences between advertising and public relations, but also how they work in conjunction with one another. "When we worked for Taster's Choice, we were responsible for obtaining publicity surrounding the debut of each execution in the 'Coffee Couple romance' series of commercials, working with both broadcast and print media, creating a buzz to get viewers excited to see what happened after the last commercial ended." A new execution debuted approximately every six months, and DeVries was responsible for obtaining publicity for the Coffee Couple, and the commercials, during the hiatus. This involved the development and execution of several consumer promotions. One promotion, "Coffee Talk," let consumers call an 800 number to cast their ballots on their thoughts about the couple and received a coveted Bronze Anvil Award from the Public Relations Society of America (PRSA).

Sonja's day-to-day activities include program development, client relations, research, media relations, event planning, press kit writing, and results reporting. She is responsible for pitching stories about her clients in a variety of media, including magazines, newspapers, trade publications, and television. She stresses that it is extremely important to know the media you are pitching and to adjust your approach accordingly. For the launch of new SnackWell's Chocolate Nonfat Yogurt, DeVries staged a wedding between Mr. Chocolate and Ms. Yogurt, portrayed by actors dressed in full costume, complete with a ceremony and wedding toast with the yogurt. The clever stunt resulted in national coverage on NBC's "The Today Show" and countless other local news stations.

"Public relations is such an exciting field to work in," notes Sonja. "One of the interesting aspects of working at a public relations agency is that you have the opportunity to work on a variety of accounts, which is great for the learning process." For anyone interested in pursuing a career in public relations, Sonja highly recommends internships and having a related major in college. "The practical experience learned during an internship is the perfect complement to course work in the field," says Sonja. She also recommends involvement in communications/journalism organizations such as the Public Relations Student Society of America (PRSSA) and the Society of Professional Journalists.

Sonja joined DeVries as an account assistant in 1993 after graduating Magna Cum Laude from Ball State University with a BA in Journalism and minors in marketing and German. She has rapidly risen through the ranks with four promotions in four years. In 1997 she received the Ball State University Department of Journalism Outstanding Young Alumnus Award given to an alumnus under the age of 30 who has accomplished a great deal in his/her related field of journalism. Sonja is an active member of the Public Relations Society of America, and serves as an award judge for several PRSSA competitions.

IMC Perspective 16–2
O. J. Simpson and the Power of Publicity

By now we all know how many people and companies were able to capitalize on the O. J. Simpson trial. Many of the participants wrote books, O. J. sold videotapes, and Kato Kaelin got his own radio talk show. What you may not realize is the growth spurt many products experienced even without any marketing efforts behind them. For example:

- *Bruno Magli.* The murderer allegedly wore a pair of Bruno Magli shoes. After 30 pictures of Simpson wearing Bruno Maglis were introduced as evidence in the civil trial, sales of the shoe brand increased by 30 percent.
- *BackSaver.* The ergonomic chair gained notoriety when Judge Ito requested a special chair to use during the trial. When the attorneys saw the chair they all wanted one as well (Simpson was not allowed to have one). Due to TV exposure and some associated public relations efforts, the $2,000 chair saw sales increase more than 42 percent over the previous six months in certain parts of the country, including Los Angeles, Washington, D.C., and Austin, Texas.
- *Juice Plus.* This Memphis-based product was thrust into the spotlight when Simpson said it helped his arthritis pain. Prosecutors issued a subpoena for the videotape in which Simpson makes the claim. While the company made no efforts to capitalize on the publicity, it received thousands of inquiries about the product.

Of course not all publicity comes from marathon trials, nor is all publicity desirable. For example, when *Consumer Reports* warned buyers to stay away from the Isuzu Trooper sports utility vehicle, sales plunged 83 percent from the same period a year earlier. When Calvin Klein ran an ad that included prepubescent models in sexy poses, so much publicity resulted that many magazines refused to run the campaign. Calvin Klein eventually had to pull the ads from those media that did accept them. When fashion retailer Clothestime attempted to gain publicity through controversial advertising, the networks saw through it and refused to run the ads. The campaign never got off the ground.

The recipients of the publicity have taken different perspectives on its value. As noted, the agency for Clothestime (Mendelshon/Zien) is believed to have put the ads together specifically to gain publicity. Relax the Back, the chain store that distributes the "Judge Ito chair," wants the world to know that the participants were in its chair, and has taken efforts to capitalize on it. (Its PR firm, Fishman Public Relations, sent a press release to media in the 22 markets where Relax the Back is located.) Both Sony (on the TV display monitors) and IBM (Ito's notebook) made sure their names were prominently displayed.

On the other hand, NordicTrack, which donated exercise equipment for the jurors to use during their sequestration, wanted no publicity and asked for the equipment to be donated to charity when it was no longer needed. Both Juice Plus and Bruno Magli attempted to disassociate themselves from the publicity altogether. The president of National Safety Associates, the manufacturer of Juice Plus, was adamant that the company did not want publicity and called the case a tragedy. And a spokesperson for Bruno Magli says the company will be glad when its shoes are associated with someone else. By the way, Hillary Clinton's been known to wear a pair or two.

Sources: A. Scott Walton, "Bruno Magli: Sales Are Up because of Ad Campaign," *Atlanta Constitution*, January 16, 1997, p. 3G; Kathy Tyrer, "Retailer Puts on the Schock," *Adweek*, March 18, 1996, p. 2; Earle Eldridge, "Trooper Sales Skid on *CR* Report," *USA Today*, October 8, 1996, p. 2b; Margaret Carlson, "Where Calvin Crossed the Line," *Time*, September 11, 1995; Cindy Wolff, "All the O. J. Court Is a Stage to Product Positioners," *The Commercial Appeal*, April 2, 1995, p. 1c.

---

brand share had been regained. Unfortunately, a marketer cannot always capitalize on positive publicity or control the effects of negative publicity so effectively.

Why is publicity so much more powerful than advertising or sales promotion—or even other forms of public relations? First, publicity is highly credible. Unlike advertising and sales promotions, publicity is not usually perceived as being sponsored by the company (in the negative instances, it never is). So consumers perceive this information as more objective and place more confidence in it. In fact, *Consumer Reports*, the medium responsible for one of the examples previously cited, recently ran an ad campaign designed to promote its credibility by noting it does not accept advertising and therefore can be objective in its evaluations.

Publicity information may be perceived as endorsed by the medium in which it appears. For example, publicity regarding a breakthrough in the durability of golf balls will go far to promote them if it is reported by *Golf* magazine. *Car & Driver*'s award for car of the year reflects the magazine's perception of the quality of the auto selected.

Still another reason for publicity's power is its news value and the frequency of exposure it generates. When basketball stars Larry Bird and Kareem Abdul-Jabbar appeared together in a commercial for Lay's potato chips, the ad appeared on every major TV network and many cable sports programs, both as a paid commercial and free as the media publicized the campaign. When Lay's introduced its campaign for Doritos Tortilla Thins featuring comedian Chevy Chase, TV reporters aired 1,734 stories about the ads using footage provided by Frito-Lay.[19]

The bottom line is that publicity is news, and people like to pass on information that has news value. Publicity thus results in a significant amount of free, credible, word-of-mouth information regarding the firm and its products.

The Control and Dissemination of Publicity

In some of the examples cited earlier, the control of publicity was not in the hands of the company. While in some instances it is the firm's own blunder to allow information to leak out, Texaco and Isuzu could do nothing to stop the media from releasing negative information. When publicity becomes news, it is reported by the media, sometimes despite the efforts of the firm. In these instances, the organization needs to react to the potential threat created by the news.

A good example of one company's efforts to respond to adverse publicity is shown in Exhibit 16–10. Tree Top's problems began when all the major news media reported that the chemical Alar, used by some growers to regulate the growth of apples, might cause cancer in children. Despite published statements by reliable scientific and medical authorities (including the surgeon general) that Alar does not cause cancer, a few special-interest groups were able to generate an extraordinary amount of adverse publicity, causing concern among consumers and purchasing agents. A few school districts took apples off their menus, and even applesauce and juice were implicated. Tree Top ran the ad in Exhibit 16–10 to state its position and alleviate consumers' fears. It also sent a direct mailing to nutritionists and day care operators. The campaign was successful in assuring consumers of the product's safety and rebuilding their confidence.

In other instances, however, publicity must be managed like any other promotional tool. For example, when the FDA instructed P&G to stop using "fresh" claims in its Citrus Hill orange juice, the company refused to do so. After a lengthy confrontation, the FDA im-

EXHIBIT 16–10
Tree Top responds to the threat of negative publicity

pounded thousands of gallons of the product, and the resulting publicity reflected negatively on both the brand and the organization.

Publicity can also work for marketers. The Cabbage Patch Kids and Tickle Me Elmo dolls achieved significant sales due to high levels of positive publicity and word-of-mouth advertising. Sales of Cabernet Sauvignon increased an average of 45 percent in the month after a CBS "60 Minutes" report that daily moderate consumption of red wine can reduce the risk of heart disease. There are many more examples of the positive impact publicity can have.

Marketers like to have as much control as possible over the time and place where information is released. One way to do this is with the **video news release** (VNR), a publicity piece produced by publicists so that stations can air it as a news story. The videos almost never mention that they are produced by the subject organization, and most news stations don't mention it either. The Doritos Tortilla Thins ad was a subject of a VNR, as were stories about Elizabeth Taylor's 60th birthday party at Disneyland, the making of a Pepsi commercial featuring Shaquille O'Neal, and Jessica Little (a child who got lost at night in Ripley, Tennessee, and was found when searchers saw the lights on her L.A. Gear shoes).[20] Many companies have made significant use of video news releases.

In their efforts to manage publicity and public relations, marketers are continuously learning more about these activities. Courses are offered and books written on how to manage publicity. These books cover how to make a presentation, whom to contact, how to issue a press release, and what to know about each medium addressed, including TV, radio, newspapers, magazines, and direct-response advertising. They discuss such alternative media as news conferences, seminars, events, and personal letters, as well as insights on how to deal with government and other legislative bodies. Because this information is too extensive to include as a single chapter in this text, we suggest you peruse one of the many books available on this subject for additional insights.

Advantages and Disadvantages of Publicity

Publicity offers the advantages of credibility, news value, significant word-of-mouth communications, and a perception of being endorsed by the media. Beyond the potential impact of negative publicity, two major problems arise from the use of publicity: timing and accuracy.

TIMING

Timing of the publicity is not always completely under the control of the marketer. Unless the press thinks the information has very high news value, the timing of the press release is entirely up to the media—if it gets released at all. Thus, the information may be released earlier than desired or too late to make an impact.

ACCURACY

A major way to get publicity is the press release. Unfortunately, the information sometimes gets lost in translation—that is, it is not always reported the way the provider wishes it to be. As a result, inaccurate information, omissions, or other errors may result. Sometimes when you see a publicity piece that was written based on a press release, you wonder if they are even talking about the same topic.

Measuring the Effectiveness of Publicity

The methods for measuring the effects of publicity are essentially the same as those discussed earlier under the broader topic of public relations. Rather than reiterate them here, we thought it would be more interesting to show you an actual example. Figure 16–6 is a model developed by Ketchum Public Relations for tracking the effects of publicity. (I guess we just provided Ketchum with some free publicity.)

CORPORATE ADVERTISING

One of the more controversial forms of advertising is **corporate advertising**. Actually an extension of the public relations function, corporate advertising does not promote any one specific product or service. Rather, it is designed to promote the firm overall, by en-

FIGURE 16–6   The Ketchum publicity tracking model

Paul H. Alvarez, chair and chief executive officer of Ketchum Public Relations, describes his firm's publicity tracking model as follows:

We have done a pretty good job in educating clients on what publicity programs can and cannot do, and what can be realistically expected. But true accountability requires measured results. Is publicity measurable?

Up to now, perhaps not. But Ketchum Public Relations has been working for three years on the Ketchum publicity tracking model, the first computer-based measurement system designed specifically to evaluate publicity programs. It goes beyond traditional accounting methods such as reporting to the client the number of column inches or the amount of broadcast time obtained and the total audiences reached. It evaluates, via a publicity exposure index, the amount of target audience exposure received and the degree to which planned messages were delivered to the target audience.

In planning a campaign to be evaluated by the model, the client and the firm agree upon standards of performance in two areas: the number of gross impressions to be achieved within the target audience, and the key messages to be delivered to that audience. The firm's computer is programmed with audience statistics from media in 120 top national markets. Performance standards for a given program are also programmed into the computer along with campaign results.

Results are then printed out by media category, target audience reached, and the quality (based on numerical values assigned to various "selling" points in the copy) of the message delivered to the audience. The computer then produces two evaluative numbers: an overall exposure index and an overall value index. Taking 1.00 as a standard index for the campaign, the degree to which the index is above or below this figure shows to what extent performance was above or below the norm.

In the accompanying sample tracking report, based on a campaign in Orlando, Florida, the exposure index (1.08) and the value index (1.48) indicate that the program overall met expectations and exceeded the established norms.

The first column of figures in the report shows media exposure among designated market area (DMA) audiences. The second column records average size/length of exposure for each medium, which is translated into average media units (based on a norm of 1.00) and publicity exposure units.

The columns for average impact factor and publicity value units indicate the degree to which key "selling" points in the copy were mentioned in the exposures. Note that the average impact factor for network television is low (0.81). The reason is that although the subject of the campaign (a special event) was mentioned fairly often (1.93 average media units), mention of specific dates and other key copy points did not meet expectations.

The tracking model also demonstrates in advance what a publicity program will do. Thus it is a tool for deciding whether or not a program is worth carrying out. If the decision is "go," it then reports how well objectives were met. Instead of guesswork, we now have a method for placing accountability to the client on a factual basis.

Sample Tracking Report						
Placement Type	DMA Target Audience (thousands)	Average Size/ Length	Average Media Units	Publicity Exposure Units (thousands)	Average Impact Factor	Publicity Value Units (thousands)
Newspapers	4,552	1/9 page	0.93	4,233	1.26	5,334
Magazines	268	1/2 page	1.66	455	1.47	656
TV (network)	95	5:10 min	1.93	183	0.81	149
TV (local)	504	6:05 min	2.13	1,073	1.81	1,946
Radio (local)	200	10:00	2.60	520	1.40	728
Totals	5,619		1.15	6,454	1.37	8,813

Publicity exposure norm = 5,960,000

Publicity exposure index (6,454 ÷ 5,960) = 1.08

Publicity value index (8,813 ÷ 5,960) = 1.48

The publicity exposure norm is established by estimating the target audiences (adults 18–49, weighted 60 percent male, 40 percent female) and an exposure of a "good" hypothetical placement schedule.

The publicity exposure index suggests the campaign's exposure was 1.08, as good as expected on a normal (= 1.00) basis.

The publicity value index suggests the impact value of the campaign was 1.48 times as good as expected on a normal (= 1.00) basis.

hancing its image, assuming a position on a social issue or cause, or seeking direct involvement in something. Why is corporate advertising controversial? A number of reasons are offered:

1. *Consumers are not interested in this form of advertising.* A Gallup and Robinson study reported in *Advertising Age* found consumers were 35 percent less interested in corporate ads than in product-oriented advertising.[21] This may be because consumers do not understand the reasons behind such ads. Of course, much of this confusion results from ads that are not very good from a communications standpoint.

2. *It's a costly form of self-indulgence.* Firms have been accused of engaging in corporate image advertising only to satisfy the egos of top management. This argument stems from the fact that corporate ads are not easy to write. The message to be communicated is not as precise and specific as one designed to position a product, so the top managers often dictate the content of the ad, and the copy reflects their ideas and images of the corporation.

3. *The firm must be in trouble.* Some critics believe the only time firms engage in corporate advertising is when they are in trouble—either in a financial sense or in the public eye—and are advertising to attempt to remedy the problem. There are a number of forms of corporate advertising, each with its own objectives. These critics argue that these objectives have become important only because the firm has not been managed properly.

4. *Corporate advertising is a waste of money.* Given that the ads do not directly appeal to anyone, are not understood, and do not promote anything specific, critics say the monies could be better spent in other areas. Again, much of this argument has its foundation in the fact that corporate image ads are often intangible. They typically do not ask directly for a purchase; they do not ask for investors. Rather, they present a position or try to create an image. Because they are not specific, many critics believe their purpose is lost on the audience and these ads are not a wise investment of the firm's resources.

Despite these criticisms and others, corporate advertising has increased in use. It's been estimated that more than 7 percent of all advertising dollars spent are for corporate advertising, meaning billions of dollars are spent on this form of communication.[22]

While corporate advertising has generally been regarded as the domain of companies such as USX, Kaiser Aluminum, and Boise Cascade (that is, companies with no products to sell directly to the consumer market) this is no longer the case. Beatrice Foods, BASF, and Procter & Gamble are just a few consumer products companies running corporate image ads, and IBM and AT&T have also increased expenditures in this area.

Since the term *corporate advertising* tends to be used as a catchall for any type of advertising run for the direct benefit of the corporation rather than its products or services, much advertising falls into this category. For purposes of this text (and to attempt to bring some perspective to the term), we use it to describe any type of advertising designed to promote the organization itself rather than its products or services.

Objectives of Corporate Advertising

Corporate advertising may be designed with two goals in mind: (1) creating a positive image for the firm and (2) communicating the organization's views on social, business, and environmental issues. More specific applications include:

- Boosting employee morale and smoothing labor relations.
- Helping newly deregulated industries ease consumer uncertainty and answer investor questions.
- Helping diversified companies establish an identity for the parent firm rather than relying solely on brand names.[23]

As these objectives indicate, corporate advertising is targeted at both internal and external audiences and involves the promotion of the organization as well as its ideas.

Types of Corporate Advertising

Marketers seek attainment of corporate advertising's objectives by implementing image, advocacy, or cause-related advertising. Each form is designed to achieve specific goals.

IMAGE ADVERTISING

One form of corporate advertising is devoted to promoting the organization's overall image. **Image advertising** may accomplish a number of objectives, including creating goodwill both internally and externally, creating a position for the company, and generating resources, both human and financial. A number of methods are used.

1. *General image or positioning ads.* As shown in Exhibit 16–11, ads are often designed to create an image of the firm in the public mind. The exhibit shows how Tyco is attempting to create an image of itself as a market leader and acquisitions expert, not a *toy* company.

Other companies have used image advertising to attempt to change an existing image. The American Medical Association (AMA), responding to its less than positive image among many Americans who perceived doctors as inattentive money-grubbers, ran a series of ads portraying doctors in a more sensitive light. It spent over $1.75 million to highlight the caring, sharing, and sensitive side of AMA members.[24] *Penthouse* magazine attempted to change its image with advertisers by running ads in trade magazines that showed *Penthouse* was not just a magazine with pictures of nude females.

2. *Sponsorships.* A firm often runs corporate image advertising on TV programs or specials. For example, the Hallmark or IBM specials and documentaries on network TV and Mobil and Gulf Oil program sponsorships on public TV are designed to promote the corporation as a good citizen. By associating itself with high-quality or educational programming, the firm hopes for a carryover effect that benefits its own image.

Other examples of sponsorships include those run by Amoco (Fishers of Men, a project to help disadvantaged black youths in Chicago), Dutch Boy paints and the National Basketball Association to raise funds to fight child abuse, *Family Circle* magazine and JCPenney's to support "Sesame Street," and Budget Rent-a-Car's sponsorship of women's sports (Ladies' Professional Golf Association, Women's Tennis Association, and Women's Sports Foundation). Exhibit 16–12 shows the variety of companies sponsoring the America's Cup sailing races.

EXHIBIT 16–11   Tyco uses image advertising to avoid confusion

EXHIBIT 16–12   A variety of companies sponsor the America's Cup races

Visa considers sponsorships an important part of its integrated marketing communications. It has sponsored the Olympics, the U.S. decathlon team, U.S. basketball's dream team, the U.S. Gymnastics Federation, the U.S. Open Tennis Championships, and Major League Baseball's All-Star game. According to John Bennett, senior VP for international marketing communications, the sponsorships are designed to fulfill specific business objectives while providing support for the recipients.[25] Figure 16–7 shows a few of the companies that decided an Olympic sponsorship would be good for them.

3. *Recruiting.* The promotional piece for Deloitte & Touche presented here is a good example of corporate image advertising designed to attract new employees. If you are a graduating senior considering a career in accounting, this ad, promoting a corporate image for the company, will interest you.

The Sunday employment section of most major metropolitan newspapers is an excellent place to see this form of corporate image advertising at work. Notice the ads in these papers and consider the images the firms are presenting.

4. *Generating financial support.* Some corporate advertising is designed to generate investments in the corporation. By creating a more favorable image, the firm makes itself attractive to potential stock purchasers and investors. More investments mean more working capital, more monies for research and development, and so on. In this instance, corporate image advertising is almost attempting to make a sale; the product is the firm.

While there is no concrete evidence that corporate image advertising leads directly to increased investment, at least one study shows a correlation between the price of stock and the amount of corporate advertising done.[26] Firms that spend more on corporate advertising also tend to have higher-priced stocks (though a direct relationship is very difficult to substantiate).

This thing called image is not unidimensional. Many factors affect it. Exhibit 16–13 shows the results of a survey conducted by *Fortune* magazine on the most and least admired firms in the United States. The most admired firms did not gain their positions merely by publicity and word of mouth (nor, we guess, did the least admired).

A positive corporate image cannot be created just from a few advertisements. Quality of products and services, innovation, sound financial practices, good corporate citizenship, and wise marketing are just a few of the factors that contribute to overall image.

ADVOCACY ADVERTISING

A second major form of corporate advertising addresses social, business, or environmental issues. Such **advocacy advertising** is concerned with propagating ideas and elucidating controversial social issues of public importance in a manner that supports the interests of the sponsor.[27]

While still portraying an image for the company or organization, advocacy advertising does so indirectly, by adopting a position on a particular issue rather than promoting the organization itself. An example is shown in Exhibit 16–14. Advocacy advertising has increased in use over the past few years and has also met with increased criticism. The ads may be sponsored by a firm or by a trade association and are designed to tell readers how the firm operates or management's position on a particular issue.

Sometimes the advertising is a response to negative publicity or to the firm's inability to place an important message through public relations channels. Sometimes the firm just wants to get certain ideas accepted or have society understand its concerns.

Advocacy advertising has been criticized by a number of sources (including consumer advocate Ralph Nader). But as you can see in Exhibit 16–15, this form of communication

FIGURE 16–7 Many companies paid big bucks to share in Olympic glory

Companies/brands that paid cash, products and services to be category-exclusive sponsors of the 1996 Summer Olympics in Atlanta.

Worldwide Partners: $40 million for global rights (includes 1994 Winter Olympics in Lillehammer, Norway)

Bausch & Lomb Optical product/dental care	**IBM** Information technology	**Sports Illustrated/ Time** Magazines	**Visa** Payment systems
Coca-Cola Soft drinks	**Kodak** Still imaging	**UPS** Package delivery	**Xerox** Document processing
John Hancock Life insurance	**Matsushita/Panasonic** TV/audio/video equipment		

Centennial Partners: $40 million for domestic rights

Anheuser-Busch Malt beverages/theme parks/salty snacks	**Home Depot** Retail home improvement	**Motorola** Wireless communications	**Sara Lee** Activewear/select food products
AT&T Telecommunications	**IBM** Information technology	**NationsBank** Banking services	**Swatch** Timing and scoring
Delta Air Lines Travel	**McDonald's** Restaurants		

Centennial Sponsors: $5 million to $15 million for domestic rights

American Gas Association Fueling/vehicle maintenance	**Dial Corp.** Soap/laundry/household cleaning	**Merrill Lynch** Investment banking	**Texaco** Petroleum
Avon Cosmetics/skincare	**General Mills** Cereals/food products	**Nissan** Import trucks, sport-utility vehicles, minivans	**Textron** Personnel/cargo carrier
BellSouth Local telecommunications	**General Motors** Domestic cars/trucks	**Randstad** Staffing services	**Worldtravel** Travel services
Blue Cross/Blue Shield Health insurance	**Georgia Power** Power source/electrical services	**Reebok International** Footwear supplier/home video licensee	**York** Air conditioning systems
BMW Import cars/motorcycles/ mountain bikes	**Holiday Inn** Hotel accommodations	**Scientific Atlanta** Broadband TV distribution systems	**"Wheel of Fortune"/ "Jeopardy"** Promotional support
Borg-Warner Security Protective services	**International Paper** Paper products	**Sensormatic** Electronic security systems	**WXIA-TV Atlanta** NBC affiliate
Brunswick Corp. Yachting equip./Olymp. village bowling center			

has been around for a long time. AT&T engaged in issues-oriented advertising way back in 1908 and has continued to employ this form of communication throughout the 20th century. Critics contend that companies with large advertising budgets purchase too much ad space and time and that advocacy ads may be misleading, but the checks and balances of regular product advertising also operate in this area.

For example, an ad run by the seven regional Bell operating companies that addressed the threat of Japanese technologies in the telecommunications industry was perceived by some members of Congress (the group the ads were designed to influence) as Japan-bashing and offensive. When the ad backfired, the campaign was immediately halted and the agency that developed it was fired.[28] The ultimate judge, of course, is always the reader.

CAUSE-RELATED ADVERTISING

An increasingly popular method of image building is **cause-related marketing**, in which companies link with charities or nonprofit organizations as contributing sponsors. The company benefits from favorable publicity, while the charity receives much-needed funds. This

Coca-Cola repeats this year as America's most admired company, garnering praise for its financial soundness, management quality, and investment value.

PHILIPPE HOUZE

THE MOST ADMIRED

RANK	1995	COMPANY	SCORE
1	1	**Coca-Cola** Beverages	8.87
2	7	**Mirage Resorts** Hotels, casinos, resorts	8.44
3	6	**Merck** Pharmaceuticals	8.34
4	25	**United Parcel Service** Mail, pkg. & freight delivery	8.31
5	7	**Microsoft** Computer & data services	8.29
6	4	**Johnson & Johnson** Pharmaceuticals	8.27
7	5	**Intel** Electronics	8.27
8	12	**Pfizer** Pharmaceuticals	8.23
9	2	**Procter & Gamble** Soaps, cosmetics	8.18
10	17	**Berkshire Hathaway** Diversified financial	8.18

THE LEAST ADMIRED

RANK	1995	COMPANY	SCORE
431	417	**TWA** Airlines	3.42
430	408	**Standard Commercial** Tobacco	3.76
429	415	**Kmart** General merchandise	3.82
428	•	**Canandaigua Wine** Beverages	4.03
427	416	**Morrison Knudsen** Engineering, construction	4.05
426	401	**Flagstar** Food services	4.07
425	414	**USAir Group** Airlines	4.13
424	399	**Beverly Enterprises** Health care	4.31
423	411	**Amerco** Trucking	4.44
422	407	**Cal Fed Bancorp** Savings institutions	4.44

apparent win/win situation is not always as good as it seems, however; some companies have found that thier support may have hurt sales. For example, Starkist believes that its support of dolphin-safe tuna has led consumers to switch to cheaper brands.[29] In many cases, consumers believe that the company has ulterior motives (that is, generating sales) beyond supporting the cause.[30]

Advantages and Disadvantages of Corporate Advertising

A number of reasons for the increased popularity of corporate advertising become evident when you examine the advantages of this form of communication.

1. *It is an excellent vehicle for positioning the firm.* Firms, like products, need to establish an image or position in the marketplace. Corporate image ads are one way to accomplish this objective. A well-positioned product is much more likely to achieve success than is one with a vague or no image. The same holds true of the firm. Stop and think for a moment about the image that comes to mind when you hear the name IBM, Apple, Johnson & Johnson, or Procter & Gamble.

Now what comes to mind when you hear Unisys, USX, or Navistar? How many consumer brands can you name that fall under Beatrice Foods' corporate umbrella? (Swiss Miss, Tropicana, Cutty Sark, and many others.) While we are not saying these latter companies are not successful—because they certainly are—we are suggesting their corporate identities (or positions) are not as well entrenched as the identities of those first cited. Companies with strong positive corporate images have an advantage over competitors that may be enhanced when they promote the company overall.

2. *It takes advantage of the benefits derived from public relations.* As the PR efforts of firms have increased, the attention paid to these events by the media has lessened (not because they are of any less value, but because there are more events to cover). The net result is that when a company engages in a public relations effort, there is no guarantee it will receive press coverage and publicity. Corporate image advertising gets the message out, and though consumers may not perceive it as positively as information from an objective source, the fact remains that it can communicate what has been done.

EXHIBIT 16—14   Advocacy ads take a position on an issue

EXHIBIT 16—15   Advocacy ads have been used for years

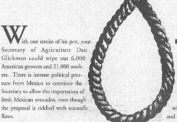

Dear Mr. President:

The USDA is about to sign the death warrant for a billion dollar American industry.

With one stroke of his pen, your Secretary of Agriculture Dan Glickman could wipe out 6,000 American growers and 21,000 workers. There is intense political pressure from Mexico to convince the Secretary to allow the importation of fresh Mexican avocados, even though the proposal is riddled with scientific flaws.

Without your help, the U. S. avocado industry could be sentenced to death by a USDA decision to allow importation of Mexican avocados. Scientists say some of these Mexican avocados will carry pests that can destroy entire groves — entire businesses — if they infest America's bountiful agricultural areas.

Secretary Glickman has repeatedly promised he will decide this issue based on science and not politics. However, he is being misled on the state of the science. The Department *doesn't have* solid data and its method of analysis is highly flawed.

Here are the *facts* on an issue clouded by politics and rhetoric:

■ Independent scientific experts from Cornell, Boston University, Oregon State and the Universities of California and Illinois have uniformly criticized the limited research procedures and findings on which the USDA is relying in its formulation of the proposed rule. Each and every independent scientist has concluded that the proposal should be delayed pending the development of a more thorough and unbiased scientific review.

■ Harvard University's Center for Risk Analysis has invited the USDA to participate in a symposium later this year, the purpose of which is "to assist...in the understanding, development and application of proper quantitative risk assessment principles." The USDA should accept Harvard's invitation, withhold issuance of the proposed rule and use information developed in this neutral forum to ensure that the interests of American agriculture are served.

■ This issue is not about economics. American agriculture has competed successfully with foreign-grown avocados for decades. *We fear for the health of our groves.* The nine quarantine pests of economic significance listed by USDA that are commonly found in Mexican avocados would have a devastating impact on not only the avocado industry, but also on citrus, grapes, apples and numerous other products that are grown throughout the country.

PLEASE, MR. PRESIDENT, DON'T COMPROMISE THE SCIENCE! Your leadership and your decision on Mexican avocados will help define whether or not your Administration will be known as the one that stands up for American agriculture or the one that ignored the facts and sacrificed American growers just to help Mexico. PLEASE, MR. PRESIDENT, WE NEED YOUR HELP.

Mark Affleck
President, California Avocado Commission
Representing America's 6,000 avocado growers

California Avocado Commission • 1251 E. Dyer Rd. #200 • Santa Ana, CA 92705

★
SHE'S A PARTNER IN A GREAT AMERICAN BUSINESS

She is one of 850,000 owners of Bell System securities. They are typical Americans—some young, some middle age, some old. They live in every part of the nation.

One may be a housewife in Pennsylvania. Another a physician in Oregon—a clerk in Illinois—an engineer in Texas—a merchant in Massachusetts—a miner in Nevada—a stenographer in Missouri—a teacher in California—or a telephone employee in Michigan.

For the most part, Bell System stockholders are men and women who have put aside small sums for saving. More than half of them have held their shares for five years or longer. More than 650,000 of these 850,000 security holders own stock in the American Telephone and Telegraph Company—the parent company of the Bell System. More than 225,000 own five shares or less. Over fifty per cent are women. No one owns as much as one per cent of the stock of A. T. & T. In a very real sense, the Bell System is a democracy in business—owned by the people it serves.

More than 270,000 men and women work for the Bell System. One person out of every 150 in this country owns A. T. & T. securities or stock and bonds of associated companies in the Bell System.

BELL TELEPHONE SYSTEM

3. *It reaches a select target market.* Corporate image advertising should not be targeted to the general public. It is often targeted to investors and managers of other firms rather than to the general public. It doesn't matter if the general public does not appreciate this form of communication, as long as the target market does. In this respect, this form of advertising may be accomplishing its objectives.

Some of the disadvantages of corporate advertising were alluded to earlier in the chapter. To these criticisms, we can add the following.

1. *Questionable effectiveness.* There is no strong evidence to support the belief that corporate advertising works. Many doubt the data cited earlier that demonstrated a correlation between stock prices and corporate image advertising. A study by Bozell & Jacobs Advertising of 16,000 ads concluded that corporate advertising contributed to only 4 percent of the variability in the company's stock price, compared with a 55 percent effect attributable to financial factors.[31] A second study also casts doubts on earlier studies that concluded that corporate advertising worked.[32]

2. *Constitutionality and/or ethics.* Some critics contend that since larger firms have more money, they can control public opinion unfairly. This point was resolved in the courts in favor of the advertisers. Nevertheless, many consumers still see such advertising as unfair and immediately take a negative view of the sponsor.

A number of valid points have been offered for and against corporate advertising. Two things are certain: (1) no one knows who is right and (2) the use of this communications form continues to increase.

Measuring the Effectiveness of Corporate Advertising

As you can tell from our discussion of the controversy surrounding corporate advertising, there need to be methods for evaluating whether or not such advertising is effective.

- *Attitude surveys.* One way to determine the effectiveness of corporate advertising is conducting attitude surveys to gain insights into both the public's and investors' reactions to ads. The Phase II study conducted by market research firm Yankelovich, Skelly & White is one of the best-known applications of this measurement method.[33] The firm measured recall and attitudes toward corporate advertisers and found that corporate advertising is more efficient in building recall for a company name than is product advertising alone. Frequent corporate advertisers rated better on virtually all attitude measures than those with low corporate ad budgets.
- *Studies relating corporate advertising and stock prices.* The Bozell & Jacobs study is one of many that have examined the effect of various elements of corporate advertising (position in the magazine, source effects, etc.) on stock prices. These studies have yielded conflicting conclusions, indicating that while the model for such measures seems logical, methodological problems may account for at least some of the discrepancies.
- *Focus group research.* Focus groups have been used to find out what investors want to see in ads and how they react after the ads are developed. As with product-oriented advertising, this method has limitations, although it does allow for some effective measurements.

While the effectiveness of corporate advertising has been measured by some of the methods used to measure product-specific advertising, research in this area has not kept pace with that of the consumer market. (One study reported that only 35 of the Fortune 500 companies ever attempted to measure performance of their annual reports.[34]) The most commonly offered reason for this lack of effort is that corporate ads are often the responsibility of those in the highest management positions in the firm, and these parties do not wish to be held accountable. Interestingly, those who should be most concerned with accountability are the most likely to shun this responsibility!

SUMMARY

This chapter examined the role of the promotional elements of public relations, publicity, and corporate advertising. We noted that these areas are all significant to the marketing and communications effort and are usually considered differently from the other promotional elements. The reasons for this special treatment stem from the facts that (1) they are typically not designed to promote a specific product or service and (2) in many instances it is harder for the consumer to make the connection between the communication and its intent.

Public relations was shown to be useful in its traditional responsibilities as well as in a more marketing-oriented role. In many firms, PR is a separate department operating independently of marketing; in others, it is considered a support system. Many large firms have an external public relations agency, just as they have an outside ad agency.

In the case of publicity, another factor enters the equation: lack of control over the communication the public will receive. In public relations and corporate advertising, the organization remains the source and retains much more control. Publicity often takes more of a reactive than a proactive approach, yet it may be more instrumental (or detrimental) to the success of a product or organization than all other forms of promotion combined.

While not all publicity can be managed, the marketer must nevertheless recognize its potential impact. Press releases and the management of information are just two of the factors under the company's control. Proper reaction and a strategy to deal with uncontrollable events are also responsibilities.

Corporate advertising was described as controversial, largely because the source of the message is top management, so the rules for other advertising and promoting forms are often not applied. This element of communication definitely has its place in the promotional mix. But to be effective, it must be used with each of the other elements, with specific communications objectives in mind.

Finally, we noted that measures of evaluation and control are required for each of these program elements, just as they are for all others in the promotional mix. We presented some methods for taking such measurements and some evidence why it is important to use them. As long as the elements of public relations, publicity, and corporate advertising are considered integral components of the overall communications strategy, they must respect the same rules as the other promotional mix elements to ensure success.

KEY TERMS

public relations, 514
marketing public relations
   (MPR), 516
internal audiences, 518
external audiences, 518

press release, 523
press conference, 523
exclusive, 523
team approach, 528
internal audits, 528

external audits, 528
publicity, 528
video news release, 532
corporate advertising, 532

image advertising, 535
advocacy advertising, 536
cause-related marketing,
   537

DISCUSSION QUESTIONS

1. Explain what is meant by the terms *cause-related advertising* and *advocacy advertising*. Cite some organizations that have used this strategy. Does it work?

2. Give examples of companies that are pursuing traditional public relations activities and those that are employing the new role.

3. What are MPR's functions? How might they benefit the organization's marketing program?

4. Why is publicity so powerful? Give examples of how it has worked for and against companies.

5. Some people believe firms should not adopt the new marketing-oriented role for public relations. Argue for and against this position.

6. Many companies are now taking the position that their charitable contributions should lead to something in re-

turn—for example, sales or increased visibility. Discuss the pros and cons of this position.

7. Many companies are now trying to generate as much free publicity as they can. Cite some examples of this and discuss the advantages and disadvantages associated with this strategy.

8. Describe some of the problems that might result from boycotts. Discuss strategies for combating boycotts.

9. Discuss the ethics involved in using situations like the O. J. Simpson case to gain publicity for one's products and services.

10. The text discussed the negative publicity and PR problem facing Texaco after executives were taped allegedly making discriminatory remarks about minorities. What would you do if you were the head of Texaco?

CHAPTER 17

Personal Selling

Chapter Objectives

- To discuss the role of personal selling in the integrated marketing communications program.

- To examine the advantages and disadvantages of personal selling as a promotional program element.

- To demonstrate how personal selling is combined with other elements in an IMC program.

- To consider ways to determine the effectiveness of the personal selling effort.

THE BEST SALES FORCES REFLECT AN IMC APPROACH

Sales & Marketing Management magazine ranks the top 25 sales forces in the United States. One factor common to all the selections is their increasing reliance on other marketing program elements. In short, effective salespeople are becoming more marketing (and more IMC) oriented. According to *S&MM*, "Adapt or die" is the main lesson to be learned from the top sales forces. Each has successfully evolved to meet the ever-changing requirements of the global marketplace. Procter & Gamble, Frito–Lay, and 3M all radically reorganized their sales departments to meet customer needs. Motorola and Merck rolled out new products to help their sales forces remain ahead of the competition, and American Express relied on market segmentation to discover a whole new market for its cards. Other companies have specifically employed an IMC approach to achieve this lofty ranking. For example:

- Northwestern Mutual Life Insurance (NML) ran a nationwide contest to assist its agencies in recruiting "the perfect rep." The contest was presented through the company's newsletter and attracted 100 of NML's 300 agencies. The criteria for winning involved the number of contacts made, the adaptability of the promotional efforts to other agencies, and the program's cost effectiveness. One of the winning agencies hosted a career fair that featured mock interviews and resume critiques. Recruitment was up 23 percent over the previous year, and over 56 percent on college campuses.
- Walt Disney Co. reps are getting the message out to their clients by incorporating packages for seniors and young adults into all of their presentations. The reps

S&MM profiles the Northwestern's "consistently successful sales force"

'Devotion, products, & pride'

Judging from her article in the November issue of *Sales & Marketing Management* magazine, **Ginger Conlon** left Milwaukee overwhelmed by the Northwestern, its agents and the career. A few excerpts:

"His fervor is shared...": "Don't be fooled by (College Agent **Glenn**) **Starfield's** youth: His fervor is shared by most of NML's 7,300 agents. The devotion they feel for NML, the belief they have in its products, and pride they take in their jobs are what make the company's sales force consistently successful.
"The challenge for NML is finding energetic self-starters like Starfield, who are committed to a lifelong career in insurance sales, because unlike most products, insurance is a lifetime investment."

"People with the courage...": "We need people with the courage to build a career that's not just what will come the first year, but what will come in twenty to thirty years," says **Dennis Tamcsin**, Senior Vice President – Agencies, of the Milwaukee-based company.
"We provide support, but agents will rise or fall, succeed or fail on their own. Few other jobs have this level of autonomy, so we attract people who are driven to succeed."

"Customer service driven...": "NML also looks for people who will fit into its customer-service-driven, 'we're-one-big-happy-family' culture.

"Strong business values...": "People with strong business values are drawn to Northwestern because it's driven to produce long-term value for policy owners," says **Ruble Hord** of Richmond, Virginia, NML's top producer for 1995.
"I'm able to express my business values because they're the same as Northwestern Mutual's."

"Keeping the fabric strong...": "Why all the hoopla over finding the 'perfect' rep? Keeping the fabric of the company strong is as important to NML as is increasing sales."

"The best candidates...": "As agent **Walter Putnam** of Charlotte, North Carolina, puts it, 'it's our responsibility to find the best candidates to replace ourselves, because the only way to help ourselves succeed is to help others succeed.'"

are supported by an extensive database, advertising, and tailored pitches that include brochures, videos, and other promotional materials.

- The Coca-Cola Co. dominates the soda fountain business, showing growth rates of 16 and 11 percent respectively in the past two years. Part of the reason is that Coke's salespeople are referred to as account managers. They are armed with reams of information about potential and existing clients' business, supported by marketing teams that conduct in-depth consumer behavior studies of trade channels. They act as partners with their clients in a strong relationship marketing approach. The Coke reps make recommendations about adding new products as well as advertising and promoting them. They also provide strong merchandising support.
- Also on the list of the top 25 are two traditional "selling" companies: Mary Kay and Amway. Unlike the other companies, which both represent and sell, these two direct marketers have focused their efforts on selling. Both are now engaged in what they refer to as "consulting" with their clients and have increased their use of promotions and other marketing tools.

These are just a few example of how top-rated sales teams are using IMC tools. Each of the other companies cited shows a strong IMC orientation as selling efforts are replaced by marketing efforts. Maybe someday sales reps will all be called marketing reps.

Geoffrey Brewer and Christine Galea, "The Top," *Sales & Marketing Management*, November 1996, pp. 38–75.

THE SCOPE OF PERSONAL SELLING

The examples in the chapter opener demonstrate just a few of the ways organizations are integrating the personal selling function into the overall marketing communications program. They also reflect the complementary role of each of these elements in a field previously dominated by personal sales. In Chapter 1, we stated that while we recognize the importance of personal selling and the role it plays in the overall marketing and promotions effort, it is not emphasized in this text. Personal selling is typically under the control of the sales manager, not the advertising and promotions department. But personal selling does make a valuable contribution to the promotional program. To develop a promotional plan effectively, a firm must integrate the roles and responsibilities of its sales force into the communications program. Strong cooperation between the departments is also necessary.

This chapter focuses on the role personal selling assumes in the IMC program, the advantages and disadvantages of this program element, and the basis for evaluating its contributions to attaining communications objectives. In addition, we explore how personal selling is combined with other program elements, both to support them and to receive support from them.

Personal selling involves selling through a person-to-person communications process. The emphasis placed on personal selling varies from firm to firm depending on a variety of factors, including the nature of the product or service being marketed, size of the organization, and type of industry. Personal selling often plays the dominant role in industrial firms, while in other firms, such as makers of low-priced consumer nondurable goods, its role is minimized. In many industries, these roles are changing to a more balanced use of promotional program elements. In an integrated marketing communications program, personal selling is a partner with, not a substitute for, the other promotional mix elements.

Figure 17–1 shows the results of a survey of marketing managers' perceptions of how the various elements of the promotional mix were expected to change over the years. The managers interviewed expect sales management and personal selling to increase in importance more than any other element of the promotional mix. Note, however, that other elements are expected to gain in importance as well, indicating an enhanced overall promotional program.

FIGURE 17–1 Change in relative importance of components of the promotional mix

Strategy Statement	Change in Relative Importance					
	Greatly Decreased	Moderately Decreased	Same	Moderately Increased	Greatly Increased	Mean Rating*
Promotional strategy						
Special promotional activities such as promotional warranties, trade shows, dealer aids, and product displays	0.0%	12.6%	48.5%	35.0%	3.9%	3.3
Public relations, public affairs, and community relations	0.0	7.8	43.7	33.8	9.7	3.5
Product branding and promotional packaging	0.0	8.7	47.6	35.0	8.7	3.4
Sales management and personal selling, including all sales management activities (e.g., training, supervision) and the sales efforts of company management personnel	1.0	2.9	28.4	52.9	14.7	3.8
Print media advertising in newspapers, magazines, and brochures	0.0	17.6	52.0	24.5	5.9	3.2
Broadcast media advertising on radio/TV	0.0	15.8	51.5	25.7	6.9	3.2
Media advertising on cable TV, over-the-air pay TV, and videodisk	1.0	7.9	29.7	49.5	11.9	3.6

*1 = Greatly decreased, 2 = Moderately decreased, 3 = Same, 4 = Moderately increased, 5 = Greatly increased.

THE ROLE OF PERSONAL SELLING IN THE IMC PROGRAM

Manufacturers may promote their products *directly* to consumers through advertising and promotions and/or direct-marketing efforts or *indirectly* through resellers and salespeople. (A sales force may call on customers directly—for example, in the insurance industry or real estate. But this chapter focuses on the personal selling function as it exists in most large corporations or smaller companies—that is, as a link to resellers or dealers in business-to-business transactions.) Depending on the role defined by the organization, the responsibilities and specific tasks of salespeople may differ, but ultimately these tasks are designed to help attain communications and marketing objectives.

Personal selling differs from the other forms of communication presented thus far in that messages flow from a sender (or group of senders) to a receiver (or group of receivers) directly (usually face to face). This *direct* and *interpersonal communication* lets the sender immediately receive and evaluate feedback from the receiver. This communications process, known as **dyadic communication** (between two people or groups), allows for more specific tailoring of the message and more personal communications than do many of the other media discussed. The message can be changed to address the receiver's specific needs and wants.

In some situations, this ability to focus on specific problems is mandatory; a standard communication would not suffice. Consider an industrial buying situation in which the salesperson is an engineer. To promote the company's products and/or services, the salesperson must understand the client's specific needs. This may mean understanding the tensile strength of materials or being able to read blueprints or plans to understand the requirements. Or say a salesperson represents a computer graphics firm. Part of his or her responsibility for making a sale may involve the design of a software program to solve a problem unique to this customer. Mass communications cannot accomplish these tasks. Personal selling plays a critical role not just in industrial settings but in the consumer market as well.

The great entrepreneur Marshall Field said, "The distance between the salesperson and the potential buyer is the most important three feet in business."[1] Personal selling is important in selling to consumers and resellers. Consumer products companies must secure distribution, motivate resellers to stock and promote the product, and so on.

Why is personal selling so important? Let's examine its role with respect to other promotional program elements.

Determining the Role of Personal Selling

The first questions a manager needs to ask when preparing the promotional program are what the specific responsibilities of personal selling will be and what role it will assume relative to the other promotional mix elements. To determine its role, management should be guided by four questions:

1. What specific information must be exchanged between the firm and potential customers?
2. What are the alternative ways to carry out these communications objectives?
3. How effective is each alternative in carrying out the needed exchange?
4. How cost effective is each alternative?[2]

• *Determining the information to be exchanged.* In keeping with the objectives established by the communications models in Chapter 5, the salesperson may have a variety of messages to communicate, such as creating awareness of the product or service offering, demonstrating product benefits for evaluation, initiating trial, and/or closing the sale. It may also be necessary to answer questions, counter misconceptions, and discover potentially unmet needs.

• *Examining promotional mix alternatives.* In previous chapters, we discussed the roles of advertising and sales promotion, direct marketing, and public relations/publicity. Each of these program elements offers specific advantages and disadvantages, and each needs to be considered when the promotional mix is developed. Personal selling is an alternative that offers distinct advantages in some situations but is less appropriate in others, as evidenced in Figure 17–2.

FIGURE 17–2   When the sales force is a major part of the IMC mix

Product or Service	Channels
Complex products requiring customer application assistance (computers, pollution control system, steam turbines) Major purchase decisions, such as food items purchased by supermarket chains Features and performance of the product requiring personal demonstration and trial by the customer (private aircraft)	Channel system relatively short and direct to end users Product and service training and assistance needed by channel intermediaries Personal selling needed to push product through channel Channel intermediaries available to perform personal selling function for supplier with limited resources and experience (brokers or manufacturer's agents)
Price	**Advertising**
Final price is negotiated between buyer and seller (appliances, cars, real estate) Selling price or quality purchased enables an adequate margin to support selling expenses (traditional department store compared to discount house)	Advertising media do not provide effective link with market targets Information needed by buyer cannot be provided entirely through advertising and sales promotion (life insurance) Number and dispersion of customers will not enable acceptable advertising economies

- *Evaluating the relative effectiveness of alternatives.* The effectiveness of each program element must be evaluated based on the target market and the objectives sought. Personal selling is effective in many situations, but other program elements may be more attractive in other cases. For example, advertising may do a better job of repeating messages or reaching a large number or people with one distinct, consistent message.
- *Determining cost effectiveness.* One of the major disadvantages of personal selling is the cost involved. (Cahners Research estimates the average cost per sales call could be as high as $332.)[3] While the cost of a personal sales call may not be prohibitive in industrial settings where a single purchase can be worth millions of dollars, the same cost may be unfeasible in a consumer market. Other media may be able to communicate the required message at a much lower cost.

The Nature of Personal Selling

To integrate the personal selling effort into the overall promotional program, we must understand the nature of this tool. Let us look at how personal selling has evolved over the years and then examine some of its characteristics.

The personal selling task encompasses a variety of responsibilities (some of which we discuss in the next section). Like other aspects of the promotional mix, these responsibilities are constantly changing. As noted by Thomas Wotruba, the personal selling area is constantly evolving as the marketing environment itself evolves.[4] Wotruba identifies five distinct stages of personal selling evolution, shown in Figure 17–3.

1. *Provider stage.* Selling activities are limited to accepting orders for the supplier's available offering and conveying it to the buyer.
2. *Persuader stage.* Selling involves an attempt to persuade market members to buy the supplier's offerings.
3. *Prospector stage.* Activities include seeking out selected buyers who are perceived to have a need for the offering as well as the resources and authority to buy it.
4. *Problem-solver stage.* Selling involves obtaining the participation of buyers to identify their problems, which can be translated into needs, and then presenting a selection from the supplier's offerings that corresponds with those needs and can solve those problems.
5. *Procreator stage.* Selling defines the buyer's problems or needs and their solutions through active buyer-seller collaboration and then creates a market offering uniquely tailored to the customer.

According to Wotruba, firms evolving through these five stages have to assume different market orientations, as well as different organizational designs, staffing, and compensation

FIGURE 17–3   The stages in the evolution of selling

Stages and Description	Characteristics of Stages			
	Customer Needs	Type of Market	Nature and Intensity of Competition	Examples
1. *Provider:* accepts orders and delivers to buyer.	Assumed to exist; not a concern	Sellers'	None	Route salespeople/drivers; some retail salesclerks
2. *Persuader:* attempts to convince anyone to buy available offerings.	Created, awakened	Buyers'	Undifferentiated; slight intensity	Telemarketers for photo studio; many new car dealers
3. *Prospector:* seeks out prospects with need for available offering and resources to buy.	Considered but inferred	Segmented	Differentiated; growing	Car insurance salespeople calling on new car buyers; office supplies sellers calling on small businesses
4. *Problem-solver:* matches available offerings to solve customer-stated problems.	Diagnosed, with attention to customer input	Participative	Responsive and counteractive with increasing resources	Communication systems salespeople for a telephone company; architectural services sellers calling on building contractors
5. *Procreator:* creates a unique offering to match the buyer's needs as mutually specified, involving any or all aspects of the seller's total marketing mix.	Mutually defined; matched with tailored offering	Coactive	Focused; growing in breadth of market and service offerings	Materials handling equipment salespeople who design and sell a system to fit a buyer's manufacturing facility

programs. The different stages require different promotional strategies, each integrated with personal selling to achieve the maximum communications effect.

RELATIONSHIP MARKETING

As noted in the introduction to this chapter, personal selling has evolved from persuasive techniques used to sell a product or service to a much more marketing-oriented *partnership* with the customer. This new role requires much broader thinking and expertise on the part of the seller and a more extensive use of the various promotional tools. The modern salesperson is attempting to establish a long-term, symbiotic relationship with the client, along the lines of stages 4 and 5 of Wotruba's model.

Relationship marketing is defined as "an organization's effort to develop a long-term, cost-effective link with individual customers for mutual benefit."[5] Rather than focusing on a short-term sale, the sales rep tries to establish a long-term bond. And rather than just selling, the sales department works with marketing to use techniques like database marketing, message differentiation to different target markets, and tracking of promotional effects to improve the relationship. As noted by Copulsky and Wolf, such marketing uses a more personalized form of communication that crosses the previous boundaries between personal selling and the other promotional tools.[6] Kimberly-Clark, Porsche, and MCI are just a few of the companies now involving the salesperson in the integrated marketing communications program.

THE COSTS OF PERSONAL SELLING.

In some industries, personal selling constitutes a substantial portion of the communications effort and may account for most of the promotional budget. This is true because (1) much attention is devoted to this function due to its advantages over other communication methods and (2) it is an expensive form of communication. As demonstrated by Figure 17–4, the average cost per sales call varies by industry, ranging from a low of $235 to $332 in the manufacturing sector. Communication does not come cheap!

FIGURE 17–4

Average cost per sales call by industry

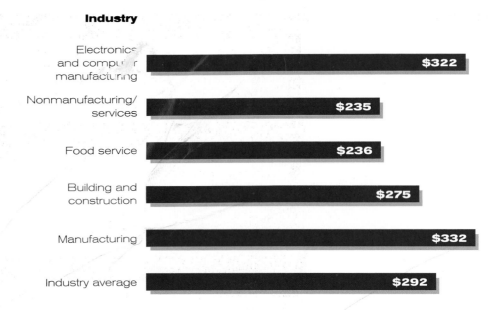

Industry	
Electronics and computer manufacturing	$322
Nonmanufacturing/services	$235
Food service	$236
Building and construction	$275
Manufacturing	$332
Industry average	$292

When the cost per sales call is compared with the cost per message delivered through other media, this figure seems outrageous. We saw in earlier chapters that these costs could be as low as 3 cents. But taking these numbers at face value may lead to unfair comparisons. In evaluating the costs of personal selling, we must consider the nature of the call, the objectives sought, and whether other program elements could deliver the message as effectively. It may be that the higher costs cannot be avoided.

The costs of personal selling are even higher when you consider that one sales call is not likely to be enough to close a deal. This is particularly true in the industrial market; while it may take (on the average) only 2.7 sales calls to close a deal in a services industry, the same close in manufacturing may require 4.4 visits.[7] As you can see through simple multiplication, the cost per sale is now even more intimidating (though in industrial markets the returns may easily warrant the expense).

Overall, personal selling is an expensive way to communicate. Yet it does usually involve more than just communicating, and the returns (more direct sales) may be greater than for the other program elements.

PERSONAL SELLING RESPONSIBILITIES

Sales & Marketing Management uses three categories to classify salespeople: **order taking**, **creative selling**, and **missionary sales**[8] (see Figure 17–5). Of course, not all firms treat each of these responsibilities the same, nor are their salespeople limited to only these tasks. Personal selling has evolved responsibilities beyond these. Job requirements may include (1) locating prospective customers; (2) determining customers' needs and wants that are not being satisfied; (3) recommending a way to satisfy these needs and/or wants; (4) demonstrating the capabilities of the firm and its products for providing this satisfaction; (5) closing the sale and taking the order; and (6) following up and servicing the account. Let's discuss these job classifications and some of the responsibilities assigned to each.

1. *Locating prospective customers.* The process of locating new customers (often referred to as **prospecting**) involves the search for and qualification of prospective customers. Salespeople must follow up on **leads** (those who may become customers) and **prospects** (those who need the product or service). They must also determine whether these prospects are **qualified prospects**—that is, able to make the buying decision and pay for the product. Exhibit 17–1 is an ad for a company that helps sales forces identify qualified leads.

2. *Determining customers' needs and wants.* At this stage, the salesperson gathers more information on the prospect and decides the best way to approach him or her. The rep must

FIGURE 17–5
Types of sales jobs

Creative Selling

Creative selling jobs may require the most skill and preparation. In addition to prospecting, the salesperson must assess the situation, determine the needs to be met, present the capabilities for satisfying these needs, and get an order. The salesperson is often the "point person" who has established the initial contact on behalf of the firm and who is primarily responsibile for completing the exchange. He or she is, in fact, the order getter.

Order Taking

Once the initial sale has taken place, the creative seller may be replaced (not physically!) by an order taker, whose role is much more casual. It may simply involve a straight rebuy—that is, the order does not change much. (A bottled-water delivery person is an example.) When a slight change is considered, the order taker may be involved in a modified rebuy, which may require some creative selling (for example, a salesperson calling on a wholesale food company may have a list of products to sell). If a major purchase decision is required, however, the role of making the sale may again be turned over to the creative seller.

Missionary Sales Reps

The missionary representative is essentially a support role. While performing many of the tasks assumed in creative selling, the missionary rep may not actually take the order. He or she introduces new products, new promotions, and/or new programs, with the actual order to be taken by the company's order taker or by a distributor representing the company's goods. The missionary sales rep may have additional account service responsibilities. Missionary reps are most often employed in industries where the manufacturer uses a middleperson to distribute the product (for example, food products or pharmaceuticals).

EXHIBIT 17–1
Giltspur offers salespeople expertise on how to qualify leads

determine what the customer needs or wants and make certain the person being approached is capable of making the purchase decision.

3. *Recommending a way to satisfy the customers' needs and wants.* Here the salesperson recommends a possible solution to the problem and/or needs of the potential customer. This may entail providing information the prospect had not considered or identifying alternative solutions that might work.

4. *Demonstrating the capabilities of the firm and its products.* At this stage, the salesperson demonstrates the capabilities of the firm and shows the prospect why that firm is the obvious choice. As you might expect, corporate image (created through advertising and other promotional tools) is important to the salesperson.

5. *Closing the sale.* The key ingredient in any sales presentation is the **close**—getting the prospect's commitment. For many salespeople, this is the most difficult task. Many reps are adept at prospecting, identifying customer needs, and making presentations, but they are reluctant to ask for the sale. Most managers work with their sales forces to close the sale and help reluctant or uncertain buyers make a decision.

6. *Following up and servicing the account.* The responsibilities of the sales force do not end once the sale has been made. It is much easier to keep existing customers than to attract new ones. Maintaining customer loyalty, generating repeat sales, and getting the opportunity to **cross sell**—that is, sell additional products and services to the same customer—are some of the advantages of keeping customers satisfied through follow-up activities.

A primary advantage a salesperson offers is the opportunity to assess the situation first-hand and adapt the sales message accordingly (a *direct feedback* network). No other promotional element provides this opportunity. The successful salesperson constantly analyzes the situation, reads the feedback provided by the receiver, and shapes the message to specifically meet the customer's needs.

While you might expect this to be an easy task, it isn't always the case. Sometimes buyers will not or cannot express their needs accurately. Other times, the salesperson must become a problem solver for the client. More and more, salespeople are being asked to assist in the buyers' decision-making process. The more salespeople can become involved in planning and decision making, the more confidence the buyer places in them, and the more bonding the relationship becomes.

Sometimes the true motivation for purchasing is not the one the customer gives. You might expect buyers to base their decisions on rational, objective factors, but this is not always the case. Even in industrial markets (where product specifications may be critical) or reseller markets (where product movements and/or profits are important), many purchase decisions are made on what might be called nonrational criteria (not irrational, but involving factors beyond cost or other product benefits). Since it is generally believed these purchase situations involve less emotion and more rational thinking than many consumer purchases, this is an important insight.

Consider the marketer's dilemma. If a firm provides advertising and promotions that speak only to the rational purchase motives, it may not be able to make the sale. On the other hand, how could an advertiser possibly know all the emotional or nonrational criteria influencing the decision, let alone integrate this information into its messages? The personal sales effort may be the only way to uncover the many motivations for purchasing and address them.

When you review this list of responsibilities, it becomes clear that the salesperson of today is no mere huckster. Global Perspective 17–1 demonstrates the fact that to sell in the international community may even require more sophistication, while Figure 17–6 provides a few dos and don'ts for the effective international salesperson (as reported by Francisco Javier Perez, who logs over 300,000 miles a year selling around the world).

The importance of personal selling in the integrated marketing communications program should now be clear. This program element provides opportunities that no other form of message delivery does. But while the tasks performed by salespeople offer some distinct advantages to the marketing program, they may also constitute disadvantages, as you will now see.

Global Perspective 17-1
Selling Overseas: A Different Way to Do Business

While personal selling requires more and more sophistication to be successful in U.S. markets, for companies that compete globally the U.S. market seems like kids' stuff. As more companies look to foreign markets for new business, they are being confronted with a whole new set of rules and problems. Consider the following examples:

- Millions of people are not consumers by American standards. In India, 70 percent of the country's 900 million people live in rural areas. Only one-third have TV sets and more than half are illiterate. Many have never seen such products as shampoo and toothpaste.
- Each country has a unique way of doing business. In Korea, there is a hierarchy of buyers. Salespeople must first present to the lower hierarchies, then present the same information again to upper-level managers (if they make the cut). In Spanish-speaking countries, socializing is much more important; people want to know personally who they are buying from and feel comfortable with them first.
- Time perspectives are different. Says Gareth Taube, VP of marketing and business development for Praxix International, "Most foreign countries are about six months behind the United States when it comes to product rollouts. You relive the anxiety of the product rollout six months after you have lived it here." Systems and Computer Technology Corp. worked on an account in Singapore for two years before getting the bid.

What this means to the sales force is that they have to adapt. Strategies and procedures that work in the United States may not fly in foreign markets, due to either legal or cultural issues. For example, Praxis learned that it is imperative to use formal names in Asian countries and to be more familial in Latin American countries. Veson had to rethink its negotiation strategy when selling computers to Korea to avoid making too many concessions in the early presentations. The Logical Choice, a New York-based company, increased its socializing time when doing business in Mexico and Puerto Rico.

But perhaps the biggest adaptation of all is demonstrated by Colgate-Palmolive's selling approach in India. Colgate created a video van in the shape of a toothpaste tube. The vehicle is driven around rural India. Groups of people are greeted with a 27-minute infomercial explaining the benefits of using toothpaste (social and functional) and given free samples and toothbrushes. Sales have doubled since 1990 and as Harish Manwani, director of personal products says, "There isn't any alternative."

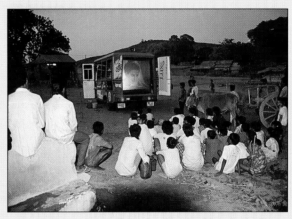

Sources: Deidra-Ann Parrish, "Selling Overseas—Small Steps Lead to Big Business for VARs who Learn to Break through the Cultural Barriers", *VAR-Business*, August 1, 1996, p. 67; Miriam Jordan, "In Rural India, Video Vans Sell Toothpaste and Shampoo," *The Wall Street Journal*, January 10, 1996.

Advantages and Disadvantages of Personal Selling

The nature of personal selling positions this promotional tool uniquely among those available to marketers. Its advantages include the following.

- *Allowing for two-way interaction.* The ability to interact with the receiver allows the sender to determine the impact of the message. Problems in comprehension or objections can be resolved and in-depth discussions of certain selling points can be provided immediately. In mass communications this direct feedback is not available and such information cannot be obtained immediately (if at all).
- *Tailoring of the message.* Because of the direct interaction, messages can be tailored to the receiver. This more precise message content lets the sender address the consumer's specific concerns, problems, and needs. The sales rep can also determine when to move on to the next selling point, ask for the sale, or close the deal.
- *Lack of distraction.* In many personal selling situations, a one-to-one presentation is conducted. The likelihood of distractions is minimized and the buyer is generally paying close attention to the sales message. Even when the presentation is made by a group of salespeople or more than one decision maker is present, the setting is less distracting than those in which nonpersonal mass media are used.

FIGURE 17–6
The dos and don'ts of selling globally

Do Your Homework

"It's so basic," says Francisco Javier Perez (chosen as one of *Selling*'s top salespeople in the world). "Before I set foot in a foreign country, I learn as much as I can about the people and the potential market for my company, Bobby Jones (a sportswear division of Hartmarx). Even so, I still end up getting some things wrong. But not as many."

Don't Dictate

Avoid imposing your beliefs and ways of doing business, he says. "At least not at first. Give people a chance to succeed on their own terms."

Do Listen to the Customer

"If they don't speak English," advises Perez, "watch their eyes and body language."

Don't Take It for Granted

"Remember," says Perez, "details that aren't spelled out in person will have to be hammered out later over the phone—and possibly in a foreign language."

Do Sell Yourself

"In an established market, you judge a salesperson by the brand he carries," explains Perez. "But in a new market, it's the reverse. Your manner and appearance are especially important here."

Don't Eliminate Possibilities

"Remember, the world goes round," he says. "A partner who isn't right this year could be next year."

- *Involvement in the decision process.* Through consultative selling and relationship marketing, the seller becomes more of a partner in the buying decision process, acting in conjunction with the buyer to solve problems. This leads the buyer to rely more on the salesperson and his or her products and services. An added benefit may be increasing the involvement of the organization's own employees.

As you can see, the advantages of personal selling focus primarily on the dyadic communications process, the ability to alter the message, and the opportunity for direct feedback. Sometimes, however, these potential advantages are not always realized. In fact, they may become disadvantages.

Disadvantages associated with personal selling include the following.

- *Inconsistent messages.* Earlier we stated that the ability to adapt the message to the receiver is a distinct advantage of personal selling. But the lack of a standardized message can become a disadvantage. The message to be communicated is generally designed by the marketing staff with a particular communications objective in mind. Once this message has been determined, it is communicated to all receivers. But the salesperson may alter this message in ways the marketer did not intend. Thus, the marketing staff is at the mercy of the sales force with respect to what exactly is communicated. (Sales communications aids can offset this problem to some degree, as you will see later in this chapter.)

- *Sales force/management conflict.* Unfortunately, there are situations in even the best companies when one wonders if the sales staff and marketing staff know they work for the same company and for the same goals. Because of failure to communicate, corporate politics, and myriad other reasons, the sales force and marketing may not be working as a team. The marketing staff may not understand the problems faced by the sales staff, or the salespeople may not understand why marketing people do things the way they do. The result is that the sales force may not use materials provided from marketing, marketing may not be responsive to the field's assessment of customer needs, and so forth. The bottom line is that the communications process is not as effective as it could be due to faulty internal communications and/or conflicts.

• *High cost.* We discussed earlier the high cost of personal selling. As the cost per sales call continues to climb, the marketer may find mass communications a more cost-effective alternative.

• *Poor reach.* Personal selling cannot reach as many members of the target audience as other elements. Even if money were no object (not a very likely scenario!), the sales force has only so many hours and so many people it can reach in a given time. Further, the frequency with which these accounts are reached is also low.

• *Potential ethical problems.* Because the manager does not have complete control over the messages the salespeople communicate and because income and advancement are often directly tied to sales, sometimes sales reps bend the rules. They may say and do things they know are not entirely ethical or in the best interest of the firm in order to get a sale. The potential for this problem has led to a renewed emphasis on ethics in the marketplace.

COMBINING PERSONAL SELLING WITH OTHER PROMOTIONAL TOOLS
Combining Personal Selling and Advertising

Like the other program elements, personal selling is usually one component of the integrated marketing communications program. Rarely, if ever, is it used alone. Rather, this promotional tool both supports and is supported by other program elements.

With specific market situations and communications objectives, the advantages of advertising make it more effective in the early stages of the response hierarchy (for example, in creating awareness and interest), whereas personal selling is more likely to be used in the later stages (for example, stimulating trial and getting the order). Thus, each may be more or less appropriate depending on the objectives sought. These elements can be combined in the promotional mix to compensate for each other's weaknesses and complement each other.

Consider a new product introduction. Given an adequate budget, the initial objective might be to reach as many people in the target market as quickly and cost effectively as possible. Since the primary objective is awareness and a simple message will suffice, advertising will likely be the most appropriate medium.

Now suppose specific benefits must be communicated that are not very obvious or easy to comprehend, and a product demonstration would be useful. Or consider a situation in which the objective is to ask for the sale and/or to establish a relationship. Here personal selling is a more appropriate tool than advertising. In common marketing situations like these, you can see how well advertising and personal selling work together to attain the objectives sought.

A number of studies bear out this complementary relationship. A study by Theodore Levitt showed that sales reps from well-known companies are better received than those from companies that do not spend advertising dollars to create awareness.[9] (Once they are in the door, however, the buyer expects the salesperson to perform better than those from lesser-known companies.) If a salesperson from a lesser-known company can get in to see the buyer, he or she is as likely to make the sale. But in risky situations, the well-advertised company rep has the advantage.

In other studies, John Morrill found that selling costs were 2 percent to 28 percent lower if the buyer had received an advertising message before the salesperson's arrival.[10] McGraw-Hill Corp., in a review of 54 studies, concluded the combination of advertising and personal selling is important since "less than 10 percent of industrial decision makers had been called upon by a salesperson from a specific company about a specific product in the previous two months."[11]

The studies suggest that combining advertising and personal selling is likely to improve reach, reduce costs, and increase the probability of a sale (assuming the advertising is effective, a concern reflected in Exhibit 17–2).

Combining Personal Selling and Public Relations

The job descriptions presented earlier demonstrate that personal selling involves much more than just selling products and/or services. The personal selling agent is often the firm's best source of public relations. In their day-to-day duties, salespeople represent the

EXHIBIT 17–2
Advertising and personal selling
should be designed to work together

firm and its products. Their personalities, servicing of the account, cooperation, and empathy not only influence sales potential but also reflect on the organizations they represent.

The salesperson may also be used directly in a PR role. Many firms encourage sales reps to participate in community activities like the Jaycees and Little League. Sometimes sales reps, in conjunction with the company, sacrifice time from their daily duties to help people in need. For example, after the Los Angeles earthquake, local companies donated food and their sales forces' time to aid quake victims. Computer salespeople devoted much of their time to getting customers and noncustomers back online. After a catastrophic flood, a beer company in the Northeast had its sales reps distribute water in its cans to flood victims. Coors provided free water in its cans to Pittsburghers when a barge break contaminated the drinking water. After floods ravished the Midwest in 1997, Provident Bank of Cincinnati, Ohio, had its tellers sell blue ribbons for $1 apiece, with proceeds going to flood victims. Thriftway Food Stores and a number of organizations also helped rebuild the ravaged community. Such actions result in goodwill toward both the company and its products while at the same time benefiting society.

Combining Personal Selling and Direct Marketing

Companies have found that integrating direct marketing, specifically telemarketing, into their field sales operations makes their sales efforts more effective. The cost of a sales call and the cost associated with closing the sale are already very high and on the increase. Many marketers have reduced these costs by combining telemarketing and sales efforts (a typical telesales call costs about $15).[12] A number of companies now offer consulting services to help organizations in that endeavor, as shown in Exhibit 17–3.

The telemarketing department is used to screen leads and—after qualifying potential buyers on the basis of interest, credit ratings, and the like—pass them on to the sales force. The net result is a higher percentage of sales closings, less wasted time by the sales force, and a lower average cost per sale. For example, IBM has teamed up with Zacson Corp. to open an integrated teleservices center for its Northern California territory. The group han-

dles inquiries, lead generation, and qualification; develops promotional campaigns; distributes PR materials; and does problem solving for IBM clients. The new relationship reduced
IBM's customer contact costs by 97 percent, lowered sales visit costs from $500 to $15, and
exceeded customer expectations 78 percent of the time.[13]

As shown in Figure 17–7, there has been a rapid growth in the use of the telemarketing/
sales combination for other firms as well. They have determined the phone can be used effectively for service and follow-up functions as well as for growth-related activities. Supplementing personal selling efforts with phone calls frees the sales force to spend more time selling.

In addition to selling and supporting the sales efforts, the telemarketing staff provides a
public relations dimension. Communicating with buyers more often creates goodwill, improving customer satisfaction and loyalty.

In addition to telemarketing, other forms of direct marketing have been combined successfully with personal selling. For example, many companies send out lead cards to screen
prospective customers. The salesperson follows up on those who express a genuine interest,

FIGURE 17–7
The growth of telemarketing as a
sales function: reasons for growth
(in percent)

	Telephone Sales and Service	Field Sales
Total growth related	58.0	61.8
Overall business growth or expansion	44.7	43.1
Adding product lines	10.2	8.0
Adding territories	3.1	10.7
Total system related	20.8	7.5
Added centralized telemarketing dept.	11.5	1.8
Added/changed computer system	6.2	4.4
Centralized sales and marketing	3.1	1.3
Customer demand	10.5	10.2
Cost efficiencies	1.4	0
Other	2.0	2.2
Can't tell/no response	9.8	18.2

Note: Adds to more than 100 percent due to multiple mentions.

IMC Perspective 17–2
Auto Dealers Find a New Way to Sell Cars—by Marketing

One year before the new Mercedes sport utility vehicle would be on the market, the $30,000-plus light truck was already being sold—or should we say marketed. Mercedes' goal was that before the SUV was even available in showrooms, the entire allotment of 35,000 units would be sold. These preselling efforts reflect a different orientation in the automobile industry to market new and used cars rather than just selling them.

The Saturn division of General Motors Corporation was actually one of the innovators in this new approach to marketing. Based on research findings that car buyers' perceptions of the personal selling experience was less than desirable (to put it mildly), Saturn initiated a number of programs to remedy the situation, including one price, no haggling. Other GM lines followed with their own programs, including a recruiting and training school for the "new salesperson."

Another automaker, Infiniti, offered lower sticker prices, full refunds within three days, price protection for 30 days, and greater security for used-car buyers.

The most marketing-oriented program of all, however, was that instituted by Mercedes-Benz. Well before the new utility vehicle even had a name, Mercedes was contacting prospective buyers. In an attempt to instill "yearning," it undertook an extensive $12 million direct-marketing program. It bought a list of 770,000 names of Mercedes owners and owners of other brands of sport utility vehicles and hired the direct-marketing agency Rapp Collins to ask whether those on the list would be willing to have a two-year dialogue by mail with Mercedes. About 94,000 agreed, and 10,000 more names were added from other sources.

Mailings contained a detailed questionnaire asking about everything from styling preferences to how many beverage cup holders were preferred. The completed surveys were tabulated according to customers' preferences and concerns. Prospects concerned about safety received a letter explaining the value of side airbags and crumple zones. Those with interior room issues were told how favorably the new Mercedes would compare with the competitive models. In return, prospects' desires were included into the new product's design.

Although a $12 million direct-mail campaign isn't cheap, Mercedes-Benz of North America's president Mike Jackson says, "Mass selling has been a tremendous strain on our resources . . . the world is not exactly waiting for a new sports utility vehicle from Mercedes-Benz." Something had to be done to stimulate excitement. Did it work? At least one Mercedes-Benz passenger car dealer thinks so. He received over 1,000 serious inquiries about ordering from eager buyers, even though he didn't have any vehicles yet or know if he would be one of the dealers who would meet all the requirements to be a Mercedes-Benz light truck dealer.

Sources: Joshua Levine, "Give Me One of Those," *Forbes*, June 3, 1996, p. 134; Robert Simison, "Infiniti Adopts New Sales Strategy to Polish Its Brand," *The Wall Street Journal*, June 10, 1996, p. B1.

saving valuable time and increasing the potential for a sale. IMC perspective 17–2 reports on a direct-marketing campaign used by Mercedes to help its dealers sell their new sport utility vehicle.

Combining Personal Selling and Sales Promotion

The program elements of sales promotion and personal selling also support each other. For example, many of the sales promotions targeted to resellers are presented by the sales force, who will ultimately be responsible for removing or replacing them as well.

While trade sales promotions are designed to support the reseller and are often targeted to the ultimate consumer, many other promotional tools are designed to assist the sales staff. Flip charts, leave-behinds, and specialty ads may be designed to assist salespeople in their presentations, serve as reminders, or just create goodwill. The number of materials available may range from just a few to hundreds, depending on the company. (If you ever get the chance, look into the trunk of a consumer products salesperson's car. You will find everything from pens to calendars to flip charts to samples to lost baseball mitts—all but the last of which are used in the selling effort.)

Likewise, many sales promotions are targeted at the sales force itself. Incentives such as free trips, cash bonuses, or gifts are often used to stimulate sales efforts. And, as we saw with resellers, contests and sweepstakes may also be used.

It is important that the elements of the promotional program work together, as each has its specific advantages and disadvantages. While personal selling is valuable in accomplishing certain objectives and supporting other promotional tools, it must be supported by the other elements. Ads, sales promotions, and the like may be targeted to the ultimate user, resellers, or the organization's sales force.

EVALUATING THE PERSONAL SELLING EFFORT

Like all other elements of the promotional mix, personal selling must be evaluated based on its contribution to the overall promotional effort. The costs of personal selling are often high, but the returns may be just as high.

Because the sales force is under the supervision of the sales manager, evaluations are typically based on sales criteria. Sales may be analyzed by total sales volume, territories, product line, customer type, or sales rep.[14] Other sales-related criteria such as new account openings and personal traits are also sometimes considered, as shown in Figure 17–8.

From a promotional perspective, sales performance is important, as are the contributions of individuals in generating these sales. On the other hand, the promotions manager must evaluate the performance of personal selling as one program element contributing to the overall promotional program. So he or she needs to use different criteria in determining its effectiveness.

Criteria for Evaluating Personal Selling

A number of criteria may be used to evaluate the contribution of the personal selling effort to the promotional program. They include the following.

* *Provision of marketing intelligence.* The ability of the sales force to feed back information regarding competitive programs, customer reactions, market trends, and other factors that may be important in the development of the promotional program.
* *Follow-up activities.* The use and dissemination of promotional brochures and correspondences with new and existing customers; providing feedback on the effectiveness of various promotional programs.
* *Program implementations.* The number of promotional programs implemented; the number of shelf and/or counter displays used and so forth; the implementation and assessment of cooperative advertising programs.
* *Attainment of communications objectives.* The number of accounts to whom presentations were made (awareness, evaluation), the number of trial offers accepted, and the like.

Combining these criteria with those used by the sales department, the promotions manager should be able to accurately assess the effectiveness of the personal selling program. Making these evaluations requires a great deal of cooperation between the departments.

FIGURE 17–8

Criteria used to evaluate sales forces

Sales Results	Sales Efforts
Quantitative Measures	

Orders

Number of orders obtained

Average order size (units or dollars)

Batting average (orders ÷ sales calls)

Number of orders canceled by customers

Sales volume

Dollar sales volume

Unit sales volume

By customer type

By product category

Translated into market share

Percentage of sales quota achieved

Margins

Gross margin

Net profit

By customer type

By product category

Customer accounts

Number of new accounts

Number of lost accounts

Percentage of accounts sold

Number of overdue accounts

Dollar amount of accounts receivable

Collections made of accounts receivable

Sales calls

Number made on current customers

Number made on potential new accounts

Average time spent per call

Number of sales presentations

Selling time versus nonselling time

Call frequency ratio per customer type

Selling expenses

Average per sales call

As percentage of sales volume

As percentage of sales quota

By customer type

By product category

Direct-selling expense ratios

Indirect-selling expense ratios

Customer service

Number of service calls

Displays set up

Delivery cost per unit sold

Months of inventory held, by customer type

Number of customer complaints

Percentage of goods returned

Qualitative Measures

Selling skills

Knowing the company and its policies

Knowing competitors' products and sales strategies

Use of marketing and technical backup teams

Understanding of selling techniques

Customer feedback (positive and negative)

Product knowledge

Customer knowledge

Execution of selling techniques

Quality of sales presentations

Communication skills

Sales-related activities

Territory management: sales call preparation, scheduling, routing, and time utilization

Marketing intelligence: new product ideas, competitive activities, new customer preferences

Follow-ups: use of promotional brochures and correspondence with current and potential accounts

Customer relations

Report preparation and timely submission

Personal characteristics

Cooperation, human relations, enthusiasm, motivation, judgment, care of company property, appearance, self-improvement efforts, patience, punctuality, initiative, resourcefulness, health, sales management potential, ethical and moral behavior

SUMMARY

This chapter discussed the nature of personal selling and the role this program element plays in the promotional mix. The role of personal selling in the IMC program varies depending on the nature of the industry, competition, and market conditions. In many industries (for example, industrial markets) the personal selling component may receive the most attention, while in others (for example, consumer nondurables) it plays a minor role. However, managers in most industries believe the importance of this program element will continue to increase over the next few years.

Personal selling offers the marketer the opportunity for a dyadic communications process (a two-way exchange of information). The salesperson can instantly assess the situation and the effects of the communication and adapt the message if necessary.

While this exchange lets the sales rep tailor the message specifically to the needs and wants of the receiver, its disadvantage is a nonstandardized message, since the final message communicated is under the salesperson's control. In an attempt to develop a standard communication, marketers provide their reps with flip charts, leave-behinds, and other promotional pieces.

Evaluation of the personal selling effort is usually under the control of the sales department, since sales is the most commonly used criterion. The promotions manager must assess the contribution of personal selling with nonsales-oriented criteria as well.

KEY TERMS

personal selling, 544	prospector stage, 546	order taking, 548	prospects, 548
dyadic communication, 545	problem-solver stage, 546	creative selling, 548	qualified prospects, 548
provider stage, 546	procreator stage, 546	missionary sales, 548	close, 550
persuader stage, 546	relationship marketing, 547	prospecting, 548	cross sell, 551
		leads, 548	

DISCUSSION QUESTIONS

1. Explain how Mercedes' "preselling" of its new sport utility vehicle reflects an IMC approach to marketing.
2. What is relationship marketing? Give examples of how companies might employ this strategy.
3. Give examples of companies' public relations efforts that may have required the efforts of their sales force.
4. In what situations, and for what types of products, might personal selling be effective? Give examples.
5. What questions must a company ask to determine the role of personal selling in integrated marketing communications?
6. Describe the five stages in the evolution of selling. Explain the salesperson's role at each stage.

7. Many marketing students' first job is in personal selling. Explain why Fortune 500 companies typically require entry-level marketing people to start off in sales.
8. Explain how a personal sales agent might use the Internet to become a more effective marketer.
9. Explain why the sales force might be one of the more vulnerable areas of the firm in respect to ethics. Discuss some of the problems that might arise from unethical behaviors.
10. Explain why the salesperson's ability to tailor the message to the receiver can be both an advantage and a disadvantage.

Monitoring, Evaluation, and Control

18

Measuring the Effectiveness of the Promotional Program

18

Measuring the Effectiveness of the Promotional Program

Chapter Objectives

- To discuss reasons for measuring promotional program effectiveness.

- To examine the various measures used in assessing promotional program effectiveness.

- To evaluate alternative methods for measuring promotional program effectiveness.

- To review the requirements of proper effectiveness research.

NASCAR, STADIUMS, AND COLLEGE BOWL GAMES: SPONSORSHIPS TAKE OFF

It seems that everywhere you look these days, a sponsor has its name attached to sports. It's the Nokia Sugar Bowl, Qualcomm Stadium, and the United (Airlines) Arena. It's Square D sponsoring a NASCAR auto and Tiger Woods sporting a Titleist visor. And it's not just in the United States. From Nynex Arena in Manchester, England, to GM Place in Vancouver, British Columbia, Canada, sponsorships have become a popular means of corporate identification. One estimate places corporate sponsorships of U.S. events alone at over $5 billion in 1996.

With all this money being spent to have companies' names associated with sporting events, the logical question to ask is, "Is it worth it?" That is, are these sponsorships effective? The sponsors seem to think so and cite a variety of measures to support their beliefs.

- *Media equivalencies.* One of the more common measures equates the exposure time for the name to how much it would cost to advertise for the same period of time. For example, if Tiger Woods appears with his Titleist visor for 30 seconds, the value is the cost for a 30-second ad on the same event.
- *Exposures.* Sybase, a software company, signed on as the official software for the 1998 World Cup in France, with total viewership estimated at over 38 billion persons. More than 150,000 fans attend the Daytona 500 NASCAR race.
- *Image.* For many companies, association with a top-notch sporting event may lead to an improved image in the marketplace. James H. Warsaw of the University of Oregon Sports Marketing Center says, "Sponsorship is a form of affinity marketing" that allows the organization to distinguish itself and show off its capabilities.
- *Brand awareness.* Companies like 3Com (placing its name on Candlestick Park in San Francisco) and Qualcomm (on Jack Murphy stadium in San Diego) hope to achieve brand awareness for products that do not typically come to the minds of consumers.

The list of reasons why corporations buy sponsorships also includes creating goodwill, motivating the sales force, creating positive feelings about the company internally and externally, and so on.

Jed Pearsall, president of Performance Research—an Atlanta-based marketing firm that measures the value of sponsorships for clients—says most of his clients do not look at the direct impact on sales; they focus on brand awareness and image shift, and they've been very pleased with the results. Nokia (Sugar Bowl) and CompUSA (Florida Citrus Bowl) both believe that they have higher brand awareness as a result of their associations, and CompUSA says December and January sales have increased each year since its sponsorship began. The Corel Centre—home of the Ottawa Senators of the National Hockey League—has resulted in over 400 million media impressions annually, according to Canada's largest software company. L. M. Ericsson, the Swedish telecom company, believes the only way it could compete for name recognition was through sponsorship of the Carolina Panthers of the NFL. Qualcomm estimates that the $18 million it paid to put its name on Jack Murphy Stadium was worth $45 million in exposures.

Perhaps the most lucrative sponsorships of all come with association with NASCAR, according to Performance Research. Fans are so brand loyal that 72 percent buy products made by NASCAR sponsors (the next closest sport is tennis at 52 percent). Caterpillar's exposure of its logo on TV was worth over $5 million of advertising according to sports marketing director Greg Towles. Kellogg repainted Terry Labonte's No. 5 car (which had a hood that looked like a Kellogg's Corn Flakes box) with a label for Honey Crunch Corn Flakes to introduce the brand to the marketplace. Kellogg believes the sponsorship was successful by every barometer; LaBonte even won the race.

The old days of sponsoring a golf tournament because the CEO liked to hack around on weekends are apparently gone. In his place are Bud, Miller, Nike, Reebok, Coke, and Pepsi—with a large waiting list of other media-savvy marketers.

Sources: Jim Morrison, "The Skybox Syndrome," *Marketing Computers*, June 1996, pp. 38–41; Mark Lewyn, "See a Game, Shop for a Car, Surf the Net," *Business Week*, January 29, 1996, p. 53; Brian Trusdell, "Fast Lane," *Sales & Marketing Management*, February 1997, pp. 67–76.

As marketers spend their communications dollars in diverse areas, the need to determine the effectiveness of these expenditures becomes increasingly important. As you can see by the lead-in to this chapter, several methods for evaluating the effectiveness of these programs are used. Both clients and agencies are continually striving to determine whether their communications are working and how well they are working relative to other options. Unfortunately, there seems to be little agreement on the best measures to use. Almost everyone agrees that research is required, but they disagree on how it should be conducted and how the results should be used.

Measuring the effectiveness of the promotional program is a critical element in the promotional planning process. Research allows the marketing manager to evaluate the performance of specific program elements and provides input into the next period's situation analysis. It is a necessary ingredient to a continuing planning process, yet it is often not carried out.

In this chapter, we discuss some reasons firms should measure the effectiveness of their IMC programs, as well as why many decide not to. We also examine how, when, and where such measurements can be conducted. Most of our attention is devoted to measuring the effects of advertising because much more time and effort have been expended developing evaluation measures in advertising than in the other promotional areas. We will, however, discuss measurement in other areas of the IMC program as well. (In some of these areas, the measures are more directly observable—for example, direct marketing and personal selling.) You'll recall that we addressed the methods used to evaluate many of the other promotional elements in previous chapters.

It is important to understand that in this chapter we are concerned with research that is conducted in an evaluative role—that is, to measure the effectiveness of advertising and promotion and/or to assess various strategies before implementing them. This is not to be confused with research discussed earlier in the text to help develop the promotional program. While evaluative research may occur at various times throughout the promotional process (including the development stage), it is conducted specifically to assess the effects of various strategies. We begin our discussion with the reasons effectiveness should be measured as well as some of the reasons firms do not do so.

ARGUMENTS FOR AND AGAINST MEASURING EFFECTIVENESS

Almost any time one engages in a project or activity, whether for work or fun, some measure of performance occurs. In sports you may compare your golf score against par or your time on a ski course to other skiers' performance. In business, employees are generally given objectives to accomplish, and their job evaluations are based on their ability to achieve these objectives. Advertising and promotion should not be an exception. It is important to determine how well the communications program is working and to measure this performance against some standards.

Reasons to Measure Effectiveness

Assessing the effectiveness of ads both before they are implemented and after the final versions have been completed and fielded offers a number of advantages.

1. *Avoiding costly mistakes.* The top three advertisers in the United States spent over $7.2 billion in advertising and promotion in 1996. The top 10 spent a total of over $35

billion. This is a lot of money to be throwing around without some understanding of how well it is being spent. If the program is not achieving its objectives, the marketing manager needs to know so he or she can stop spending (wasting) money on it.

Just as important as the out-of-pocket costs is the opportunity loss due to poor communications. If the advertising and promotions program is not accomplishing its objectives, not only is the money spent lost but so too is the potential gain that could result from an effective program. Thus, measuring the effects of advertising does not just save money. It also helps the firm maximize its investment.

2. *Evaluating alternative strategies.* Typically a firm has a number of strategies under consideration. For example, there may be some question as to which medium should be used or whether one message is more effective than another. Or the decision may be between two promotional program elements. For example, should research be spent on sponsorships or on advertising? Research may be designed to help the manager determine which strategy is most likely to be effective. Companies often test alternate versions of their advertising in different cities to determine which ad communicates most effectively. They may also explore different forms of couponing.

3. *Increasing the efficiency of advertising in general.* You may have heard the expression "can't see the forest for the trees." Sometimes advertisers get so close to the project they lose sight of what they are seeking, and because they know what they are trying to say, they expect their audience will also understand. They may use technical jargon that not everyone is familiar with. Or the creative department may get too creative or too sophisticated and lose the meaning that needs to be communicated. How many times have you seen an ad and asked yourself what it was trying to say? Conducting research helps companies develop more efficient and effective communications. An increasing number of clients are demanding accountability for their promotional programs and putting more pressure on the agencies to produce.

Reasons Not to Measure Effectiveness

Companies give a number of reasons for not measuring the effectiveness of advertising and promotions strategies.

1. *Cost.* Perhaps the most commonly cited reason for not testing (particularly among smaller firms) is the expense. Good research can be expensive, in terms of both time and money. Many managers decide that time is critical and they must implement the program while the opportunity is available. Many believe the monies spent on research could be better spent on improved production of the ad, additional media buys, and the like.

While the first argument may have some merit, the second does not. Imagine what would happen if a poor campaign were developed or the incentive program did not motivate the target audience. Not only would you be spending money without the desired effects, but the effort could do more harm than good. Spending more money to buy media does not remedy a poor message or substitute for an improper promotional mix. For example, one of the nation's leading brewers watched its test-market sales for a new brand of beer fall short of expectations. The solution, it decided, was to buy all the TV time available that matched its target audience. After two months sales had not improved, and the product was abandoned in the test market. Analysis showed the problem was not in the media but rather in the message, which communicated no reason to buy. Research would have identified the problem, and millions of dollars and a brand might have been saved. The moral: spending research monies to gain increased exposure to the wrong message is not a sound management decision.

2. *Research problems.* A second reason cited for not measuring effectiveness is that it is difficult to isolate the effects of promotional elements. Each variable in the marketing mix affects the success of a product or service. Because it is rarely possible to measure the contribution of each marketing element directly, some managers become frustrated and decide not to test at all. They say, "If I can't determine the specific effects, why spend the money?"

This argument also suffers from weak logic. While we agree that it is not always possible to determine the dollar amount of sales contributed by promotions, research can provide useful results.

3. *Disagreement on what to test.* The objectives sought in the promotional program may differ by industry, by stage of the product life cycle, or even for different people within the firm. The sales manager may want to see the impact of promotions on sales, top management may wish to know the impact on corporate image, and those involved in the creative process may wish to assess recall and/or recognition of the ad. Lack of agreement on what to test often results in no testing.

Again, there is little rationale for this position. With the proper design, many or even all of the above might be measured. Since every promotional element is designed to accomplish its own objectives, research can be used to measure its effectiveness in doing so.

4. *The objections of creative.* It has been argued by many (and denied by others) that the creative department does not want its work to be tested and many agencies are reluctant to submit their work for testing. This is sometimes true. Ad agencies' creative departments argue that tests are not true measures of the creativity and effectiveness of ads; applying measures stifles their creativity; and the more creative the ad, the more likely it is to be successful. They want permission to be creative without the limiting guidelines marketing may impose. The Chiat/Day ad shown here reflects how many people in the advertising business feel about this subject.

At the same time, the marketing manager is ultimately responsible for the success of the product or brand. Given the substantial sums being allocated to advertising and promotion, it is the manager's right, and responsibility, to know how well a specific program—or a specific ad—will perform in the market. IMC Perspective 18–1 discusses the creativity–effectiveness controversy in more detail.

5. *Time.* A final reason given for not testing is a lack of time. Managers believe they already have too much to do and just can't get around to testing, and they don't want to wait to get the message out because they might miss the window of opportunity.

Planning might be the solution to the first problem. While many managers are overworked and time-poor, research is just too important to skip.

The second argument can also be overcome with proper planning. While timeliness is critical, getting the wrong message out is of little or no value and may even be harmful. There will be occasions where market opportunities require choosing between testing and immediate implementation. But even then some testing may help avoid mistakes or improve effectiveness. In most instances, proper planning and scheduling will allow time for research.

To advertisers interested in 'day after recall', we submit a case history:

"*My friends... each of you is a single cell in the great body of the State. And today, that great body has purged itself of parasites.*"

"*We have triumphed over the unprincipled dissemination of facts. The thugs and wreckers have been cast out. And the poisonous weeds of disinformation have*"

"*been consigned to the dustbin of history... Let each and every cell rejoice! For today we celebrate the first glorious anniversary of the Information Purification Directives.*"

"*We have created, for the first time in all history, a garden of pure ideology, where each worker may bloom secure from the pests of contradictory and confusing truths.*"

"*Our Unification of Thought is more powerful a weapon than any fleet or army on earth. We are one people. With one will.*"

"*Our resolve. Our cause. Our enemies shall talk themselves to death. And we will bury them with their own confusion.*"

"*We shall prevail!*"

Title and Voice Over: On January 24, Apple Computer will introduce Macintosh.

And you'll see why 1984 won't be like "1984"

On January 22, 1984, one commercial for Apple Computer ran on network television.

With all due respect to Burke, we didn't bother to test it.

Unlike a lot of advertising agencies, we prefer a different form of measurement:

When the product mentioned in the commercial, Apple's new Macintosh,' was unveiled on January 24, over 200,000 people lined up to see it in person.

Within 6 hours, they bought $3,500,000 worth of Macintosh computers. And left cash deposits for $1,000,000 more.

ABC, CBS, NBC and CNN featured the commercial in network news segments.

Dan Rather covered it at night. Bryant Gumbel covered it at dawn.

The BBC ran it in England.

Associated Press put it on the wire.

27 TV stations in major U.S. markets

ran it on local news programs.

Steven Spielberg called.

As did *The New York Times, The Wall Street Journal, The Washington Post,* the *Philadelphia Inquirer, USA Today,* the *Boston Globe,* the *Los Angeles Times,* the *San Francisco Chronicle* and, of course, the *San Jose Mercury News.*

Not to mention *Time, Newsweek, Fortune, Forbes, Business Week* and, of course, *Advertising Age.*

Apple is now producing one Macintosh every 27 seconds. And selling one every 20 seconds.

Not bad for one 60-second spot on the Super Bowl.

Chiat/Day

Los Angeles, San Francisco, New York

CONDUCTING RESEARCH TO MEASURE ADVERTISING EFFECTIVENESS
What to Test

We now examine how to measure the effects of communications. This section considers what elements to evaluate, as well as where and how such evaluations should occur.

In Chapter 5, we discussed the components of the communications model (source, message, media, receiver) and the importance of each in the promotional program. Marketers need to determine how each is affecting the communications process. Other decisions made in the promotional planning process must also be evaluated.

IMC Perspective 18–1
Creativity or Effectiveness?

For as long as almost anyone can remember, the camps have been split regarding attempts to measure advertising creativity. Tom Robinson, market research director for *The Wall Street Journal*, says the phrase "We need to conduct some research to prove that our advertising campaign is working" strikes fear into the hearts of many ad people and raises the ire of many more. On the client side, however, the pressures for accountability continue to increase. Therein lies the controversy. Creatives are interested in developing and producing exciting, entertaining, and memorable ads—forms of art. Businesses are looking for ads that work, as measured by sales and/or market share increases, recall, recognition, or other more quantifiable measures.

Why don't copywriters like research? Arthur Kover of Fordham University cites a number of reasons: (1) research is not human—that is, it is numbers and science, not warm human beings relating to warm human beings; (2) research is political—the design and interpretation of research is based on internal political needs of the parties involved; (3) the research methods currently employed are not accurate enough to tell if an ad really works; and (4) copywriters believe researchers don't understand what they do (as one copywriter says, "Don't tell me that you with your little questions and statistics can pinpoint the complexity and richness of how people respond to my work.")

Clients, on the other hand, want accountability—usually through quantitative measures. They cite multiple examples of award-winning advertising campaigns that did little or nothing to improve sales. They say, "I'm not interested in winning advertising awards, I'm interested in generating sales."

Is it possible for ads to be both creative and effective? Some advertisers (on both sides) think so. Tom Robinson and Arthur Kover both believe the solution is more effective measurement tools. They argue that traditional measures need to be updated to include more of the receivers' emotional reactions—something the creatives have argued for years. The need, they say, is to determine what kind of advertising works and to get away from traditional quantitative measures that reflect "organizational structures." Effective advertising is that which provides "personal enhancement" for the receiver. Research offered by Max Blackston provides additional support, concluding that the "feel-good" effect of the advertising leads to increased brand value.

So the answer, at least according to these researchers, is to create advertising that consumers like, that makes them feel good, and that leads to personal enhancement. Isn't this what the copywriters have said all along? Now, say the researchers, "If only we could measure it!"

Sources: Thomas Robinson, "The Age of Accountability," *Marketing Tools*, June 1996, p. 4; Arthur J. Kover, "Why Copywriters Don't Like Advertising Research—and What Kind of Research Might They Accept," *Journal of Advertising Research*, March/April 1996, pp. RC8–10; Arthur J. Kover, Stephen M. Goldberg, and William L. James, "Creativity vs. Effectiveness?" *Journal of Advertising Research*, Novermber/December, 1995, p. 29–38.

SOURCE FACTORS

An important question is whether the spokesperson being used is effective and how the target market will respond to him or her. For example, John McEnroe, considered the bad boy of tennis because of his abrasive on-court antics, proved to be an extremely successful spokesperson for Dunlop, Nike, and Bic. Or a product spokesperson may be an excellent source initially but, owing to a variety of reasons, may lose impact over time. Bill Cosby is a spokesperson for Kodak. At one time or another, he has also done ads for Ford, Jell-O, Texas Instruments, and E. F. Hutton, among others—which might bring his credibility into question (as discussed in Chapter 6). In other instances, changes in the source's attractiveness or likability or other external factors may lead to changes in source effectiveness.

MESSAGE VARIABLES

Both the message and the means by which it is communicated are bases for evaluation. For example, in the beer example discussed earlier, the message never provided a reason for consumers to try the new product. In other instances, the message may not be strong enough to pull readers into the ad by attracting their attention or clear enough to help them evaluate the product. Sometimes the message is memorable but doesn't achieve the other goals set by management. A recent study showed that 7 of the 25 products that scored highest on interest and memorability in Video Storyboard Tests' ad test had flat or declining sales.[1] A number of factors regarding the message and its delivery may have an impact on its effectiveness, including the headline, illustrations, text, and layout.

Many ads are never seen by the public because of the message they convey. For example, an ad in which Susan Anton ate a slice of Pizza Hut pizza was considered too erotic for the company's small-town image. Likewise, an ad created for General Electric in which Uncle

Sam got slapped in the face (to demonstrate our growing trade imbalance) was killed by the company's chair.[2]

MEDIA STRATEGIES

Media decisions need to be evaluated. Research may be designed to determine which media class (for example, broadcast versus print), subclass (newspaper versus magazines), or specific vehicles (which newspapers or magazines) generate the most effective results. The location within a particular medium (front page versus back page) and size of ad or length of commercial also merit examination. For example, research has demonstrated that readers pay more attention to larger ads.[3] Similarly, direct-response advertisers on TV have found that some programs are more effective than others. One successful direct marketer found that old TV shows yield more responses than first runs:

> The fifth rerun of "Leave It to Beaver" will generate much more response than will the first run of a prime-time television program. Who cares if you miss something you have seen four times before? But you do care when it's the first time you've seen it.[4]

Another factor is the **vehicle option source effect**, "the differential impact that the advertising exposure will have on the same audience member if the exposure occurs in one media option rather than another."[5] People perceive ads differently depending on their context.[6]

A final factor in media decisions involves scheduling. The evaluation of flighting versus pulsing or continuous schedules is important, particularly given the increasing costs of media time. Likewise, there may be opportunities associated with increasing advertising weights in periods of downward sales cycles or recessions. The manager experimenting with these alternative schedules and/or budget outlays should attempt to measure their differential impact.[7]

BUDGETING DECISIONS

A number of studies have examined the effects of budget size on advertising effectiveness and the effects of various ad expenditures on sales. Many companies have also attempted to determine whether increasing their ad budget directly increases sales. This relationship is often hard to determine, perhaps because using sales as an indicator of effectiveness ignores the impact of other marketing mix elements. More definitive conclusions may be possible if other dependent variables, such as the communications objectives stated earlier, are used.

When to Test

Virtually all test measures can be classified according to when they are conducted. **Pretests** are measures taken before the campaign is implemented; **posttests** occur after the ad or commercial has been in the field. A variety of pretests and posttests are available to the marketer, each with its own methodology designed to measure some aspect of the advertising program. Figure 18–1 classifies these testing methods.

FIGURE 18–1
Classification of testing methods

Pretests		
Laboratory Methods		
Consumer juries	Theater tests	Readability tests
Portfolio tests	Rough tests	Comprehension and reaction tests
Physiological measures	Concept tests	
Field Methods		
Dummy advertising vehicles	On-air tests	
Posttests		
Field Methods		
Recall tests	Single-source systems	Recognition tests
Association measures	Inquiry tests	Tracking studies

PRETESTING

Pretests may occur at a number of points, from as early on as idea generation to rough execution to testing the final version before implementing it. More than one type of pretest may be used. For example, concept testing (which is discussed later in this chapter) may take place at the earliest development of the ad or commercial, when little more than an idea, basic concept, or positioning statement is under consideration. In other instances, layouts of the ad campaign that include headlines, some body copy, and rough illustrations are used. For TV commercials, storyboards and animatics may be tested.

The methodologies employed to conduct pretests vary. In focus groups, participants freely discuss the meanings they get from the ads, consider the relative advantages of alternatives, and even suggest improvements or additional themes. In addition to or instead of the focus groups, consumers are asked to evaluate the ad on a series of rating scales. (Different agencies use different measures.) In-home interviews, mall intercept, or laboratory methods may be used to gather the data.

The advantage of pretesting at this stage is that feedback is relatively inexpensive. Any problems with the concept or the way it is to be delivered are identified before large amounts of money are spent in development. Sometimes more than one version of the ad is evaluated to determine which is most likely to be effective.

A study of 4,637 on-air commercials designed to build normative intelligence conducted by McCollum Spielman Worldwide (MSW) found that only 19 percent were considered outstanding or really good. Nearly twice as many (34 percent) were failures. On the other hand, of those spots that were pretested before the final form was aired, the share of good to outstanding rose to 37 percent, while the failure rate fell to 9 percent.[8] This is certainly a testimonial to the value of pretesting.

The disadvantage is that mock-ups, storyboards, or animatics may not communicate nearly as effectively as the final product. The mood-enhancing and/or emotional aspects of the message are very difficult to communicate in this format. Another disadvantage is time delays. Many marketers believe being first in the market offers them a distinct advantage over competitors, so they forgo research to save time and ensure this position.

POSTTESTING

Posttesting is also common among both advertisers and ad agencies (with the exception of testing commercials for wearout). Figure 18–2 presents the results of a study that examined ad agencies' and advertisers' use of various advertising research methods. The percentage of organizations that evaluate finished commercials and TV campaigns is very high. Posttest-

FIGURE 18—2 General findings about copy research

	Total		Agencies		Advertisers	
	Number	Percent	Number	Percent	Number	Percent
Total respondents	112	100.0	39	100.0	73	100.0
Undertake preliminary, background, or strategic research in preparation for advertising campaigns	104	92.9	39	100.0	65	89.0
Evaluate copy ideas, storyboards, other formats before rough commercial	85	75.9	34	87.2	51	69.9
Evaluate rough commercial execution of other formats before finished commercial	102	91.1	38	97.4	64	87.7
Evaluate finished commercials	105	93.8	35	89.7	70	95.9
Evaluate TV campaigns	98	87.5	37	94.9	61	83.6
Test competitive commercials	73	65.2	27	69.2	46	63.0
Test commercials for wearout	29	25.9	9	23.1	20	27.4

ing is designed to (1) determine if the campaign is accomplishing the objectives sought and (2) serve as input into the next period's situation analysis. A variety of posttest measures are available, most of which involve survey research methods.

Where to Test

In addition to when to test, decisions must be made as to *where*. These tests may take place in either laboratory or field settings.

LABORATORY TESTS

In **laboratory tests**, people are brought to a particular location where they are shown ads and/or commercials. The testers either ask questions about them or measure participants' responses by other methods—for example, pupil dilation, eye tracking, or galvanic skin response.

The major advantage of the lab setting is the *control* it affords the researcher. Changes in copy, illustration, formats, colors, and the like can be manipulated inexpensively and the differential impact of each assessed. This makes it much easier for the researcher to isolate the contribution of each factor.

The major disadvantage is the lack of *realism*. Perhaps the greatest effect of this lack of realism is a **testing bias**. When people are brought into a lab (even if it has been designed to look like a living room), they may scrutinize the ads much more closely than they would at home. A second problem with this lack of realism is that it cannot duplicate the natural viewing situation, complete with the distractions or comforts of home. Looking at ads in a lab setting may not be the same as viewing at home on the couch, with the spouse, kids, dog, cat, and parakeet chirping in the background. (A bit later you will see that some testing techniques have made progress in correcting this deficiency. No, they did not bring in the dogs and the parakeets.) Overall, however, the control offered by this method probably outweighs the disadvantages, which accounts for the frequent use of lab methods.

FIELD TESTS

Field tests are tests of the ad or commercial under natural viewing situations, complete with the realism of noise, distractions, and the comforts of home. Field tests take into account the effects of repetition, program content, and even the presence of competitive messages.

The major disadvantage of field tests is the lack of control. It may be impossible to isolate causes of viewers' evaluations. If atypical events occur during the test, they may bias the results. Competitors may attempt to sabotage the research. And field tests usually take more time and money to conduct, so the results are not available to be acted on quickly. Thus, realism is gained at the expense of other important factors. It is up to the researcher to determine which trade-offs to make.

How to Test

Our discussion of what should be tested, when, and where was general and designed to establish a basic understanding of the overall process as well as some key terms. In this section, we discuss more specifically some of the methods commonly used at each stage. First, however, it is important to establish some criteria by which to judge ads and commercials.

Conducting evaluative research is not easy. In 1982, 21 of the largest U.S. ad agencies endorsed a set of principles aimed at "improving the research used in preparing and testing ads, providing a better creative product for clients, and controlling the cost of TV commercials."[9] This set of nine principles, called **PACT (Positioning Advertising Copy Testing)**, defines *copy testing* as research "which is undertaken when a decision is to be made about whether advertising should run in the marketplace. Whether this stage utilizes a single test or a combination of tests, its purpose is to aid in the judgment of specific advertising executions."[10] The nine principles of good copy testing are shown in Figure 18–3.

As you can see, advertisers and their clients are concerned about developing *appropriate* testing methods. Adherence to these principles may not make for perfect testing, but it goes a long way toward improving the state of the art and alleviates at least one of the testing problems cited earlier.

FIGURE 18–3
Positioning Advertising Copy Testing
(PACT)

1. Provide measurements that are relevant to the objectives of the advertising.
2. Require agreement about how the results will be used in advance of each specific test.
3. Provide multiple measurements (because single measurements are not adequate to assess ad performance).
4. Be based on a model of human response to communications—the reception of a stimulus, the comprehension of the stimulus, and the response to the stimulus.
5. Allow for consideration of whether the advertising stimulus should be exposed more than once.
6. Require that the more finished a piece of copy is, the more soundly it can be evaluated and require, as a minimum, that alternative executions be tested in the same degree of finish.
7. Provide controls to avoid the biasing effects of the exposure context.
8. Take into account basic considerations of sample definition.
9. Demonstrate reliability and validity.

THE TESTING PROCESS

Testing may occur at various points throughout the development of an ad or a campaign: (1) concept generation research, (2) rough, prefinished art, copy, and/or commercial testing, (3) finished art or commercial pretesting, and (4) market testing of ads or commercials (posttesting).

Concept Generation and Testing

Figure 18–4 describes the process involved in advertising **concept testing**, which is conducted very early in the campaign development process in order to explore the targeted consumer's response to a potential ad or campaign or have the consumer evaluate advertising alternatives. Positioning statements, copy, headlines, and/or illustrations may all be under scrutiny. The material to be evaluated may be just a headline or a rough sketch of the ad. The colors used, typeface, package designs, and even point-of-purchase materials may be evaluated.

One of the more commonly used methods for concept testing is focus groups, which usually consist of 8 to 10 people in the target market for the product. For example, in testing new concepts for Jell-O gelatin, Young & Rubicam assessed reactions of mothers and children (the mothers being the buyers; the children, the ultimate consumers). The number of focus groups used varies depending on group consensus, strength of response, and/or the degree to which participants like or dislike the concepts. Some companies use 50 or more groups to develop a campaign, although fewer than 10 are usually needed to test a concept sufficiently.

While focus groups continue to be a favorite of marketers, they are often overused. The methodology is attractive in that results are easily obtained, directly observable, and immediate. A variety of issues can be examined, and consumers are free to go into depth in areas they consider important. Also, focus groups don't require quantitative analysis. Unfortunately, many managers are uncertain about research methods that require statistics, and focus groups, being qualitative in nature, don't demand much skill in interpretation. Weaknesses with focus groups are shown in Figure 18–5. Clearly, there are appropriate and inappropriate circumstances for employing this methodology.

FIGURE 18–4
Concept testing

Objective: Explores consumers' responses to various ad concepts as expressed in words, pictures, or symbols.

Method: Alternative concepts are exposed to consumers who match the characteristics of the target audience. Reactions and evaluations of each are sought through a variety of methods, including focus groups, direct questioning, and survey completion. Sample sizes vary depending on the number of concepts to be presented and the consensus of responses.

Output: Qualitative and/or quantitative data evaluating and comparing alternative concepts.

FIGURE 18–5
Weaknesses associated with focus group research

- The results are not quantifiable.
- Sample sizes are too small to generalize to larger populations.
- Group influences may bias participants' responses.
- One or two members of the group may steer the conversation or dominate the discussion.
- Consumers become instant "experts."
- Members may not represent the target market. (Are focus group participants a certain type of person?)
- Results may be taken to be more representative and/or definitive than they really are.

Another way to gather consumers' opinions of concepts is mall intercepts, where consumers in shopping malls are approached and asked to evaluate rough ads and/or copy. Rather than participating in a group discussion, individuals assess the ads via questionnaires, rating scales, and/or rankings.

Rough Art, Copy, and Commercial Testing

Because of the high cost associated with the production of an ad or commercial (many network commercials cost hundreds of thousands of dollars to produce), advertisers are increasingly spending more monies testing a rendering of the final ad at early stages. Slides of the artwork posted on a screen or animatic and photomatic roughs may be used to test at this stage. (See Figure 18–6 for an explanation of terminology.) Because such tests can be conducted for about $3,000, research at this stage is becoming ever more popular.

But cost is only one factor. The test is of little value if it does not provide relevant, accurate information. Rough tests must indicate how the finished commercial would perform. Some studies have demonstrated that these testing methods are reliable and the results typically correlate well with the finished ad.[11]

Most of the tests conducted at the rough stage involve lab settings, although some on-air field tests are also available. Popular tests include comprehension and reaction tests and consumer juries.

1. *Comprehension and reaction tests.* One key concern for the advertiser is whether the ad or commercial conveys the meaning intended. The second concern is the reaction the ad generates. Obviously, the advertiser does not want an ad that evokes a negative reaction or offends someone. **Comprehension and reaction tests** are designed to assess these responses (which makes you wonder why some ads are ever brought to the marketplace).

    Tests of comprehension and reaction employ no one standard procedure. Personal interviews, group interviews, and focus groups have all been used for this purpose, and sample sizes vary according to the needs of the client; they typically range from 50 to 200 respondents.

FIGURE 18–6
Rough testing terminology

A rough commercial is an unfinished execution that may fall into three broad categories:

Animatic rough	**Live-action rough**
Succession of drawings/cartoons	Live motion
Rendered artwork	Stand-in/nonunion talent
Still frames	Nonunion crew
Simulated movement:	Limited props/minimal opticals
Panning/zooming of frame/rapid sequence	Location settings
Photomatic rough	**A finished commercial uses**
Succession of photographs	Live motion/animation
Real people/scenery	Highly paid union talent
Still frames	Full union crew
Simulated movements:	Exotic props/studio sets/special effects
Panning/zooming of frame/rapid sequence	

FIGURE 18–7
Consumer juries

Objective:	Potential viewers (consumers) are asked to evaluate ads and give their reactions to and evaluation of them. When two or more ads are tested, viewers are usually asked to rate or rank order the ads according to their preferences.
Method:	Respondents are asked to view ads and rate them according to either (1) the order of merit method or (2) the paired comparison method. In the former, the respondent is asked to view the ads, then rank them from one to *n* according to their perceived merit. In the latter, ads are compared only two at a time. Each ad is compared to every other ad in the group, and the winner is listed. The best ad is that which wins the most times. Consumer juries typically employ 50 to 100 participants.
Output:	An overall reaction to each ad under construction as well as a rank ordering of the ads based on the viewers' perceptions.

2. *Consumer juries.* This method uses consumers representative of the target market to evaluate the probable success of an ad. **Consumer juries** may be asked to rate a selection of layouts or copy versions presented in pasteups on separate sheets. The objectives sought and methods employed in consumer juries are shown in Figure 18–7.[12] Sample questions asked of jurists are shown in Figure 18–8.

While the jury method offers the advantages of control and cost effectiveness, serious flaws in the methodology limit its usefulness.

• *The consumer may become a self-appointed expert.* One of the benefits sought from the jury method is the *objectivity* and *involvement* in the product or service that the targeted consumer can bring to the evaluation process. Sometimes, however, knowing they are being asked to critique ads, participants try to become more *expert* in their evaluations, paying more attention and being more critical than usual. The result may be a less than objective evaluation or an evaluation on elements other than those intended.

• *The number of ads that can be evaluated is limited.* Whether *order of merit* or *paired comparison* methods are used, the ranking procedure becomes tedious as the number of alternatives increases. Consider the ranking of 10 ads. While the top two and the bottom two may very well reveal differences, those ranked in the middle may not yield much useful information.

In the paired comparison method, the number of evaluations required is calculated by the formula

$$\frac{n(n-1)}{2}$$

If six alternatives are considered, 15 evaluations must be made. As the number of ads increases, the task becomes even more unmanageable.

• *A halo effect is possible.* Sometimes participants rate an ad good on all characteristics because they like a few and overlook specific weaknesses. This tendency, called the **halo effect,** distorts the ratings and defeats the ability to control for specific components. (Of course, the reverse may also occur—rating an ad bad overall due to only a few bad attributes.)

• *Preferences for specific types of advertising may overshadow objectivity.* Ads that involve emotions or pictures may receive higher ratings or rankings than those employing copy, facts, and/or rational criteria. Even though the latter are often more effective in the marketplace, they may be judged less favorably by jurists who prefer emotional appeals.

FIGURE 18–8
Questions asked in a consumer jury test

1. Which of these ads would you most likely read if you saw it in a magazine?
2. Which of these headlines would interest you the most in reading the ad further?
3. Which ad convinces you most of the quality or superiority of the product?
4. Which layout do you think would be most effective in causing you to buy?
5. Which ad did you like best?
6. Which ad did you find most interesting?

Some of the problems noted here can be remedied by the use of ratings scales instead of rankings. But ratings are not always valid either. Thus, while consumer juries have been used for years, questions of bias have led researchers to doubt their validity. As a result, a variety of other methods (discussed later in this chapter) are more commonly employed.

Pretesting of Finished Ads

Figure 18–2 showed that pretesting finished ads receives the most attention and participation among marketing researchers and their agencies. At this stage, a finished advertisement or commercial is used; since it has not been presented to the market, changes can still be made.

Many researchers believe testing the ad in final form provides better information. Several test procedures are available for print and broadcast ads, including both laboratory and field methodologies.

Print methods include portfolio tests, analyses of readability, and dummy advertising vehicles. Broadcast tests include theater tests and on-air tests. Both print and broadcast may use physiological measures.

PRETESTING FINISHED PRINT MESSAGES

A number of methods for pretesting finished print ads are available. One is *Diagnostic Research Inc.'s Copytest System*, described in Figure 18–9. The most common of these methods are portfolio tests, readability tests, and dummy advertising vehicles.

Portfolio Tests

Portfolio tests are a laboratory methodology designed to expose a group of respondents to a portfolio consisting of both control and test ads. Respondents are then asked what information they recall from the ads. The assumption is that the ads that yield the *highest recall* are the most effective.

While portfolio tests offer the opportunity to compare alternative ads directly, a number of weaknesses limit their applicability.

1. Factors other than advertising creativity and/or presentation may affect recall. Interest in the product or product category, the fact that respondents know they are participating in a test, or interviewer instructions (among others) may account for more differences than the ad itself.
2. Recall may not be the best test. Some researchers argue that for certain types of products (those of low involvement) ability to recognize the ad when shown may be a better measure than recall.

One way to determine the validity of the portfolio method is to correlate its results with readership scores once the ad is placed in the field. Whether such validity tests are being conducted or not is not readily known, although the portfolio method remains popular in the industry.

Readability Tests

The communications efficiency of the copy in a print ad can be tested without reader interviews. This test uses the **Flesch formula**, named after its developer, Rudolph Flesch, to assess readability of the copy by determining the average number of syllables per 100 words.

FIGURE 18–9
Reflections: Diagnostic Research Inc.'s print test

Objective:	Tests recall and readers' impressions of print ads.
Method:	Mall intercepts in two or more cities are used to screen respondents and have them take home "test magazines" for reading. Participants are phoned the next day to determine opinions of the ads, recall of ad contents, and other questions of interest to the sponsor. Approximately 225 people constitute the sample.
Output:	Scores reported include related recall of copy and visual elements, sales messages, and other nonspecific elements. Both quantitative (table) scores and verbatim responses are reported.

Human interest appeal of the material, length of sentences, and familiarity with certain words are also considered and correlated with the educational background of target audiences. Test results are compared to previously established norms for various target audiences. The test suggests that copy is best comprehended when sentences are short, words are concrete and familiar, and personal references are drawn.

This method eliminates many of the interviewee biases associated with other tests and avoids gross errors in understanding. The norms offer an attractive standard for comparison.

Disadvantages are also inherent, however. The copy may become too mechanical, and direct input from the receiver is not available. Without this input, contributing elements like creativity cannot be addressed. To be effective, this test should be used only in conjunction with other pretesting methods.

Dummy Advertising Vehicles

In an improvement on the portfolio test, ads are placed in "dummy" magazines developed by an agency or research firm. The magazines contain regular editorial features of interest to the reader, as well as the test ads, and are distributed to a *random sample* of homes in predetermined geographic areas. Readers are told the magazine publisher is interested in evaluations of editorial content and asked to read the magazines as they normally would. Then they are interviewed on their reactions to both editorial content and ads. Recall, readership, and interest-generating capabilities of the ad are assessed.

The advantage of this method is that it provides a more natural setting than the portfolio test. Readership occurs in the participant's own home, the test more closely approximates a natural reading situation, and the reader may go back to the magazine, as people typically do.

But the dummy magazine shares the other disadvantages associated with portfolio tests. The testing effect is not eliminated, and product interest may still bias the results. Thus, while this test offers some advantages over the portfolio method, it is not a guaranteed measure of the advertising's impact.

PRETESTING FINISHED BROADCAST ADS

A variety of methods for pretesting broadcast ads are available. The most popular are theater tests, on-air tests, and physiological measures.

Theater Tests

One of the most popular laboratory methods for pretesting finished commercials is **theater testing,** in which participants are invited by telephone, mall intercepts, and/or tickets in the mail to view pilots of proposed TV programs. In some instances, the show is actually being tested, but more commonly a standard program is used so audience responses can be compared with normative responses established by previous viewers. Sample sizes range from 250 to 600 participants.

On entering the theater, viewers are told a drawing will be held for gifts and asked to complete a product preference questionnaire asking which products they would prefer if they win. This form also requests demographic data. Participants may be seated in specific locations in the theater to allow observation by age, sex, and so on. They view the program and commercials, and a form asking for evaluations is distributed. Participants are then asked to complete a second form for a drawing so that changes in product preference can be noted. In addition to product/brand preference, the form may request other information:

1. Interest in and reaction to the commercial.
2. Overall reaction to the commercial as measured by an adjective checklist.
3. Recall of various aspects of the commercial.
4. Interest in the brand under consideration.
5. Continuous (frame-by-frame) reactions throughout the commercial.

The methods of theater testing operations vary, though all measure brand preference changes. Some do not take all the measures listed here; others ask the consumers to turn dials or push buttons on a keypad to provide the continual responses. An example of one methodology is shown in Figure 18–10.

FIGURE 18–10
The ACT theater methodology

- Advertising Control for Television (ACT), a lab procedure of McCollum Spielman Worldwide, uses about 400 respondents representing four cities. It measures initial brand preference by asking participants which brands they most recently purchased. Respondents are then divided into groups of 25 to view a 30-minute program with seven commercials inserted in the middle. Four are test commercials; the other three are control commercials with established viewing norms. After viewing the program, respondents are given a recall test of the commercials. After the recall test, a second 30-minute program is shown, with each test commercial shown again. The second measure of brand preference is taken at this time, with persuasion measured by the percentage of viewers who switched preferences from their most recently purchased brand to one shown in the test commercials.

Those opposed to theater tests cite a number of disadvantages. First, they say the environment is too artificial. The lab setting is bad enough, but asking respondents to turn dials or, as one service does, wiring people for physiological responses takes them too far from a natural viewing situation. Second, the contrived measure of brand preference change seems too phony to believe. Critics contend that participants will see through it and make changes just because they think they are supposed to. Finally, the group effect of having others present and overtly exhibiting their reactions may influence viewers who did not have any reactions themselves.

Proponents argue that theater tests offer distinct advantages. In addition to control, the established norms (averages of commercials' performances) indicate how one's commercial will fare against others in the same product class that were already tested. Further, advocates say the brand preference measure is supported by actual sales results.

Despite the limitations of theater testing, most major consumer product companies have used it to evaluate their commercials. This method may have shortcomings, but it allows them to identify strong or weak commercials and to compare them to other ads.

On-Air Tests

Some of the firms conducting theater tests also insert the commercials into actual TV programs in certain test markets. Typically, the commercials are in finished form, although the testing of ads earlier in the developmental process is becoming more common. This is referred to as an **on-air test** and often includes single-source ad research (discussed later in this chapter). Information Resources, ASI Market Research, Inc., McCollum Spielman Worldwide (MSW), and Nielsen are well-known providers of on-air tests. Figure 18–11 describes one of these services, ASI's recall-plus test.

On-air testing techniques offer all the advantages of field methodologies, as well as all the disadvantages. Further, there are negative aspects to the specific measures taken through the on-air systems. One concern is associated with **day-after recall scores**, the primary measure used in these tests. Lyman Ostlund notes that measurement errors may result from the natural environment—the position of the ad in the series of commercials shown, the adjacent program content, and/or the number of commercials shown.[13] While the testing services believe their methods overcome many of these criticisms, each still uses

FIGURE 18–11
ASI Market Research's recall-plus test

Objective: Tests finished or rough commercials to allow day-after recall and verbatim reactions.

Method: One control and four test commercials are inserted into new 30-minute family TV programs. The commercials and program are sent to two geographically dispersed cities and aired on CATV during prime-time viewing hours. Approximately 200 female viewers between the ages of 18 and 65 are randomly selected from all homes on the CATV system in the area. Commercials are then reexposed to viewers who recalled the ad, and more diagnostic questions are administered.

Output: Day-after recall scores, verbatim responses to the commercials, and test–retest reliability scores are provided. Scores on competing commercials (if used) are also provided.

recall as a primary measure of effectiveness. Since recall tests best reflect the degree of attention and interest in an ad, claims that the tests predict the ad's impact on sales may be going too far. (In 28 studies reviewed by Jack Haskins, only two demonstrated that factual recall could be related to sales.)[14] Joel Dubow's research indicates that recall is a necessary but not sufficient measure, while research by Jones and Blair was even more demonstrative, noting that "it is unwise to look to recall for an accurate assessment of a commercial's sales effect" (p. 42).[15]

On the plus side, most of the testing services have offered evidence of both validity and reliability for on-air pretesting of commercials. Both ASI and MSW claim their pretest and posttest results yield the same recall scores 9 out of 10 times—a strong indication of reliability and a good predictor of the effect the ad is likely to have when shown to the population as a whole.

In summary, on-air pretesting of finished or rough commercials offers some distinct advantages over lab methods and some indications of the ad's likely success. Whether the measures used are as strong an indication as the providers say still remains in question.

Physiological Measures

A less common method of pretesting finished commercials involves a laboratory setting in which physiological responses are measured. These measures indicate the receiver's *involuntary* response to the ad, theoretically eliminating biases associated with the voluntary measures reviewed to this point. (Involuntary responses are those over which the individual has no control, such as heartbeat and reflexes.) Physiological measures used to test both print and broadcast ads include pupil dilation, galvanic skin response, eye tracking, and brain waves.

1. *Pupil dilation.* Research in **pupillometrics** is designed to measure dilation and constriction of the pupils of the eyes in response to stimuli. Dilation is associated with action; constriction involves the body's conservation of energy.

Advertisers have used pupillometrics to evaluate product and package design as well as to test ads. Pupil dilation suggests a stronger interest in (or preference for) an ad or implies arousal or attention-getting capabilities. Other attempts to determine the affective (liking or disliking) responses created by ads have met with less success.

Because of high costs and some methodological problems, the use of pupillometrics has waned over the past decade. But it can be useful in evaluating certain aspects of advertising.

2. *Galvanic skin response.* Also known as **electrodermal response**, GSR measures the skin's resistance or conductance to a small amount of current passed between two electrodes. Response to a stimulus activates sweat glands, which in turn increases the conductance of the electrical current. Thus, GSR/EDR activity might reflect a reaction to advertising. In their review of the research in this area, Paul Watson and Robert Gatchel concluded that GSR/EDR (1) is sensitive to affective stimuli, (2) may present a picture of attention, (3) may be useful to measure long-term advertising recall, and (4) is useful in measuring ad effectiveness.[16] In interviews with practitioners and reviews of case studies, Priscilla LaBarbera and Joel Tucciarone also concluded that GSR is an effective measure and is useful for measuring affect, or liking, for ads.[17] While a number of companies have offered skin response measures, this research methodology is not commonly used now, and LaBarbera and Tucciarone believe that it is underused, given its potential.

3. *Eye tracking.* A methodology that is more commonly employed is **eye tracking** (Figure 18–12), in which viewers are asked to view an ad while a sensor aims a beam of infrared light at the eye. The beam follows the movement of the eye and shows the exact spot on which the viewer is focusing. The continuous reading of responses demonstrates which elements of the ad are attracting attention, how long the viewer is focusing on them, and the sequence in which they are being viewed.

Eye tracking can identify strengths and weaknesses in an ad. For example, attractive models or background action may distract the viewer's attention away from the brand or product being advertised. The advertiser can remedy this distraction before fielding the ad. In other instances, colors or illustrations may attract attention and create viewer interest in the ad.

FIGURE 18–12
Eye movement research

Objective:	Tracks viewers' eye movements to determine what viewers read or view in print ads and where their attention is focused in TV commercials or billboards.
Method:	Fiber optics, digital data processing, and advanced electronics are used to follow eye movements of viewers and/or readers as they process an ad.
Output:	Relationship among what readers see, recall, and comprehend. Scan paths on print ads, billboards, commercials, and print materials. (Can also be used to evaluate package designs.)

4. *Brain waves.* **Electroencephalographic (EEG) measures** can be taken from the skull to determine electrical frequencies in the brain. These electrical impulses are used in two areas of research, alpha waves and hemispheric lateralization.

• **Alpha activity** refers to the degree of brain activation. People are in an alpha state when they are inactive, resting, or sleeping. The theory is that a person in an alpha state is less likely to be processing information (recall correlates negatively with alpha levels) and that attention and processing require moving from this state. By measuring a subject's alpha level while viewing a commercial, researchers can assess the degree to which attention and processing are likely to occur.
• **Hemispheric lateralization** distinguishes between alpha activity in the left and right sides of the brain. It has been hypothesized that the right side of the brain processes visual stimuli and the left processes verbal stimuli. The right hemisphere is thought to respond more to emotional stimuli, while the left responds to logic. The right determines recognition, while the left is responsible for recall.[18] If these hypotheses are correct, advertisers could design ads to increase learning and memory by creating stimuli to appeal to each hemisphere. However, some researchers believe the brain does not function laterally and an ad cannot be designed to appeal to one side or the other.

While EEG research has engaged the attention of academic researchers, it has been much less successful in attracting the interest of practitioners.

Market Testing of Ads

The fact that the ad and/or campaign has been implemented does not mean there is no longer a need for testing. The pretests were conducted on smaller samples and may in some instances have questionable merit, so the marketer must find out how the ad is doing in the field. In this section, we discuss methods for posttesting an ad. Some of the tests are similar to the pretests discussed in the previous section and are provided by the same companies.

POSTTESTS OF PRINT ADS

A variety of print posttests are available, including inquiry tests, recognition tests, and recall tests.

Inquiry Tests

Used in both consumer and business-to-business market testing, **inquiry tests** are designed to measure advertising effectiveness on the basis of inquiries generated from ads appearing in various print media. The inquiry may take the form of the number of coupons returned, phone calls generated, or direct inquiries through reader cards (Exhibit 18–1). For example, if you called in response to an ad in a local medium recently, perhaps you were asked how you found out about the company or product or where you saw the ad. This is a very simple measure of the ad's or medium's effectiveness.

More complex methods of measuring effectiveness through inquiries may involve (1) running the ad in successive issues of the same medium, (2) running **split-run tests**, in which variations of the ad appear in different copies of the same newspaper or magazine, and/or (3) running the same ad in different media. Each of these methods yields information on different aspects of the strategy. The first measures the *cumulative* effects of the campaign; the second examines specific elements of the ad or variations on it. The final method measures the effectiveness of the medium rather than the ad itself.

While inquiry tests may yield useful information, weaknesses in this methodology limit its effectiveness. For example, inquiries may not be a true measure of the attention-getting or information-providing aspects of the ad. The reader may be attracted to an ad, read it, and even store the information but not be motivated to inquire at that particular time. Time constraints, lack of a need for the product or service at the time the ad is run, and other factors may limit the number of inquiries. But a small number of inquiries doesn't mean the ad was not effective; attention, attitude change, awareness, and recall of copy points may all have been achieved. At the other extreme, a person with a particular need for the product may respond to any ad for it, regardless of specific qualities of the ad.

Major advantages of inquiry tests are that they are inexpensive to implement and they provide some feedback with respect to the general effectiveness of the ad or medium used. But they are usually not very effective for comparing different versions or specific creative aspects of an ad.

FIGURE 18–13
The *Starch Readership Report*

Objective: Determining recognition of print ads and comparing them to other ads of the same variety or in the same magazine.

Method: Samples are drawn from 20 to 30 urban areas reflecting the geographic circulation of the magazine. Personal interviewers screen readers for qualifications and determine exposure and readership. Samples include a minimum of 200 males and females, as well as specific audiences where required. Participants are asked to go through the magazines, looking at the ads, and provide specific responses.

Output: *Starch Readership Reports* generate three recognition scores:

- Noted score—the percentage of readers who remember seeing the ad.
- Seen-associated score—the percentage of readers who recall seeing or reading any part of the ad identifying the product or brand.
- Read-most score—the percentage of readers who report reading at least half of the copy portion of the ad.

Recognition Tests

Perhaps the most common posttest of print ads is the **recognition method**, most closely associated with Roper Starch Worldwide. The *Starch Readership Report* lets the advertiser assess the impact of an ad in a single issue of a magazine, over time, and/or across different magazines (see Figure 18–13). Starch measures over 75,000 ads in more than 1,000 issues representing more than 100 consumer, farm, and business magazines and newspapers per year and provides a number of measures of the ad's effectiveness. An example of a Starch-scored ad is shown in Exhibit 18–2.

Starch also offers the *Starch Impression Study* and the *Starch Ballot Readership Study*. The impression study provides consumers' qualitative impressions of ads (for example, company image and important features); the readership study measures readership in business magazines.

EXHIBIT 18–2
Example of a Starch-scored ad

Starch claims that (1) the pulling power of various aspects of the ad can be assessed through the control offered, (2) the effectiveness of competitors' ads can be compared through the norms provided, (3) alternative ad executions can be tested, and (4) readership scores are a useful indication of consumers' *involvement* in the ad or campaign. (The theory is that a reader must read and become involved in the ad before the ad can communicate. To the degree that this readership can be shown, it is a direct indication of effectiveness.)

Of these advantages, perhaps the most valid is the ability to judge specific aspects of the ad. Many researchers have criticized other aspects of the Starch recognition method (as well as other recognition measures) based on the problems of false claiming, interviewer sensitivities, and unreliable scores.

1. *False claiming.* Research shows that in recognition tests, respondents may claim to have seen an ad when they did not. False claims may be a result of having seen similar ads elsewhere, expecting that such an ad would appear in the medium, or wanting to please the questioner. Interest in the product category also increases reporting of ad readership. Whether this false claiming is deliberate or not, it leads to an overreporting of effectiveness. On the flip side, factors such as interview fatigue may lead to an underreporting bias—that is, respondents not reporting an ad they did see.

2. *Interviewer sensitivities.* Any time research involves interviewers, there is a potential for bias. Respondents may want to impress the interviewer or fear looking unknowledgeable if they continually claim not to recognize an ad. There may also be variances associated with interviewer instructions, recordings, and so on, regardless of the amount of training and sophistication involved.

3. *Reliability of recognition scores.* Starch admits that the reliability and validity of its readership scores increase with the number of insertions tested, which essentially means that to test just one ad on a single exposure may not produce valid or reliable results.

In sum, despite critics, the Starch readership studies continue to dominate the posttesting of print ads. The value provided by norms and the fact that multiple exposures can improve reliability and validity may underlie the decisions to employ this methodology.

Recall Tests

There are several tests to measure recall of print ads. Perhaps the best known of these are the ASI Print Plus Test and the Gallup & Robinson Impact Test (described in Figure 18–14). These **recall tests** are similar to those discussed in the section on pretesting broadcast ads in that they attempt to measure recall of specific ads.

In addition to the same interviewer problems as recognition tests, recall tests have other disadvantages. The reader's degree of involvement with the product and/or the distinctiveness of the appeals and visuals may lead to higher than accurate recall scores, although in general the method may lead to lower levels of recall than actually exist (an error the advertiser would be happy with). Critics contend the test is not strong enough to reflect recall ac-

FIGURE 18–14
Gallup & Robinson magazine impact research service

Objective: Tracking recall of advertising (and client's ads) appearing in magazines to assess performance and effectiveness.

Method: Test magazines are placed in participants' homes and respondents are asked to read the magazine that day. A telephone interview is conducted the second day to assess recall of ads, recall of copy points, and consumers' impressions of the ads. Sample size is 150 people.

Output: Three measurement scores are provided:

- Proven name registration—the percentage of respondents who can accurately recall the ad.
- Idea communication—the number of sales points the respondents can recall.
- Favorable buying attitude—the extent of favorable purchase reaction to the brand or corporation.

curately, so many ads may score as less effective than they really are, and advertisers may abandon or modify them needlessly.

On the plus side, it is thought that recall tests can assess the ad's impact on memory. Proponents of recall tests say the major concern is not the results themselves but how they are interpreted.

POSTTESTS OF BROADCAST COMMERCIALS

A number of methods exist for posttesting broadcast commercials. The most common are day-after recall tests, test marketing, single-source tracking, and other tracking studies.

Day-After Recall Tests

The most popular method of posttesting employed in the broadcast industry is the ASI recall-plus test (formerly known as the *Burke test*) (Figure 18–15). While recall-plus is actually a specific test provided by ASI Market Research, the *day-after recall (DAR) test* is almost generic for all recall tests. It is important to recognize, however, that other firms provide the same services. In addition, variations and extensions on the basic DAR test are available.

While different organizations offer their own methodologies, the effectiveness measure is always the number of people able to *recall* the ad. For example, the ASI and Gallup & Robinson tests use different markets, use different numbers of respondents, and select respondents differently. (ASI calls the day after the ad until 200 people are found who saw the program, whereas Gallup & Robinson prerecruits viewers.) Yet both tests provide scores reporting two basic factors, unaided and aided recall.

1. *Unaided recall.* Respondents are asked a simple question such as, "While watching [program] last night, did you see a commercial for [product category]?" The unaided recall score reflects the percentage of respondents who recall a particular commercial on their own—a strong measure of memory.
2. *Aided recall.* Aids are given, such as, "While watching [program] last night, did you see a commercial for [brand name]?" The percentage of respondents who can then recall the commercial is reported as an aided score.

Because of advertisers' reliance on the measure, the day-after recall score can make or break an ad—sometimes erroneously. Like the other methodologies discussed, recall tests are not without their critics. In addition to those problems cited earlier, the following disadvantages have been suggested.

1. DAR tests may favor unemotional appeals because respondents are asked to verbalize the message. Thinking messages may be easier to recall than emotional communications, so recall scores for emotional ads may be lower.[19] A number of other studies have also indicated that emotional ads may be processed differently from thinking ones; some ad agencies, for example, Leo Burnett and BBDO Worldwide, have gone so far as to develop their own methods of determining emotional response to ads.[20]
2. Program content may influence recall. The programs in which the ad appears may lead to different recall scores for the same brand. The net result is a potential inaccuracy in the recall score and in the norms used to establish comparisons.[21]

FIGURE 18–15
ASI Market Research day-after recall test

Objective: Determining the ability of the commercial to gain viewer attention, communicate an intended message, associate the brand name with the message, and affect purchase behavior.

Method: Interviews take place the day after the commercial airs in numerous cities throughout the United States. The sample is 200 people who confirm that they watched the program in which the ad was placed. All individuals are asked if they remember a commercial, then what they can remember about it.

Output: Scores reflecting unaided and aided recall, indicating that viewers remember the commercial and can relate details about it.

3. A prerecruited sample (Gallup & Robinson) may pay increased attention to the program and the ads contained therein because the respondents know they will be tested the next day. This effect would lead to a higher level of recall than really exists.

The major advantage of day-after recall tests is that they are field tests. The natural setting is supposed to provide a more realistic response profile. These tests are also popular because they provide norms that give advertisers a standard for comparing how well their ads are performing.

Test Marketing

Many companies conduct tests designed to measure their advertising effects in specific test markets before releasing them nationally. The markets chosen are representative of the target market. For example, a company may test its ads in Portland, Oregon; San Antonio, Texas; or Buffalo, New York, if the demographic and socioeconomic profiles of these cities match the product's market. A variety of factors may be tested, including reactions to the ads (for example, alternative copy points), the effects of various budget sizes, or special offers. The ads run in finished form in the media where they might normally appear, and effectiveness is measured after the ads run.

The advantage of test marketing of ads is realism. Regular viewing environments are used and the testing effects are minimized. A high degree of control can be attained if the test is designed successfully. For example, an extensive test market study was designed and conducted by Seagram and Time, Inc., over three years to measure the effects of advertising frequency on consumers' buying habits. This study demonstrated just how much could be learned from research conducted in a field setting but with some experimental controls. It also showed that proper research can provide strong insights into the impact of ad campaigns. (Many advertising researchers consider this study one of the most conclusive ever conducted in the attempt to demonstrate the effects of advertising on sales.)

The Seagram study also reveals some of the disadvantages associated with test market measures, not the least of which are cost and time. Few firms have the luxury to spend three years and hundreds of thousands of dollars on such a test. In addition, there is always the fear that competitors may discover and intervene in the research process.

Test marketing can provide substantial insight into the effectiveness of advertising if care is taken to minimize the negative aspects of such tests.

Single-Source Tracking Studies

Single-source tracking methods track the behaviors of consumers from the television set to the supermarket checkout counter. Participants in a designated area who have cable TV and agree to participate in the studies are given a card (similar to a credit card) that identifies their household and gives the research company their demographics. The households are split into matched groups; one group receives an ad while the other does not, or alternate ads are sent to each. Their purchases are recorded from the bar codes of the products bought. Commercial exposures are then correlated with purchase behaviors.

Earlier we mentioned the use of single-source ad research in pretesting commercials. A recent study demonstrates that the single-source method can also be used effectively to posttest ads, allowing for a variety of dependent measures and tracking the effects of increased ad budgets and different versions of ad copy—and even ad effects on sales.[22]

A 10-year study conducted by Information Resources' BehaviorScan service demonstrated long-term effects of advertising on sales. The study examined copy, media schedules, ad budgets, and the impact of trade promotions on sales in 10 markets throughout the United States and concluded that advertising can produce sales growth as long as two years after a campaign ends.[23] (The study also concluded that results of copy recall and persuasion tests were unlikely to predict sales reliably.) As shown in Figure 18–16, a number of single-source methods have been used, among them BehaviorScan (Information Resources), AdTel (SAMI-Burke), and ERIM (A. C. Nielsen).

Many advertisers believe these single-source measures will change the way research is conducted due to the advantages of control and the ability to measure directly the ads' effects on

FIGURE 18—16   Single-source ad tracking systems

BehaviorScan
1. Ten geographically dispersed test communities. Examples: Pittsfield, MA; Rome, GA; Eau Claire, WI; and Visalia, CA
2. About 30,000 panel households
3. Requires cable TV system

AdTel
1. Five geographically dispersed test communities. Examples: Portland, ME; the Quad Cities (Davenport, IA; Moline, IL; etc.); and Boise, ID
2. About 12,000 panel households
3. Requires cable TV system

ERIM
1. Two test communities: Sioux Falls, SD; and Springfield, MO
2. About 6,000 panel households
3. No requirement for cable TV

Roper CollegeTrack
1. College students' product usage, purchases, and media habits
2. Combines Roper and CollegeTrack surveys on national samples

MarketSource
1. College and high school campuses
2. 1,600 locations throughout 500 college campuses
3. 500 high schools

sales. A number of major corporations and ad agencies are now employing this method, including Campbell Soup, Colgate-Palmolive, Nestlé, General Foods, P&G, Pepsi-Cola, Leo Burnett, and J. Walter Thompson. After using scanner data to review the advertising/sales relationship for 78 brands, John Jones concluded that single-source data are beginning to fulfill their promise now that more measurements are available.[24]

While single-source testing is a valuable tool, it still has some problems. One researcher says, "Scanner data focus on short-term sales effects, and as a result capture only 10 to 30 percent of what advertising does."[25] Others complain that the data are too complicated to deal with, as an overabundance of information is available. Still another disadvantage is the high cost of collecting single-source data.

Tracking Print/Broadcast Ads

One of the more useful and adaptable forms of posttesting involves tracking the effects of the ad campaign by taking measurements at regular intervals. **Tracking studies** have been used to measure the effects of advertising on awareness, recall, interest, and attitudes toward the ad and/or brand as well as purchase intentions. (Ad tracking may be applied to both print and broadcast ads but is much more common with the latter.) Personal interviews, phone surveys, mall intercepts, and even mail surveys have been used. Sample sizes typically range from 250 to 500 cases per period (usually quarterly or semiannually). Tracking studies yield perhaps the most valuable information available to the marketing manager for assessing current programs and planning for the future.

The major advantage of tracking studies is that they can be tailored to each specific campaign and/or situation. A standard set of questions can track effects of the campaign over time. The effects of various media can also be determined, although with much less effectiveness. Tracking studies have also been used to measure the differential impact of different budget sizes, the effects of flighting, brand or corporate image, and recall of specific copy points. Finally, when designed properly, as shown in Figure 18–17, tracking studies offer a high degree of reliability and validity.[26]

Some of the problems of recall and recognition measures are inherent in tracking studies, since many other factors may affect both brand and advertising recall. Despite these limitations, however, tracking studies are a very effective way to assess the effects of advertising campaigns.

In summary, you can see that each of the testing methods considered in this chapter has its strengths and its limitations. You may wonder: Can we actually test advertising effectiveness? What can be done to ensure a valid, reliable test? The next section of this chapter suggests some answers.

FIGURE 18–17
Factors that make or break tracking studies

1. Properly defined objectives
2. Alignment with sales objectives
3. Properly designed measures (e.g., adequate sample size, maximum control over interviewing process, adequate time between tracking periods)
4. Consistency through replication of the sampling plan
5. Random samples
6. Continuous interviewing (that is, not seasonal)
7. Evaluative measures related to behavior (attitudes meet this criterion; recall of ads does not)
8. Critical evaluative questions asked early to eliminate bias
9. Measurement of competitors' performance
10. Skepticism about questions that ask where the advertising was seen or heard (TV always wins)
11. Building of news value into the study
12. "Moving averages" used to spot long-term trends and avoid seasonality
13. Data reported in terms of relationships rather than as isolated facts
14. Integration of key marketplace events with tracking results (e.g., advertising expenditures of self and competitors, promotional activities associated with price changes in ad campaigns, introductions of new brands, government announcements, changes in economic conditions)

ESTABLISHING A PROGRAM FOR MEASURING ADVERTISING EFFECTS
Problems with Current Research Methods

There is no surefire way to test advertising effectiveness. However, in reponse to pressures to determine the contribution of ads to the overall marketing effort, steps are being taken to improve this measurement task. Let's begin by reviewing the major problems with some existing methods and then examine possible improvements.

When current testing methods are compared to the criteria established by PACT (see Figure 18–3), it is clear that some of the principles important to good copy testing can be accomplished readily, whereas others require substantially more effort. For example, principle 6 (providing equivalent test ads) should require a minimum of effort. The researcher can easily control the state of completion of the test communications. Also fairly easy are principles 1 and 2 (providing measurements relative to the objectives sought and determining a priori how the results will be used).

We have seen throughout this text that each promotional medium, the message, and the budget all consider the marketing and communications objectives sought. The integrated marketing communications planning model establishes the roles of these elements. So by the time one gets to the measurement phase, the criteria by which these programs will be evaluated should simply fall into place.

Slightly more difficult are principles 3, 5, and 8, although again these factors are largely in the control of the researcher. Principle 3 (providing multiple measurements) may require little more than budgeting to make sure more than one test is conducted. At the most, it may require considering two similar measures to ensure reliability. Likewise, principle 5 (exposing the test ad more than once) can be accomplished with a proper research design. Finally, principle 8 (sample definition) requires little more than sound research methodology; any test should use the target audience to assess an ad's effectiveness. You would not use a sample of nondrinkers to evaluate new liquor commercials.

The most difficult factors to control—and the principles that may best differentiate between good and bad testing procedures—are PACT requirements 4, 7, and 9. Fortunately, however, addressing each of these contributes to the attainment of the others.

The best starting point is principle 4, which states the research should be guided by a model of human response to communications that encompasses reception, comprehension, and behavioral response. It is the best starting point, in our opinion, because it is the principle least addressed by practicing researchers. If you recall, Chapter 5 proposed a number of models that could fulfill this principle's requirements. Yet even though these models have existed for quite some time, few if any common research methods attempt to integrate them into their methodologies. Most current methods do little more than provide recall scores, despite the fact many researchers have shown that recall is a poor measure of effectiveness. Models that do claim to measure such factors as attitude change or brand preference change are often fraught with problems that severely limit their reliability. An effective measure must include some relationship to the communications process.

It might seem at first glance that principle 7 (providing a nonbiasing exposure) would be easy to accomplish. But lab measures, while offering control, are artificial and vulnerable to testing effects. And field measures, while more realistic, often lose control. The Seagram and Time study may have the best of both worlds, but it is too large a task for most firms to undertake. Some of the improvements associated with the single-source systems help to solve this problem. In addition, properly designed ad tracking studies provide truer measures of the impact of the communication. As technology develops and more attention is paid to this principle, we expect to see improvements in methodologies soon.

Last but not least is principle 9, the concern for reliability and validity. Most of the measures discussed are lacking in at least one of these criteria, yet these are two of the most critical distinctions between good and bad research. If a study is properly designed, and by that we mean it addresses principles 1 through 8, it should be both reliable and valid.

Essentials of Effective Testing

Simply put, good tests of advertising effectiveness must address the nine principles established by PACT. One of the easiest ways to accomplish this is by following the decision sequence model in formulating promotional plans.

- *Establish communications objectives.* We have stated that except for a few instances (most specifically direct-response advertising), it is nearly impossible to show the direct impact of advertising on sales. So the marketing objectives established for the promotional program are not good measures of communication effectiveness. For example, it is very difficult (or too expensive) to demonstrate the effect of an ad on brand share or on sales. On the other hand, attainment of communications objectives can be measured and leads to the accomplishment of marketing objectives.
- *Use a consumer response model.* Early in this text we reviewed hierarchy of effects models and cognitive response models, which provide an understanding of the effects of communications and lend themselves to achieving communications goals.
- *Use both pretests and posttests.* From a cost standpoint—both actual cost outlays and opportunity costs—pretesting makes sense. It may mean the difference between success or failure of the campaign or the product. But it should work in conjunction with posttests, which avoid the limitations of pretests, use much larger samples, and take place in more natural settings. Posttesting may be required to determine the true effectiveness of the ad or campaign.
- *Use multiple measures.* Many attempts to measure the effectiveness of advertising focus on one major dependent variable—perhaps sales, recall, or recognition. As noted earlier in this chapter, advertising may have a variety of effects on the consumer, some of which can be measured through traditional methods, others that require updated thinking (recall the discussion on physiological responses). For a true assessment of advertising effectiveness, a number of measures may be required. IMC Perspective 18–2 offers some additional insights into this area.
- *Understand and implement proper research.* It is critical to understand research methodology. What constitutes a good design? Is it valid and reliable? Does it measure what we need it to? There is no shortcut to this criterion, and there is no way to avoid it if you truly want to measure the effects of advertising.

A major study sponsored by the Advertising Research Foundation (ARF), involving interviews with 12,000 to 15,000 people, addressed some of these issues.[27] While we do not have the space to analyze this study here, note that the research was designed to evaluate measures of copy tests, compare copy testing procedures, and examine some of the PACT

IMC Perspective 18–2
Measuring Effectiveness: Science or Art?

Much has been made of the need to measure the effectiveness of IMC elements and the fact that too many companies do not do so. Some companies' award-winning programs seem to translate directly into sales and/or brand share. Others are not so fortunate—or are they? Consider this: Video Storyboard Tests makes awards based on which ads consumers like best. Among recent winners, seven of the top 25 finishers had flat or declining sales, including Pepsi and Energizer. Others, like Kodak, Doritos, and Coke showed increases. The inconsistencies of these results lend support to advertisers' claims that the effects of advertising cannot be measured. The results are equally inconsistent among academic researchers. Some provide results of an advertising/sales relationship, but others say there is none, or if there is, it cannot be accurately measured.

Maybe the problem is not in the measures themselves but in the outcomes expected. Perhaps measuring effectiveness isn't a science after all, but a combination of science and art. In other words, maybe the ads are working but the measures that we use to determine this are not the right ones—or as noted by the creative types, there is too much reliance on numbers and statistics.

Consider these success stories relating to advertising and public relations programs:

Grey Poupon. Before the "Pardon me do you have any Grey Poupon?" campaign, the brand was an also-ran in the mustard category. Competitor French's controlled over half of the market. The new ad campaign positioned the brand as an upscale, sophisticated product, not what one would put on hot dogs. It led to a number of positive things:(1) an entirely new segment of mustard was created, with Grey Poupon as the leader; (2) the campaign, developed for a few test markets, was adapted nationwide; (3) French's developed its own brand to compete in the new segment (and failed); and (4) price elasticity was forgotten. With some variations, the campaign has now been running for over a decade and has been imitated and adopted by other product categories. (Mercedes has run ads that say "It even comes with its own Grey Poupon".)

Grammercy Press. MCI's 12-episode miniseries of TV commercials about a fictional downtown Manhattan publishing company featured an old codger editor resisting new technology, an egotistical head of sales, a yuppie owner, and a gossipy, beautiful receptionist in an attempt to promote MCI's business unit. Taking a page from Taster's Choice, MCI hoped to break through the clutter and to humanize business services. The results were astonishing: thousands of people called MCI asking when the next episode could be expected, the ad won *Advertising Age*'s best commercial spot for the year, awareness scores rose significantly, and the MCI website had over 6 million hits. MCI also believes the ads were responsible for reenergizing the sales staff.

General Mills. In a different approach, General Mills has achieved success by cutting advertising expenditures and focusing on public relations. Some of the strategies and results:

- Surreptitiously stuffing 162 boxes of Cheerios into Seattle Mariner Jay Buhner's locker and filming his surprise when he opened it. Shown by TV stations in 12 major markets.
- Offering a free food column by Betty Crocker. Carried by 700 newspapers under the Betty Crocker logo.
- Painting Cheerios boxes red, white, and blue for the 1996 Olympics (they sold out so quickly the company had to scramble to replace them) and initiating the Wheaties watch (which Olympic winner would appear on the next Wheaties box?). The national media debated the issue for two weeks before the new box introduction. According to Prudential Securities analyst John McMillin, "General Mills got more bang for its buck than any other Olympic sponsor"—including significant sales increases. George L. Staphos, analyst at PaineWebber, says, "Any way you measure it, the promotional effectiveness of General Mills is two to three times that of its competitors."

While these examples no doubt contributed to sales increases, they were also effective in other ways, only some of them quantifiable. Which suggests that advertisers who focus only on the quantitative aspects of effectiveness may not be able to see the forest for the trees!

Sources: Kevin Helliker, "Old-Fashioned PR Gives General Mills Advertising Bargains," *The Wall Street Journal*, March 20, 1997, p. A1; Bob Garfield, "Best Reel: Fictitious Grammercy," *Advertising Age*, December 19, 1994, p. 23; Advertising Educational Foundation, 1997.

principles. Information on this study has been published in a number of academic and trade journals and by the ARF.

MEASURING THE EFFECTIVENESS OF OTHER PROGRAM ELEMENTS
Measuring the Effectiveness of Sales Promotions

Throughout this text, we have discussed how and when promotional program elements should be used, the advantages and disadvantages of each, and so on. In many chapters we have discussed measures of effectiveness used to evaluate these programs. In the final section of this chapter, we add a few measures that were not discussed earlier.

Sales promotions are not limited to retailers and resellers of products. Sports marketers have found them a very effective way to attract crowds and have been able to measure their relative effectiveness by the number of fans attending games. Major League Baseball teams have seen their attendance increase for those games in which promotions are offered.

A number of organizations measure sales promotions. One firm, MarketSource, provides marketers with a basis for measuring the effectiveness of their sampling programs. While too involved to discuss in detail here, the program calculates a breakeven rate by dividing the sampling investment by the profit for the user. If the conversions exceed the breakeven rate, the sampling program is successful.[28] Promotion Decisions Inc. examines the impact of freestanding inserts (FSIs) (Figure 18–18).

Other measures of sales promotions are also available. Schnucks (St. Louis), Smitty's Super Valu (Phoenix), and Vons (Los Angeles) have all used pretests with effects measured through scanner data. Others have employed this methodology to examine brand and store switching, alternative promotions, price discounts, and merchandising techniques.[29] Other advertisers use awareness tracking studies and count the number of inquiries, coupon redemptions, and sweepstakes entries. They also track sales during promotional and nonpromotional periods while holding other factors constant.

One recent technological development designed to track the effectiveness of sales promotions at the point of sale is offered by Datatec Industries. This automated system, called Shopper Trak, places sensors in the store that track whether a person is coming or going, calculate the shopper's height (to differentiate between adults and children), and gauge traffic patterns. The system helps retailers evaluate the effectiveness of promotions or displays located throughout the store.[30]

Measuring the Effectiveness of Nontraditional Media

In Chapter 13, we noted that one of the disadvantages of employing nontraditional media is that it is usually difficult to measure the effectiveness of the programs. But some progress has been made, as shown in these examples:

- *The effects of shopping cart signage.* Earlier we discussed sales increases that occurred when shopping cart signage was used. We have also noted throughout this chapter that

---

FIGURE 18–18
Measuring the effects of FSIs

A study by Promotion Decisions Inc. examined the actual purchase data of users and nonusers of 27 coupon promotions in its National Shopper Lab (75,000 households) over a period of 18 months. The findings:

- FSI coupons generated significant trial by new and lapsed users of a product (53%).
- Repeat purchase rates were 11.8% higher among coupon redeemers than nonredeemers.
- 64.2% of repeat volume among coupon redeemers was without a coupon.
- There was no significant difference in share of volume between buyers who used coupons versus those who did not.
- Coupons returned between 71 and 79% of their cost within 12 weeks.
- Full-page ads provided higher redemption rates, incremental volume, redemption by new users, and a higher number of repeat buyers than half-page ads.
- Consumers who used coupons were brand loyal.

Source: Promotion Decisions Inc., *PR Newswire*, March 17, 1997.

while increasing sales is a critical goal, many other factors may contribute to or detract from this measure. (It should also be noted that these results are provided by the companies that sell these promotional media.) At least one study has examined the effectiveness of shopping cart signage on data besides sales.[31] This study used personal interviews in grocery stores to measure awareness of, attention to, and influence of this medium. Interestingly, it suggests shopping carts are much less effective than the sign companies claim.

• *The effectiveness of ski-resort-based media.* In Chapter 13, we discussed advertising on ski chair lifts and other areas to attempt to reach selective demographic groups. Now the Traffic Audit Bureau (TAB) is tracking the effectiveness of this form of advertising to give advertisers more reliable criteria on which to base purchase decisions. The TAB data verify ad placements, while the media vendors have employed Simmons Market Research Bureau and Nielsen Media Research to collect ad impressions and advertising recall information.[32] These measures are combined with sales tracking data to evaluate the medium's effectiveness.

Measuring the Effectiveness of Sponsorships

At the beginning of this chapter we discussed the growth in sponsorships and the reasons why organizations have increased their investments in this area. Along with the increased expenditures have come a number of methods for measuring the impact of sponsorships.

A number of companies now measure the effectiveness of sports sponsorships. For example, Events Marketing Research of New York specializes in custom research projects that perform sales audits in event areas, participant exit surveys, and economic impact studies. Joyce Julius & Associates of Ann Arbor, Michigan, assigns a monetary value to the amount of exposure the sponsor receives during the event. It reviews broadcasts and adds up the number of seconds a sponsor's product name or logo can be seen clearly (for example, on signs or shirts). A total of 30 seconds is considered the equivalent of a 30-second commercial.[33] (Such measures are of questionable validity.)

Performance Research in Newport, Rhode Island, measures impact on brand awareness and image shifts. PS Productions, a Chicago-based research organization, provides clients with a measure of event sponsorships based on increased sales. PS calculates sales goals based on the cost of the event and the value of extras like donated media, customized displays, ads for key retailers, and tickets given away. An event is a success if it brings in at least that amount in additional sales (Figure 18–19).

While each of these measures has its advantages and disadvantages, we suggest using several in assessing the impact of sponsorships. In addition to those mentioned here and in the lead-in, the eight-step process suggested in Figure 18–20 could be used to guide these evaluations.

FIGURE 18–19
Sales impact of concert sponsorships (average 4–6 weeks)

Product	Market	Sales during Event (dollar or volume)	Percent Change from Average Sales
Snacks	Louisville	$119,841	+52%
	Salt Lake City	$135,500	+47%
	Indianapolis	$ 347,940	+105%
Soap	Atlanta	950 cases	+375%
	Minneapolis	880 cases	+867%
	Cleveland	972 cases	+238%
	Portland, OR	580 cases	+580%
	St. Louis	1,616 cases	+1,454%
Salad dressing	Atlanta	NA	+175%
	Salt Lake City	NA	+143%

Source: Betsy Spethmann, "Sponsors Sing a Profitable Tune in Concert with Event Promos," *Brandweek*, January 1, 1994, pp. 21–22. ©1994 BRANDWEEK Magazine. Used with permission from ASM Communications, Inc.

FIGURE 18–20
Eight steps to measuring event sponsorship

1. Narrowly define objectives with specifics.
2. Establish solid strategies against which programming will be benchmarked and measure your programming and effectiveness against the benchmark.
3. Set measurable and realistic goals; make sure everything you do supports them.
4. Enhance, rather than just change, other marketing variables.
5. Don't pull Marketing Plan 101 off the shelf. Programming should be crafted to reflect the particulars of your company's constituencies and target audiences.
6. Define the scope of your involvement. Will it involve multiple areas within the company? Who internally and externally comprises the team?
7. Think "long term." It takes time to build brand equity. Also, think of leveraging your sponsorship through programming for as long as possible, before and after the event.
8. Build evaluation and a related budget into your overall sponsoring program. Include items such as pre- and post-event attitude surveys, media analysis, and sales results.

Source: Mara Heffler, "Making the Sponsorships Meet all the Parameters," *Brandweek*, May 16, 1994, p. 16. ©1994 BRANDWEEK Magazine. Used with permission from ASM Communications, Inc.

Measuring the Effectiveness of other IMC Program Elements

Many of the organizations mentioned in this chapter offer research services to measure the effectiveness of promotional program elements. We do not have the space to discuss them all, but Figure 18–21 mentions a few to show you that these options exist.

All the advertising effectiveness measures discussed here have their inherent strengths and weaknesses. They offer the advertiser some information that may be useful in evaluating the effectiveness of promotional efforts. While not all promotional efforts can be evaluated effectively, at least the first step has been taken.

FIGURE 18–21
A sampling of measures of effectiveness of promotional program elements

Company	Effectiveness Measure Provided
Perception Research Services, Inc.	Package design; out-of-home media; point-of-purchase displays; logos; corporate identity
McCollum Spielman Worldwide	Impact of celebrity presenters
Competitive Media Reporting	Business-to-business advertising; media effects
The PreTesting Company, Inc.	Package design; P-O-P displays; billboards; direct mail
Gallup & Robinson	Radio advertising recall; trade show exhibit measures
TransWestern Publishing	Telephone directory advertising effectiveness

SUMMARY

This chapter introduced you to issues involved in measuring the effects of advertising and promotions. These issues include reasons for testing, reasons companies do not test, and the review and evaluation of various research methodologies. We arrived at a number of conclusions: (1) advertising research to measure effectiveness is important to the promotional program, (2) not enough companies test their ads, and (3) problems exist with current research methodologies. In addition, we reviewed the criteria for sound research and suggested some ways to accomplish effective studies.

All marketing managers want to know how well their promotional programs are working. This information is critical to planning for the next period, since program adjustments and/or maintenance are based on evaluation of current strategies. Problems often result when the measures taken to determine such effects are inaccurate or improperly used.

This chapter demonstrated that testing must meet a number of criteria (defined by PACT) to be successful. These evaluations should occur both before and after the campaigns are implemented.

A variety of research methods were discussed, many provided by syndicated research firms such as ASI, MSW, Arbitron, and A. C. Nielsen. Many companies have developed their own testing systems.

Single-source research data such as BehaviorScan, ERIM, and AdTel were discussed for measuring the effects of advertising. These single-source systems offer strong potential for improving the effectiveness of ad measures in the future, since commercial exposures and reactions may be correlated to actual purchase behaviors.

It is important to recognize that different measures of effectiveness may lead to different results. Depending on the criteria used, one measure may show that an ad or promotion is effective while another states that it is not. This is why clearly defined objectives and the use of multiple measures are critical to determining the true effects of an IMC program.

KEY TERMS

vehicle option source effect, 568
pretests, 568
posttests, 568
laboratory tests, 570
testing bias, 570
field tests, 570
PACT (Positioning Advertising Copy Testing), 570

concept testing, 571
comprehension and reaction tests, 572
consumer juries, 573
halo effect, 573
portfolio tests, 574
Flesch formula, 574
theater testing, 575
on-air test, 576

day-after recall scores, 576
pupillometrics, 577
electrodermal response, 577
eye tracking, 577
EEG measures, 578
alpha activity, 578
hemispheric lateralization, 578

inquiry tests, 578
split-run tests, 578
recognition method, 580
recall tests, 581
single-source tracking methods, 583
tracking studies, 584

DISCUSSION QUESTIONS

1. Discuss some of the reasons copywriters and researchers are often at odds regarding the creative aspects of the campaign. What steps might be taken to reduce this conflict?

2. A great deal of money is being spent on sponsorships. Discuss why organizations are increasing their expenditures in this area, and how they can measure the effectiveness of these investments.

3. The bottom line for advertisers is to evoke some behavior—for example, sales. Explain why it may be difficult to use sales to measure advertising effectiveness.

4. Describe some of the effectiveness measures that might be used to get at nonquantifiable aspects of advertising and promotions.

5. Describe some of the methods used to test other elements of the promotional mix.

6. What are some of the problems associated with recognition tests?

7. Discuss how tracking studies might be tied into the hierarchy of effects models.

8. Describe some physiological measures of advertising effectiveness. Give examples of companies that might find these measures useful.

9. What is a theater test? What measures do these tests provide?

10. Discuss the concept of single-source research. What advantages does it offer the marketer?

Special Topics and Perspectives

PART

7

19

Business-to-Business Communications

Chapter Objectives

- To understand the differences between business-to-business and consumer product advertising and promotions.

- To consider the objectives of business-to-business communications.

- To recognize the roles of various program elements in the business-to-business promotional program.

- To examine the methods for evaluating promotional program effectiveness in business-to-business communications.

When you think of Chrysler, Holiday Inn, and General Electric, what usually comes to mind? You probably said cars, hotels, and home appliances—and you are right. What you may not realize is that these companies, along with many others that market consumer products, derive a substantial portion of their income from business-to-business markets as well.

Take GE, for example. Few companies enjoy such strong brand name identity and slogan recall ("Better living . . ."). That has resulted from years of integrated marketing; over $1 billion has been spent on advertising the slogan alone since 1979. GE products ranging from toasters to TV sets to dishwashers are common features in homes throughout the world. But few people know that about 80 percent of GE's $70 billion a year in revenue is from nonconsumer businesses. GE Capital Services, GE Medical Systems, GE Aircraft Engines, and GE Power Systems are not household names, but the brand name and extensive marketing programs are no less important in the business-to-business community. By combining the power of the GE brand with one-to-one marketing, the company continues to grow in this important market.

A company that has increased its marketing efforts in nonconsumer markets is Chrysler. The car manufacturer's business-to-business marketing efforts were minimal in the early 1990s. Now, backed by a strong corporate image campaign—"What's new in your world from Chrysler"—the automaker has taken its message to new markets.

For example, business vehicle sales were formerly a low-priority, low-profit part of the corporation. Then the Dodge division started signing deals with regional companies to cus-

Our Business Is Helping Yours® See More Clearly Than The Competition.

WE CAN HELP U IMPROVE YOUR VISION AND YOUR COMPETITIVE EDGE.

Both you and your competition have similar goals in sight. And who gets there first will depend on who has a sharper vision of the future.

GE Capital Services can help you provide your customers with more value–giving you the competitive edge. Like helping a major auto company develop a nationwide leasing program within 60 days, which involved the successful training of 54 dealers. Or helping a membership warehouse club achieve growth through sales while allowing commercial customers to buy on credit for the first time.

At GE Capital Services, we're 26 diversified businesses. Each one is dedicated to developing and delivering products and services that help you see opportunities before the competition. Give us a call at 1-800-243-2222. And see what the competition can't.

GE Capital Services
Our Business Is Helping Yours®

tomize pickups and vans sold to commercial customers. The result was a market share increase from 6 percent to nearly 16.5 percent, and expectations for 1997 are in the neighborhood of 20 percent. Commercial trucks now account for 40 percent of all new Dodge vehicle sales. Over 100 types of small businesses are targeted, with leads generated through toll-free numbers in print ads appearing in trade media like *Progressive Farmer* and *Tow Times*. Direct mail and trade shows also play a significant role in the IMC program.

In the past few years, you may have noticed two new hotels bearing the Holiday Inn name: Holiday Inn Select and Crowne Plaza. Both are specifically designed with business travelers in mind and are marketed separately and distinctly from the consumer and resort products. A full 25 percent of Holiday Inn's marketing budget is targeted to the business segment, which constitutes 50 percent of most hotels' occupancies. HI uses radio, trade shows, and direct marketing as well as more traditional advertising. It emphasizes direct sales targeted to businesses with 500 or fewer employees. Business-to-business group travel (35 percent), airline crew rooms (15 percent) and other business travel have responded favorably to these efforts, resulting in significant growth for Holiday Inns.

A number of other companies that you are familiar with in the consumer market derive significant sales from the business-to-business segments, including MCI, Du Pont, and Intuit. And, you probably didn't even know it!

Sources: Kathy Jackson, "Chrysler Readies Major Corporate Ad Campaign," *Advertising Age*, September 9, 1996, p. 62; Alan Salomon, "Holiday Inn Makes Room for Businesses," *Business Marketing*, June 1996, p. S–7; Jean Halliday, "Chrysler Accelerates Commercial Sales," *Business Marketing*, June 1996, p. S–11; Laura Loro, "GE Puts Power of Brand behind B-to-B Effort," *Business Marketing*, June 1996, p. S–16.

When we think of advertising and promotions, it is usually in regard to consumer products or resellers of these products. But about $138 billion a year is spent on promoting products used in business and industrial markets.[1] The objectives of these communications and the strategies designed to achieve them often differ from those we discussed in earlier chapters.

The lead-in to this chapter describes just a few of the companies that earn a significant portion of their incomes from business-to-business markets. As providers of consumer products and services as well, they have had to adapt their marketing efforts to these nonconsumer markets. While business-to-business marketers may have been considered unidimensional, plain, or even boring in the past, this is certainly no longer the case.

Business-to-business advertising is becoming more creative, more innovative, more emotional, more interesting—and more effective. Holiday Inn and Chrysler are just a few of the many examples of how companies are discovering this market (GE has been there for a long time) and how traditionally consumer-oriented firms are adapting to the b-to-b world. The result is a changing marketplace for business-to-business marketers in general. As you will see in this chapter, business-to-business communications are becoming more sophisticated and, in many ways, more similar to the consumer market.

BUSINESS-TO-BUSINESS COMMUNICATIONS

Before we discuss how business-to-business communications are used, it is important to clarify exactly what the term refers to. Had you opened an advertising or promotions text just a few years ago, you probably would not have found a chapter titled "Business-to-Business Communications." Rather, you would have seen the title "Industrial Marketing" or "Industrial Advertising." Much of the material would have dealt with advertising in the industrial sector and advertising to manufacturers.

As the United States has moved from an industrial to a service economy (now accounting for about two-thirds of the national economy), a new and different target market has evolved. This market still includes those involved in the industrial sector but has broadened to include a nation of office workers.

Along with this new market came the need to broaden the title given to advertising and promotions used to communicate with it. The term *industrial advertising* was somewhat misleading; it did not represent the true nature of the industry, and it was not current with the profession. So a few years ago, the industry began to refer to itself as *business-to-business*. For this text, we use the term **business-to-business communications**, although we want you to recognize that this term still includes communications targeted to the industrial sector. (When it is important to distinguish between industrial and service sectors, we will specify which market we are referring to.)

Differences between Business and Consumer Communications

The primary difference between business-to-business and consumer-oriented communications is that the latter are generally targeted at those consumers who will actually use the product or service in its final form, while b-to-b communications are directed at companies that produce goods or services designed to facilitate the operation of the enterprise. These products are typically thought of as having a **derived demand**—that is, their demand is generated by the need for other goods or services. Intel is one of the first to target end users as well as original equipment manufacturers (OEMs) and, as Global Perspective 19–1 shows, the campaign has been extremely successful worldwide.

To understand the role of business-to-business communications, consider what is involved in manufacturing an automobile. While the car is the final consumer product, the materials used to manufacture it—steel, rubber, leather, plastic, and so on—must be purchased, as must the building, equipment, and products used to market it. There is competition among suppliers to gain the auto manufacturers' business. Goodyear and Firestone may compete for the tire business, USX and Wheeling–Pittsburgh may want to sell the steel, and so on. All the elements of the promotional mix are employed in an attempt to sell these products to carmakers.

There are a number of differences between business-to-business and consumer communications. Perhaps nine key characteristics best differentiate the areas.[2]

Global Perspective 19–1
Intel Takes Its Successful Campaign Worldwide

In 1991 Intel announced the launch of a $250 million advertising campaign that has a familiar logo, flashy TV commercials, and attention-getting print ads. The campaign was the talk of Madison Avenue. What's so unusual about that? Well, for one thing, Intel makes microprocessors, a component part of computers. And two, the campaign is targeted to computer buyers, not the manufacturers.

So why would a company that sells to original equipment manufacturers spend so much money to make its brand known to consumers? Why would end users care whose chip is inside their PC? Intel says that being number one always attracts a crowd and that in a highly competitive market where decisions are often made on price alone, the need to differentiate is critical. Inducing consumers to ask for Intel should help pull the product through the channels. Increasing knowledge of the importance of the chip in running software also helps to create brand preference.

The "Intel Inside" campaign actually involved much more than advertising—and many believe much more than $300 million was actually spent. TV campaigns using dazzling special effects, print ads scrawling the Intel logo over 8,000 pages per month in Intel's own ads as well as those of OEMs like Dell and Compaq, and over $150 million in merchandising support led a varied effort. Much of the advertising cost was picked up by cooperative advertising partners, and more and more companies jumped on the bandwagon. (Intel reported that 1,200 manufacturers signed on to the co-branding program.) But did it work? Well, brand preference increased by 20 percent, the number of consumers who specified a chip brand rose from 5

percent to 23 percent, worldwide market share increased by 5 percent, and sales rose 63 percent. Intel is now considered one of the most valuable brands in the United States.

But it didn't stop there. In 1996 Intel expanded its co-op ad program by adding more media outlets worldwide. The chip maker tripled the number of participants in the international program by adding 800 print and 220 broadcast participants in 40 countries, and the co-op ad budget now exceeds $500 million. Intel says every major publication now participates in the "Intel Inside" program, and over 1,880 PC marketers will receive rebates.

After a two-year hiatus, Compaq Computer Corp., the world's largest PC manufacturer, returned to the Intel program. In 1996 IBM signed on as well. That just about wraps up the world.

Sources: Bradley Johnson, "'Intel Inside' Program Expands Global Reach," *Advertising Age*, January 29, 1996, p.9; Nancy Arnott, "Inside Intel's Marketing Coup," *Sales & Marketing Management*, February 1994, pp. 78–81; "There's No Down-Time for No. 1 in the Process of Staying on Top," March 14, 1994, pp. 26–27.

1. *The decision maker.* While in consumer markets the consumer and decision maker may be the same person, this is usually not the case in the business-to–business setting. Here the buying decision is typically made by a **buying center** or committee. The buying center is often formalized and includes individuals from throughout the organization, as shown in Figure 19–1.

All members of the buying center must be reached and influenced; different message and media strategies may be required for each. Sometimes the decision maker's identity is not readily apparent to the marketer.

2. *Communications.* Communications are designed to support the sales effort. As elements of the promotional mix, advertising and promotions may take on a major role or a supportive one. In b-to-b marketing, advertising is usually supportive. Communications tend to be information based, rational, and designed to generate leads or inquiries in support of the sales staff. Says one business-to-business agency: "Each ad should make it desirable for the potential customer to contact the manufacturer, all inquiries should be responded to in the same day, and all information should help the customer sell the product or service to their management."[3]

FIGURE 19—1
Participants in a buying center

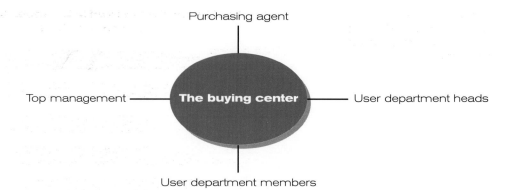

3. *Purchase decisions.* While purchase decisions may be made quickly in the consumer market, a long-range perspective is more common in the b-to-b setting. Immediate sales are rare because committee decisions, budgetary considerations, and buying formulas may need to be addressed before the actual purchase is made. In some industrial situations, it is not uncommon to operate on three- to five-year purchase cycles. Since many of the products have long life cycles, decisions are much less frequent and much more involved.

4. *Buyer involvement.* The buyer is generally involved in the decision to purchase a consumer product. If the product does not live up to expectations, the buyer suffers the consequences. If a poor decision is made in an industrial setting, the entire organization may suffer—and more than the buyer's personal satisfaction is at stake. The buyer may lose his or her job or the firm may experience other consequences, as demonstrated in the ad for Brock Control Systems in Exhibit 19–1.

5. *Integration of communications elements.* While business-to-business marketing efforts are improving rapidly, many marketers consider this sector less sophisticated than consumer marketing. Advertising and marketing have commonly not been well integrated in industrial firms.

In a survey of b-to-b marketers conducted by *Business Marketing* magazine and *Advertising Age*, nearly two-thirds of the respondents said they contracted with an outside agency to handle their creative messages. As Figure 19–2 shows, a number of other services are being outsourced as well.

At least some of the reason that business marketers are seeking outside assistance is the lack of in-house expertise in this area. However, many of these problems are being overcome as business-to-business marketers become more sophisticated and begin to apply methods from the consumer market. For example, just as the consumer market once relied mainly on demographic and geographic segmentation, so too, until recently,

EXHIBIT 19—1
Brock Control Systems ads show consequences of the wrong decision

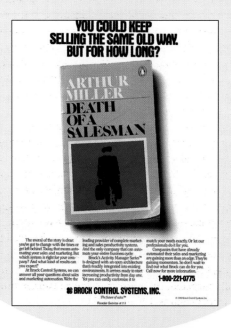

FIGURE 19–2
Outside vendors used in business-to-business marketing (percent of respondents)

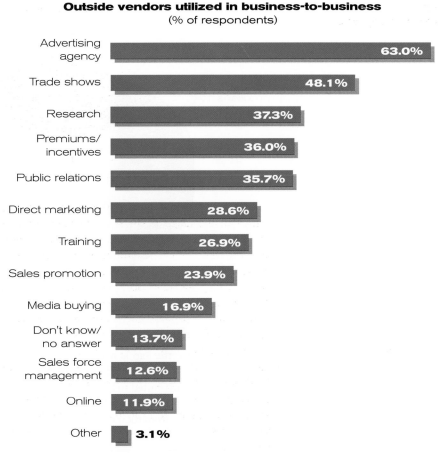

Outside vendors utilized in business-to-business
(% of respondents)

Source: Reprinted with permission from the June 1996 issue of "Outfront Marketing," in *Advertising Age*. Copyright Crain Communications, Inc. 1996.

did business-to-business marketers. Now psychographics is supplementing demographic segmentation. Business marketers are using behavioral models like the **social style model**, which suggests people's social styles influence how they react on the job, and the **CUBE model** (Comprehensive Understanding of Business Environments), which details values and lifestyles of corporate buying groups.[4]

6. *Budget allocations.* The bulk of marketing monies in business-to-business sectors has traditionally been allocated to support the sales organization. Advertising and promotions often receive less of the marketing budget. Likewise, market research is used extensively by consumer products firms but receives much less support in the industrial sector (constituting only about 5 percent of the overall budget) (Figure 19–3).[5]

7. *Evaluation measures.* In Chapter 18, we discussed the measures of advertising effectiveness employed by consumer products firms. Later in this chapter, you will see that the industrial sector uses different measures that are usually tied directly to sales rather than to communications objectives.

8. *Message content.* The communications message of consumer products advertisers may be designed to create awareness, interest, or other communications objectives and may employ both rational and emotional approaches. While the use of emotional appeals has increased recently, business-to-business communications tend to focus on information presented in a logical format or on testimonials. Humor, sex, and other forms of emotional appeals are rarely used; most ads tend to be very technical and factual. Many b-to-b marketers recognize this lack of creativity and have attempted to jazz up their messages.

9. *Media use.* As you would expect, the media used in business-to-business advertising are often very different from the media employed in the consumer products sector. (We will discuss business-to-business media later in the chapter.) Media here tend to be more specifically targeted, in contrast to the consumer products market, which relies heavily on mass media such as TV and radio.

FIGURE 19–3
Business-to-business category spending of firms with over $100 million in sales/revenue

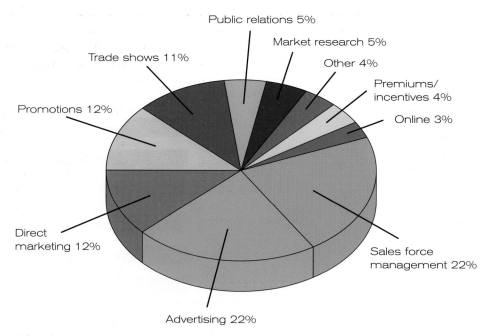

Source: Reprinted from the June 1996 issue of *Advertising Age*. Copyright Crain Communications, Inc. 1996.

In summary, while the gap is narrowing, there are obviously many differences between the communications strategies of business-to-business and consumer products companies. Much of this can be attributed to the nature of the industries; some may be a result of marketing sophistication. Also, b-to-b marketers may define the objectives of advertising and promotions differently from their consumer market counterparts.

ESTABLISHING BUSINESS-TO-BUSINESS COMMUNICATIONS OBJECTIVES

The objectives that were established in Chapter 7 are just as relevant for business-to-business marketers as for consumer products firms. Obviously, b-to-b advertisers have marketing objectives, and they should establish communications objectives to attain these goals. Likewise, establishing a *corporate image* is no less important for industrial firms than for their consumer counterparts.

However, since business-to-business marketers often concentrate their efforts directly on achieving sales, the emphasis in advertising and promotions has been to support sales efforts, and sales have been used as the measure of their success. In this text, we take the position that communications and sales objectives need not be independent. That is, business-to-business marketers need to achieve the same objectives as consumer marketers to reach sales goals. These objectives include creating awareness; establishing a favorable image or position in the marketplace; and generating consumer interest, knowledge, and trial of the product, among others. Figure 19–4 shows the objectives 3M has established for its selling process and the relative roles of marketing communications (Marcomm), the sales force, and the product or service at each stage.

FIGURE 19–4
3M establishes objectives for the five stages of its selling process

Stage of Selling Process	Marcomm Role	Sales Force Role	Product or Service Role
Awareness	Very high	Relatively low	None
Comprehension	High	Relatively low	None
Preference	Medium	High	Some
Trial	Low	Medium	High
Satisfaction	Almost none	Very little	Very high

Source: Jack Edmonston, "Practical Tips to Measure Advetising's Performance," *Business Marketing*, April 1996, p. 26. Reprinted with permission from the April 1996 issue of *Business Marketing*. Copyright Crain Communications, Inc.

DEVELOPING AND IMPLEMENTING THE BUSINESS-TO-BUSINESS PROGRAM
Developing Business-to-Business Promotional Strategies

Just as the objectives of business-to-business programs have been different from those of consumer markets, so too have been the strategies employed to achieve them. (Figure 19–3 showed where these monies are being spent throughout the industry.) These differences are becoming less distinct, however.

Personal selling has always been the primary promotional tool used by business-to-business marketers. In the past, much less emphasis was placed on the development of advertising and promotional programs. Advertising was used almost exclusively to create awareness of products, and the messages were typically rational, information laden, and somewhat unexciting. Recently the role of advertising in the b-to-b promotional program has changed, in respect to both expenditures and the types of ads themselves. For example, color, illustrations, models, and emotional appeals have become more common as this promotional element has expanded. As Exhibit 19–2 shows, attractive, interesting ads are no longer the exclusive domain of consumer products marketers.

This change in advertising strategy does not reflect a reduced emphasis on providing information. Rather, it stems from the realization that to be read, the ad must first gain the attention of the receiver. It must cut through the clutter of competing ads and assist in the attainment of communications objectives such as knowledge, evaluation, and attitude formation. More attractive and creative advertising is designed to accomplish these objectives.

Likewise, advertising strategies designed to achieve trial have increased. As you can see in Exhibit 19–3, the Nomadic Display ad goes beyond providing product information and ac-

EXHIBIT 19–2 Business-to-business ads are becoming more interesting

EXHIBIT 19–3 This business-to-business ad is designed to stimulate trial

tually attempts to move the reader to action—in this case, asking for more information or a trial demonstration.

Business-to-business marketers have realized the importance of other promotional program elements besides advertising and promotions programs. While personal selling continues to play a significant role in the promotional mix, direct-marketing and public relations efforts have increased. Direct-marketing tools have helped reduce selling costs by screening prospects, determining interest levels and qualifications, and disseminating information to prospective customers more cost effectively. Public relations programs have been designed to achieve better customer relations and to manage publicity. A variety of support media have also been employed.

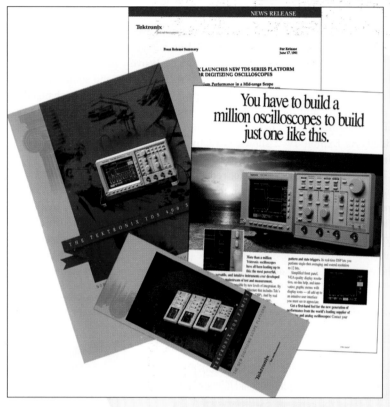

Sales promotions, like advertising, have become more creative and have taken on a support role. An excellent example of this is provided in this display of Tektronix promotional materials. In addition to the ad, a direct-mail brochure, a leave-behind promotional piece, and a demo disk are all used to promote the product. (These promotional materials generated the best response Tektronix has had in years.)

Given the high costs of personal sales calls, support provided by advertising and promotions is a direct benefit for industrial firms. Studies conducted by the American Business Press (ABP) and the Forsyth Group estimate that business publication advertising enhances personal selling efforts at only 31 cents per contact—far less than the $292 cost per sales call.[6] Sales inquiries from these activities may also generate leads from sources the sales force previously had no knowledge of or time to explore, increasing market coverage.

Implementing the Business-to-Business Program

As noted, business-to-business marketers spent over $138 billion to advertise and promote their products, services, and corporate images in 1996. Figure 19–5 yields some interesting insights into the allocation of the business-to-business promotional budget. Program elements that lead to the closest contact with the buyer and are most directly related to selling (for example, trade shows, catalogs, and direct mail) are most frequently used. The largest percentage of the budget is typically allocated to advertising in specialized business publications. Let us examine these allocations in more detail.

ADVERTISING

Because their reach is too broad, many of the media used to reach the consumer market receive less of the budget in the business-to-business sector. Advertising tends to be concentrated in business publications that reach specific markets. Figure 19–6 shows the 30 leading advertisers in specialized business publications. (Figure 19–5 showed that 80 percent advertised in one of the many trade publications available, while only 17 percent used general business publications.) Much less of the advertising dollar is spent on broadcast, outdoor, or other media that do not allow for specific targeting.

While broadcast media have not been used extensively in the past, this trend is changing. As Figure 19–7 demonstrates, when used properly, even TV, the broadest-reaching medium, may be effective. IMC Perspective 19–2 demonstrates that the use of this medium by business-to-business advertisers is on the increase.

In fact, many of the mass media are experiencing an increase in b-to-b ads owing to an increase in the b-to-b mass market. With so many people employed in service businesses, marketers find that mass media have significantly less waste coverage than expected. This

FIGURE 19–5   Promotional allocations of business-to-business marketers

	Total	Average Percent of Budget		
	Percent Using	Average Percent of Budget	Up to $500 M	$500–999 M	$1M and Over
Special business publications	80%	26.9%	34.1%	23.1%	23.4%
General business publications	17	3.9	2.0	3.8	5.2
Farm publications	3	0.1	–	.1	0.2
Medical publications	7	1.3	–	2.4	1.6
Consumer publications	6	0.8	0.1	2.1	0.5
Newspapers	8	1.1	.8	.2	1.9
Telemarketing	11	1.1	1.9	.9	0.7
Direct mail	66	7.5	6.8	6.4	8.4
Network TV	1	0.1	–	–	0.3
Spot TV	4	1.0	0.3	0.1	2.0
Spot radio	5	0.8	0.9	–	1.3
Directories	29	1.9	2.0	2.0	1.9
Company catalogs	61	16.7	13.8	20.9	16.4
Trade shows/exhibits	74	14.5	15.6	16.2	12.8
Dealer/distributor aids	25	2.8	1.7	3.2	3.3
Internal house organs	23	1.5	2.0	1.9	1.0
External house organs	23	2.3	2.4	1.7	2.7
AV (slide, movie, etc.)	36	2.1	1.7	2.5	2.2
Specialty advertising	27	1.5	1.3	2.0	1.3
Outdoor transit	3	0.2	0.4	–	0.2
Publicity/PR	60	5.2	4.6	4.9	5.7
Research	18	0.6	0.3	0.5	0.9
Videos	35	2.5	3.2	2.4	2.1
Other	22	3.6	4.1	2.5	3.8

is particularly true given the ability to narrowcast through cable TV. Channels and programs that reach specific audiences—the Financial News Network, "Moneyline," and so on—allow advertisers to reach specific business audiences through broadcast media (an example of which is shown in Exhibit 19–4). The next time you watch TV, notice the increasing number of ads for copy machines, computers, and other office equipment in prime time.

Radio also has seen an increase in business-to-business ads. Advertisers find it effective in reaching business audiences during drive time and news segments. A study by the Radio Advertising Bureau showed that as much as 53 percent of the work force listens to the radio while at work.[7] Certain radio formats tend to have a higher business listening audience.

DIRECT MARKETING

Just as consumer marketers have discovered the advantages of direct marketing, so too have business-to-business marketers—particularly the benefits associated with telemarketing. Two-thirds of the firms in Figure 19–5 said they use direct mail in their promotional mix, and 11 percent use telemarketing. Figure 19–8 shows where these monies are being spent. While the telemarketing expenditure was estimated to account for an average of only 1 percent of the overall budget(another study has estimated this figure could be as high as 6 percent), it must be remembered that the costs of telemarketing are very low. And many of the firms surveyed may not have considered sales calls as a direct part of telemarketing, which would make their cost estimates unrealistically low. Nevertheless, the use of telemarketing

FIGURE 19—6 1996 Top 30 business-to-business advertisers

Company	Total $000	Company	Total $000
1. AT&T Co	$248,345	16. Federal Express Corp.	45,428
2. IBM Corp	228,054	17. Xerox Corp.	45,372
3. Microsoft Corp	124,221	18. Intel Corp.	38,281
4. MCI Communications Corp.	108,208	19. Toshiba of America	35,492
5. Hewlett-Packard Co	84,181	20. National Assoc. of Security Dealers	32,566
6. Sprint Corp.	77,340	21. Novell	30,463
7. United Parcel Service of America	66,838	22. Texas Instruments	29,330
8. Compaq Computer Corp.	59,185	23. Acer International	29,217
9. American Express Co.	58,430	24. E.I. du Pont de Nemours & Co.	28,247
10. Canon	55,056	25. American Plastics Council	27,967
11. Apple Computer	52,346	26. GTE Corp.	26,898
12. Digital Equipment Corp.	52,099	27. Micron Technology	26,575
13. NEC Corp.	49,841	28. Computer Associates International	25,150
14. Gateway 2000	49,706	29. ITT Corp.	24,866
15. Dell Computer Corp.	45,765	30. America Online	24,450

Note: Figures measured by ad spending in business trade publications.

Source: Ad expenditure totals were compiled by *Business Marketing* based on data provided by MMS–Rome Reports, a New York-based market research company.

among business-to-business marketers is increasing. Reasons for the increasing attractiveness of this medium include the following.

1. *Coverage.* Telemarketing efforts can lead to significantly more contact with customers and potential customers. More people can be exposed to the marketing communication and be reached in much less time.
2. *Costs.* We have already discussed the high cost per sales call of field sales reps. Add in telemarketing's benefits as a prescreening device and as a follow-up strategy, and it becomes even more attractive.
3. *Sales.* Business-to-business sales account for approximately 80 percent of the sales generated through telemarketing. At an average sale of $1,500, this effort is well spent.[8]

FIGURE 19—7 Using TV in business-to-business advertising

While most business-to-business advertisers use little or no TV, Jeffrey W. Kaumeyer of Hammond Farrell, Inc., a New York ad agency specializing in industrial marketing, notes that given three essential conditions, a number of possibilities for TV exist.

The Essential Conditions

1. The prospects must be concentrated geographically.
2. The sales pitch must be boiled down to one simple, compelling human message.
3. TV must be complemented by the other, more basic components in a complete marketing communications plan.

The Possibilities

Ten other situations where TV should be considered:

1. A first-class memorable spot can be produced for less than $197,000.
2. Purchase patterns are cyclical or heavily seasonal.
3. Buying influences are large in number and growing.
4. The most important buying influencers are hard to get in to see.
5. Speed of communication is essential.
6. The objective is to breathe life into a tired product and/or sales force.
7. Competitors' spending is drowning out your message.
8. You can continue to maintain at least a modest national presence.
9. Your marketing effort could use the support of indirect influences.
10. Your agency is making a good profit on your business (spot TV buying is not lucrative to the agency).

IMC Perspective 19—2
TV Gains Popularity with Business Marketers

An ad for Hewlett-Packard LaserJet printers targeted to business buyers ran on "60 Minutes" and "Seinfeld." Haven't these media buyers ever heard of waste coverage? HP thinks it knows what it's doing, as do a variety of other advertisers, including Xerox, Siemens, ADM, Microsoft, Sun Microsystems, Apple, Packard Bell, and IBM. All these and many other business-to-business marketers are increasing their advertising expenditures on television. Computer hardware, software, and other technology companies alone spend over $492 million on TV commercials, a 23 percent increase over 1995 and more than a $208 million jump from just two years earlier.

Many high-tech companies like Microsoft (Wieden & Kennedy), IBM (Ogilvy & Mather), and Apple (Chiat/Day) have hired ad agencies that specialize in consumer advertising to develop their creative strategies. These agencies like to use broad-based appeals employing humor and cutting-edge executions. Others employ a variety of celebrities, from comedian Dennis Leary (Lotus) to astronaut Sally Ride (US Robotics). Intelliquest, Inc., has even started a poll among high-technology agency executives to determine the best advertising campaigns (Microsoft, IBM, and Intel have all been in the top five).

How can media buyers justify such a strategy? Analysts suggest a number of reasons:

1. Costs are becoming more affordable.
2. Cable allows for improved targeting.
3. TV lets the marketer endow the brand with a personality.
4. Competition has forced reluctant advertisers to respond.
5. There is spillover into the home buyer market.
6. The products are similar and creating an image is an important objective.
7. The early adopters' market has been penetrated, so the mass market is now being targeted.

Additional reasons are also offered, but the most important one seems to be the fact that television provides reach and the ability to generate emotional appeals and name recognition, unequaled by any other media. Because of TV advertising even the casual viewer knows that Xerox is "the document company" and ADM is "the supermarket to the world."

Terry O'Connor, director of marketing at BASF, notes that TV constitutes the backbone of his company's marketing efforts, representing 85 percent of all corporate ad spending and as much as 40 percent of overall ad spending. He says, "TV is as efficient at reaching our target audience as many of the business books [magazines]." He points out that seven years ago his company was unknown, but TV has changed all that. Digital Equipment agrees and says TV is an effective medium for creating an image for business-to-business companies. Others agree on the effectiveness of this medium. Packard Bell took pre- and post-measures of their $13 million TV campaign. The results show an 11 percent increase in brand awareness and "the next intended purchase" scores. Auto-by-Tel Corp., a $5 million company that brokers cars on the Web, placed an ad on the Super Bowl and saw purchase requests increase 66 percent over the first 25 days in January.

Of course, not everyone is sold on TV yet. James Garrity, director of communications for Compaq, thinks that more audience segmentation is required and TV isn't suited to a narrow audience. Others also mention lack of specificity and audience waste. They believe TV will never rival trade publications as the medium of choice for business marketers. This is just fine with those people at Intel, Digital, and Packard Bell. You'll see them on "Seinfeld."

Sources: "Cars, Beer, and Web Browsers," *Business Week*, May 12, 1997, pp. 113–14; Edmund O. Lawler, "Microsoft's Campaign Takes No.1; IBM a Close No. 2 among Ad Agencies" *Business Marketing*, September 1995, p. A8; Joe Mullich, "TV Gets Top Ratings from Business Marketers," *Business Marketing*, January 1993, pp. 62–4.

4. *Market research.* The telephone allows the business-to-business marketer to engage in instant market research. The direct contact this medium provides between marketer and customer allows the marketer to gain the customer's insights almost immediately, gauge the response, and follow up or probe.

As Figure 19–9 shows, direct-marketing methods, particularly telemarketing, are being applied to a number of sales and marketing functions. This trend is likely to continue and probably increase as personal selling and other media costs continue to climb.

EXHIBIT 19–4
Business-to-business ads are
becoming more common on TV

The use of database marketing has also been on the increase. It now constitutes about 20 percent of the direct-marketing budget.[9] Companies like Sherwin-Williams, Compaq, and Hoechst-Celanese have implemented effective database marketing programs. Richard Gillespie, head of the Gillespie Organization, a database marketing agency, says that database marketing will soon "become so commonplace it will simply be called 'marketing.'"[10] Many experts agree as more and more firms employ this marketing approach.

THE INTERNET

As noted earlier in this text, the Internet is particularly appealing to business-to-business marketers. A recent study by Cahners revealed that an estimated 60 percent of all b-to-b marketers planned to have a website by 1997, with another 7 percent expected to establish

FIGURE 19–8
Direct-marketing tools used in
business-to-business marketing

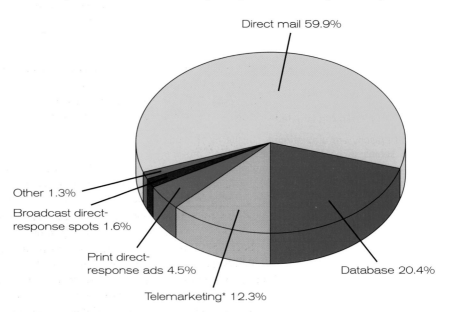

Direct mail 59.9%

Other 1.3%

Broadcast direct-
response spots 1.6%

Print direct-
response ads 4.5%

Telemarketing* 12.3%

Database 20.4%

*Excludes compensation and commissions.

Source: Reprinted with permission from the June 1996 issue of *Advertising Age*. Copyright Crain Communications, Inc. 1996.

FIGURE 19–9   Applications of telemarketing in business-to-business communications

Application/Integration	Percentage	Application/Integration	Percentage
Customer Service	83.5	**Lead Qualification**	75.0
Customer discretion or whoever is available to the customer at the time	31.5	Phone reps qualify leads, then hand them off to the field for follow-up	34.4
Phone representatives refer service requests to the field	24.7	Field reps qualify leads, then hand them off to phone reps for follow-up	28.1
Field reps refer service requests to phone reps	23.2	Marketing/advertising services assign lead follow-up to both	12.5
Separate field and phone accounts/territories	4.1		
Order Taking	88.8	**Prospecting**	78.6
Field reps refer orders to phone reps	30.7	Phone reps refer prospects to the field for follow-up	38.5
Customer discretion or whoever is available at the time	28.3	Field reps refer orders to phone reps for follow-up	29.3
Phone reps refer orders to the field	26.7	Marketing/advertising services assign prospects to both	10.8
Separate field and phone accounts/territories	3.1		
Handling Complaints	84.7	**Full Account Management**	97.6
Field reps refer complaints to phone reps	31.1	Shared accounts: Phone and field reps exchange information on sales/service activity by phone, fax, mail, and e-mail	92.4
Customer discretion or whoever is available at the time	24.5		
Phone reps refer complaints to the field	21.1	Separate phone and field accounts/territories	5.2
Separate field and phone accounts/territories	7.8	**Dealer Locator**	79.3
Product Prepurchase Information	87.4	Customer discretion or whoever is available at the time	29.2
Field reps refer inquiries to phone reps	32.9		
Customer discretion or whoever is available at the time	26.6	Phone reps refer inquiries to the field	25.0
Phone reps refer inquiries to the field	24.1	Field reps refer inquiries to phone reps	20.9
Separate field and phone accounts/territories	3.8	Separate field and phone accounts/territories	4.2
Lead Generation	99.9		
Phone reps refer leads to field for follow-up	40.0		
Marketing/advertising services assign leads to both	37.7		
Field reps refer leads to phone reps for follow-up	22.2		

Note: Only integration methods mentioned by a significant number of respondents are listed above.

one in the near future.[11] Other studies have estimated these percentages to be even higher, with some industries (high technology) reporting that over 90 percent of the firms have a website.[12] Regardless of which figures one believes, there is no doubt about the attractiveness of the Net and the rapid adoption of this medium.

TRADE SHOWS

As shown in Figure 19–5, after specialized business advertising, the business-to–business marketer is most likely to use trade shows as a means of communication. Three-quarters of the firms said they had employed this medium, allocating an estimated 14.5 percent of the budget to this communications tool. (As the Impact Exhibits, Inc. ad on the next page reveals, the trade show exhibit is an important part of this expenditure.) Studies by the Trade Show Bureau project growth in trade show activity in the 1990s to exceed 35 percent, with over 1.3 million companies exhibiting their wares.[13]

The reasons for the extensive use of trade shows are many. First, the *cost per contact* is significantly lower than it would be through the field sales force. Equally important is the quality of the sales contact; the majority of those attending trade shows have some influence in the purchase decision process, and most are there specifically to seek new ideas or suppliers. The net result of this cost/contact combination is that the estimate to close a sale at a trade

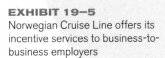
show is approximately $142, versus over $1,100 to do the same through the sales force.[14] In addition, a study by Gopalakrishna and colleagues found that trade shows generate awareness and interest and result in positive economic returns for the firm.[15] Given these numbers, you can see why firms use this communications medium.

SALES PROMOTIONS

Business-to-business marketers spend approximately 10 percent of their promotional budgets on sales promotions.[16] These promotions include video materials, point-of-sale materials, and permanent display racks, among others. More than one-third of the firms in Figure 19–5 reported using videos, constituting an average 2.5 percent of the promotional budget.

Earlier we said the use of videotapes in the consumer market was increasing, particularly in the automotive industry. Business-to-business marketers are also finding video an extremely beneficial medium because it allows for product introductions and demonstrations at a far lower cost than a personal sales call. Videos can also increase the reach to the target market in much less time. The role of many of these materials is to aid sales reps in the selling effort and provide a leave-behind to reinforce the selling effort. A variety of other sales promotions tools are also used, including allowances, contests, and sweepstakes.

INCENTIVES

Incentives are an important part of the business-to-business communications budget. The majority of that money is spent on merchandise incentives provided to the company's sales force, dealers, distributors, and customers. This merchandise includes specialty advertising materials as well as TVs, VCRs, radios, computers, and even trips (see Exhibit 19–5) that are given as motivational tools. Another category is cash incentives, most of which are provided directly to the firm's own sales force.

EXHIBIT 19–5
Norwegian Cruise Line offers its incentive services to business-to-business employers

FIGURE 19–10
Top marketers place major emphasis
on public relations programs

	Percent Responding
Marketing/product support	85%
Corporate image building	19
Employee communications	11
Community relations	6
Special events	6
Financial/investor tours	5

Note: Responses add to more than 100% due to multiple mentions.

PUBLIC RELATIONS

Eight out of 10 industrial companies report they have a formalized public relations function, although it constitutes only 4 to 5 percent of the budget.[17] Because typical public relations media include business paper articles, trade magazines, and journals, PR has been used much more for marketing than for other reasons mentioned in Chapter 16 (as demonstrated in Figure 19–10). The use of articles and press releases to detail product innovations and developments is common in this market. Many customers rely on these articles to keep abreast of new developments in the marketplace.

INTERACTIVE MEDIA

Earlier in this book, we observed that the use of interactive media is on the increase. This is also true in the business-to-business market. Well-known companies such as IBM, Digital Equipment Corp., AT&T, and Honeywell are already driving the information highway very successfully. Given the large volumes of specific information industrial firms often require, the capabilities of many interactive media make them a viable tool. For example, E. I. du Pont de Nemours envisions the information highway as a new way of segmenting business-to-business markets by determining customers' specific needs and communicating with them directly. Digital's remote communications access division was designed specifically to help home and remote office workers tie into the network.

One market in which e-mail is common is the government sector. Information regarding new laws, changes in product specifications, or contracts open for bid is very quickly and effectively communicated. Since government decisions are typically (at least in theory) based on comparative bids for products or services, information relevant to the structuring of the bid is important, and timing is critical.

In summary, the relative use of each of the program elements discussed here varies from one firm to the next. The use of each tool is dictated by the objectives to be accomplished as well as the budgets provided, just as in consumer-oriented companies. Another similarity is that market research is needed in designing the promotional program and evaluating its effectiveness. Such research is discussed in the next section.

THE ROLE OF RESEARCH IN BUSINESS-TO-BUSINESS PROMOTION

Throughout this text, we have discussed the contribution of research to the promotional process—both as an *input* into decision making and as a *measure of the effectiveness* of various programs. As you saw in Figures 19–3 and 19–5, marketing research constitutes only a small portion of the business-to-business marketing budget This section examines b-to-b marketers' use of research as an aid to identify and enter various markets. In the final section, we examine the use of research to measure the effectiveness of the promotional effort.

Research Input into the Decision Process

One factor that makes business-to-business marketing different is that there are often **multiple buying influences**. The same person is not always influencer, decision maker, purchaser, and user. The marketing manager must identify all those involved in the purchase decision process, perhaps by industry, size of plant, and title or job function. Otherwise, the advantages of specialized business media are lost, because the message will go unseen by potential buyers. To assist in this task, the manager can turn to a number of secondary sources.

SIC DATA

Standard Industrial Classification (SIC) data, provided by the U.S. Office of Management and Budget, describe a company numerically based on the product it produces. Companies carry a four- to seven-digit code, with each additional code number more specifically identifying the manufactured product or service. Most major libraries contain SIC classification data. They can also be acquired from the U.S. Government Printing Office in Washington, DC.

DUN & BRADSTREET

Dun & Bradstreet publishes a plant list index based on SIC codes. While the government lists the products made by plants, it does not carry the reverse information—that is, the names and number of plants manufacturing SIC code products.

MCC MEDIA DATA FORM

The MCC Media Data Form provides information regarding an industry publication's circulation as well as its universe, or number of companies engaged in the business this medium is addressing.

CENSUS OF MANUFACTURERS

The Census of Manufacturers provides reports on 452 SIC manufacturing industries in the United States, including the number of establishments, employment, payrolls, hours worked, value added by manufacturing, quantity and value of products shipped, materials consumed, and capital expenditures.

U.S. INDUSTRIAL OUTLOOK

U.S. Industrial Outlook is a yearly report from the U.S. government detailing sales, shipments, and forecasts for selected industries. The report also identifies key trends, innovations, and foreign impacts on the market.

BUSINESS INFORMATION NETWORK

The Business Information Network (BIN) reports advertiser page volume and expenditures in as many as 1,000 business-to-business publications covering dozens of market niches. This publication is the business equivalent of the Publishers Information Bureau (PIB) available to consumer marketers.

TRADE PUBLICATIONS

Business-to-business marketers also rely on an estimated 3,000 trade publications. Each provides information of interest to its own specific audience, as shown in Exhibit 19–6. Some trade magazines have a more general appeal.

Of course, business-to-business marketers also engage in *primary* research, which may serve as an input to the planning process or a measure of effectiveness. Many of the methodologies used in the consumer market have been adopted by business marketers, including focus groups, interviewing, and surveys.

Evaluating Promotional Efforts

While nine out of 10 business-to-business marketers consider marketing research important in their communications programs, Figure 19–11 suggests this importance is based on research input more than evaluation. None of the top 10 research studies used is specifically oriented to measuring the effects of advertising and promotions. (While focus groups are also cited, these groups are primarily used to provide in-depth views of sales prospects' attitudes rather than to evaluate ads.) Of the 5 percent or so of the promotional budget spent specifically on advertising research, approximately 23 percent is used to pretest ads or follow up the effects once the ad campaign has begun.[18] The remaining 77 percent is again used as input into the advertising program.

Interestingly, even though the amount spent on evaluative research appears low, a number of research services are available to business-to-business advertisers, as shown in Figure 19–12. These services provide a variety of effectiveness measures.

We have said repeatedly that business-to-business marketers tend to use advertising and promotional tools to assist in the sales support effort. It should come as no surprise, then, that the measures most commonly employed to evaluate the effectiveness of these programs also assess contribution to the selling effort (Figure 19–13). In addition to criteria often used in the general-interest and/or consumer market (read most, awareness, attention, recall), b-to-b criteria include more behavioral (and sales-oriented) items such as readership by purchase decision, built preference, kept customers sold, referred ad to someone else, and specified or purchased product.

FIGURE 19–11
Research studies used by business-to-business marketers

	Percent Responding
Market position studies	56%
Readership studies	46
Customer attitude studies	42
Focus groups	37
New product feasibility studies	37
Competitive environment analyses	35
Brand preference studies	33
Market potential studies	31
Company image studies	27
Prospect feedback studies	20

Note: Responses add to more than 100% due to multiple mentions.

FIGURE 19—12
A sampling of effectiveness measures available to business-to-business advertisers

Ad-Sell Performance Study	McGraw-Hill telephone survey of 100 magazine readers. Scores: established contact; created awareness; aroused interest; built preference; kept customers sold
Ad-Chart	Chilton Marketing Research Co. survey of 100 readers. Scores: % who noticed ad; % started to read; % read half or more; total readership index; informativeness index; cost-effectiveness index
Beta Research	Studies in health care field. Scores: likelihood of reading; changes in opinion of product as a result of ad; informativeness of ad; believability of ad
Fosdick Ad Evaluation	Survey of 100 respondents. Scores: buyers who read ad; buyers who did not read ad; nonbuyers who read ad; nonbuyers who did not read ad
Gallup & Robinson	Report on 150 respondents. Scores: proved name registration; idea communication; favorable attitude
Starch Readership Reports	Readership of ads. Scores: noted; associated; read most
Advalue	Readership by 100 people. Scores: recall seeing; readership; ad effect; action taken; future purchase; salesperson contact; ad comparisons
Ad Lab	Mail survey sent to 750–1,500 subscribers. Scores: total sample noting; total sample who started to read; total sample reading more than half; total finding ad informative/useful; buyers noting/specified; buyers/specifiers starting to read; buyers/specifiers reading more than half; buyers/specifiers finding ad or editorial informative/useful

In Figure 19–14, the criteria used by Copy Chasers (a panel of experts who evaluate business-to-business ads for *Business Marketing* magazine) provide insight into what is considered necessary to communicate effectively in this market. As you can see, the role advertising is supposed to play is somewhat different from in the consumer market. Should advertising be expected to generate such results? Or is this one reason so little is spent on measuring advertising effectiveness in the business-to-business market?

In sum, marketing and advertising research in business markets tends to be oriented to providing input into the marketing and promotional programs. As the role of advertising continues to expand in this area, the amount and types of research used may follow.

FIGURE 19—13
How business-to-business marketers assess the effectiveness of their programs

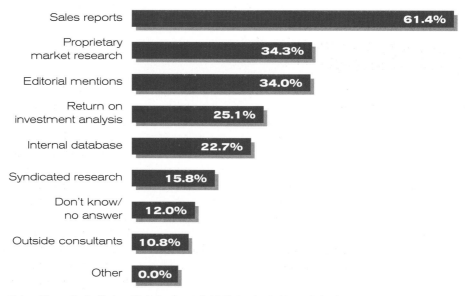

Sales reports	61.4%
Proprietary market research	34.3%
Editorial mentions	34.0%
Return on investment analysis	25.1%
Internal database	22.7%
Syndicated research	15.8%
Don't know/ no answer	12.0%
Outside consultants	10.8%
Other	0.0%

Source: "Factors Used to Evaluate Marketing Success," p. S-13. Reprinted with permission from the June 1996 issue of *Business Marketing*. Copyright, Crain Communications, Inc.

FIGURE 19—14
The Copy Chasers criteria for evaluating business-to-business ads

1. The successful ad has a high degree of visual magnetism.
2. The successful ad selects the right audience.
3. The successful ad promises a reward.
4. The successful ad backs up the promise.
5. The successful ad talks person to person.
6. The successful ad presents the selling proposition in logical sequence.
7. The successful ad invites the reader into the scene.
8. Successful advertising is easy to read.
9. Successful advertising has been purged of nonessentials.
10. Successful advertising emphasizes the service, not the source.

SUMMARY

Business-to-business advertisers view the role of advertising and promotions somewhat differently from those in the consumer products industries. While the latter may expect advertising and promotions to meet communications objectives, in the business-to-business sector it is generally considered a sales support.

Because of the role advertising and promotions are asked to assume, the message and media strategies designed to accomplish the sales support objectives are again different from those in the consumer products market. Messages tend to be more information laden, to the point, and designed to elicit inquiries or answer questions. Illustrations, humor, and/or sex appeals are much less commonly employed.

The media used by industrial advertising are also different. No fewer than 3,000 trade journals exist in this country, and the vast majority of firms use the ones in their field. Trade shows and sales incentives are popular. Interactive electronic media—in something of an infant stage in the consumer products market—have found a great reception in the industrial sector.

Finally, the measures used to determine the effectiveness of business-to-business strategies are also designed to support sales. Criteria such as number of inquiries generated, referrals, and actual purchases are often used to determine the relative effectiveness of various strategies.

KEY TERMS

business-to-business communications, 596

derived demand, 596
buying center, 597

social style model, 599
CUBE model, 599

multiple buying influences, 609

DISCUSSION QUESTIONS

1. Explain some of the reasons consumer-oriented marketing companies have now begun to target the business-to-business market. Can you think of any companies that previously focused on the b-to-b market that now target consumer markets?

2. What are some of the factors that may underlie business-to-business advertisers' attempts to instill more creativity into their advertising? What are some of the reasons many continue to use more rational, informative appeals?

3. It has been said that the Internet is especially well suited for business-to-business marketers. Explain why.

4. Discuss some of the criteria used to evaluate business-to-business ads. How do they differ from those used in the consumer products market?

5. Why are trade shows likely to be an effective way for business-to-business marketers to communicate with their markets?

6. Why has the use of mass media such as TV and consumer magazines for advertising business-to-business products and services been increasing?

7. Why would corporate image advertising be important to business-to-business advertisers? Cite examples of companies using this strategy.

8. Give examples of how business-to-business advertisers might employ an integrated marketing communications program.

9. The text cites an example of 3M's objectives in the five stages of the selling process. Compare this approach to communications hierarchies discussed in Chapter 5 of the text.

10. Explain how a business-to-business marketer might use sales promotions similar to those used in the consumer market as part of the IMC mix.

20

International Advertising and Promotion

Chapter Objectives

- To examine the importance of international marketing and the role of international advertising and promotion.

- To review the various factors in the international environment and how they influence advertising and promotion decisions.

- To consider the pros and cons of global versus localized marketing and advertising.

- To examine the various decision areas of international advertising.

- To understand the role of other promotional mix elements in the international marketing program.

GLOBAL MARKETERS GO WITH ONE IMAGE, ONE AGENCY

Traditionally, most large multinational corporations maintained a network of ad agencies around the world to handle their advertising in various countries. For example, 3M, which operates in more than 70 countries, ran its global advertising through 34 separate agencies based in 23 countries. Germany's Bayer AG maintained a network of some 50 agencies around the world to handle advertising for its various brands, which include Bayer aspirin and Alka-Seltzer. Recently, however, both 3M and Bayer consolidated their global advertising: 3M chose Grey Advertising, which has 278 offices in 70 countries, to handle most of its corporate and consumer advertising, while Bayer consolidated the bulk of its $300 million global consumer products advertising with BBDO Worldwide.

Bayer and 3M joined a growing list of major companies who have pared their agency rosters to a single source. The consolidation trend began in May 1994, when IBM dismissed 40 agencies around the world and awarded its $450 million account to Ogilvy & Mather Worldwide. In December 1995, Colgate-Palmolive consolidated more than $500 million in global advertising with New York-based Young & Rubicam. The move, which followed the worldwide restructuring of Colgate's manufacturing and distribution system, marked the first time a large multibrand advertiser put all of its billings with one agency. Other companies that have gone the consolidation route recently include Frito-Lay, Campbell Soup, Kodak, and Citibank.

A number of factors are driving the consolidation trend. Most major corporations recognize they must develop a consistent global image for the company and/or its brands and speak with one coordinated marketing voice around the world. For example, IBM officials felt the company had been projecting too many images with its advertising divided among so many agencies. The consolidation enabled IBM to present a single brand identity around the world while taking advantage of one of the world's best-known brand names. Ogilvy & Mather developed the popular "Solutions for a small planet" global campaign, whose message is that IBM delivers solutions that are both simple and powerful enough to manage information anywhere, anytime, and for anyone. The commercials developed for the campaign use the same imagery but are varied for each country by the use of subtitles in the local language.

Companies are also consolidating their global advertising in an effort to increase efficiency and save money. Colgate, for example, has moved into 25 new countries in the past five years and increased its advertising spending at a compounded rate of about 10 percent. The company faces a tremendous demand for resources as new markets open in countries such as China and Vietnam. It believes consolidation will generate savings that can be invested in additional advertising.

3M's director of corporate advertising says consolidation will help the company enhance its global competitive advantage in bringing new products to market quickly: "It's difficult to roll out new products with one global voice when you have 25 different agencies." The chair and CEO of Grey Advertising says, "If a client wants to export a product it has already successfully launched in, say, the U.S., the client doesn't want to hire small agencies in country after country, each with their own egos who want to reinvent the creative."

Consolidation also gives advertisers greater leverage over their agencies. When a major client puts all of its advertising with one agency, that company often becomes the agency's most important account. And, as one IBM executive says, "You become a magnet for talent and attention."

Advertising executives also note that agencies now have the ability to communicate and manage globally. Fax machines, e-mail, and airline connections make it much easier to manage accounts around the globe. Of course, placing an entire global advertising account with one agency can be risky. If the agency fails to deliver an effective campaign, the client has no backup agency to make a fast rebound, and the search for a new agency can be very time consuming. Clients who consolidate also face the problem of selling the idea to regional offices, which often previously enjoyed their own local agency relationship. However, it appears that more and more companies are finding that the rewards outweigh these risks. They are relying on one agency to handle their advertising around the world.

Source: Noreen O'Leary, "World Tours with a Single Client," *Adweek*, August 5, 1996, pp. 34–37; Sally Goll Beatty, "Young & Rubicam Is Only One for Colgate," *The Wall Street Journal*, December 1, 1995, p. B6; Kevin Goldman, "Global Companies Hone Agency Rosters," *The Wall Street Journal*, July 25, 1995, p. B8.

The primary focus of this book so far has been on integrated marketing communications programs for products and services sold in the U.S. market. Many American companies have traditionally devoted most of their marketing efforts to the domestic market, since they often lack the resources, skills, or incentives to go abroad. This is changing rapidly, however, as U.S. corporations recognize the opportunities that foreign markets offer for new sources of sales and profits as well as the need to market their products internationally. Many companies are striving to develop global brands that can be advertised and promoted the world over.

In this chapter, we look at international advertising and promotion and the various issues marketers must consider in communicating with consumers around the globe. We examine the environment of international marketing and how companies often must adapt their promotional programs to conditions in each country. We reveiw the debate over whether a company should use a global marketing and advertising approach or tailor it specifically for various countries.

We also examine how firms organize for international advertising, select agencies, and consider various decision areas such as research, creative strategy, and media selection. While the focus of this chapter is on international advertising, we also consider other promotional mix elements in international marketing, including sales promotion, personal selling, and publicity/public relations. Let's begin by discussing some of the reasons international marketing has become so important to companies.

THE IMPORTANCE OF INTERNATIONAL MARKETING

U.S. companies are focusing on international markets for a number of reasons. Many recognize that the national market offers them limited opportunity for expansion because of slow population growth, saturated markets, intense competition, and an unfavorable marketing environment. For example, U.S. tobacco companies face declining domestic consumption as a result of restrictions on their marketing and advertising efforts and the growing antismoking sentiment in this country. Companies such as R. J. Reynolds and Philip Morris are turning to Asia and South America, where there are fewer restrictions and cigarette consumption is growing.[1] Many U.S.-based brewers, among them Anheuser-Busch, Miller, and Coors, are looking to international markets to sustain growth as beer sales in this country decline and regulatory pressures increase.[2] Anheuser-Busch is targeting fast-growing beer markets in Asia, South America (especially Argentina, Brazil and Chile), and China.[3]

Companies are also pursuing international markets because of the opportunities they offer for growth and profits. The dramatic economic, social, and political changes around the world in recent years have opened markets in Eastern Europe and China. The growing markets of the Far East, Latin America, and other parts of the world present tremendous opportunities to marketers of consumer products and services as well as business-to-business marketers.

The importance and potential profitability of international marketing have long been recognized by many U.S. companies. IBM, Ford, General Motors, Exxon, Du Pont, and Colgate-Palmolive generate much of their sales and profits from foreign markets. Gillette sells over 800 products in more than 200 countries; Procter & Gamble markets 165 products overseas and had international sales of $18 billion in 1996. Kellogg earns 35 percent of its

profits outside the United States and has nearly 50 percent of the European cereal market. Coca-Cola, Pepsi, IBM, Reebok, KFC, Compaq Computer, McDonald's, and many other U.S. companies and brands are known all over the world (Exhibit 20–1).

Many U.S.-based companies have formed joint ventures or strategic alliances with foreign companies to market their products internationally. For example, General Mills and Swiss-based Nestlé entered into a joint venture to create Cereal Partners Worldwide (CPW), taking advantage of General Mills' popular product line and Nestlé's powerful distribution channels in Europe, Asia, Latin America, and Africa.[4] Nestlé has also begun joint ventures with Coca-Cola to have the beverage giant distribute its instant coffee and tea throughout the world. Häagen-Dazs entered into a joint venture in Japan with Suntory Ltd., and its sales in Asia have doubled since 1989.[5]

International markets are important to small and mid-size companies as well as the large multinational corporations. Many of these firms can compete more effectively in foreign markets, where they may face less competition or appeal to specific market segments or where products have not yet reached the maturity stage of their life cycle. For example, the WD-40 Co. has saturated the U.S. market with its lubricant product and now gets much of its sales growth from Europe, Canada, and Japan (Exhibit 20–2).

Another reason it is increasingly important for U.S. companies to adopt an international marketing orientation is that imports are taking a larger and larger share of the domestic market for many products. The United States has been running a continuing **balance-of-trade deficit**; the monetary value of our imports exceeds that of our exports. American companies are realizing that we are shifting from being an isolated, self-sufficient, national economy to being part of an interdependent *global economy*. This means U.S. corporations must defend against foreign inroads into the domestic market as well as learn how to market their products and services to other countries.[6]

While many U.S. companies are becoming more aggressive in their pursuit of international markets, they face stiff competition from large multinational corporations from other countries. Some of the world's most formidable marketers are European companies such as Unilever, Nestlé, Siemens, Philips, and Renault, as well as the various Japanese car and electronic manufacturers and package-goods companies such as Suntory, Shiseido, and Kao.

THE ROLE OF INTERNATIONAL ADVERTISING AND PROMOTION

Advertising and promotion are important parts of the marketing program of firms competing in the global marketplace. While more than $174 billion is spent on advertising in the United States each year, advertising expenditures outside the United States have increased dramatically over the past decade and now exceed $220 billion annually.[7] Global marketers based in the United States as well as European and Asian countries are increasing their worldwide advertising spending.[8] Figure 20–1 shows the top 25 companies in terms of advertising spending outside the United States.

FIGURE 20–1   Top 25 companies by ad spending outside of the United States in 1995

Rank	Advertiser	Headquarters	Ad Spending Outside the U.S.	U.S. Ad Spending	Worldwide Ad Spending
1	Procter & Gamble	Cincinnati	$2,559.6	$2,777.1	$5,336.7
2	Unilever	Rotterdam/London	2,410.1	858.3	3,268.4
3	Nestlé SA	Vevey, Switzerland	1,415.8	487.3	1,903.1
4	Toyota Motor Corp.	Toyota City, Japan	1,081.9	733.4	1,815.3
5	PSA Peugeot-Citroen SA	Paris	881.2	0.0	881.2
6	Nissan Motor Co.	Tokyo	869.4	466.4	1,335.8
7	Philip Morris Cos.	New York	835.7	2,576.9	3,412.6
8	General Motors Corp.	Detroit	812.5	2,046.9	2,859.4
9	Volkswagen AG	Wolfsburg, Germany	797.8	135.2	933.0
10	Mars Inc.	McLean, VA.	734.9	416.1	1,151.0
11	Ford Motor Co.	Dearborn, MI	725.4	1,149.2	1,874.6
12	Coca-Cola Co.	Atlanta	713.4	433.2	1,146.6
13	L'Oreal	Paris	619.7	480.9	1,100.6
14	Sony Corp.	Tokyo	602.9	674.3	1,277.2
15	Kao Corp.	Tokyo	586.8	28.7	615.5
16	Renault SA	Paris	566.0	0.0	566.0
17	Fiat SpA	Turin Italy	563.9	1.5	565.5
18	Colgate-Palmolive Co.	New York	560.7	313.0	873.7
19	Mitsubishi Motor Co.	Tokyo	545.1	168.8	713.9
20	Honda Motor Co.	Tokyo	542.8	534.2	1,077.0
21	Ferrero SpA	Perugia, Italy	539.5	15.9	555.4
22	Matsushita Electric Industrial Co.	Osaka	508.1	29.1	537.2
23	Henkel Group	Duesseldorf	488.2	0.0	488.2
24	McDonald's Corp.	Oak Brook, IL	473.1	880.0	1,353.1
25	Philips NV	Eindhoven, The Netherlands	449.6	169.4	619.0

Source: Reprinted with permission from the November 1996 issue of *Ad Age International*, p. i15. Copyright Crain Communications, Inc. 1996.

More and more companies recognize that an effective promotional program is important for companies competing in foreign markets. As one international marketing scholar notes:

> Promotion is the most visible as well as the most culture bound of the firm's marketing functions. Marketing includes the whole collection of activities the firm performs in relating to its market, but in other functions the firm relates to the market in a quieter, more passive way. With the promotional function, however, the firm is standing up and speaking out, wanting to be seen and heard.[9]

Many companies have run into difficulties developing and implementing advertising and promotion programs for international markets. Companies that promote their products or services abroad face an unfamiliar marketing environment and customers with different sets of values, customs, consumption patterns, and habits, as well as differing purchase motives and abilities. Languages vary from country to country and even within a country, such as India or Switzerland. Media options are quite limited in many countries, owing to lack of availability or limited effectiveness. These factors demand different creative and media strategies as well as changes in other elements of the advertising and promotional program for foreign markets.

THE INTERNATIONAL ENVIRONMENT

Just as with domestic marketing, companies engaging in international marketing must carefully analyze the major environmental factors of each market in which they compete, including economic, demographic, cultural, and political/legal variables. Figure 20–2 shows some of the factors marketers must consider in each category when analyzing the environment of each country or market. These factors are important in evaluating the potential of each country as well as designing and implementing a marketing and promotional program.

The Economic Environment

A country's economic conditions indicate its present and future potential for consuming, since products and services can be sold only to countries where there is enough income to buy them. This is generally not a problem in developed countries such as the United States,

FIGURE 20–2
Forces in the international marketing environment

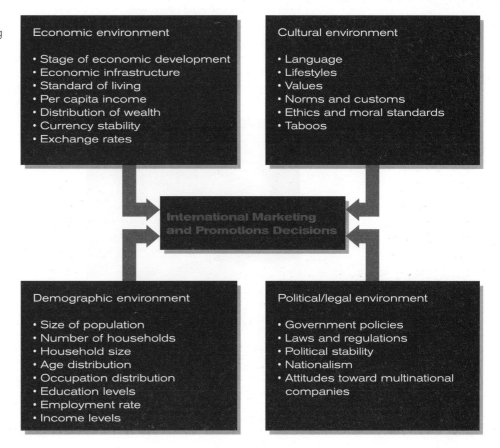

Economic environment

- Stage of economic development
- Economic infrastructure
- Standard of living
- Per capita income
- Distribution of wealth
- Currency stability
- Exchange rates

Cultural environment

- Language
- Lifestyles
- Values
- Norms and customs
- Ethics and moral standards
- Taboos

International Marketing and Promotions Decisions

Demographic environment

- Size of population
- Number of households
- Household size
- Age distribution
- Occupation distribution
- Education levels
- Employment rate
- Income levels

Political/legal environment

- Government policies
- Laws and regulations
- Political stability
- Nationalism
- Attitudes toward multinational companies

Canada, Japan, and most of Western Europe, where consumers generally have higher incomes and standards of living. Thus, they can and want to purchase a variety of products and services. Developed countries have the **economic infrastructure** in terms of the communications, transportation, financial, and distribution networks needed to conduct business in these markets effectively. By contrast, many developing countries lack purchasing power and have limited communications networks available to firms that want to promote their products or services to these markets.

For most companies, industrialized nations represent the greatest marketing and advertising opportunities. But most of these countries have stable population bases, and their markets for many products and services are already saturated. Many marketers are turning their attention to parts of the world whose economies and consumer markets are growing. For example, the "four tigers" of Asia—South Korea, Singapore, Hong Kong, and Taiwan—continue to be among the fastest-growing markets in the world. It is predicted that these countries will account for nearly a quarter of the world's gross domestic product by the turn of the century, and increases in per capita income are expected to follow.[10] Many U.S. companies already have a strong presence in these countries (including Colgate-Palmolive, Du Pont, Quaker Oats, and Coca-Cola).

Marketers are also focusing on developing countries that have expanding populations and future growth opportunities. For example, Nestlé, the world's largest food company, estimates that 20 percent of the world's population in Europe and North America consumes 80 percent of its products. While Nestlé continues to target the European and American markets with ads such as Exhibit 20–3, it is also focusing on Third World nations as the market of tomorrow.[11]

The Demographic Environment

Major demographic differences exist among countries as well as within them. Marketers must consider income levels and distribution, age and occupation distributions of the population, household size, education, and employment rates. In some countries, literacy rates are also a factor; people who cannot read will not respond well to print ads. Demographic data can provide insight into the living standards and lifestyles in a particular country to help companies plan ad campaigns.

Demographic information can reveal the market potential of various foreign markets. For example, by the year 2000, the population of India is expected to reach nearly 1 billion.[12] Latin America remains one of the world's largest potential markets, although the meager income of most consumers in the region is still a problem. Brazil, the largest consumer market in South America, is expected to have a population of 200 million by the year 2000 and is a

EXHIBIT 20–3
Nestlé advertises its products to countries all over the world

growing market for many products and services. Indonesia has more people under the age of 16 than the United States, and they are very receptive to Western ways and products. For example, Tower Records, a California-based chain of music stores, recently opened stores in Bangkok that are nearly identical to its U.S. outlets and are very popular with the youth in Thailand.[13] Global Perspective 20–1 discusses how opportunities in international markets have become a key part of Nike's growth strategy.

The Cultural Environment

Another important aspect of the international marketing environment is the culture of each country. Cultural variables marketers must consider include language, customs, tastes, attitudes, lifestyles, values, and ethical/moral standards. Nearly every country exhibits cultural traits that influence not just the needs and wants of consumers but how they go about satisfying them.

Marketers must be sensitive not only in determining what products and services they can sell foreign cultures but also in communicating with them. Advertising is often the most effective way to communicate with potential buyers and create markets in other countries. But it can also be one of the most difficult aspects of the international marketing program because of problems in developing messages that will be understood in various countries.

International advertisers often have problems with language. The advertiser must know not only the native tongue of the country but also its nuances, idioms, and subtleties. International marketers must be aware of the connotations of words and symbols used in their messages and understand how advertising copy and slogans are translated. In Global Perspective 5–1, we discussed some of the problems marketers encounter in translating their advertising messages and brand names into various languages. The Heineken ad in Exhibit 20–4 is one example. Although this ad worked well in the United States and other English-speaking countries, the line "you don't have to make a great fuss" could not be translated in a meaningful way into many other languages.

Advertisers can also encounter problems with the connotative meaning of signs and symbols used in their messages. For example, Pepsodent toothpaste was unsuccessful in Southeast Asia because it promised white teeth to a culture where black and yellow teeth are symbols of prestige. An American ad campaign using various shades of green was a disaster in Malaysia, where the color symbolizes death and disease.

Problems arising from language diversity and differences in signs and symbols can usually be best solved with the help of local expertise. Marketers should consult local employees or use an ad agency knowledgeable in the local language that can help verify that the adver-

EXHIBIT 20–4
This Heineken ad did not translate well into some languages

Brewers don't have to be good talkers.

When you make a great beer, you don't have to make a great fuss.

Global Perspective 20–1
Just Doing It Globally

Most athletes or companies would give anything to have the hot streak that Nike, Inc., has enjoyed for the past two decades. Nike took advantage of the fitness boom in the U.S. market with innovative products like its Air Trainers and Air 180 running shoes, cross-training shoes, and Air Jordans for basketball. The Nike ethos of pure, brash performance was captured in the "Just do it" slogan, which became a catch phrase for the sports world and is personified in advertising featuring Michael Jordan, Tiger Woods, Ben Johnson, and many other star athletes. The company's omnipresent "swoosh logo" is so well-known that the Nike brand name need not appear in its ads around the world.

Nike has emerged as one of the world's great brand names and most profitable companies. The company quadrupled its sales from 1987 to 1993 and ran past all of its competitors to become the world's largest shoe company, with nearly $4 billion in annual sales. In 1996 Nike sold $6.5 billion worth of sneakers, apparel, and sports equipment and became the world's largest athletic apparel company. It leads the U.S. athletic market with a 36 percent share (versus 20 percent for archrival Reebok). However, like many other companies, Nike has found that it cannot rely on the U.S. market to sustain its strong growth. Many of the teenagers and twenty-somethings responsible for Nike's growth over the past few years have turned away from sneakers in droves.

Nike is responding to the changing U.S. market by selling hiking boots and other rugged footwear through its outdoor division and focusing more on the apparel market. But, Nike also recognizes that markets outside the United States are critical to its goal of reaching $12 billion in sales by the year 2000. Nike's international sales hit $2.33 billion in 1996 and the company expects its international sales to be at least even with domestic sales by the end of the decade.

International expansion is a key element of the company's corporate strategy. In Europe, Nike has overcome 30 percent European Community duties and is stealing sales from Adidas and Puma, the German companies that dominated the European market for decades. Nike has used nearly $100 million in advertising, appealing designs, and European youth's fascination with American products to surge to a 25 percent market share in Europe, versus less than 5 percent 15 years ago. It has exploited basketball's surging popularity in Europe. NBA stars Charles Barkley and Michael Jordan appear in Nike ads as well as company-sponsored basketball clinics and other promotional events there. Along with Reebok, Nike also helped expand the overall market by taking sneakers from the playing field into the street and making them fashionable footwear.

The company is also expanding its business in China, Japan, Mexico, and Brazil. Advertising in these countries will be more tightly focused on sports and Nike has launched market-specific sneakers such as badminton shoes for Asia. Nike's strategy in these countries includes producing, promoting, and sponsoring global sporting events that feature its growing stable of superstars. For example, in late 1996 Nike paid a record-setting $200 million to sponsor the Brazilian soccer team for the next 10 years.

Nike's advertising agency, Wieden & Kennedy, is helping the company develop strength across a diversity of sports segments for both men and women. The "If you let me play" campaign underscored its push into women's sports. The award-winning "Nike vs. Evil" spot from the agency's Amsterdam office, in which Nike's soccer endorsers do battle with Satan, reflects Nike's belief that it must dominate soccer to have global credibility. In 1996 Nike added golf phenom Tiger Woods to its stable of superstar endorsers to help penetrate the golfing market in both the United States and Asia.

With respect to its worldwide ad strategy, Liz Dolan, Nike's vice president of global marketing communications, says, "We have to approach our brand marketing from a global point of view but also must devise a country-by-country plan to make the brand part of the cultural fabric." Both Nike and Wieden & Kennedy have formed global marketing management and account teams to serve this approach. It appears that Nike's global marketing is working very well and the company is on its way to getting consumers around the world to "Just do it."

Sources: Linda Himelstein, "The Game's the Thing at Nike Now," *Business Week*, January 27, 1997, p. 88 ; Jeff Jensen, "Marketer of the Year," *Advertising Age*, December 16, 1996, pp. 1, 16; Randall Lane, "You Are What You Wear," *Forbes*, October 14, 1996, pp. 42–46.

tiser is saying what it wants to say. Many companies turn to agencies that specialize in translating advertising slogans and copy into foreign languages.

Tastes, traditions, and customs are also an important part of cultural considerations. The customs of a society affect what products and services it will buy and how they must be marketed. In France, cosmetics are used heavily by men as well as women, and advertising to the male market is common. There are also cultural differences in grooming and hygiene habits of consumers in various countries. For example, though many U.S. consumers use products like deodorant and shampoo daily, consumers in many other Western countries are not as fanatical about personal hygiene, so consumption of products such as deodorants and mouthwash is much lower than in the United States.

Japan is one of the more difficult markets for many American advertisers to understand because of its unique values and customs.[14] For example, the Japanese have a very strong commitment to the group; social interdependence and collectivism are as important to them as individualism is to most Americans. Ads stressing individuality and nonconformity have traditionally not done well in Japan, but Westernized values have become more prevalent in Japanese advertising in recent years.[15] However, the Japanese dislike ads that confront or disparage the competition and tend to prefer soft rather than hard sells.[16] Figure 20–3 lists advertising appeals one copywriter suggests would not work well in Japan, along with some appeals that would help sell a product.

Religion is another aspect of culture that affects norms, values, and behaviors. For example, in many Arab countries, advertisers must be aware of various taboos resulting from conservative applications of the Islamic religion. Alcohol and pork cannot be advertised. Human nudity is forbidden, as are pictures of anything sacred, such as images of a cross or photographs of Mecca. The faces of women may not be shown in photos, so cosmetics use drawings of women's faces in ads.[17] In conservative Islamic countries, many religious authorities are opposed to advertising on the grounds that it promotes Western icons and culture and the associated non-Islamic consumerism.[18]

The Political/Legal Environment

The political and legal environment in a country is one of the most important factors influencing the advertising and promotional programs of international marketers. Regulations differ owing to economic and national sovereignty considerations, nationalistic and cultural factors, and the goal of protecting consumers not only from false or misleading advertising but, in some cases, from advertising in general. It is difficult to generalize about advertising regulation at the international level, since some countries are increasing government control of advertising while others are decreasing it. Government regulations and restrictions can affect various aspects of a company's advertising program, including:

- The types of products that may be advertised.
- The content or creative approach that may be used.
- The media that all advertisers (or different classes of advertisers) are permitted to employ.
- The amount of advertising a single advertiser may use in total or in a specific medium.
- The use of foreign languages in ads.
- The use of advertising material prepared outside the country.
- The use of local versus international advertising agencies.
- The specific taxes that may be levied against advertising.[19]

A number of countries ban or restrict the advertising of various products. Cigarette advertising is banned in some or all media in numerous countries besides the United States, including Argentina, Canada, France, Italy, Malaysia, Norway, Sweden, and Switzerland. In 1993 the Australian government limited tobacco advertising to point of purchase. The ban also excludes tobacco companies from sponsoring sporting events.[20] Tobacco ads were banned from TV in the United Kingdom in 1991, although they are still permitted on radio and other media. In China, tobacco and liquor advertising are banned except in hotels for foreigners. In Hong Kong, which reverted to Chinese control in July 1997, a total ban on tobacco advertising is being considered, although it faces strong opposition from the tobacco and advertising industries.[21]

FIGURE 20–3
Advertising appeals for the Japanese market

Appeals That Do Not Work in Japan

A copywriter who wishes to appeal to a Japanese audience would be wise to forget the following fundamental American appeals:

- *Be the first person in your neighborhood to own the Frammis washing machine . . .*

(Japanese buyers would never want to be out of step with their neighbors. Nor would they wish to appear superior. This is considered to be very bad taste.)

- *FREE . . . this $4.96 volume, no strings attached . . .*

(The average Japanese buyer would simply not believe that something is given for nothing.)

- *Less work for mother . . .*

(Japanese mothers want their families to know that they have personally prepared every bite of food. TV dinners are virtually unknown in Japan. Several years ago, food processors were introduced. They were a dismal failure, because Japanese women want to do all that chopping and blending by hand. Anything less would be considered an insult to the family.)

- *Act today and save 10 percent off the price of this brand-new model stereo . . .*

(Price is not a significant appeal to Japanese buyers. They are more concerned with the dependability and reliability of the company.)

- *Here's a great way to express your individuality and set yourself apart from the crowd . . .*

(The Japanese consider individuality a bad thing. A saying Japanese children learn almost from the first day of school is "The nail that stands highest gets hammered.")

The Art of Selling—Japanese Style

So what appeals does a copywriter use when attempting to sell something to a Japanese audience? Bruce Guilfoile is a Japanese-American account executive at McCann-Erickson Hakuhodo, Inc., one of Tokyo's major advertising agencies (also one of the major agencies specializing in Japanese direct response). Guilfoile suggests that copywriters in Japan use these appeals:

- *Our company has been in business for over 35 years . . .*

(Stability is considered a great virtue in Japan, and this appeal is viewed as very important.)

- *Our TV set is guaranteed to last longer than any other TV set on the market . . .*

(Reliability is the major value the Japanese look for when buying a product.)

- *Our company has the strength of the Rock of Gibraltar . . .*

(Image is very important to the Japanese.)

- *This is an idea whose time has come . . .*

(The Japanese are great believers in timing. Even if an idea seems incredibly hot, they will wait until the time is right. Once they are committed to a course of action, it would take wild horses to get them to change.)

- *Buy this product. It will bring greater harmony to your life at home and at the office . . .*

(Beyond a doubt, this is the most appealing thing you could say to a Japanese audience. Any product that claims to improve human relations is guaranteed to sell.)

Source: Milton Pierce, "Direct Response in Japan," *Direct Marketing*, November 1986, p. 160.

While international marketers are accustomed to restrictions on the advertising of cigarettes, liquor, and pharmaceuticals, they are often surprised by restrictions on other products or services. For example, margarine cannot be advertised in France, nor can restaurant chains. For many years, the French government restricted travel advertising because it encourages the French to spend their francs outside the country.[22]

Many countries restrict the media advertisers can use. Some of the most stringent advertising regulations in the world are found in Scandinavian countries. Commercial TV advertising did not begin in Sweden until 1992 and both Sweden and Denmark limit the amount of time available for commercials.[23] Saudi Arabia opened its national TV system to commercial advertising in 1986 but advertising is not permitted on the state-run radio system. Advertising in magazines and newspapers in the country is subject to government and religious restrictions.[24]

Many governments have rules and regulations that affect the advertising message. Brazil's self-regulatory advertising codes are so strict that no advertiser has been able to cre-

ate a comparative message that has been approved.[25] Many countries restrict the types of claims advertisers can make, the words they can use, and the way products can be represented in ads. In Greece, specific claims for a product, such as "20 percent fewer calories" are not permitted in an advertising message.[26] Copyright and other legal restrictions make it difficult to maintain the same name from market to market. For example as shown in this ad, Diet Coke is known as Coca-Cola Light in Germany, France, and many other countries because of legal restrictions prohibiting the word *diet*.

Government restrictions can influence the use of foreign languages in advertising as well as the production of the ad. Most countries permit the use of foreign languages in print ads and direct mail. However, some do not allow foreign-language commercials on TV or radio or in cinema ads, and some restrict foreign-language ads to media targeted to foreigners in their country.[27] Some countries also restrict the use of foreign-produced ads and foreign talent. For example, with few exceptions, such as travel advertising, all commercials aired on Malaysian television must be made in Malaysia. However, the Asian country is considering changing its rules to allow foreign commercials to air on the new legalized satellite signals into the country.[28]

These restrictions are motivated primarily by economic considerations. Many countries require local production of at least a portion of commercials to build local film industries and create more jobs for local producers of print and audiovisual materials. Nationalistic and cultural factors also contribute to these restrictions, along with a desire to prevent large foreign ad agencies from dominating the advertising business in a country and thus hampering its development.

In some countries, steps are being taken to ease some of the legal restrictions and other barriers facing international advertisers. For example, the Maastricht Treaty on European Union was designed to create a single European market and remove many of the barriers to trade among the 12 member nations of the European Community. One of the goals of this plan was a single advertising law throughout the EC, but when the treaty was ratified in November 1993, many of the advertising directives were not agreed upon—so many advertising regulations are still decided by each country. For example, the directive aimed at prohibiting tobacco advertising everywhere within the EC (excluding point-of-purchase ads in tobacco specialty shops) was opposed by many countries and withdrawn, leaving the handling of the matter to each individual country.[29] However, antismoking sentiment is building in Europe and the European Commission continues to push for an EU-wide ban on tobacco advertising and on smoking in public places.[30] TV ads for cigarettes have been illegal in the EU since 1989.

GLOBAL VERSUS LOCALIZED ADVERTISING

The discussion of differences in the marketing environments of various countries suggests that each market is different and requires a distinct marketing and advertising program. However, in recent years a great deal of attention has focused on the concept of **global marketing**, where a company uses a common marketing plan for all countries in which it operates, thus selling the product in essentially the same way everywhere in the world. **Global advertising** falls under the umbrella of global marketing as a way to implement this strategy by using the same basic advertising approach in all markets.

The debate over standardization versus localization of marketing and advertising programs began years ago.[31] But the idea of global marketing was popularized by Professor Theodore Levitt, who says the worldwide marketplace has become homogenized and consumers' basic needs, wants, and expectations transcend geographic, national, and cultural boundaries.[32] One writer described Levitt's position on global marketing as follows:

Levitt's vision of total worldwide standardization is global marketing at the extreme. He argues that, thanks to cheap air travel and new telecommunications technology, consumers the world over are thinking—and shopping—increasingly alike. According to Levitt, the New Republic of Technology homogenizes world tastes, wants, and possibilities into global marketing proportions, which allows for world standardized products.[33]

Not everyone agrees with Levitt's global marketing theory, particularly with respect to advertising. Many argue that products and advertising messages must be designed or at least adapted to meet the differing needs of consumers in different countries.[34] We will consider the arguments for and against global marketing and advertising, as well as situations where it is most appropriate.

Advantages of Global Marketing and Advertising

A global marketing strategy and advertising program offer certain advantages to a company, including the following.

- Economies of scale in production and distribution.
- Lower marketing and advertising costs as a result of reductions in planning and control.
- Lower advertising production costs.
- Abilities to exploit good ideas on a worldwide basis and introduce products quickly into various world markets.
- A consistent international brand and/or company image.
- Simplification of coordination and control of marketing and promotional programs.

Advocates of global marketing and advertising contend that standardized products are possible in all countries if marketers emphasize quality, reliability, and low prices. They say people everywhere want to buy the same products and live the same way. Product standardization results in lower design and production costs as well as greater marketing efficiency, which translates into lower prices for consumers. Product standardization and global marketing also enable companies to roll out products faster into world markets, which is becoming increasingly important as product life cycles become shorter and competition increases.

A number of companies have been very successful using a global advertising approach, including Coca-Cola, Merrill Lynch, Xerox, American Express, and British Airways. Gillette used global advertising to launch its Sensor shaving system, which has become one of the most successful new products in the company's history. The advertising theme for the global campaign was "The best a man can get." Exhibit 20–5 shows a Sensor ad used in France, where the theme was translated into *La perfection au masculin,* or "perfection, male style."

Problems with Global Advertising

Opponents of the standardized global approach argue that very few products lend themselves to global advertising.[35] Differences in culture, market, and economic development; consumer needs and usage patterns; media availabilities; and legal restrictions make it extremely difficult to develop an effective universal approach to marketing and advertising. Advertising may be particularly difficult to standardize because of cultural differences in circumstances, language, traditions, values, beliefs, lifestyle, music, and so on. Moreover, some experts argue that cultures around the world are becoming more diverse, not less so. Thus, advertising's job of informing and persuading consumers and moving them toward using a particular brand can be done only within a given culture.

Consumer usage patterns and perceptions of a product may vary from one country to another, so advertisers must adjust their marketing and advertising approaches to different problems they may face in different markets. For example, when Nestlé introduced its Nescafé instant coffee brand, the company faced at least five different situations in various parts of the world.

1. In the United States, the idea of instant coffee had great penetration but Nescafé had the minor share.
2. In continental Europe, Nescafé had the major share of the market, but the idea of instant coffee was in the early stages.
3. In the tea-drinking countries, such as the United Kingdom and Japan, tea drinkers had to be converted not just to coffee but to instant coffee.

EXHIBIT 20—5   Gillette used global advertising to launch its Sensor shaving system

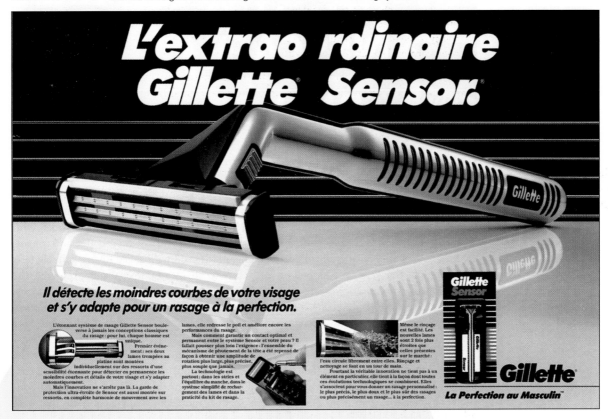

4. In Latin America, the preferred coffee was a heavy one that could not be duplicated with an instant version.
5. In Scandinavia, Nestlé had to deal with the ingrained custom of keeping a pot of coffee on the stove from early morning until late at night.

Nestlé had to use different advertising strategies for each market; a global campaign would not have been able to address the varying situations adequately. Exhibit 20–6 shows Nescafé ads used in Japan and Norway. Nestlé encountered yet another challenge when it

EXHIBIT 20—6

A. Nescafé instant coffee ad used in Japan   B. Nescafé instant coffee ad used in Norway

entered the Israeli market in 1995. *Nescafe* was the generic word for instant coffee as Israelis assumed that it was an abbreviation of the Hebrew word *namess* (dissolving). Israeli consumers were also not very demanding with respect to the quality of their coffee and considered the low-quality powdered coffee, or *nescafe*, produced by a local company, suitable fare. To overcome the generic connotation of Nescafé, all of the advertising presented the Nescafé Classic brand as "Nescafé of Nestlé" and portrayed it as the coffee choice of people all around the world (Exhibit 20–7). The company also relied on taste-testing at the points of sale so consumers could experience Nescafé Classic's superior quality. Within one year Nestlé had 30 percent of the instant coffee market in Israel.[36]

Many experts believe that marketing a standardized product the same way all over the world can turn off consumers, alienate employees, and blind a company to diversities in customer needs. For example, when McDonald's expanded to Puerto Rico, it alienated consumers by using American TV ads dubbed in Spanish and then using Hispanic ads that were brought in from New York, which subsequent research showed looked too Mexican.[37]

Parker Pen also encountered problems when it attempted to use global advertising in the mid-1980s. Local managers in its foreign branches resented the home office centralizing the advertising function with one worldwide agency and mandating the type of advertising appeal used in their markets.[38]

Such problems have led some major companies to move away from a completely standardized approach. For example, the Colgate-Palmolive Co. has used global advertising for many of its brands, including the Colgate, Palmolive, Fab, and Ajax product lines, and continues to endorse the use of global appeals. Under its current marketing strategy, however, advertising is often modified for a specific country or region, particularly where local creativity can improve the advertising over the global standard.[39] An example of this approach is the advertising used for Colgate toothpaste (see Exhibit 20–8). The globe/smile image is used as the visual in nearly every country where Colgate is marketed, but the copy varies. This ad for the Russian market appeared in the Moscow edition of *Reader's Digest*.

Some marketing experts claim much of the attention to the advantages of global advertising stems from large ad agencies trying to increase business by encouraging clients to use one agency to handle their marketing communications worldwide.[40] As discussed in the opening vignette, many large multinational companies are indeed consolidating their business with one or a few agencies who have offices around the world and offer international advertising capabilities. However, the consolidations are often driven by the client's increasing emphasis on global markets.[41]

When Is Globalization Appropriate?

While globalization of advertising is viewed by many in the advertising industry as a difficult task, some progress has been made in learning what products and services are best suited to worldwide appeals.[42]

1. Brands that can be adapted for a visual appeal, avoiding the problems of trying to translate words into dozens of languages.
2. Brands that are promoted with image campaigns that play to universal appeals such as sex or wealth.

МИР ГОВОРИТ «КОЛГЕЙТ»–
ПОДРАЗУМЕВАЕТ ЗУБНАЯ ПАСТА.
МИР ГОВОРИТ ЗУБНАЯ ПАСТА–
ПОДРАЗУМЕВАЕТ «КОЛГЕЙТ».

Для людей в более чем 160 странах мира зубная паста «Колгейт» вот уже 100 лет является синонимом высочайшего качества. Люди больше доверяют пасте «Колгейт», чем другим пастам, потому что она содержит кальций и фтор, которые способствуют укреплению зубов и защищают их от кариеса.

С помощью пасты «Колгейт» вы и ваша семья смогут сохранить зубы здоровыми. Вашей семье также понравится освежающий вкус ментола.

Чистите зубы пастой «Колгейт» и вы убедитесь сами, что «Колгейт» означает качество.

ЗУБНАЯ ПАСТА НОМЕР ОДИН В МИРЕ.

Translation:

COLGATE. WHAT THE WORLD CALLS TOOTHPASTE.

THE WORLD SAYS COLGATE, THE WORLD MEANS TOOTHPASTE.
THE WORLD SAYS TOOTHPASTE, THE WORLD MEANS COLGATE.

In the 100 years since it was first introduced, Colgate toothpaste has come to mean superior quality to people in over 160 countries. In fact, more families trust Colgate than any other toothpaste in the world because it contains calcium and fluoride for stronger teeth and unsurpassed cavity protection. Colgate will also help keep your family's teeth healthy. And it has a fresh, minty taste they'll love. Brush with Colgate. And see for yourself that, when the world says "Colgate," they mean quality.

THE NUMBER ONE TOOTHPASTE IN THE WORLD.

3. High-tech products and new products coming to the world for the first time, not steeped in the cultural heritage of the country.
4. Products with nationalistic flavor if the country has a reputation in the field.
5. Products that appeal to a market segment with universally similar tastes, interests, needs, and values.

Many companies and brands rely heavily on visual appeals that are easily adapted for use in global advertising campaigns. For example, Nike used global advertising to launch the Air 180 running shoe, its first worldwide product launch. The commercials contained no spoken language and relied on visual imagery. International airlines such as British Airways and Singapore Airlines also use global corporate image ads that rely heavily on visual appeals (Exhibit 20–9).

Products such as jewelry, liquor, cosmetics, and cigarettes can be promoted using image advertising, the second category. Marlboro uses its cowboy/western imagery around the world, and many cosmetic companies use similar image campaigns in different countries.

EXHIBIT 20–9
Visual appeals work well in global advertising

Levitt, like many advertisers, believes that joy, sentiment, excitement, and many other emotions are universal. Thus, it is common for global advertising campaigns to use emotional and image appeals. One advertising executive said:

> What it all boils down to is that we are all human. We share the gift of emotional response. We feel things. And we feel them in remarkably similar ways. We speak different languages, we observe different customs, but we are wired to each other and to an ultimate power source that transcends us in a way that makes us subject to a common emotional spectrum.[43]

High-tech consumer products such as personal computers, calculators, VCRs, TVs, and audio equipment are in the third category, as are various types of business-to-business products and services such as computer systems. Business-to-business marketers like Digital Equipment Corp. and Xerox have begun using global advertising campaigns, as have Compaq and IBM (recall IBM's "Solutions for a small planet" campaign, discussed in the opening vignette).

Products in the fourth category are those whose national reputation for quality can be the basis for a global advertising campaign. Examples include Swiss watches, French wine, and German beer or automobiles. Many U.S. companies are taking advantage of the cachet American products have acquired among consumers in Europe and other international markets.[44] For example, Jeep promotes itself as "the American legend" in Europe and Japan. Brown-Forman has been using an American theme for its Jack Daniel's and Southern Comfort liquor brands since it began selling them in foreign markets more than two decades ago.

In the final category for which globalization is appropriate are products and services that can be sold to common market segments around the world, such as those identified by Salah Hassan and Lea Katsansis.[45] One such segment is the world's *elite*—people who, by reason of their economically privileged position, can pursue a lifestyle that includes fine jewelry, expensive clothing, quality automobiles, and the like. Marketers of high-quality products such as Bally leather goods, Cartier jewelry, Godiva chocolates, and Louis Vuitton luggage can use global advertising to appeal to the elite market segment around the world. Seagram launched a global billboard advertising campaign for its expensive Chivas Regal scotch based on the idea that "the rich all over the world will sip the tony brand, no matter where they made their fortune."[46] Well-known international brands competing in the luxury goods marketplace often present a singular image of prestige and style to the entire world.

Teenagers around the world are becoming increasingly similar. Global Perspective 20–2 discusses how they are another global market segment that many companies are pursuing.

Global Perspective 20–2
Teens: A New Global Market Segment

Marketers are continually searching for global consumer market segments to whom products and services can be advertised and promoted in a similar fashion all over the world. Many marketers are heralding the arrival of the most global market segment of all—teenagers. They believe the global teens are a new breed of youth who show amazing similarities in taste, interests, language, and attitude. Teens in Latin America, Asia, Europe, and America are zipping up their Levi's, lacing up their Nikes and Reeboks, drinking Coke and Pepsi, dancing to the Red Hot Chili Peppers, watching MTV, and playing Sega and Nintendo video games.

Multinational companies recognize that one of their major global marketing challenges is tapping into the billions being spent by teens around the world. In 1996, America's teens spent an estimated $60 billion of their own money. And although the teen business is good in the United States, it may be even better abroad. There are over 200 million teens in Europe, Latin America, and the Pacific Rim countries of Asia who are converging with the 28 million in the United States to create a vast, free-spending global market.

The New York City ad agency BSB Worldwide videotaped teenagers' bedrooms in 25 countries. It's hard to tell whether the rooms are those of American, Japanese, or German teens. Basketballs sit next to soccer balls and closets overflow with staples from an international, unisex uniform that includes Levi's or Diesel jeans, NBA jackets, and rugged Doc Martens or Timberland shoes.

The convergence in teens' tastes, attitudes, and product preferences is being driven by several factors. The most powerful unifying force among teens is television, including TV advertising. Television helped create a vast single market in the United States, and satellite TV is helping to do the same elsewhere. Companies run European- or Asian-wide campaigns by using similar ads in a series of national markets. MTV, the New York-based video music network, is watched in nearly 100 countries and is tremendously popular in Europe, reaching almost 60 million households. The network synonymous with rock music is capitalizing on its hip image with young people by launching a clothing line in the United States, Europe, and Israel.

Music and sports are universal languages for teens. The hip-hop style in fashion and music was first popularized by African-Americans and is now popular among teens around the world. So is the grunge culture, which includes harsh, angst-ridden music and an outdoor, back-to-basics style of dress (torn jeans, flannel shirts, and hiking boots). Basketball is gaining in popularity in Europe as well as Asia, and Michael Jordan, Charles Barkley, and Shaquille O'Neal are popular product endorsers the world over for companies like Nike, McDonald's, Pepsi, and Reebok.

Some companies are developing new products for the global teen market. PepsiCo is attempting to gain ground in foreign markets with Pepsi Max, a sugar-free drink that it hopes will appeal to teens in Asian and European markets where diet soft drinks are not very popular. The new brand is being promoted with commercials aimed at those who like to live on the wild side, showing a quartet of thrill-seeking teens skydiving from Big Ben, rollerblading off the Sphinx, and surfing the dunes of the Sahara desert. The path to popularity for teenage girls in Japan and other countries is to have their pictures taken with friends by a Print Club machine (found in video arcades). The sheet of self-portrait stickers is then divided among the girls. SEGA Enterprises and Atlus, joint developers of Print Club, expect to sell 10,000 of the machines in Japan alone in 1997.

The advertising sales director of MTV Europe says, "An 18-year-old boy in France has more in common with another 18-year-old in Germany than he does his own parents. We consider them as one nation." To many marketers, teens are an important global market segment.

Sources: Laurel Wentz, "Japan: The Ultimate Buyer's Market," *Advertising Age International*, January 1997, p. I35; Juliana Koranteng, "MTV Europe Takes Turn on the Runway," *Advertising Age International*, March 1997, p. I14; Shawn Tully, "Teens: The Most Global Market of All," *Fortune*, May 16, 1994, pp. 90–97.

Global Products, Local Messages

While the pros and cons of global marketing and advertising continue to be debated, many companies are taking an in-between approach by standardizing their products and basic marketing strategy but localizing their advertising messages. This approach recognizes similar desires, goals, needs, and uses for products and services but tailors advertising to the local cultures and conditions in each market. Some agencies call this approach "Think globally, act locally." Grey Advertising describes it as "global vision with a local touch."[47]

Although some marketers use global ads with little or no modification, most companies adapt their messages to respond to differences in language, market conditions, and other factors. Many global marketers use a strategy called **pattern advertising**; their ads follow a basic approach, but themes, copy, and sometimes even visual elements are adapted to differences in local markets. For example, Unilever's Dove soap uses the same basic advertising and positioning theme globally, but models from Australia, France, Germany, and Italy are used to appeal to women in those countries. Continental Airlines uses pattern advertising to promote its BusinessFirst class of service in various countries. Exhibit 20–10 shows Continental ads used in Spain and France. You may recall that the U.S. version of this was discussed as a feature appeal in Chapter 9 (see Exhibit 9–2).

Another way global marketers adapt their campaigns to local markets is by producing a variety of ads with a similar theme and format and allowing managers in various countries or regions to select those messages they believe will work best in their markets. Seagram used this approach in a worldwide campaign for Chivas Regal scotch.[48] It tested four campaigns in seven countries and decided on the theme "There will always be a Chivas Regal." A series of ads using universal images and a Chivas crest was created and translated into 15 languages. Marketing executives in the 34 countries where the campaign was running could choose specific ads in the series.

Although many marketers are striving to develop global brands, research suggests most are doing so by using a localized approach. A study of international advertising strategies of successful U.S. multinational corporations found that only 9 percent used totally standardized global advertising for all foreign markets, while 37 percent used all localized advertising. The remaining 54 percent used a combination strategy, standardizing portions of their advertising but adapting it for local markets.[49] Marketers said a major risk of the global approach was a lack of communication owing to cultural differences. Another study found that most U.S. consumer durable goods manufacturers used a localized advertising approach—but most used some standardized messages.[50]

A more recent study of international advertising decision makers sponsored by *Advertising Age International* found that "think globally, act locally" still appears to be the dominant strategy of international advertisers, but with a slight revision: "Think globally, act regionally."[51] Most of the respondents in this survey said their companies' worldwide headquarters play a dominant role in determining their international advertising messages so they are consistent worldwide. However, there is a trend toward giving regional offices the autonomy to adapt the global theme for their local markets.

Most managers believe it is important to adapt components of their advertising messages—such as the language, models, scenic backgrounds, message content, and symbols—to reflect the culture and frame of reference of consumers in various countries. Many companies are making these tactical adjustments to their advertising messages while still

EXHIBIT 20–10
Continental Airlines uses pattern advertising to promote its BusinessFirst class in various countries

pursuing global strategies that will help them project a consistent global image and turn their products and services into global brands.

DECISION AREAS IN INTERNATIONAL ADVERTISING

Companies developing advertising and promotional programs for international markets must make certain organizational and functional decisions similar to those for domestic markets. These decisions include organization style, agency selection, advertising research, creative strategy and execution, and media strategy and selection.

Organizing for International Advertising

One of the first decisions a company must make when it decides to market its products to other countries is how to organize the international advertising and promotion function. This decision is likely to depend on how the company is organized overall for international marketing and business. Three basic options are centralization at the home office or headquarters, decentralization of decision making to local foreign markets, or a combination of the two.

CENTRALIZATION

Many companies prefer to *centralize* the international advertising and promotion function so that all decisions about agency selection, research, creative strategy and campaign development, media strategy, and budgeting are made at the firm's home office.

Complete centralization is likely when market and media conditions are similar from one country to another, when the company has only one or a few international agencies handling all of its advertising, when the company can use standardized advertising, or when it desires a consistent image worldwide. Centralization may also be best when a company's international business is small and it operates through foreign distributors or licensees who do not become involved in the marketing and promotional process.

Many companies prefer the centralized organizational structure to protect their foreign investments and keep control of the marketing effort and corporate and/or brand image. Centralization can save money, since it reduces the need for staff and administration at the local subsidiary level. As the trend toward globalized marketing and advertising strategies continues, more companies are likely to move more toward centralization of the advertising function to maintain a unified world brand image rather than presenting a different image in each market. Some foreign managers may actually prefer centralized decision making, as it removes them from the burden of advertising and promotional decisions and saves them from defending local decisions to the home office.

However, many marketing and advertising managers in foreign markets oppose centralized control. They say the structure is too rigid and makes it difficult to adapt the advertising and promotional program to local needs and market conditions. As noted earlier, Parker Pen encountered such resistance when it attempted to implement a global advertising strategy.

DECENTRALIZATION

Under a *decentralized* organizational structure, marketing and advertising managers in each market have the authority to make their own advertising and promotional decisions. Local managers can select ad agencies, develop budgets, conduct research, approve creative themes and executions, and select advertising media. Companies using a decentralized approach put a great deal of faith in the judgment and decision-making ability of personnel in local markets. This approach is often used when companies believe local managers know the marketing situation in their countries the best. They may also be more effective and motivated when given responsibility for the advertising and promotional program in their markets. Decentralization also works well in small or unique markets where headquarters' involvement is not worthwhile or advertising must be tailored to the local market.

International fragrance marketer Chanel, Inc., uses a decentralized strategy. Chanel found that many of its fragrance concepts do not work well globally and decided to localize advertising. For example, the U.S. office has the option of using ads created by the House of Chanel in Paris or developing its own campaigns for the U.S. market. Chanel executives in the United States think that the French concept of prestige is not the same as Americans' and the artsy ads created in France do not work well in this country.[52]

Another company that uses a decentralized structure with multiple advertising agencies is Compaq Computer. When Compaq began its first global advertising campaign in 1996, it decided to have the agencies representing its two biggest regions—North America and Europe—develop distinct brand campaigns.[53] Compaq then gave the two agencies' work to managers in the other regions to test and decide which campaign they wanted to run.

COMBINATION

While there is an increasing trend toward centralizing the international advertising function, many companies combine the two approaches. The home office, or headquarters, has the most control over advertising policy, guidelines, and operations in all markets. The international advertising manager works closely with local or regional marketing managers and personnel from the international agency (or agencies) and sets advertising and promotional objectives, has budgetary authority, approves all creative themes and executions, and approves media selection decisions, especially when they are made on a regional basis or overlap with other markets.

Advertising managers in regional or local offices submit advertising plans and budgets for their markets, which are reviewed by the international advertising manager. Local managers play a major role in working with the agency to adapt appeals to their particular markets and select media.

The combination approach allows for consistency in a company's international advertising yet permits local input and adaptation of the promotion program. Most consumer product companies find that local adaptation of advertising is necessary for foreign markets or regions, but they want to maintain control of the overall worldwide image they project. Eastman Kodak, for example, provides central strategy and support to local offices and acts as consultant to them. Although each country is autonomous, the main office controls the quality of advertising and advertising policy. Media buying is done on a local level, but the main office becomes involved in special media opportunities and overall strategy for events such as Olympic sponsorship and regionalized campaigns. Global Perspective 20–3 discusses how Levi Strauss & Co. has recently restructured its international marketing efforts to use the combination approach. Levi's created a centralized vice president of global marketing position to oversee the company's marketing in over 60 countries but still provides a great deal of autonomy to regional marketing directors.

Agency Selection

One of the most important decisions for a firm engaged in international marketing is the choice of an advertising agency. The company has three basic alternatives in selecting an agency to handle its international advertising. First, it can choose a major agency with both domestic and overseas offices. Many large agencies have offices all over the world and have become truly international operations. Some Western agencies have opened offices in Eastern Europe and Russia to create ads for the multinational companies participating in the free-market economies that are developing in these countries. (Exhibit 20–11).[54]

Many American companies prefer to use a U.S.-based agency with foreign offices; this gives them greater control and convenience and also facilitates coordination of overseas advertising. For example, one of the reasons Colgate consolidated all of its worldwide advertising with Young & Rubicam was the unique fit with Y&R's worldwide agency network.[55] Young & Rubicam is one of the few U.S. agencies that owns agencies in virtually every country where they operate. Companies often use the same agency to handle international and domestic advertising. As discussed in Chapter 3, the flurry of mergers and acquisitions in the ad agency business in recent years, both in the United States and in other countries, has created large global agencies that can meet the international needs of global marketers. As the opening vignette discussed, a number of multinational companies are consolidating their advertising with one large agency.

A second alternative for the international marketer is to choose a domestic agency that, rather than having its own foreign offices or branches, is affiliated with agencies in other countries or belongs to a network of foreign agencies. An agency may acquire an interest in

Global Perspective 20–3
Levi Strauss Begins to Think Globally

To most people, Levi Strauss & Co. (LS&CO.) seems as all-American as the California gold rush that spawned its rugged-looking blue denims. In fact, LS&CO. has become a global company whose goal is to lead apparel markets around the world. The company began selling outside the U.S. in the 1950s but did not become ambitious in its overseas efforts until the 1970s. Today, however, LS&CO. is the world's largest apparel company, with half of its $7.1 billion in revenue coming from international sales. The company is the market leader in the United States, Europe, and many Far East markets.

Levi Strauss & Co. is taking steps maintain its worldwide leadership position and enhance its global image. In January 1996 the company hired Robert Holloway as its first vice president of global marketing. Holloway and his team are transforming LS&CO.'s culture by transporting ads and product ideas across borders, building websites, reviewing its worldwide media mix, appointing hot new agencies, and launching a global brand equity measurement system.

As part of its makeover, LS&CO. has replaced its international division with three divisions: the Americas, Europe, and Asia. Previously, each of the company's four regional marketing directors (for Asia, Europe, Latin America, and the U.S.) developed their own advertising and marketing strategies with little thought about exporting their ideas elsewhere. The result was a "think locally, act locally" approach to international marketing. Now Holloway is moving the company toward a "think globally, act locally" approach with campaigns that carry a unified message, but whose look mirror their individual markets. He says global marketing brings very powerful benefits to the brand and is also important to the bottom line, since global images can be more cost efficient than local ones. Using the same campaign in multiple markets saves production costs of $100,000 to $1 million for a 30-second commercial. However LS&CO. is careful not to let costs drive its communication decisions.

Holloway has already begun moving successful local Levi's ads across borders and turning them into global campaigns. The most prominent example is the Claymation commercial that Bartle Bogle Hegarty of London (BBH) developed for European markets and was used in Asia, Latin America, and the U.S. The animated spot features a character called Nick Clayman, who rescues a woman from a burning building by taking off his Levi's® 501® jeans and using the strong, durable jeans to parachute through an adjacent building's window to a bathroom where the two bump into an elderly man sitting on the toilet. The agency's chair and creative director notes: "We want to talk to people on a global scale with ads that are distinct, not bland. We want the ads to be relevant whether you are in Idaho or China. I think we are good at producing nonverbal global narrative that can travel around the world."

The campaign developed by BBH has helped Levi's® 501® jeans record double-digit sales growth in Europe.

The brand outsells rivals Lee and Wrangler, even though its $70-plus price is 10–15% higher than the nearest competitor's. LS&CO. recently moved its Dockers® European account to BBH as well as its Levi Strauss Asia/Pacific advertising. However, Holloway downplays any notion that Levi's ultimately wants to use fewer agencies or perhaps consolidate all of its global advertising with BBH. He says, "We want the local managers to select their own ad agencies with no pressure from me. How can I possibly know all the local markets?" In Asia, several local and regional agencies handle LS&CO.'s marketing, while BBH works at a regional level developing the TV spots. Latin America is on a fast-track development and imports work from around the globe that is most relevant. LS&CO. is in the process of making agency appointments a local decision there.

As part of its global transformation, Levi Strauss & Co. is also examining its worldwide media mix, 75% of which goes to television. It plans on spending fewer TV ad dollars in mature markets (where TV is losing share) and allocating more in emerging markets, where the medium is most efficient. Holloway has also hired a digital media director to oversee LS&CO. websites that feature everything from the history of the brand to fashion, tips, games, and youth trends. They plan on keeping the websites regularly updated and relevant for consumers. Holloway sees the Internet as a key component of LS&CO.'s media mix in the future, and more spending is also on the way as reaction to the current sites has surpassed the company's expectations.

To leverage LS&CO.'s global presence, Holloway leads a global marketing council and has begun holding forums where the company's top marketers address strategic issues. It appears the old approach of "think locally, act locally" has given way to global thinking at Levi Strauss & Co.

Sources: Rebecca A. Fannin, "Levi's Global Guru Shakes Up Culture," *Advertising Age International*, November 1996, pp. I20, I23; Juliana Koranteng, "Dockers Tailors Retail Agenda for European Growth," *Advertising Age*, September 16, 1996, p. 17.

EXHIBIT 20—11   Agencies are creating ads for clients targeting the expanding economies in Russia and Eastern Europe

several foreign agencies or become part of an organization of international agencies. The agency can then sell itself as an international agency offering multinational coverage and contacts. For example, many U.S. agencies are expanding into Latin America by forming associations with regional agencies and acquiring partial or full ownership of agencies in various countries. Leo Burnett has majority stakes in agencies in 11 Latin American countries and minority ownership or associations in seven others.[56]

The advantage of this arrangement is that the client can use a domestic-based agency yet still have access to foreign agencies with detailed knowledge of market conditions, media, and so on in each local market. There may be problems with this approach, however. The local agency may have trouble coordinating and controlling independent agencies, and the quality of work may vary among network members. Companies considering this option must ask the local agency about its ability to control the activities of its affiliates and the quality of their work in specific areas such as creative and media.

The third alternative for the international marketer is to select a local agency for each national market in which it sells its products or services. Since local agencies often have the best understanding of the marketing and advertising environment in their country or region, they may be able to develop the most effective advertising.

Some companies like local agencies because they may provide the best talent in each market. In many countries, smaller agencies may, because of their independence, be more willing to take risks and develop the most effective, creative ads. Choosing local agencies also increases the involvement and morale of foreign subsidiary managers by giving them responsibility for managing the promotion function in their markets. Some companies have the subsidiary choose a local agency, since it is often in the best position to evaluate the agency and will work closely with it.

CRITERIA FOR AGENCY SELECTION

The selection of an agency to handle a company's international advertising depends on how the firm is organized for international marketing and the type of assistance it needs to meet its goals and objectives in foreign markets. Figure 20–4 lists some criteria a company might use in selecting an agency.

FIGURE 20–4
Criteria for selecting an agency to handle international advertising

- Ability of agency to cover relevant markets
- Quality of agency work
- Market research, public relations, and other services offered by agency
- Relative roles of company advertising department and agency
- Level of communication and control desired by company
- Ability of agency to coordinate international campaign
- Size of company's international business
- Company's desire for local versus international image
- Company organizational structure for international business and marketing (centralized versus decentralized)
- Company's level of involvement with international operations

Some companies choose a combination of the three alternatives just discussed because their involvement in each market differs, as do the advertising environment and situation in each country. Several experts in international marketing and advertising advocate the use of international agencies by international companies, particularly those firms moving toward global marketing and striving for a consistent corporate or brand image around the world.[57] The trend toward mergers and acquisitions and the formation of mega-agencies with global marketing and advertising capabilities suggests the international agency approach will become the preferred arrangement among large companies.

Advertising Research

Research plays the same important role in the development of international advertising and promotion programs that it does domestically—helping managers make better, more informed decisions. However, many companies do not conduct advertising research in international markets. Probably the main reason for this is the high cost of conducting research in foreign markets, coupled with the limited budgets many firms have for international advertising and promotion. When international markets represent a small percentage of overall sales, investments in research are difficult to justify. Rather than quality marketing information, generalizations based on casual observations of foreign markets have guided the promotional process.

As companies increase their investment in international marketing, they are recognizing the importance of conducting marketing and advertising research to better understand the characteristics and subtleties of consumers in foreign markets. There are a number of areas where research on foreign markets can help firms make better advertising decisions.

- Information on demographic characteristics of markets.
- Information on cultural differences such as norms, lifestyles, and values.
- Information on consumers' product usage, brand attitudes, and media preferences.
- Information on media usage and audience size.
- Copy testing to determine reactions to different types of advertising appeals and executions.
- Research on the effectiveness of advertising and promotional programs in foreign markets.

A great deal of information on international markets is available through secondary sources. One of the most valuable sources of information for companies based in this country is the U.S. Department of Commerce, which works closely with American companies to help them sell their products overseas through its International Trade Administration (ITA) division. The ITA publishes a series of *Overseas Business Reports* that provide valuable information on most major world markets, including economic and marketing data as well as laws and regulations. Information on markets is sometimes available from other countries' government agencies, embassies, or consulates.

The *United Nations Statistical Yearbook*, which is published annually, provides demographic and economic data on more than 200 countries. Yearbooks and other reports are also available for regions such as Latin America, Europe, and Asia. Other international organiza-

ROBERT HOLLOWAY

When Robert Holloway entered college at Wolverhampton University in England, he had no interest in a career in business. However, after taking a retailing course from a particularly inspiring professor he found himself turned on by marketing. He graduated from Wolverhampton with a major in business with a specialization in marketing. After teaching for a year and traveling around the world, Holloway accepted a marketing position with Levi Strauss & Co. (LS&CO.) in London. He thought it would be interesting to work for a few

years for a well-known American company that was making one of the most popular brands in the world. Fifteen years later, he is the vice president of global marketing for LS&CO. and is leading the development of global strategies for the world's largest apparel company.

Robert began his career with LS&CO. in 1982 as a marketing assistant in the youth wear division. He was promoted to a product manager trainee and moved quickly through the product management ranks, becoming the senior product manager for the United Kingdom and then for Brussels. In 1991 he was promoted to a position as the European marketing manager and three years later became the director of marketing for Europe. In 1996 he was transferred from Brussels to LS&CO.'s San Francisco headquarters as the company's first vice president of global marketing.

As VP-global marketing, Robert Holloway supports LS&CO.'s marketing in 60 countries and works with regional marketing vice presidents for the company's three divisions—the Americas, Europe, and Asia/Pacific. He and his global marketing team are responsible for leading the development of global initiatives and strategies for LS&CO. and its powerful brand franchises such as Levis® and Dockers®. They are helping the company leverage effective advertising and marketing strategies developed in local markets by exporting these ideas. Holloway notes, "What we are doing is transferring best practices from local marketing to global markets. We're trying to eliminate the 'not invented here' syndrome and bringing a different perspective to the individual and local businesses that previously didn't exist at Levi Strauss & Co."

"What we are doing is transferring best practices from local markets to global markets."

Holloway passionately believes in the strength of global marketing, noting it not only brings very powerful benefits to the brand but is important to the bottom line. However, he is quick to point out the dangers of becoming obsessed with globalization and ignoring the differences in regional and local markets. He feels that many companies try to globalize too quickly and often ignore differences in culture and economic development for various markets as well as the experience, knowledge, and morale of local managers. Holloway notes there are still major differences in the way consumers in different countries respond to marketing communications and says, "companies that ignore local culture do so at their own peril."

Robert Holloway feels one of the major challenges he faces is getting senior management to envision a future that will be very different and allow him and his global marketing team to develop strategies to compete effectively in the rapidly changing markets. He feels that the rapid growth of the Internet in particular will have a major impact as it is making consumers better informed and more powerful.

As part of his mission to globalize Levi Strauss & Co.'s marketing efforts, Holloway has begun forums where the company's marketing managers from around the world can exchange marketing and product ideas. He has also initiated benchmarking sessions with marketing counterparts from companies outside the apparel industry to seek out ideas for product development, marketing research, and advertising in global markets.

Robert Holloway is recognized as a visionary who is helping transform Levi Strauss & Co. into a truly global company. It's been quite a successful career thus far for someone who had no interest in business.

EXHIBIT 20–12
NCH Promotional Services is a
source of information on coupon
distribution and use in various
countries

tions that can provide valuable information on world markets include the International Monetary Fund and regional organizations like the Japanese External Trade Organization and the European Community.

Information on product and brand attitudes, usage patterns, and media habits is generally more difficult to find, particularly in developing countries. However, more information is becoming available. A. C. Nielsen has developed an international database that tracks purchase patterns of over 2,000 product classes in 25 countries, and Predicast has a foreign intelligence syndicated service. NCH Promotional Services now collects information on coupon distribution and redemption patterns in the United States and a number of European countries (Exhibit 20–12). Data on media usage in European countries have increased tremendously over the past decade.[58] However, information on TV audiences is still lacking in many countries.

Much of the information advertisers need must be gathered from research generated by the company and/or ad agency. Consumer needs and wants, purchase motives, and usage patterns often vary from one country to another, and research is needed to understand these differences. Some companies and their agencies conduct psychographic research in foreign markets to determine activities, interests, and opinions as well as product usage patterns. A recent survey conducted by *Advertising Age International* and the research firm of Yankelovich, Clancy, Shulman looked at purchase habits and brand loyalty of consumers in the United Kingdom, France, and Germany. As Figure 20–5 shows, consumers in all three countries said value for their money was the most important factor in their purchase decisions and were very open to buying products from other countries. The survey also found that consumers in the United Kingdom are most loyal to a brand.[59]

A number of agencies and market research firms are now studying China to better understand what consumers in the world's most populous market want to buy. Global Perspective 20–4 discusses some of their findings.

Advertisers should also research consumers' reactions to the advertising appeal and execution style they plan to use in foreign markets. One agency researcher recommends testing the basic premise and/or selling idea to be used in a global campaign first to be sure it is relevant to the target audiences in the markets where it will appear.[60]

Creative Decisions

Another decision facing the international advertiser is determining the appropriate advertising messages for each market. Creative strategy development for international advertising is basically similar in process and procedure to that for domestic advertising. Advertising and communications objectives should be based on the marketing strategy and market conditions in foreign markets. Major selling ideas must be developed and specific appeals and execution styles chosen.

FIGURE 20–5 Importance of purchase criteria in the United Kingdom, France, and Germany

Value Tops Purchase Priorities

"Which of the following do you think is the single most important consideration when considering the purchase of a product?"

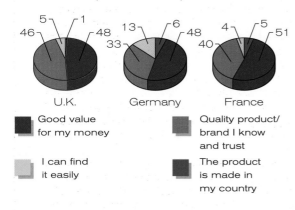

■ Good value for my money

■ I can find it easily

■ Quality product/ brand I know and trust

■ The product is made in my country

Germans Indifferent to Well-Known Brands

"How much does the fact that it is a known and trusted brand name influence your decision?"

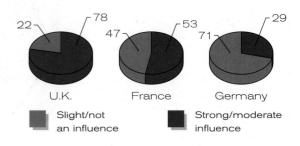

■ Slight/not an influence

■ Strong/moderate influence

Brits Pledge Brand Loyalty . . .

"Once I find a brand, it is very difficult to get me to change brands."

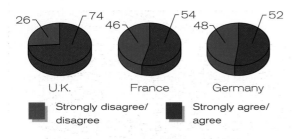

■ Strongly disagree/ disagree

■ Strongly agree/ agree

. . . but Are Blind to Brand Differences

"There is usually not much difference between competing brands. They are all about the same."

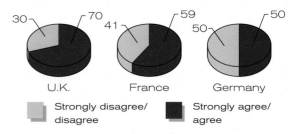

■ Strongly disagree/ disagree

■ Strongly agree/ agree

An important factor in the development of creative strategy is the issue of global versus localized advertising. If the standardized approach is taken, the creative team must develop advertising that will transcend cultural differences and communicate effectively in every country. For example, Tropicana Products Inc. uses a global advertising campaign for its pure premium orange juice. Its ads, though tailored a bit for each market, stress the superior, nearly fresh-squeezed taste of its juice over local brands that are often reconstituted from concentrates.[61]

When companies follow a **localized advertising strategy**, the creative team must determine what type of selling idea, ad appeal, and execution style will work in each market. A product may have to be positioned differently in each market depending on consumers' usage patterns and habits. For example, General Foods found that in France, people drink very little orange juice and almost none at breakfast. Thus, when the company decided to market its Tang instant breakfast drink in France, the agency developed ads positioning the brand as a refreshment for any time of day rather than as a substitute for orange juice (the approach used in the United States).[62]

Marketers must also figure out what type of advertising appeal or execution style will be most effective in each market. Emotional appeals such as humor may work well in one country but not in another because of differences in cultural backgrounds and consumer perceptions of what is or is not funny. While humorous appeals are popular in the United States and Britain, they are not used often in Germany, where consumers do not respond favorably to them.

France, Italy, and Brazil are more receptive to sexual appeals and nudity in advertising than are most other societies. Grey Advertising found that an ad it developed for Camay

Global Perspective 20–4
What Do a Half Billion Chinese Consumers Want to Buy?

For many years marketers could only dream of selling their products to China's more than 1 billion consumers. But with the end of the cultural revolution in 1979 and its massive modernization drive over the past two decades, China has become one of the fastest-growing consumer markets in the world. A number of multinational companies—including Coca-Cola, Procter & Gamble, Kodak, Unilever, Gillette, Kellogg, and Nike—are marketing their products to the world's largest potential mass market. However, the marketing and advertising industry is still working to answer one of the world's highest-stakes questions: What does China's massive consumer market want to buy?

Studying China's shopping and consumption habits has become a boom industry, attracting some of Madison Avenue's global giants. Grey Advertising, along with Nielsen SRG China, recently fielded a small army of pollsters to sample consumer attitudes on everything from price sensitivity to the most popular computer brands. Leo Burnett tracks Chinese consumers with bimonthly surveys in six cities, while the Gallup Organization in Beijing recently conducted the largest of all the China surveys, covering every province except Tibet.

China's middle class is just under 10 percent of the population and represents more than 100 million people. The composite portrait presented by these surveys shows China's middle-class consumer households earning about $225 a month, with most of it disposable, since housing, transportation, and medical care are usually benefits that come with a job. Nearly everyone in the middle class watches television, but the viewers aren't jaded by advertising because the commercials are more interesting than the TV programming they sponsor. In fact, the surveys find that Chinese consumer trust in advertising is among the highest anywhere in the world.

Leo Burnett is using its research results to help clients like Kellogg and McDonald's adapt their advertising and marketing positioning to speak to Chinese consumers. For instance, in a commercial for McDonald's, a grandfather uses chopsticks to sample french fries for the first time as his family looks on. Leo Burnett's worldwide head of planning says, "The commercial creates a bond with the Chi-

nese because it shows respect for the elderly, and it also shows the family eating together—both of which have an impact."

The agency also used the research results to market a new brand called Wheat Flakes to the southern areas of China with a campaign touting the cereal's nutritional benefits, including a recommendation by the Chinese Institute of Nutrition. The positioning was designed to speak to Chinese mothers who desire to make their children strong and healthy. This message works well in China, where families are limited to one child. The family revolves around the child, who represents an insurance policy that parents will be taken care of in their old age. The child also ensures that the family line will continue, which is crucial to the Chinese culture.

Marketers still face many challenges in marketing and advertising their products in China—such as choosing media in a country that has about 700 TV stations, 900 newspapers, and 7,000 magazines with provincial or national coverage. There is also a multitiered rate structure that is discriminatory toward foreign companies. However, despite these limitations, many marketers are anxious to advertise to the nearly 400 million Chinese who now have purchasing power.

Sources: Rebecca A. Fannin, "Burnett Tracks Shifts in Norms Shaping China," *Advertising Age International*, March 1997, p. I32; Craig Smith, "China's Huge Consumer Potential Prompts Industry Survey Boom," *The Wall Street Journal*, March 20, 1996, p. B8; and Michael Laris, "China: The World's Most Populous Market," *Advertising Age*, May 15, 1996, p. I11.

soap in the United States, which featured a man touching a woman's skin while she bathed, would be a disaster in Japan. Even the idea of a man being in the bathroom with a female is considered taboo there.[63]

International marketers sometimes find they can change consumer purchasing patterns by taking a creative risk. For example, Häagen-Dazs broke through cultural barriers in Britain, where ice cream consumption is only a third as great as in the United States and consumers usually purchase low-grade, low-priced local brands. A sexy advertising campaign showing seminude couples feeding each other the ice cream helped get British con-

It is the

intense

flavour of
the finest ingredients
combined with

fresh

cream that is
essentially Häagen-Dazs

Häagen-Dazs

FRESH CREAM ICE CREAM
Dedicated to Pleasure

sumers to pay premium prices for Häagen-Dazs. The company also used an avant-garde billboard campaign in Japan showing a young couple kissing in public, a near-taboo. The posters were so popular that many were stolen.[64]

Media Selection

One of the most difficult decision areas for the international advertiser is media strategy and selection. U.S. firms generally find major differences in the media outside the United States, and media conditions may vary considerably from one area to another, particularly in developing countries. Media planners face a number of problems in attempting to communicate advertising messages to consumers in foreign countries.

First, the types of media available are different in different countries. Many homes in developing countries do not have TV sets. For example, in many South and Central African nations (such as Uganda, Tanzania, Kenya, and Zimbabwe), radio is the dominant medium and access to TV sets is very limited.[65]

In some countries, TV advertising is not accepted or the amount of commercial time is severely limited. For example, in Germany, TV advertising is limited to 20 minutes a day on each of the government-owned channels (four 5-minute breaks) and banned on Sundays and holidays. Germany's two privately owned television stations, however, are permitted to devote up to 20 percent of their air time to commercials. In the Netherlands, TV spots are limited to 5 percent of air time and must be booked up to a year in advance. Programs also do not have fixed time slots for ads, making it impossible to plan commercial buys around desired programs.

The number of TV sets is increasing tremendously, but there is still controversy over TV advertising. In India, for example, commercials are restricted to only 10 percent of programming time and must appear at the beginning or end of a program.[66] Australia just recently lifted a ban on cable TV advertising. However, some cable channels won't accept any advertising and some media directors predict that Australian consumers will not tolerate as much advertising on cable channels as on free TV networks.[67]

The characteristics of media differ from country to country in terms of coverage, cost, quality of reproduction, restrictions, and the like. In some countries, media rates are negotiable or may fluctuate owing to unstable currencies, economic conditions, or government regulations. For example, in China TV stations charge a local rate for Chinese advertisers, a foreign rate, and a joint venture rate.[68]

Another problem international advertisers face is obtaining reliable media information such as circulation figures, audience profiles, and costs. Many countries that had only state-owned TV channels are now experiencing a rapid growth in commercial channels, which is providing more market segmentation opportunities. However, reliable audience measurement data are not available and media buyers often rely on their instincts when purchasing TV time. A number of research companies are developing audience measurement systems for countries in Eastern Europe, Russia, and China.[69] International advertising and television trade groups are also working to develop standardized measurement principles for global TV advertising.[70]

The goal of international advertisers is to select media vehicles that reach their target audience most effectively and efficiently. Media selection is often localized even for a centrally planned, globalized campaign. Local agencies or media buyers generally have more knowledge of local media and better opportunities to negotiate rates, and subsidiary operations can maintain control and adapt to media conditions and options in their market. Media planners have two options: using national or local media or using international media.

LOCAL MEDIA

Many advertisers choose the local media of a country to reach its consumers. Print is the most used medium worldwide, since TV commercial time and the number of homes with TV sets are limited in many countries. Many countries have magazines that are circulated nationwide as well as national or regional newspapers that carry advertising directed to a national audience. Most countries also have magazines that appeal to special interests or activities, allowing for targeting in media selection.

Although restrictions and regulations have limited the development of TV as a dominant advertising medium in many countries, it is a primary medium for obtaining nationwide coverage in most developed countries and offers tremendous creative opportunities. Restrictions on television may be lessening in some countries, and time availability may increase. For example, the number of TV stations and television advertising in Italy have exploded in the past decade since government restrictions against private broadcasting were lifted.[71] Advertising groups are using economic, legal, and political pressure to get more television commercial time from reluctant European governments. The increase in TV channels through direct broadcasting by satellite to many European households (discussed later in this section) is hastening this process.

In addition to print and television, local media available to advertisers include radio, direct mail, billboards, cinema, and transit advertising. These media give international advertisers great flexibility and the opportunity to reach specific market segments and local markets within a country. Most international advertisers rely heavily on national and local media in their media plans for foreign markets.

INTERNATIONAL MEDIA

The other way for the international advertiser to reach audiences in various countries is through international media that have multimarket coverage. The primary focus of international media has traditionally been magazines and newspapers. A number of U.S.-based consumer-oriented publications have international editions, including *Time, Newsweek, Reader's Digest*, and *National Geographic* as well as the newspaper *USA Today*. *Cosmopolitan* publishes 29 international editions that reach over 30 million readers in various countries (Exhibit 20–13). U.S.-based business publications with foreign editions include *Business Week, Fortune, Harvard Business Review*, and *The Wall Street Journal*.

International publications offer advertisers a way to reach large audiences on a regional or worldwide basis. Readers of these publications are usually upscale, high-income individuals who are desirable target markets for many products and services. There are, however, several problems with these international media that can limit their attractiveness to many advertisers. Their reach in any one foreign country may be low, particularly for specific segments of a market. Also, while they deliver desirable audiences to companies selling business or upscale consumer products and services, they do not cover the mass consumer markets or specialized market segments very well. Other U.S.-based publications in foreign markets do offer advertisers ways to reach specific market segments.

While print remains the dominant medium for international advertising, many companies are turning their attention to international commercial TV. Package-goods companies in particular, such as Gillette, McDonald's, Pepsi, and Coca-Cola, view TV advertising as the best way to reach mass markets and effectively communicate their advertising messages. Satellite technology has helped spread the growth of cable TV in other countries and made global television networks a reality.

A major development affecting broadcasting in Europe, Asia, and Latin America is **direct broadcast by satellite (DBS)** to homes and communities equipped with small, low-cost receiving dishes. A number of satellite networks operate in these regions and beam entertainment programming across several countries. For example, media baron Rupert

Murdoch's News Corp. owns 40 percent of British Sky Broadcasting (BSkyB), which was formed by the merger of Sky Television and British Satellite Broadcasting and beams 40 channels to 6 million subscribers in the United Kingdom. In 1993 News Corp. purchased Satellite Television Asian Region (STAR TV), which beams 15 advertising-supported channels and nine subscription movie channels to over 60 million Asian households, hotels, and restaurants equipped with satellite dishes. STAR TV has a potential market of 3 billion people (two-thirds of the world's population) as satellite dishes become more common in this region.[72] In 1996 News Corp. launched Sky Entertainment in Brazil and Mexico and expects to have nearly 5 million subscribers by the end of the decade in Brazil alone.[73]

The main incentive to the growth of these satellite networks has been the severely limited program choices and advertising opportunities on government-controlled stations in many countries. However, many European and Asian governments are moving to preserve cultural values and protect advertising revenues from going to foreign-based networks. In India, for example, advertising revenue has been shifting to ISkyB, a subsidiary of STAR TV, from Doordarshan, the state-run television network.[74] The Indian government is considering legislation that would regulate foreign satellite channels and advertisers and favor the Doordarshan. India's minister for information and broadcasting says foreign satellite channels are a threat to India's cultural fabric and should be curbed. He cites offensive program content and the amount of nudity on foreign channels as reasons why the Indian government needs to regulate satellite channels.

Advances in satellite and communications technology, the expansion of multinational companies with global marketing perspectives, and the development of global ad agencies mean advertisers' use of television as a global medium is likely to increase.

THE ROLES OF OTHER PROMOTIONAL MIX ELEMENTS IN INTERNATIONAL MARKETING

This chapter has focused on advertising, since it is usually the primary element in the promotional mix of the international marketer. However, as in domestic marketing, promotional programs for foreign markets generally include such other elements as sales promotion, personal selling, public relations, and websites on the Internet. The roles of these other promotional mix elements vary depending on the firm's marketing and promotional strategy in foreign markets.

Sales promotion and public relations can support and enhance advertising efforts; the latter may also be used to create or maintain favorable images for companies in foreign markets. For some firms, personal selling may be the most important promotional element and advertising may play a support role. This final section considers the roles of some of these other promotional mix elements in the international marketing program.

Sales Promotion

As we saw in Chapter 15, sales promotion is one of the fastest-growing areas of marketing in the United States. Companies increasingly rely on consumer- and trade-oriented sales promotion to help sell their products in foreign markets as well. Many of the promotional tools that are effective in the United States, such as free samples, premiums, event sponsorships, contests, coupons, and trade promotions, are also used in foreign markets. For example, Häagen-Dazs estimates it gave out more than 5 million free tastings of its ice cream as part of its successful strategy for entering the European market. Since taste is the major benefit of this premium product, sampling was an appropriate sales promotion tool for entering foreign markets.

A form of sales promotion that has become very popular in foreign markets is event sponsorship. Many companies sponsor sporting events, concerts, and other activities in foreign countries to promote their products and enhance corporate image. For example, Pepsi and Visa have sponsored worldwide concert tours for rock stars Michael Jackson, Elton John, and Tina Turner in numerous countries, and Coke set up a pan-European sponsorship department to oversee its music-related marketing efforts. Visa sponsors World Cup Cricket matches as part of its promotional strategy for introducing its credit card to India; MasterCard, Gillette, and Canon sponsor Asian soccer.[75]

Unlike advertising, which can be done on a global basis, sales promotions must be adapted to local markets. Kamran Kashani and John Quelch noted several important differences among countries that marketers must consider in developing a sales promotion program.[76] They include the stage of economic development, market maturity, consumer perceptions of promotional tools, trade structure, and legal restrictions and regulations.

• *Economic development.* In highly developed countries such as the United States, Canada, Japan, and Western European nations, marketers can choose from a wide range of promotional tools. But in developing countries they must be careful not to use promotional tools such as in- or on-package premiums that would increase the price of the product beyond the reach of most consumers. Free samples and demonstrations are widely used, effective promotional tools in developing countries. But coupons, which are so popular with consumers in the United States, are rarely used because of problems with distribution and resistance from retailers. In the United States and Britain, most coupons are distributed through newspapers (including FSIs) or magazines. Low literacy rates in some countries make print media an ineffective coupon distribution method, so coupons are delivered door to door, handed out in stores, or placed in or on packages. Figure 20–6 shows the total number of coupons redeemed in various countries in 1995.

• *Market maturity.* Marketers must also consider the stage of market development for their product or service in various countries when they design sales promotions. To introduce a product to a country, consumer-oriented promotional tools such as sampling, high-value coupons, and cross-promotions with established products and brands are often effective. The competitive dynamics of a foreign market are also often a function of its stage of development. More competition is likely in well-developed mature markets, which will influence the types of sales promotion tools used. For example, there may be competitive pressure to use trade allowances to maintain distribution or consumer pro-

FIGURE 20–6
Number of coupons redeemed in
various countries

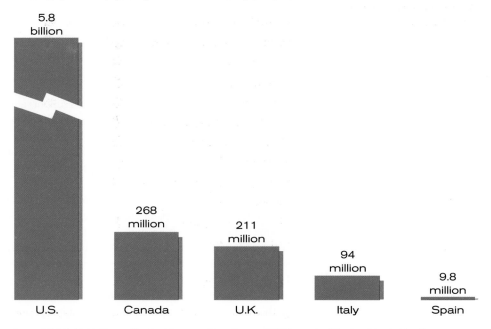

Number of Coupons Redeemed in Various Countries in 1995

Source: 1996 Worldwide Coupon Trends of Consumer Usage Patterns, NHC Promotional Services, Lincolnshire, IL.

motions that will maintain customer loyalty, such as bonus packs, price-off deals, or coupons.

• *Consumer perceptions.* An important consideration in the design of sales promotion programs is how they are perceived by consumers as well as the trade. Consumer perceptions of various sales promotion tools vary from market to market. For example, Japanese women are less likely to take advantage of contests, coupons, or other promotions than are women in the United States.[77] Premium offers in particular must be adapted to the tastes of consumers in various markets.

• *Trade structure.* In areas with highly concentrated retailing systems, such as northern Europe, the trade situation is becoming much like the United States and Canada as pressure grows for more price-oriented trade and in-store promotions. In southern Europe, the retail industry is highly fragmented and there is less trade pressure for promotions. The willingness and ability of channel members to accommodate sales promotion programs must also be considered. Retailers in many countries do not want to take time to process coupons, post promotional displays, or deal with premiums or packaging that require special handling or storage. In countries like Japan or India, where retailing structures are highly fragmented, stores are too small for point-of-purchase displays or in-store sampling.

• *Regulations.* An important factor affecting the use of sales promotions in foreign countries is the presence of legal restrictions and regulations. Laws affecting sales promotions are generally more restrictive in other countries than in the United States. Some countries ban contests, games, or lotteries, while others restrict the size or amount of a sample, premium, or prize. For example, fair-trade regulations in Japan limit the maximum value of premiums to 10 percent of the retail price; in France the limit is 5 percent. In some countries, a free premium must be related to the nature of the product purchased. Many countries have strict rules when it comes to premium offers for children, and some ban them altogether. Figure 20–7 shows how restrictions on promotions vary among five European countries.

Variations in rules and regulations mean marketers must often develop separate consumer sales promotion programs for each country. Many companies have found it difficult to do any promotions throughout Europe because sales promotion rules differ so from one country to another. While the treaty on European Union may result in a more

FIGURE 20–7
Which European countries allow which promotions?

Promotion	U.K.	Spain	Germany	France	Italy
In-pack premiums	●	●	⬤	△	●
Multiple-purchase offers	●	●	△	●	●
Extra product	●	●	△	●	●
Free product	●	●	●	●	●
Mail-in offers	●	●	●	●	●
Purchase-with-purchase	●	●	●	●	●
Cross-promotions	●	●	⬤	●	●
Contests	●	●	△	●	●
Self-liquidating premiums	●	●	●	●	●
Sweepstakes	△	△	●	△	△
Money-off coupons	●	●	●	●	△
Next-purchase coupons	●	●	●	●	△
Cash rebates	●	●	△	●	⬤
In-store demos	●	●	●	●	●

● Permitted   ⬤ Not permitted   △ May be permitted

standardized legal environment in Europe, laws regarding sales promotion are still likely to vary. This is why many companies use local agencies or international sales promotion companies to develop sales promotion programs for foreign markets.

MANAGEMENT OF SALES PROMOTION IN FOREIGN MARKETS

Although sales promotion programs of multinational companies have traditionally been managed locally, this is changing somewhat as marketers create global brands. Many global marketers recognize the importance of giving local managers the autonomy to design and execute their own sales promotion programs. However, the ways local promotions influence and contribute to global brand equity must also be considered.

Kashani and Quelch developed a framework for analyzing the role of centralized (head-quarters) versus local management in sales promotion decisions based on various stages of globalization (Figure 20–8). This model suggests headquarters' influence will be greatest for global brands and least for local brands. Since global brands require uniformity in marketing communications, the promotional program should be determined at the headquarters level.

FIGURE 20–8
Central versus local roles in international sales promotion

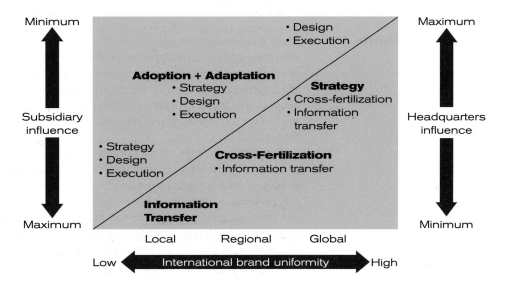

Decisions regarding overall promotional strategy—including international communications objectives, positioning, allocation of the communications budget to sales promotion versus advertising, and weight of consumer versus trade promotions—are made at the headquarters level.[78]

While the promotional strategy for global brands is determined by global product managers at headquarters, implementation of the programs should be left to local management. It is important to make the promotional strategy broad enough to allow for differences in diverse local markets. Headquarters is also responsible for encouraging the cross-fertilization of ideas and practices among local managers and facilitating the transfer of information.

Regional brands usually do not require the same level of standardization as global brands, and the promotional strategy can be developed by regional offices and carried out at the local level. However, regional promotions should avoid contradictory brand communications and promotional activities that might upset local activities in nearby markets. The role of national-level brand managers is adoption and adaptation. They determine what promotional ideas to adopt from the region and adapt them to local conditions.

For local brands, decisions regarding promotional strategy, program design, and execution are left to local managers. Of course, local managers may benefit from information about the promotions used in other local markets.

Personal Selling

As a company's most direct contact with its customers in foreign markets, personal selling is an important part of the marketing and promotional process. Companies selling industrial and high-tech products generally rely heavily on personal selling as the primary method for communicating with their customers, internationally as well as domestically. Consumer products firms may also use personal selling to call on distributors, wholesalers, or major retailing operations in foreign markets. Due to low wages in many developing countries, some companies hire large sales staffs to perform missionary activities and support selling and advertising efforts. For example, Citibank launched its credit cards in many Asian countries using a multifaceted marketing program that included advertising, direct mail, and personal selling. The company found personal selling a very focused and cost-effective way to reach prospective credit-card applicants in countries such as India, Malaysia, and Thailand. Citibank captured 40 percent of Thailand's credit-card market, relying primarily on a sales force of 600 part-timers who were paid a fee for each applicant approved.[79]

Because it involves personal contact and communication, personal selling is generally even more culture bound than advertising. So most companies use sales reps from the host country and adapt personal selling activities and sales programs to each market. Management of the sales force is usually decentralized to the local subsidiaries, although the international marketer sets the general sales policy and advises foreign managers on the role personal selling should play in their market, the development of the sales program, and various aspects of sales management.

Public Relations

Many companies involved in international marketing are recognizing the importance of using public relations to support and enhance their marketing and advertising efforts.[80] Public relations activities are needed to deal with local governments, media, trade associations, and the general public, any of which may feel threatened by the presence of a foreign multinational. The job of PR agencies in foreign markets is not only to help the company sell its products or services but also to present the firm as a good corporate citizen concerned about the future of the country.

Companies generally need a favorable image to be successful in foreign markets. Those perceived negatively may face pressure from the media, local governments, or other relevant publics, or even boycotts by consumers. Often, public relations is needed to deal with specific problems a company faces in international markets. For example, the G. D. Searle Co. had problems getting its NutraSweet low-calorie sweetener into some markets because of strong sugar lobbies in Australia, Canada, and Europe. These lobbies encouraged the foreign press to pick up some unfavorable news about the product from the U.S. media. Searle retained Burson-Marsteller, the second-largest PR company in the world, to help design factual ads about the product and to conduct other PR activities to counter the problems and get the facts out about NutraSweet.

Public relations can play an important role in helping companies pursue business in foreign markets. Acustar, Inc., a U.S. automotive component manufacturer, used its PR firm to increase its visibility before negotiating contracts with Japanese automakers. The PR campaign included an executive reception to introduce the company and its products, press interviews, and presentations to senior executives of several Japanese car manufacturers. The PR firm also distributed a news release to Japanese news media before the Acustar executives' visit and arranged interviews with the company's chair for the leading business and trade publications in Japan. Stories about Acustar appeared in more than 10 national and regional newspapers, *The Asian Wall Street Journal*, two TV networks, and several domestic publications. The PR campaign helped the company win contracts with several Japanese auto manufacturers.[81]

Like advertising, public relations is becoming more of a global activity. Like ad agencies, PR firms are merging with and/or acquiring overseas offices so clients can use one firm to communicate with appropriate parties all over the world

The Internet

The use of the Internet around the globe continues to grow; predictions are that the number of online homes worldwide will increase from 23 million in 1996 to 67 million by the year 2000. Use of the Internet by consumers as well as marketers is highest in the United States and Western Europe. In other regions of the world there is tremendous variation in consumer usage as well as in the level of marketing activity occurring on the World Wide Web.

In the Asia/Pacific region, Internet use is high in Hong Kong and Thailand. Both markets have considerable numbers of high-end users and several domestic service providers. By contrast, India, the world's second-largest country, has only about 2,000 Internet users and only one state-run access provider. The number of Internet users is still relatively small in most Latin American countries, and marketers' understanding and use of the Internet is rather limited. Mexico is giving more attention to online services and the Internet, but the number of users and local Web pages is still very limited.[82]

EXHIBIT 20–14
IBM offers country-specific information in several languages on its website

The use of the Internet as a marketing tool by local companies in many countries is limited by a lack of understanding of the medium and the challenge of developing and maintaining a website. However, many multinational companies are using the Internet, particularly to support their advertising programs. IBM, Hewlett-Packard, Levi Strauss & Co., Swatch, AT&T, and Samsung Electronics are among the global advertisers that are using TV advertising to raise brand awareness and providing more detailed information to consumers through their websites.[83] IBM has a multicultural website that offers country-specific information in several languages including Japanese (Exhibit 20–14). A number of global marketers are also using websites to target businesspeople.

The Internet is also a potential new ad stream for cable and satellite TV. A number of international satellite and cable TV operators are developing websites that advertisers can use to complement their international TV campaigns. For example, CNN Interactive has been established as a separate service independent from CNN International. CNN Interactive plans to offer regional as well as localized Internet packages to advertisers.

Internet use in international markets is still limited by low numbers of consumers with Internet access, but Internet growth is expected to develop quickly as telecommunications companies move into emerging markets such as Eastern Europe and Latin America and improve the communications infrastructure. As this occurs, marketers are likely to make greater use of the Internet in their international promotional mix.

SUMMARY

Many U.S. companies are recognizing not only the opportunities but also the necessity of marketing their products and services internationally because of saturated markets and intense competition from both domestic and foreign competitors. Advertising and promotion are important parts of the international marketing program of a multinational corporation. Advertising is generally the most cost-effective way to communicate with buyers and create a market in other countries.

International marketers must carefully analyze the major environmental forces in each market where they compete, including economic, demographic, cultural, and political/legal factors. These factors are important not only in assessing the potential of each country as a market but also in designing and implementing advertising and promotional programs.

In recent years, much attention has focused on global marketing, where a standard marketing program is used in all markets. Part of global marketing is global advertising, where the same basic advertising approach is used in all markets. Opponents of the global (standardized) approach argue that differences in culture, market and economic conditions, and consumer needs and wants make a universal approach to marketing and advertising impractical. Many companies use an in-between approach, standardizing their basic marketing strategy but localizing advertising messages to fit each market.

There are a number of important decision areas in the development of advertising and promotional programs for international markets. These include organization, agency selection, advertising research, creative strategy and execution, and media strategy and selection.

Sales promotion, personal selling, public relations, and Internet websites are also part of the promotional mix of international marketers. Sales promotion programs usually must be adapted to local markets. Factors to consider include stage of market development, market maturity, consumer perceptions of promotional tools, trade structure, and legal restrictions and regulations. Personal selling is the most important element of some companies' international marketing programs, since it is their main form of contact with foreign customers. PR programs are also important to help international marketers develop and maintain favorable relationships with governments, media, and consumers in foreign countries. The use of the Internet as a marketing tool varies by region. In many countries, there are few Internet users and few local companies with websites. But as the numer of consumers online grows, so too does the number of large international marketers using the Internet to support their ad campaigns.

KEY TERMS

balance-of-trade deficit, 618
economic infrastructure, 620
global marketing, 625

global advertising, 625
pattern advertising, 632

localized advertising
    strategy, 640

direct broadcast by
    satellite (DBS), 643

DISCUSSION QUESTIONS

1. The opening vignette describes the way many large multinational companies are consolidating all of their worldwide advertising with one large agency. Evaluate the pros and cons of this approach.

2. Why are international markets becoming so important to companies like Anheuser-Busch and Compaq Computer? Discuss the role of advertising and other forms of promotion in these firms' international marketing programs.

3. Global Perspective 20–1 discusses how sales from international markets have become a major part of Nike's growth strategy. What are some of the major advertising and promotional challenges facing Nike as it strives to meet its goal of becoming a $12 billion company by the year 2000 with sales split evenly between domestic and foreign markets?

4. Choose two foreign countries and discuss the problems a U.S. consumer package-goods company might encounter in developing an advertising and promotion program in these markets.

5. In 1983, Theodore Levitt argued that the worldwide marketplace is becoming homogenized and the basic needs, wants, and expectations of consumers transcend geographic, national, and cultural boundaries. Do you think the global village has arrived and a single advertising campaign can be used for all countries? What has happened since to either support or refute Levitt's position?

6. What is meant by a global market segment? Provide several examples of companies that advertise their products the same way around the world to a global market segment.

7. Discuss the pros and cons of global advertising. What types of products and services lend themselves to global advertising?

8. What are some of the problems international marketers face in developing media strategies for foreign markets?

9. Discuss the various factors involved in developing sales promotion programs in foreign markets. How would the planning and implementation of a sales promotion program differ for global brands versus regional or local brands?

10. Evaluate the use of the Internet by global marketers. What factors will affect its use as a marketing tool for international advertising and promotion?

21

Regulation of Advertising and Promotion

Chapter Objectives

- To examine how advertising is regulated, including the role and function of various regulatory agencies.

- To examine self-regulation of advertising and evaluate its effectiveness.

- To consider how advertising is regulated by federal and state government agencies, including the Federal Trade Commission.

- To examine rules and regulations that affect sales promotion and direct marketing.

For more than five decades, distilled spirits were not advertised on television or radio because of a self-imposed ban by members of the Distilled Spirits Council of the United States (DIS-CUS). Council members agreed in 1936 to avoid radio advertising and extended the ban to TV in 1948. But Seagram, the second-largest distiller in the world, ended the U.S. spirits industry's long-standing ban on broadcast advertising in June 1996 by airing commercials for its Crown Royal Canadian whiskey brand on an NBC affiliate in Corpus Christi, Texas.

Seagram issued a statement that it was ending the liquor industry's decades-old practice of not advertising on TV because DISCUS's voluntary code of good practice placed spirits at a competitive disadvantage to beer and wine. Arthur Shapiro, Seagram's vice president for marketing and strategy, said, "Wine and beer face no restrictions on advertising. That inequity creates an unfair situation as far as promotion of spirits is concerned. We have a right to examine and test television as a viable communications medium." Seagram also argued that the ban has become outdated as radio and TV have become more targeted media, which means they can pinpoint their advertising message to people of legal drinking age.

Initial reactions within the liquor industry were mixed. Some companies were upset because Seagram made its move before the industry had time to reach a coordinated stand on the sensitive subject of TV advertising. The vice president of public relations for Heublin Inc. expressed concern that Seagram had acted rashly. He said, "We are not convinced that there has been enough research done into the attitudes of lawmakers, regulators, consumer groups, and the public at large regarding their attitudes toward distilled spirits broadcast advertising. We're concerned there could be backlash against the industry."

A number of distillers, eager to turn around the long, slow decline in hard liquor sales, watched Seagram test the water with its TV ads before rolling out their own commercials. Some, such as Hiram Walker and Brown-Forman, held discussions with broadcast outlets but waited for a formal amendment to the DISCUS code of good practice before proceeding. The amendment came on November 7, 1996, when DISCUS members voted unanimously to overturn the self-imposed ban on broadcast ads. DISCUS president and CEO Fred A. Meister noted that spirits marketers want to break down the public perception that spirits are stronger or more dangerous than beer and wine and thus deserving of harsher social and political treatment.

A number of liquor companies have followed Seagram's lead and are running ads on television. Although the three major networks say they will continue to refuse liquor ads, they cannot control the practices of affiliate stations they do not own. Advertising industry executives expect to see a lot of liquor ads on cable TV, where guidelines are often looser and executives are hungrier for new sources of advertising revenue. For now, liquor companies that want to air TV commercials do not face any serious government obstacles. Officials at the Federal Trade Commission, which oversees advertising, and the Bureau of Alcohol, Tobacco and Firearms, which regulates the spirits industry, say federal law does not give either agency the authority to ban liquor ads. In fact, the First Amendment protects this type of commercial speech.

As might be expected, many consumer and public interest groups are very upset over the liquor industry's decision to run ads on TV. Critics fear that viewers will be overwhelmed with liquor advertising. Of particular concern is the opening of TV, the most youth-oriented medium, to liquor ads. Some predict that the controversy created by airing liquor ads will result in government regulations that ultimately force all al-

cohol advertising off TV. Meanwhile, viewers can expect to see ads for Crown Royal, Chivas Regal, and many other brands.

Sources: Ian P. Murphy, "Competitive Spirits: Liquor Industry Turns to TV Ads," *Marketing News*, December 2, 1996, pp. 1, 17; Sally Goll Beatty and Yumiko Ono, "Liquor Industry Is Divided over Use of TV Ads," *The Wall Street Journal*, June 12, 1996, pp. B1, 9; and Sally Goll Beatty, "Seagram Flouts Ban on TV Ads Pitching Liquor," *The Wall Street Journal*, June 11, 1996, pp. B1, 6.

Suppose you are the advertising manager for a consumer products company and have just reviewed a new commercial your agency created. You are very excited about the ad. It presents new claims about your brand's superiority that should help differentiate it from the competition. However, before you approve the commercial you need answers. Are the claims verifiable? Did researchers use proper procedures to collect and analyze the data and present the findings? Do research results support the claims? Were the right people used in the study? Could any conditions have biased the results?

Before approving the commercial, you have it reviewed by your company's legal department and by your agency's attorneys. If both reviews are acceptable, you send the ad to the major networks, which have their censors examine it. They may ask for more information or send the ad back for modification. (No commercial can run without approval from a network's Standards and Practices Department.)

Even after approval and airing, your commercial is still subject to scrutiny from such state and federal regulatory agencies as the state attorney general's office and the Federal Trade Commission. Individual consumers or competitors who find the ad misleading or have other concerns may file a complaint with the National Advertising Division of the Council of Better Business Bureaus. Finally, disparaged competitors may sue if they believe your ad distorts the facts and misleads consumers. If you lose the litigation, your company may have to retract the claims and pay the competitor damages, sometimes running into millions of dollars.

After considering all these regulatory issues, you must ask yourself if the new ad can meet all these challenges and is worth the risk. Maybe you ought to continue with the old approach that made no specific claims and simply said your brand was great.

Regulatory concerns can play a major role in the advertising decision-making process. Advertisers operate in a complex environment of local, state, and federal rules and regulations. Additionally, a number of advertising and business-sponsored associations, consumer groups and organizations, and the media attempt to promote honest, truthful, and tasteful advertising through their own self-regulatory programs and guidelines. The legal and regulatory aspects of advertising are very complex. Many parties are concerned about the nature and content of advertising and its potential to offend, exploit, mislead, and/or deceive consumers.

Numerous guidelines, rules, regulations, and laws constrain and restrict advertising. These regulations primarily influence individual advertisers, but they can also affect advertising for an entire industry. For example, cigarette advertising was banned from the broadcast media in 1970, and many groups are pushing for a total ban on the advertising of tobacco products.[1] Legislation now being considered would further restrict the advertising of alcoholic beverages, including beer and wine.[2] Advertising is controlled by internal self-regulation and by external state and federal regulatory agencies such as the Federal Trade Commission (FTC), the Federal Communications Commission (FCC), the Food and Drug Administration (FDA), and the U.S. Postal Service. And recently state attorneys general have become more active in advertising regulation. While only government agencies (federal, state, and local) have the force of law, most advertisers also abide by the guidelines and decisions of internal regulatory bodies. In fact, internal regulation from such groups as the media and the National Advertising Review Board probably has more influence on advertisers' day-to-day operations and decision making than government rules and regulations.

Decision makers on both the client and agency side must be knowledgeable about these regulatory groups: including the intent of their efforts, how they operate, and how they influence and affect advertising and other promotional mix elements. In this chapter, we examine the major sources of advertising regulation, including efforts by the industry at voluntary self-regulation and external regulation by government agencies. We also examine regulations involving sales promotion and direct marketing.

SELF-REGULATION

For many years, the advertising industry has practiced and promoted voluntary **self-regulation**. Most advertisers, their agencies, and the media recognize the importance of maintaining consumer trust and confidence. Advertisers also see self-regulation as a way to limit government interference, which, they believe, results in more stringent and troublesome regulations. Self-regulation and control of advertising emanate from all segments of the advertising industry, including individual advertisers and their agencies, business and advertising associations, and the media.

Self-Regulation by Advertisers and Agencies

Self-regulation begins with the interaction of client and agency when creative ideas are generated and submitted for consideration. Most companies have specific guidelines, standards, and policies to which their ads must adhere. Recognizing that their ads reflect the company, advertisers carefully scrutinize all messages to ensure they are consistent with the image the firm wishes to project. Companies also review their ads to be sure any claims made are reasonable and verifiable and do not mislead or deceive consumers. Ads are usually examined by corporate attorneys to avoid potential legal problems and their accompanying time, expense, negative publicity, and embarrassment.

Internal control and regulation also come from advertising agencies. Most have standards regarding the type of advertising they either want or are willing to produce, and they try to avoid ads that might be offensive or misleading. Agencies are responsible for verifying product claims made by the advertiser and for ensuring that adequate documentation or substantiation is available. Agencies can be held legally responsible for fraudulent or deceptive claims and in some cases have been fined when their clients were found guilty of engaging in deceptive advertising. Many agencies have a creative review board or panel composed of experienced personnel who examine ads for content and execution as well as for their potential to be perceived as offensive, misleading, and/or deceptive. Most agencies also employ or retain lawyers who review the ads for potential legal problems. Exhibit 21–1 shows an ad for a legal firm specializing in advertising law.

EXHIBIT 21–1
The Kinney & Lange firm specializes in advertising law

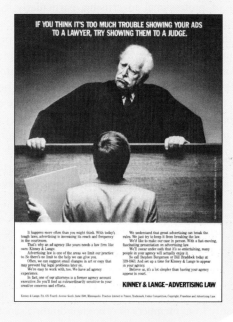

Self-Regulation by Trade Associations

Like advertisers and their agencies, many industries have also developed self-regulatory programs. This is particularly true in industries whose advertising is prone to controversy, such as liquor and alcoholic beverages, drugs, and various products marketed to children. Many trade and industry associations develop their own advertising guidelines or codes that member companies are expected to abide by.

The Wine Institute, the U.S. Brewers Association, and the Distilled Spirits Council of the United States all have guidelines that member companies are supposed to follow in advertising alcoholic beverages. As discussed in the opening vignette, no specific law prohibits the advertising of hard liquor on radio or television. However, such advertising was effectively banned for over five decades as a result of a code provision of the National Association of Broadcasters and by agreements of liquor manufacturers and their self-governing body, the Distilled Spirits Council. Other industry trade associations with advertising guidelines and programs include the Toy Manufacturers Association, the Motion Picture Association of America, the Pharmaceutical Manufacturers Association, and the Proprietary Association (the trade association for nonprescription drug makers).[3]

Many professions also maintain advertising guidelines through local, state, and national organizations. For years professional associations like the American Medical Association (AMA) and the American Bar Association (ABA) restricted advertising by their members on the basis that such promotional activities lowered members' professional status and led to unethical and fraudulent claims. However, such restrictive codes have been attacked by both government regulatory agencies and consumer groups. They argue that the public has a right to be informed about a professional's services, qualifications, and background and that advertising will improve professional services as consumers become better informed and are better able to shop around.[4]

In 1977, the Supreme Court held that state bar associations' restrictions on advertising are unconstitutional and that attorneys have First Amendment freedom of speech rights to advertise.[5] Many professional associations subsequently removed their restrictions, and advertising by lawyers and other professionals is now common (Exhibit 21–2).[6] In 1982, the Supreme Court upheld an FTC order permitting advertising by dentists and physicians.[7]

Research shows that consumers generally favor increased use of professional advertising. However, professionals continue to have reservations. They worry that advertising has a negative impact on their image, credibility, and dignity and see benefits to consumers as unlikely.[8] Still, advertising by professionals is increasing, particularly among newcomers to medicine, dentistry, and law. Associations such as the AMA and the ABA developed guidelines for members' advertising to help maintain standards and guard against misleading, deceptive, or offensive ads.

The issue of professional advertising, particularly by attorneys, is still hotly debated. Some traditional law firms resist using advertising, particularly on TV, due to concern that it might hurt the profession's image. Many in the legal profession worry that ads soliciting personal injury victims only worsen the public's perception of attorneys. A sizable faction within the American Bar Association blames the legal profession's image problem on sleazy ads. The ABA's Commission on Advertising recently held a series of public hearings on what, if any, restrictive measures to recommend to state ethics panels. Some states, such as Iowa and Florida, already restrict the content of attorney ads and the way they can be delivered. For example, Iowa lawyers are limited to "tombstone" print ads that merely list their name, location, and objective qualifications. And all ads require a disclaimer urging consumers not to base their attorney selection on an advertisement. Florida attorneys cannot use testimonials or endorsements, dramatizations, self-laudatory statements, illustrations, or photos.[9]

Many attorneys are incensed over efforts to restrict their rights to promote themselves because they use advertising to help build their practices. Several cases are currently being litigated, but ultimately the Supreme Court may have to decide just how far states can go in curtailing advertising.

Although industry associations are concerned with the impact and consequences of members' advertising, they have no legal way to enforce their guidelines. They can only rely on peer pressure from members or other nonbinding sanctions to get advertisers to comply.

EXHIBIT 21—2   Advertising by lawyers has become more common as the result of a 1977 Supreme Court ruling

Man: We were being strangled by our debts. We couldn't sleep, our work suffered . . . We'd heard about bankruptcy, but didn't know much about it.

Lawyer: By the time the Brills came to Jacoby & Meyers, they were being harassed by their creditors, their wages were attached and their home was in foreclosure. We stopped all that.

Man: We figured, our creditors were using lawyers to protect their rights. Why shouldn't we?

Lawyer: The Brills just needed a chance to get a fresh start. Jacoby & Meyers. When it's time to call a lawyer about a bankruptcy.

Self-Regulation by Businesses

A number of self-regulatory mechanisms have been established by the business community in an effort to control advertising practices. The largest and best known is the **Better Business Bureau** (BBB), which promotes fair advertising and selling practices across all industries. The BBB was established in 1916 to handle consumer complaints about local business practices and particularly advertising. Local BBBs are located in most large cities throughout the United States and supported entirely by dues of the more than 100,000 member firms.

Local BBBs receive and investigate complaints from consumers and other companies regarding the advertising and selling tactics of businesses in their area. Each local office has its own operating procedures for handling complaints; generally, the office contacts the violator and, if the complaint proves true, requests that the practice be stopped or changed. If the violator does not respond, negative publicity may be used against the firm or the case may be referred to appropriate government agencies for further action.

While BBBs provide effective control over advertising practices at the local level, the parent organization, the **Council of Better Business Bureaus**, plays a major role at the national level. The council assists new industries in developing advertising codes and standards, and it provides information about advertising regulations and legal rulings to advertisers, agencies, and the media. The council also plays an important self-regulatory role through its National Advertising Division (NAD) and Children's Advertising Review Unit (CARU). The NAD works closely with the **National Advertising Review Board** (NARB) to sustain truth, accuracy, and decency in national advertising.

The NAD/NARB

In 1971 four associations—the American Advertising Federation (AAF), the American Association of Advertising Agencies (AAAA), the Association of National Advertisers (ANA), and the Council of Better Business Bureaus—joined forces to establish the **National Advertising Review Council** (NARC). The NARC's mission is to sustain high standards of truth, accuracy, and social responsibility in national advertising. The council has two operating arms, the National Advertising Division of the Council of Better Business Bureaus and the National Advertising Review Board. The NAD/NARB has become the advertising industry's primary self-regulatory mechanism.

The NAD's advertising monitoring program is the source of many of the cases it reviews (Figure 21–1). It also reviews complaints from consumers and consumer groups, local BBBs, and competitors. IMC Perspective 21–1 discusses a complaint BMW filed with the NAD over a recent Volvo commercial claiming its 850 Turbo Sportswagon accelerates faster than a BMW 328i.[10] The NAD acts as the investigative arm of the NARC. After initiating or receiving a complaint, it determines the issue, collects and evaluates data, and makes the initial decision on whether the advertiser's claims are substantiated. The NAD may ask the advertiser to supply substantiation for the claim in question. If this is done, the case is deemed

IMC Perspective 21-1
Volvo and BMW Battle over Whose Car Is Faster

In 1990, Swedish automaker Volvo was involved in a major controversy over its infamous "monster truck" commercial which showed a pickup truck with huge, oversize tires driving over the top of a row of cars, crushing the roofs of all of them except the Volvo. An investigation by the Texas Attorney General's office found that the commercial was deceptive: the roof of the Volvo used in the spot had been reinforced with steel and plywood, while the rival vehicles' roof supports had been weakened. The Federal Trade Commission penalized Volvo for using deceptive advertising methods and the scandal led to the dismissal of Volvo's longtime agency, Scali, McCabe, Sloves.

Six years after being banged up by the monster truck ad scandal, Volvo found itself in the middle of another flap, this time over a commercial showing its 850 turbo Sportswagon going from zero to 60 in less time than a BMW 328i. Actor Donald Sutherland does the voiceover in the spot, saying: "The ultimate driving machine, outdone by a Volvo. Is nothing sacred?" BMW of North America claims the ad is deceptive. It says Volvo's testing was invalid and conflicted with its own tests and those of other independent sources. But Volvo's agency, Messner Vetere Berger McNamee Schmetterer/ Euro RSCG, New York, is standing behind the commercial. An agency partner/account director on Volvo said, "Our position is we developed advertising to explain the results of independent research that found the Volvo 850 turbo Sportswagon was faster than the 328i in acceleration. The results are quite unexpected, which is the whole point of the commercial."

When creating comparative ads, most car companies hire a recognized vendor to conduct the tests, then have the results sanctioned by one of several auto-related bodies, like the U.S. Auto Club. Volvo did not go that route. It hired a former automotive engineer, who is now a freelance journalist, to do the tests. BMW is upset with a number of aspects of his testing methods. The German automaker argues that the Volvo's engine may have benefited because it was more broken in (with 9,150 miles on the odometer) than the 328i (with 1,091 miles). The BMW transmission was tested in economy mode while the Volvo was in sport mode, and the Volvo was driven 12 times versus BMW's five. BMW argues that none of these qualifiers was mentioned in the commercial.

BMW had its own tests conducted by a well-known testing company, Automotive Marketing Consultants, a month before Volvo's. The company tested the zero to 60 acceleration of the 328i versus the Volvo 850 turbo sedan (not the station wagon shown in the ad) and two other competitors. Each vehicle was tested 24 times and used the average of the fastest 16 runs. All four cars had the same mileage and each was driven in the highest gear available. The BMW was the fastest of all four vehicles tested and none of the Volvo's single times beat any of BMW's—although the report noted that the 850 turbo beat the 328i in a quarter-mile test.

In June 1996 BMW filed a complaint with the National Advertising Division of the Council of Better Business Bureaus calling the Volvo ad deceptive, misleading, inaccurate, and biased. However, two months later the NAD ruled in favor of Volvo. While saying that Volvo's ad should have more clearly communicated its testing methodology, the NAD ruled that the commercial was based on testing "conducted in a reasonable manner." The NAD ruled, "While it was shown there are certainly accepted (auto) industry guidelines, it was also established that there are no required testing standards the advertiser is mandated to follow."

Volvo viewed the NAD ruling as a victory, noting that when the NAD was done evaluating the facts, it said the testing was fair and unbiased. However, Volvo did agree to take into consideration all of the NAD's concerns in its future comparative advertising for the 850 Sportswagon.

BMW initially said it would appeal the NAD ruling to the National Advertising Review Board. BMW's director of corporate communications argued, "There has to be standardized (testing) methodology so the consumer can make a true comparison. If this stands, it opens the door for all sorts of subjective testing to be used." However, BMW did not appeal the ruling.

Some advertising experts have questioned the logic of Volvo's decision to move into the gray area of comparative ad claims as it tries to move beyond its safety image and toward a performance-based positioning. They point out that it took a long time for Volvo to regain consumer trust after the monster truck fiasco and that the risk of the comparative claims outweighs the potential rewards.

Sources: Jean Halliday, "BMW to Appeal NAD Vindication of Volvo Spot," *Advertising Age*, August 19, 1996, pp. 4, 32; Jean Halliday, "Volvo's Ad Claims Questioned—Again," *Advertising Age*, June 10, 1996, pp. 1, 44; Steven W. Colford and Raymond Serafin, "Scali Pays for Volvo Ad: FTC," *Advertising Age*, August 26, 1991, p. 4.

FIGURE 21-1   Sources of NAD cases and decisions, 1996

Sources	Number	Percent	Decisions	Number	Percent
Competitor challenges	67	70%			
NAD monitoring	16	17	Modified/discontinued	75	78%
Local BBB challenges	9	9	Substantiated	16	17
Consumer challenges	4	4	Referred to government	5	5
Total	96	100%	Total	96	100%

substantiated. If the substantiation is unsatisfactory, the NAD negotiates with the advertiser to modify or discontinue the advertising. For example, ConAgra agreed to modify advertising for its Healthy Choice fat-free cheese after competitor Kraft General Foods challenged five ConAgra claims. The claims included "So Healthy Choice took out the fat by pouring in skim milk, for more flavor" and "Never settle for less." Since ConAgra failed to provide consumer perception studies, comparative taste tests, or a nutritional analysis, the NAD ruled the claims could not be substantiated, except for "Never settle for less," which was interpreted as permissible puffery.[11]

If the NAD and the advertiser fail to resolve the controversy, either can appeal to a five-person panel from the National Advertising Review Board. The NARB is composed of 85 advertising professionals and prominent public-interest members. If the NARB panel agrees with the NAD and rules against the advertiser, the advertiser must discontinue the advertising. If the advertiser refuses to comply, the NARB refers the matter to the appropriate government agency and indicates the fact in its public record. Figure 21–2 shows a flowchart of the steps in the NAD/NARB review process.

Although the NARB has no power to order an advertiser to modify or stop running an ad and no sanctions it can impose, advertisers who participate in an NAD investigation and NARB appeal rarely refuse to abide by the panel's decision.[12] Most cases do not even make it to the NARB panel. For example, in 1996, of the 96 NAD investigations, 16 ad claims were substantiated, 5 were referred to the government, and 75 were modified or discontinued (Figure 21–1). Of the 75 cases where the advertising claims were modified or discontinued, in only four did the advertiser appeal to the NARB for resolution.[13]

In 1993, for the first time in its history, the NARB referred a matter to the Federal Trade Commission following an advertiser's refusal to modify a commercial in accordance with an NARB decision The case involved advertising for Eggland's Best eggs and is discussed in IMC Perspective 21–2 later in this chapter.[14]

The NAD/NARB is a valuable and effective self-regulatory body. Cases brought to it are handled at a fraction of the cost (and with much less publicity) than those brought to court and are expedited more quickly than those reviewed by a government agency such as the FTC. The system also works because judgments are made by the advertiser's peers, and most companies feel compelled to comply. Firms may prefer self-regulation rather than government intervention in part because they can challenge competitors' unsubstantiated claims through groups like the NARB.[15]

ADVERTISING ASSOCIATIONS

Various groups in the advertising industry also favor self-regulation. The two major national organizations, the American Association of Advertising Agencies and the American Advertising Federation, actively monitor and police industrywide advertising practices. The AAAA, which is the major trade association of the ad agency business in the United States, has established standards of practice and its own creative code. It also issues guidelines for specific types of advertising such as comparative messages (Figure 21–3). The AAF consists of advertisers, agencies, media, and numerous advertising clubs. The association has standards for truthful and responsible advertising, is involved in advertising legislation, and actively influences agencies to abide by its code and principles.

Self-Regulation by Media

The media are another important self-regulatory mechanism in the advertising industry. Most media maintain some form of advertising review process and, except for political ads, may reject any they regard as objectionable. Some media exclude advertising for an entire product class; others ban individual ads they think offensive or objectionable. For example, *Reader's Digest* does not accept advertising for tobacco or liquor products. A number of magazines in the United States and other countries refused to run some of Benetton's shock ads (discussed in Ethical Perspective 8–1) on the grounds that their readers would find them offensive or disturbing (Exhibit 21–3).

Newspapers and magazines have their own advertising requirements and restrictions, which often vary depending on the size and nature of the publication. Large, established publications, such as major newspapers or magazines, often have strict standards regarding

FIGURE 21–2   Council of Better Business Bureaus, National Advertising Division resolution process

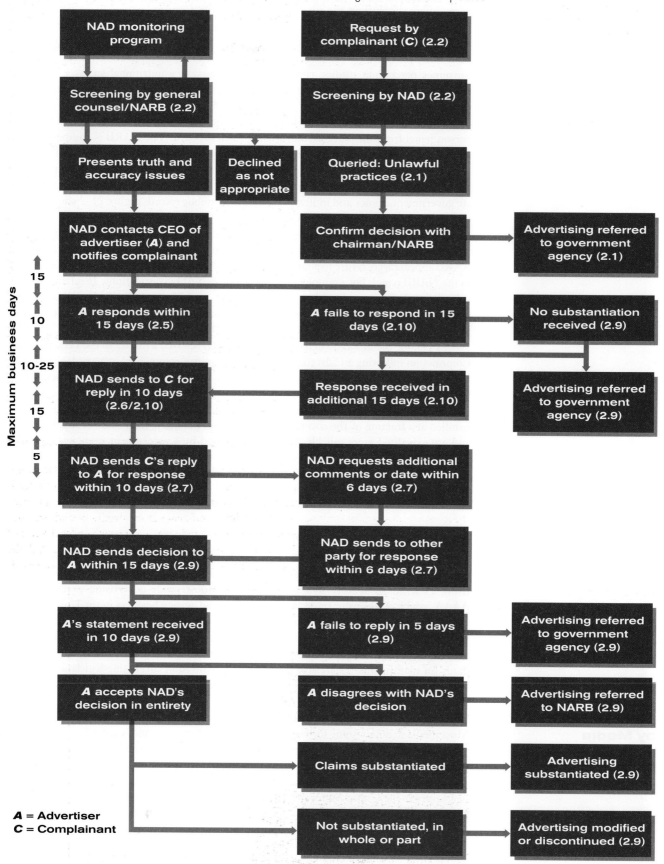

FIGURE 21—3
AAAA policy statement and guidelines for comparative advertising

The Board of Directors of the American Association of Advertising Agencies recognizes that when used truthfully and fairly, comparative advertising provides the consumer with needed and useful information.

However, extreme caution should be exercised. The use of comparative advertising, by its very nature, can distort facts and, by implication, convey to the consumer information that misrepresents the truth.

Therefore, the Board believes that comparative advertising should follow certain guidelines:

1. The intent and connotation of the ad should be to inform and never to discredit or unfairly attack competitors, competing products, or services.

2. When a competitive product is named, it should be one that exists in the marketplace as significant competition.

3. The competition should be fairly and properly identified but never in a manner or tone of voice that degrades the competitive product or service.

4. The advertising should compare related or similar properties or ingredients of the product, dimension to dimension, feature to feature.

5. The identification should be for honest comparison purposes and not simply to upgrade by association.

6. If a competitive test is conducted, it should be done by an objective testing source, preferably an independent one, so that there will be no doubt as to the veracity of the test.

7. In all cases the test should be supportive of all claims made in the advertising that are based on the test.

8. The advertising should never use partial results or stress insignificant differences to cause the consumer to draw an improper conclusion.

9. The property being compared should be significant in terms of value or usefulness of the product to the consumer.

10. Comparatives delivered through the use of testimonials should not imply that the testimonial is more than one individual's thought unless that individual represents a sample of the majority viewpoint.

the type of advertising they accept. Some magazines, such as *Parents* and *Good Housekeeping*, regularly test the products they advertise and offer a "seal of approval" and refunds if the products are later found to be defective. Such policies are designed to enhance the credibility of the publication and increase the reader's confidence in the products it advertises.

Advertising on television and radio has been regulated for years through codes developed by the industry trade association, the National Association of Broadcasters (NAB). Both the radio code (established in 1937) and the television code (1952) provided standards for broad-

EXHIBIT 21—3
A number of magazines refused to run this Benetton ad

cast advertising for many years. Both codes prohibited the advertising of certain products, such as hard liquor. They also affected the manner in which products could be advertised. However, in 1982, the NAB suspended all of its code provisions after the courts found that portions (dealing with time standards and required length of commercials in the TV code) were in restraint of trade. While the NAB codes are no longer in force, many individual broadcasters, such as the major TV networks, have incorporated major portions of the code provisions into their own standards.[16]

The three major television networks have the most stringent review process of any media. All three networks maintain standards and practices divisions, which carefully review all commercials submitted to the network or individual affiliate stations. Advertisers must submit for review all commercials intended for airing on the network or an affiliate.

A commercial may be submitted for review in the form of a script, storyboard, animatic, or finished commercial (when the advertiser believes there is little chance of objection). Network reviewers consider whether the proposed commercial meets acceptable standards and is appropriate for certain audiences. For example, different standards are used for ads designated for prime-time versus late-night spots or for children's versus adults' programs (see Figure 21–4). Although most of these guidelines remain in effect, ABC and NBC recently loosened their rules on celebrity endorsements.[17]

The three major networks receive over 50,000 commercials a year for review; nearly two-thirds are accepted and only 3 percent are rejected. Most problems with the remaining 30 percent are resolved through negotiation, and the ads are revised and resubmitted.[18]

Network standards regarding acceptable advertising change constantly. The networks first allowed lingerie advertisers to use live models rather than mannequins in 1987. Advertising for contraceptives is now appearing on some stations. The networks also loosened long-standing restrictions on endorsements and competitive advertising claims.[19] Network standards will continue to change as society's values and attitudes toward certain issues and products change. Also, many advertising people believe these changes are a response to com-

FIGURE 21—4 A sampling of the TV networks' guidelines for children's advertising

Each of the major TV networks has its own set of guidelines for children's advertising, although the basics are very similar. A few rules, such as the requirement of a static "island" shot at the end, are written in stone; others, however, can sometimes be negotiated. Many of the rules below apply specifically to toys. The networks also have special guidelines for kids' food commercials and for kids' commercials that offer premiums.

	ABC	CBS	NBC
Must not overglamorize product	✓	✓	✓
No exhortative language, such as "Ask Mom to buy …"	✓	✓	✓
No realistic war settings	✓		✓
Generally no celebrity endorsements	✓	Case-by-case	✓
Can't use "only" or "just" in regard to price	✓	✓	✓
Show only two toys per child or maximum of six per commercial	✓		✓
Five-second "island" showing product against plain background at end of spot	✓	✓	✓ (4 to 5)
Animation restricted to one-third of a commercial	✓		✓
Generally no comparative or superiority claims	Case-by-case	Handle w/care	✓
No costumes or props not available with the toy	✓		✓
No child or toy can appear in animated segments	✓		✓
Three-second establishing shot of toy in relation to child	✓	✓ (2.5 to 3)	
No shots under one second in length		✓	
Must show distance a toy can travel before stopping on its own		✓	

Source: "Kid Advertising Guidelines: Double Standard for Kid's TV Ads," *The Wall Street Journal*, June 10, 1988, p. 25.

petition from independent and cable stations, which tend to be much less stringent in their standards and practices. However, since television is probably the most carefully scrutinized and frequently criticized of all forms of advertising, the networks must be careful not to offend their viewers and detract from advertising's credibility.

Appraising Self-Regulation

The three major participants in the advertising process—advertisers, agencies, and the media—work individually and collectively to encourage truthful, ethical, and responsible advertising. The advertising industry views self-regulation as an effective mechanism for controlling advertising abuses and avoiding the use of offensive, misleading, or deceptive practices, and it prefers this form of regulation to government intervention. Self-regulation of advertising has been effective and in many instances probably led to the development of more stringent standards and practices than those imposed by or beyond the scope of legislation.

In a speech to the American Advertising Federation, then FTC Commissioner Mary Azuenaga commented on the fact that the Eggland's Best eggs case marked the first time in its 22-year history the NARB referred a matter to the FTC. She said, "Although it was unfortunate that such a referral was necessary, the very novelty of the referral underscores the important contribution of NARB and other self-regulatory groups in addressing questions of deceptive advertising."[20]

There are, however, limitations to self-regulation, and the process has been criticized in a number of areas. For example, the NAD may take six months to a year to resolve a complaint, during which time a company often stops using the commercial anyway. Budgeting and staffing constraints may limit the number of cases the NAD/NARB system investigates and the speed with which it resolves them.[21] And some critics believe that self-regulation is self-serving to the advertisers and advertising industry and lacks the power or authority to be a viable alternative to federal or state regulation.

Many do not believe advertising can or should be controlled solely by self-regulation. They argue that regulation by government agencies is necessary to ensure that consumers get accurate information and are not misled or deceived. Moreover, since advertisers do not have to comply with the decisions and recommendations of self-regulatory groups, it is sometimes necessary to turn to the federal and/or state government.

FEDERAL REGULATION OF ADVERTISING

The government controls and regulates advertising through federal, state, and local laws and regulations enforced by various government agencies. The federal government, through the **Federal Trade Commission (FTC)**, is the most important source of external regulation.

Background on Federal Regulation of Advertising

Federal regulation of advertising originated in 1914 with the passage of the **Federal Trade Commission Act** (FTC Act), which created the FTC, the agency that is today the most active in, and has primary responsibility for, controlling and regulating advertising. The FTC Act was originally intended to help enforce antitrust laws, such as the Sherman and Clayton acts, by helping to restrain unfair methods of competition. The main focus of the first five-member commission was to protect competitors from one another; the issue of false or misleading advertising was not even mentioned. In 1922, the Supreme Court upheld an FTC interpretation that false advertising was an unfair method of competition, but in the 1931 case *FTC v. Raladam Co.*, the Court ruled the commission could not prohibit false advertising unless there was evidence of injury to a competitor.[22] This ruling limited the power of the FTC to protect consumers from false or deceptive advertising and led to a consumer movement that resulted in an important amendment to the FTC Act.

In 1938, Congress passed the **Wheeler-Lea Amendment**. It amended section 5 of the FTC Act to read: "Unfair methods of competition in commerce and unfair or deceptive acts or practices in commerce are hereby declared to be unlawful." The amendment empowered the FTC to act if there was evidence of injury to the public; proof of injury to a competitor was not necessary. The Wheeler-Lea Amendment also gave the FTC the power to issue cease-and-desist orders and levy fines on violators. It extended the FTC's jurisdiction over false advertising of foods, drugs, cosmetics, and therapeutic devices. And it gave the FTC access to the injunctive power of the federal courts, initially only for food and drug products but expanded in 1972 to include all products in the event of a threat to the public's health and safety.

In addition to the FTC, numerous other federal agencies are responsible for, or involved in, advertising regulation. The authority of these agencies is limited, however, to a particular product area or service, and they often rely on the FTC to assist in handling false or deceptive advertising cases.

The Federal Trade Commission

The FTC is responsibile for protecting both consumers and businesses from anticompetitive behavior and unfair and deceptive practices. The major divisions of the FTC include the bureaus of competition, economics, and consumer protection (Figure 21–5). The Bureau of Competition enforces antitrust laws. The Bureau of Economics aids and advises the commission on the economic aspects of its activities and prepares economic reports and surveys. The Bureau of Consumer Protection investigates and litigates cases involving acts or practices alleged to be deceptive or unfair to consumers. The National Advertising Division

FIGURE 21–5 The Federal Trade Commission organization

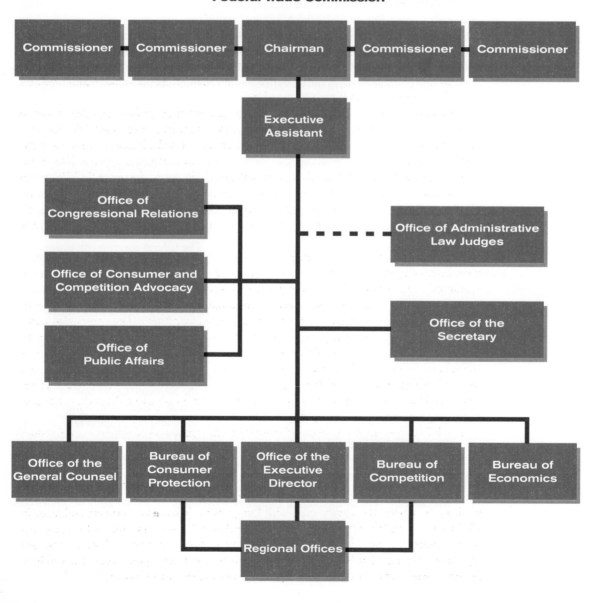

Federal Trade Commission

of the Bureau of Consumer Protection enforces those provisions of the FTC Act that forbid misrepresentation, unfairness, and deception in national advertising.

The FTC has had the power to regulate advertising since passage of the Wheeler-Lea Amendment. However, not until the early 1970s—following criticism of the commission in a book by "Nader's Raiders" and a special report by the American Bar Association citing its lack of action against deceptive promotional practices—did the FTC become active in regulating advertising.[23] The authority of the FTC was increased considerably throughout the 1970s. The Magnuson–Moss Act of 1975, an important piece of legislation, dramatically broadened the FTC's powers and substantially increased its budget. The first section of the act dealt with consumers' rights regarding product warranties; it allowed the commission to require restitution for deceptively written warranties where the consumer lost more than $5. The second section, the FTC Improvements Act, empowered the FTC to establish **trade regulation rules** (TRRs), industrywide rules that define unfair practices before they occur.

During the 1970s, the FTC made enforcement of laws regarding false and misleading advertising a top priority. Several new programs were instituted, budgets were increased, and the commission became a very powerful regulatory agency. However, many of these programs, as well as the expanded powers of the FTC to develop regulations on the basis of "unfairness," became controversial. At the root of this controversy is the fundamental issue of what constitutes unfair advertising.

The Concept of Unfairness

Under section 5 of the FTC Act, the Federal Trade Commission has a mandate to act against unfair or deceptive advertising practices. However, this statute does not define the terms *unfair* and *deceptive*, and the FTC has been criticized for not doing so itself. While the FTC has taken steps to clarify the meaning of *deception*, people have been concerned for years about the vagueness of the term "unfair."

Controversy over the FTC's authority to regulate unfair advertising practices began in 1978, when the agency relied on this mandate to formulate its controversial "kid vid" rule restricting advertising to children.[24] This interpretation caused widespread concern in the business community that the term *unfair* could be used to encompass anything FTC commissioners might find objectionable. For example, in a 1980 policy statement the FTC noted that "the precise concept of consumer unfairness is one whose precise meaning is not immediately obvious." Consequently, in 1980 Congress responded by suspending the children's advertising rule and banning the FTC from using unfairness as a legal basis for advertising rulemaking.

The FTC responded to these criticisms in December 1980 by sending Congress a statement containing an interpretation of unfairness. According to FTC policy, the basis for determining **unfairness** is that a trade practice (1) causes substantial physical or economic injury to consumers, (2) could not reasonably be avoided by consumers, and (3) must not be outweighed by countervailing benefits to consumers or competition. The agency also stated that a violation of public policy (such as of other government statutes) could, by itself, constitute an unfair practice or could be used to prove substantial consumer injury. Practices considered unfair are claims made without prior substantiation, claims that might exploit such vulnerable groups as children and the elderly, and instances where consumers cannot make a valid choice because the advertiser omits important information about the product or competing products mentioned in the ad.[25]

The FTC's statement was intended to clarify its interpretation of unfairness and reduce ambiguity over what might constitute unfair practices. However, efforts by the FTC to develop industrywide trade regulation rules that would define unfair practices and have the force and effect of law were limited by Congress in 1980 with the passage of the FTC Improvements Act. Amidst calls to end the stalemate over the FTC's regulation of unfair advertising by having the agency work with Congress to define its advertising authority, in 1994 Congress and the advertising industry agreed on a definition of unfair advertising that is very similar to the FTC's 1980 policy statement discussed earlier. However, the new agreement requires that before the FTC can initiate any industrywide rule, it has to have reason to believe that the unfair or deceptive acts or practices are prevalent.[26]

The FTC does have specific regulatory authority in cases involving deceptive, misleading, or untruthful advertising. The vast majority of advertising cases that the FTC handles concern deception and advertising fraud, which usually involve knowledge of a false claim.

Deceptive Advertising

In most economies, advertising provides consumers with information they can use to make consumption decisions. However, if this information is untrue or misleads the consumer, advertising is not fulfilling its basic function. But what constitutes an untruthful or deceptive ad? Deceptive advertising can take a number of forms, ranging from intentionally false or misleading claims to ads that, although true, leave some consumers with a false or misleading impression.

The issue of deception, including its definition and measurement, receives considerable attention from the FTC and other regulatory agencies. One of the problems regulatory agencies deal with in determining deception is distinguishing between false or misleading messages and those that, rather than relying on verifiable or substantiated objective information about a product, make subjective claims or statements, a practice known as puffery. **Puffery** has been legally defined as "advertising or other sales presentations which praise the item to be sold with subjective opinions, superlatives, or exaggerations, vaguely and generally, stating no specific facts."[27] The use of puffery in advertising is common. For example, Bayer aspirin calls itself the "wonder drug that works wonders," Nestlé claims "Nestlé makes the very best chocolate," and Healthy Choice foods tell consumers "Never settle for less." Superlatives such as *greatest*, *best*, and *finest* are puffs that are often used.

Puffery has generally been viewed as a form of poetic license or allowable exaggeration. The FTC takes the position that because consumers expect exaggeration or inflated claims in advertising, they recognize puffery and don't believe it. But some studies show that consumers may believe puffery and perceive such claims as true.[28] One study found that consumers could not distinguish between a verifiable fact-based claim and puffery and were just as likely to believe both types of claims.[29] Ivan Preston argues that puffery has a detrimental effect on consumers' purchase decisions by burdening them with untrue beliefs and refers to it as "soft-core deception" that should be illegal.[30]

Advertisers' battle to retain the right to use puffery was supported in the latest revision of the Uniform Commercial Code in 1996. The revision switches the burden of proof to consumers from advertisers in cases pertaining to whether certain claims were meant to be taken as promises. The revision states that the buyer must prove that an affirmation of fact (as opposed to puffery) was made, that the buyer was aware of the advertisement, and that the affirmation of fact became part of the agreement with the seller.[31]

Since unfair and deceptive acts or practices have never been precisely defined, the FTC is continually developing and refining a working definition in its attempts to regulate advertising. The traditional standard used to determine deception was whether a claim had the "tendency or capacity to deceive." However, this standard was criticized for being vague and all-encompassing.

In 1983 the FTC, under Chair James Miller III, put forth a new working definition of **deception**: "The commission will find deception if there is a misrepresentation, omission, or practice that is likely to mislead the consumer acting reasonably in the circumstances to the consumer's detriment."[32] Under this definition, the representation, omission, or practice must be a "material" one, meaning it is likely to affect the consumer's conduct or decision with regard to a product or service. If so, consumer injury is likely because the consumer might have chosen differently but for the deception.[33]

Miller's goal was to help the commission determine which cases were worth pursuing and which were trivial. Miller argued that for an ad to be considered worthy of FTC challenge, it should be seen by a substantial number of consumers, it should lead to significant injury, and the problem should be one that market forces are not likely to remedy. However, the revised definition may put a greater burden on the FTC to prove that deception occurred and that the deception influenced the consumers' decision-making process in a detrimental way.

Determining what constitutes deception is still a gray area. Two of the factors the FTC considers in evaluating an ad for deception are (1) whether there are significant omissions of important information and (2) whether advertisers can substantiate the claims made for the product or service. The FTC has developed several programs to address these issues.

AFFIRMATIVE DISCLOSURE

An ad can be literally true yet leave the consumer with a false or misleading impression if the claim is true only under certain conditions or circumstances or if there are limitations to what the product can or cannot do. Thus, under its **affirmative disclosure** requirement, the FTC may require advertisers to include certain types of information in their ads so consumers will be aware of all the consequences, conditions, and limitations associated with the use of a product or service. The goal of affirmative disclosure is to give consumers sufficient information to make an informed decision. An ad may be required to define the testing situation, conditions, or criteria used in making a claim. For example, fuel mileage claims in car ads are based on Environmental Protection Agency (EPA) ratings since they offer a uniform standard for making comparisons. Cigarette ads must contain a warning about the health risks associated with smoking.

An example of an affirmative disclosure ruling is the FTC's 1989 case against Campbell Soup for making deceptive and unsubstantiated claims. Campbell's ads, run as part of its "Soup is good food" campaign, linked the low fat and cholesterol content of its soup with a reduced risk of heart disease. However, the advertising failed to disclose that the soups are high in sodium, which may increase the risk of heart disease. In a consent agreement accepted in 1991, Campbell agreed that, for any soup containing more than 500 milligrams of sodium in an eight-ounce serving, it will disclose the sodium content in any advertising that directly or by implication mentions heart disease in connection with the soup. Campbell also agreed it would not imply a connection between soup and a reduction in heart disease in future advertising.[34]

Another area where the Federal Trade Commission is seeking more specificity from advertisers is in regard to country of origin claims. The FTC has been working with marketers and trade associations to develop a better definition of what the "Made in the USA" label means. The 50-year-old definition currently used requires full manufacturing in the United States, using U.S. labor and parts, with only raw materials from overseas.[35] Many companies argue that in an increasingly global economy, it is becoming very difficult to have 100 percent U.S. content and remain price competitive. However, the FTC argues that advertising or labeling a product as "Made in the USA" can provide a company with a competitive advantage. For many products some consumers do respond to the claim, as they trust the quality of domestic made products and/or feel patriotic when they buy American.

In 1995 the FTC issued a complaint against two athletic-shoe companies, New Balance and Hyde Athletic Industries Inc., the maker of Saucony shoes, arguing that the companies' "Made in the USA" claims were deceptive since they both used imported components.[36] Hyde, which imported both the soles and upper part of its shoes, agreed to a settlement and accepted a compromise label reading: "Made in the USA from domestic and imported components." However, New Balance argued that 75 percent of the cost of its shoes is derived from U.S. content and appealed the FTC ruling. The FTC held public workshops on the issue and is developing guidelines for using "Made in the USA" claims and labels that will take into consideration the percentage of domestic content as well as where the components are assembled into the finished product.

ADVERTISING SUBSTANTIATION

A major area of concern to regulatory agencies is whether advertisers can support or substantiate their claims. For many years, there were no formal requirements concerning substantiation of advertising claims. Many companies made claims without any documentation or support such as laboratory tests and clinical studies. In 1971, the FTC's **advertising substantiation** program required advertisers to have supporting documentation for their claims and to prove the claims are truthful.[37] Broadened in 1972, this program now requires advertisers to substantiate their claims before an ad appears. Substantiation is required for all claims involving safety, performance, efficacy, quality, or comparative price.

The FTC's substantiation program has had a major effect on the advertising industry, because it shifted the burden of proof from the commission to the advertiser. Before the substantiation program, the FTC had to prove that an advertiser's claims were unfair or deceptive.

Ad substantiation seeks to provide a basis for believing advertising claims so consumers can make rational and informed decisions and to deter companies from making claims they cannot adequately support. The FTC takes the perspective that it is illegal and unfair to consumers for a firm to make a claim for a product without having a "reasonable basis" for the claim. In their decision to require advertising substantiation, the commissioners made the following statement:

> Given the imbalance of knowledge and resources between a business enterprise and each of its customers, economically it is more rational and imposes far less cost on society, to require a manufacturer to confirm his affirmative product claims rather than impose a burden on each individual consumer to test, investigate, or experiment for himself. The manufacturer has the ability, the know-how, the equipment, the time and resources to undertake such information, by testing or otherwise, . . . the consumer usually does not.[38]

Many advertisers respond negatively to the FTC's advertising substantiation program. They argue it is too expensive to document all their claims and most consumers either won't understand or aren't interested in the technical data. Some advertisers threaten to avoid the substantiation issue by using puffery claims, which do not require substantiation.

Generally, advertisers making claims covered by the substantiation program must have available prior substantiation of all claims. However, in 1984, the FTC issued a new policy statement that suggested after-the-fact substantiation might be acceptable in some cases and it would solicit documentation of claims only from advertisers that are under investigation for deceptive practices.

In a number of cases, the FTC orders advertisers to cease making inadequately substantiated claims. In 1993, the FTC obtained relief against Union Oil of California and its agency for making unsubstantiated claims in advertising for Unocal's 89 and 92 octane gasoline. According to the FTC complaint, Unocal lacked adequate scientific evidence for its claims that the higher-octane gasolines increased engine performance and longevity. Yet, the FTC argued, many consumers believe that higher-octane gasoline improves an engine's performance and the advertising played into this belief. In settling with the FTC, Unocal and its agency agreed that, lacking better scientific evidence, they would stop making claims that drivers could get better performance by exceeding auto manufacturers' recommendations for fuel use.[39]

In the same year the FTC also took on the weight-loss industry when it filed a complaint charging that none of five large, well-known diet program marketers had sufficient evidence to back up claims that their customers achieved their weight-loss goals or maintained the loss (Exhibit 21–4). Three of the companies agreed to publicize the fact that most weight loss is temporary and to disclose how long their customers kept off the weight they lost. The agreement required the companies to substantiate their weight-loss claims with scientific data and to document claims that their customers keep off the weight by monitoring a group of them for two years.[40]

In 1997 the FTC challenged advertising claims made by Abbott Laboratories for its Ensure brand nutritional beverage. The FTC charged that Abbott made false and unsubstantiated claims that many doctors recommend Ensure as a meal supplement and replacement for healthy adults, including those in their 30s and 40s. The agency complaint said Abbott relied on a survey of doctors that wasn't designed to determine *whether* many doctors actually recommended Ensure as a meal replacement for healthy adults. Rather, according to the FTC complaint, the survey asked doctors to assume that they would recommend a supplement for adults who were not ill and then merely select which brand they would suggest. The FTC ruled that Abbott went too far when it suggested that doctors recommend Ensure for healthy, active people like those pictured in its ads, in order to stay healthy and active. Abbott agreed to settle the charges and stop using endorsements from medical professionals unless it could produce reliable scientific evidence to substantiate the claims.[41]

The FTC's Handling of Deceptive Advertising Cases

CONSENT AND CEASE-AND-DESIST ORDERS

Allegations of unfair or deceptive advertising come to the FTC's attention from a variety of sources, including competitors, consumers, other government agencies, or the commission's own monitoring and investigations. Once the FTC decides a complaint is justified and warrants further action, it notifies the offender, who then has 30 days to respond. The advertiser can agree to negotiate a settlement with the FTC by signing a **consent order**, which is an agreement to stop the practice or advertising in question. This agreement is for settlement purposes only and does not constitute an admission of guilt by the advertiser. Most FTC inquiries are settled by consent orders because they save the advertiser the cost and possible adverse publicity that might result if the case went further.

If the advertiser chooses not to sign the consent decree and contests the complaint, a hearing can be requested before an administrative law judge employed by the FTC but not under its influence. The judge's decision may be appealed to the full five-member commission by either side. The commission either affirms or modifies the order or dismisses the case. If the complaint has been upheld by the administrative law judge and the commission, the advertiser can appeal the case to the federal courts.

The appeal process may take some time, during which the FTC may want to stop the advertiser from engaging in the deceptive practice. The Wheeler-Lea Amendment empowers the FTC to issue a **cease-and-desist order**, which requires that the advertiser stop the specified advertising claim within 30 days and prohibits the advertiser from engaging in the objectionable practice until after the hearing is held. Violation of a cease-and-desist order is punishable by a fine of up to $10,000 a day. Figure 21–6 summarizes the FTC complaint procedure.

CORRECTIVE ADVERTISING

By using consent and cease-and-desist orders, the FTC can usually stop a particular advertising practice it believes is unfair or deceptive. However, even if an advertiser ceases using a deceptive ad, consumers may still remember some or all of the claim. To address the problem of residual effects, in the 1970s the FTC developed a program known as **corrective advertis-**

FIGURE 21—6 FTC complaint procedure

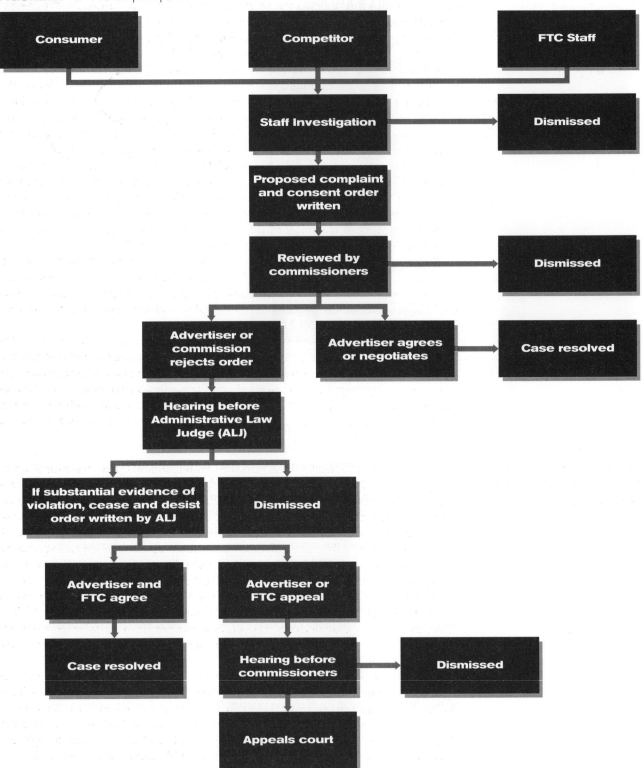

ing. An advertiser found guilty of deceptive advertising can be required to run additional advertising designed to remedy the deception or misinformation contained in previous ads.

The impetus for corrective advertising was another case involving Campbell Soup, which placed marbles in the bottom of a bowl of vegetable soup to force the solid ingredients to the surface, creating a false impression that the soup contained more vegetables than it really did. (Campbell Soup argued that if the marbles were not used, all the ingredients would settle to the bottom, leaving an impression of fewer ingredients than actually existed!) While Campbell Soup agreed to stop the practice, a group of law students calling themselves SOUP (Students Opposed to Unfair Practices) argued to the FTC that this would not remedy false impressions created by prior advertising and contended Campbell Soup should be required to run advertising to rectify the problem.[42]

Although the FTC did not order corrective advertising in the Campbell case, it has done so in many cases since then. Profile Bread ran an ad stating each slice contained fewer calories than other brands—but the ad did not mention that slices of Profile bread were thinner than those of other brands. Ocean Spray cranberry juice was found guilty of deceptive advertising because it claimed to have more "food energy" than orange or tomato juice but failed to note it was referring to the technical definition of food energy, which is calories. In each case, the advertisers were ordered to spend 25 percent of their annual media budget to run corrective ads. The STP Corporation was required to run corrective advertising for claims regarding the ability of its oil additive to reduce oil consumption. Many of the corrective ads run in the STP case appeared in business publications to serve notice to other advertisers that the FTC was enforcing the corrective advertising program. The texts of the corrective messages required in each of these cases are shown in Figure 21–7.

The consent order signed by Unocal as part of its 1993 settlement with the FTC also included a corrective advertising provision. Unocal agreed to mail a corrective notice to all of its active credit-card customers in its primary marketing area stating that most cars do not need a high-octane gasoline to perform properly and reminding them to check their owner's manual for the recommended fuel octane level.

Corrective advertising is probably the most controversial of all the FTC programs. Advertisers argue that corrective advertising infringes on First Amendment rights of freedom of speech. The effectiveness of corrective advertising campaigns is also being questioned, as is the FTC's involvement in the business of creating ads through requiring particular content in corrective messages.[43] IMC Perspective 21–2 discusses a case involving Listerine mouthwash, which tested the FTC's legal power to order corrective advertising, as well as a more recent controversial case involving Eggland's Best eggs.

Current Status of Federal Regulation by the FTC

By the end of the 1970s, the FTC had become a very powerful and active regulator of advertising. However, Congress was concerned about the FTC's broad interpretation of unfairness, which led to the restrictive legislation of the 1980 FTC Improvements Act. During the 1980s, the FTC became less active and cut back its regulatory efforts, due in large part to the Reagan administration's laissez-faire attitude toward the regulation of business in general. Some feared that the FTC had become too narrow in its regulation of national advertising, forcing companies and consumer groups to seek relief from other sources such as state and federal courts or through self-regulatory groups such as the NAD/NARB.[44]

In 1988–89, an 18-member panel chosen by the American Bar Association undertook a study of the FTC as a 20-year follow-up to the 1969 report used by President Richard Nixon to overhaul the commission. The panel's report expressed strong concern over the FTC's lack of sufficient resources and staff to regulate national advertising effectively and called for more funding.

After more than a decade of relative inactivity, the Federal Trade Commission has once again become active in the regulation of advertising. The commission has shown particular interest in cracking down on misleading advertising in areas such as health, nutrition, weight loss, and environmental claims as well as advertising directed to children and the elderly.[45] The FTC has also become more involved with potential fraud and deception through various other promotional methods such as telemarketing, 900 numbers, and infomercials.

While the FTC is the major regulator of advertising for products sold in interstate commerce, several other federal agencies and departments also regulate advertising and promotion.

Additional Federal Regulatory Agencies

THE FEDERAL COMMUNICATIONS COMMISSION

The FCC, founded in 1934 to regulate broadcast communication, has jurisdiction over the radio, television, telephone, and telegraph industries. The FCC has the authority to license

FIGURE 21–7 Examples of corrective advertising messages

Profile Bread

"Hi, [celebrity's name] for Profile Bread. Like all mothers, I'm concerned about nutrition and balanced meals. So, I'd like to clear up any misunderstanding you may have about Profile Bread from its advertising or even its name.

"Does Profile have fewer calories than any other breads? No. Profile has about the same per ounce as other breads. To be exact, Profile has seven fewer calories per slice. That's because Profile is sliced thinner. But eating Profile will not cause you to lose weight. A reduction of seven calories is insignificant. It's total calories and balanced nutrition that count. And Profile can help you achieve a balanced meal because it provides protein and B vitamins as well as other nutrients.

"How does my family feel about Profile? Well, my husband likes Profile toast, the children love Profile sandwiches, and I prefer Profile to any other bread. So you see, at our house, delicious taste makes Profile a family affair."

(To be run in 25 percent of brand's advertising, for one year.)

Ocean Spray

"If you've wondered what some of our earlier advertising meant when we said Ocean Spray Cranberry Juice Cocktail has more food energy than orange juice or tomato juice, let us make it clear: we didn't mean vitamins and minerals. Food energy means calories. Nothing more.

"Food energy is important at breakfast since many of us may not get enough calories, or food energy, to get off to a good start. Ocean Spray Cranberry Juice Cocktail helps because it contains more food energy than most other breakfast drinks.

"And Ocean Spray Cranberry Juice Cocktail gives you and your family Vitamin C plus a great wake-up taste. It's ... the other breakfast drink."

(To be run in one of every four ads for one year.)

STP

As a result of an investigation by the Federal Trade Commission into certain allegedly inaccurate past advertisements for STP's oil additive, STP Corporation has agreed to a $700,000 settlement. With regard to that settlement, STP is making the following statement:

"It is the policy of STP to support its advertising with objective information and test data. In 1974 and 1975 an independent laboratory ran tests of the company's oil additive which led to claims of reduced oil consumption. However, these tests cannot be relied on to support the oil consumption reduction claim made by STP.

"The FTC has taken the position that, in making the claim, the company violated the terms of a consent order. When STP learned that the test did not support the claim, it stopped advertising containing that claim. New tests have been undertaken to determine the extent to which the oil additive affects oil consumption. Agreement to this settlement does not constitute an admission by STP that the law has been violated. Rather, STP has agreed to resolve the dispute with the FTC to avoid protracted and prohibitively expensive litigation."

broadcast stations as well as to remove a license or deny renewal to stations not operating in the public's interest. The FCC's authority over the airways gives it the power to control advertising content and to restrict what products and services can be advertised on radio and TV. The FCC can eliminate obscene and profane programs and/or messages and those it finds in poor taste. While the FCC can purge ads that are deceptive or misleading, it generally works closely with the FTC in the regulation of advertising.

Many of the FCC's rules and regulations for TV and radio stations have been eliminated or modified. The FCC no longer limits the amount of television time that can be devoted to commercials. (But in 1991 the Children's Television Act went into effect. The act limits advertising during children's programming to 10.5 minutes an hour on weekends and 12 minutes an hour on weekdays.)

Under the Reagan administration, the controversial *Fairness Doctrine*, which required broadcasters to provide time for opposing viewpoints on important issues, was repealed on the grounds that it was counterproductive. It was argued that the Fairness Doctrine actually reduced discussion of important issues because a broadcaster might be afraid to take on a paid controversial message in case it might be required to provide equal free exposure for

IMC Perspective 21–2
The Debate over Corrective Advertising Continues

One of the most publicized corrective advertising cases ever, and the first to test the FTC's legal power to order corrective messages, involved Warner-Lambert's Listerine mouthwash. For more than 50 years, Warner-Lambert had advertised that gargling with Listerine helped prevent colds and sore throats or lessened their severity because it killed the germs that caused these illnesses. In 1975, the FTC ruled these claims could not be substantiated and ordered Listerine to stop making them. In addition the FTC argued that corrective advertising was needed to rectify the erroneous beliefs Listerine had created with its large advertising expenditures over the prior 50 years.

Warner-Lambert argued that the advertising was not misleading and, further, that the FTC did not have the power to order corrective advertising. Listerine appealed the FTC decision all the way to the Supreme Court, which rejected the argument that corrective advertising violates advertisers' First Amendment rights. The powers of the FTC in the areas of both claim substantiation and corrective advertising were upheld. Warner-Lambert was required to run $10 million worth of corrective ads over a 16-month period stating, "Listerine does not help prevent colds or sore throats or lessen their severity."

The "Warner-Lambert test" was used in a 1993 FTC decision to order corrective advertising. The case involved ads for Eggland's Best eggs claiming "You can eat eggs again . . . and not increase your serum cholesterol" and "They're special eggs from specially fed hens." The FTC argued that the company's ads and promotional materials deceptively represented that Eggland's eggs do not increase consumers' serum cholesterol and are superior to regular eggs in this respect. In a settlement with the FTC, Eggland's Best agreed not to misrepresent the absolute or comparative amount of cholesterol, total fat, saturated fat, or any other nutrient or ingredient or to make any claims about the health benefits of its eggs.

The settlement also included a provision for corrective advertising. The commissioners, by a 3 to 2 margin, voted to require Eggland's Best to place a "clear and prominent" notice on the package label for its eggs specifying that "There are no studies showing that these eggs are different from other eggs in their effect on serum cholesterol." The corrective notice was to continue for one year and cover specified geographic areas where the ads had been shown for 12 weeks or more.

The two dissenting commissioners argued that corrective advertising was unwarranted under the Warner-Lambert test. One noted there was no direct evidence, as there was in Warner-Lambert, that Eggland's ads created a lingering false impression about its eggs' effects on serum cholesterol. The other commissioner argued that there was no evidence that Eggland's campaign was so similarly saturated or that a substantial portion of the public would continue to believe the challenged claims in the absence of corrective advertising.

However, the commissioner whose vote broke the tie noted that Eggland's ability to charge about 200 percent of the typical price per dozen eggs constituted strong evidence that the company's ads had been successful in making consumers believe that Eggland's eggs were meaningfully superior. He argued, "Common sense tells me that this belief is not going to disappear overnight simply because the advertising making the claim ceases."

Some legal experts think that despite the closeness of the vote in this case, the FTC will place more emphasis on corrective advertising in the future. For example, in 1996 the FTC warned the Swiss pharmaceutical giant Ciba-Geigy that it might require the company to run corrective ads for falsely claiming that its Doan's pills are more effective than other pain relievers in combating back pain.

Sources: Sally Goll Beatty, "FTC Sues Doan's Pill Maker over Claim," *The Wall Street Journal*, June 28, 1996, p. B2; "Settlement of FTC Charges over Deceptive Cholesterol Claims Sparks Corrective Advertising Controversy," *WR&F Advertising Law Update* 7, no. 1, pp. 3, 7; *Warner-Lambert Co. v. Federal Trade Commission*, CCH P61, 563A-D.C., August 1977 and CCH P61, 646 CA-D.C., September 1977.

opposing viewpoints. It was under this doctrine that the FCC required stations to run commercials about the harmful effects of smoking before passage of the Public Health Cigarette Smoking Act of 1970, which banned broadcast advertising of cigarettes. Many stations still provide time for opposing viewpoints on controversial issues as part of their public service requirement, not necessarily directly related to fairness.

Several pieces of legislation passed in recent years involve the FCC and have an impact on advertising and promotion. The Cable Television Consumer Protection and Competition Act, passed in 1992, allows the FCC and local governments to regulate basic cable TV rates and forces cable operators to pay licensing fees for local broadcast programming they did retransmit for free. One purpose of this bill is to improve the balance between cable rates and rapidly escalating advertising revenue. FCC rules affecting telemarketing will be discussed toward the end of this chapter.

THE FOOD AND DRUG ADMINISTRATION

Now under the jurisdiction of the Department of Health and Human Services, the FDA has authority over the labeling, packaging, branding, ingredient listing, and advertising of packaged foods and drug products. The FDA is authorized to require caution and warning labels on potentially hazardous products and also has limited authority over nutritional claims made in food advertising. This agency has the authority to set rules for promoting these products and the power to seize food and drugs on charges of false and misleading advertising.

Like the FTC, the Food and Drug Administration has become a very aggressive regulatory agency in recent years, particularly since David A. Kessler's stint as commissioner beginning in 1991. The FDA has cracked down on a number of commonly used descriptive terms it believes are often abused in the labeling and advertising of food products—for example, *natural*, *light*, *no cholesterol*, and *fat free*. The FDA has also become tougher on nutritional claims implied by brand names that might send a misleading message to consumers. For example, Great Foods of America was not permitted to continue using the HeartBeat trademark under which it sold most of its foods. The FDA argued the trademark went too far in implying the foods have special advantages for the heart and overall health.

Many changes in food labeling are a result of the Nutritional Labeling and Education Act, which Congress passed in 1990. Under this law the FDA established legal definitions for a wide range of terms (such as *low fat*, *light*, and *reduced calories*) and required straightforward labels for all foods beginning in early 1994 (Exhibit 21–5). In its current form the act applies only to food labels, but it may soon affect food advertising as well. The FTC would be asked to ensure that food ads comply with the new FDA standards.

In 1996 President Clinton signed an executive order declaring that nicotine is an addictive drug and giving the Food and Drug Administration broad jurisdiction to regulate cigarettes and smokeless tobacco. IMC Perspective 21–3 discusses the new regulations the FDA hopes to enact, most of which are designed to keep teenagers from smoking.

THE U.S. POSTAL SERVICE

Many marketers use the U.S. mail to deliver advertising and promotional messages. The U.S. Postal Service has control over advertising involving the use of the mail and ads that involve lotteries, obscenity, or fraud. The regulation against fraudulent use of the mail has been used to control deceptive advertising by numerous direct-response advertisers. These firms advertise on TV or radio or in magazines and newspapers and use the U.S. mail to receive orders and payment. Many have been prosecuted by the Post Office Department for use of the mail in conjunction with a fraudulent or deceptive offer.

BUREAU OF ALCOHOL, TOBACCO, AND FIREARMS

The Bureau of Alcohol, Tobacco, and Firearms (BATF) is an agency within the Treasury Department that enforces laws, develops regulations, and is responsible for tax collection for the liquor industry. The BATF regulates and controls the advertising of alcoholic beverages. The agency determines what information can be provided in ads as well as what constitutes false and misleading advertising. It is also responsible for including warning labels on alcohol advertising and banning the use of active athletes in beer commercials. The BATF can impose strong sanctions for violators.

The Lanham Act

While most advertisers rely on self-regulatory mechanisms and the FTC to deal with deceptive or misleading advertising by their competitors, many companies are filing lawsuits against competitors they believe are making false claims. One piece of federal legislation that

IMC Perspective 21–3
New Regulations Try to Curb Teen Smoking

For more than 30 years the tobacco industry has been following a strategy of seeking compromise laws to avoid more stringent regulations. In the mid-1960s cigarette makers forestalled Federal Trade Commission regulations of their ads by agreeing to put warning labels on their packs. They also successfully weakened the FTC's proposed language. The labels became a powerful industry defense in liability lawsuits by smokers, as lawyers for tobacco companies argued that the risks of smoking were publicized. A few years later, the tobacco companies asked Congress to ban them from advertising on television. The ban reduced a wave of antismoking commercials that got on TV under the equal time provision of the Fairness Doctrine—and cigarette consumption rose.

Michael Pertschuk, a former FTC commissioner and longtime tobacco opponent, says the tobacco industry "has always had a strategy of giving just what they had to give to head off something worse." However, the tobacco industry may have little room to compromise over the latest round of regulations announced by the federal government. In August 1996, President Clinton signed an executive order that defines nicotine as an addictive drug and gives the Food and Drug Administration broad jurisdiction to regulate cigarettes and smokeless tobacco.

Under its new authority, the FDA is enacting sweeping new rules designed to keep teenagers from smoking. The new rules include requiring that anyone younger than 27 show proof of age before buying cigarettes; banning most vending machine sales, except in places frequented by adults, such as bars; banning brand-name tobacco sponsorship of sporting events; eliminating brand-name tobacco logos on baseball caps, T-shirts, and other merchandise; and in the most controversial provision of all, restricting advertising in publications read by a significant number of young people to a black-and-white, text-only format with no photographs. This format also applies to billboards, which will be banned entirely within 1,000 feet of schools and playgrounds.

The new rules will enable the FDA to insert itself between consumers and a product the government says kills more than 400,000 Americans each year. Their goal is to keep teens from ever starting to smoke. Studies show that 90 percent of adults who smoke began before they turned 18. Underage smoking has been rising since 1992, reversing a 16-year decline, even though all 50 states outlaw the sale of cigarettes to minors. In announcing the new FDA regulations, President Clinton said the smoking epidemic among young people is no accident: "Children are bombarded daily by massive marketing campaigns that play on their vulnerabilities, their insecurities, their longings to be something in the world. Joe Camel promises that smoking will make you cool. Virginia Slims models whisper that smoking will help you stay thin."

Clinton declared, "Joe Camel and the Marlboro Man will be out of our children's reach forever." However, it may not be as easy as he thinks. Although the new rules are to be implemented over a two-year period, they are likely to be tied up in the courts for years. A spokeswoman for the Tobacco Institute, the industry's lobbying arm, says, "We have no choice but to fight the FDA rules. They are illegal and they will not work to reduce youth smoking." Advertising and publishing trade associations are also suing to block the rules, which they say would cost them $1 billion a year. Citing a recent Supreme Court ruling that overturned a ban on liquor price advertising, the Freedom to Advertise Coalition contends that the regulations violate the Constitution's First Amendment guarantee of freedom of speech.

In keeping with its past, the tobacco industry has tried to come up with a compromise to counter the biggest legal and regulatory attack it has ever faced. Philip Morris Cos. and other tobacco companies asked Congress to impose a more limited set of restrictions on cigarette sales and advertising aimed at curbing youth smoking. However, the proposal had a giant string attached: The FDA would be blocked from ever regulating tobacco products. Antismoking advocates argue that the tobacco industry knows it needs some form of legislation to stop the FDA from enacting its new regulations. But this time it may find the government very unwilling to compromise.

Sources: Sheryl Stolberg, "Clinton Imposes Wide Crackdown on Tobacco Firms," *Los Angeles Times*, August 24, 1996, pp. A1, 10; Richard Lacayo, "Put Out the Butt, Junior," *Time*, September 2, 1996, p. 51; Suein L. Hwang, Timothy Noah, and Laurie McGinley, "Philip Morris Proposes Curbs on Sales to Kids," *The Wall Street Journal*, May 16, 1996, pp. B1, 5.

has become increasingly important in this regard is the Lanham Act. This act was originally written in 1947 as the Lanham Trade-Mark Act to protect words, names, symbols, or other devices adopted to identify and distinguish a manufacturer's products. The **Lanham Act** was amended to encompass false advertising by prohibiting "any false description or representation including words or other symbols tending falsely to describe or represent the same." While the FTC Act did not give individual advertisers the opportunity to sue a competitor for deceptive advertising, civil suits are permitted under the Lanham Act.

More and more companies are using the Lanham Act to sue competitors for their advertising claims, particularly since comparative advertising has become so common. For example, a U.S. district court fined Jartran a record $20 million in punitive damages on top of the $20 million awarded to U-Haul International to compensate for losses resulting from ads comparing the companies' prices and equipment that were ruled deceptive. In several recent cases, companies have sued a competitor for damages resulting from false advertising claims. A court ordered Ralston Purina to pay Alpo Petfoods $12 million for damages it caused by making false claims that its Purina Puppy Chow dog food could ameliorate and help prevent joint disease. The court ruled that the claim was based on faulty data and that the company continued the campaign after learning its research was in error. Alpo was awarded the money as compensation for lost revenue and for the costs of advertising it ran in response to the Puppy Chow campaign.[46]

Wilkinson Sword and its advertising agency were found guilty of false advertising and ordered to pay $953,000 in damages to the Gillette Co. Wilkinson had run TV and print ads claiming its Ultra Glide razor and blades produced shaves "six times smoother" than Gillette's Atra Plus blades. This case marked the first time an agency was held liable for damages in connection with false claims made in a client's advertising.[47] Although the agency was later found not liable, the case served as a sobering reminder to agencies that they can be drawn into litigation over advertising they create for their clients. To deal with this problem, many agencies insist on indemnification clauses in contracts with their clients.

Suing competitors for false claims was made even easier with passage of the Trademark Law Revision Act of 1988. According to this law, anyone is vulnerable to civil action who "misrepresents the nature, characteristics, qualities, or geographical origin of his or her or another person's goods, services, or commercial activities." This wording closed a loophole in the Lanham Act, which prohibited only false claims about one's own goods or services. While many disputes over comparative claims are never contested or are resolved through the NAD, more companies are turning to lawsuits for several reasons: the broad information discovery powers available under federal civil procedure rules, the speed with which a competitor can stop the offending ad through a preliminary injunction, and the possibility of collecting damages.[48] However, companies do not always win their lawsuits. And when they lose, a competitor may take advantage of its victory in future ads, as discussed in IMC Perspective 21–4.

STATE REGULATION

In addition to the various federal rules and regulations, advertisers must also concern themselves with numerous state and local controls. An important early development in state regulation of advertising was the adoption in 44 states of the *Printers Ink* model statutes as a basis for advertising regulation. These statutes were drawn up in 1911 by *Printers Ink*, for many years the major trade publication of the advertising industry. Many states have since modified the original statutes and adopted laws similar to those of the Federal Trade Commission Act for dealing with false and misleading advertising.

In addition to recognizing decisions by the federal courts regarding false or deceptive practices, many states have special controls and regulations governing the advertising of specific industries or practices. As the federal government became less involved in the regulation of national advertising during the 1980s, many state attorneys general (AGs) began to enforce state laws regarding false or deceptive advertising. For example, the attorneys general in New York and Texas initiated investigations of Kraft ads claiming the pasteurized cheese used in Cheez Whiz was real cheese.[49] The well-publicized "monster truck" decep-

IMC Perspective 21–4
The Battle of the Spaghetti Sauces

Marketers often use comparative advertising when introducing a new product to position their brand directly against a market leader and promote its advantages. When the Campbell Soup Co. introduced its Prego spaghetti sauce in 1988, Van Den Bergh Foods' Ragú brand was the market leader with a nearly 50 percent market share. Campbell's agency, FCB/Leber Katz partners, knew it had to find a way to convince consumers that Prego was better than Ragú. One of the most important attributes of a spaghetti sauce is thickness, so the agency decided that the best way to convince consumers that Prego was thicker was to show them. Based on the old idea that seeing is believing, the agency created commercials showing side-by-side comparisons of Prego's regular version and Ragú Old World Style spaghetti sauce. In several executions, some of which show the two brands being poured over spaghetti and through slotted spoons, Ragú is portrayed as thin and runny compared to a thicker, slower-pouring Prego.

Van Den Bergh challenged the Prego commercials before the television networks and the National Advertising Division of the Council of Better Business Bureaus. When the appeals to the self-regulatory bodies failed, the company took Campbell Soup Co. to court in 1993. In March 1995, the U.S. District Court in New York dismissed Van Den Bergh's suit to have Campbell's comparative ads for Prego halted. Van Den Bergh continued the legal battle and appealed the lower court's decision. However, in September 1996, the U.S. Court of Appeals ruled that Van Den Bergh had waited too long to sue. An attorney specializing in advertising said the court was essentially wondering how false the Prego ads could be if Van Den Bergh waited five years to sue.

Campbell capitalized on its first-round victory in 1995 by creating a new ad based on the district court's decision. The ad tweaks Ragú by showing snippets of the compari-

son ads and then a shot of Prego with a breadstick standing up in the sauce. The tagline: "Ragú took us to court. . . . We made our case stand. Just like our breadstick." Campbell also ran this spot following its victory in the appellate court in late 1996.

The legal battle appears to have reached its final turn and the rulings have vindicated Campbell's use of pointedly comparative advertising. Van Den Bergh Foods has one more level of appeal available—the U.S. Supreme Court—although it's unlikely that the company will appeal the case that far. The Prego–Ragú spaghetti sauce battle is a classic example of how comparative advertising is used to distinguish an upstart brand from an established market leader. Since the campaign began in 1988, Prego's share of the spaghetti sauce category has climbed to 26 percent, while Ragú's share has fallen to 37 percent. Campbell is likely to continue using the comparative messages to differentiate Prego from Ragú. An agency executive says the marketer and agency "are constantly working on evolving that simple idea." Van Den Bergh Foods may have to become thicker, either in the skin or with Ragú.

Source: Judann Pollack, "Prego Prevails in Battle over Comparative Ad," *Advertising Age*, September 16, 1996, p. 12.

tive advertising case involving Volvo and its advertising agency discussed in IMC Perspective 21–1 was initiated by the attorney general's office in the state of Texas.

The **National Association of Attorneys General** (NAAG) moved against a number of national advertisers as a result of inactivity by the FTC during the Reagan administration. In 1987, the NAAG developed enforcement guidelines on airfare advertising that were adopted by more than 40 states. The NAAG has also been involved in other regulatory areas, including car-rental price advertising as well as advertising dealing with nutrition and health claims in food ads.[50] In the early 1990s, a group of attorneys general from various states reached an agreement with Pfizer Corp. and its ad agency to stop making deceptive claims regarding the ability of Pfizer's Plax mouthwash to reduce plaque.[51]

The NAAG's foray into regulating national advertising raises the issue of whether the states working together can create and implement uniform national advertising standards that will, in effect, supersede federal authority. An American Bar Association panel concluded that the Federal Trade Commission is the proper regulator of national advertising and recommended the state AGs focus on practices that harm consumers within a single state.[52] This report also called for cooperation between the FTC and the state attorneys general.

Advertisers are concerned about the trend toward increased regulation of advertising at the state and local levels because it could mean that national advertising campaigns would have to be modified for every state or municipality. Yet the FTC takes the position that businesses that advertise and sell nationwide need a national advertising policy. While the FTC recognizes the need for greater cooperation with the states, the agency believes regulation of national advertising should be its responsibility.[53] Just in case, the advertising industry is still keeping a watchful eye on changes in advertising rules, regulations, and policies at the state and local levels.

REGULATION OF OTHER PROMOTIONAL AREAS

So far we've focused on the regulation of advertising. However, other elements of the promotional mix also come under the surveillance of federal, state, and local laws and various self-regulatory bodies. This section examines some of the rules, regulations, and guidelines that affect sales promotion, direct marketing, and marketing on the Internet.

Sales Promotion

Both consumer- and trade-oriented promotions are subject to various regulations. The Federal Trade Commission regulates many areas of sales promotion through the Marketing Practices Division of the Bureau of Consumer Protection. Many promotional practices are also policed by state attorneys general and local regulatory agencies. Various aspects of trade promotion, such as allowances, are regulated by the Robinson-Patman Act, which gives the FTC broad powers to control discriminatory pricing practices.

CONTESTS AND SWEEPSTAKES

As noted in Chapter 15, numerous legal considerations affect the design and administration of contests and sweepstakes, and these promotions are regulated by a number of federal and state agencies. There are two important considerations in developing contests (including games) and sweepstakes. First, marketers must be careful to ensure their contest or sweepstakes is not classified as a *lottery*, which is considered a form of gambling and violates the Federal Trade Commission Act and many state and local laws. A promotion is considered a lottery if a prize is offered, if winning a prize depends on chance and not skill, and if the participant is required to give up something of value in order to participate. The latter requirement is referred to as *consideration* and is the basis on which most contests, games, and sweepstakes avoid being considered lotteries. Generally, as long as consumers are not required to make a purchase to enter a contest or sweepstakes, consideration is not considered to be present and the promotion is not considered a lottery.

The second important requirement in the use of contests and sweepstakes is that the marketer provide full disclosure of the promotion. Regulations of the FTC, as well as many state and local governments, require marketers using contests, games, and sweepstakes to make certain all of the details are given clearly and to follow prescribed rules to ensure the fairness of the game.[54] Disclosure requirements include the exact number of prizes to be awarded and the odds of winning, the duration and termination dates of the promotion, and the availability of lists of winners of various prizes (Exhibit 21–6). The FTC also has specific rules governing the way games and contests are conducted, such as requirements that game pieces be randomly distributed, that a game not be terminated before the distribution of all game pieces, and that additional pieces not be added during the course of a game.

Recently a number of states have responded to what they believe is widespread fraud on the part of some contest and sweepstakes operators. In 1995, at least 13 states either passed or tightened prize notification laws, requiring fuller disclosure of rules, odds, and the retail value of prizes. And many of the states are following through with tougher enforcement of these laws. For example, Publishers Clearing House, known for its million-dollar giveaways, agreed to pay $490,000 to 14 states and to change some of its language, better defining terms like "finalist" and "tie breaker." It also began to disclose the odds of winning prizes. Some of the most ambitious legal actions are taking place in individual states such as West Virginia

EXHIBIT 21—6
Marketers are required to provide
consumers with full details of a
contest or sweepstakes

and Iowa, where prosecutors are taking sweepstakes and contest companies to court for misleading and deceptive practices.[55]

PREMIUMS

Another sales promotion area subject to various regulations is the use of premiums. A common problem associated with premiums is misrepresentation of their value. Marketers that make a premium offer should list its value as the price at which the merchandise is usually sold on its own. Marketers must also be careful in making premium offers to special audiences such as children. While premium offers for children are legal, their use is controversial; many critics argue that they encourage children to request a product for the premium rather than for its value. The Children's Advertising Review Unit has voluntary guidelines concerning the use of premium offers. However, a recent study of children's advertising commissioned by CARU found the single most prevalent violation involved devoting virtually an entire commercial message to information about a premium. CARU guidelines state that advertising targeted to children must emphasize the product rather than the premium offer.[56]

TRADE ALLOWANCES

Marketers using various types of trade allowances must be careful not to violate any stipulations of the Robinson-Patman Act, which prohibits price discrimination. Certain sections of the Robinson-Patman Act prohibit a manufacturer from granting wholesalers and retailers various types of promotional allowances and/or payments unless they are made available to all customers on proportionally equal terms.[57] Another form of trade promotion regulated by the Robinson-Patman Act is vertical cooperative advertising. The FTC monitors cooperative advertising programs to ensure that co-op funds are made available to retailers on a proportionally equal basis and that the payments are not used as a disguised form of price discrimination.

DIRECT MARKETING

As we saw in Chapter 14, direct marketing is growing rapidly. Many consumers now purchase products directly from companies in response to TV and print advertising or direct selling. The Federal Trade Commission enforces laws related to direct marketing, including mail-order offers, the use of 900 telephone numbers, and direct-response TV advertising. The U.S. Postal Service enforces laws dealing with the use of the mail to deliver advertising and promotional messages or receive payments and orders for items advertised in print or broadcast media.

A number of laws govern the use of mail-order selling. The FTC and the Postal Service police direct-response advertising closely to ensure the ads are not deceptive or misleading and do not misrepresent the product or service being offered. Laws also forbid mailing unordered merchandise to consumers, and rules govern the use of "negative option" plans whereby a company proposes to send merchandise to consumers and expects payment unless the consumer sends a notice of rejection or cancellation.[58] FTC rules also encourage direct marketers to ship ordered merchandise promptly. Companies that cannot ship merchandise within the time period stated in the solicitation (or 30 days if no time is stated) must give buyers the option to cancel the order and receive a full refund.[59]

Another area of direct marketing facing increased regulation is telemarketing. With the passage of the Telephone Consumer Protection Act of 1991, marketers who use telephones to contact consumers must follow a complex set of rules developed by the Federal Communications Commission. These rules require telemarketers to maintain an in-house list of residential telephone subscribers who do not want to be called. Consumers who continue to receive unwanted calls can take the telemarketer to state court for damages of up to $500. The rules also ban telemarketing calls to homes before 8:00 A.M. and after 9:00 P.M., automatic dialer calls, and recorded messages to emergency phones, health care facilities, and numbers for which the call recipient may be charged. They also ban unsolicited junk fax ads and require that fax transmissions clearly indicate the sender's name and fax number.[60]

The direct-marketing industry is also scrutinized by various self-regulatory groups, such as the Direct Marketing Association and the Direct Selling Association, that have specific guidelines and standards member firms are expected to adhere to and abide by. Exhibit 21–7 shows part of the Code of Ethics of the Direct Selling Association.

EXHIBIT 21–7 The Direct Selling Association has a Code of Ethics for companies engaged in direct selling

**DIRECT SELLING
ASSOCIATION**

**CODE
OF
ETHICS**

PREAMBLE

The Direct Selling Association, recognizing that companies engaged in direct selling assume certain responsibilities toward consumers arising out of the personal-contact method of distribution of their products and services, hereby sets forth the basic fair and ethical principles and practices to which member companies of the association will continue to adhere in the conduct of their business.

INTRODUCTION

The Direct Selling Association is the national trade association of the leading firms that manufacture and distribute goods and services sold directly to consumers. The Association's mission is "to protect, serve and promote the effectiveness of member companies and the independent businesspeople marketing their products and to assure the highest level of business ethics and service to consumers." The cornerstone of the Association's commitment to ethical business practices and consumer service is its Code of Ethics. Every member company pledges to abide by the Code's standards and procedures as a condition of admission and continuing membership in the Association. Consumers can rely on the extra protection provided by the Code when they purchase products or services from a salesperson associated with a member company of the Direct Selling Association. For a current list of Association members, contact DSA, 1776 K St., N.W., Washington, DC 20006, (202) 293-5760.

A. CODE OF CONDUCT

1. Deceptive or Unlawful Consumer Practices

No member company of the Association shall engage in any deceptive or unlawful consumer practice.

2. Products or Services

The offer of products or services for sale by member companies of the Association shall be accurate and truthful as to price, grade, quality, make, value, performance, quantity, currency of model, and availability.

3. Terms of Sale

A written order or receipt shall be delivered to the customer at the time of sale, which sets forth in language that is clear and free of ambiguity:

A. All the terms and conditions of sale, with specification of the total amount the customer will be required to pay, including all interest, service charges and fees, and other costs and expenses as required by federal and state law;

B. The name and address of the salesperson or the member firm represented.

4. Warranties and Guarantees

The terms of any warranty or guarantee offered by the seller in connection with the sale shall be furnished to the buyer in a manner that fully conforms to federal and state warranty and guarantee laws and regulations. The manufacturer, distributor and/or seller shall fully and promptly perform in accordance with the terms of all warranties and guarantees offered to consumers.

5. Pyramid Schemes

For the purpose of this Code, pyramid or endless chain schemes shall be considered consumer transactions actionable under this Code. The Code Administrator shall determine whether such pyramid or endless chain schemes constitute a violation of this Code in accordance with applicable federal, state and/or local law or regulation.

Marketing on the Internet

The rapid growth of the Internet as a marketing tool is creating a new area of concern for regulators. Currently marketing on the Internet is not subject to any formal government regulation, and many consumer and industry groups are concerned that some marketers will use the new medium to get around regulations and restrictions on other promotional areas. Two major areas of concern with regard to marketing on the Internet are privacy issues and online marketing to children.

With regard to privacy, several consumer and industry groups have proposed significant restrictions in the way marketers use the World Wide Web to get information from consumers, the types of information they can get, and what they do with this information.[61] The restrictions that have been proposed include:

- Banning unsolicited e-mail that cannot be automatically screened out. The Direct Marketing Association and the Interactive Services Association propose requiring marketers who send unsolicited e-mail messages to use coding that will allow mail systems to automatically remove such messages.
- Disclosing fully and prominently both the marketer's identity and the use for which information is being gathered in every communication.
- Giving consumers the right to bar marketers from selling or sharing any information collected from them as well as to review the personal information collected.

While these proposals are aimed at protecting the privacy rights of adults, one of the biggest concerns is how to restrict marketers whose activities or websites are targeted at children. A number of children's advocacy groups have been critical of online marketing to children. In 1996 the Center for Media Education, in cooperation with the National Parent-Teachers Association (PTA), the Consumer Federation of America, and several other groups, issued a report entitled the "Web of Deception."[62] The report criticized marketers' online activities in a number of areas, including seeking household information from kids, sending direct mail, offering prizes, using advertising characters to reach children, and mixing advertising and nonadvertising content in websites.

The report called for strict rules that would virtually eliminate the websites for children presently offered by some marketers and media companies and urged the FTC to adopt guidelines and restrictions. The restrictions being sought include prohibiting marketers from obtaining any personal information, including the age and e-mail address of children; forcing the clear labeling of advertising and promotion and its clear separation from other content; banning product mascots as spokespeople for websites; barring hypertext links jumping from content areas to advertising; and banning any microtargeting of children and direct-response marketing based on website-gathered data.

Following a Federal Trade Commission hearing in 1996, chair Robert Pitofsky issued a plea for voluntary industry codes rather than FTC rules and regulations. He noted that the commission's legal authority is limited to the areas of unfair or deceptive promotional practices, and many potential abuses may not fall into these categories. Extending the FTC's legal authority would require congressional action.

As the use of the Internet as a commercial medium increases, the need for ethical standards by marketers and voluntary industry codes and guidelines will become greater. If they fail to respond, intervention by the FTC or other regulatory agencies is likely.

◆ SUMMARY

Regulation and control of advertising stem from internal or self-regulation as well as from external control by federal, state, and local regulatory agencies. For many years the advertising industry has promoted the use of voluntary self-regulation to regulate advertising and limit government interference with and control over advertising. Self-regula-

tion of advertising emanates from all segments of the advertising industry, including advertisers and their agencies, business and advertising associations, and the media.

The NAD/NARB, the primary self-regulatory mechanism for national advertising, has been very effective in achieving its goal of voluntary regulation of advertising. Various media also have their own advertising guidelines. The major television networks maintain the most stringent review process and restrictions.

Traditionally, the federal government has been the most important source of external regulation, with the Federal Trade Commission serving as the major watchdog of advertising in the United States. The FTC protects both consumers and businesses from unfair and deceptive practices and anticompetitive behavior. The FTC became very active in the regulation of advertising during the 1970s when it began several new programs and policies, including affirmative disclosure, advertising substantiation, and corrective advertising. Since 1980 the FTC has not been allowed to implement industrywide rules that would define unfair advertising practices. However, the advertising industry and Congress are nearing agreement on a definition of unfairness, and this power may be restored to the FTC.

In 1983 the FTC developed a new working definition of deceptive advertising. Recently the FTC has become more active in policing false and deceptive advertising. Under the Lanham Act, many companies are taking the initiative by suing competitors that make false claims. Many states, as well as the National Association of Attorneys General, are also ac-

tive in exercising their jurisdiction over false and misleading advertising.

A number of laws also govern the use of other promotional mix elements, such as sales promotion and direct marketing. The Federal Trade Commission regulates many areas of sales promotion as well as direct marketing. Various consumer-oriented sales promotion tools such as contests, games, sweepstakes, and premiums are subject to regulation. Recently many states have become very active in the regulation of contests and sweepstakes. Trade promotion practices, such as the use of promotional allowances and vertical cooperative advertising, are regulated by the Federal Trade Commission under the Robinson–Patman Act. The FTC also enforces laws in a variety of areas that relate to direct marketing and mail-order selling, while the FCC has rules governing telemarketing companies.

Currently there are no specific laws governing marketing practices on the Internet. However, two major areas of concern with regard to marketing on the Internet are privacy and online marketing to children. The Federal Trade Commission has called for voluntary industry codes rather than FTC rules to govern marketers' use of the Internet.

KEY TERMS

self-regulation, 655
Better Business Bureau, 657
Council of Better Business
    Bureaus, 657
National Advertising
    Review Board, 657
National Advertising
    Review Council, 657

Federal Trade
    Commission, 663
Federal Trade
    Commission Act, 663
Wheeler–Lea
    Amendment, 663
trade regulation rules, 665

unfairness, 665
puffery, 666
deception, 666
affirmative disclosure, 667
advertising
    substantiation, 667
consent order, 669

cease-and-desist orders,
    669
corrective advertising,
    669–670
Lanham Act, 676
National Association of
    Attorneys General, 677

DISCUSSION QUESTIONS

1. Analyze the decision by the Distilled Spirits Council of the United States to overturn its self-imposed ban on broadcast advertising. Do you agree with the industry's argument that it is at a competitive disadvantage because beer and wine are advertised on TV and hard liquor is not?

2. Discuss the pros and cons of self-regulation of advertising through organizations such as the NAD/NARB. What are the incentives for advertisers to cooperate with self-regulatory bodies?

3. IMC Perspective 21–1 discusses the controversy between BMW and Volvo regarding proper testing methods for determining acceleration. Based on the information provided, which company's testing methods appear to be more reliable? Do you agree with BMW's arguments that the Volvo ad was biased, inaccurate, and misleading?

4. Although it is legal, do you think advertising by professionals such as doctors, lawyers, and dentists is ethical? Defend your position.

5. Discuss the FTC definition of unfairness. Why do you think there has been so much opposition to having the FTC use unfairness as a legal foundation for regulating advertising?

6. Do you agree with marketers and trade associations that argue that the FTC's definition of "Made in the USA," which requires full manufacturing in the United States using U.S. labor and parts, with only raw materials from overseas, is out of date? What restrictions should the FTC put on marketers such as New Balance who want to use "Made in the USA" in their advertising claims?

7. What is meant by puffery? Find examples of several ads that use puffery. Should advertisers be permitted to use puffery? Why or why not?

8. What is meant by advertising substantiation? Should advertisers be required to substantiate their claims before running an ad, or should they need to provide documentation only if their advertising claims are challenged?

9. IMC Perspective 21–3 discusses the new FDA restrictions imposed on the tobacco industry that are designed to curb smoking by teens and children. Do you think these new regulations will be effective? Why or why not?

10. Discuss some rules and regulations that affect the use of nonadvertising elements of the promotional mix, such as sales promotion, direct marketing, and marketing on the Internet. Do these promotional areas require as much regulatory attention as advertising? Why or why not?

22

Evaluating the Social, Ethical, and Economic Aspects of Advertising and Promotion

Chapter Objectives

- To consider various perspectives concerning the social, ethical, and economic aspects of advertising and promotion.

- To evaluate the social criticisms of advertising.

- To examine the economic role of advertising and its effects on consumer choice, competition, and product costs and prices.

USING ADVERTISING TO PROMOTE WORTHY CAUSES

Consumers are bombarded with advertising messages designed to sell them all types of products and services. Ad agencies make their money by creating these ads, and the media generate income by selling ad time and space to run them. However, the advertising community also devotes considerable time, effort, services, and money to develop messages to promote worthy causes or deal with societal problems such as AIDS, drug abuse, or drunk driving. Much of this work is done through the Advertising Council, a nonprofit educational organization supported by advertisers, ad agencies, and the media that creates more than $1 billion of free advertising each year.

Many agencies work on these campaigns on a pro bono basis, donating the time, talent, and services of some of their creative staff. Local TV and radio stations as well as the major networks donate media time for public service announcements (PSAs), while magazines and newspapers donate space. Many pro bono campaigns address well-publicized problems. For example, the Partnership for a Drug-Free America is a nonprofit collation of professionals from the communications industry whose collective mission is to reduce demand for illicit drugs in America. To date, nearly 400 commercials have been created by partnership volunteers and more than $1 billion of media time has been donated to run the messages.

In early 1997 the Clinton administration proposed a $350 million antidrug advertising program, with half of the costs coming from contributions of space and time by the media and half from ads paid for by the government. It would be one

Denzel Washington

Put this card in the hands of a child and there'll be no room for a gun. A needle. Or a knife.

It's only a piece of paper, but that little membership card has helped keep millions of kids off drugs, out of gangs and in school. To learn how you can help the Boys & Girls Clubs, call: **1-800-854-Club.**

BOYS & GIRLS CLUBS OF AMERICA

of the biggest advertising programs ever undertaken by the federal government and would be in addition to the antidrug PSAs run by the Partnership for a Drug-Free America.

Agencies also do pro bono work for causes or groups that are not well known but are important in their own right. For example, Wieden & Kennedy, the agency best known for its outstanding creative work for Nike, does a pro bono campaign for the American Indian College Fund (AICF). The AICF was founded to raise monies to help the 27 tribal colleges in the United States that are members of the American Indian Higher Education Consortium. Most of these tribal colleges are located on Native American reservations, such as the Crow reservation in Montana, which is the home of Little Big Horn College.

The AICF campaign is somewhat different from the typical cause campaign. The ads stress the importance of a college education in helping American Indians achieve success and improve their economic opportunities. But they also focus on the preservation of Native American culture. With the theme "Help save the cultures that could save ours," the campaign promotes support for the AICF as support for the traditional values of American Indians. Donations to the AICF are up significantly and the series has won awards as one of the best pro bono campaigns.

Another public service campaign that has been very successful is for the Boys & Girls Clubs of America and features actor Denzel Washington. The campaign, done pro bono by the New York agency Ammirati Puris Lintas, is designed to establish an image to distinguish the Boys & Girls Clubs from other public service groups and to encourage adults to organize clubs. Washington is a very credible spokesperson since he was a club member for 12 years of his childhood; the agency has turned his real-life Boys & Girls Clubs experience into a poignant, multiphase campaign. The campaign's PSAs received 35,000 airings in 1996, nearly six times the number for the typical nonprofit group. Since the campaign began, the number of Boys & Girls Clubs opened each year has nearly tripled and the organization's vice president of marketing and communications says existing clubs are "jam-packed."

Sources: Ira Teinowitz, "$175 Mil in Anti-drug Ads Urged," *Advertising Age*, February 17, 1997, p. 37; Pamela Sebastian, "Boys & Girls Club Featuring Denzel Washington Is a Standout," *The Wall Street Journal*, July 8, 1996, p. B7; "The Best of Pro Bono 1993," *Adweek*, December 20, 1993, p. 28.

> If I were to name the deadliest subversive force within capitalism, the single greatest source of its waning morality—I would without hesitation name advertising. How else should one identify a force that debases language, drains thought, and undoes dignity?[1]

The primary focus of this text has been on the role of advertising and other promotional variables as marketing activities used to convey information to, and influence the behavior of, consumers. We have been concerned with examining the advertising and promotion function in the context of a business and marketing environment and from a perspective that assumes these activities are appropriate. However, as you can see in this quote from economist Robert Heilbroner, not everyone shares this viewpoint. Advertising and promotion are the most visible of all business activities and are prone to scrutiny by those who are concerned about the methods marketers use to sell their products and services.

Proponents of advertising argue that it is the lifeblood of business—it provides consumers with information about products and services and encourages them to improve their standard of living. They say advertising produces jobs and helps new firms enter the marketplace. Companies employ people who make the products and provide the services that advertising sells. Free market economic systems are based on competition, which revolves around information, and nothing delivers information better and at less cost than advertising.

Not everyone, however, is sold on the value of advertising. Critics argue that most advertising is more propaganda than information; it creates needs and faults consumers never knew they had. Ads suggest that children won't succeed without a computer, that our bodies should be leaner, our faces younger, and our houses cleaner. They point to the sultry, scantily clad bodies used in ads to sell everything from perfume to beer to power tools and argue that advertising promotes materialism, insecurity, and greed.

Because of its high visibility and pervasiveness, along with its persuasive character, advertising has been the subject of a great deal of controversy and criticism. Numerous books are critical of not only advertising's methods and techniques but also its social consequences. Various parties—including scholars, economists, politicians, sociologists, government agencies, social critics, special-interest groups, and consumers—have attacked advertising for a variety of reasons, including its excessiveness, the way it influences society, the methods it uses, its exploitation of consumers, and its effect on our economic system.

Advertising is a very powerful force, and this text would not be complete without a look at the criticisms regarding its social and economic effects as well as some defenses against these charges. We consider the various criticisms of advertising from an ethical and societal perspective and then appraise the economic effects of advertising.

ADVERTISING AND PROMOTION ETHICS

In the previous chapter, we examined the regulatory environment in which advertising and promotion operate. While many laws and regulations determine what advertisers can and cannot do, not every issue is covered by a rule. Marketers must often make decisions regarding appropriate and responsible actions based on ethical considerations rather than on what is legal or within industry guidelines. **Ethics** are moral principles and values that govern the actions and decisions of an individual or group.[2]

A particular action may be within the law and still not be ethical. A good example of this involves target marketing. No laws restrict tobacco companies from targeting advertising and

Good Example.

promotion for new brands to African-Americans. However, given the high levels of lung cancer and smoking-related illnesses among the black population, many people would consider this an unethical business practice.

Throughout this text we have presented a number of ethical perspectives to show how various aspects of advertising and promotion often involve ethical considerations. Ethical issues must be considered in integrated marketing communications decisions. And advertising and promotion are areas where a lapse in ethical standards or judgment can result in actions that are highly visible and often very damaging to a company. The controversy over Volvo's monster truck commercial discussed in IMC Perspective 21–1 is an example of this.

eg.

The role of advertising in society is controversial and has sometimes resulted in attempts to restrict or ban advertising and other forms of promotion to certain groups or for certain products. College students are one such group. A study by Columbia University's Center on Addiction and Substance Abuse a few years ago concluded that America's colleges are witnessing a major increase in binge drinking, particularly among women, and as many as one in three students abuses alcohol. The study advocated a ban on alcohol-related advertising and promotions.[3] In 1996 legislation was proposed to Congress that would stringently restrict alcohol advertising. Among the proposed restrictions are banning sponsorship or support of any athletic, musical, cultural, or social event at colleges by any alcoholic beverage company and limiting college newspaper advertising to no more than price and product information.[4] Ethical Perspective 22–1 discusses whether beer companies are purposely targeting underage drinkers.

Decisions to ban the advertising of alcohol or tobacco involve very complex economic considerations as well as social issues. Companies such as Joseph E. Seagram & Sons recognize the need to reduce alcohol abuse and drunken driving, particularly among young people. The company has produced a number of ads designed to address this problem (Exhibit 22–1). The ads promote responsible behavior among adults of legal drinking age and are intended for that audience.

Criticism often focuses on the actions of specific advertisers. Groups like the National Organization for Women and Women Against Pornography have been critical of advertisers such as Calvin Klein for promoting sexual permissiveness and objectifying women in their ads (Exhibit 22–2). The company was heavily criticized and even boycotted over the controversial "kiddie porn" ads it ran a few years ago featuring intimate snapshots of teenagers in provocative states of undress.[5] As we will see later in this chapter, a number of advertisers have been criticized for running ads that are insensitive to certain segments of society.

As you read this chapter, remember that the various perspectives presented reflect judgments of people with different backgrounds, values, and interests. You may see nothing

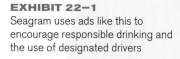

EXHIBIT 22–1
Seagram uses ads like this to encourage responsible drinking and the use of designated drivers

IT HAD EVERY SAFETY FEATURE. IN THE WORLD. EXCEPT A DESIGNATED DRIVER.

SOMETIMES DRINKING RESPONSIBLY MEANS NOT DRINKING AT ALL. DESIGNATE A DRIVER.

JOSEPH E. SEAGRAM & SONS, INC.
Those who appreciate quality enjoy it responsibly.

Ethical Perspective 22–1
Do Beer Companies Target Underage Drinkers?

On July 6, 1996, a commercial for Stroh Brewing Co.'s Schlitz Malt Liquor brand aired on an episode of MTV's "My So-Called Life," a program targeted at teens. Both MTV and Stroh were quick to explain that the airing of the spot was unintentional. Stroh said it had a long-time policy of targeting ads only at adults of legal drinking age; MTV said the ad ran by mistake due to a last-minute programming switch.

Stroh claims that the airing of a beer commercial on a program with a predominantly teen audience was an aberration. But the fact is that it was hardly an isolated event. Despite the beer industry's insistence that it doesn't target teens, its commercials regularly reach a large number of underage viewers. A survey conducted by Competitive Media Reporting for *The Wall Street Journal* showed that during one arbitrarily chosen week, the first week of September 1996, youths under the legal drinking age made up the majority of the audience for beer commercials for a number of shows (see the "Who's Watching" chart).

The airing of beer commercials on these shows appears to be in clear violation of the advertising and marketing guidelines published by the Beer Institute, the industry's chief trade association. According to these guidelines, "Beer advertising should not be placed in magazines, newspapers, television programs, or other media where most of the audience is reasonably expected to be below the legal purchase age." The industry has been pointing to these guidelines in an aggressive lobbying effort against proposed new federal restrictions on beer and liquor advertising.

The issue of whether brewers are targeting teens comes at a time when a great deal of attention is being focused on the problem of underage drinking. The actions of beer, wine, and liquor marketers are being closely scrutinized in Washington in the wake of the distilled spirits industry's decision to reverse a long-standing ban on TV and radio advertising. In late 1996 the Federal Trade Commission launched a probe into alcohol advertising to children. The director of the FTC's Bureau of Consumer Protection says the number of ads reaching kids is very troubling. However, she notes that in any investigation, the commission would first look at whether alcohol advertisers are following their own industry guidelines. And she says the commission "would never act on just one episode or one mistake—we would act on the pattern."

Beer companies and TV executives insist that it doesn't make sense to evaluate beer ads on a single night's audience or on a one-week period. For example, the Miller Brewing Co., which markets Molson in the United States, issued a statement in response to *The Wall Street Journal* survey saying: "Any attempt to analyze the beer industry's media buying practice by examining only selected broadcast media buys during a one-week period is misleading and simplistic." Miller officials noted that more than 75 percent of the broadcast audience reached by the programming it buys is over 21. Stroh's officials argue that there is a difference between putting ads in front of kids and targeting them explicitly. The company's general counsel says: "We understand that when an ad is run it's going to be seen by some people who are under 21 years of age, whether it's a billboard, in a magazine, or on TV. That does not mean we target the group that is under 21."

While brewers argue they are not targeting underage drinkers, they are concerned about the FTC investigation and the possibility of stronger government regulations. In December 1996 Anheuser-Busch, the best-selling brewer, pulled all of its beer advertising from MTV. A spokesman said, "We feel it's important that people understand our intentions and that they are not misrepresented. We do not target underage drinkers." Miller pulled its ads off of MTV in May 1997 noting that it was too difficult to control where its ads aired on the cable network.

TV executives said that Anheuser-Busch's move confirmed their fear that the controversy over the airing of liquor commercials on TV will ultimately affect ads for beer and wine. Many feel the liquor industry's push to join beer and wine advertisers on TV is testing public attitudes and may lead to support for more government regulation. Their concern is that the FTC will use protection of underage drinkers to justify a wider effort to curtail alcoholic beverage ads in general.

Sources: Ira Teinowitz, "Miller Joins Exodus of Beer Ads from MTV," *Advertising Age*, May 26, 1997, pp. 1, 84; Sally Goll Beatty, "Are Beer Ads on 'Beavis and Butt-Head' Aimed at Kids?" *The Wall Street Journal*, January 6, 1997, pp. B1, 5; Chuck Ross, "Anheuser-Busch Pulls Beer Ads Off MTV Network," *Advertising Age*, December 23, 1996, pp. 1, 27.

Who's Watching–Highlights of a Week's Worth of Beer Advertising			
Advertiser	Show (Network)	Date (Time)	Percent Viewers under 21
Coors Light	Hit List (BET)	Sept. 2 (8–10 P.M.)	51%
Molson	Singled Out (MTV)	Sept. 2 (7 P.M.)	52
Molson Ice	Beavis and Butt-head (MTV)	Sept. 2 (11:30 P.M.)	48
Foster's	Singled Out (MTV)	Sept. 3 (11 P.M.)	46
Molson	Real World (MTV)	Sept. 3 (8:30 P.M.)	45
Foster's	Melrose Place (E!)	Sept. 2 (7–8 P.M.)	41
Miller	Unreal (BET)	Sept. 5 (8–10 P.M.)	65
Schlitz	Yo MTV (MTV)	Sept. 5 (10 P.M.)	50
Molson	Beavis and Butt-head (MTV)	Sept. 6 (10:30 P.M.)	69
Budweiser	Video Music Awards (MTV)	Sept. 7 (8:30 P.M.)	46

Sources: Competitive Media Reporting (ad placement), Nielsen Media Research (viewer demographics) in *The Wall Street Journal*, January 6, 1997, p. B1.

EXHIBIT 22–2
Ads by Calvin Klein have been the target of criticism by women's groups and others

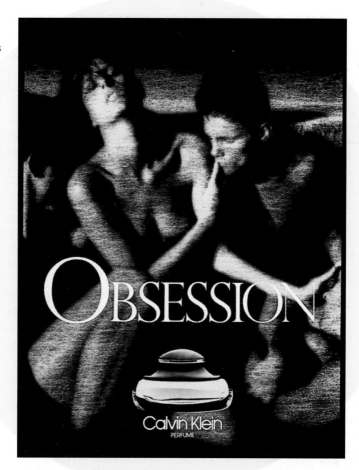

wrong with the ads for cigarettes or beer or sexually suggestive ads. Other students, however, may oppose these actions on moral and ethical grounds. While we attempt to present the arguments on both sides of these controversial issues, you will have to draw your own conclusions as to who is right or wrong.

SOCIAL AND ETHICAL CRITICISMS OF ADVERTISING

Much of the controversy over advertising stems from the ways many companies use it as a selling tool and from its impact on society's tastes, values, and lifestyles. Specific techniques used by advertisers are criticized as deceptive or untruthful, offensive or in bad taste, and exploitative of certain groups, such as children. We discuss each of these criticisms, along with advertisers' responses. We then turn our attention to criticisms concerning the influence of advertising on values and lifestyles, as well as charges that it perpetuates stereotyping and that advertisers exert control over the media.

Advertising as Untruthful or Deceptive

One of the major complaints against advertising is that many ads are misleading or untruthful and deceive consumers. Attempts by industry and government to regulate and control deceptive advertising were discussed in Chapter 21. We noted that advertisers should have a reasonable basis for making a claim about product performance and may be required to provide evidence to support their claims. However, deception can occur more subtly as a result of how consumers perceive the ad and its impact on their beliefs.[6] The difficulty of determining just what constitutes deception, along with the fact that advertisers have the right to use puffery and make subjective claims about their products, tends to complicate the issue. But a concern of many critics is the extent to which advertisers are *deliberately* untruthful or misleading.

Creating wants based on untruths →

Sometimes advertisers have made overtly false or misleading claims or failed to award prizes promoted in a contest or sweepstakes. However, these cases usually involve smaller companies and a tiny portion of the hundreds of billions of dollars spent on advertising and promotion each year. Most advertisers do not design their messages with the intention to mislead or deceive consumers or run sweepstakes with no intention of awarding prizes. Not only are such practices unethical, but the culprits would damage their reputation and risk prosecution by regulatory groups or government agencies. National advertisers in particular invest large sums of money to develop loyalty to, and enhance the image of, their brands. These companies are not likely to risk hard-won consumer trust and confidence by intentionally deceiving consumers.

The problem of untruthful or fraudulent advertising and promotion exists more at the local level and in specific areas such as mail order, telemarketing, and other forms of direct marketing. Yet there have been many cases where large companies were accused of misleading consumers with their ads or promotions. Some companies test the limits of industry and government rules and regulations to make claims that will give their brands an advantage in highly competitive markets.

While many critics of advertising would probably agree that most advertisers are not out to deceive consumers deliberately, they are still concerned that consumers may not be receiving enough information to make an informed choice. They say advertisers usually present only information that is favorable to their position and do not always tell consumers the whole truth about a product or service.

Many believe advertising should be primarily informative in nature and should not be permitted to use puffery or embellished messages. Others argue that advertisers have the right to present the most favorable case for their products and services and should not be restricted to just objective, verifiable information.[7] They note that consumers can protect themselves from being persuaded against their will and that the various industry and government regulations suffice to keep advertisers from misleading consumers. Figure 22–1 shows the advertising principles of the American Advertising Federation, which many advertisers use as a guideline in preparing and evaluating their ads.

Advertising as Offensive or in Bad Taste

Another common criticism of advertising, particularly by consumers, is that ads are offensive, tasteless, irritating, boring, obnoxious, and so on. In a study by Ogilvy & Mather, half of the consumers surveyed considered most ads to be in poor taste.[8]

SOURCES OF DISTASTE

Consumers can be offended or irritated by advertising in a number of ways. Some object when a product or service like contraceptives or personal hygiene products is advertised at all. Only in the last few years have media begun accepting ads for condoms, as the AIDS cri-

FIGURE 22–1
Advertising principles of the American Advertising Federation

1. *Truth.* Advertising shall reveal the truth, and shall reveal significant facts, the omission of which would mislead the public.

2. *Substantiation.* Advertising claims shall be substantiated by evidence in possession of the advertiser and the advertising agency prior to making such claims.

3. *Comparisons.* Advertising shall refrain from making false, misleading, or unsubstantiated statements or claims about a competitor or his products or service.

4. *Bait advertising.* Advertising shall not offer products or services for sale unless such offer constitutes a bona fide effort to sell the advertised products or services and is not a device to switch consumers to other goods or services, usually higher priced.

5. *Guarantees and warranties.* Advertising of guarantees and warranties shall be explicit, with sufficient information to apprise consumers of their principal terms and limitations or, when space or time restrictions preclude such disclosures, the advertisement shall clearly reveal where the full text of the guarantee or warranty can be examined before purchase.

6. *Price claims.* Advertising shall avoid price claims that are false or misleading, or savings claims that do not offer provable savings.

7. *Testimonials.* Advertising containing testimonials shall be limited to those of competent witnesses who are reflecting a real and honest opinion or experience.

8. *Taste and decency.* Advertising shall be free of statements, illustrations, or implications that are offensive to good taste or public decency.

EXHIBIT 22–3
Many magazines and TV stations now accept ads for condoms

sis forced them to reconsider their restrictions (Exhibit 22–3). The major TV networks gave their affiliates permission to accept condom advertising in 1987, but the first condom ad did not appear on network TV until 1991, when Fox broadcast a spot.

In 1994 the U.S. Department of Health's Centers for Disease Control and Prevention (CDC) began a new HIV prevention campaign that includes radio and TV commercials urging sexually active people to use latex condoms. The commercials prompted strong protests from conservative and religious groups, which argue that the government should stress abstinence in preventing the spread of AIDS among young people. NBC and ABC agreed to broadcast all the commercials, while CBS said it would air certain spots.[9]

A study of prime-time TV commercials found a strong product class effect with respect to the types of ads consumers perceived as distasteful or irritating. The most irritating commercials were for feminine hygiene products; ads for women's undergarments and hemorrhoid products were close behind.[10] Another study found that consumers are more likely to dislike ads for products they do not use and for brands they would not buy.[11] Ads for personal products have become more common on television and in print, and the public is more accepting of them.[12] However, advertisers must still be careful of how these products are presented and the language and terminology used. There are still many rules, regulations, and taboos advertisers must deal with to have their TV commercials approved by the networks.[13]

Another way advertising can offend consumers is by the type of appeal or the manner of presentation. For example, many people object to appeals that exploit consumer anxieties. Fear appeal ads, especially for products such as deodorants, mouthwash, and dandruff shampoos, are criticized for attempting to create anxiety and using a fear of social rejection to sell these products. Some ads for home computers were also criticized for attempting to make parents think that if their young children couldn't use a computer, they would fail in school.

SEXUAL APPEALS

The advertising appeals that have received the most criticism for being in poor taste are those using sexual appeals and/or nudity. These techniques are often used to gain consumers' attention and may not even be appropriate to the product being advertised. Even if the sexual appeal relates to the product, people may be offended by it. Many people object to both nudity in advertising and sexually suggestive ads.

Advertising critics are particularly concerned about the use of sexual appeals to glorify the image of cigarettes, liquor, and beer or to suggest they can enhance one's own attractiveness. For example, the Center for Science in the Public Interest, a consumer advocacy group, gave one of its recent Lemon Awards to an ad for Kool cigarettes featuring attractive women dressed in provocative clothing and high heels next to the headline "Totally Kool." Center officials said the ad implies that smoking adds to sexual attraction.[14]

Another common criticism of sexual appeals is that they can demean women (or men) by depicting them as sex objects (Exhibit 22–4). Ads for cosmetics, lingerie, beer, and liquor are among the most criticized for their portrayal of women as sex objects. Stroh Brewing Co. ignited a major controversy a few years ago with an ad campaign for Old Milwaukee beer featuring the Swedish Bikini Team, a group of Scandinavian-looking women wearing blue bikinis who appeared out of nowhere in front of groups of beer-drinking men. A number of consumer groups were very critical of the ads, and female employees at the company even sued Stroh's because they said the ads contributed to an atmosphere that was conducive to sexual harassment in the workplace.[15]

Many advertisers are being much more careful not to portray women as sex objects. A few years ago Anheuser-Busch announced that it was committed to portraying women with more respect and in more equal roles with men (Exhibit 22–5). Other beer companies, such as Miller and Stroh's, are also more careful about the way they portray women in their ads.[16]

Some advertisers complain about the double standard: even the most suggestive commercials are bland compared with the content of many TV programs. The networks say they have to scrutinize commercials more carefully because ads encourage people to imitate behaviors, while programs are merely meant to entertain. Network executives also note the complaints of parents who are concerned about their children seeing these ads since they cannot always be there to change the channel or turn off the TV.

Because of the increasing clutter in the advertising environment, advertisers will probably continue to use sexual appeals and other techniques that offend many people but catch the attention of consumers in their target audience. How far the advertisers can go with these appeals will probably depend on the public's reactions. When consumers think they have gone too far, they are likely to pressure the advertisers to change their ads and the media to stop accepting them.

EXHIBIT 22–4 Sexual appeals are often criticized for portraying women as sex objects

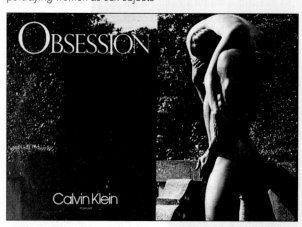

EXHIBIT 22–5 Anheuser-Busch is sensitive to the way women are portrayed in ads for the company's products

Advertising and Children

One of the most controversial topics advertisers must deal with is the issue of advertising to children. TV is a vehicle through which advertisers can reach children easily. Children between the ages of 2 and 11 watch an average of 21.5 hours of TV a week and may see between 22,000 and 25,000 commercials a year.[17] Studies show that television is an important source of information for children about products.[18] Concern has also been expressed about marketers' use of other promotional vehicles and techniques such as radio ads, point-of-purchase displays, premiums in packages, and the use of commercial characters as the basis for TV shows.

Critics argue that children, particularly young ones, are especially vulnerable to advertising because they lack the experience and knowledge to understand and evaluate critically the purpose of persuasive advertising appeals. Research has shown that preschool children cannot differentiate between commercials and programs, do not perceive the selling intent of commercials, and cannot distinguish between reality and fantasy.[19] Research has also shown that children need more than a skeptical attitude toward advertising; they must understand how advertising works in order to use their cognitive defenses against it effectively.[20] Because of children's limited ability to interpret the selling intent of a message or identify a commercial, critics charge that advertising to them is inherently unfair and deceptive and should be banned or severely restricted.

At the other extreme are those who argue that advertising is a part of life and children must learn to deal with it in the **consumer socialization process** of acquiring the skills needed to function in the marketplace.[21] They say existing restrictions are adequate for controlling children's advertising.

This issue received a great deal of attention in 1979 when the Federal Trade Commission held hearings on proposed changes in regulations regarding advertising to children. An FTC staff report recommended banning all TV advertising for any product directed to or seen by audiences composed largely of children under age 8 because they are too young to understand the selling intent of advertising.[22]

The FTC proposal was debated intensely. The advertising industry and a number of companies argued strongly against it, based on factors including advertisers' right of free speech under the First Amendment to communicate with those consumers who make up their primary target audience.[23] They also said parents should be involved in helping children interpret advertising and can refuse to purchase products they believe are undesirable for their children.

The FTC proposal was defeated, and changes in the political environment resulted in less emphasis on government regulation of advertising. But parent and consumer groups like the Center for Science in the Public Interest are still putting pressure on advertisers regarding what they see as inappropriate or misleading ads for children. One activist group, Action for Children's Television (ACT), was disbanded in 1992, but first it was instrumental in getting Congress to approve the Children's Television Act in October 1990. The act limits the amount of commercial time in children's programming to 10.5 minutes per hour on weekends and 12 minutes on weekdays.[24]

In 1996 broadcasters, children's advocates, and the federal government reached an agreement requiring TV stations to air three hours of children's educational shows a week.[25] Many believe advertisers will play a major role in implementing the new initiative by providing financial backing for the educational shows—which have long had trouble luring sponsors.[26]

Children are also protected from the potential influences of commercials by network censors and industry self-regulatory groups such as the Council of Better Business Bureaus' Children's Advertising Review Unit (CARU). CARU has strict self-regulatory guidelines regarding the type of appeals, product presentation and claims, disclosures and disclaimers, the use of premiums, safety, and techniques such as special effects and animation. The CARU guidelines for advertising addressed to children under 12 are presented in Figure 22–2.

As we saw in Chapter 21, the major networks also have strict guidelines for ads targeted to children. For example, in network TV ads, only 10 seconds can be devoted to animation and special effects; the final five seconds are reserved for displaying all the toys shown in the ad

FIGURE 22–2   Children's Advertising Review Unit principles

Five basic principles underlie these guidelines for advertising directed to children:

1. Advertisers should always take into account the level of knowledge, sophistication, and maturity of the audience to which their message is primarily directed. Younger children have a limited capability for evaluating the credibility of what they watch. Advertisers, therefore, have a special responsibility to protect children from their own susceptibilities.

2. Realizing that children are imaginative and that make-believe play constitutes an important part of the growing-up process, advertisers should exercise care not to exploit that imaginative quality of children. Unreasonable expectations of product quality or performance should not be stimulated either directly or indirectly by advertising.

3. Recognizing that advertising may play an important part in educating the child, information should be communicated in a truthful and accurate manner with full recognition by the advertiser that the child may learn practices from advertising that can affect his or her health and well-being.

4. Advertisers are urged to capitalize on the potential of advertising to influence social behavior by developing advertising that, wherever possible, addresses itself to social standards generally regarded as positive and beneficial, such as friendship, kindness, honesty, justice, generosity, and respect for others.

5. Although many influences affect a child's personal and social development, it remains the prime responsibility of the parents to provide guidance for children. Advertisers should contribute to this parent–child relationship in a constructive manner.

and disclosing whether they are sold separately and whether accessories such as batteries are included. Networks also require three seconds of every 30-second cereal ad to portray a balanced breakfast, usually by showing a picture of toast, orange juice, and milk.[27]

Advertising to children will remain a controversial topic. A recent study found that marketers of products targeted to children believe advertising to them provides useful information on new products and does not disrupt the parent–child relationship. However, the general public did not have such a favorable opinion. Older consumers and those from households with children had particularly negative attitudes toward children's advertising.[28]

It is important to many companies to communicate directly with children. However, only by being sensitive to the naiveté of children as consumers will they be able to do so freely and avoid potential conflict with those who believe children should be protected from advertising.

Social and Cultural Consequences

Concern is often expressed over the impact of advertising on society, particularly on values and lifestyles. While a number of factors influence the cultural values, lifestyles, and behavior of a society, the overwhelming amount of advertising and its prevalence in the mass media lead many critics to argue that advertising plays a major role in influencing and transmitting social values. In his book *Advertising and Social Change*, Ronald Berman says:

> The institutions of family, religion, and education have grown noticeably weaker over each of the past three generations. The world itself seems to have grown more complex. In the absence of traditional authority, advertising has become a kind of social guide. It depicts us in all the myriad situations possible to a life of free choice. It provides ideas about style, morality, behavior.[29]

While there is general agreement that advertising is an important social influence agent, opinions as to the value of its contribution are often negative. Advertising is criticized for encouraging materialism, manipulating consumers to buy things they do not really need, perpetuating stereotypes, and controlling the media.

ADVERTISING ENCOURAGES MATERIALISM

Many critics claim advertising has an adverse effect on consumer values by encouraging **materialism**, a preoccupation with material things rather than intellectual or spiritual concerns. The United States is undoubtedly the most materialistic society in the world, which many critics attribute to advertising that

- Seeks to create needs rather than merely showing how a product or service fulfills them.
- Surrounds consumers with images of the good life and suggests the acquisition of material possessions leads to contentment and happiness and adds to the joy of living.

- Suggests material possessions are symbols of status, success, and accomplishment and/or will lead to greater social acceptance, popularity, sex appeal, and so on.

The ad shown in Exhibit 22–6 for Rolls-Royce automobiles is an example of how advertising can promote materialistic values.

This criticism of advertising assumes that materialism is undesirable and is sought at the expense of other goals. But many believe materialism is an acceptable part of the **Protestant ethic**, which stresses hard work and individual effort and initiative and views the accumulation of material possessions as evidence of success. Others argue that the acquisition of material possessions has positive economic impact by encouraging consumers to keep consuming after their basic needs are met. Many Americans believe economic growth is essential and materialism is both a necessity and an inevitable part of this progress.

Economist John Kenneth Galbraith, often a vocal critic of advertising, describes the role advertising plays in industrialized economies by encouraging consumption:

> Advertising and its related arts thus help develop the kind of man the goals of the industrial system require—one that reliably spends his income and works reliably because he is always in need of more. In the absence of the massive and artful persuasion that accompanies the management of demand, increasing abundance might well have reduced the interest of people in acquiring more goods. Being not pressed by the need for these things, they would have spent less reliably to get more. The consequence—a lower and less reliable propensity to consume—would have been awkward for the industrial system.[30]

It has also been argued that an emphasis on material possessions does not rule out interest in intellectual, spiritual, or cultural values. Defenders of advertising say consumers can be more interested in higher-order goals when basic needs have been met. Raymond Bauer and Stephen Greyser point out that consumers may purchase material things in the pursuit of nonmaterial goals.[31] For example, a person may buy an expensive stereo system to enjoy music rather than simply to impress someone or acquire a material possession.

Even if we assume materialism is undesirable, there is still the question of whether advertising is responsible for creating and encouraging it. While many critics argue that advertising is a major contributing force to materialistic values, others say advertising merely reflects the values of society rather than shaping them.[32] They argue that consumers' values are defined by the society in which they live and are the results of extensive, long-term socialization or acculturation.

The argument that advertising is responsible for creating a materialistic and hedonistic society is addressed by Stephen Fox in his book *The Mirror Makers: A History of American*

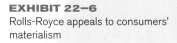

EXHIBIT 22–6
Rolls-Royce appeals to consumers' materialism

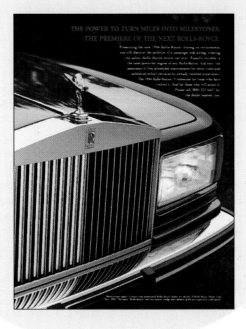

Advertising and Its Creators. Fox concludes advertising has become a prime scapegoat for our times and merely reflects society. Regarding the effect of advertising on cultural values, he says:

> To blame advertising now for those most basic tendencies in American history is to miss the point. It is too obvious, too easy, a matter of killing the messenger instead of dealing with the bad news. The people who have created modern advertising are not hidden persuaders pushing our buttons in the service of some malevolent purpose. They are just producing an especially visible manifestation, good and bad, of the American way of life.[33]

Some people say that advertising determines America's tastes.
Which is another way of saying that advertising determines *your* tastes.
Which is, in turn, another way of saying that you don't have a mind of your own.
Well, time and time again the advertising industry has found that you do have a mind of your own. If a product doesn't interest you, you simply don't buy it.
And if the product's advertising doesn't interest you, you don't buy that either.
Think of it as a sort of natural selection.

Good products and good advertising survive. Bad products and bad advertising perish. All according to the decisions you make in the marketplace.
So we've concluded that advertising is a mirror of society's tastes. Not vice versa.
Our conclusion is based on a great deal of thought. And many years of reflection.

ADVERTISING.
ANOTHER WORD FOR FREEDOM OF CHOICE.
American Association of Advertising Agencies

This ad developed by the American Association of Advertising Agencies suggests that advertising is a reflection of society's tastes and values, not vice versa. The ad was part of a campaign that addressed criticisms of advertising.

Advertising does contribute to our materialism by portraying products and services as symbols of status, success, and achievement and by encouraging consumption. As Richard Pollay says, "While it may be true that advertising reflects cultural values, it does so on a very selective basis, echoing and reinforcing certain attitudes, behaviors, and values far more frequently than others."[34]

The extent to which advertising is responsible for materialism and the desirability of such values are deep philosophical issues that will continue to be part of the debate over the societal value and consequences of advertising.

ADVERTISING MAKES PEOPLE BUY THINGS THEY DON'T NEED

A common criticism of advertising is that it manipulates consumers into buying things they do not need. Many critics say advertising should just provide information useful in making purchase decisions and should not persuade. They view information advertising (which reports price, performance, and other objective criteria) as desirable but persuasive advertising (which plays on consumers' emotions, anxieties, and psychological needs and desires such as status, self-esteem, and attractiveness) as unacceptable. Persuasive advertising is criticized for fostering discontent among consumers and encouraging them to purchase products and services to solve deeper problems. Critics say advertising exploits consumers and persuades them to buy things they don't need.

Defenders of advertising offer a number of rebuttals to these criticisms. First, they point out that a substantial amount of advertising is essentially informational in nature.[35] Also, it is difficult to separate desirable informational advertising from undesirable persuasive advertising. Shelby Hunt, in examining the *information–persuasion dichotomy*, points out that even advertising that most observers would categorize as very informative is often very persuasive.[36] He says, "If advertising critics really believe that persuasive advertising should not be permitted, they are actually proposing that no advertising be allowed, since the purpose of all advertising is to persuade."[37]

Defenders of advertising also take issue with the argument that it should be limited to dealing with basic functional needs. In our society, most lower-level needs recognized in Maslow's hierarchy, such as the need for food, clothing, and shelter, are satisfied for most people. It is natural to move from basic needs to higher-order ones such as self-esteem and status or self-actualization. Consumers are free to choose the degree to which they attempt to satisfy their desires, and wise advertisers associate their products and services with the satisfaction of higher-order needs.

Proponents of advertising offer two other defenses against the charge that advertising makes people buy things they do not really need. First, this criticism attributes too much power to advertising and assumes consumers have no ability to defend themselves against it.

Second, it ignores the fact that consumers have the freedom to make their own choices when confronted with persuasive advertising. While they readily admit the persuasive intent of their business, advertisers are quick to note it is extremely difficult to make consumers purchase a product they do not want or for which they do not see a personal benefit. For example, the "green" marketing movement has not gotten consumers to forgo low prices in favor of products that make environmental claims. The market research firm of Roper Starch Worldwide conducted an extensive study of 300 green ads that appeared in magazines between 1991 and 1994 and found that most were not effective. The study concluded that too many green ads failed to make the connection between what the company is doing for the environment and how it affects individual consumers.[38]

If advertising were as powerful as the critics claim, we would not see products with multi-million-dollar advertising budgets failing in the marketplace. The reality is that consumers do have a choice, and they are not being forced to buy. Consumers ignore ads for products and services they do not really need or that fail to interest them (see Exhibit 22–7).

ADVERTISING AND STEREOTYPING

Advertising is often accused of creating and perpetuating stereotypes through its portrayal of women, ethnic minorities, and other groups.

Women

Advertising has received much criticism for stereotyping women. Critics charge that advertising has failed to acknowledge the changing role of women in our society. It generally depicts women as homemakers or mothers or shows them as decorative objects or sexually provocative figures. A number of studies have examined advertising's portrayal of women. In 1980, Alice Courtney and Thomas Whipple reviewed the findings of nearly 70 studies in this area and concluded that women were typically portrayed in traditional roles such as housewives and mothers, as dependent on men and sometimes subservient. They also noted that women were often used as sexual or decorative objects in advertising but were seldom shown in authoritative roles.[39]

While sexism and stereotyping still exist, advertising's portrayal of women is improving in many areas.[40] Many advertisers have begun to recognize the importance to their bottom line

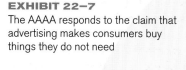

EXHIBIT 22–7
The AAAA responds to the claim that advertising makes consumers buy things they do not need

of portraying women realistically. The increase in the number of working women has resulted not only in women having more influence in family decision making but also in more single-female households, which means more independent purchasers. Many advertisers are trying to depict women in a diversity of roles that reflect their changing place in society.[41]

Some advertisers have found that being more sensitive to women customers can influence their purchase behavior. For example, a few years ago Maidenform began a campaign critical of negative stereotyping of women that significantly increased sales (Exhibit 22–8). Nike saw its sales to women increase 28 percent as a result of its "Empathy" campaign, which directly targeted women and issues that are relevant to them.[42] Feminist groups such as the National Organization for Women (NOW) argue that advertising that portrays women as sex objects contributes to violence against women. NOW and other groups often protest to advertisers and their agencies about ads they find insulting to women and have even called for boycotts against offending advertisers.

Blacks and Hispanics

African-Americans and Hispanics have also been the target of stereotyping in advertising. For many years, advertisers virtually ignored all nonwhite ethnic groups as identifiable subcultures and viable markets. Ads were rarely targeted to these ethnic groups, and the use of blacks and Hispanics as spokespeople, communicators, models, or actors in ads was very limited.[43]

Several studies have examined the incidence of minorities in advertising. One study reported that 11 percent of the people in commercials were African-Americans.[44] Another just two years later found that blacks appeared in 26 percent of all ads on network TV that used live models, but Hispanics appeared in only 6 percent of the commercials with live models.[45] A study by Thomas Stevenson found that the number of trade journal ads depicting blacks increased from 4.9 percent in 1966 to 10.6 percent in 1976 and stayed at the same level to

EXHIBIT 22–8 Maidenform's campaign lamenting the stereotyping of women resulted in a significant increase in sales

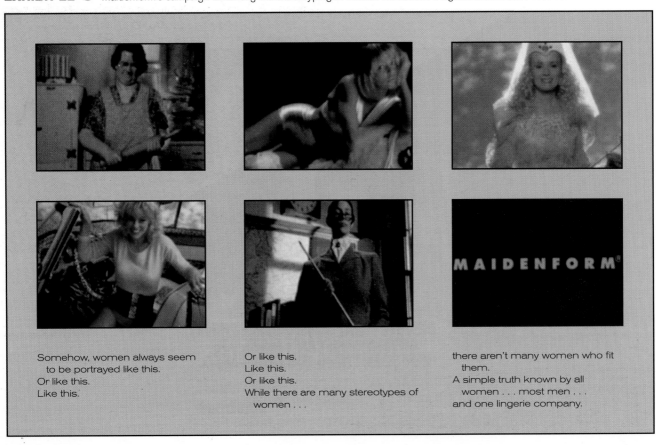

Somehow, women always seem
  to be portrayed like this.
Or like this.
Like this.

Or like this.
Like this.
Or like this.
While there are many stereotypes of
  women . . .

there aren't many women who fit
  them.
A simple truth known by all
  women . . . most men . . .
and one lingerie company.

1986.[46] However, this study also found that the percentage of blacks shown in business ads did not increase significantly over the 20 years.

In recent years, not only has the sheer number of African-Americans in ads increased, but so has their social and role status. For example, blacks are increasingly being shown in executive positions in many ads. FedEx said that a recent commercial featuring a black female executive beating out her white male adversaries in a conference call showdown over a high-stakes business deal was one of its most successful ads in the last 10 years.[47]

Ads are increasingly likely to be racially integrated. Recently some advertisers have begun breaking the taboo against suggesting interracial attraction. For example, a Diet Pepsi commercial placed the popular black Uh-Huh Girls in bikinis on a beach, where they were approached by two white men.[48] Furniture retailer Ikea recently ran a TV commercial showing an interracial couple shopping for a "daddy chair" and discussing their plans to conceive[49] (Exhibit 22–9).

There is little question that advertising has been guilty of stereotyping women and ethnic groups in the past and, in some cases, still does so. But as the role of women changes, advertisers are changing their portrayals to remain accurate and appeal to their target audience. Advertisers are also trying to increase the incidence of minority groups in ads while avoiding stereotypes and negative role portrayals. They are being careful to avoid ethnic stereotyping and striving to develop advertising that has specific appeals to various ethnic groups as shown in this Mattel ad.

Other Groups

While the focus here has been on women and ethnic minorities, some other groups feel they are victims of stereotyping by advertisers. For example, some advertisers have been criticized for portraying senior citizens as feeble, foolish,

inept, or in desperate need of help.[50] Advocates for the mentally ill objected to a Nike ad campaign featuring actor Dennis Hopper, who is best known for playing eccentric and sometimes violent characters. In the commercials he plays the ultimate football fanatic—an ex-referee who is obsessed with the game—and his performance includes twitches, tics, and maniacal laughter that some suggest portray a mentally ill person.[51]

Many groups in our society are battling against stereotyping and discrimination, and companies must consider whether their ads might offend them. It is increasingly difficult not to offend some segment of the public. Creative personnel in agencies are feeling restricted as their ideas are squelched out of concern that they might offend someone or be misinterpreted.[52] However, advertisers must be sensitive to the portrayal of specific types of people in their ads, for both ethical and commercial reasons.

One area where significant changes have taken place recently is in advertising targeted to gay consumers. In 1995 Ikea broke new ground with a TV commercial featuring a gay couple shopping for furniture. For years beer companies targeted this market by placing ads in local gay media to support or sponsor AIDS awareness, Gay Pride festivals, and the Gay Games. Recently a number of beer companies, including Anheuser-Busch and Miller Brewing Co., have begun placing gay-specific, brand-specific ads in national gay publications.[53] Exhibit 22–10 shows an ad Miller used to target gay readers as part of its "Life is good" campaign for its Lite beer brand.

ADVERTISING AND THE MEDIA

The fact that advertising plays such an important role in financing the media has led to concern that advertisers may influence or even control the media. It is well documented that *economic censorship* occurs, whereby the media avoid certain topics, or even present biased news coverage, in acquiescence to advertiser demands.[54] In fact, Professors Lawrence Soley and Robert Craig say, "The assertion that advertisers attempt to influence what the public sees, hears, and reads in the mass media is perhaps the most damning of all criticisms of advertising, but this criticism isn't acknowledged in most advertising textbooks."[55] We will address this important issue in this book by considering arguments on both sides.

EXHIBIT 22–10
Miller targets gay consumers in this Lite beer ad

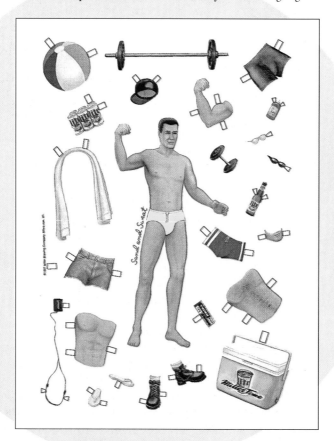

Ethical Perspective 22-2
Do Advertisers Get Favorable Treatment from Magazines?

Advertising is the primary source of revenue for nearly all of the news and entertainment media in the United States. And because advertising pays the bills, newspaper and magazine publishers as well as TV and radio networks and station executives must keep their advertisers happy. Professors Jef Richards and John Murphy call it a "task not unlike feeding crocodiles." They note the inherent danger is that advertisers might use their economic influence to act as unofficial censors of the media, banning them from publishing or broadcasting certain material.

It is well recognized that advertisers systematically avoid TV shows that deal with certain controversial issues, such as abortion and homosexuality. Most advertisers also have contract stipulations allowing them to cancel a media purchase if, after prescreening a show, they are uncomfortable with its content or feel it may reflect poorly on their company. And TV is not the only medium that must deal with the threats of advertiser defection or attempts to influence content. Advertisers can also influence the editorial content of magazines and newspapers by pressuring them to run only positive stories about their products or services.

Most magazines and newspaper publishers insist that they do not allow advertiser pressure to influence their editorial content. For example, editors of major personal finance magazines such as *Money*, *Kiplinger's Personal Finance*, *SmartMoney*, and *Worth* insist they protect the integrity of their stories by keeping the editorial side (the people who write and edit articles) separate from the publishing side (the people who sell the ads and generally run the business). This can be done by separating editorial and advertising offices, barring the ad sales force from reading articles before they are printed, and prohibiting editorial employees from participating in advertising sales calls.

Journalists agree that giving favorable editorial consideration to a company simply because it advertises in the publication would be a cardinal sin. Yet critics argue that this does sometimes occur. For example, a controversy arose recently in business publishing when one magazine accused another of cozying up to advertisers. In 1996 *Fortune* published an article accusing its fierce rival *Forbes* of "turning downbeat stories into upbeat stories in order to keep advertisers happy—even at the risk of misleading their own readers." *Fortune* charged that *Forbes* "systematically allows its advertising executives to see stories—and command changes—before they run."

Forbes issued a statement saying, "The *Forbes* advertising department has no input in the *Forbes* editorial process." However, the magazine also noted that its publisher sees all stories before they go into print and that "if he does not like what he sees, he can complain to a top editor. Very occasionally, these queries lead to changes in these stories." The editor in chief of another rival magazine, *Business Week*, thinks *Forbes*'s procedures invite trouble: "The major sin that Forbes commits is that they routinely send articles to the ad side for vetting."

Most magazines are members of the American Society of Magazine Editors (ASME), which issues voluntary guidelines designed to help them maintain their objectivity. These guidelines also cover special advertising sections and *advertorials* (ads designed to look like articles). The guidelines dictate that ads that could be mistaken for stories must be clearly labeled and the appearance of ad pages should be "distinctly different" from that of articles.

Magazines can and do take steps to separate their editorial judgments from their advertising sales goals. Not only is it the ethical thing to do, it is in their own self-interest. Most advertisers support this goal, as do virtually all the journalists whose names appear above the stories. As one freelance writer says, "Journalists don't want to kowtow to advertisers—that's why they're journalists, not selling ads."

Sources: Steven T. Goldberg, "Do the Ads Tempt the Editors?" *Kiplinger's Personal Finance*, May 1996, pp. 45–49; Jef I. Richards and John H. Murphy II, "Economic Censorship and Free Speech: The Circle of Communication between Advertisers, Media, and Consumers," *Journal of Current Issues and Research in Advertising*, 18, no. 1 (Spring 1996), pp. 21–34.

Arguments Supporting Advertiser Control

Some critics charge the media's dependence on advertisers' support makes them susceptible to various forms of influence, including exerting control over the editorial content of magazines and newspapers; biasing editorial opinions to favor the position of an advertiser; limiting coverage of a controversial story that might reflect negatively on a company; and influencing the program content of television. Ethical Perspective 22–2 considers whether the editorial content of magazines is influenced by advertisers.

Newspapers and magazines receive nearly 70 percent of their revenue from advertising; commercial TV and radio derive virtually all their income from advertisers. Small, financially insecure newspapers, magazines, or broadcast stations are the most susceptible to pressure from advertisers, particularly companies that account for a large amount of the media outlet's advertising revenue. A local newspaper may be reluctant to print an unfavorable story about a car dealer or supermarket chain on whose advertising it depends. For example, a few years ago more than 40 car dealers canceled their ads in the *San Jose Mercury News* when the paper printed an article titled "A Car Buyer's Guide to Sanity." The dealers objected to the tone of the article, which they felt implied consumers should consider car dealers unethical adversaries in the negotiation process.[56] A recent survey of 147 daily newspapers found that more than 90 percent of editors have been pressured by advertisers and more than one-third of them said advertisers had succeeded in influencing news at their papers.[57]

While larger, more financially stable media should be less susceptible to an advertiser's influence, they may still be reluctant to carry stories detrimental to companies that purchase large amounts of advertising time or space.[58] For example, since cigarette commercials were taken off radio and TV in 1970, tobacco companies have allocated most of their budgets to the print media. The tobacco industry outspends all other national advertisers in newspapers, and cigarettes constitute the second-largest category of magazine advertising (behind transportation). This has led to charges that magazines and newspapers avoid articles on the hazards of smoking to protect this important source of ad revenue.[59] A study by Joanne Lipman found that magazines relying on cigarette advertising are far less likely than others to publish stories about the health hazards associated with smoking.[60]

Individual TV stations and even the major networks also can be influenced by advertisers. Programming decisions are made largely on the basis of what shows will attract the most viewers and thus be most desirable to advertisers. Critics say this often results in lower-quality television as educational, cultural, and informative programming is usually sacrificed for shows that get high ratings and appeal to the mass markets.

Advertisers have also been accused of pressuring the networks to change their programming. Many advertisers have begun withdrawing commercials from programs that contain too much sex or violence, often in response to threatened boycotts of their products by consumers if they advertise on these shows. For example, groups such as the American Family Association have been fighting sex and violence in TV programs by calling for boycotts. Recently a number of companies, including Procter & Gamble, Mars Inc., and Kraft Foods, pulled their advertising from certain talk shows, like those of Jenny Jones and Ricki Lake, because of some of their incendiary topics.[61]

It has been speculated that the new rating system developed by the networks may result in advertisers avoiding programs with adult content labels. This could result in a drop in advertising rates for these programs and greater demand for shows rated as suitable for family viewing.[62]

Arguments against Advertiser Control

The commercial media's dependence on advertising means advertisers can exert influence on their character, content, and coverage of certain issues. However, media executives offer several reasons why advertisers do not exert undue influence over the media.

First, they point out it is in the best interest of the media not to be influenced too much by advertisers. To retain public confidence, they must report the news fairly and accurately without showing bias or attempting to avoid controversial issues. Media executives point to the vast array of topics they cover and the investigative reporting they often do as evidence of their objectivity. They want to build a large audience for their publications or stations so they can charge more for advertising space and time.

Media executives also note that an advertiser needs the media more than they need any individual advertiser, particularly when the medium has a large audience or does a good job of reaching a specific market segment. Many publications and stations have a very broad base of advertising support and can afford to lose an advertiser that attempts to exert too much influence. This is particularly true for the larger, more established, financially secure media. For example, a consumer products company would find it difficult to reach its target audience without network TV and could not afford to boycott a network if it disagreed with a station's editorial policy or program content. Even the local advertiser in a small community may be dependent on the local newspaper, since it may be the most cost-effective media option available.

The media in the United States are basically supported by advertising, which means we can enjoy them for free or for a fraction of what they would cost without advertising. The alternative to an advertiser-supported media system is support by users through higher sub-

scription costs for the print media and a fee or pay-per-view system with TV. The ad in Exhibit 22–11, part of a campaign by the International Advertising Association, explains how advertising lowers the cost of print media for consumers. Another alternative is government-supported media like those in many other countries, but this runs counter to most people's desire for freedom of the press. Although not perfect, our system of advertising-supported media provides the best option for receiving information and entertainment.

Summarizing Social Effects

We have examined a number of issues and have attempted to analyze the arguments for and against them. Many people have reservations about the impact of advertising and promotion on society. The numerous rules, regulations, policies, and guidelines marketers comply with do not cover every advertising and promotional situation. Moreover, what one individual views as distasteful or unethical may be acceptable to another.

Negative opinions regarding advertising and other forms of promotion have been around almost as long as the field itself, and it is unlikely they will ever disappear. However, the industry must address the various concerns about the effects of advertising and other forms of promotion on society. Advertising is a very powerful institution, but it will remain so only as long as consumers have faith in the ads they see and hear every day. Many of the problems discussed here can be avoided if individual decision makers make ethics an important element of the IMC planning process.

The primary focus of this discussion of social effects has been on the way advertising is used (or abused) in the marketing of products and services. It is important to note that advertising and other IMC tools, such as direct marketing and public relations, are also used to promote worthy causes and to deal with problems facing society (drunk driving, drug abuse, and the AIDS crisis, among others). As discussed in the opening vignette, campaigns for nonprofit organizations and worthy causes are often developed pro bono by advertising agencies and free advertising time and space are donated by the media.

ECONOMIC EFFECTS OF ADVERTISING

Advertising plays an important role in a free-market system like ours by making consumers aware of products and services and providing them with information for decision making. Advertising's economic role goes beyond this basic function, however. It is a powerful force that can affect the functioning of our entire economic system.

Advertising can encourage consumption and foster economic growth. It not only informs customers of available goods and services but also facilitates entry into markets for a firm or a new product or brand; leads to economies of scale in production, marketing, and distribution, which in turn lead to lower prices; and hastens the acceptance of new products and the rejection of inferior products.

Critics of advertising view it as a detrimental force that not only fails to perform its basic function of information provision adequately but also adds to the cost of products and services and discourages competition and market entry, leading to industrial concentration and higher prices for consumers.

In their analysis of advertising, economists generally take a macroeconomic perspective: they consider the economic impact of advertising on an entire industry or on the economy as a whole rather than its effect on an individual company or brand. Our examination of the economic impact of advertising focuses on these broader macro-level issues. We consider its effects on consumer choice, competition, and product costs and prices.

Effects on Consumer Choice

Some critics say advertising hampers consumer choice, as large advertisers use their power to limit our options to a few well-advertised brands. Economists argue that advertising is used to achieve (1) **differentiation**, whereby the products or services of large advertisers are perceived as unique or better than competitors', and (2) brand loyalty, which enables large national advertisers to gain control of the market, usually at the expense of smaller brands.

Larger companies often end up charging a higher price and achieve a more dominant position in the market than smaller firms that cannot compete against them and their large advertising budgets. When this occurs, advertising not only restricts the choice alternatives to a few well-known, heavily advertised brands but also becomes a substitute for competition based on price or product improvements.

Heavily advertised brands dominate the market in certain product categories, such as soft drinks, beer, and cereals.[63] But advertising generally does not create brand monopolies and reduce the opportunities for new products to be introduced to consumers. In most product categories, a number of different brands are on the store shelves and thousands of new products are introduced every year. The opportunity to advertise gives companies the incentive to develop new brands and improve their existing ones. When a successful new product such as a personal computer is introduced, competitors quickly follow and use advertising to inform consumers about their brand and attempt to convince them it is superior to the original. Companies like Virgin Atlantic Airways recognize that advertising has been an important part of their success (Exhibit 22–12).

Effects on Competition

One of the most common criticisms economists have about advertising concerns its effects on competition. They argue that power in the hands of large firms with huge advertising budgets creates a **barrier to entry**, which makes it difficult for other firms to enter the market. This results in less competition and higher prices. Economists note that smaller firms already in the market find it difficult to compete against the large advertising budgets of the industry leaders and are often driven out of business. For example, in the U.S. beer industry, the number of national brewers has declined dramatically. In their battle for market share, industry giants Anheuser-Busch and Miller increased their ad budgets substantially and reaped market shares that total over 60 percent. Anheuser-Busch alone spent nearly $600 million on advertising in 1996. However, these companies are spending much less per barrel than smaller firms, making it very difficult for the latter to compete.

Large advertisers clearly enjoy certain competitive advantages. First, there are **economies of scale** in advertising, particularly with respect to factors such as media costs. Firms such as Procter & Gamble and Philip Morris, which spend over $2 billion a year on advertising and promotion, are able to make large media buys at a reduced rate and allocate them to their various products.

Large advertisers usually sell more of a product or service, which means they may have lower production costs and can allocate more monies to advertising, so they can afford the costly but more efficient media like network television. Their large advertising outlays also give them more opportunity to differentiate their products and develop brand loyalty. To the extent that these factors occur, smaller competitors are at a disadvantage and new competitors are deterred from entering the market.

While advertising may have an anticompetitive effect on a market, there is no clear evidence that advertising alone reduces competition, creates barriers to entry, and thus in-

EXHIBIT 22–12

Virgin Atlantic Airways chair Richard Branson acknowledges the importance of advertising

creases market concentration. Lester Telser noted that high levels of advertising are not always found in industries where firms have a large market share. He found an inverse relationship between intensity of product class advertising and stability of market share for the leading brands.[64] These findings run contrary to many economists' belief that industries controlled by a few firms have high advertising expenditures, resulting in stable brand shares for market leaders.

Defenders of advertising say it is unrealistic to attribute a firm's market dominance and barriers to entry solely to advertising. There are a number of other factors, such as price, product quality, distribution effectiveness, production efficiencies, and competitive strategies. For many years, products such as Coors beer and Hershey chocolate bars were dominant brands even though these companies spent little on advertising. Hershey did not advertise at all until 1970. For 66 years, the company relied on the quality of its products, its favorable reputation and image among consumers, and its extensive channels of distribution to market its brands. Industry leaders often tend to dominate markets because they have superior product quality and the best management and competitive strategies, not simply the biggest advertising budgets.[65]

While market entry against large, established competitors is difficult, companies with a quality product at a reasonable price often find a way to break in. Moreover, they usually find that advertising actually facilitates their market entry by making it possible to communicate the benefits and features of their new product or brand to consumers. For example, South Korea's Kia Motors Corp. entered the U.S. car market in the mid-1990s using ads like Exhibit 22–13 to tell consumers about the features of its low-priced compact cars.

Effects on Product Costs and Prices

A major area of debate among economists, advertisers, consumer advocates, and policymakers concerns the effects of advertising on product costs and prices. Critics argue that advertising increases the prices consumers pay for products and services. First, they say the large sums of money spent advertising a brand constitute an expense that must be covered, and

the consumer ends up paying for it through higher prices. This is a common criticism from consumer advocates. Several studies show that firms with higher relative prices advertise their products more intensely than do those with lower relative prices.[66]

A second way advertising can result in higher prices is by increasing product differentiation and adding to the perceived value of the product in consumers' minds. Paul Farris and Mark Albion note that product differentiation occupies a central position in theories of advertising's economic effects.[67] The fundamental premise is that advertising increases the perceived differences between physically homogeneous products and enables advertised brands to command a premium price without an increase in quality.

Critics of advertising generally point to the differences in prices between national brands and private-label brands that are physically similar, such as aspirin or tea bags, as evidence of the added value created by advertising. They see consumers' willingness to pay more for heavily advertised national brands rather than purchasing the lower-priced, nonadvertised brand as wasteful and irrational. However, consumers do not always buy for rational, functional reasons. The emotional, psychological, and social benefits derived from purchasing a national brand are important to many people. Moreover, say Albion and Farris,

> Unfortunately there seems to be no single way to measure product differentiation, let alone determine how much is excessive or attributable to the effects of advertising. . . . Both price insensitivity and brand loyalty could be created by a number of factors such as higher product quality, better packaging, favorable use experience and market position. They are probably related to each other but need not be the result of advertising.[68]

Proponents of advertising offer several other counterarguments to the claim that advertising increases prices. They acknowledge that advertising costs are at least partly paid for by consumers. But advertising may help lower the overall cost of a product more than enough to offset them. For example, advertising may help firms achieve economies of scale in production and distribution by providing information to and stimulating demand among mass markets. These economies of scale help cut the cost of producing and marketing the product, which can lead to lower prices—if the advertiser chooses to pass the cost savings on to the consumer. The ad in Exhibit 22–14, from a campaign sponsored by three major advertising trade associations, emphasizes this point.

Advertising can also lower prices by making a market more competitive, which usually leads to greater price competition. A study by Lee Benham found that prices of eyeglasses were 25 to 30 percent higher in states that banned eyeglass advertising than in those that permitted it.[69] Robert Steiner analyzed the toy industry and concluded that advertising resulted in lower consumer prices. He argued that curtailment of TV advertising would drive up consumer prices for toys.[70] Finally, advertising is a means to market entry rather than a

EXHIBIT 22–14
This ad refutes the argument that reducing advertising expenditures will lead to lower prices

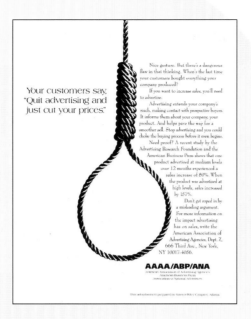

deterrent and helps stimulate product innovation, which makes markets more competitive and helps keep prices down.

Overall, it is difficult to reach any firm conclusions regarding the relationship between advertising and prices. After an extensive review of this area, Farris and Albion concluded, "The evidence connecting manufacturer advertising to prices is neither complete nor definitive . . . consequently, we cannot say whether advertising is a tool of market efficiency or market power without further research."[71]

Economist James Ferguson argues that advertising cannot increase the cost per unit of quality to consumers because if it did, consumers would not continue to respond positively to advertising.[72] He believes advertising lowers the costs of information about brand qualities, leads to increases in brand quality, and lowers the average price per unit of quality.

Summarizing Economic Effects

Albion and Farris suggest that economists' perspectives can be divided into two principal schools of thought that make different assumptions regarding the influence of advertising on the economy.[73] Figure 22–3 summarizes the main points of the "advertising equals market power" and "advertising equals information" perspectives.

ADVERTISING EQUALS MARKET POWER

The belief that advertising equals market power reflects traditional economic thinking and views advertising as a way to change consumers' tastes, lower their sensitivity to price, and build brand loyalty among buyers of advertised brands. This results in higher profits and market power for large advertisers, reduces competition in the market, and leads to higher prices and fewer choices for consumers. Proponents of this viewpoint generally have negative attitudes regarding the economic impact of advertising.

ADVERTISING EQUALS INFORMATION

The belief that advertising equals information takes a more positive view of advertising's economic effects. This model sees advertising as providing consumers with useful information, increasing their price sensitivity (which moves them toward lower-priced products), and increasing competition in the market. Advertising is viewed as a way to communicate with consumers and tell them about a product and its major features and attributes. More informed and knowledgeable consumers pressure companies to provide high-quality products at lower prices. Efficient firms remain in the market, whereas inefficient firms leave as new entrants appear. Proponents of this model believe the economic effects of advertising are favorable and think it contributes to more efficient and competitive markets.

FIGURE 22–3   Two schools of thought on advertising's role in the economy

Advertising = Market Power		Advertising = Information
Advertising affects consumer preferences and tastes, changes product attributes, and differentiates the product from competitive offerings.	Advertising	Advertising informs consumers about product attributes but does not change the way they value those attributes.
Consumers become brand loyal and less price sensitive and perceive fewer substitutes for advertised brands.	Consumer buying behavior	Consumers become more price sensitive and buy best "value." Only the relationship between price and quality affects elasticity for a given product.
Potential entrants must overcome established brand loyalty and spend relatively more on advertising.	Barriers to entry	Advertising makes entry possible for new brands because it can communicate product attributes to consumers.
Firms are insulated from market competition and potential rivals; concentration increases, leaving firms with more discretionary power.	Industry structure and market power	Consumers can compare competitive offerings easily and competitive rivalry increases. Efficient firms remain, and as the inefficient leave, new entrants appear; the effect on concentration is ambiguous.
Firms can charge higher prices and are not as likely to compete on quality or price dimensions. Innovation may be reduced.	Market conduct	More informed consumers pressure firms to lower prices and improve quality; new entrants facilitate innovation.
High prices and excessive profits accrue to advertisers and give them even more incentive to advertise their products. Output is restricted compared with conditions of perfect competition.	Market performance	Industry prices decrease. The effect on profits due to increased competition and increased efficiency is ambiguous.

It is unlikely the debate over the economic effects and value of advertising will be resolved soon. Many economists will continue to take a negative view of advertising and its effects on the functioning of the economy, while advertisers will continue to view it as an efficient way for companies to communicate with their customers and an essential component of our economic system. Global Perspective 22–3 discusses a campaign the International Advertising Association has been running for several years to convince consumers around the world of the economic value of advertising.

Figure 22–4, excerpts from a speech given by famous adman Leo Burnett, summarizes the perspective of most advertising people on the economic effects of advertising. Perhaps the only area of agreement is that advertising has a significant effect on the functioning of our economy.

FIGURE 22–4

This message describes the positive economic effects of advertising

To me it means that if we believe to any degree whatsoever in the economic system under which we live, in a high standard of living and in high employment, advertising is the most efficient known way of moving goods in practically every product class.

My proof is that millions of businessmen have chosen advertising over and over again in the operations of their business. Some of their decisions may have been wrong, but they must have thought they were right or they wouldn't go back to be stung twice by the same kind of bee.

It's a pretty safe bet that in the next 10 years many Americans will be using products and devices that no one in this room has even heard of. Judging purely by past performance, American advertising can be relied on to make them known and accepted overnight at the lowest possible prices.

Advertising, of course, makes possible our unparalleled variety of magazines, newspapers, business publications, and radio and television stations.

It must be said that without advertising we would have a far different nation, and one that would be much the poorer—not merely in material commodities, but in the life of the spirit.

Leo Burnett

These excerpts are from a speech given by Leo Burnett on the American Association of Advertising Agencies' 50th anniversary, April 20, 1967.

Global Perspective 22–3
Telling Consumers around the World about the Economic Value of Advertising

The use of advertising and other forms of promotion is increasing around the world. The former communist countries of Eastern Europe are striving to develop Western-style free-market economies, and even China is trying to develop more of a capitalist system, albeit state controlled. Governments and companies are recognizing that advertising plays an important role in a free and open marketplace of ideas and products and makes important contributions to their economic well-being.

However, not everyone is sold on the value of advertising. Consumers in the United States and many other countries view advertising as a social menace that promotes materialism, encourages them to buy products they don't really need, and insults their intelligence. Some believe advertising for many, if not all, products and services should be banned.

The advertising industry in the United States continually promotes the value of advertising. Trade associations like the AAAA and the AAF run campaigns highlighting advertising's contributions to the economy as well as to consumers' social well-being. As advertising becomes more prevalent globally, there is a need to remind consumers in other countries of the benefits of advertising. In 1992 the International Advertising Association (IAA) began a global campaign to convince the general public of the value of advertising. The IAA has more than 3,200 members in 87 countries that account for 97 percent of global ad expenditures.

The IAA campaign uses two approaches, depending on how developed the market is. In markets such as China and Russia, where the concept of advertising is unfamiliar, the tagline is "Advertising. That's the way it works." In markets such as France or the United States, where the role of advertising is understood, the campaign theme is "Advertising. The right to choose." The IAA campaign includes print messages and TV spots that are seen all over the world. When the campaign first broke, CNN ran a 12-day blitz showing the commercials in 122 countries. One TV spot shows how limiting corporate sponsorships of sports events could hurt fans: As a voiceover says, "It would be, as they say, a whole new ball game," one of two teams playing a soccer match vanishes.

Gallup International conducted a global study to provide the IAA with baseline information for its campaign. The study surveyed 22,000 consumers in 22 countries about their attitudes toward advertising. Individuals in former communist countries were among the most enthusiastic

supporters of advertising, which may reflect their desire to embrace consumer-oriented capitalism.

Consumers in the former East Germany were an exception. They were more negative toward advertising than people in either West Germany or other former communist countries. Consumers in Japan, Uruguay, and Bulgaria had the most favorable attitudes toward advertising. The Japanese were the least inclined to believe that advertising insults consumers' intelligence and the most likely to say they would miss advertising if it were banned. Egypt was the only country where respondents were consistently anti-advertising, an attitude IAA officials attributed to the rise of religious fundamentalism there.

According to Norman Vale, director general of the IAA, the campaign is not a magic bullet that will make everyone love advertising. However, it may reassure people in healthy and emerging economies that advertising has value and is not a social menace.

WHEN ADVERTISING DOES ITS JOB, MILLIONS OF PEOPLE KEEP THEIRS.

Good advertising doesn't just inform. It sells. It helps move product and keep businesses in business. Every time an ad arouses a consumer's interest enough to result in a purchase, it keeps a company going strong. And it helps secure the jobs of the people who work there.

Advertising. That's the way it works.

INTERNATIONAL
ADVERTISING
ASSOCIATION

The global partnership of advertisers, agencies and media

Sources: Laurel Wentz, "Major Global Study Finds Consumers Support Ads," *Advertising Age International*, October 11, 1993, pp. 11, 21; Cyndee Miller, "The Marketing of Advertising," *Marketing News*, December 7, 1992, pp. 1, 2.

SUMMARY

Advertising is a very powerful institution and has been the target of considerable criticism regarding its social and economic impact. The criticism of advertising concerns the specific techniques and methods used as well as its effect on societal values, tastes, lifestyles, and behavior. Critics argue that advertising is deceptive and untruthful; that it is often offensive, irritating, or in poor taste; and that it exploits certain groups, such as children. Many people believe advertising should be informative only and advertisers should not use subjective claims, puffery, embellishment, or persuasive techniques.

Advertising often offends consumers by the type of appeal or manner of presentation used; sexually suggestive ads and nudity receive the most criticism. Advertisers say their ads are consistent with contemporary values and lifestyles and are appropriate for the target audiences they are attempting to reach. Advertising to children is an area of particular concern, since critics argue that children lack the experience, knowledge, and ability to process and evaluate persuasive advertising messages rationally. Although an FTC proposal to severely restrict advertising to children was defeated, it remains an issue.

The pervasiveness of advertising and its prevalence in the mass media have led critics to argue that it plays a major role in influencing and transmitting social values. Advertising has been charged with encouraging materialism, manipulating consumers to buy things they do not really want or need, perpetuating stereotypes through its portrayal of certain groups such as women, minorities, and the elderly, and controlling the media.

Advertising has also been scrutinized with regard to its economic effects. The basic economic role of advertising is to give consumers information that helps them make consumption decisions. Some people view advertising as a detrimental force that has a negative effect on competition, product costs, and consumer prices. Economists' perspectives regarding the effects of advertising follow two basic schools of thought: the advertising equals market power model and the advertising equals information model. Arguments consistent with each perspective were considered in analyzing the economic effects of advertising.

KEY TERMS

ethics, 686

consumer socialization process, 693

materialism, 694

Protestant ethic, 695

differentiation, 704

barrier to entry, 704

economies of scale, 704

DISCUSSION QUESTIONS

1. The federal government plans to spend $175 million per year for the next five years on an antidrug advertising program. The Partnership for a Drug Free America runs the equivalent of nearly $300 million of antidrug messages each year. Do you feel advertising is effective in deterring drug use? Defend your position.

2. Discuss the role of ethics in advertising and promotion. How do ethical considerations differ from legal considerations?

3. Ethical Perspective 22–1 discusses the issue of whether beer companies and other alcoholic beverage marketers purposely target underage drinkers with their media purchases. Evaluate the arguments on both sides of this controversial issue.

4. Should networks run commercials from the HIV prevention campaign developed by the Centers for Disease Control and Prevention that promote the use of latex condoms, or are they inappropriate for TV? Defend your position.

5. Find examples of three ads that you find irritating, offensive, or in bad taste. Discuss the basis of your objections to these ads.

6. New government regulations will require TV networks to air three hours a week of educational programming. Do you feel advertisers should be allowed to sponsor this programming or should it be commercial free? Defend your position.

7. A common criticism of advertising is that it stereotypes women. Discuss how advertising might stereotype men as well. Find an example of an ad that does this.

8. With which position do you agree? "Advertising determines American consumers' tastes and values and is responsible for creating a materialistic society." "Advertising is a reflection of society and mirrors its tastes and values."

9. Do you feel a publication such as a newspaper or magazine can avoid having its editorial content influenced by advertisers? What factors might affect a publication's ability to avoid being influenced by advertisers?

10. Evaluate the efforts of the International Advertising Association to convince consumers around the world of the value of advertising. Why would the advertising industry support such a campaign? Do you think it will be effective?

Glossary of Advertising and Promotion Terms

80/20 rule (2)   The principle that 80 percent of sales volume for a product or service is generated by 20 percent of the customers.

5-W's model of communication (5)   A model of the communications process that contains five basics elements: who? (source), says what? (message), in what way? (channel), to whom? (receiver), and with what effect? (feedback).

A

AIDA model (5)   A model that depicts the successive stages a buyer passes through in the personal selling process including: attention, interest, desire, and action.

ASI Recall Plus Test (18)   A day-after recall test of television commercials (formerly known as the Burke Test).

absolute costs (10)   The actual total cost of placing an ad in a particular media vehicle.

account executive (3)   The individual who serves as the liaison between the advertising agency and the client. The account executive is responsible for managing all of the services the agency provides to the client and representing the agency's point of view to the client.

account specific marketing (15)   Development of customized promotional programs for individual retail accounts by marketers.

adjacencies (11)   Commercial spots purchased from local television stations that generally appear during the time periods adjacent to network programs.

ad execution-related thoughts (5)   A type of thought or cognitive response a message recipient has concerning factors related to the execution of the ad such as creativity, usual effects, color, and style.

advertising (1)   Any paid form of nonpersonal communication about an organization, product, service, or idea by an identified sponsor.

advertising agency (3)   A firm that specializes in the creation, production, and placement of advertising messages and may provide other services that facilitate the marketing communications process.

advertising appeal (9)   The basis or approach used in an advertising message to attract the attention or interest of consumers and/or influence their feelings toward the product, service, or cause.

advertising campaign (8)   A comprehensive advertising plan that consists of a series of messages in a variety of media that center on a single theme or idea.

advertising creativity (8)   The ability to generate fresh, unique, and appropriate ideas that can be used as solutions to communication problems.

advertising manager (3)   The individual in an organization who is responsible for the planning, coordinating, budgeting, and implementing of the advertising program.

advertising specialties (13)   Items used as giveaways to serve as a reminder or stimulate remembrance of a company or brand such as calendars, T-shirts, pens, key tags, and the like. Specialties are usually imprinted with a company or brand name and other identifying marks such as an address and phone number.

advertising substantiation (21)   A Federal Trade Commission regulatory program that requires advertisers to have documentation to support the claims made in their advertisements.

advocacy advertising (16)   Advertising that is concerned with the propagation of ideas and elucidation of social issues of public importance in a manner that supports the position and interest of the sponsor.

aerial advertising (13)   A form of outdoor advertising where messages appear in the sky in the form of banners pulled by airplanes, skywriting, and on blimps.

affect referral decision rule (4)   A type of decision rule where selections are made on the basis of an overall impression or affective summary evaluation of the various alternatives under consideration.

affiliates (11)   Local television stations that are associated with a major network. Affiliates agree to preempt time during specified hours for programming provided by the network and carry the advertising contained in the program.

affirmative disclosure (21)   A Federal Trade Commission program whereby advertisers may be required to include certain types of information in their advertisements so consumers will be aware of all the consequences, conditions, and limitations associated with the use of the product or service.

affordable method (7)   A method of determining the budget for advertising and promotion where all other budget areas are covered and remaining monies are available for allocation.

agate line (12)   Unit of newspaper space measurement, 1 column wide by 1/14 inch deep. (Thus, 14 agate lines = 1 column inch.)

agency evaluation process (3)   The process by which a company evaluates the performance of its advertising agency. This process includes both financial and qualitative aspects.

alpha activity (18)   A measure of the degree of brain activity that can be used to assess an individual's reactions to an advertisement.

alternative media (13)   A term commonly used in advertising to describe support media.

animatic (8)   A preliminary version of a commercial whereby a videotape of the frames of a storyboard is produced along with an audio soundtrack.

arbitrary allocation (7)   A method for determining the budget for advertising and promotion based on arbitrary decisions of executives.

Note: Numbers in parentheses after term indicate chapter(s) where term is discussed.

area of dominant influence (ADI) (11) A geographic survey area created and defined by Arbitron. Each county in the nation is assigned to an ADI, which is an exclusive geographic area consisting of all counties in which the home market stations receive a preponderance of viewing.

attitude toward the ad (5) A message recipient's affective feelings of favorability or unfavorability toward an advertisement.

attractiveness (6) A source characteristic that makes him or her appealing to a message recipient. Source attractiveness can be based on similarity, familiarity, or likability.

audimeter (11) An electric measurement device that is hooked to a television set to record when the set is turned on and the channel to which it is tuned.

audiotex (13) The use of telephone and voice information services to market, advertise, promote, entertain, and inform consumers.

average frequency (10) The number of times the average household reached by a media schedule is exposed to a media vehicle over a specified period.

average quarter-hour figure (AQH) (11) The average number of persons listening to a particular station for at least five minutes during a 15-minute period. Used by Arbitron in measuring the size of radio audiences.

average quarter-hour rating (11) The average quarter-hour figure estimate expressed as a percentage of the population being measured. Used by Arbitron in measuring the size of radio audiences.

average quarter-hour share (11) The percentage of the total listening audience tuned to each station as a percentage of the total listening audience in the survey area. Used by Arbitron in measuring the size of radio audiences.

B

balance-of-trade deficit (20) A situation where the monetary value of a country's imports exceeds its exports.

barrier to entry (22) Conditions that make it difficult for a firm to enter the market in a particular industry, such as high advertising budgets.

barter syndication (11) The offering of television programs to local stations free or at a reduced rate but with some of the advertising time presold to national advertisers. The remaining advertising time can be sold to local advertisers.

behavioristic segmentation (2) A method of segmenting a market by dividing customers into groups based on their usage, loyalties, or buying responses to a product or service.

benchmark measures (7) Measures of a target audience's status concerning response hierarchy variables such as awareness, knowledge, image, attitudes, preferences, intentions, or behavior. These measures are taken at the beginning of an advertising or promotional campaign to determine the degree to which a target audience must be changed or moved by a promotional campaign.

benefit segmentation (2) A method of segmenting markets on the basis of the major benefits consumers seek in a product or service.

Better Business Bureau (BBB) (21) An organization established and funded by businesses that operates primarily at the local level to monitor activities of companies and promote fair advertising and selling practices.

big idea (8) A unique or creative idea for an advertisement or campaign that attracts consumers' attention, gets a reaction, and sets the advertiser's product or service apart from the competition.

billings (3) The amount of client money agencies spend on media purchases and other equivalent activities. Billings are often used as a way of measuring the size of advertising agencies.

bleed pages (12) Magazine advertisements where the printed area extends to the edge of the page, eliminating any white margin or border around the ad.

body copy (9) The main text portion of a print ad. Also often referred to as copy.

bonus packs (15) Special packaging that provides consumers with extra quantity of merchandise at no extra charge over the regular price.

bounce-back coupon (15) A coupon offer made to consumers as an inducement to repurchase the brand.

brand development index (BDI) (10) An index that is calculated by taking the percentage of a brand's total sales that occur in a given market as compared to the percentage of the total population in the market.

brand equity (2) The intangible asset of added value or goodwill that results from the favorable image, impressions of differentiation, and/or the strength of consumer attachment of a company name, brand name, or trademark.

brand loyalty (4) Preference by a consumer for a particular brand that results in continual purchase of it.

brand manager (3) The person responsible for the planning, implementation, and control of the marketing program for an individual brand.

broadcast media (12) Media that use the airwaves to transmit their signal and programming. Radio and television are examples of broadcast media.

build-up approach (7) A method of determining the budget for advertising and promotion by determining the specific tasks that have to be performed and estimating the costs of performing them. See objective and task method.

Burke Test (18) A method of posttesting television commercials using a day-after recall test (now known as ASI Recall Plus Test).

business-to-business advertising (19) Advertising used by one business to promote the products and/or services it sells to another business.

buying center (5, 19) A committee or group of individuals in an organization who are responsible for evaluating products and services and making purchase decisions.

C

cable television (11) A form of television where signals are carried to households by wire rather than through the airways.

carryover effect (7) A delayed or lagged effect whereby the impact of advertising on sales can occur during a subsequent time period.

category development index (CDI) (10) An index that is calculated by taking the percentage of a product category's total sales that occur in a given market area as compared to the percentage of the total population in the market.

category extension (2) The strategy of applying an existing brand name to a new product category.

category management (3) An organizational system whereby managers have responsibility for the marketing programs for a particular category or line of products.

cease and desist order (21) An action by the Federal Trade Commission that orders a company to stop engaging in a practice that is considered deceptive or misleading until a hearing is held.

central route to persuasion (5) One of two routes to persuasion recognized by the elaboration likelihood model. The central route to persuasion views a message recipient as very active and involved in the communications process and as having the ability and motivation to attend to and process a message.

centralized organizational structure (20) A method of organizing for international advertising and promotion whereby all decisions are made in a company's home office.

centralized system (3) An organizational system whereby advertising along with other marketing activities such as sales, marketing research, and planning are divided along functional lines and are run from one central marketing department.

channel (5) The method or medium by which communication travels from a source or sender to a receiver.

city zone (12) A category used for newspaper circulation figures that refers to a market area composed of the city where the paper is published and contiguous areas similar in character to the city.

classical conditioning (4) A learning process whereby a conditioned stimulus that elicits a response is paired with a neutral stimulus that does not elicit any particular response. Through repeated exposure, the neutral stimulus comes to elicit the same response as the conditioned stimulus.

classified advertising (12) Advertising that runs in newspapers and magazines that generally contains text only and is arranged under subheadings according to the product, service, or offering. Employment, real estate, and automotive ads are the major forms of classified advertising.

clients (3) The organizations with the products, services, or causes to be marketed and for which advertising agencies and other marketing promotional firms provide services.

clipping service (7) A service which clips competitors' advertising from local print media allowing the company to monitor the types of advertising that are running or to estimate their advertising expenditures.

close (17) Obtaining the commitment of the prospect in a personal selling transaction.

clutter (6, 11) The nonprogram material that appears in a broadcast environment, including commercials, promotional messages for shows, public service announcements, and the like.

cognitive dissonance (4) A state of psychological tension or postpurchase doubt that a consumer may experience after making a purchase decision. This tension often leads the consumer to try to reduce it by seeking supportive information.

cognitive processing (4) The process by which an individual transforms external information into meanings or patterns of thought and how these meanings are used to form judgments or choices about behavior.

cognitive responses (5) Thoughts that occur to a message recipient while reading, viewing, and/or hearing a communication.

collateral services (3) Companies that provide companies with specialized services such as package design, advertising production, and marketing research.

combination rates (12) A special space rate or discount offered for advertising in two or more periodicals. Combination rates are often offered by publishers who own both morning and evening editions of a newspaper in the same market.

commission system (3) A method of compensating advertising agencies whereby the agency receives a specified commission (traditionally 15 percent) from the media on any advertising time or space it purchases.

communication (5) The passing of information, exchange of ideas, or process of establishing shared meaning between a sender and a receiver.

communication objectives (1, 7) Goals that an organization seeks to achieve through its promotional program in terms of communication effects such as creating awareness, knowledge, image, attitudes, preferences, or purchase intentions.

communication task (7) Under the DAGMAR approach to setting advertising goals and objectives, something that can be performed by and attributed to advertising such as awareness, comprehension, conviction, and action.

comparative advertising (6, 9) The practice of either directly or indirectly naming one or more competitors in an advertising message and usually making a comparison on one or more specific attributes or characteristics.

compensatory decision rule (4) A type of decision rule for evaluating alternatives where consumers consider each brand with respect to how it performs on relevant or salient attributes and the importance of each attribute. This decision rule allows for a negative evaluation or performance on a particular attribute to be compensated for by a positive evaluation on another attribute.

competitive advantage (2) Something unique or special that a firm does or possesses that provides an advantage over its competitors.

competitive parity method (7) A method of setting the advertising and promotion budget based on matching the absolute level of percentage of sales expenditures of the competition.

compliance (6) A type of influence process where a receiver accepts the position advocated by a source to obtain favorable outcomes or to avoid punishment.

computer simulation models (7) Quantitative-based models that are used to determine the relative contribution of advertising expenditures on sales response.

concave downward function (7) An advertising/sales response function that views the incremental effects of advertising on sales as decreasing.

concentrated marketing (2) A type of marketing strategy whereby a firm chooses to focus its marketing efforts on one particular market segment.

concept testing (18) A method of pretesting alternative ideas for an advertisement or campaign by having consumers provide their responses and/or reactions to the creative concept.

conditioned response (4) In classical conditioning, a response that occurs as a result of exposure to a conditioned stimulus.

conditioned stimulus (4) In classical conditioning, a stimulus that becomes associated with an unconditioned stimulus and capable of evoking the same response or reaction as the unconditioned stimulus.

conjunctive decision rule (4) A type of decision rule for evaluating alternatives where consumers establish minimally acceptable levels of performance for each important product attribute and accept an alternative only if it meets the cutoff level for each attribute.

consent order (21) A settlement between a company and the Federal Trade Commission whereby an advertiser agrees to stop the advertising or practice in question. A consent order is for settlement purposes only and does not constitute an admission of guilt.

consumer behavior (4) The process and activities that people engage in when searching for, selecting, purchasing, using, evaluating, and disposing of products and services so as to satisfy their needs and desires.

consumer franchise-building promotions (15) Sales promotion activities that communicate distinctive brand attributes and contribute to the development and reinforcement of brand identity.

consumer juries (18) A method of pretesting advertisements by using a panel of consumers who are representative of the target audience and provide ratings, rankings, and/or evaluations of advertisements.

consumer-oriented sales promotion (15) Sales promotion techniques that are targeted to the ultimate consumer such as coupons, samples, contests, rebates, sweepstakes, and premium offers.

consumer socialization process (22) The process by which an individual acquires the skills needed to function in the marketplace as a consumer.

contest (15) A promotion whereby consumers compete for prizes or money on the basis of skills or ability, and winners are determined by judging the entries or ascertaining which entry comes closest to some predetermined criteria.

continuity (10) A media scheduling strategy where a continuous pattern of advertising is used over the time span of the advertising campaign.

contribution margin (7) The difference between the total revenue generated by a product or brand and its total variable costs.

controlled circulation basis (12) Distribution of a publication free to individuals a publisher believes are of importance and responsible for making purchase decisions or are prescreened for qualification on some other basis.

cooperative advertising (2, 15) Advertising program in which a manufacturer pays a certain percentage of the expenses a retailer or distributor incurs for advertising the manufacturer's product in a local market area.

copy platform (8) A document that specifies the basic elements of the creative strategy such as the basic problem or issue the advertising must address, the advertising and communications objectives, target audience, major selling idea or key benefits to communicate, campaign theme or appeal, and supportive information or requirements.

copywriter (3, 8) Individual who helps conceive the ideas for ads and commercials and writes the words or copy for them.

corporate advertising (16) Advertising designed to promote overall awareness of a company or enhance its image among a target audience.

corrective advertising (21) An action by the Federal Trade Commission whereby an advertiser can be required to run advertising messages designed to remedy the deception or misleading impression created by its previous advertising.

cost per customer purchasing (14) A cost effectiveness measure used in direct marketing based on the cost per sale generated.

cost per order (CPO) (13) A measure used in direct marketing to determine the number of orders generated relative to the cost of running the advertisement.

cost per ratings point (10) A computation used by media buyers to compare the cost efficiency of broadcast programs that divides the cost of commercial time on a program by the audience rating.

cost per thousand (10) A computation used in evaluating the relative cost of various media vehicles that represents the cost of exposing 1,000 members of a target audience to an advertising message.

cost plus system (3) A method of compensating advertising agencies whereby the agency receives a fee based on the cost of the work it performs plus an agreed-on amount for profit.

Council of Better Business Bureaus (21) The parent office of local offices of the Better Business Bureau. The council assists in the development of codes and standards for ethical and responsible business and advertising practices.

counterargument (5) A type of thought or cognitive response a receiver has that is counter or opposed to the position advocated in a message.

coverage (10) A measure of the potential audience that might receive an advertising message through a media vehicle.

creative boutique (3) An advertising agency that specializes in and provides only services related to the creative aspects of advertising.

creative execution style (9) The manner or way in which a particular advertising appeal is transformed into a message.

creative selling (17) A type of sales position where the primary emphasis is on generating new business.

creative strategy (8) A determination of what an advertising message will say or communicate to a target audience.

creative tactics (8) A determination of how an advertising message will be implemented so as to execute the creative strategy.

creativity (8) A quality possessed by persons that enables them to generate novel approaches, generally reflected in new and improved solutions to problems.

credibility (6) The extent to which a source is perceived as having knowledge, skill, or experience relevant to a communication topic and can be trusted to give an unbiased opinion or present objective information on the issue.

cross-media advertising (12) An arrangement where opportunities to advertise in several different types of media are offered by a single company or a partnership of various media providers.

cross/multimagazine deals (12) An arrangement where two or more publishers offer their magazines to an advertiser as one media package.

cross-ruff coupon (15) A coupon offer delivered on one product that is redeemable for the purchase of another product. The other product is usually one made by the same company but may involve a tie-in with another manufacturer.

cross sell (17) A term used in personal selling that refers to the sale of additional products and/or services to the same customer.

CUBE Model (19) Acronym for Comprehensive Understanding of Business Environments, a model in which values and lifestyles of corporate buying groups are detailed.

culture (4, 19) The complexity of learned meanings, values, norms, and customs shared by members of a society.

cume (11) A term used for cumulative audience, which is the estimated total number of different people who listened to a radio station for a minimum of five minutes during a particular daypart.

D

DAGMAR (7) An acronym that stands for defining advertising goals for measured advertising results. An approach to setting advertising goals and objectives developed by Russell Colley.

daily inch rate (10) A cost figure used in periodicals based on an advertisement placed one inch deep and one column wide (whatever the column inch).

database (14) A listing of current and/or potential customers for a company's product or service that can be used for direct-marketing purposes.

database marketing (14) The use of specific information about individual customers and/or prospects to implement more effective and efficient marketing communications.

day-after recall scores (18) A measure used in on-air testing of television commercials by various marketing research companies. The day-after recall score represents the percentage of viewers surveyed who can remember seeing a particular commercial.

dayparts (10, 11) The time segments into which a day is divided by radio and television networks and stations for selling advertising time.

decentralized organizational structure (20) A method of organizing for international advertising and promotion where managers in each market or country have decision-making authority.

decentralized system (3) An organizational system whereby planning and decision-making responsibility for marketing, advertising, and promotion lies with a product/brand manager or management team rather than a centralized department.

deception (21) According to the Federal Trade Commission, a misrepresentation, omission, or practice that is likely to mislead the consumer acting reasonably in the circumstances to the consumer's detriment.

decoding (5) The process by which a message recipient transforms and interprets a message.

demographic segmentation (2) A method of segmenting a market based on the demographic characteristics of consumers.

departmental system (3) The organization of an advertising agency into departments based on functions such as account services, creative, media, marketing services, and administration.

derived demand (19) A situation where demand for a particular product or service results from the need for other goods and/or services. For example, demand for aluminum cans is derived from consumption of soft drinks or beer.

designated market area (DMA) (11) The geographic areas used by the Nielsen Station Index in measuring audience size. DMAs are nonoverlapping areas consisting of groups of counties from which stations attract their viewers.

differentiated marketing (2) A type of marketing strategy whereby a firm offers products or services to a number of market segments and develops separate marketing strategies for each.

differentiation (22) A situation where a particular company or brand is perceived as unique or better than its competitors.

direct-action advertising (1) Advertising designed to produce an immediate effect such as the generation of store traffic or sales.

direct broadcast by satellite (DBS) (20) A television signal delivery system whereby programming is beamed from satellites to special receiving dishes mounted in the home or yard.

direct channel (2) A marketing channel where a producer and ultimate consumer interact directly with one another.

direct headline (9) A headline that is very straightforward and informative in terms of the message it is presenting and the target audience it is directed toward. Direct headlines often include a specific benefit, promise, or reason for a consumer to be interested in a product or service.

direct marketing (1, 14) A system of marketing by which an organization communicates directly with customers to generate a response and/or transaction.

direct-marketing media (14) Media that are used for direct-marketing purposes including direct mail, telemarketing, print, and broadcast.

direct-response agencies (3) Companies that provide a variety of direct-marketing services to their clients including database management, direct mail, research, media service, and creative and production capabilities.

direct-response advertising (1, 14) A form of advertising for a product or service that elicits a sales response directly from the advertiser.

direct selling (1, 14) The direct personal presentation, demonstration, and sale of products and services to consumers usually in their homes or at their jobs.

directional medium (13) Advertising media that are not used to create awareness or demand for products or services but rather to inform customers as to where purchases can be made once they have decided to buy. The Yellow Pages are an example of a directional medium.

display advertising (12) Advertising in newspapers and magazines that uses illustrations, photos, headlines, and other visual elements in addition to copy text.

dissonance/attribution model (5) A type of response hierarchy where consumers first behave, then develop attitudes or feelings as a result of that behavior, and then learn or process information that supports the attitude and behavior.

diverting (15) A practice whereby a retailer or wholesaler takes advantage of a promotional deal and then sells some of the product purchased at the low price to a store outside of their area or to a middleman who will resell it to other stores.

duplicated reach (10) Audience members' exposure to a message as a result of messages having appeared in two or more different media vehicles.

dyadic communication (17) A process of direct communication between two persons or groups such as a salesperson and a customer.

E

economic infrastructure (20) A country's communications, transportation, financial, and distribution networks.

economies of scale (7, 22) A decline in costs with accumulated sales or production. In advertising, economies of scale often occur in media purchases as the relative costs of advertising time and/or space may decline as the size of the media budget increases.

effective reach (10) A measure of the percentage of a media vehicle's audience reached at each effective frequency increment.

elaboration likelihood model (ELM) (5) A model that identifies two processes by which communications can lead to persuasion—central and peripheral routes.

electrodermal response (18) A measure of the resistance the skin offers to a small amount of current passed between two electrodes. Used as a measure of consumers' reaction level to an advertisement.

electroencephalographic (EEG) measures (18) Measures of the electrical impulses in the brain that are sometimes used as a measure of reactions to advertising.

electronic teleshopping (14) Online shopping and information retrieval service that is accessed through a personal computer.

emotional appeals (6, 9) Advertising messages that appeal to consumers' feelings and emotions.

encoding (5) The process of putting thoughts, ideas, or information into a symbolic form.

ethics (22) Moral principles and values that govern the actions and decisions of an individual or group.

evaluative criteria (4) The dimensions or attributes of a product or service that are used to compare different alternatives.

event sponsorship (15) A type of promotion whereby a company develops sponsorship relations with a particular event such as a concert, sporting event, or other activity.

evoked set (4) The various brands identified by a consumer as purchase options and that are actively considered during the alternative evaluation process.

exchange (1) Trade of something of value between two parties such as a product or service for money. The core phenomenon or domain for study in marketing.

exclusive (16) A public relations tactic whereby one particular medium is offered exclusive rights to a story.

expertise (6) An aspect of source credibility where a communicator is perceived as being knowledgeable in a given area or for a particular topic.

external analysis (1) The phase of the promotional planning process that focuses on factors such as the characteristics of an organization's customers, market segments, positioning strategies, competitors, and marketing environment.

external audiences (16) In public relations, a term used in reference to individuals who are outside of or not closely connected to the organization such as the general public.

external audits (16) Evaluations performed by outside agencies to determine the effectiveness of an organization's public relations program.

external search (4) The search process whereby consumers seek and acquire information from external sources such as advertising, other people, or public sources.

eye tracking (18) A method for following the movement of a person's eyes as he or she views an ad or commercial. Eye tracking is used for determining which portions or sections of an ad attract a viewer's attention and/or interest.

F

failure fee (15) A trade promotion arrangement whereby a marketer agrees to pay a penalty fee if a product stocked by a retailer does not meet agreed-upon sales levels.

Fairness Doctrine (21) A Federal Communications Commission program that required broadcasters to provide time for opposing viewpoints on important issues.

fear appeals (6) An advertising message that creates anxiety in a receiver by showing negative consequences that can result from engaging in (or not engaging in) a particular behavior.

Federal Trade Commission (FTC) (21) The federal agency that has the primary responsibility for protecting consumers and businesses from anticompetitive behavior and unfair and deceptive practices. The FTC regulates advertising and promotion at the federal level.

Federal Trade Commission Act (21) Federal legislation passed in 1914 that created the Federal Trade Commission and gave it the responsibility to monitor deceptive or misleading advertising and unfair business practices.

fee-commission combination (3) A type of compensation system whereby an advertising agency establishes a fixed monthly fee for its services to a client and media commissions received by the agency are credited against the fee.

feedback (5) Part of message recipient's response that is communicated back to the sender. Feedback can take a variety of forms and provides a sender with a way of monitoring how an intended message is decoded and received.

field of experience (5) The experiences, perceptions, attitudes, and values that senders and receivers of a message bring to a communication situation.

field tests (18) Tests of consumer reactions to an advertisement that are taken under natural viewing situations rather than in a laboratory.

financial audit (3) An aspect of the advertising agency evaluation process that focuses on how the agency conducts financial affairs related to serving a client.

first-run syndication (11) Programs produced specifically for the syndication market.

fixed-fee arrangement (3) A method of agency compensation whereby the agency and client agree on the work to be done and the amount of money the agency will be paid for its services.

flat rates (12) A standard newspaper advertising rate where no discounts are offered for large-quantity or repeated space buys.

Flesch formula (18) A test used to assess the difficulty level of writing based on the number of syllables and sentences per 100 words.

flighting (10) A media scheduling pattern in which periods of advertising are alternated with periods of no advertising.

focus groups (8) A qualitative marketing research method whereby a group of 10–12 consumers from the target market are led through a discussion regarding a particular topic such as a product, service, or advertising campaign.

forward buying (15) A practice whereby retailers and wholesalers stock up on a product being offered by a manufacturer at a lower deal or off-invoice price and resell it to consumers once the marketer's promotional period has ended.

frequency (10) The number of times a target audience is exposed to a media vehicle(s) in a specified period.

full-service agency (3) An advertising agency that offers clients a full range of marketing and communications services including the planning, creating, producing, and placing of advertising messages and other forms of promotion.

functional consequences (4) Outcomes of product or service usage that are tangible and can be directly experienced by a consumer.

G

game (15) A promotion that is a form of sweepstakes because it has a chance element or odds of winning associated with it. Games usually involve game card devices that can be rubbed or opened to unveil a winning number or prize description.

gatefolds (12) An oversize magazine page or cover that is extended and folded over to fit into the publication. Gatefolds are used to extend the size of a magazine advertisement and are always sold at a premium.

general preplanning input (8) Information gathering and/or market research studies on trends, developments, and happenings in the marketplace that can be used to assist in the initial stages of the creative process of advertising.

geographical weighting (10) A media scheduling strategy where certain geographic areas or regions are allocated higher levels of advertising because they have greater sales potential.

geographic segmentation (2) A method of segmenting a market on the basis of different geographic units or areas.

global advertising (20) The use of the same basic advertising message in all international markets.

global marketing (20) A strategy of using a common marketing plan and program for all countries in which a company operates, thus selling the product or services the same way everywhere in the world.

green marketing (22) The marketing and promotion of products on the basis of environmental sensitivity.

gross ratings points (GRPs) (10)   A measure that represents the total delivery or weight of a media schedule during a specified time period. GRPs are calculated by multiplying the reach of the media schedule by the average frequency.

group system (3)   The organization of an advertising agency by dividing it into groups consisting of specialists from various departments such as creative, media, marketing services, and other areas. These groups work together to service particular accounts.

H

halo effect (18)   The tendency for evaluations of one attribute or aspect of a stimulus to distort reactions to its other attributes or properties.

headline (9)   Words in the leading position of the advertisement; the words that will be read first or are positioned to draw the most attention.

hemisphere lateralization (18)   The notion that the human brain has two relatively distinct halves or hemispheres with each being responsible for a specific type of function. The right side is responsible for visual processing while the left side conducts verbal processing.

heuristics (4)   Simplified or basic decision rules that can be used by a consumer to make a purchase choice, such as buy the cheapest brand.

hierarchy of effects model (5)   A model of the process by which advertising works that assumes a consumer must pass through a sequence of steps from initial awareness to eventual action. The stages include awareness, interest, evaluation, trial, and adoption.

hierarchy of needs (4)   Abraham Maslow's theory that human needs are arranged in an order or hierarchy based on their importance. The need hierarchy includes physiological, safety, social/love and belonging, esteem, and self-actualization needs.

horizontal cooperative advertising (15)   A cooperative advertising arrangement where advertising is sponsored in common by a group of retailers or other organizations providing products or services to a market.

households using television (HUT) (11)   The percentage of homes in a given area that are watching television during a specific time period.

I

identification (6)   The process by which an attractive source influences a message recipient. Identification occurs when the receiver is motivated to seek some type of relationship with the source and adopt a similar position in terms of beliefs, attitudes, preferences, or behavior.

image advertising (8)   Advertising that creates an identity for a product or service by emphasizing psychological meaning or symbolic association with certain values, lifestyles, and the like.

image transfer (11)   A radio advertising technique whereby the images of a television commercial are implanted into a radio spot.

incentive-based system (3)   A form of compensation whereby an advertising agency's compensation level depends on how well it meets predetermined performance goals such as sales or market share.

index numbers (10)   A ratio used to describe the potential of a market. The index number is derived by dividing the percentage of users in a market segment by the percentage of population in the same segment and multiplying by 100.

indirect channels (2)   A marketing channel where intermediaries such as wholesalers and retailers are utilized to make a product available to the customer.

indirect headlines (9)   Headlines that are not straightforward with respect to identifying a product or service or providing information regarding the point of an advertising message.

in-flight advertising (13)   A variety of advertising media targeting air travelers while they are in flight.

infomercials (11, 14)   Television commercials that are very long, ranging from several minutes to an hour. Infomercials are designed to provide consumers with detailed information about a product or service.

information processing model (5)   A model of advertising effects developed by William McGuire that views the receiver of a message as an information processor and problem solver. The model views the receiver as passing through a response hierarchy that includes a series of stages including message presentation, attention, comprehension, acceptance or yielding, retention, and behavior.

informational/rational appeals (9)   Advertising appeals that focus on the practical, functional, or utilitarian need for a product or service and emphasize features, benefits, or reasons for owning or using the brand.

ingredient sponsored cooperative advertising (15)   Advertising supported by raw material manufacturers with the objective being to help establish end products that include materials and/or ingredients supplied by the company.

inherent drama (8)   An approach to advertising that focuses on the benefits or characteristics that lead a consumer to purchase a product or service and uses dramatic elements to emphasize them.

in-house agency (3)   An advertising agency set up, owned, and operated by an advertiser that is responsible for planning and executing the company's advertising program.

ink-jet imaging (12)   A printing process where a message is reproduced by projecting ink onto paper rather than mechanical plates. Ink-jet imaging is being offered by many magazines to allow advertisers to personalize their messages.

innovation-adoption model (5)   A model that represents the stages a consumer passes through in the adoption process for an innovation such as a new product. The series of steps includes: awareness, interest, evaluation, trial, and adoption.

inquiry tests (18)   Tests designed to measure advertising effectiveness on the basis of inquiries or responses generated from the ad such as requests for information, number of phone calls, or number of coupons redeemed.

inside cards (13)   A form of transit advertising where messages appear on cards or boards inside of vehicles such as buses, subways, or trolleys.

instant coupon (15)   Coupons attached to a package that can be removed and redeemed at the time of purchase.

in-store couponing (15)   The distribution of coupons in retail stores through various methods such as tear-off pads, handouts, and on-shelf or electronic dispensers.

in-store media (13)   Advertising and promotional media that are used inside of a retail store such as point-of-purchase displays, ads on shopping carts, coupon dispensers, and display boards.

integrated information response model (5)   A model of the response process or sequence advertising message recipients go through which integrates concepts from the traditional and low-involvement response hierarchy perspectives.

integrated marketing communication objectives (7)   Statements of what various aspects of the integrated marketing communications program will accomplish with respect to factors such as communication tasks, sales, market share, and the like.

integrated marketing communications (1)   A concept of marketing communications planning that recognizes the added value of a comprehensive plan that evaluates the strategic roles of a variety of communication disciplines—for example, general advertising, direct response, sales promotion, and public relations—and combines these disciplines to provide clarity, consistency, and maximum communications impact.

integration processes (4)   The way information such as product knowledge, meanings, and beliefs is combined to evaluate two or more alternatives.

interactive agency (3)   An organization that specializes in the creation of interactive media such as CD-roms, kiosks, and websites.

interactive media (10)   A variety of media that allows the consumer to interact with the source of the message, actively receiving information and altering images, responding to questions, and so on.

interconnects (11)   Groups of cable systems joined together for advertising purposes.

internal analysis (1)   The phase of the promotional planning process that focuses on the product/service offering and the firm itself including the capabilities of the firm and its ability to develop and implement a successful integrated marketing communications program.

internal audiences (16)   In public relations, a term used to refer to individuals or groups inside of the organization or with a close connection to it.

internal audits (16)   Evaluations by individuals within the organization to determine the effectiveness of a public relations program.

internalization (6)   The process by which a credible source influences a message recipient. Internalization occurs when the receiver is motivated to have an objectively correct position on an issue and the receiver will adopt the opinion or attitude of the credible communicator if he or she believes the information from this source represents an accurate position on the issue.

internal search (4)   The process by which a consumer acquires information by accessing past experiences or knowledge stored in memory.

international media (20)   Advertising media that have multicountry coverage and can be used to reach audiences in various countries.

Internet (14)   A worldwide means of exchanging information and communicating through a series of interconnected computers.

J

jingles (9)   Songs about a product or service that usually carry the advertising theme and a simple message.

L

laboratory tests (18)   Tests of consumer reactions to advertising under controlled conditions.

Lanham Act (21)   A federal law that permits a company to register a trademark for its exclusive use. The Lanham Act was recently amended to encompass false advertising and prohibits any false description or representation including words or other symbols tending falsely to describe or represent the same.

layout (9)   The physical arrangement of the various parts of an advertisement including the headline, subheads, illustrations, body copy, and any identifying marks.

lexicographic decision rule (4)   A type of decision rule where choice criteria are ranked in order of importance and alternatives are evaluated on each attribute or criterion beginning with the most important one.

local advertising (11)   Advertising done by companies within the limited geographic area where they do business.

localized advertising strategy (20)   Developing an advertising campaign specifically for a particular country or market rather than using a global approach.

low involvement hierarchy (5)   A response hierarchy whereby a message recipient is viewed as passing from cognition to behavior to attitude change.

M

magazine networks (12)   A group of magazines owned by one publisher or assembled by an independent network that offers advertisers the opportunity to buy space in a variety of publications through a package deal.

mailing list (14)   A type of database containing names and addresses of present and/or potential customers who can be reached through a direct-mail campaign.

major selling idea (8)   The basis for the central theme or message idea in an advertising campaign.

marginal analysis (7)   A principle of resource allocation that balances incremental revenues against incremental costs.

market opportunities (2)   Areas where a company believes there are favorable demand trends, needs, and/or wants that are not being satisfied, and where it can compete effectively.

market segmentation (2)   The process of dividing a market into distinct groups that have common needs and will respond similarly to a marketing action.

market segments (2)   Identifiable groups of customers sharing similar needs, wants, or other characteristics that make them likely to respond in a similar fashion to a marketing program.

marketing (1, 2)   The process of planning and executing the conception, pricing, promotion, and distribution of ideas, goods, and services to create exchanges that satisfy individual and organizational objectives.

marketing channels (2)   The set of interdependent organizations involved in the process of making a product or service available to customers.

marketing mix (1, 2)   The controllable elements of a marketing program including product, price, promotion, and place.

marketing objectives (1, 7)   Goals to be accomplished by an organization's overall marketing program such as sales, market share, or profitability.

marketing plan (1)   A written document that describes the overall marketing strategy and programs developed for an organization, a particular product line, or a brand.

marketing public relations function (MPR) (16)   Public relations activities designed to support marketing objectives and programs.

mass media (5)   Nonpersonal channels of communication that allow a message to be sent to many individuals at one time.

materialism (22) A preoccupation with material things rather than intellectual or spiritual concerns.

media buying services (3) Independent companies that specialize in the buying of media, particularly radio and television time.

media objectives (10) The specific goals an advertiser has for the media portion of the advertising program.

media organizations (3) One of the four major participants in the integrated marketing communications process whose function is to provide information or entertainment to subscribers, viewers, or readers while offering marketers an environment for reaching audiences with print and broadcast messages.

media plan (10) A document consisting of objectives, strategies, and tactics for reaching a target audience through various media vehicles.

media planning (10) The series of decisions involved in the delivery of an advertising message to prospective purchasers and/or users of a product or service.

media strategies (10) Plans of action for achieving stated media objectives such as which media will be used for reaching a target audience, how the media budget will be allocated, and how advertisements will be scheduled.

media vehicle (10) The specific program, publication, or promotional piece used to carry an advertising message.

medium (10) The general category of communication vehicles that are available for communicating with a target audience such as broadcast, print, direct mail, and outdoor.

message (5) A communication containing information or meaning that a source wants to convey to a receiver.

missionary sales (17) A type of sales position where the emphasis is on performing supportive activities and services rather than generating or taking orders.

mnemonics (4) Basic cues such as symbols, rhymes, and associations that facilitate the learning and memory process.

mobile billboards (13) An out-of-home medium in which advertisements are able to be transported to different locations (signs painted on automobiles, trailers pulling billboards, and the like).

motivation research (4) Qualitative research designed to probe the consumer's subconscious and discover deeply rooted motives for purchasing a product.

motive (4) Something that compels or drives a consumer to take a particular action.

multiattribute attitude model (4) A model of attitudes that views an individual's evaluation of an object as being a function of the beliefs that he or she has toward the object on various attributes and the importance of these attributes.

multimagazine deals (12) Arrangements whereby two to more publishers offer advertisers the opportunity to buy space in their magazines with one single media buy.

multiple buying influences (19) The idea that a number of different individuals may influence the purchase process for a product or service within an organization.

multiplexing (11) An arrangement where multiple channels are transmitted by one cable network.

N

narrowcasting (11) The reaching of a very specialized market through programming aimed at particular target audiences. Cable television networks offer excellent opportunities for narrowcasting.

national advertisers (2) Companies that advertise their products or services on a nationwide basis or in most regions of the country.

National Advertising Review Board (NARB) (21) A part of the National Advertising Division of the Council of Better Business Bureaus. The NARB is the advertising industry's primary self-regulatory body.

National Advertising Review Council (NARC) (21) An organization founded by the Council of Better Business Bureaus and various advertising industry groups to promote high standards of truth, accuracy, morality, and social responsibility in national advertising.

National Association of Attorneys General (21) An organization consisting of state attorneys general that is involved in the regulation of advertising and other business practices.

national spot (11) All non-network advertising done by a national advertiser in local markets.

negotiated commission (3) A method of compensating advertising agencies whereby the client and agency negotiate the commission structure rather than relying on the traditional 15 percent media commission.

noise (5) Extraneous factors that create unplanned distortion or interference in the communications process.

noncompensatory integration strategies (4) Types of decision rules used to evaluate alternatives that do not allow negative evaluation or performance on a particular attribute to be compensated for by positive evaluation or performance on some other attribute.

nonfranchise-building promotions (15) Sales promotion activities that are designed to accelerate the purchase decision process and generate an immediate increase in sales but do little or nothing to communicate information about a brand and contribute to its identity and image.

nonmeasured media (13) A term commonly used in the advertising industry to describe support media.

nonpersonal channels (5) Channels of communication that carry a message without involving interpersonal contact between sender and receiver. Nonpersonal channels are often referred to as mass media.

nontraditional media (13) A term commonly used in the advertising industry to describe support media.

O

objective and task method (7) A build-up approach to budget setting involving a three-step process: (1) determining objectives, (2) determining the strategies and tasks required to attain these objectives, and (3) estimating the costs associated with these strategies and tasks.

off-invoice allowance (15) A promotional discount offered to retailers or wholesalers whereby a certain per-case amount or percentage is deducted from the invoice.

off-network syndication (11) Reruns of network shows bought by individual stations.

on-air tests (18) Testing the effectiveness of television commercials by inserting test ads into actual TV programs in certain test markets.

one-sided message (6) Communications in which only positive attributes or benefits of a product or service are presented.

one-step approach (14) A direct-marketing strategy in which the medium is used directly to obtain an order (for example, television direct-response ads).

open rate structure (12) A rate charged by newspapers in which discounts are available based on frequency or bulk purchases of space.

operant conditioning (instrumental conditioning) (4) A learning theory that views the probability of a behavior as being dependent on the outcomes or consequences associated with it.

order taking (17) A personal selling responsibility in which the salesperson's primary responsibility is taking the order.

out-of-home advertising (13) The variety of advertising forms including outdoor, transit, skywriting, and other media viewed outside the home.

outside posters (13) Outdoor transit posters appearing on buses, taxis, trains, subways, and trolley cars.

P

PACT (Positioning Advertising Copy Testing) (18) A set of principles endorsed by 21 of the largest U.S. ad agencies aimed at improving the research used in preparing and testing ads, providing a better creative product for clients, and controlling the cost of TV commercials.

participations (11) The situation where several advertisers buy commercial time or spots on network television.

pass-along rate (10) An estimate of the number of readers of a magazine in addition to the original subscriber or purchaser.

pass-along readership (12) The audience that results when the primary subscriber or purchaser of a magazine gives the publication to another person to read, or when the magazine is read in places such as waiting rooms in doctors' offices, etc.

pattern advertising (20) Advertisements that follow a basic global approach although themes, copy, and sometimes even visual elements may be adjusted.

payout plan (7) A budgeting plan that determines the investment value of the advertising and promotion appropriation.

people meter (11) An electronic device that automatically records a household's television viewing, including channels watched, number of minutes of viewing, and members of the household who are watching.

percentage charges (3) The markups charged by advertising agencies for services provided to clients.

percentage of projected future sales method (7) A variation of the percentage of sales method of budget allocation in which projected future sales are used as the base.

percentage of sales method (7) A budget method in which the advertising and/or promotions budget is set based on a percentage of sales of the product.

perception (4) The process by which an individual receives, selects, organizes, and interprets information to create a meaningful picture of the world.

perceptual map (2) A "map" of perceptions of the positions of brands or products as received by consumers.

peripheral route to persuasion (5) In the elaboration likelihood model, one of two routes to persuasion in which the receiver is viewed as lacking the ability or motivation to process information and is not likely to be engaging in detailed cognitive processing.

personal selling (1) Person-to-person communication in which the seller attempts to assist and/or persuade prospective buyers to purchase the company's product or service or to act on an idea.

persuasion matrix (6) A communications planning model in which the stages of the response process (dependent variables) and the communications components (independent variables) are combined to demonstrate the likely effect that the independent variables will have on the dependent variables.

phased processing strategy (4) An information processing strategy in which more than one decision rule is applied during the purchase decision process.

planograms (15) A planning configuration of products that occupy a shelf section in a store that is used to provide more efficient shelf space utilization.

portfolio tests (18) A laboratory methodology designed to expose a group of respondents to a portfolio consisting of both control and test print ads.

positioning (2) The art and science of fitting the product or service to one or more segments of the market in such a way as to set it meaningfully apart from competition.

positioning strategies (2) The strategies used in positioning a brand or product.

posttests (18) Ad effectiveness measures that are taken after the ad has appeared in the marketplace.

preferred position rate (12) A rate charged by newspapers that ensures the advertiser the ad will appear in the position required and/or in a specific section of the newspaper.

premium (15) An offer of an item of merchandise or service either free or at a low price that is used as an extra incentive for purchasers.

preprinted inserts (12) Advertising distributed through newspapers that is not part of the newspaper itself, but is printed by the advertiser and then taken to the newspaper to be inserted.

press release (16) Factual and interesting information released to the press.

pretests (18) Advertising effectiveness measures that are taken before the implementation of the advertising campaign.

price elasticity (2) The responsiveness of the market to change in price.

price-off deal (15) A promotional strategy in which the consumer receives a reduction in the regular price of the brand.

primacy effect (6) A theory that the first information presented in the message will be the most likely to be remembered.

primary circulation (12) The number of copies of a magazine distributed to original subscribers.

problem detection (8) A creative research approach in which consumers familiar with a product (or service) are asked to generate an exhaustive list of problems encountered in its use.

problem recognition (4) The first stage in the consumer's decision-making process in which the consumer perceives a need and becomes motivated to satisfy it.

problem-solver stage (17) A stage of personal selling in which the seller obtains the participation of buyers in identifying their problems, translates these problems into needs, and then presents a selection from the supplier's offerings that can solve those problems.

procreator stage (17) A stage of personal selling in which the seller defines the buyer's problems or needs and the solutions to those problems or needs through active buyer-seller collaboration, thus creating a market offering tailored to the customer.

product manager (3) The person responsible for the planning, implementation, and control of the marketing program for an individual brand.

product placement (13) A form of advertising and promotion in which products are placed in television shows and/or movies to gain exposure.

product-specific preplanning input (8) Specific studies provided to the creative department on the product or service, the target audience, or a combination of the two.

product symbolism (2) The meaning that a product or brand has to consumers.

program rating (11) The percentage of TV households in an area that are tuned to a program during a specific time period.

promotion (1) The coordination of all seller-initiated efforts to set up channels of information and persuasion to sell goods and services or to promote an idea.

promotional management (1) The process of coordinating the promotional mix elements.

promotional mix (1) The tools used to accomplish an organization's communications objective. The promotional mix includes advertising, direct marketing, sales promotion, publicity/public relations, and personal selling.

promotional plan (1) The framework for developing, implementing, and controlling the organization's communications program.

promotional products marketing (13) The advertising or promotional medium or method that uses promotional products such as ad specialties, premiums, business gifts, awards, prizes, or commemoratives.

promotional pull strategy (2) A strategy in which advertising and promotion efforts are targeted at the ultimate consumers to encourage them to purchase the manufacturer's brand.

promotional push strategy (2) A strategy in which advertising and promotional efforts are targeted to the trade to attempt to get them to promote and sell the product to the ultimate consumer.

prospector stage (17) A selling stage in which activities include seeking out selected buyers who are perceived to have a need for the offering as well as the resources to buy it.

Protestant ethic (22) A perspective of life which stresses hard work and individual effort and initiative and views the accumulation of material possessions as evidence of success.

psychoanalytic theory (4) An approach to the study of human motivations and behaviors pioneered by Sigmund Freud.

psychographic segmentation (2) Dividing the product on the basis of personality and/or lifestyles.

psychosocial consequences (4) Purchase decision consequences that are intangible, subjective, and personal.

public relations (1, 16) The management function that evaluates public attitudes, identifies the policies and procedures of an individual or organization with the public interest, and executes a program to earn public understanding and acceptance

public relations firm (3) An organization that develops and implements programs to manage a company's publicity, image, and affairs with consumers and other relevant publics.

publicity (1, 16) Communications regarding an organization, product, service, or idea that is not directly paid for or run under identified sponsorship.

puffery (21) Advertising or other sales presentations that praise the item to be sold using subjective opinions, superlatives, or exaggerations, vaguely and generally, stating no specific facts.

pulsing (10) A media scheduling method that combines flighting and continuous scheduling.

pupillometrics (18) An advertising effectiveness methodology designed to measure dilation and constriction of the pupils of the eye in response to stimuli.

purchase intention (4) The predisposition to buy a certain brand or product.

push money (15) Cash payments made directly to the retailers' or wholesalers' sales force to encourage them to promote and sell a manufacturer's product.

Q

qualified prospects (17) Those prospects that are able to make the buying decision.

qualitative audit (3) An audit of the advertising agency's efforts in planning, developing, and implementing the client's communications programs.

qualitative media effect (6) The positive or negative influence the medium may contribute to the message.

R

ratings point (11) A measurement used to determine television viewing audiences in which one ratings point is the equivalent of 1 percent of all of the television households in a particular area tuned to a specific program.

rational appeal (6) Communications in which features and/or benefits are directly presented in a logical, rational method.

reach (10) The number of different audience members exposed at least once to a media vehicle (or vehicles) in a given period.

readers per copy (10) A cost comparison figure used for magazines that estimates audience size based on pass-along readership.

recall tests (18) Advertising effectiveness tests designed to measure advertising recall.

receiver (5) The person or persons with whom the sender of a message shares thoughts or information.

recency effect (6) The theory that arguments presented at the end of the message are considered to be stronger and therefore are more likely to be remembered.

recognition method (18) An advertising effectiveness measure of print ads that allows the advertiser to assess the impact of an ad in a single issue of a magazine over time and/or across alternative magazines.

reference group (4) A group whose perspectives, values, or behavior is used by an individual as the basis for his or her judgments, opinions, and actions.

refutational appeal (6) A type of message in which both sides of the issure are presented in the communication, with arguments offered to refute the opposing viewpoint.

regional networks (11) A network that covers only a specific portion of the country. Regional network purchases are based in proportion to the percentage of the country receiving the message.

reinforcement (4) The rewards or favorable consequences associated with a particular response.

relationship marketing (1, 17) An organization's effort to develop a long-term, cost-effective link with individual customers for mutual benefit.

relative cost (10) The relationship between the price paid for advertising time or space and the size of the audience delivered; it is used to compare the prices of various media vehicles.

reminder advertising (9) Advertising designed to keep the name of the product or brand in the mind of the receiver.

repositioning (2) The changing of a product or brand's positioning.

resellers (2) Intermediaries in the marketing channel such as wholesalers, distributors, and retailers.

response (5) The set of reactions the receiver has after seeing, hearing, or reading a message.

retail trading zone (12) The market outside the city zone whose residents regularly trade with merchants within the city zone.

ROI budgeting method (return on investment) (7) A budgeting method in which advertising and promotions are considered investments, and thus measurements are made in an attempt to determine the returns achieved by these investments.

rolling boards (13) Advertising painted or mounted on cars, trucks, vans, trailers, etc., so the exposure can be mobile enough to be taken to specific target market areas.

run of paper (ROP) (12) A rate quoted by newspapers that allows the ad to appear on any page or in any position desired by the medium.

S

S-shaped response curve (7) A sales response model that attempts to show sales responses to various levels of advertising and promotional expenditures.

sales-oriented objectives (7) Budgeting objectives related to sales effects such as increasing sales volume.

sales promotion (1, 15) Marketing activities that provide extra value or incentives to the sales force, distributors, or the ultimate consumer and can stimulate immediate sales.

sales promotion agency (3) An organization that specializes in the planning and implementation of promotional programs such as contests, sweepstakes, sampling, premiums, and incentive offers for its clients.

sales promotion trap (15) A spiral that results when a number of competitors extensively use promotions. One firm uses sales promotions to differentiate its product or service and other competitors copy the strategy, resulting in no differential advantage and a loss of profit margins to all.

salient beliefs (4) Beliefs concerning specific attributes or consequences that are activated and form the basis of an attitude.

sampling (15) A variety of procedures whereby consumers are given some quantity of a product for no charge to induce trial.

scatter market (11) A period for purchasing television advertising time that runs throughout the TV season.

schedules of reinforcement (4) The schedule by which a behavioral response is rewarded.

script (9) A written version of the commercial that provides a detailed description of its video and audio content.

selective attention (4) A perceptual process in which consumers choose to attend to some stimuli and not others.

selective binding (12) A computerized production process that allows the creation of hundreds of copies of a magazine in one continuous sequence.

selective comprehension (4) The perceptual process whereby consumers interpret information based on their own attitudes, beliefs, motives, and experiences.

selective demand advertising (2) Advertising that focuses on stimulating demand for a specific manufacturer's product or brand.

selective exposure (4) A process whereby consumers choose whether or not to make themselves available to media and message information.

selective learning (5) The process whereby consumers seek information that supports the choice made and avoid information that fails to bolster the wisdom of a purchase decision.

selective perception (4) The perceptual process involving the filtering or screening of exposure, attention, comprehension, and retention.

selective retention (4) The perceptual process whereby consumers remember some information but not all.

selectivity (12) The ability of a medium to reach a specific target audience.

self-liquidating premiums (15) Premiums that require the consumer to pay some or all of the cost of the premium plus handling and mailing costs.

self-paced media (6) Media that viewers and/or readers can control their exposure time to, allowing them to process information at their own rate.

self-regulation (21) The practice by the advertising industry of regulating and controlling advertising to avoid interference by outside agencies such as the government.

semiotics (5) The study of the nature of meaning.

sensation (4) The immediate and direct response of the senses (taste, smell, sight, touch, and hearing) to a stimulus such as an advertisement, package, brand name, or point-of-purchase display.

shaping (4) The reinforcement of successive acts that lead to a desired behavior pattern or response.

share-of-audience (11) The percentage of households watching television in a special time period that are tuned to a specific program.

showing (13) The percentage of supplicated audience exposed to an outdoor poster daily.

similarity (6) The supposed resemblance between the source and the receiver of a message.

single-source tracking (18) A research method designed to track the behaviors of consumers from the television set to the supermarket checkout counter.

situational determinants (4) Influences originating from the specific situation in which consumers are to use the product or brand.

sleeper effect (6) A phenomenon in which the persuasiveness of a message increases over time.

slotting allowance (15) Fees that must be paid to retailers to provide a "slot" or position to accommodate a new product on the store shelves.

social class (4) Relatively homogeneous divisions of society into which people are grouped based on similar lifestyles, values, norms, interests, and behaviors.

social style model (19) A model that suggests businesspersons' "social styles" will influence how they react on the job.

source (5, 6) The sender—person, group, or organization—of the message.

source bolsters (5) Favorable cognitive thoughts generated toward the source of a message.

source derogations (5) Negative thoughts generated about the source of a communication.

source power (6) The power of a source as a result of his or her ability to administer rewards and/or punishments to the receiver.

specialized marketing communication services (3) Organizations that provide marketing communication services in their areas of expertise including direct marketing, public relations, and sales promotion firms.

specialty advertising (13) An advertising, sales promotion, and motivational communications medium that employs useful articles of merchandise imprinted with an advertiser's name, message, or logo.

split runs (12) Two or more versions of a print ad are printed in alternative copies of a particular issue of a magazine.

split run test (18) An advertising effectiveness measure in which different versions of an ad are run in alternate copies of the same newspaper and/or magazine.

split 30s (11) 30-second TV spots in which the advertiser promotes two different products with two different messages during a 30-second commercial.

sponsorship (11) When the advertiser assumes responsibility for the production and usually the content of the program as well as the advertising that appears within it.

spot advertising (11) Commercials shown on local television stations, with the negotiation and purchase of time being made directly from the individual stations.

standard advertising unit (SAU) (12) A standard developed in the newpaper industry to make newspaper purchasing rates more comparable to other media that sell space and time in standard units.

standard learning model (5) Progression by the consumers through a learn-feel-do hierarchical response.

station reps (11) Individuals who act as sales representatives for a number of local stations and represent them in dealings with national advertisers.

storyboard (8) A series of drawings used to present the visual plan or layout of a proposed commercial.

strategic marketing plan (2) The planning framework for specific marketing activities.

subcultures (4) Smaller groups within a culture that possess similar beliefs, values, norms, and patterns of behavior that differentiate them from the larger cultural mainstream.

subheads (9) Secondary headlines in a print ad.

subliminal perception (4) The ability of an individual to perceive a stimulus below the level of conscious awareness.

superagencies (3) Large external agencies that offer integrated marketing communications on a worldwide basis.

superstations (11) Independent local stations that send their signals via satellite to cable operators that, in turn, make them available to subscribers (WWOR, WPIX, WGN, WSBK, WTBS).

support advertising (14) A form of direct marketing in which the ad is designed to support other forms of advertising appearing in other media.

support argument (5) Consumers' thoughts that support or affirm the claims being make by a message.

support media (13) Those media used to support or reinforce messages sent to target markets through other more "dominant" and/or more traditional media.

sweeps periods (10) The times of year in which television audience measures are taken (February, May, July, and November).

sweepstakes (15) A promotion whereby consumers submit their names for consideration in the drawing or selection of prizes and winners are determined purely by chance. Sweepstakes cannot require a proof of purchase as a condition for entry.

syndicated programs (11) Shows sold or distributed to local stations.

T

target marketing (2) The process of identifying the specific needs of segments, selecting one or more of these segments as a target, and developing marketing programs directed to each.

target ratings points (TRPs) (10) The number of persons in the primary target audience that the media buy will reach—and the number of times.

team approach (16) A method of measuring the effectiveness of public relations programs whereby evaluators are actually involved in the campaign.

teaser advertising (9) An ad designed to create curiosity and build excitement and interest in a product or brand without showing it.

telemarketing (14) Selling products and services by using the telephone to contact prospective customers.

tele-media (14) The use of telephone and voice information services (800, 900, 976 numbers) to market, advertise, promote, entertain, and inform.

television households (11) The number of households in a market that own a television set.

television network (11) The provider of news and programming to a series of affiliated local television stations.

terminal posters (13) Floor dislays, island showcases, electronic signs, and other forms of advertisements that appear in train or subway stations, airline terminals, etc.

testing bias (18) A bias that occurs in advertising effectiveness measures because respondents know they are being tested and thus alter their responses.

tests of comprehension and reaction (18) Advertising effectiveness tests that are designed to assess whether the ad conveyed the desired meaning and is not reacted to negatively.

theater testing (18) An advertising effectiveness pretest in which consumers view ads in a theater setting and evaluate these ads on a variety of dimensions.

top-down approaches (7) Budgeting approaches in which the budgetary amount is established at the executive level and monies are passed down to the various departments.

total audience (television) (11) The total number of homes viewing any five-minute part of a television program.

total audience/readership (12) A combination of the total number of primary and pass-along readers multiplied by the circulation of an average issue of a magazine.

tracking studies (18) Advertising effectiveness measures designed to assess the effects of advertising on awareness, recall, interest, and attitudes toward the ad as well as purchase intentions.

trade advertising (2) Advertising targeted to wholesalers and retailers.

trademark (2) An identifying name, symbol, or other device that gives a company the legal and exclusive rights to use.

trade-oriented sales promotion (15) A sales promotion designed to motivate distributors and retailers to carry a product and make an extra effort to promote or "push" it to their customers.

trade regulation rules (TRRs) (21) Industrywide rules that define unfair practices before they occur. Used by the Federal Trade Commission to regulate advertising and promotion.

trade show (15) A type of exhibition or forum where manufacturers can display their products to current as well as prospective buyers.

transformational advertising (9) An ad that associates the experience of using the advertised brand with a unique set of psychological characteristics that would not typically be associated with the brand experience to the same degree without exposure to the advertisement.

transit advertising (13) Advertising targeted to target audiences exposed to commercial transportation facilities, including buses, taxis, trains, elevators, trolleys, airplanes, and subways.

trustworthiness (6) The honesty, integrity, and believability of the source of a communication.

two-sided message (6) A message in which both good and bad points about a product or claim are presented.

two-step approach (14) A dierct-marketing strategy in which the first effort is designed to screen or qualify potential buyers, while the second effort has the responsibility of generating the response.

U

undifferentiated marketing (2) A strategy in which market segment differences are ignored and one product or service is offered to the entire market.

unduplicated reach (10) The number of persons reached once with a media exposure.

unfairness (21) A concept used by the Federal Trade Commission to determine unfair or deceptive advertising practices. Unfairness occurs when a trade practice causes substantial physical or economic injury to consumers, could not be avoided by consumers, and must not be outweighed by countervailing benefits to consumers or competition.

unique selling proposition (8) An advertising strategy that focuses on a product or service attribute that is distinctive to a particular brand and offers an important benefit to the customer.

up-front market (11) A buying period that takes place prior to the upcoming television season when the networks sell a large part of their commercial time.

V

values and lifestyles program (VALS) (2) Stanford Research Institute's method for applying lifestyle segmentation.

vehicle option source effect (18) The differential impact the advertising exposure will have on the same audience member if the exposure occurs in one media option rather than another.

vertical cooperative advertising (13) Advertisements appearing in movie theaters and on videotapes.

video news release (16) News stories produced by publicists so that television stations may air them as news.

voiceover (9) Action on the screen in a commercial that is narrated or described by a narrator who is not visible.

W

want (4) A felt need shaped by a person's knowledge, culture, and personality.

waste coverage (10) A situation where the coverage of the media exceeds the target audience.

webcasting (14) A system for pushing out site information to Web users rather than waiting for them to find the site on their own. (Often referred to as push technologies).

Wheeler-Lea Amendment (21) An act of Congress passed in 1938 that amended section 5 of the FTC Act to read that unfair methods of competition in commerce and unfair or deceptive acts or practices in commerce are declared unlawful.

word-of-mouth communications (5) Social channels of communication such as friends, neighbors, associates, coworkers, or family members.

World Wide Web (WWW) (14) Commonly referred to as the Web, a service provided on the Internet.

Y

Yellow Pages advertising (13) Advertisements that appear in the various Yellow Pages-type phone directories.

Z

zapping (11) The use of a remote control device to change channels and switch away from commercials.

zero-based communications planning (7) An approach to planning the integrated marketing communications program that involves determining what tasks need to be done and what marketing communication functions should be used to accomplish them and to what extent.

zipping (11) Fast-forwarding through commercials during the playback of a program previously recorded on a VCR.

Endnotes

Chapter 1

1. Robert J. Cohen, "'96 Expected to Deliver Energetic Ad Growth," *Advertising Age*, May 20, 1996, p. 22.
2. Sally Goll Beatty, "Record Ad Spending Projected for 1996," *The Wall Street Journal*, December 5, 1995, p. B8.
3. "AMA Board Approves New Marketing Definition," *Marketing News*, March 1, 1985, p. 1.
4. Richard P. Bagozzi, "Marketing as Exchange," *Journal of Marketing* 39 (October 1975), pp. 32–39.
5. Leonard L. Berry, "Relationship Marketing of Services—Growing Interest, Emerging Perspectives," *Journal of the Academy of Marketing Science*, 23, no. 4, 1995, pp. 236–245; Jonathan R. Capulsky and Michael J. Wolfe, "Relationship Marketing: Positioning for the Future," *Journal of Business Strategy*, July–August 1991, pp. 16–26.
6. B. Joseph Pine II, Don Peppers, and Martha Rogers, "Do You Want to Keep Your Customers Forever?" *Harvard Business Review*, March–April 1995, p. 103–14.
7. Adrienne Ward Fawcett, "Integrated Marketing-Marketers Convinced: Its Time Has Arrived," *Advertising Age*, November 6, 1993, pp. S1–2.
8. "Do Your Ads Need a SuperAgency?" *Fortune*, April 27, 1997, p. 81–85; Faye Rice, "A Cure for What Ails Advertising?" *Fortune*, December 16, 1991, pp. 119–22.
9. Scott Hume, "Campus Adopts 'New' Advertising," *Advertising Age*, September 23, 1991, p. 17.
10. Don E. Schultz, "Integrated Marketing Communications: Maybe Definition Is in the Point of View," *Marketing News*, January 18, 1993, p. 17.
11. Ibid.
12. John Deighton, "The Future of the Marketing Communications Industry: Implications of Integration and Interactivity," presented to Marketing Science Institute Conference on Marketing Communications Strategies Today and Tommorrow: Interaction, Allocation, and Interactive Technologies, March 1994, Boston, MA; Thomas R. Duncan and Stephen E. Everett, "Client Perception of Integrated Marketing Communications," *Journal of Advertising Research*, May/June 1993, pp. 30–39.
13. Anthony J. Tortorici, "Maximizing Marketing Communications through Horizontal and Vertical Orchestration," *Public Relations Quarterly* 36, no. 1 (1991), pp. 20–22.
14. Robert H. Ducoffe, Dennis Sandler, and Eugene Secunda, "A Survey of Senior Agency, Advertiser, and Media Executives on the Future of Advertising," *Journal of Current Issues and Research in Advertising* 18, no. 1, Spring 1996.
15. Joe Cappo, "Agencies: Change or Die," *Advertising Age*, December 7, 1992, p. 26.
16. Michael L. Ray, *Advertising and Communication Management* (Englewood Cliffs, NJ: Prentice Hall, 1982).
17. Ralph S. Alexander, ed., *Marketing Definitions* (Chicago: American Marketing Association, 1965), p. 9.
18. "Trends in Media," research report by Television Bureau of Advertising, New York, June 1997.
19. "The $70 Billion Promotion Engine Rolls On," The 1996 Annual Report on the Promotion Industry, *Promo*, July 1996, p. 35.
20. *Cox Direct 19th Annual Survey of Promotional Practices* (Largo, FL: Cox Direct 1997).
21. Judann Dagnoli, "Sorry Charlie, Heinz Puts Promos First," *Advertising Age*, March 30, 1992, p. 3.
22. Jefferson Graham, "Abs Machine Sales Go Flabby," *USA Today*, October 22, 1996, p. D1.
23. H. Frazier Moore and Bertrand R. Canfield, *Public Relations: Principles, Cases, and Problems*, 7th ed. (Burr Ridge, IL: Richard D. Irwin, 1977), p. 5.
24. Art Kleiner, "The Public Relations Coup," *Adweek's Marketing Week*, January 16, 1989, pp. 20–23.
25. Anne B. Fisher, "Spiffing Up the Corporate Image," *Fortune*, July 21, 1986, pp. 68–72.

Chapter 2

1. Geoffrey Smith, "Reebok Is Tripping Over Its Own Laces," *Business Week*, February 26, 1996, pp. 62–66.
2. Ibid.
3. Spencer L. Hapoinen, "The Rise of Micromarketing," *The Journal of Business Strategy*, November/December 1990, pp. 37–42.
4. "What Happened to Advertising?" *Business Week*, September 23, 1991, pp. 66–72.
5. Cyndee Miller, "Liz Claiborne Throws a Curve with New Brand for Gen Xers," *Marketing News*, July 1, 1996, pp. 1, 10.
6. Pat Sloan, "L'Oreal Preens for Sales with $32 Mil Budget," *Advertising Age*, March 11, 1996, p.3.
7. "Last Minute News," *Advertising Age*, November 28, 1996, p. 60.
8. Eric N. Berkowitz, Roger A. Kerin, and William Rudelius, *Marketing*, 2nd ed. (Burr Ridge, IL: Richard D. Irwin, 1989).
9. Edward M. Tauber, "Research on Food Consumption Values Finds Four Market Segments: Good Taste Still Tops," *Marketing News*, May 15, 1981, p. 17; Rebecca C. Quarles, "Shopping Centers Use Fashion Lifestyle Research to Make Marketing Decisions, "*Marketing News*, January 22, 1982, p. 18; and "Our Auto, Ourselves," *Consumer Reports*, June 1985, p. 375.

10. Judith Graham, "New VALS 2 Takes Psychological Route," *Advertising Age*, February 13, 1989, p. 24.

11. *Ayer's Dictionary of Advertising Terms* (Philadelphia: Ayer Press, 1976).

12. Davis A. Aaker and John G. Myers, *Advertising Management*, 3rd ed. (Englewood Cliffs, NJ: Prentice Hall, 1987, p. 125.

13. Jack Trout and Al Ries, "Positioning Cuts through Chaos in the Marketplace," *Advertising Age*, May 1, 1972, pp. 51–53.

14. Ibid.

15. David A. Aaker and J. Gary Shansby, "Positioning Your Product," *Business Horizons*, May–June 1982, pp. 56–62.

16. Aaker and Myers, *Advertising Management*.

17. Trout and Ries, "Positioning Cuts through Chaos."

18. Aaker and Myers, *Advertising Management*.

19. J. Paul Peter and Jerry C. Olson, *Consumer Behavior* (Burr Ridge, IL: Richard D. Irwin, 1987), p. 505.

20. Michael R. Solomon, "The Role of Products as Social Stimuli: A Symbolic Interactionism Perspective," *Journal of Consumer Research*, December 1983, pp. 319–29.

21. Don. E. Schultz, Stanley I. Tannenbaum, and Robert F. Lauterborn, "Integrated Marketing Communications: Putting It Together and Making It Work" (Lincolnwood, IL: NTC Publishing Group) p. 72.

22. Peter and Olson, *Consumer Behavior*, p. 571.

23. Paul W. Farris and David J. Reibstein, "How Prices, Ad Expenditures, and Profits Are Linked," *Harvard Business Review*, November–December 1979, pp. 172–84.

24. David W. Stewart, Gary L. Frazier, and Ingrid Martin, "Integrated Channel Management: Merging the Communication and Distribution Functions of the Firm," in *Integrated Communication: Synergy of Persuasive Voices*, pp. 185–215, Esther Thorson & Jeri Moore (eds), Lawrence Earlbaum Associates, 1996, Mahwah, NJ.

Chapter 3

1. Thomas J. Cosse and John E. Swan, "Strategic Marketing Planning by Product Managers—Room for Improvement?" *Journal of Marketing* 47 (Summer 1983), pp. 92–102.

2. "Behind the Tumult at P&G," *Fortune*, March 7, 1994, pp.74–82; "The Marketing Revolution at Procter & Gamble," *Business Week*, July 25, 1988, pp. 72–76; "Category Management: New Tools Changing Life for Manufacturers, Retailers," *Marketing News*, September 25, 1989, pp. 2, 19.

3. Cosse and Swan, "Strategic Marketing Planning by Product Managers—Room for Improvement?"

4. Victor P. Buell, *Organizing for Marketing/Advertising Success* (New York: Association of National Advertisers, 1982).

5. M. Louise Ripley, "What Kind of Companies Take Their Advertising In-House?" *Journal of Advertising Research*, October/November 1991, pp. 73–80.

6. Bruce Horovitz, "Some Companies Say the Best Ad Agency Is No Ad Agency at All," *Los Angeles Times*, July 19, 1989, Sec. IV, p. 5.

7. Ibid.

8. "Do Your Ads Need a Superagency?" *Fortune*, April 27, 1987, p. 81.

9. Kevin Goldman, "Interpublic Group Nears Acquisition of Ammirati & Puris," *The Wall Street Journal*, July, 11, 1994, p. B5.

10. Sally Goll Beatty, "Global Needs Challenge Midsize Agencies," *The Wall Street Journal*, December 14, 1995, p. B9.

11. Bob Lammons, "A Good Account Exec Makes a Big Difference," *Marketing News*, June 3, 1996, p. 12.

12. Bradley Johnson, "Nestlé U.S. Units Join for Media Clout," *Advertising Age*, January 14, 1991, p. 3.

13. Sally Goll Beattty, "Media Planners to Draw Straws for Coke," *The Wall Street Journal*, February 14, 1996, p. B8; Kevin Goldman, "GM Merging Media Buying at Interpublic," *The Wall Street Journal*, December 8, 1993, p. B3.

14. Joe Mandese, "Buyers' Boom Costs Ad Agencies," *Advertising Age*, September 16, 1991, p. 3.

15. "Achenbaum Puts His Cards on the Table," *Advertising Age*, May 9, 1988, p. 3.

16. Quote in: Patricia Sellers, "Do You Need Your Ad Agency?" *Fortune*, November 15, 1993, pp. 47–61.

17. Mark Gleason, "Role of Performance Gains in Agency Pay," *Advertising Age*, November 27, 1995, pp. 3, 44.

18. Laurie Peterson, "Pursuing Results in the Age of Accountability," *Adweek's Marketing Week*, November 19, 1990, pp. 20–22.

19. Faye Rice, "A Cure for What Ails Advertising?" *Fortune*, December 16, 1991, pp. 119–22.

20. Melanie Wells, "Calet Will 'Guarantee Results'," *Advertising Age*, June 6, 1993, pp. 1, 44.

21. Gleason, "Role of Performance Gains in Agency Pay."

22. Raymond Serafin, "GM Tests Fee-Based Compensation System," *Advertising Age*, February 19, 1996, pp. 3, 41.

23. Rebecca Blumenstein, "GM Shifts Gears on Ad Strategy, Aims at Entertaining Customers," *The Wall Street Journal*, August 8, 1996, p. B5.

24. Laurel Wentz, "Cost-Cutting About Face," *Advertising Age*, July 15, 1991, pp. 1, 38.

25. Nancy Giges, "Reviewing the Review: Borden Likes System of Agency Evaluation," *Advertising Age*, April 18, 1977, p. 3.

26. Mark Gleason, "MIA on Madison Avenue: Agency, client loyalty," *Advertising Age*, January 27, 1997, pp. 3, 42.

27. Fred Beard, "Marketing Client Role Ambiguity As A Source Of Dissatisfaction In Client-Ad Agency Relationships," *Journal of Advertising Research*, September/October 1996, pp. 9–20; Paul Michell, Harold Cataquet, and Stephen Hague, "Establishing the Causes of Disaffection in Agency-Client Relations," *Journal of Advertising Research*, 32, 2, 1992, pp. 41–48; "Peter Doyle, Marcel Corstiens, and Paul Michell, "Signals of Vulnerability in Agency-Client Relations," *Journal of Marketing* 44 (Fall 1980), pp. 18–23; and Daniel B. Wackman, Charles Salmon, and Caryn C. Salmon, "Developing an Advertising Agency-Client Relationship," *Journal of Advertising Research* 26, no. 6 (December 1986/January 1987), pp. 21–29.

28. Sallly Goll Beatty, "AT&T Sends Agencies to Drawing Board," *The Wall Street Journal*, August 5, 1996, p. B6.

29. Sally Goll Beatty, "Blockbuster Puts Agencies in a Permanent Shootout," *The Wall Street Journal*, October 2, 1996, pp. B1, 8; and "Big Agencies Starting to Call for End to Costly Free Pitches," *The Wall Street Journal*, February 22, 1989, p. B7.

30. "A Potent New Tool for Selling: Database Marketing," *Business Week*, September 5, 1994, pp. 56–62.; Bradley Johnson, "In a Millisecond, Microsoft

Boots Up Marketing Database," *Advertising Age*, November 6, 1993, p. S–6.

31. Prema Nakra, "The Changing Role of Public Relations in Marketing Communications," *Public Relations Quarterly* 1 (1991), pp. 42–45.

32. Mark Gleason and Debra Aho Williamson, "The New Interactive Agency," *Advertising Age*, February 2, 1996, pp. S1–11.

33. "Do Your Ads Need a Superagency?"

34. Sally Goll Beatty, "Interpublic Diversifies Further With Purchase of Direct Marketer," *The Wall Street Journal*, May 17, 1996, p. B5.

35. "It's All Advertising," *PROMO Magazine*, October 1991, pp. 6, 7, 32.

36. Anders Gronstedt and Esther Thorson, "Five Approaches to Organize an Integrated Marketing Communications Agency," *Journal of Marketing Research*, March/April 1996, pp. 48–58.

37. "Ad Firms Falter on One-Stop Shopping," *The Wall Street Journal*, December 1, 1988, p. 81; and "Do Your Ads Need a Superagency?" *Fortune*, April 27, 1987, p. 81.

38. Rice, "A Cure for What Ails Advertising?" p. 122.

39. Adrienne Ward Fawcett, "Integrated Marketing-Marketers Convinced: Its Time Has Arrived," *Advertising Age*, November 6, 1993, pp. S1–2.

40. Adrienne Ward Fawcett, "Integrated Marketing Door Open for Experts," *Advertising Age*, November 6, 1993, p. S2.

Chapter 4

1. Russell W. Belk, "Possessions and the Extended Self," *Journal of Consumer Research*, September 1988, pp. 139–68.

2. Eric N. Berkowitz, Roger A. Kerin, Steven W. Hartley, and William Rudelius, *Marketing*, 3rd ed. (Burr Ridge, IL: Richard D. Irwin, 1992), p. 14.

3. A. H. Maslow, "'Higher' and 'Lower' Needs," *Journal of Psychology* 25 (1948), pp. 433–36.

4. Morton Deutsch and Robert M. Krauss, *Theories in Social Psychology* (New York: Basic Books, 1965).

5. Jagdish N. Sheth, "The Role of Motivation Research in Consumer Psychology" (Faculty Working Paper, University of Illinois, Champaign: 1974); Bill Abrams, "Charles of the Ritz Discovers What Women Want," *The Wall Street Journal*, August 20, 1981, p. 29; and Ernest Dichter, *Getting Motivated* (New York: Pergamon Press, 1979).

6. Ronald Alsop, "Advertisers Put Consumers on the Couch," *The Wall Street Journal*, May 13, 1988, p. 19.

7. For an excellent discussion of memory and consumer behavior, see James R. Bettman, "Memory Factors in Consumer Choice: A Review," *Journal of Marketing* 43 (Spring 1979), pp. 37–53.

8. Gilbert Harrell, *Consumer Behavior* (San Diego: Harcourt Brace Jovanovich, 1986), p. 66.

9. Raymond A. Bauer and Stephen A. Greyser, *Advertising in America: The Consumer View* (Boston: Harvard Business School, 1968).

10. Neal Santelmann, "Color That Yells 'Buy Me'," *Forbes*, May 2, 1988, p. 110.

11. J. Paul Peter and Jerry C. Olson, *Consumer Behavior*, 2nd ed. (Burr Ridge, IL: Richard D. Irwin, 1990), p. 73.

12. Gordon W. Allport, "Attitudes," in *Handbook of Social Psychology*, ed. C. M. Murchison (Winchester, MA: Clark University Press, 1935), p. 810.

13. Robert B. Zajonc and Hazel Markus, "Affective and Cognitive Factors in Preferences," *Journal of Consumer Research* 9 (1982), pp. 123–31.

14. Alvin Achenbaum, "Advertising Doesn't Manipulate Consumers," *Journal of Advertising Research*, April 2, 1970, pp. 3–13.

15. William D. Wells, "Attitudes and Behavior: Lessons from the Needham Lifestyle Study," *Journal of Advertising Research*, February–March 1985, pp. 40–44; and Icek Ajzen and Martin Fishbein, "Attitude-Behavior Relations: A Theoretical Analysis and Review of Empirical Research," *Psychological Bulletin*, September 1977, pp. 888–918.

16. For a review of multiattribute models, see William L. Wilkie and Edgar A. Pessemier, "Issues in Marketing's Use of Multiattribute Models," *Journal of Marketing Research* 10 (November 1983), pp. 428–41.

17. Joel B. Cohen, Paul W. Minniard, and Peter R. Dickson, "Information Integration: An Information Processing Perspective," in *Advances in Consumer Research*, vol. 7, ed. Jerry C. Olson (Ann Arbor, MI: Association for Consumer Research, 1980), pp. 161–70.

18. Peter and Olson, *Consumer Behavior*, p. 182.

19. Peter L. Wright and Fredric Barbour, "The Relevance of Decision Process Models in Structuring Persuasive Messages," *Communications Research*, July 1975, pp. 246–59.

20. James F. Engel, "The Psychological Consequences of a Major Purchase Decision," in *Marketing in Transition*, ed. William S. Decker (Chicago: American Marketing Association, 1963), pp. 462–75.

21. John A. Howard and Jagdish N. Sheth, *The Theory of Consumer Behavior* (New York: John Wiley & Sons, 1969).

22. Leon G. Schiffman and Leslie Lazar Kannuk, *Consumer Behavior*, 4th ed. (Englewood Cliffs, NJ: Prentice Hall, 1991), p. 192.

23. I. P. Pavlov, *The Work of the Digestive Glands*, 2nd ed., trans. W. N. Thompson (London: Griffin, 1910).

24. Gerald J. Gorn, "The Effects of Music in Advertising on Choice: A Classical Conditioning Approach," *Journal of Marketing* 46 (Winter 1982), pp. 94–101.

25. James J. Kellaris, Anthony D. Cox, and Dena Cox, "The Effect of Background Music on Ad Processing: A Contingency Explanation," *Journal of Marketing*, 57, no. 4 (Fall 1993), p. 114.

26. Brian C. Deslauries and Peter B. Everett, "The Effects of Intermittent and Continuous Token Reinforcement on Bus Ridership," *Journal of Applied Psychology* 62 (August 1977), pp. 369–75.

27. Michael L. Rothschild and William C. Gaidis, "Behavioral Learning Theory: Its Relevance to Marketing and Promotions," *Journal of Marketing Research* 45, no. 2 (Spring 1981), pp. 70–78.

28. For an excellent discussion of social class and consumer behavior, see Richard P. Coleman, "The Continuing Significance of Social Class to Marketing," *Journal of Consumer Research* 10, no. 3 (December 1983), pp. 265–80.

29. Lyman E. Ostlund, *Role Theory and Group Dynamics in Consumer Behavior: Theoretical Sources*, ed. Scott Ward and Thomas S. Robertson (Englewood Cliffs, NJ: Prentice Hall, 1973), pp. 230–75.

30. James Stafford and Benton Cocanougher, "Reference Group Theory," in *Perspective in Consumer Behavior*, ed. H. H. Kassarjian and T. S. Robertson (Glenview, IL: Scott, Foresman, 1981), pp. 329–43.

31. Jagdish N. Sheth, "A Theory of Family Buying Decisions," in *Models of Buying Behavior*, ed. Jagdish N. Sheth (New York: Harper & Row, 1974), pp. 17–33.

32. Ibid.

33. Russell Belk, "Situational Variables and Consumer Behavior," *Journal of Consumer Research*, December 1975, pp. 157–64.

Chapter 5

1. Wilbur Schram, *The Process and Effects of Mass Communication* (Urbana: University of Illinois Press, 1955).
2. Ibid.
3. Joseph Ransdell, "Some Leading Ideas of Peirce's Semiotic," *Semiotica* 19 (1977), pp. 157–78.
4. Ronald Alsop, "Agencies Scrutinize Their Ads for Psychological Symbolism," *The Wall Street Journal*, June 11, 1987, p. 25.
5. For an excellent article on the application of semiotics to consumer behavior and advertising, see David G. Mick, "Consumer Research and Semiotics: Exploring the Morphology of Signs, Symbols, and Significance," *Journal of Consumer Research* 13, no. 2 (September 1986), pp. 196–213; and Edward F. McQuarrie and David Glen Mick, "Figures of Rhetoric in Advertising Language," *Journal of Consumer Research*, 22, March 1996, pp. 424–38.
6. Barry L. Bayus, "Word of Mouth: The Indirect Effect of Marketing Efforts," *Journal of Advertising Research*, June/July 1985, pp. 31–39.
7. Quote by Gorden S. Bower in *Fortune*, October 14, 1985, p. 11.
8. Thomas V. Bonoma and Leonard C. Felder, "Nonverbal Communication in Marketing: Toward Communicational Analysis," *Journal of Marketing Research*, May 1977, pp. 169–80.
9. Jacob Jacoby and Wayne D. Hoyer, "Viewer Miscomprehension of Televised Communication: Selected Findings," *Journal of Marketing*, Fall 1982, pp. 12–26; Jacoby and Hoyer, "The Comprehension and Miscomprehension of Print Communications: An Investigation of Mass Media Magazines" (New York: Advertising Education Foundation study, 1987).
10. E. K. Strong, *The Psychology of Selling* (New York: McGraw-Hill, 1925), p. 9.
11. Robert J. Lavidge and Gary A. Steiner, "A Model for Predictive Measurements of Advertising Effectiveness," *Journal of Marketing* 24 (October 1961), pp. 59–62.
12. Everett M. Rogers, *Diffusion of Innovations* (New York: Free Press, 1962), pp. 79–86.
13. William J. McGuire, "An Information Processing Model of Advertising Effectiveness," in *Behavioral and Management Science in Marketing*, ed. Harry J. Davis and Alvin J. Silk (New York: Ronald Press, 1978), pp. 156–80.
14. Michael L. Ray, "Communication and the Hierarchy of Effects," in *New Models for Mass Communication Research*, ed. P. Clarke (Beverly Hills, Calif.: Sage Publications, 1973), pp. 147–75.
15. Herbert E. Krugman, "The Impact of Television Advertising: Learning without Involvement," *Public Opinion Quarterly* 29 (Fall 1965), pp. 349–56.
16. Scott A. Hawkins and Stephen J. Hoch, "Low-Involvement Learning: Memory without Evaluation," *Journal of Consumer Research*, 19, no. 2 (September 1992), pp. 212–25.
17. Harry W. McMahan, "Do Your Ads Have VIP?" *Advertising Age*, July 14, 1980, pp. 50–51.
18. Robert E. Smith and William R. Swinyard, "Information Response Models: An Integrated Approach," *Journal of Marketing* 46, no. 2 (Winter 1982), pp. 81–93.
19. Ibid., p. 90.
20. Ibid., p. 86.
21. Robert E. Smith, "Integrating Information from Advertising and Trial: Processes and Effects on Consumer Response to Product Information," *Journal of Marketing Research* 30 (May 1993), pp. 204–19.
22. Harold H. Kassarjian, "Low Involvement: A Second Look," in *Advances in Consumer Research*, 8 (Ann Arbor: Association for Consumer Research, 1981), pp. 31–34; also see Anthony G. Greenwald and Clark Leavitt, "Audience Involvement in Advertising: Four Levels," *Journal of Consumer Research* 11, no. 1 (June 1984), pp. 581–92.
23. Judith L. Zaichkowsky, "Conceptualizing Involvement," *Journal of Advertising* 15, no. 2 (1986), pp. 4–14.
24. Richard Vaughn, "How Advertising Works: A Planning Model," *Journal of Advertising Research* 20, no. 5 (October 1980), pp. 27–33.
25. Richard Vaughn, "How Advertising Works: A Planning Model Revisited," *Journal of Advertising Research* 26, no. 1 (February/March 1986), pp. 57–66.
26. Jerry C. Olson, Daniel R. Toy, and Philip A. Dover, "Mediating Effects of Cognitive Responses to Advertising on Cognitive Structure," in *Advances in Consumer Research* 5, ed. H. Keith Hunt (Ann Arbor: Association for Consumer Research, 1978), pp. 72–78.
27. Anthony A. Greenwald, "Cognitive Learning, Cognitive Response to Persuasion and Attitude Change," in *Psychological Foundations of Attitudes*, ed.
A. G. Greenwald, T. C. Brock, and T. W. Ostrom (New York: Academic Press, 1968); Peter L. Wright, "The Cognitive Processes Mediating Acceptance of Advertising," *Journal of Marketing Research* 10 (February 1973), pp. 53–62; Brian Wansink, Michael L. Ray, and Rajeev Batra, "Increasing Cognitive Response Sensitivity," *Journal of Advertising* 23, no. 2, June 1994, pp. 65–76.
28. Peter Wright, "Message Evoked Thoughts, Persuasion Research Using Thought Verbalizations," *Journal of Consumer Research* 7, no. 2 (September 1980), pp. 151–75.
29. Scott B. Mackenzie, Richard J. Lutz, and George E. Belch, "The Role of Attitude toward the Ad as a Mediator of Advertising Effectiveness: A Test of Competing Explanations," *Journal of Marketing Research* 23 (May 1986), pp. 130–43; Rajeev Batra and Michael L. Ray, "Affective Responses Mediating Acceptance of Advertising," *Journal of Consumer Research* 13 (September 1986), pp. 234–49.
30. Ronald Alsop, "TV Ads that Are Likeable Get Plus Rating for Persuasiveness," *The Wall Street Journal*, February 20, 1986, p. 23.
31. David J. Moore and William D. Harris, "Affect Intensity and the Consumer's Attitude toward High-Impact Emotional Advertising Appeals," *Journal of Advertising* 25, no. 2 (Summer 1996), pp. 37–50; Andrew A. Mitchell and Jerry C. Olson, "Are Product Attribute Beliefs the Only Mediator of Advertising Effects on Brand Attitude?" *Journal of Marketing Research* 18 (August 1981), pp. 318–32.
32. David J. Moore, William D. Harris and Hong C. Chen, "Affect Intensity: An Individual Difference Response to Advertising Appeals," *Journal of Consumer Research* 22, September 1995, pp. 154–64; Julie Edell and Marian C. Burke, "The Power of Feelings in Understanding Advertising Effects," *Journal of Consumer Research* 14 (December 1987), pp. 421–33.
33. Richard E. Petty and John T. Cacioppo, "Central and Peripheral Routes to Persuasion: Application to Advertising," in *Advertising and Consumer Psychology*, ed. Larry Percy and Arch Woodside (Lexington, MA: Lexington Books, 1983), pp. 3–23.
34. David A. Aaker, Rajeev Batra, and John G. Myers, *Advertising Management*, 4th ed. (Englewood Cliffs, NJ: Prentice Hall, 1992).

35. Richard E. Petty, John T. Cacioppo, and David Schumann, "Central and Peripheral Routes to Advertising Effectiveness: The Moderating Role of Involvement," *Journal of Consumer Research* 10 (September 1983), pp. 135–46.

Chapter 6

1. William J. McGuire, "An Information Processing Model of Advertising Effectiveness," in *Behavioral and Management Science in Marketing*, ed. Harry J. Davis and Alvin J. Silk (New York: Ronald Press, 1978), pp. 156–80.

2. Herbert C. Kelman, "Processes of Opinion Change," *Public Opinion Quarterly* 25 (Spring 1961), pp. 57–78.

3. William J. McGuire, "The Nature of Attitudes and Attitude Change," in *Handbook of Social Psychology*, 2nd ed., ed. G. Lindzey and E. Aronson (Cambridge, Mass.: Addison-Wesley, 1969), pp. 135–214; Daniel J. O'Keefe, "The Persuasive Effects of Delaying Identification of High- and Low-Credibility Communicators: A Meta-analytic Review," *Central States Speech Journal* 38, 1987, pp. 63–72.

4. Roobina Ohanian, "The Impact of Celebrity Spokespersons' Image on Consumers' Intention to Purchase," *Journal of Advertising Research*, February/March 1991, pp. 46–54.

5. "Business Celebrities," *Business Week*, June 23, 1986, pp. 100–107.

6. Bill McDowell, "Wendy's Won't Dump Dave Ads—For Now," *Advertising Age*, December 23, 1996, p. 8.

7. Eric Reidenback and Robert Pitts, "Not All CEOs Are Created Equal as Advertising Spokespersons: Evaluating the Effective CEO Spokesperson," *Journal of Advertising* 20, no. 3, 1986, pp. 35–50; Roger Kerin and Thomas E. Barry, "The CEO Spokesperson in Consumer Advertising: An Experimental Investigation," in *Current Issues in Research in Advertising*, ed. J. H. Leigh and C. R. Martin (Ann Arbor: University of Michigan, 1981), pp. 135–48; J. Poindexter, "Voices of Authority," *Psychology Today*, August 1983.

8. A. Eagly and S. Chaiken, "An Attribution Analysis of the Effect of Communicator Characteristics on Opinion Change," *Journal of Personality and Social Psychology* 32 (1975), pp. 136–44.

9. For a review of these studies, see Brian Sternthal, Lynn Phillips, and Ruby Dholakia, "The Persuasive Effect of Source Credibility: A Situational Analysis," *Public Opinion Quarterly* 42 (Fall 1978), pp. 285–314.

10. Brian Sternthal, Ruby Dholakia, and Clark Leavitt, "The Persuasive Effects of Source Credibility: Tests of Cognitive Response," *Journal of Consumer Research* 4, no. 4 (March 1978), pp. 252–60; and Robert R. Harmon and Kenneth A. Coney, "The Persuasive Effects of Source Credibility in Buy and Lease Situations," *Journal of Marketing Research* 19 (May 1982), pp. 255–60.

11. For a review, see Noel Capon and James Hulbert, "The Sleeper Effect: An Awakening," *Public Opinion Quarterly* 37 (1973), pp. 333–58.

12. Darlene B. Hannah and Brian Sternthal, "Detecting and Explaining the Sleeper Effect," *Journal of Consumer Research* 11, no. 2 (September 1984), pp. 632–42.

13. H. C. Triandis, *Attitudes and Attitude Change* (New York: John Wiley & Sons, 1971).

14. J. Mills and J. Jellison, "Effect on Opinion Change Similarity between the Communicator and the Audience He Addresses," *Journal of Personality and Social Psychology* 9, no. 2 (1969), pp. 153–56.

15. Arch G. Woodside and J. William Davenport, Jr., "The Effect of Salesman Similarity and Expertise on Consumer Purchasing Behavior," *Journal of Marketing Research* 11 (May 1974), pp. 198–202; Paul Busch and David T. Wilson, "An Experimental Analysis of a Salesman's Expert and Referent Bases of Social Power in the Buyer-Seller Dyad," *Journal of Marketing Research* 13 (February 1976), pp. 3–11.

16. Randall Lane and Peter Spiegel, "The Year of the Michaels," *Forbes*, December 16, 1996, pp. 244–52.

17. Bruce Horowitz, "Mazda Drops Garner to Try New Route in Commercials," *Los Angeles Times*, February 10, 1989, pt. IV, p. 1.

18. Valerie Folkes, "Recent Attribution Research In Consumer Behavior: A Review and New Directions," *Journal of Consumer Research*, 14, March 1988, pp. 548–65; John C. Mowen and Stephen W. Brown, "On Explaining and Predicting the Effectiveness of Celebrity Endorsers," in *Advances in Consumer Research*, 8 (Ann Arbor: Association for Consumer Research, 1981), pp. 437–41.

19. Stephen Rae, "How Celebrities Make Killings on Commercials," *Cosmopolitan*, January 1997, pp. 164–67.

20. Charles Atkin and M. Block, "Effectiveness of Celebrity Endorsers," *Journal of Advertising Research* 23, no. 1 (February/March 1983), pp. 57–61.

21. Study by Total Research Corp. cited in: Bruce Horowitz, "Wishing on a Star," *Los Angeles Times*, November 7, 1993, pp. D1, 7.

22. Bruce Horowitz, "Sneaker Firms, Pitchmen Not Always in Step," *Los Angeles Times*, November 7, 1993, pp. D1, 8.

23. Rae, "How Celebrities Make Killings on Commercials."

24. James R. Schiffman, "PepsiCo Cans TV Ads with Madonna, Pointing Up Risks of Using Superstars," *The Wall Street Journal*, April 5, 1989, p. B11.

25. Bruce Horowitz, "It May Be Hard to Swallow Some Endorsements," *Los Angeles Times*, February 11, 1992, p. D1.

26. Michael A. Kamins, "An Investigation into the 'Match-up' Hypothesis in Celebrity Advertising," *Journal of Advertising* 19, no. 1 (1990), pp. 4–13.

27. Grant McCracken, "Who Is the Celebrity Endorser? Cultural Foundations of the Endorsement Process," *Journal of Consumer Research* 16, no. 3 (December 1989), pp. 310–21.

28. Ibid., p. 315.

29. Raymond Serafin, "Subaru Outback Taps Crocodile Dundee," *Advertising Age*, September 15, 1995, p. 38; Steve Geisi, "Dundee Returns to Extend Outback into Entry Level," *Brandweek*, September 2, 1996, pp. 1, 6.

30. For an excellent review of these studies, see W. B. Joseph, "The Credibility of Physically Attractive Communicators," *Journal of Advertising* 11, no. 3 (1982), pp. 13–23.

31. Michael Solomon, Richard Ashmore and Laura Longo, "The Beauty Match-Up Hypothesis: Congruence between Types of Beauty and Product Images in Advertising," *Journal of Advertising* 21, no. 4, pp. 23–34; M. J. Baker and Gilbert A. Churchill, Jr., "The Impact of Physically Attractive Models on Advertising Evaluations," *Journal of Marketing Research* 14 (November 1977), pp. 538–55.

32. Robert W. Chestnut, C. C. La Chance, and A. Lubitz, "The Decorative Female Model: Sexual Stimuli and the Recognition of the Advertisements," *Journal of Advertising* 6 (Fall 1977), pp. 11–14; Leonard N. Reid and Lawrence C.

Soley, "Decorative Models and Readership of Magazine Ads," *Journal of Advertising Research* 23, no. 2 (April/May 1983), pp. 27–32.

33. Herbert E. Krugman, "On Application of Learning Theory to TV Copy Testing," *Public Opinion Quarterly* 26 (1962), pp. 626–39.

34. C. I. Hovland and W. Mandell, "An Experimental Comparison of Conclusion Drawing by the Communicator and by the Audience," *Journal of Abnormal and Social Psychology* 47 (July 1952), pp. 581–88.

35. Alan G. Sawyer and Daniel J. Howard, "Effects of Omitting Conclusions in Advertisements to Involved and Uninvolved Audiences," *Journal of Marketing Research* 28 (November 1991), pp. 467–74.

36. Paul Chance, "Ads without Answers Make Brain Itch," *Psychology Today* 9 (1975), p. 78.

37. George E. Belch, "The Effects of Message Modality on One- and Two-Sided Advertising Messages," in *Advances in Consumer Research*, 10, ed. Richard P. Bagozzi and Alice M. Tybout (Ann Arbor: Association for Consumer Research, 1983), pp. 21–26.

38. Robert E. Settle and Linda L. Golden, "Attribution Theory and Advertiser Credibility," *Journal of Marketing Research* 11 (May 1974), pp. 181–85; Edmund J. Faison, "Effectiveness of One-Sided and Two-Sided Mass Communications in Advertising," *Public Opinion Quarterly* 25 (Fall 1961), pp. 468–69.

39. Alan G. Sawyer, "The Effects of Repetition of Refutational and Supportive Advertising Appeals," *Journal of Marketing Research* 10 (February 1973), pp. 23–37; George J. Szybillo and Richard Heslin, "Resistance to Persuasion: Inoculation Theory in a Marketing Context," *Journal of Marketing Research* 10 (November 1973), pp. 396–403.

40. Andrew A. Mitchell, "The Effect of Verbal and Visual Components of Advertisements on Brand Attitudes and Attitude toward the Advertisement," *Journal of Consumer Research* 13 (June 1986), pp. 12–24; and Julie A. Edell and Richard Staelin, "The Information Processing of Pictures in Advertisements," *Journal of Consumer Research* 10, no. 1 (June 1983), pp. 45–60; Elizabeth C. Hirschmann, "The Effects of Verbal and Pictorial Advertising Stimuli on Aesthetic, Utilitarian and Familiarity Perceptions," *Journal of Advertising* 15, no. 2 (1986), pp. 27–34.

41. Jolita Kisielius and Brian Sternthal, "Detecting and Explaining Vividness Effects in Attitudinal Judgments," *Journal of Marketing Research* 21, no. 1 (1984), pp. 54–64.

42. H. Rao Unnava and Robert E. Burnkrant, "An Imagery-Processing View of the Role of Pictures in Print Advertisements," *Journal of Marketing Research* 28 (May 1991), pp. 226–31.

43. Susan E. Heckler and Terry L. Childers, "The Role of Expectancy and Relevancy in Memory for Verbal and Visual Information: What Is Incongruency?" *Journal of Consumer Research* 18, no. 4, March 1992, pp. 475–92.

44. Michael J. Houston, Terry L. Childers, and Susan E. Heckler, "Picture–Word Consistency and the Elaborative Processing of Advertisements," *Journal of Marketing Research*, November 1987, pp. 359–69.

45. William L. Wilkie and Paul W. Farris, "Comparative Advertising: Problems and Potential," *Journal of Marketing* 39 (1975), pp. 7–15.

46. For a review of comparative advertising studies, see Cornelia Pechmann and David W. Stewart, "The Psychology of Comparative Advertising," in *Attention, Attitude and Affect in Response to Advertising*, ed. E. M. Clark, T. C. Brock, and D. W. Stewart (Hillsdale, NJ: Lawrence Erlbaum Associates, 1994), pp. 79–96.

47. Michael L. Ray and William L. Wilkie, "Fear: The Potential of an Appeal Neglected by Marketing," *Journal of Marketing* 34 (January 1970), pp. 54–62.

48. Brian Sternthal and C. Samuel Craig, "Fear Appeals Revisited and Revised," *Journal of Consumer Research* 1 (December 1974), pp. 22–34.

49. Punam Anand-Keller and Lauren Goldberg Block, "Increasing the Persuasiveness of Fear Appeals: The Effect of Arousal and Elaboration," *Journal of Consumer Research* 22, no. 4, March 1996, pp. 448–60.

50. John F. Tanner Jr., James B. Hunt, and David R. Eppright, "The Protection Motivation Model: A Normative Mode of Fear Appeals," *Journal of Marketing* 55 (July 1991), pp. 36–45.

51. Ibid.

52. Sternthal and Craig, "Fear Appeals Revisited and Revised."

53. For a discussion of the use of humor in advertising, see C. Samuel Craig and Brian Sternthal, "Humor in Advertising," *Journal of Marketing* 37 (October 1973), pp. 12–18.

54. Yong Zhang, "Responses to Humorous Advertising: The Moderating Effect of Need for Cognition," *Journal of Advertising* 25, no. 1 (Spring 1996), pp. 15–32; Marc G. Weinberger and Charles S. Gulas, "The Impact of Humor in Advertising: A Review," *Journal of Advertising* 21, December 1992, pp. 35–59.

55. Marc G. Weinberger and Leland Campbell, "The Use of Humor in Radio Advertising," *Journal of Advertising Research* 31, December/January 1990–91, pp. 44–52.

56. Thomas J. Madden and Marc C. Weinberger, "Humor in Advertising: A Practitioner View," *Journal of Advertising Research* 24, no. 4 (August/September 1984), pp. 23–26.

57. Harold C. Cash and W. J. E. Crissy, "Comparison of Advertising and Selling: The Salesman's Role in Marketing," *The Psychology of Selling* 12 (1965), pp. 56–75.

58. Marshall McLuhan, *Understanding Media: The Extensions of Man* (New York: McGraw-Hill, 1966).

59. Marvin E. Goldberg and Gerald J. Gorn, "Happy and Sad TV Programs: How They Affect Reactions to Commercials," *Journal of Consumer Research* 14, no. 3 (December 1987), pp. 387–403.

60. Peter H. Webb, "Consumer Initial Processing in a Difficult Media Environment," *Journal of Consumer Research* 6, no. 3 (December 1979), pp. 225–36.

61. Kevin Goldman, "TV Promotional Clutter Irks Ad Industry," *The Wall Street Journal*, February 11, 1994, p. B6.

62. For a review of marketing communications studies involving source, message, channel, and receiver factors, see George E. Belch, Michael A. Belch, and Angelina Villarreal, "Effects of Advertising Communications: Review of Research," in *Research in Marketing* 9 (Greenwich, Conn.: JAI Press, 1987), pp. 59–117.

Chapter 7

1. Michael Wilke, "Delta Ad Spending Plummets," *Advertising Age*, January 22, 1996, p. 8.

2. Robert A. Kriegel, "How to Choose the Right Communications Objectives," *Business Marketing*, April 1986, pp. 94–106.

3. 1993 Effies, New York Chapter of the American Marketing Association, New York, 1993, p. 10.

4. Donald S. Tull, "The Carry-Over Effect of Advertising," *Journal of Marketing*, April 1965, pp. 46–53.

5. Darral G. Clarke, "Econometric Measurement of the Duration of Advertising Effect on Sales," *Journal of Marketing Research* 23 (November 1976), pp. 345–57.

6. Philip Kotler, *Marketing Decision Making: A Model Building Approach* (New York: Holt, Rinehart & Winston, 1971), ch. 5.

7. Kathy Rebello, with Mary Kuntz, "Feel the Buzz," *Business Week*, August 28, 1995, p. 31.

8. For a more detailed discussion of this, see William M. Weilbacher, *Advertising*, 2nd ed. (New York: Macmillan, 1984), p. 112.

9. Courtland I. Bovee and William F. Arens, *Advertising*, 3rd ed. (Burr Ridge, IL: Richard D. Irwin, 1989).

10. 1993 Effies, p. 6.

11. Russell H. Colley, *Defining Advertising Goals for Measured Advertising Results* (New York: Association of National Advertisers, 1961).

12. Ibid., p. 21.

13. Don E. Schultz, Dennis Martin, and William Brown, *Strategic Advertising Campaigns*, 2nd ed. (Lincolnwood, IL: Crain Books, 1984).

14. Michael L. Ray, "Consumer Initial Processing: Definitions, Issues, Applications," in *Buyer/Consumer Information Processing*, ed. G. David Hughes (Chapel Hill: University of North Carolina Press, 1974); David A. Aaker and John G. Myers, *Advertising Management*, 2nd ed. (Englewood Cliffs, NJ: Prentice Hall, 1982), pp. 122–23.

15. Sandra Ernst Moriarty, "Beyond the Hierarchy of Effects: A Conceptual Framework," in *Current Issues and Research in Advertising*, ed. Claude R. Martin, Jr., and James H. Leigh (Ann Arbor, MI: University of Michigan, 1983), pp. 45–55.

16. Aaker and Myers, *Advertising Management*.

17. Kristian S. Palda, "The Hypothesis of a Hierarchy of Effects: A Partial Evaluation," *Journal of Marketing Research* 3 (February 1966), pp. 13–24.

18. Stewart H. Britt, "Are So-Called Successful Advertising Campaigns Really Successful?" *Journal of Advertising Research* 9, no. 2 (1969), pp. 3–9.

19. Steven W. Hartley and Charles H. Patti, "Evaluating Business-to-Business Advertising: A Comparison of Objectives and Results," *Journal of Advertising Research* 28 (April/May 1988), pp. 21–27.

20. Ibid., p. 25.

21. Study cited in Robert F. Lauterborn, "How to Know If Your Advertising Is Working," *Journal of Advertising Research* 25 (February/March 1985), pp. RC 9–11.

22. Don E. Schultz, " Integration Helps You Plan Communications from Outside-In," *Marketing News*, March 15, 1993, p. 12.

23. Thomas R. Duncan, "To Fathom Integrated Marketing, Dive!" *Advertising Age*, October 11, 1993, p. 18.

24. Robert L. Steiner, "The Paradox of Increasing Returns to Advertising," *Journal of Advertising Research*, February/March 1987, pp. 45–53.

25. Frank M. Bass, "A Simultaneous Equation Regression Study of Advertising and Sales of Cigarettes," *Journal of Marketing Research* 6, no. 3 (August 1969), p. 291.

26. David A. Aaker and James M. Carman, "Are You Overadvertising?" *Journal of Advertising Research* 22, no. 4 (August/September 1982), pp. 57–70.

27. Julian A. Simon and Johan Arndt, "The Shape of the Advertising Response Function," *Journal of Advertising Research* 20, no. 4 (1980), pp. 11–28.

28. Paul B. Luchsinger, Vernan S. Mullen, and Paul T. Jannuzzo, "How Many Advertising Dollars Are Enough?" *Media Decisions* 12 (1977), p. 59.

29. Paul W. Farris, *Determinants of Advertising Intensity: A Review of the Marketing Literature* (Report no. 77–109, Marketing Science Institute, Cambridge, MA, 1977).

30. Melvin E. Salveson, "Management's Criteria for Advertising Effectiveness" (Proceedings 5th Annual Conference, Advertising Research Foundation, New York, 1959), p. 25.

31. Robert Settle and Pamela Alreck, "Positive Moves for Negative Times," *Marketing Communications*, January 1988, pp. 19–23.

32. James O. Peckham, "Can We Relate Advertising Dollars to Market Share Objectives?" in *How Much to Spend for Advertising*, ed. M. A. McNiven (New York: Association of National Advertisers, 1969), p. 30.

33. "Marketers Fuel Promotion Budgets," *Marketing and Media Decisions*, September 1984, p. 130.

34. Ibid.

35. Mary Welch, "Upbeat Marketers, Bigger Budgets, Shift Marketing Mix," *Business Marketing*, February 1993, p. 23.

36. John P. Jones, "Ad Spending: Maintaining Market Share," *Harvard Business Review*, January/February 1990, pp. 38–42; and James C. Schroer, "Ad Spending: Growing Market Share," *Harvard Business Review*, January/February 1990, pp. 44–48.

37. Randall S. Brown, "Estimating Advantages to Large-Scale Advertising," *Review of Economics and Statistics* 60 (August 1978), pp. 428–37.

38. Kent M. Lancaster, "Are There Scale Economies in Advertising?" *Journal of Business* 59, no. 3 (1986), pp. 509–26.

39. Johan Arndt and Julian Simon, "Advertising and Economies of Scale: Critical Comments on the Evidence," *Journal of Industrial Economics* 32, no. 2 (December 1983), pp. 229–41; Aaker and Carman, "Are You Overadvertising?"

40. George S. Low and Jakki J. Mohr, "The Budget Allocation between Advertising and Sales Promotion: Understanding the Decision Process," 1991 AMA Educators' Proceedings: Chicago, IL: Summer 1991, pp. 448–57.

Chapter 8

1. Jeanne Whalen, "BK Caters to Franchisees with New Review," *Advertising Age*, October 25, 1993, p. 3.

2. Judann Pollack, "Burger King Sizzles in Wake of Arch Deluxe," *Advertising Age*, June 17, 1996, pp. 3, 41.

3. Joshua Levine, "Fizz, Fizz—Plop, Plop," *Fortune*, June 21, 1993, p. 139.

4. Bill Abrams, "What Do Effie, Clio, Addy, Andy and Ace Have in Common?" *The Wall Street Journal*, July 16, 1983, p. 1; Jennifer Pendleton, "Awards—Creatives Defend Pursuit of Prizes," *Advertising Age*, April 25, 1988, p. 1; David Herzbrun, "The Awards Awards," *Advertising Age*, May 2, 1988, p. 18.

5. Elizabeth C. Hirschman, "Role-Based Models of Advertising Creation and Production," *Journal of Advertising* 18, no. 4 (1989), pp. 42–53.

6. Ibid., p. 51.

7. Ronald Alsop, "TV Ads That Are Likeable Get Plus Rating for Persuasiveness," *The Wall Street Journal*, February 20, 1986, p. 23; and Cyndee Miller, "Study Says 'Likability' Sur-

...ss,"

...on the em-
...messages, see
..., *Advertising*,
...macmillan, 1984),

...
9. Davi... ...fessions of an Advertis-
ing Man (... ...fork: Atheneum
Publishers, 1963); and Hanley Norins,
The Compleat Copywriter (New York:
McGraw-Hill, 1966).

10. Hank Sneiden, *Advertising Pure and
Simple* (New York: ANACOM, 1977).

11. Quoted in Valerie H. Free, "Absolut
Original," *Marketing Insights*, Summer
1991, p. 65.

12. Jeff Jensen, "Marketer of the Year,"
Advertising Age, December 16, 1996, pp.
1, 16; Cathy Taylor, "Risk Takers:
Wieden & Kennedy," *Adweek*'s *Marketing Week*, March 23, 1992, pp. 26, 27.

13. James Webb Young, *A Technique for
Producing Ideas*, 3rd ed. (Chicago: Crain
Books, 1975), p. 42.

14. Sandra E. Moriarty, *Creative Advertising: Theory and Practice* (Englewood
Cliffs, NJ: Prentice Hall, 1986).

15. E. E. Norris, "Seek Out the Consumer's
Problem," *Advertising Age*, March 17,
1975, pp. 43–44.

16. Thomas L. Greenbaum, "Focus
Groups Can Play a Part in Evaluating
Ad Copy," *Marketing News*, September
13, 1993, pp. 24–25.

17. William D. Wells, Clark Leavitt, and
Maureen McConville, "A Reaction Profile for Commercials," *Journal of Advertising Research* 11 (December 1971), pp.
11–17.

18. Eben Shapiro, "Campbell Shifts Famil-
iar Slogan to Back Burner," *The Wall
Street Journal*, September 9, 1993, pp.
B1, 5.

19. A. Jerome Jeweler, *Creative Strategy in
Advertising* (Belmont, CA: Wadsworth,
1981).

20. John O'Toole, *The Trouble with Advertising*, 2nd ed. (New York: Random
House, 1985), p. 131.

21. David Ogilvy, *Ogilvy on Advertising*
(New York: Crown, 1983), p. 16.

22. Rosser Reeves, *Reality in Advertising*
(New York: Knopf, 1961), pp. 47, 48.

23. Bill Abrams, "Ad Constraints Could
Persist Even If the FTC Loosens Up,"
The Wall Street Journal, December 10,
1981, p. 33.

24. Alecia Swasy, "How Innovation at P&G
Restored Luster to Washed-Up Pert

and Made It No. 1," *The Wall Street
Journal*, December 6, 1990, p. B1.

25. Ogilvy, *Confessions*.

26. Martin Mayer, *Madison Avenue, U.S.A.*
(New York: Pocket Books, 1958).

27. Jack Trout and Al Ries, "The Positioning Era Cometh," *Advertising Age*, April
24, 1972, pp. 35–38; May 1, 1972, pp.
51–54; May 8, 1972, pp. 114–16.

28. Rajeev Batra, John G. Myers, and
David A. Aaker, *Advertising Manage-
ment*, 5th ed. (Upper Saddle River, NJ:
Prentice Hall, 1996).

Chapter 9

1. Sandra E. Moriarty, *Creative Advertising: Theory and Practice*, 2nd ed.
(Englewood Cliffs, NJ: Prentice Hall,
1991), p. 76.

2. William M. Weilbacher, *Advertising*,
2nd ed. (New York: Macmillan, 1984),
p. 197.

3. William Wells, John Burnett, and Sandra Moriarty, *Advertising* (Englewood
Cliffs, NJ: Prentice Hall, 1989), p. 330.

4. Stuart J. Agres, "Emotion in Adver-
tising: An Agency Point of View," in
*Emotion in Advertising: Theoretical and
Practical Explorations*, ed. Stuart J.
Agres, Julie A. Edell, and Tony M.
Dubitsky, (Westport, CT: Quorom
Books, 1991).

5. Edward Kamp and Deborah J. Macinnis, "Characteristics of Portrayed Emotions in Commercials: When Does
What Is Shown in Ads Affect Viewers?"
Journal of Advertising Research (Novem-
ber/December 1995), pp. 19–28.

6. For a review of research on the effect of
mood states on consumer behavior, see
Meryl Paula Gardner, "Mood States
and Consumer Behavior: A Critical Review," *Journal of Consumer Research* 12,
no. 3 (December 1985), pp. 281–300.

7. Cathy Madison, "Researchers Work
Advertising into an Emotional State,"
Adweek, November 5, 1990, p. 30.

8. Christopher P. Puto and William D.
Wells, "Informational and Transformational Advertising: The Different
Effects of Time," in *Advances in Consumer Research*, vol. 11, ed. Thomas C.
Kinnear (Ann Arbor, MI: Association
for Consumer Research, 1984), p. 638.

9. Ibid.

10. David Ogilvy and Joel Raphaelson,
"Research on Advertising Techniques
That Work and Don't Work," *Harvard
Business Review*, July–August 1982,
p. 18.

11. *Topline*, No. 4, McCann-Erickson (September 1989) New York.

12. Dottie Enrico, "Teaser Ads Grab Spotlight on Madison Ave.," *USA Today*,
July 6, 1995, pp. 1,2B.

13. Jacqueline Mitchell, "New Jeep to Roll
Out with 'Teaser' Ads," *The Wall Street
Journal*, February 6, 1992, p. B7.

14. "Infiniti Ads Trigger Auto Debate,"
Advertising Age, January 22, 1990, p. 49.

15. Quote by Irwin Warren cited in Enrico,
"Teaser Ads Grab Spotlight on Madison Avenue."

16. Martin Mayer, *Madison Avenue, U.S.A.*
(New York: Pocket Books, 1958), p. 64.

17. Kevin Goldman, "Slim-Fast Ads Use
Brooke Shields to Appeal to the Low-
Fat Dieter," *The Wall Street Journal*,
January 10, 1994, p. B7.

18. Alecia Swasy, "P&G Tries Bolder
Ads—With Caution," *The Wall Street
Journal*, May 7, 1990, pp. B1, 7.

19. Lynn Coleman, "Advertisers Put Fear
into the Hearts of Their Prospects,"
Marketing News, August 15, 1988, p. 1.

20. Kevin Goldman, "Chips Ahoy! Ad
Uses Spin on Claymation," *The Wall
Street Journal*, February 9, 1994, p. B5.

21. Bill McDowell, "Jack in the Box Battles
Back with Some Help from a Clown,"
Advertising Age, November 25, 1996,
p.11.

22. Barbara B. Stern, "Classical and
Vignette Television Advertising: Struc-
tural Models, Formal Analysis, and
Consumer Effects," *Journal of
Consumer Research* 20, no. 4 (March
1994), pp. 601–15; and John Deighton,
Daniel Romer, and Josh McQueen,
"Using Drama to Persuade," *Journal of
Consumer Research* 15, no. 3 (December
1989), pp. 335–43.

23. Moriarty, *Creative Advertising*, p. 77.

24. Courtland L. Bovee and William F.
Arens, *Contemporary Advertising*, 4th
ed. (Burr Ridge, IL: Richard D. Irwin,
1992), p. 292.

25. W. Keith Hafer and Gordon E. White,
Advertising Writing, 3rd ed. (St. Paul,
MN: West Publishing, 1989), p. 98.

26. "How Much Should a Commercial
Cost?" *Marketing Communications*, June
1983, p. 41.

27. Wendy Brandes, "Star Power Leaves
Some Voice-Over Artists Speechless,"
The Wall Street Journal, June 2, 1995,
p. B6.

28. Linda M. Scott, "Understanding
Jingles and Needledrop: A Rhetorical
Approach to Music in Advertising,"
Journal of Consumer Research 17, no. 2
(September 1990), pp. 223–36.

29. Ibid., p. 223.
30. Russell I. Haley, Jack Richardson, and Beth Baldwin, "The Effects of Nonverbal Communications in Television Advertising," *Journal of Advertising Research* 24, no. 4, pp. 11–18.
31. Gerald J. Gorn, "The Effects of Music in Advertising on Choice Behavior: A Classical Conditioning Approach," *Journal of Marketing* 46 (Winter 1982), pp. 94–100.
32. "A Few Rockers Give Ad Makers No Satisfaction," *The Wall Street Journal*, August 25, 1995, p. B1.
33. Sally Goll Beatty, "Staid Brands Put New Spin on Old Jingles," *The Wall Street Journal*, July 19, 1996, p. B5.
34. Swasy, "P&G Tries Bolder Ads," p. B1.
35. Eva Pomice, "Madison Avenue's Blind Spot," *U.S. News & World Report*, October 3, 1988, p. 49.
36. Bruce Horowitz, "TV Spots for Light Bulbs, Diet Pepsi This Year's Big Clio Award Winners," *Los Angeles Times*, June 21, 1988, pt. IV, p. 6.

Chapter 10

1. John P Cortez, "Flowers Flourish through Interactive Media," *Advertising Age*, July 12, 1993, p. 12.
2. Patricia Sellers, "The Best Way to Reach Buyers," *Fortune*, Autumn/Winter 1993, pp. 14–17.
3. Michael J. Naples, *Effective Frequency: The Relationship between Frequency and Advertising Effectiveness* (New York: Association of National Advertisers, 1979).
4. Joseph W. Ostrow, "Setting Frequency Levels: An Art or a Science?" *Journal of Advertising Research* 24 (August/September 1984), pp. i9–11.
5. David Berger, "How Much to Spend" (Foote, Cone & Belding Internal Report), in Michael L. Rothschild, *Advertising* (Lexington, MA: D. C. Heath, 1987), p. 468.
6. David W. Olson, "Real World Measures of Advertising Effectiveness for New Products" (Speech to the 26th Annual Conference of the Advertising Research Foundation, New York, March 18, 1980).
7. Naples, *Effective Frequency*.
8. Joseph W. Ostrow, "What Level Frequency?" *Advertising Age*, November 1981, pp. 13–18.
9. Ibid.
10. Louisa Ha, "Media Models and Advertising Effects: Conceptualization and Theoretical Implications," *Journal of Current Issues and Research in Advertising*, Fall 1995, pp. 1–15.
11. Ibid.
12. Hanna Liebman, "2002: Interactive Adland?" *MediaWeek*, May 17, 1993, p. 14.
13. Tara Parker-Pope, "Interactive Offerings Have Less Appeal in Europe than in U.S., Survey Says," *The Wall Street Journal*, June 20, 1995, p. A7.

Chapter 11

1. *Radio Marketing Guide and Fact Book for Advertisers* (New York: Radio Advertising Bureau, Inc., 1997).
2. Nielsen Station Index, DM Market Rank and Demographic Rank Report: TV Household and Demographic Universe Estimates (New York: Nielsen Media Research, September 1996).
3. *Trends in Media* (New York: Television Bureau of Advertising, Inc., June 1997).
4. John J. Cronin, "In-Home Observations of Commercial Zapping Behavior," *Journal of Current Issues and Research in Advertising* 17, no. 2 (Fall 1995), pp. 69–75; Dennis Kneale, "Zapping of TV Ads Appears Pervasive," *The Wall Street Journal*, April 25, 1988, p. 27.
5. Laura Petrecca, "4A's: Production Cost for TV Spots Up by 6%," *Advertising Age*, August 18, 1997, p. 30.
6. Bruce Horovitz, "More Advertisers Are Tailoring TV Spots to Ethnicity of Viewers," *Los Angeles Times*, May 3, 1994, pp. D1, 3.
7. Wayne Waley, "Popularity of :15s Falls," *Advertising Age*, January 14, 1991, pp. 1, 41.
8. Kevin Goldman, "TV Promotional Clutter Irks Ad Industry," *The Wall Street Journal*, February 11, 1994, p. B6.
9. Dennis Kneale, "Zapping of TV Ads Appears Pervasive."
10. John J. Cronin and Nancy Menelly, "Discrimination vs. Avoidance: 'Zipping' of Television Commercials," *Journal of Advertising* 21 (2), June 1992, pp. 1–7.
11. John J. Cronin, "In-Home Observations of Commercial Zapping Behavior."
12. Carrie Heeter and Bradley S. Greenberg, "Profiling the Zappers," *Journal of Advertising Research*, April/May 1985, pp. 9–12; Fred S. Zufryden, James H. Pedrick, and Avu Sandaralingham, "Zappping and Its Impact on Brand Purchase Behavior," *Journal of Advertising Research* 33 (January/February 1993), pp. 58–66; Patricia Orsini, "Zapping: A Man's World," Spring Television Report, *Adweek's Marketing Week*, April 8, 1991, p. 3.
13. Linda F. Alwitt and Parul R. Prabhaker, "Identifying Who Dislikes Television Advertising: Not by Demographics Alone," *Journal of Advertising Research*, 32, no. 5, 1992, pp. 30–42.
14. Ernest F. Larkin, "Consumer Perceptions of the Media and Their Advertising Content," *Journal of Advertising* 8 (1979), pp. 5–7.
15. Lucy L. Henke, "Young Children's Perceptions of Cigarette Brand Advertising Symbols: Awareness, Affect, and Target Market Identification," *Journal of Advertising* 24, no. 4 (Winter 1995), pp. 13–28.
16. John Helyar, Meg Cox, and Elizabeth Jensen, "How Fox Stole the Football away from CBS," *The Wall Street Journal*, December 20, 1993, p. B1.
17. Joe Mandese, "NBC's 'Seinfeld,' 'ER' Hit Record $1 Million Minute," *Advertising Age*, September 16, 1996, pp. 1, 52.
18. "And Now, a Show from Your Sponsor," *Business Week*, May 22, 1995, pp. 100–102.
19. *1997 Cable TV Facts* (New York: Cable Advertising Bureau).
20. Sally Goll Beatty, "MSNBC Already Waging Marketing War," *The Wall Street Journal*, July 9, 1996, p. B8.
21. *1997 Cable TV Facts.*
22. Chuck Ross, "Cable TV," *Advertising Age*, March 25, 1996, pp. 23–24.
23. David Leonhardt, "The Real Super Bowl," *Business Week*, February 3, 1997, pp. 118–19.
24. Gary Levin, "Arbitron Exits from Ratings Race," *Advertising Age*, October 25, 1993, p. 4.
25. Elizabeth Jensen, "Networks Blast Nielsen, Blame Faulty Ratings for Drop in Viewership," *The Wall Street Journal*, November 22, 1996, pp. A1, 10.
26. David J. Wallace, "Changes at Oft-Maligned Nielsen," *Advertising Age*, July 22, 1996, p. S16.
27. Chuck Ross, "Nielsen Explores Switch to Continuous Measurement," *Advertising Age*, April 8, 1996, p. 10.
28. David J. Wallace, "High Hopes for Smart Rating Service, but Promises Need to Be Fulfilled," *Advertising Age*, July 22, 1996, p. S16.
29. "A Big Step for Smart-TV," *Advertising Age*, February 24, 1997, p. 24.

30. Quote by William Staklein, head of Radio Advertising Bureau, cited in "More Firms Tune into Radio to Stretch Their Ad Budgets," *The Wall Street Journal*, July 17, 1986, p. 27.

31. *Radio Marketing Guide and Fact Book*.

32. Ibid.

33. Verne Gay, "Image Transfer: Radio Ads Make Aural History," *Advertising Age*, January 24, 1985, p. 1.

34. Avery Abernethy, "Differences between Advertising and Program Exposure for Car Radio Listening," *Journal of Advertising Research* 31, no. 2 (April/May 1991) pp. 33–42.

35. Howard Schlossberg, "New Radio Ratings Services Zero in on Moving Cars and Smaller Markets," *Marketing News*, April 26, 1993, pp. 1, 7.

36. Michael Wilke, "Arbitron May Offer Net Ratings," *Advertising Age*, May 27, 1996, p. 28.

Chapter 12

1. *The Magazine Handbook* 68 (New York: Magazine Publishers Association, 1996).

2. Herbert E. Krugman, "The Measurement of Advertising Involvement," *Public Opinion Quarterly* 30 (Winter 1966–67), pp. 583–96.

3. Jerry Schlosberg, "The Glittering City Magazines," *American Demographics*, July 1986, pp. 22–25.

4. Scott Donaton and Pat Sloan, "Ad 'Printaculars' under Scrutiny," *Advertising Age*, February 12, 1990, p. 3.

5. *Magazine Audiences* 2 (New York: Mediamark Research Inc., Spring 1982).

6. Ibid.

7. Steve Fajen, "Numbers Aren't Everything." *Media Decisions* 10 (June 1975), pp. 65–69.

8. *A Study of Media Involvement* (New York: Magazine Publishers of America, 1996).

9. Ibid.

10. *The Magazine Handbook*.

11. Garfield Ricketts, "The ABCs of ABC Statements," *Marketing & Media Decisions*, November 1988, p. 84.

12. Study cited in Jim Surmanek, *Media Planning: A Practical Guide* (Lincolnwood, IL: Crain Books, 1985).

13. "How Advertising Readership Is Influenced by Ad Size" Cahners Advertising Research Report no. 110.1 (Newton, MA: Cahners Publishing Company); "Larger Advertisements Get Higher Readership," (New York: McGraw-Hill Research, LAP Report no. 3102).

14. "Effect of Size, Color and Position on Number of Responses to Recruitment Advertising," (New York: McGraw-Hill Research, LAP Report no. 3116).

15. *The Magazine Handbook*.

16. Keith J. Kelly, "Magazines Stay on Downward Course in First Half," *Advertising Age*, August 29, 1996, p. 25.

17. Eric Garland, "The Road to Recovery," *Adweek Special Report: Consumer Magazines*, February 17, 1992, pp. 4, 5.

18. "Magazine of the Year," *Advertising Age*, March 11, 1996, pp. S1,11.

19. Andrew Wallenstein, "Men's *Journal* Shift in Focus Looking Good," *Advertising Age*, March 11, 1996, p. S10.

20. "Magazines Stay on Downward Course in First Half."

21. Joe Mandese, "Strong Roots for Cross-Media," *Advertising Age*, October 6, 1991, pp. 34, 35.

22. *The Magazine Handbook*.

23. Junu Bryan Kim, "Cracking the Barrier of Two Dimensions," *Advertising Age*, October 6, 1991, pp. 32, 34.

24. *Facts about Newspapers 1996* (New York: Newspaper Association of America, 1996).

25. Survey by Newspaper Advertising Bureau, October 1988.

26. Hanna Liebman, "NAA Network Ready to Roll," *MediaWeek*, December 13, 1993, p. 18.

27. Thomas B. Rosentiel, "Newspapers Fear Being Bypassed by Advertisers," *Los Angeles Times*, April 27, 1989, pt. IV, p. 1.

28. Lisa Benenson, "The Data Chase," *Adweek Special Report: The Newspaper Business*, May 4, 1992, pp. 6–7.

29. Studies cited in *Facts about Newspapers 1996*.

30. Daniel Pearl, "Newspapers Strive to Win Back Women," *The Wall Street Journal*, May 4, 1992, pp. B1, 12.

31. Jane Hodges, "Newspapers Plug Along in Quest for Web Answer," *Advertising Age*, April 29, 1996, p. S6.

32. Jane Hodges, "NCN Trying New Web Model," *Advertising Age*, April 29, 1996, p. 4.

Chapter 13

1. "OAAA Special Report" (New York: Outdoor Advertising Association of America, 1996).

2. Ibid.

3. John Medearis, "Ads on Wheels Run into Flak," *Los Angeles Times*, July 11, 1984, p. IV–2.

4. David Kalish, "Supermarket Sweepstakes," *Marketing & Media Decisions*, November 1988, p. 34.

5. Adam Snyder, "Outdoor Forecast: Sunny, Some Clouds," *Adweek's Marketing Week*, July 8, 1991, p. 18–19.

6. Laurie Freeman and Alison Fahey, "Package Goods Ride with Transit," *Advertising Age*, April 23, 1990, p. 28.

7. *Advertisers Take the City Bus to Work* (New York: Winston Network, 1988), p. 13.

8. *Transit Fact Book* (New York: American Public Transit Association, 1996).

9. Promotional Products Association International (Irving, TX: 1996).

10. Ibid.

11. George L. Herpel and Steve Slack, *Specialty Advertising: New Dimensions in Creative Marketing* (Irving, TX: Specialty Advertising Association, 1983), pp. 76, 79–80.

12. Ibid., p. 78.

13. M. J. Caballero and J. B. Hunt, *Smilin' Jack: Measuring Goodwill*. An unpublished research report from the Center for Professional Selling, Baylor University, 1989; M. J. Cooper and J. B. Hunt, *How Speciality Advertising Affects Goodwill*. A research report of Specialty Advertising Association International (now PPAI), Irving, TX, 1992.

14. George L. Herpel and Steve Slack, *Specialty Advertising: New Dimensions in Creative Marketing* (Irving, TX: Specialty Advertising Association, 1983), p. 75.

15. Joel J. Davis, *Understanding Yellow Pages* (Troy, MI: Yellow Pages Publishers Association), 1995.

16. Carol Hall, "Branding the Yellow Pages," *Marketing & Media Decisions*, April 1989, p. 59.

17. Ibid., p. 3.

18. Ibid.

19. Ibid., p. 5.

20. Ibid.

21. Ibid., p. 8.

22. Joel J. Davis, *Understanding Yellow Pages*.

23. Adam Snyder, "Are Spots on Home Video Badvertising?" *Brandweek*, January 29, 1996, p. 40.

24. Scott Hume, "Consumers Pan Ads on Video Movies," *Advertising Age*, May 28, 1990, p. 8.

25. Joanne Lipman and Kathleen A. Hughes, "Disney Prohibits Ads in Theaters Showing Its Movies," *The Wall Street Journal*, February 9, 1990, p. B1.

26. Adam Snyder, "Are Spots on Home Video Badvertising?" *Brandweek*, January 29, 1996, p. 40.

27. Ibid.

28. Motion Picture Association of America, 1996.

29. Betsy Baurer, "New Quick Flicks: Ads at the Movies," *USA Today*, March 13, 1986, p. D1.

30. Ibid.

31. Michael A. Belch and Don Sciglimpaglia, "Viewers' Evaluations of Cinema Advertising," Proceedings of the American Institute for Decision Sciences, March 1979, pp. 39–43.

32. Adam Snyder, "Are Spots on Home Video Badvertising?" *Brandweek*, January 29, 1996, p. 40.

33. "Hershey Befriends Extra-terrestrial," *Advertising Age*, July 19, 1982, p. 1.

34. J. D. Reed, "Plugging away in Hollywood," *Time*, January 2, 1998, p. 103.

35. Motion Picture Association of America, 1996.

36. Damon Darlin, "Highbrow Hype," *Forbes*, April 12, 1993, pp. 126–27.

37. Randall Rothenberg, "Is It a Film? Is It an Ad? Harder to Tell, *New York Times*, March 13, 1990, p. D23.

38. Laurie Mazur, "Screenland's Dirty Little Secret," *E* magazine, May/June 1996, p. 38.

39. "Consumer Products become Movie Stars," *The Wall Street Journal*, February 29, 1988, p. 23.

40. Damon Darlin, "Highbrow Hype," *Forbes*, April 12, 1993, pp. 126–27.

41. Mendelsohn Media Research, New York, 1993.

42. Jennifer Lawrence, "In-Flight Gets above Turbulence," *Advertising Age*, August 19, 1991, p. 32.

43. Ibid.

44. Joann S. Lublin, "In-Flight TV Commercials Are Booming," *The Wall Street Journal*, September 19, 1990, p. B6.

45. Dean Takahashi, "Intel Plans a Major Blitz through Kiosks," *The Wall Street Journal*, August 30, 1996, p. B2.

Chapter 14

1. Stan Rapp and Thomas I. Collins, *Maximarketing* (New York: McGraw-Hill, 1987).

2. Peter D. Bennett, ed., *Dictionary of Marketing Terms* (Chicago: American Marketing Association, 1988), p. 58.

3. *Direct Marketing Association Statistical Fact Book 1997* (New York, NY: Direct Marketing Association, 1997).

4. *Federal Reserve Bulletin—Annual Statistical Digest*, 1993, p. 516.

5. Jagdish N. Sheth, "Marketing Megatrends," *Journal of Consumer Marketing* 1, no. 1 (June 1983), pp. 5–13.

6. *Statistical Abstract of the United States* (Washington, DC: U.S. Bureau of Labor Statistics, 1996).

7. *Direct Marketing Association Statistical Fact Book 1997*.

8. William Dunn, "Pushing the Envelope," *Marketing Tools*, September 1995, pp. 20–23.

9. "A Potent New Tool for Selling: Database Marketing," *Business Week*, September 5, 1994, pp. 56–59.

10. Herbert Kanzenstein and William S. Sachs, *Direct Marketing*, 2nd ed. (New York: Macmillan, 1992).

11. *Direct Marketing Association Statistical Fact Book 1997*.

12. Ibid.

13. Ibid.

14. Cleveland Horton, "Porsche 300,000: The New Elite," *Advertising Age*, February 5, 1990, p. 8.

15. *Direct Marketing Association Statistical Fact Book 1997*.

16. Ibid.

17. Laura Bird, "Forget Ties; Catalogs Now Sell Mansions," *The Wall Street Journal*, November 7, 1996, p. B1.

18. Elaine Underwood, "Is There a Future for the TV Mall?" *Brandweek*, March 25, 1996, pp. 24–26.

19. Ibid.

20. "Infomercial 96 and Direct Response Television: The Entertainment Industry's Use of Infomercials," Supplement to *Adweek*, *Brandweek*, and *MediaWeek*, 1996.

21. Chad Rubel, "Infomercials Evolve as Major Firms Join Successful Format," *Marketing News*, January 2, 1995, p. 1.

22. Elaine Underwood, "Is There a Future for the TV Mall?"

23. Ibid.

24. *Direct Marketing Association Statistical Fact Book 1996*.

25. Ibid.

26. Ibid.

27. Ibid.

28. Ibid.

29. Tom Eisenhart, "Tele-media: Marketing's New Dimension," *Business Marketing*, February 1991, pp. 50–53.

30. *Direct Marketing Association Statistical Fact Book 1996*.

31. "New Tally of Online Subscribers," *Advertising Age*, February 10, 1997, p. 41.

32. America Online *Annual Report*, 1996, http://www.pls.aol.com/plweb-cgi/fastweb?getdoc+view1+Tour_AOL+93+1+wAAA+Marketplace

33. Direct Selling Association, 1994.

34. Paul Hughes, "Profits Due," *Entrepreneur*, February 1994, pp. 74–78.

35. Jon Berry, "The TV Shopping Future: It's Further than You Think," *Brandweek*, October 4, 1993, p. 16.

36. Michael J. Major, "Videotex Never Really Left, but It's Not All Here," *Advertising Age*, November 12, 1990, p. 2.

37. *The Economist*, September 16, 1995.

38. Andrew Kantor and Michael Neubarth, "Off the Charts: The Internet 1996," *Internet World*, December 1996, pp. 44–51.

39. Ibid.

40. Robert H. Ducoffe, "Advertising Value and Advertising on the Web," *Journal of Advertising Research*, September/October 1996, pp. 21–35; and New Media Pathfinder Study, Arbitron, 1995.

41. Robert H. Ducoffe, "Advertising Value and Advertising on the Web."

42. Pierre Berthon, Leyland Pitt, and Richard Watson, "The World Wide Web as an Advertising Medium: Toward an Understanding of Conversion Efficiency," *Journal of Advertising Research*, January/February 1996, pp. 43–53.

43. Robert D. Hof, "Don't Surf to Us, We'll Surf to You," *Business Week*, September 9, 1996, pp. 108–9.

44. Debra Aho Williamson, "P & G Clicks with New Web Pricing," *Advertising Age*, May 13, 1996, p. 12.

45. Debra Aho Williamson, "Web Ad Spending at $66.7 Mil in 1st Half," *Advertising Age*, September 1996, http://www.adage.com.

46. *Internet Marketing and Technology Report*, May 1996.

47. Debra Aho Williamson, "Web Ad Spending at $66.7 Mil in 1st Half."

48. Debra Aho Williamson, "Outlook '97: Will Web Ads Go Mainstream?" *Advertising Age*, October 1996, http://www.adage.com.

49. Berthon, Pitt, and Watson, "The World Wide Web as an Advertising Medium."

Chapter 15

1. Louis J. Haugh, "Defining and Redefining," *Advertising Age*, February 14, 1983, p. M44.

2. Scott A. Nielsen, John Quelch, and Caroline Henderson, "Consumer

Promotions and the Acceleration of Product Purchases," in *Research on Sales Promotion: Collected Papers*, ed. Katherine E. Jocz (Cambridge, MA: Marketing Science Institute, 1984).

3. J. Jeffrey Inman and Leigh McAlister, "Do Coupon Expiration Dates Affect Consumer Behavior?" *Journal of Marketing Research* 31, August 1994, pp. 423–28.

4. The Wall Street Journal Centennial Survey, cited in Ron Alsop, "Brand Loyalty Is Rarely Blind Loyalty," *The Wall Street Journal*, October 19, 1989, p. B1.

5. Todd Johnson, NPD Research Inc., "Declining Brand Loyalty Trends: Fact or Fiction?" (Paper presented at the Fourth Annual AMA Marketing Research Conference, October 5, 1983.)

6. Bob Schmitz and Keith Jones, "The New Retailer/Marketer: Friend or Foe?" in *Looking at the Retail Kaleidoscope*, Forum IX (Stamford, Conn.: Donnelley Marketing, 1988).

7. Scott Hume, "Coupons Score with Consumers," *Advertising Age*, February 15, 1988, p. 40.

8. Robert B. Settle and Pamela L. Alreck, "Hyperchoice in the Marketplace," *Marketing Communications*, May 1988, p. 15.

9. *1996 Trend Report* (Anaheim, CA: Actmedia, Inc., 1996).

10. Leigh McAlister, "A Model of Consumer Behavior," *Marketing Communications*, April 1987, p. 27.

11. Study cited in "Make It Simple," *Business Week*, September 9, 1996, p. 98.

12. Ruth M. McMath, "Winning the Space Wars," *Marketing Communications*, May 1988, pp. 55–58.

13. Lynn G. Coleman, "Marketers Advised to Go Regional," *Marketing News*, May 8, 1989, p. 1.

14. "What Happened to Advertising?" *Business Week*, September 23, 1991, pp. 66–72.

15. Richard Gibson, "How Products Check Out Helps Determine Pay," *The Wall Street Journal*, August 1, 1991, p. B1.

16. Betsy Spethmann, "Account Specific Comes Due," *Promo*, November 1996, pp. 39–48.

17. *NCH Reporter*, no. 1 (Nielsen Clearing House, 1983).

18. *The Magazine Handbook*, no. 59 (New York: Magazine Publishers of America, 1991).

19. Judann Dagnoli, "Jordan Hits Ad Execs for Damaging Brands," *Advertising Age*, November 4, 1991, p. 47.

20. Study cited in "What Happened to Advertising," *Business Week*.

21. R. M. Prentice, "How to Split Your Marketing Funds between Advertising and Promotion Dollars," *Advertising Age*, January 10, 1977, pp. 41–42, 44.

22. Betsy Spethmann, "Money and Power," *Brandweek*, March 15, 1993, p. 21.

23. Quote by Vincent Sottosanti, president of Council of Sales Promotion Agencies, in "Promotions that Build Brand Image," *Marketing Communications*, April 1988, p. 54.

24. "Fast Food Chains Start to Tune in on Frequency," *Brandweek*, March 21, 1994, pp. 36–38.

25. Jeffrey K. McElenea and Michael J. Enzer, "Building Brand Franchises," *Marketing Communications*, April 1986, pp. 42–64.

26. Raymond Sefafin, "Upscale Drivers," *Advertising Age*, February 26, 1996, pp. 30–31.

27. Reference cited in John P. Rossiter and Larry Percy, *Advertising and Promotion Management* (New York: McGraw-Hill, 1987), p. 360.

28. Glenn Heitsmith, "Something for Nothing," *Promo*, September 1993, pp. 30–36.

29. *1996 Worldwide Coupon Trends and Consumer Usage Patterns*, (Lincolnshire, IL: NCH Promotional Services, 1996).

30. Raju Narisetti, "Many Companies Are Starting to Wean Consumers Off Coupons," *The Wall Street Journal*, January 22, 1997, pp. B1, 10.

31. J. Jeffrey Inman and Leigh McAlister, "Do Coupon Expiration Dates Affect Consumer Behavior?"

32. Betsy Spethmann, "A Wake-Up Call at Breakfasttime," *Promo*, December 1996, pp. 27–28.

33. Jack Neff, "P&G Extends Co-branded Coupons," *Advertising Age*, June 3, 1996, p. 9.

34. "Romancing the Net," *Promo*, August 1996, pp. N4–N8.

35. Survey by Oxtoby-Smith, Inc., cited in "Many Consumers View Rebates as a Bother," *The Wall Street Journal*, April 13, 1989, p. B1.

36. William R. Dean, "Irresistible but Not Free of Problems," *Advertising Age*, October 6, 1980, pp. S1–12.

37. Eric Schmuckler, "Two Action Figures To Go, Hold the Burger," *Brandweek*, April 1, 1996, pp. 38–39.

38. "Mickey May Be the Big Winner in Disney–McDonald's Alliance," *The Wall Street Journal*, May 24, 1996, p. B5.

39. William A. Robinson, "What Are Promos' Weak and Strong Points?" *Advertising Age*, April 7, 1980, p. 54.

40. Betsy Spethmann, "The Perils of Promotion," *Promo*, November 1996, pp. 22, 134.

41. "Sweepstakes Fever," *Forbes*, October 3, 1988, pp. 164–66.

42. Maxine S. Lans, "Legal Hurdles Big Part of Promotions Game," *Marketing News*, October 24, 1994, pp. 15–16.

43. Russell D. Bowman, *Couponing and Rebates: Profits on the Dotted Line* (New York: Lebhar-Friedman Books, 1980).

44. Survey by Oxtoby-Smith, Inc., "Many Consumers View Rebates as a Bother."

45. Peter Tat, William A. Cunningham III, and Emin Babakus, "Consumer Perceptions of Rebates," *Journal of Advertising Research*, August/September 1988, pp. 45–50.

46. Martha Graves, "Mail-in Rebates Stirring Shopper, Retailer Backlash," *Los Angeles Times*, January 11, 1989, pt. IV, p. 1.

47. Edward A. Blair and E. Lair Landon, "The Effects of Reference Prices in Retail Advertisements," *Journal of Marketing* 45, no. 2 (Spring 1981), pp. 61–69.

48. Shav Glick, "Takeovers, Mergers Take Their Toll, Too," *Los Angeles Times*, March 27, 1989, pt. III, p. 14.

49. Brian Trusdell, "Will a Cigarette Ban Stall Nascar's Growth?" *Sales & Marketing Management*, February 1997, pp. 67–75.

50. Frank Green, "Battling for Shelf Control," *San Diego Union*, November 19, 1996, pp. C1, 6, 7.

51. "Want Shelf Space at the Supermarket? Ante Up," *Business Week*, August 7, 1989, pp. 60–61.

52. Melissa Campanelli, "What's in Store for EDLP?" *Sales & Marketing Management*, August 1993, pp. 56–59; "Procter & Gamble Hits Back," *Business Week*, July 19, 1993, pp. 20–22.

53. Amy Barone and Laurel Wentz, "Artzt Steering Barilla into EDLP Strategy," *Advertising Age*, February 26, 1996, p. 10.

54. Tom Steinhagen, "Space Management Shapes Up with Planograms," *Marketing News*, November 12, 1990, p. 7.

55. Srinath Gopalakrishna, Gary L. Lilien, Jerome D. Williams, and Ian K. Sequeria, "Do Trade Shows Pay Off?" *Journal of Marketing* 59, July 1995, pp. 75–83.

56. Cynthia Rigg, "Hard Times Means Growth for Co-op Ads," *Advertising Age*, November 12, 1990, p. 24.

57. Edwin L. Artzt, "The Lifeblood of Brands," *Advertising Age*, November 4, 1991, p. 32.

58. "Everyone Is Bellying Up to This Bar," *Business Week*, January 27, 1992, p. 84.

59. Benson P. Shapiro, "Improved Distribution with Your Promotional Mix," *Harvard Business Review*, March/April 1977, p. 116; and Roger A. Strang, "Sales Promotion—Fast Growth, Faulty Management," *Harvard Business Review*, July/August 1976, p. 119.

60. Quote by Thomas E. Hamilton, director of sales promotion services, William Esty Advertising, cited in Felix Kessler, "The Costly Couponing Craze," *Fortune*, June 9, 1986, p. 84.

61. Alan G. Sawyer and Peter H. Dickson, "Psychological Perspectives on Consumer Response to Sales Promotion," in *Research on Sales Promotion: Collected Papers*, ed. Katherine E. Jocz (Cambridge, MA: Marketing Science Institute, 1984).

62. William E. Myers, "Trying to Get Out of the Discounting Box," *Adweek*, November 11, 1985, p. 2.

63. Leigh McAlister, "Managing the Dynamics of Promotional Change," in *Looking at the Retail Kaleidoscope*, Forum IX (Stamford, CT: Donnelley Marketing, April 1988).

64. "Promotions Blemish Cosmetic Industry," *Advertising Age*, May 10, 1984, pp. 22–23, 26.

65. Richard Green, "Worried McDonald's Plans Dramatic Shifts and Big Price Cuts," *The Wall Street Journal*, February 26, 1997, pp. A1, 6.

Chapter 16

1. Judann Pollack, "New Marketing Spin: The PR 'Experience'." *Advertising Age*, August 5, 1996, p. 33.

2. Raymond Simon, *Public Relations, Concept and Practices*, 2nd ed. (Columbus, OH: Grid Publishing, 1980), p. 8.

3. William N. Curry, "PR Isn't Marketing," *Advertising Age*, December 18, 1991, p. 18.

4. Martha M. Lauzen, "Imperialism and Encroachment in Public Relations," *Public Relations Review* 17, no. 3 (Fall 1991), pp. 245–55.

5. Philip Kotler and William Mindak, "Marketing and Public Relations," *Journal of Marketing* 42 (October 1978), pp. 13–20.

6. Thomas L. Harris, "How MPR Adds Value to Integrated Marketing Communications," *Public Relations Quarterly*, Summer 1993, pp. 13–18.

7. Sally Goll Beatty, "Texaco's Effort to Repair Image Comes under Fire after First Ad," *The Wall Street Journal*, November 27, 1996, p. B7.

8. Simon, *Public Relations*, p. 164.

9. Bob Donath, "Corporate Communications," *Industrial Marketing*, July 1980, pp. 53–57.

10. Scott M. Cutlip, Allen H. Center, and Glenn M. Broom, *Effective Public Relations*, 6th ed. (Englewood Cliffs, NJ: Prentice Hall, 1985), p. 200.

11. John E. Marston, *Modern Public Relations* (New York: McGraw-Hill, 1979).

12. Joe Agnew, "Marketers Find the Antidrug Campaign Addictive," *Marketing News*, October 9, 1987, p. 12.

13. Raymond Serafin, "Cars Squeeze Mileage from Awards," *Advertising Age*, June 4, 1990, p. 36.

14. Jeffrey M. O'Brien, "H-P Heads for Home," *Marketing Computers*, July/August 1996, pp. 55–58.

15. Raymond Simon, *Public Relations, Concepts and Practices*, 3rd ed. (New York: John Wiley & Sons, 1984), p. 291.

16. Harold Mendelsohn, "Some Reasons Why Information Campaigns Can Succeed," *Public Opinion Quarterly*, Spring 1973, p. 55.

17. Walter K. Linermann, "An Effectiveness Yardstick to Measure Public Relations Success," *Public Relations Quarterly* 38, no. 1 (Spring 1993), pp. 7–10.

18. Deborah Holloway, "How to Select a Measurement System That's Right for You," *Public Relations Quarterly* 37, no. 3 (Fall 1992), pp. 15–18.

19. J. Lawrence, "New Doritos Gets the Star Treatment," *Advertising Age*, March 29, 1993, p. 64.

20. Adam Shell, "VNRs Are the Right Thing, Uh-huh!" *Public Relations Journal* 49, no. 8 (August 1993), p. 6.

21. Jaye S. Niefeld, "Corporate Advertising," *Industrial Marketing*, July 1980, pp. 64–74.

22. Tom Garbett, "What Companies Project to Public," *Advertising Age*, July 6, 1981, p. 51.

23. Ed Zotti, "An Expert Weighs the Prose and Yawns," *Advertising Age*, January 24, 1983, p. M-11.

24. Bob Seeter, "AMA Hopes New Ads Will Cure Image Problem," *Los Angeles Times*, August 14, 1991, p. A-5.

25. John Burnett, "Shopping for Sponsorships? Integration Is Paramount," *Brandweek*, February 14, 1994, p. 18.

26. Ed Zotti, "An Expert Weighs the Prose and Yawns," *Advertising Age*, January 24, 1983, p. M-11.

27. Prakash Sethi, *Advertising and Large Corporations* (Lexington, MA: Lexington Books, 1977), pp. 7–8.

28. Janet Myers, "JWT Anti-Japan Ad Is a Bomb," *Advertising Age*, April 2, 1990, p. 4.

29. Niefeld, "Corporate Advertising," p. 64.

30. Geoffrey Smith and Ron Stodgill, "Are Good Causes Good Marketing?" *Business Week*, March 21, 1994, pp. 64–65.

31. Karen Benezra, "Cause and Effects Marketing," *Brandweek*, April 22, 1996, p. 38.

32. Donath, "Corporate Communications," p. 52.

33. Ibid., p. 53.

34. Ibid., p. 52.

Chapter 17

1. Carl G. Stevens and David P. Keane, "How to Become a Better Sales Manager: Give Salespeople How to, Not Rah Rah," *Marketing News*, May 30, 1980, p. 1.

2. Tom Wotruba and Edwin K. Simpson, *Sales Management* (Boston: Kent Publishing, 1989).

3. Cahners Publishing Co., a division of Reed Elsevier, Inc., 1996, http://www.cahners.com/research/5425d.htm.

4. Thomas R. Wotruba, "The Evolution of Personal Selling," *Journal of Personal Selling & Sales Management* 11, no. 3 (Summer 1991), pp. 1–12.

5. Jonathan R. Copulsky and Michael J. Wolf, "Relationship Marketing: Positioning for the Future," *Journal of Business Strategy*, July/August 1990, pp. 16–20.

6. Ibid.

7. Cahners Publishing Co., 1996, http://www.cahners.com/research/5425d.htm.

8. Thayer C. Taylor, "A Letup in the Rise of Sales Call Costs," *Sales & Marketing Management*, February 25, 1980, p. 24.

9. Theodore Levitt, "Communications and Industrial Selling," *Journal of Marketing* 31 (April 1967), pp. 15–21.

10. John E. Morrill, "Industrial Advertising Pays Off," *Harvard Business Review*, March/April 1970, p. 4.

11. "Salespeople Contact Fewer than 10 Percent of Purchase Decision Makers over a Two-Month Period," McGraw-

Hill LAP Report no. 1029.3 (New York: McGraw-Hill, 1987).

12. Peggy Moretti, "Telemarketers Serve Clients," *Business Marketing*, April 1994, pp. 27–29.

13. Ibid.

14. Rolph E. Anderson, Joseph F. Hair, and Alan J. Bush, *Professional Sales Management* (New York: McGraw-Hill, 1988).

Chapter 18

1. Laura Bird, "Loved the Ad. May (or May Not) Buy the Product," *The Wall Street Journal*, April 7, 1994, p. B1.

2. Bruce Horowitz, "TV Ads the Public Will Never See," *Los Angeles Times*, August 3, 1988, p. 1.

3. McGraw-Hill Lap Report no. 3151 (New York: McGraw-Hill, 1988); Alan D. Fletcher, *Target Marketing through the Yellow Pages* (Troy, MI: Yellow Pages Publishers Association, 1991), p. 23.

4. Personal interview with Jay Khoulos, president of World Communications, Inc., 1988.

5. David A. Aaker and John G. Myers, *Advertising Management*, 3rd ed. (Englewood Cliffs, NJ: Prentice Hall, 1987), p. 474.

6. Joel N. Axelrod, "Induced Moods and Attitudes toward Products," *Journal of Advertising Research* 3 (June 1963), pp. 19–24; Lauren E. Crane, "How Product, Appeal, and Program Affect Attitudes toward Commercials," *Journal of Advertising Research* 4 (March 1964), p. 15.

7. Robert Settle, "Marketing in Tight Times," *Marketing Communications* 13, no. 1 (January 1988), pp. 19–23.

8. "What Is Good Creative?" *Topline*, no. 41 (New York: McCollum Spielman Worldwide, 1994), p. 4.

9. "21 Ad Agencies Endorse Copy-Testing Principles," *Marketing News* 15, no. 17 (February 19, 1982), p. 1.

10. Ibid.

11. John M. Caffyn, "Telepex Testing of TV Commercials," *Journal of Advertising Research* 5, no. 2 (June 1965), pp. 29–37; Thomas J. Reynolds and Charles Gengler, "A Strategic Framework for Assessing Advertising: The Animatic vs. Finished Issue," *Journal of Advertising Research*, October/November 1991, pp. 61–71; Nigel A. Brown and Ronald Gatty, "Rough vs. Finished TV Commercials in Telepex Tests," *Journal of*

Advertising Research 7, no. 4 (December 1967), p. 21.

12. Charles H. Sandage, Vernon Fryburger, and Kim Rotzoll, *Advertising Theory and Practice*, 10th ed. (Burr Ridge, IL: Richard D. Irwin, 1979).

13. Lyman E. Ostlund, "Advertising Copy Testing: A Review of Current Practices, Problems and Prospects," *Current Issues and Research in Advertising*, 1978, pp. 87–105.

14. Jack B. Haskins, "Factual Recall as a Measure of Advertising Effectiveness," *Journal of Advertising Research* 4, no. 1 (March 1964), pp. 2–7.

15. John Philip Jones and Margaret H. Blair, "Examining 'Conventional Wisdoms' about Advertising Effects with Evidence from Independent Sources," *Journal of Advertising Research*, November/December 1996, pp. 37–52.

16. Paul J. Watson and Robert J. Gatchel, "Autonomic Measures of Advertising," *Journal of Advertising Research* 19 (June 1979), pp. 15–26.

17. Priscilla A. LaBarbera and Joel D. Tucciarone, "GSR Reconsidered: A Behavior-based Approach to Evaluating and Improving the Sales Potency of Advertising," *Journal of Advertising Research*, September/October 1995, pp. 33–40.

18. Flemming Hansen, "Hemispheric Lateralization: Implications for Understanding Consumer Behavior," *Journal of Consumer Research* 8 (1988), pp. 23–36.

19. Hubert A. Zielske, "Does Day-after Recall Penalize 'Feeling Ads'?" *Journal of Advertising Research* 22, no. 1 (1982), pp. 19–22.

20. Arthur J. Kover, "Why Copywriters Don't Like Advertising Research—and What Kind of Research Might They Accept," *Journal of Advertising Research*, March/April 1996, pp. RC8–RC10; Gary Levin, "Emotion Guides BBDO's Ad Tests," *Advertising Age*, January 29, 1990, p.12.

21. Terry Haller, "Day-after Recall to Persist Despite JWT Study; Other Criteria Looming," *Marketing News*, May 18, 1979, p. 4.

22. Dave Kruegel, "Television Advertising Effectiveness and Research Innovations," *Journal of Consumer Marketing* 5, no. 3 (Summer 1988), pp. 43–52.

23. Gary Levin, "Tracing Ads' Impact," *Advertising Age*, November 12, 1990, p. 49.

24. John Philip Jones, "Single-source Research Begins to Fulfill Its Promise," *Journal of Advertising Research*, May/June 1995, pp. 9–16.

25. Jeffrey L. Seglin, "The New Era of Ad Measurement," *Adweek's Marketing Week*, January 23, 1988, p. 24.

26. James F. Donius, "Marketing Tracking: A Strategic Reassessment and Planning Tool," *Journal of Advertising Research* 25, no. 1 (February/March 1985), pp. 15–19.

27. Russell I. Haley and Allan L. Baldinger, "The ARF Copy Research Validity Project," *Journal of Advertising Research*, April/May 1991, pp. 11–32.

28. Glenn Heitsmith, "Something for Nothing," *Promo*, September 1993, pp. 30, 31, 93.

29. Ibid.

30. "Journeying Deeper into the Minds of Shoppers," *Business Week*, February 4, 1991, p. 85.

31. David W. Schumann, Jennifer Grayson, Johanna Ault, Kerri Hargrove, Lois Hollingsworth, Russell Ruelle, and Sharon Seguin, "The Effectiveness of Shopping Cart Signage: Perceptual Measures Tell a Different Story," *Journal of Advertising Research*, February/March 1991, pp. 17–22.

32. June Bryan Kim, "Research Makes Ski Run Easier," *Advertising Age*, August 18, 1991, p. 30.

33. Scott Hume, "Sports Sponsorship Value Measured," *Advertising Age*, August 6, 1990, p. 22.

Chapter 19

1. Char Kosek, "Business-to-Business Captures 37.4% of All Marketing Spending," *Advertising Age*, June 3, 1996, p. 46.

2. Yolanda Brugaletta, "What Business-to-Business Advertisers Can Learn from Consumer Advertisers," *Journal of Advertising Research* 25, no. 3 (June/July 1985), pp. 8–9.

3. Anderson & Lembke, Inc., Stamford, Conn., 1985 sales promotion literature.

4. Tom Eisenhart, "How to Really Excite Your Prospects," *Business Marketing*, July 1988, pp. 44–55.

5. Business Marketing Association, 1994.

6. *Carr Reports* (Newton, Mass.: Cahners Publishing Co., 1991).

7. Tom Eisenhart, "What's Right, What's Wrong with Each Medium," *Business Marketing*, April 1990, pp. 40–47.

8. National Telemarketing Association, 1992.
9. Outfront Marketing Study, *Business Marketing*, June 1996, p. S16.
10. David Atkins, "Reeling in the Prospects," *Business Marketing*, February 2, 1994, pp. 27–31.
11. Cahners Publishing Company, a division of Reed Elsevier, Inc., 1996, http://www.cahners.com/research/5425d.htm.
12. Kim Cleland, "High Tech Concerns only Wet Their Toes in Interactive Pool," Technology Agency Media & Marketing Survey, *Advertising Age*, September 1995, p. A6.
13. Srinath Gopalakrishna, Gary L. Lilien, Jerome D. Williams, and Ian K. Sequereira, "Do Trade Shows Pay Off?" *Journal of Marketing*, July 1995, pp. 75–83.
14. Trade Show Bureau, 1992.
15. Srinath Gopalakrishna, Gary L. Lilien, Jerome D. Williams, and Ian K. Sequereira, "Do trade shows pay off?"
16. Business Marketing Association, 1994.
17. 1986 Starmark Report, *Business Marketing*, p. 17.
18. Business Marketing Association, 1994.

Chapter 20

1. Fara Warner, "Tobacco Brands Outmaneuver Asian Ad Bans," *The Wall Street Journal*, August 6, 1996, pp. B1, 3; Bill Saporito, "Where the Global Action Is," *Fortune*, Special Issue, Autumn/Spring 1993, pp. 63–65.
2. "Anheuser-Busch Says Skoal, Salud, Prosit," *Business Week*, November 20, 1993, pp. 76–77.
3. Jonathan Friedland and Michael J. McCarthy, "Pairing Bud with Sushi in South America," *The Wall Street Journal*, February 20, 1997, pp. B1, 6.
4. Christopher Knowlton, "Europe Cooks Up a Cereal Brawl," *Fortune*, June 3, 1991, pp. 175–78.
5. "They're All Screaming for Haagen-Dazs," *Business Week*, October 14, 1991, p. 121.
6. Martha T. Moore, "New Breed CEO Markets Locally—Worldwide," *USA Today*, February 7, 1996, pp. 1, 2B.
7. Sally Goll Beatty, "Record Ad Spending Projected for 1996," *The Wall Street Journal*, December 5, 1995, p. B8.
8. "Global Marketers," *Advertising Age International*, November 1996, pp. i15, i19.

9. Vern Terpstra, *International Marketing*, 4th ed. (New York: Holt, Rinehart & Winston/Dryden Press, 1987), p. 427.
10. "Asian Horizons," *Sales & Marketing Management*, August 1996, pp. 64–68.
11. Carla Rapoport, "Nestlé's Brand Building Machine," *Fortune*, September 19, 1994, pp. 147–56.
12. Mir Maqbool Alan Khan, "Enormity Tempts Marketers to Make a Passage to India," *Advertising Age International*, May 15, 1995, p. i12.; Cyndee Miller, "India Opening Up to Western Marketers, but Challenges Abound," *Marketing News*, November 6, 1995, pp. 1, 2.
13. G. Pascal Zachary, "Major U.S. Companies Expand Efforts to Sell to Consumers Abroad," *The Wall Street Journal*, June 13, 1996, pp. A1, 6.
14. For an excellent discussion of various elements of Japanese culture such as language and its implications for promotion, see John F. Sherry, Jr., and Eduardo G. Camargo, "May Your Life Be Marvelous: English Language Labelling and the Semiotics of Japanese Promotion," *Journal of Consumer Research* 14 (September 1987), pp. 174–88.
15. Barbara Mueller, "Reflections on Culture: An Analysis of Japanese and American Advertising Appeals," *Journal of Advertising Research*, June/July 1987, pp. 51–59.
16. Barbara Mueller, "Standardization vs. Specialization: An Examination of Westernization in Japanese Advertising," *Journal of Advertising Research*, January/February 1992, pp. 15–24; Johny K. Johanson, "The Sense of Nonsense: Japanese TV Advertising," *Journal of Advertising* 23, no. 1 (March 1994) pp. 17–26.
17. Marian Katz, "No Women, No Alcohol; Learn Saudi Taboos before Placing Ads," *International Advertiser*, February 1986, pp. 11–12.
18. Safran S. Al-Makaty, G. Norman van Tubergen, S. Scott Whitlow, and Douglas A. Boyd, "Attitudes toward Advertising in Islam," *Journal of Advertising Research*, May/June 1996, pp. 16–26.
19. Dean M. Peebles and John K. Ryans, *Management of International Advertising* (Newton, MA: Allyn & Bacon, 1984).
20. Geoffrey Lee Martin, "Tobacco Sponsors Fear Aussie TKO," *Advertising Age International*, April 27, 1992, p. i8.
21. Jane Blennerhassett, "Hong Kong Ban May Be Tougher than China's," *Advertising Age International*, July 1996, p. I6.

22. Laurel Wentz, "Local Laws Keep International Marketers Hopping," *Advertising Age*, July 11, 1985, p. 20.
23. David Bartel and Laurel Wentz, "Danes Phase in TV Spots," *Advertising Age*, November 23, 1987, p. 65.
24. Safran S. Al-Makaty et al., "Attitudes toward Advertising in Islam."
25. Derek Turner, "Coke Pops Brazilian Comparative Ad," *Advertising Age*, September 9, 1991, p. 24.
26. J. Craig Andrews, Steven Lysonski, and Srinivas Durvasula, "Understanding Cross-Cultural Student Perceptions of Advertising in General: Implications for Advertising Educators and Practitioners," *Journal of Advertising* 20, no. 2 (June 1991), pp. 15–28.
27. J. J. Boddewyn and Iris Mohr, "International Advertisers Face Government Hurdles," *Marketing News*, May 8, 1987, pp. 21–22.
28. Tze Yee-Lin, "Malaysia May Allow Foreign Commercials," *Advertising Age International*, March 1997, p. i22.
29. Amy Haight, "EC Ad Ban May Go Up in Smoke," *Advertising Age International*, January 17, 1994, p. i8.
30. Martin Du Bois, "Philip Morris Campaign Stirs Uproar in Europe," *The Wall Street Journal*, July 1, 1996, pp. B1, 2; Martin Du Bois, "Europe's Anti-smoking Sentiments Heat Up as Talk of Bans Increases," *The Wall Street Journal*, June 6, 1995, p. B5.
31. Robert D. Buzzell, "Can You Standardize Multinational Marketing?" *Harvard Business Review*, November/December 1968, pp. 102–13; Ralph Z. Sorenson and Ulrich E. Wiechmann, "How Multinationals View Marketing," *Harvard Business Review*, May/June 1975, p. 38.
32. Theodore Levitt, "The Globalization of Markets," *Harvard Business Review*, May/June 1983, pp. 92–102; Theodore Levitt, *The Marketing Imagination* (New York: Free Press, 1986).
33. Anne B. Fisher, "The Ad Biz Gloms onto Global," *Fortune*, November 12, 1984, p. 78.
34. Keith Reinhard and W. E. Phillips, "Global Marketing: Experts Look at Both Sides," *Advertising Age*, April 15, 1988, p. 47; Anthony Rutigliano, "The Debate Goes On: Global vs. Local Advertising," *Management Review*, June 1986, pp. 27–31.
35. Kevin Goldman, "Professor Who Started Debate on Global Ads Still

Backs Theory," *The Wall Street Journal*, October 13, 1992, p. B8.

36. Example from speech by Eugene H. Kummel, chair emeritus of McCann-Erickson Worldwide, and Koji Oshita, president and CEO of McCann-Erickson Hakuhodo, Japan, in San Diego, October 19, 1988; Margo Sugarman, "Nescafé's Israel Entry Redefines Coffee Market,"*Advertising Age International*, April 1997, p. i12.

37. Joanne Lipman, "Marketers Turn Sour on Global Sales Pitch," *The Wall Street Journal*, May 12, 1988, p. 1.

38. Joseph M. Winski and Laurel Wentz, "Parker Pens: What Went Wrong?" *Advertising Age*, June 2, 1986, p. 1.

39. Laurie Freeman, "Colgate Axes Global Ads, Thinks Local," *Advertising Age*, November 26, 1990, pp. 1, 59.

40. Lipman, "Marketers Turn Sour."

41. Sally Goll Beatty, "Global Needs Challenge Midsize Agencies," *The Wall Street Journal*, December 14, 1995, p. B9.

42. Criteria cited by Edward Meyer, CEO of Grey Advertising, in Rebecca Fannin, "What Agencies Really Think of Global Theory," *Marketing & Media Decisions*, December 1984, p. 74.

43. Quote cited in Reinhard and Phillips, "Global Marketing," p. 47.

44. Dana Ilbank, "Made in America Becomes a Boast in Europe," *The Wall Street Journal*, January 19, 1994, pp. B1, 12.

45. Salah S. Hassan and Lea P. Katsansis, "Identification of Global Consumer Segments: A Behavioral Framework," *Journal of International Consumer Marketing* 3, no. 2, 1991, pp. 11–28.

46. Goldman, "Professor Who Started Debate."

47. Fannin, "What Agencies Really Think of Global Theory," p. 75.

48. Gary Levin, "Ads Going Global," *Advertising Age*, July 22, 1991, pp. 4, 42.

49. Robert E. Hite and Cynthia L. Fraser, "International Advertising Strategies of Multinational Corporations," *Journal of Advertising Research*, August/September 1988, pp. 9–17.

50. Ali Kanso, "International Advertising Strategies: Global Commitment to Local Vision," *Journal of Advertising Research*, January/February 1992, pp. 10–14.

51. Jan Jaben, "Ad Decision-Makers Favor Regional Angle," *Advertising Age International*, May 1995, pp i3, 16.

52. Penelope Rowlands, "Global Approach Doesn't Always Make Scents," *Advertising Age International*, January 17, 1994, pp. 1, 38.

53. Bradley Johnson, "It's a Small World for Compaq Campaign,"*Advertising Age International*, November 1996, p. i4.

54. Tara Parker-Pope, "Ad Agencies Are Stumbling in Eastern Europe," *The Wall Street Journal*, May 10, 1996, pp. B1, 3.

55. Sally Goll Beatty, "Young & Rubicam Is Only One for Colgate," *The Wall Street Journal*, December 1, 1995, p. B6.

56. Calmetta Y. Coleman, "U.S. Agencies Expand in Latin America," *The Wall Street Journal*, January 3, 1996, p. B8.

57. Terpstra, *International Marketing*; Dean M. Peebles and John K. Ryans, Jr., *Management of International Advertising*.

58. Normandy Madden and Sheryl R. Lee, "Demand for Viewer Data Going Up," *Advertising Age International*, July 1996, p. i16.

59. Nancy Giges, "Europeans Buy Outside Goods, but Like Local Ads," *Advertising Age International*, April 27, 1992, pp. i1, 26.

60. Joseph T. Plummer, "The Role of Copy Research in Multinational Advertising," *Journal of Advertising Research*, October/November 1986, p. 15.

61. Yumiko Ono, "Tropicana Is Trying to Cultivate a Global Taste for Orange Juice," *The Wall Street Journal*, March 28, 1994, p. B2.

62. Ron Alsop, "Efficacy of Global Ad Projects Is Questioned in Firm's Survey," *The Wall Street Journal*, September 13, 1984, p. 31.

63. Fannin, "What Agencies Really Think."

64. "They're All Screaming for Haagen-Dazs."

65. Karen Yates, "Advertising's Heart of Darkness,"*Advertising Age International*, May 15, 1995, p. i10, 15.

66. Mir Maqbool Alam Kahn, "TV Ad Spending Could Suffer under Pro-India Politicking," *Advertising Age International*, March 1997, p. i22.

67. Rochell Burbury, "Australia Ends Ban on Cable TV Spots," *Advertising Age International*, March 1997, p. i22.

68. Michael Laris, "China: The World's Most Populous Market,"*Advertising Age International*, May 15, 1995, p. i11.

69. Fara Warner, "Sofres Group Faces Daunting Task of Rating China's TV Audience," *The Wall Street Journal*, August 1, 1996, p. B7; Normandy Madden and Sheryl R. Lee, "Demand for Viewer Data Going Up," *Advertising Age International*, July 1996, pp. i16, 22.

70. Chuck Ross, "Global Rules Are Proposed for Measuring TV," *Advertising Age*, August 12, 1996, pp. 3, 28.

71. James H. Rosenfield, "The Explosion of Worldwide Media," *Marketing Communications*, September 1987, p. 65.

72. Thomas McCarroll, "New Star over Asia," *Time*, August 9, 1993, p. 53.

73. Juliana Koranteng, "Sky TV Tries to Repeat U.K. Success," *Advertising Age International*, March 1997, pp. i18, 20.

74. Mir Magbool Alam Khan, "TV Ad Spending Could Suffer under Pro-India Politicking,"*Advertising Age International*, March 1997, p. i22.

75. "Stickey Wickets, but What a Future," *Business Week*, August 7, 1995, pp. 72–73.

76. Kamran Kashani and John A. Quelch, "Can Sales Promotion Go Global?" *Business Horizons*, May/June 1990, pp. 37–43.

77. "What You Should Know about Advertising in Japan," *Advertising World*, April 1985, pp. 18, 42.

78. Kashani and Quelch, "Can Sales Promotion Go Global?"

79. Andrew Tanzer, "Citibank Blitzes Asia," *Forbes*, May 6, 1995, p.44.

80. "Foreign Ads Go Further with PR," *International Advertiser*, December 1986, p. 30.

81. Anne Roman, "Ohio Firm Breaks International Ice," *Public Relations Journal* 47, no. 5 (May 1991), pp. 40–42.

82. Todd Pruzan, "Internet Foreign Turf to Some Marketers," *Advertising Age International*, March 11, 1996, p. i12.

83. Juliana Koranteng, "Global Advertisers Value On-air, Online Combination," *Advertising Age International*, March 1997, p. i10.

Chapter 21

1. Ira Teinowitz, "'Historic' Attack on Cig Marketing," *Advertising Age*, August 26, 1996, pp. 1, 28; Sheryl Stolberg, "Clinton Imposes Wide Crackdown on Tobacco Firms," *Los Angeles Times*, August 24, 1996, pp. A1, 10.

2. Ira Teinowitz, "Rep. Kennedy Hits Alcohol Ads," *Advertising Age*, May 13, 1996, pp. 1, 52.

3. Priscilla A. LaBarbera, "Analyzing and Advancing the State of the Art of Advertising Self-Regulation," *Journal of Advertising* 9, no. 4 (1980), p. 30.

4. John F. Archer, "Advertising of Professional Fees: Does the Consumer Have a

Right to Know?" *South Dakota Law Review* 21 (Spring 1976), p. 330.

5. *Bates v. State of Arizona*, 97 S.Ct. 2691. 45, U.S. Law Week 4895 (1977).

6. Charles Laughlin, "Ads on Trial," *Link*, May 1994, pp. 18–22; "Lawyers Learn the Hard Sell—and Companies Shudder," *Business Week*, June 10, 1985, p. 70.

7. Bruce H. Allen, Richard A. Wright, and Louis E. Raho, "Physicians and Advertising," *Journal of Health Care Marketing* 5 (Fall 1985), pp. 39–49.

8. Robert E. Hite and Cynthia Fraser, "Meta-Analyses of Attitudes toward Advertising by Professionals," *Journal of Marketing* 52, no. 3 (July 1988), pp. 95–105.

9. "Ads on Trial," *Link*, May 1994.

10. Volvo Cars of North America, Inc./ Volvo Sportswagon (National Advertising Division, Council of Better Business Bureaus, Inc.) *NAD Case Reports* 26, no. 6 (August 1996), pp. 221–26.

11. *NAD Case Reports* 23, no. 4 (June 1993), p. 27.

12. Gary M. Armstrong and Julie L. Ozanne, "An Evaluation of NAD/ NARB Purpose and Performance," *Journal of Advertising* 12, no. 3 (1983), pp. 15–26.

13. National Advertising Division, Council of Better Business Bureaus, Inc., *NAD Case Reports: Analysis of 1996 Decisions* 26, no. 10 (January 1997), p. 343.

14. *NAD Case Reports* 23, no. 4 (June 1993), p. 23.

15. Dorothy Cohen, "The FTC's Advertising Substantiation Program," *Journal of Marketing* 44, no. 1 (Winter 1980), pp. 26–35.

16. Lynda M. Maddox and Eric J. Zanot, "The Suspension of the National Association of Broadcasters' Code and Its Effects on the Regulation of Advertising," *Journalism Quarterly* 61 (Summer 1984), pp. 125–30, 156.

17. Joe Mandese, "ABC Loosens Rules," *Advertising Age*, September 9, 1991, pp. 2, 8.

18. Eric Zanot, "Unseen but Effective Advertising Regulation: The Clearance Process," *Journal of Advertising* 14, no. 4 (1985), p. 48.

19. Mandese, "ABC Loosens Rules."

20. Azuenga quote cited in *Advertising Topics*, Supplement 533, March/April 1994 (Council of Better Business Bureaus, Inc., Arlington, VA), p. 3.

21. Steven W. Colford, "Speed Up the NAD, Industry Unit Told," *Advertising Age*, May 1, 1989, p. 3.

22. *FTC v. Raladam Co.*, 258 U.S. 643 (1931).

23. Edward Cox, R. Fellmeth, and J. Schultz, *The Consumer and the Federal Trade Commission* (Washington, DC: American Bar Association, 1969); American Bar Association, *Report of the American Bar Association to Study the Federal Trade Commission* (Washington, DC: The Association, 1969).

24. *FTC Staff Report on Advertising to Children* (Washington, DC: Government Printing Office, 1978).

25. Federal Trade Commission Improvements Act of 1980, P.L. No. 96–252, 94 Stat. 374 (May 28, 1980).

26. Bruce Silverglade, "Does FTC Have an 'Unfair' Future?" *Advertising Age*, March 26, 1994, p. 20.

27. Ivan L. Preston, *The Great American Blow-Up: Puffery in Advertising and Selling* (Madison: University of Wisconsin Press, 1975), p. 3.

28. Isabella C. M. Cunningham and William H. Cunningham, "Standards for Advertising Regulation," *Journal of Marketing* 41 (October 1977), pp. 91–97; Herbert J. Rotfeld and Kim B. Rotzell, "Is Advertising Puffery Believed?" *Journal of Advertising* 9, no. 3 (1980), pp. 16–20.

29. Herbert J. Rotfeld and Kim B. Rotzell, "Puffery vs. Fact Claims—Really Different?" in *Current Issues and Research in Advertising*, ed. James H. Leigh and Claude R. Martin, Jr. (Ann Arbor: University of Michigan, 1981), pp. 85–104.

30. Preston, *The Great American Blow-Up.*

31. Chuck Ross, "Marketers Fend Off Shift in Rules for Ad Puffery," *Advertising Age*, February 19, 1996, p. 41.

32. Federal Trade Commission, "Policy Statement on Deception," 45 ATRR 689 (October 27, 1983), p. 690.

33. Gary T. Ford and John E. Calfee, "Recent Developments in FTC Policy on Deception," *Journal of Marketing* 50, no. 3 (July 1986), pp. 86–87.

34. Ray O. Werner, ed. "Legal Developments in Marketing," *Journal of Marketing* 56 (January 1992), p. 102.

35. Ira Teinowitz, "FTC Strives to Clarify 'Made in USA' Rules," *Advertising Age*, April 29, 1996, p. 12.

36. Michael Oneal, "Does New Balance Have an American Soul?" *Business Week*, December 12, 1994, pp. 86, 90.

37. Cohen, "The FTC's Advertising Substantiation Program."

38. Trade Regulation Reporter, Par. 20,056 at 22,033, 1970–1973 Transfer Binder, Federal Trade Commission, July 1972.

39. Michael Parrish, "Unocal, FTC Settle over Premium Gas Claims," *Los Angeles Times*, December 31, 1993, p. D1.

40. John E. Califee, "FTC's Hidden Weight-Loss Ad Agenda," *Advertising Age*, October 25, 1993, p. 29.

41. Michael J. McCarthy, "Abbott Will Settle FTC Charges Linked to Ensure Endorsement," *The Wall Street Journal*, January 2, 1997, p. B2.

42. For an excellent description of the Campbell Soup corrective advertising case, see Dick Mercer, "Tempest in a Soup Can," *Advertising Age*, October 17, 1994, pp. 25, 28–29.

43. William L. Wilkie, Dennis L. McNeill, and Michael B. Mazis, "Marketing's 'Scarlet Letter': The Theory and Practice of Corrective Advertising," *Journal of Marketing* 48 (Spring 1984), pp. 11–31.

44. "Deceptive Ads: The FTC's Laissez-Faire Approach Is Backfiring," *Business Week*, December 2, 1985, p. 136.

45. Joanne Lipman, "FTC Puts Advertisers on Notice of Crackdown on Misleading Ads," *The Wall Street Journal*, February 4, 1991, p. B6.

46. Steven W. Colford, "$12 Million Bite," *Advertising Age*, December 2, 1991, p. 4.

47. Jan Joben, "A Setback for Competitive Ads?" *Business Marketing*, October 1992, p. 34.

48. Bruce Buchanan and Doron Goldman, "Us vs. Them: The Minefield of Comparative Ads," *Harvard Business Review*, May/June 1989, pp. 38–50.

49. "Deceptive Ads: The FTC's Laissez-Faire Approach."

50. Jennifer Lawrence, "State Ad Rules Face Showdown," *Advertising Age*, November 28, 1988, p. 4.

51. "Ally in Plax Settlement," *The Wall Street Journal*, February 12, 1991, p. B4.

52. Steven Colford, "ABA Panel Backs FTC over States," *Advertising Age*, April 10, 1994, p. 1.

53. S. J. Diamond, "New Director Putting Vigor Back into FTC," *Los Angeles Times*, March 29, 1991, pp. D1, 4.

54. Federal Trade Commission, "Trade Regulation Rule: Games of Chance in the Food Retailing and Gasoline Industries," 16 CFR, pt. 419 (1982).

55. Mark Pawlosky, "States Rein in Sweepstakes, Game Operators," *The Wall Street Journal*, July 3, 1995, pp. B1, 3.

56. Steven W. Colford, "Top Kid TV Offender: Premiums," *Advertising Age*, April 29, 1991, p. 52.

57. Federal Trade Commission, "Guides for Advertising Allowances and Other

Merchandising Payments and Services," 16 CFR, pt. 240 (1983).

58. Federal Trade Commission, "Trade Regulation Rule: Use of Negative Option Plans by Sellers in Commerce," 16 CFR, pt. 42 (1982).

59. For a more thorough discussion of legal aspects of sales promotion and mail-order practices, see Louis W. Stern and Thomas L. Eovaldi, *Legal Aspects of Marketing Strategy* (Englewood Cliffs, NJ: Prentice Hall, 1984).

60. Mary Lu Carnevale, "FTC Adopts Rules to Curb Telemarketing," *The Wall Street Journal*, September 18, 1992, pp. B1, 10.

61. Ira Teinowitz,"FTC Plans to Zoom in on Kids Online Issues," *Advertising Age*, April, 1, 1996, p. 60.

62. Ira Teinowitz, "FTC Chairman Seeking Voluntary Web Rules," *Advertising Age*, June 10, 1996, p. 42.

Chapter 22

1. Robert L. Heilbroner, "Demand for the Supply Side," *New York Review of Books* 38 (June 11, 1981), p. 40.

2. Eric N. Berkowitz et al., *Marketing*, 2nd ed. (Burr Ridge, IL: Richard D. Irwin, 1992), p. 90.

3. Willam J. Eaton, "College Binge Drinking Soars, Study Finds," *The Los Angeles Times*, June 8, 1994, p. A21.

4. Ira Teinowitz, "Rep. Kennedy Hits Alcohol Ads," *Advertising Age*, May 13, 1996, pp. 1, 52.

5. "Calvin's World," *Newsweek*, September 11, 1995, pp. 60–66.

6. J. Edward Russo, Barbara L. Metcalf, and Debra Stephens, "Identifying Misleading Advertising," *Journal of Consumer Research* 8 (September 1981), pp. 119–31.

7. Shelby D. Hunt, "Informational vs. Persuasive Advertising: An Appraisal," *Journal of Advertising*, Summer 1976, pp. 5–8.

8. Study cited in Ron Alsop, "Advertisers Find the Climate Less Hostile Outside the U.S.," *The Wall Street Journal*, December 10, 1987, p. 29.

9. Helen Cooper, "CDC Advocates Use of Condoms in Blunt AIDS-Prevention Spots," *The Wall Street Journal*, January 5, 1994, p. B1.

10. David A. Aaker and Donald E. Bruzzone, "Causes of Irritation in Advertising," *Journal of Marketing* 5 (Spring 1985), pp. 47–57.

11. Stephen A. Greyser, "Irritation in Advertising," *Journal of Advertising Research* 13 (February 1973), pp. 3–10.

12. Ron Alsop, "Personal Product Ads Abound as Public Gets More Tolerant," *The Wall Street Journal*, April 14, 1986, p. 19.

13. Joanne Lipman, "Censored Scenes: Why You Rarely See Some Things in Television Ads," *The Wall Street Journal*, August 17, 1987, p. 17.

14. Bruce Horowitz, "Taking Aim at the Bad Ads," *The Los Angeles Times*, January 28, 1994, pp. D1, 4.

15. John P. Cortez and Ira Teinowitz, "More Trouble Brews for Stroh Bikini Team," *Advertising Age*, December 9, 1991, p. 45.

16. Ira Teinowitz, "Days of 'Beer and Babes' Running Out," *Advertising Age*, October 4, 1993, p. S-5.

17. David Lieberman, "Broadcasters Crowd the Playground," *USA Today*, February 7, 1996, pp. 1, 2B.

18. Scott Ward, Daniel B. Wackman, and Ellen Wartella, *How Children Learn to Buy: The Development of Consumer Information Processing Skills* (Beverly Hills, CA: Sage, 1979).

19. Thomas S. Robertson and John R. Rossiter, "Children and Commercial Persuasion: An Attribution Theory Analysis," *Journal of Consumer Research* 1, no. 1 (June 1974), pp. 13–20; Scott Ward and Daniel B. Wackman, "Children's Information Processing of Television Advertising," in *New Models for Communications Research*, ed. G. Kline and P. Clark (Beverly Hills, CA: Sage, 1974), pp. 81–119.

20. Merrie Brucks, Gary M. Armstrong, and Marvin E. Goldberg, "Children's Use of Cognitive Defenses against Television Advertising: A Cognitive Response Approach," *Journal of Consumer Research* 14, no. 4 (March 1988), pp. 471–82.

21. For a discussion on consumer socialization, see Scott Ward, "Consumer Socialization," *Journal of Consumer Research* 1, no. 2 (September 1974), pp. 1–14.

22. *FTC Staff Report on Advertising to Children* (Washington, DC: Government Printing Office, 1978).

23. Ben M. Enis, Dale R. Spencer, and Don R. Webb, "Television Advertising and Children: Regulatory vs. Competitive Perspectives," *Journal of Advertising* 9, no. 1 (1980), pp. 19–25.

24. Richard Zoglin, "Ms. Kidvid Calls It Quits," *Time*, January 20, 1992, p. 52.

25. Elizabeth Jensen and Albert R. Karr, "Summit on Kids' TV Yields Compromise," *The Wall Street Journal*, July 30, 1996, p. B12.

26. Sally Goll Beatty, "White House Pact on TV for Kids May Prove a Marketing Bonanza," *The Wall Street Journal*, August 2, 1996, p. B2.

27. Ronald Alsop, "Watchdogs Zealously Censor Advertising Targeted to Kids," *The Wall Street Journal*, September 5, 1985, p. 35.

28. Robert E. Hite and Randy Eck, "Advertising to Children: Attitudes of Business vs. Consumers," *Journal of Advertising Research*, October/November 1987, pp. 40–53.

29. Ronald Berman, *Advertising and Social Change* (Beverly Hills, CA: Sage, 1981), p. 13.

30. John K. Galbraith, *The New Industrial State* (Boston: Houghton Mifflin, 1967), cited in Richard W. Pollay, "The Distorted Mirror: Reflections on the Unintended Consequences of Advertising," *Journal of Marketing*, August 1986, p. 25.

31. Raymond A. Bauer and Stephen A. Greyser, "The Dialogue that Never Happens," *Harvard Business Review*, January/February 1969, pp. 122–28.

32. Morris B. Holbrook, "Mirror Mirror on the Wall, What's Unfair in the Reflections on Advertising," *Journal of Marketing* 5 (July 1987), pp. 95–103; Theodore Levitt, "The Morality of Advertising," *Harvard Business Review*, July/August 1970, pp. 84–92.

33. Stephen Fox, *The Mirror Makers: A History of American Advertising and Its Creators* (New York: Morrow, 1984), p. 330.

34. Richard W. Pollay, "The Distorted Mirror: Reflections on the Unintended Consequences of Advertising," *Journal of Marketing* 50 (April 1986), p. 33.

35. Jules Backman, "Is Advertising Wasteful?" *Journal of Marketing* 32 (January 1968), pp. 2–8.

36. Hunt, "Informational vs. Persuasive Advertising."

37. Ibid., p. 6.

38. Kevin Goldman, "Survey Asks Which 'Green' Ads Are Read," *The Wall Street Journal*, April 11, 1994, p. B5.

39. Alice E. Courtney and Thomas W. Whipple, *Sex Stereotyping in America: An Annotated Bibliography* (Cambridge, MA: Marketing Science Institute), Report no. 80-100, February 1980, p. v.

40. Cyndee Miller, "Liberation for Women in Ads," *Marketing News*, August 17, 1992, p. 1; Adrienne Ward-Fawcett, "Narrowcast in Past, Women Earn Revised Role in Advertising," *Advertising Age*, October 4, 1993, p. S-1.

41. Basil Englis, Michael Solomon, and Richard Ashmore, "Beauty before the Eyes of Beholders: The Cultural Encoding of Beauty Types in Magazine Advertising and Music Television," *Journal of Advertising*, 23 (June 1994), pp. 49–64.

42. Miller, "Liberation for Women in Ads."

43. Helen Czepic and J. Steven Kelly, "Analyzing Hispanic Roles in Advertising," in *Current Issues and Research in Advertising*, ed. James H. Leigh and Claude Martin (Ann Arbor: University of Michigan, 1983), pp. 219–40; R. F. Busch, Allan S. Resnik, and Bruce L. Stern, "A Content Analysis of the Portrayal of Black Models in Magazine Advertising," in American Marketing Association Proceedings: *Marketing in the 1980s*, ed. Richard P. Bagozzi (Chicago: American Marketing Association, 1980); and R. F. Busch, Allan S. Resnik, and Bruce L. Stern, "There Are More Blacks in TV Commercials," *Journal of Advertising Research* 17 (1977), pp. 21–25.

44. James Stearns, Lynette S. Unger, and Steven G. Luebkeman, "The Portrayal of Blacks in Magazine and Television Advertising," in *AMA Educator's Proceedings*, ed. Susan P. Douglas and Michael R. Solomon (Chicago: American Marketing Association, 1987).

45. Robert E. Wilkes and Humberto Valencia, "Hispanics and Blacks in Television Commercials," *Journal of Advertising* 18, no. 1 (1989), pp. 19–26.

46. Thomas H. Stevenson, "How Are Blacks Portrayed in Business Ads?" *Industrial Marketing Management* 20 (1991), pp. 193–99.

47. Leon E. Wynter, "Minorities Play the Hero in More TV Ads as Clients Discover Multicultural Sells," *The Wall Street Journal*, December 24, 1993, pp. B1, 6.

48. Ibid.

49. Bob Garfield, " Ikea again Furnishes Ad Breakthrough," *Advertising Age*, April 1, 1996, p. 61.

50. Kevin Goldman, "Seniors Get Little Respect on Madison Avenue," *The Wall Street Journal*, September 20, 1993, p. B8.

51. Laura Bird, "Critics Cry Foul at Nike Spots with Actor," *The Wall Street Journal*, December 16, 1993, p. B8.

52. Jon Berry, "Think Bland," *Adweek's Marketing Week*, November 11, 1991, pp. 22–24.

53. Todd Pruzan, "Brewing New Ties with Gay Consumers," *Advertising Age*, April 8, 1996, p. 13.

54. Jef I. Richards and John H. Murphy, II, "Economic Censorship and Free Speech: The Circle of Communication betweeen Advertisers, Media, and Consumers," *Journal of Current Issues and Research in Advertising* 18, no. 1 (Spring 1996), pp. 21–33.

55. Lawrence C. Soley and Robert L. Craig, "Advertising Pressure on Newspapers: A Survey," *Journal of Advertising* 21 (December 1992), pp. 1–10.

56. Mark Simon, "Mercury News Ad Dispute Cooling Off: Advertisers Return while Reporters Stew," *San Francisco Chronicle*, July 15, 1994, p. B1.

57. Soley and Craig, "Advertising Pressure on Newspapers: A Survey."

58. Steven T. Goldberg, "Do the Ads Tempt the Editors?" *Kiplinger's*, May 1996, pp. 45–49.

59. Janet Guyon, "Do Publications Avoid Anti-Cigarette Stories to Protect Ad Dollars?" *The Wall Street Journal*, November 22, 1982, pp. 1, 20; Elizabeth M. Whelan, "When *Newsweek* and *Time* Filtered Cigarette Copy," *The Wall Street Journal*, November 1, 1984, p. 3; "RJR Swears Off Saatchi and Nabisco Is in a Sweat," *Business Week*, April 18, 1988, p. 36.

60. Joanne Lipman, "Media Content Is Linked to Cigarette Ads," *The Wall Street Journal*, January 30, 1992, p. B5.

61. Laurie Freeman, "Pillsbury Re-evaluates Ads on Violent Shows," *Advertising Age*, January 15, 1996, p. 6.

62. Sally Goll Beatty, "If TV Gets Ratings, Risque Could Be Passe," *The Wall Street Journal*, February 16, 1996, p. B11.

63. For a discussion of monopolies in the cereal industry, see Paul N. Bloom, "The Cereal Industry: Monopolists or Super Marketers?" *MSU Business Topics*, Summer 1978, pp. 41–49.

64. Lester G. Telser, "Advertising and Competition," *Journal of Political Economy*, December 1964, pp. 537–62.

65. Robert D. Buzzell, Bradley T. Gale, and Ralph G. M. Sultan, "Market Share—A Key to Profitability," *Harvard Business Review*, January/February 1975, pp. 97–106.

66. Robert D. Buzzell and Paul W. Farris, *Advertising Cost in Consumer Goods Industries* (Cambridge, MA: Marketing Science Institute), Report no. 76, p. 111, August 1976; Paul W. Farris and David J. Reibstein, "How Prices, Ad Expenditures, and Profits Are Linked," *Harvard Business Review*, November/December 1979, pp. 173–84.

67. Paul W. Farris and Mark S. Albion, "The Impact of Advertising on the Price of Consumer Products," *Journal of Marketing* 44, no. 3 (Summer 1980), pp. 17–35.

68. Ibid., p. 19.

69. Lee Benham, "The Effect of Advertising on the Price of Eyeglasses," *Journal of Law and Economics* 15 (October 1972), pp. 337–52.

70. Robert L. Steiner, "Does Advertising Lower Consumer Prices?" *Journal of Marketing* 37, no. 4 (October 1973), pp. 19–26.

71. Farris and Albion, "The Impact of Advertising," p. 30.

72. James M. Ferguson, "Comments on 'The Impact of Advertising on the Price of Consumer Products,'" *Journal of Marketing* 46, no. 1 (Winter 1982), pp. 102–5.

73. Farris and Albion, "The Impact of Advertising."

Credits and Acknowledgments

Chapter 7

Chapter opener: POST is a registered trademark of Kraft Foods, Inc. Photo used with permission. **Page 198, wrapped photo:** Courtesy of Volvo. **Exhibit 7–1:** Courtesy Georgia-Pacific Corp. **Exhibit 7–2:** Courtesy Pace. **Exhibit 7–3:** Reprinted with permission of Del Monte Foods. **Exhibit 7–4:** Reuters/Jeff Vinnick/Archive Photos. **Exhibit 7–5:** Courtesy FasTrak Fitness, a division of American Harvest, Inc. **Page 205, wrapped photo:** Courtesy Service Merchandise. **Exhibit 7–6:** Courtesy Dooney & Bourke. **Exhibit 7–7:** Courtesy Midwest Express Airlines. **Exhibit 7–8:** ©Sonance, a Division of Dana Innovations, Kevin W. Topp, art director. **IMC Perspective 7–2:** Courtesy Wolverine World Wide, Inc. **Page 215, wrapped photo:** Courtesy of the Zoological Society of San Diego. **Exhibit 7–9:** ©American Association of Advertising Agencies. **Exhibit 7–10:** Courtesy of International Business Machines Corporation.

Chapter 8

Chapter opener: Copyright, Nissan 1996. All rights reserved. Nissan and the Nissan logo are registered trademarks of Nissan. **Exhibit 8–1:** Courtesy Fallon McElligott for BMW of North America, Inc. **Exhibit 8–2:** Courtesy Consumer Healthcare Products, Miles Inc. **Global Perspective 8–1:** Courtesy Nestlé Beverage Co. **IMC Perspective 8–2:** Courtesy TBWA Chiat/Day, Inc. **Exhibit 8–3:** Courtesy Nike, Inc. **Exhibit 8–4:** Reprinted with permission of *Advertising Age.* Copyright 1997 Crain Communications Inc. **Exhibit 8–5:** Courtesy Westin Hotels & Resorts. **IMC Perspective 8–3:** Courtesy California Milk Processor Board. **Exhibit 8–6:** Used by permission of San Diego Trust & Savings Bank. **Exhibit 8–7:** Army materials courtesy of the U.S. Government, as represented by the Secretary of the Army. **Page 257, wrapped photo:** Courtesy Easterby & Associates. **Exhibit 8–8:** Courtesy Castrol North America Automotive Inc. **Page 259, wrapped photo:** Courtesy No Fear. **Exhibit 8–9:** Courtesy Leo Burnett Company, Inc. as agent for Hallmark Cards, Incorporated. **Exhibit 8–10:** Courtesy Copper Mountain Resort, Colorado. **Ethical Perspective 8–4:** United Colors of Benetton advertising campaign: Concept & Photo—O. Toscani.

Chapter 9

Chapter opener: Courtesy Chevrolet Division General Motors and Campbell-Ewald Advertising. **Exhibit 9–1:** Courtesy The Quaker Oats Company. **Exhibit 9–2:** Courtesy Continental Airlines, Inc. **Exhibit 9–3:** Courtesy of DFO, Inc. **Exhibit 9–4:** Courtesy Minolta. **IMC Perspective 9–1:** Courtesy Norwegian Cruise Line and Goodby, Silverstein & Partners. **Exhibit 9–5:** Courtesy Team One Advertising for LEXUS. **Exhibit 9–6:** Courtesy Hershey Foods Corporation. AMERICAN BEAUTY, HERSHEY'S, and HERSHEY'S KISSES are trademarks of Hershey Foods Corporation. **Global Perspective 9–2:** Courtesy Nestlé USA, Inc. **Exhibit 9–7:** Courtesy Taco Bell Corp. **Exhibit 9–8:** Courtesy Valvoline, Inc. **Exhibit 9–9:** The DERMASIL print ad was reproduced courtesy Chesebrough–Pond's USA Co. **Exhibit 9–10:** Courtesy DuPont. Teflon® is a registered trademark of DuPont. **Exhibit 9–11:** Courtesy Sybase, Inc. **Exhibit 9–12:** Courtesy AT&T Advertising Department. **Page 278, wrapped photo:** Used with permission of ©Nabisco, Inc. **Exhibit 9–13:** Courtesy Maytag Company. **Exhibit 9–14:** Courtesy Foodmaker Incorporated. **Exhibit 9–15:** Courtesy BASF Corporation. **Page 282, wrapped photo:** Courtesy AT&T Corp. Copyright 1997 AT&T Corp. All rights reserved. **Exhibit 9–16:** Courtesy The Coca-Cola company. FRESCA is a trademark of The Coca-Cola Company. **Exhibit 9–17:** Courtesy British Airways and Saatchi & Saatchi, New York, New York. **Exhibit 9–18:** Reproduced with permission of PepsiCo, Inc. 1994, Purchase, New York. **IMC Perspective 9–4:** Courtesy Apple Computer, Inc. **Exhibit 9–19:** Courtesy Philips Lighting Company.

Chapter 10

Chapter opener: Courtesy WebTV Networks, Inc. **Figure 10–4:** Simmons Market Research Bureau, Inc. 1994. **Figure 10–8:** Reprinted with permission of *Sales & Marketing Management.* **Figure 10–9:** Reprinted with permission of *Sales & Marketing Management.* **Figure 10–10:** Reprinted with permission of *Sales & Marketing Management.* **IMC Perspective 10–2:** TM & ©Marvel Characters, Inc. All rights reserved.

Chapter 11

Chapter opener: Courtesy ESPN, Inc. **Exhibit 11–1:** Courtesy Porsche Cars of North America. **Exhibit 11–2:** Courtesy The Discovery Channel. **Exhibit 11–3:**

Copyright, Nissan 1996. All rights reserved. Nissan and the Nissan logo are registered trademarks of Nissan. **Exhibit 11–4:** ©1997 Fox Broadcasting Company. All rights reserved. **Figure 11–3:** Reprinted with permission from the September 16, 1996 issue of *Advertising Age,* Copyright Crain Communications, Inc. 1996. **Page 351, wrapped photo:** Courtesy All American Television, Inc. **Exhibit 11–5:** Courtesy Nickelodeon. Used by Permission. **IMC Perspective 11–2:** Photo by Tom Casaleni; Courtesy of U.S. Satellite Broadcasting^{SM}. **Exhibit 11–6:** ©1996 Cable News Network, Inc. A Time Warner Company. All Rights Reserved. **Exhibit 11–7:** Courtesy A.C. Nielsen Company. **Exhibit 11–8:** Courtesy KFMB-TV 8/Midwest Television Inc. **Page 367, wrapped photo:** Courtesy Radio Advertising Bureau. **Exhibit 11–9:** Courtesy Banana Boat of California, Inc. **Exhibit 11–10:** Courtesy KCEO Radio. **Figure 11–13:** Reprinted with permission of XHTZ 90.3 FM.

Chapter 12

Chapter opener: Reprinted with permission from *Spin.* **Page 380, wrapped photo:** Courtesy Surfer Publications, Inc. **Exhibit 12–2:** Courtesy *Beef* Magazine. **Exhibit 12–3:** Courtesy *Newsweek* Magazine. **Exhibit 12–4:** Courtesy *Newsweek* Magazine. **Exhibit 12–5:** Courtesy Transamerica Corporation. **Exhibit 12–6:** Used by permission of WD-40 Company. **Exhibit 12–7:** Courtesy Magazine Publishers of America. **Ethical Perspective 12–1:** Courtesy Bausch & Lomb Healthcare and Optics Worldwide. **Exhibit 12–8:** Courtesy Audit Bureau of Circulations. **Exhibit 12–9:** Courtesy Petersen Publishing Company. **IMC Perspective 12–2:** Courtesy Ivy League Magazine Network. **Exhibit 12–10:** Courtesy *Newsweek* Magazine. **Exhibit 12–11:** Courtesy *Newsweek* Magazine. **Exhibit 12–12:** Reprinted by permission of *The Wall Street Journal.* ©1996 Dow Jones & Company, Inc. All Rights Reserved. **Page 399, wrapped photo:** Courtesy *The Daily Aztec.* **Exhibit 12–13:** Courtesy CompuServe, Inc. **Exhibit 12–14:** Courtesy *The Chicago Tribune.* **Exhibit 12–15:** Courtesy Union-Tribune Publishing Company. **Figure 12–4:** Reprinted with permission of Newspaper Association of America from "1997 Newspaper Association of America Report." **Exhibit 12–16:** Courtesy Cathay Pacific Airways and McCann-Erickson. **Exhibit 12–17:** Courtesy National Newspaper Network. **Figure 12–5:** Courtesy Newspaper Advertising Bureau, Inc. **IMC Perspective 12–3:** Reprinted with permission of *The Miami Herald.* **Exhibit 12–18:** Courtesy *Newsweek* Magazine.

Chapter 13

Chapter opener: Photofest. **Exhibit 13–1:** Courtesy Atomic Props & Effects Ltd. **Exhibit 13–2:** Courtesy of Inflatable Images, Brunswick, Ohio. **Exhibit 13–3:** Courtesy AVIAD. **Exhibit 13–5:** Courtesy United Airlines, AT&T/Young & Rubicam. **Page 423, wrapped photo:** Courtesy TDI. **Exhibit 13–6:** Courtesy Gannett Transit. **Exhibit 13–7:** Courtesy Promotional Products Association International. **Page 428, wrapped photo:** Courtesy Bell Atlantic Directory Services, Bell Atlantic Corporation. **Figure 13–8:** National Yellow Pages Monitor, a division of NFD Research, Inc. **Exhibit 13–8:** Paramount/Shooting Star. **Exhibit 13–9:** Courtesy of Halsey Publishing Co., publishers of Delta Air Lines *SKY* Magazine. Photography by Brian W. Robb.

Chapter 14

Chapter opener: This material originally appeared on the cover of *INTERNET SHOPPER* magazine, Volume 1, Issue 1, Spring 1997. Copyright ©1997 Mecklermedia Corporation, 20 Ketchum Street, Westport, CT 06880; (203)341-2802; info@mecklermedia.com; http://www.iworld.com. All rights reserved. Reprinted with permission. **Exhibit 14–1:** Courtesy Cox Direct. **Exhibit 14–2:** Courtesy LEXUS. Photography by Doug Taub. **Page 447, wrapped photo:** Courtesy Porsche Cars North America/Heiman & Associates. **Exhibit 14–4:** Courtesy Bennett Kuhn Varner, Inc. **Exhibit 14–5:** Courtesy Volvo Cars of North America. **Exhibit 14–6:** Courtesy The GM Card. **Exhibit 14–7:** Courtesy America Online. Please note that AOL software, which was glued on to this ad, has been removed for illustrative purposes. **Exhibit 14–8:** Courtesy Tupperware. **Page 456, wrapped photo:** Sharon Hoogstraten. **Exhibit 14–9:** Courtesy DoubleClick. **Exhibit 14–10:** Courtesy of International Business Machines Corporation. **Exhibit 14–11:** Image provided courtesy of Silicon Graphics, Inc. **Exhibit 14–12:** Reprinted by permission of Levi Strauss & Co. **Exhibit 14–13:** Reprinted from *Inc.,* October 1995, pp. 84–85, with permission of Hot Hot Hot. **Global Perspective 14–2:** Remy de la Mauviniere: AP/Wide World Photos.

Chapter 15

Chapter opener: Reprinted from September 9, 1996 issue of *Business Week* by special permission, copyright ©1996 by The McGraw-Hill Companies, Inc. **Exhibit 15–1:**

Courtesy General Mills, Inc. Photography by Sharon Hoogstraten. **Exhibit 15–2:** Used with permission of ©Nabisco, Inc. **Exhibit 15–3:** Courtesy Cox Direct. **Page 477, wrapped photo:** Courtesy Ryan Partnership. **Exhibit 15–4:** Courtesy The Colgate-Palmolive Company. **Exhibit 15–5:** Courtesy Burson Marsteller for Church & Dwight Company, Inc. **Exhibit 15–6:** Reproduced with permission of PepsiCo, Inc. 1994, Purchase, New York. **Exhibit 15–7:** Courtesy Cadillac Motor Car Division General Motors. **IMC Perspective 15–2:** J.J. Warner/Courtesy Sears. **Exhibit 15–8:** Sharon Hoogstraten. **Exhibit 15–9:** Courtesy ArmorAll Products Corporation. **IMC Perspective 15–3:** POST is a registered trademark of Kraft Foods, Inc. Photo used with permission. **Page 489, wrapped photo:** Courtesy Kellogg Company. Eggo®, Common Sense®, and Kellogg's® are registered trademarks of Kellogg Company. All rights reserved. **Exhibit 15–10:** Courtesy Catalina Marketing. **Exhibit 15–11:** Courtesy Catalina Marketing. **Exhibit 15–12:** Courtesy McDonald's Corporation. **Exhibit 15–13:** Courtesy The Gillette Company. **Exhibit 15–14:** Courtesy ArmorAll Products Corporation. **Exhibit 15–15:** Courtesy Bristol-Myers Company. **Exhibit 15–16:** Courtesy Van Camp Seafood Company. **Exhibit 15–17:** Courtesy Van Camp Seafood Company. **Exhibit 15–18:** Courtesy Spalding Sports Worldwide. **Exhibit 15–19:** Courtesy Cadillac Motor Car Division General Motors. **Exhibit 15–20:** Courtesy Ski the Summit Colorado - Arapahoe Basin, Breckenridge, Copper Mountain, & Keystone. **Exhibit 15–21:** Courtesy New Balance Athletic Shoe, Inc. **Exhibit 15–22:** Courtesy of Taster's Choice. **Exhibit 15–23:** Courtesy Lever Brothers Company.

Chapter 16

Chapter opener: Ray Stubblebine: AP/Wide World Photos. **Exhibit 16–1:** Courtesy Texaco. **Exhibit 16–2:** Courtesy Brunswick Corporation. **Exhibit 16–3:** Courtesy Campbell Soup Company. **Exhibit 16–4:** Courtesy Chevron Corporation. **Page 521, wrapped photo:** Courtesy Yellow Pages Publishers Association. **Exhibit 16–5:** Courtesy KXAS-TV. **Exhibit 16–6:** Courtesy Sears. **Exhibit 16–7:** CLIENT: Olympus America Inc. AGENCY: McCaffery & Ratner Gottlieb Lane. **Exhibit 16–8:** Courtesy HP—Home Products Division. **Exhibit 16–9:** ©1991 Dow Jones & Company, Publisher of *The Wall Street Journal*. All Rights Reserved. **Exhibit 16–10:** Used by permission of Tree Top, Inc. **Exhibit 16–11:** Courtesy Tyco International Ltd. **Exhibit 16–12:** Robert Burroughs/Gamma Liaison. **Page 536, wrapped photo:** Courtesy Deloitte & Touche. **Exhibit 16–13:** ©1997 Time, Inc. Reprinted by permission. **Exhibit 16–14:** Courtesy California Avocado Commission. **Exhibit 16–15:** Courtesy AT&T Advertising.

Chapter 17

Chapter opener: Courtesy Northwestern Mutual Life. **Exhibit 17–1:** Courtesy Giltspur, Inc./Haddon Advertising. **Global Perspective 17–1:** Raghu Rai/Magnum. **Exhibit 17–2:** Courtesy Gordon Publications, Inc. **Exhibit 17–3:** Courtesy Targetbase Marketing. **IMC Perspective 17–2:** Courtesy Mercedes-Benz of North America, Inc.

Chapter 18

Chapter opener: Courtesy Kellogg Company. **Page 566, wrapped photo:** Courtesy Chiat/Day/Mojo Inc. Advertising. **Exhibit 18–1:** Reprinted from *Business Week* with special permission. **Exhibit 18–2:** Courtesy Roper Starch Worldwide Inc. **IMC Perspective 18–2:** Courtesy General Mills.

Chapter 19

Chapter opener: Courtesy GE Capital Services. **Global Perspective 19–1:** Courtesy Intel Corporation. **Exhibit 19–1:** Courtesy Brock Control Systems, Inc.

Exhibit 19–2: Courtesy NEC America, Inc. **Exhibit 19–3:** Advertisement provided courtesy Nomadic Display. **Page 602, wrapped photo:** Courtesy Tektronix, Inc. **IMC Perspective 19–1:** Courtesy Xerox Corporation. **Exhibit 19–4:** Courtesy Fallon McElligott for Continental Bank. **Page 608, wrapped photo:** Courtesy Impact Exhibits, Inc. **Exhibit 19–5:** Courtesy Norwegian Cruise Line. **Exhibit 19–6:** Courtesy Chilton Company.

Chapter 20

Chapter opener: Courtesy of International Business Machines Corporation. **Exhibit 20–1:** Courtesy Kentucky Fried Chicken (KFC) Corporation. **Exhibit 20–2:** Used by permission of WD-40 Company. **Exhibit 20–3:** Courtesy Nestlé. **Exhibit 20–4:** Courtesy Heineken Breweries. **Global Perspective 20–1:** Courtesy Nike, Inc. **Page 625, wrapped photo:** Coca-Cola and Coca-Cola Light are registered trademarks of The Coca-Cola Company. Permission granted by The Coca-Cola Company. **Exhibit 20–5:** Courtesy The Gillette Company. **Exhibit 20–6:** Courtesy Nestlé. **Exhibit 20–7:** Courtesy Nestlé. **Exhibit 20–8:** Courtesy The Colgate-Palmolive Company. **Exhibit 20–9:** Courtesy Singapore Airlines. **Global Perspective 20–2:** Reproduced with permission of PepsiCo, Inc. 1997, Purchase, New York. **Exhibit 20–10:** Courtesy Continental Airlines. **Global Perspective 20–3:** Courtesy Levi Strauss & Co. **Exhibit 20–11:** Courtesy Merrill Lynch & Company, Inc. **Exhibit 20–12:** Courtesy NCH Promotional Services. **Global Perspective 20–4:** Used with permission from McDonald's Corporation. **Page 642, wrapped photo:** Courtesy Häagen-Dazs. **Exhibit 20–13:** Courtesy of Hearst Magazines International. **Exhibit 20–14:** Courtesy of International Business Machines Corporation.

Chapter 21

Chapter opener: Courtesy Center for Science in the Public Interest. **Exhibit 21–1:** Reprinted with permission of Kinney & Lange. All Rights Reserved. **Exhibit 21–2:** Courtesy Jamko Advertising (in-house agency for Jacoby & Meyers Law Offices). **Exhibit 21–3:** Courtesy Benetton Cosmetics Corporation. Photo by O. Toscani. **Figure 21–4:** Reprinted by permission of *The Wall Street Journal*, ©1988 Dow Jones & Company, Inc. All Rights Reserved Worldwide. **Exhibit 21–4:** Courtesy Jenny Craig Weight Loss Centres, Inc. **Exhibit 21–5:** Courtesy Van Camp Seafood Company. **IMC Perspective 21–3:** Courtesy Campaign for Tobacco-Free Kids. **IMC Perspective 21–4:** Courtesy Campbell Soup Company. **Exhibit 21–6:** ©1992 Wildcraft® Herbs, Santa Cruz, CA 95060. **Exhibit 21–7:** Courtesy Direct Selling Association.

Chapter 22

Chapter opener: Courtesy Boys & Girls Clubs of America. **Exhibit 22–1:** Reprinted with permission of Joseph E. Seagram & Sons, Inc. **Exhibit 22–2:** Used by permission of Calvin Klein. **Exhibit 22–3:** Courtesy Ansell. **Exhibit 22–4:** Used by permission of Calvin Klein. **Exhibit 22–5:** Courtesy Fleishman Hillard Inc. for Anheuser-Busch. **Exhibit 22–6:** Reprinted by permission of Rolls-Royce Motor Cars Inc. **Page 696, wrapped photo:** ©American Association of Advertising Agencies. **Exhibit 22–7:** ©American Association of Advertising Agencies. **Exhibit 22–8:** Courtesy Maidenform, Inc./Agency—Levine, Huntley, Schmidt & Beaver; Creative—Rochelle Klein, Michael Vitiello; Director—Mark Coppos, Coppos Films. **Exhibit 22–9:** Courtesy Ikea and Deutsch Inc. **Page 699, wrapped photo:** Courtesy Mattel. **Exhibit 22–10:** Courtesy Miller Brewing Company. **Exhibit 22–11:** Courtesy International Advertising Association. **Exhibit 22–12:** ©American Association of Advertising Agencies. **Exhibit 22–13:** Courtesy Kia Motors America, Inc. **Exhibit 22–14:** ©American Association of Advertising Agencies. **Global Perspective 22–3:** Courtesy International Advertising Association.

Name/Company/ Brand Index

Subject Index

Advertising and Promotion

An Integrated Marketing Communications Perspective

The Irwin/McGraw-Hill Series in Marketing